THE GUILD® SOURCEBOOK OF ARCHITECTURAL & INTERIOR ART 22

THE GUILD® SOURCEBOOK OF ARCHITECTURAL & INTERIOR ART 22

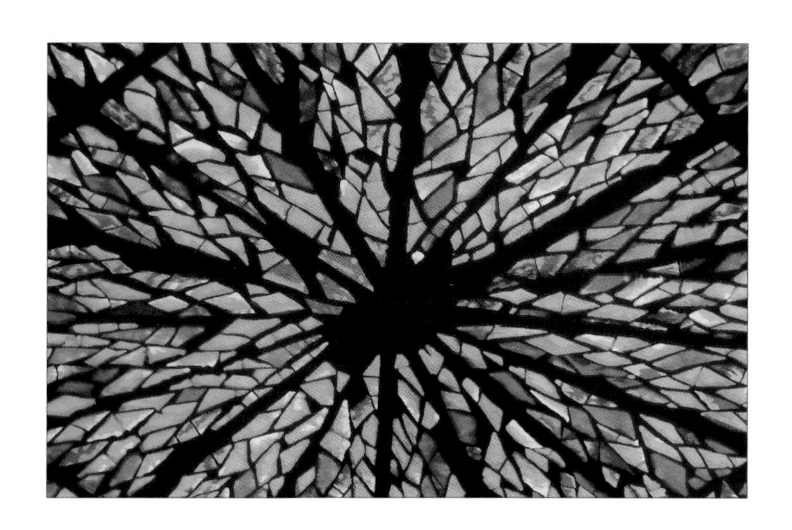

Guild Sourcebooks
Madison, Wisconsin
USA

THE GUILD SOURCEBOOK OF ARCHITECTURAL & INTERIOR ART 22

Guild Sourcebooks
An imprint of The Guild, Inc.
931 East Main Street
Madison, Wisconsin 53703-2955
TEL 800-930-1856 ■ TEL 877-284-8453

ADMINISTRATION
Toni Sikes, CEO and Founder
Michael Baum, President
Annik Lott, Manager of Sourcebook Sales
Elizabeth Tucker, Manager of Trade Relations
Jenna Brandt, Administrative Assistant

DESIGN, PRODUCTION, AND EDITORIAL
Jill Schaefer, Director of Editorial & Production, Writer
Laura Grady, Project Designer & Production Artist
Barbara Hatley, Production Coordinator & Image Specialist
Laura Beausire, Writer
Melita Schuessler, Proofreader

ARTIST MARKETING CONSULTANTS
Nicole Carroll • Dana Jansen
Amy Lambright • Laura Marth • Paul Murphy

Copyright ©2007 The Guild, Inc.
ISBN-13 (hardcover) 978-1-880140-63-5
ISBN-13 (softcover) 978-1-880140-64-2

Printed in China by Global PSD

All rights reserved. Artwork in this publication is protected by copyright and may not be reproduced in any form without permission of the artist. No part of this publication may be reproduced or transmitted in any form or by any means, electronic or mechanical, including photocopy, recording, or any other information storage and retrieval system without prior permission in writing from the publisher.

COVER ART and PAGE 1: Public Art Commissions, Aubusson-style tapestry, see page 100.

Special thanks to our 2007 Review Committee:
Robert D. Cooper, AIA , Design Principal, Eppstein Uhen Architects
Karen J. Darcy-Dominguez, Owner, Archisphere Design Studio LLC
Catherine Davidson, Owner, CR Davidson Art
Sharon Devenish, President, Devenish Associates, Inc.
Michael Monroe, Executive Director, Bellevue Arts Museum
Thomas K. Nisbet, AIA, Nisbet/Architects
Brenda B. Trier, Owner, Trier Design LLC

■

The Guild is the Internet's leading retailer of original art and fine craft.
Visit www.guild.com.

TABLE OF CONTENTS

LISTING OF ART CONSULTANTS 313
As the scope of commissioned art has grown, so has the need for the technical expertise required to find, select, and place art. Our state-by-state directory includes client lists and business descriptions.

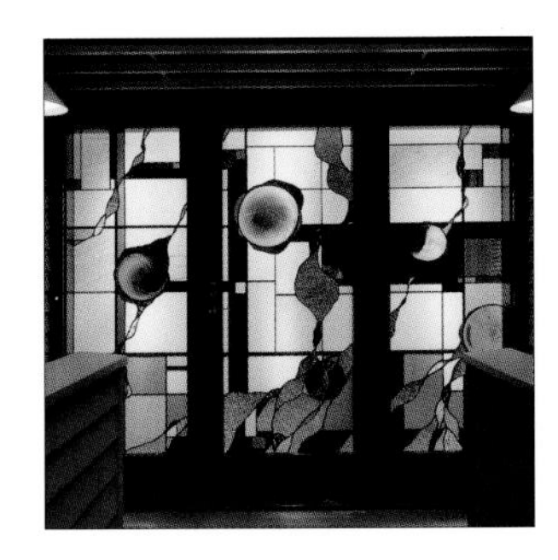

Architectural Glass
Page 22

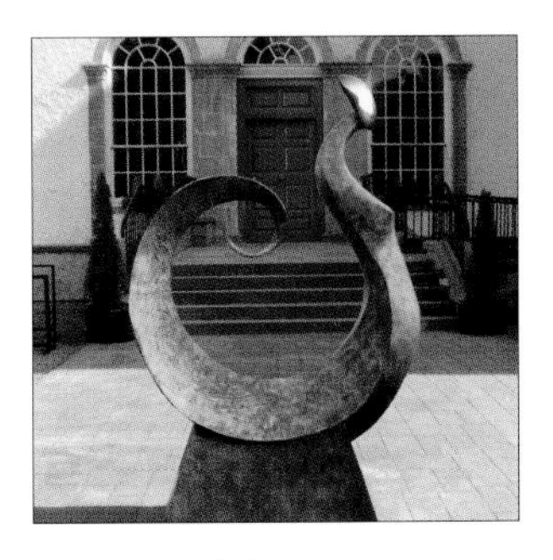

Public Art
Page 76

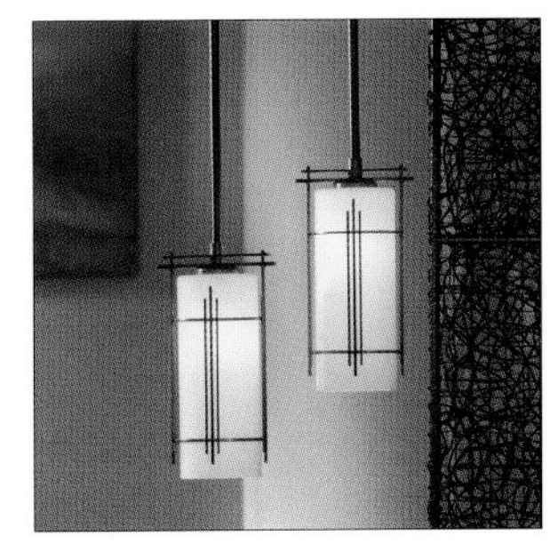

Lighting
Page 180

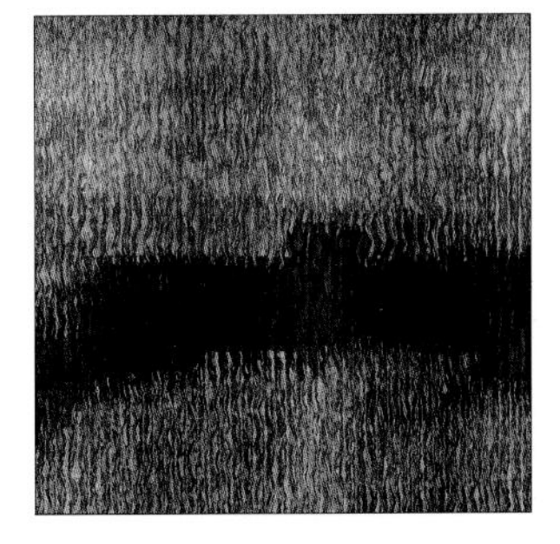

Fiber Wall Art
Page 286

The Guild Sourcebook of Architectural & Interior Art 22 shows artwork of enduring value—we think you'll refer to it for years to come. If at any time you're unable to reach an artist through contact information included in this book, call The Guild at 1-800-930-1856. We keep track of updated phone numbers and the like, and we are glad to share our most current information.

ARTISTS BY SECTION

ARCHITECTURAL GLASS

ATRIUM SCULPTURE

PUBLIC ART

NON-REPRESENTATIONAL SCULPTURE

REPRESENTATIONAL SCULPTURE

ARTISTS BY SECTION

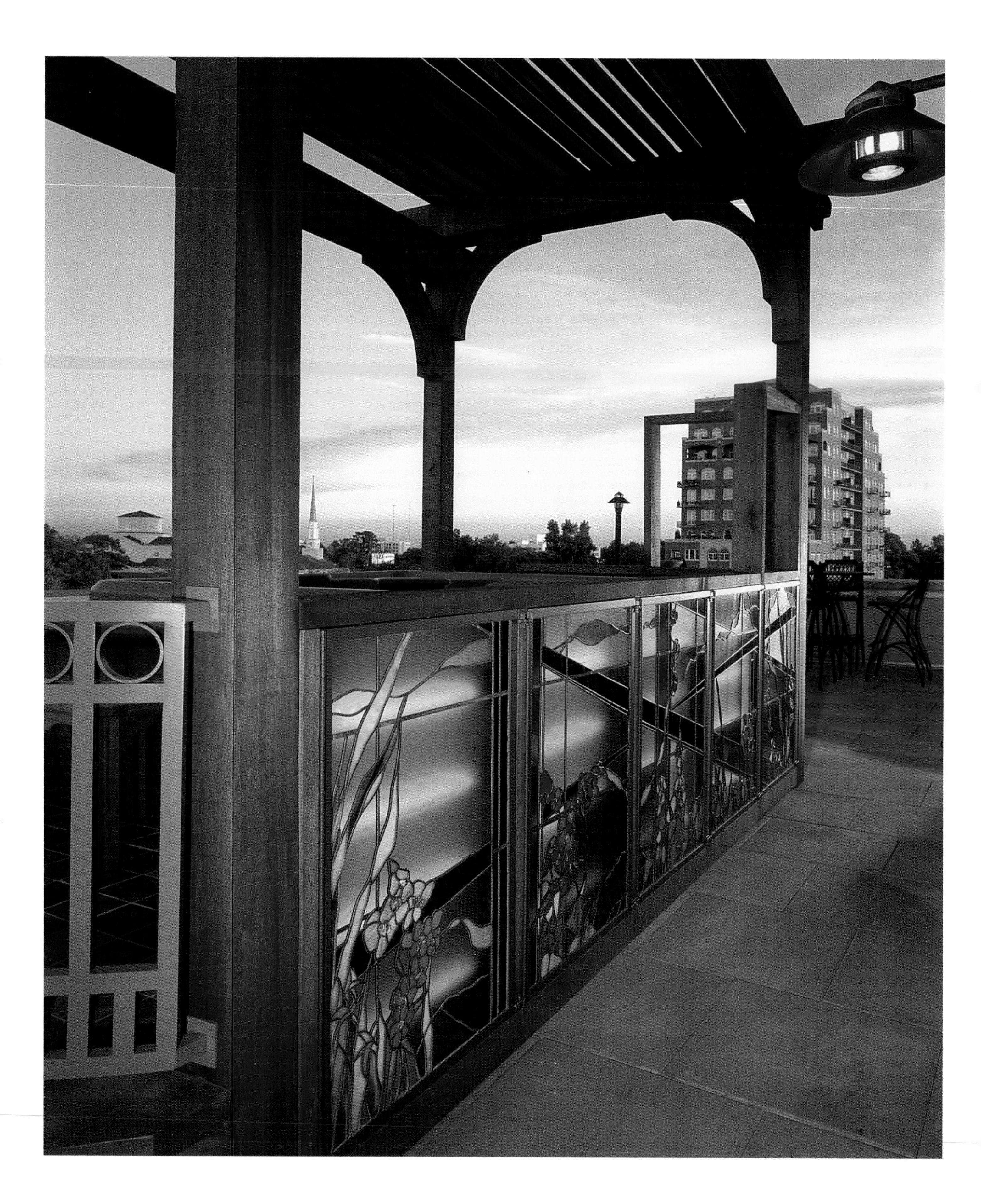

THE AESTHETIC SIGNATURE

When it comes to making large-scale artwork, the number of decisions required, the physical limitations of the media, and the sheer logistics of transportation and installation are enough to terrify the faint of heart. And that's only after the project has been conceived.

It all begins with an idea.

The conception of a work of art—its form, imaginative content, and expressiveness—is the concern of the creator, and should be distinguished from the execution of the work in a particular technique and material.

The highest level of accomplishment in the art world occurs when design and craftsmanship are intimately fused. The artist who begins with an artistic vision, and has the skills in a certain medium to accomplish his or her vision, can play an important role in complicated design projects.

This twenty-second annual publication of *The Guild Sourcebook of Architectural & Interior Art* is filled with such artists—top-notch professionals, juried for their experience in site-specific, architectural installations. Each has a distinct aesthetic signature, and the expertise to apply that signature to a wide variety of projects.

We hope that the aesthetic signatures you find within these pages will inspire you to enter into a creative relationship with a talented artist. Your own imaginative designs will love the company.

Toni Sikes
Publisher

Opposite: *Garden Wall* by Seranda Vespermann, see page 58. Photograph: Brian Gassel.

GREAT WAYS TO USE SOURCEBOOK 22

1 QUALITY CONTROL. This book begins with an assurance that these artists are reliable and professional. Artists featured by The Guild have been juried in on the basis of their experience, quality of work, and solid reputation for working with architects and designers.

2 MOTIVATION. Taking your copy of *The Guild Sourcebook of Architectural & Interior Art* to client meetings is highly recommended. Clients have been known to reach levels of extreme excitement upon viewing the artistic possibilities showcased here.

3 DEEPEN YOUR UNDERSTANDING. We believe a picture is worth a thousand words. But words provide the information you need to pursue your dreams. In the Artist Statements section (pages 326–365), our artists describe their inspiration, technique, training, and professional experience so that you can proceed with confidence.

4 GO AHEAD AND CALL. If something intrigues you while perusing *The Guild Sourcebook of Architectural & Interior Art*—a shape, a form, or an exotic use of the commonplace—please, give the artist a call. Serendipity often leads to a wonderful creation.

5 DESKTOP DIRECTORY. *The Guild Sourcebook of Architectural & Interior Art* is designed for quick reference as well as leisurely browsing. Looking for an artist nearby? Check the Location Index, which lists our artists by state. The Index of Artists and Companies will direct you to all the artists featured in the full-color pages, so finding a current phone number or checking product information is easily done. The information in your PDA may grow stale; *The Guild Sourcebook of Architectural & Interior Art* is fresh each year.

6 BE INSPIRED. So many wonderful commissions have come about through The Guild over these twenty-two years, and behind every one is a story of creativity, teamwork, and dedicated effort. We've featured some of our favorites in these pages to inspire, intrigue, and encourage you.

7 FOLLOW OUR ARTISTS' WORK. We've published books for architects, designers, and art consultants for more than twenty years. Many of the artists whose work you see in this volume were also featured in earlier Guild publications. These are listed at the end of each artist's statement for easy reference.

8 DESIGN OPTIONS. The feature article that follows highlights the myriad design services artists can offer. Collaboration is always welcome, but if your own creative juices aren't flowing, we'd like to remind you that artists are ready to jump in with their own ideas, sketches, models, and more.

9 EXPLORE EVEN MORE. This sourcebook is just the beginning of what The Guild can offer. All of the artists included here—and many more—can be reached through our Custom Design Center at www.guild.com. Our design consultants will work with you to make the commission process both painless and satisfying.

10 OUR NEXT LANDMARK. The Guild will be twenty-five in the year 2010. We'd like to feature your project in that anniversary edition. Please take a minute and daydream about the artwork you'll commission in the next three years!

THE ARTIST AS DESIGNER

The are many skills an artist brings to a collaborative project, but none is more important than his or her overall vision, the aesthetic signature that marks the work as the artist's own. Before an idea is realized in glass, or metal, or granite, or paint, it exists in its creator's mind. At this point, before the artistic vision becomes a reality, or perhaps even before it is committed to paper or maquette, what is its value? In other words, what is an idea worth?

Because architects and other trade professionals are creative people who live by the power of their ideas, they recognize—in theory, at least—that an artist's unique vision is valuable indeed. But when it comes down to a specific project, and when they are focused on issues of control and responsibility, they may be reluctant to use an artist's skills as fully as they might. For both the artist and the client, an opportunity is lost when the artist is hired merely as the maker and supplier of a product, rather than a knowledgeable partner whose ideas can be a vital part of creative design solutions.

At The Guild we see impressive partnerships between trade professionals and artists that are getting better and more productive every year. What most of these satisfying working relationships share is a true collaborative spirit, where the artist's design ideas, as well as his or her completed work, are both solicited and respected.

But because the area of design is both the most intangible and the most creative part of any project—whether it's creating a building, designing a particular interior, or envisioning a specific work of art—this is a place in the collaborative process where there's plenty of room for misunderstanding. There are few clear standards about procedures and fees during the initial design stages of a project; later on, there are firm contracts, tangible work, and more fully articulated schedules and responsibilities.

In an effort to help make the partnerships between clients, design professionals, and artists most rewarding to everyone involved, we've put together a short checklist based on interviews with artists who work extensively on

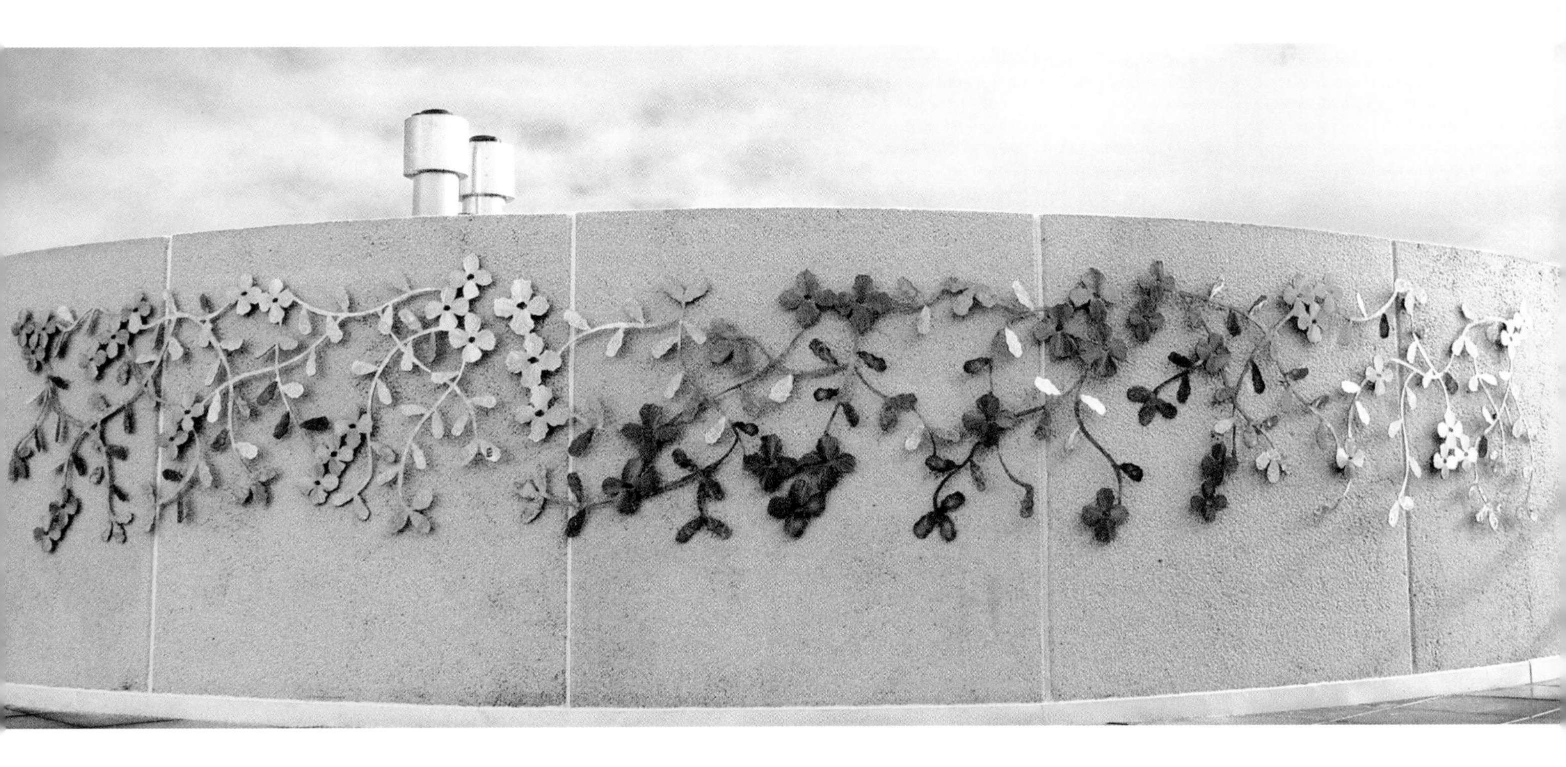

Above: Martin Sturman, exterior wall hanging, Royal Caribbean Cruise Lines, Springfield, OR. Photograph: Barry Michlin.

MARTIN STURMAN

Royal Caribbean Cruise Lines, Eugene, OR

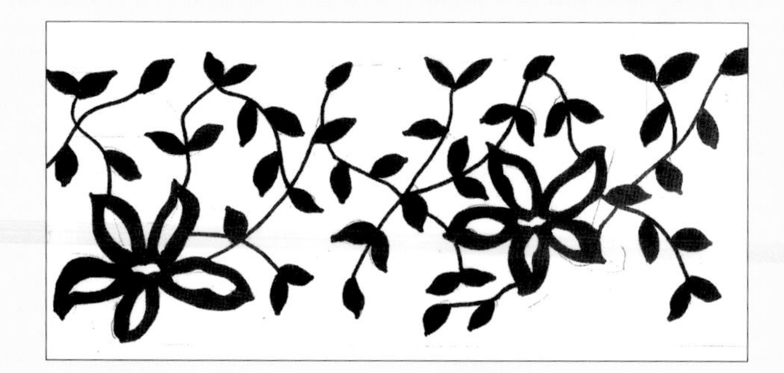

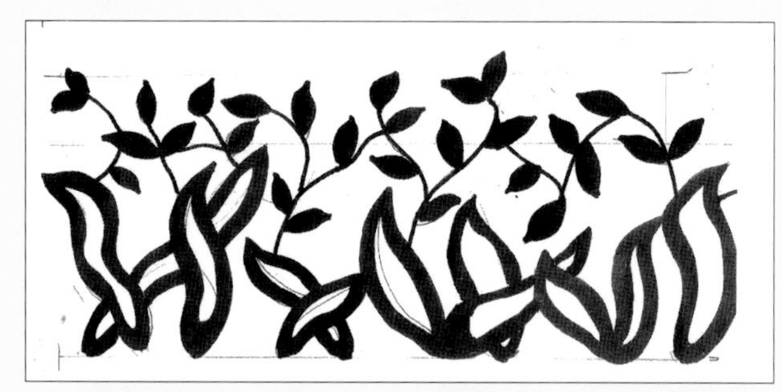

It could be argued that one indicator of a great designer is the willingness to proceed with a concept even though it will mean executing a medium in a completely new way, because it's what the design requires.

When Martin Sturman received a phone call from art consultant Dana Bailey about creating some large metal wall hangings for Royal Caribbean's Eugene, Oregon, office, he knew some new technical skills would be required.

"Dana asked me about creating three twenty-foot interior wall pieces and one thirty-foot exterior piece [see page 11]," Sturman recalls. "The interior pieces had to bend to match the exterior curve of the round conference rooms, and that was something I had never done before."

It didn't deter the artist, however, whose designs immediately appealed to the client. "I didn't have to do much back-and-forth with Martin on this," Bailey notes. "Royal Caribbean's Eugene office is a very modern, green building. Much of the artwork in the building has to do with nature and the environment. They wanted three-dimensional wall pieces that would continue this theme while also providing visual stimulation for the employees who work there."

Sturman's concept of showing three of the four seasons seemed like a good way to meet the client's theme without showing identical pieces of artwork. "I showed Dana some sketches," the artist says, "which she modified only slightly by making the leaf tips more rounded, so that no one would risk getting caught up or injured on sharp metal edges."

"The client was great," Bailey concludes. "They trusted me, they were very decisive, and they could envision from Martin's sketches what the final piece would look like. These pieces were also easy to install. Everyone was thrilled with the outcome."

Dana Bailey owns ArtFolio, an art consulting business in Wellington, FL, tel: 561-753-8494; e-mail artfodb@bellsouth.net.

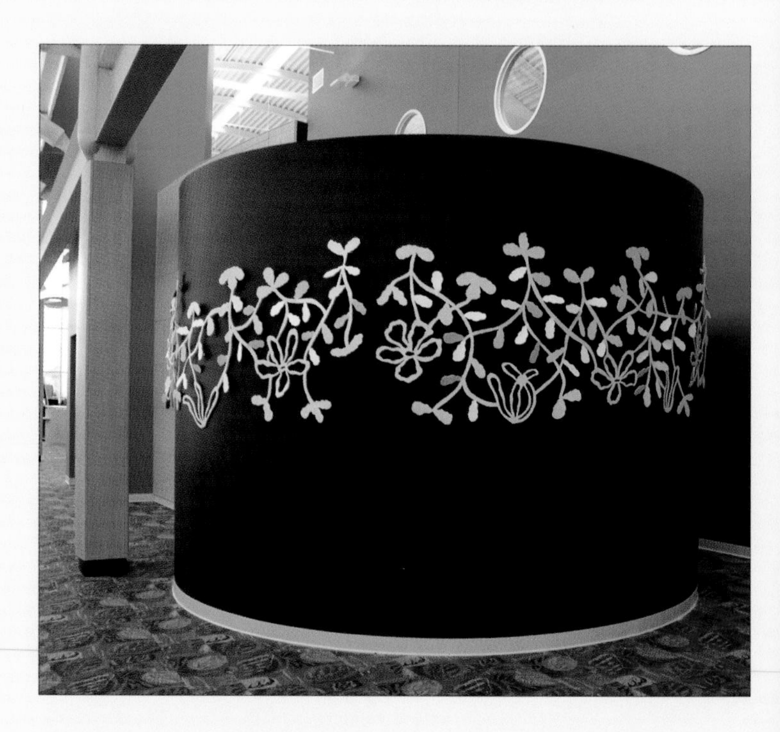

See more of Martin Sturman's work on page 168. Photograph: Barry Michlin.

collaborative projects. While each artist has an individual way of working, this list includes the design issues that most agree should be addressed for a truly successful creative relationship.

We also share a few collaboration stories, where the artist had a starring role in the project's design, thanks to the support and confidence of the trade professional, who was thus able to exceed client expectations. We hope you'll find these stories both enjoyable and inspiring.

1. EXPECT TO PAY FOR DESIGN

We should say up front that not every artist charges a design fee. Some consider preliminary sketches a part of their marketing effort and figure they will be compensated for their time by the client once the project is approved. But it's more common for an artist to require a design fee of 5%-10% of the final project budget. In some cases, especially when the artist has considerable experience and a strong reputation in a specialized area, the design fee may be as high as 25% of the project budget. That's most likely if the artist is asked to provide specific solutions to complicated architectural problems. Obviously, in this kind of situation, the artist is not merely asked to supply a product, but rather is expected to contribute a significant part of the design solution, when ideas and experience are as important as his or her tangible work.

2. CONSIDER A SEPARATE DESIGN BUDGET FOR YOUR PROJECT

A design budget is particularly helpful when you:

- want to get lots of ideas from an artist;
- need site-specific ideas that involve significant research;
- require a formal presentation with finished drawings, blueprints, or maquettes.

To evaluate designs for a project from several artists, consider having a competition with a small design fee for each artist.

3. RESPECT THE ARTIST'S IDEAS AND VISION

When we hire a doctor, we want a thoughtful, intelligent diagnosis, not just a course of treatment. The same should be true when we hire an artist to work with a design team. Most Guild artists have become successful through many years of experience, and because of their excellence in technique and aesthetic imagination. Take advantage of that by bringing the artist into the project early, and asking him or her for ideas.

4. DESIGN IDEAS ARE THE ARTIST'S PROPERTY

It should go without saying that it is highly unethical, as well as illegal, to take an artist's designs—even very preliminary or non-site-specific sketches—and use them without the artist's permission. Some artists may include specific language about ownership of ideas, models, sketches, etc., in their contracts or letters of agreement. Even if an artist does not use a written agreement, be sure you are clear at the outset about what you are paying for and what rights the artist retains.

5. KEEP THE ARTIST INFORMED OF CHANGES

Tell the artist about changes—even seemingly minor details—that may have a significant impact on the project design. A change in location or materials, or a change in the area surrounding the artist's work may be critical to the way the design is developed, or the work is actually created. If the artist is working as a member of the design team, it's easier to include him or her in the ongoing dialogue about the overall project and the details that make things go smoothly.

It comes down to an issue of professionalism. Artists today have the technical skills to do wonderful and amazing things with simple materials. But they also have sophisticated conceptual and design talents. By making use of these talents and skills, and being willing to pay for them, trade professionals add vision and variety to their creative products. In such a partnership, both parties gain, and the ultimate result is a client who is delighted by the outcome of the collaboration.

ULRICH PAKKER

Everett Event Center, Everett, WA

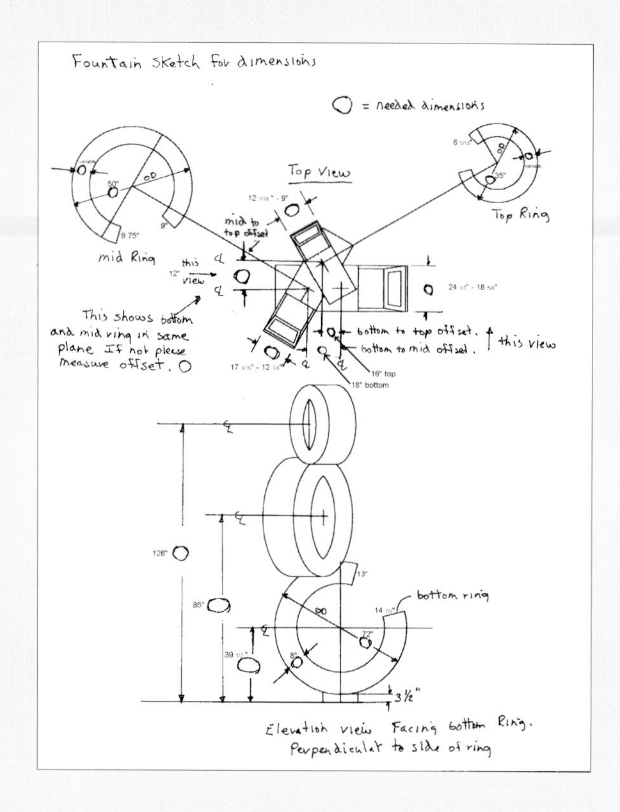

The nice thing about a good design is that once you have one, you can use it and modify it over and over again without ever creating exactly the same piece.

When the Everett Events Center in Everett, Washington, held a competition for an iconic public art sculpture/fountain, Ulrich Pakker, with help from his wife, Pamela, went to work on a design that had already been percolating in his mind.

"Ulrich was thinking about ways to minimize or eliminate the open basin at the bottom of his fountains so that viewers could instead really focus on the design of the piece," Pamela Pakker-Kozicki reports. "It just so happened that the Everett Event Center was looking for the same design for this piece."

"We were interested in having a water feature to encourage community members to use and gather at the building," notes project engineer Hal Gausman. "Ulrich's proposal was selected from three finalists because we really liked the monumental scale of his piece and how he incorporated the water element. It really seemed to capture the energy of the events center."

To create the design, Pamela took photos of existing pieces, which had been photographed from all angles, and put them together for Ulrich to modify. They began with a simple circular element, and their masterpiece grew from there.

Trained as a journeyman sheet metal worker at the age of seventeen, Ulrich calculated measurements and angles to ensure the mathematics and physics would support his artistic vision. He immediately went to work on a ten-foot version of the piece. "He was eager to get

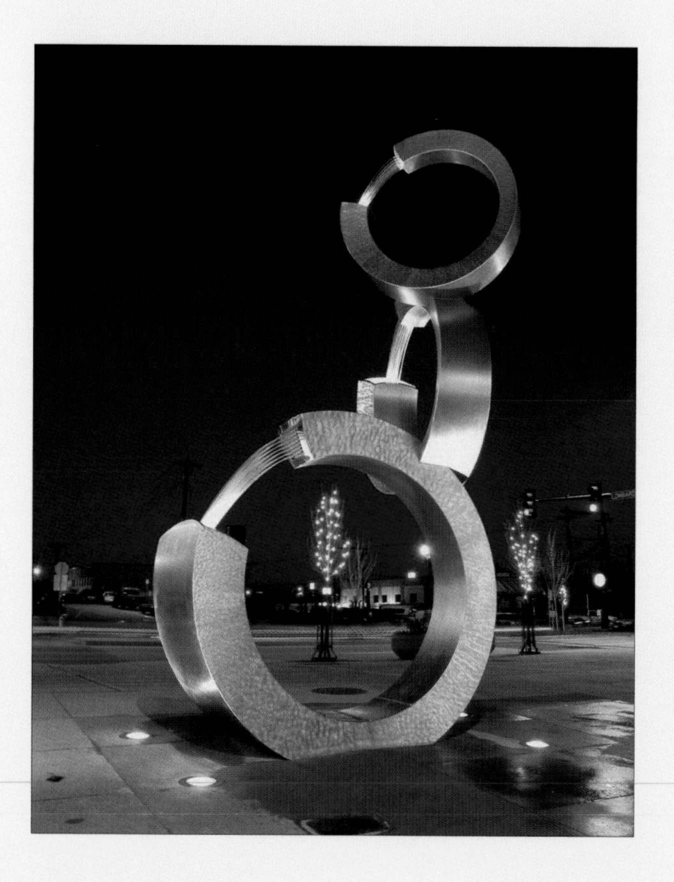

See more of Ulrich Pakker's work on page 97.

his hands on the metal and start working," Pamela recalls. "He's not much of a 'sketch guy.'"

In creating the piece, Ulrich was determined that the piece function as much as a sculpture as it did as a fountain. "It's something he does innately with all of his designs," his wife explains. "If it doesn't work as a sculpture for him, it can't work as a fountain."

This philosophy was evident once the installation took place. The twenty-foot *Trivergence* was installed in late October, but because of the center's plumbing and electrical issues, they weren't able to turn on the water until March. "People really seemed to love it as a sculpture—they didn't even realize it was a fountain," she reports. "When we turned on the water in March, it was like icing on the cake."

"The piece is great," Gausman adds. "The community loves it, and visitors always want to have their picture taken in front of it."

Pakker has since repeated variations of the design in other works—in all sizes and formations [see below]. "It's all about the design," Pakker-Kozicki concludes. "They have to have the engineering to be graceful and successful works of art."

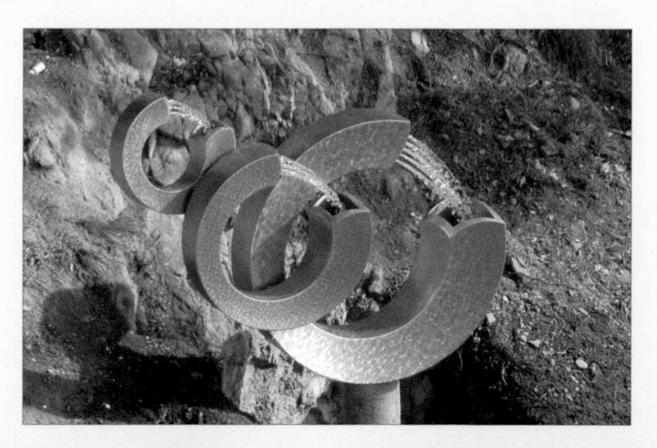

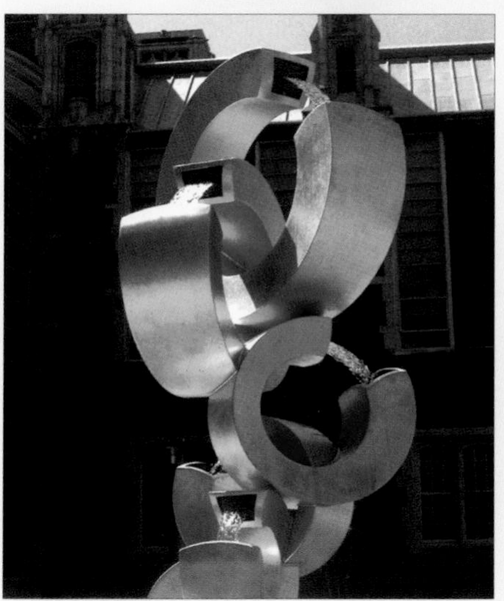

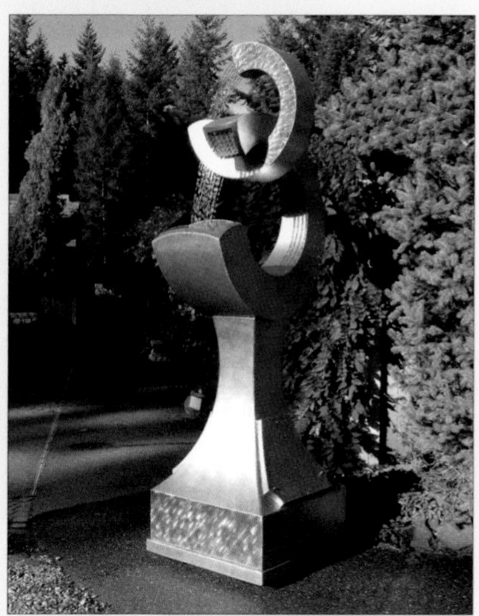

Above: Ulrich Pakker, top: *Bouncing Rolling,* 5'H x 6'W x 2'D; bottom left: *Ascending Waters,* 9'H x 5'W x 4'D; bottom right: *Divergence,* 8'H x 3'W x 3.5'D.

ELLEN MANDELBAUM

Holy Spirit Catholic Community Church, Naperville, IL

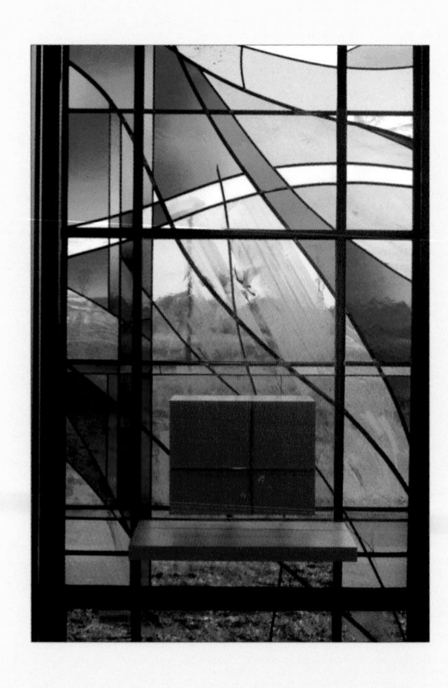

Good design can elicit more than a beautifully crafted piece of artwork; it also has the power to lift spirits. A few years ago, glass artist Ellen Mandelbaum was contacted by liturgical consultants from INAI Studio of Adrian, MI, about creating a stained glass window for the new Blessed Sacrament Chapel of the Holy Spirit Catholic Community Church in Naperville, IL.

"My inspiration for the design of that window, *Wind of the Spirit,* came from a variety of sources," Mandelbaum recalls. "During the design process, I visited with Father Richard Bennett and the liturgical designers, who were looking for a meditative piece. The committee mentioned that the church often incorporated banners into their religious celebrations, and I really loved the idea of including a banner design in my piece, one that would lift the eyes, and spirit, upward."

"We were attracted to Ellen's work for its elusive painterly effect," reports INAI liturgical designer Barbara Chenicek, OP. (Mandelbaum often uses a technique of painting her glass with metal oxides, then firing the glass again to make these brushstrokes permanent.)

In 2006, INAI Studio was honored with a Merit Award for Liturgical/Interior Design from Faith & Form for their work on the Holy Spirit Catholic Community Church. INAI (it means "within") has worked strictly with the design of sacred spaces for over thirty years.

Ellen Mandelbaum has since followed up with the church about adding more windows to her original creation. "The church was so excited about that original piece that I created a sketch of what some additional windows might look like. I really want the motion to flow from one window to the next, and I think I will accomplish that in my final design."

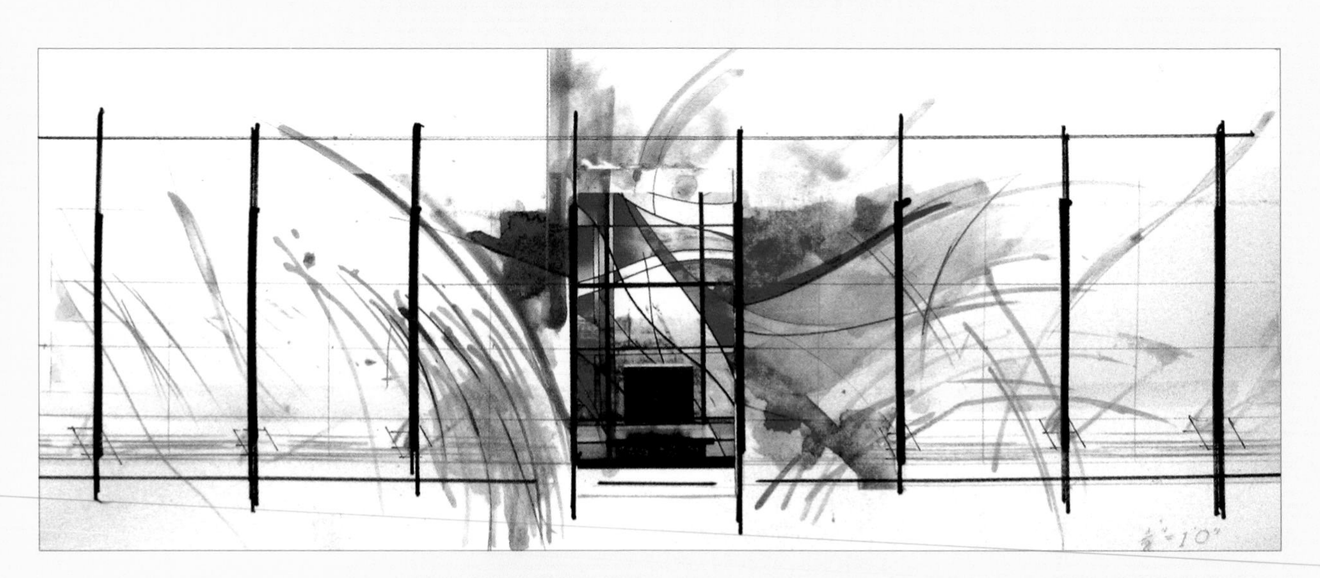

See more of Ellen Mandelbaum's work on page 47. Photograph: Scott Pfeiffer.

THE COMMISSION PROCESS

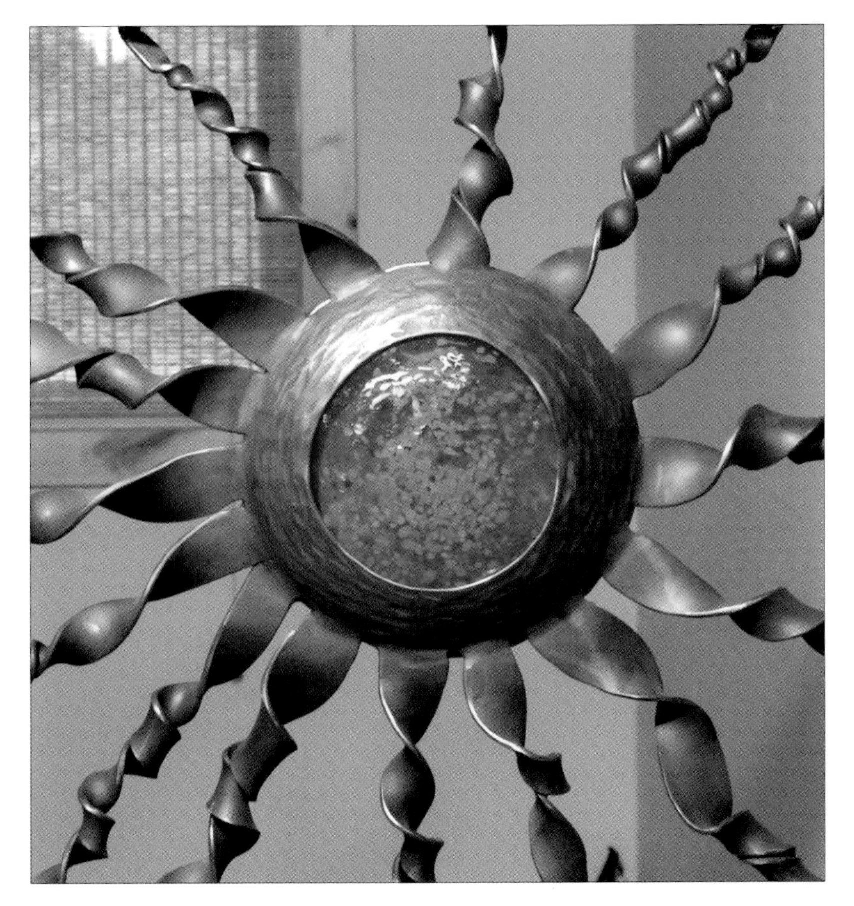

By far the most important step in a successful commission is choosing the right artist for your particular project and budget. The right choices at this early stage will make things go more smoothly later on.

The more than two hundred artists featured in *The Guild Sourcebook of Architectural & Interior Art 22* represent a remarkable spectrum of artistic talent and vision. Whether you're looking for a large-scale public sculpture or a residential accessory, this book can put you directly in touch with highly qualified artists throughout North America. Any one of these artists can be commissioned to create a unique work of art—but with so many exceptional artists to choose from, finding the right one for your specific project can be a challenge. Once the artist has been selected, careful planning and communication can help ensure a great outcome.

Having watched art commissions unfold since the first Guild Sourcebook was published in 1986, we can suggest steps to ensure successful partnerships between artists and trade professionals. We especially want to reassure those who have been reluctant to try such a collaboration because of questions about how the process works.

This article is a how-to guide to the art commissioning process. It suggests strategies to help selection and hiring go smoothly. It also describes steps that can help establish shared (and realistic) expectations on the part of artists and clients, and explains the advantages of including the artist in the design team early in the planning process.

FINDING THE ARTIST

By far the most important step in a successful commission is choosing the right artist for your particular project and budget. This choice is the decision from which all others will flow, so it's worth investing time and energy in the selection process and seasoning the search with both wild artistic hopes and hard-nosed realism. The right choices at this early stage will make things go more smoothly later on.

Some clients will want to help select and work with the artist. Others will want only minimal involvement, leaving most of the decision-making to the design team.

Above: Lee Proctor, *Sun Railings* (detail), see page 193. Photograph: Nicole Holdener.

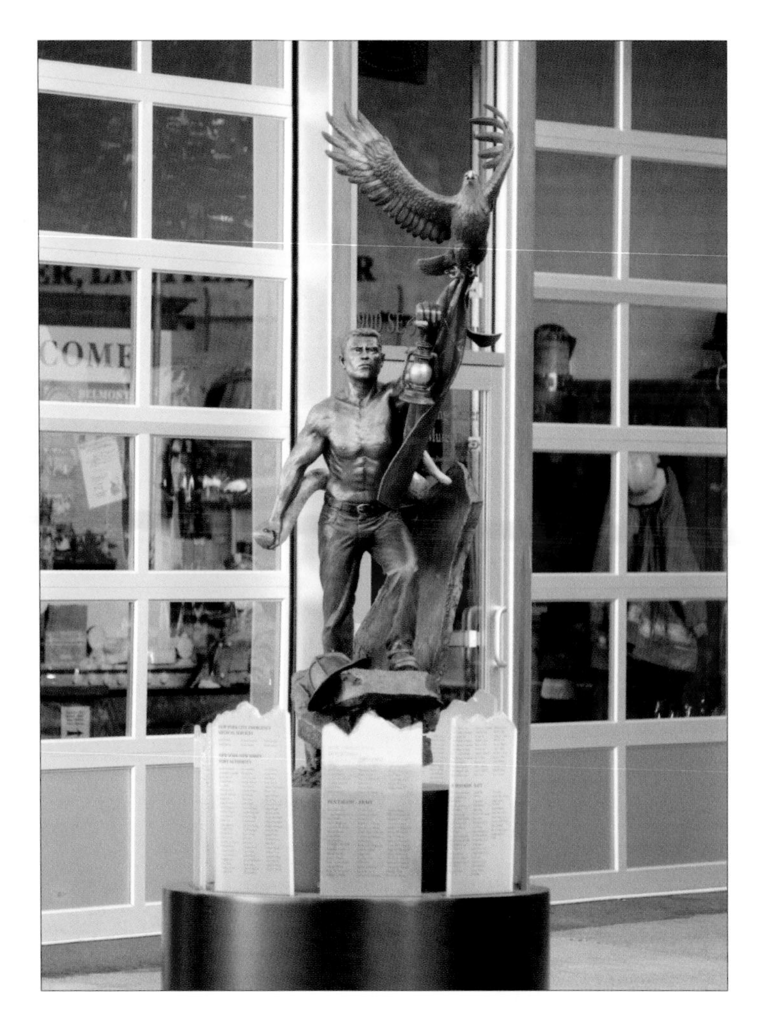

No matter who makes the decisions, there are several ways to find the right artist. Obviously, we recommend browsing through *The Guild Sourcebook of Architectural & Interior Art 22*. Every artist featured on these pages is actively seeking commission projects—that's why they're included in the book. Many of these artists have already established strong track records working with designers, architects, and art consultants; you will gain from their professionalism and experience. Others are newer in their field; their determination to prove themselves can fuel an exciting and successful collaboration.

NARROWING THE FIELD

Once your A-list is narrowed down to two or three names, it's time to schedule meetings, either face-to-face or by phone. As you talk, try to determine the artist's interest in your project, and pay attention to your own comfort level with the artist. Try to find out if the chemistry is right—whether you have the basis to build a working relationship. This is also the time to confirm that the artist has the necessary skills to undertake your project. Be thorough and specific when asking questions. Is the artist excited about the project? What does he or she see as the most important issues or considerations? Will your needs be a major or minor concern? Evaluate the artist's style, approach, and personality.

If it feels like you might have trouble working together, take heed. But if all goes well and it feels like a good fit, ask for a list of references. These are important calls; don't neglect to make them! Ask about the artist's work habits, communication style, and, of course, the success of the artwork. You should also ask whether the project was delivered on time and within budget. If you like what you hear, you'll be one important step closer to hiring your artist.

EXPECT PROFESSIONALISM

If this is an expensive or complicated project, you may want to request preliminary designs. Since most artists charge a design fee whether or not they're ultimately hired for the project, start by asking for sketches from your top candidate. If you're unhappy with the designs submitted, you can go to your second choice. But if the design is what you'd hoped for, it's time to finalize your working agreement with this artist.

As you discuss contract details, be resolved that silence is not golden and ignorance is not bliss! Be frank. Discuss the budget and timetable, and tell the artist what you expect. Now is the time for possible misunderstandings to be brought up and resolved—not later, when the work is half done and deadlines loom.

WORKING WITH AN ART CONSULTANT

As your project gains definition, you'll need to pay attention to its technical aspects, including building codes, lighting specifications, and details related to zoning and installation. Most designers find the artist's knowledge and understanding of materials, code, safety, and en-

Above: *Strength of America* by Rip Caswell, see pages 144-145. Photograph: Timothy J. Park.

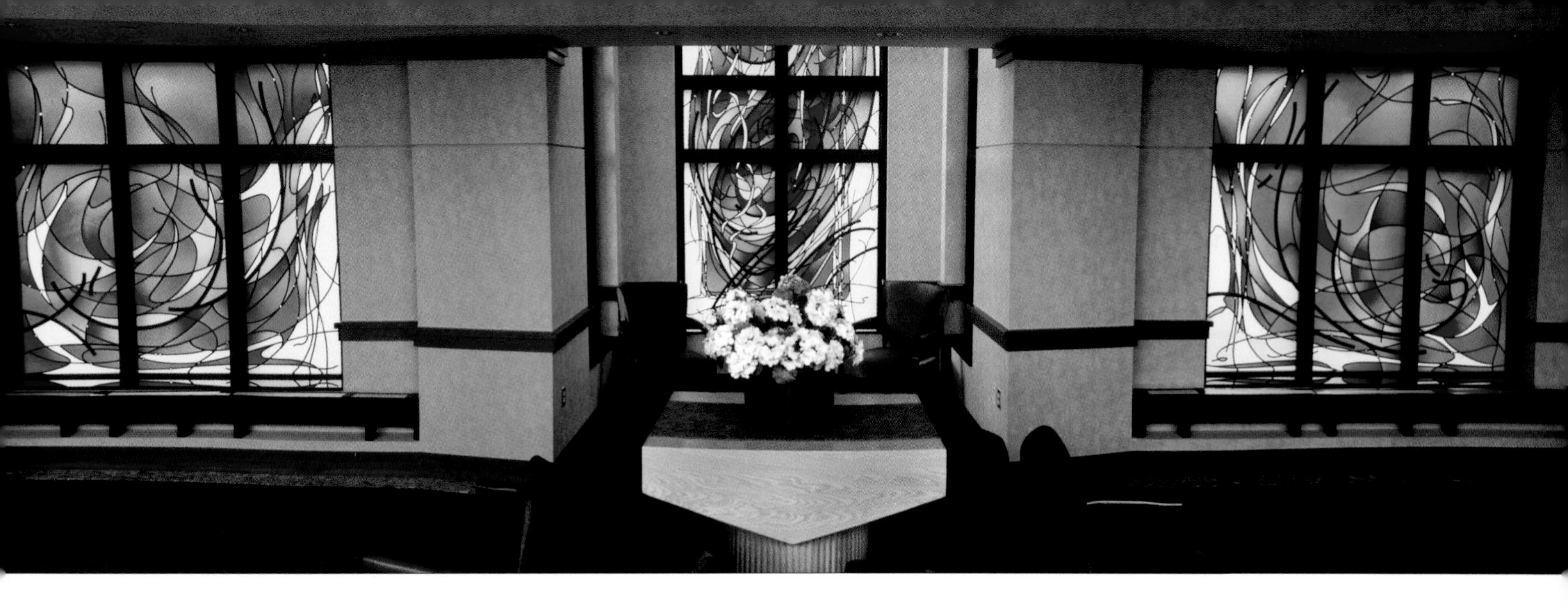

gineering complete and reassuring. However, complex projects may warrant hiring an art consultant to help with these details, as well as the initial selection of art and artists. Just as you would when hiring any other professional, call references to be sure the consultant you hire is sophisticated and experienced enough to provide real guidance with your project. This means the ability to help negotiate the technical aspects of a very specific contract, including issues like installation, insurance, storage, transportation, and engineering costs.

PUTTING IT IN WRITING

It is a truism in any kind of business that it is much cheaper to get the lawyers involved at the beginning of a process rather than after something goes wrong. A signed contract or letter of agreement commits the artist to completing his or her work on time and to specifications. It also assures the artist that he or she will get paid the right amount at the right time.

Contracts should be specific to the job. Customarily, artists are responsible for design, production, shipping, and installation. If someone else will install the artwork, be sure you specify who will coordinate and pay for the installation; if not the artist, it's usually the client. With a large project, it's helpful to identify the tasks that, if delayed for any reason, would set back completion of the project. These should be discussed up front to ensure that both parties agree on requirements and expectations.

Most trade professionals recognize that adequately compensating artists ensures the level of service needed to fulfill the client's expectations. The more complex the project, the more you should budget for the artist's work and services.

PAYMENT SCHEDULE

Payments are usually tied to specific milestones in the process. These serve as checkpoints and confirm that work is progressing in a satisfactory manner, on time, and on budget. Payment is customarily made in three stages, although this will certainly depend on the circumstances, scope, and complexity of the project. The first payment is usually made when the contract is signed. It covers the artist's time and creativity in developing a detailed design specific to your needs. You can expect to go through several rounds of trial and error in the design process, but at the end of this stage you will have detailed drawings (and, for three-dimensional work, a maquette, or model) that everyone agrees upon. The cost of the maquette and the design time are usually factored into the artist's fee.

The second payment is generally set for a point midway through the project and is for work completed to date. If the materials are expensive, the client may be asked to advance money at this stage to cover costs. If the commission is canceled during this period, the artist keeps the money already paid for work performed.

Final payment is usually due when the work is installed. If the piece is finished on time but the building or project is delayed, the artist is customarily paid on delivery, but still has the obligation to oversee installation.

Above: Cindy Kessler, Central DuPage Hospital Chapel windows, see page 43.

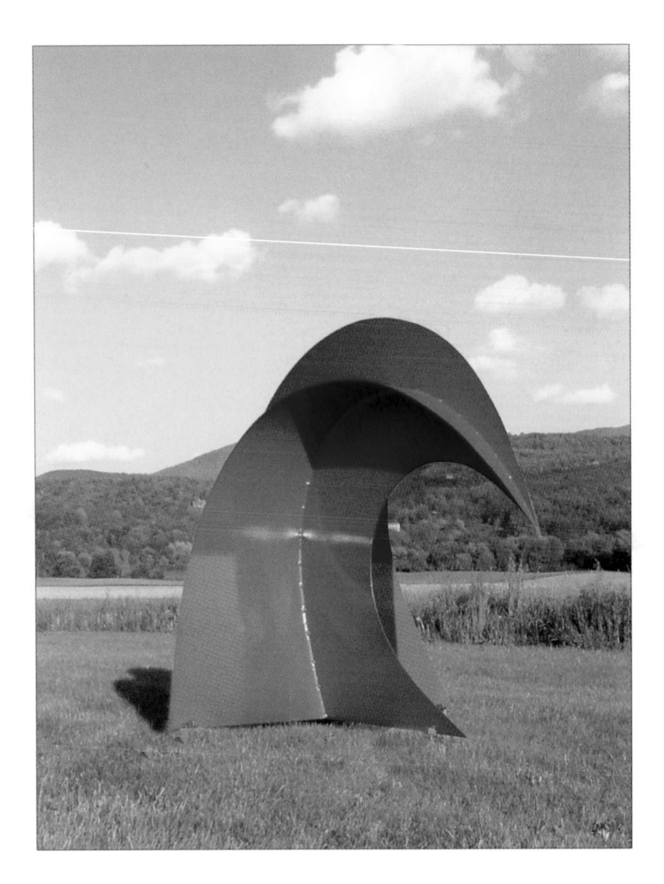

You will find that most artists keep tabs on the project budget. Be sure that the project scope does not deviate from what was agreed upon at the outset. If the scope changes, amend the agreement to reflect the changes.

A COLLABORATIVE ATMOSPHERE

With most commission projects, it's best to bring the artist into the process at about the same time you hire a general contractor. By involving the artist at this early stage, the space will be designed with the art in mind, and the art will be designed to enhance the space. As a result, there will be no unpleasant surprises about size or suitability of artwork. Furthermore, when art is planned for early on and included as a line item in the budget, it's far less likely to be cut at the end of the project, when money is running low.

Early inclusion of the artist also helps ensure that the collaborative effort will flow smoothly throughout all phases of the project. If the artist is respected as part of the team, his or her work can benefit the project's overall design.

Naturally, the scope of the project will determine the number of players to be involved with the artist. How will decisions be made? Who is the artist's primary liaison? Will a single person sign off on designs and recommendations? Are committees necessary? It's important that all individuals understand both their own responsibilities and the responsibilities of their collaborators.

SEEK TWO-WAY UNDERSTANDING

Be sure the artist understands the technical requirements of the job, including traffic flow, intended use of space, building structure, maintenance, lighting, and environmental concerns. By fully explaining these details, you'll ensure that the artist's knowledge, experience, and skills inform the project.

Keep the artist apprised of any changes that will affect the work in progress. Did you find a specified material unavailable and replace it with something else? Did the available space become bigger or smaller? These changes could have a profound impact on an artist's planning.

At the same time, the artist should let you know of any special requirements that his or her work will place on the space. Is it especially heavy? Does it need to be mounted in a specific way? Must it be protected from theft or vandalism? What kind of lighting is best? You may need to budget funds for these kinds of installation or maintenance expenses.

Most artists experienced with commissioned projects factor the expense of a continuing design dialog into their fee. There is an unfortunate belief harbored by some trade professionals (and yes, artists too) that a willingness to develop and adapt a design based on discussions with the client or design team somehow indicates a lack of commitment or creativity. On the contrary. The ability to modify design or execution without compromising artistic quality is a mark of professionalism. We recommend looking for this quality in the artist you choose, and then respecting it by treating the artist as a partner in any decisions that will affect his or her work.

Of course, part of working together is making clear who is responsible for what. Since few designers and architects (and even fewer contractors) are accustomed to working with artists, the relationship is ripe for misun-

Above: Gordon Auchincloss, *Red Wave*, see page 67. Photograph: Reid Bailey.

derstanding. Without constant communication, things can easily fall through the cracks.

FORGING A PARTNERSHIP

The partnership between artists and trade professionals is an old and honorable one. Many venerable blueprints indicate, for example, an architect's detail for a ceiling with the scrawled note: "Finish ceiling in this manner." The assumption, of course, is that the artisan working on the ceiling has both the technical mastery and the aesthetic skill to create a whole expanse of space based on a detail sketched by the architect's pen.

The artists whose work fills these pages—and with whom we work every day at The Guild—are capable of interactive relationships like those described here. We're delighted to see increasing numbers of trade professionals include artists on their design teams. After seeing the arts separated from architectural and interior design for too many years, we're happy to be part of a renewed interest in collaboration.

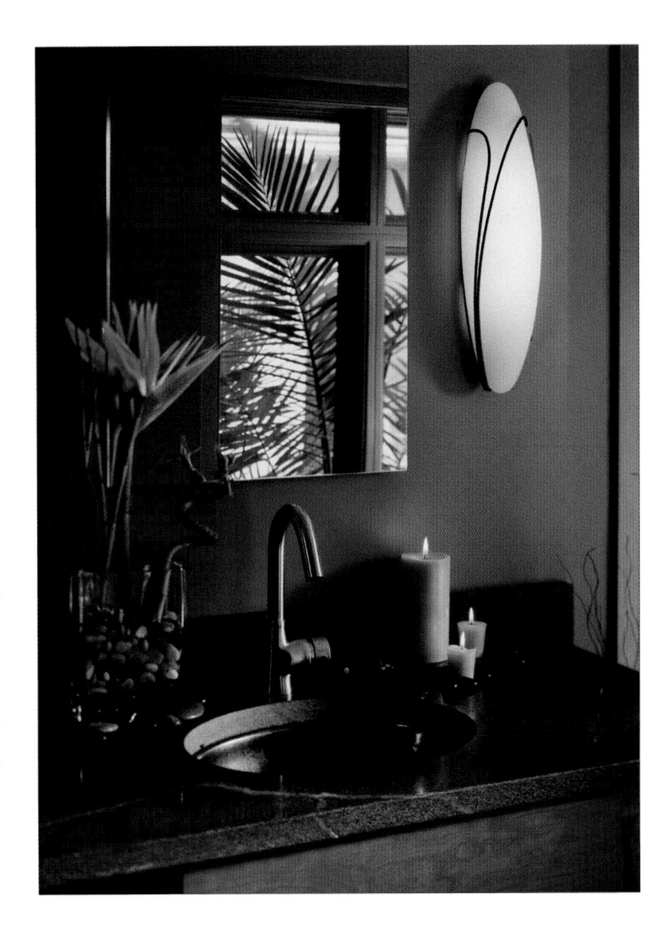

COMMISSION GUIDELINES

- Bring the artist into the project as early as possible.
- Be as specific as possible about the scope and range of the project, even in early meetings before the artist is selected.
- Be honest and realistic when discussing deadlines, responsibilities, and specific project requirements—and expect the same from the artist. Don't avoid discussing areas where there seem to be questions.
- For larger projects, use specific milestones to assure continuing consensus on project scope and budget. It may also be necessary to make adjustments at these points.
- Choose an artist based on a solid portfolio of previous work and excellent references. It's less risky to use an artist who has worked on projects of similar size and scope, who can handle the demands of your specific job.
- Consider hiring an art consultant if the commission is particularly large or complex. The consultant should help with complicated contract arrangements and make certain that communication between artists and support staff (including subcontractors and engineers) is thoroughly understood.
- Trust your instincts when choosing an artist. Like selecting an advertising agency or an architect, choosing an artist is based partly on chemistry. You need to like the work and respect the artist, and you also need to be able to work together comfortably.

Above: Hubbardton Forge, *Oval Sconce*, see page 188. Photograph: Jim Westphalen Photography.

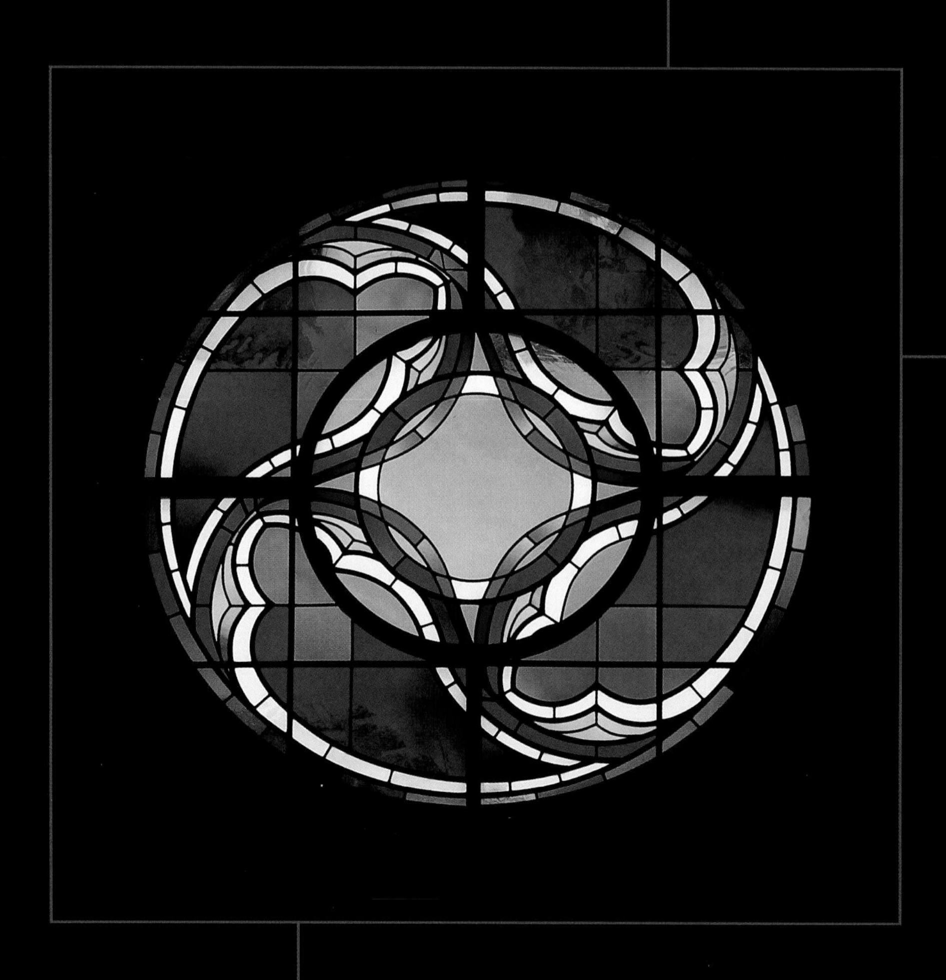

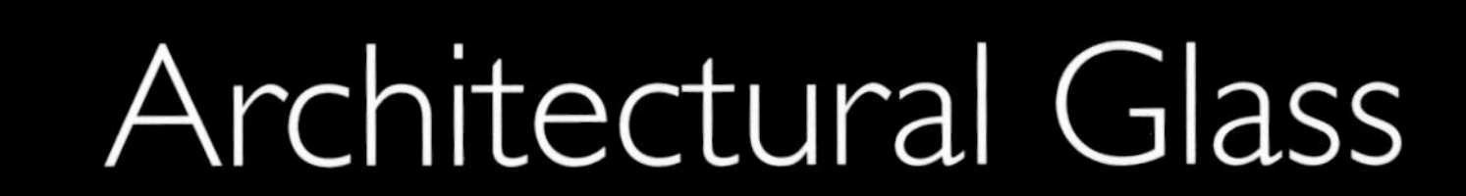

Architectural Glass

KATHY BARNARD

KATHY BARNARD STUDIO ■ 1605 LOCUST STREET ■ KANSAS CITY, MO 64108 ■ TEL 816-472-4977
FAX 816-471-0984 ■ E-MAIL KATHY@KATHYBARNARDSTUDIO.COM ■ WWW.KATHYBARNARDSTUDIO.COM

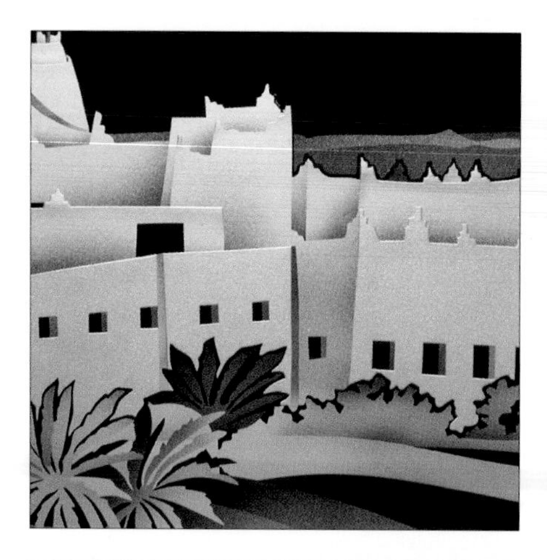

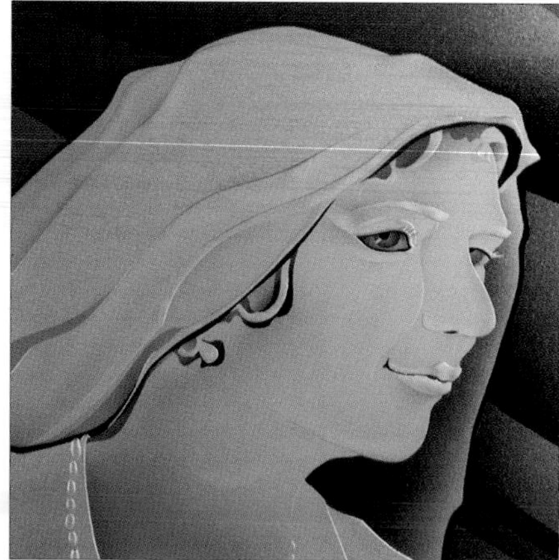

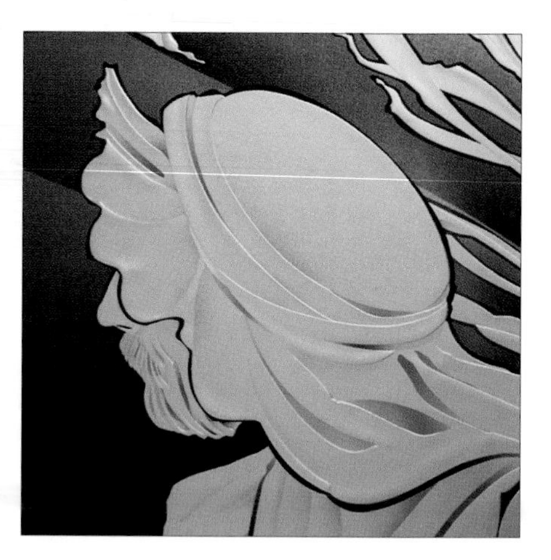

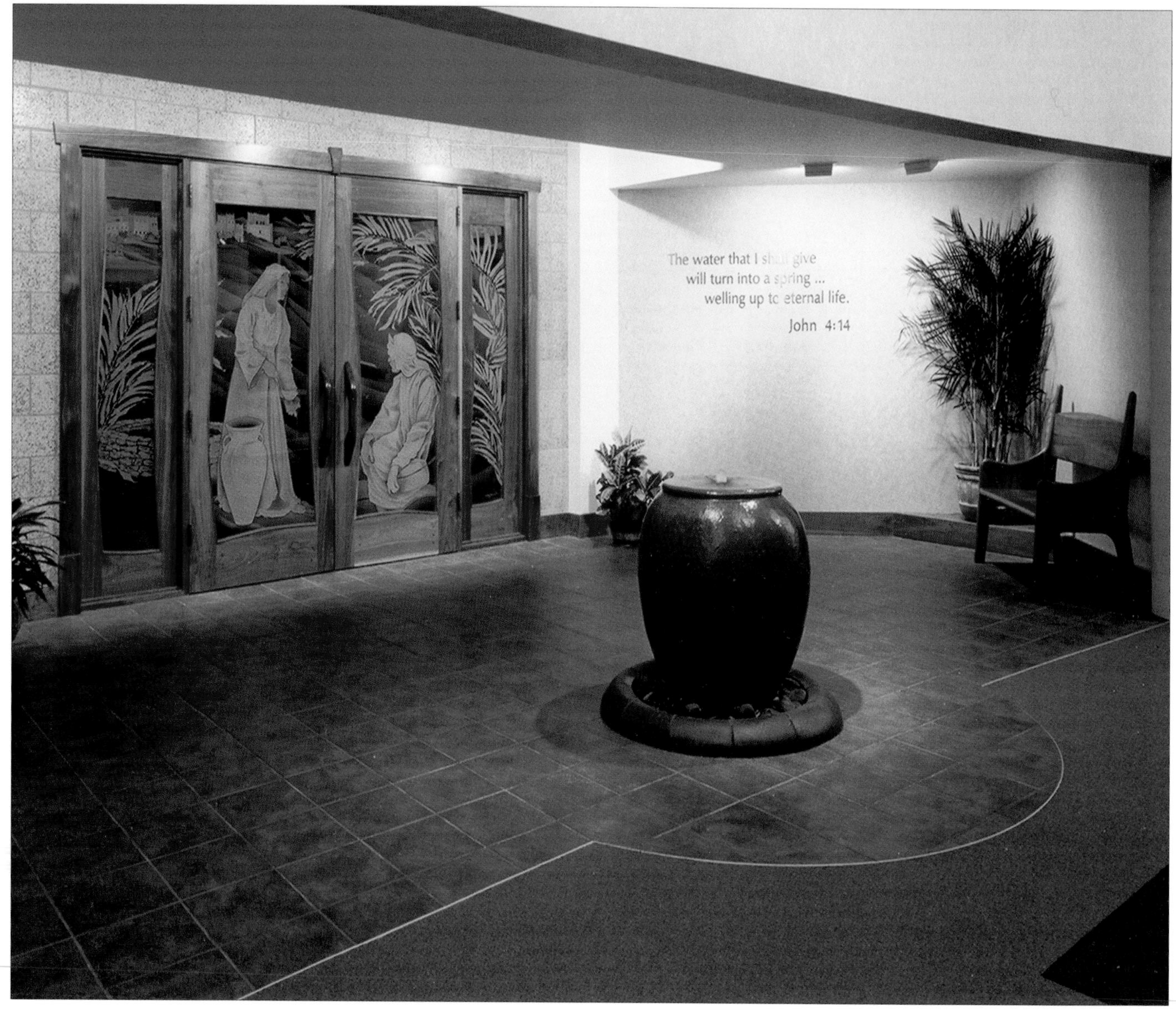

Samaritan Woman at the Well with Jesus, Chapel of Mercy, Assisted Living & Memory Care Facility, Wichita, KS, deep-carved glass, 12' x 8'.

KATHY BARNARD

KATHY BARNARD STUDIO ■ 1605 LOCUST STREET ■ KANSAS CITY, MO 64108 ■ TEL 816-472-4977
FAX 816-471-0984 ■ E-MAIL KATHY@KATHYBARNARDSTUDIO.COM ■ WWW.KATHYBARNARDSTUDIO.COM

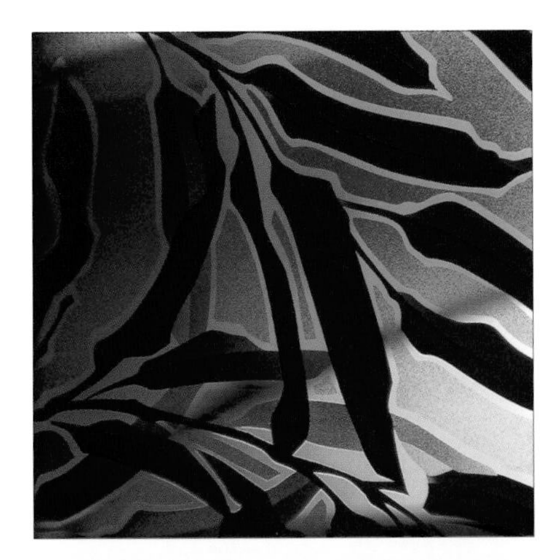

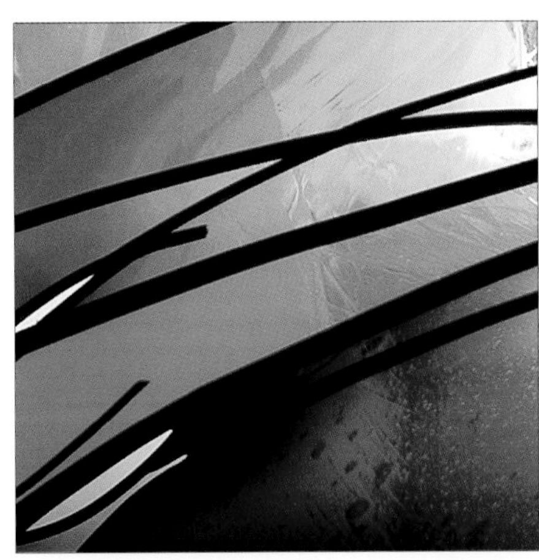

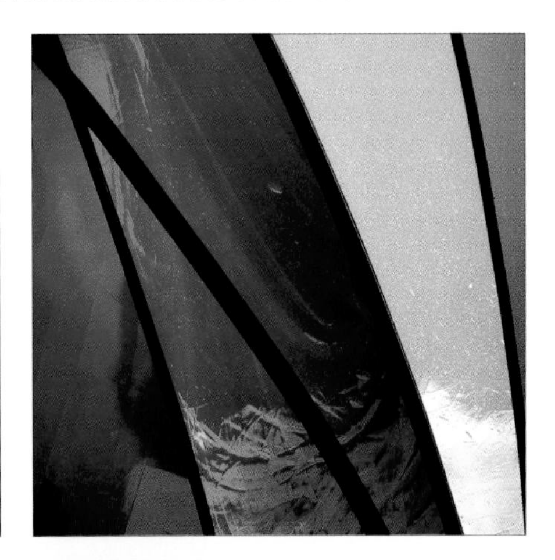

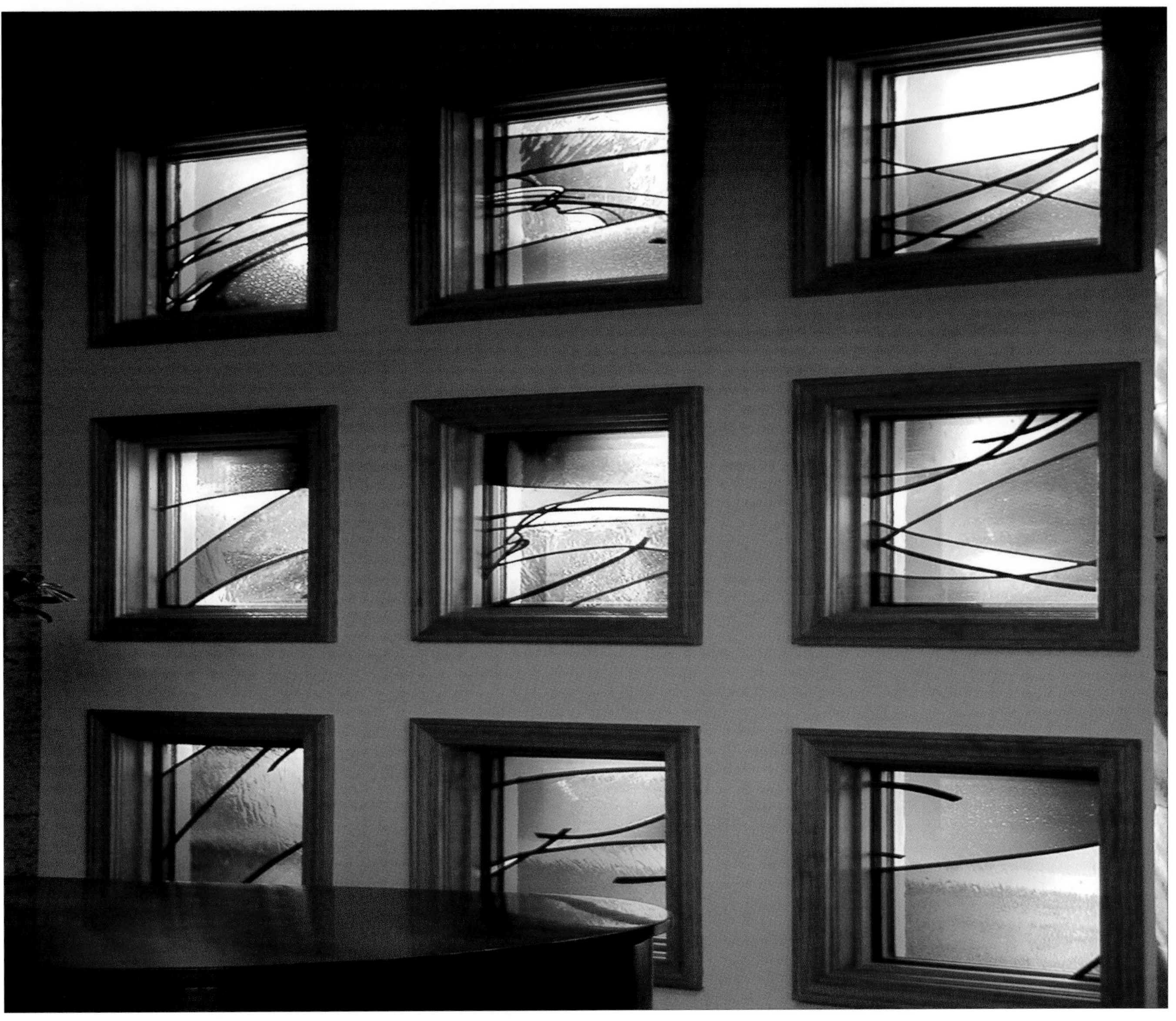

Chapel of Mercy, Assisted Living & Memory Care Facility, Wichita, KS, stained glass wall.

MATTHEW BEZARK

MOUNTAIN GLASSWORKS ■ 2777 MIDDLE FORK ROAD ■ BOULDER, CO 80302 ■ TEL 303-434-7267
FAX 303-417-1383 ■ E-MAIL MATTBEZARK@MAC.COM ■ WWW.MOUNTAINGLASSWORKS.COM

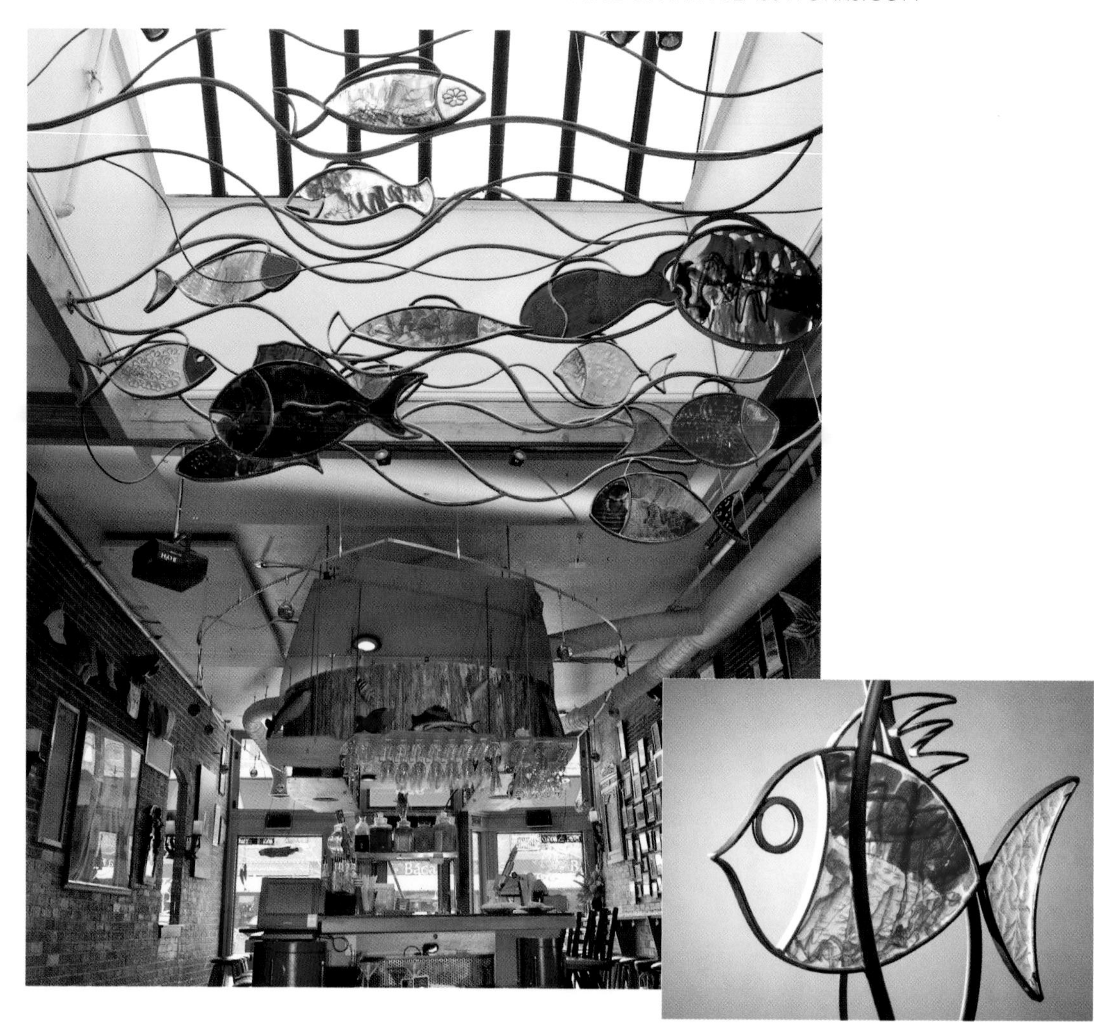

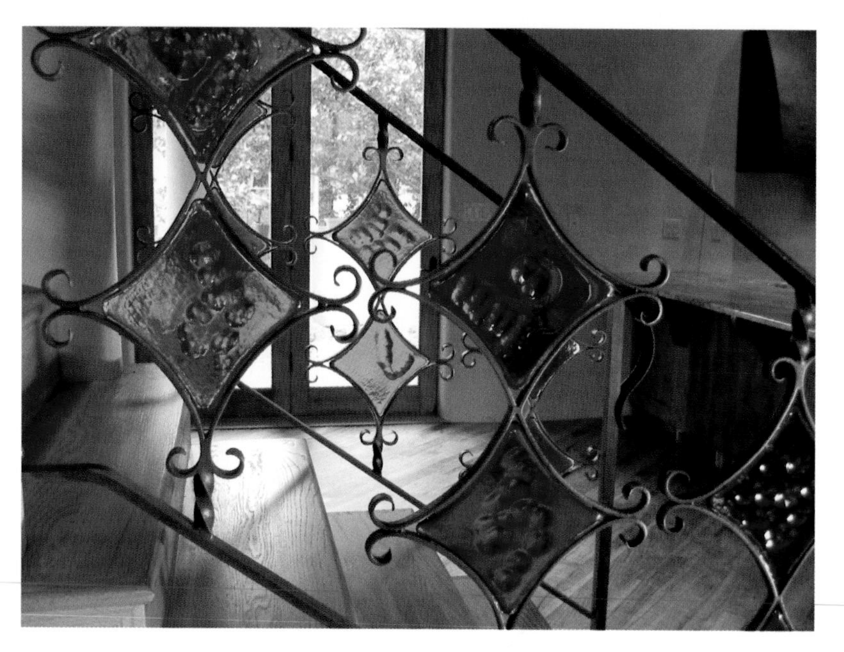

Top: Jax Fish House, Boulder, CO, hand-poured glass with steel, 6' x 12' x 12'. Photograph: Robert Kittila.
Inset: Jax Fish House. Photograph: Joshua Cohen. Bottom: Railing for private residence, hand-poured glass and hand-forged steel.

KATHY BRADFORD

NORTH STAR ART GLASS, INC. ▪ 142 WICHITA ▪ LYONS, CO 80540 ▪ TEL 303-823-6511
FAX 303-823-5350 ▪ E-MAIL KATHYBRADFORD@EARTHLINK.NET ▪ WWW.KATHYBRADFORD.COM

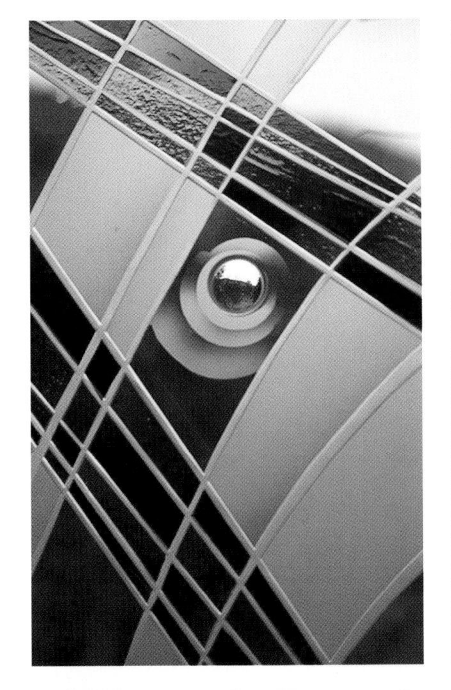

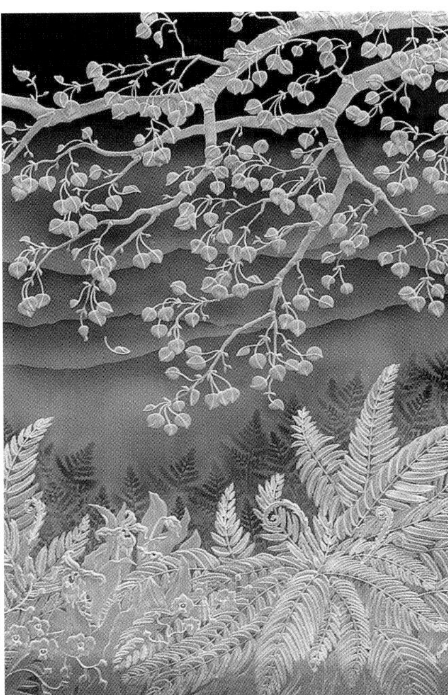

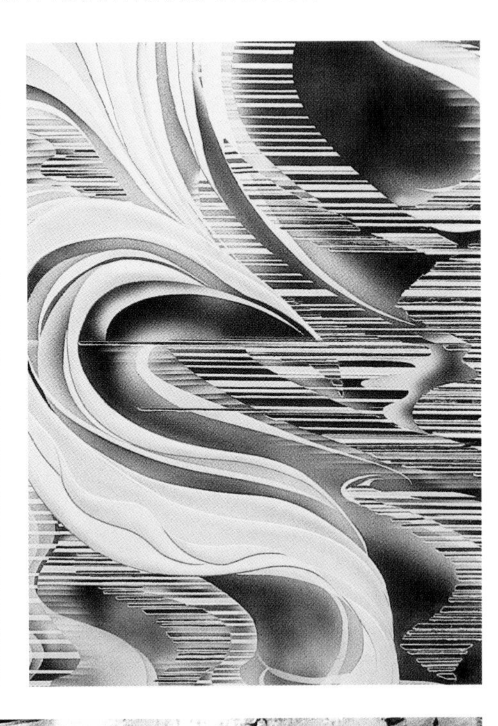

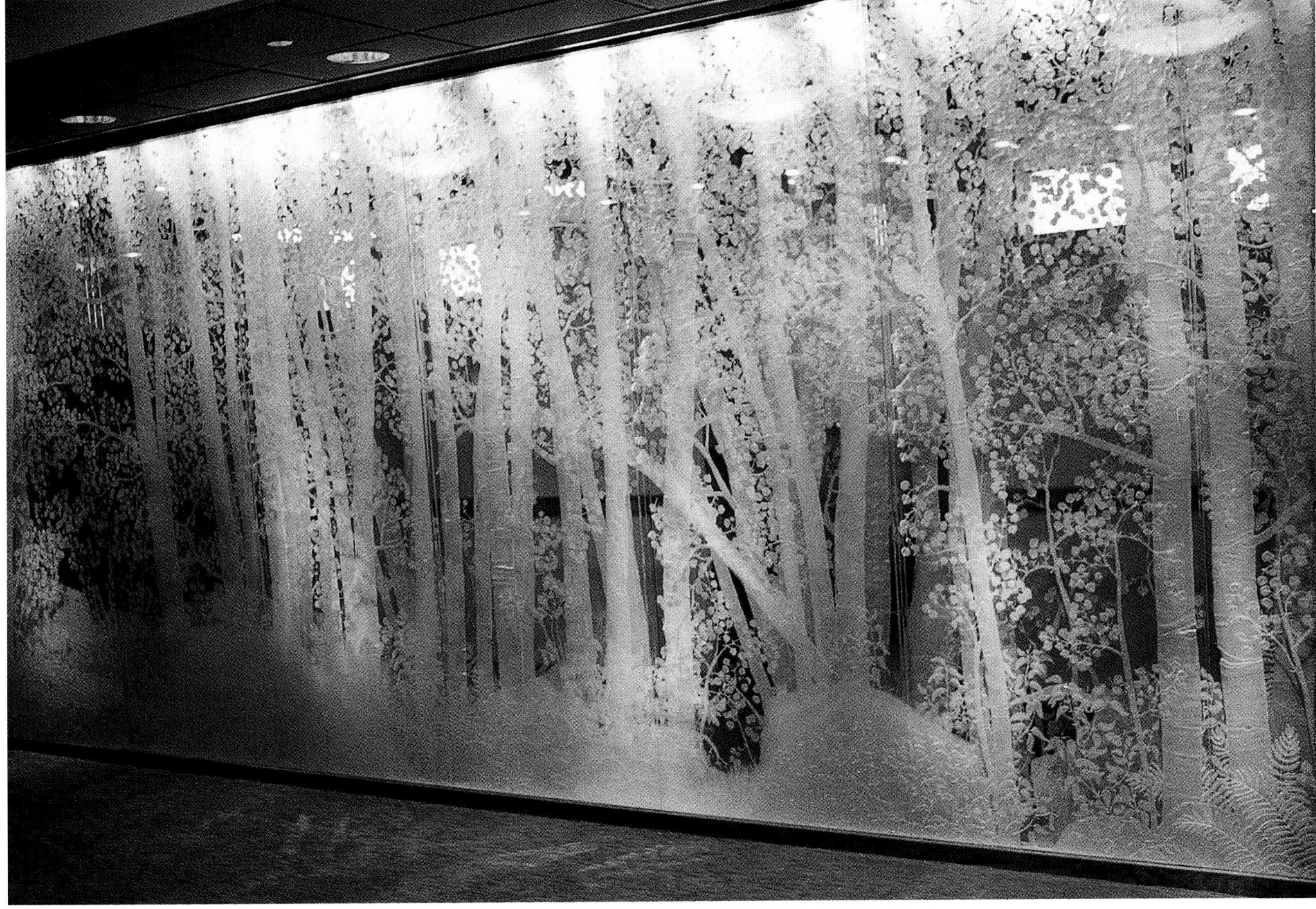

Top left: *Scottsbluff,* Scottsbluff, Nebraska, etched and sandcarved with dichroic and lenses, door entry size. Top center: *Untitled,* detail of set of two, Beavercreek, CO, etched and sandcarved, 42" x 65". Top right: *Lake Geneva,* Lake Geneva, WI, etched, sandcarved with dichroic glass, 52" x 54". Bottom: *Faces of The Forest,* Good Samaritan Hospital, Downers Grove, IL, triple-layered, etched and sandcarved.

TERESA CAMOZZI

THE CAMOZZI ART STUDIO ■ 1190 A SHAFTER AVENUE ■ SAN FRANCISCO, CA 94124
TEL 415-822-6222 ■ FAX 415-822-6322 ■ E-MAIL TCAMOZZI@COMCAST.NET ■ WWW.TERESACAMOZZI.COM

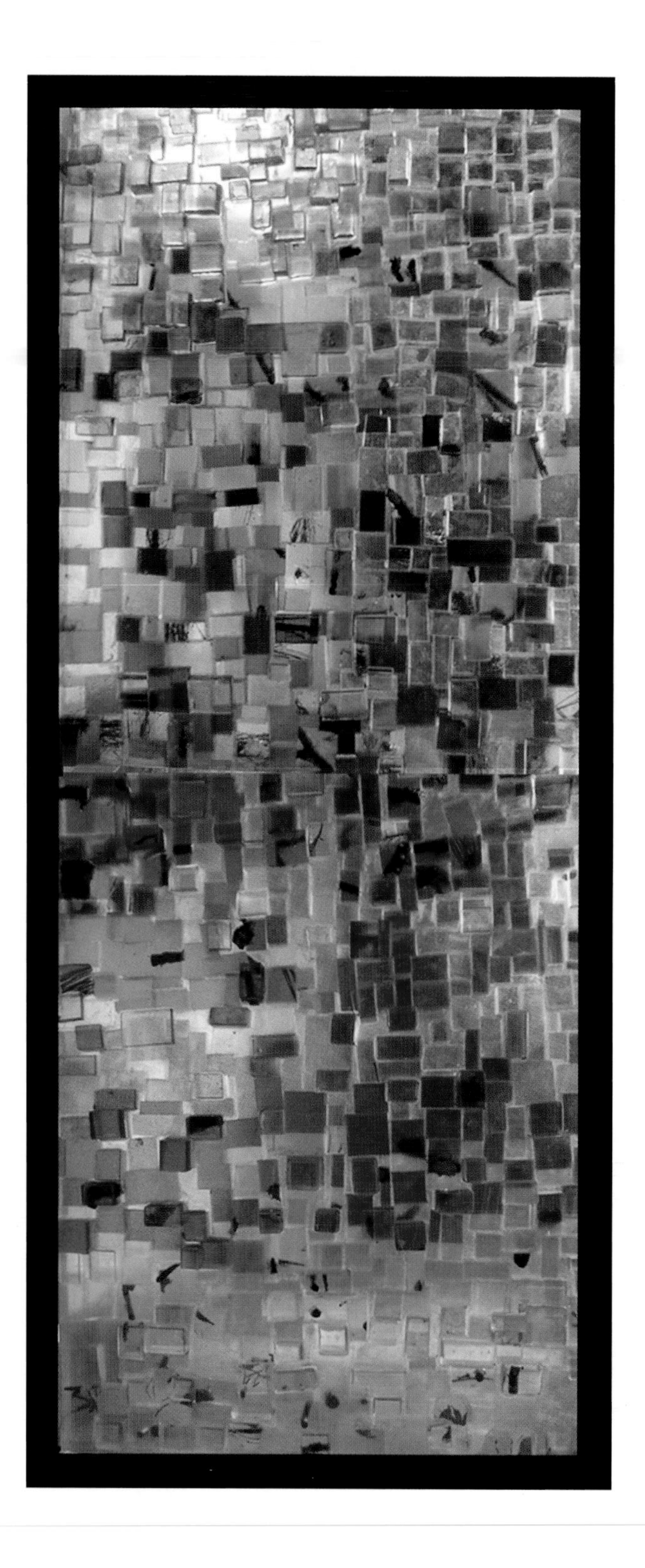

Color Study I, Metropolitan Club, Chicago, IL, tinted polyester resin with imbedded fragments of leaves and branches, 60" x 24" x 3".

DANZIGER DESIGNER GLASS STUDIO

850 17 AVENUE SW ■ CALGARY, AB T2R 0S9 ■ CANADA ■ TEL 403-777-9933
FAX 403-777-9934 ■ E-MAIL CONTACT@DANZIGERGLASS.COM ■ WWW.DANZIGERGLASS.COM

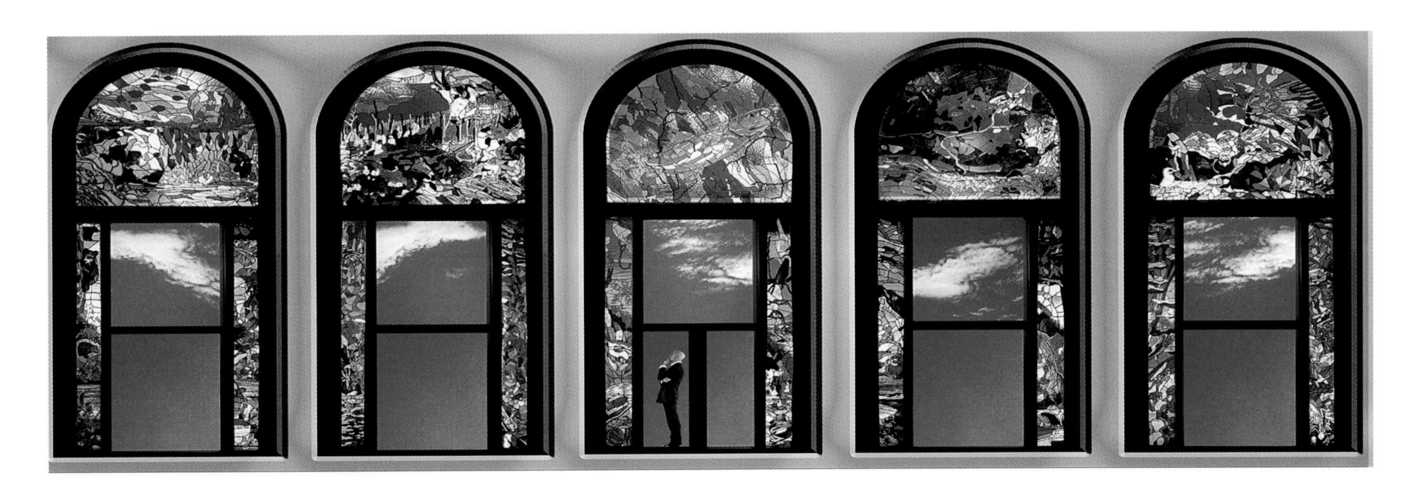

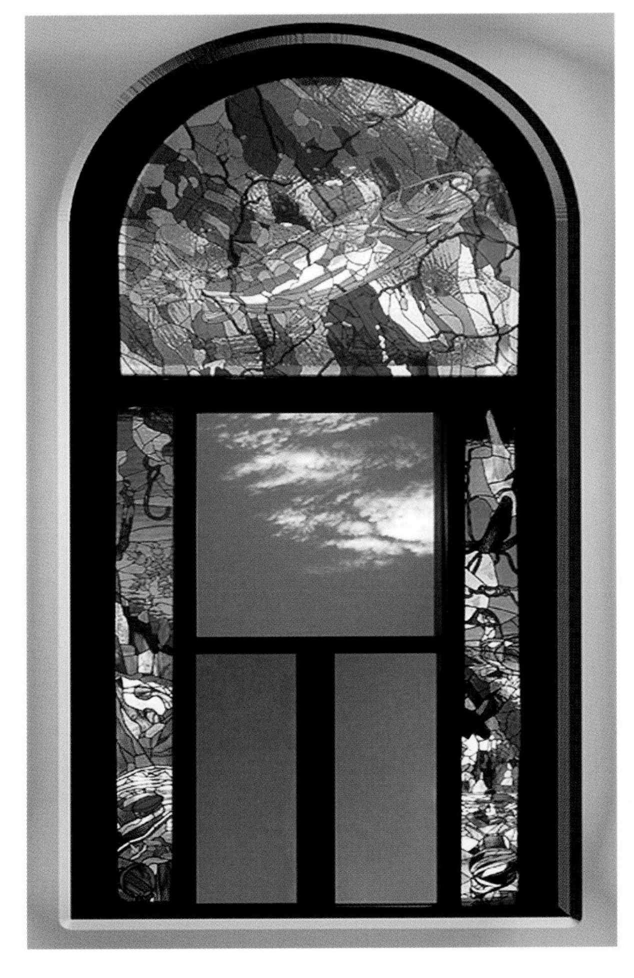

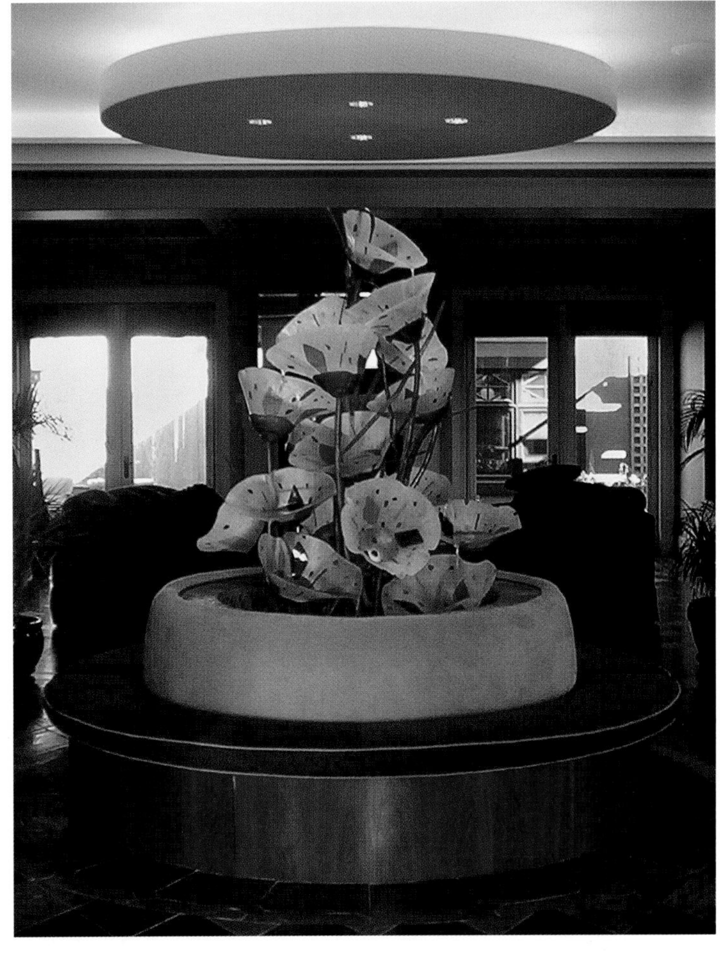

Top: Panorama of five windows, 2004, Fairmont Chateau at Lake Louise, Canada, stained glass with painted details, 23'H x 75'W.
Bottom left: Fairmont Chateau window (detail). Bottom right: *Flower Fountain,* 2005, fused and kiln-formed glass with copper structure, 8'H.

DAVID WILSON DESIGN

DAVID WILSON ▪ 202 DARBY ROAD ▪ SOUTH NEW BERLIN, NY 13843-2212 ▪ TEL 607-334-3015
FAX 607-334-7065 ▪ E-MAIL MAIL@DAVIDWILSONDESIGN.COM ▪ WWW.DAVIDWILSONDESIGN.COM

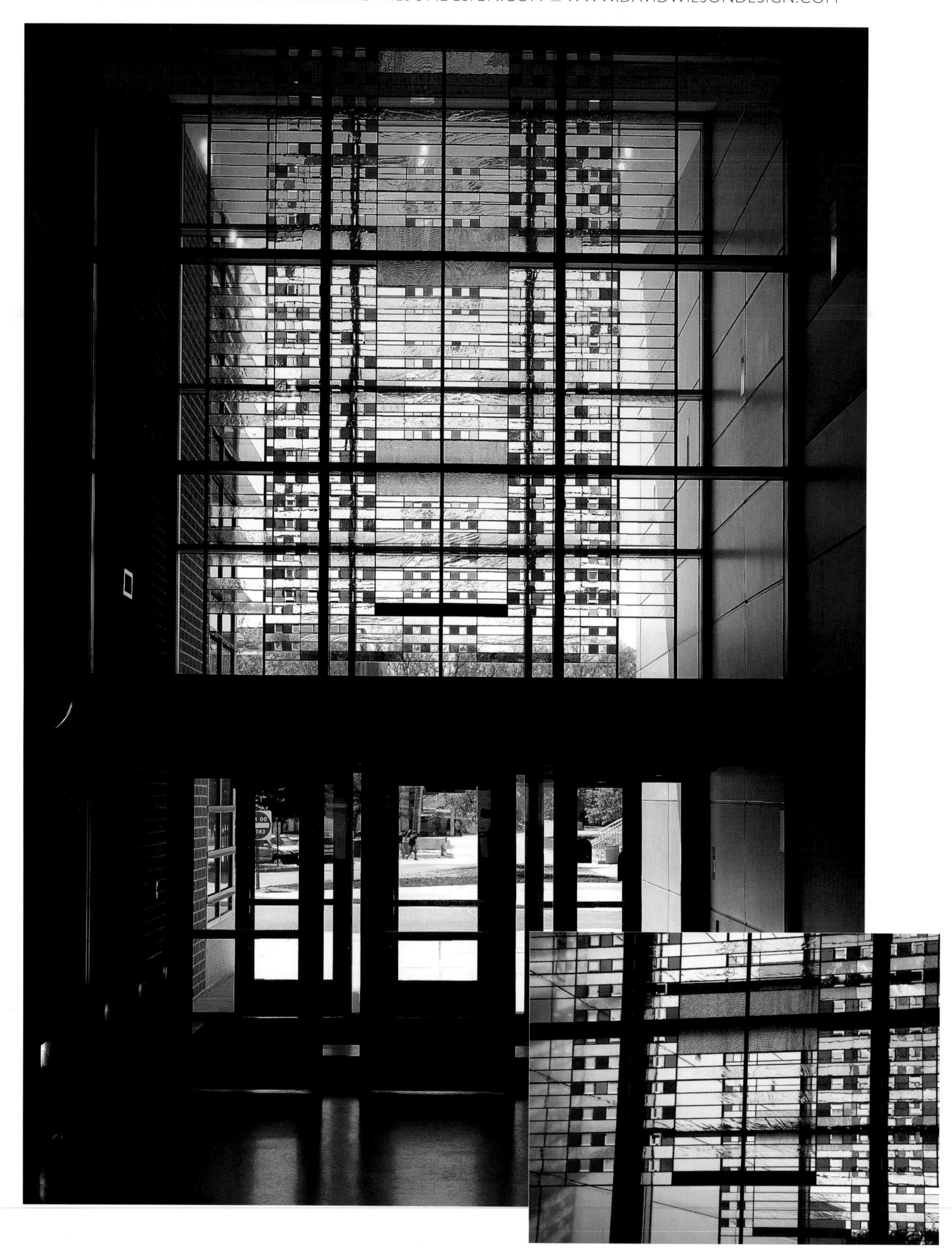

Glassboro Kaleidoscope, 2005, College of Education, Rowan University, Glassboro, NJ. A project for New Jersey State Council on the Arts. Photograph: Richard Walker.

DERIX ART GLASS CONSULTANTS

E-MAIL OFFICE@DERIXUSA.COM ■ WWW.DERIX.COM

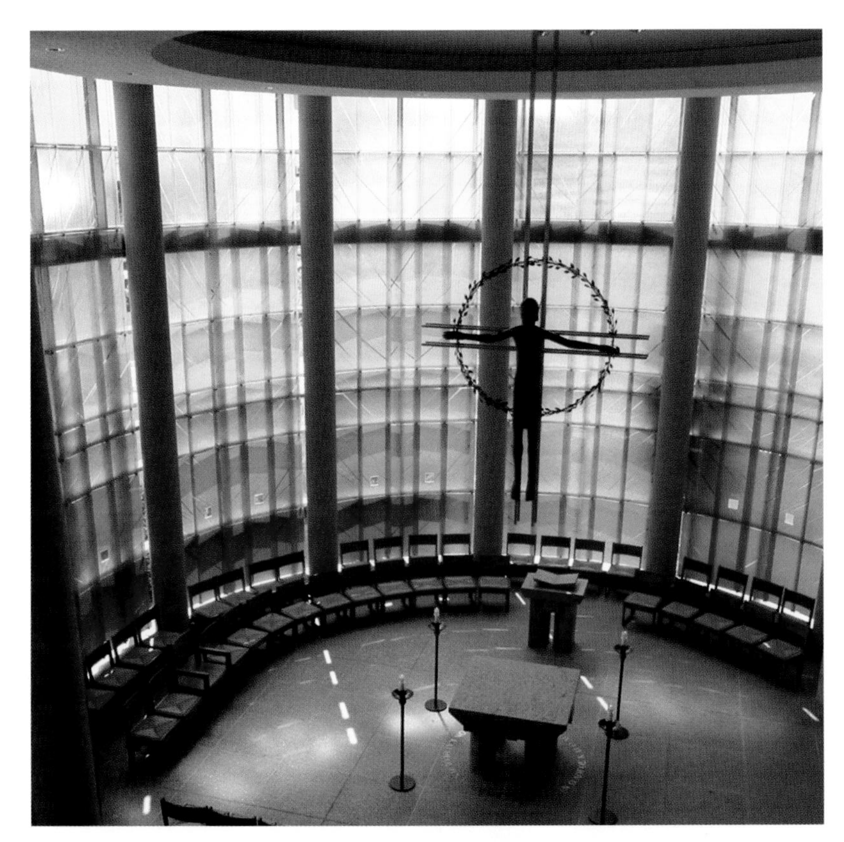

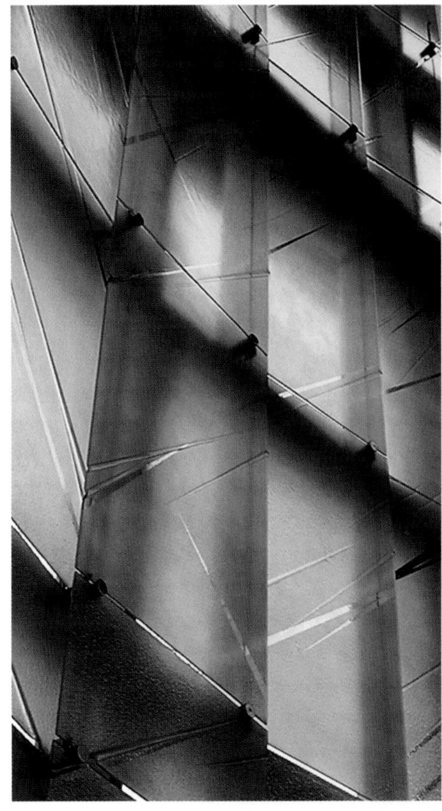

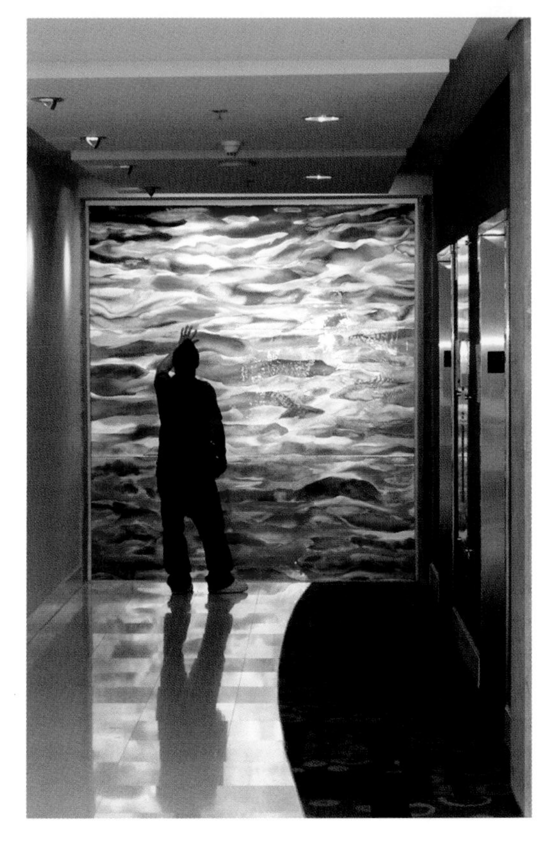

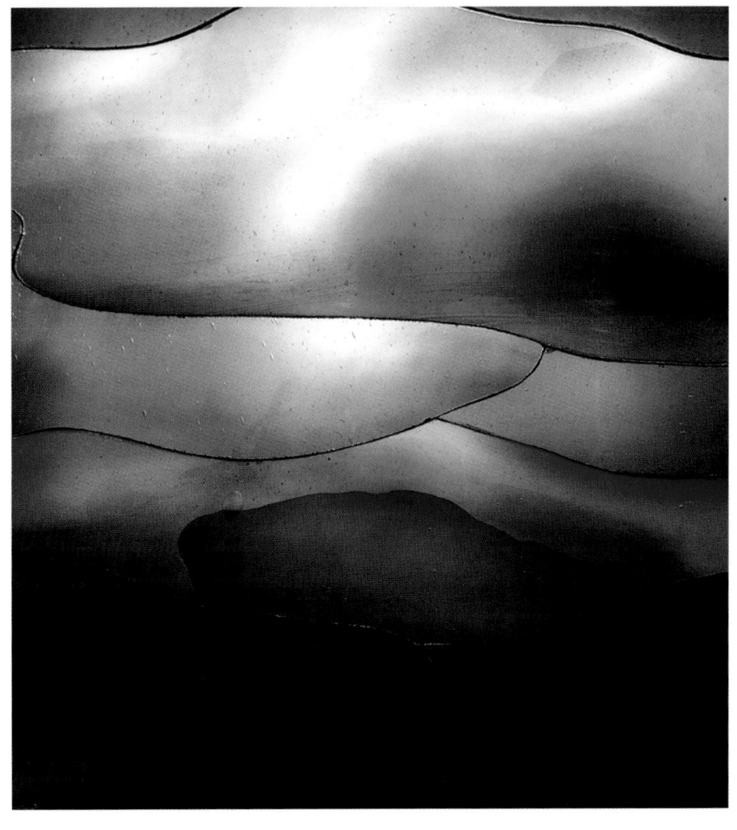

Top left and right: St. Thomas More Chapel, by Alexander Tylevich, University of St. Thomas, MN. IFFRA Award Winner.
Bottom left and right: Ashwood Commons, by Pam Beyette, Bellevue, WA.

BARBARA AND LARRY DOMSKY

DOMSKY GLASS ■ 3720 WEST OQUENDO #104 ■ LAS VEGAS, NV 89118
TEL 702-616-2830 ■ E-MAIL DOMSKYGLASS@AOL.COM ■ WWW.DOMSKYGLASS.COM

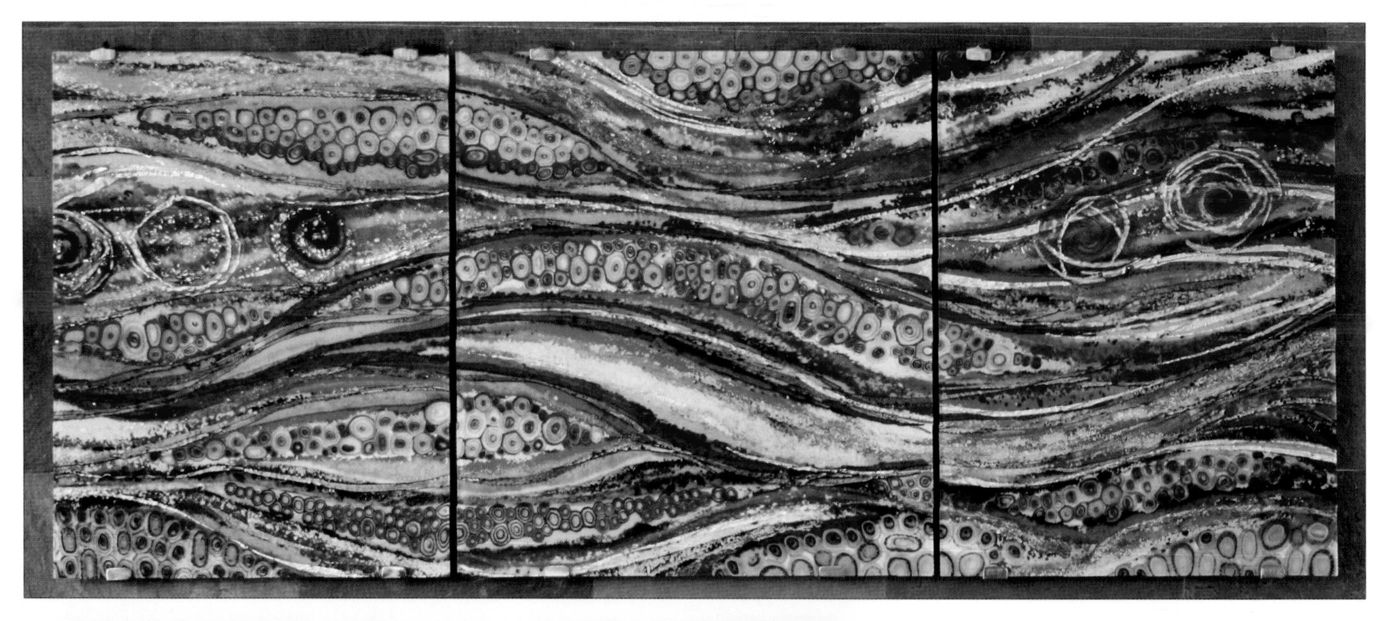

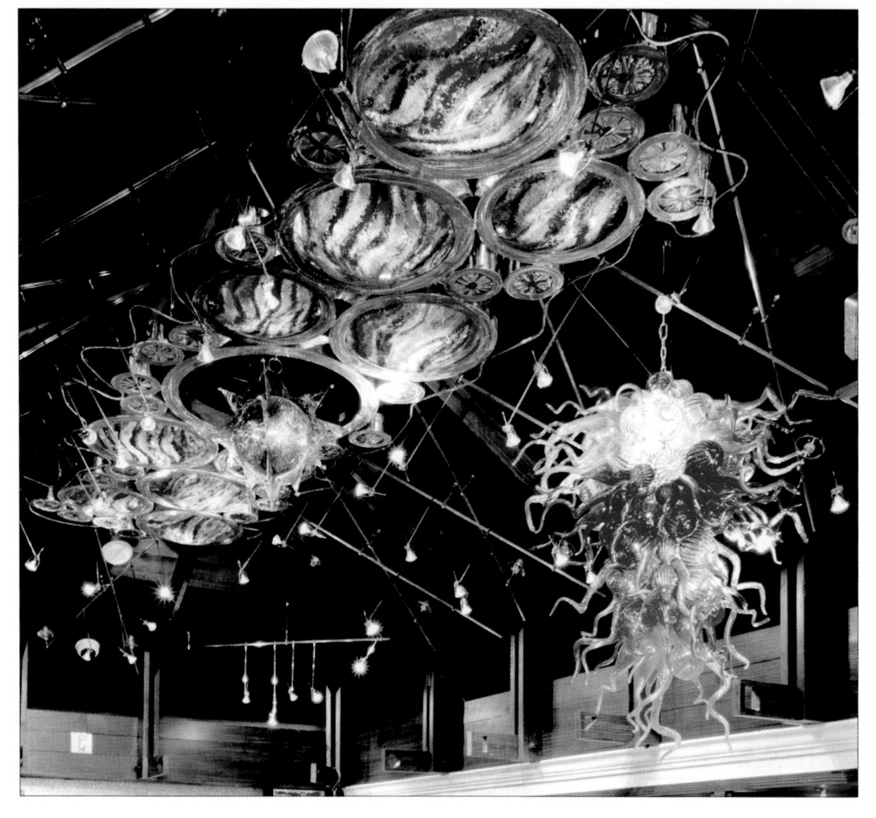

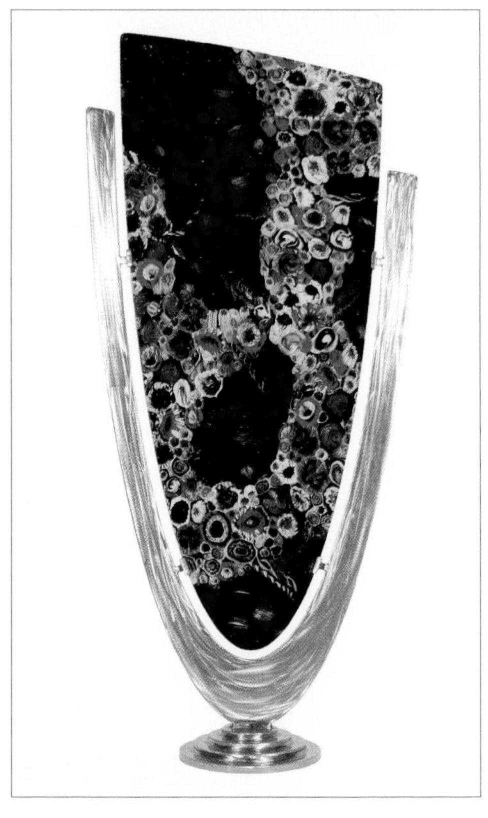

Top: *Tranquility,* private commission, hot-fusion glass painting, 48" x 102" x 1". Bottom left: Mandalay Bay Hotel, ceiling-mounted glass fusion metal chandelier: 14'L; and hanging blown glass chandelier: 4'H. Bottom right: Hot-fusion glass and steel sculpture, private commission, 5' x 23" x 1".

FUSIO STUDIO

RICHARD M. PARRISH ■ 6693 LYNX LANE #3 ■ BOZEMAN, MT 59718
TEL 406-522-9892 ■ E-MAIL GLASS@FUSIOSTUDIO.COM ■ WWW.FUSIOSTUDIO.COM

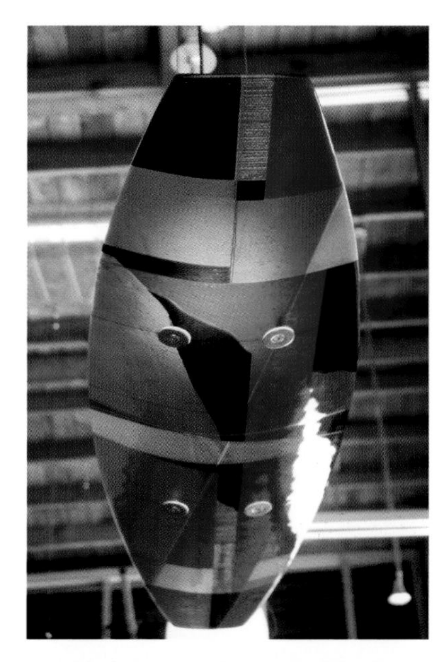

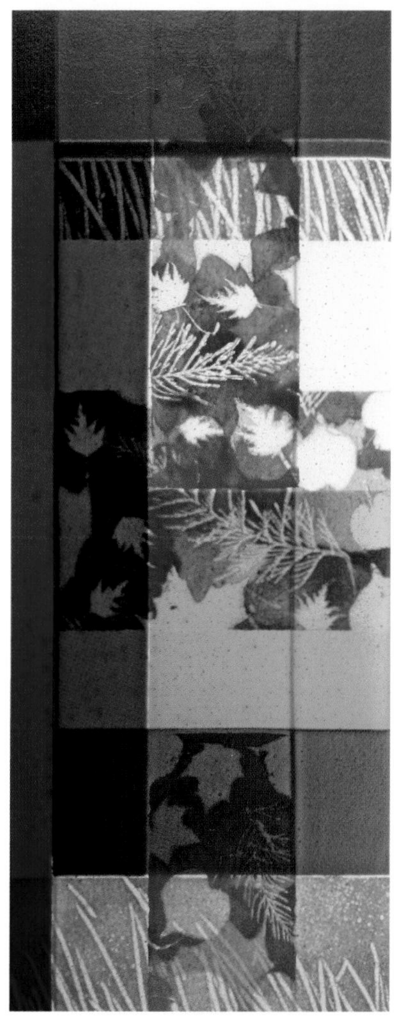

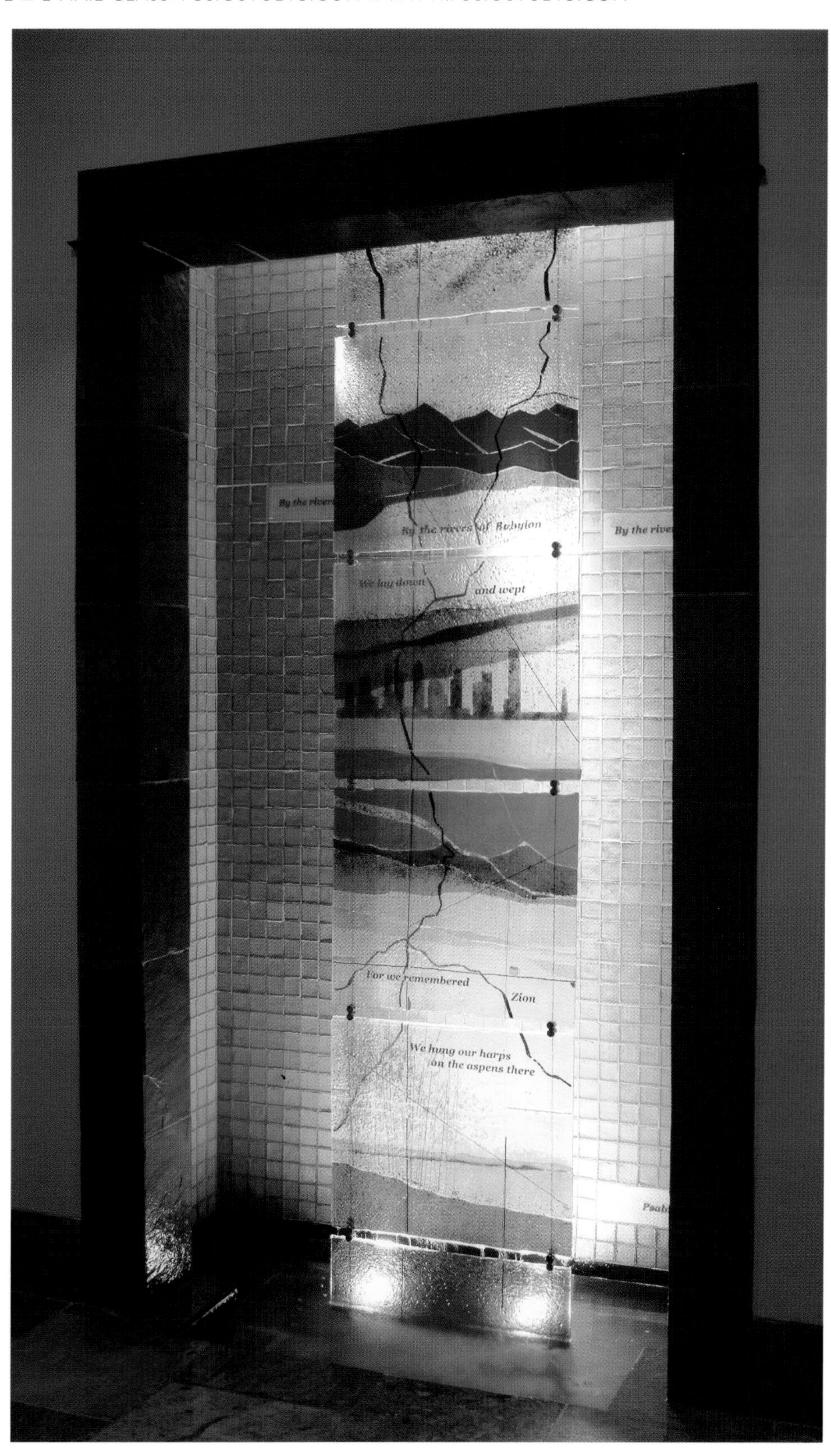

Top left: *Light Wing*, 2005, light fixture in private residence, Bozeman, MT, kiln-formed glass, cable, and remote light source, 54" x 15" x 3". Photograph: Tom Ferris.
Right: *By the Rivers of Babylon*, 2002, private residence, MT, glass panels with water element, 108" x 24". Photograph: Karl Neumann.
Bottom left: *Layered Botanical Panel* (detail), 2006, kiln-formed glass, 18" x 14.5" x 0.6". Photograph: Tom Ferris.

GRT GLASS DESIGN

GREGORY R. THOMPSON ■ 6400 BROOKVILLE ROAD SUITE B ■ INDIANAPOLIS, IN 46219 ■ TEL 317-353-6369
FAX 317-359-9630 ■ E-MAIL GREG@GRTGLASSDESIGN.COM ■ WWW.GRTGLASSDESIGN.COM

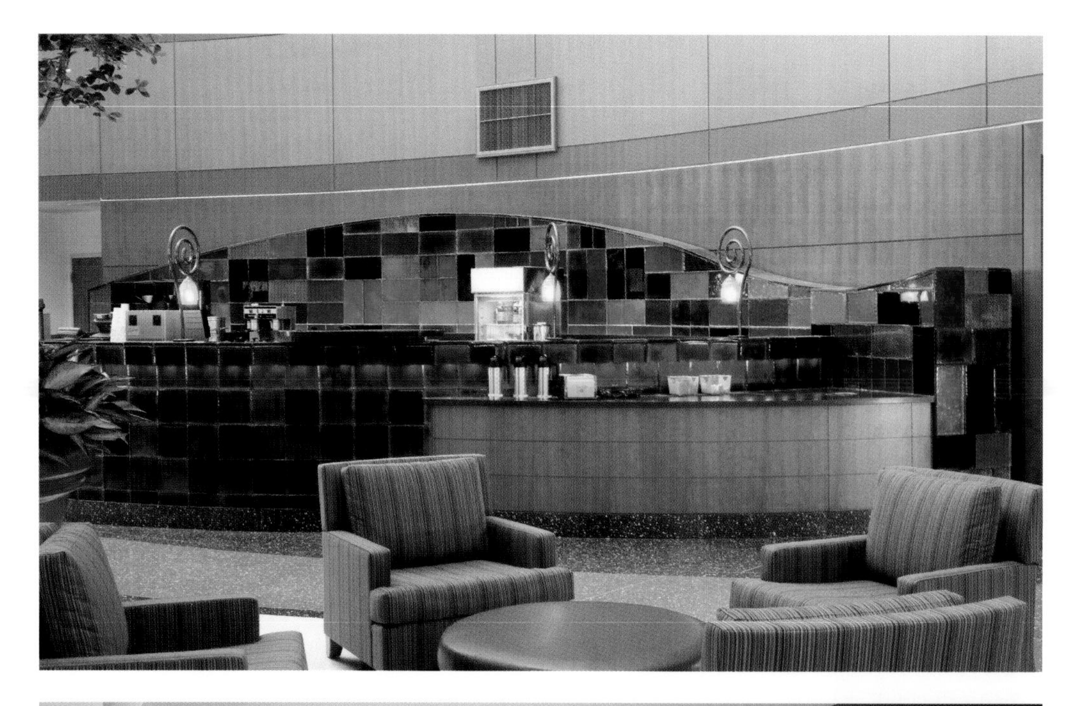

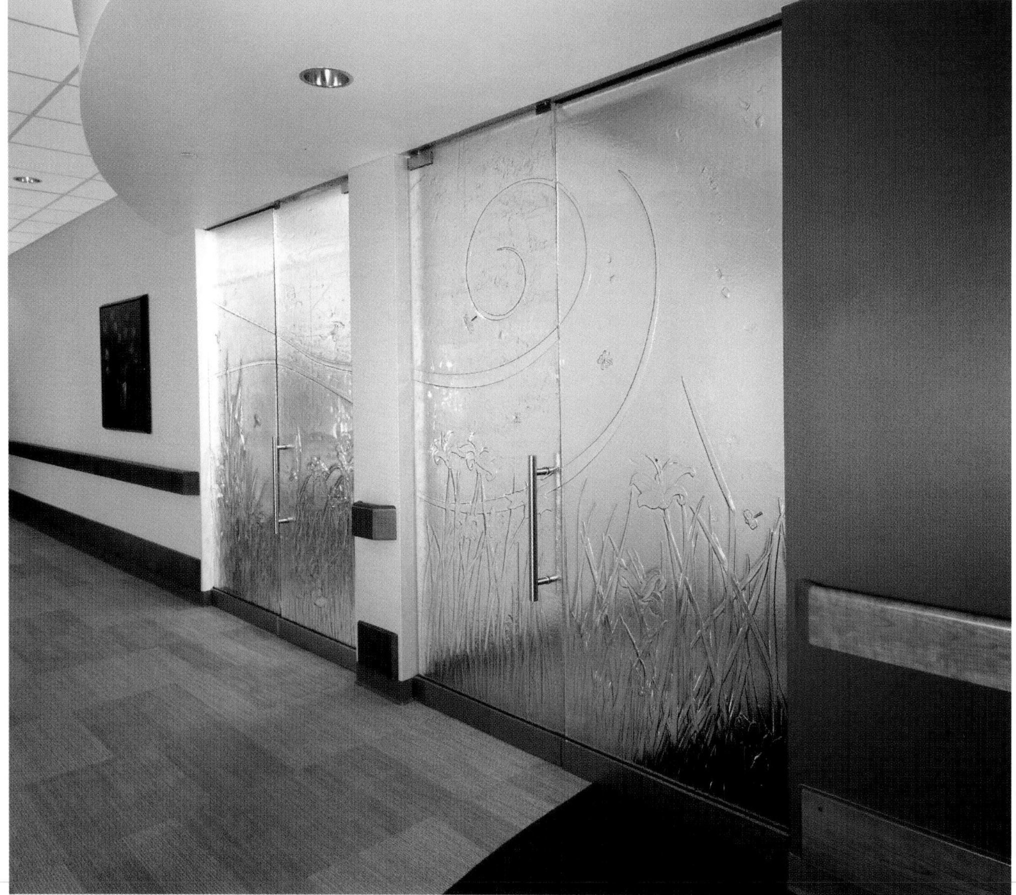

Top: *Mirrored Tiles*, 2005, Starbucks Coffee, Carmel, IN.
Bottom: *Custom Reeds and Flowers*, 2005, Clarian North Hospital, Carmel, IN.

GLASMALEREI PETERS/PETERS GLASS STUDIOS

WILHELM PETERS ▪ AM HILLIGENBUSCH 23-27 ▪ PADERBORN, 33098 ▪ GERMANY ▪ TEL +490 5251 160970
FAX +490 5251 1609799 ▪ E-MAIL INFO@GLASS-ART-PETERS.COM ▪ WWW.GLASS-ART-PETERS.COM

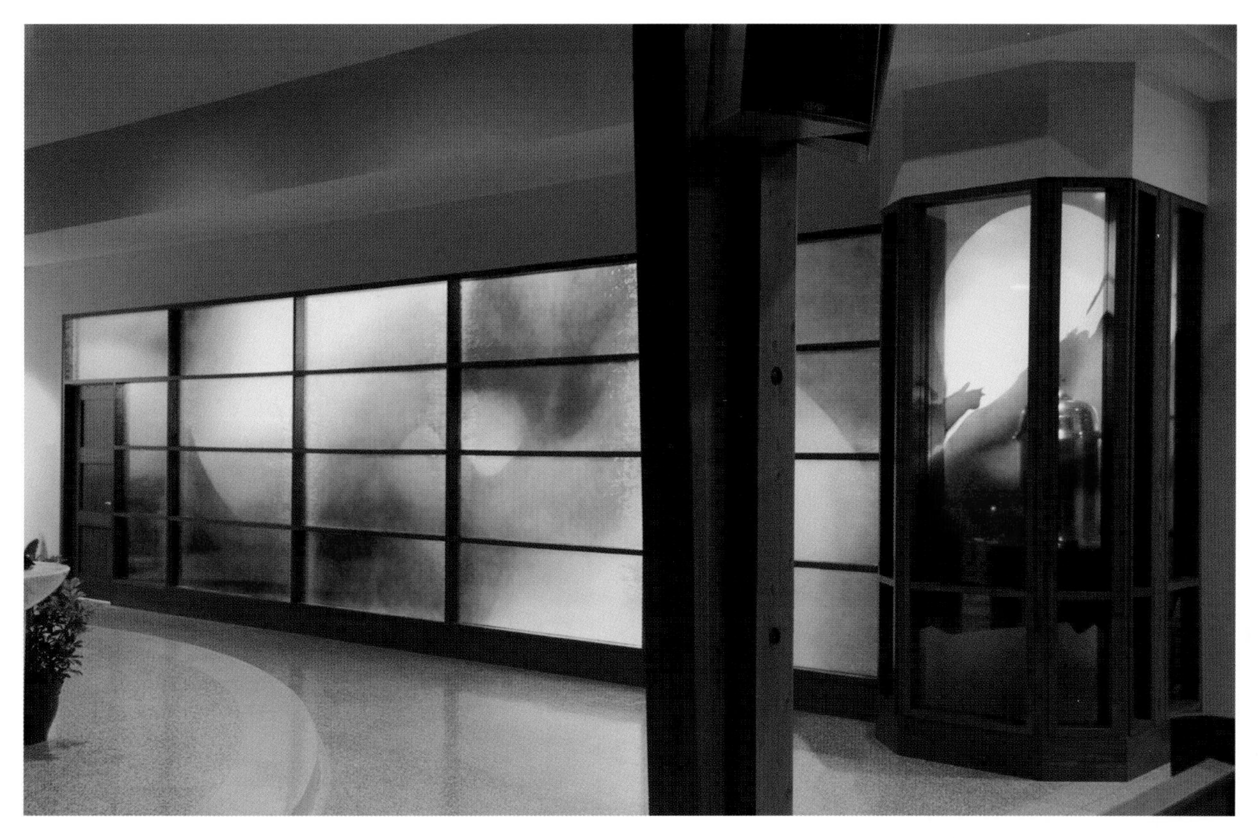

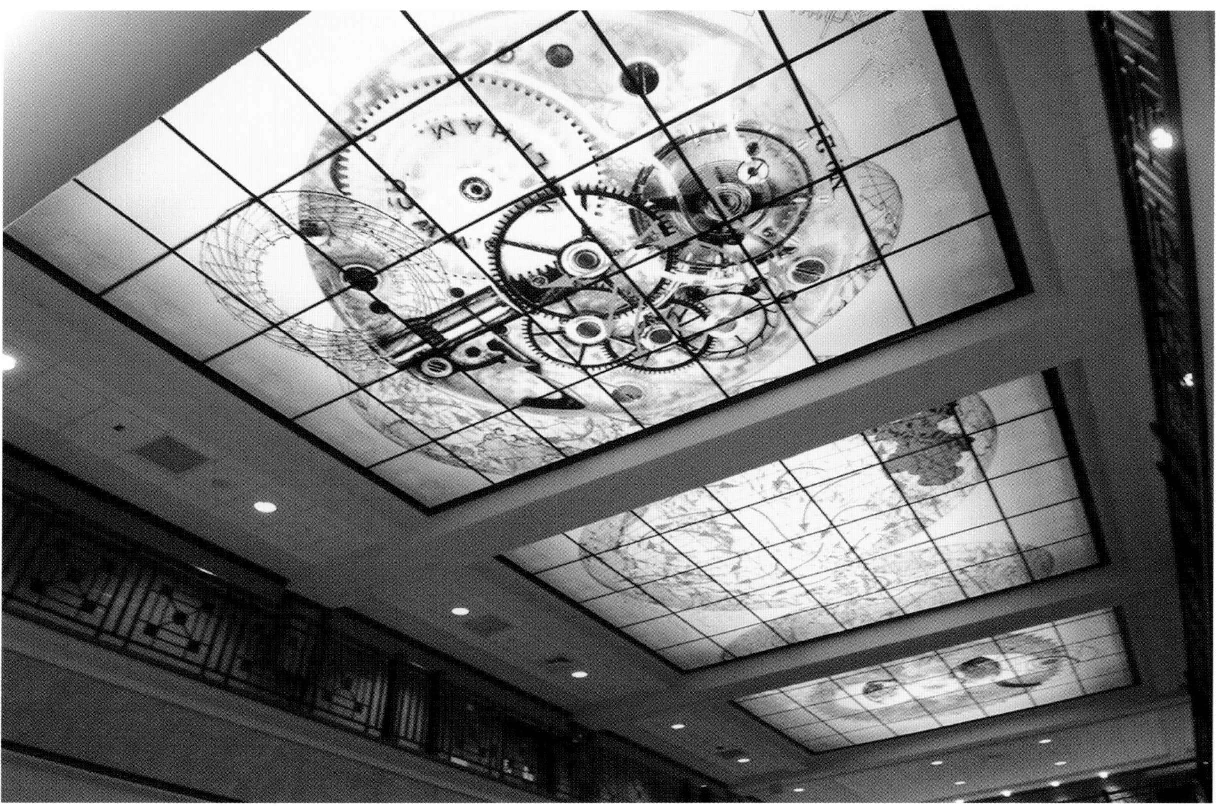

Top: *St. Rose of Lima,* Toronto, Canada, airbrush painting on toughened glass. Design: Sarah Hall, Toronto, Canada. Bottom: *Driving Force*, University of Wisconsin, Madison, USA, digital print on laminated glass. Design: Stuart Keeler & Michael Machnic, USA. Photograph: Wisconsin State Arts Board.

GLASSIC ART

LESLIE RANKIN ■ 5850 SOUTH POLARIS AVENUE #700 ■ LAS VEGAS, NV 89118
TEL/FAX 702-658-7588 ■ E-MAIL GLASSICART@GLASSICART.COM ■ WWW.GLASSICART.COM

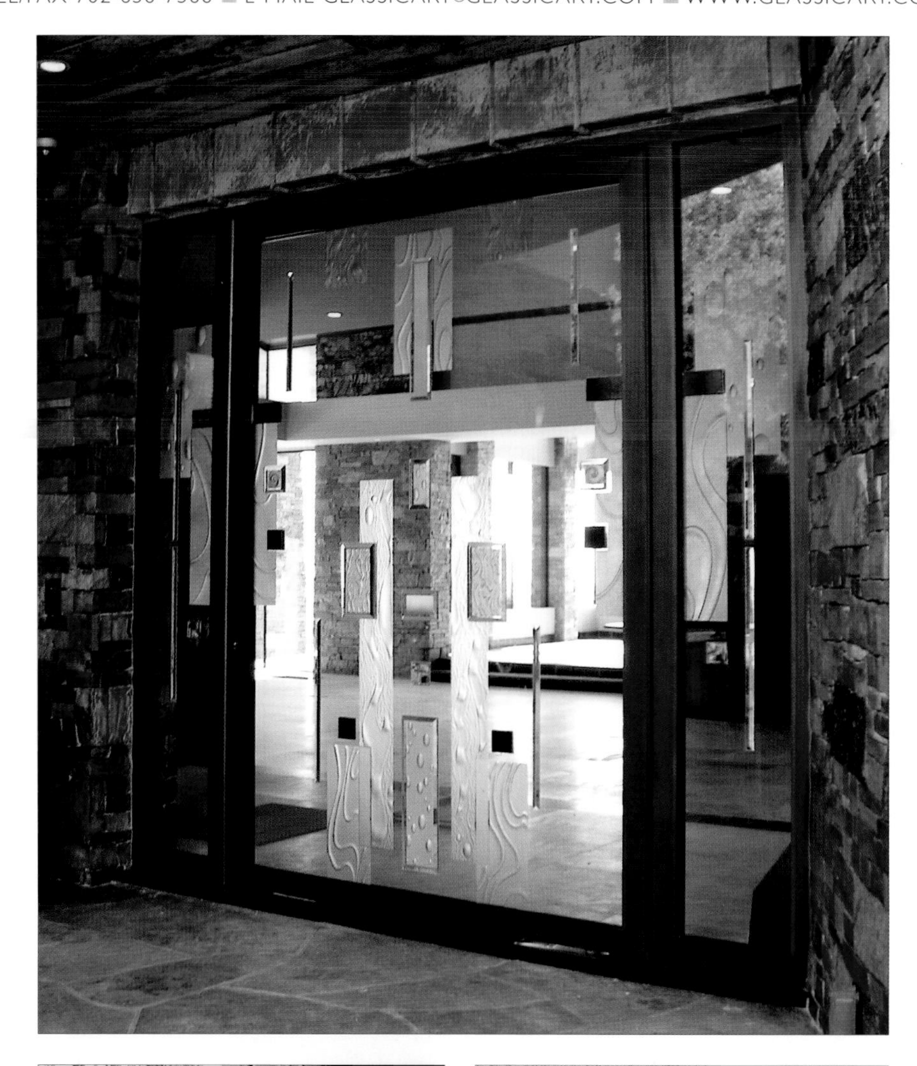

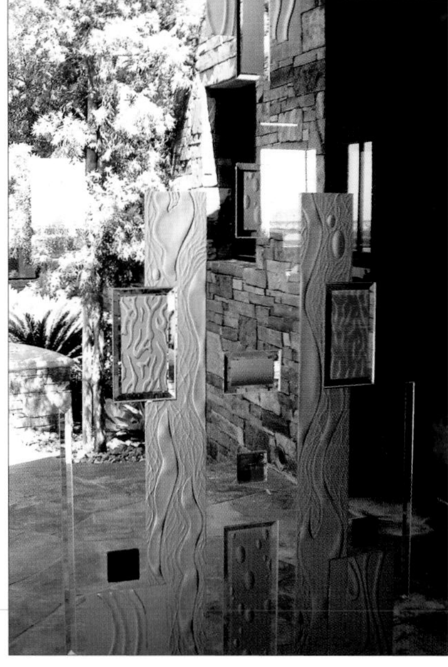

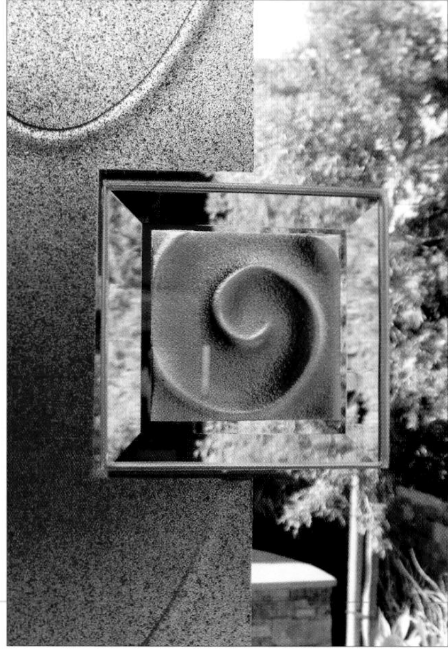

Top: Front entry *Pivot Door*—carved, colored, and welded glass. Bottom left: Detail of inside view. Bottom right: Detail of carved glass.

NANCY GONG

GONG GLASS WORKS ■ 42 PARKVIEW DRIVE ■ ROCHESTER, NY 14625-1034 ■ TEL 585-288-5520
FAX 585-288-2503 ■ E-MAIL NGONG@ROCHESTER.RR.COM ■ WWW.NANCYGONG.COM

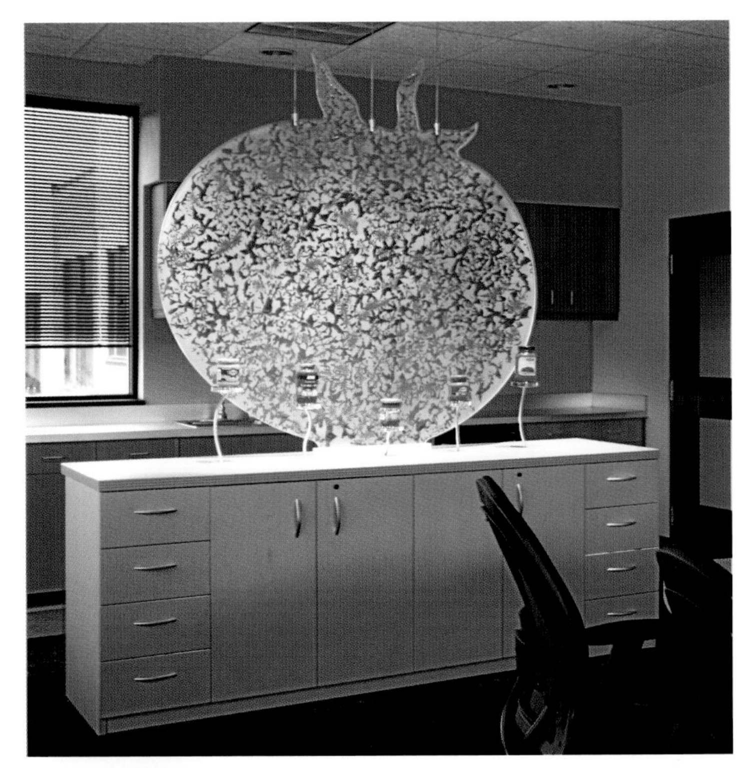

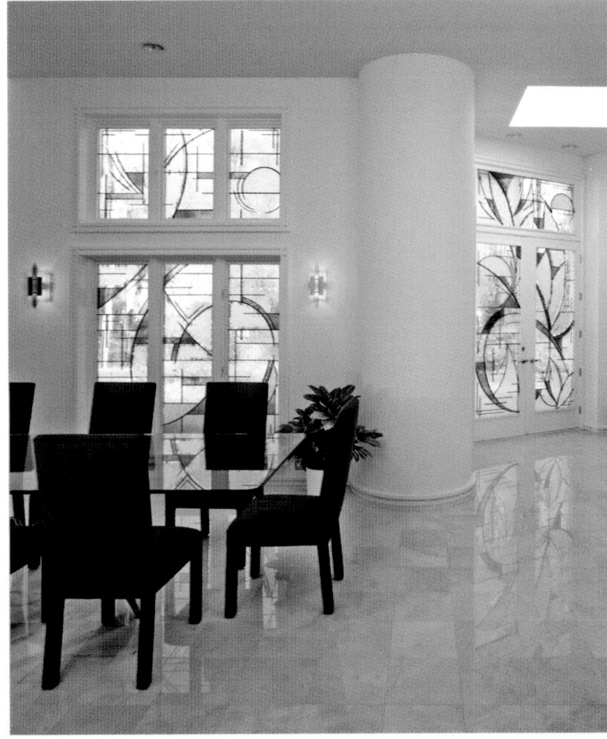

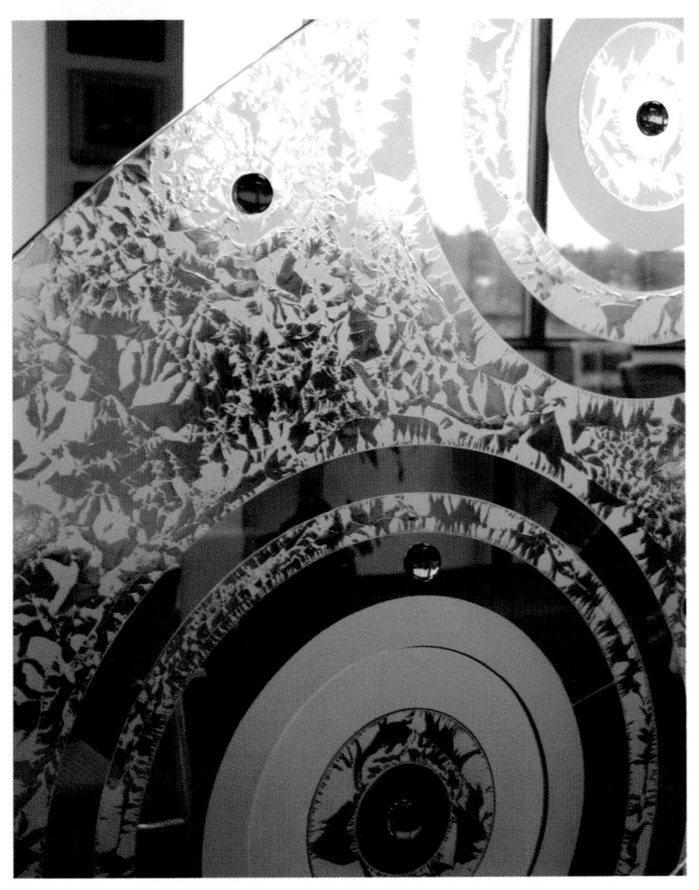

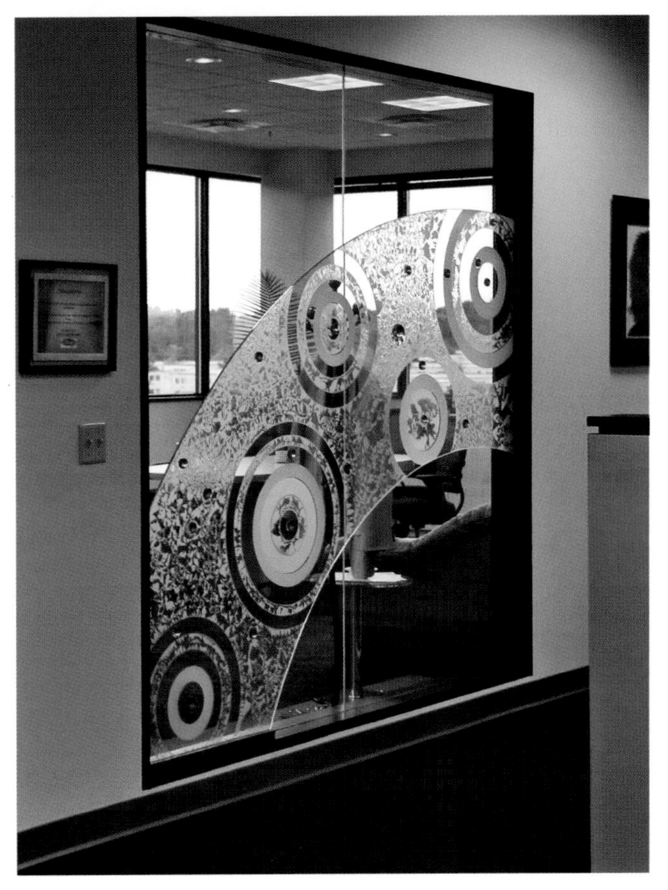

Top left: *The Big Tomato,* LiDestri Foods, Inc. boardroom. Top right: *Lyrical Illusions,* thirty-three unique leaded art glass windows. Photograph: Tim Wilkes. Bottom left: *Center of the Earth* (detail). Bottom right: *Center of the Earth,* LiDestri Foods, Inc. office.

MARK ERIC GULSRUD

ARCHITECTURAL GLASS & SCULPTURE ■ 3309 TAHOMA PLACE WEST ■ TACOMA, WA 98466
TEL 253-566-1720 ■ FAX 253-565-5981 ■ E-MAIL MARK@MARKERICGULSRUD.COM ■ WWW.MARKERICGULSRUD.COM

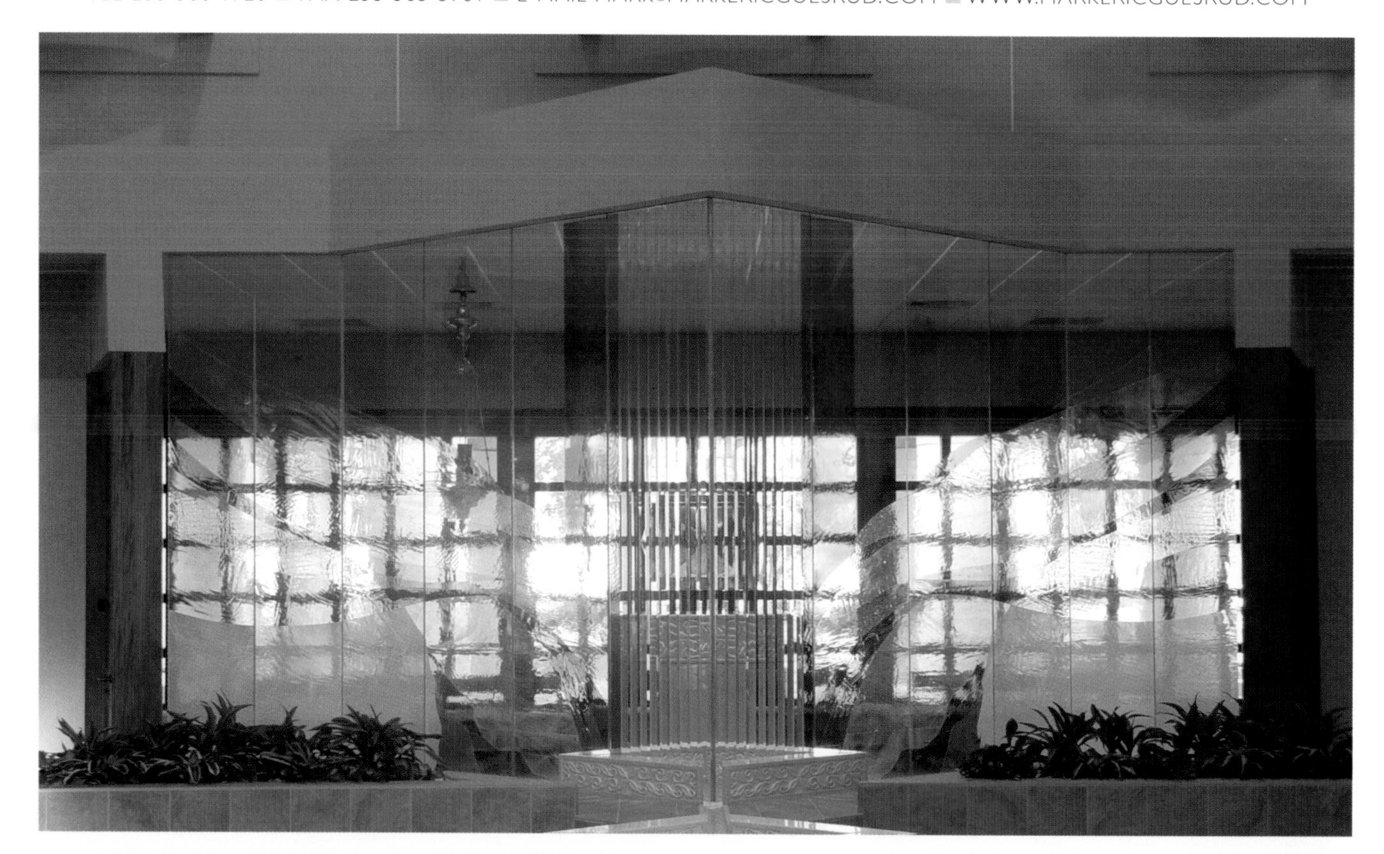

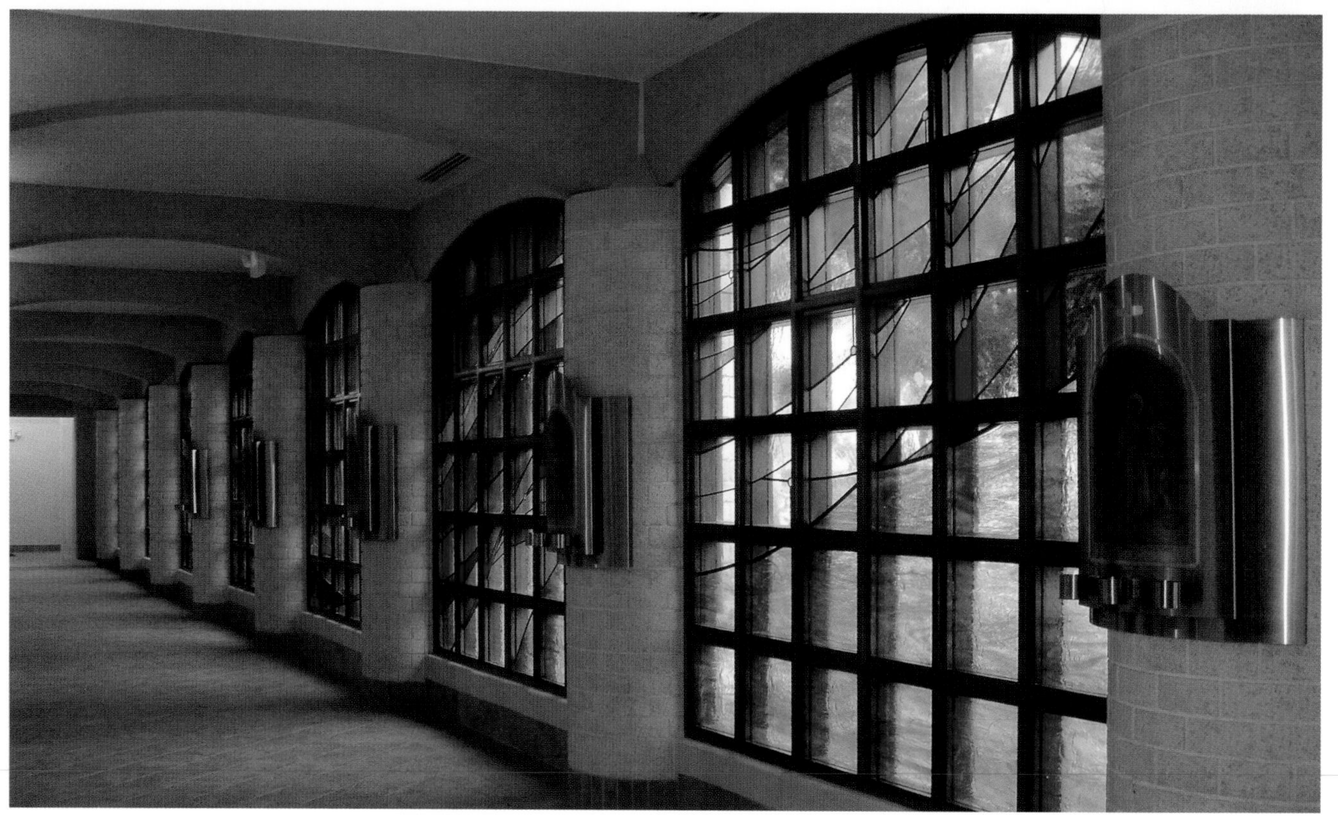

Top: Sacramental Chapel, St. Mark Catholic Church, Fort Lauderdale, FL, fabrication of laminated glass by Derix Glasstudios. Bottom: Ambulatory windows, leaded glass, Peter Kosinski, architect.

SARAH HALL

SARAH HALL STUDIO ▦ 98 BOUSTEAD AVENUE ▦ TORONTO, ON M6R 1Y9 ▦ CANADA ▦ TEL 416-532-6060
FAX 416-532-9361 ▦ E-MAIL SARAH.HALL.STUDIO@SYMPATICO.CA ▦ WWW.SARAHHALLSTUDIO.COM

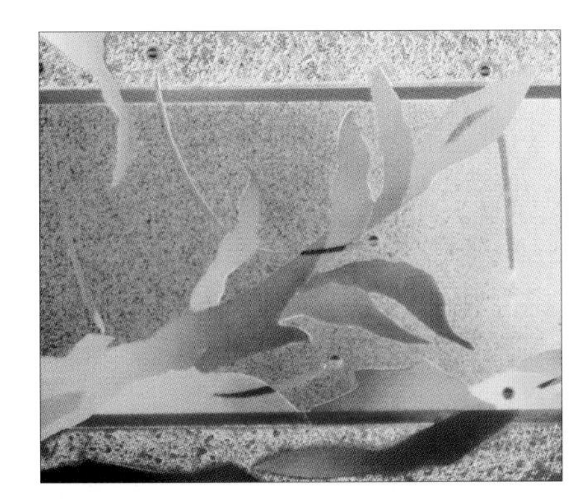

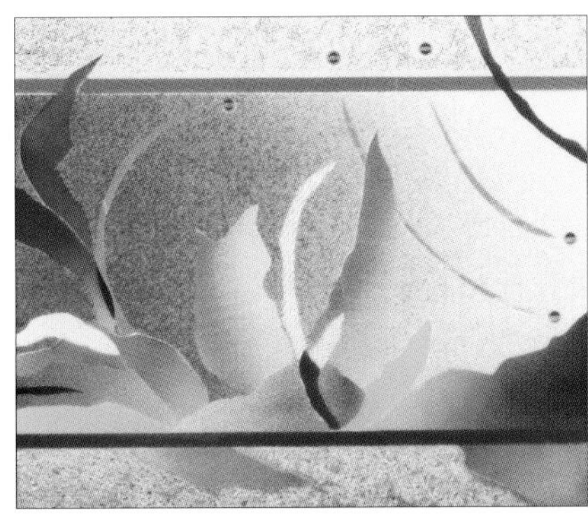

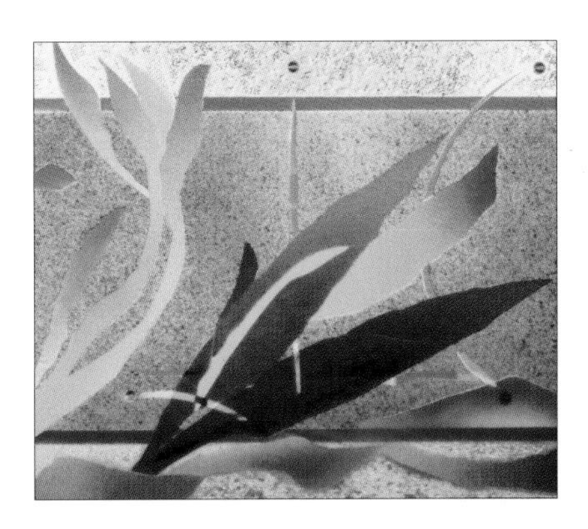

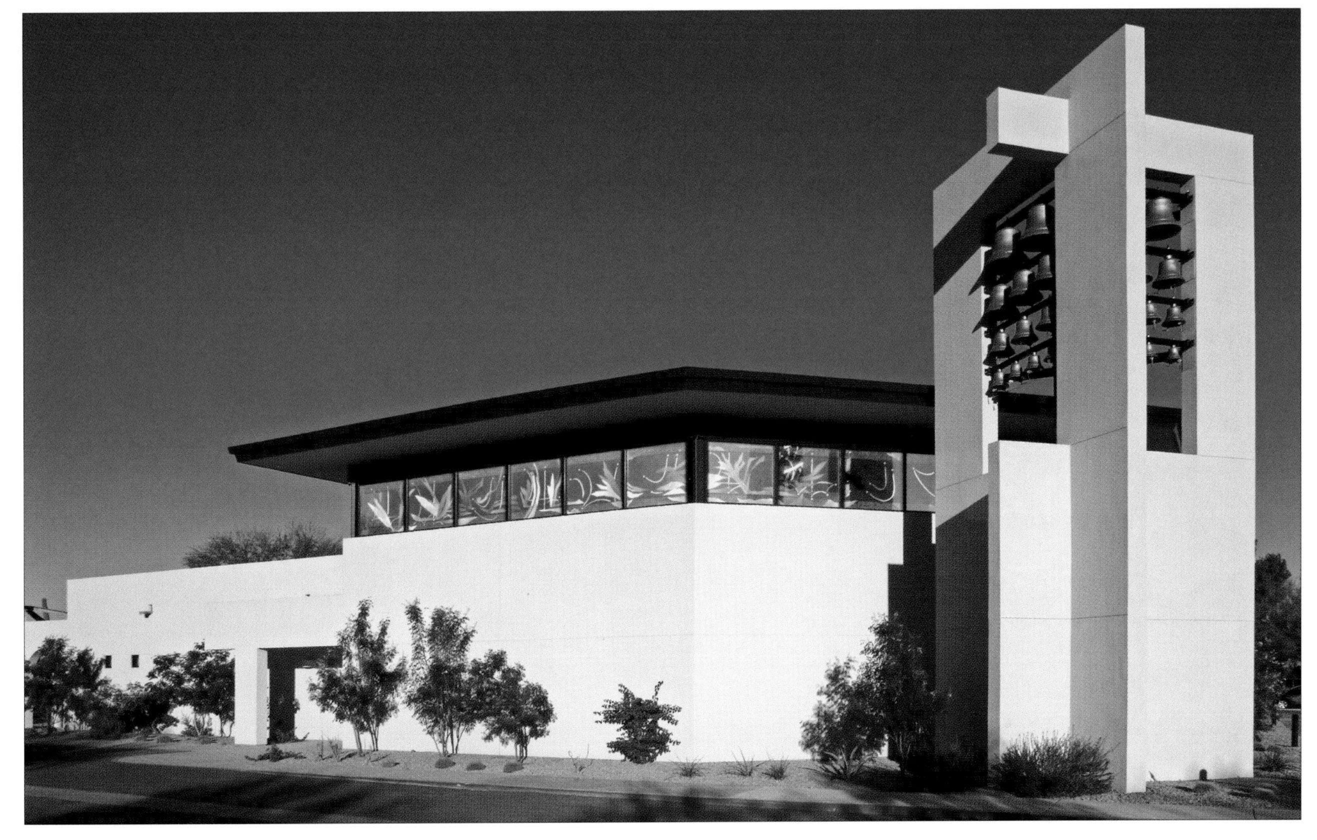

Desert Crossings—Luminous Journey, thirty-six art glass windows for the Gwen Harris Concert Hall, St. Barnabas on-the-Desert Episcopal Parish, Paradise Valley, AZ, created in collaboration with Glasmalerei Peters, Paderborn, Germany. Photograph: Knoell & Quidort Architects.

PAUL HOUSBERG

GLASS PROJECT, INC. ■ 875 NORTH MAIN ROAD ■ JAMESTOWN, RI 02835 ■ TEL 401-560-0880
FAX 401-560-0881 ■ E-MAIL INFO@GLASSPROJECT.COM ■ WWW.GLASSPROJECT.COM

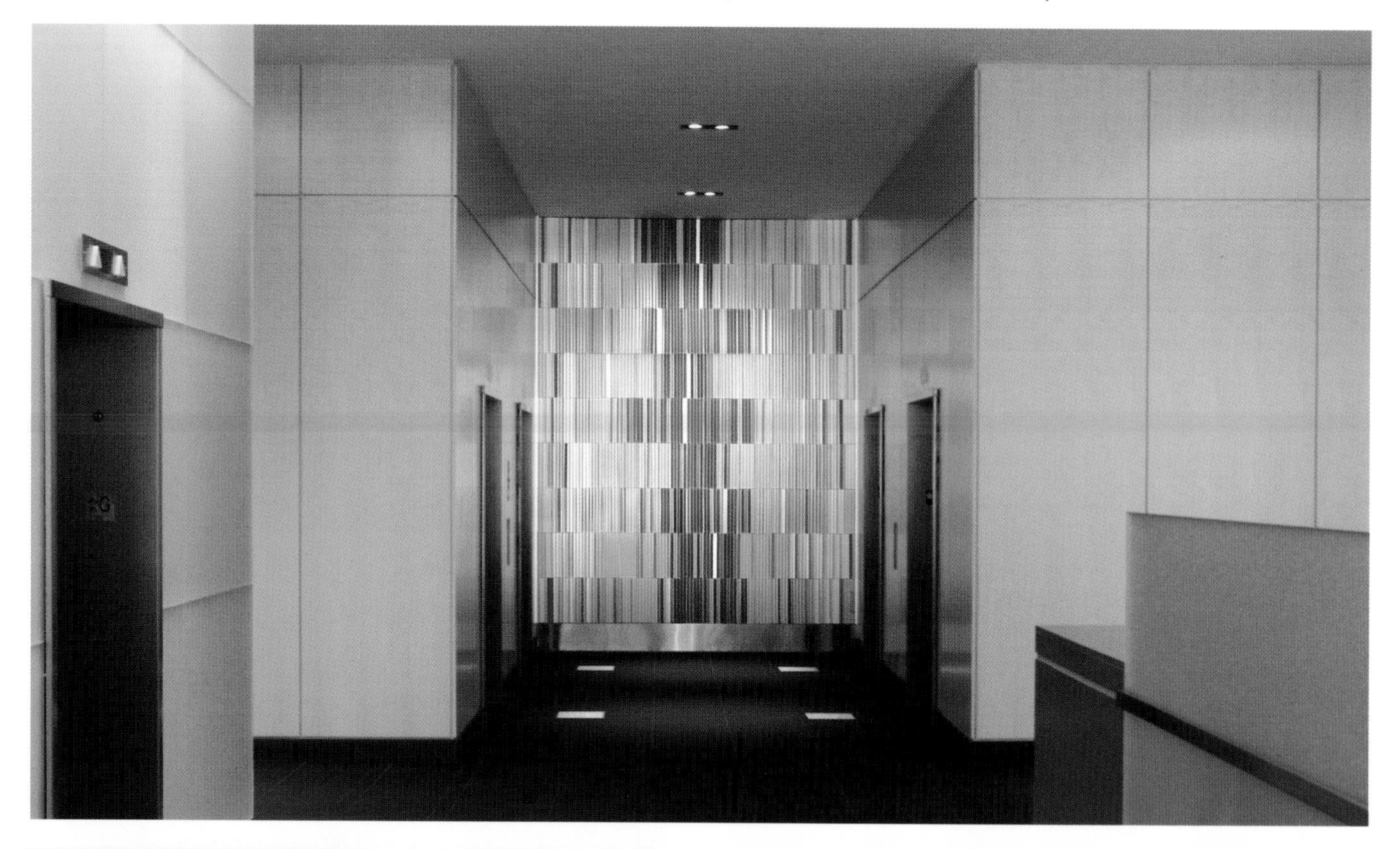

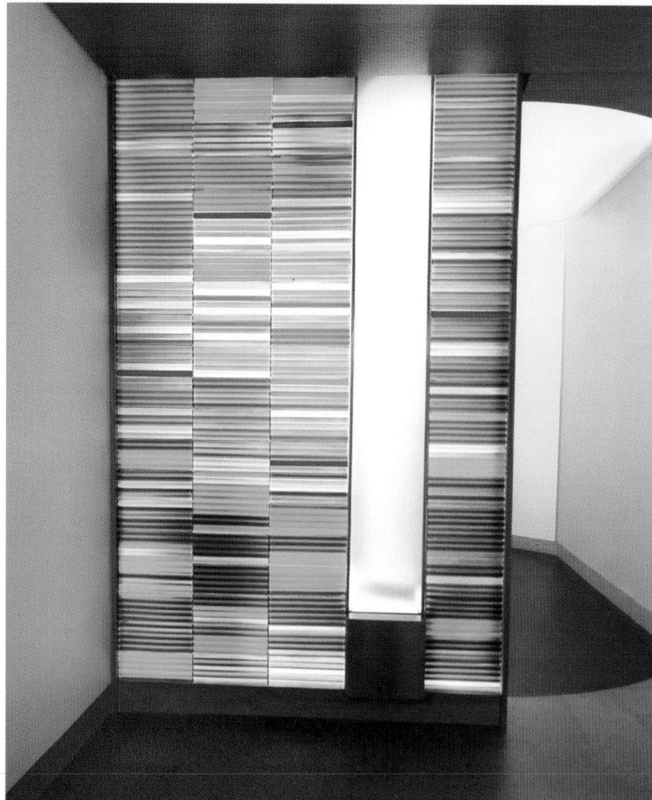

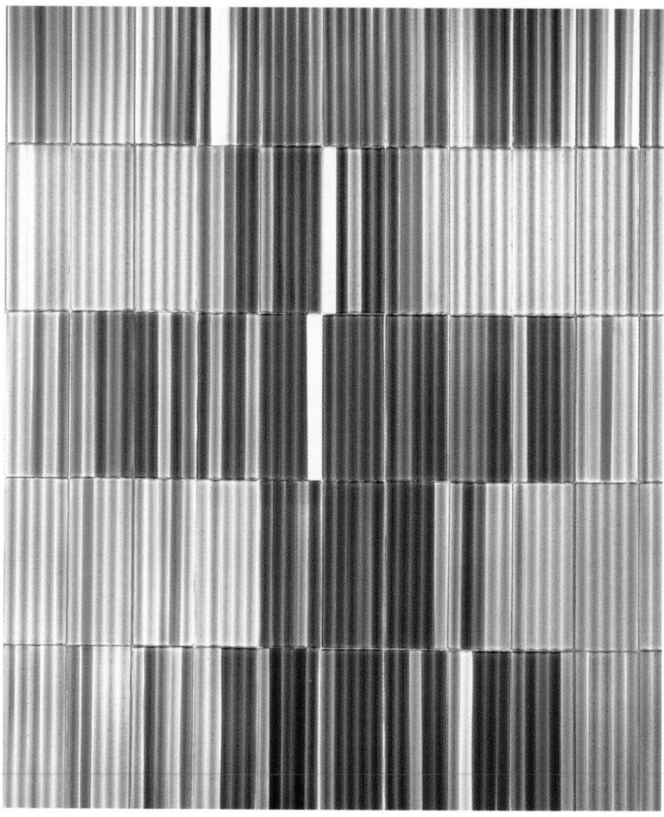

Top: GTECH Center Lobby, 2006, Providence, RI, fused/cast glass, 12'H x 9.5'W. Bottom left: Pacific Hospital Meditation Chapel, 2006, San Francisco, CA, fused/cast glass, 10'H x 5'W. Bottom right: GTECH Center Lobby (detail).

J. GORSUCH COLLINS ARCHITECTURAL GLASS

J. GORSUCH COLLINS ■ 8283 WEST ILIFF LANE ■ LAKEWOOD, CO 80227 ■ TEL 303-985-8081 ■ FAX 303-980-0692
E-MAIL JUDY@COLLINSARCHITECTURALGLASS.COM ■ WWW.COLLINSARCHITECTURALGLASS.COM

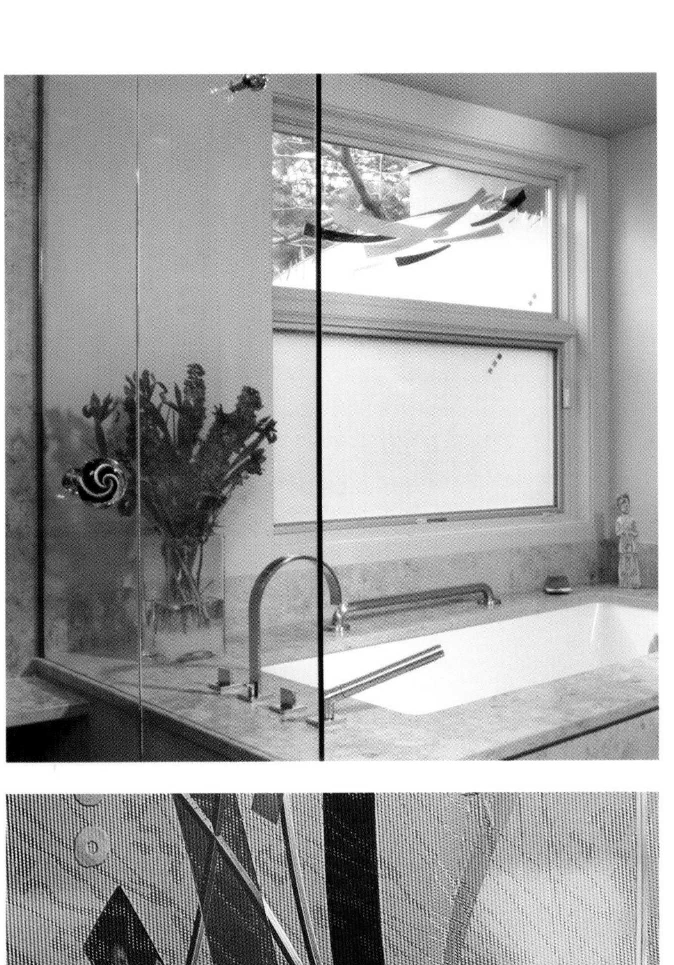

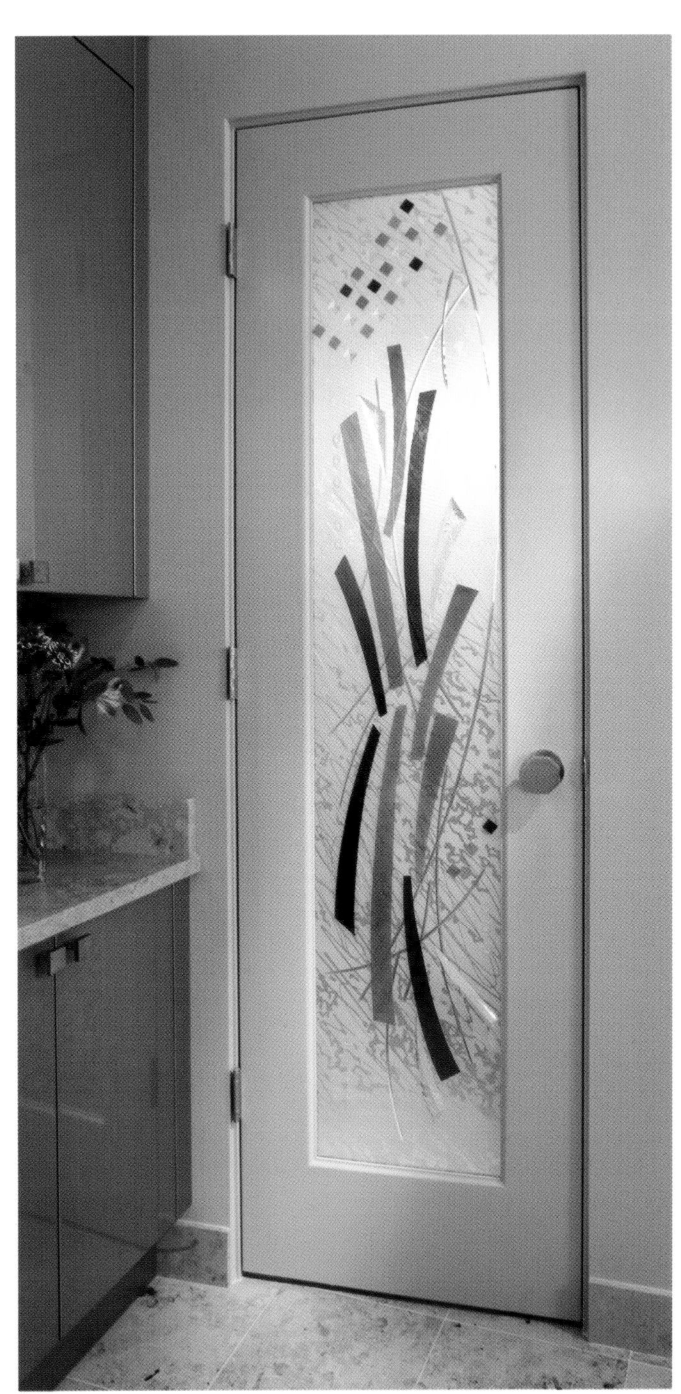

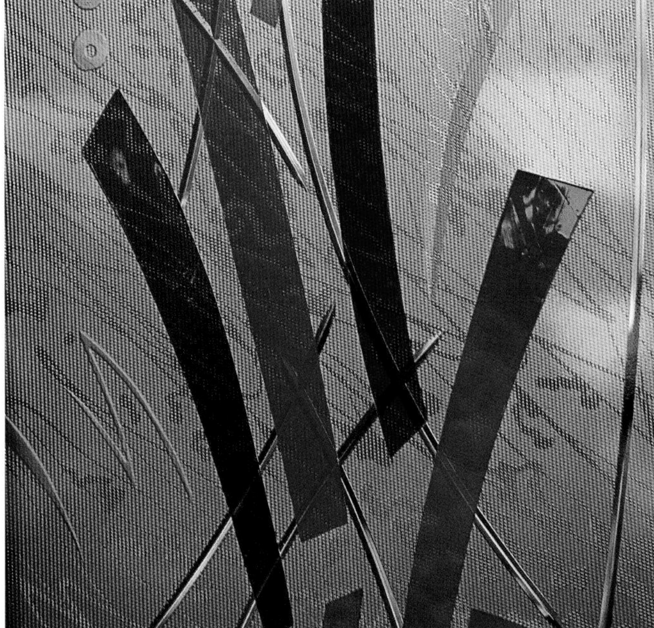

Private residence, 2006, Boulder, CO, glass appliqué. Photographs: Ron Johnson.

BJ KATZ

MELTDOWN GLASS ART & DESIGN ▪ 3225 NORTH WASHINGTON STREET ▪ CHANDLER, AZ 85225
TEL 480-633-3366 ▪ FAX 480-633-3344 ▪ E-MAIL SALES@MELTDOWNGLASS.COM ▪ WWW.MELTDOWNGLASS.COM

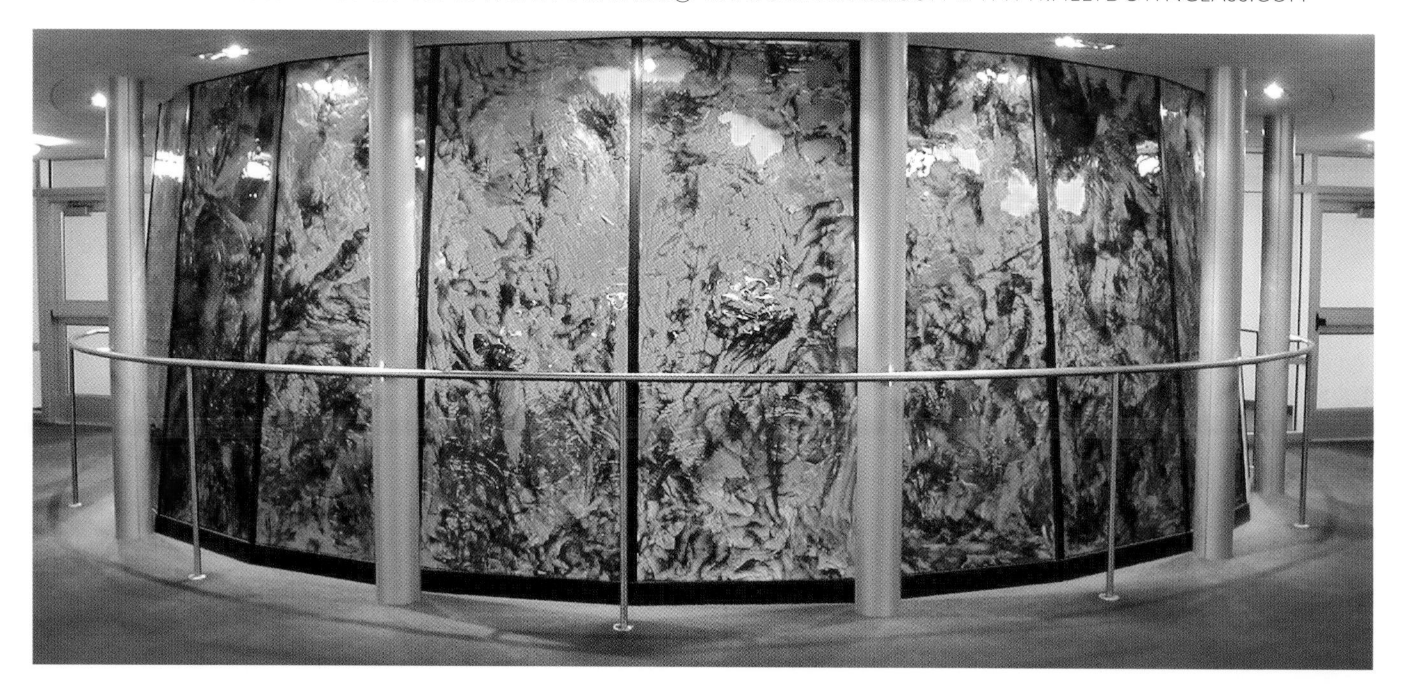

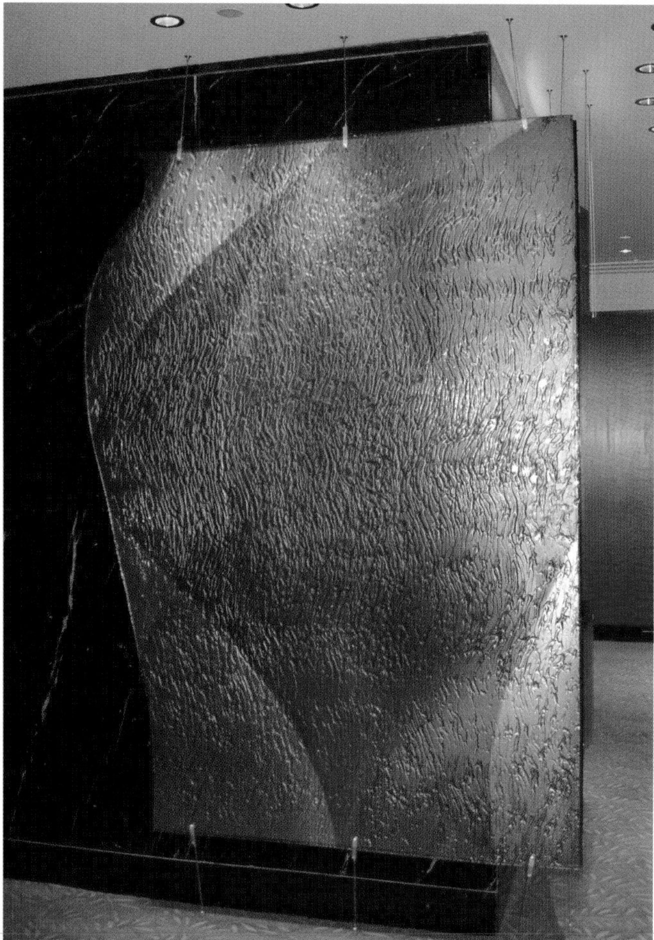

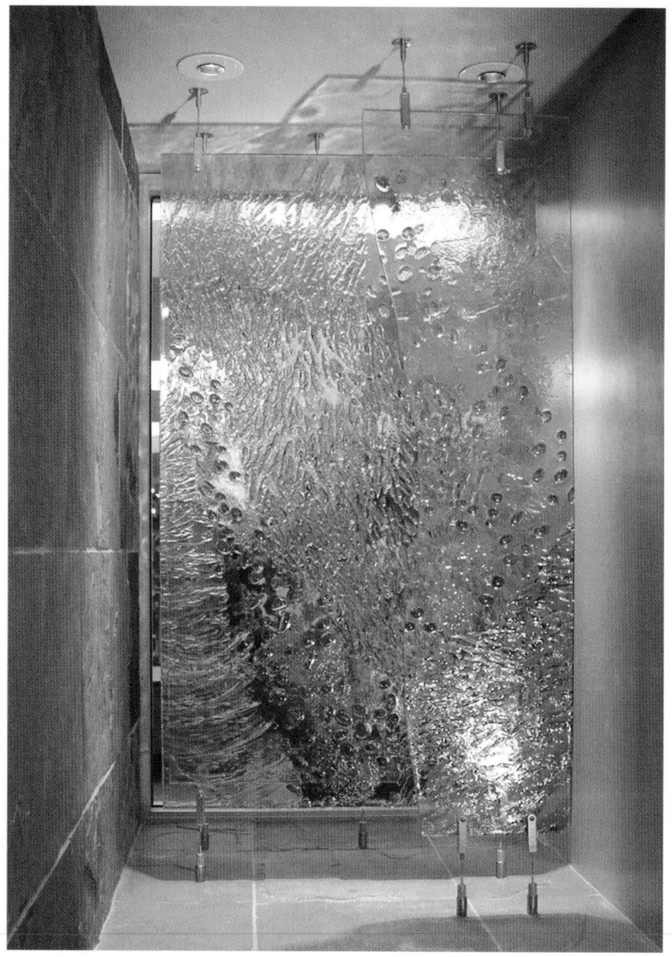

Top: Cast glass sculptural wall, Midwestern University Chapel, Downer's Grove, IL, 8'H x 84'W, custom texture and color. Photograph: Jeremy Jones.
Bottom left: Cast glass sculptural panel, Millennium Broadway Hotel, New York, NY. Photograph: Peter Hayes.
Bottom right: Cast glass sculptural panels, Banner Baywood Hospital, Mesa, AZ. Photograph: Derek Nadeau.

KESSLER STUDIOS, INC.

CINDY KESSLER ■ 273 EAST BROADWAY STREET ■ LOVELAND, OH 45140 ■ TEL 513-683-7500
FAX 513-683-7512 ■ E-MAIL INFO@KESSLERSTUDIOS.COM ■ WWW.KESSLERSTUDIOS.COM

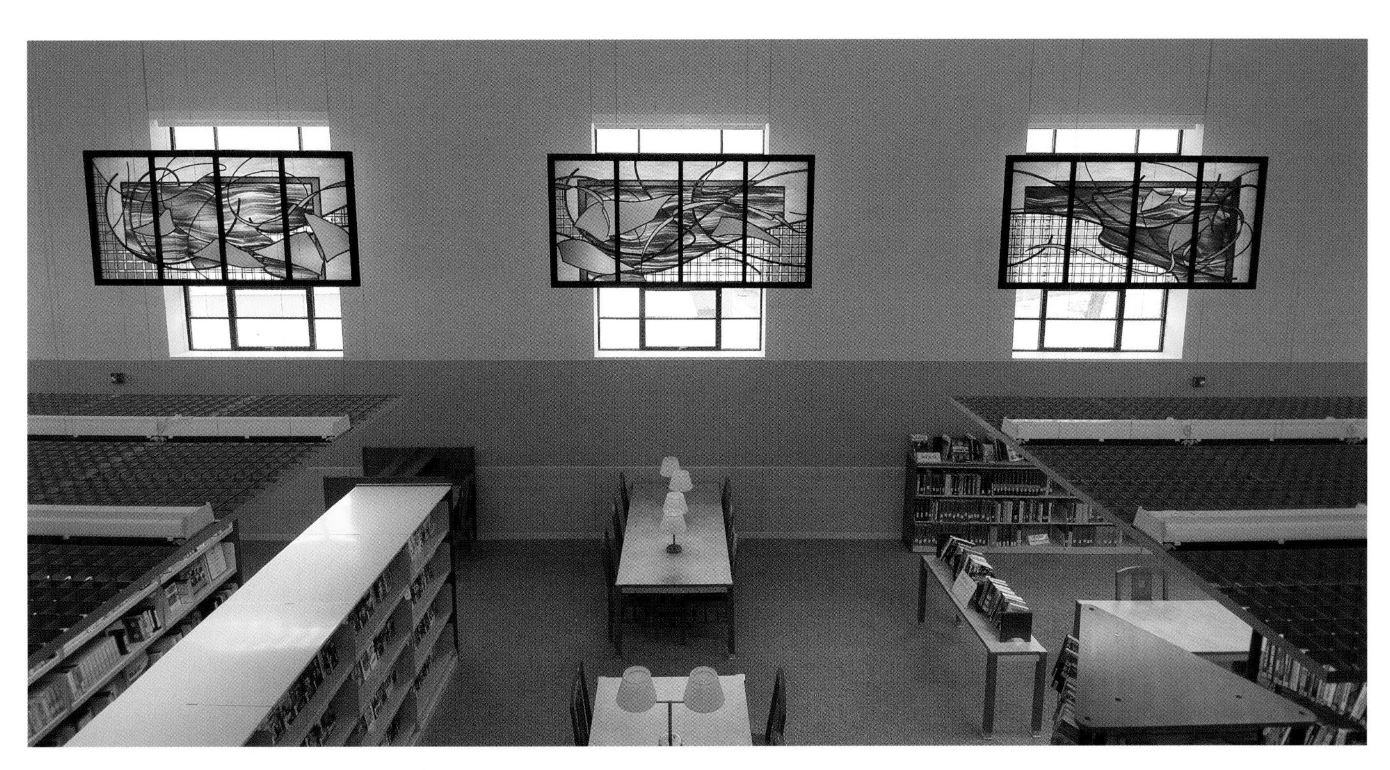

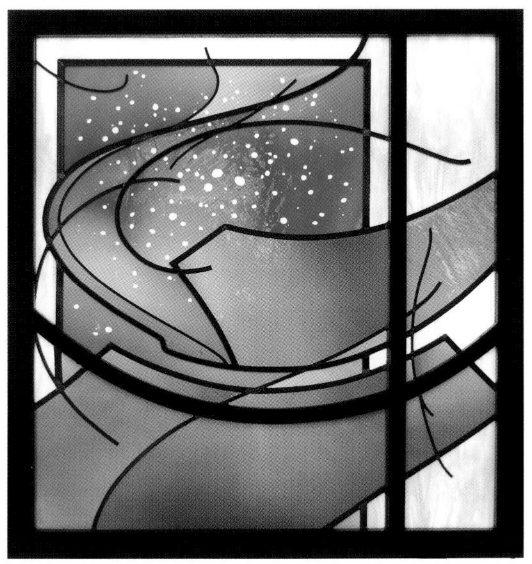

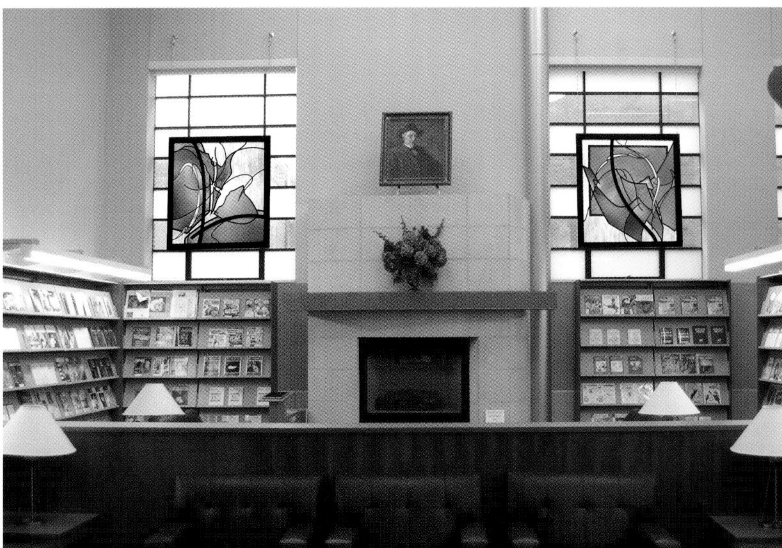

Top: *The Journey,* 2006, Peru State College Library, Peru, NE, each: 5' x 10'. Bottom left: *Roller Rink,* 2006, Peru State College Library, Peru, NE, 56" x 51".
Bottom right: *The Chapel* and *The Gymnasium,* Peru State College Library, Peru, NE, each: 56" x 51". Photographs: Bob Kessler.

MARK J. LEVY

MARK LEVY STUDIO ■ PO BOX 4722 ■ CHATSWORTH, CA 91311 ■ TEL 818-595-1195 ■ FAX 818-595-1166
E-MAIL INFO@MARKLEVYSTUDIO.NET ■ WWW.MARKLEVYSTUDIO.NET ■ WWW.MARKLEVYSTUDIO.BIZ

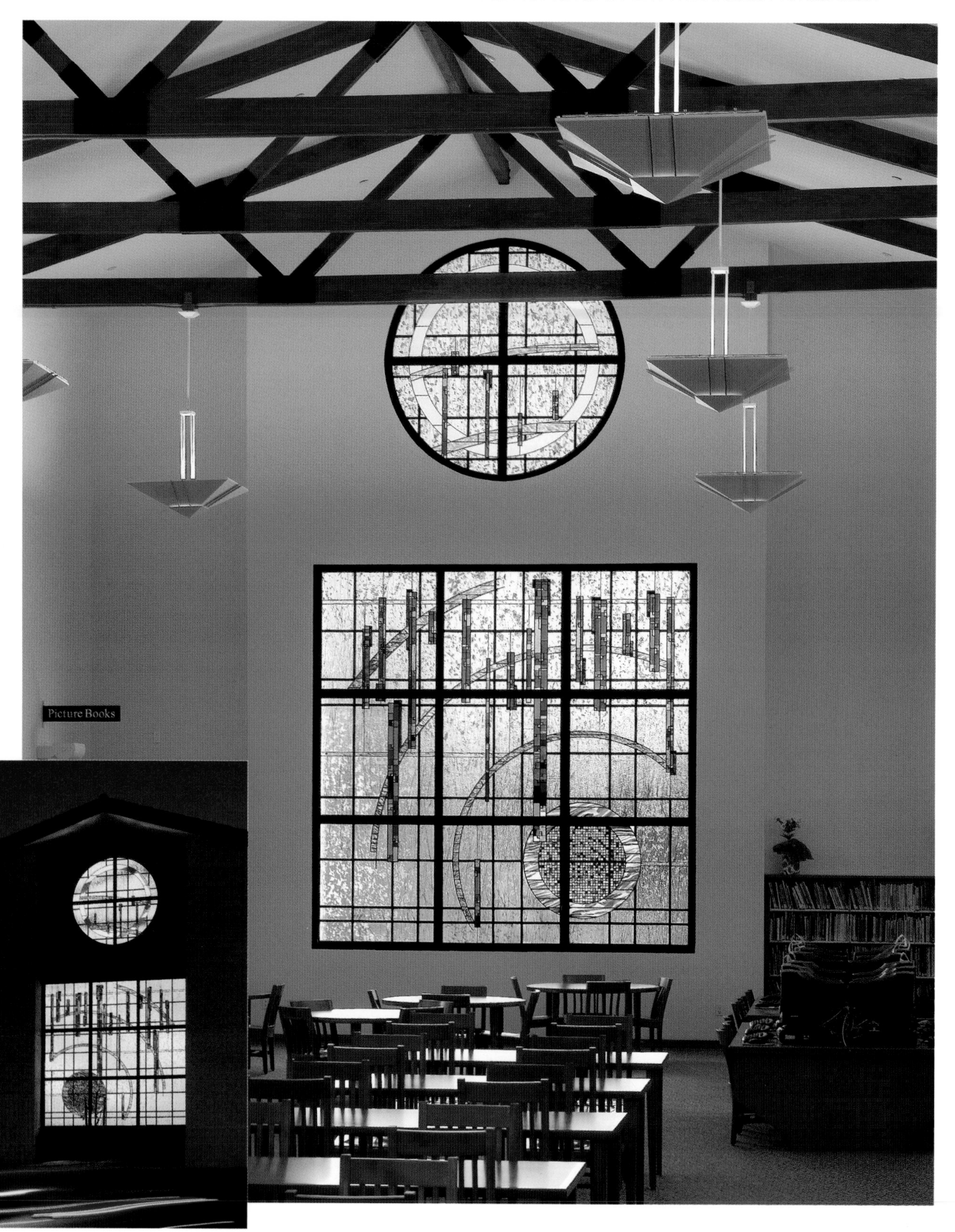

Harmonic Ascension, 2005, Los Angeles County Library, Chatsworth Branch, CA, leaded stained and fused glass in insulated glass units, 24' x 12'. Photograph: Scott Mayoral.

ALEKSANDRA LUGOWSKA

1976 SECOND AVENUE SUITE 5B ■ NEW YORK, NY 10029 ■ TEL 917-405-9502
E-MAIL OLAGLASSART@GMAIL.COM ■ WWW.OLAGLASSART.COM

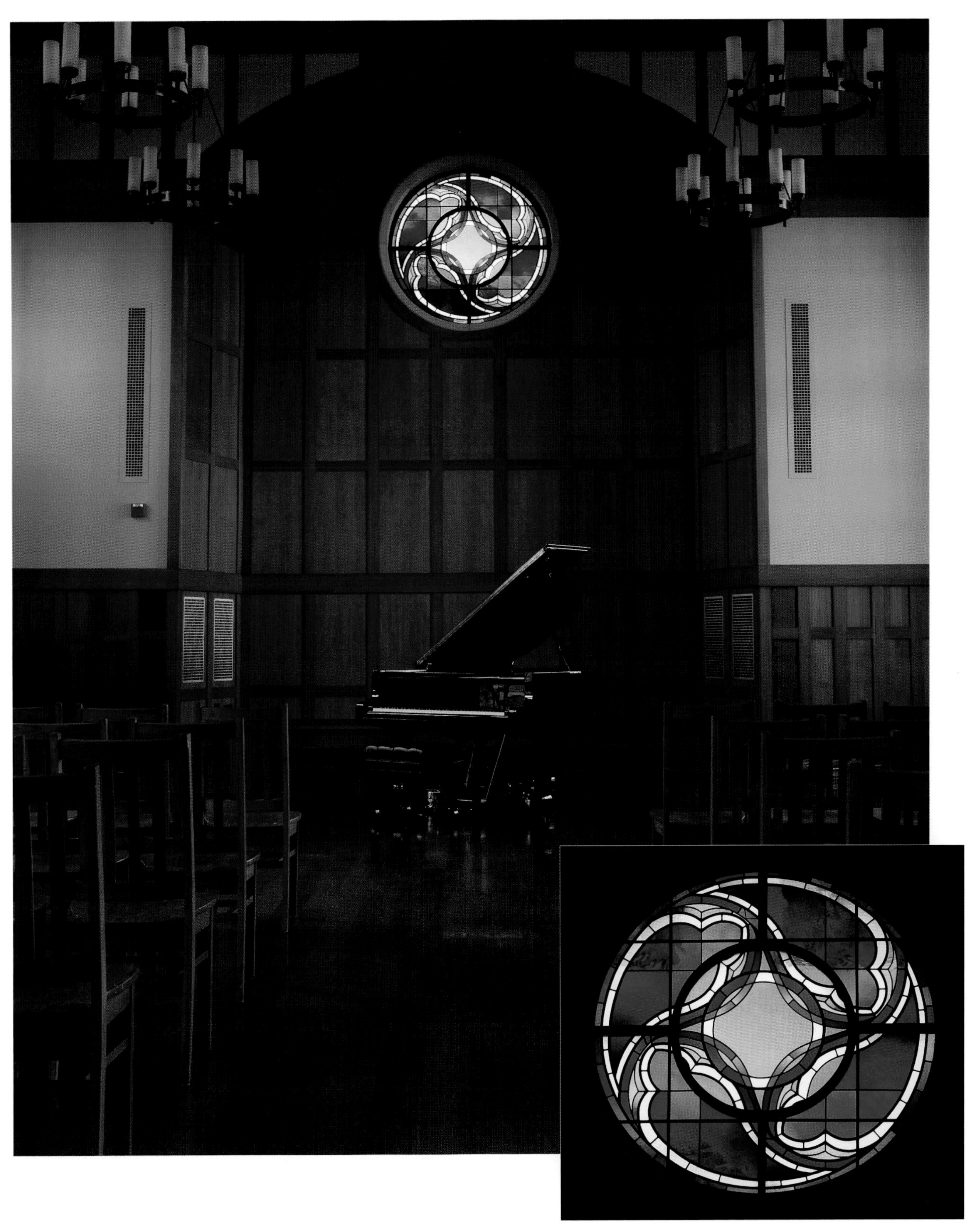

Time, Allen Memorial Hall at Hackley School, Tarrytown, NY, leaded stained glass window, 6' Dia. Photographs: Ryan Terribilini.

MICHEL MAILHOT

THINKGLASS ■ 1993 LIONEL BERTRAND ■ BOISBRIAND, QC J7H 1N8 ■ CANADA ■ TEL 450-420-1110
FAX 450-420-4010 ■ E-MAIL INFO@THINKGLASS.COM ■ WWW.THINKGLASS.COM

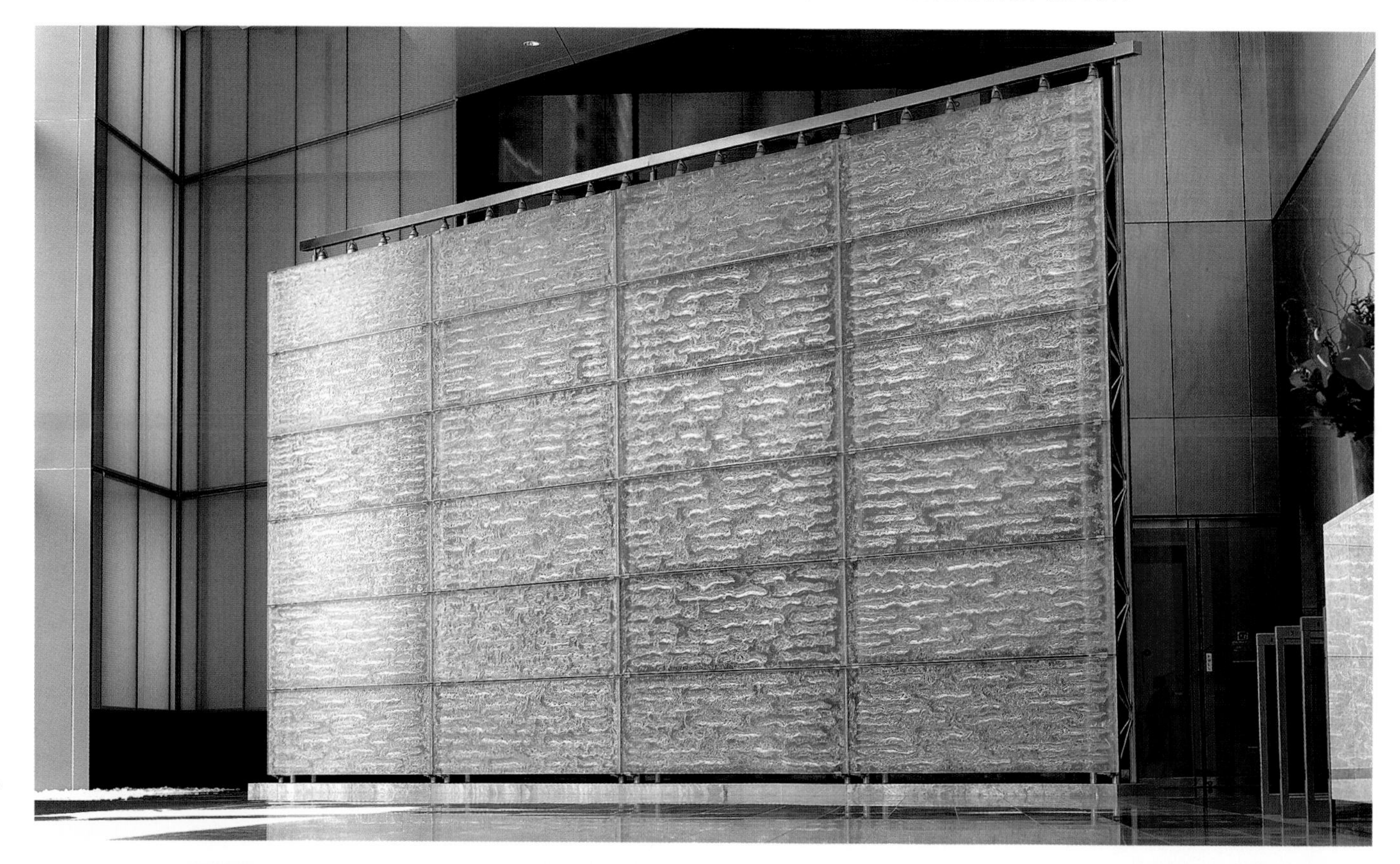

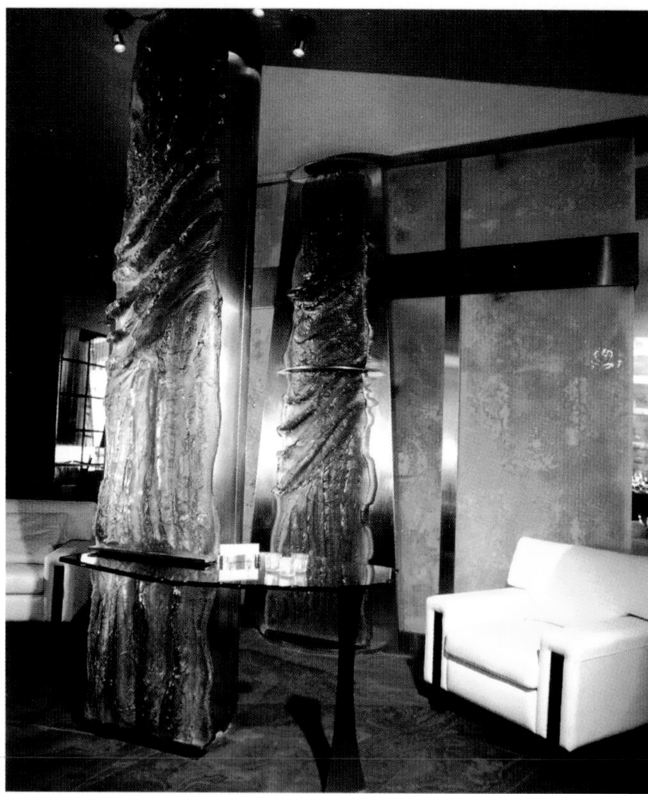

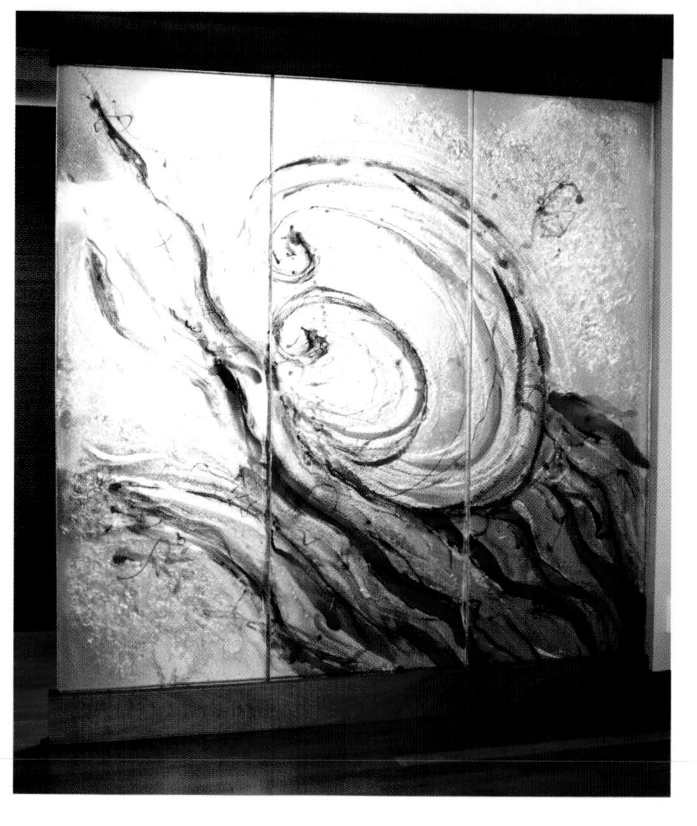

Top: Glass wall, One South Dearborn, Chicago, two walls, each: 18' x 40' x 1.5". Bottom left: Glass sculpture, California Dream, Montreal, 10' x 3' x 2". Bottom right: Glass wall, private residence, Montreal, 7' x 9' x 1.5". Photographs: Pete Morneau.

ELLEN MANDELBAUM

ELLEN MANDELBAUM GLASS ART ■ 39-49 46TH STREET ■ SUNNYSIDE, NY 11104
TEL/FAX 718-361-8154 ■ E-MAIL EMGA@EARTHLINK.NET ■ WWW.EMGLASSART.COM

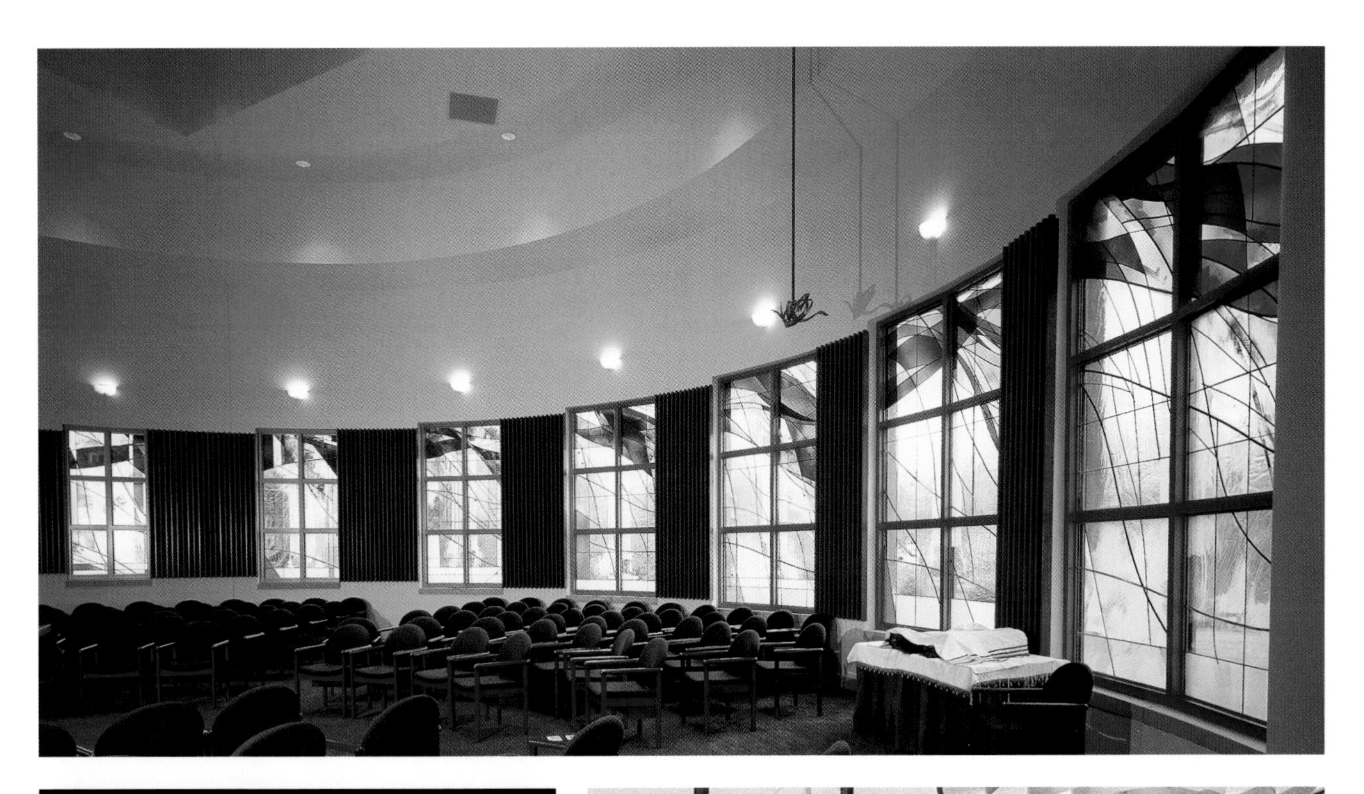

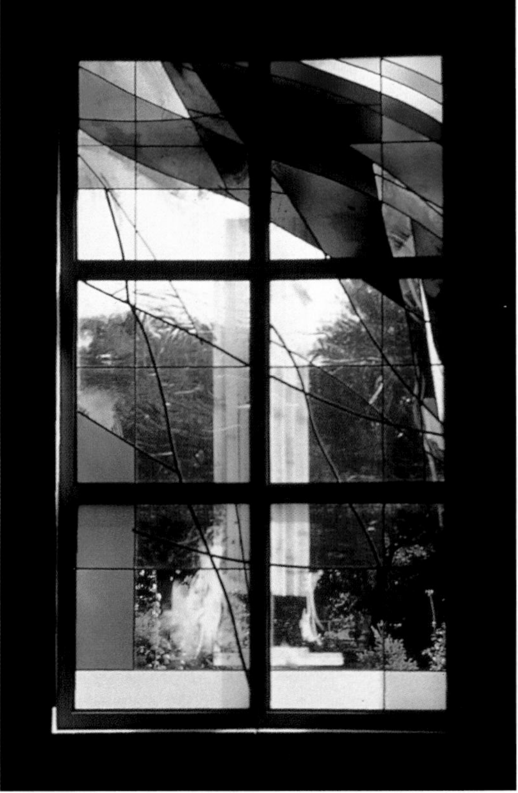

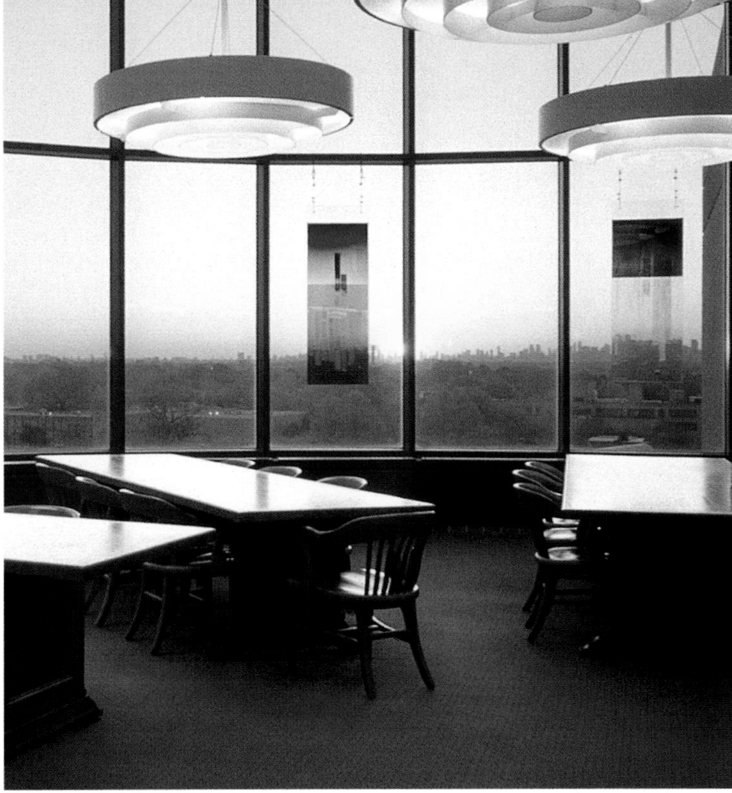

Top: Adath Jeshurun Synagogue Morning Chapel. Photograph: Saari Forrai. Bottom left: Morning Chapel (detail). Photograph: Saari Forrai.
Bottom right: *Colors of the Sky,* Queen's College Art Center, laminated, painted panels. Photograph: Elizabeth Felicella.

KARI MINNICK

KARI MINNICK ART GLASS STUDIO ■ 8230 GEORGIA AVENUE ■ SILVER SPRING, MD 20910
TEL 240-678-8649 ■ E-MAIL KARI@KARIMINNICK.COM ■ WWW.KARIMINNICK.COM

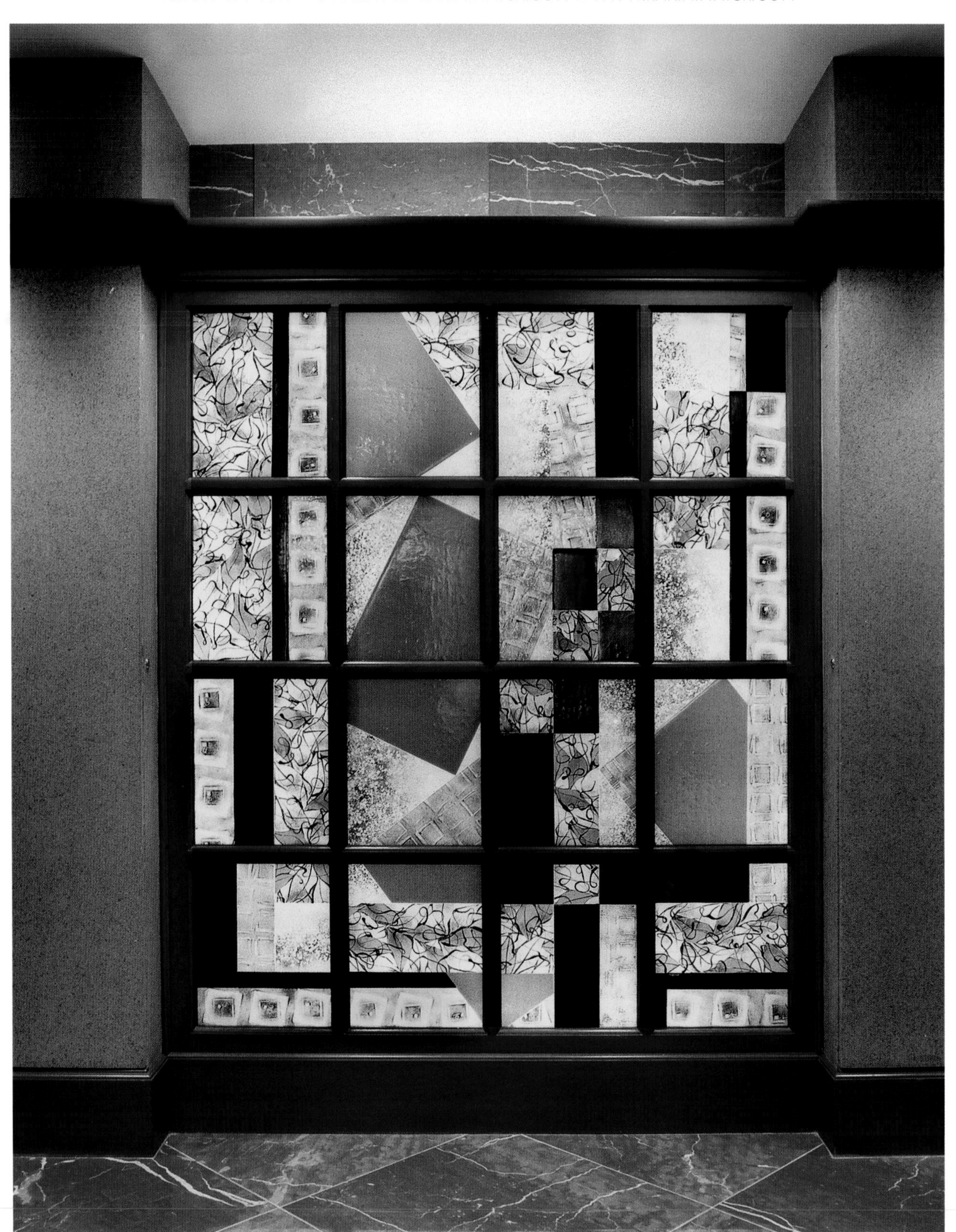

Embracing Momentum, lobby at Hampden Square, Bethesda, MD, kiln-formed glass, 64"H x 52"W. Photograph: William Geiger.

JANINE S. ODY

CRISTALLO ARCHITECTURAL GLASS ■ 333 14TH STREET SUITE 202 ■ TOLEDO, OH 43604
TEL 419-243-2717 ■ FAX 419-243-2188 ■ E-MAIL JANINEODY@CRISTALLOGLASS.COM ■ WWW.CRISTALLOGLASS.COM

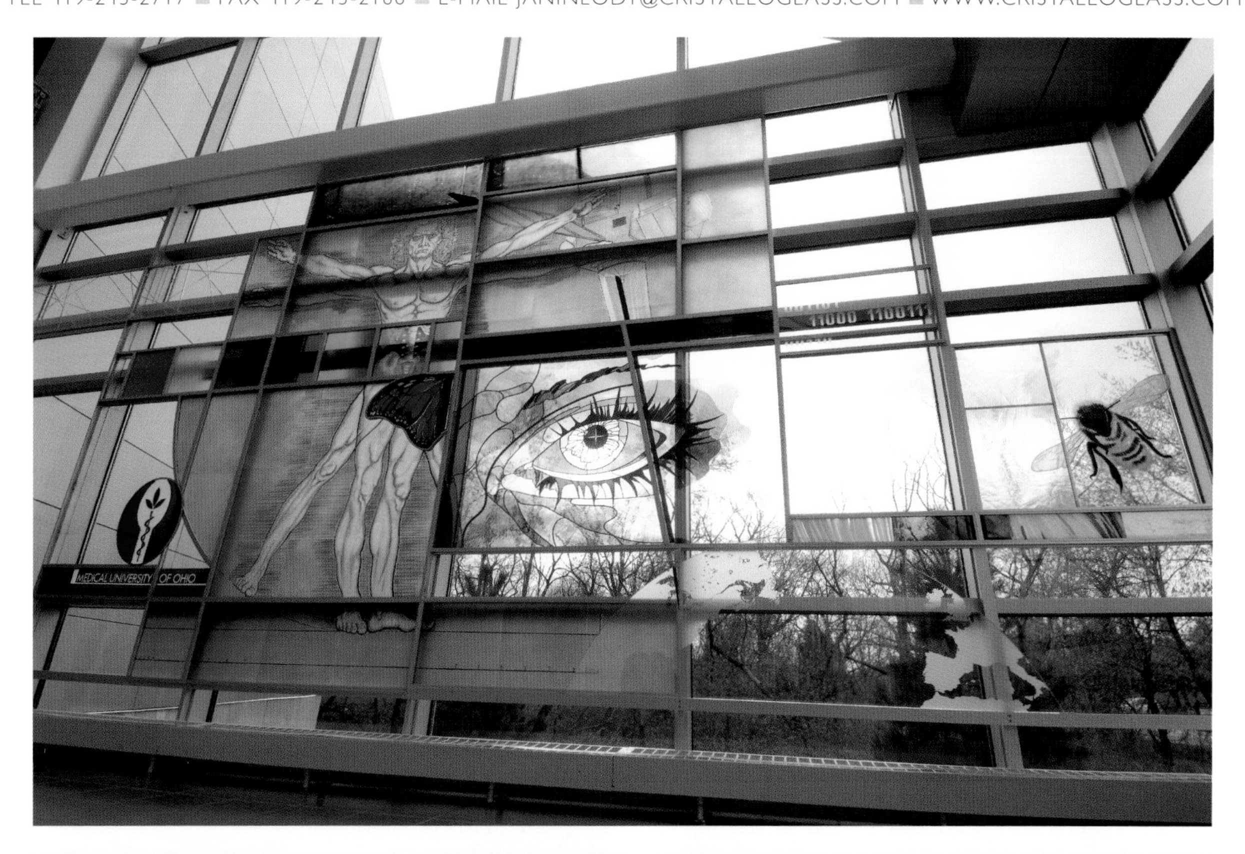

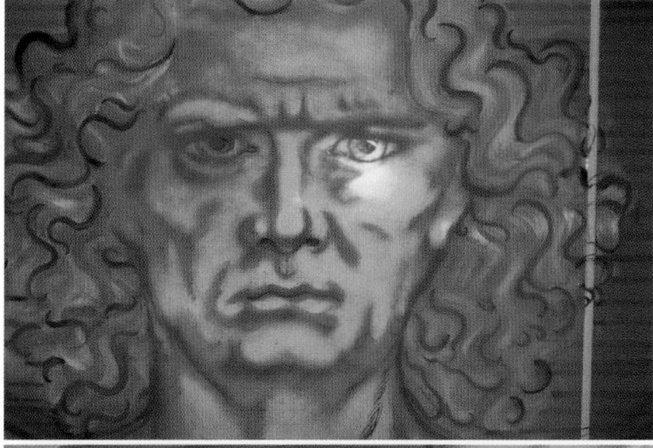

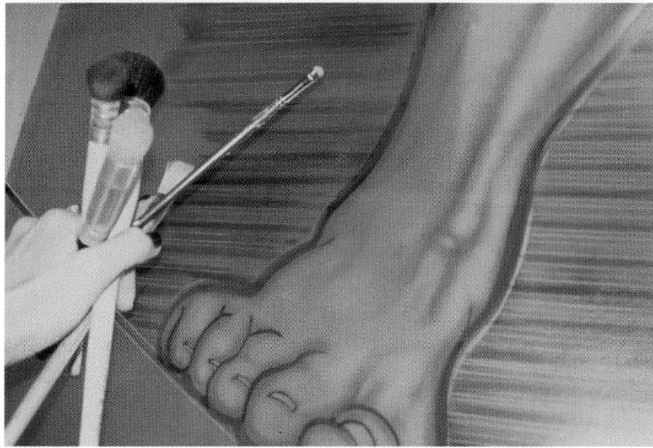

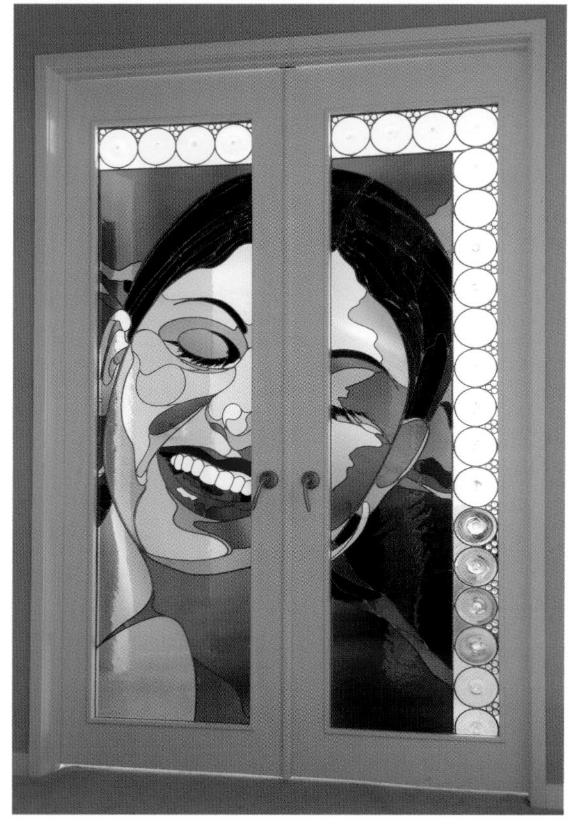

Top: Medical University of Ohio, traditionally painted and fired, laminated, leaded blown glass, fused, etched, and faceted techniques, 12'H x 25'W.
Bottom left: Medical University of Ohio (detail). Bottom right: *The Honeymoon,* leaded blown glass, 96"H x 60"W x 1.75"D. Photographs: Bruce Works Photography.

MARKIAN OLYNYK

MARKIAN STUDIOS INC. ■ 2776 WEST TENTH AVENUE ■ VANCOUVER, BC V6K 2J9 ■ CANADA
TEL 604-738-9791 ■ FAX 604-738-9722 ■ E-MAIL MARKIAN@MARKIANSTUDIOS.COM ■ WWW.MARKIANSTUDIOS.COM

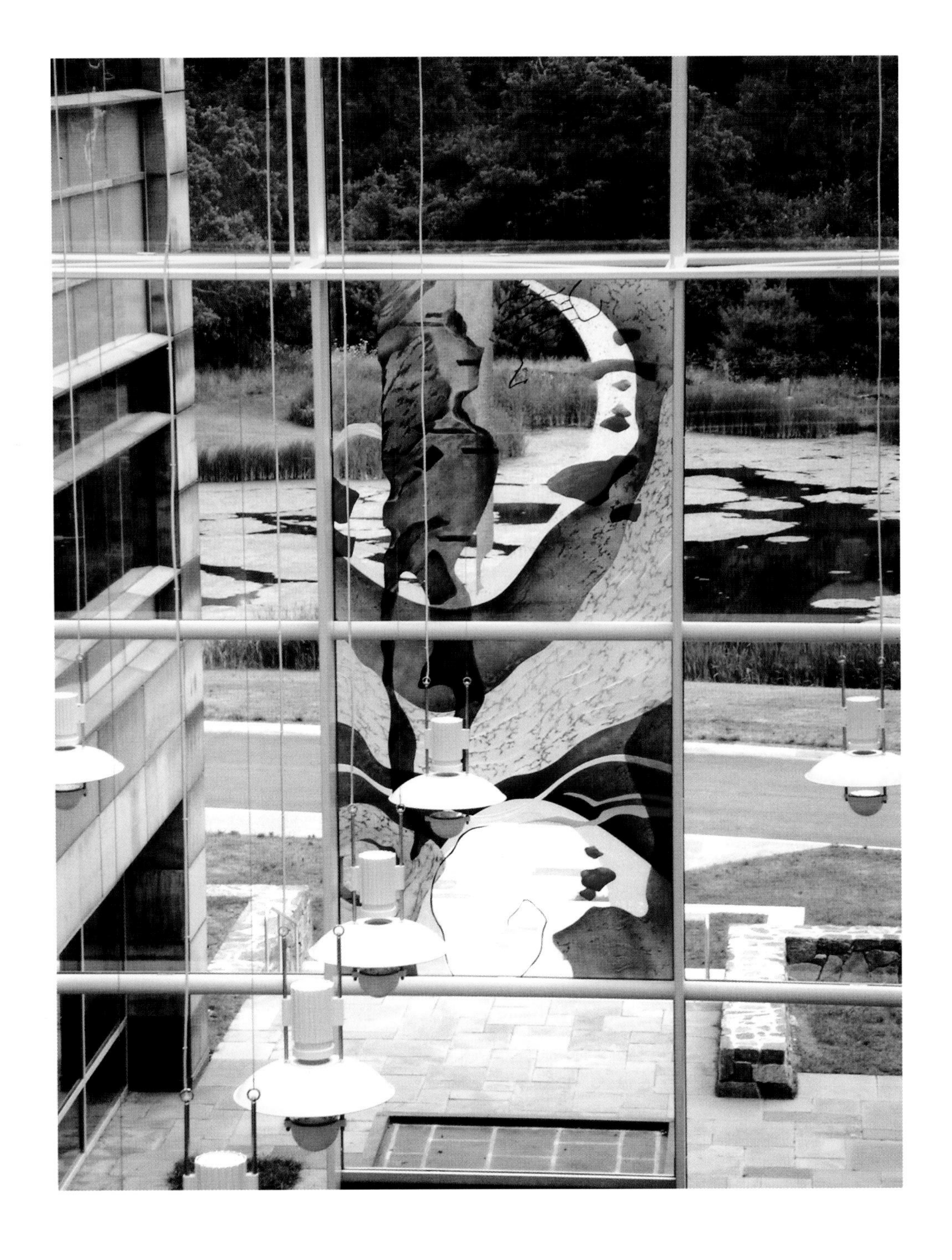

Atrium Entry Windows, New England Biolabs, Beverly, MA, 14' x 7'. Photograph: Sanjay Kumar.

PANED EXPRESSIONS STUDIOS

M.S. HANSON AND J.L. PARKER ■ 1418 TRIMBLE ROAD ■ EDGEWOOD, MD 21040 ■ TEL 410-676-1248
FAX 410-676-2112 ■ E-MAIL ARTGLASS@PANEDEXPRESSIONS.COM ■ WWW.PANEDEXPRESSIONS.COM

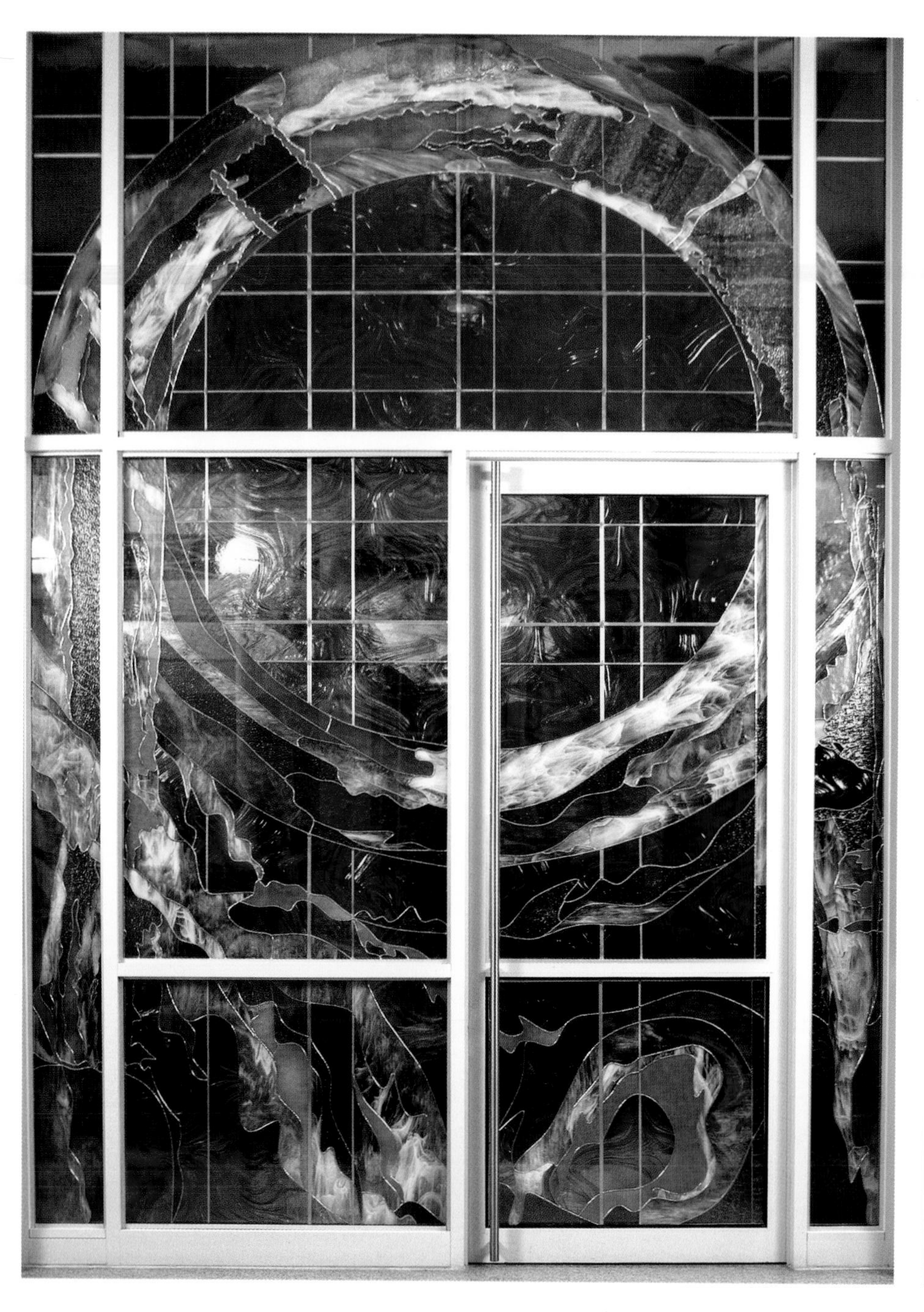

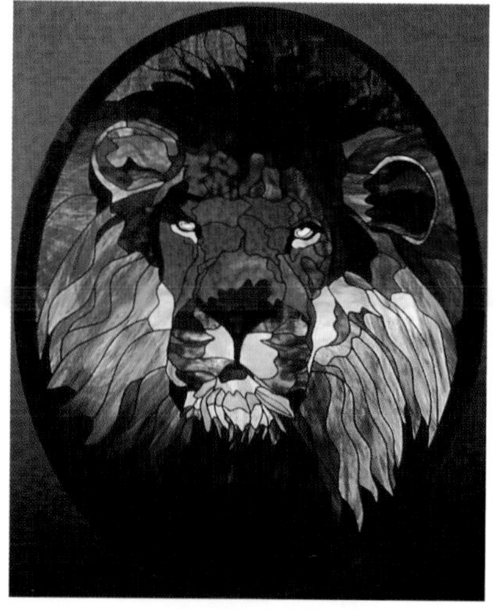

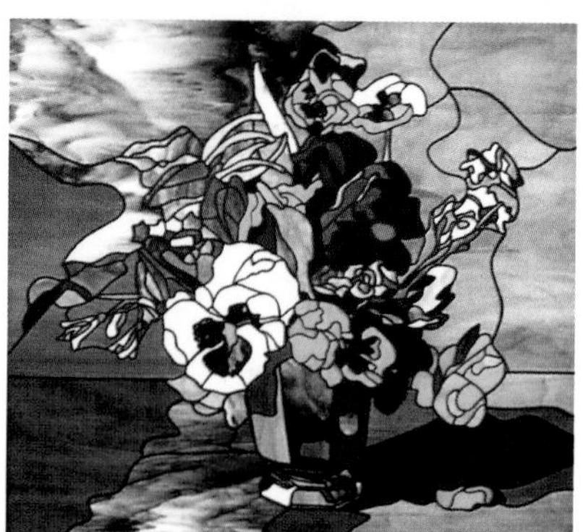

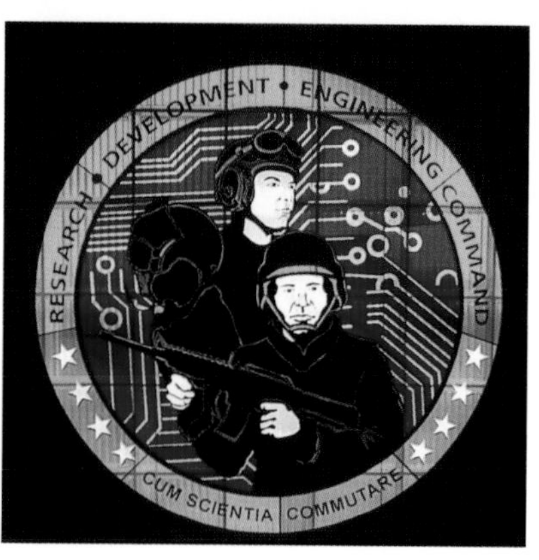

Left: *Persistence*, Weinberg Meditation Room, Kimmel Cancer Center, Johns Hopkins Hospital, Baltimore, MD, nine-panel entrance: 15' x 12'. Photograph: Dave Harp. Top right: *Arthur*, center dormer for new home, Monterey, CA, 54" x 42". Center right: *Late Summer Pansies*, foyer centerpiece, New York, 34" x 34". Bottom right: *RDE-COM Military Logo*, headquarters building, Army, MD, 72" x 72".

PEARL RIVER GLASS STUDIO

ANDREW C. YOUNG ■ 142 MILLSAPS AVENUE ■ JACKSON, MS 39202 ■ TEL 601-353-2497
TEL 800-771-3639 ■ FAX 601-969-9315 ■ E-MAIL PEARLSTUDIO@BELLSOUTH.NET ■ WWW.PRGS.COM

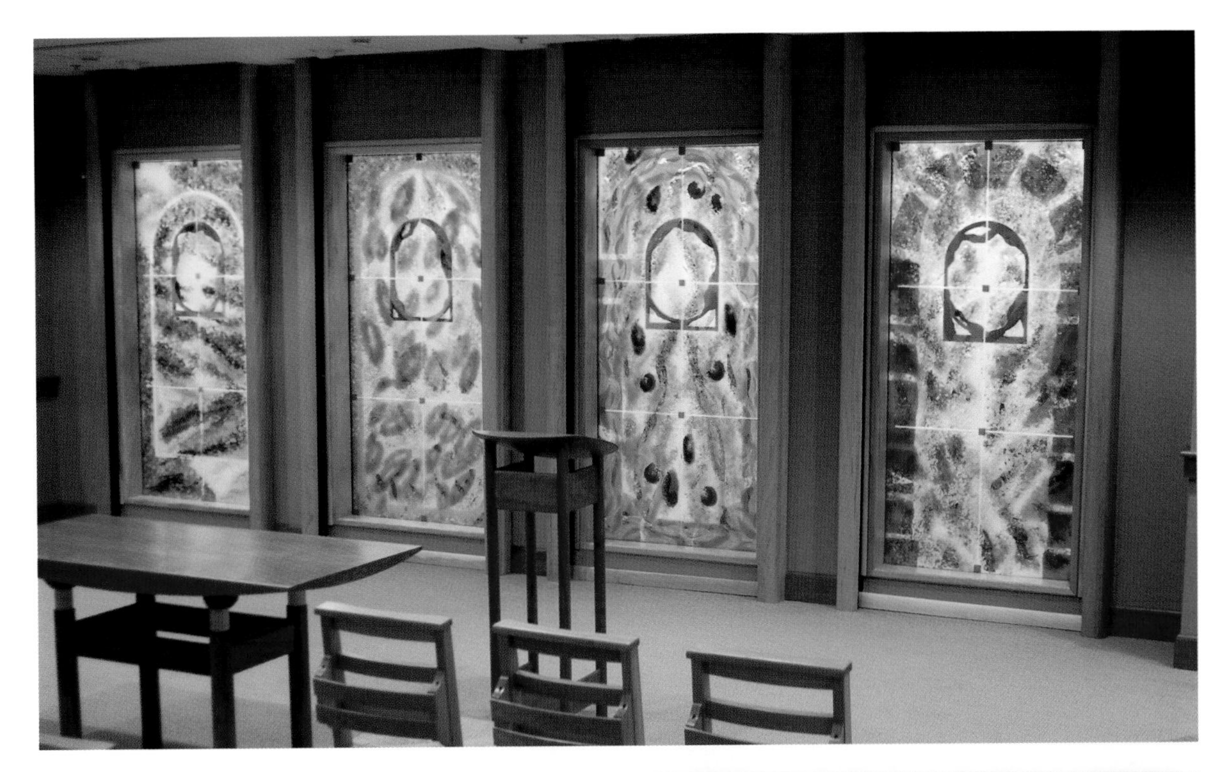

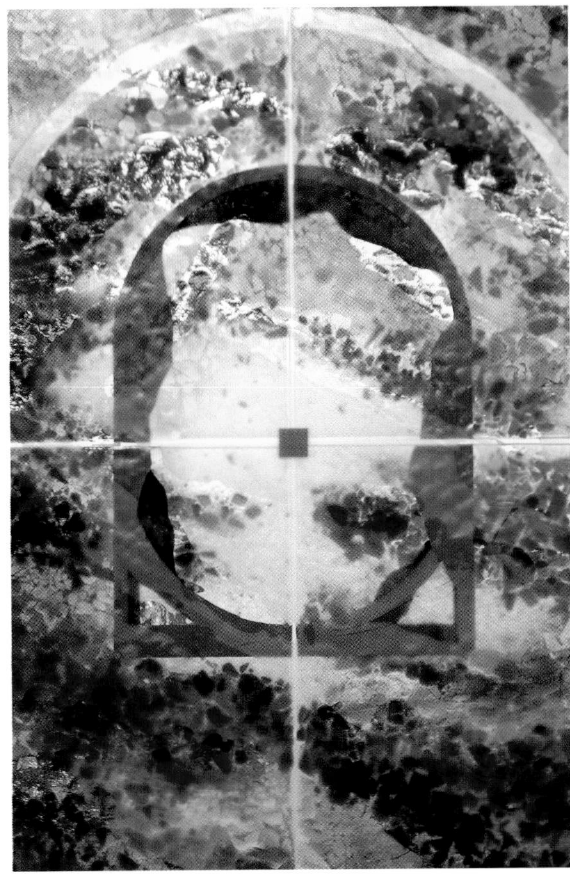

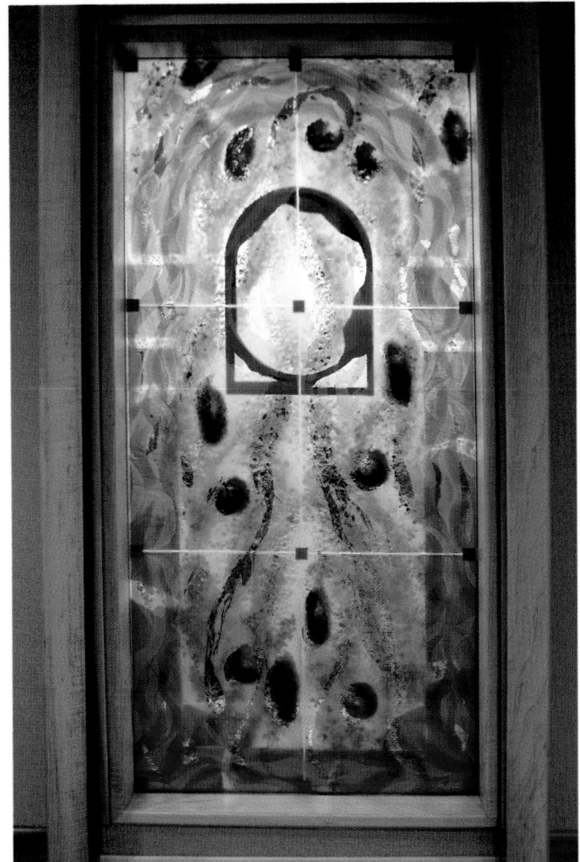

Top: *Four Seasons*, University of Mississippi Medical Center Chapel. Bottom left: *Winter*, detail.
Bottom right: *Summer*. Woodwork: Fletcher Cox. Photographs: Thomas Crouch.

TOM PHILABAUM

PHILABAUM GLASS, INC. ■ 711 SOUTH SIXTH AVENUE ■ TUCSON, AZ 85701 ■ TEL 520-884-7404
FAX 520-884-0679 ■ E-MAIL TPHILABAUM@QWEST.NET ■ WWW.PHILABAUMGLASS.COM

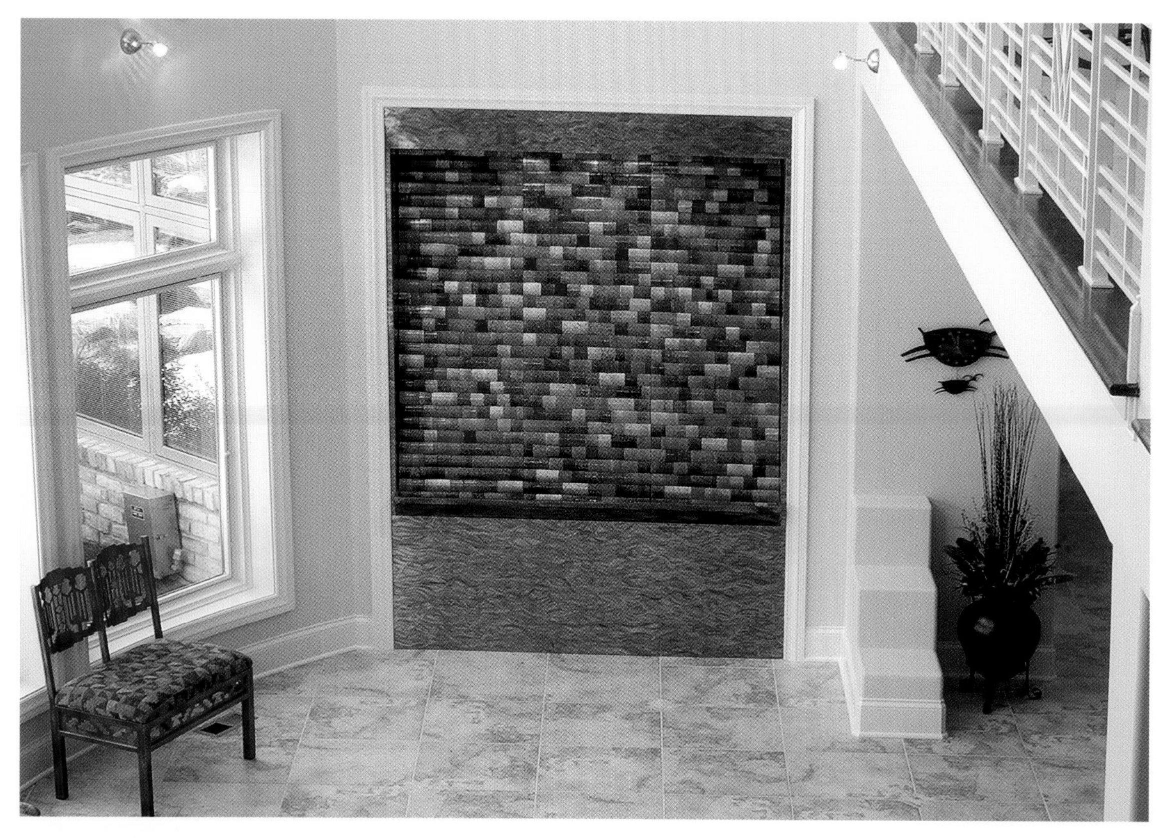

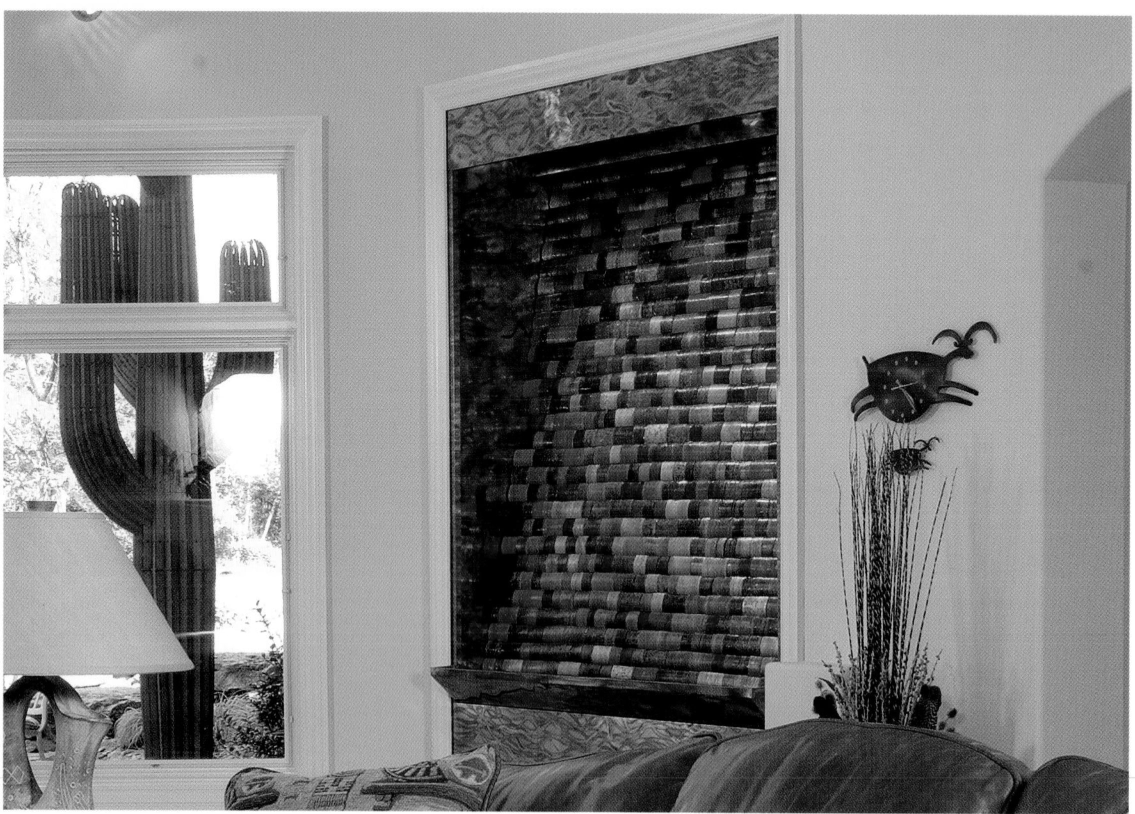

Waterfall, private residence, Indianapolis, IN, blown glass tiles, stainless steel cabinet with copper facing, 108"H x 75"W x 20"D. Photographs: Megan Van Valer.

STANTON GLASS STUDIO, LLC.

BRYANT J. STANTON ▪ 7781 GHOLSON ROAD ▪ WACO, TX. 76705 ▪ TEL 254-829-1151
FAX 254-829-2521 ▪ E-MAIL INFO@STANTONGLASS.COM ▪ WWW.STANTONGLASS.COM

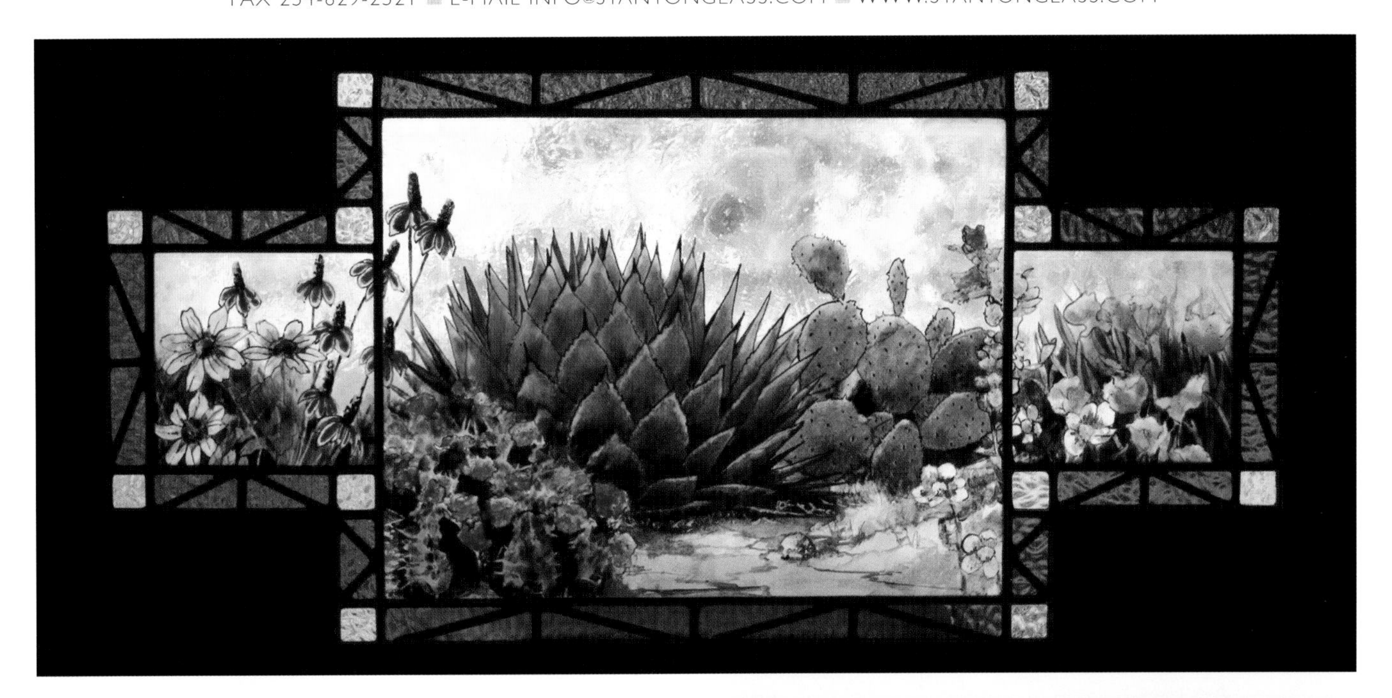

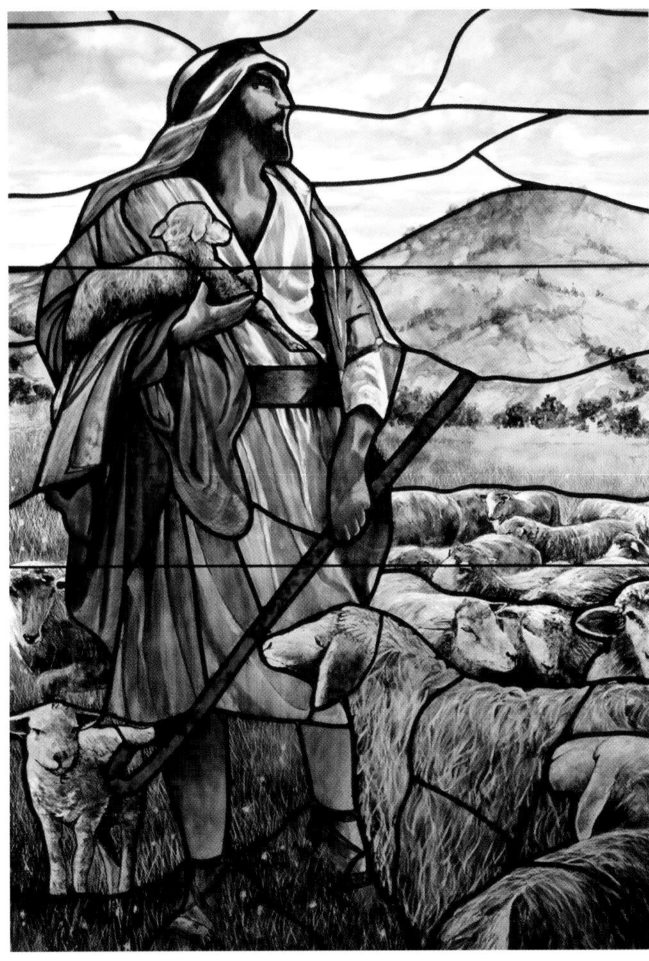

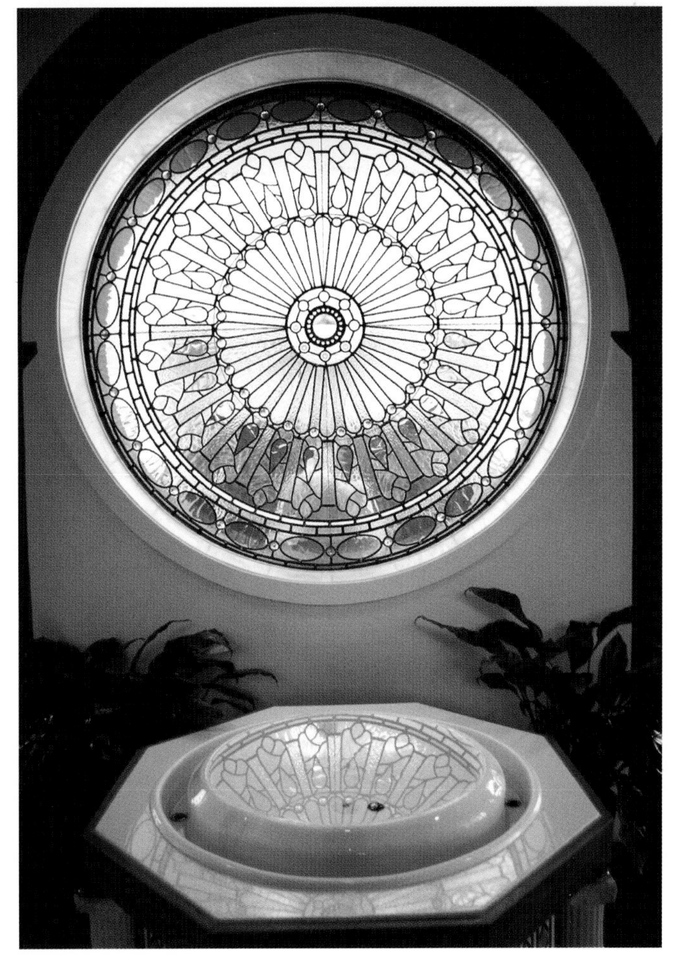

Top: *Flowering Desert Succulents*, private residence, Santa Fe, NM, leaded, stained, and hand painted kiln-fired glass, 20" x 40".
Bottom left: *The Good Shepherd*, Johnson Memorial Church, Palm Coast, FL, leaded, stained, and hand-painted kiln-fired glass, 72" x 48".
Bottom right: *Baptistery Window*, Saint Jeromes Catholic Church, Woodway, TX, leaded, clear textured glasses, 6' Dia. All designs and photos ©Stanton Glass Studio, LLC.

STANTON GLASS STUDIO, LLC.

BRYANT J. STANTON ■ 7781 GHOLSON ROAD ■ WACO, TX. 76705 ■ TEL 254-829-1151
FAX 254-829-2521 ■ E-MAIL INFO@STANTONGLASS.COM ■ WWW.STANTONGLASS.COM

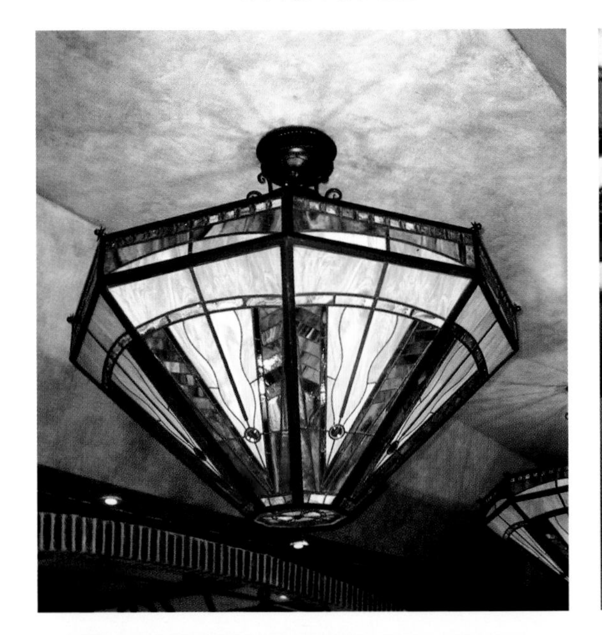

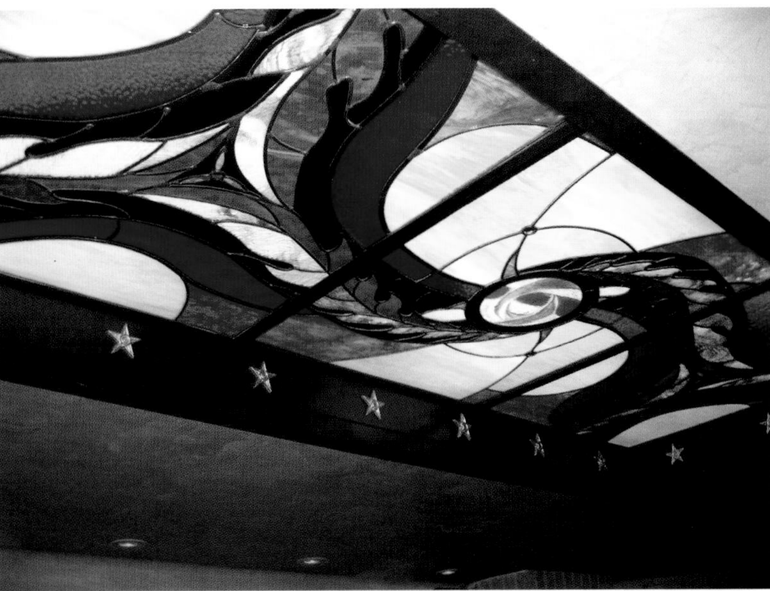

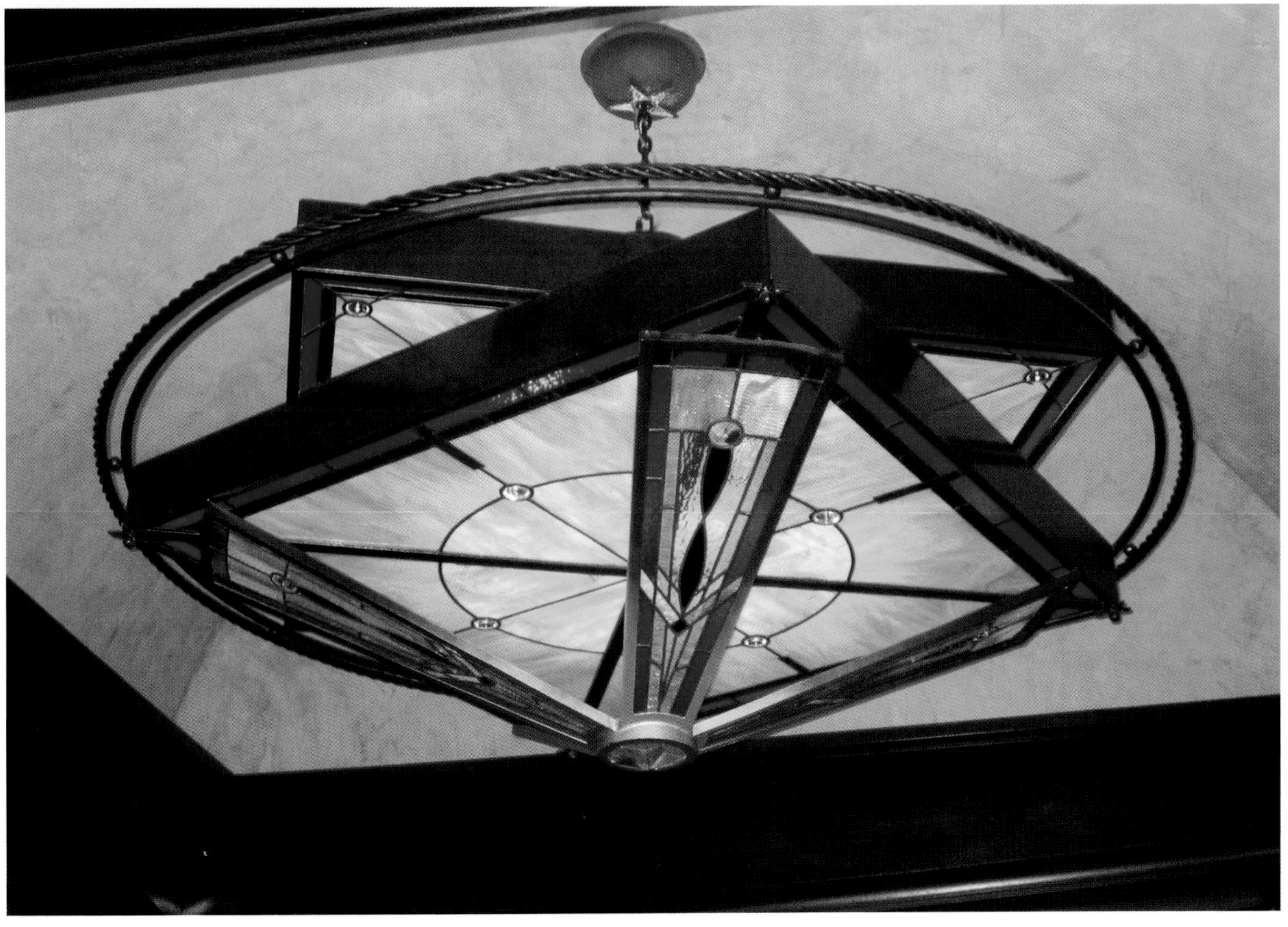

Top left: *Large Octagon Chandelier,* Vic and Anthony's Steak House, Houston, TX, leaded, stained glass with forged wrought iron fixture, 6' Dia. Top right: *Wine Cellar Lighted Ceiling,* Vic and Anthony's Steak House, Las Vegas, NV, leaded, stained, and fused glass with forged wrought iron frame and gilded stars, 4' x 12'. Bottom: *The Southern Cross© Hanging Chandelier,* Vic and Anthony's Steak House, Las Vegas, NV, and Houston, TX, leaded, stained glass with forged wrought iron fixture, 6' Dia. All designs and photos ©Stanton Glass Studio, LLC.

A Commission Story

Cindy Kessler

TITLE
Central DuPage Hospital Chapel, 2005

COMMISSIONED FOR
Central DuPage Hospital,
Chicago, IL

TIMELINE: 18 months

DIMENSIONS: *Fire Window:* 19'H x 6'W;
Transition Windows: 6.5'H x 7.5'W;
Water and *Ruah Windows:* 6.5'H x 5'W

TRADE PROFESSIONAL
Rev. Richard Lundgren
and Rev. Thomas Paul,
House of the Church
Liturgical Design Consultants

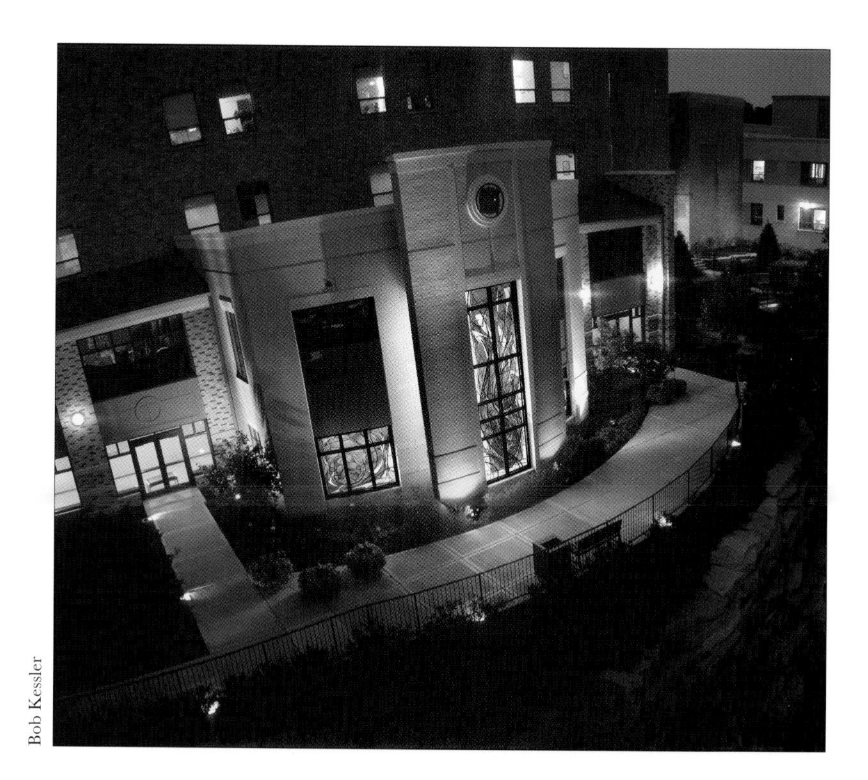

Bob Kessler

Central DuPage Hospital's Chapel Committee had a broad mandate for the window panels that would grace their new sanctuary. Reverend Richard Lundgren explains, "We wanted something that would appeal to people of varied faiths, from Judaism and Islam to various Christian denominations." Glass artist Cindy Kessler rose to the challenge. "I met with the client, the liturgical consultant, and the three chaplains. We all talked about how these windows would function. They're in the courtyard of the hospital, so if you could see through these, you'd be looking into people's rooms across the way. From a practical standpoint, the windows needed to be opaque. Then we considered theme: What did we want the windows to do?" ■ Fortunately, the building's unique site suggested a compelling solution. "The hospital is built over what is believed to be an old Indian burial site. We thought it might be appropriate to use primal symbols of nature, such as fire, water, and wind," Lundgren recalls. The glowing, otherworldly windows transport the viewer beyond the institutional setting. "Hospitals are places of change," Kessler explains. "We wanted the chapel to be a place apart, where you could leave all of that behind." By using blown German *opak* glass, Kessler protected the privacy of the space while allowing plenty of light to enter. A total of five richly colored stained glass windows are intended to flow as one, according to Kessler, who sees the series of bright panels as "a soothing embrace to all who enter." The verticality of the central two-story *Fire Window* guides eyes and thoughts heavenward while warming the viewer with recollections of campfire gatherings, hearth, and home. Kessler observes, "It's very primal, very spiritually healing. That sense of companionship, of comfort, is very important, especially in a hospital." ■ Reverend Lundgren lauds Kessler's profound interpretation. "The whole process was a journey into the creative spirit, and I believe the final result was something beautiful and prayerful."

ARTHUR STERN

ARTHUR STERN STUDIOS ■ 1075 JACKSON STREET ■ BENICIA, CA 94510 ■ TEL/FAX 707-745-8480
E-MAIL ARTHUR@ARTHURSTERN.COM ■ WWW.ARTHURSTERN.COM

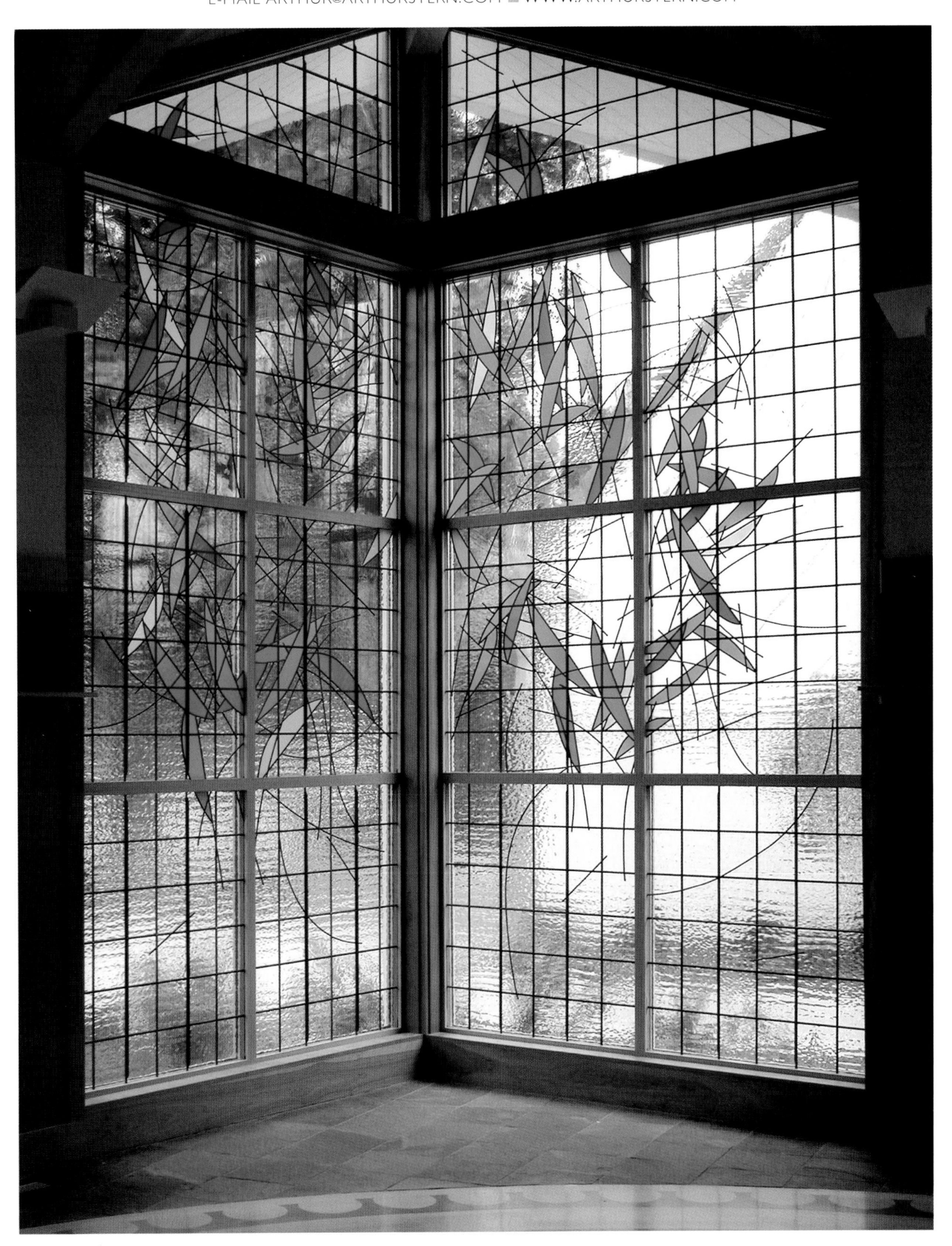

Corner window, Menlo Park, CA, leaded blown French and German glass with clear water glass, 18'H x 12'W.

SERANDA VESPERMANN

VESPERMANN GLASS GALLERY & STUDIO ■ 309 EAST PACES FERRY ROAD ■ ATLANTA, GA 30305
TEL 404-266-0102 ■ TEL 770-936-0633 ■ E-MAIL SERANDA@VESPERMANN.COM ■ WWW.VESPERMANN.COM

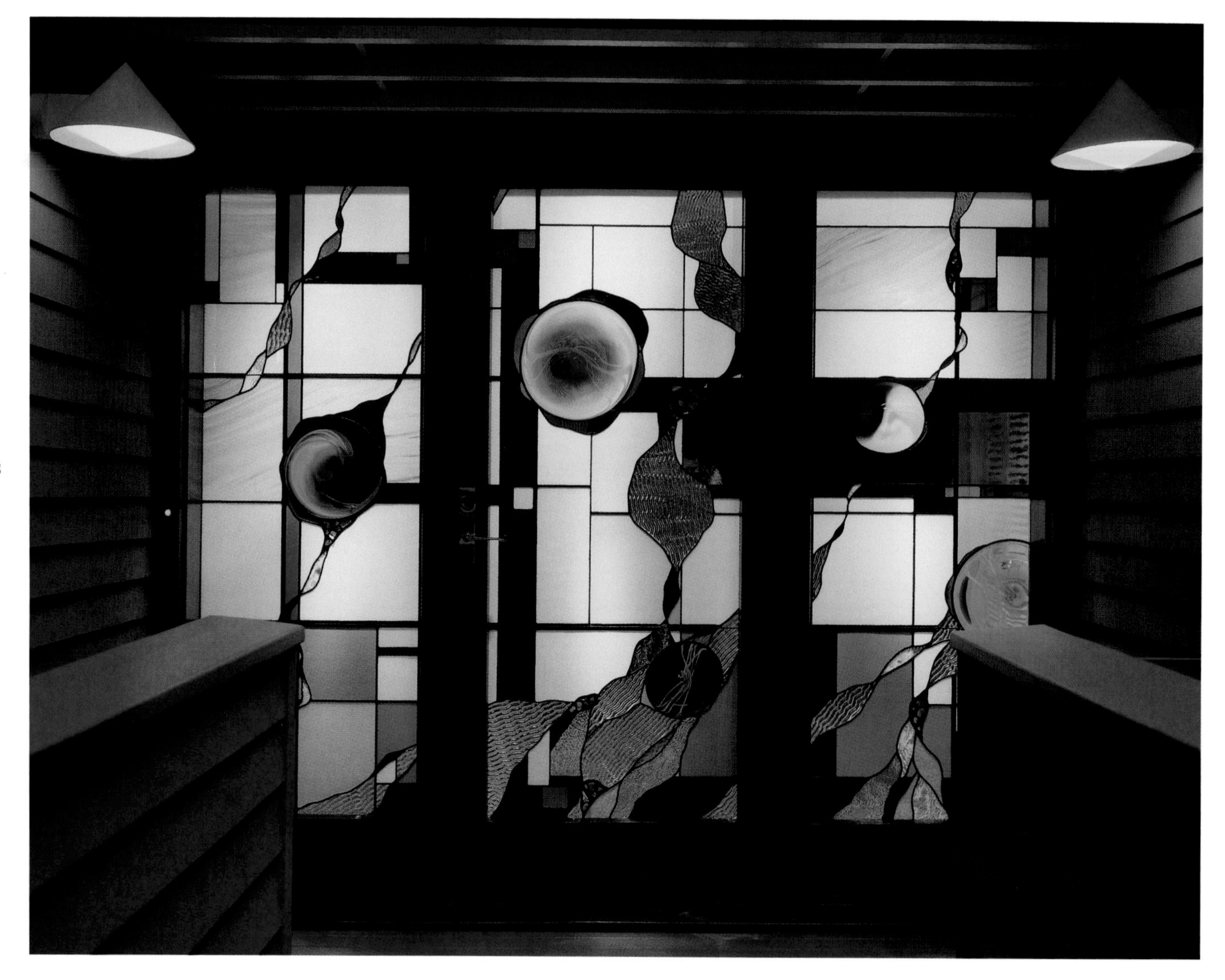

Private residence front door and sidelights, blown European stained glass, rondels, and hand-chipped dalles de verre chunks, 5.8'H x 8'W. Photograph: Bryan Gassel.

LARRY ZGODA

3932 NORTH OAKLEY AVENUE ■ CHICAGO, IL 60618 ■ TEL 773-463-3970
E-MAIL LZ@LARRYZGODASTUDIO.COM ■ WWW.LARRYZGODASTUDIO.COM

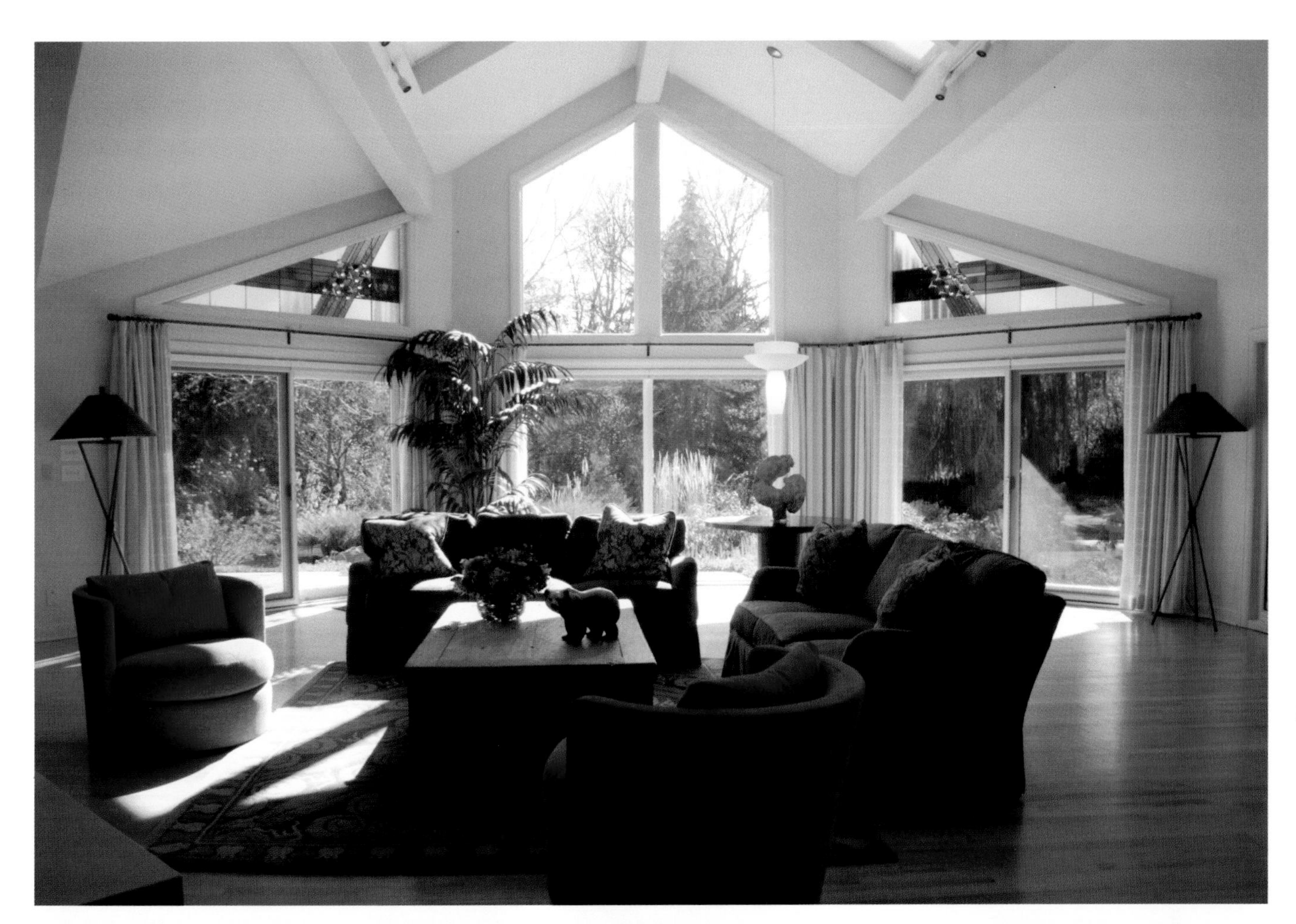

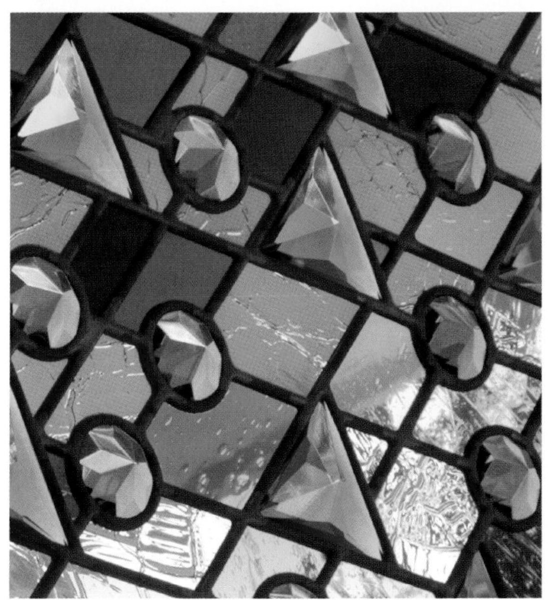

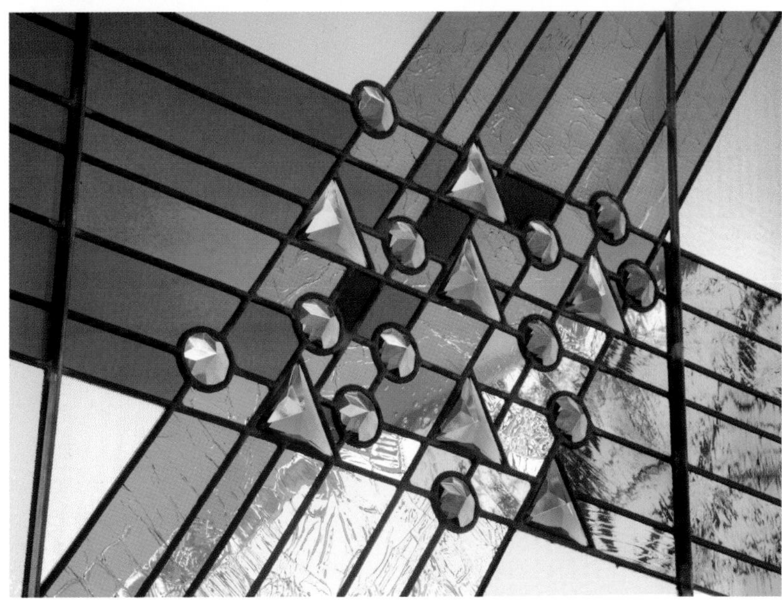

Untitled Residential Clerestories. Photographs: Richard Bruck.

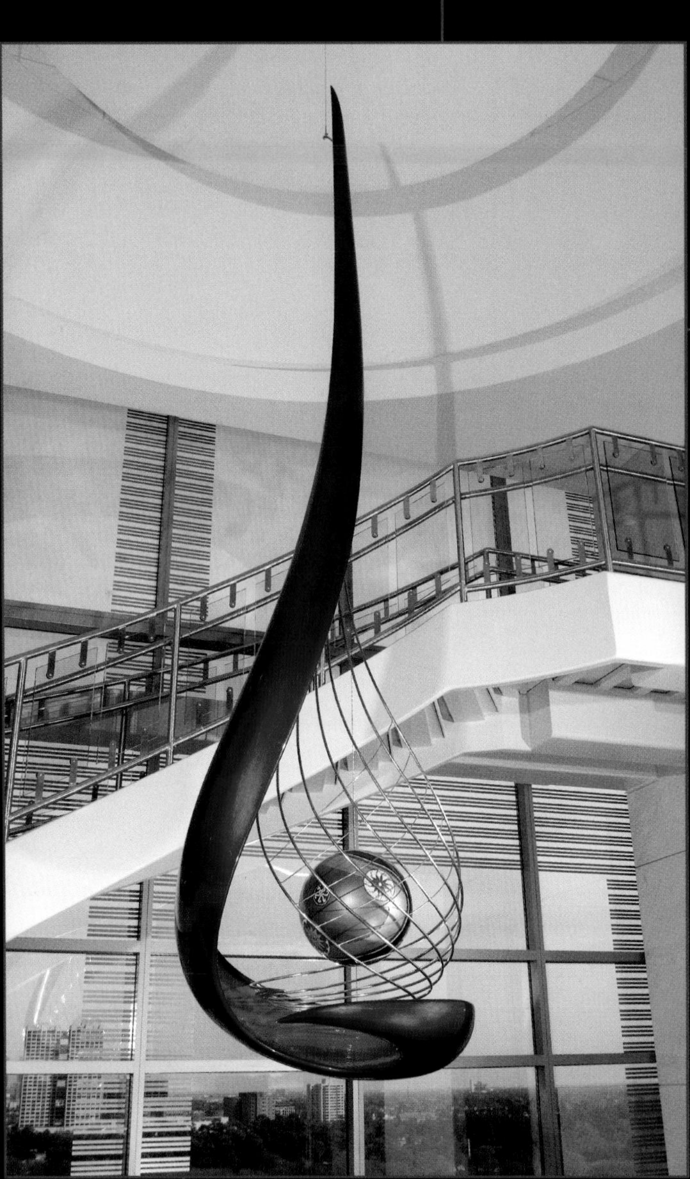

Atrium Sculpture

AIRWORKS, INC.

GEORGE PETERS AND MELANIE WALKER ■ 815 SPRUCE STREET ■ BOULDER, CO 80302
TEL/FAX 303-442-9025 ■ E-MAIL AIRWORKS@CONCENTRIC.NET ■ WWW.AIRWORKS-STUDIO.COM

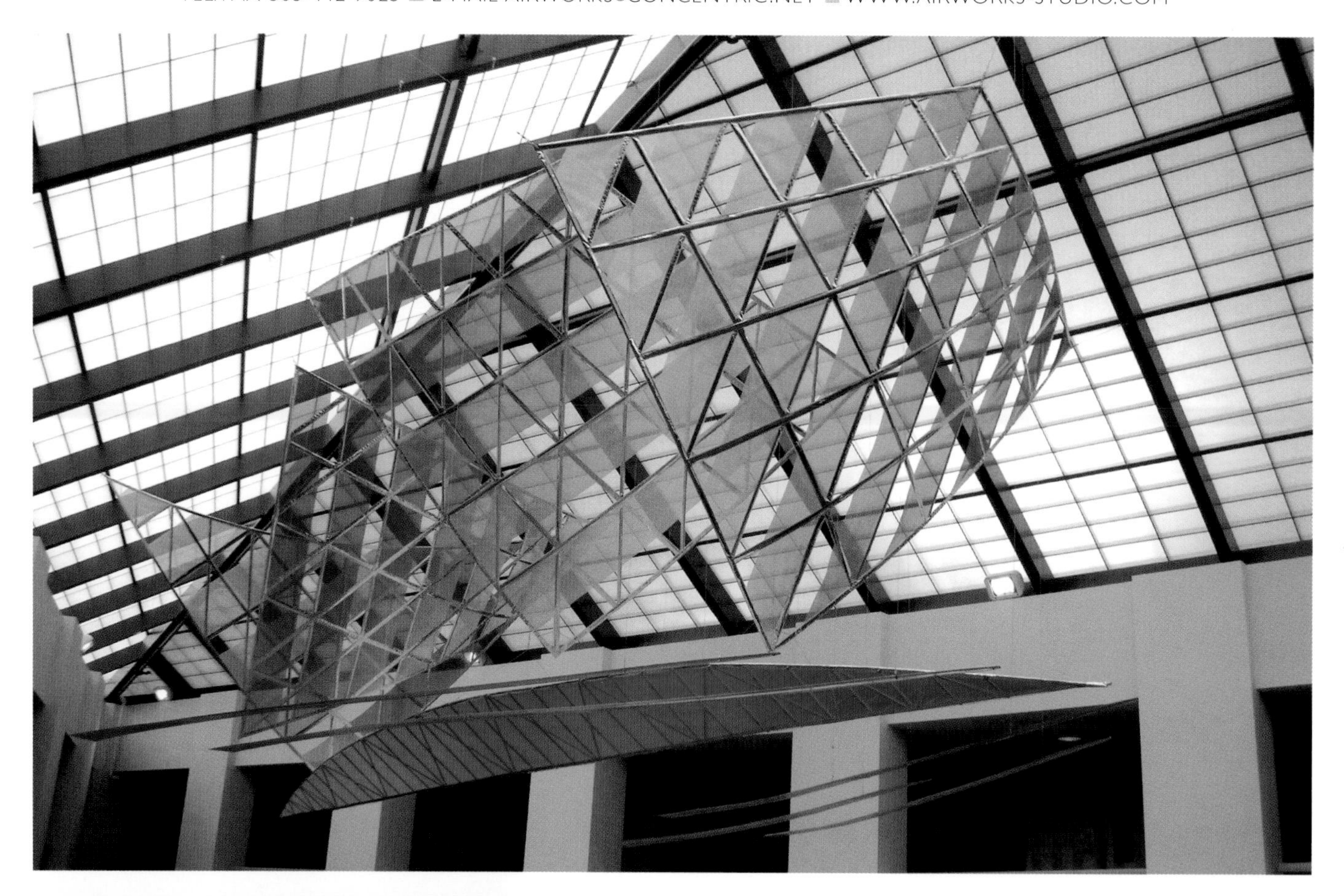

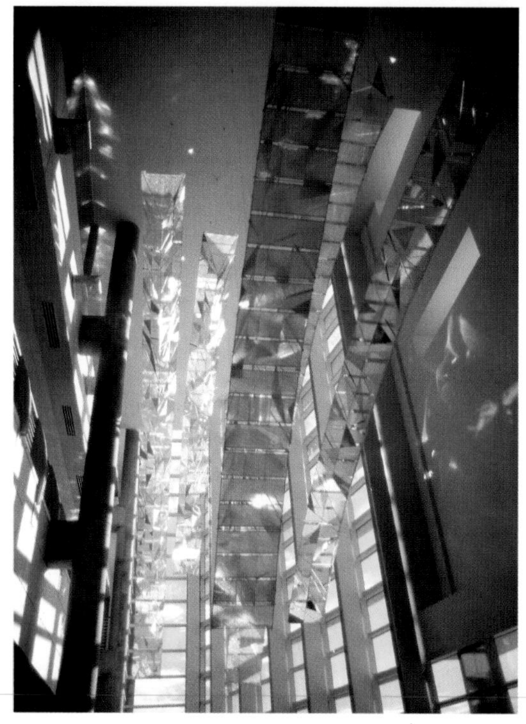

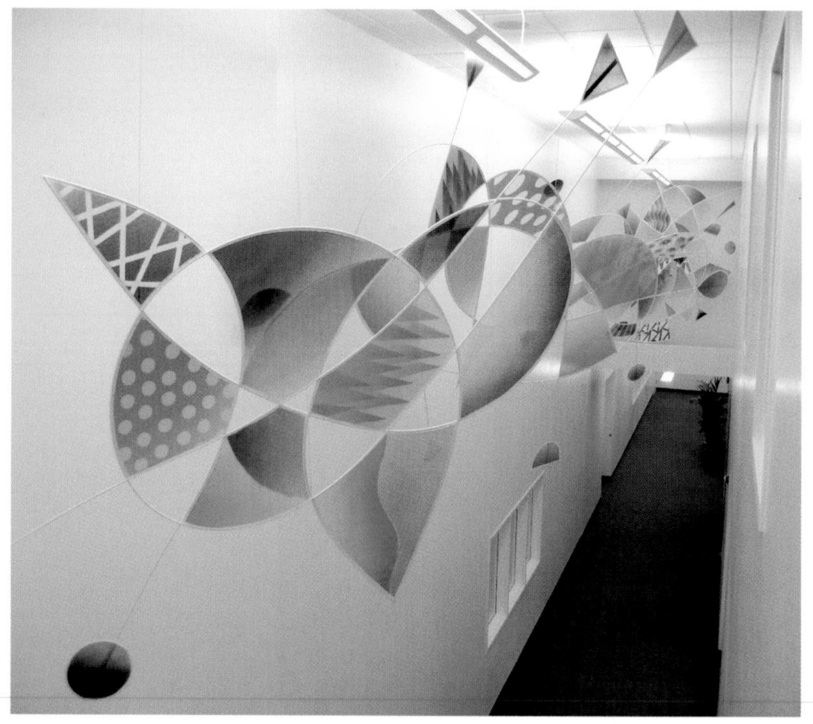

Top: *Air Ship,* 2006, Community College of Rhode Island, Newport, RI, fiberglass sunscreen, acrylic color, fiberglass bar, and mylar, 12'H x 16'W x 38'L.
Bottom left: *Light Bows,* 2001, Anchutz Cancer Pavilion, Denver Medical Center, CO, fiberglass rod, polycarbonate, prismatic mylar, and aluminum, 20'H x 20'W x 65'L.
Bottom right: *Air Jazz,* 2005, Kaiser Permanente support services building, Denver, CO, fiberglass sunscreen, acrylic color, and fiberglass rod, 10'H x 10'W x 60'L.

TERESA CAMOZZI

THE CAMOZZI ART STUDIO ■ 1190 A SHAFTER AVENUE ■ SAN FRANCISCO, CA 94124
TEL 415-822-6222 ■ FAX 415-822-6322 ■ E-MAIL TCAMOZZI@COMCAST.NET ■ WWW.TERESACAMOZZI.COM

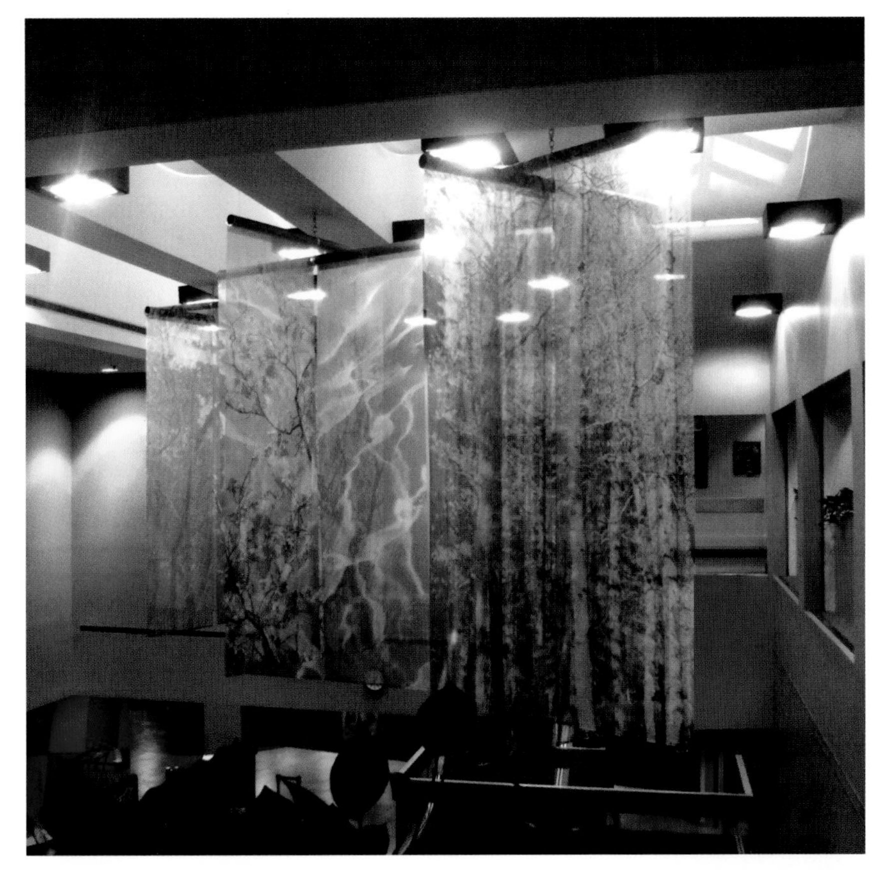

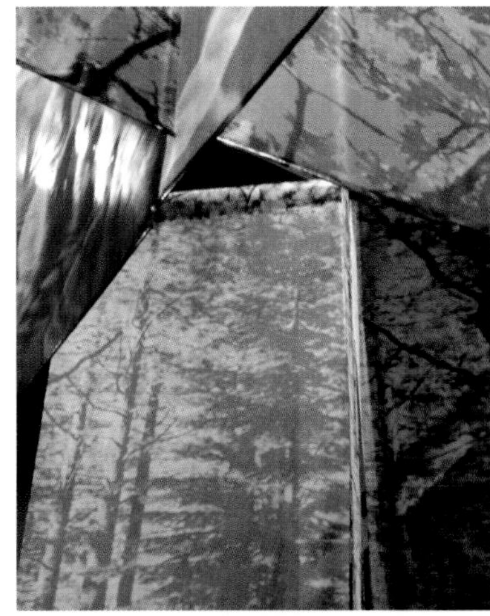

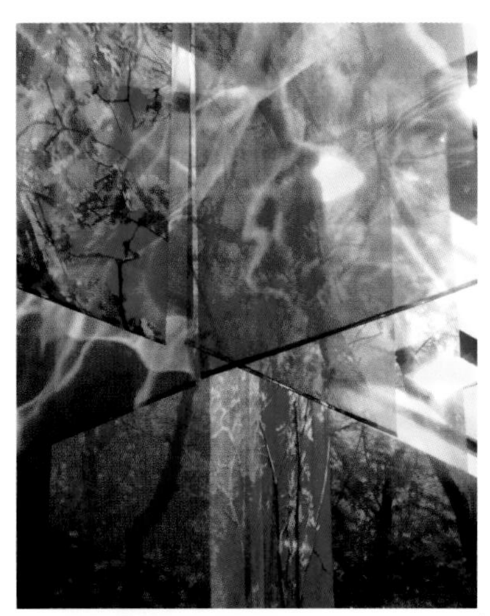

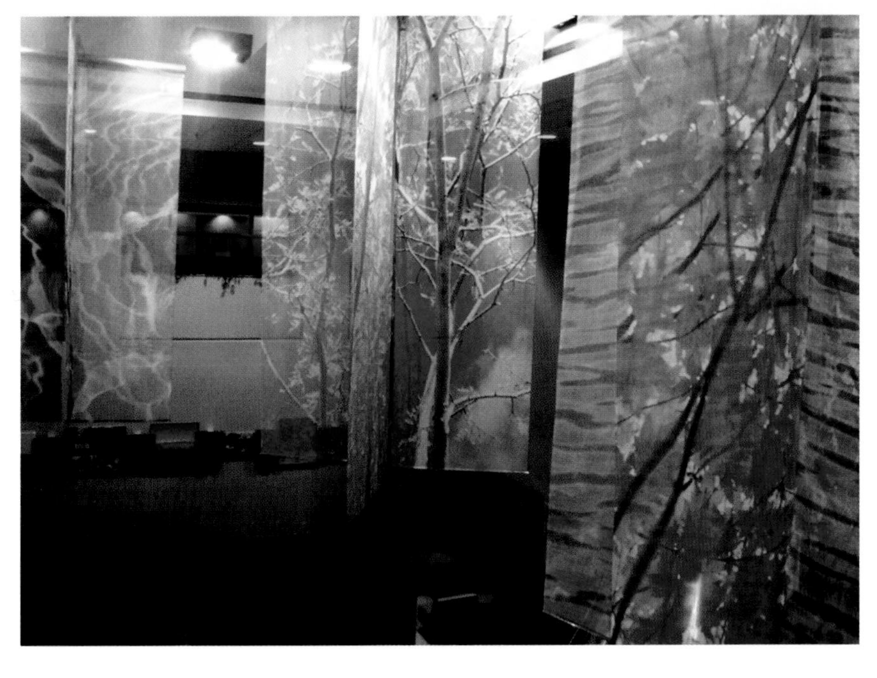

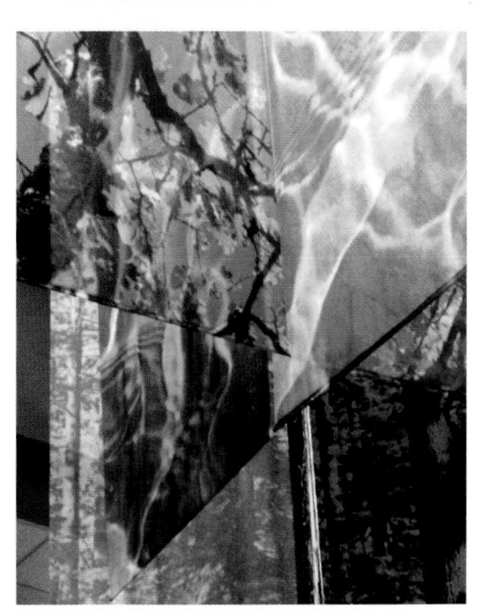

Sacred Walk, 2006, St. Vincent's Hospital, Indianapolis, mobiles comprised of 11' x 3' digitally printed chiffon.

CLOWES SCULPTURE

JONATHAN AND EVELYN CLOWES ■ 98 MARCH HILL ROAD ■ WALPOLE, NH 03608
TEL/FAX 603-756-9505 ■ E-MAIL STACEY@CLOWESSCULPTURE.COM ■ WWW.CLOWESSCULPTURE.COM

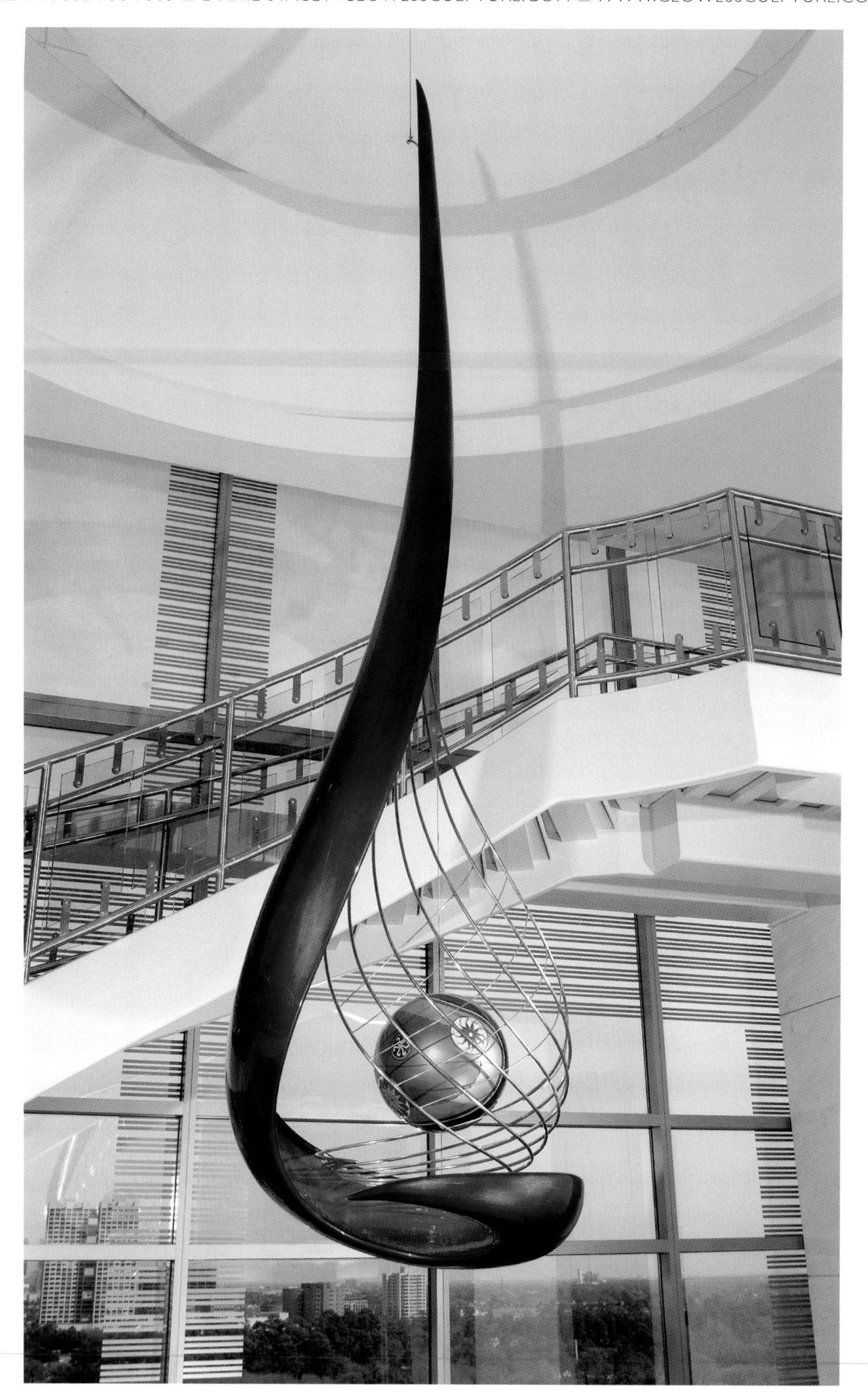

Zephyr, Memorial Hermann-Texas Medical Center, formed and painted aluminum, nickel silver rod, and spun sphere, 14'H x 4'W. Photograph: George Craig.

ERIC EHLENBERGER

GLASSLIGHT STUDIO ■ 2601 CHARTRES STREET ■ NEW ORLEANS, LA 70117
TEL 504-943-7446 ■ E-MAIL NEON@EHLENBERGER.COM ■ WWW.EHLENBERGER.COM

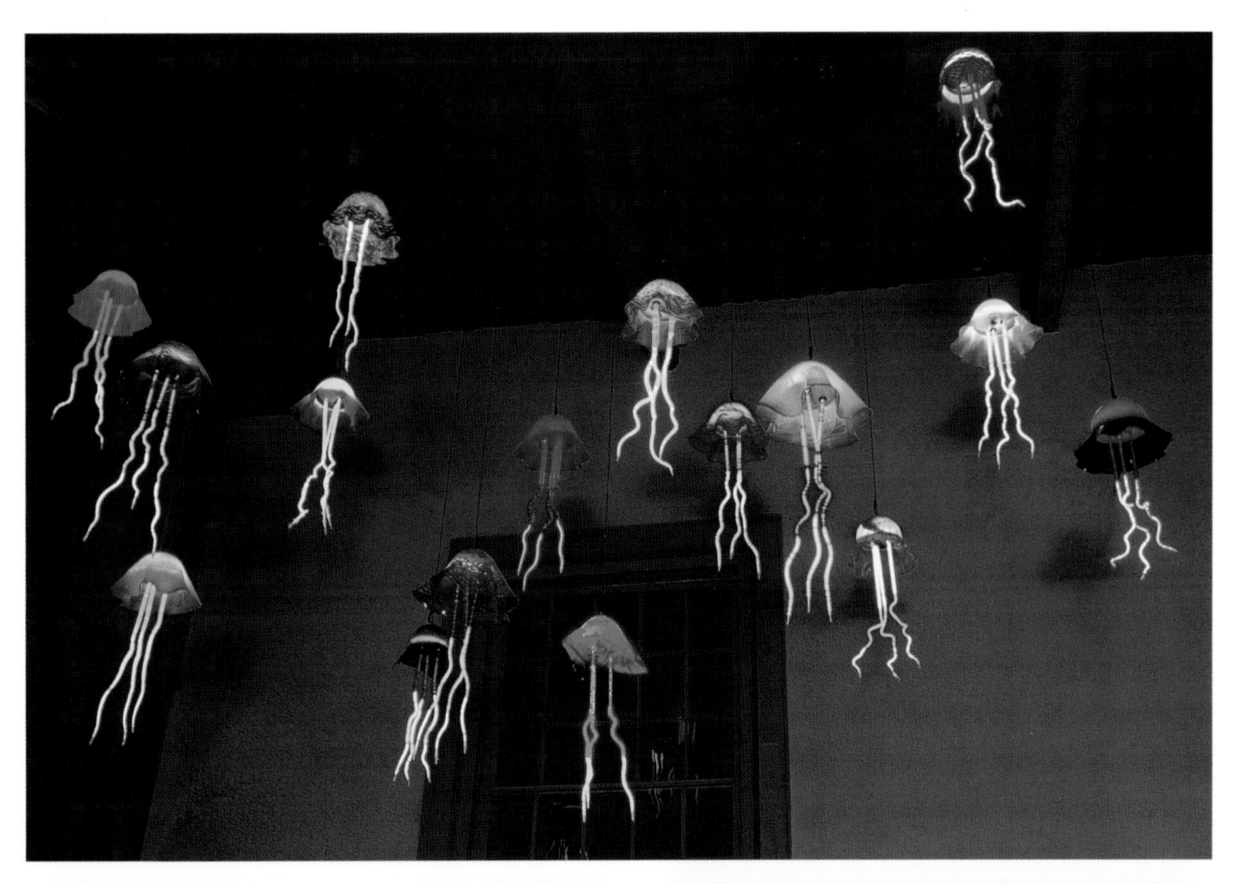

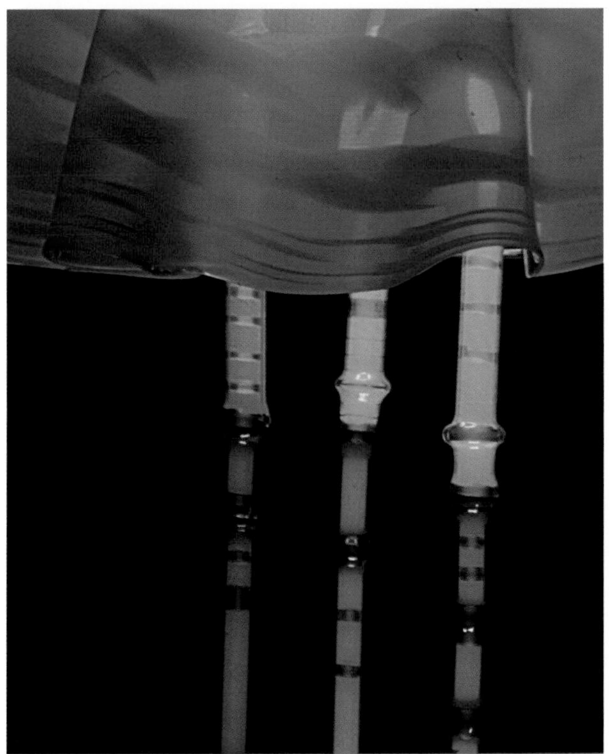

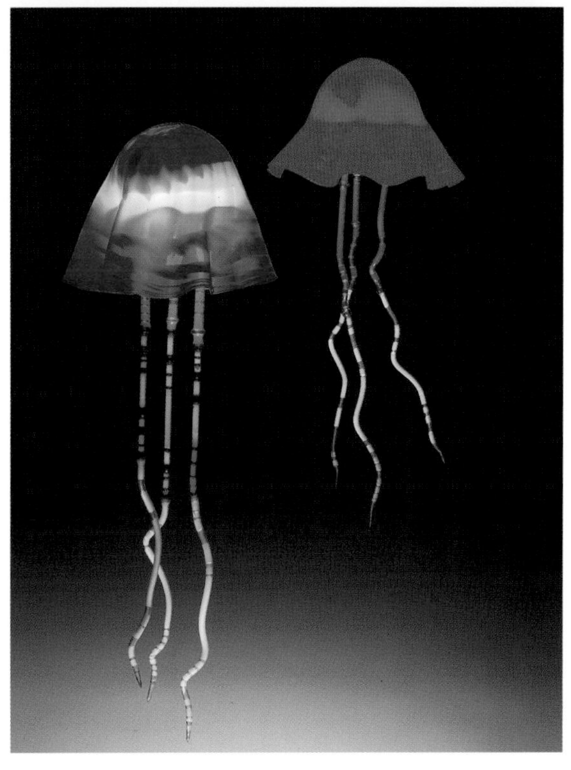

Jellyfish, blown glass and neon, sizes variable, each approx: 42" × 16" × 16".

GOLDSTEIN & KAPELLAS STUDIO

DANIEL GOLDSTEIN & JOHN KAPELLAS ■ 224 GUERRERO STREET ■ SAN FRANCISCO, CA 94103 ■ TEL 415-621-5761
FAX 415-255-2272 ■ E-MAIL DANIELJGOLDSTEIN@YAHOO.COM ■ WWW.GOLDSTEINKAPELLAS.COM

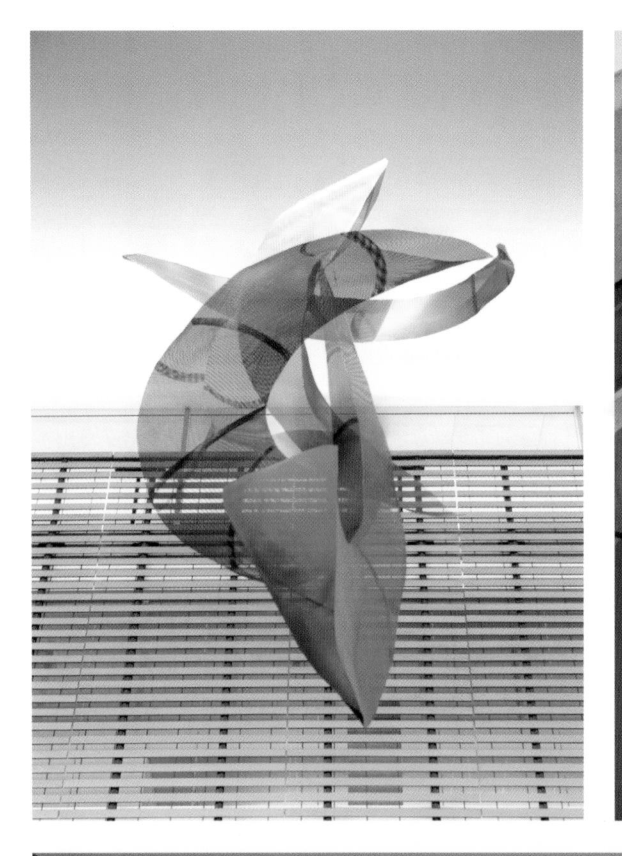

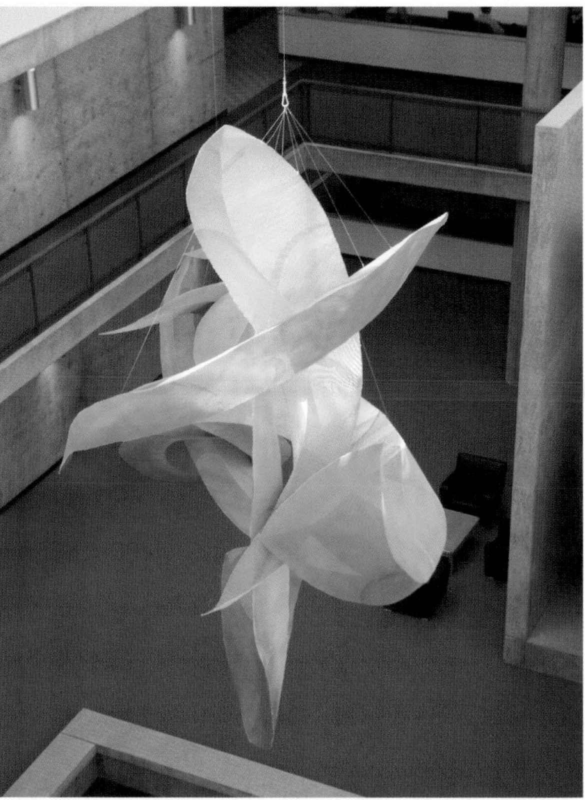

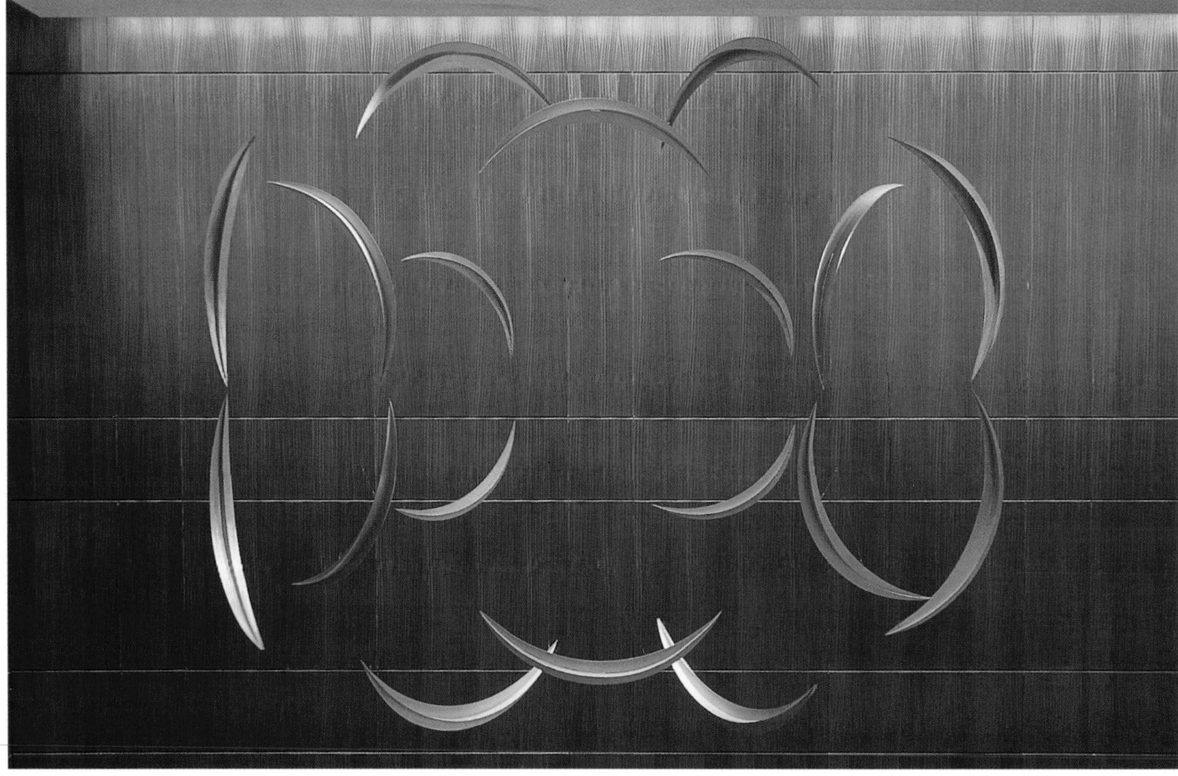

Top left: *Von Leewenhoek* (from below). Photograph: Peter Lippman. Top right: *Von Leewenhoek*, 2005, California Department of Health Services, Richmond, CA, painted expanded aluminum, 25' x 25' x 25'. Photograph: Peter Lippman.
Bottom: *Concentric*, 2004, Sallie Mae Corporation, Reston, VA, anodized aluminum, 13' x 13' x 10'. Photograph: Maxwell MacKenzie.

GORDON AUCHINCLOSS DESIGN, LLC

GORDON AUCHINCLOSS ■ 972 WEST HILL ROAD ■ HARDWICK, VT 05843
TEL 802-472-5803 ■ E-MAIL GORDON@AMBIENTFLOW.COM ■ WWW.AMBIENTFLOW.COM

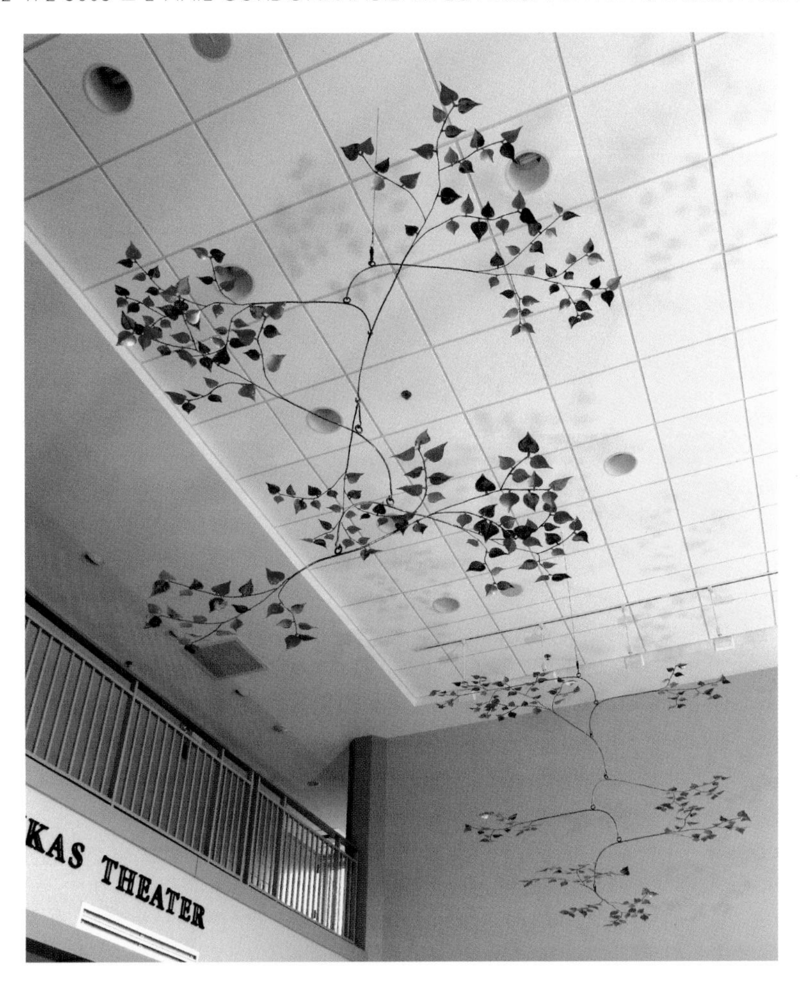

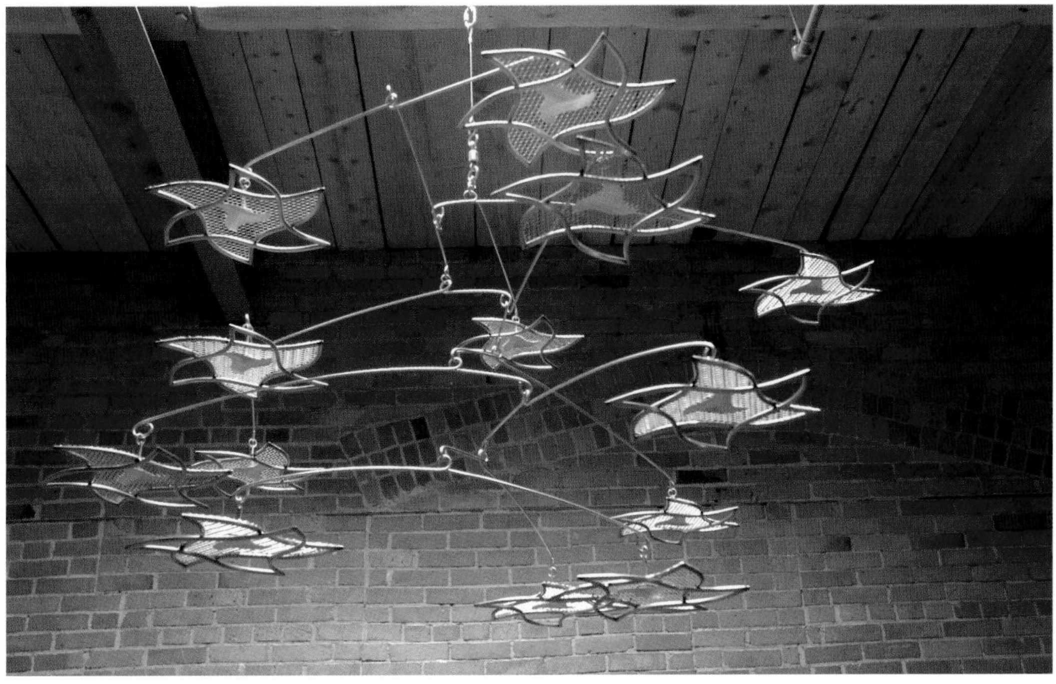

Top: *Verde and Brushed Copper Canopies*, forged steel with copper leaves, 5'H x 7'W. Photograph: William Cleary.
Bottom: *Propellers*, steel tubing, expanded metal, copper, and stainless steel armatures, 3'H x 5'W. Photograph: David Gibson.

A Commission Story

Paul Sable

TITLE
The World Within, 2005

COMMISSIONED FOR
Children's Hospital Boston,
Waltham, MA, Campus

TIMELINE: 6 weeks

DIMENSIONS: 12'Dia.

TRADE PROFESSIONAL
Pam Wilkins-Horowitz, Art Consultant,
Wilkins Art Associates, Inc.

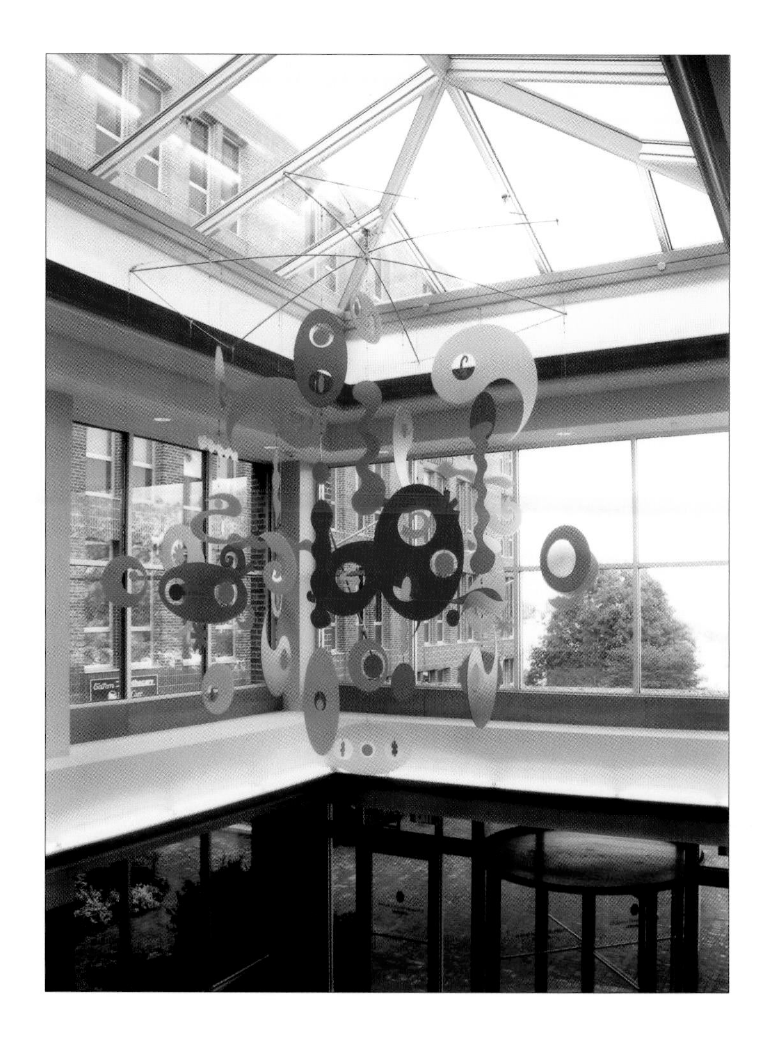

Though Paul Sable admits he's "kind of a contemplative guy," he doesn't harbor reserves of artistic angst. By refreshing contrast, Sable's inner world resembles a Technicolor amusement park. Sable confesses, "I like to think that my imagination is a child's imagination. When I look inside, I get fun colors and shapes and creativity." ■ That kind of joie de vivre was just what the doctor ordered when the Waltham campus of Children's Hospital Boston set out to commission a sculpture for their new entry atrium as the culmination of a major building renovation. Art consultant Pam Wilkins-Horowitz recalls, "The client and I wanted to create a welcoming environment with a unique, whimsical mobile. The timetable was very tight." She became aware of Paul Sable's work through The Guild. ■ The happiness of Sable's lively squiggles and spirals and circles is infectious. "Art is like being in kindergarten and just playing," he explains. "There are levels of it that are really technically complex, but the final product is all about fun and color and playfulness." ■ "Each of the ninety-odd pieces [of *The World Within*] rotates, and the entire piece rotates, so everything's built on ball-bearing swivels," Sable details. "Since there was no central place to hang it, we had to run cable from the edges of the skylight to the center of the atrium space. The balance is very subtle." Sable favors lightweight, minimalistic hanging gear: "This thing weighs less than one hundred pounds. I use really strong but really thin cables—high-end, heavy-duty fishing equipment," he explains. "They disappear." ■ The sculpture is a popular success, according to Wilkins-Horowitz. "As we hoped, the mobile is really enjoyed from many different viewpoints, from the exterior to the multiple levels of the adjacent hospital wings that overlook the glass entrance. ■ A satisfied Paul Sable reflects, "When kids and families walk in the door, they smile."

ROB FISHER SCULPTURE, LLC

TALLEY FISHER ■ 228 NORTH ALLEGHENY STREET ■ BELLEFONTE, PA 16823 ■ TEL 814-355-1458
FAX 814-353-9060 ■ E-MAIL ROBFISHERSCULPTURE@YAHOO.COM ■ WWW.ROBFISHERSCULPTURE.COM

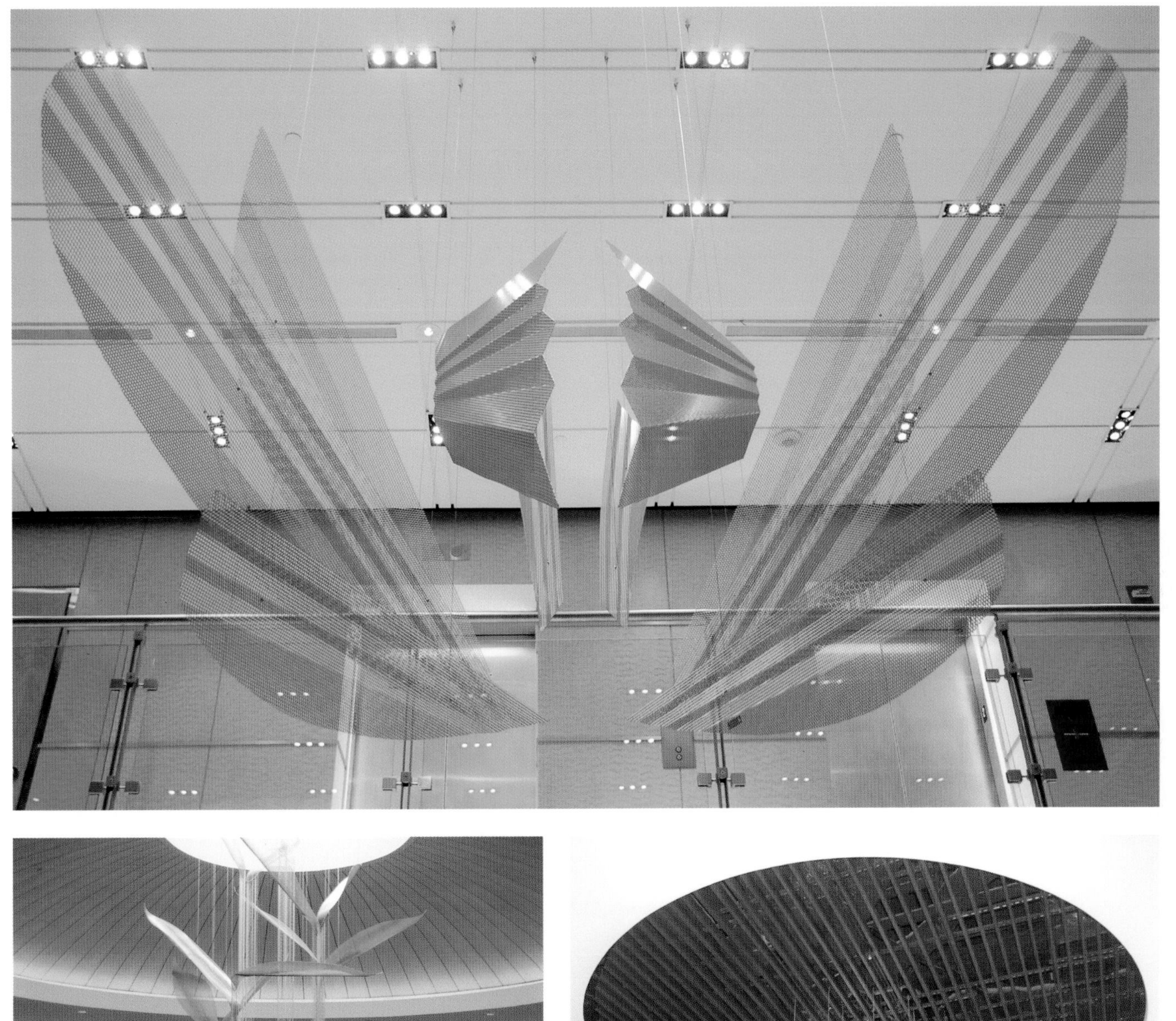

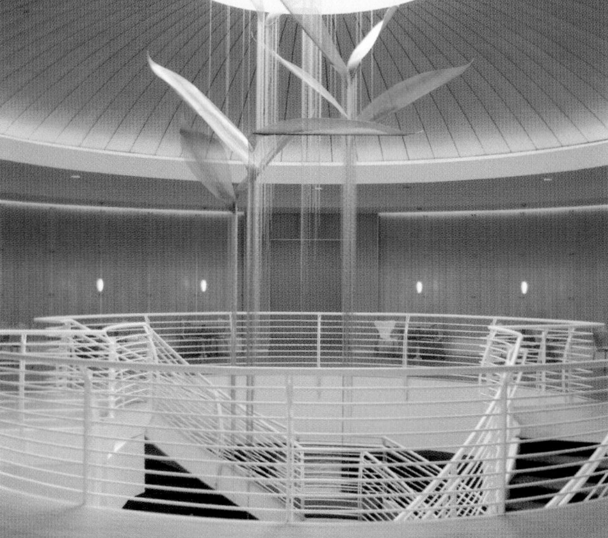

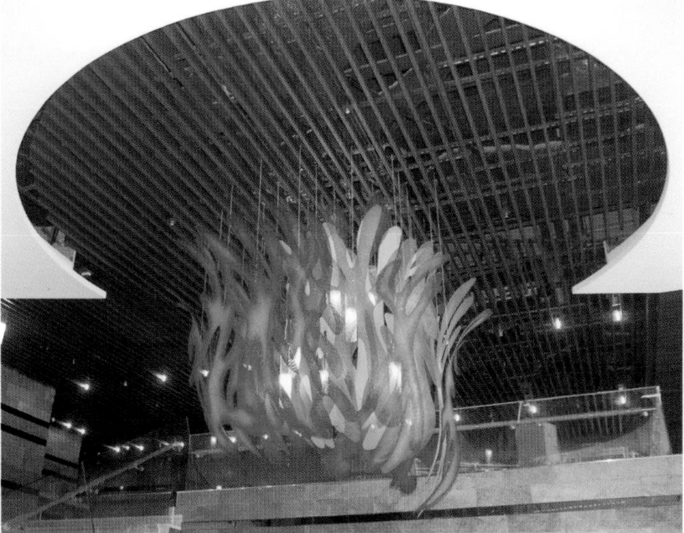

Top: *Solar Sails,* 2007, aluminum, NEST and Totah Ventures, K Street Northwest, Washington, DC. Bottom left: *Norwegian Spring,* 2006, aluminum and stainless steel, Royal Caribbean Cruise Lines, Springfield, OR. Bottom right: *Seaform,* 2006, aluminum and stainless steel, Horizon Suite Hotel, Hong Kong.

SABLE STUDIOS

PAUL SABLE ■ 100 NORTH RODEO GULCH DRIVE ■ SOQUEL, CA 95073
TEL 831-475-4012 ■ TEL 831-345-3540 ■ E-MAIL PAUL@SABLESTUDIOS.COM ■ WWW.SABLESTUDIOS.COM

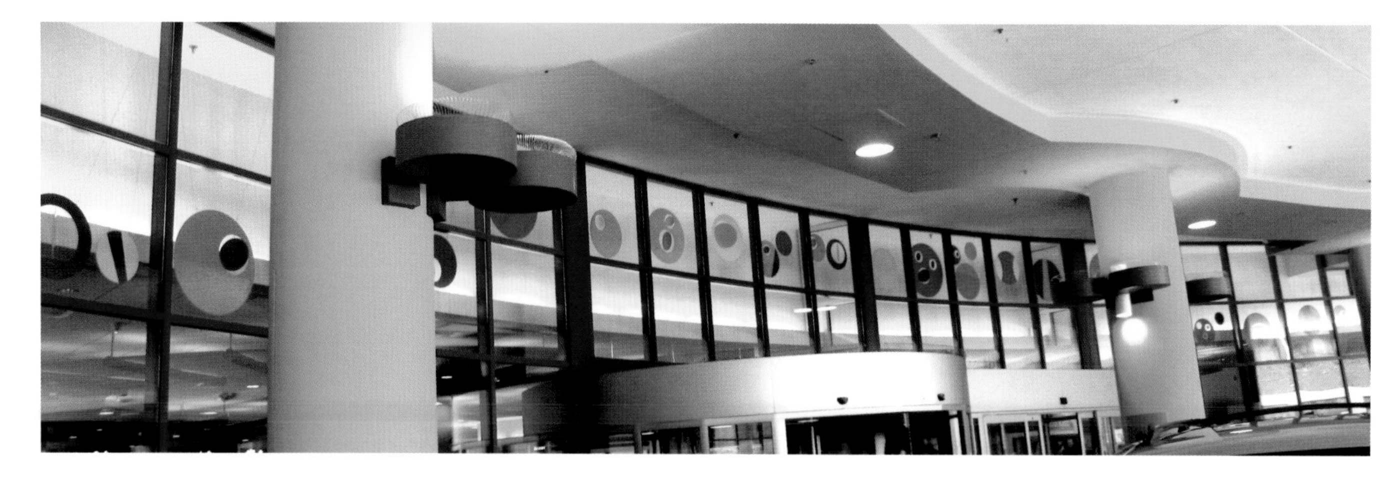

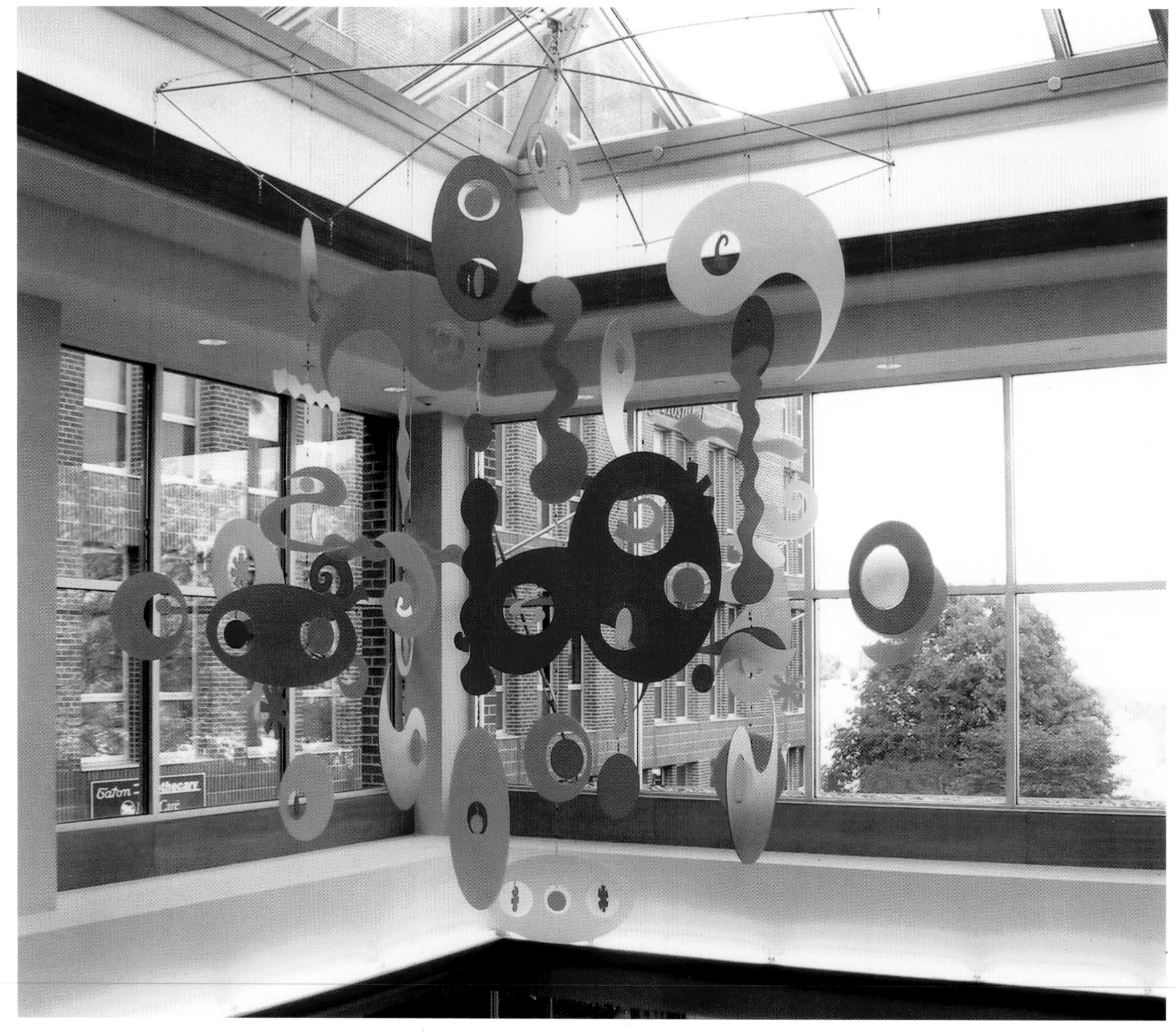

Top: *Kaliope Dance,* 2006, Children's Hospital, Boston, Sintra® and paint, 10'H x 152'L. Photograph: Kris Snibbe.
Bottom: *The World Within,* 2005, Children's Hospital, Boston, Waltham Campus, Varia™ resin panels, 12' x 12' x 12'.

SABLE STUDIOS

PAUL SABLE ■ 100 NORTH RODEO GULCH DRIVE ■ SOQUEL, CA 95073
TEL 831-475-4012 ■ TEL 831-345-3540 ■ E-MAIL PAUL@SABLESTUDIOS.COM ■ WWW.SABLESTUDIOS.COM

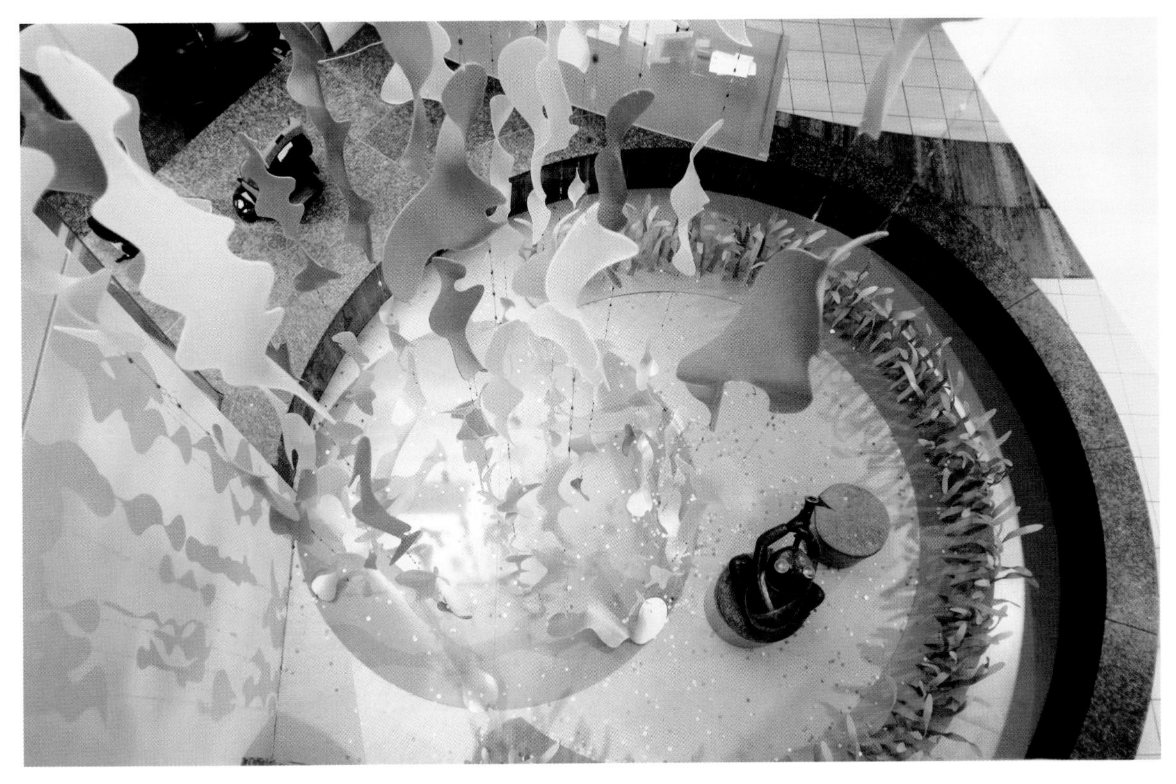

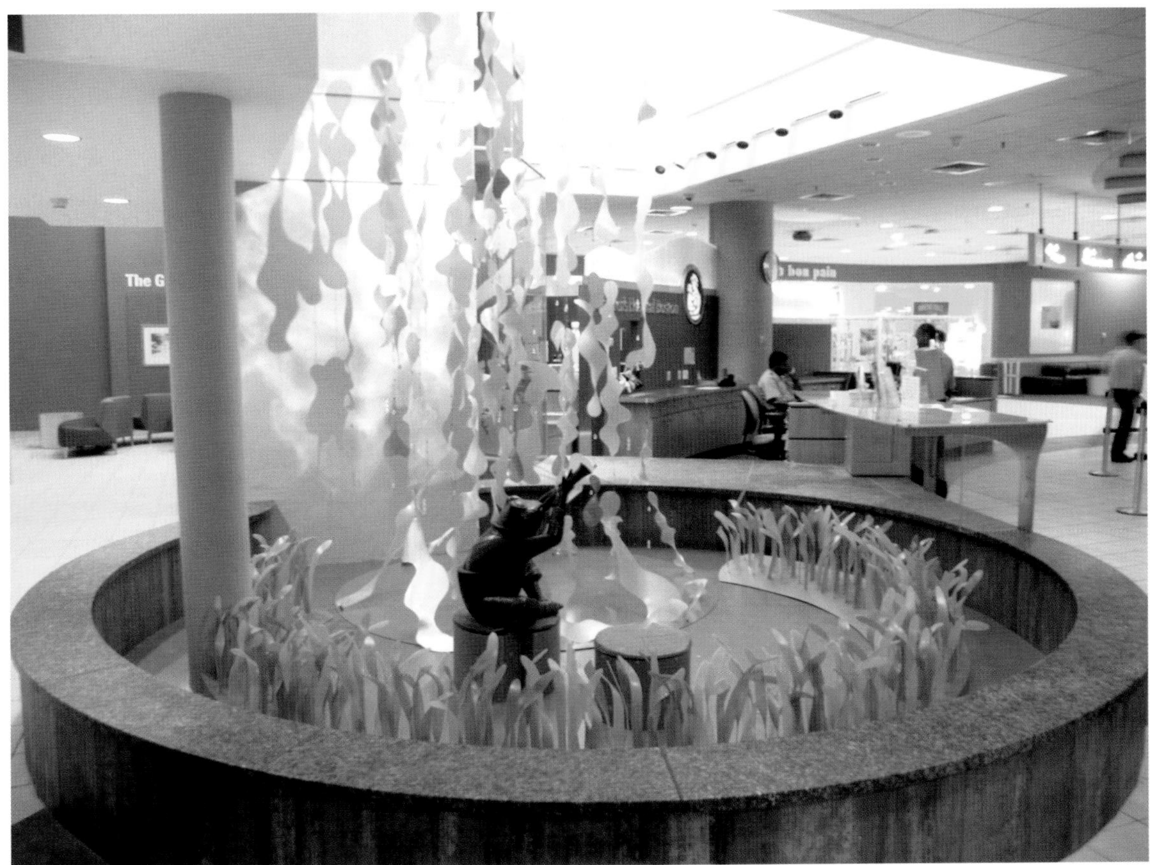

Wishing You Well, 2006, Children's Hospital, Boston, Varia™ resin panels, 30' x 16' x 16'. Photographs: Kris Snibbe.

JOANIE SAN CHIRICO

CHAPEAUX DESIGNS ■ 1064 LAKE PLACID DRIVE ■ TOMS RIVER, NJ 08753 ■ TEL 732-506-6636
FAX 732-506-0166 ■ E-MAIL JOANIE@JOANIESANCHIRICO.COM ■ WWW.JOANIESANCHIRICO.COM

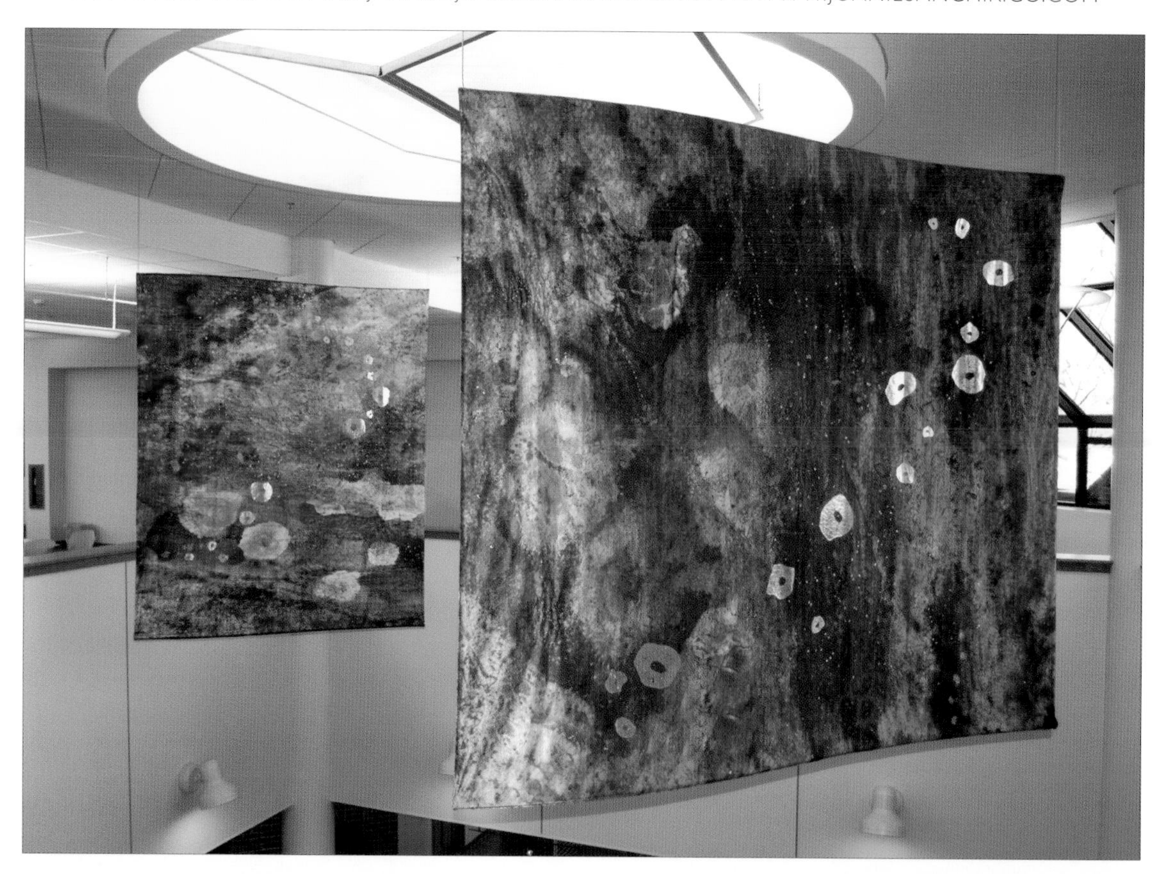

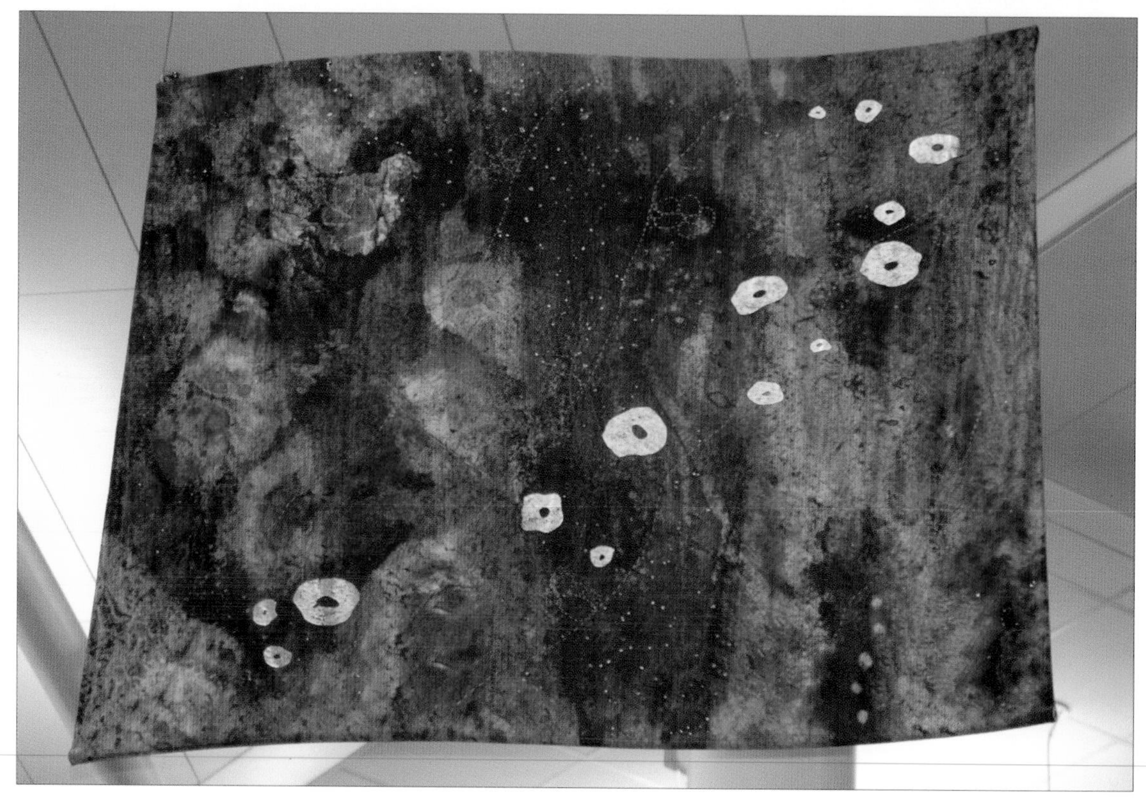

Top: *Sandbar #1* and 2, 2006, Ocean County Library Main Branch, Toms River, NJ, disperse dye on fabric, aluminum armature, and stainless steel cables, 7' × 6' and 6' × 7'. Bottom: *Sandbar #1* (detail).

KURT SHAW

PO BOX 16152 ■ PITTSBURGH, PA 15242 ■ TEL 412-921-5533
TEL 800-524-SHAW ■ E-MAIL KSFINEART@COMCAST.NET ■ WWW.KURTSHAWSTUDIO.COM

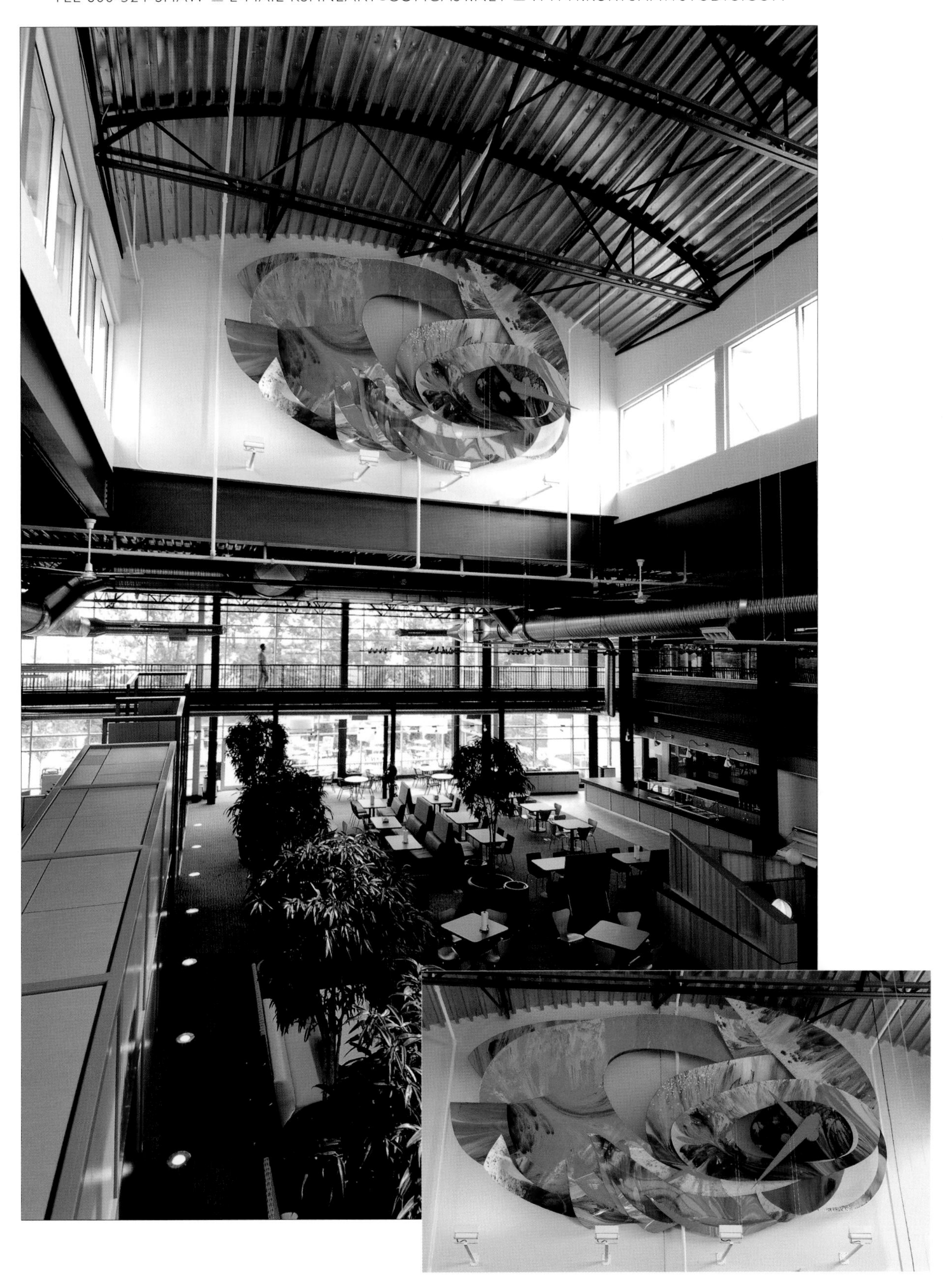

Seasonal Orb, 2006, sculptural clock created for Progressive Medical, Inc., Westerville, OH, polychrome aluminum, 13' x 22'.

METTJE SWIFT

SUSPENDED MOBILES ■ 634 GRANDE AVENUE ■ DEL NORTE, CO 81132
TEL 719-657-2967 ■ E-MAIL METTJE@BANNERART.COM ■ WWW.BANNERART.COM

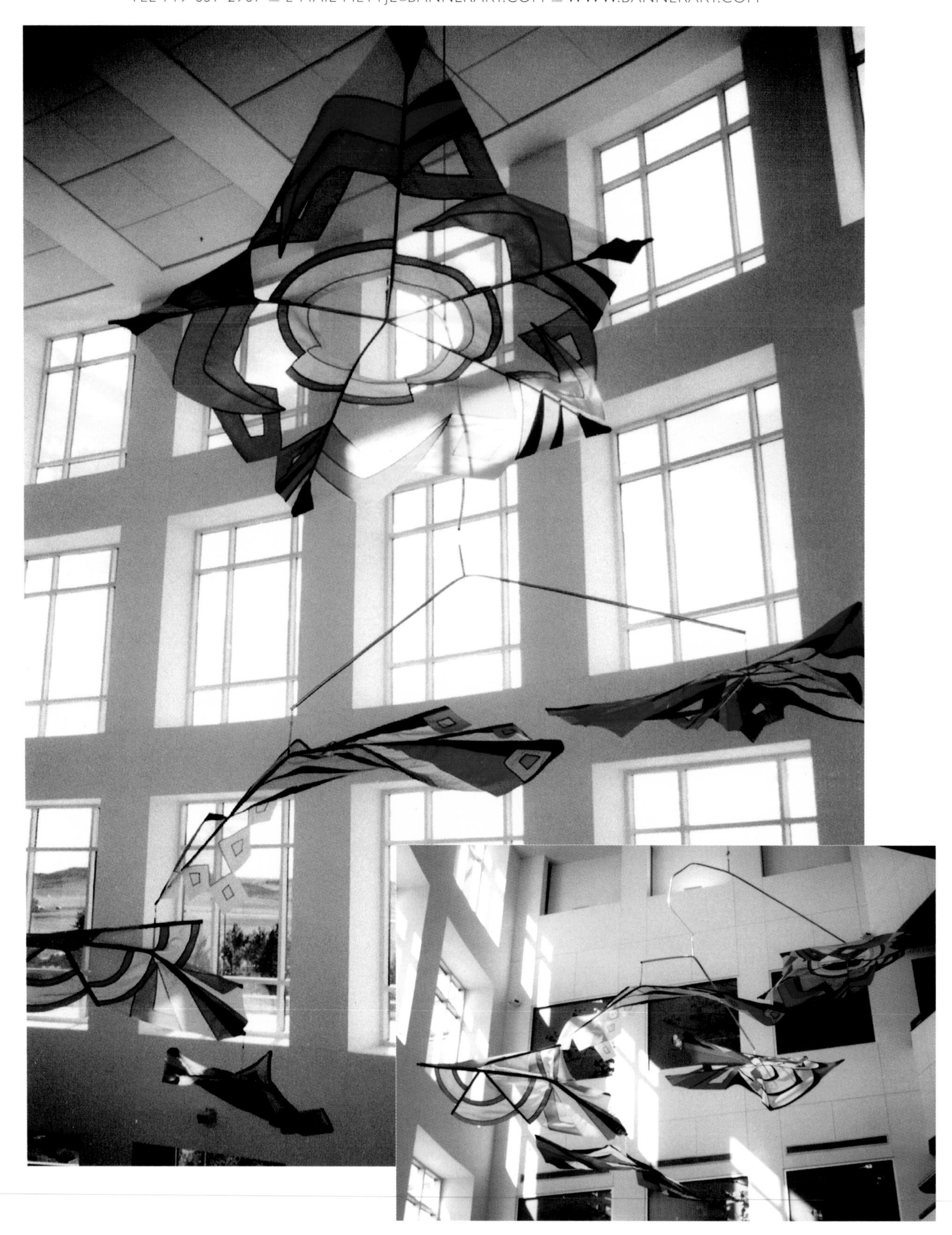

Suspended Balanced Mobile, Parker, CO, translucent nylon fabric and stainless steel tubing armatures, 20' x 24' x 24'.

KENNETH F. vonROENN, JR.

ARCHITECTURAL GLASS ART, INC. ■ 815 WEST MARKET STREET ■ LOUISVILLE, KY 40202
TEL 502-585-5421 ■ FAX 502-585-2808 ■ E-MAIL INFO@AGAINC.COM ■ WWW.AGAINC.COM

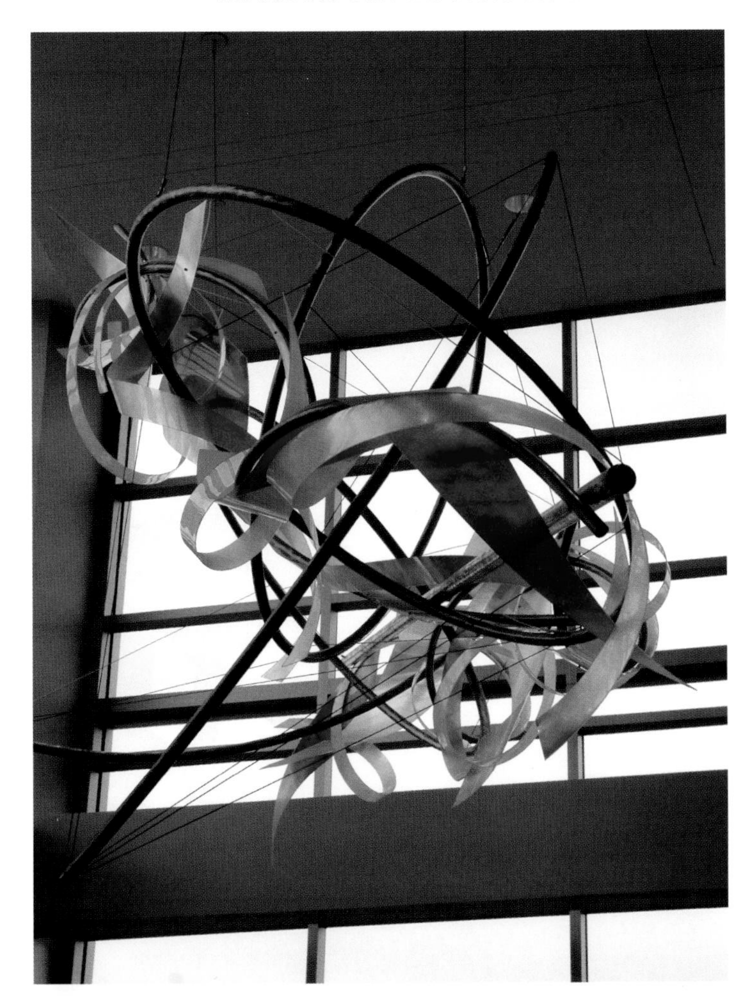

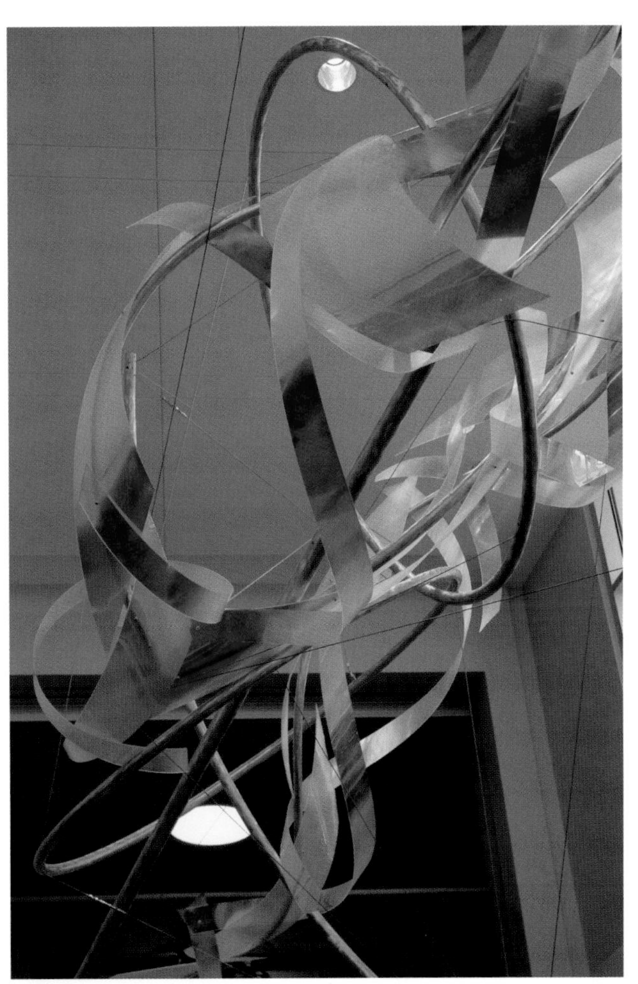

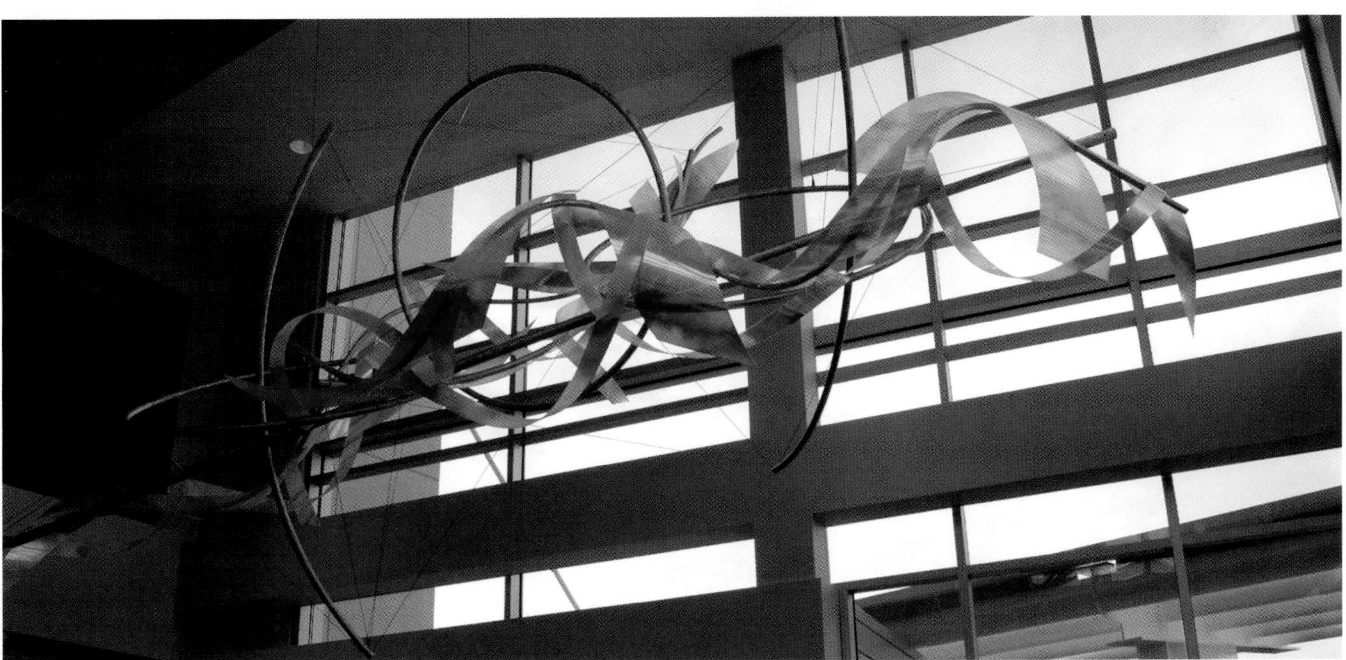

St. Mary's Hospital, Evansville, NC, aluminum tubing and stainless steel cables, forms represent the circulation of blood to and from the heart.

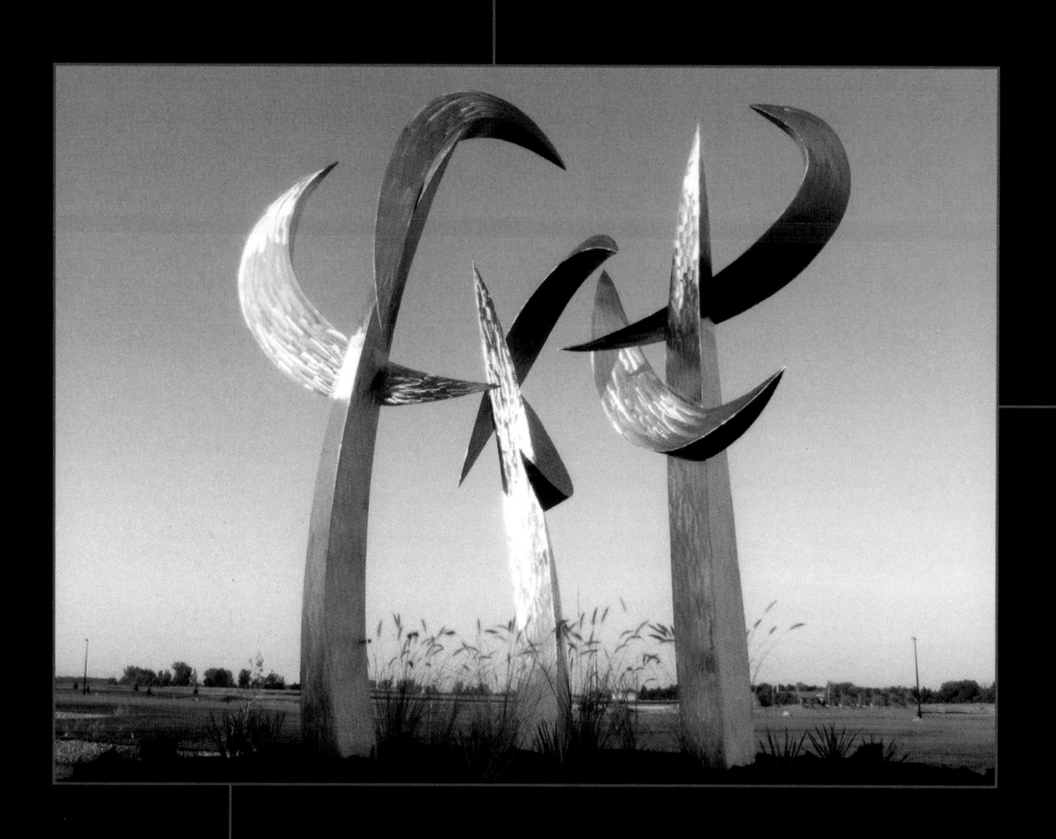

Public Art

SANDRA BELL

KEARON-HEMPENSTALL GALLERY ■ 536 BERGEN AVENUE ■ JERSEY CITY, NJ 07304
TEL 201-333-8855 ■ FAX 201-333-8488 ■ E-MAIL SUZANNE@KHGALLERY.COM ■ WWW.SANDRABELL.COM

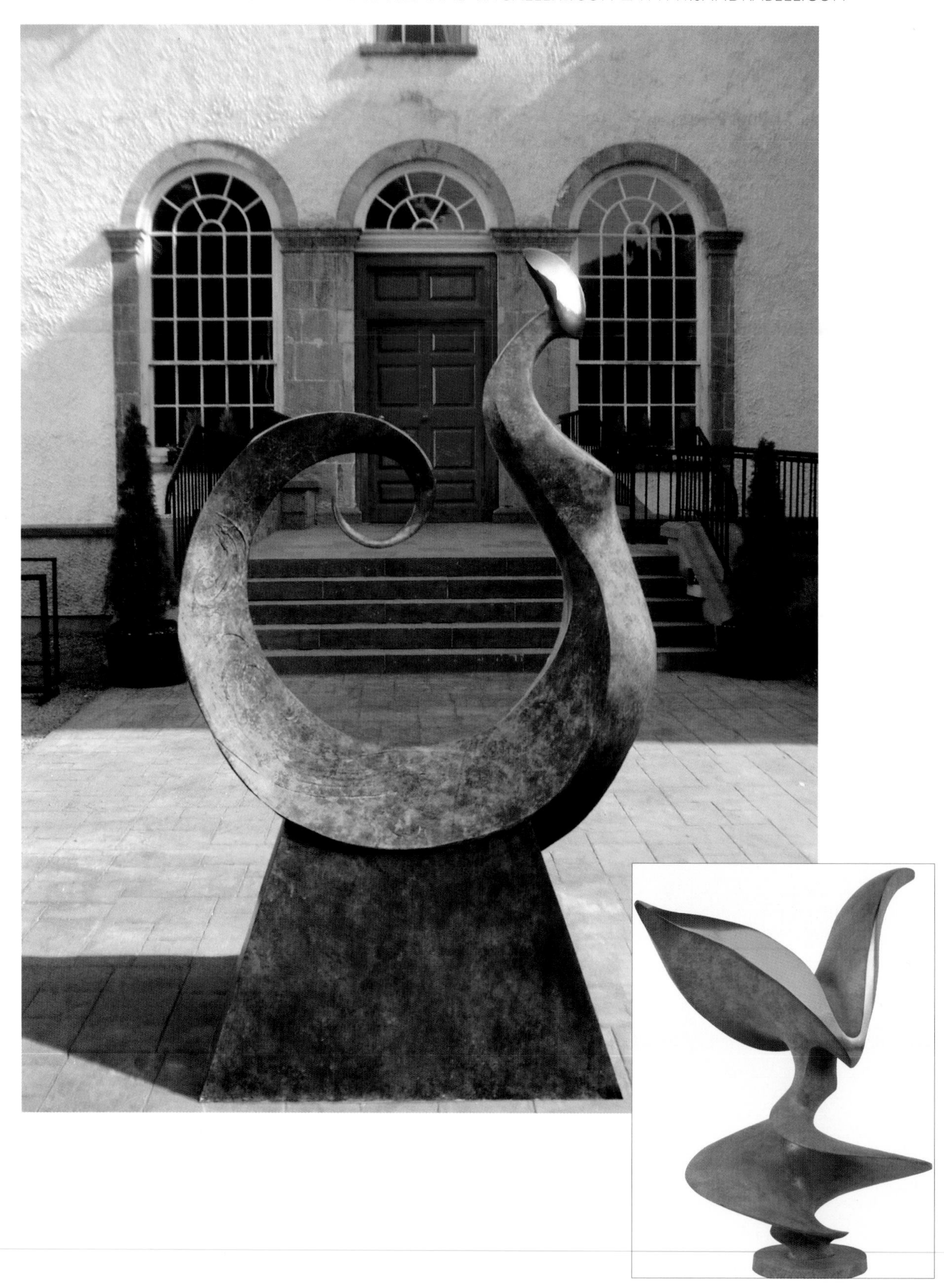

Granuaile, cast bronze, 83" x 36" x 45". Inset: *Blythe Spirit*, cast bronze, 32" x 24" x 12". Photographs: Peter Hughes.

BENNETT STUDIO

CHRIS BENNETT ■ 26983 ROUTE J40 ■ KEOSAUQUA, IA 52565 ■ TEL 319-592-3228
FAX 319-592-3463 ■ E-MAIL CBENNETT@NETINS.NET ■ WWW.BENNETTSTUDIO.COM

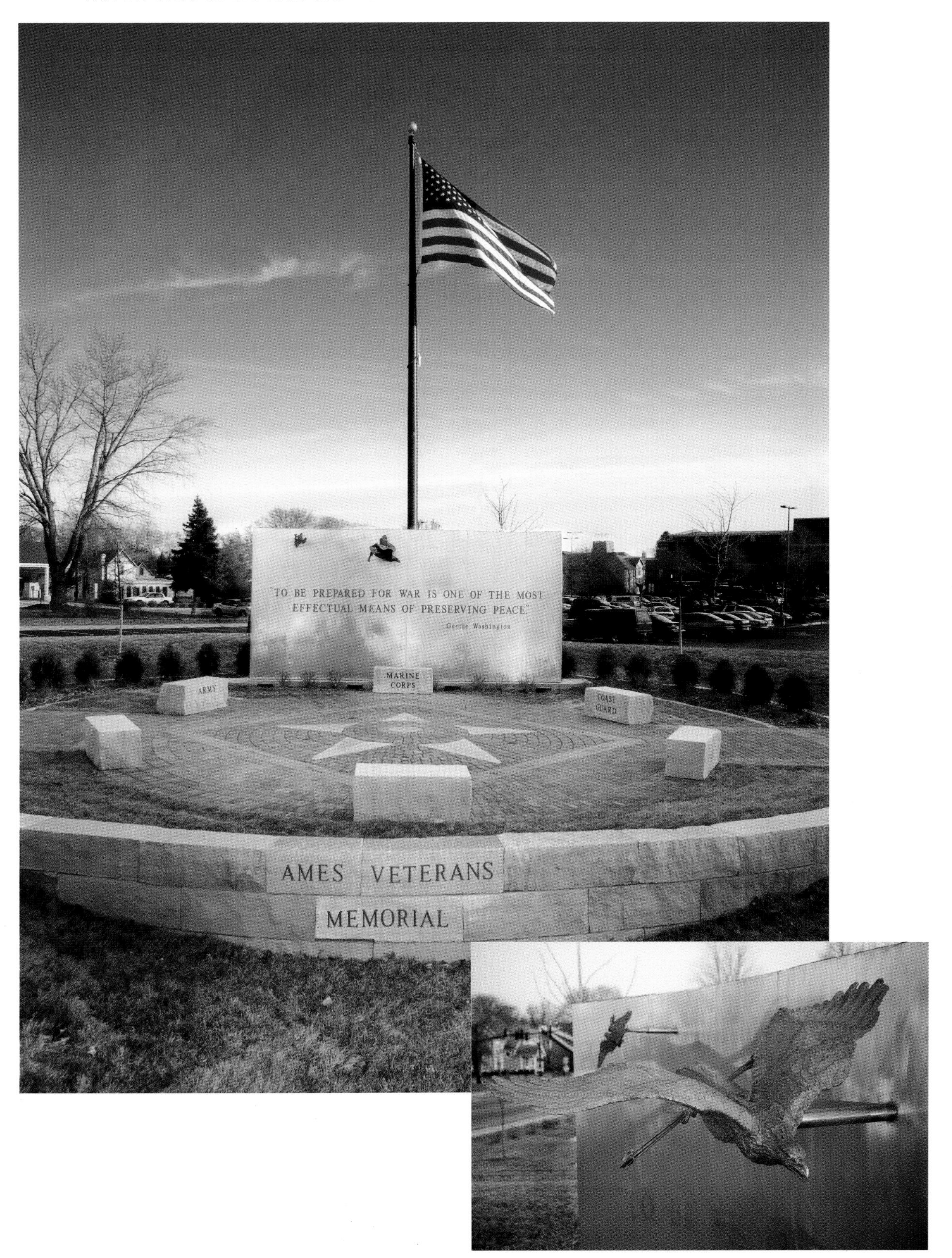

Descending Strength, Ascending Peace. Photographs: Robert Phillips.

CHARLES BIGGER

BIGGER STUDIOS ■ 4602 14TH AVENUE NW ■ SEATTLE, WA 98107 ■ TEL 206-789-3806
TEL 206-265-9605 ■ FAX 206-272-9789 ■ E-MAIL BCHARLES24@QWEST.NET ■ WWW.CHARLIEBIGGER.COM

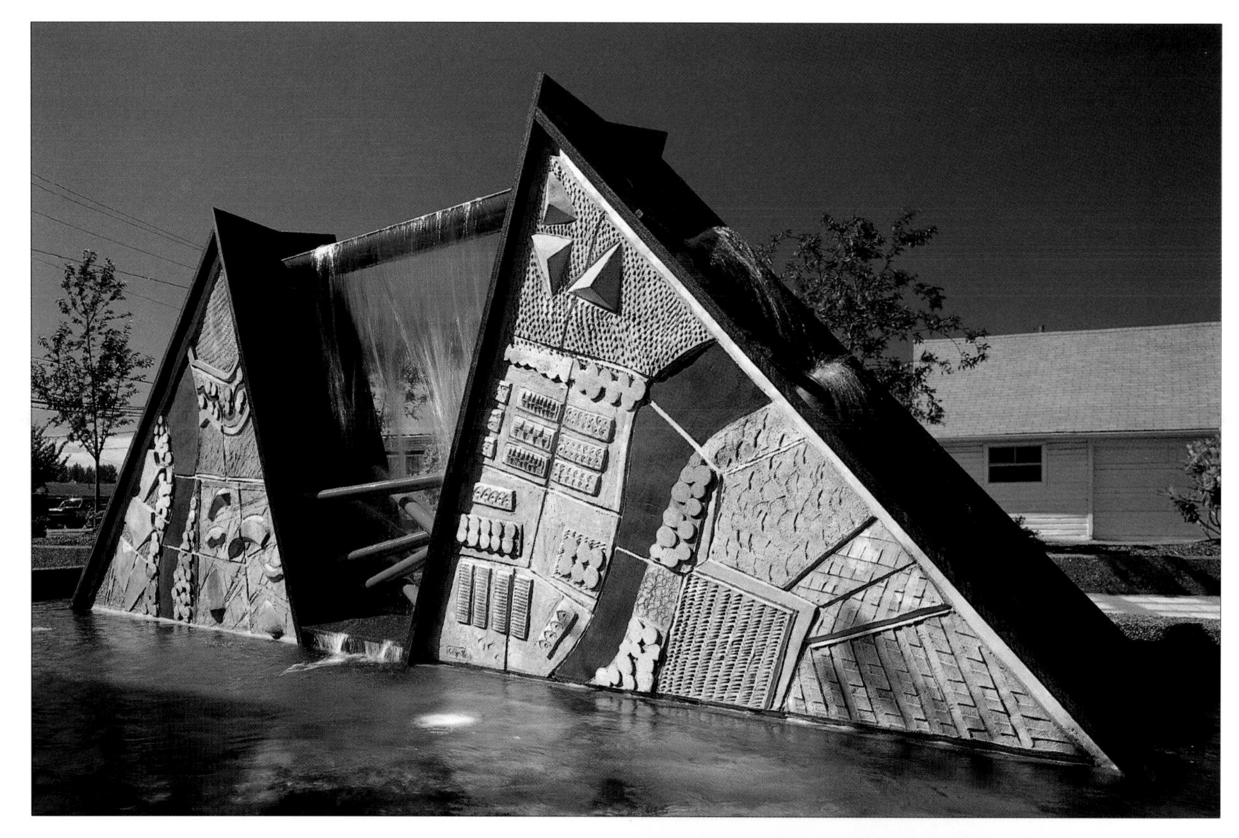

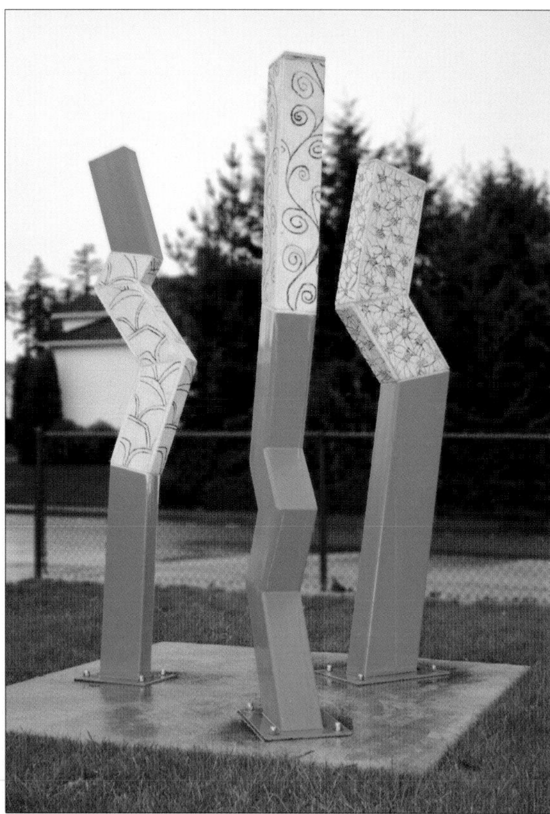

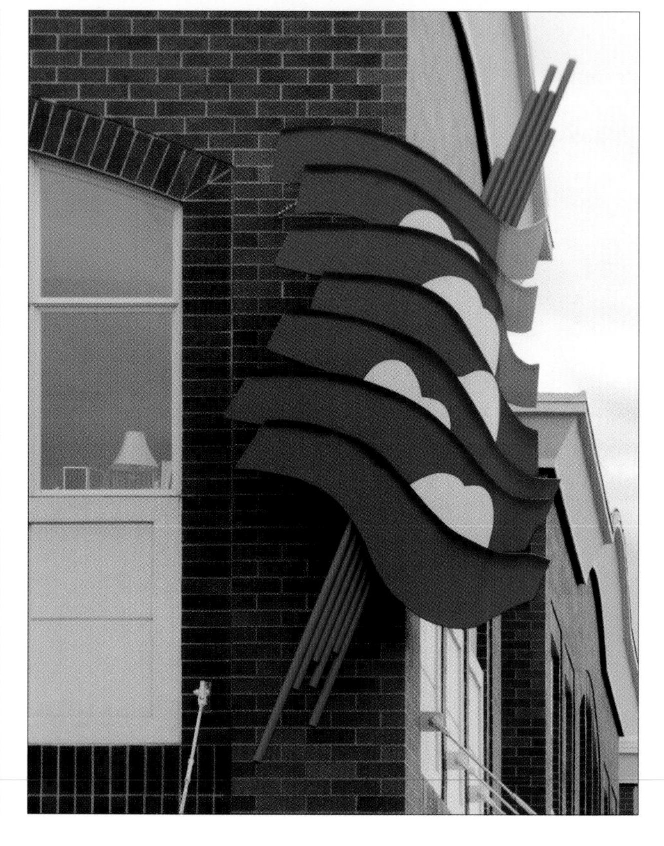

Top: *Centennial Park Water Feature*, Arlington, WA. Photograph: Dick Springate. Bottom left: *Canterbury Park*, 2004, Kent, WA. Photograph: Jim Houston. Bottom right: *Valley Financial Center*, 2005, Kent, WA. Photograph: Jim Houston.

ZACHARY COFFIN

1272 MURPHY AVENUE #300 ■ ATLANTA, GA 30310
ZACH@ZACHARYCOFFIN.COM ■ WWW.ZACHARYCOFFIN.COM

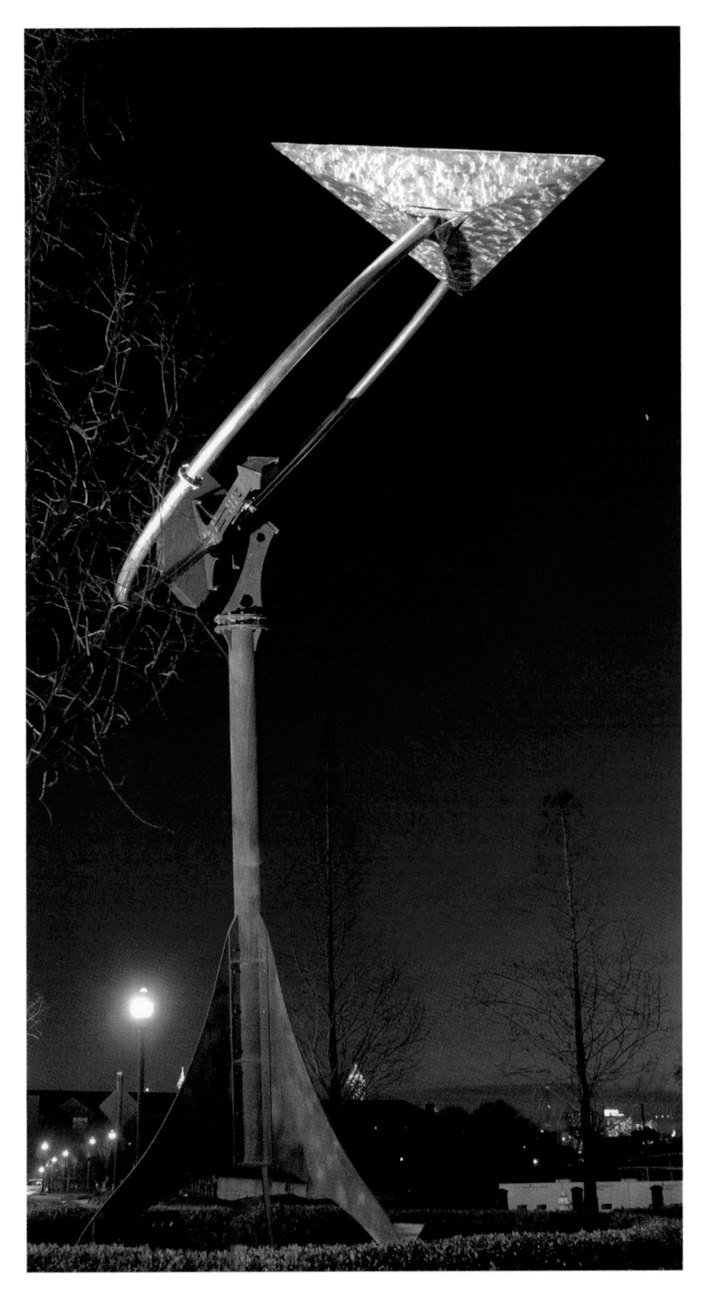

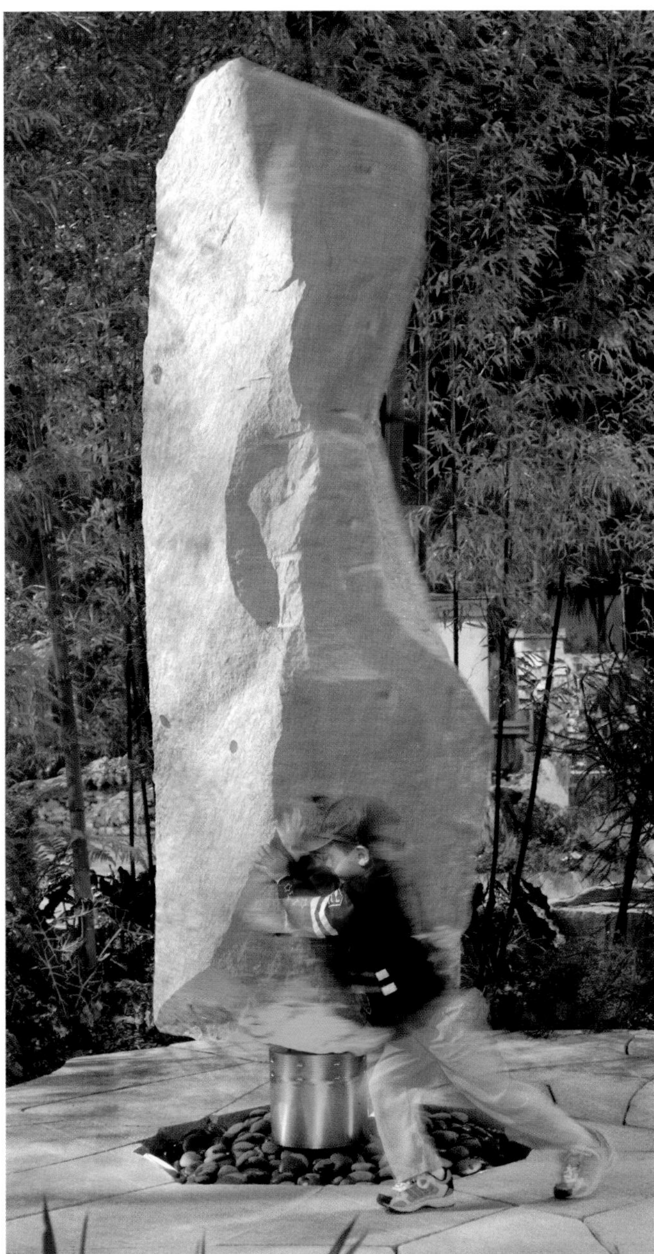

Left: *Hydrogen,* 2004, stainless steel, galvanized steel, and granite, wind powered, commissioned by Carter and Associates for Lindbergh City Center, Development, Atlanta, GA, ranging from 22'H to 32'H according to wind. Right: *Rockspinner 4,* 2007, commissioned for Tokikata Modern Gardens, granite with steel and stainless steel, approximately 10'H, 8,000lb. human-powered spinning boulder with solar-electric assist. Photograph: twmeyer.com.

EINO

EINOART, INC. ■ 3811 OPHIR AVENUE ■ PAHRUMP, NV 89048
TEL 775-727-8207 ■ TEL 770-894-1748 ■ WWW.EINO.ORG

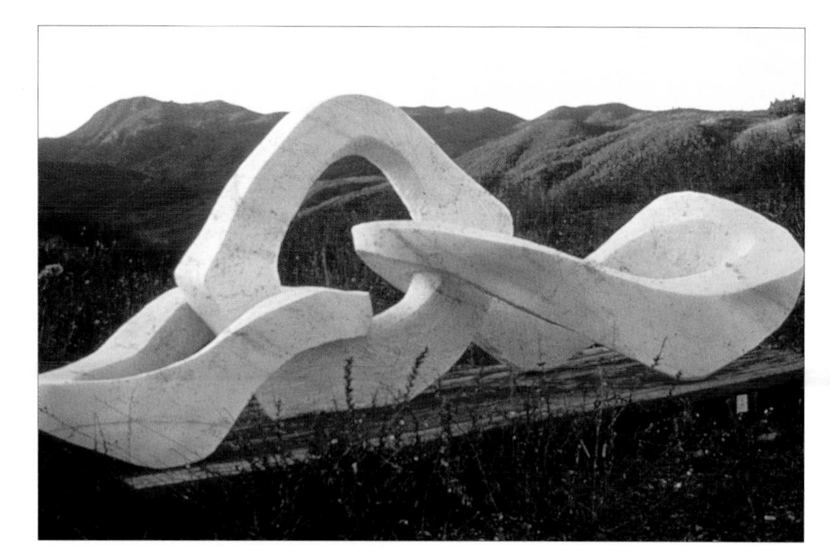

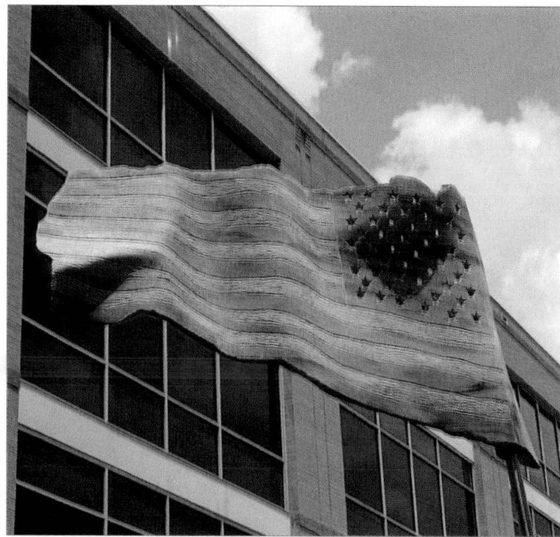

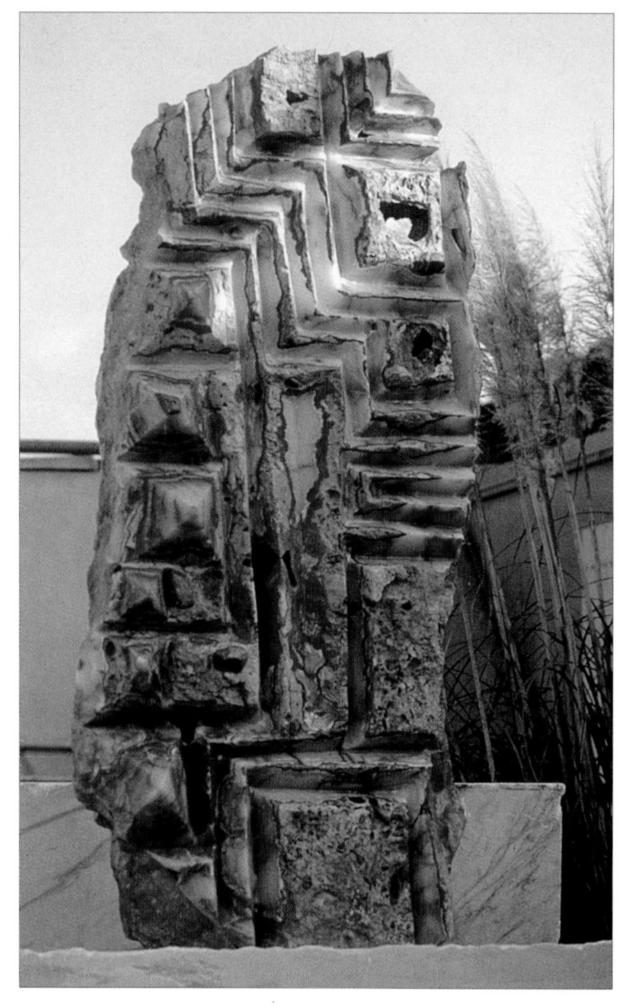

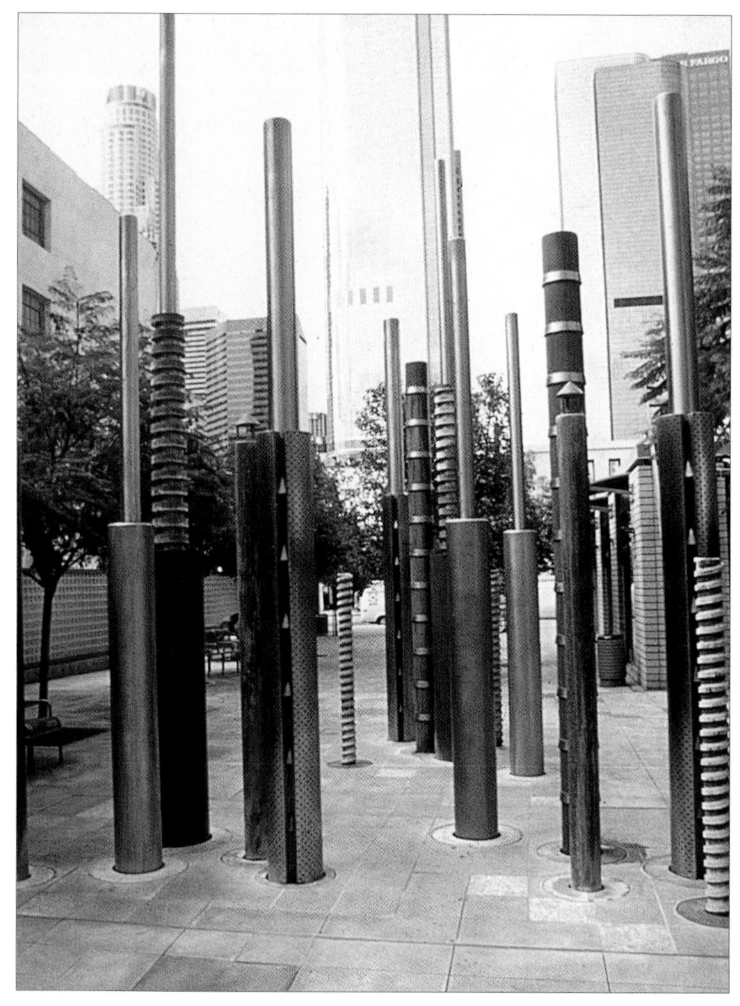

Top left: *Untitled,* 1970, Helsinki, Finland, Colorado marble, 40"H x 120"W x 36"D. Top right: *Unity,* 2002, Kennesaw State University, GA, Etowah marble, 15'H x 42"W x 4"D. Bottom left: *Zenith,* 1993, onyx, 64"H x 42"W x 11"D. Bottom right: *Untitled,* 1988, Los Angeles, CA, stainless steel and bronze, 18'H x 16'W x 14'D. Photographs: Chuck Bankuti.

DOUGLAS OLMSTED FREEMAN

DOUG FREEMAN STUDIO ■ 310 NORTH SECOND STREET ■ MINNEAPOLIS, MN 55401
TEL 612-339-7150 ■ FAX 612-339-5201 ■ E-MAIL DOUG@FREEMANSTUDIO.COM ■ WWW.FREEMANSTUDIO.COM

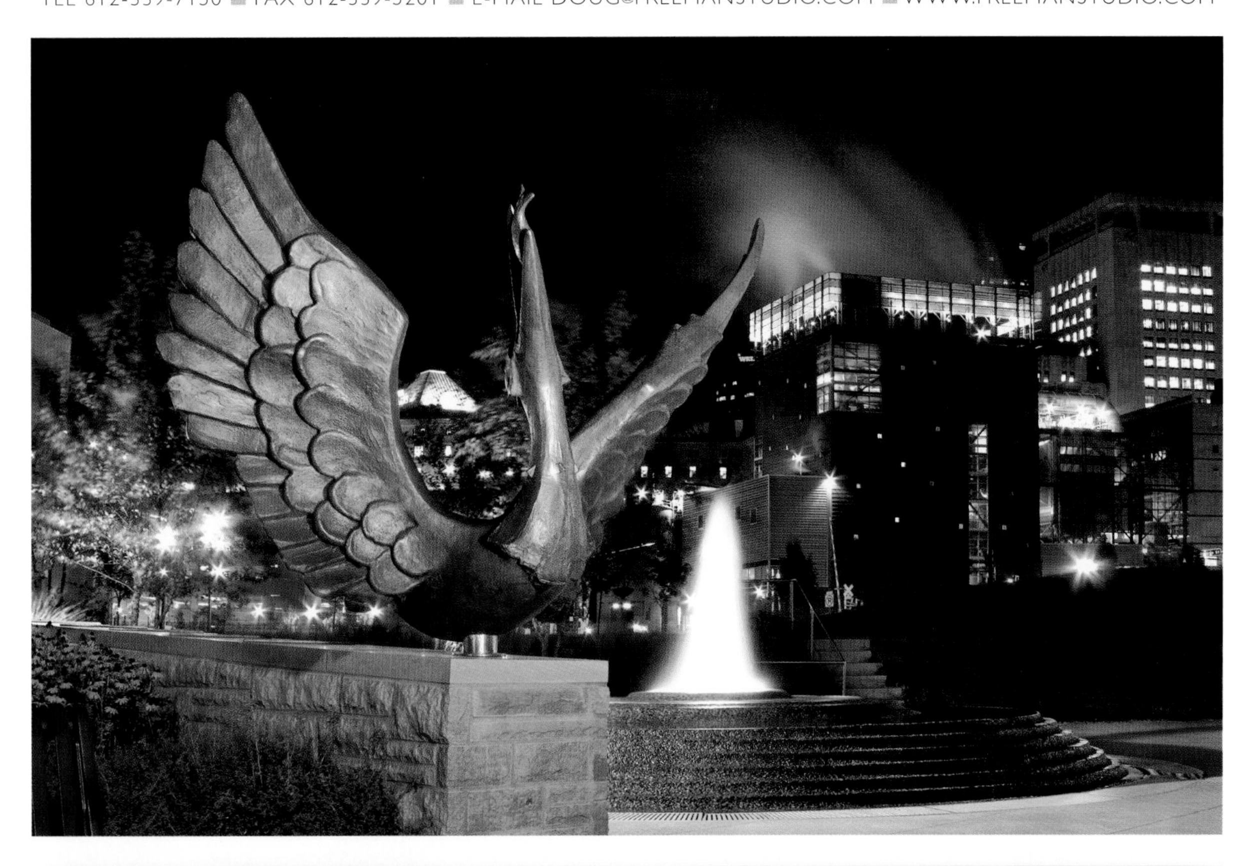

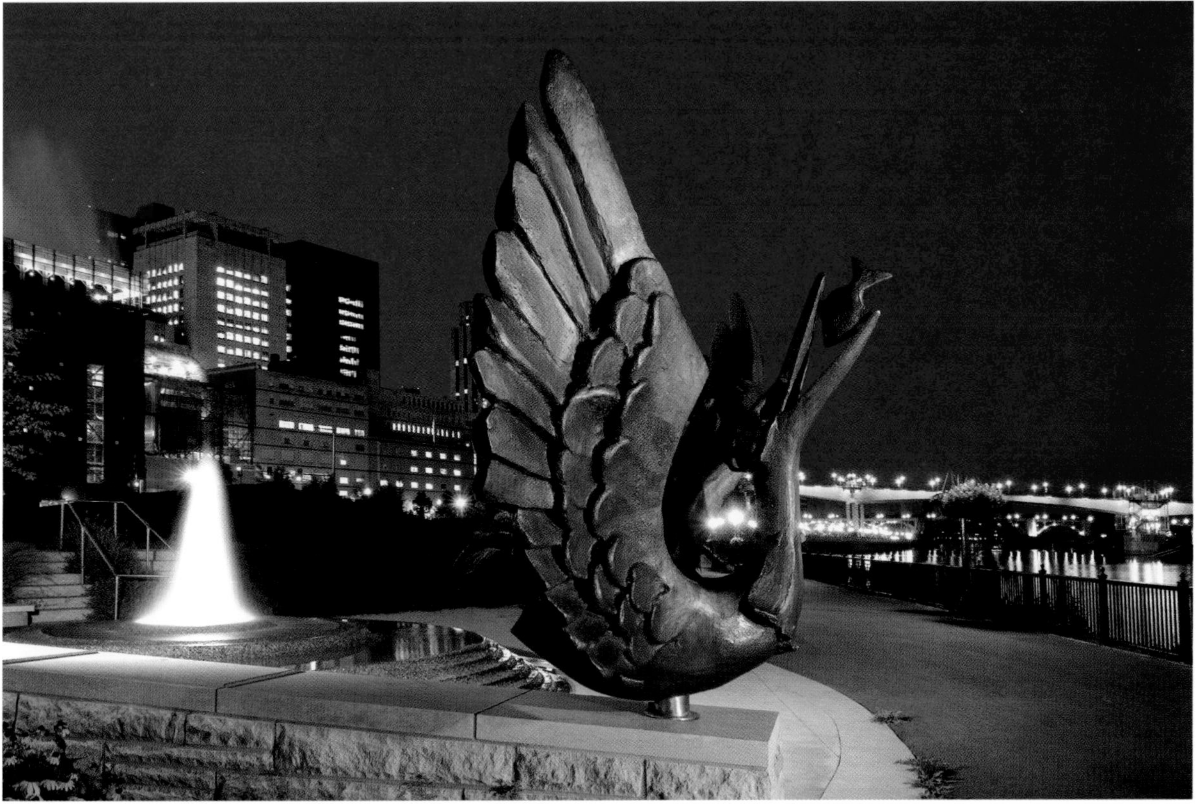

The Mississippi Guardian Birds, Saint Paul, MN. Photographs: Jerry Mathiason.

RALF GSCHWEND

RALFONSO.COM ■ 301 CLEMATIS STREET #3000 ■ WEST PALM BEACH, FL 33401
TEL 561-655-2745 ■ FAX 561-655-4158 ■ RALFONSO@RALFONSO.COM ■ WWW.RALFONSO.COM

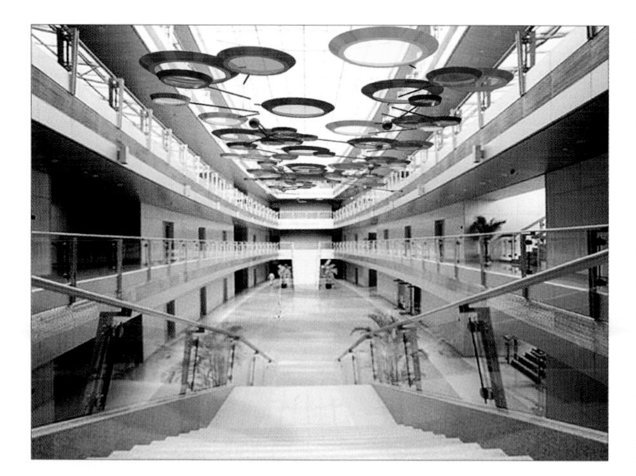

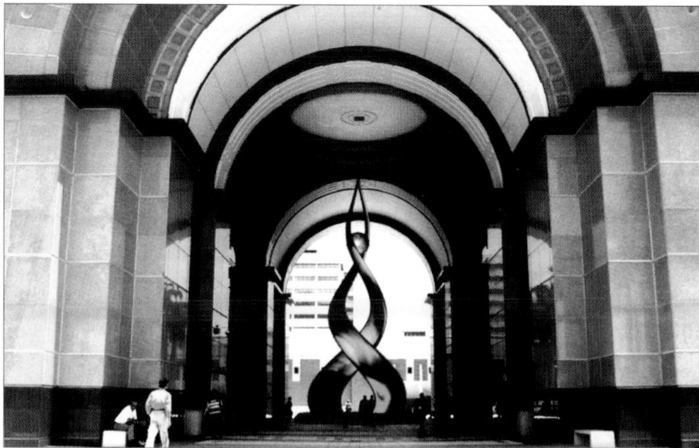

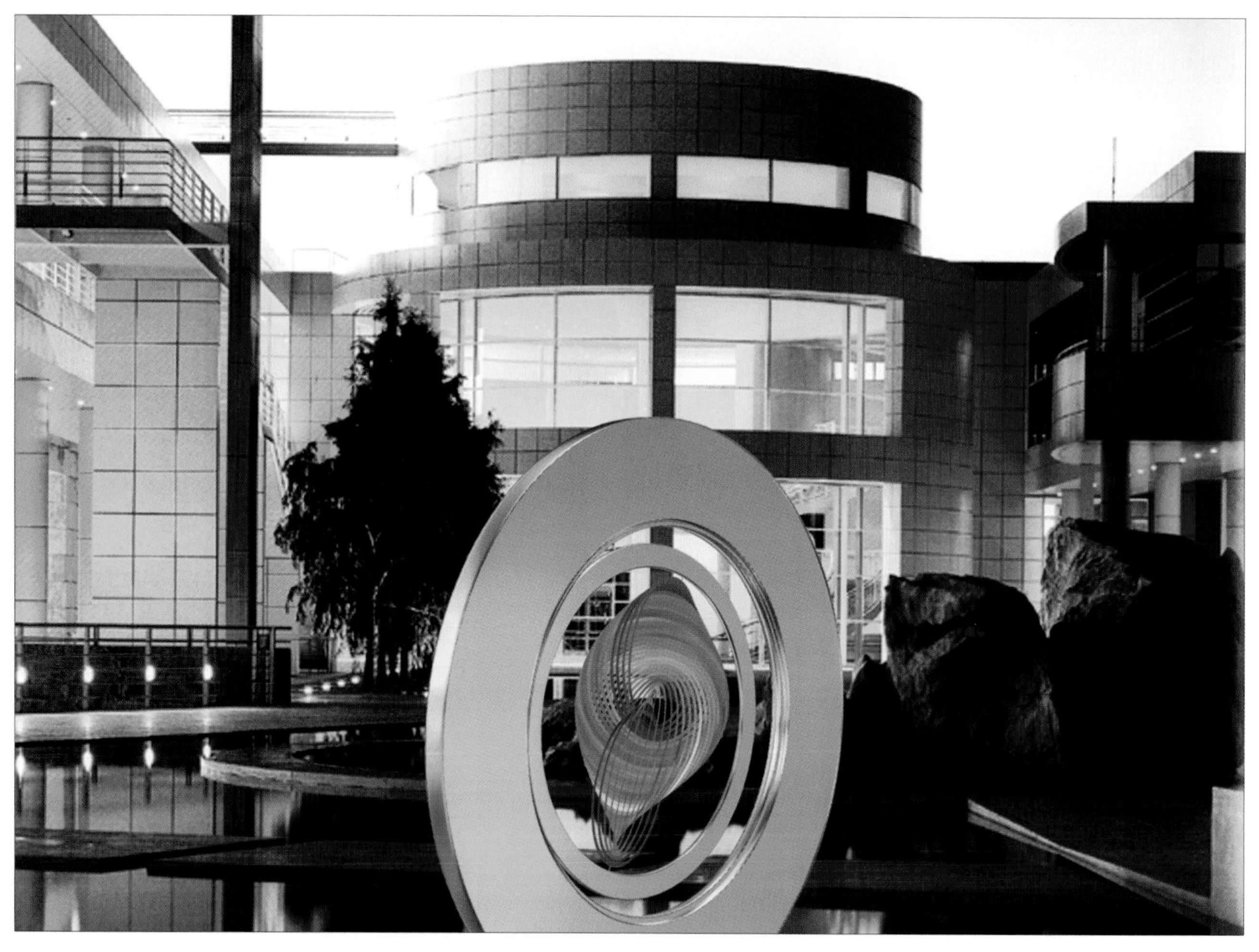

Top left: *ExoCentric Spirits*, 2003, fiberglass, seventy-disc assembly with colored lenses mobile design. Top right: *Moving on UP*, 2003, fiberglass and aluminum kinetic wind sculpture. Bottom: *Infinity 1*, 2004, anodized aluminum, kinetic, motor-driven sculpture design.

ARCHIE HELD

ARCHIE HELD STUDIO ■ #5 18TH STREET ■ RICHMOND, CA 94801 ■ TEL 510-235-8700
FAX 510-234-4828 ■ E-MAIL ARCHIEHELDSTUDIO@COMCAST.NET ■ WWW.ARCHIEHELD.COM

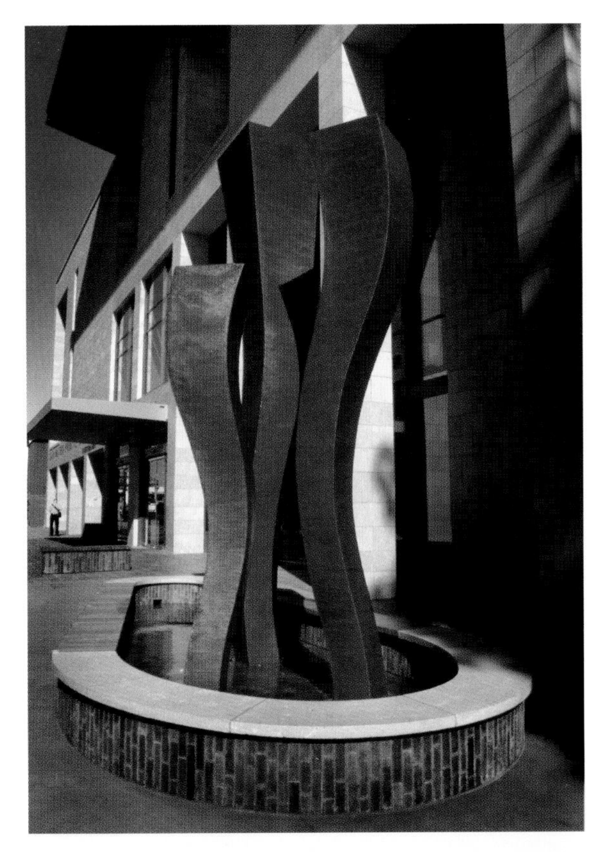

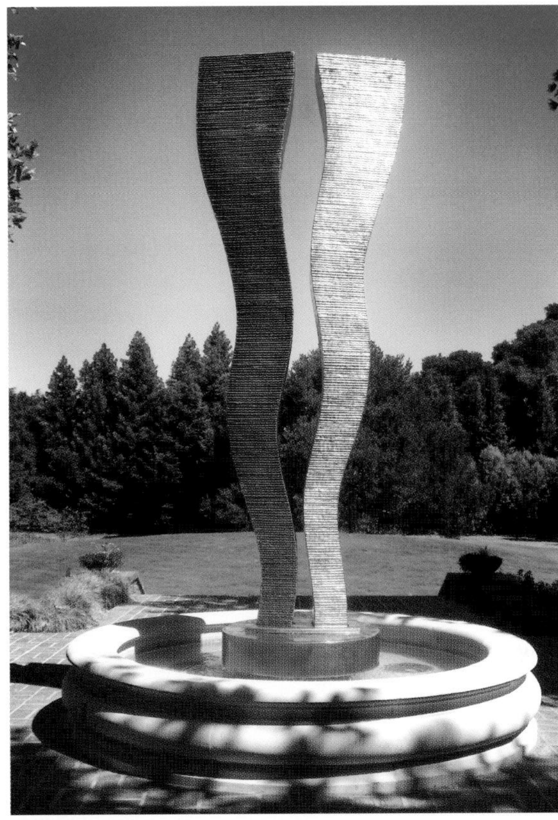

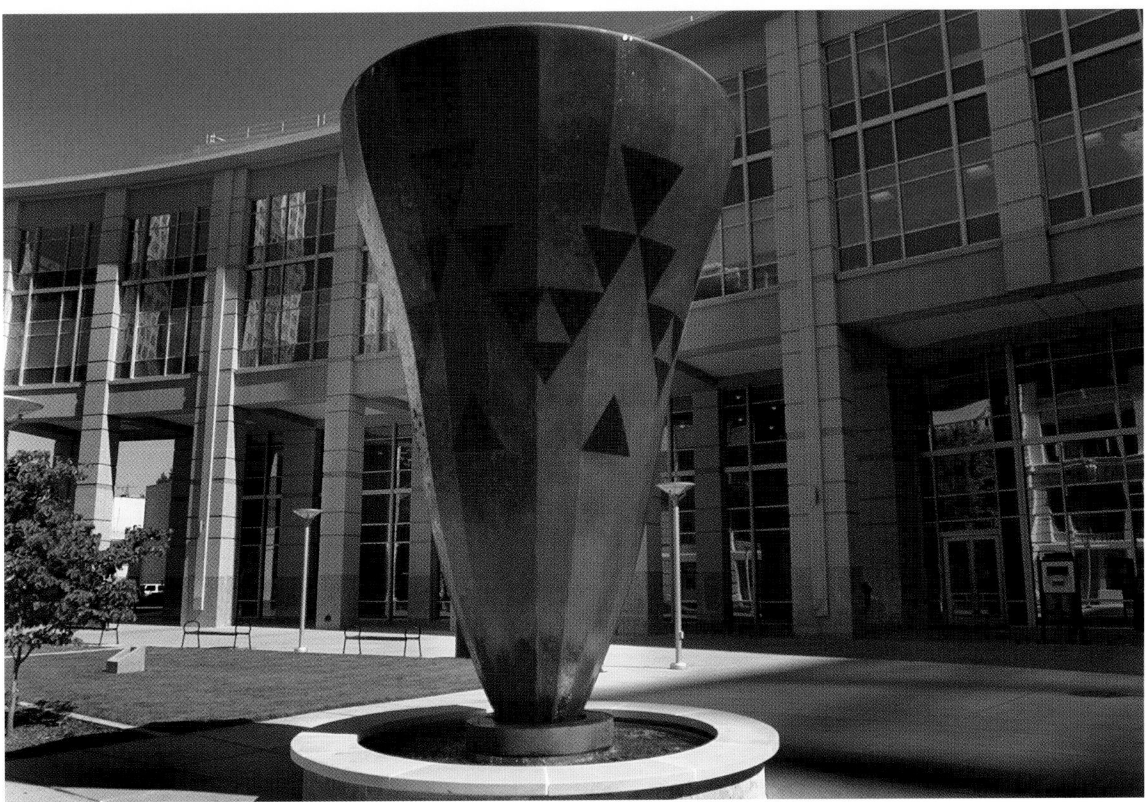

Top left: *Conversation,* 2006, San Mateo Public Library, San Mateo, CA, bronze and water, 15.6' x 11.8' x 17.6'. Top right: *Wave Columns,* 2006, private collection, Woodside, CA, stainless steel and water, 7' x 7' x 10.5'. Bottom: *Burden Basket,* 2006, Sacramento City Hall Plaza, Sacramento, CA, bronze and water, 11' x 11' x 19'. Photographs: Michael Allen Jones.

IMAGO DEI, LLC

JEREMY AND JAMIE WELLS ■ 6817 FLINTLOCK ROAD SUITE A ■ HOUSTON, TX 77040 ■ TEL 713-466-9990
FAX 713-466-9998 ■ E-MAIL INFO@IMAGODEIGALLERY.COM ■ WWW.IMAGODEIGALLERY.COM

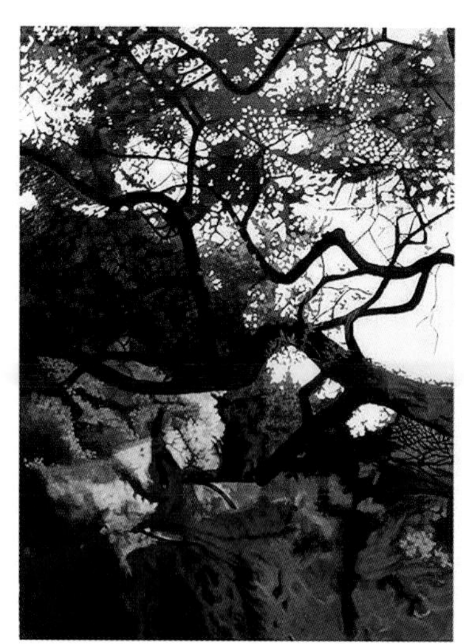
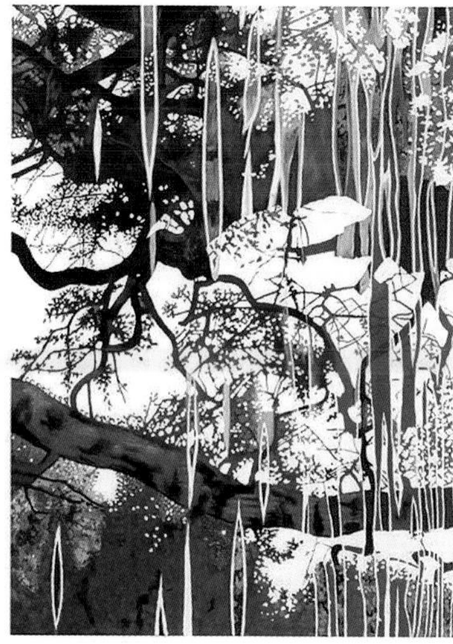
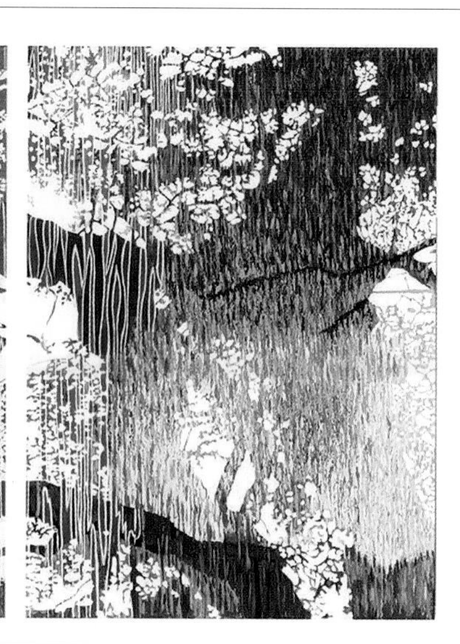

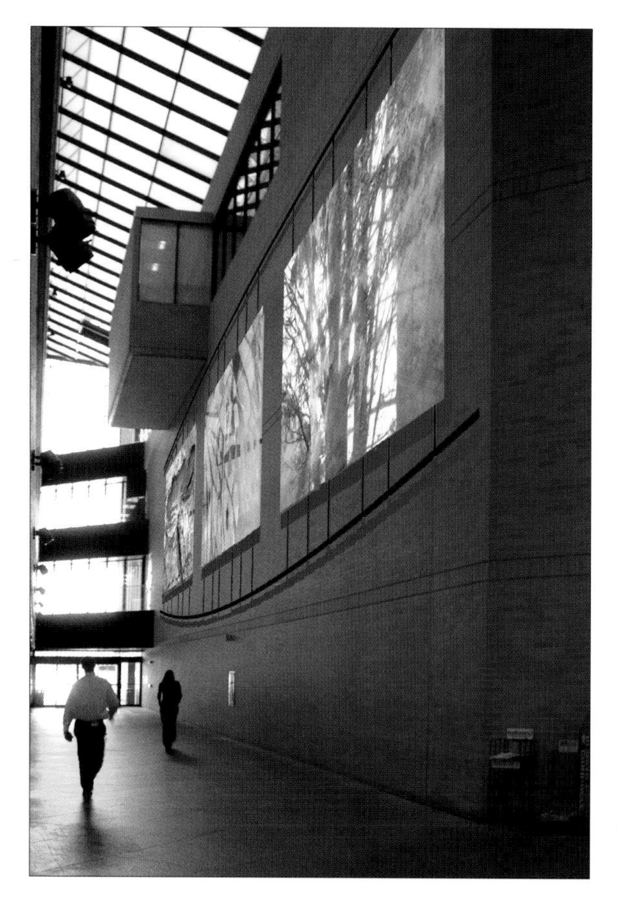
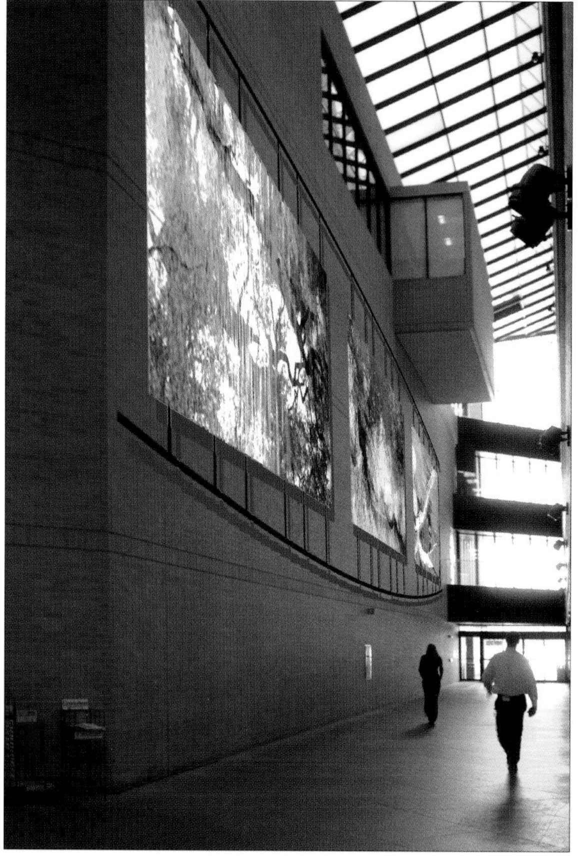

Top: *Golden Reflections* (Detail from the east wall of *Light & Life: The Texas Landscape*), 2007, acrylic on canvas, 14' x 30'.
Bottom: *Light & Life: The Texas Landscape*, 2007, Chevron Art Collection, acrylic on canvas with metal sculpture, each triptych: 14' x 30', metal sculpture: 22' x 100'.

ANTHONY KRAUSS

ANTHONY KRAUSS SCULPTURE ■ 41 LOWER BYRDCLIFFE ROAD ■ WOODSTOCK, NY 12498 ■ TEL 845-679-6360
FAX 845-679-2271 ■ E-MAIL ANTHONYKRAUSS@AOL.COM ■ WWW.FLETCHERGALLERY.COM.

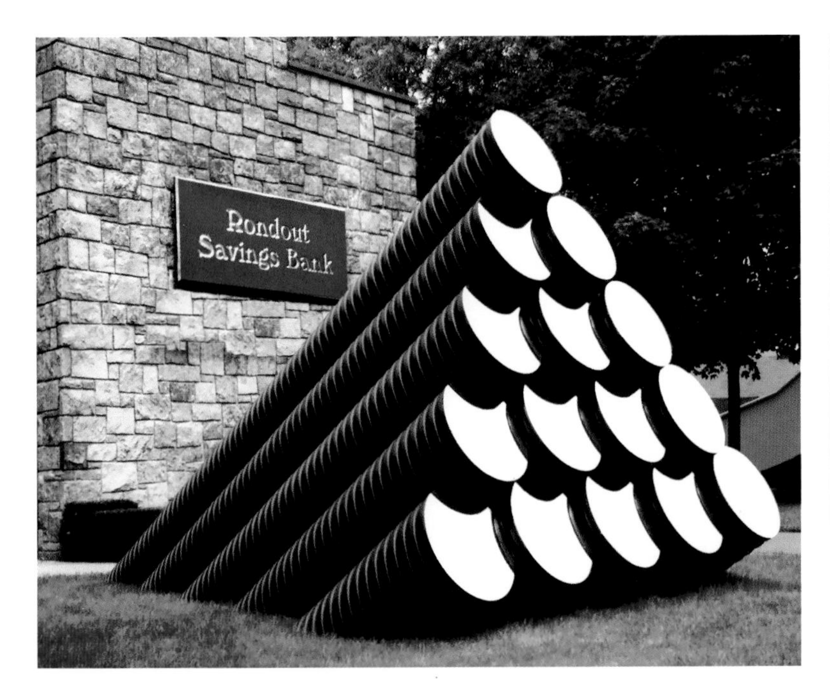

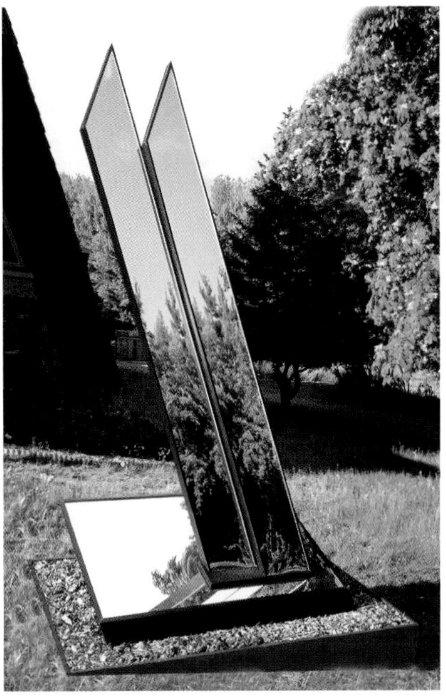

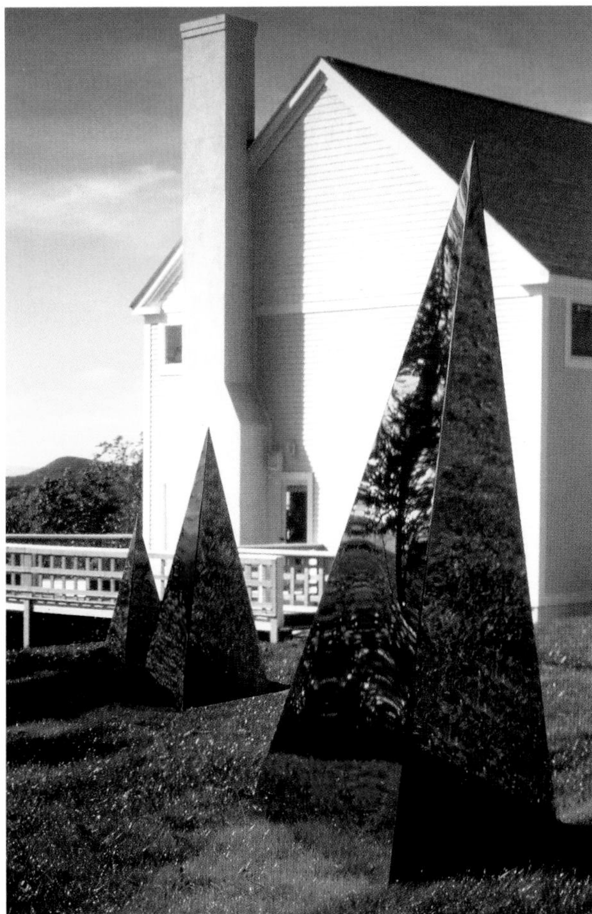

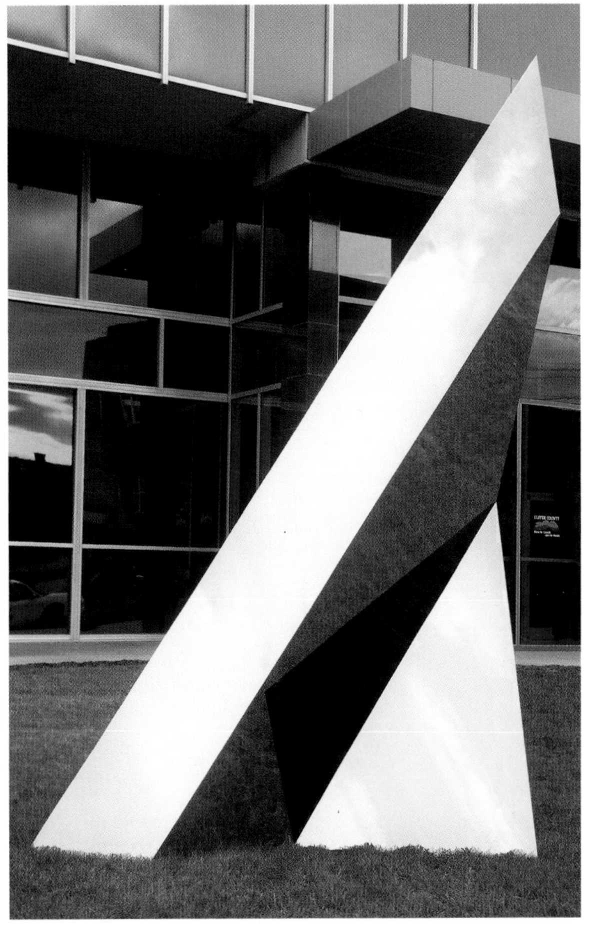

Top left: *Pyramid of Coins,* Rondout Savings Bank, Kingston, NY, mirrored aluminum and polyethylene, 9'H x 9'W x 17'D. Top right: *Twin Towers 2,* Saint Gregory's Episcopal Church, Woodstock, NY, mirrored aluminum, metal, and wood, 10'H x 5'W x 3'D. Bottom left: *Sails 3,* private commission, Monterey, MA, mirrored stainless steel, left to right: 6' x 2' x 2', 8' x 3' x 3', 10' x 4' x 4'. Photograph: John Lenz. Bottom right: *Folded Pyramid,* Ulster County Office Building, Kingston, NY, mirrored stainless steel, 10' x 6' x 2'. Photograph: Jason Zhang.

COLIN LAMBERT & PETER ADAMS

MARIPOSA STUDIO ■ 12350 RICE'S CROSSING ROAD ■ OREGON HOUSE, CA 95962 ■ TEL/FAX 530-692-0235
E-MAIL COLIN@MARIPOSASTUDIO.NET ■ WWW.MARIPOSASTUDIO.COM

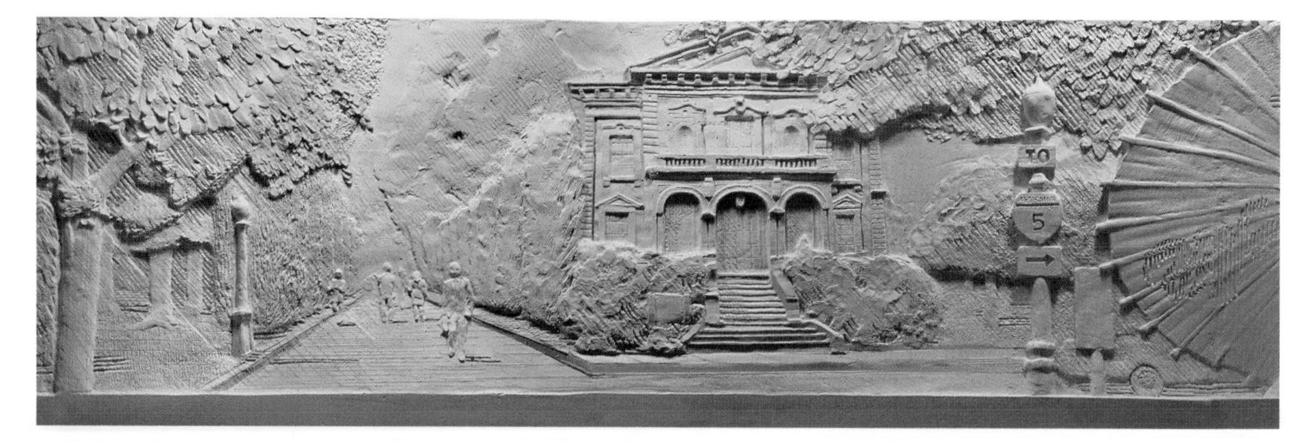

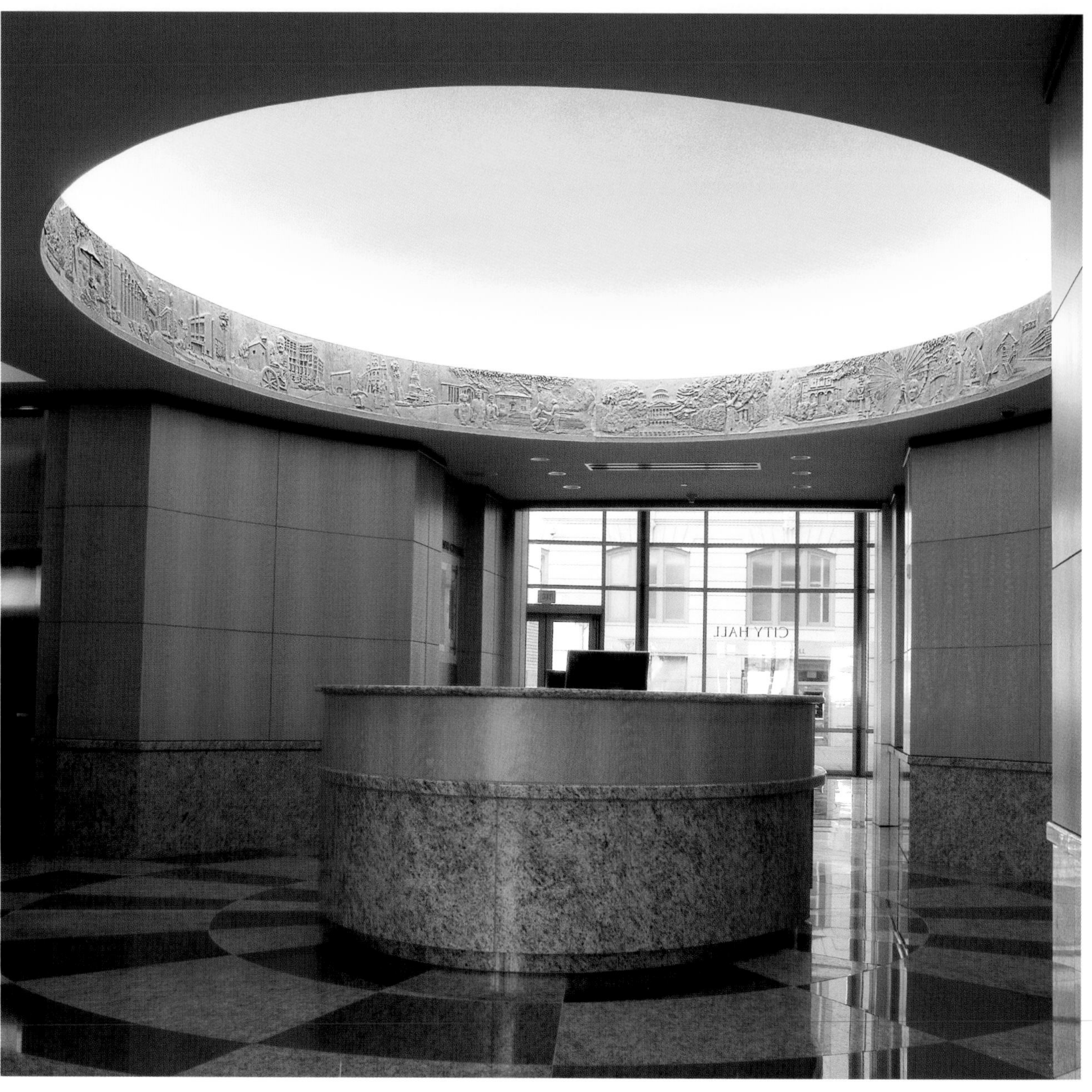

Sacremento—Here & Now, Sacramento City Hall, Sacramento, CA, cast stone, 20" × 57".

DEBORAH LEFKOWITZ

PO BOX 94 ■ RIVERSIDE, CA 92502-0094 ■ TEL/FAX 951-682-0444
E-MAIL DEBORAH@LEFKOWITZART.COM ■ WWW.LEFKOWITZART.COM

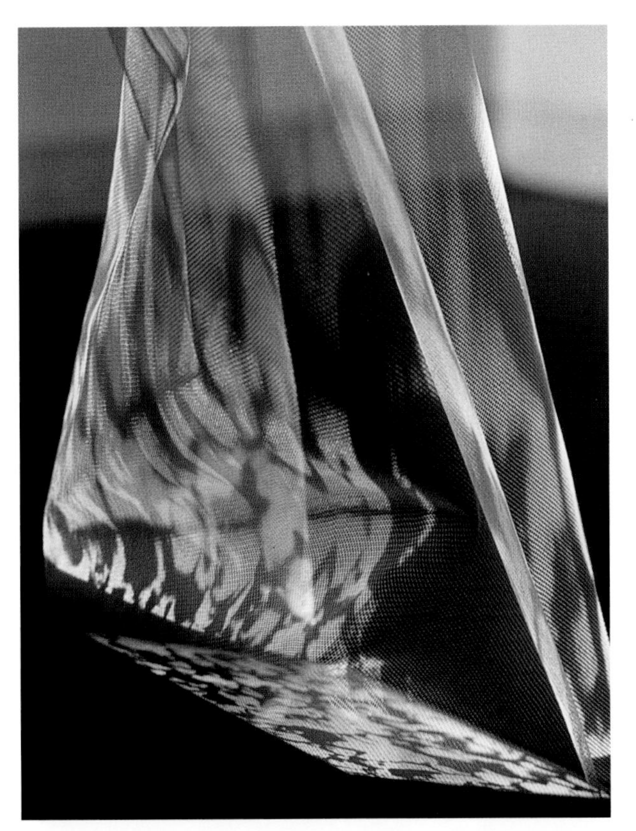

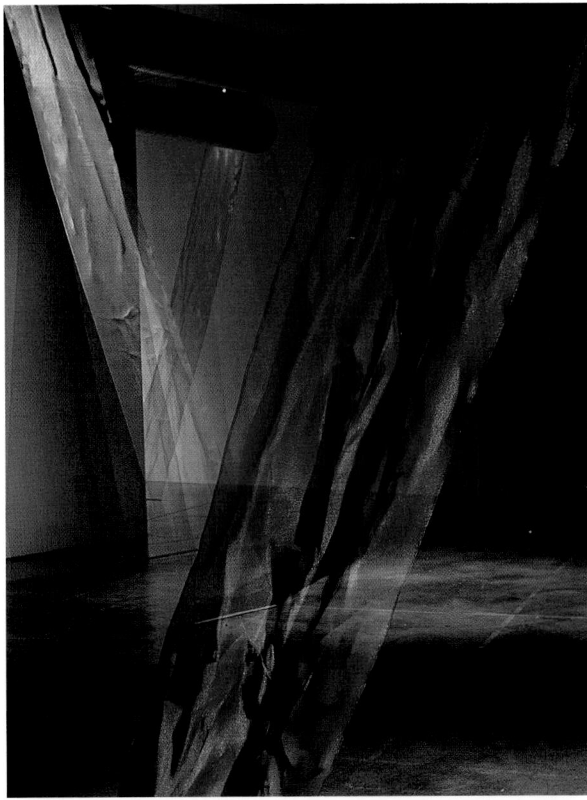

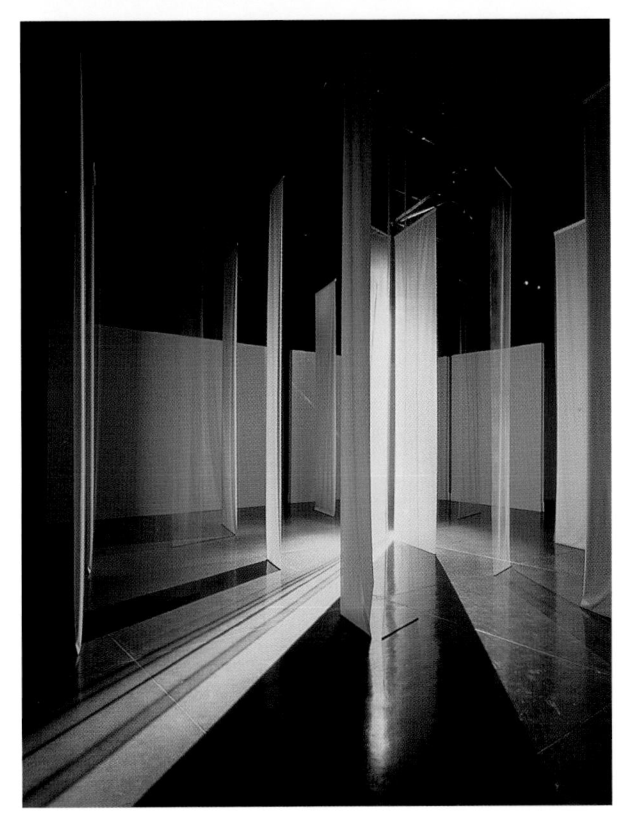

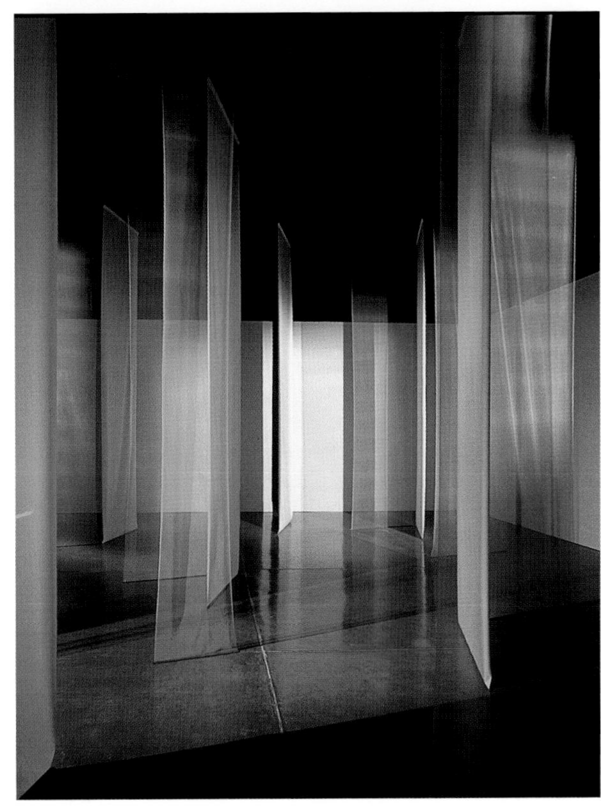

Top left: *Light Chambers* (detail), duraclear photograph on plexiglass, fabric, halogen light, and wood, 10'H x 9" x 11". Top right: Moment from *Songs of Twilight*, aluminum screening, halogen lights, dimmers, and computer-programmed lighting control, 20'H x 26' x 36'. Photograph: Robert Wedemeyer. Bottom left and right: Two moments from *In the Shadow of the Hourglass*, fabric, halogen lights, dimmers, and computer-programmed lighting control, 17'H x 48' x 48'. Photographs: Susan Einstein.

PETER W. MICHEL

PETER W. MICHEL, SCULPTOR ■ 36 KELLOGG STREET ■ CLINTON, NY 13323 ■ TEL 315-853-8146
TEL 315-663-5308 ■ FAX 315-859-1480 ■ E-MAIL PETER@PETERMICHEL.COM ■ WWW.PETERMICHEL.COM

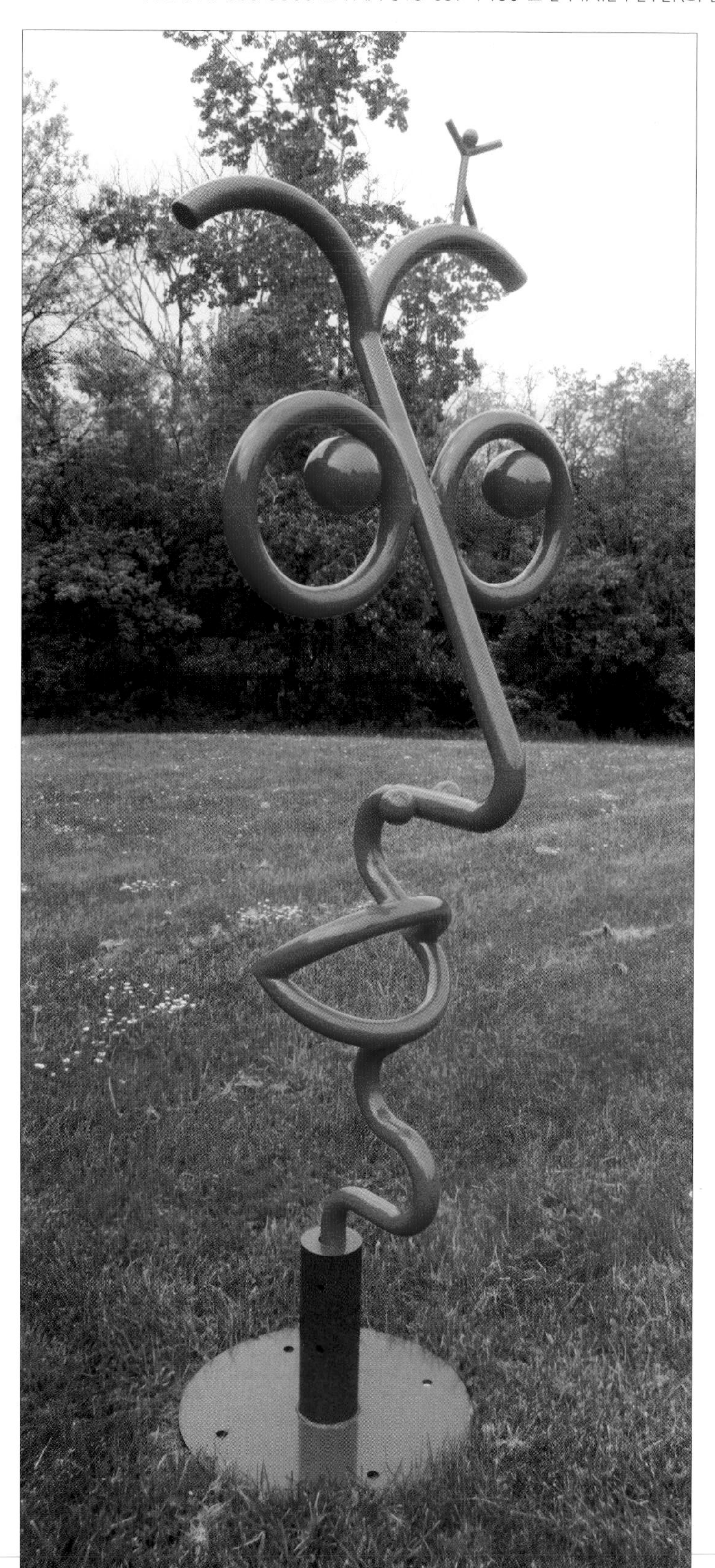

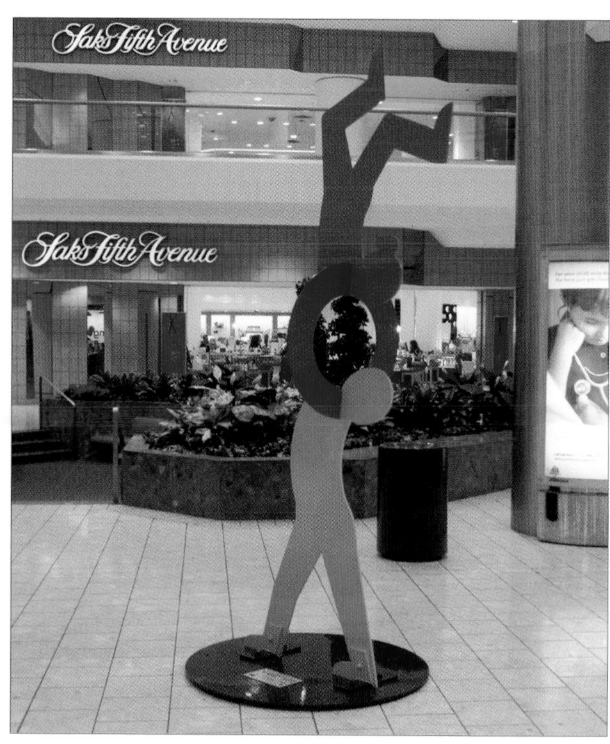

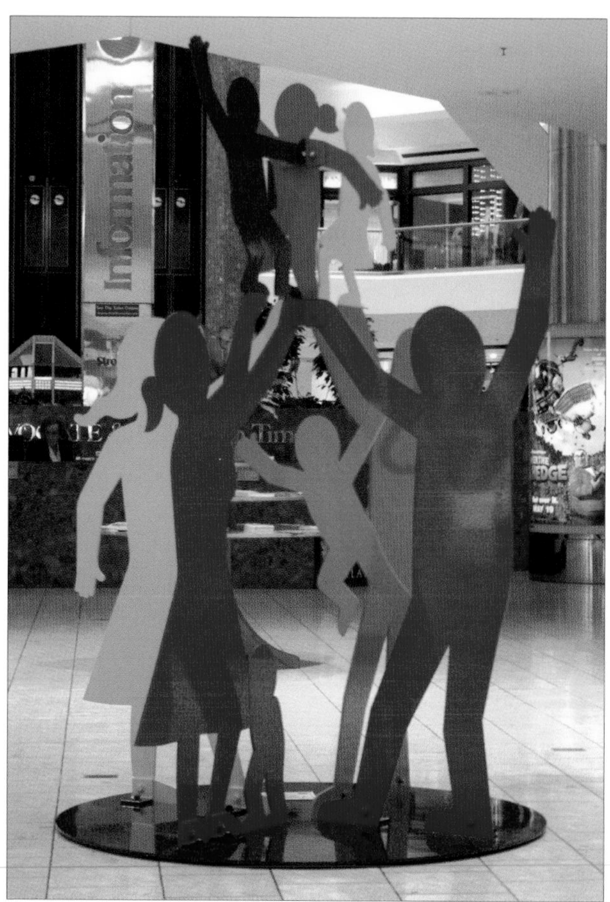

Left: *What's That Voice I Hear?*, 2006, galvanized and powder-coated steel, 78"H x 26"W x 25"D. Top right: *Two are Halves of One*, 2006, Stamford Town Center, Stamford, CT, painted aluminum, 117"H x 46"W x 50"D. Bottom right: *Family Celebration*, 2006, Stamford Town Center, Stamford, CT, painted aluminum, 93"H x 70"W x 65"D.

MONUMENTAL-SCULPTURES.COM, INC.

GARY AND ESPERANZA JACKSON ■ 13870 RIVERSIDE DRIVE ■ APPLE VALLEY, CA 92307 ■ TEL 760-946-0525
FAX 818-475-1477 ■ E-MAIL JACKSON@MONUMENTAL-SCULPTURES.COM ■ WWW.MONUMENTAL-SCULPTURES.COM

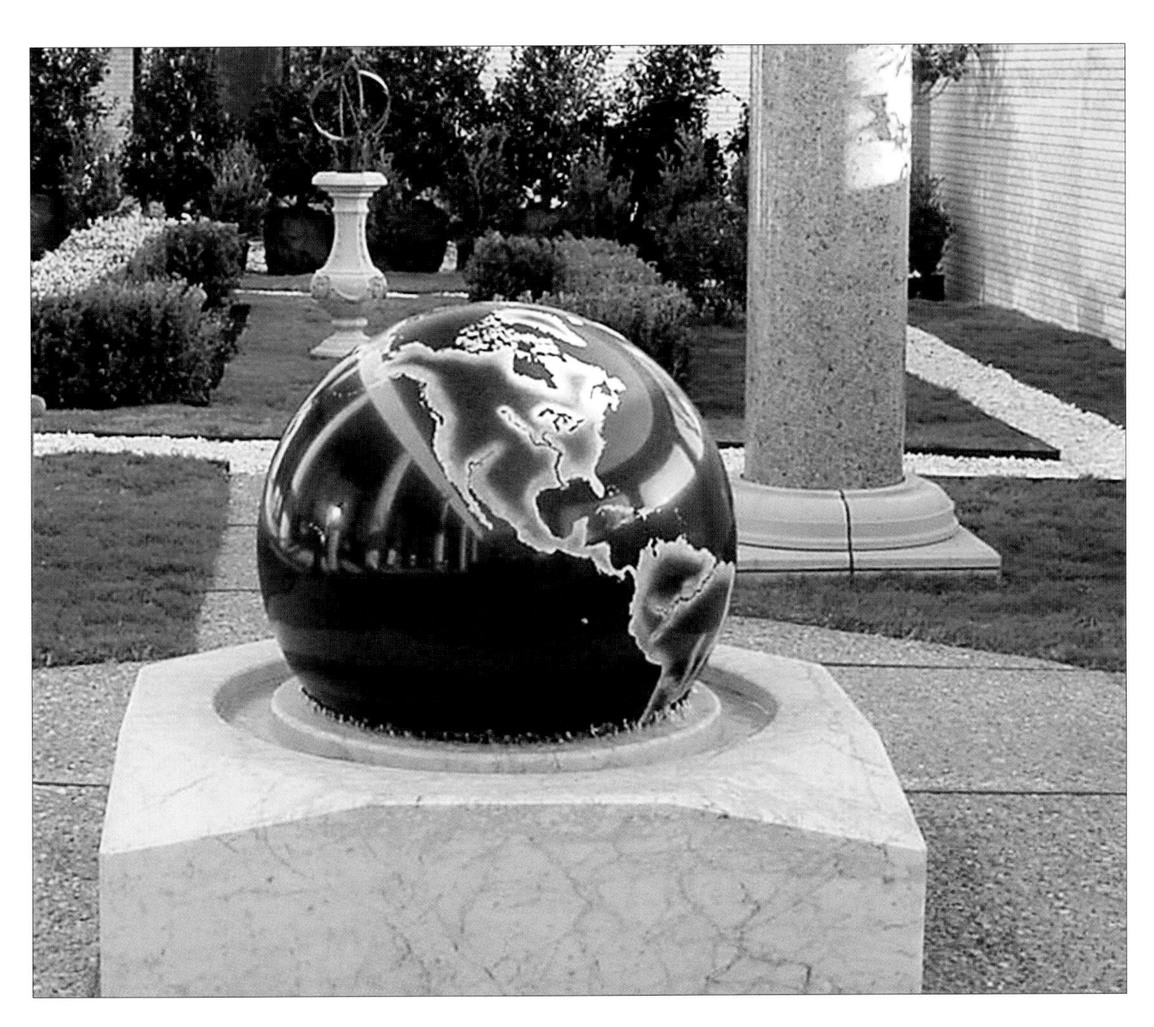

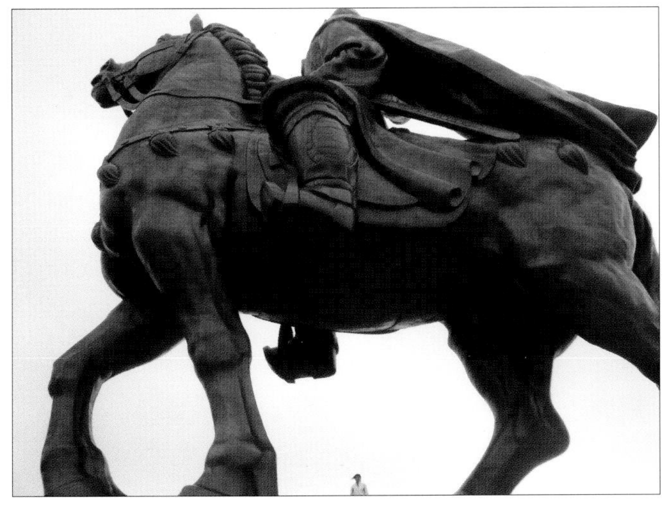

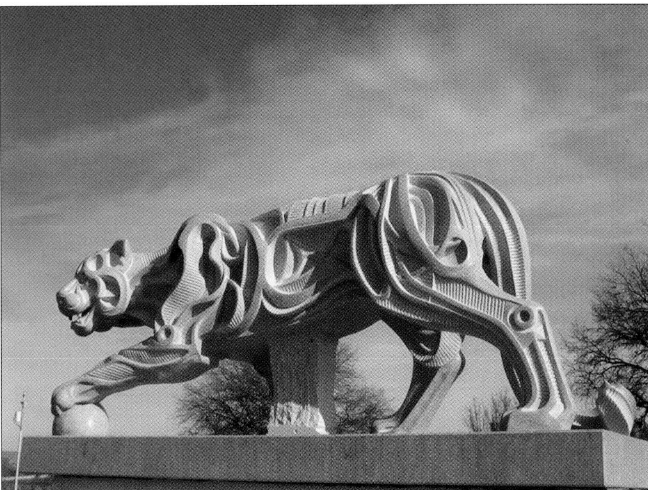

Top: *Floating Granite Sphere* and various works. Bottom left: *Heroic Bronze Horseman,* 150'H. Bottom right: *Puma,* granite, 16'L.

MERRILEE MOORE

LIFE IS BUT A DREAM ■ 13218 FOURTH AVENUE NW ■ SEATTLE, WA 98177 ■ TEL 206-365-4790
TEL 425-754-2066 ■ FAX 425-365-4790 ■ E-MAIL MERRILEE@MERRILEEMOORE.COM ■ WWW.MERRILEEMOORE.COM

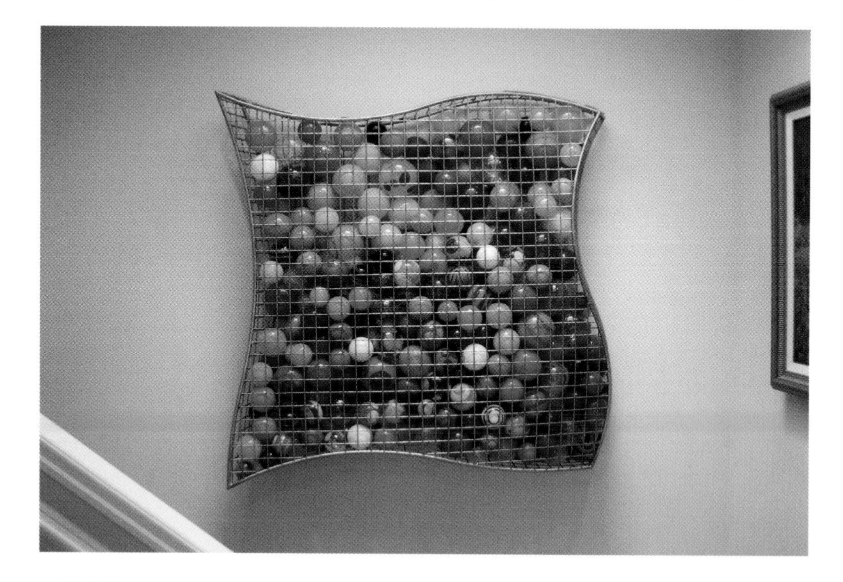

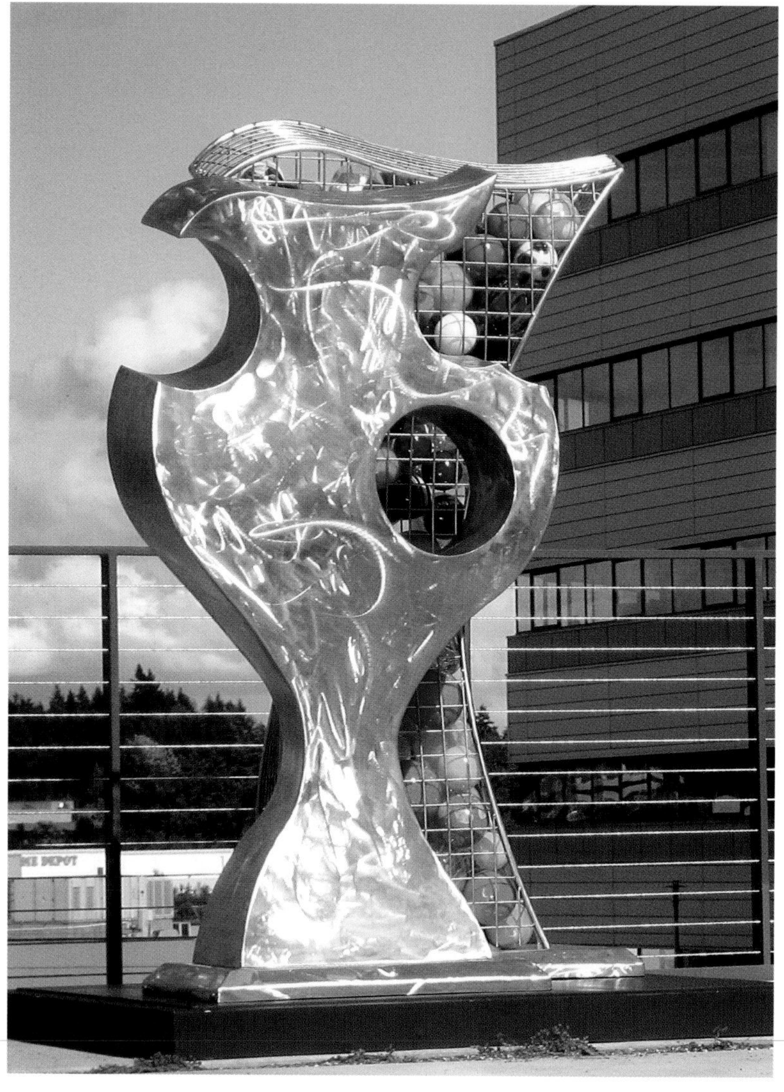

Top: *Ball Room,* 2006, private residence, Lake Sammamish, WA, stainless steel cage with blown glass balls ranging from 3"Dia. to 6"Dia., total size: 5'H x 5'W x 1'D. Bottom: *Complement,* 2006, City Hall, Bellevue, WA, stainless steel and glass, 6'H x 3'W x 1.5'D.

NATIONAL SCULPTORS' GUILD

2683 NORTH TAFT AVENUE ■ LOVELAND, CO 80538 ■ TEL 970-667-2015 ■ TEL 800-606-2015
FAX 970-667-2068 ■ E-MAIL INFO@COLUMBINENSG.COM ■ WWW.NATIONALSCULPTORSGUILD.COM

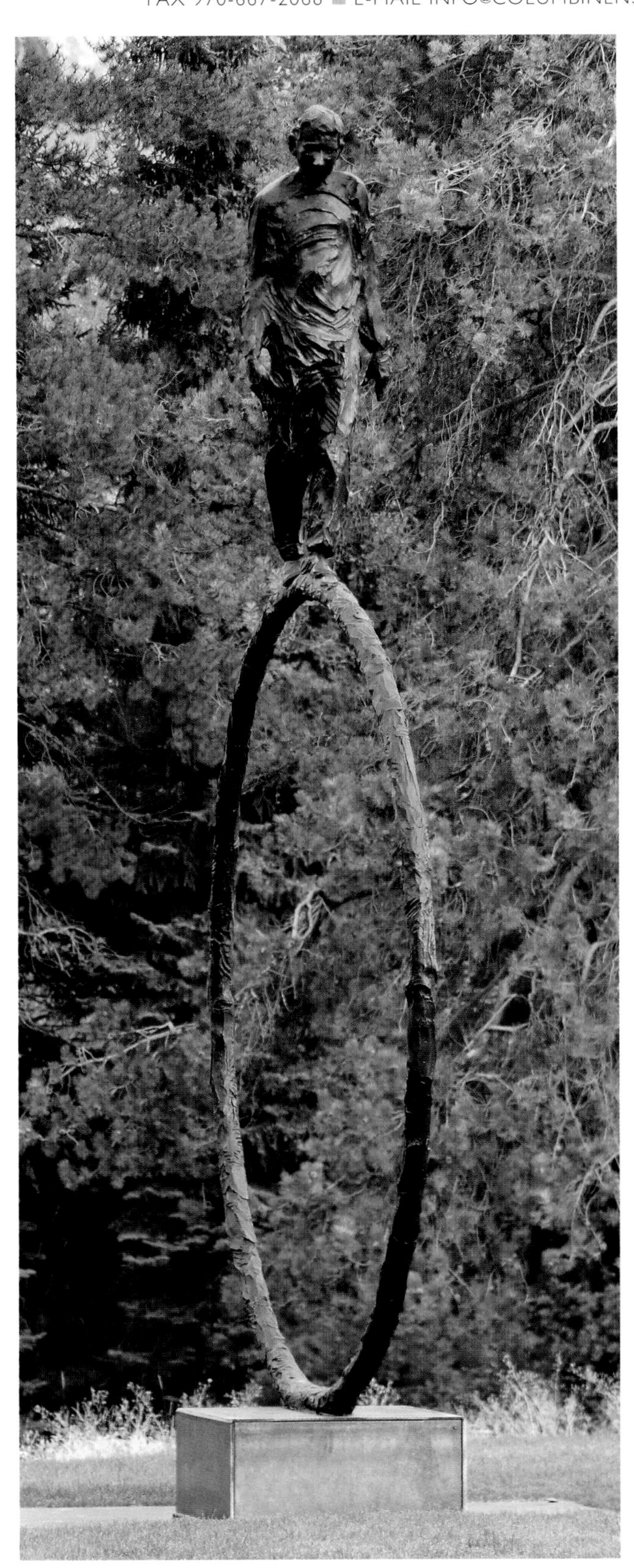

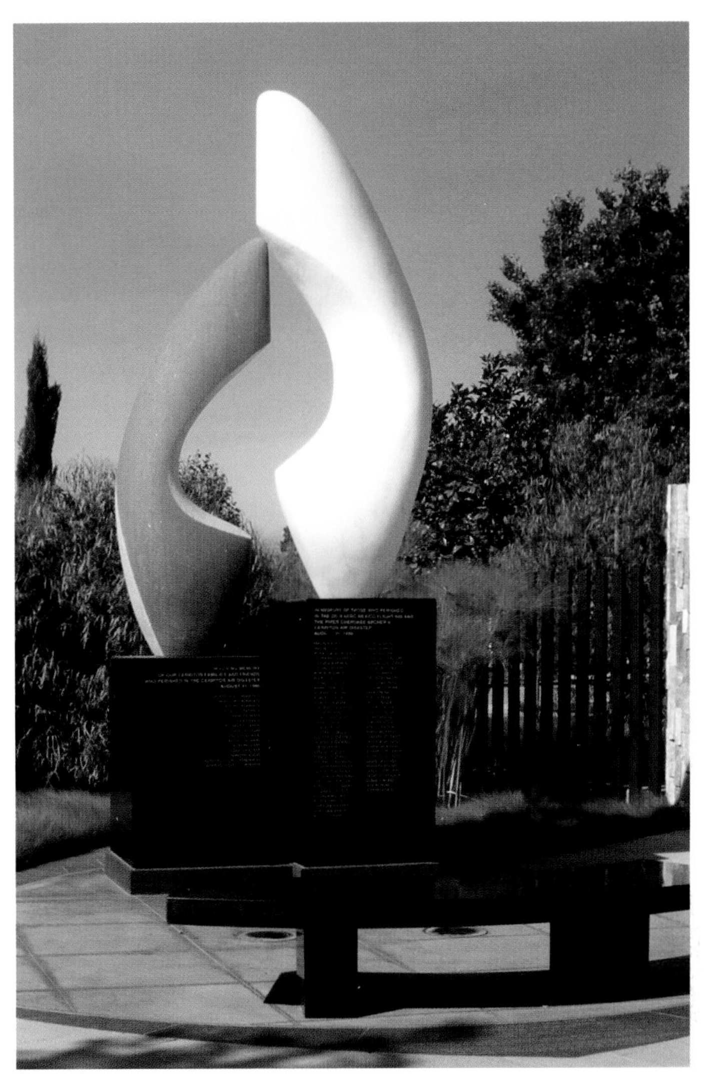

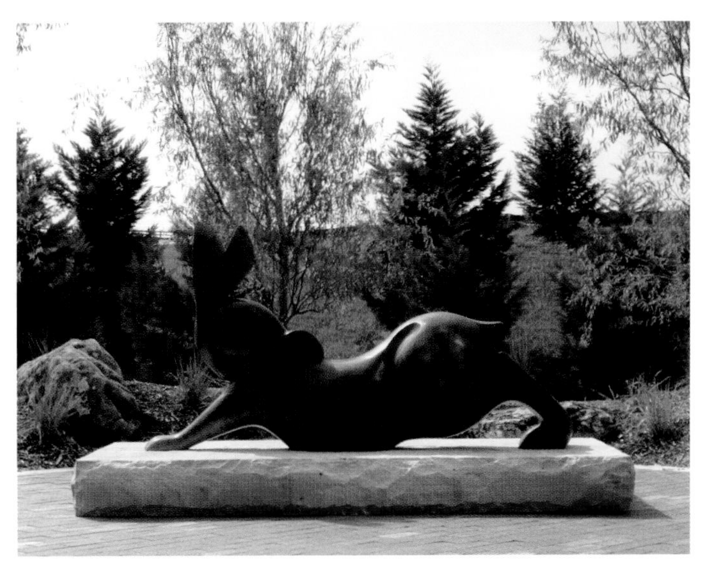

Left: *Setting the Pace* by Jane DeDecker, Art for the Mountain Community, Evergreen, CO, bronze, 16'H x 10.5'W x 2'D, edition of eleven.
Top right: Site-Specific *Air Disaster Memorial* by Kathleen Caricof, Cerritos Sculpture Garden, Cerritos, CA, granite and marble, 14'H.
Bottom right: *Rabbit Reach* by Tim Cherry, City of Little Rock, AR, bronze, 44"H x 82"W, edition of eight. Photographs: Jafe T. Parsons Photography.

BASHA RUTH NELSON

3992 ROUTE 212 ■ LAKE HILL, NY 12448 ■ TEL 845-679-2941 ■ FAX 845-679-4583
E-MAIL BASHA@BASHARUTHNELSON.COM ■ WWW.BASHARUTHNELSON.COM

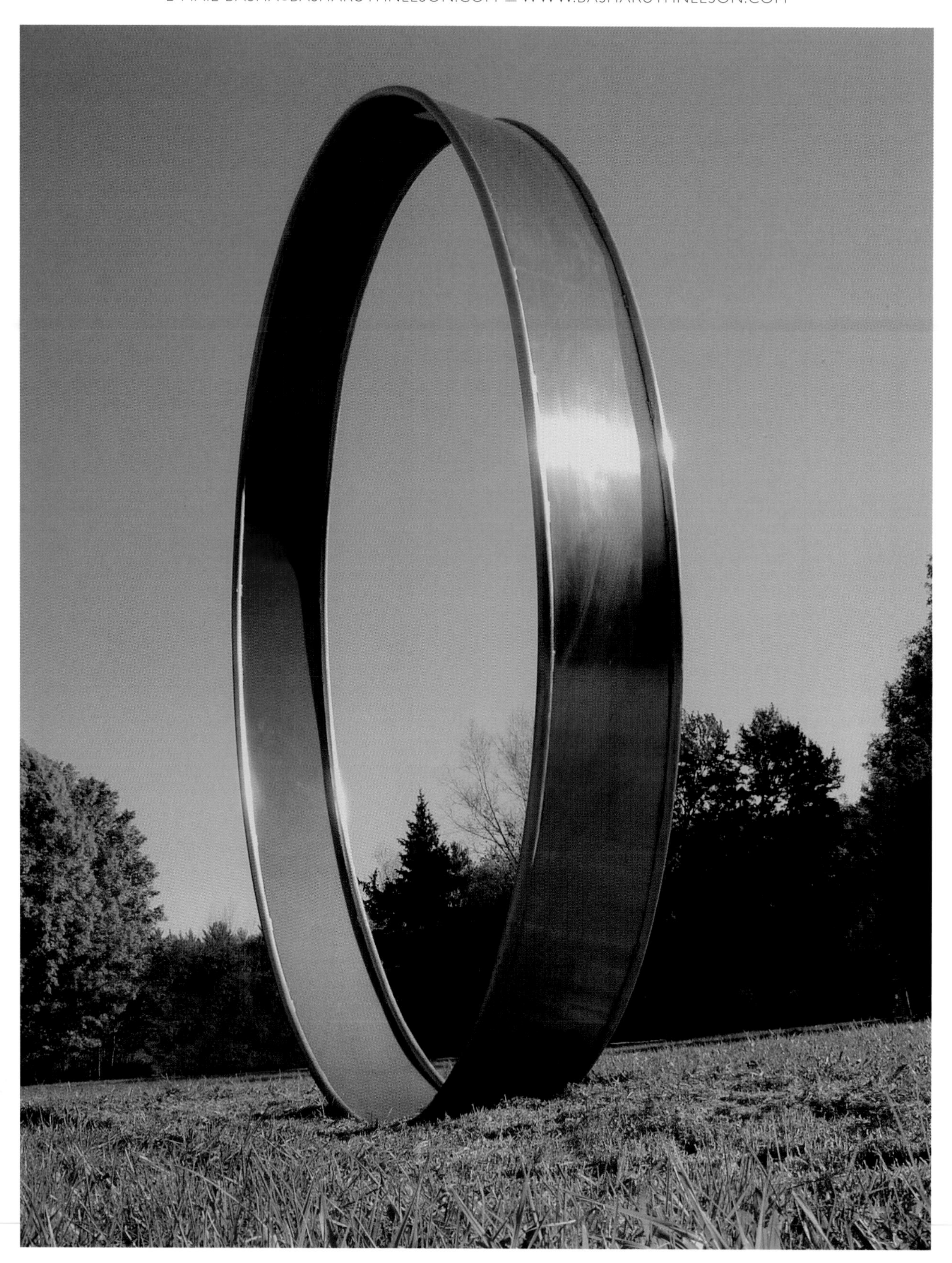

Beyond, 2006, St. Gregory's Church, Woodstock, NY, painted stainless steel, 10' x 7' x 1'. Photograph: Jason Zhang.

NORIKAZU

NORIKAZU THOMAS TSUCHIYA ■ ESSEX STUDIOS SUITE 155 ■ CINCINNATI, OH 45206
TEL 513-252-7839 ■ FAX 513-984-4270 ■ E-MAIL TOMTSUCHIYA@YAHOO.COM ■ WWW.ESSEXSTUDIOS.NET

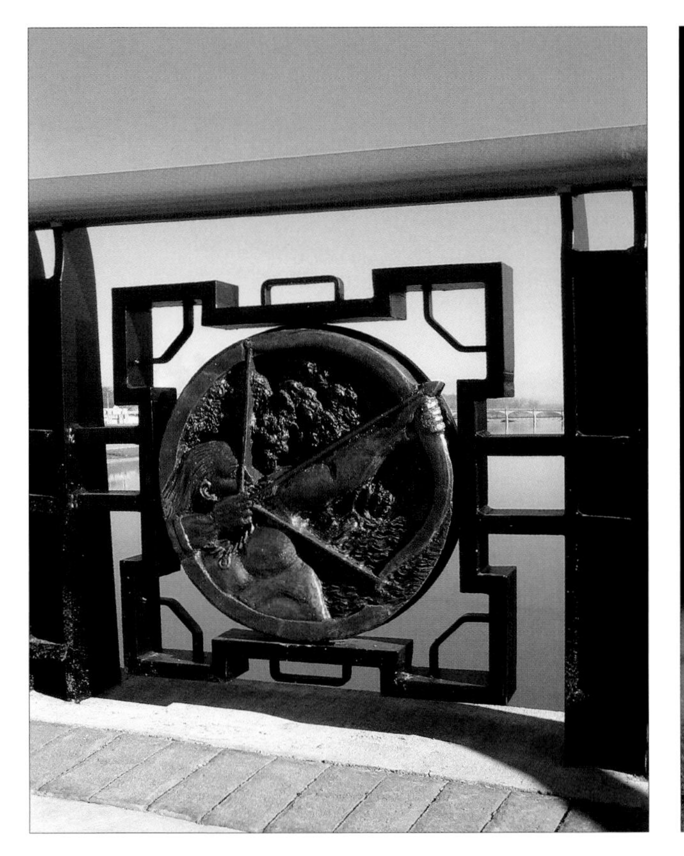

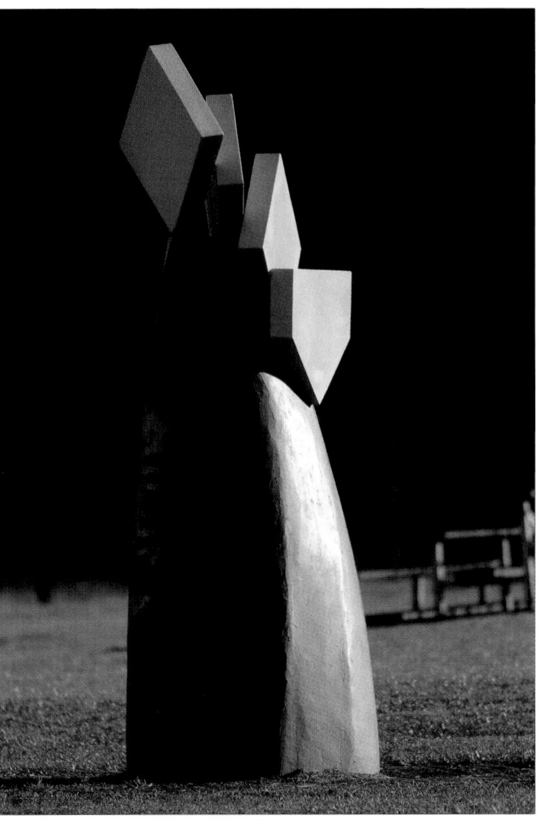

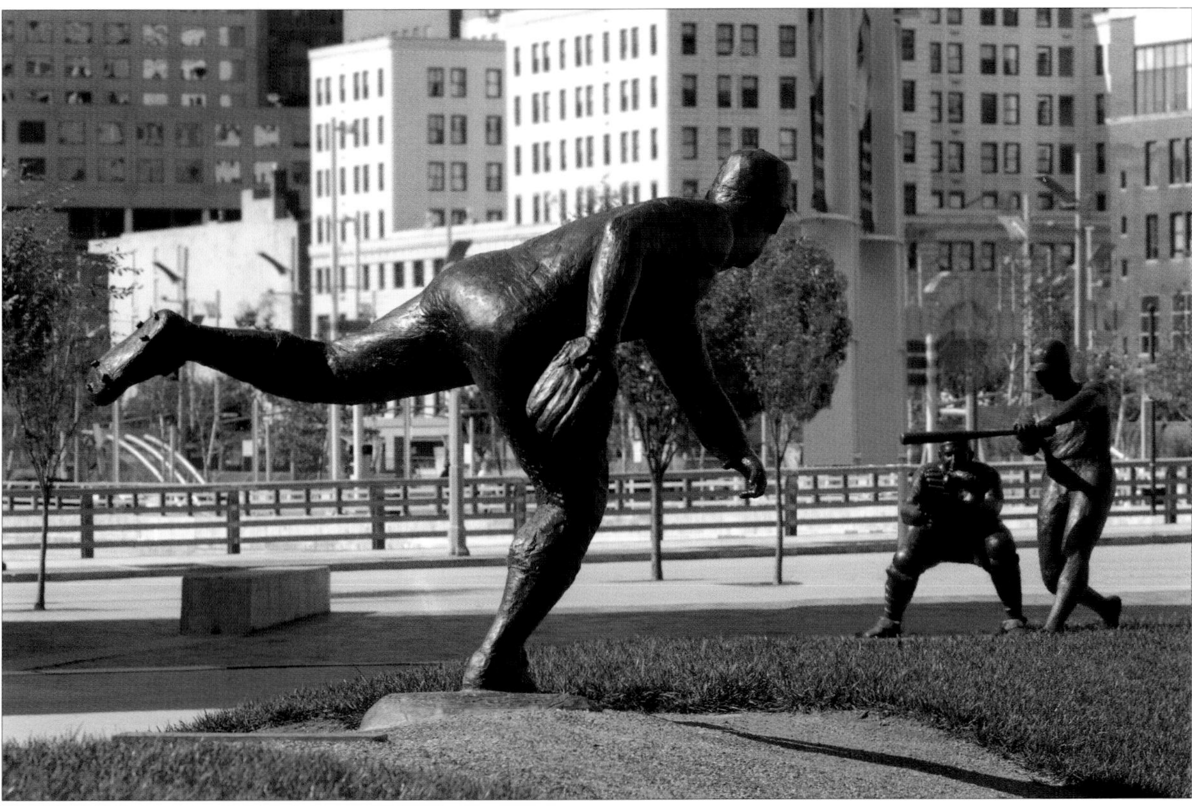

Top left: *Little Turtle,* 2006, High Street Bridge, Hamilton, OH, bronze, 2'Dia. Top right: *Cleveland Parker Memorial,* 2006, Cleveland Parker Fields, Cincinnati, OH, fiberglass, Lexan®, and LED lights, 10'H. Photograph: Gregory Rust. Bottom: *Reds Legends,* 2004, Great American Ball Park, Cincinnati, OH, bronze, life size. Photograph: Gregory Rust.

THE OLANA GROUP

ANN ADAMS ■ TWYLA ARTHUR ■ ALLISON HAYS LANE, DIRECTOR ■ 505 WEST EL PRADO DRIVE ■ SAN ANTONIO, TX 78212
TEL 210-805-9945 ■ E-MAIL ARTSOURCE@OLANAGROUP.COM ■ WWW.OLANAGROUP.COM

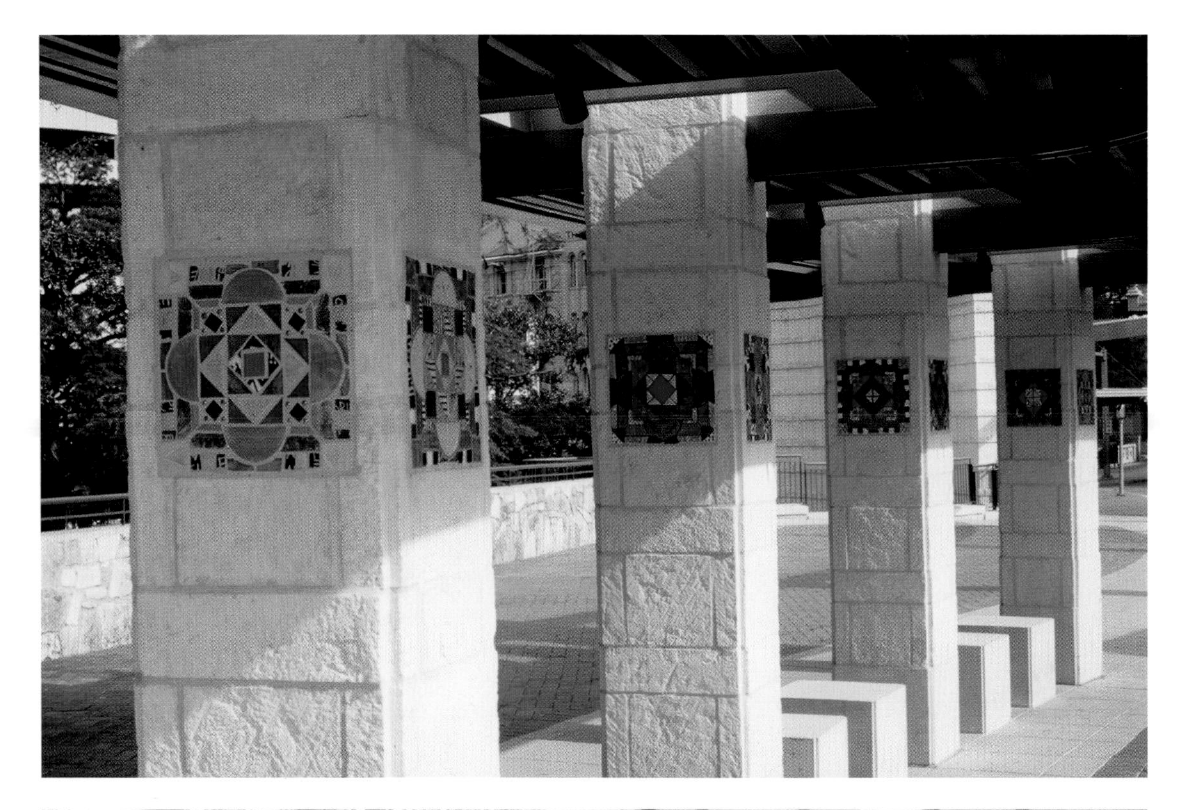

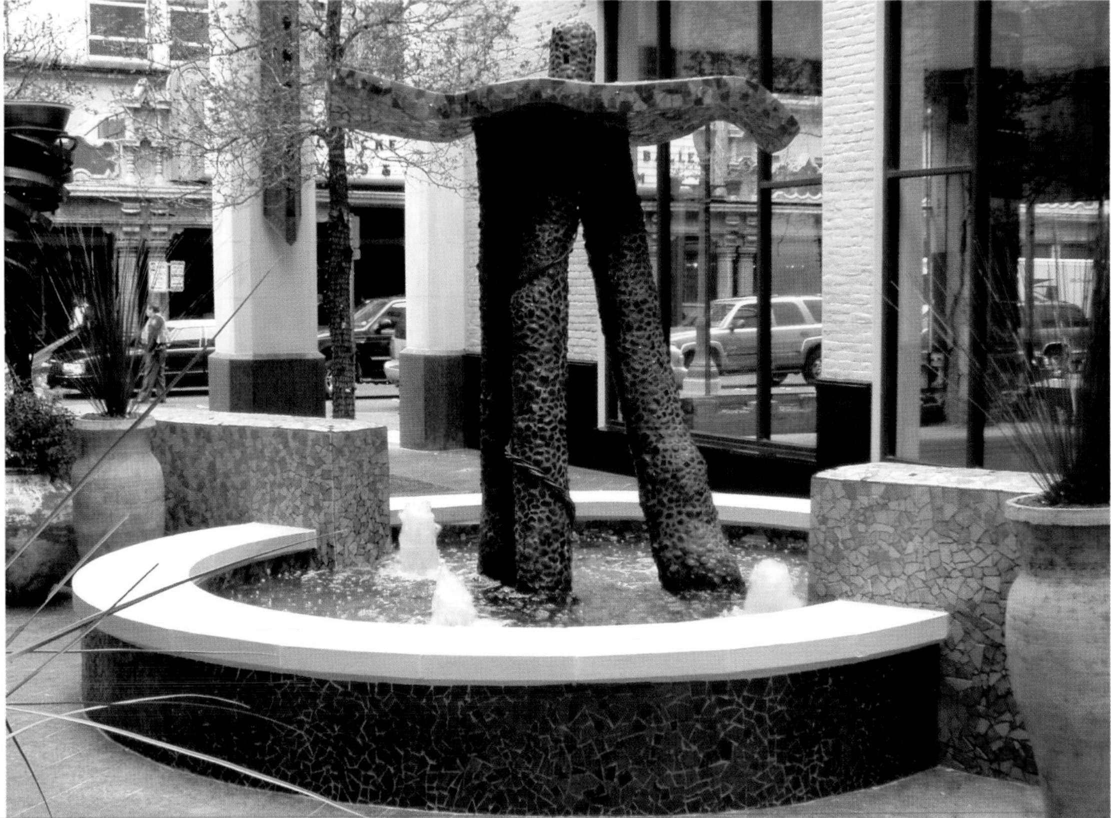

Top: *Column Treatment* by Ann Adams, 2000, Downtown Street Car Station, San Antonio, Texas, sixteen handmade ceramic tiles, each: 14" x 14".
Bottom: *Hope Springs* by Twyla Arthur, 2002, Houston Street Court Fountain, San Antonio, Texas, ceramic tile, river rocks, and glass, 9'H x 13'Dia.
Part of the Houston Street redevelopment project developed by Federal Realty Trust in partnership with the City of San Antonio.

ULRICH PAKKER

RP ART ■ 2442 NW MARKET STREET #157 ■ SEATTLE, WA 98107
TEL 206-789-7454 ■ TEL 206-380-4130 ■ E-MAIL PAMELA@RPART.COM ■ WWW.RPART.COM

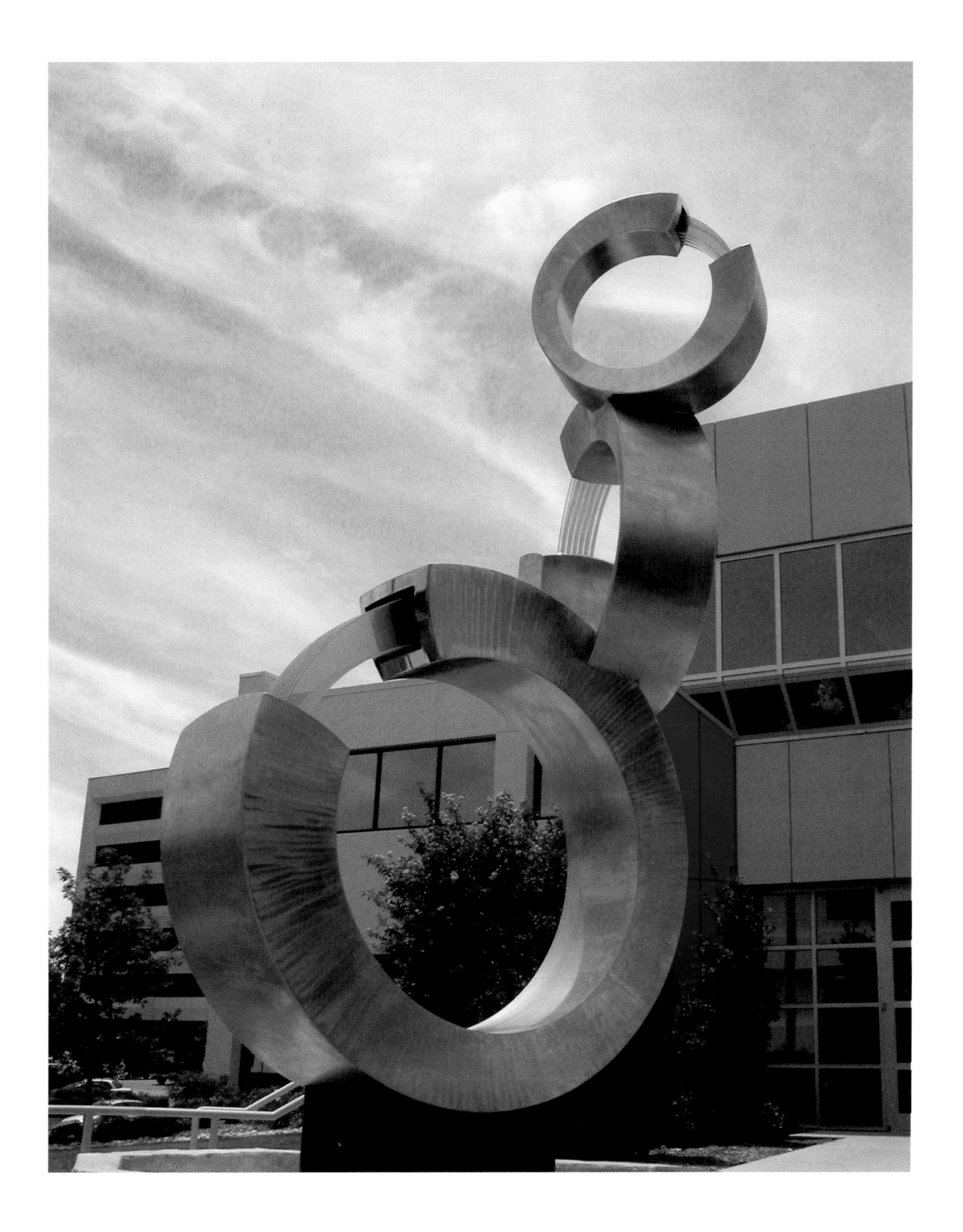

Glassflow, stainless steel and glass, 14'H x 8'W x 5.5'D.

A Commission Story

Derix Art Glass

ARTIST
Hung Liu

TITLE
Going Away, Coming Home, 2006

COMMISSIONED FOR
Port of Oakland,
Oakland International Airport, CA

TIMELINE: 4 years

DIMENSIONS: 10'H x 160'W

TRADE PROFESSIONAL
Cherie Newell,
Director, Professional Services,
Oakland Museum of California

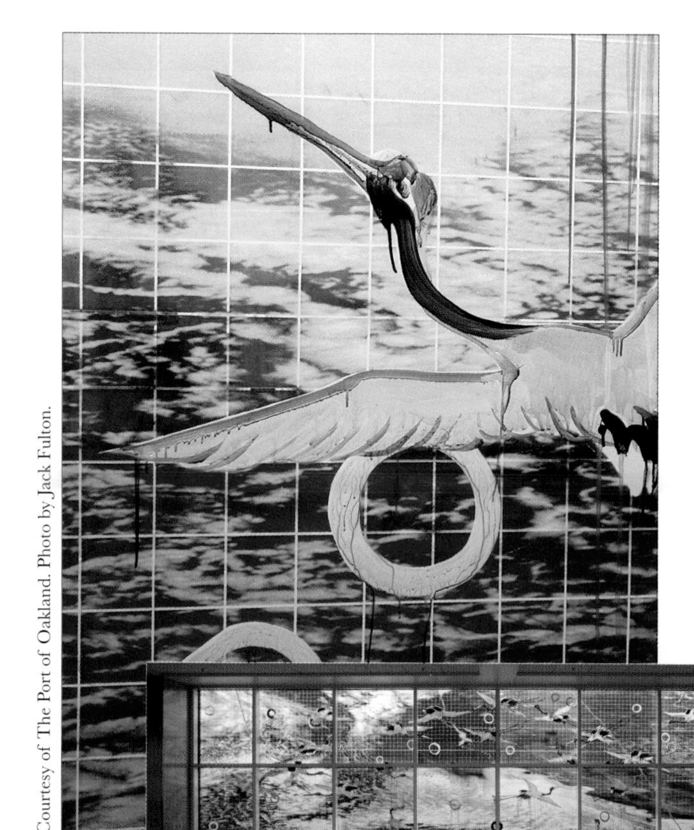

Courtesy of The Port of Oakland. Photo by Jack Fulton.

Germany's esteemed Derix Art Glass is sharing its 140-year tradition of precision glass craftsmanship with American audiences through innovative collaborations with ground-breaking contemporary artists. ■ When The Port of Oakland Public Art Initiative at Oakland International Airport launched a search for an artist to partner with Derix on a major glass installation along a 180-foot walkway, they adopted an unconventional strategy. "We wanted a painterly or photographic approach instead of a stained glass approach," Oakland Museum's Cherie Newell recalls. "Derix is all about pushing the limits of their capabilities. Working with artists who aren't glass artists by training is a great opportunity for them to expand their offerings." ■ When Chinese-born artist Hung Liu, a professor at Mills College, won the commission, she had no previous experience with glass. Barbara Derix recalls, "Hung Liu came to our studio in Germany and learned how to paint on glass using vitreous enamels, special glass colors that need to be baked into the glass surface to make them permanent." The complicated grid structure of the 160-foot *Going Away, Coming Home,* is composed of sixty-four individual insulated glass units, each five feet square. The glass panels were subjected to a complex sequence of airbrushing, firing, tempering, and sandblasting to bring the art to life. ■ Sky and land images, based on actual satellite data, correspond to a range of altitudes and distances across four sections of the mural, depicting the Bay Area, Pacific Ocean, and Asia. As each traveler walks down the corridor, he or she experiences a powerful series of conceptual images echoing the act of departure or arrival. Time-honored Chinese symbols saturate the artwork with deeper meaning. Eighty hand-painted red-crowned cranes, emblems of peace and prosperity, soar across the brilliant blue sky, while hovering circles represent the eternal universe, and the color red imparts a message of good luck. ■ The astonishingly vivid wall of glass becomes a benevolent salutation. As Barbara Derix explains, "It was Hung Liu's intention to bring blessings to the travelers."

SHELLEY PARRIOTT

3437 ROUTE 212 ■ BEARSVILLE, NY 12409 ■ TEL 845-679-6390
E-MAIL THEARTSTUDIOWDST@AOL.COM ■ WWW.SHELLEYPARRIOTT.COM

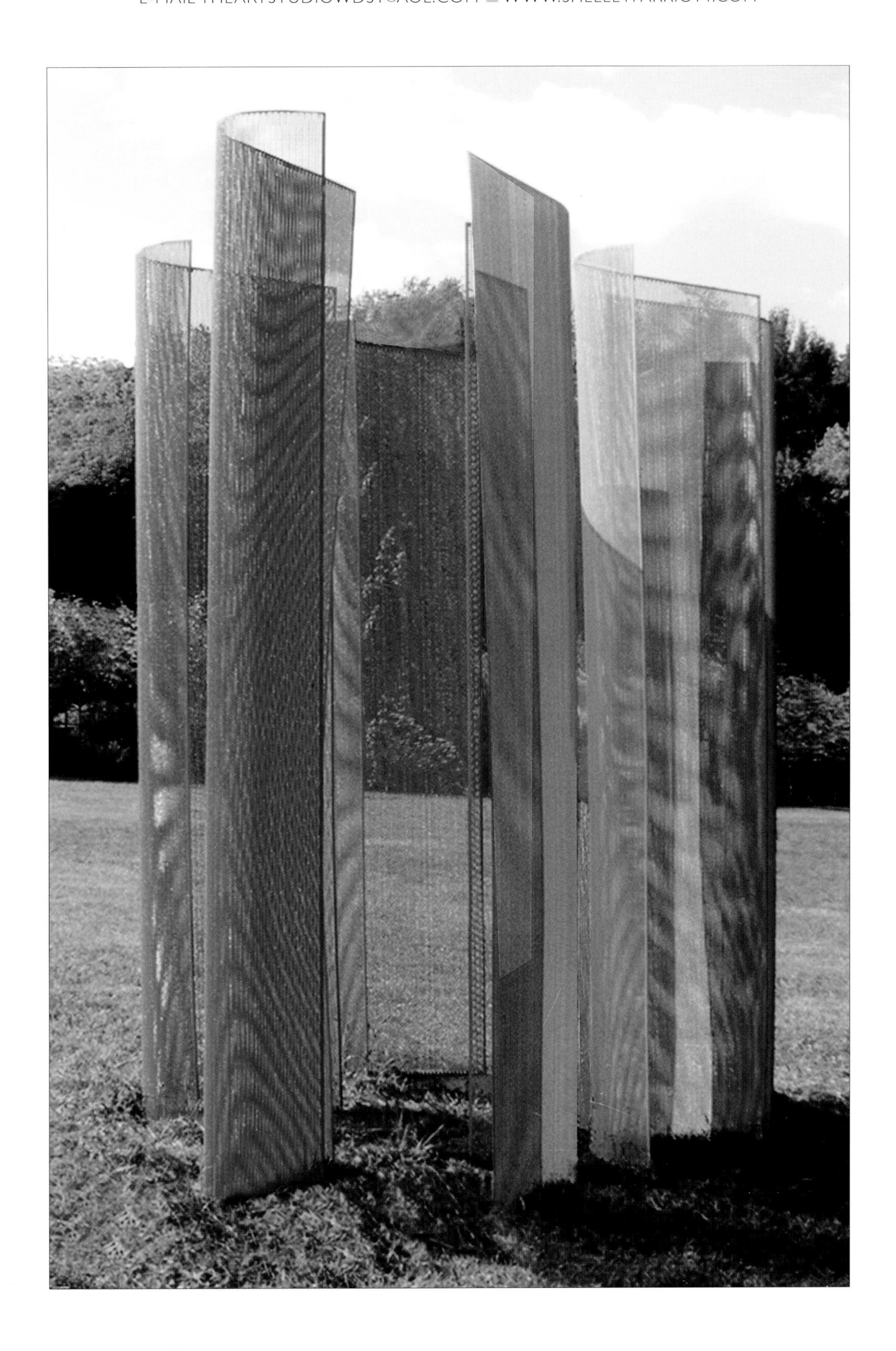

Color Field Sculpture, St. Gregory's Church, Woodstock, NY, individual overlapping layers of powder-coated perforated steel, 10'H x 10'W x 5'D. Photograph: Jason Zhang.

PUBLIC ART COMMISSIONS

CHARLES L. MADDEN, ARTIST SCULPTOR ■ 21 CONWELL DRIVE ■ MAPLE GLEN, PA 19002-3310
TEL 215-646-1599 ■ E-MAIL CHARLESLMADDEN@AOL.COM

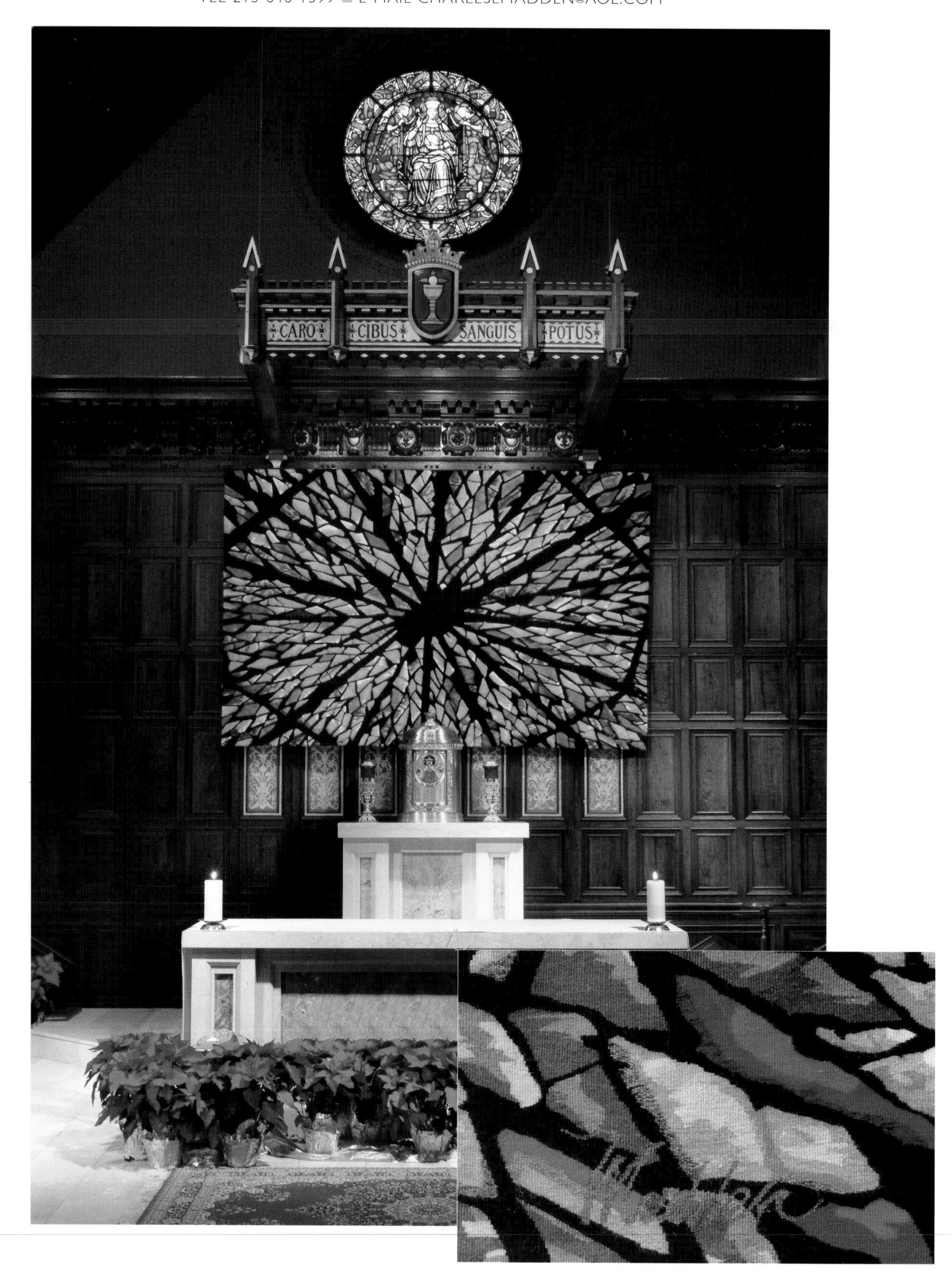

Aubusson-style tapestry, St. John Vianney Church, Gladwyne, PA, 9' × 12'.

BARTON RUBENSTEIN

RUBENSTEIN STUDIOS ■ 4819 DORSET AVENUE ■ CHEVY CHASE, MD 20815 ■ TEL 301-654-5406
FAX 301-654-5496 ■ E-MAIL BARTSHER@AOL.COM ■ WWW.RUBENSTEINSTUDIOS.COM

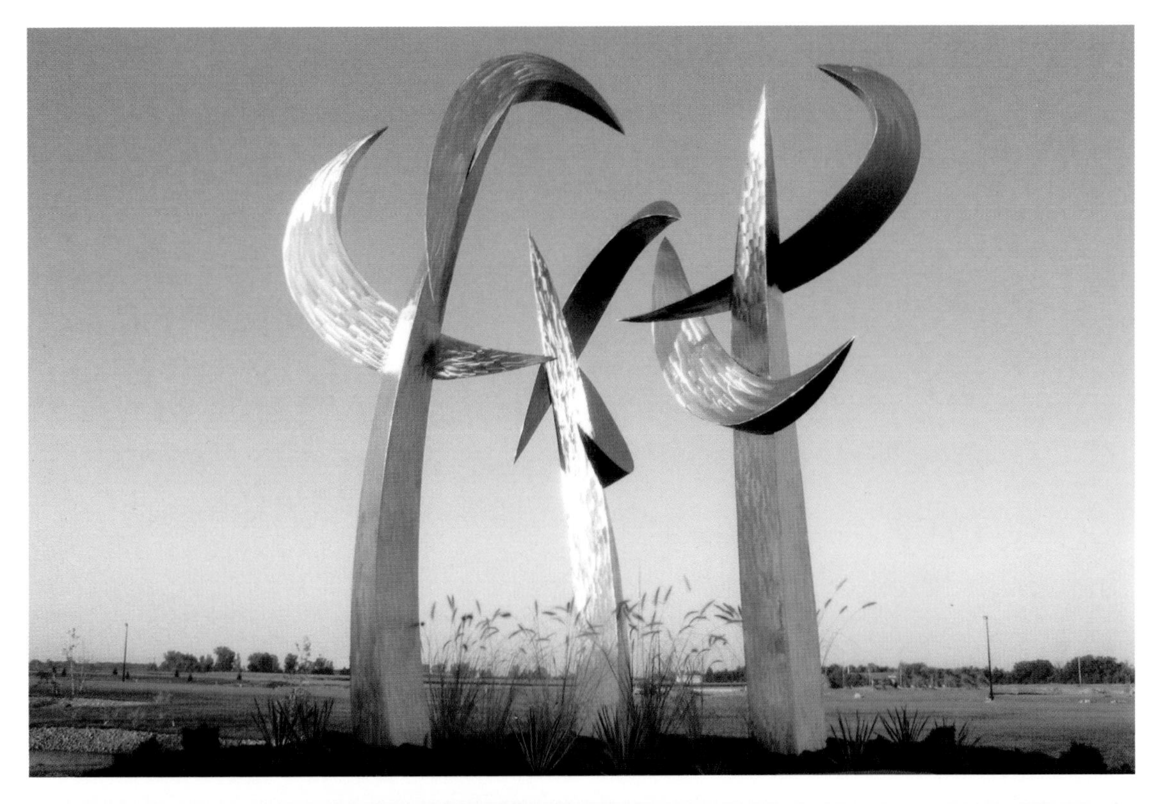

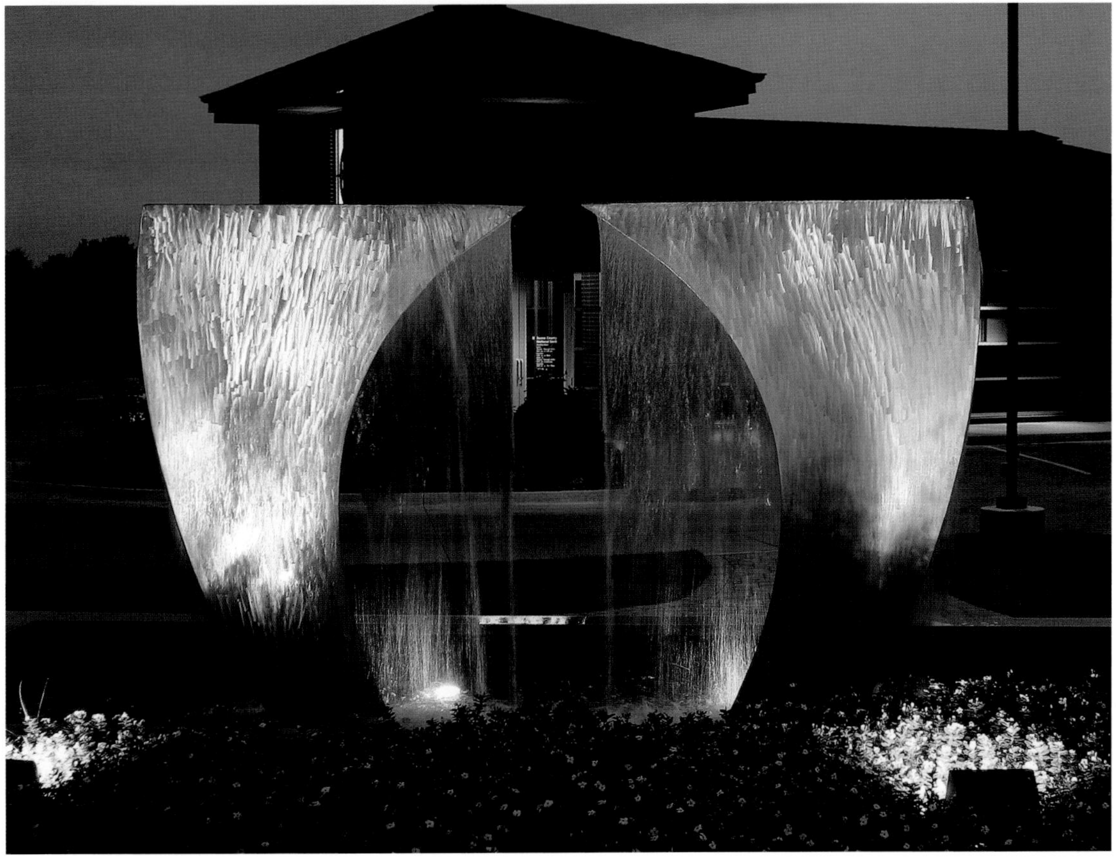

Top: *Sunburst,* 2005, Owens Community College, Findlay, OH, stainless steel, 18'H x 16'Dia. National competition-awarded commission.
Bottom: *Arch,* 2005, Boone County National Bank, Columbia, MO, stainless steel with water, 7'H x 13'W x 3'D. National competition-awarded commission.

SCOTT SNIBBE

SNIBBE INTERACTIVE ■ 1777 YOSEMITE AVENUE SUITE 315 ■ SAN FRANCISCO, CA 94124
TEL 415-822-1442 ■ E-MAIL SCOTT@SNIBBE.COM ■ WWW.SNIBBE.COM ■ WWW.SNIBBEINTERACTIVE.COM

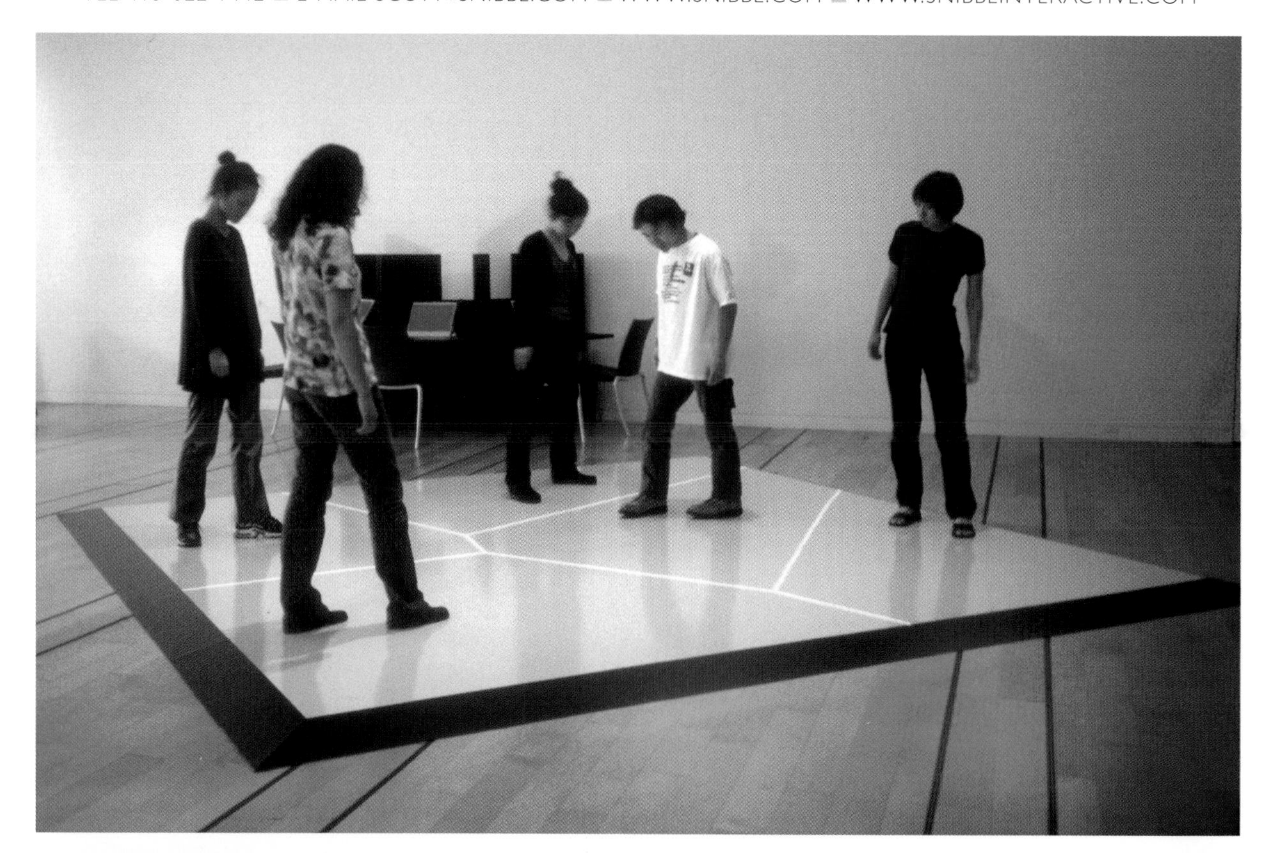

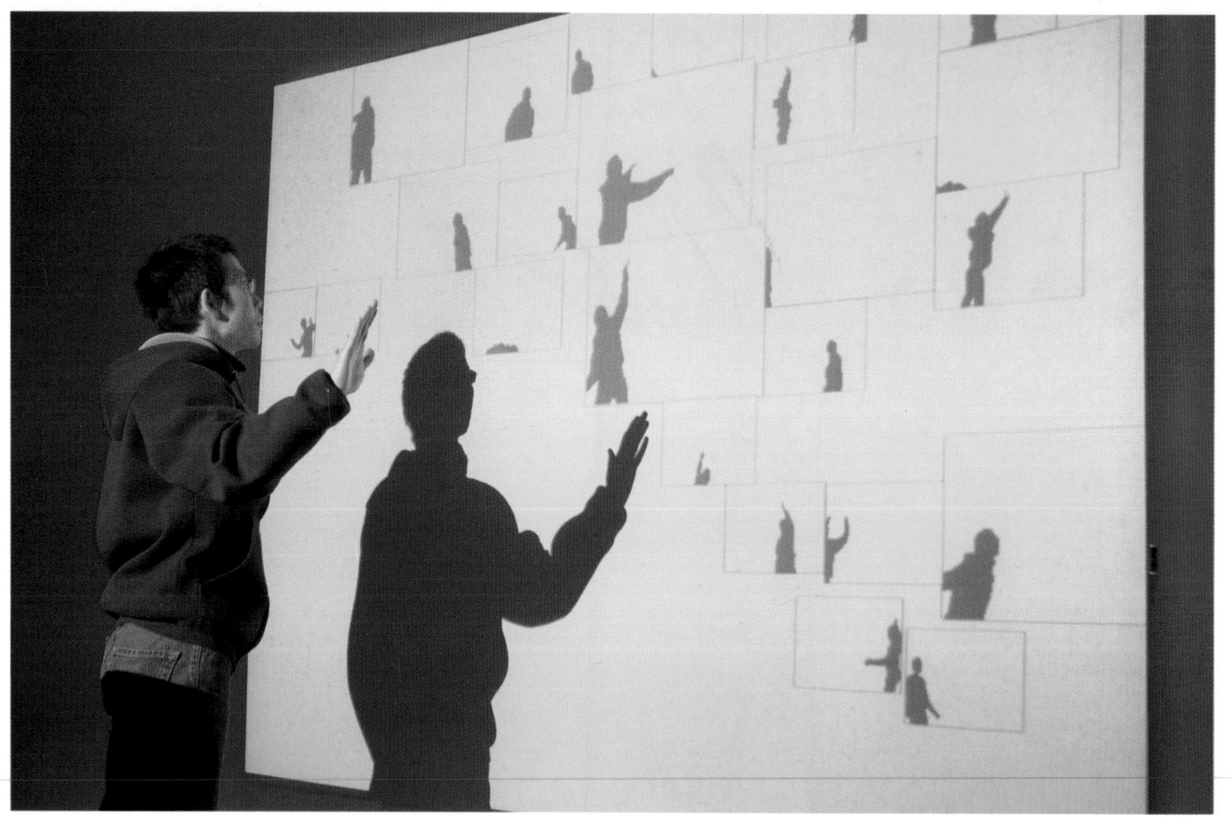

Top: *Boundary Functions*, Tokyo Intercommunications Center. Photograph: Tokyo ICC.
Bottom: *Cause and Effect*, San Francisco Exploratorium.

SCOTT WALLACE

SCOTT WALLACE STUDIO ■ PO BOX 8 ■ HENDRICKS, MN 56136 ■ TEL 507-275-3300
E-MAIL SWALLACE@ITCTEL.COM ■ WWW.SCOTTWALLACESTUDIO.COM

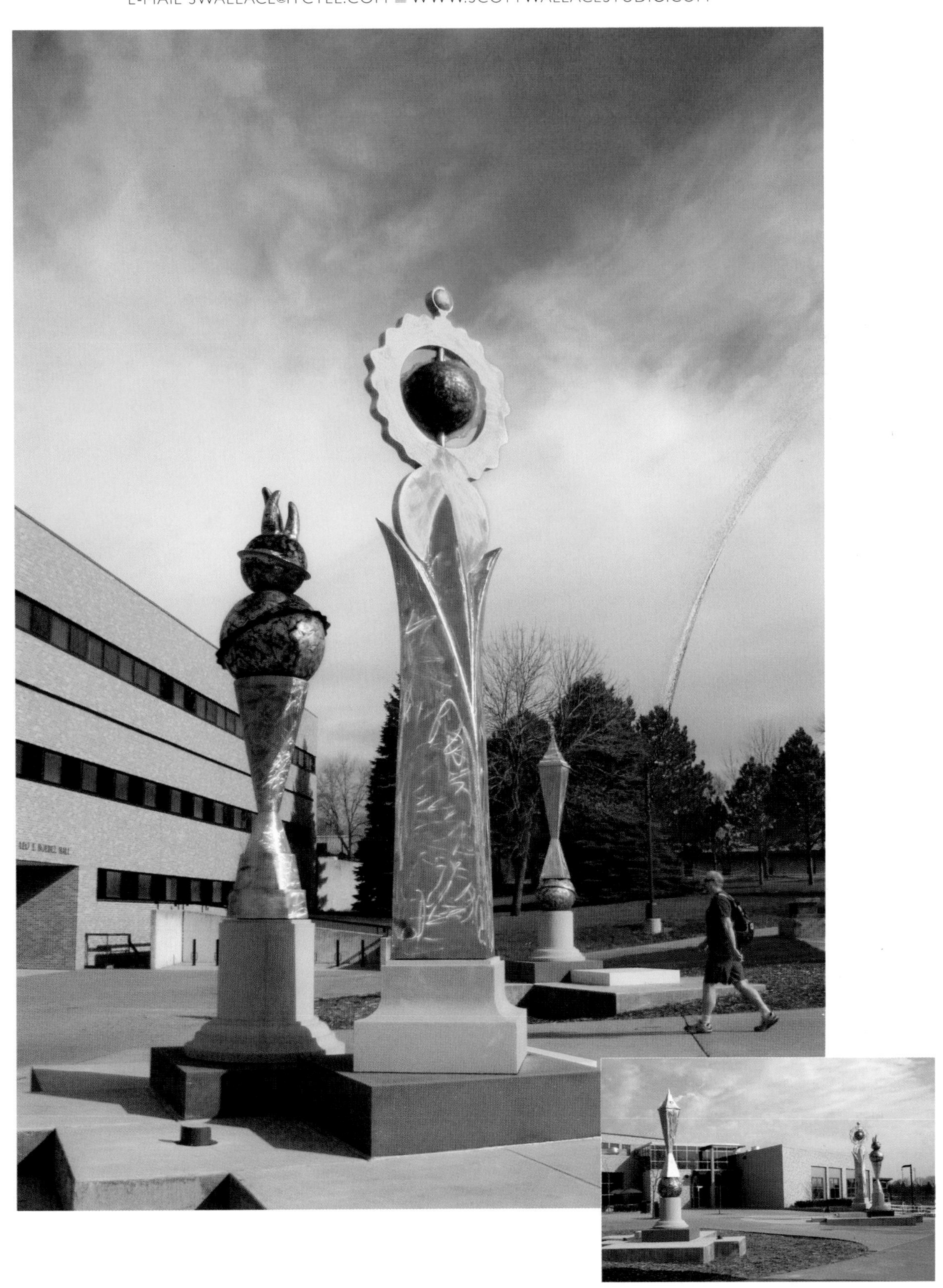

Strategem, 2006, Pioneer Student Center, University of Wisconsin–Platteville, bronze and pre-cast concrete.

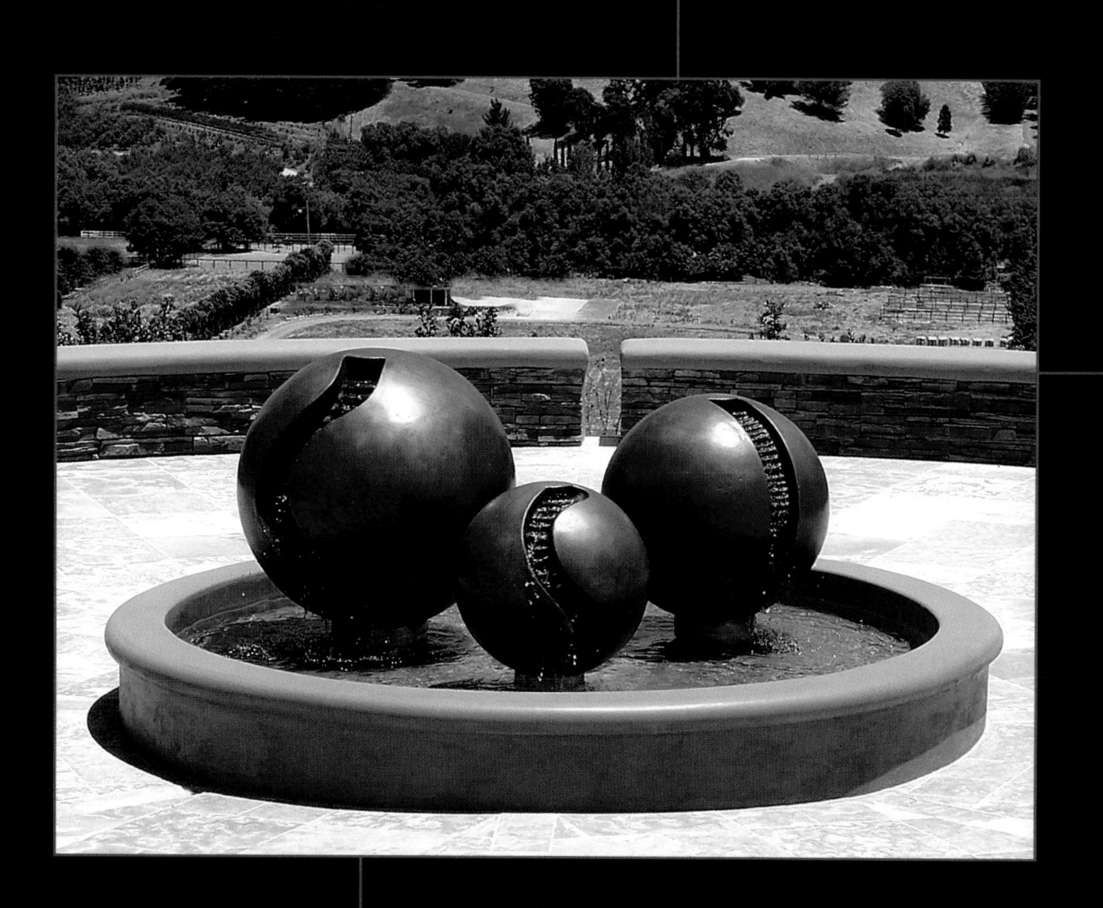

Non-Representational Sculpture

MICHAEL BAUERMEISTER

6560 AUGUSTA BOTTOM ROAD ■ AUGUSTA, MO 63332 ■ TEL/FAX 636-228-4663
E-MAIL MICHAEL@BAUERMEISTER.COM ■ WWW.MICHAELBAUERMEISTER.COM

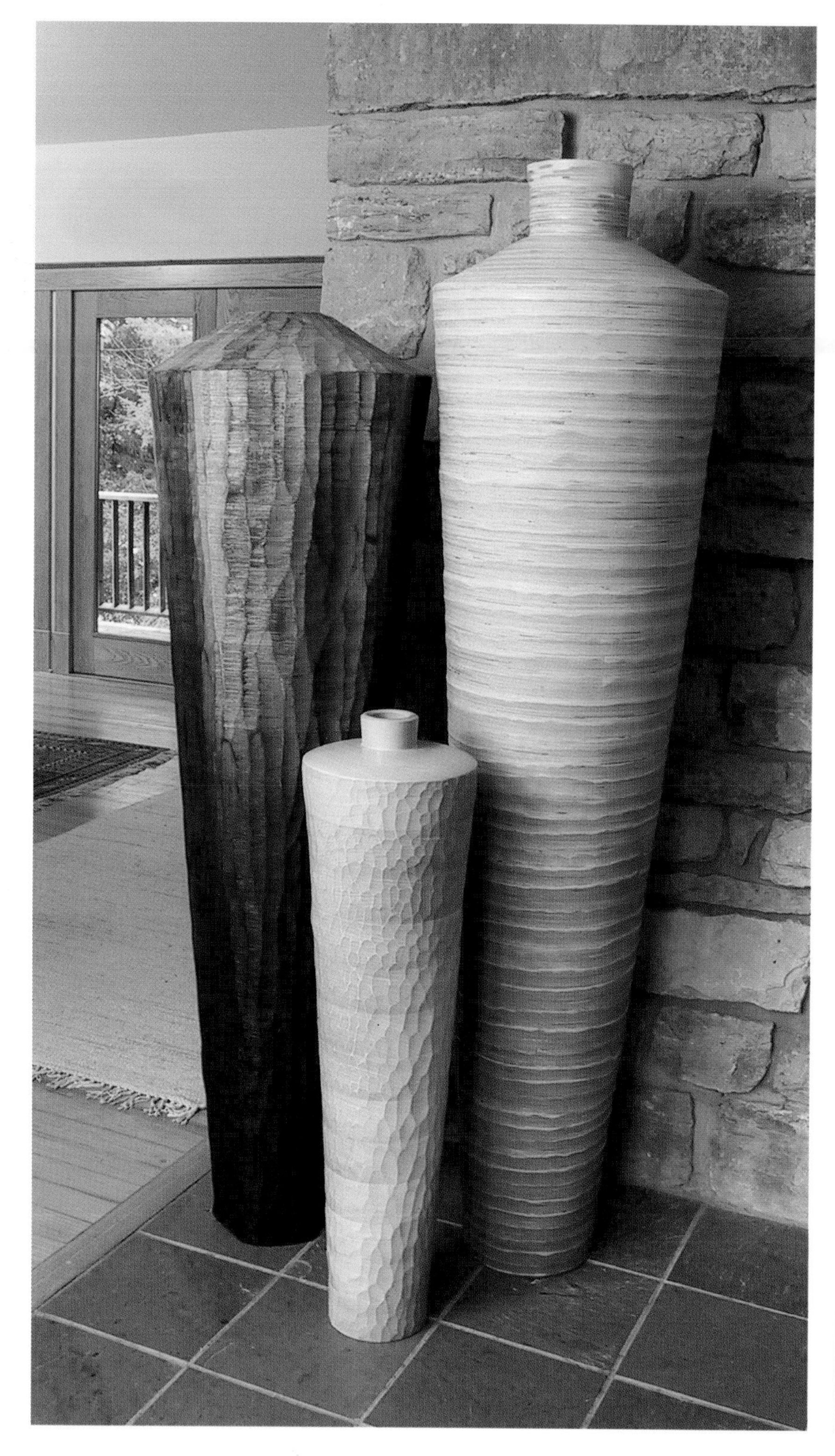

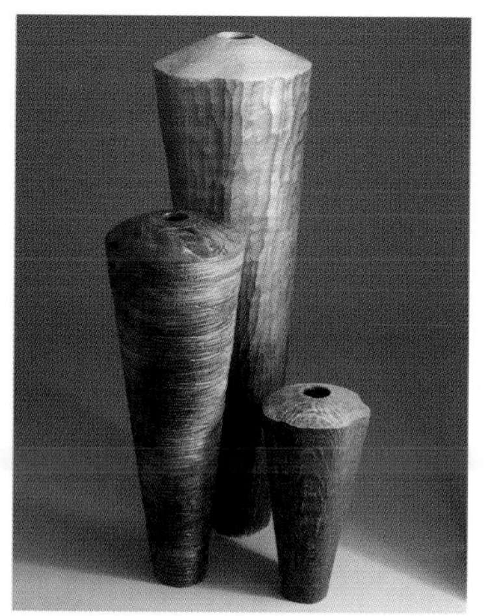

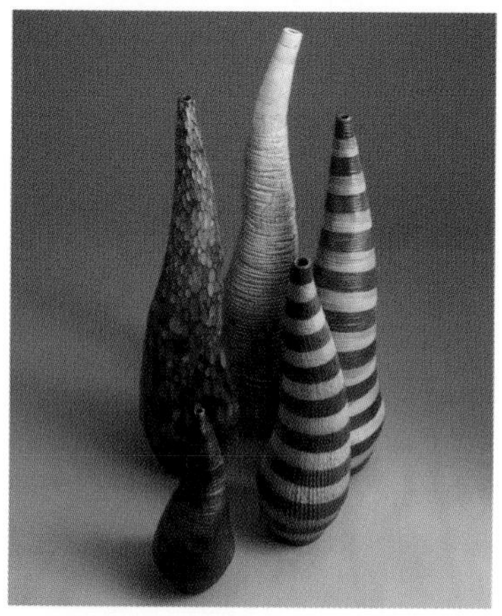

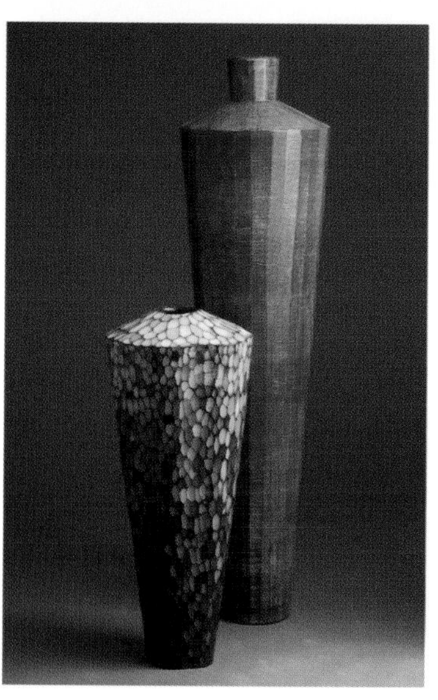

Left: *Tall Vessels* (from left to right), stained birch, 65" x 19"; linden, 40" x 11"; birch, 73" x 20". Top right: *Tall Vessels* (from left to right), walnut, 38" x 12"; oak, 50" x 14"; painted oak, 26" x 11". Center right: *Sprout Vessels*, various woods, 17"-40" tall. Bottom right: *Two Painted Vessels*, linden with paint, 34" x 14"; right, birch with paint, 56" x 15".

RIIS BURWELL

RIIS BURWELL STUDIO ■ 3815 CALISTOGA ROAD ■ SANTA ROSA, CA 95404
TEL/FAX 707-538-2676 ■ E-MAIL RIIS@RIISBURWELL.COM ■ WWW.RIISBURWELL.COM

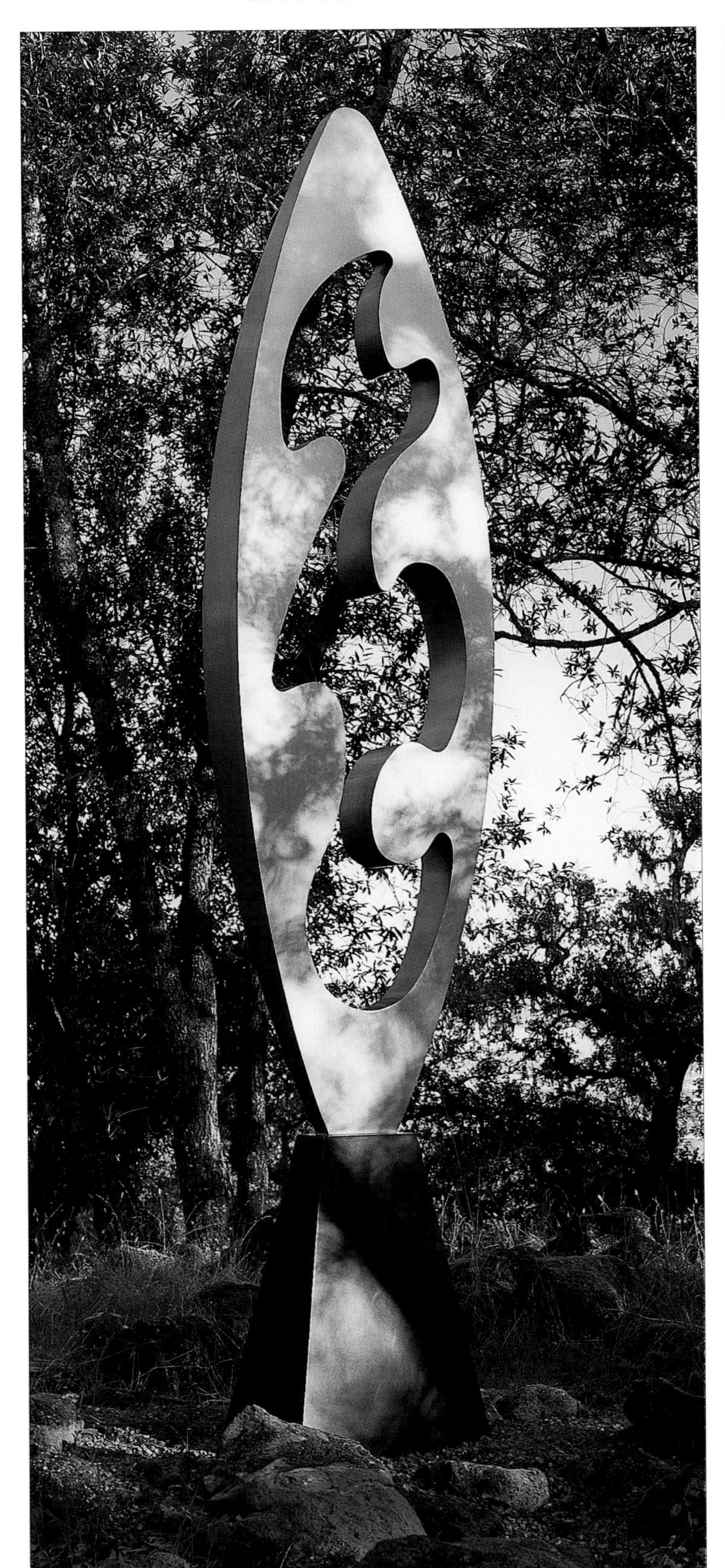

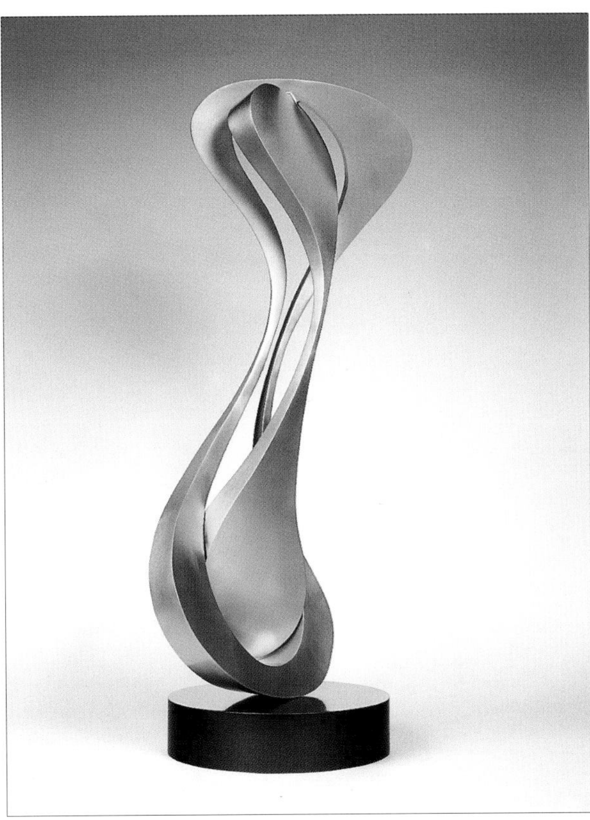

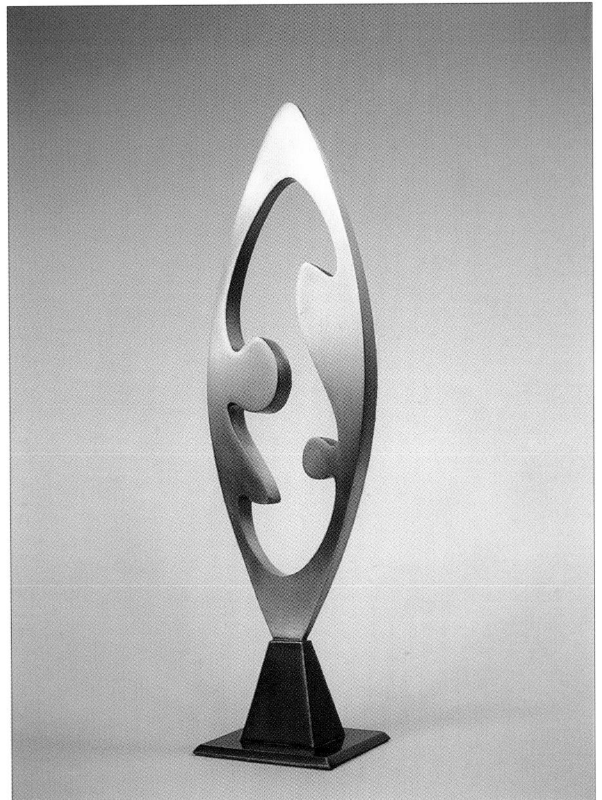

Left: *Cloud Totem 1,* 2006, Paradise Ridge Winery, Santa Rosa, CA, bronze, 10' × 3' × 2'.
Top right: *Spirit Form Var. 3,* 2006, bronze, 38" × 16" × 12". Bottom right: *Cloud Totem 2,* 2006, bronze, 20" × 5" × 4".

LUKE DAVID

LUKE DAVID SCULPTURE ■ 1230 QUAIL RIDGE ■ SOLVANG, CA 93463 ■ TEL 805-252-8864
FAX 253-399-7647 ■ E-MAIL LUKEDAVID@EARTHLINK.NET ■ WWW.LUKEDAVIDSCULPTURE.COM

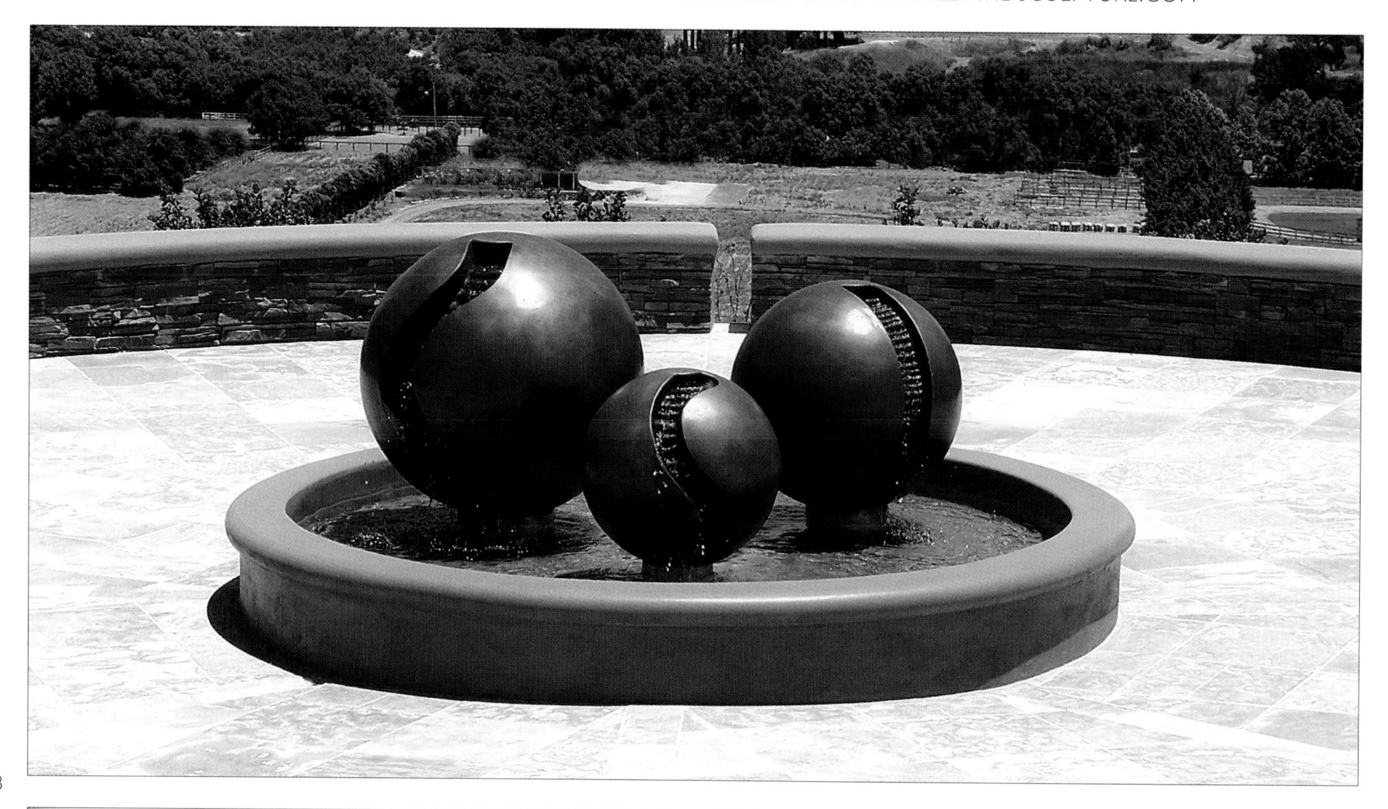

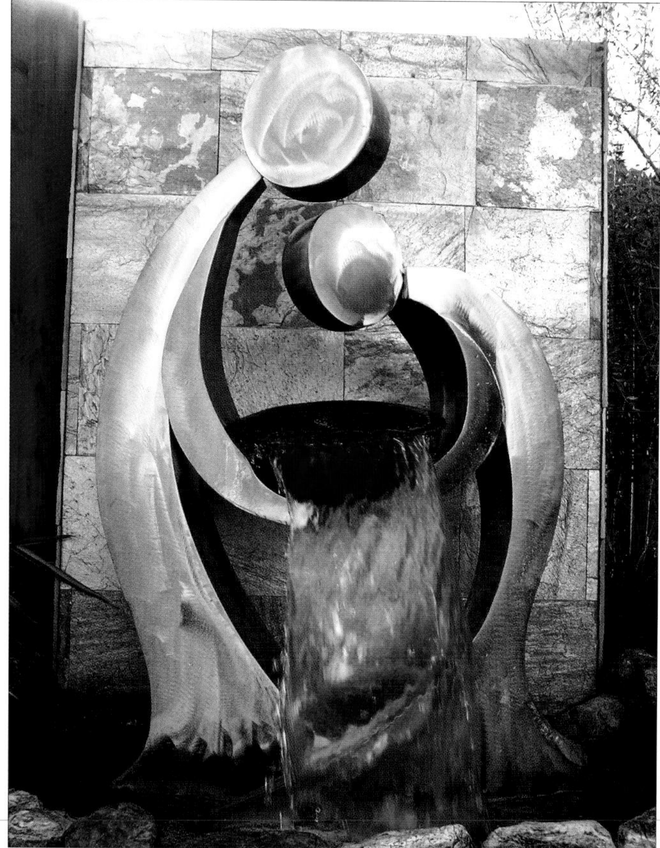

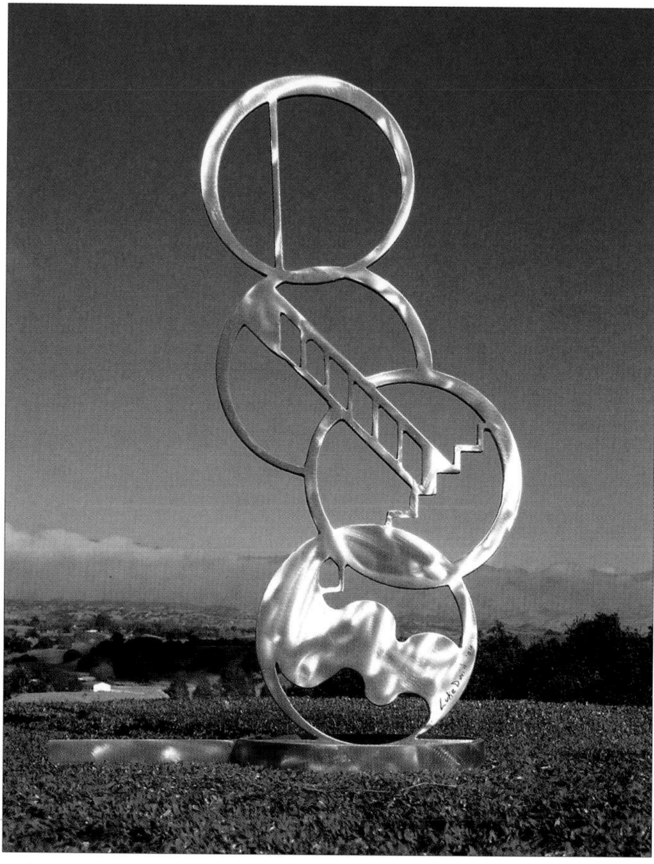

Top: *Weathered Spheres,* 2006, Santa Ynez, CA, bronze, left: 36"Dia., center: 24"Dia., right: 30"Dia.
Bottom left: *One Water,* 2006, Buellton, CA, bronze, 5'H x 4'W x 2'D. Bottom right: *Ascension,* 2006, bronze, 24"H x 18"W x 8"D.

PHILIP S. DRILL

80 MAIN STREET ■ WEST ORANGE, NJ 07052 ■ TEL 973-736-2979
FAX 973-736-3776 ■ E-MAIL PSDRILL@AOL.COM ■ WWW.PSDRILL.COM

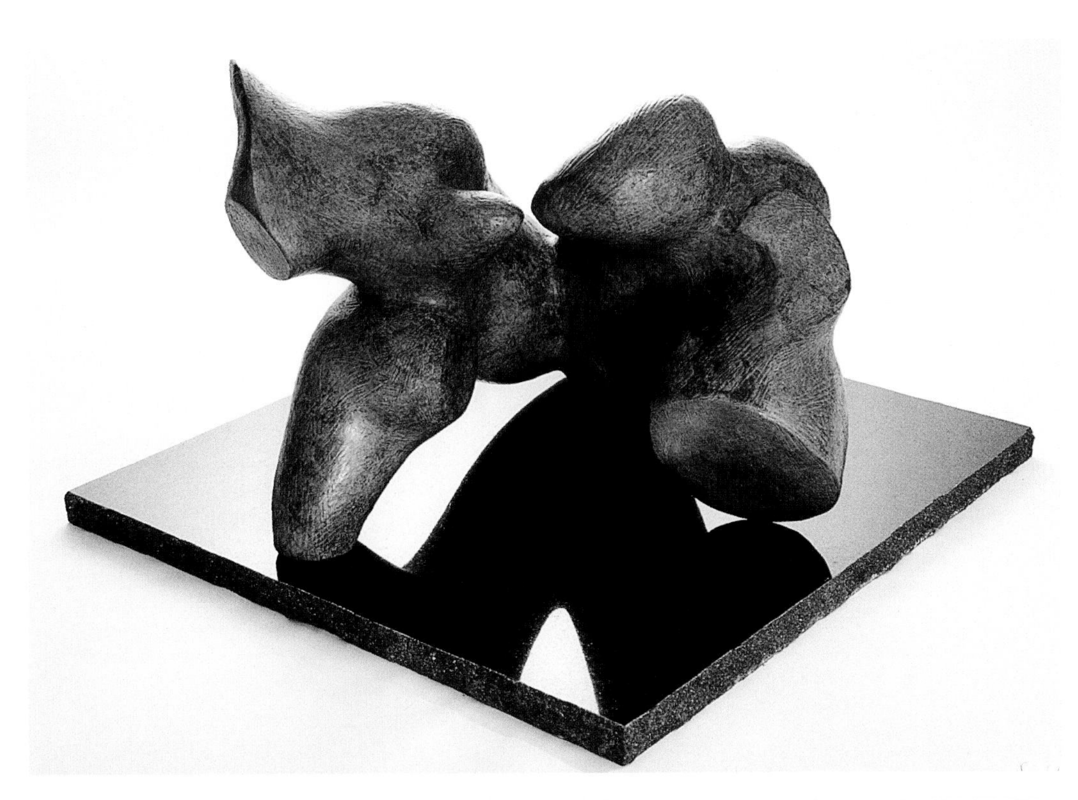

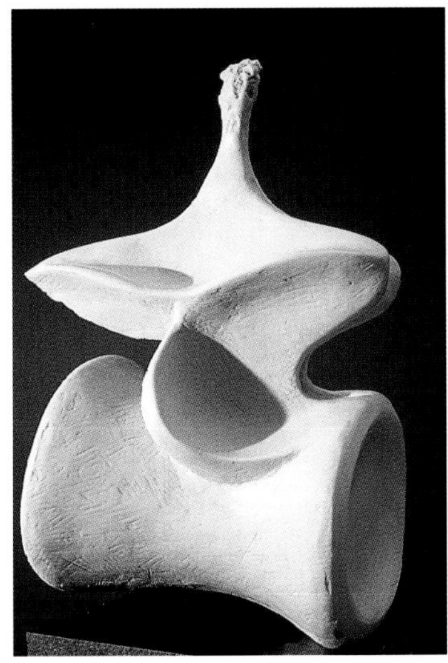

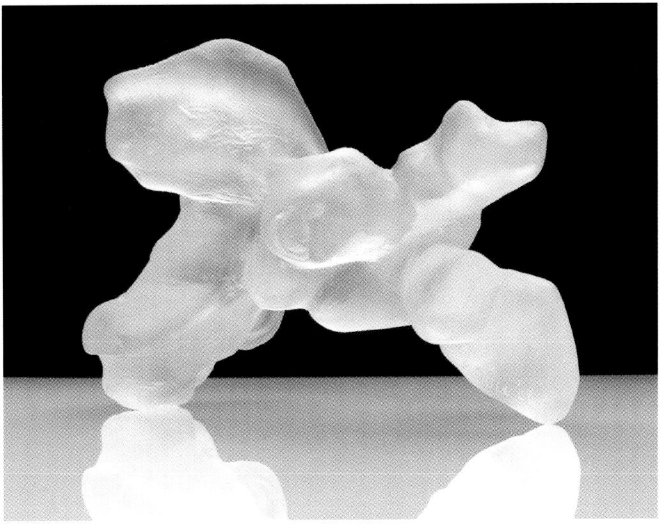

Top: *Aruba I*, bronze, 15" x 20" x 20".
Bottom left: *Dino II*, monzini, 35" x 20" x 12". Bottom right: *Halic*, cast glass, 10" x 7" x 14".

SALLY HEPLER

SALLY HEPLER STUDIO ■ PO BOX 2607 ■ SANTA FE, NM 87504 ■ TEL 505-988-3665 ■ TEL 505-577-7980
FAX 505-992-3902 ■ E-MAIL SALLY@SALLYHEPLER.COM ■ E-MAIL HEPLER3@GMAIL.COM ■ WWW.SALLYHEPLER.COM

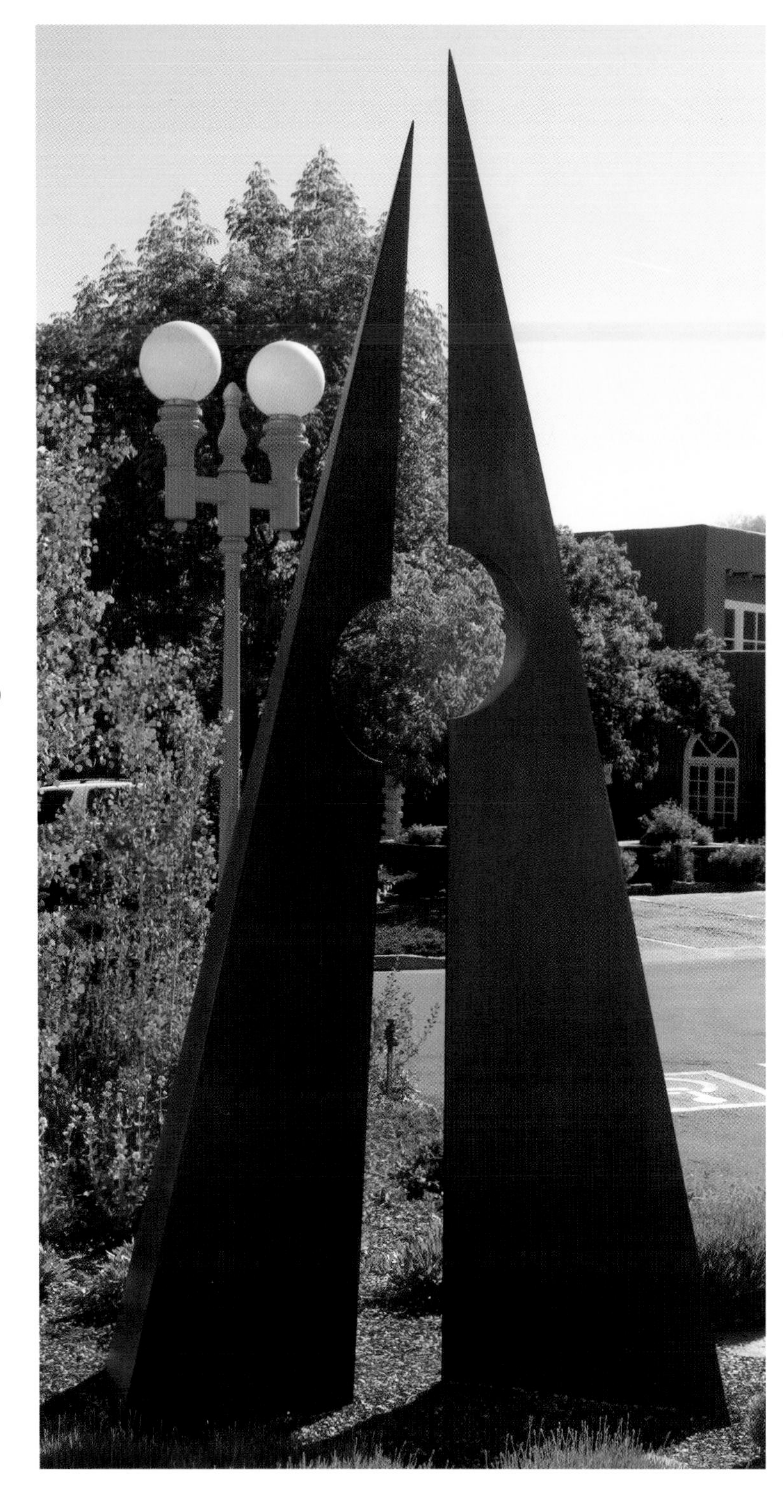

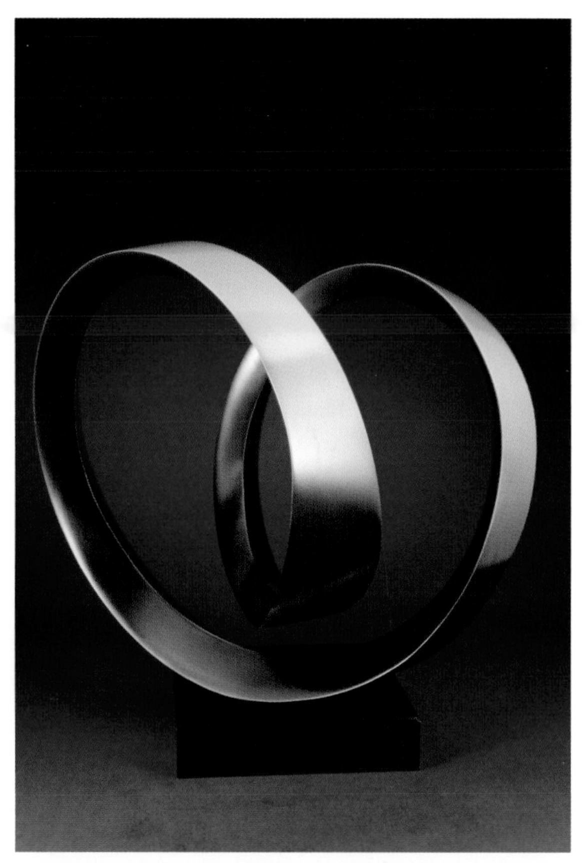

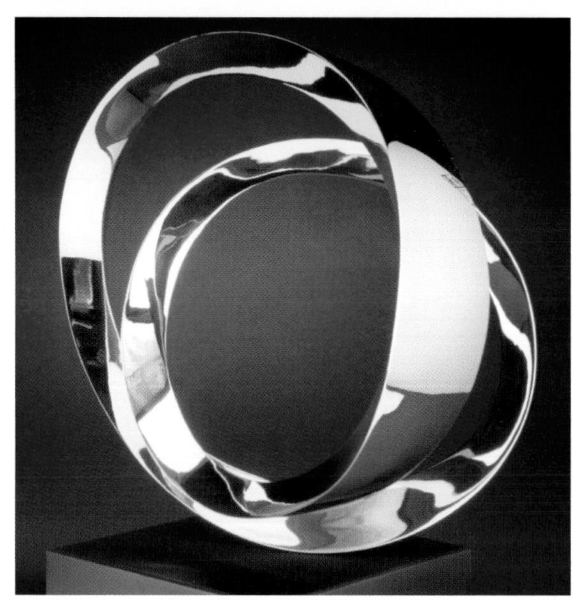

Left: *Lunar Watch,* 2006 installation, University of Oklahoma, Norman, hand-fabricated mild steel, 15' × 14'. Top right: *Imagine,* 2006, private collection, Santa Fe, NM, hand-fabricated bronze, 18" × 18" × 16". Bottom right: *Déjà Vu,* 2001, private collection, Princeton, NJ, hand-fabricated stainless steel, 14" × 13" × 10".

STEVE JENSEN

1424 TENTH ■ SEATTLE, WA 98122 ■ TEL 206-323-8020 ■ FAX 206-322-1400
E-MAIL SJWWALLPAPER@AOL.COM ■ WWW.STEVEJENSENSTUDIOS.COM

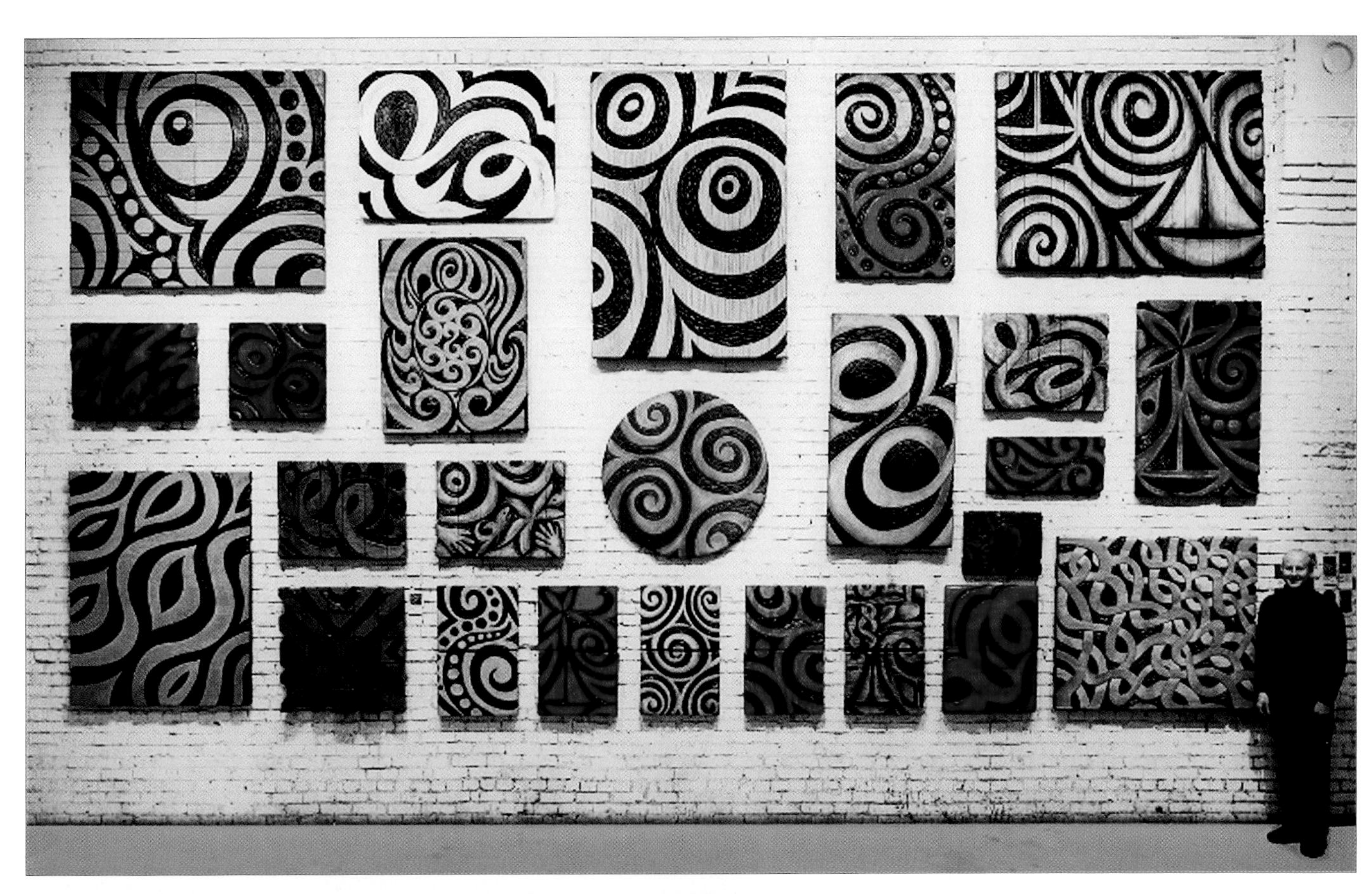

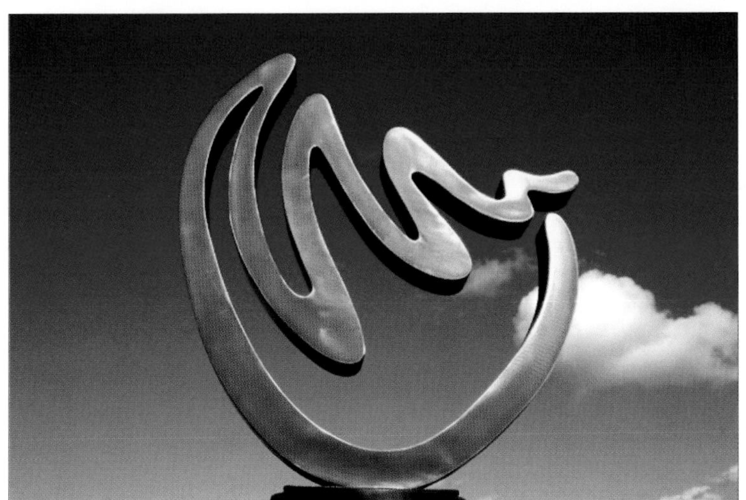

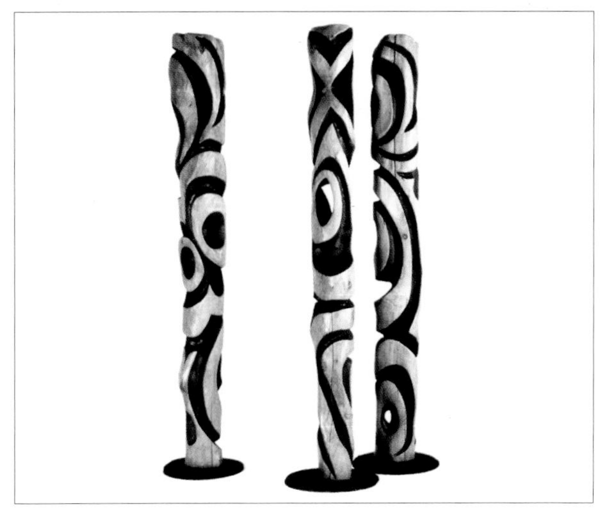

Top: *Wall Carvings*, carved recycled wood. Bottom left: *The Wave*, bronze, 36" x 36".
Bottom right: *Relics*, carved cedar (natural fallen), 96"H. Photographs: Linda Young.

PATTIE AND MARK JOHNSON

GLASS ILLUSIONS STUDIO ■ 12511 EAST SPEEDWAY ■ TUCSON, AZ 85748 ■ TEL 520-722-7847 ■ TEL 520-296-5752
E-MAIL GLASSART4U@AOL.COM ■ WWW.PATTIANDMARKJOHNSON.COM ■ WWW.GLASSILLUSIONSSTUDIO.COM

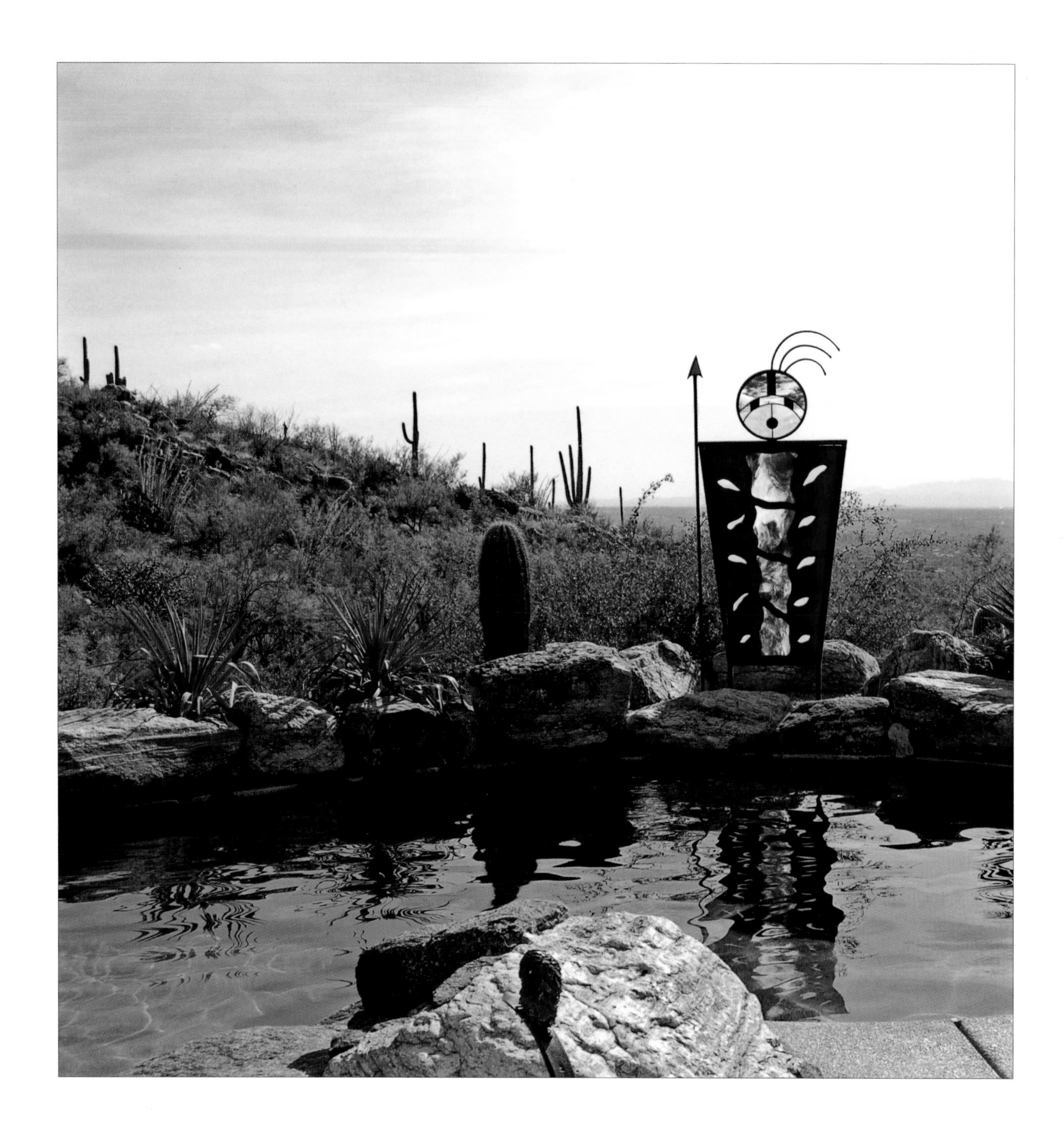

Guardian, 7.6' x 3'.

LINDA LEVITON

LINDA LEVITON SCULPTURE ▪ 1011 COLONY WAY ▪ COLUMBUS, OH 43235
TEL 614-433-7486 ▪ E-MAIL GUILD@LINDALEVITON.COM ▪ WWW.LINDALEVITON.COM

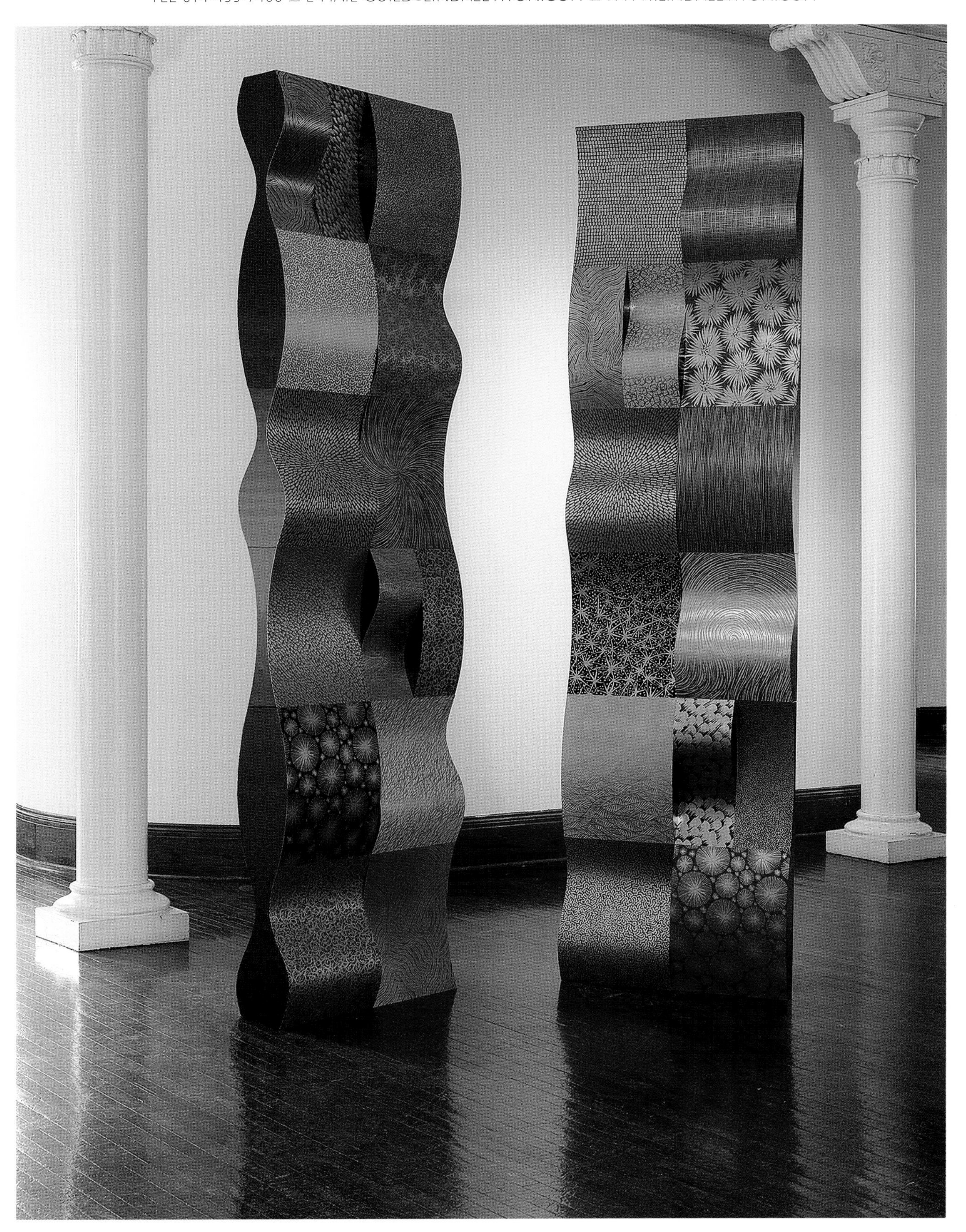

Patterns of Nature–Totem, copper, wood, paint, and patina, 10.5'H x 15"D x 34"W. Photograph: Flashback Photography.

ROB LORENSON

7 COOMBS STREET ■ MIDDLEBORO, MA 02346 ■ TEL 508-454-5478
E-MAIL RLORENSON@BRIDGEW.EDU ■ WWW.ROBLORENSON.COM

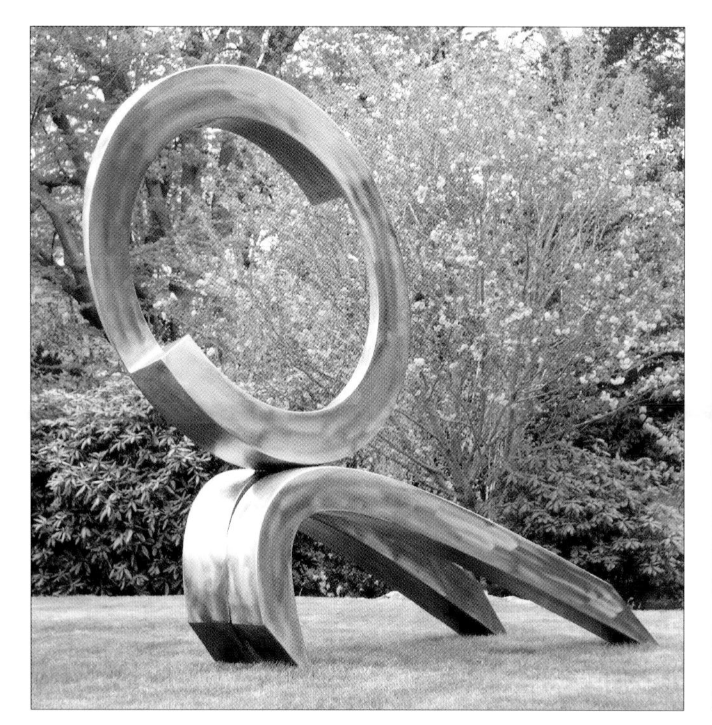

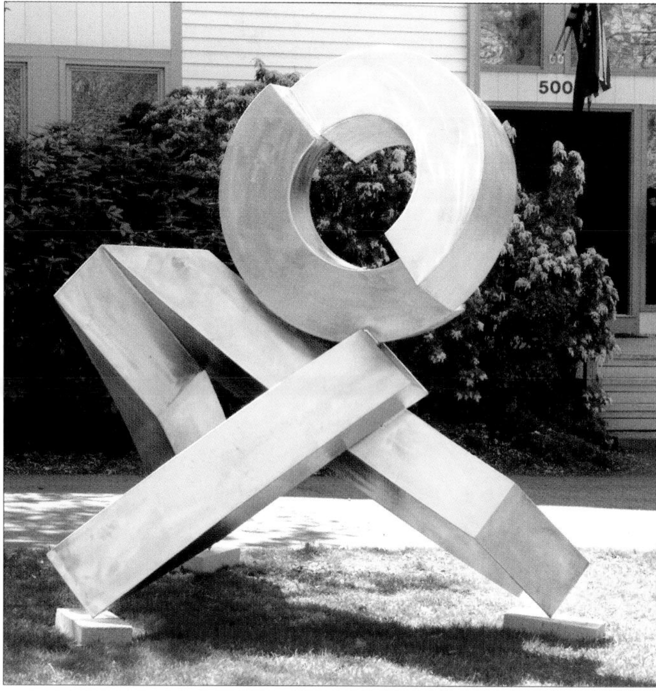

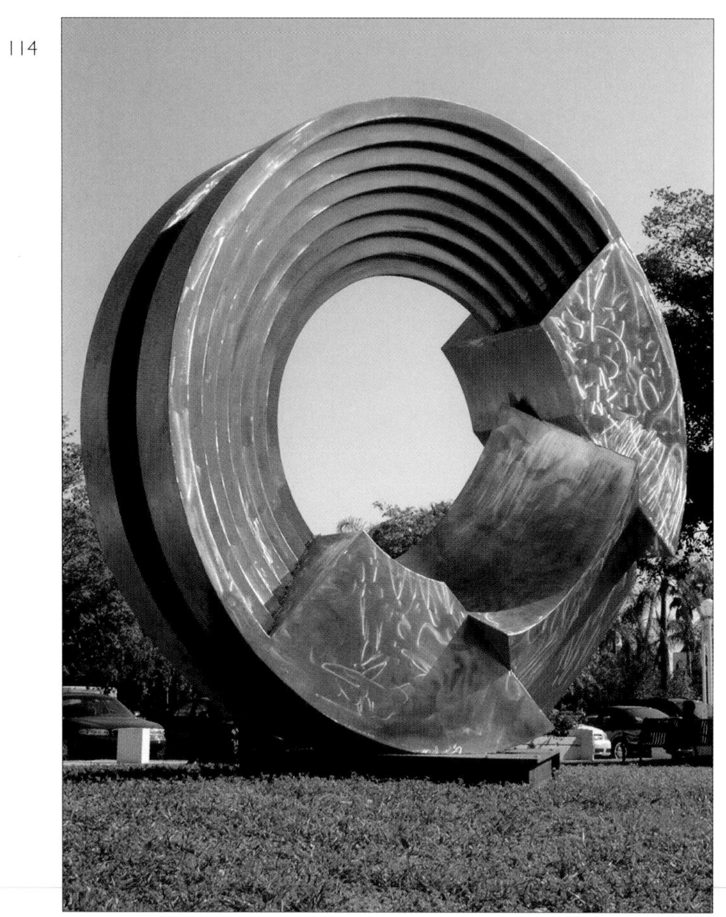

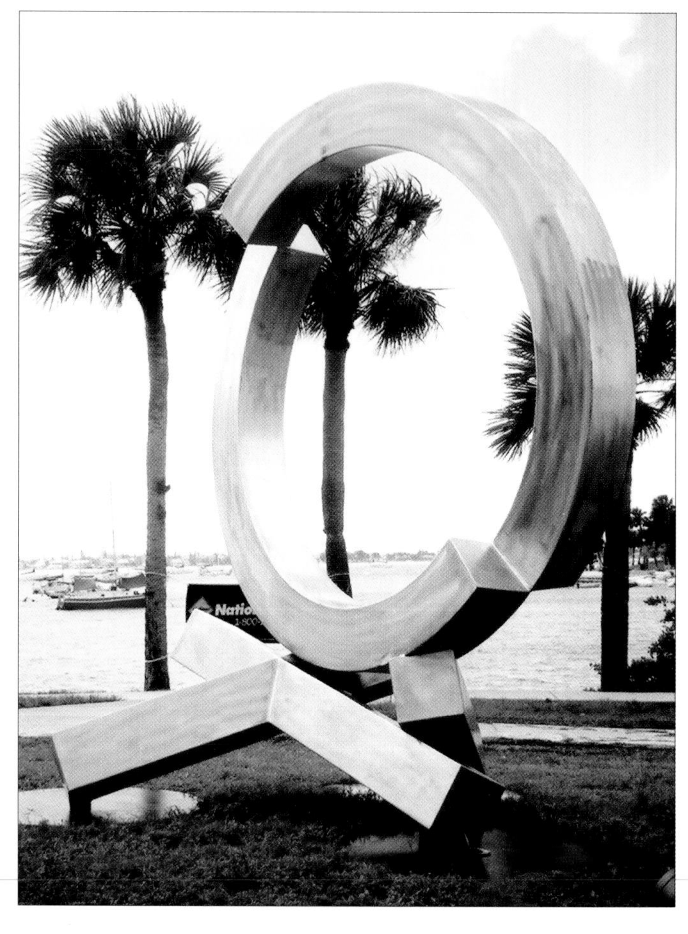

Top left: *Deuce*, 2002, stainless steel, 72" x 72" x 36". Top right: *Pulsar*, 2006, stainless steel, 96" x 96" x 85".
Bottom left: *Radio City*. Bottom right: *Split Ring in Motion*.

GRETCHEN LOTHROP

STUDIO AT ELF WAY ■ PO BOX 1562 ■ PITTSBORO, NC 27312 ■ TEL 919-545-0280
FAX 919-545-9049 ■ E-MAIL GRETCHEN@STUDIOATELFWAY.COM ■ WWW.STUDIOATELFWAY.COM

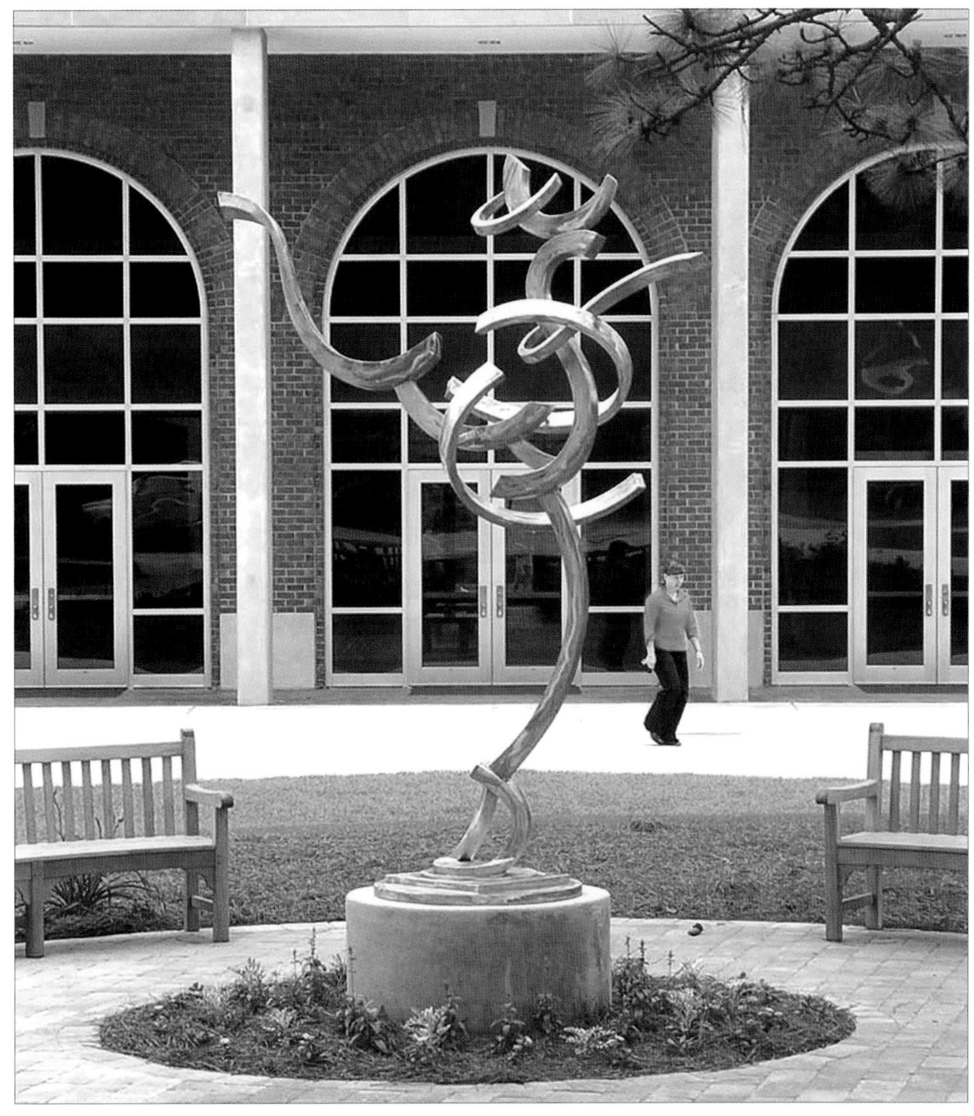

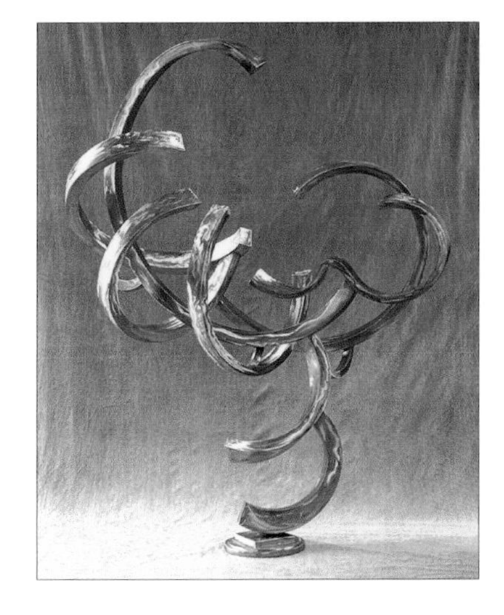

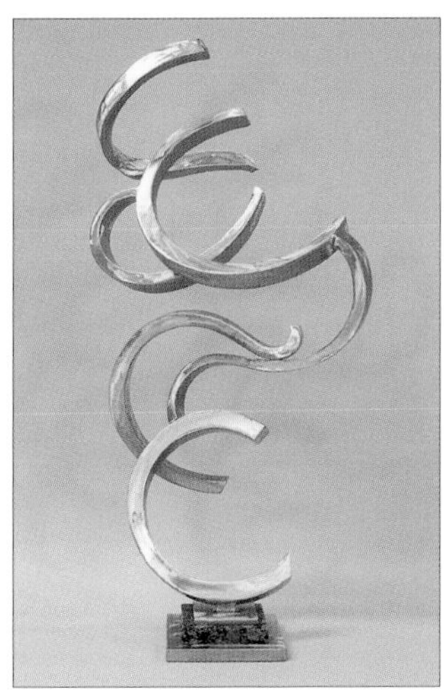

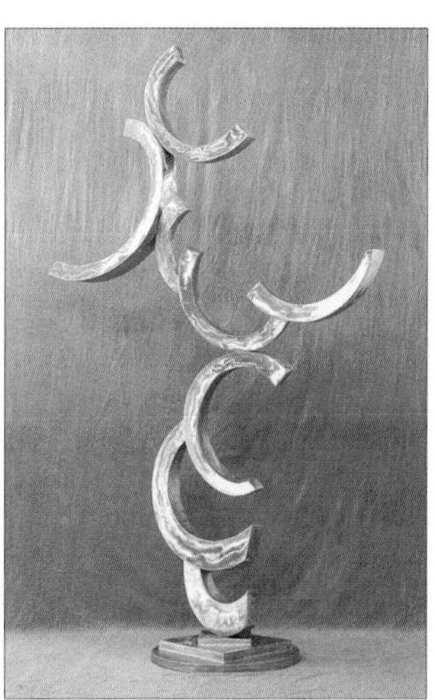

Top: *Untitled Dancing Piece*, Sandhills Community College, Pinehurst, NC, stainless steel, 8.5' x 6.3' x 2.5'. Bottom left: *The Mary Piece*, Newman Catholic Student Center, UNC, Chapel Hill, NC, stainless steel, 8.5' x 6' x 2.6'. Bottom center: *Sun Dance*, private collection, Chapel Hill, NC, bronze, 41" x 26" x 13". Bottom right: *A Subtle Miracle*, stainless steel, 10.5' x 6.1' x 2.6'.

CYNTHIA McKEAN

CMC DESIGN ■ 1000 MASON STREET ■ SAUGATUCK, MI 49453 ■ TEL 269-857-4612
E-MAIL CMCDESIGN@CYNTHIAMCKEAN.COM ■ WWW.CYNTHIAMCKEAN.COM

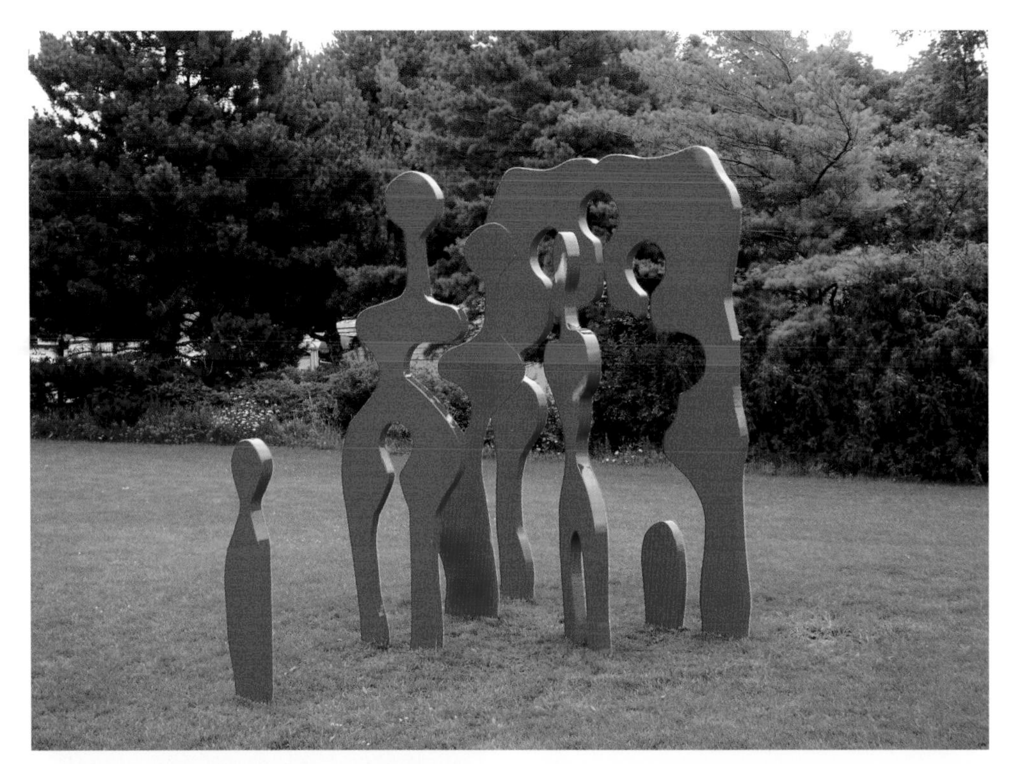

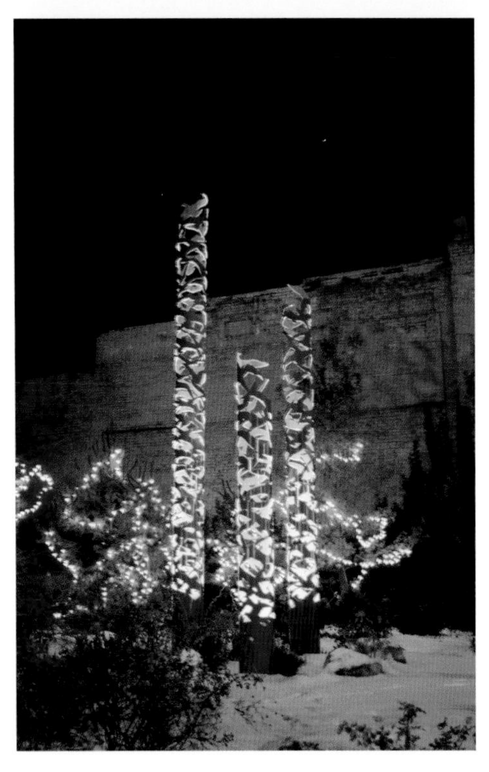

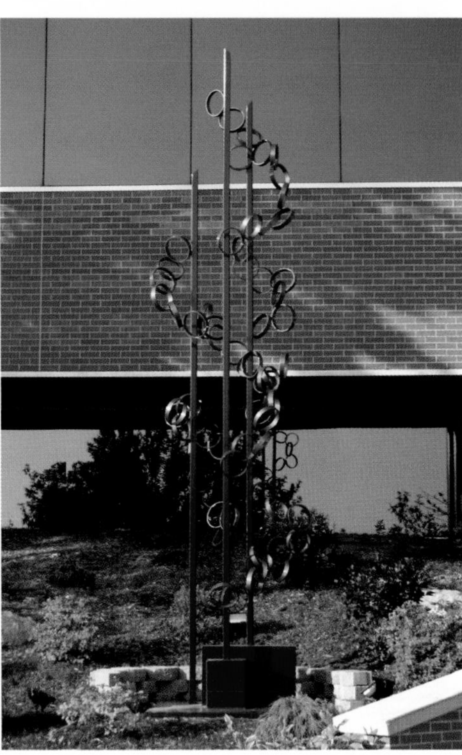

Top: *Family of Man IV.* Photograph: Gary Burmeister.
Bottom left: *Sea Gulls.* Bottom right: *Untitled.* Photograph: Julie Porter.

PETER MITTEN

PETER MITTEN STUDIOS ■ 3182 VISTA DEL RIO ■ FALLBROOK, CA 92028 ■ TEL 760-728-2416
TEL 760-525-1563 ■ E-MAIL PETERMITTEN@MAC.COM ■ WWW.PETERMITTEN.COM

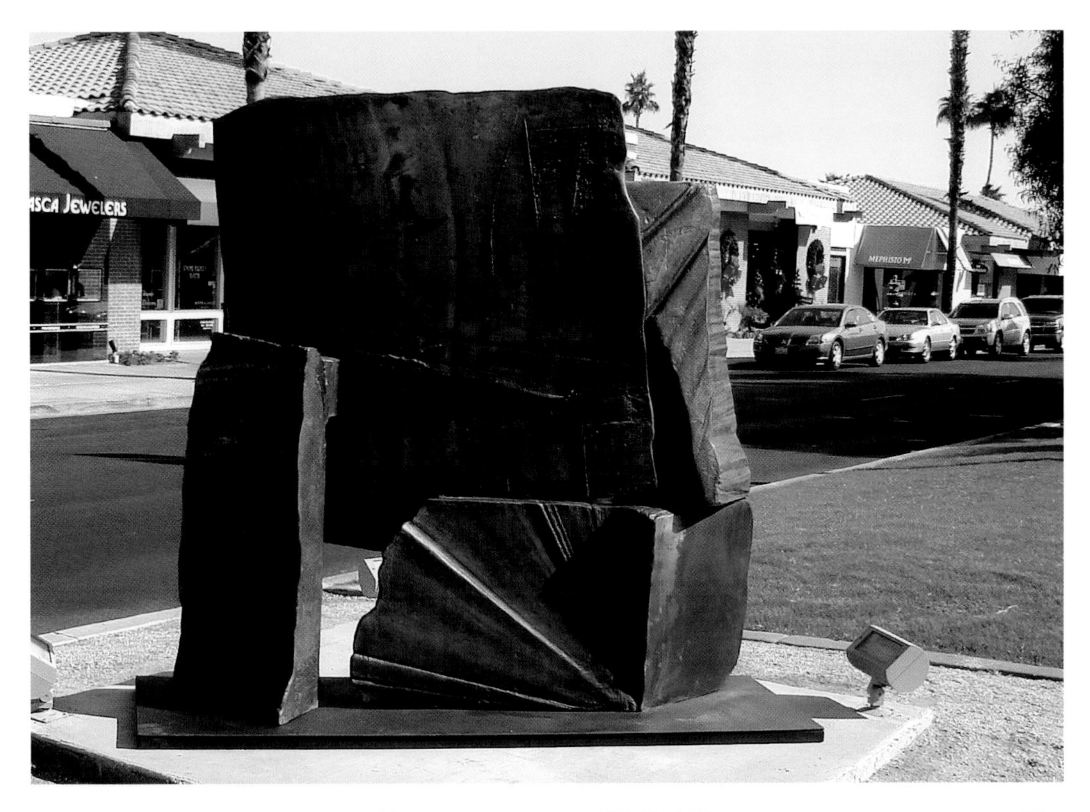

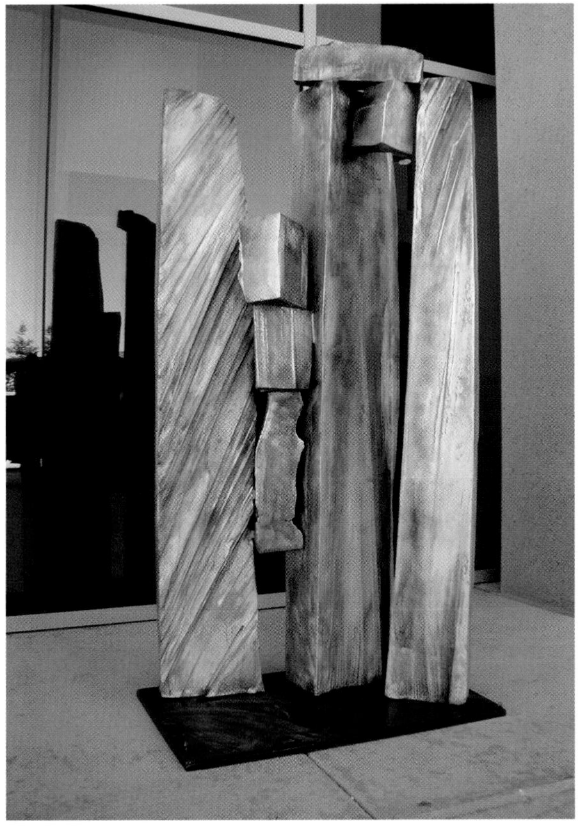

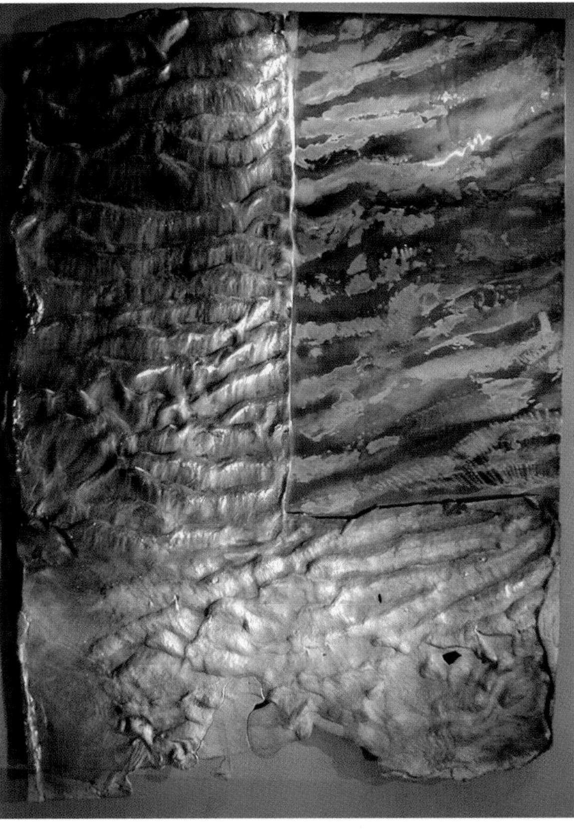

Top: *Echoes of Shawanasee*, 2003, City of Palm Desert, CA, cast bronze, 72" x 72" x 20". Bottom left: *Canyon Screen*, 2000, City of Prescott Valley, AZ, cast aluminum with acrylic wash, 90" x 48" x 24". Bottom right: *Aquifer*, 2003, private collection, Solana Beach, CA, cast and fabricated aluminum with acrylic paint, 78" x 43" x 2".

BRUCE A. NIEMI

13300 116TH STREET ■ KENOSHA, WI 53142 ■ TEL 262-857-3456 ■ TEL 847-971-0845
FAX 262-857-4567 ■ E-MAIL SCULPTURE@BRUCENIEMI.COM ■ WWW.BRUCENIEMI.COM

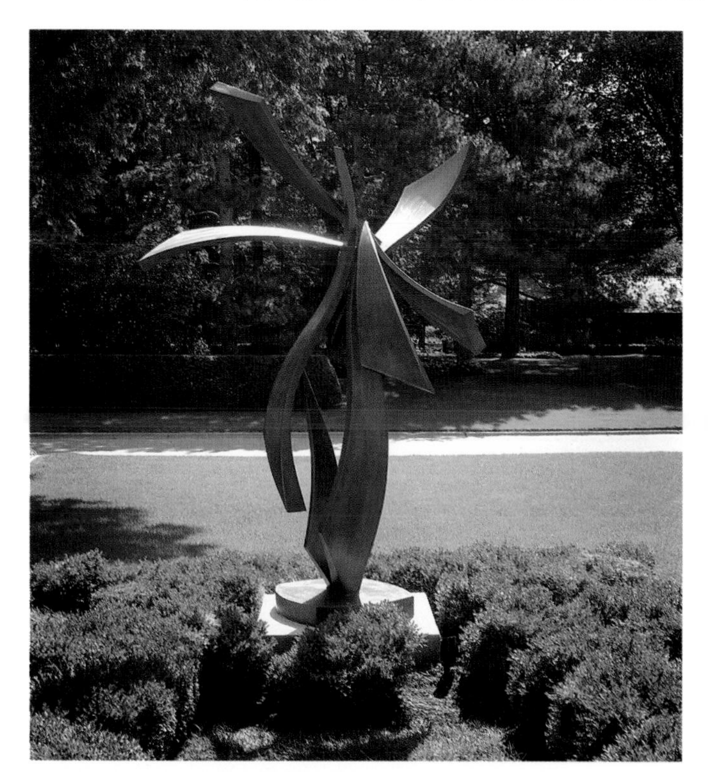

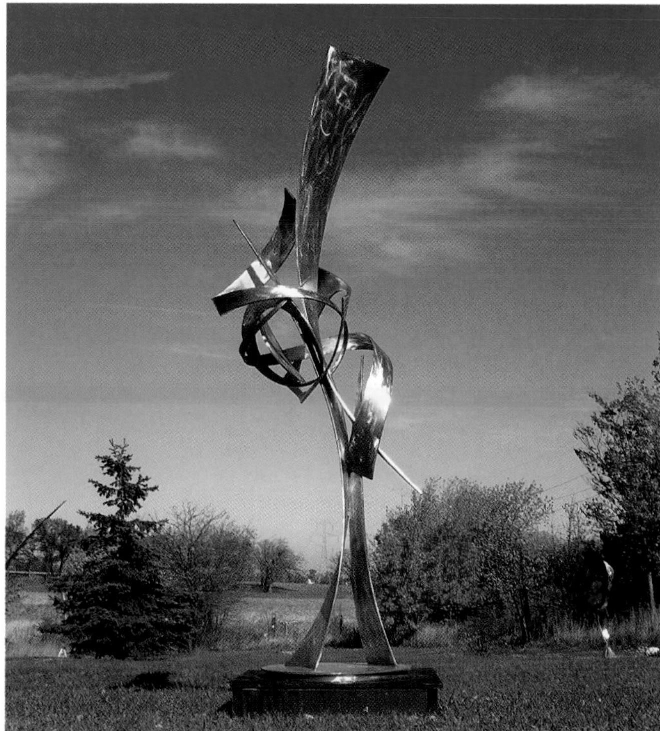

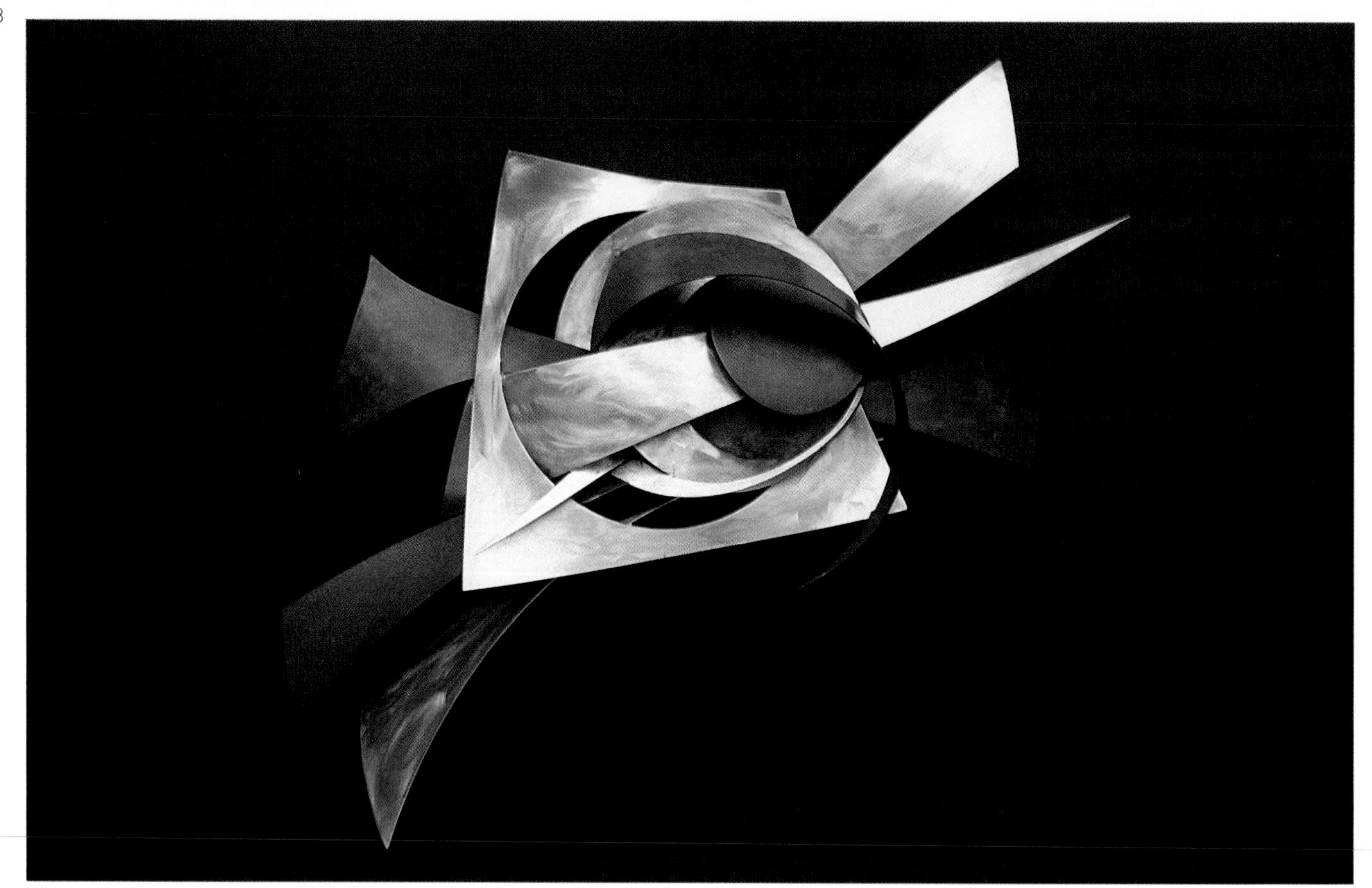

Top left: *Emergence V,* 2006, private residence, Omaha, NE, silicon bronze, 9.3'H x 7'W x 4.8'D. Top right: *To Be Held,* 2005, Niemi Sculpture Gallery, Kenosha, WI, stainless steel, 9.75'H x 3.25'W x 2.8'D. Bottom: *Breaking Free,* 2006, Niemi Sculpture Gallery, Kenosha, WI, stainless steel and bronze, 4.15'H x 4.8'W x 8'D.

DANIEL OBERTI

DANIEL OBERTI CERAMIC DESIGN ■ 3796 TWIG AVENUE ■ SEBASTOPOL, CA 95472
TEL 707-829-0584 ■ FAX 707-829-2136 ■ E-MAIL DANIEL@DANIELOBERTI.COM ■ WWW.DANIELOBERTI.COM

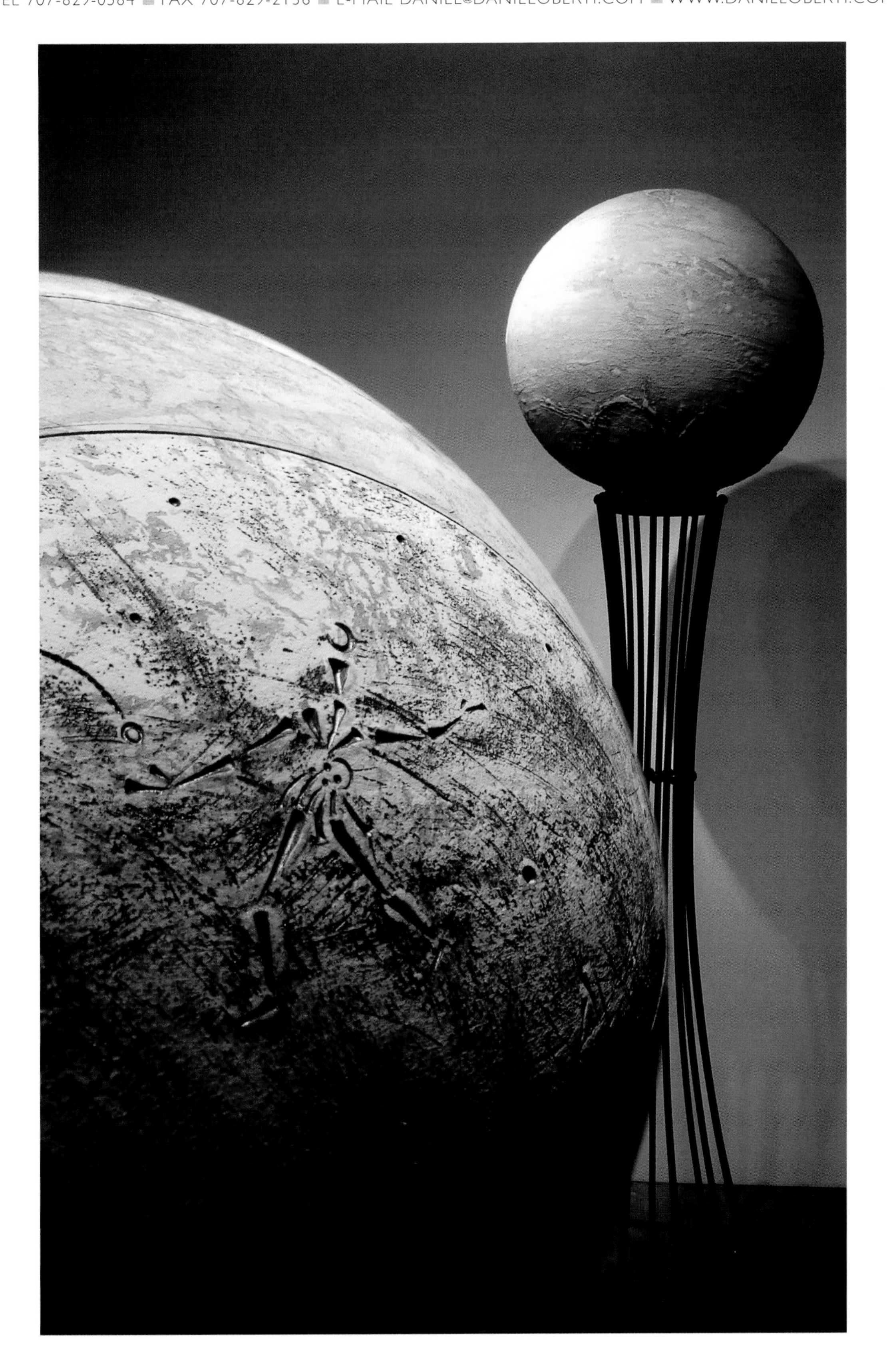

Spheres of Influence.

ERIC O'LEARY

TARIKI STUDIO ■ 12 BEAN ROAD ■ MERIDEN, NH 03770 ■ TEL 603-469-3243
FAX 603-469-3958 ■ E-MAIL INFO@TARIKI.COM ■ WWW.TARIKI.COM

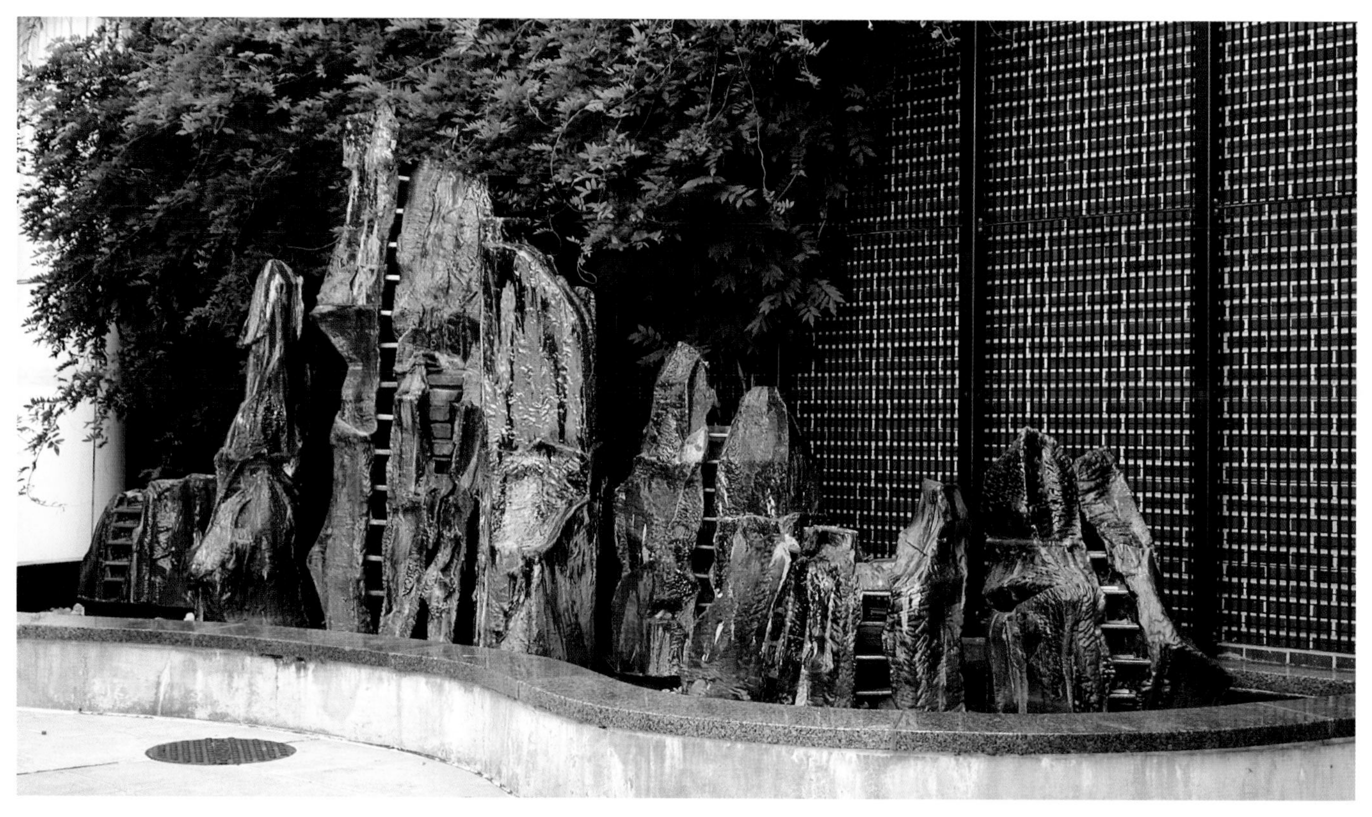

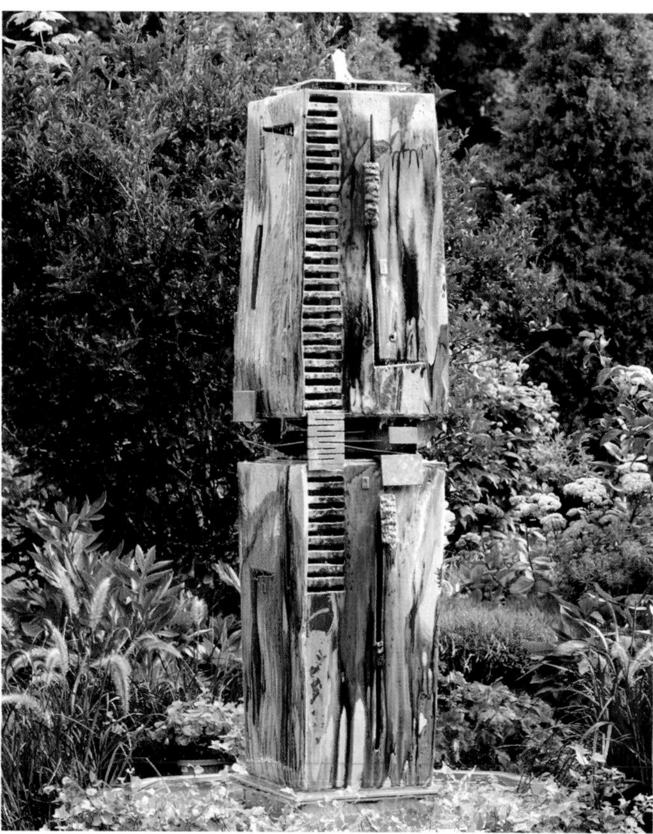

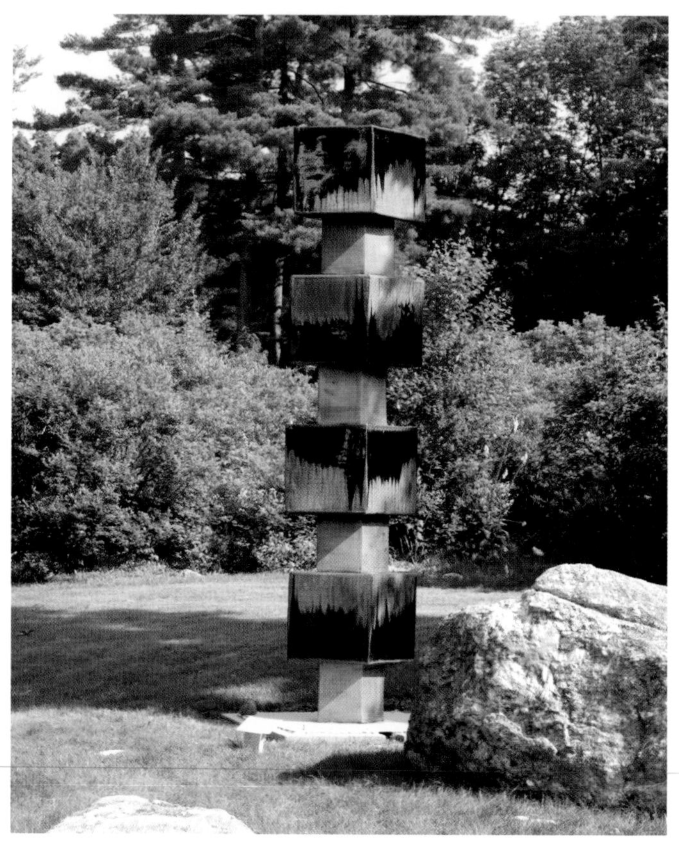

Top: *Journey Fountain,* 1995, Pinnacle Health Care courtyard, Harrisburg, PA, ceramic and stainless steel, 10' x 36' x 12'. Bottom left: *Obos II,* 2004, private collection, Scotland UK, ceramic and stainless steel, 7' x 20" x 20". Bottom right: *Black Gold,* 2005, private collection, ceramic and steel, 12' x 34" x 18". Photographs: Kevin O'Leary.

MARKIAN OLYNYK

MARKIAN STUDIOS INC. ■ 2776 WEST TENTH AVENUE ■ VANCOUVER, BC V6K 2J9 ■ CANADA
TEL 604-738-9791 ■ FAX 604-738-9722 ■ E-MAIL MARKIAN@MARKIANSTUDIOS.COM ■ WWW.MARKIANSTUDIOS.COM

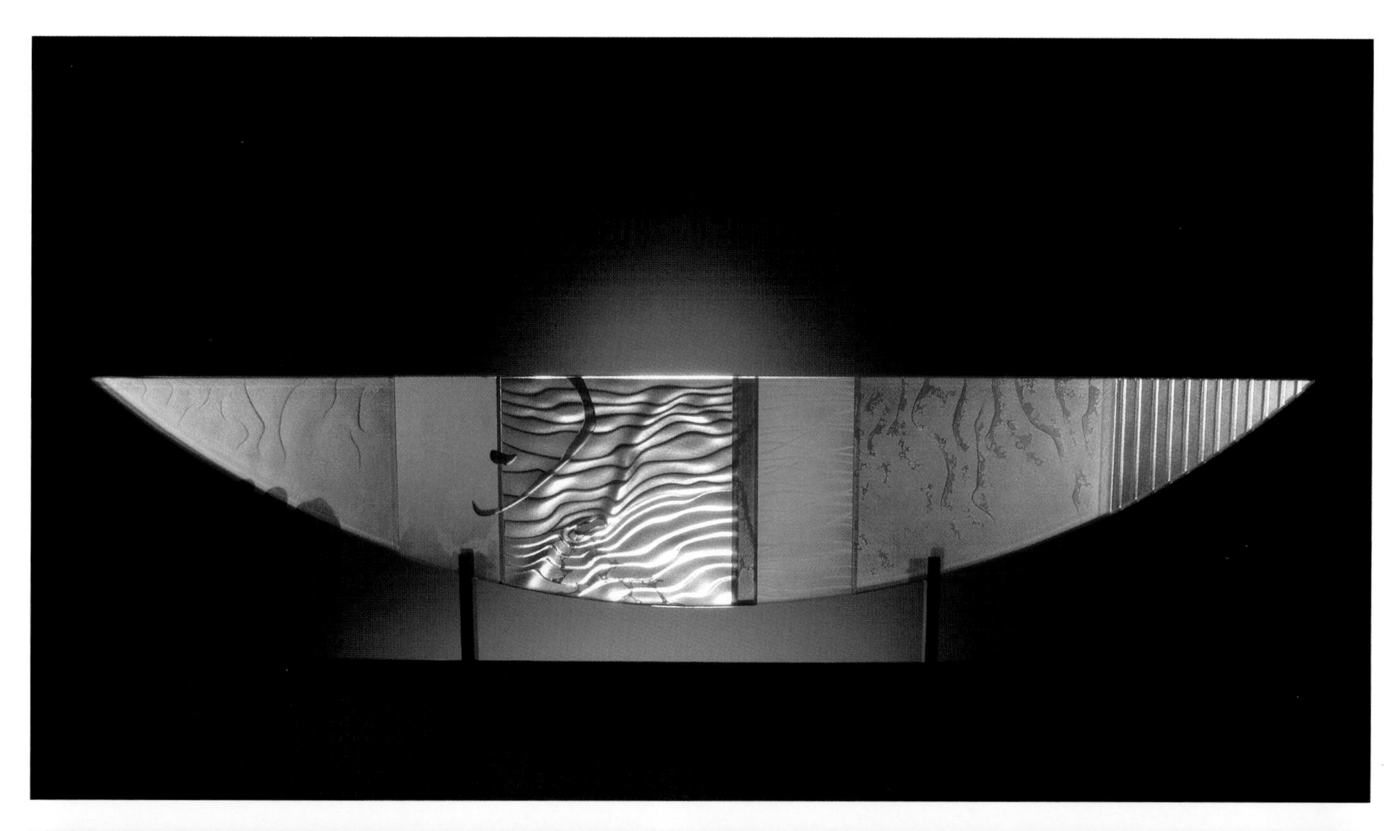

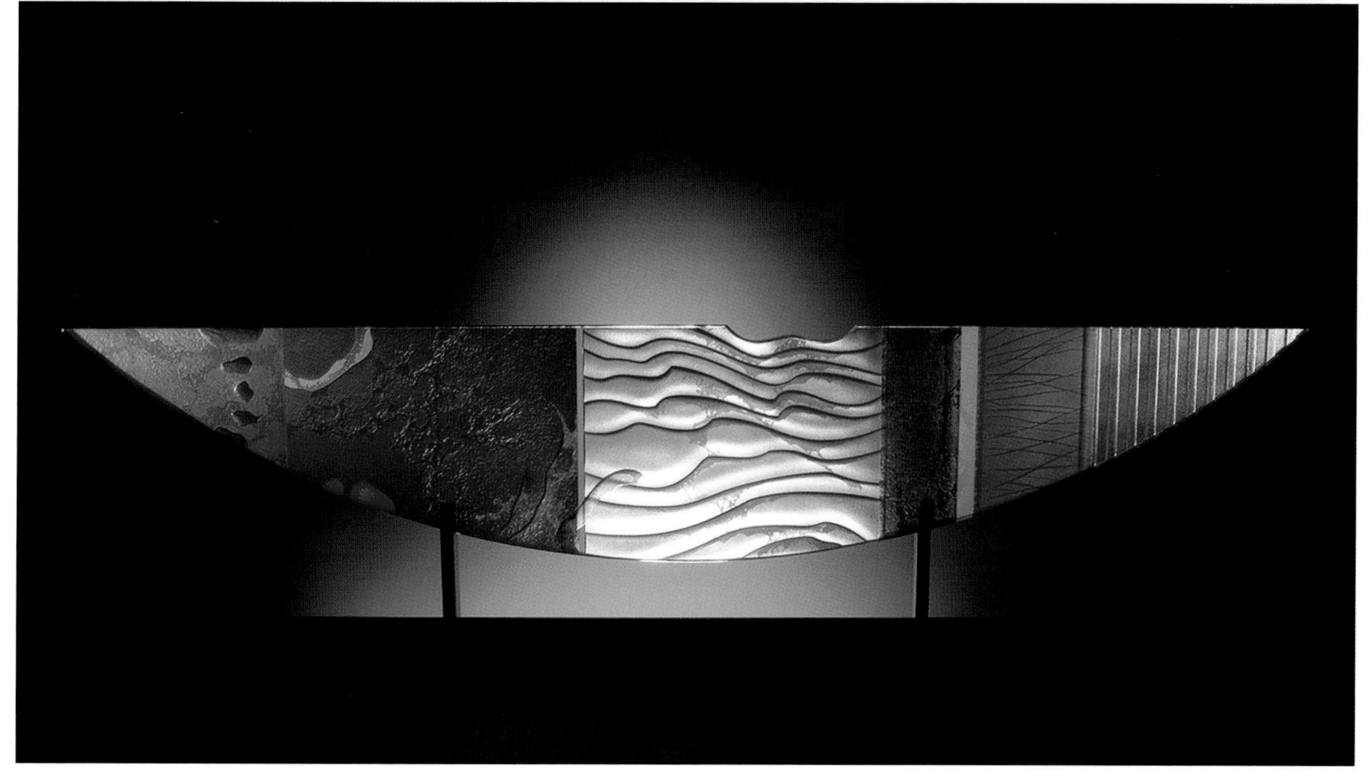

Top: *Arc Series 7ORYB5*, glass and steel, 14" x 48" x 5". Bottom: *Arc Series 7BG5*, glass and steel, 14" x 48" x 5". Photographs: Joaquin Pedrero.

ERIC PELTZER

2857 REPOSA LANE ■ ALTADENA, CA 91001
TEL 626-797-8245 ■ E-MAIL ERIC@PELTZER.NET ■ WWW.PELTZER.NET

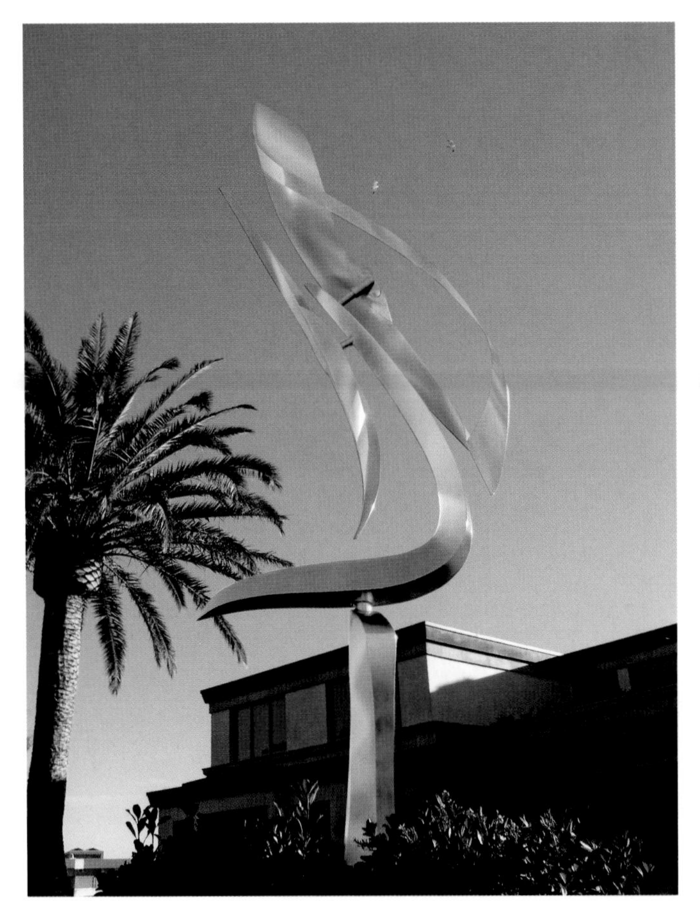

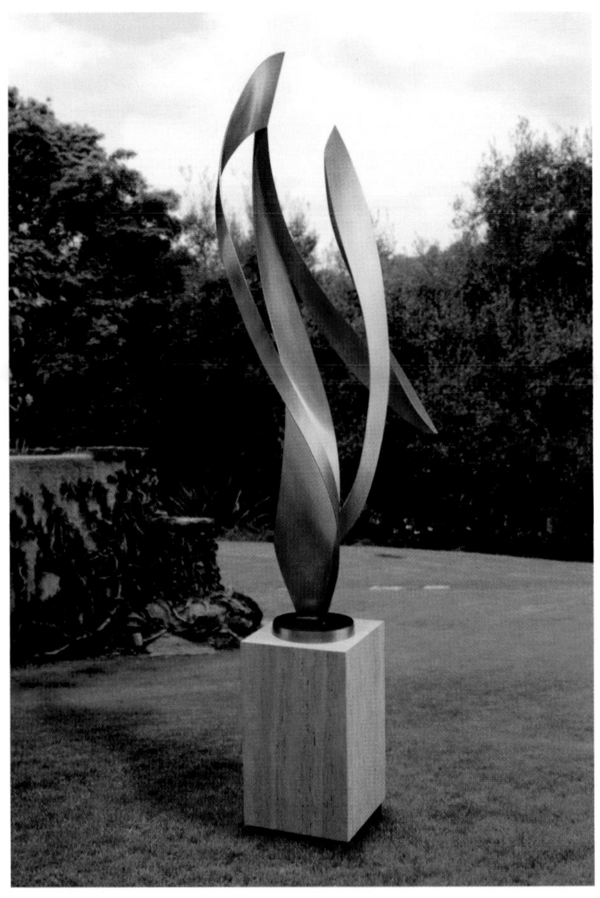

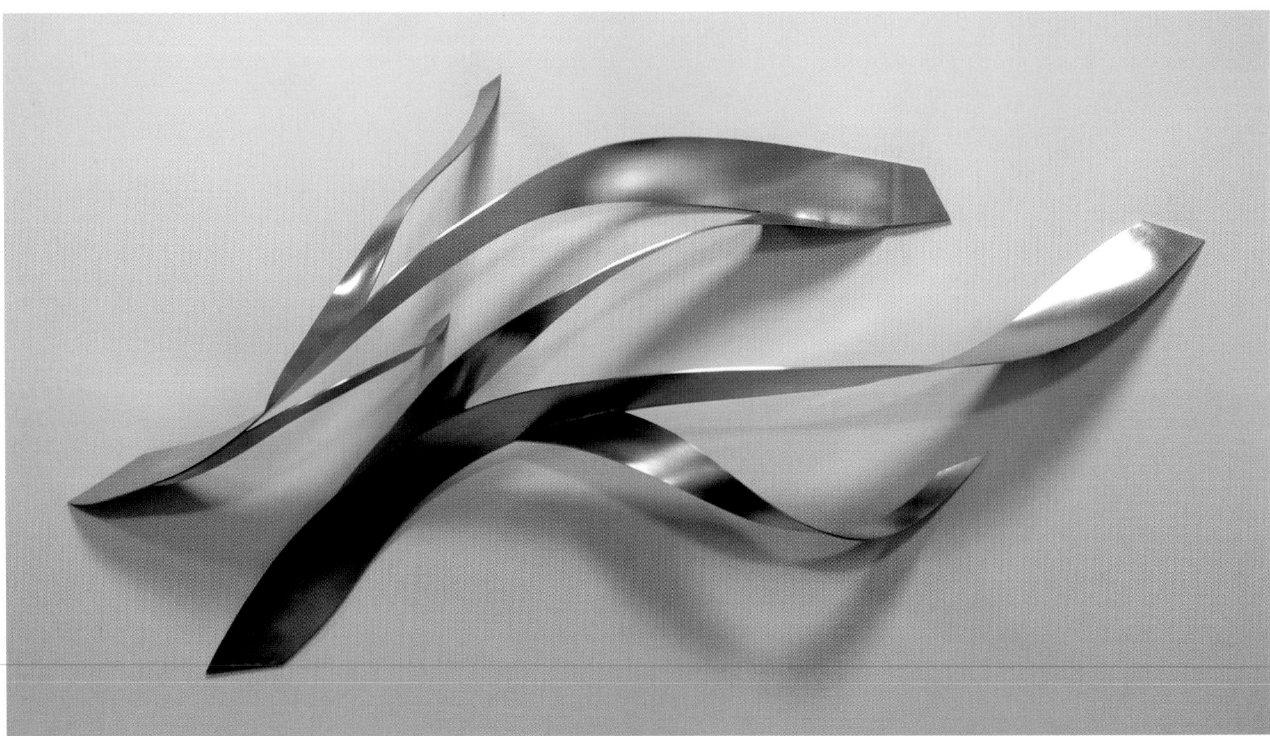

Top left: *Someone Sent Me Two Feathers,* 2004, private collection, Dana Point, CA, stainless steel kinetic wind sculpture, 12'H x 6' x 6'. Top right: *Not The Worlds We Dream,* 2003, private collection, Lakeland, FL, bronze, 61"H x 26" x 24", base: 21". Bottom: *Cloud Rivulet,* 2001, private collection, Dallas, TX, stainless steel wall sculpture, 52"W x 29"H x 9"D.

KEVIN ROBB

KEVIN ROBB STUDIOS, LLC ▪ 7001 WEST 35TH AVENUE ▪ WHEAT RIDGE, CO 80033
TEL 303-431-4758 ▪ FAX 303-425-8802 ▪ E-MAIL 3D@KEVINROBB.COM ▪ WWW.KEVINROBB.COM

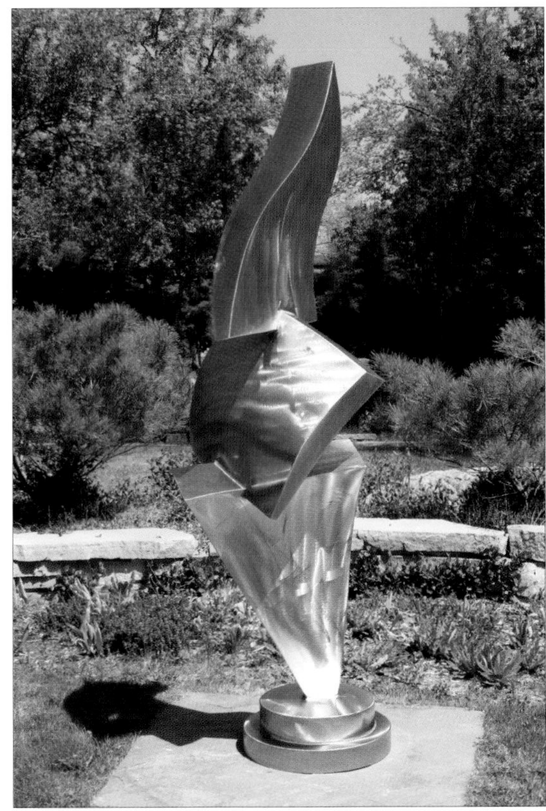

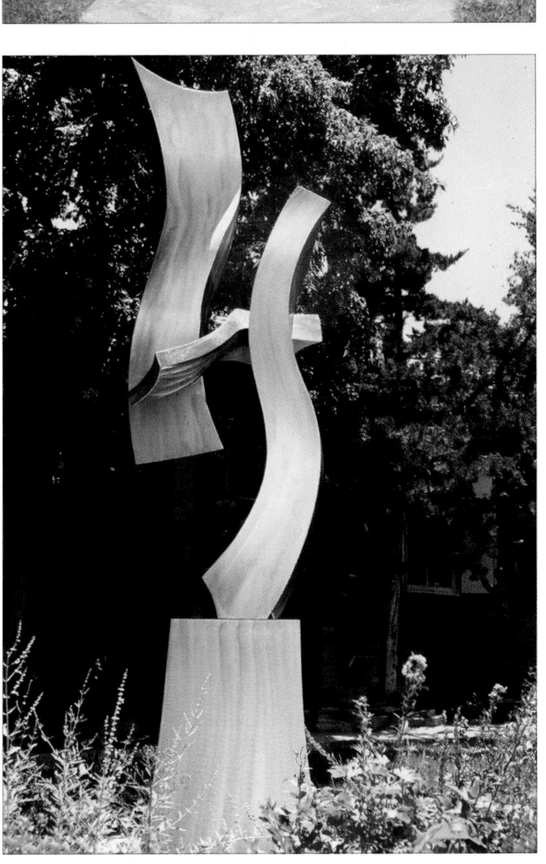

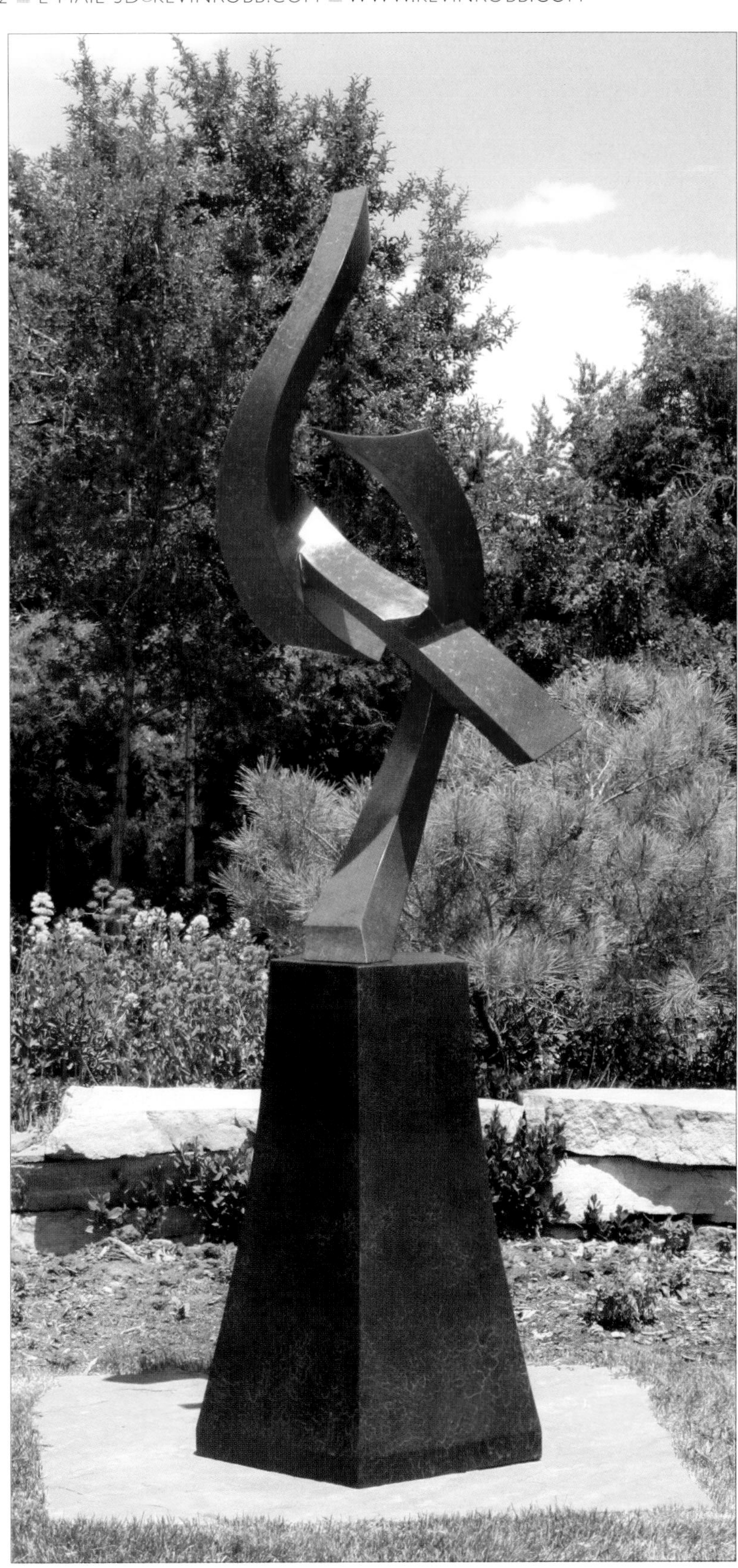

Top left: *Pieces of Sushi,* 2005, stainless steel, 76" x 27" x 22" on a 6" base. Right: *Tango,* 2006, fabricated bronze, 52" x 25" x 18" on a 32" bronze base. Bottom left: *Desert Blooms,* 2005, stainless steel, 91" x 33" x 25" on a 32" base.

BRIAN F. RUSSELL

BRIAN RUSSELL STUDIO ■ 10385 LONG ROAD ■ ARLINGTON, TN 38002 ■ TEL 901-867-7300
FAX 901-867-7843 ■ E-MAIL INFO@BRIANRUSSELLSTUDIO.COM ■ WWW.BRIANRUSSELLSTUDIO.COM

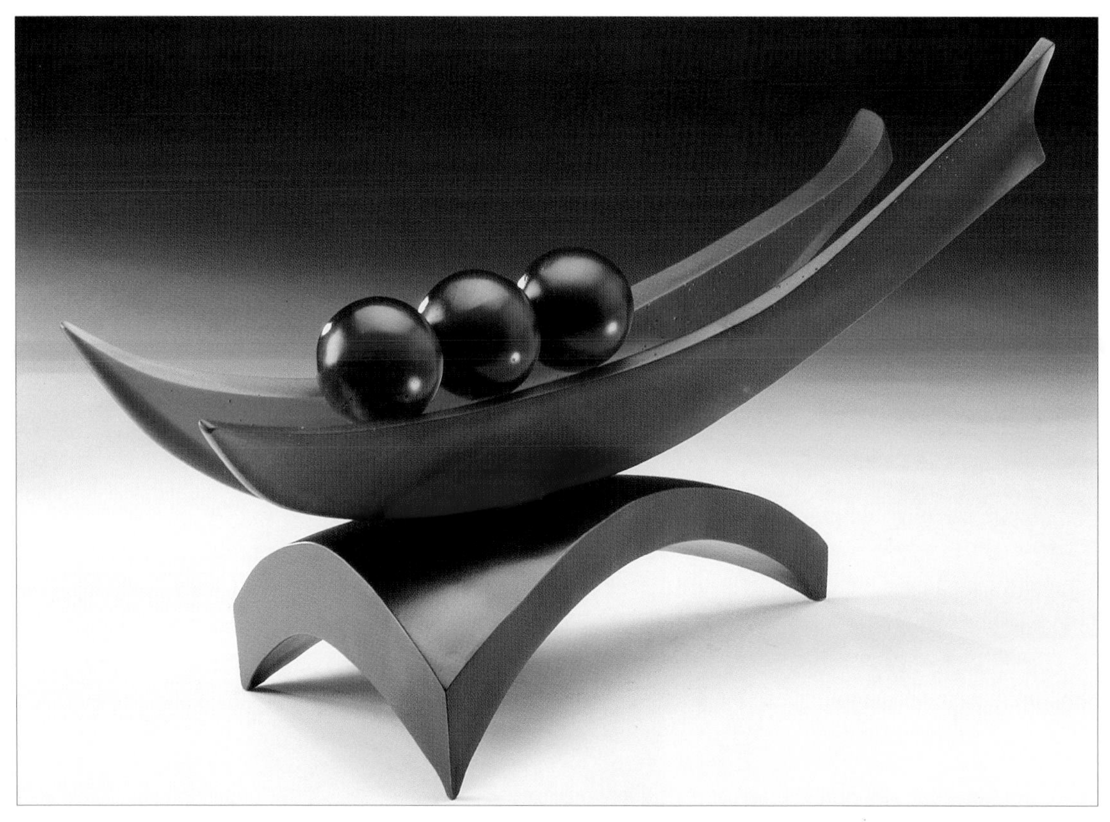

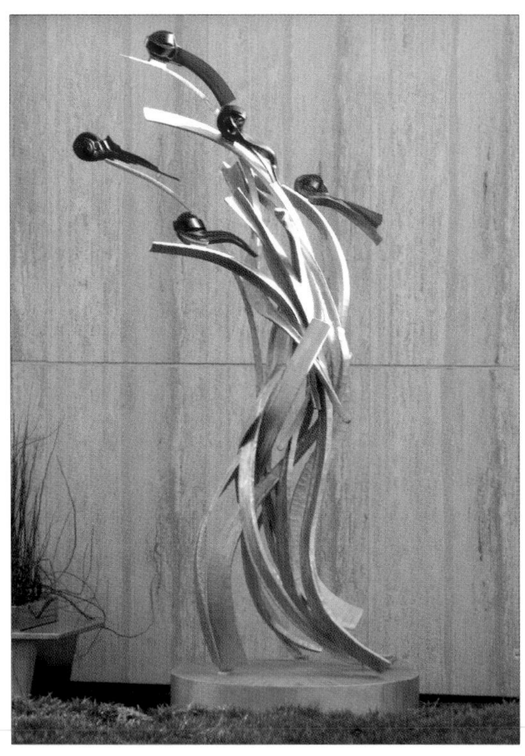

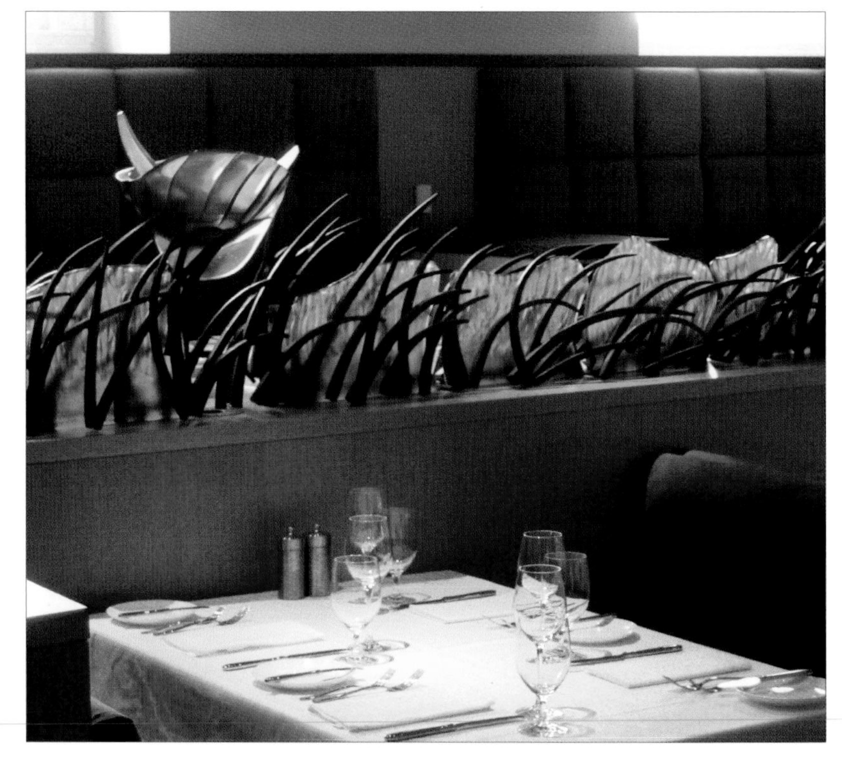

Top: *Three Peas,* 2006, cast glass and formed bronze, 16" × 28" × 12". Bottom left: *Curvilinear Motion,* 2006, First Tennessee Bank, 120"H. Bottom right: *Run Wild,* 2006, San Francisco, CA, cast glass and forged steel, 30'L.

JAMES T. RUSSELL

JAMES T. RUSSELL SCULPTURE ■ 1930 LOMITA BOULEVARD ■ LOMITA, CA 90717-1849
TEL 310-326-0785 ■ FAX 310-326-1470 ■ E-MAIL JAMES@RUSSELLSCULPTURE.COM ■ WWW.RUSSELLSCULPTURE.COM

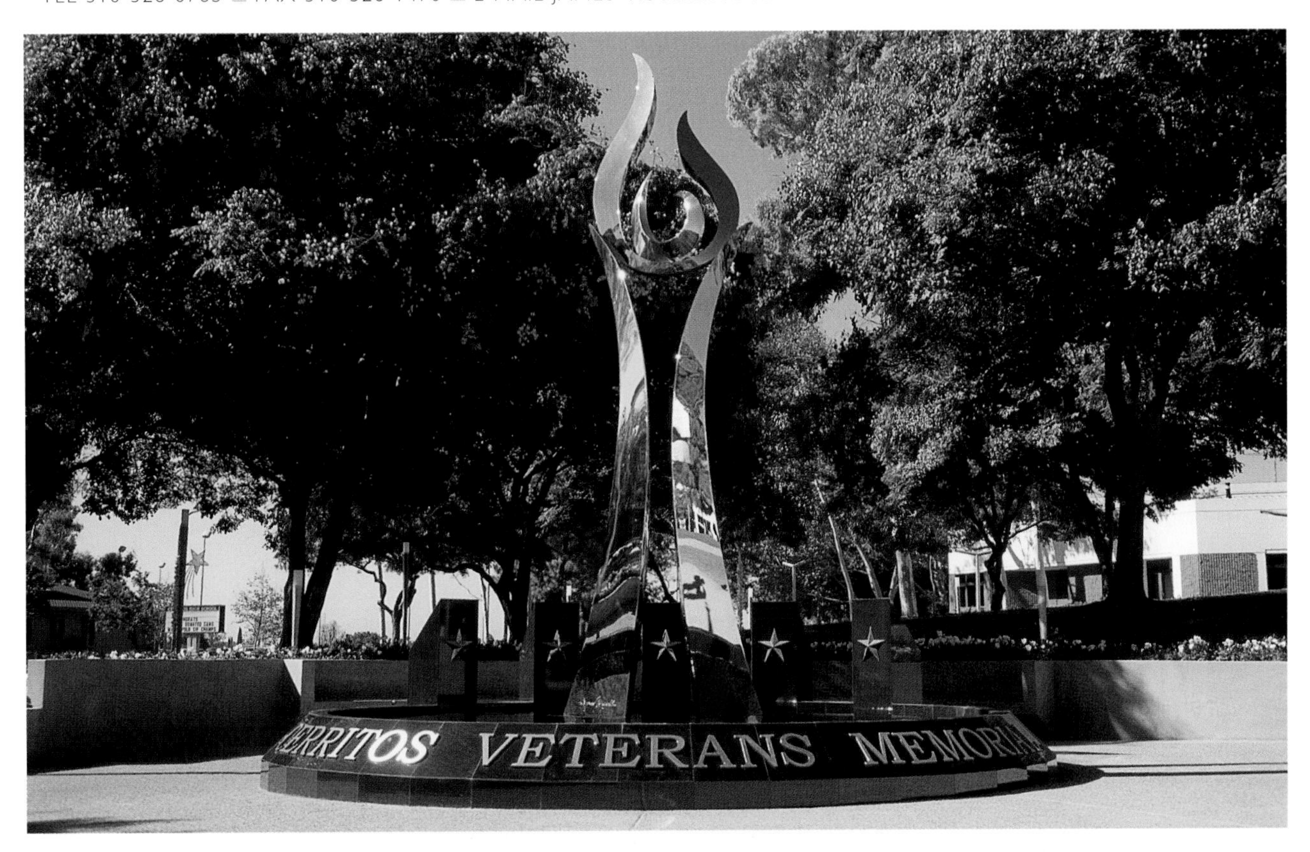

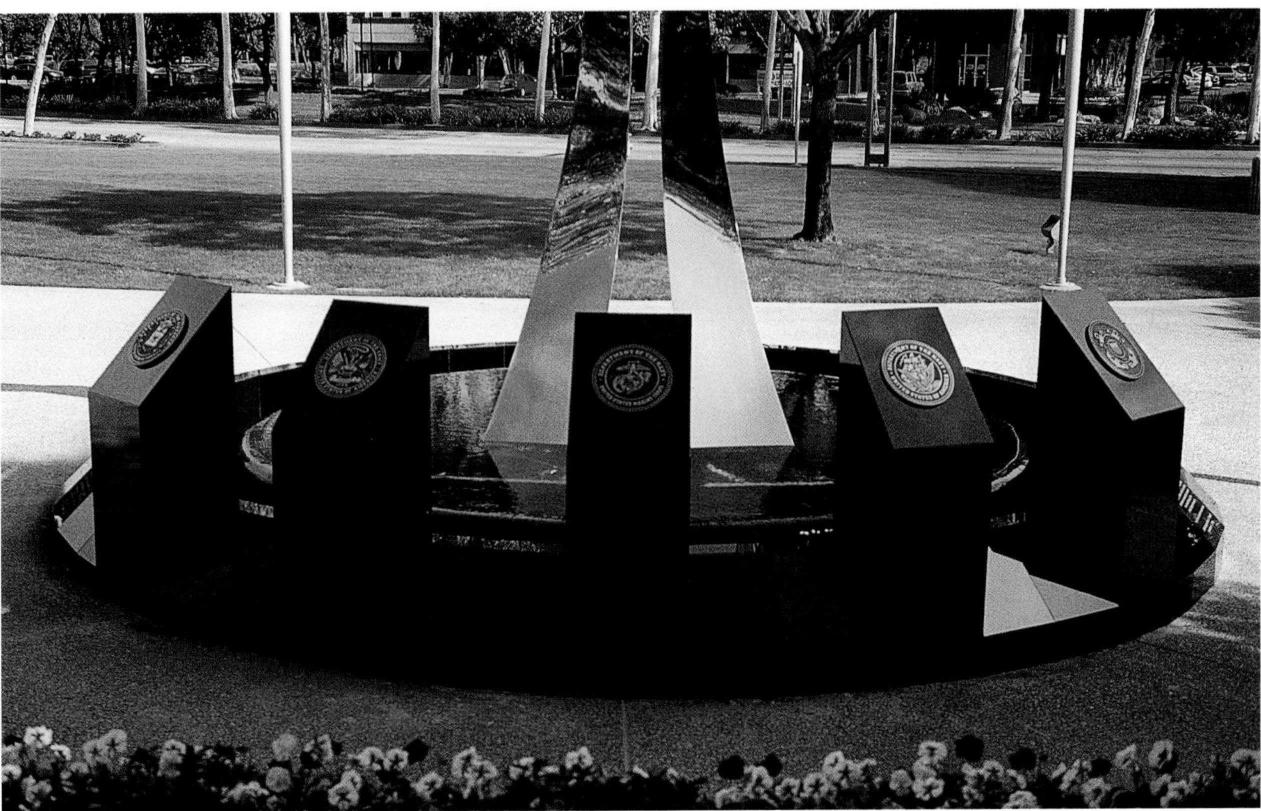

Cerritos Veterans Memorial, Cerritos Civic Center, Cerritos, CA, polished stainless steel, bronze, and absolute black granite, 20' x 20'.

CRAIG SCHAFFER

3814 JOCELYN STREET NW ■ WASHINGTON, DC 20015 ■ TEL 202-362-4507
E-MAIL SCHAFFER.SCULPTURE@GMAIL.COM ■ WWW.CRAIGSCHAFFER.COM

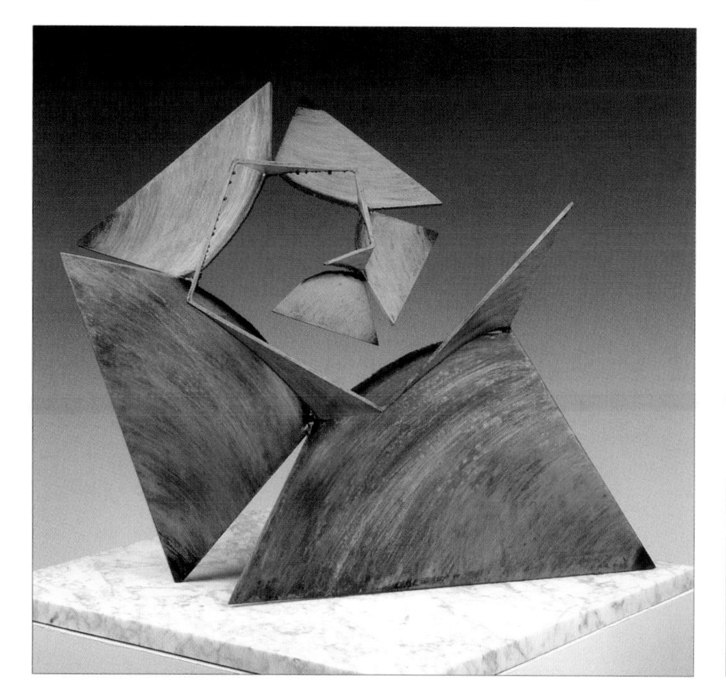

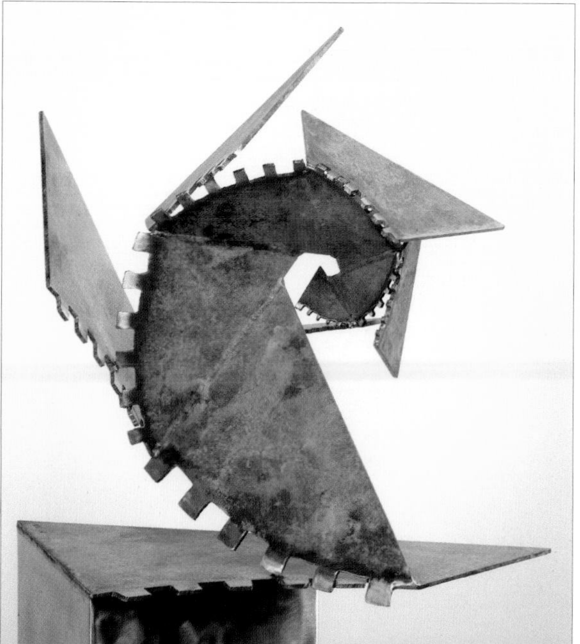

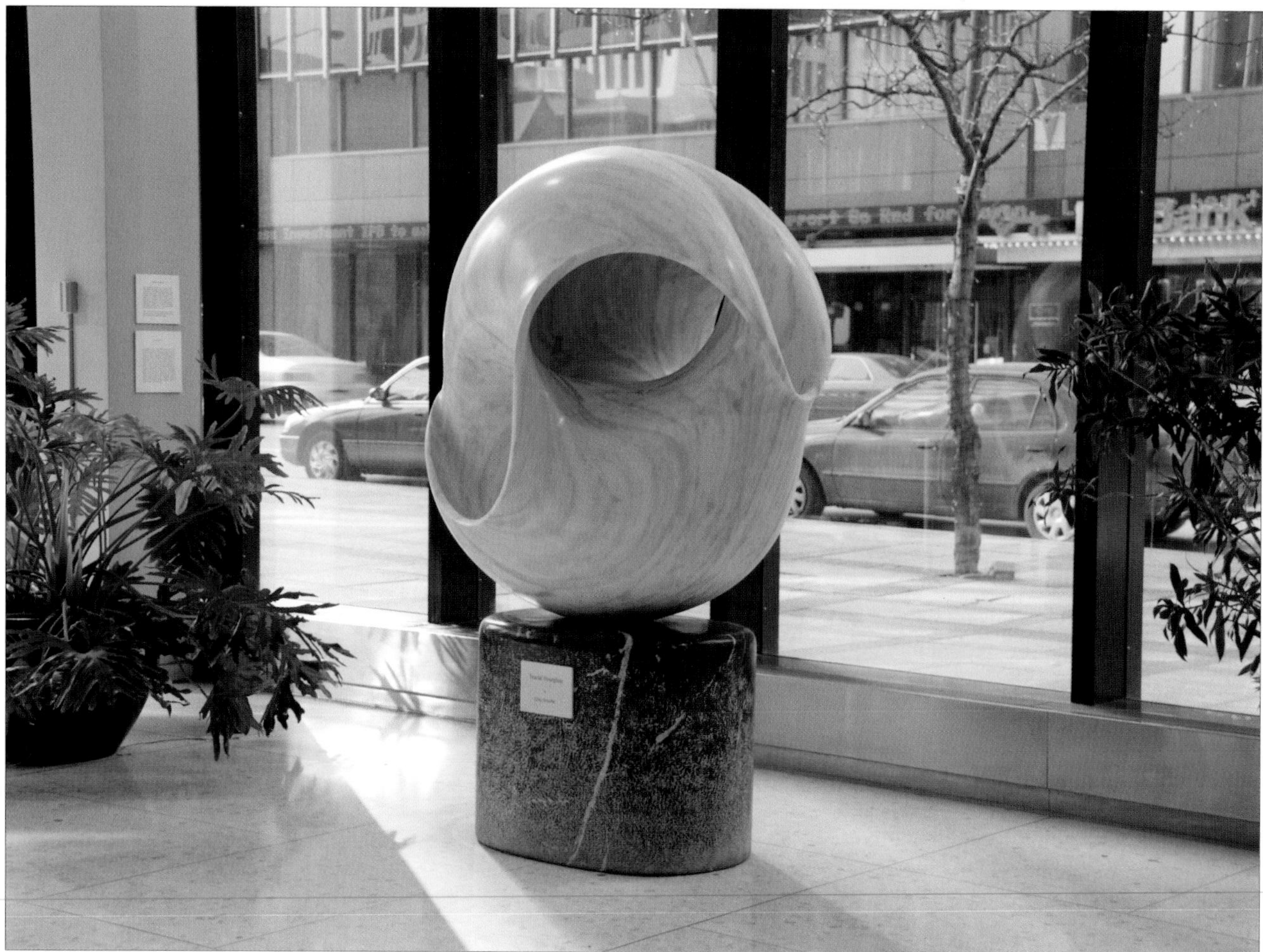

Top left: *Green Emergence*, bronze, 22" x 29" x 13". Top right: *High Gear*, bronze, 21" x 21" x 18". Bottom: *Fractal Hourglass*, marble, 50" x 50" x 32".

CRAIG SCHAFFER

3814 JOCELYN STREET NW ■ WASHINGTON, DC 20015 ■ TEL 202-362-4507
E-MAIL SCHAFFER.SCULPTURE@GMAIL.COM ■ WWW.CRAIGSCHAFFER.COM

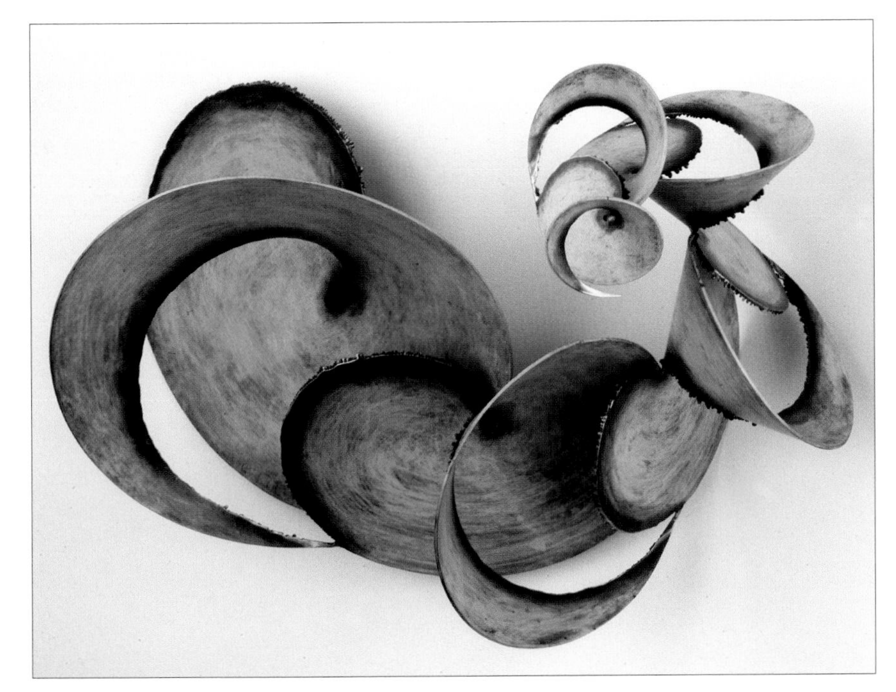

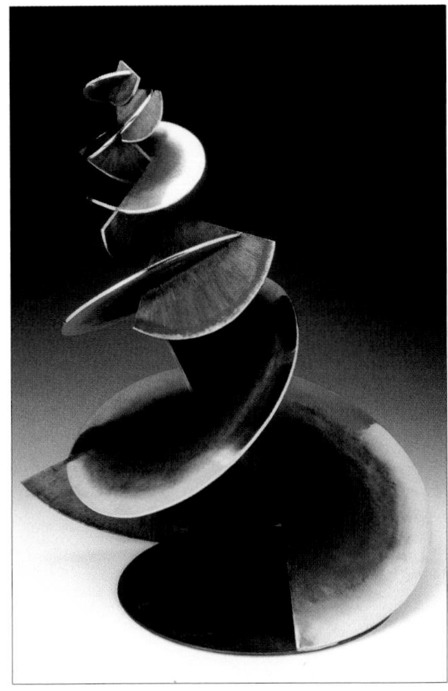

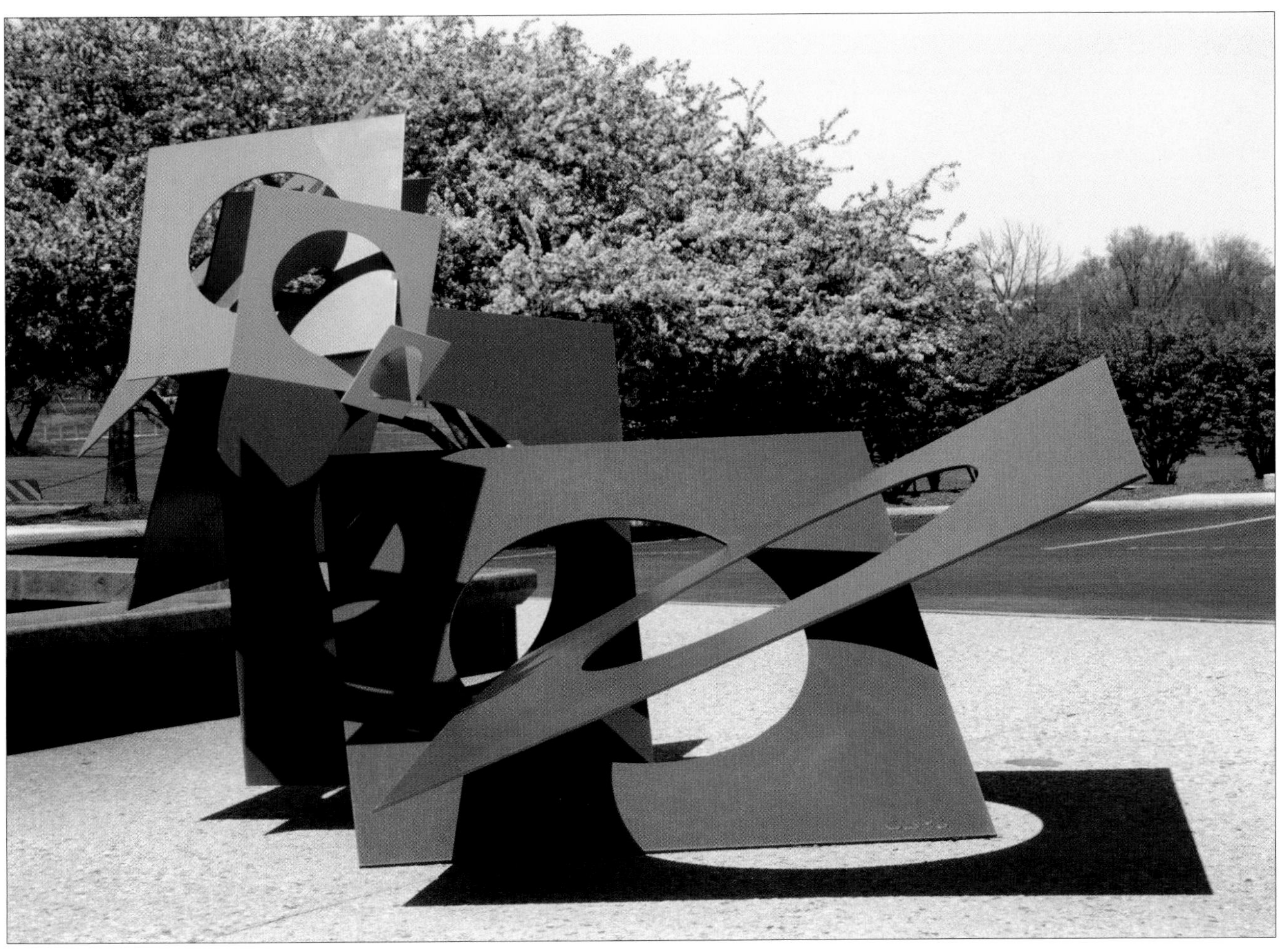

Top left: *On a Tear,* bronze, 11" x 17" x 8". Top right: *Geisha,* bronze, 33" x 26" x 21". Bottom: *Tangent,* steel, 9' x 12' x 9'.

ALI SHAHVALI

VICCOLO GLASS ■ 7740 GLORIA AVENUE ■ VAN NUYS, CA 91406 ■ TEL 818-787-7230
FAX 818-787-7306 ■ E-MAIL ALI@VICCOLOGLASS.COM ■ WWW.VICCOLOGLASS.COM

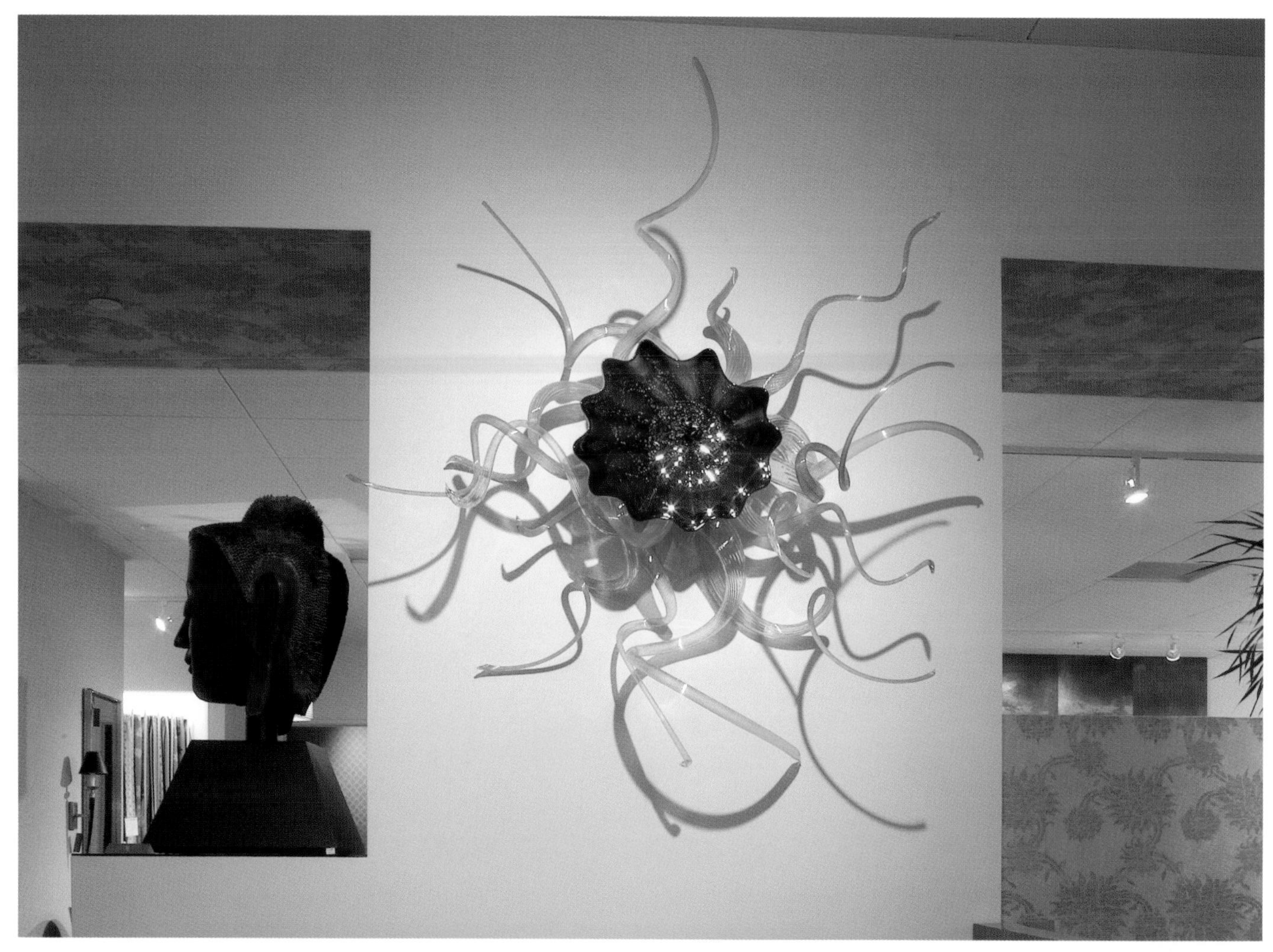

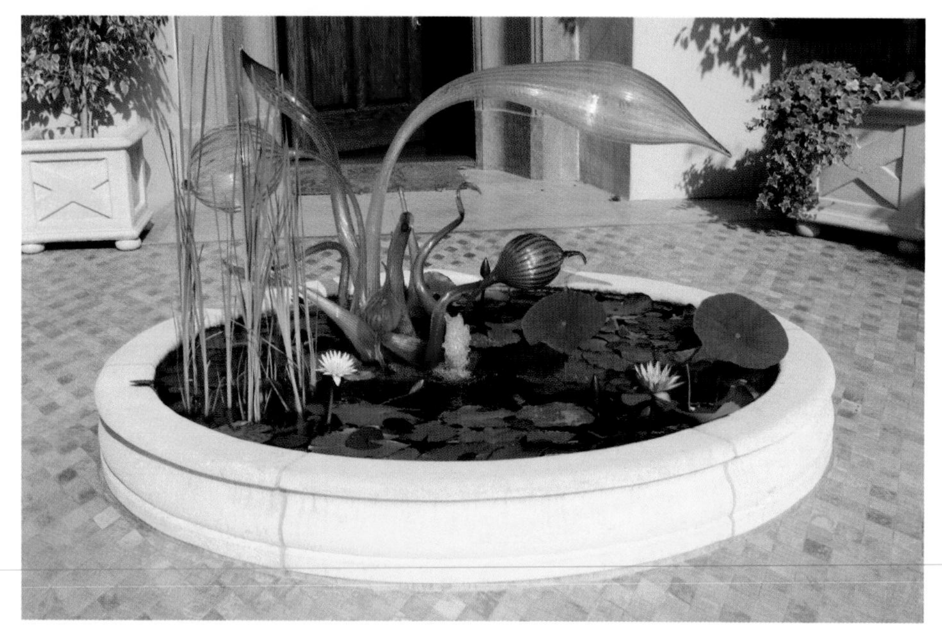

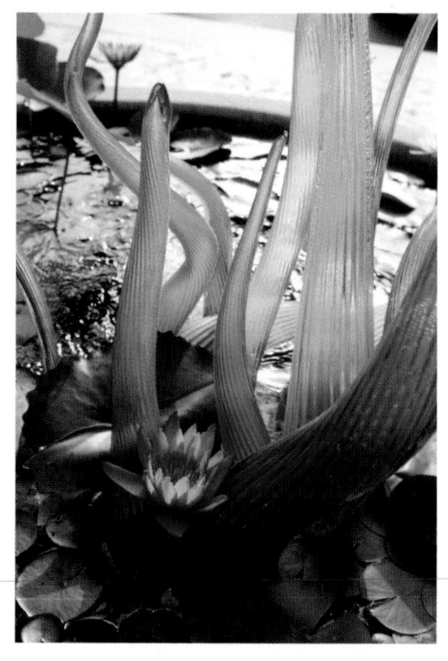

Top: *Wall Jelly,* 2006, Joanna Burke at Thomas Lavin Inc., WestWeek, West Hollywood, CA, glass sculpture. Photograph: Jason Walcot.
Bottom: *Lotus Blossom,* 2006, private collection, Pacific Palisades, CA, glass sculpture.

JOHN E. STALLINGS

STALLINGS ART ▪ 1020 WILLETT DRIVE ▪ JOHNSTOWN, PA 15905 ▪ TEL 814-255-5013
E-MAIL SCULPTURE@STALLINGSART.COM ▪ WWW.STALLINGSART.COM

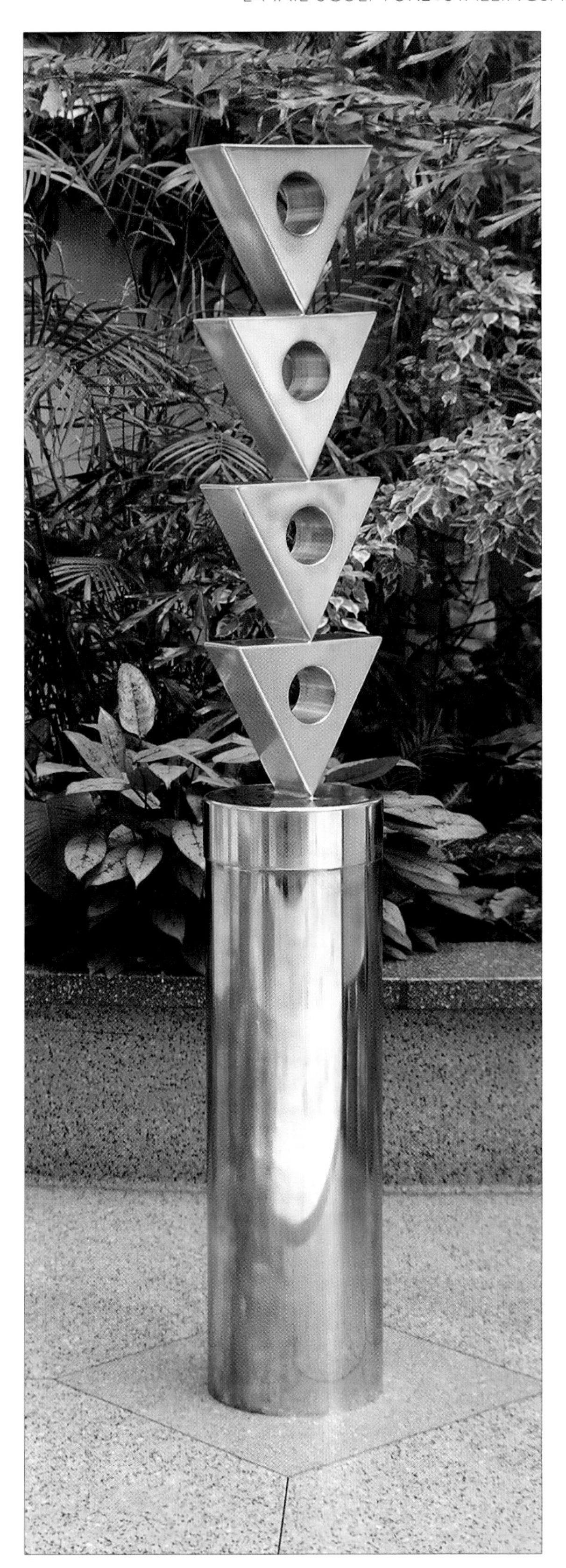

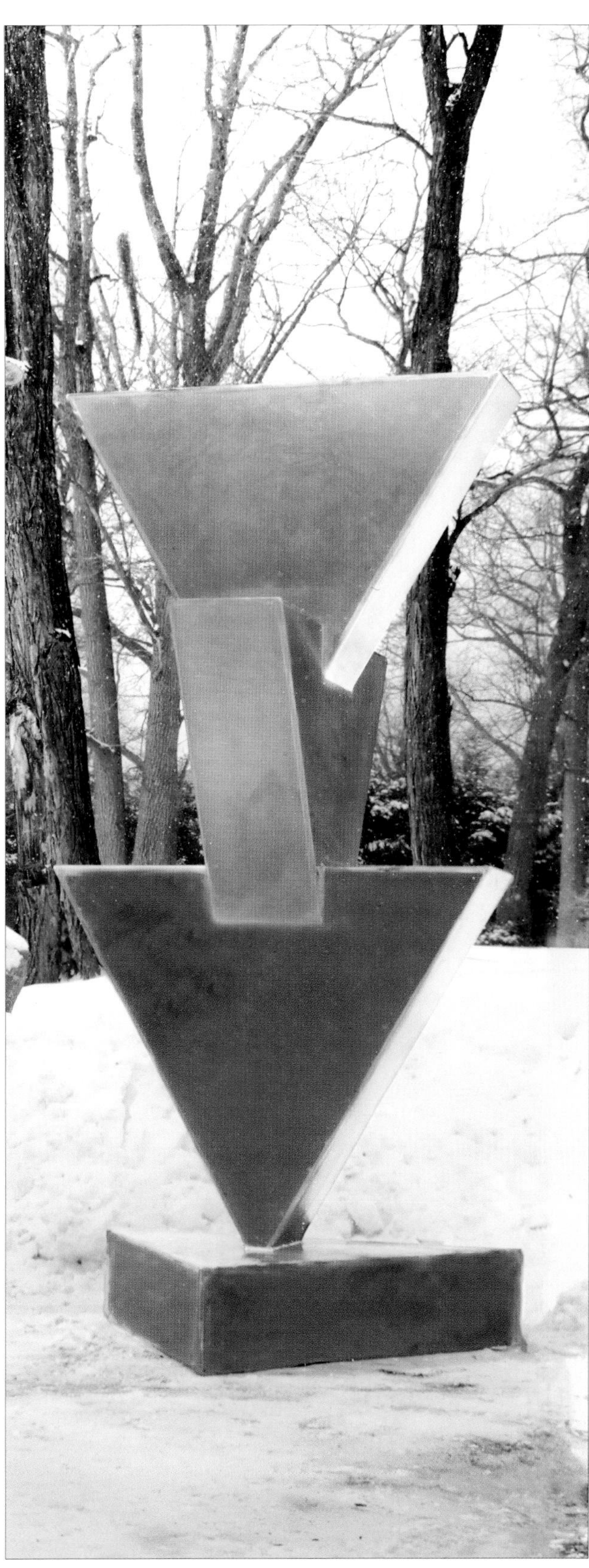

Left: *Quatri*, 2007, hand-polished aluminum, 7' × 12". Right: *Untitled*, 2006, YMCA, Johnstown, PA, corten steel, 11.5' × 4' × 4'. Photographs: J.T. Allen.

CHARLES STRAIN

7600 WEST CARR LANE ■ HARRISBURG, MO 65256 ■ TEL 573-874-3174 ■ TEL 573-268-1173
E-MAIL CSTRAIN@HOWARDELECTRICWB.COM ■ WWW.CHARLESSTRAIN.COM

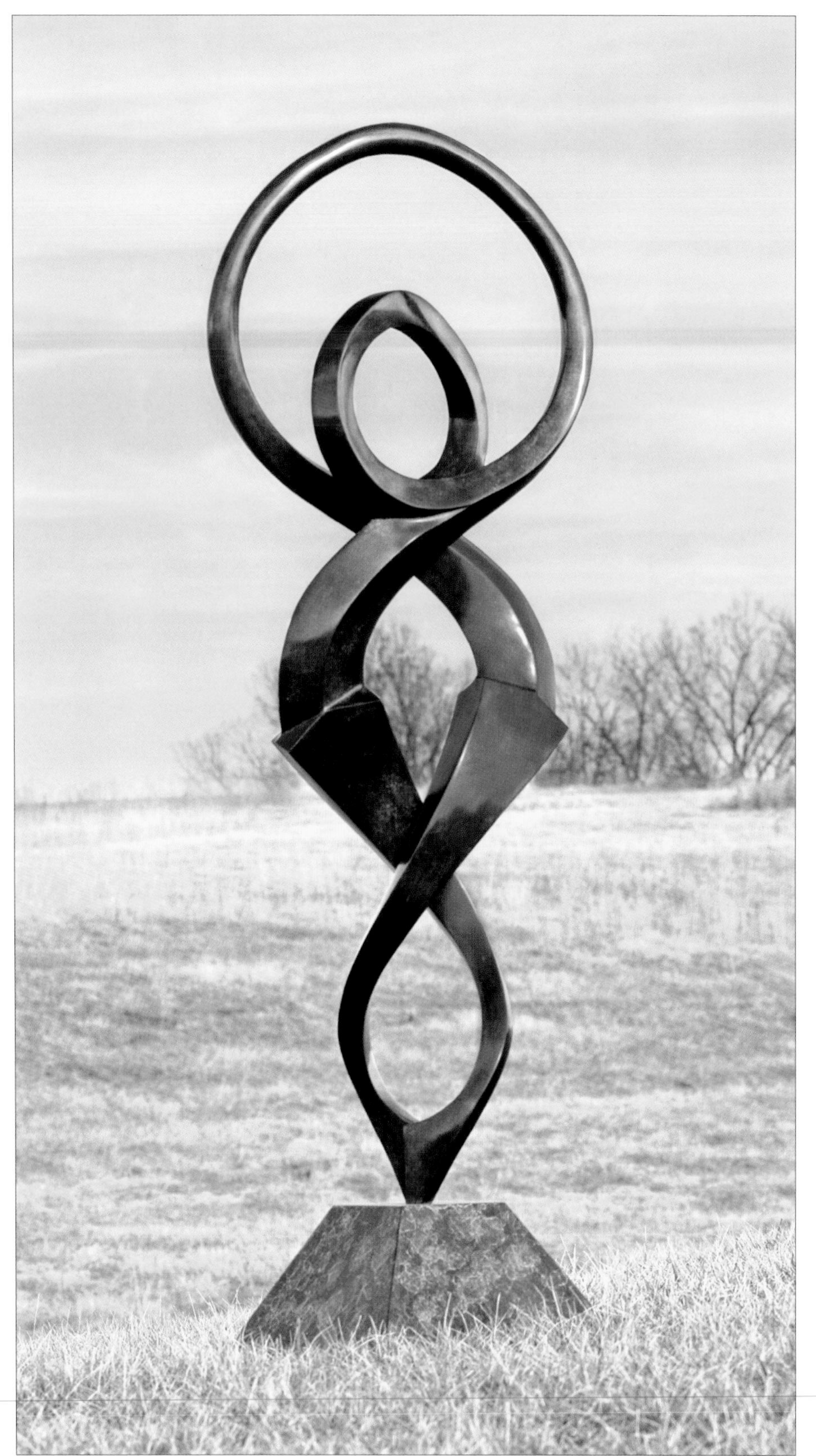

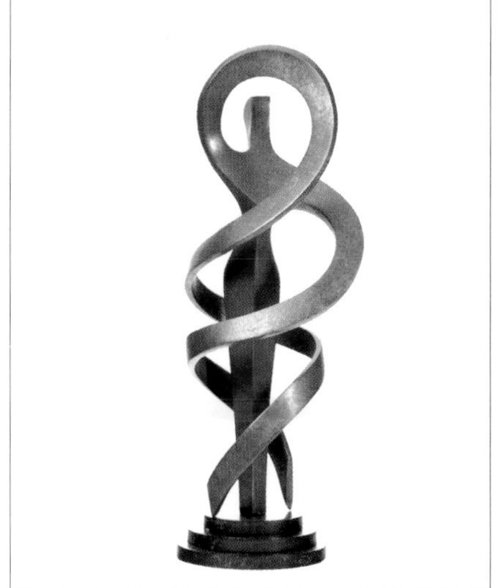

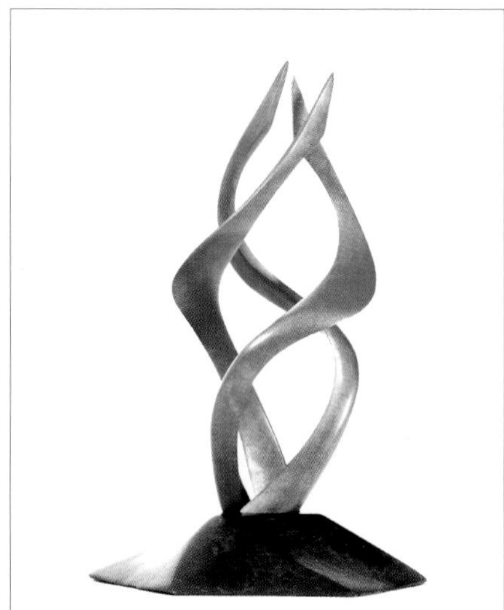

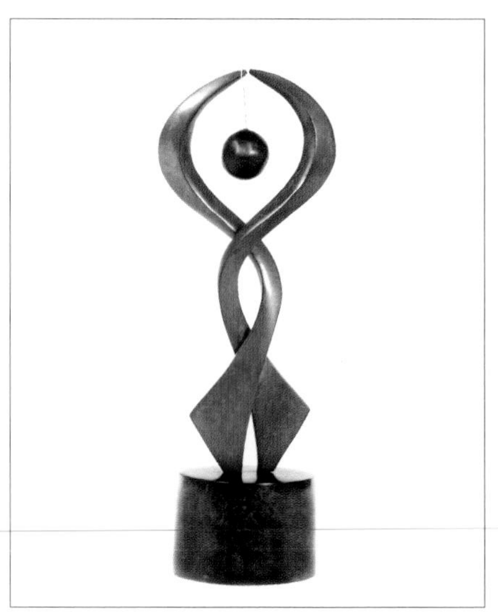

Left: *Duo,* 2004, bronze, 72" x 36". Top right: *Visionary,* 2006, bronze, 36" x 15".
Center right: *Flames,* 2006, bronze, 12" x 7". Bottom right: *Model,* 2007, bronze, 36" x 21". Photographs: Sheri Bryan.

AARON P. VAN DE KERCKHOVE

AARON P. VAN DE KERCKHOVE DESIGN ■ 2-3905 EAST CLIFF DRIVE ■ SANTA CRUZ, CA 95062
TEL 831-345-1404 ■ FAX 831-475-3471 ■ E-MAIL AARONSWORK@HOTMAIL.COM ■ WWW.APVSCULPTURE.COM

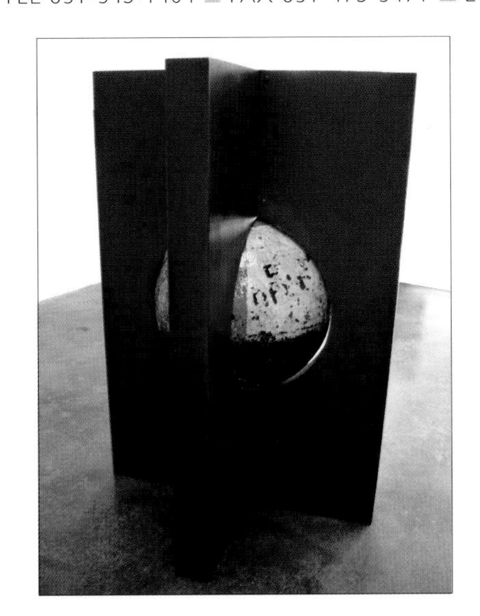

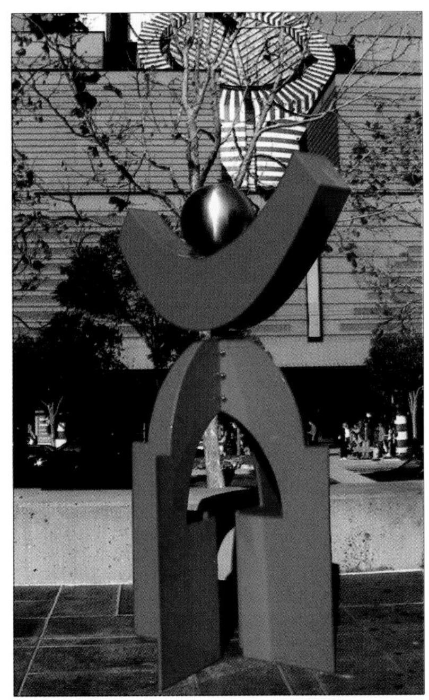

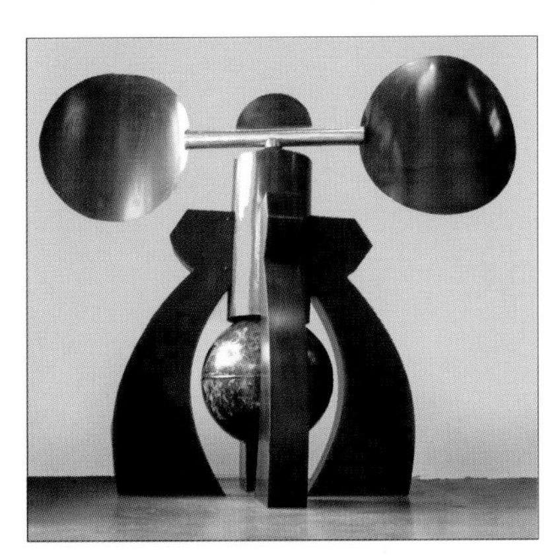

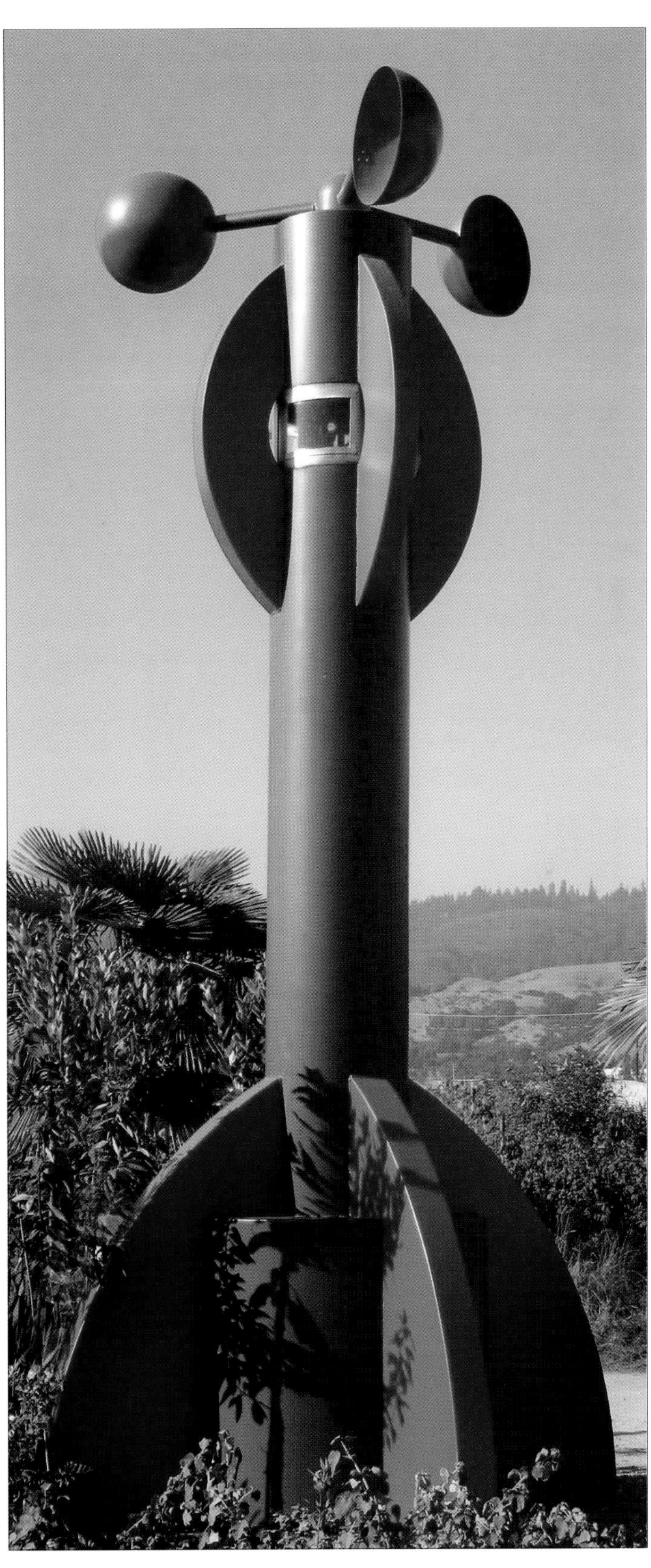

Top left: *Milestone,* 2004, spinning bouy and Cor-ten® steel, 6'H x 4'. Right: *Lighthouse,* 2005, steel, aluminum, stainless steel, glass, and electronics, 20'H x 9', produces electricity to light red beacon. Center left: *Red Pagoda,* 2003, private collection, photographed at *Red Umbrellas* exhibition, San Francisco, CA, kinetic sculpture, powder-coated steel, stainless steel bearings. Bottom left: *The Kraken,* private collection, kinetic sculpture, Cor-ten®, bouy, stainless steel, and bearings.

EDWIN C. WHITE

EDWIN WHITE DESIGNS ■ 90 KIRKMAN FORD ROAD ■ SILER CITY, NC 27344
TEL/FAX 919-742-6154 ■ E-MAIL EWDESIGNS@CENTERNET.NET ■ WWW.EDWINWHITEDESIGNS.COM

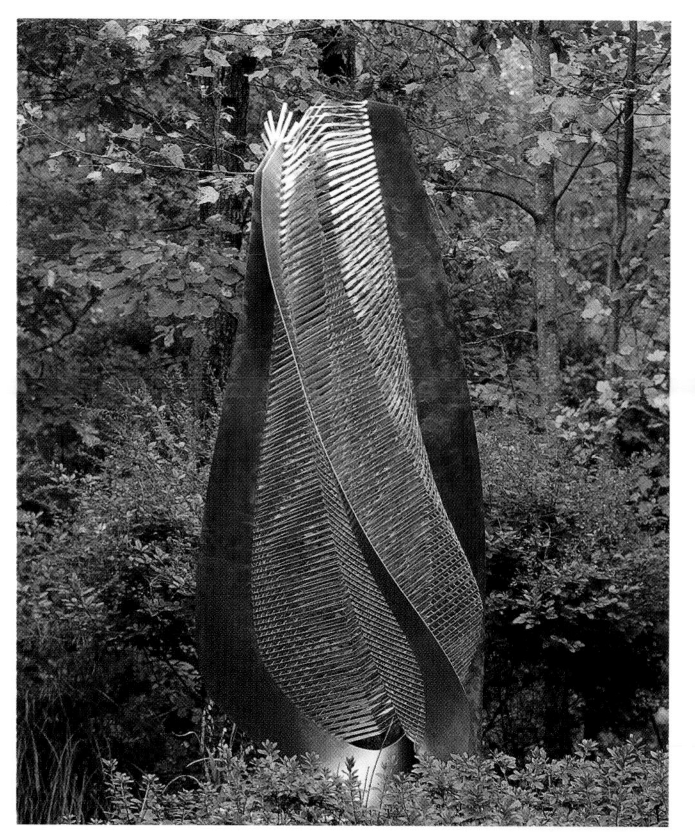

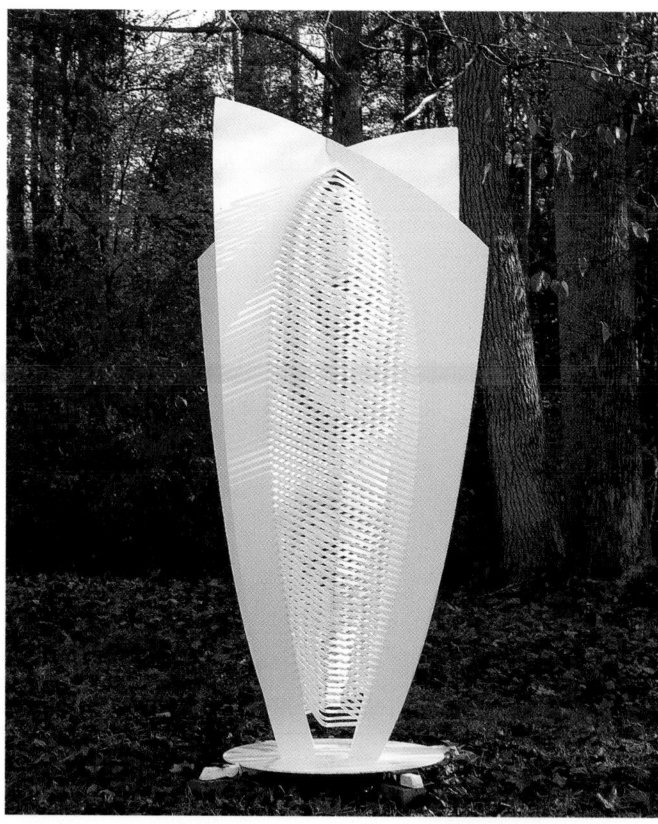

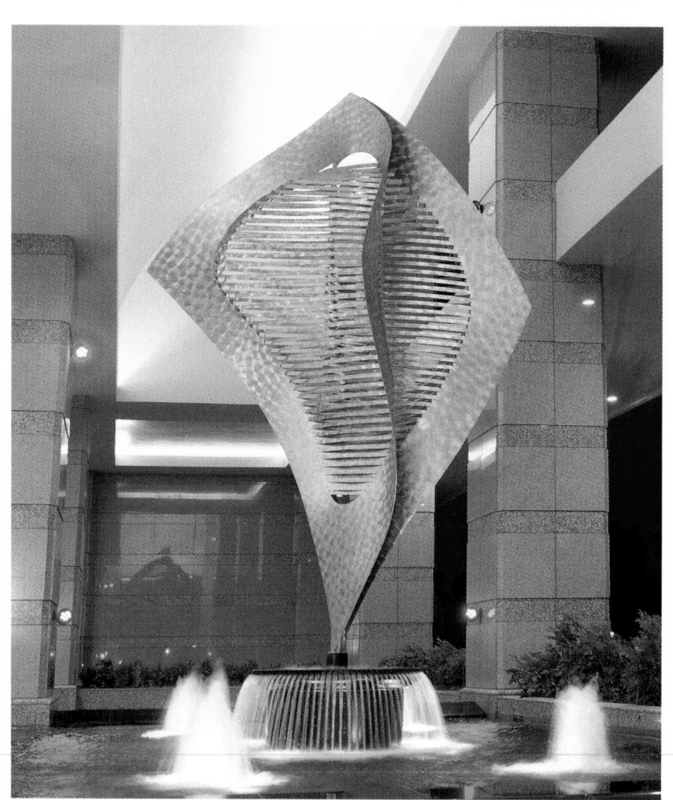

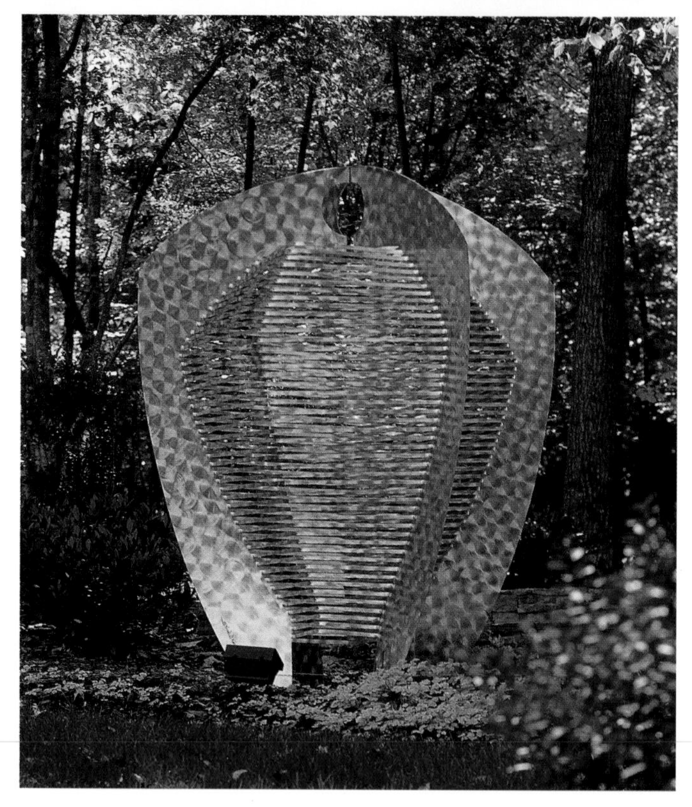

Top left: *Sterling's Grasp*, private residence, Chapel Hill, NC, stainless steel, 8.6'. Photograph: Seth Tice-Lewis. Top right: *Madison Hatches*, residence of Philip and Rhonda Szostak, Chapel Hill, NC, painted steel, 8.6'. Photograph: Seth Tice-Lewis. Bottom left: *Mengembang*, 2004, Hilton Hotel, Kuala Lumpur, Malaysia, titanium, 17' x 9.5' x 10'. Photograph: Dennis Kok. Bottom right: *Tribute*, private residence, Chapel Hill, NC, stainless steel, 7.6'. Photograph: Seth Tice-Lewis.

C.T. WHITEHOUSE

LIGHTHORSE STUDIOS ■ W61 N766 RIVEREDGE DRIVE ■ CEDARBURG, WI 53012
TEL/FAX 262-375-4834 ■ E-MAIL CTBRONZE@SBCGLOBAL.NET

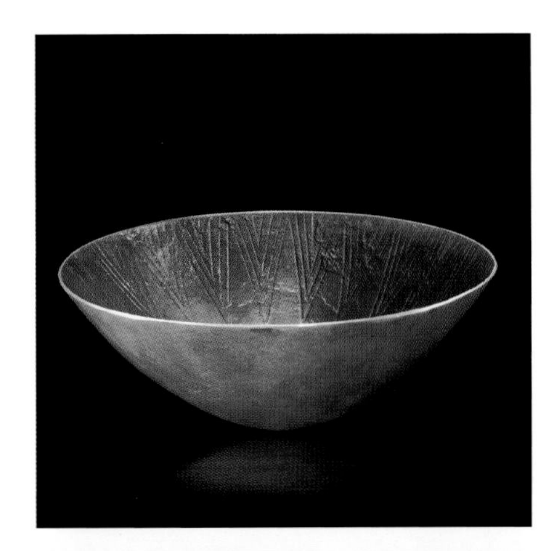

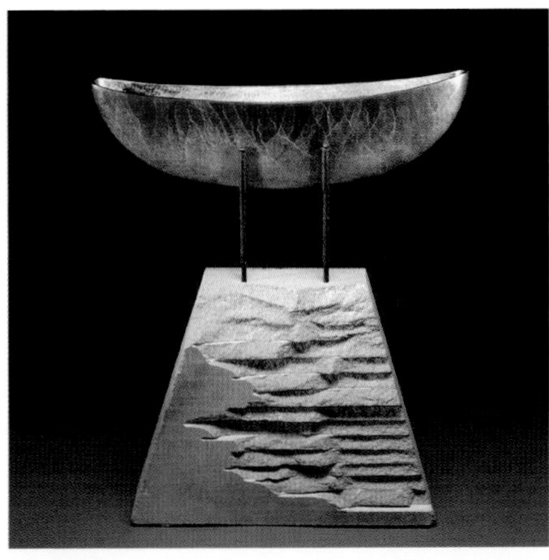

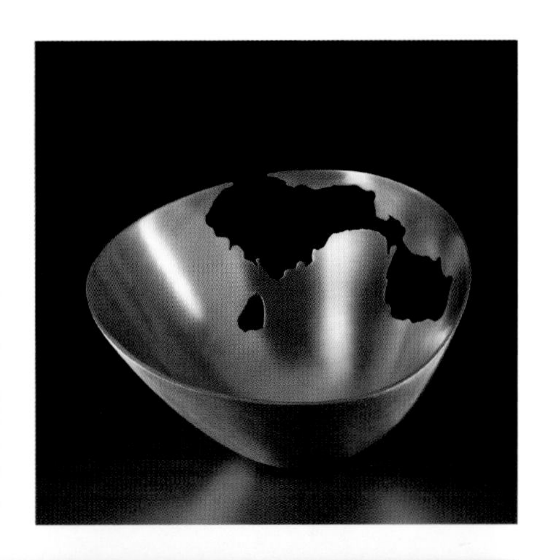

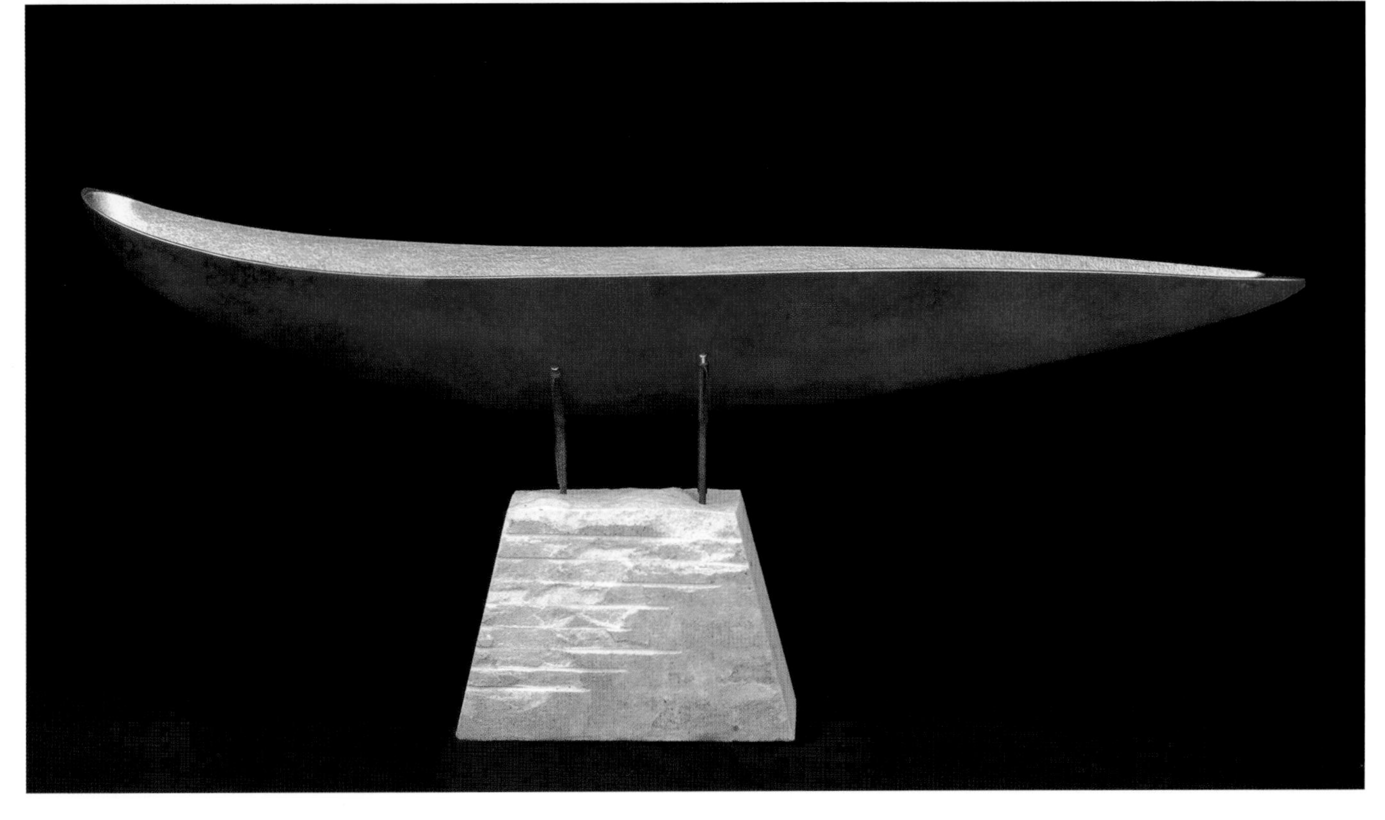

Top left: *Azteca*, bronze with patina, 5"H x 10"Dia. Top center: *Narrowed Form*, bronze, 18"H x 18"W x 3.5"D.
Top right: *Crucible*, bronze with patina, 12"Dia. Bottom: *Source*, bronze with patina, 18"H x 47"W x 5"D. Photographs: Chris Witzke.

JEAN WOLFF

1625 17TH STREET 4A ■ SANTA MONICA, CA 90404 ■ TEL 310-450-5831
FAX 310-446-1832 ■ E-MAIL SCULPTJEAN@AOL.COM ■ WWW.SCULPTJEAN.COM

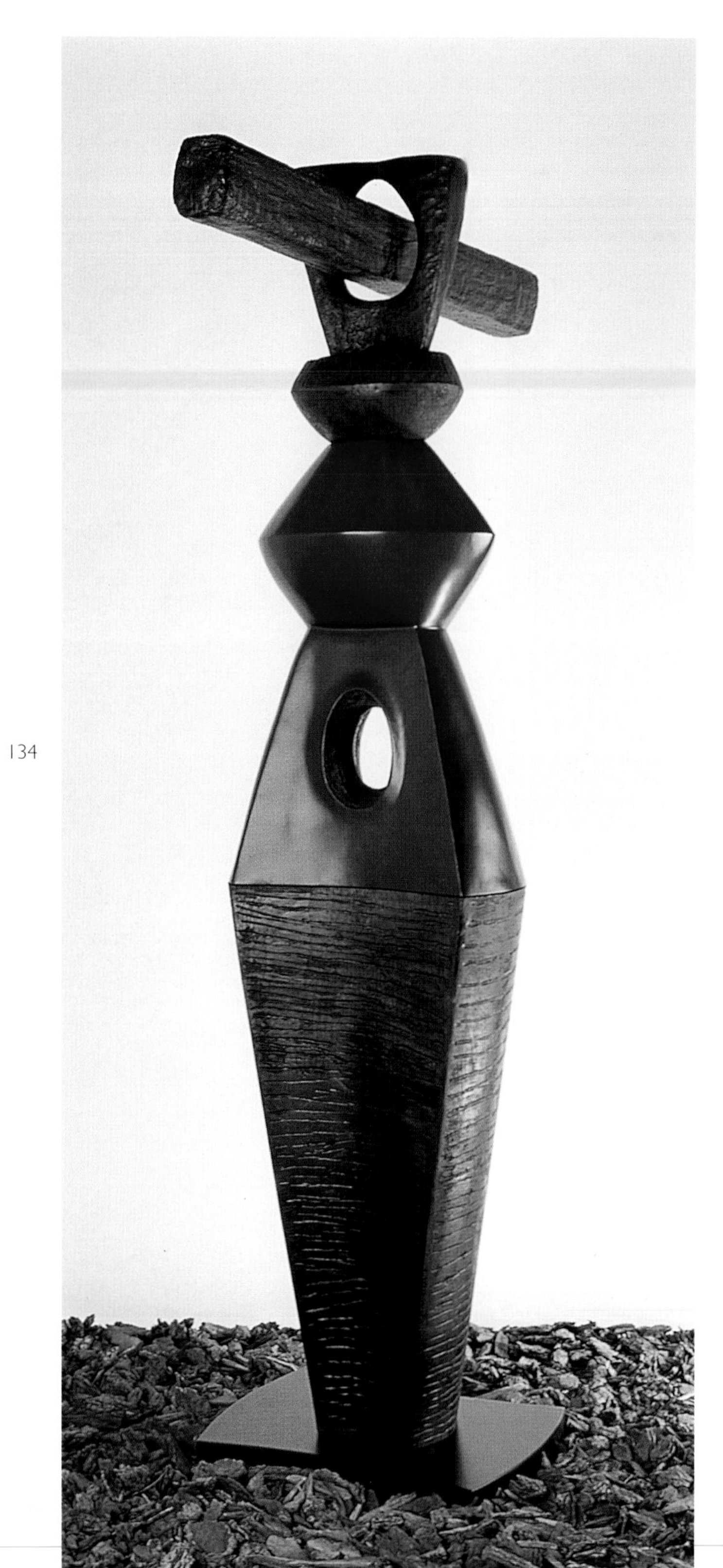

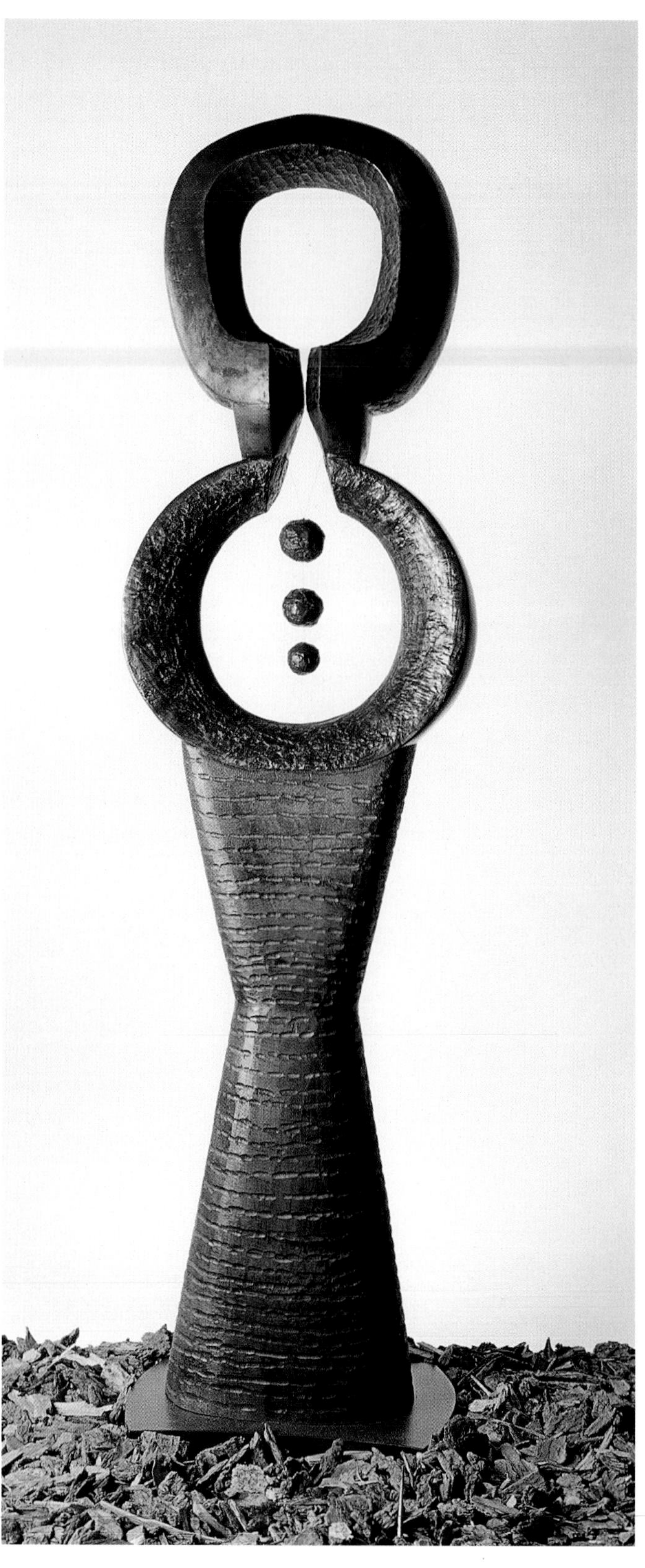

Left: *Espace Communication*, 2002, wood, bronze, and mixed media, 69" x 16.5" x 35".
Right: *Les Changements de la Vie*, 2003, wood, bronze, and mixed media, 70" x 18" x 14". Photographs: Roger Marshutz.

JEAN WOLFF

1625 17TH STREET 4A ■ SANTA MONICA, CA 90404 ■ TEL 310-450-5831
FAX 310-446-1832 ■ E-MAIL SCULPTJEAN@AOL.COM ■ WWW.SCULPTJEAN.COM

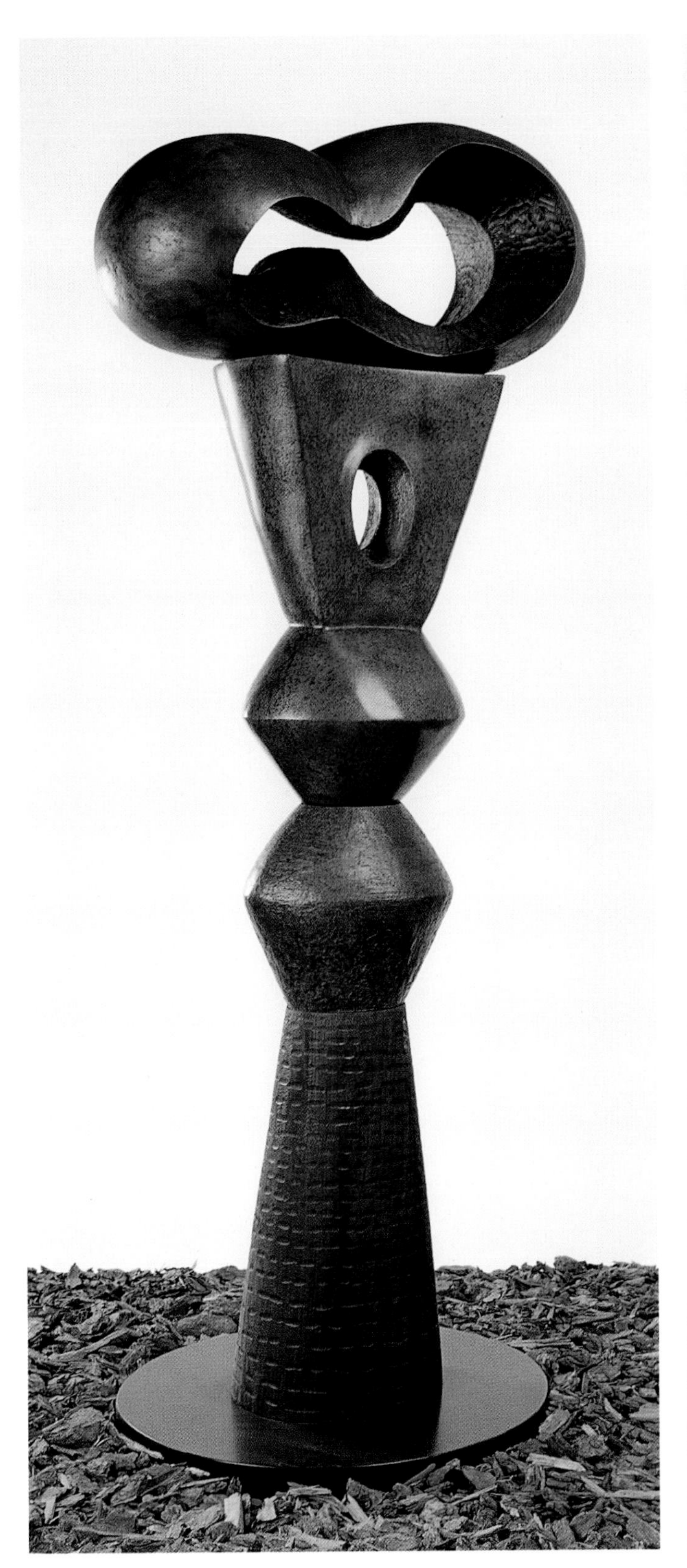

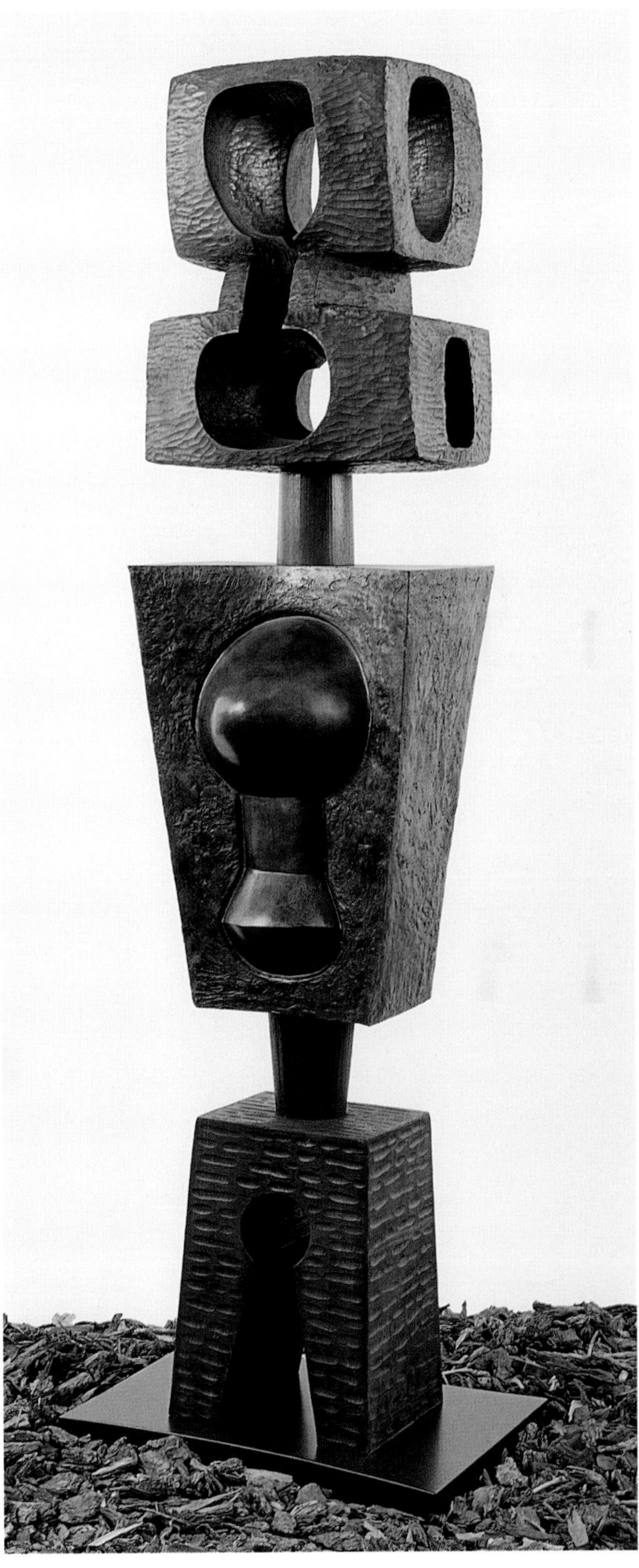

Left: *Totem de Infinite*, 2005, bronze and wood, 70" x 26.5" x 18".
Right: *Le Totem D'Emergence*, 2006, bronze and wood, 73" x 22" x 16.25". Photographs: Roger Marshutz.

A Commission Story

Markian Olynyk

TITLE
Vortex, 2005

COMMISSIONED FOR
The Attessa, private yacht

TIMELINE: 6 months

DIMENSIONS: 5'H x 5.5'Dia.

TRADE PROFESSIONAL
Nigel Walker, Nigel Walker & Associates

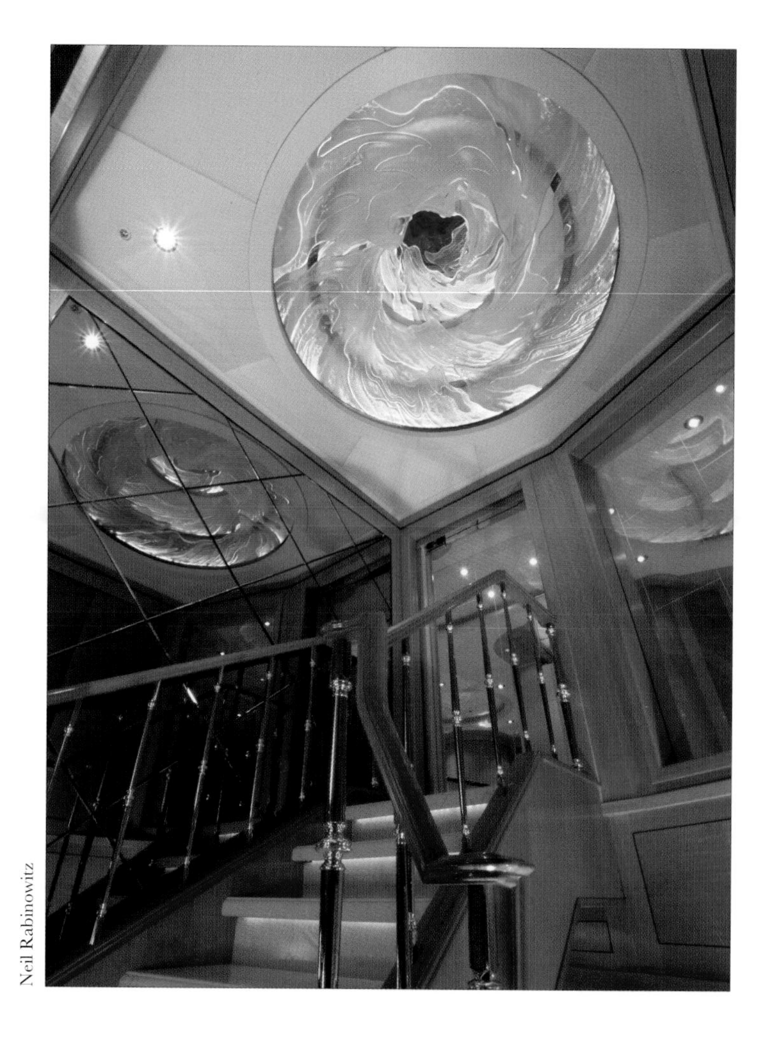

Neil Rabinowitz

When glass art virtuoso Markian Olynyk teamed up with interior designer Nigel Walker to conceive a sculptural piece for a 225-foot dream yacht, the result was nothing short of spectacular. *The Attessa* was undergoing a complete refit, which included an entirely new deck. The ship's main staircase, descending several levels, was capped by a cylindrical skylight that opened onto the upper deck, admitting an abundance of natural light. Taking advantage of the creative opportunity presented by this seven-foot light shaft, Walker and the client decided to commission a glass sculpture. ■ "The only glass artist I knew that could carry it off was Markian. He's not afraid to do different things in glass," Walker notes. The client and Walker settled on a vortex theme, inspired by whirlpools near Stuart Island, British Columbia, an area the client frequents. ■ Olynyk's painstakingly complex answer to the design challenge had a rare, ethereal beauty. Composed of six layers of limpid blue three-quarters-inch glass, the sculpture is carved, etched, shaped, textured, and tempered. "Each five-and-a-half-foot diameter glass circle is chopped into three huge chunks in that swirling vortex design," Olynyk explains. "They don't quite touch each other but are open in the middle, like a camera aperture." Moreover, the circles are offset, adding to the swirling appearance. ■ Olynyk describes the work's intense hue: "The blue is the natural color of the glass. Because the glass is so thick, there's more color—and the multiple layers add to the saturation." Each ring of glass is set into a stainless steel frame and edge-lit with LED lighting. These lights, along with the natural light that filters down through the top, give the sculpture the appearance of glowing with hypnotic intensity when viewed from either above or below. ■ Olynyk is pleased. "We wanted it to be mysterious," he admits. Nigel Walker raves, "It's just a fabulous piece. It exceeded what we had anticipated it would look like. The owner is thrilled with it."

RICHARD YASKI

6024 ALBION LITTLE RIVER ROAD ■ LITTLE RIVER, CA 95456 ■ TEL 707-937-0075
FAX 707-937-2999 ■ E-MAIL RYASKI@JUNO.COM ■ WWW.YASKI.COM

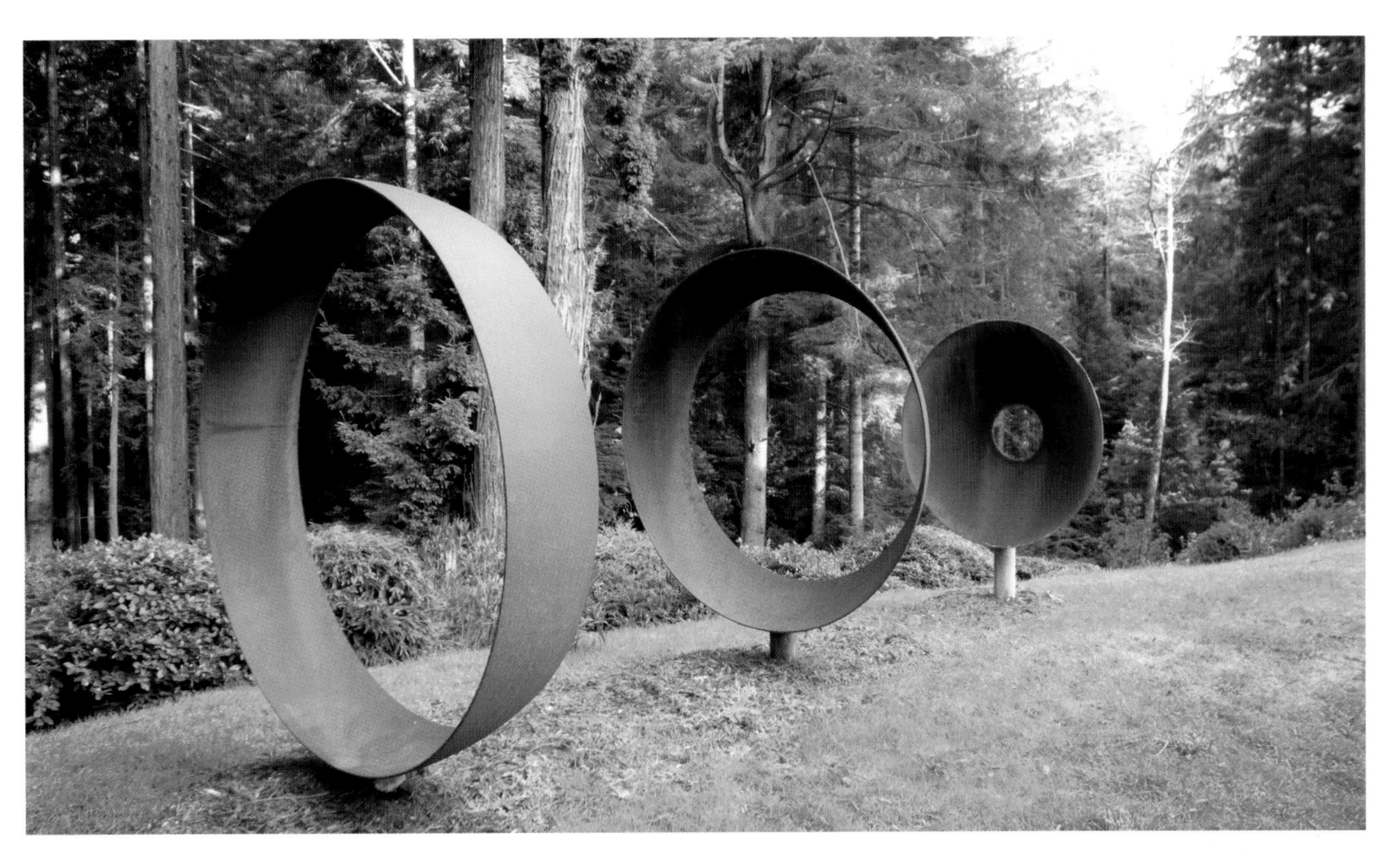

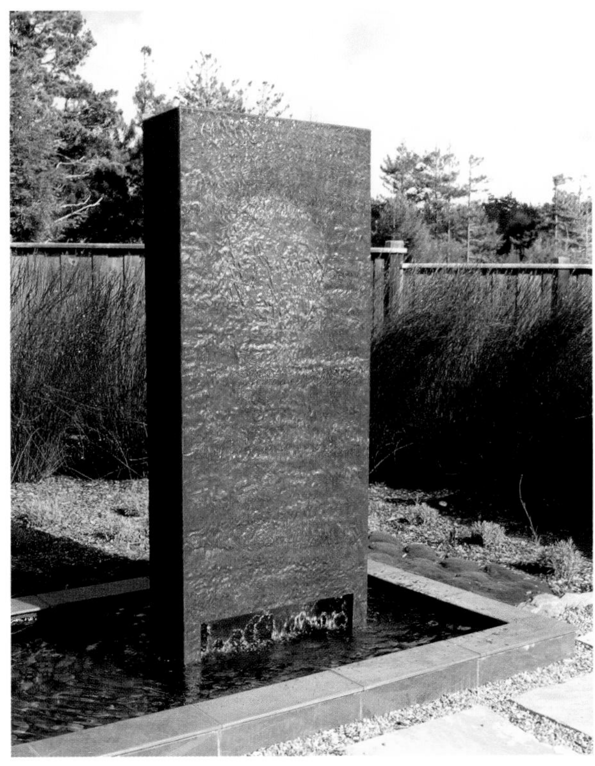

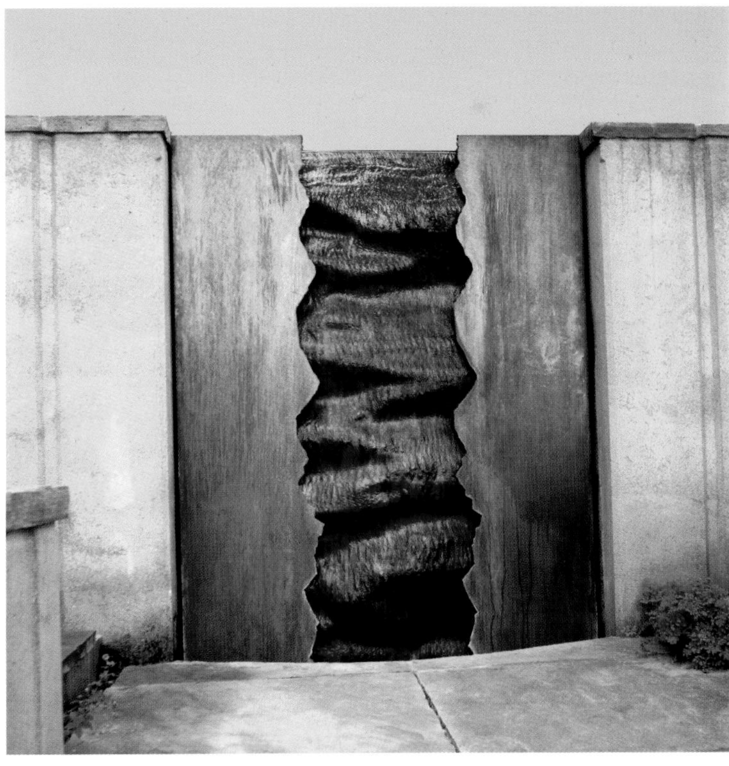

Top: *Concentric Sphere*, Shibui Sculpture Garden, Little River, CA, welded steel and bronze, 20'L x 8'Dia. Bottom left: *Primordial Monolith*, water sculpture, private residence, Mendocino, CA, welded and reticulated copper, 8'H x 3'W x 1'D. Bottom right: *Opened Earth*, water sculpture, private residence, Mendocino, CA, welded and reticulated copper, cast bronze and stainless steel, built into rammed earth wall, 8'H x 5'W x 1'D.

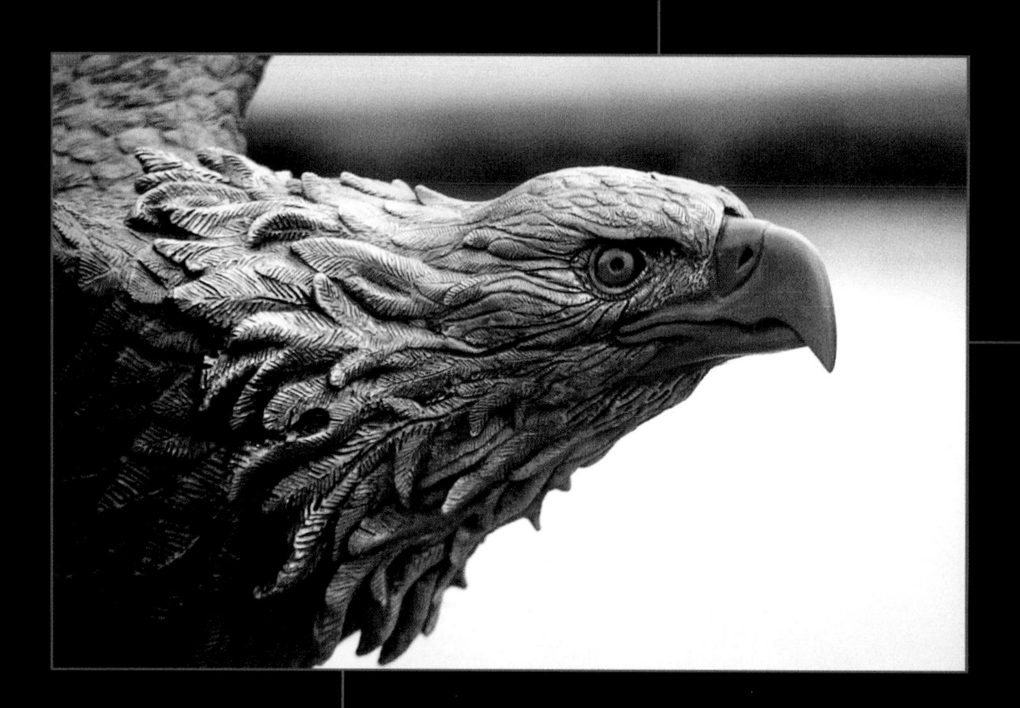

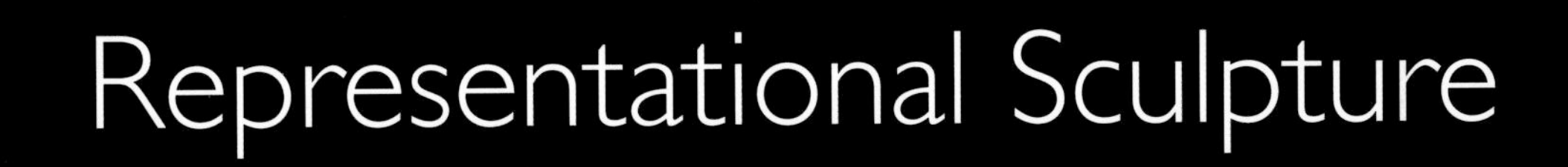

Representational Sculpture

ROBIN ANTAR

ANTAR STUDIOS INC. ■ 1485 EAST FIFTH STREET ■ BROOKLYN, NY 11230
TEL/FAX 718-375-5156 ■ E-MAIL INFO@RANTAR.COM ■ WWW.RANTAR.COM

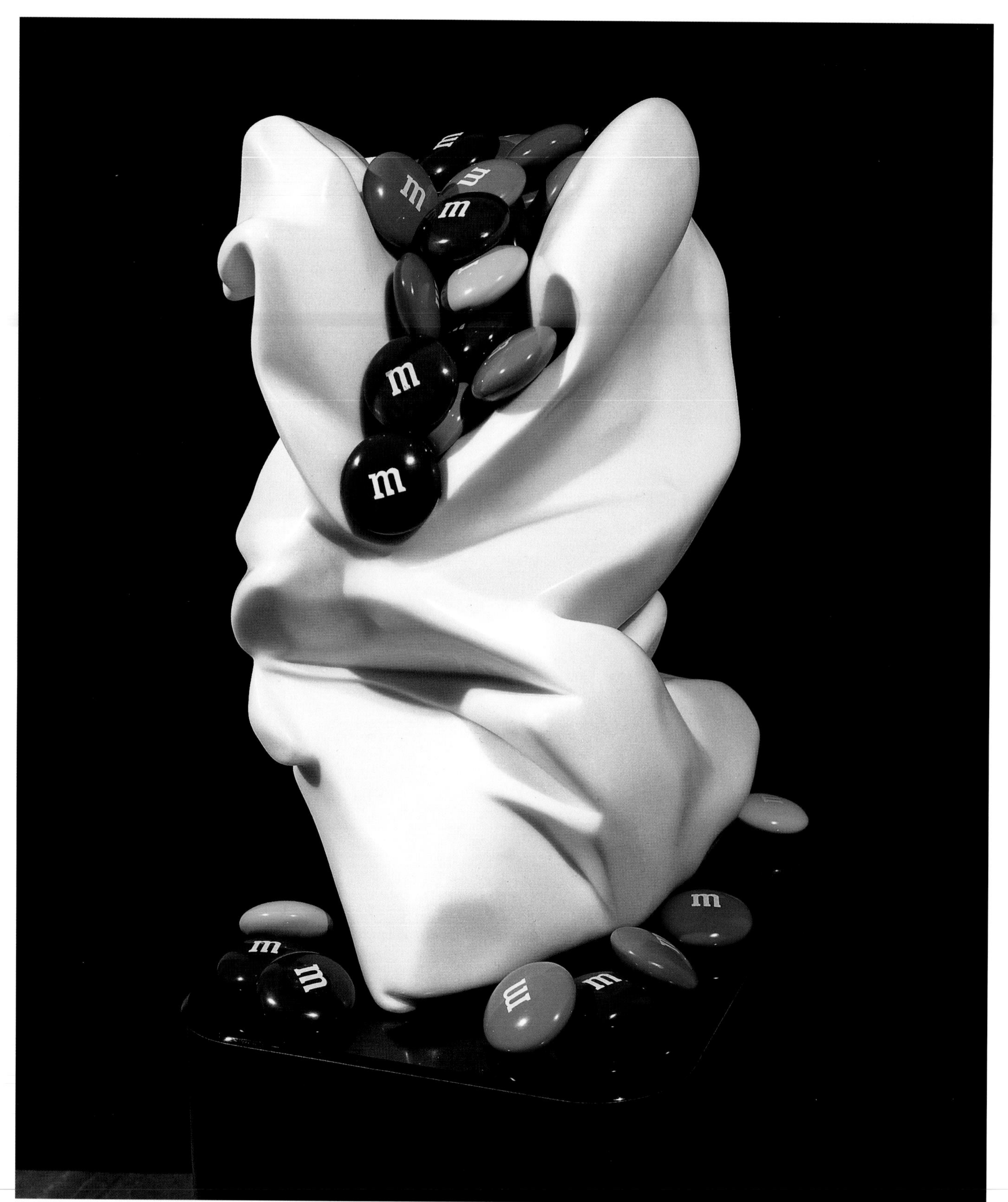

M & M Bag, carved marble and cast resin. Photograph: Edward Petterson Jr.

RENATE MARGIT BURGYAN

CHRYSALIS SCULPTURE STUDIO ■ 72 OVERBROOK DRIVE ■ COLUMBUS, OH 43214
TEL 614-832-6444 ■ E-MAIL RBURGYAN798@EARTHLINK.NET ■ WWW.CHRYSALISSCULPTURESTUDIO.COM

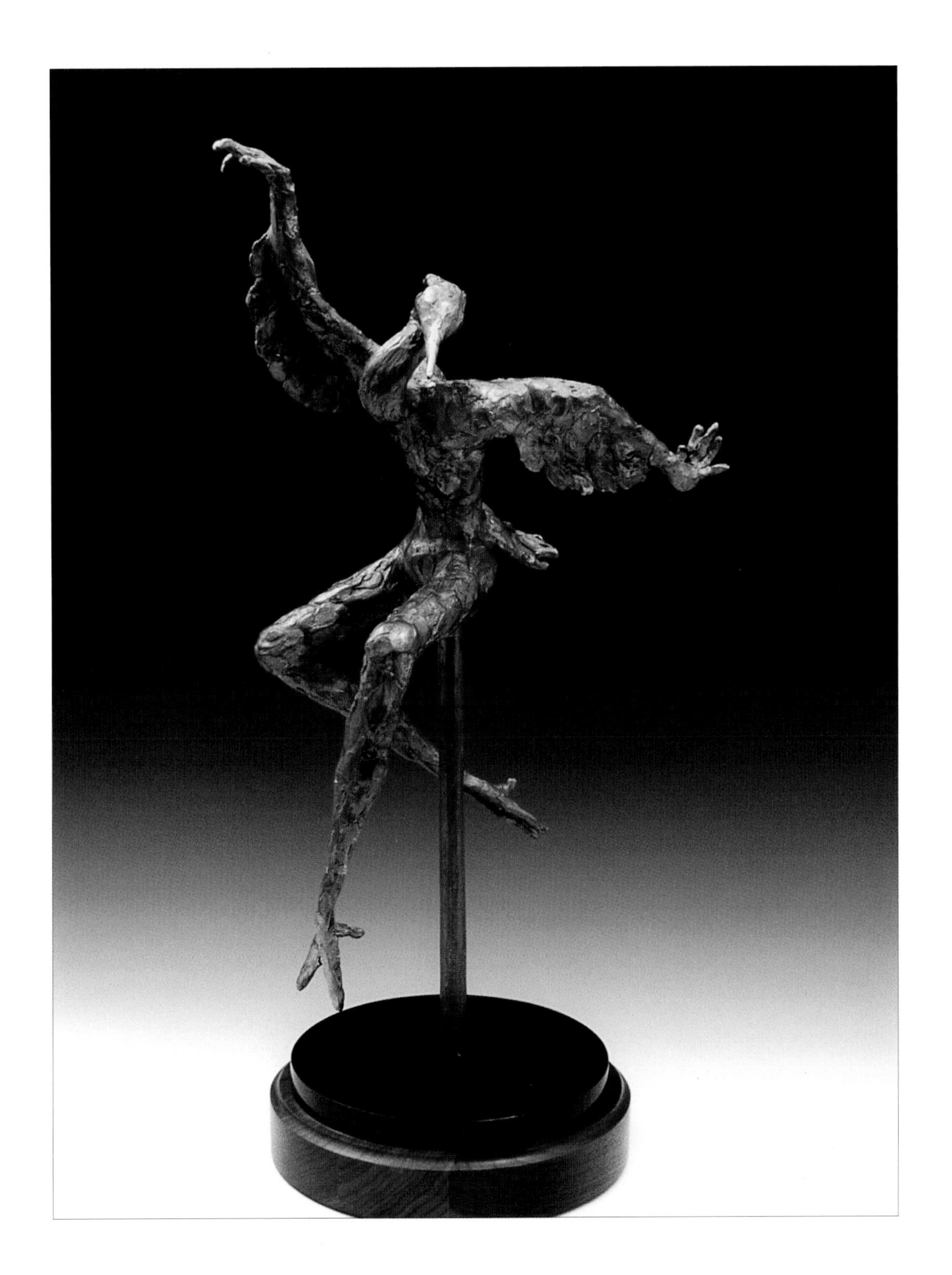

Blue Heron, 2005, bronze, 25"H x 15"W x 9"D. Photograph: Trucolor Photography Studio.

A Commission Story

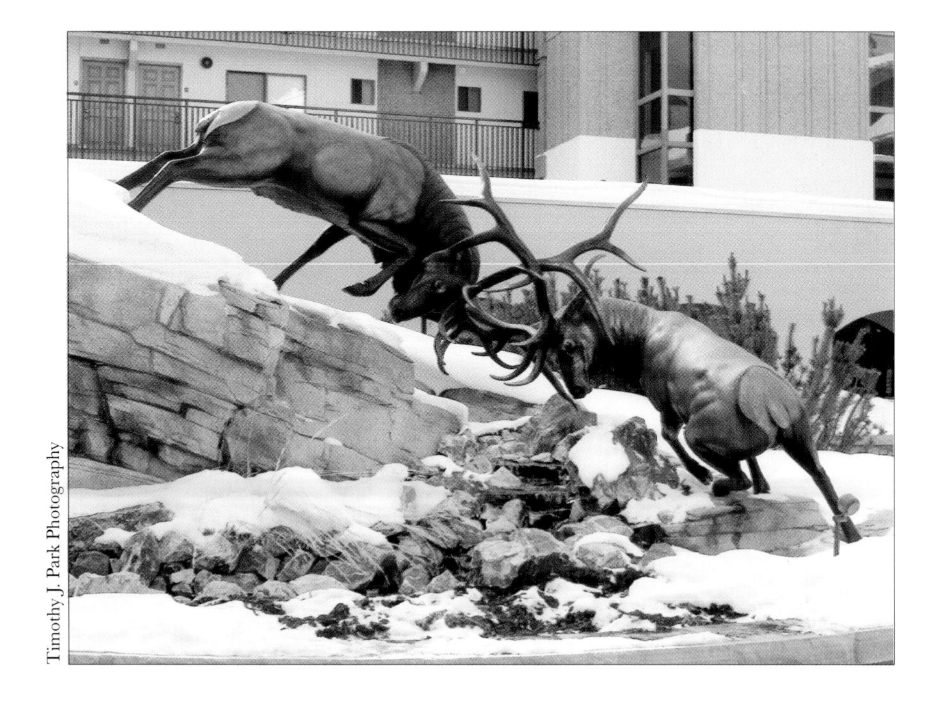

Timothy J. Park Photography

Rip Caswell

TITLE
The Battle, 2002

COMMISSIONED FOR
Antlers at Vail Condominiums
and Conference Center

TIMELINE: 1 year

DIMENSIONS: 7'H x 15'L x 4'D

TRADE PROFESSIONAL
Rob LeVine, General Manager,
Antlers at Vail Condominiums and
Conference Center

When Rob LeVine, general manager of Antlers at Vail, set eyes on the fiercely locked antlers of the two Rocky Mountain elk depicted in Rip Caswell's sculpture *The Battle,* he knew he had an answer. ■ The question had arisen during the $22 million redevelopment of the 1970s-era condominium-hotel complex, when the construction of a new underground parking garage had triggered a reevaluation of the courtyard. Vague concepts of a fountain had circulated between the architect and client, with no firm consensus on an appropriate centerpiece. ■ The enthusiastic LeVine persuaded the majority of his condo owners to take a chance on commissioning a large-scale version of Caswell's small maquette, which he had admired at the Pam Driscoll Gallery in Aspen. *The Battle* is one in a limited edition of nine monumental bronzes of stunningly realistic detail. "The two bull elk are fighting for dominance," Caswell explains. "It's very dramatic, with a lot of energy and action." ■ Installing the dynamic piece proved problematic, as the roof of the subterranean parking structure couldn't support the weight of the majestic pile of boulders planned for the sculpture's base. Instead, exhibit designers were called in to build simulated stones. ■ Once the muscular elk were positioned and welded into place, the fabricated landscape was built around them. Craftsmen interpreted the craggy hillside from Caswell's original. "I wanted to have clashing, angular lines of stone contribute to the movement and feeling in the piece," Caswell notes. Like an icy mountain stream, a fountain of water emerges from behind the upper elk, splitting into two cascading rivulets. ■ Located directly in front of the building's entrance, *The Battle* has become the signature of the complex, lending that certain, undeniable "wow" factor. The overall effect pleases Caswell, who confides, "I love incorporating bronzes in the natural habitat, whether it's purely natural landscaping or this more man-made type of setting." LeVine attests to the sculpture's success, "Hardly anyone comes in without mentioning it or admiring it. The response has been overwhelming."

BOBBIE K. CARLYLE

BOBBIE CARLYLE SCULPTURE ■ 1233 NORTH COUNTY ROAD 29 ■ LOVELAND, CO 80537 ■ TEL 970-622-0213
FAX 970-622-9904 ■ E-MAIL BOBBIECARLYLE@ATT.NET ■ WWW.BOBBIECARLYLESCULPTURE.COM

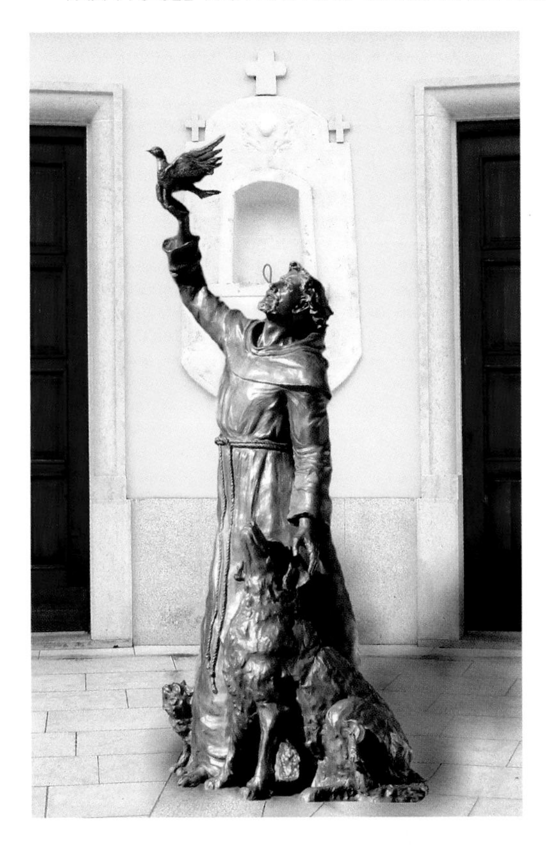

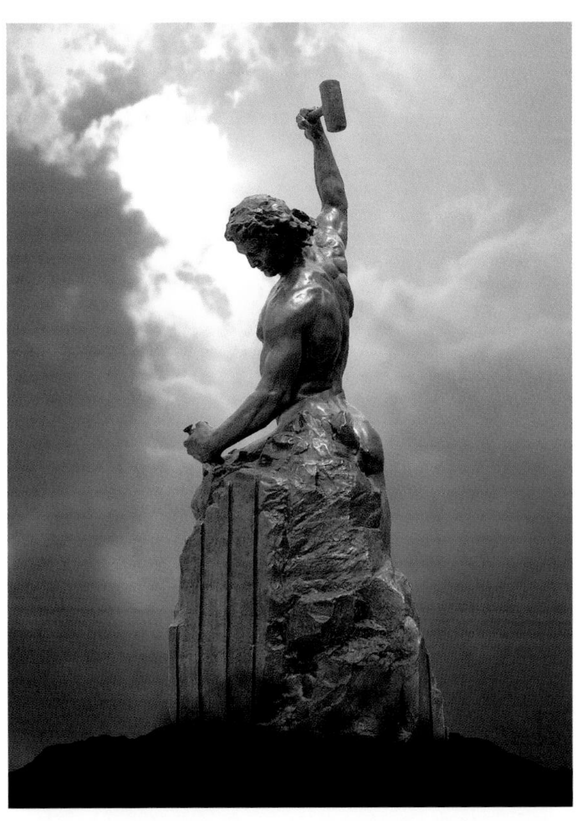

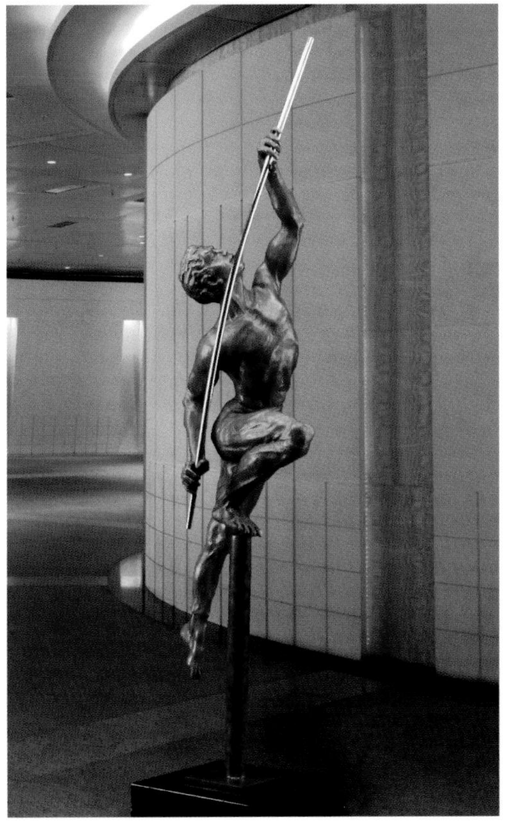

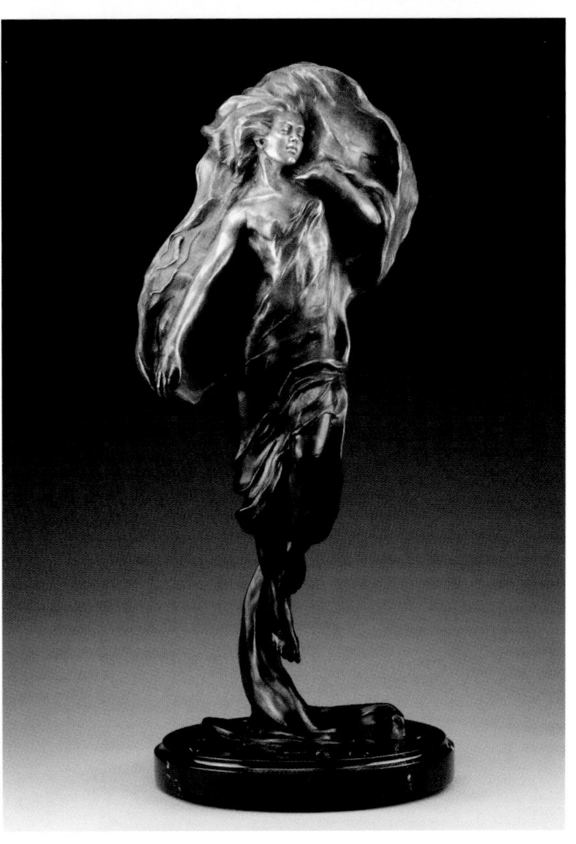

Top left: *St. Francis.* Top right: *Self-Made Man.*
Bottom left: *Endeavor.* Bottom right: *Twilight.*

RIP H. CASWELL

CASWELL GALLERY ■ 101 WEST COLUMBIA RIVER HIGHWAY ■ TROUTDALE, OR 97060
TEL 503-492-2473 ■ FAX 503-661-2946 ■ E-MAIL MAIL@CASWELLSCULPTURE.NET ■ WWW.RIPCASWELL.COM

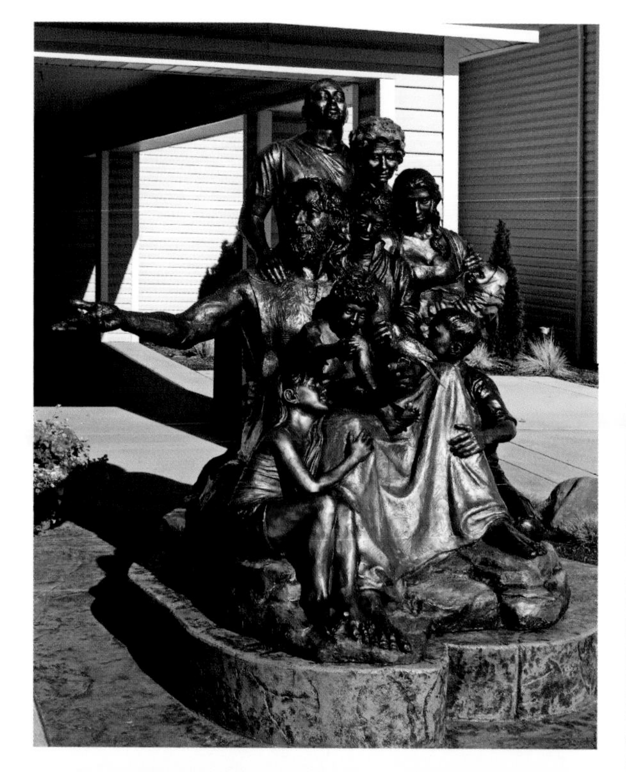

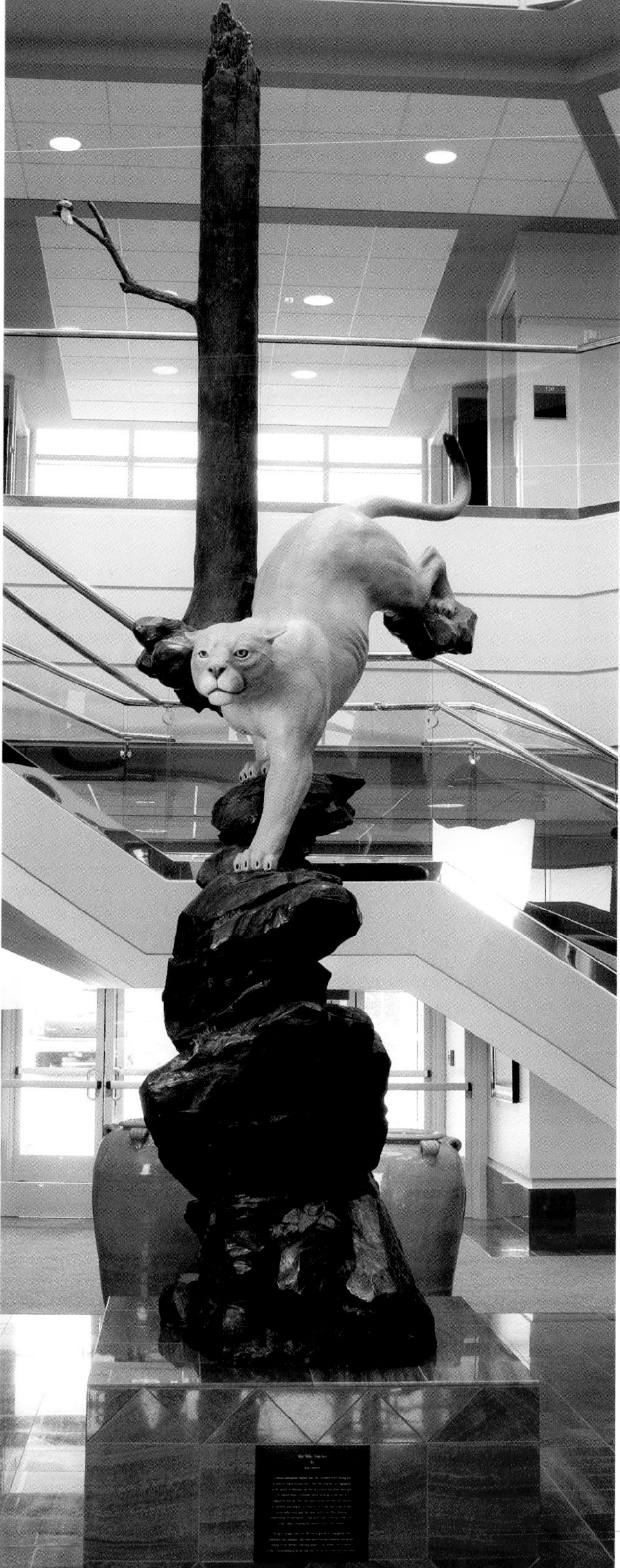

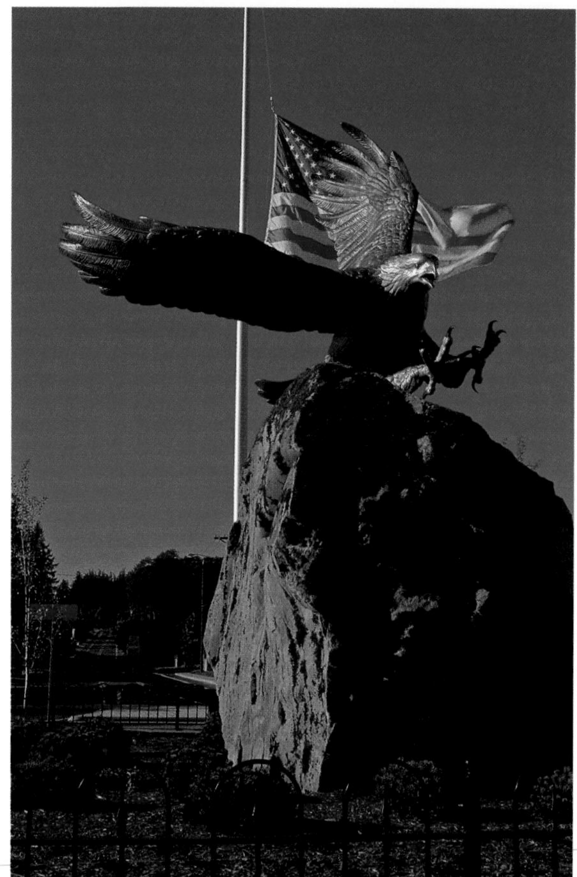

Top left: *Christ's Family*, 2006, Southlake Church, West Linn, OR, 8' monument. Right: *She Who Watches*, 2006, Park Plaza Tower, Vancouver, WA, 16' monument. Bottom left: *Guardian Spirit*, 2003, Eagle's Landing Development, Clackamas, OR, 14' monument. Photographs: Timothy J. Park.

RIP H. CASWELL

CASWELL GALLERY ■ 101 WEST COLUMBIA RIVER HIGHWAY ■ TROUTDALE, OR 97060
TEL 503-492-2473 ■ FAX 503-661-2946 ■ E-MAIL MAIL@CASWELLSCULPTURE.NET ■ WWW.RIPCASWELL.COM

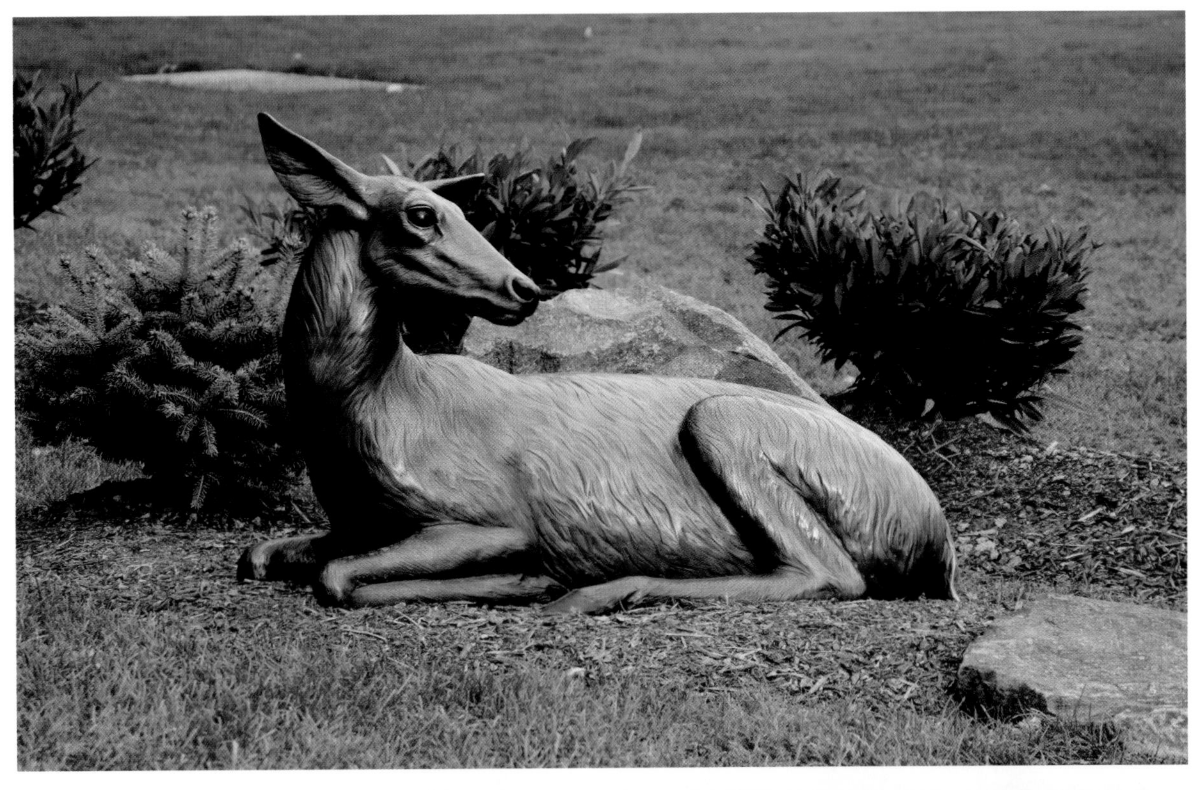

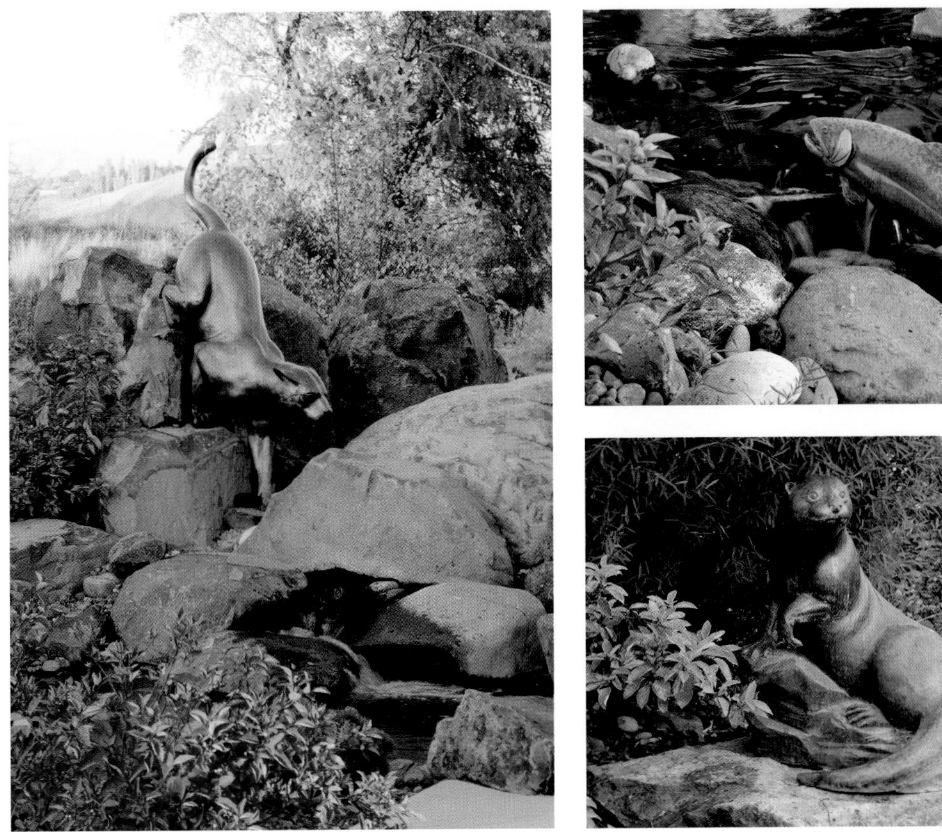

Top: *Essence of Grace,* 2003, private residence, Brush Prairie, WA, 25" x 34" x 15". Bottom left: *Cougar on the Rocks,* 2002, Hell's Gate State Park, Lewiston, ID, 79" x 32" x 18". Center right: *Upriver Challenge,* 2002, Hell's Gate State Park, Lewiston, ID. Bottom right: *Sense of Curiosity,* 2002, Hell's Gate State Park, Lewiston, ID, 38" x 18" x 18". Photographs: Timothy J. Park.

GESSO COCTEAU

45-565 WILLIAMS ROAD ■ INDIAN WELLS, CA 92210 ■ TEL 760-341-3988
TEL 760-702-5049 ■ E-MAIL GESSO@GESSOCOCTEAU.COM ■ WWW.GESSOCOCTEAU.COM

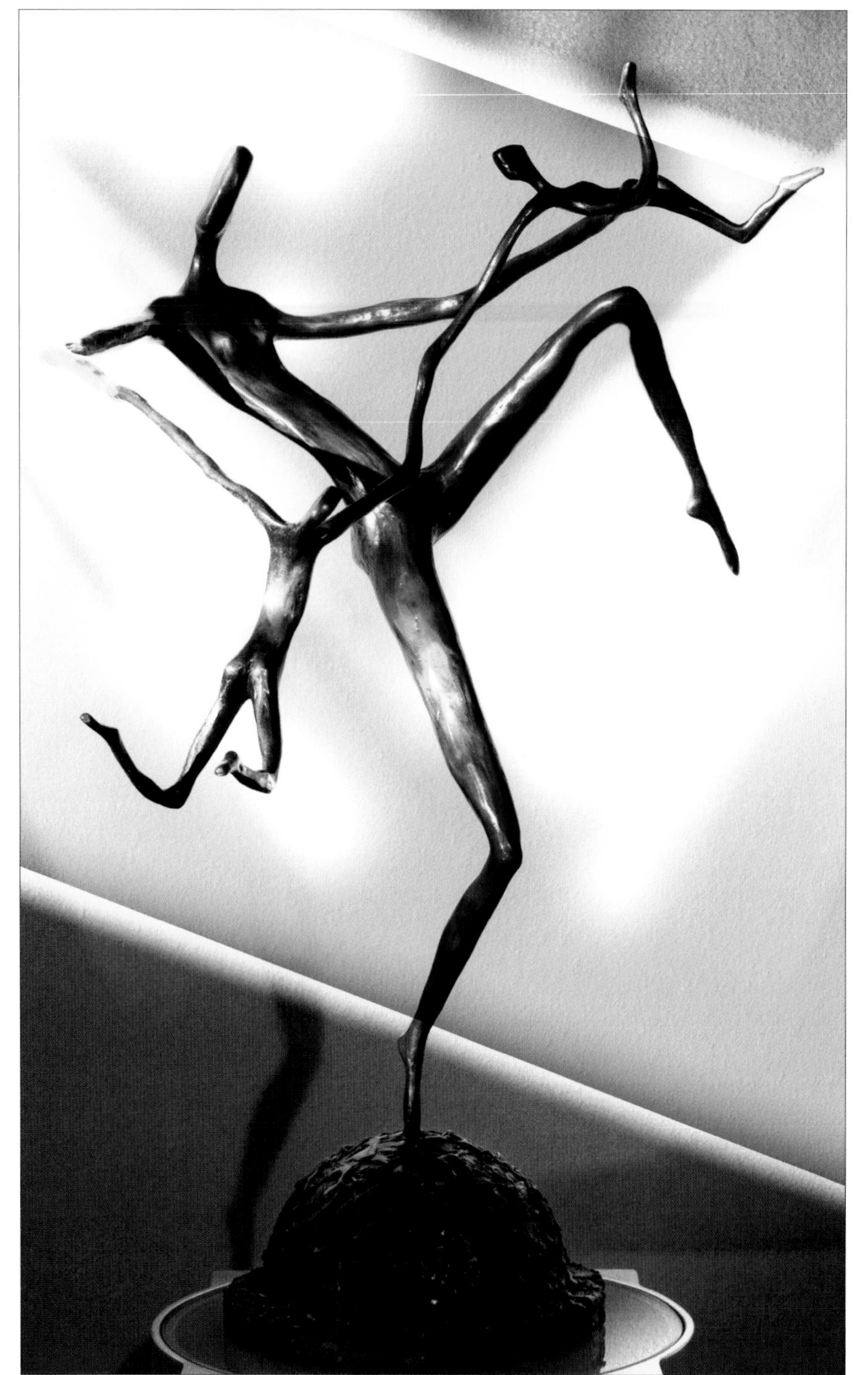

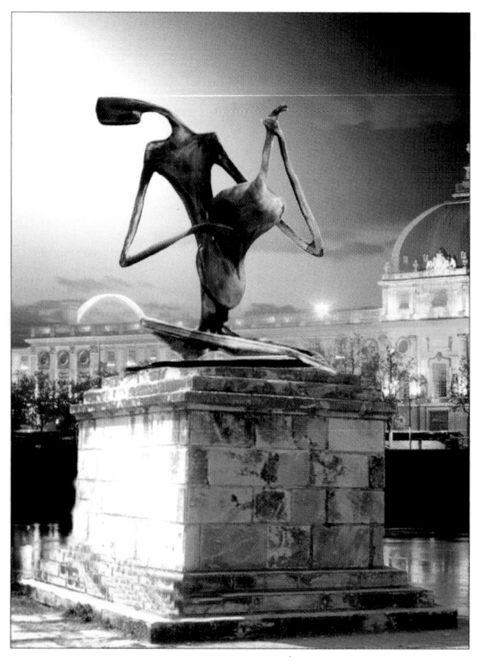

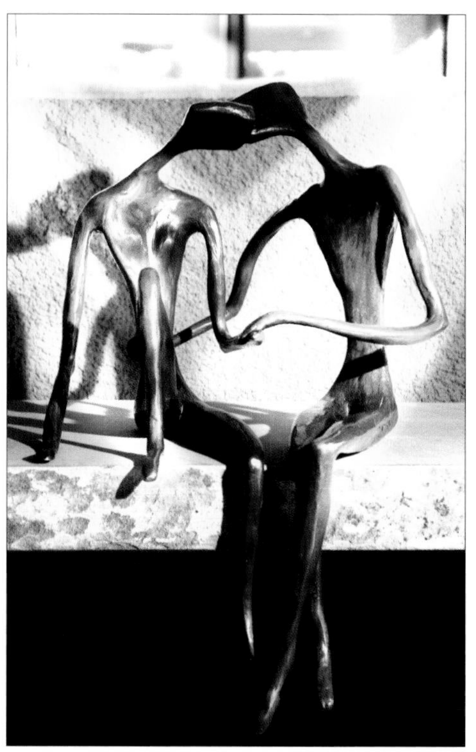

Left: *The Good Mother,* 2006, cast bronze, 34" x 22" x 22", edition of twenty-five. Top right: *Midnight Serenade,* 2007, cast bronze, 30" x 45" x 31", edition of eighteen. Bottom right: *My Beloved,* 2006, cast bronze, 13" x 15" x 9", edition of twenty-five.

GESSO COCTEAU

45-565 WILLIAMS ROAD ■ INDIAN WELLS, CA 92210 ■ TEL 760-341-3988
TEL 760-702-5049 ■ E-MAIL GESSO@GESSOCOCTEAU.COM ■ WWW.GESSOCOCTEAU.COM

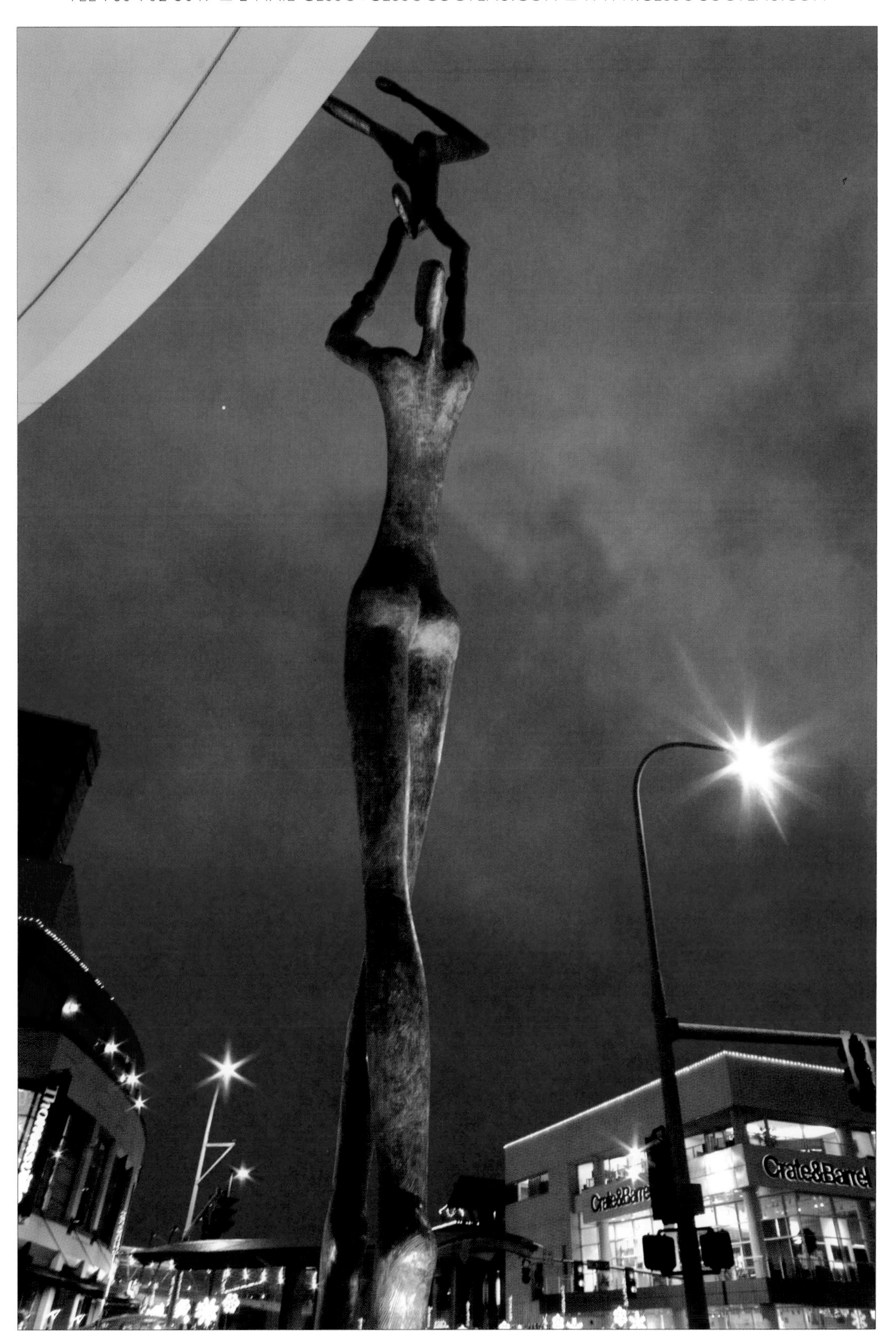

Endless Celebration, 2005, Bellevue, WA, one-of-a-kind cast bronze, 51' x 24' x 12'.

RANDY COOPER

COOPER CREATIONS, INC. ■ 130 QUINCY STREET NE ■ ALBUQUERQUE, NM 87108 ■ TEL 505-266-2781
TEL 505-463-9342 ■ FAX 505-266-5701 ■ E-MAIL RANDY@RANDYCOOPERART.COM ■ WWW.RANDYCOOPERART.COM

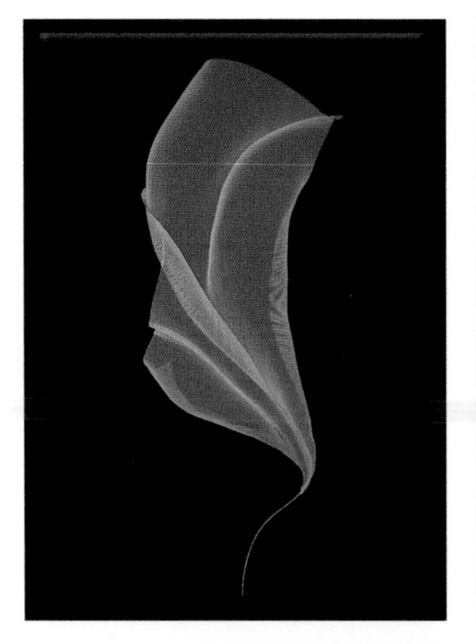

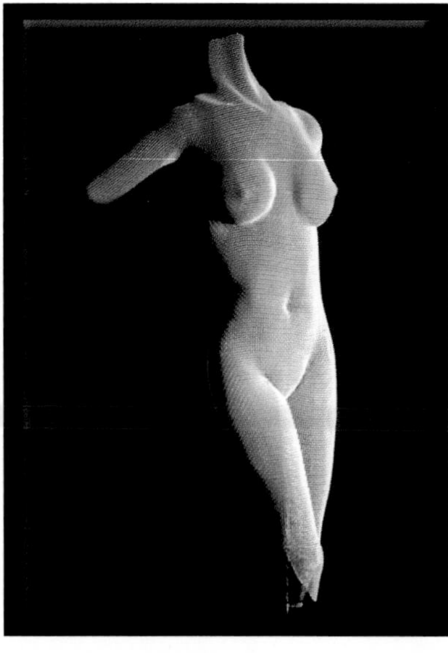

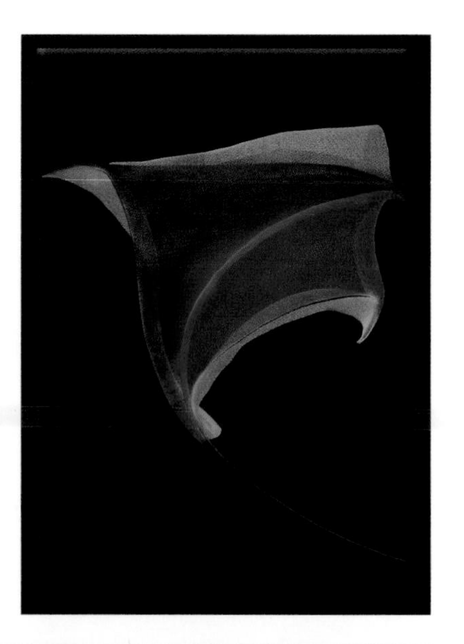

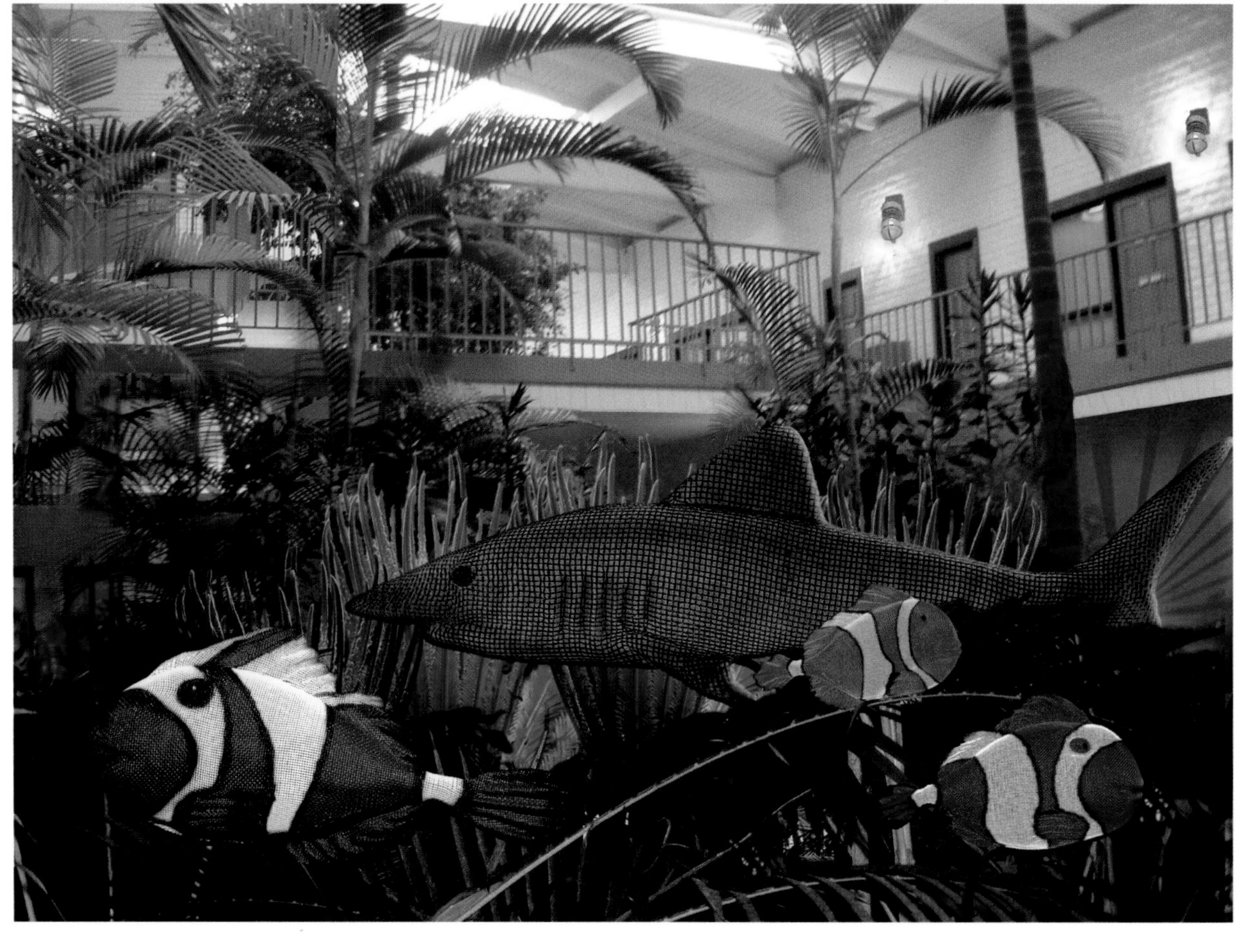

Top left: *Lily of the Vine,* 2005, steel wire mesh/powder coated, 48"H x 21"W x 10"D. Photograph: Tomar S. Flores. Top center: *Susan,* 2006, steel wire mesh/powder coated, 24"H x 16"W x 6"D. Photograph: Carol K. England. Top right: *Sailing,* 2005, steel wire mesh/powder coated, 25"H x 32"W x 5"D. Photograph: Tomar S. Flores. Bottom: *The Atrium,* 2006, steel wire mesh/powder coated, shark 96"L x 36"W x 8"D, fish 20"L x 10"W x 5"D. Photograph: Randall Quick.

LYNN CREIGHTON

369 PASEO DE PLAYA #212 ■ VENTURA, CA 93001 ■ TEL 805-652-0879
E-MAIL RSSLYNN@EARTHLINK.NET ■ WWW.SACRED-SOURCE.COM

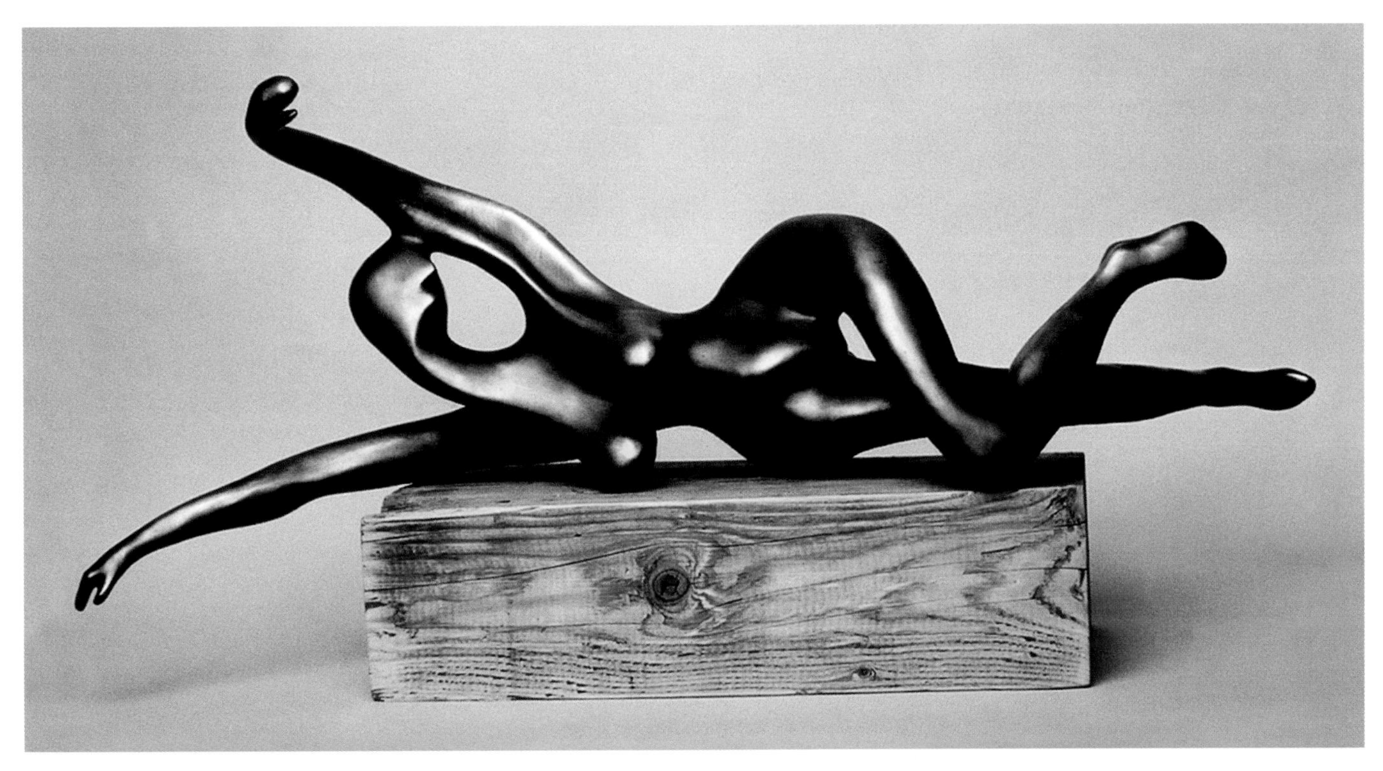

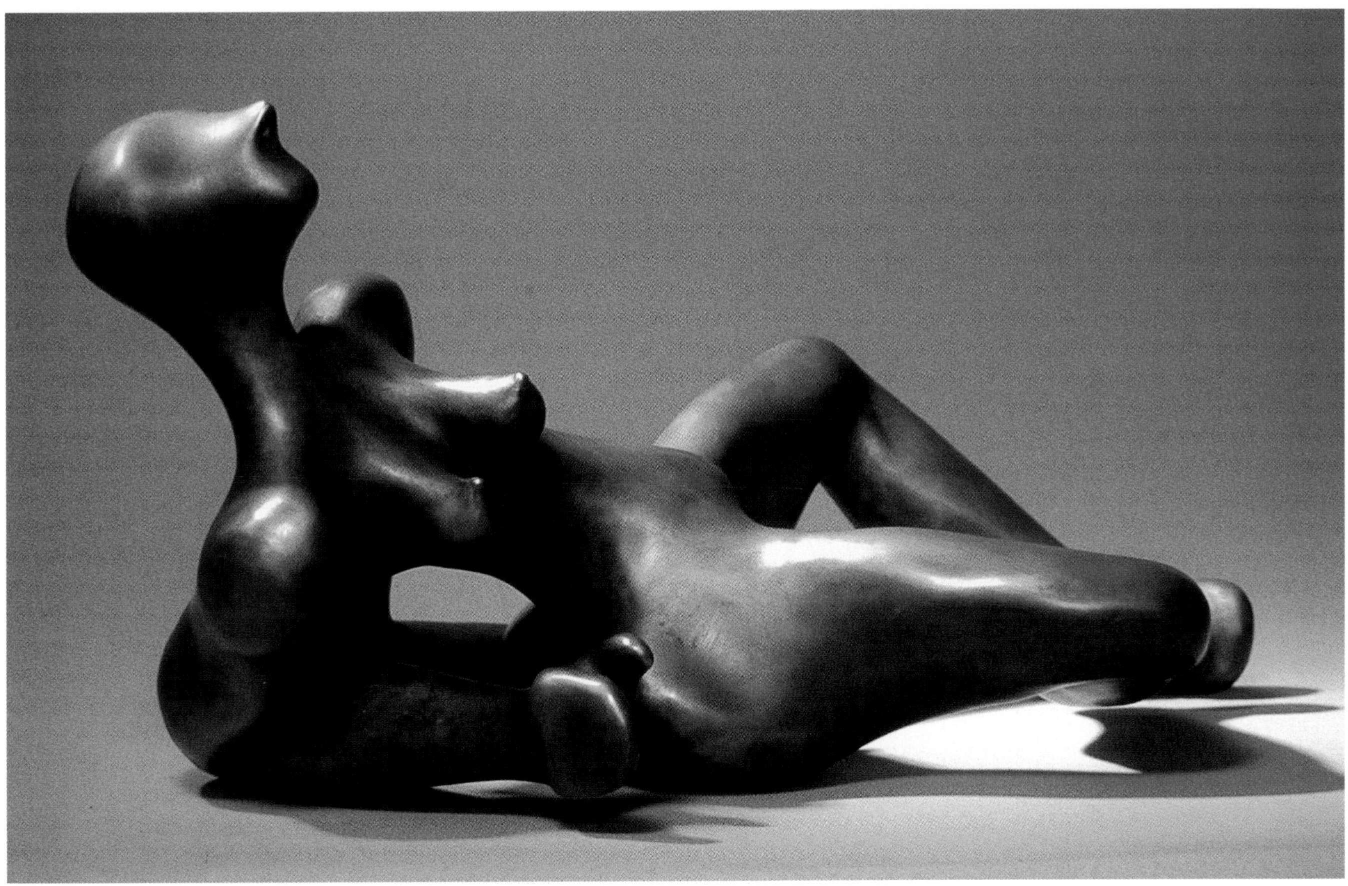

Top: *Desiree*, bronze, 15" x 33" x 15". Bottom: *Daisy*, bronze, 20" x 33" x 20".

THOMAS DONALSON

REALISTIC SCULPTURES BY THOMAS ■ PO BOX 41 ■ TOME, NM 87060
TEL 505-319-7042 ■ E-MAIL STAINLESSART@SBCGLOBAL.NET

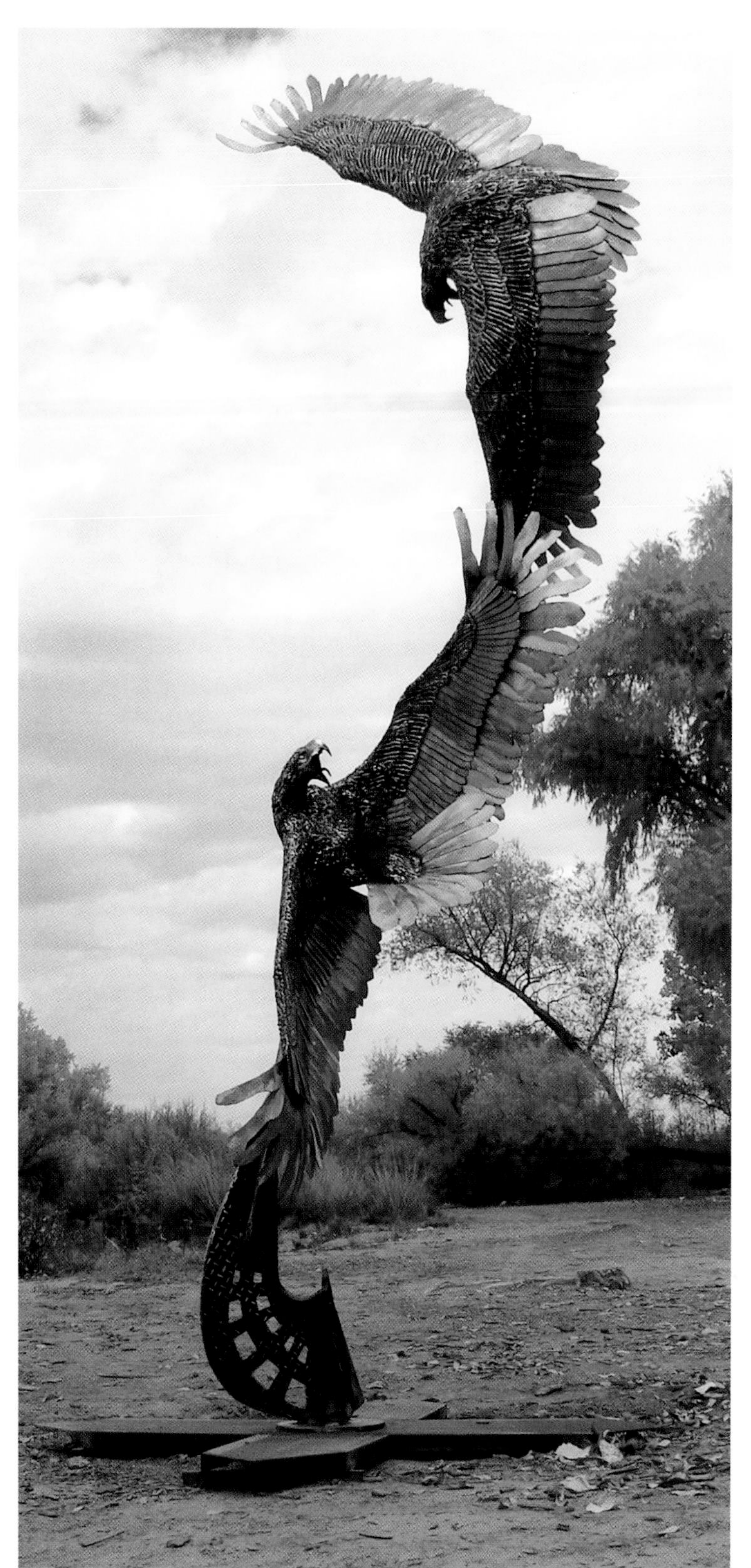

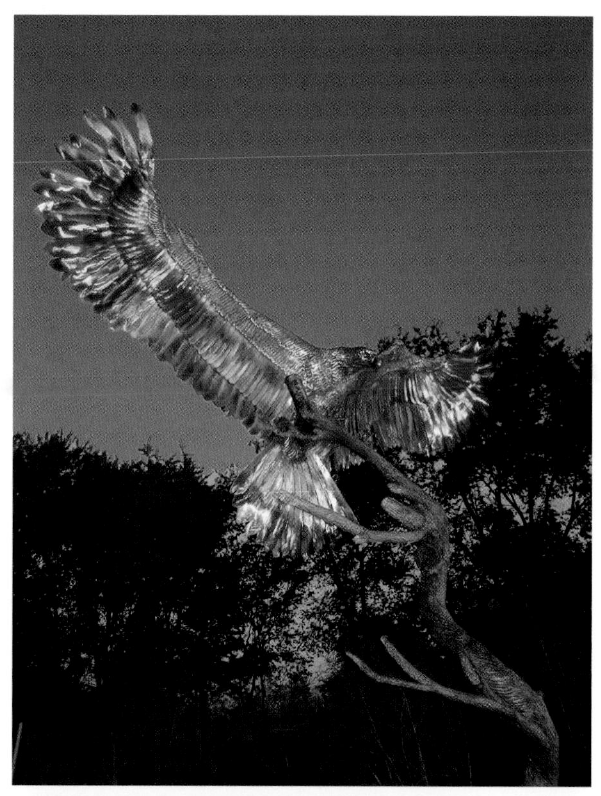

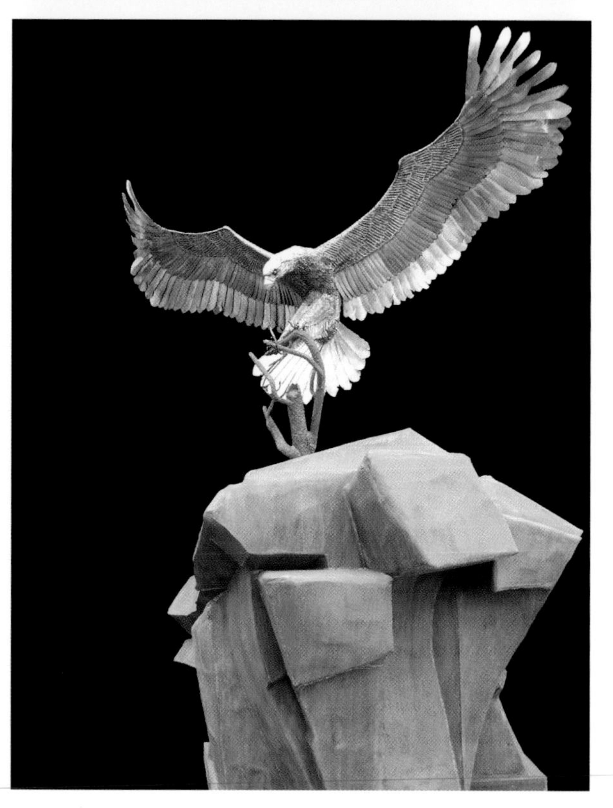

Left: *Engaging Love*, kinetic, welded stainless steel, 12.4' x 4' x 4'. Top right: *Golden Freedom*, welded stainless steel, 10' wingspan.
Bottom right: *Monumental Freedom*, welded stainless, iron, and steel, 11.5' x 6' x 5.8'.

MARTIN EICHINGER

EICHINGER SCULPTURE STUDIO ■ 2516 SE DIVISION STREET ■ PORTLAND, OR 97202
TEL 503-223-0626 ■ FAX 503-223-0454 ■ E-MAIL STUDIO@EICHINGERSCULPTURE.COM ■ WWW.EICHINGERSCULPTURE.COM

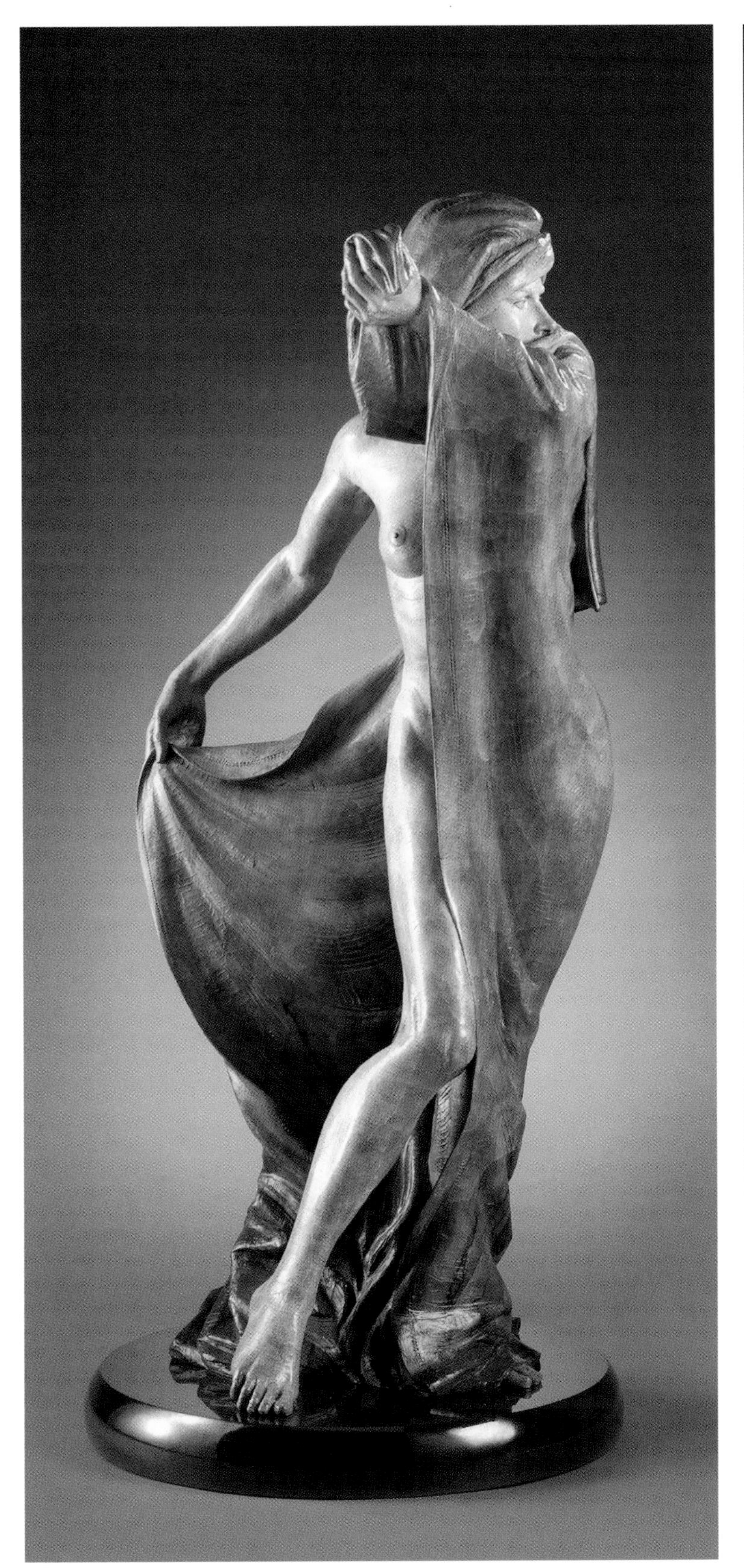

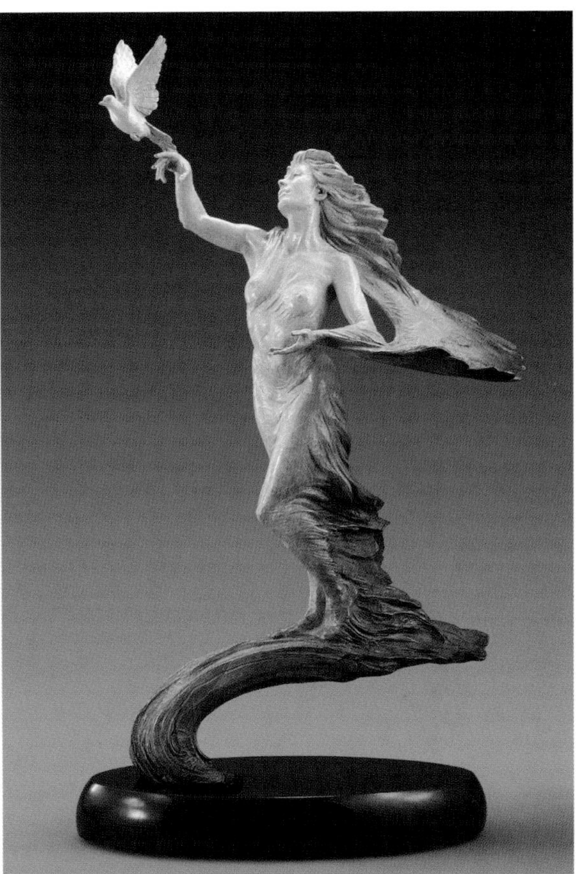

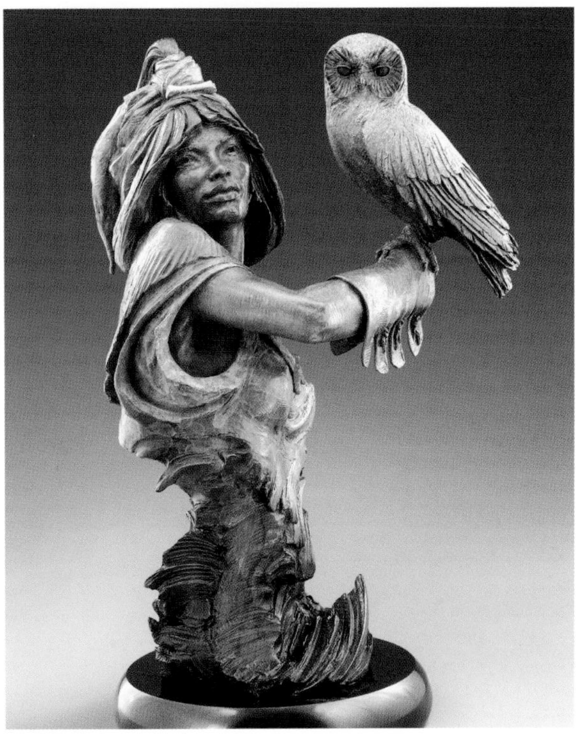

Left: *Security Blanket*, 2005, cast bronze, 56" x 24" x 22", edition of one hundred. Top right: *On Wings of Hope*, 2004, cast bronze, 41" x 24" x 13", or 28" x 16" x 8", editions of one hundred. Bottom right: *Seeing in the Dark*, 2004, cast bronze, 29" x 17" x 14", edition of one hundred.

GAIL FOLWELL

FOLWELL STUDIOS ■ 731 CRESCENT DRIVE ■ BOULDER, CO 80303 ■ TEL 720-334-1164
E-MAIL GAIL@FOLWELLSTUDIOS.COM ■ WWW.FOLWELLSTUDIOS.COM

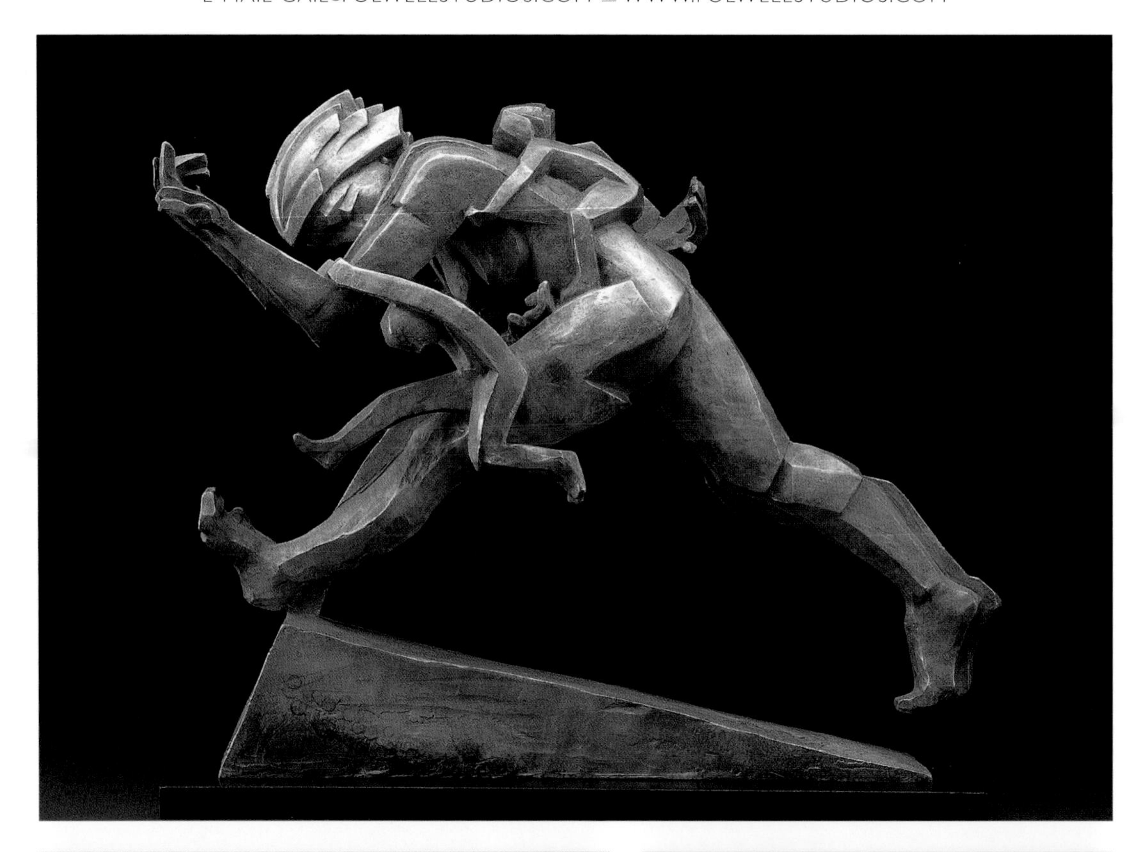

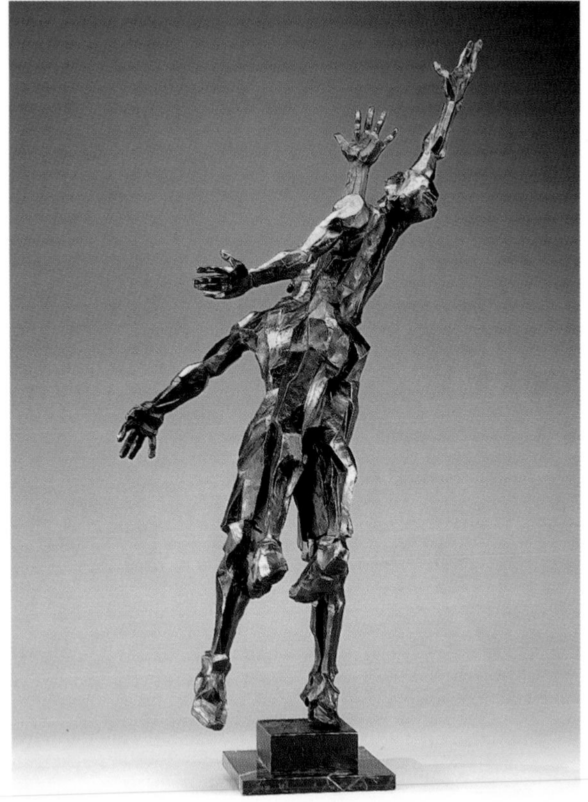

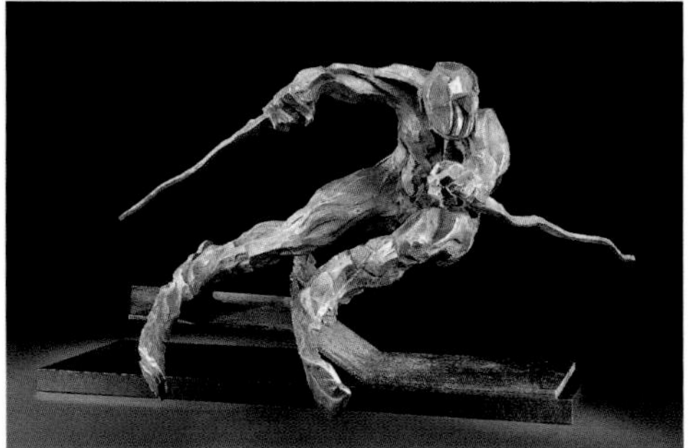

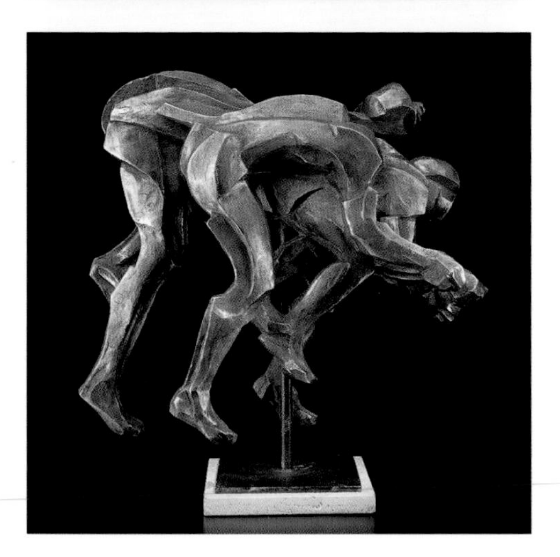

Top: *The Human Race*, 23" x 25" x 10". Bottom left: *Challenge*, 42" x 19" x 16".
Center right: *The Edge*, 31" x 31" x 19". Bottom right: *Peloton*, 19" x 17" x 10". Photographs: Mel Schockner.

MICHELLE GREGOR

MICHELLE GREGOR STUDIO ■ 812 EAST 24 STREET ■ OAKLAND, CA 94606 ■ TEL 510-834-1324
E-MAIL MICHELLE@MG3D.NET ■ WWW.GREGORSCULPTOR.NET ■ WWW.MG3D.NET

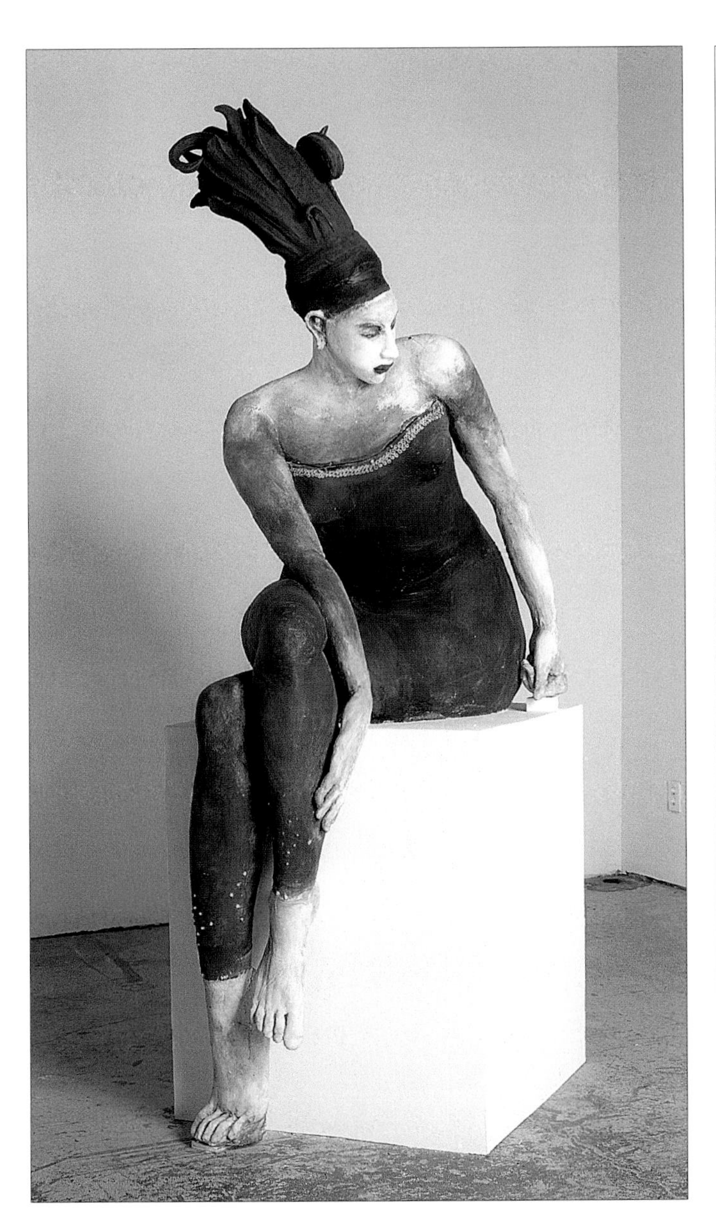

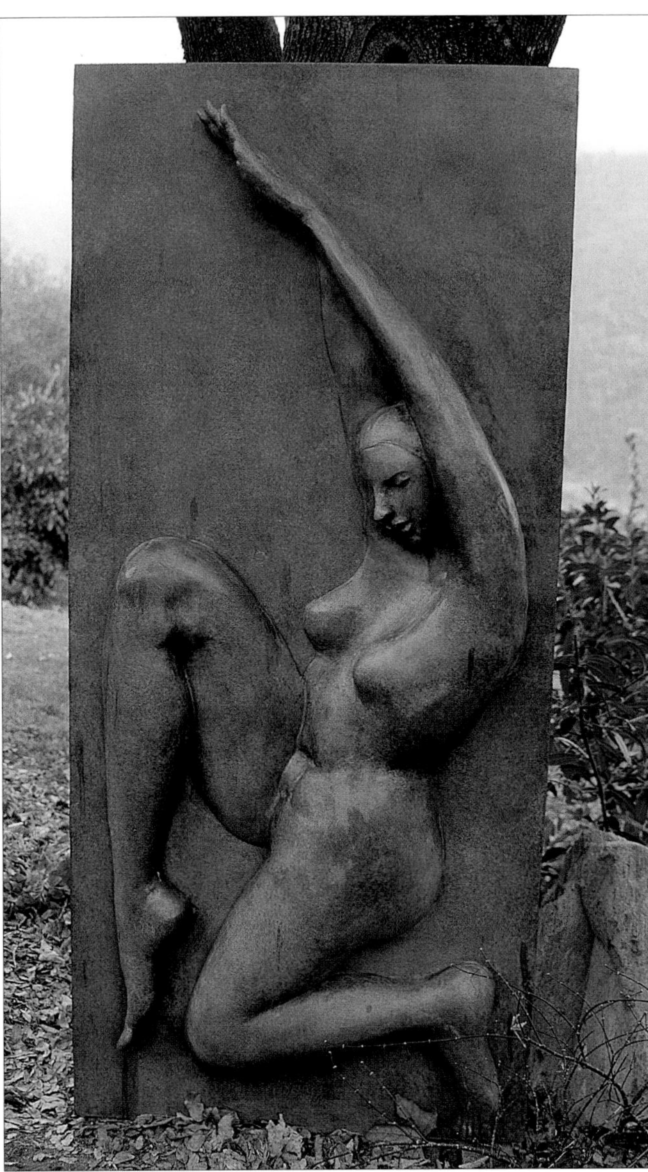

Left: *Shy Girl,* ceramic, 84"H.
Right: *Diver,* 2005, private collection, bronze, 7' x 3' x 6".

GREGORY JOHNSON

GREGORY JOHNSON FINE ART ■ 7235 SWEETGRASS COURT ■ CUMMING, GA 30041
TEL 770-887-1561 ■ E-MAIL GJHOTMETAL@BELLSOUTH.NET ■ WWW.GREGORYJOHNSON.BIZ

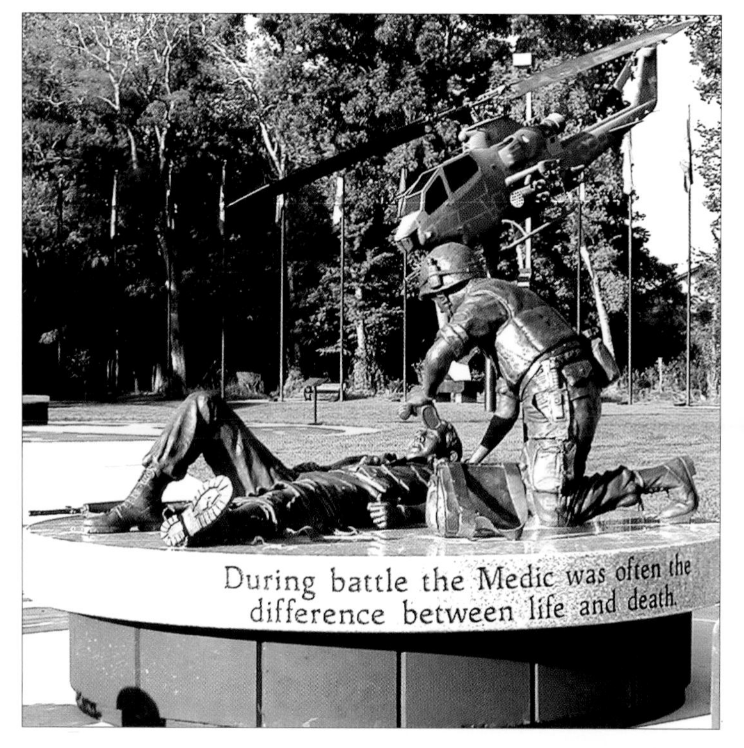

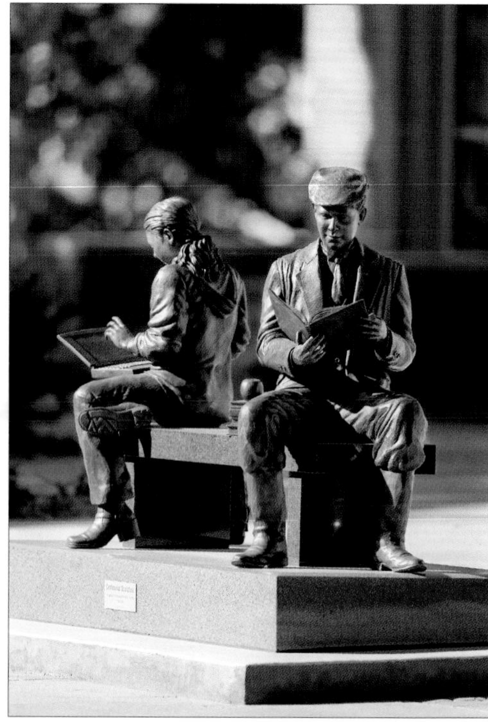

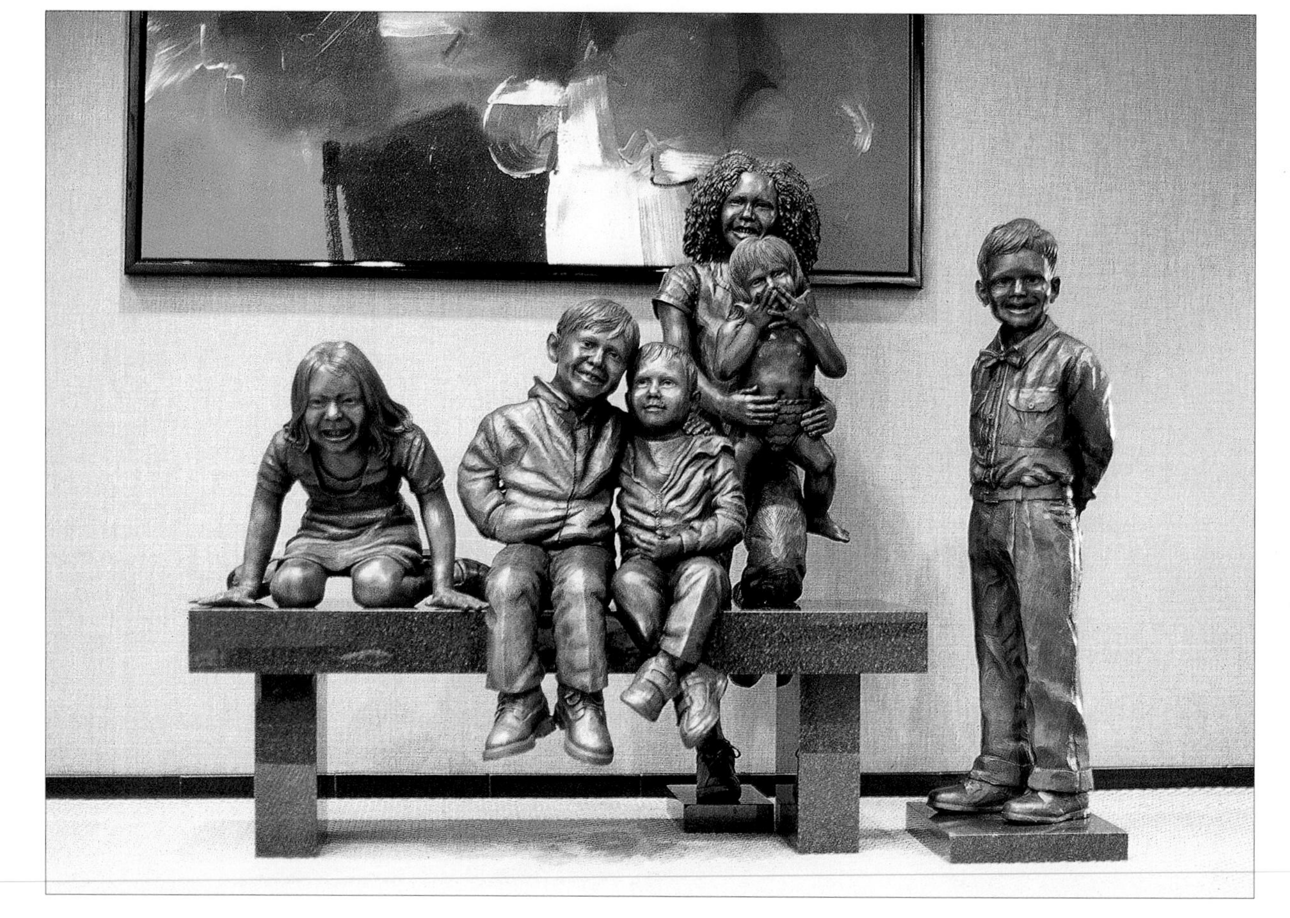

Top left: *Collegedale Medic Memorial.* Top right: *NW Missouri Centennial.* Photograph: Darren Whitley. Bottom: *Golden State Foods Foundation Kids.*

J. SEWARD JOHNSON

THE SCULPTURE FOUNDATION ■ 2525 MICHIGAN AVENUE SUITE A-6 ■ SANTA MONICA, CA 90404
TEL 310-264-2400 ■ FAX 310-264-2403 ■ E-MAIL INFO@TSFMAIL.COM ■ WWW.SEWARDJOHNSON.COM

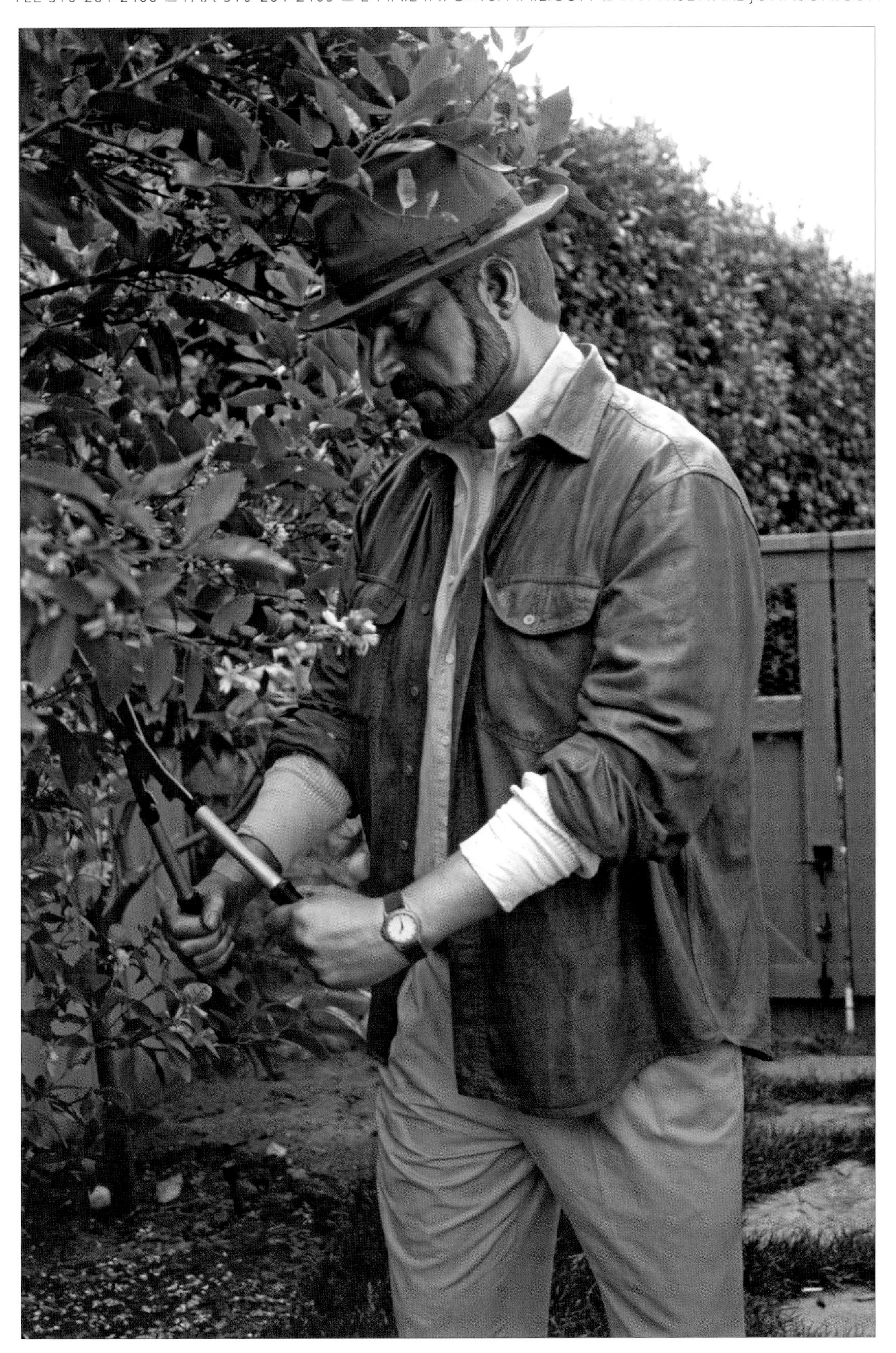

Gotcha (detail), bronze, life size. Photograph: Paula Stoeke.

BARRY WOODS JOHNSTON

SCULPTURE WORKS, INC. ■ 2423 PICKWICK ROAD ■ BALTIMORE, MD 21207 ■ TEL 410-448-1945
FAX 410-448-2663 ■ E-MAIL BARRY@SCULPTORJOHNSTON.COM ■ WWW.SCULPTORJOHNSTON.COM

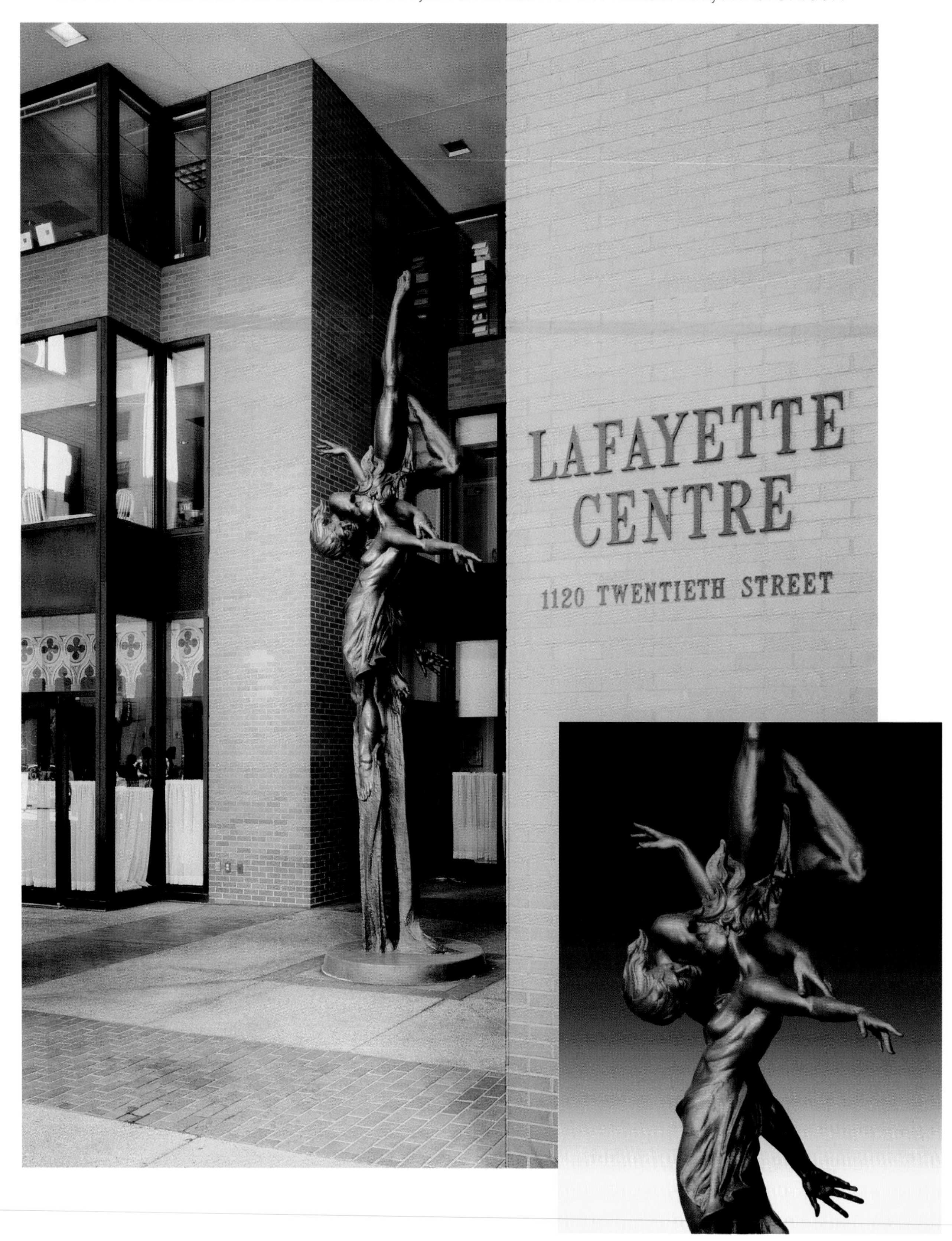

Wedlock, Lafayette Center, Washington, DC, bronze, 19.5'H. Photographs: Roy Simmons.

DAVID KLASS

136 WEST 24TH STREET ■ NEW YORK, NY 10011 ■ TEL 212-243-7633
FAX 212-924-4446 ■ E-MAIL DKLASS@VERIZON.NET ■ WWW.DAVIDKLASS.COM

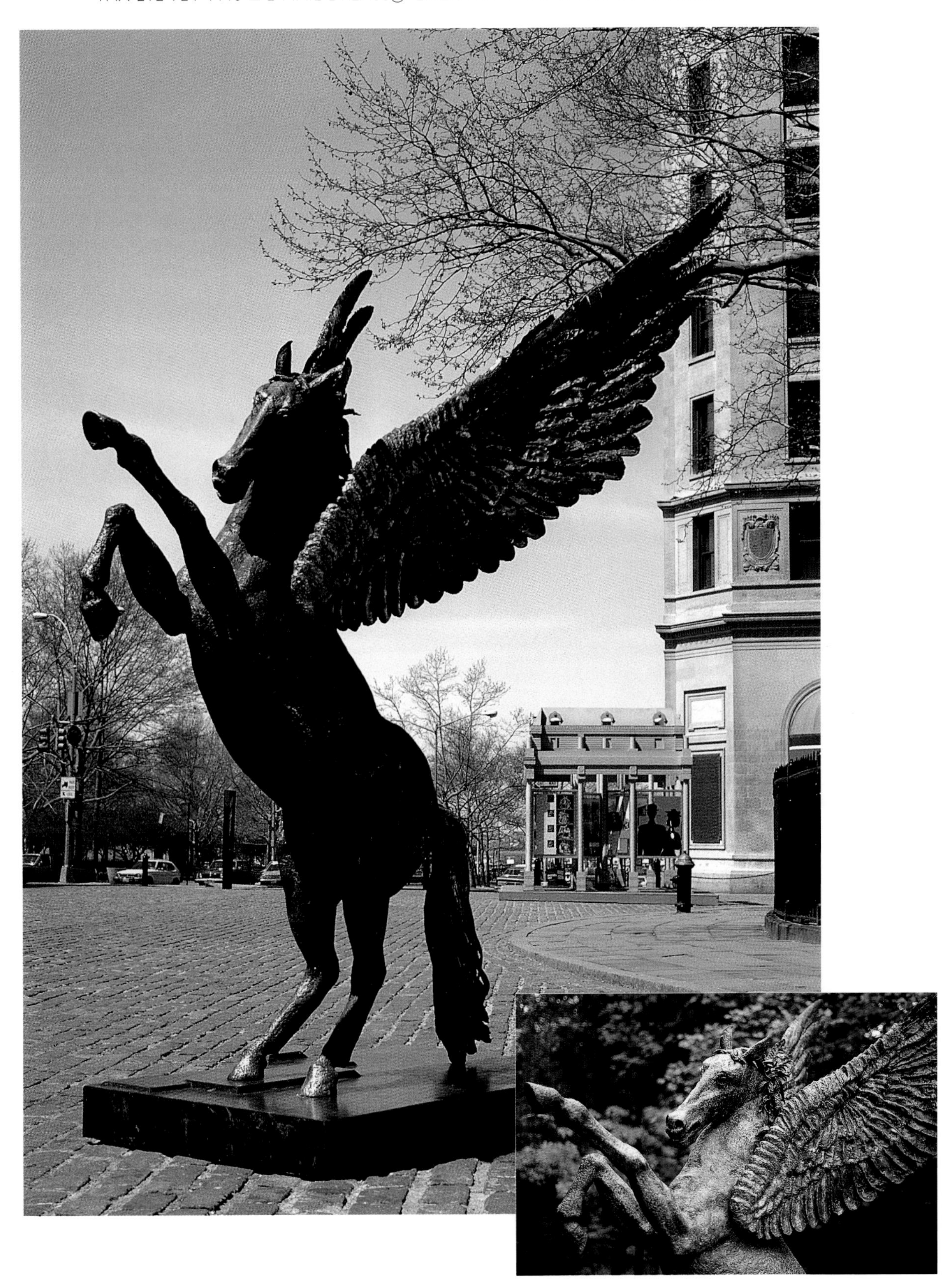

Pegasus, bronze, 120"H.

POKEY PARK

POKEY PARK STUDIOS ■ 6396 NORTH DESERT WIND CIRCLE ■ TUCSON, AZ 85750 ■ TEL 520-529-6435
TEL 520-869-6435 ■ FAX 520-529-0607 ■ E-MAIL POKEYPARKSTUDIOS@YAHOO.COM ■ WWW.POKEYPARK.COM

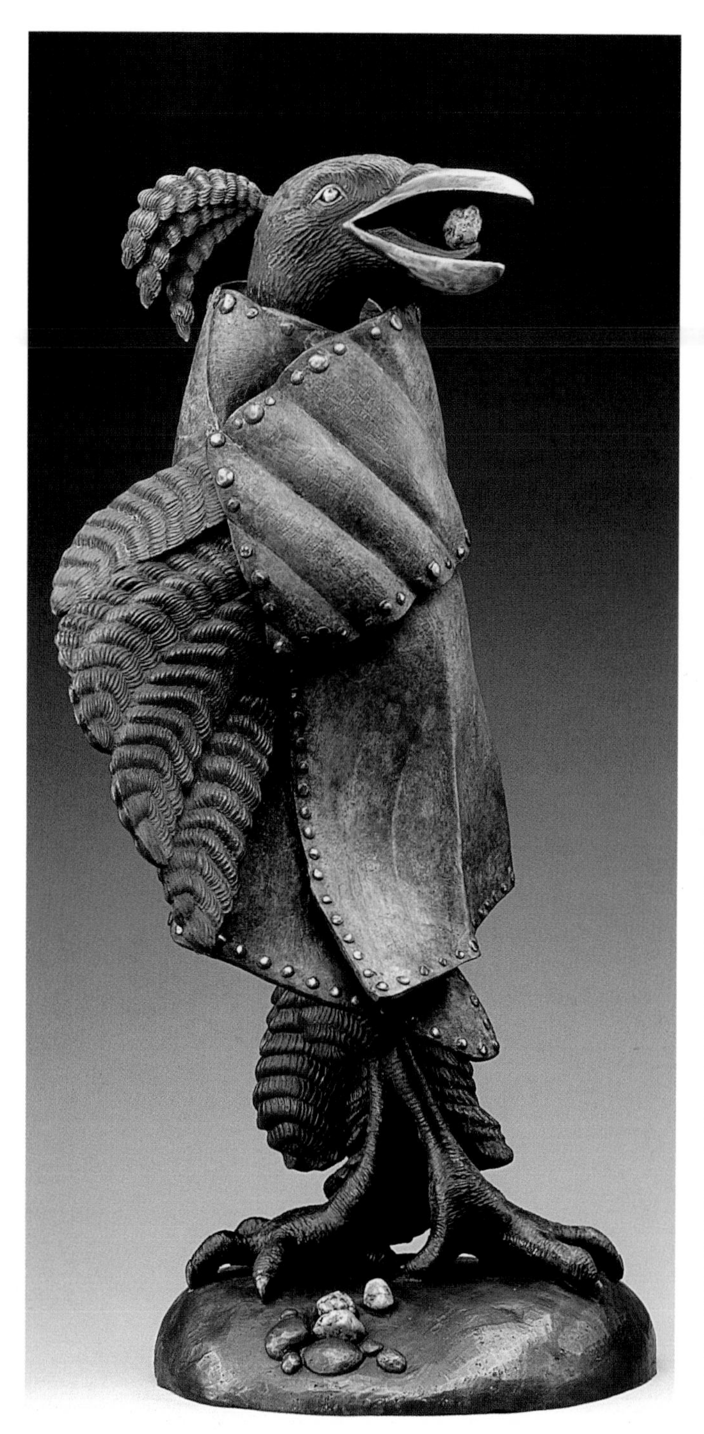

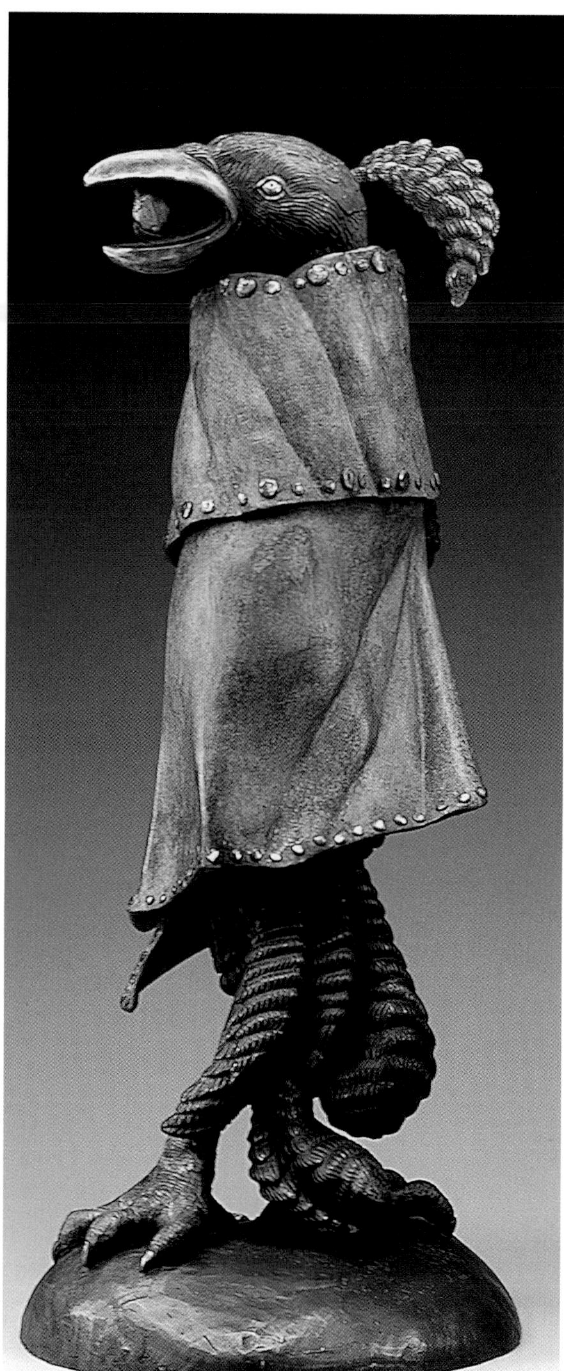

The Shaman, bronze and turquoise, 40" x 20" x 20". Photographs: Jafe Parson.

PRESCOTT STUDIOS

FREDRICK PRESCOTT ■ 3040 AGUA FRIA ■ SANTA FE, NM 87507 ■ TEL 505-424-8449
FAX 505-474-0166 ■ E-MAIL PRESCOTTPOP@GMAIL.COM ■ WWW.PRESCOTTSTUDIO.COM

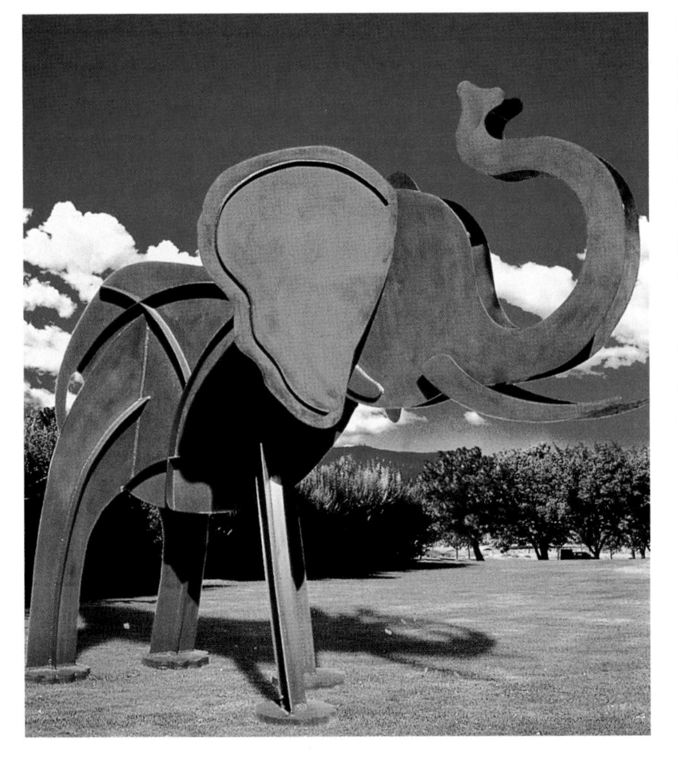

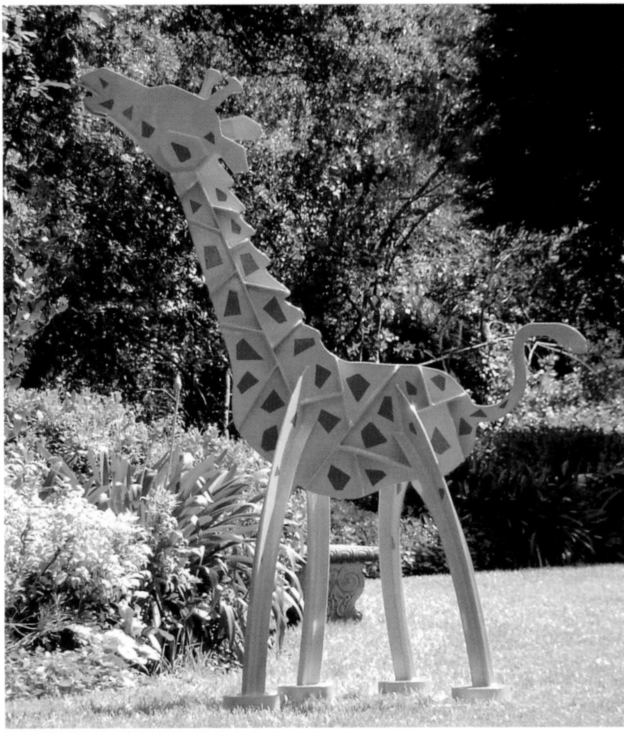

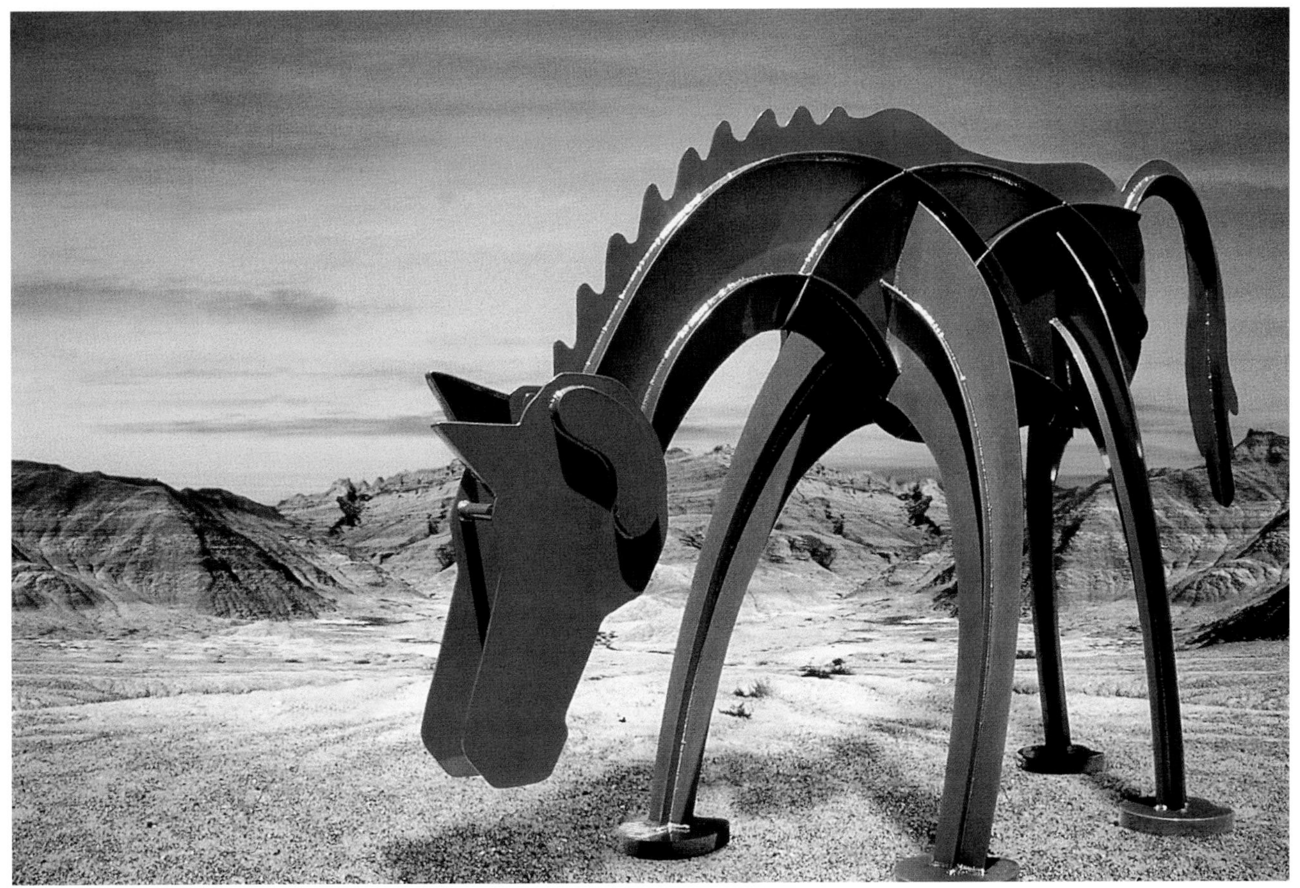

Top left: *Elephant Walk*, steel kinetic wind sculpture, 11.5'H x 12'W x 5'D. Top right: *Giraffe*, powder-coated steel, 10'H x 5.3'W x 2.6'D. Bottom: *Wild Horses*, powder-coated steel, 7.5'H x 10'W x 4.5'D.

TANYA RAGIR

TANYA RAGIR STUDIO ■ 3587 OCEAN VIEW AVENUE ■ LOS ANGELES, CA 90066
TEL 310-390-5919 ■ FAX 310-398-7965 ■ E-MAIL TANYA@TANYARAGIR.COM ■ WWW.TANYARAGIR.COM

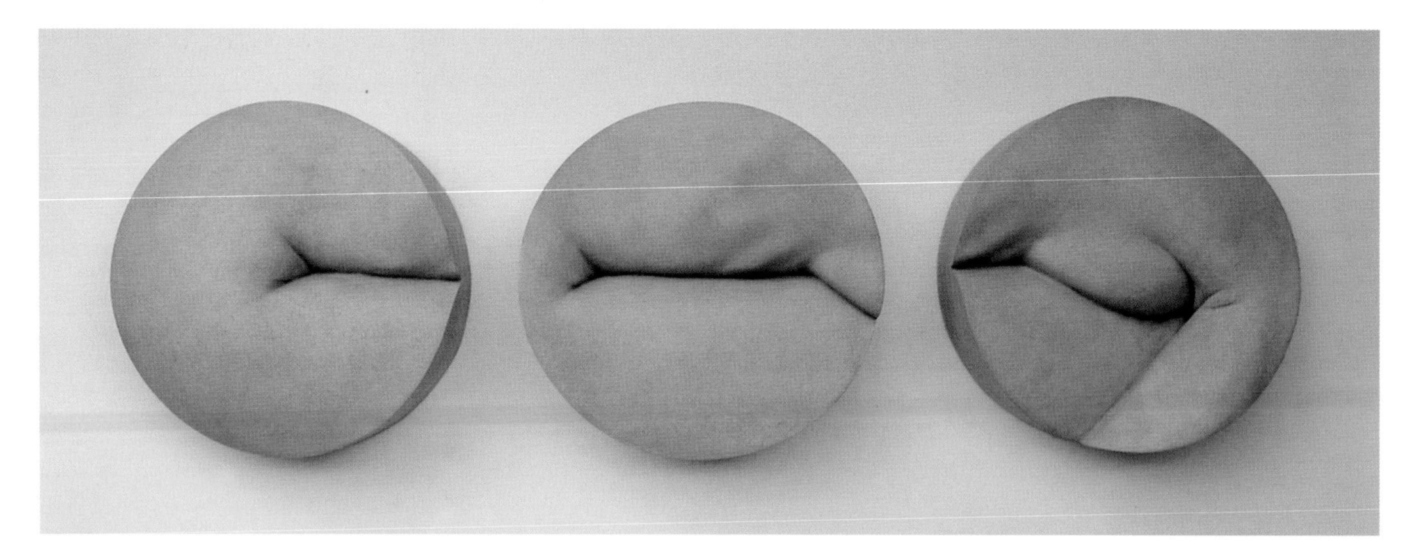

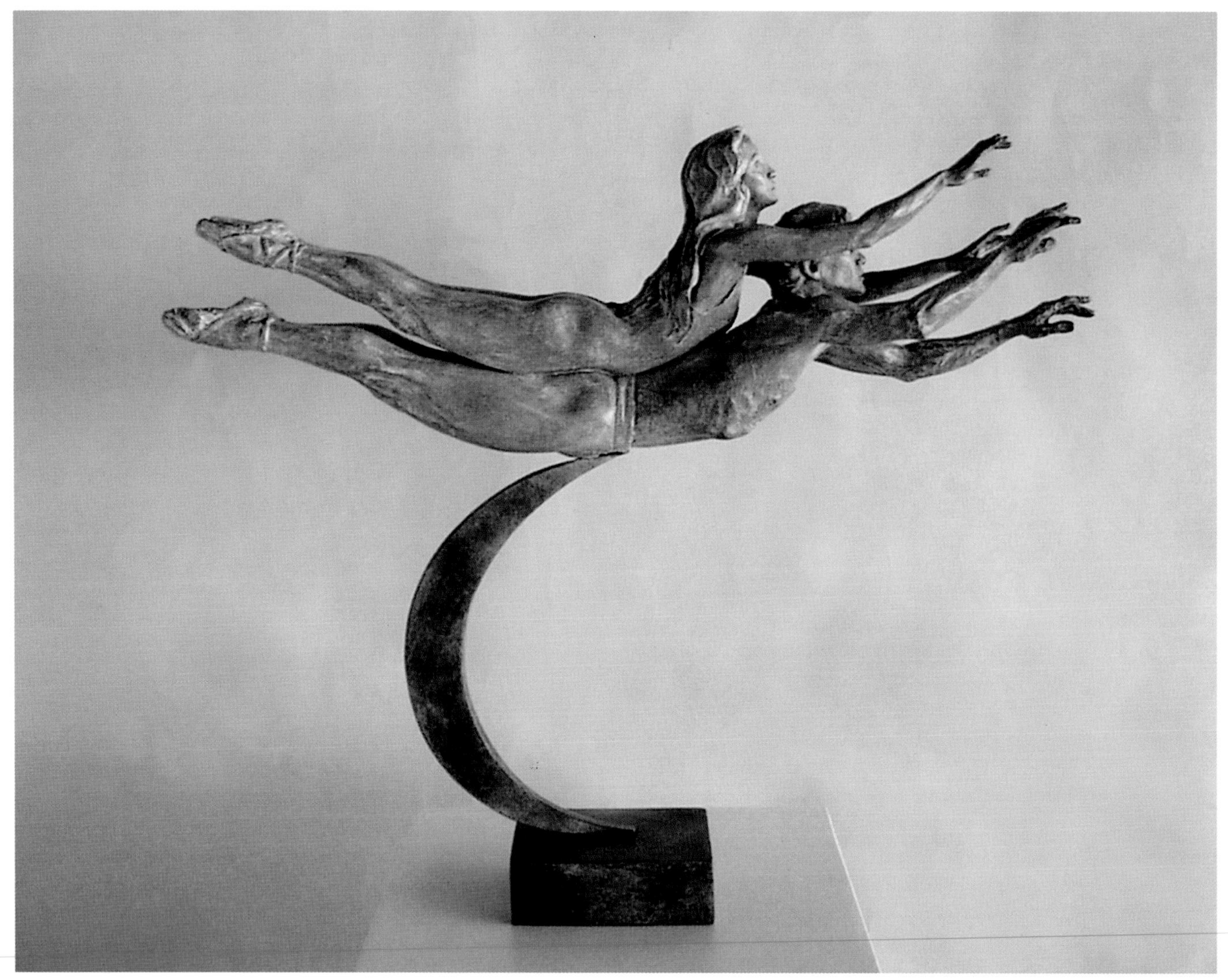

Top: *Sandscape*, 1992, painted resin, each circle: 16" x 9", edition of nine.
Bottom: *Sea Shadow*, 13" x 16" x 6", maquette for life-size sculpture for the Joffrey Ballet of Chicago, projected installation 2007-2008.

ROSETTA

405 8TH STREET SOUTHEAST #15 ■ LOVELAND, CO 80537 ■ TEL 970-667-6265
E-MAIL ROSETTASCULPTURE@EARTHLINK.NET ■ WWW.ROSETTASCULPTURE.COM

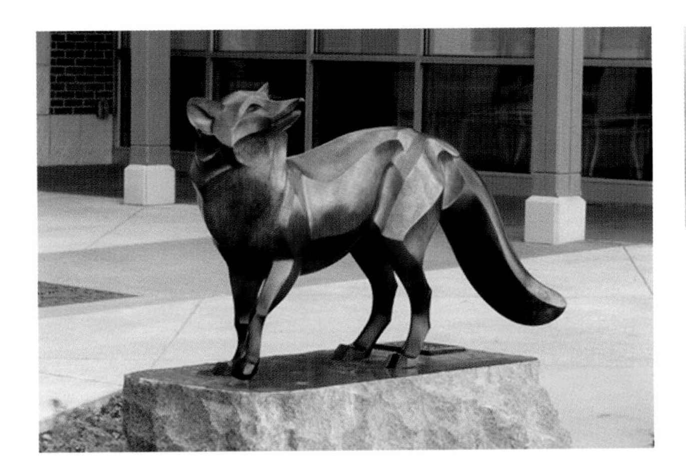

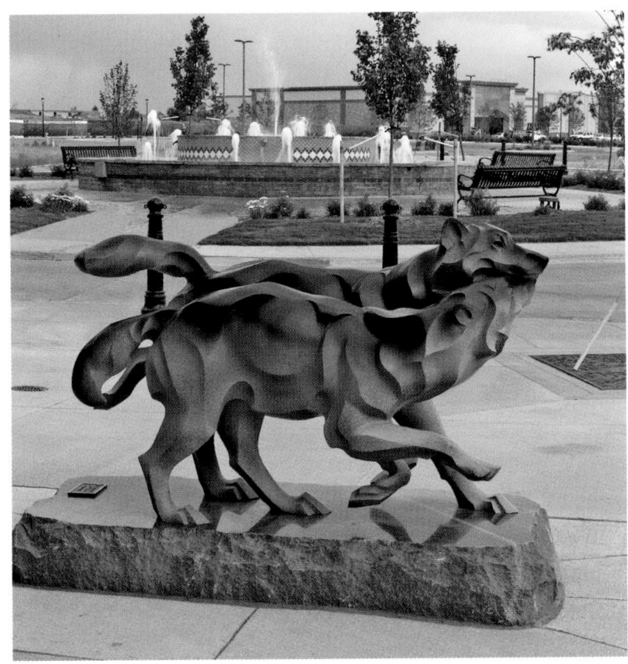

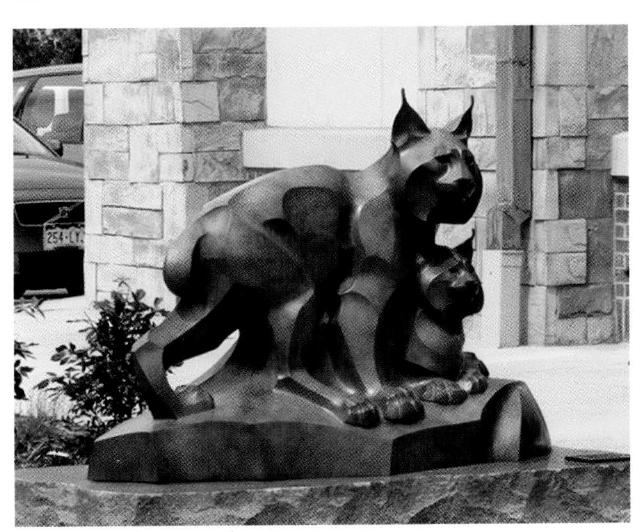

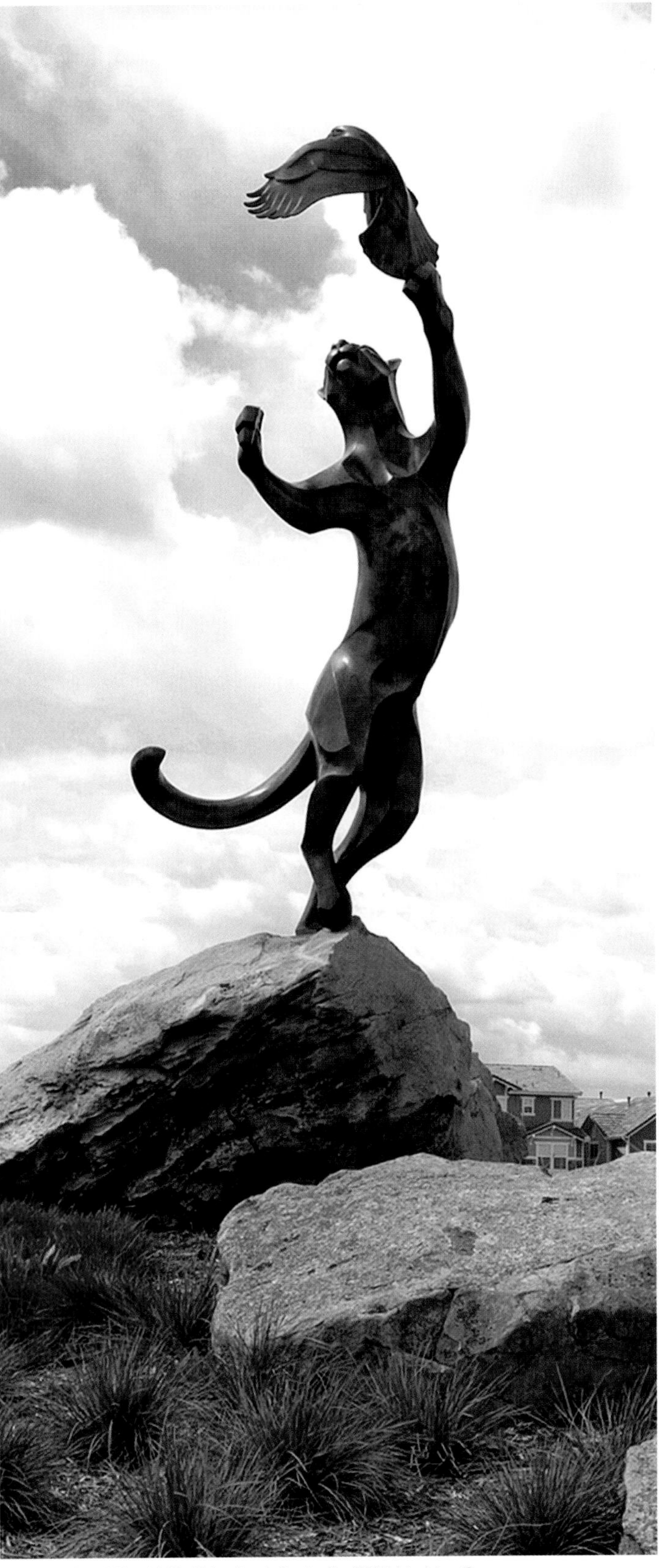

Top left: *Red Fox,* 2005, The Shops at Walnut Creek, Westminster, CO, bronze, 21.5" x 35" x 12.5". Right: *Reach for the Sky,* 2005, Meridian Commons Retail, Parker, CO, bronze, 104" x 46" x 40". Center left: *Alpha Pair,* 2005, The Shops at Walnut Creek, Westminster, CO, bronze, 40" x 70" x 26". Bottom left: *Lynx Legacy,* 2005, The Shops at Walnut Creek, Westminster, CO, bronze, 35" x 52.5" x 27". Photographs: Mel Schockner.

A Commission Story

David Klass

TITLE
Burning Bush, 2006

COMMISSIONED FOR
Northern Hills Synagogue, Cincinnati, OH

TIMELINE: 1 year

DIMENSIONS: 6'H x 4'W

TRADE PROFESSIONAL
Julie Staller-Pentelnik, Judaic Artist

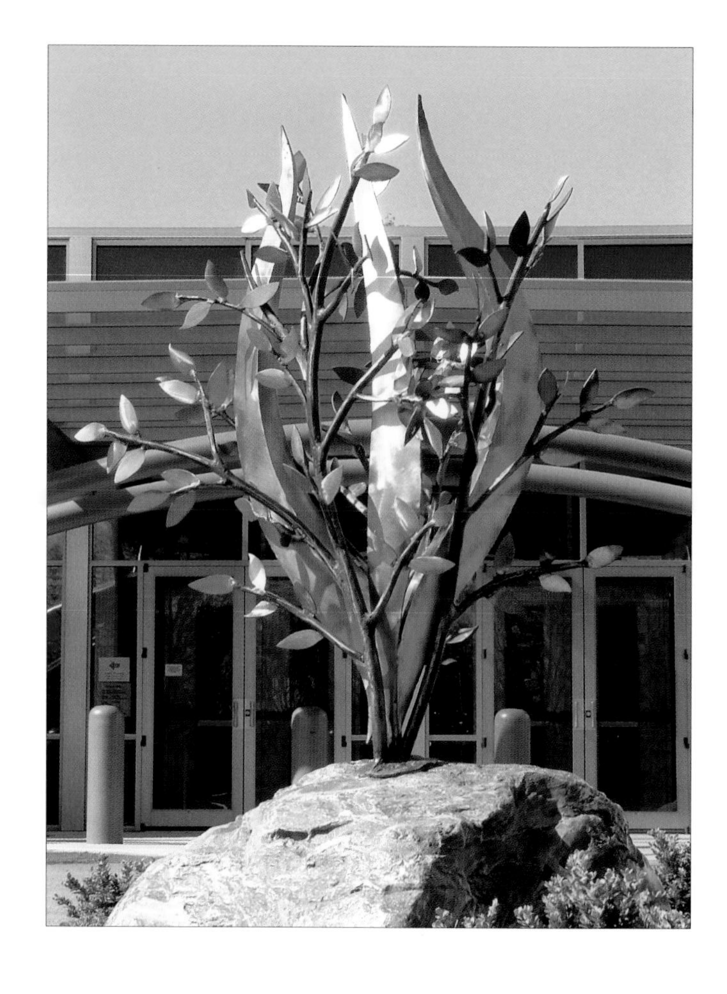

When Cincinnati's Northern Hills Synagogue constructed a new building, the circular driveway encompassed a round patch of grass ideal for an art installation. The recent death of a beloved synagogue founder inspired Sandy and Ron Richards and a committee of fellow congregants to initiate a special outdoor sculpture commission. They were searching for a piece of art that would serve both as a memorial and as an artful focal point for the entrance to the building. ■ Julie Staller-Pentelnik, a Judaic artist who also happens to be a member of the congregation, helped the committee develop a concept. "The burning bush, symbolizing God's presence, seemed very appropriate at the front of the building, and also appropriate to honor the man," she explained. After Staller-Pentelnik drafted a series of sketches, which the committee narrowed down to one, they approached a familiar artist to execute the design. ■ "I had created ark doors for their synagogue over twenty years ago," David Klass recounts. "They liked my work so much they decided they wanted me to take on this project." Klass interpreted the preliminary drawing, heeding guidance from representatives of the congregation, including Staller-Pentelnik, who appreciated Klass's collaborative spirit. "He's very creative but he was very willing to listen to my input and my ideas." ■ Back in his New York studio, Klass breathed three-dimensional life into the welded bronze piece, the symbolism of the burning bush motif becoming more resonant. Klass explains the power of fire imagery, "Flames and light are used a lot in Judaism: lighting the Sabbath candles, lighting the candles on holidays and Hanukkah, and the eternal light, which is over the ark. The three prongs of the flame form the Hebrew letter 'shin,'" Klass continues. "It's the first letter in one of the names of God. It's not just three abstract flames." Indeed, thanks to Klass's subtle interpretation of Staller-Pentelnik's design, the three distinct prongs are visible from every angle. ■ The congregation is delighted with the finished piece, describing viewer response as "overwhelming." Staller-Pentelnik is captivated by the energy of *Burning Bush*, concluding, "It's impressive, it's striking, it's spiritual."

CHERSTIN SPARKS

RUSSON STUDIOS ■ 3872 UTE MOUNTAIN TRAIL ■ CASTLE ROCK, CO 80109 ■ TEL 303-349-5514
TEL 916-847-4692 ■ E-MAIL CHERSTIN@CHERSTINSPARKS.COM ■ WWW.CHERSTINSPARKS.COM

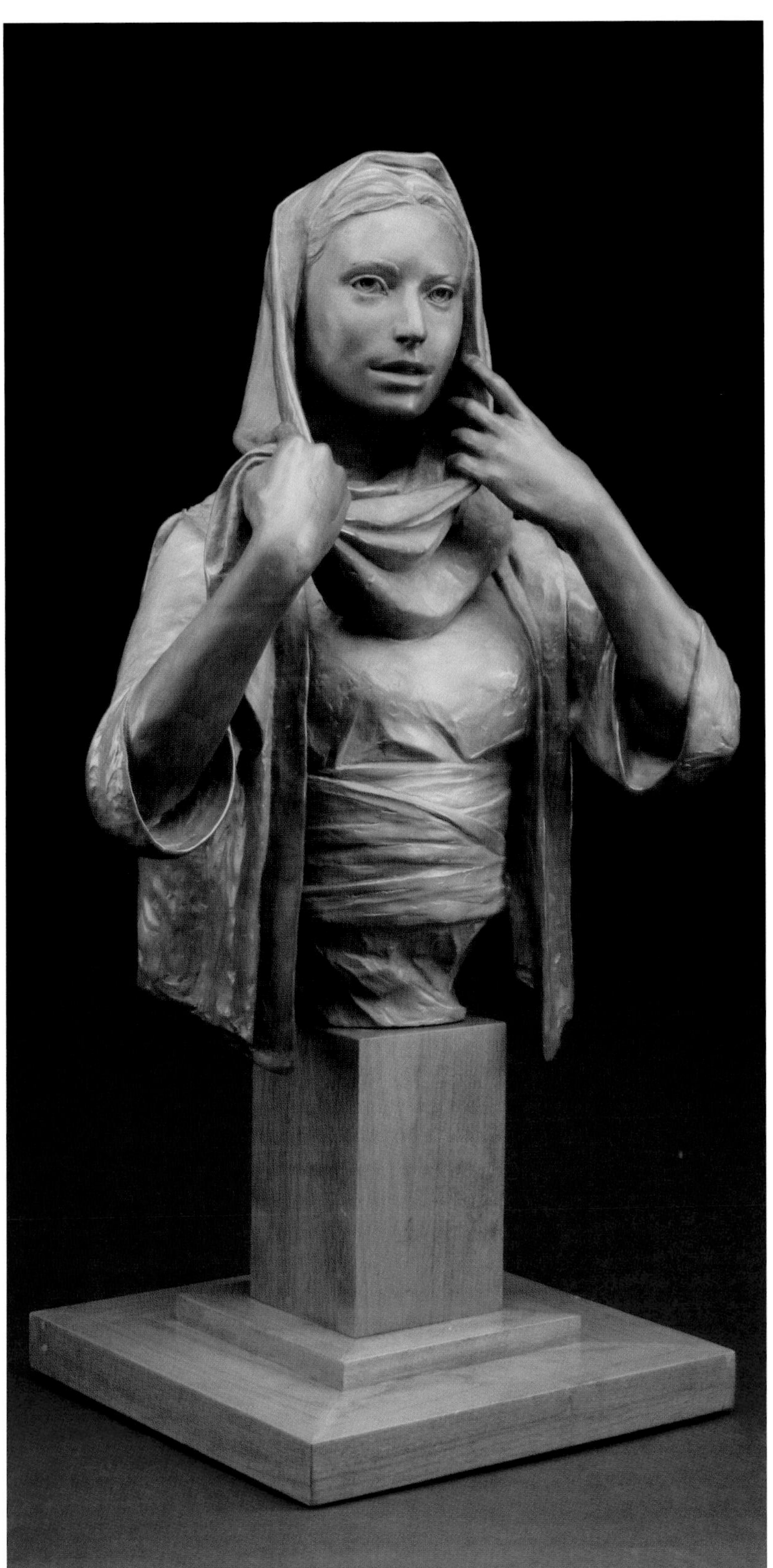

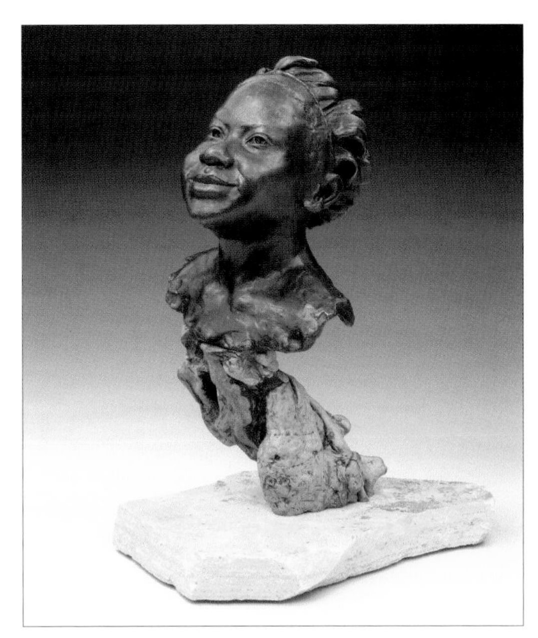

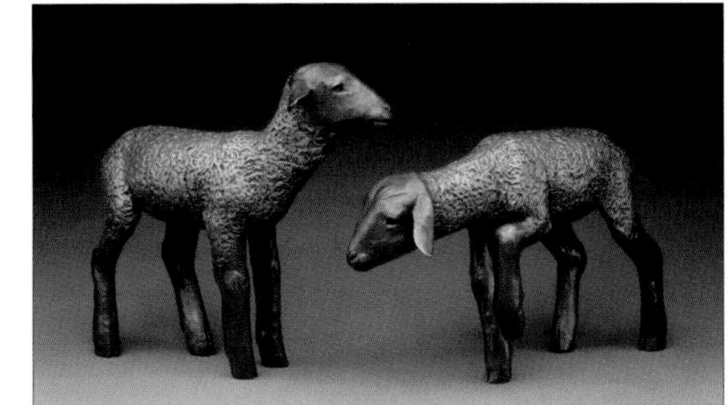

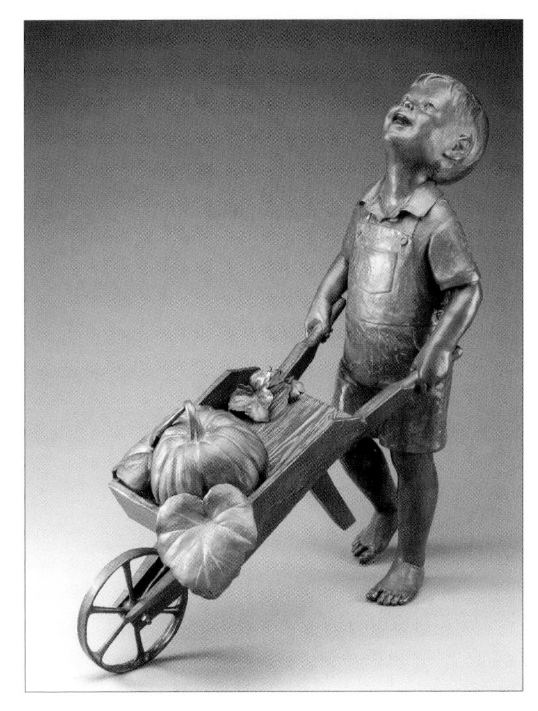

Left: *Rebekah*, bronze, 34" x 19" x 14". Top right: *Char*, bronze, 18" x 13" x 9".
Center right: *Spring Lambs*, bronze, 18" x 21" x 9", 15" x 25" x 10". Bottom right: *Farmer Jon*, bronze, 34" x 31" x 15". Photographs: Jafe Parsons.

STEVEN WHYTE SCULPTURE STUDIOS

700 CANNERY ROW SUITE GG ■ MONTEREY, CA 93940 ■ TEL/FAX 831-645-9953
TEL 831-521-6045 ■ E-MAIL SCULPTU@EARTHLINK.NET ■ WWW.STEVENWHYTESCULPTOR.COM

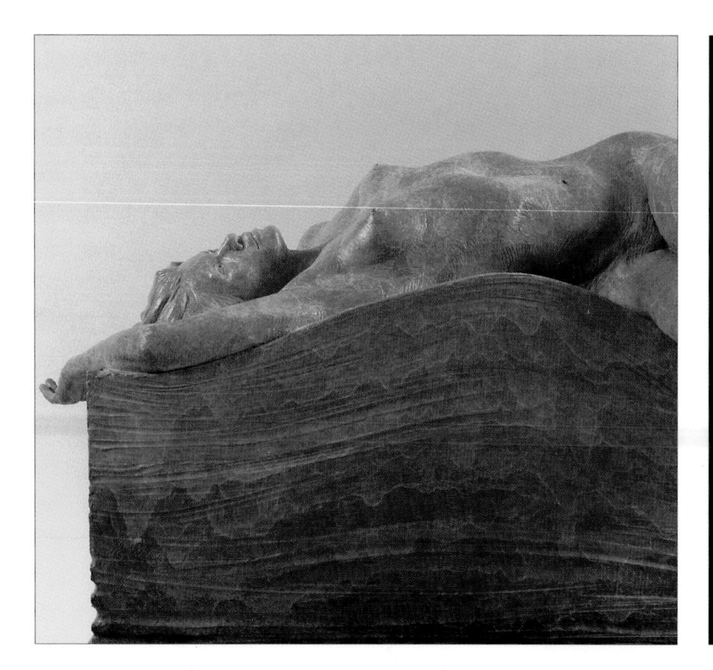

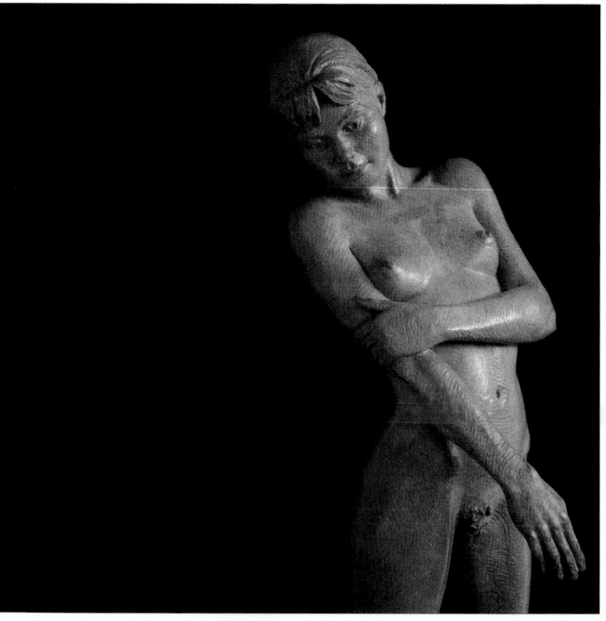

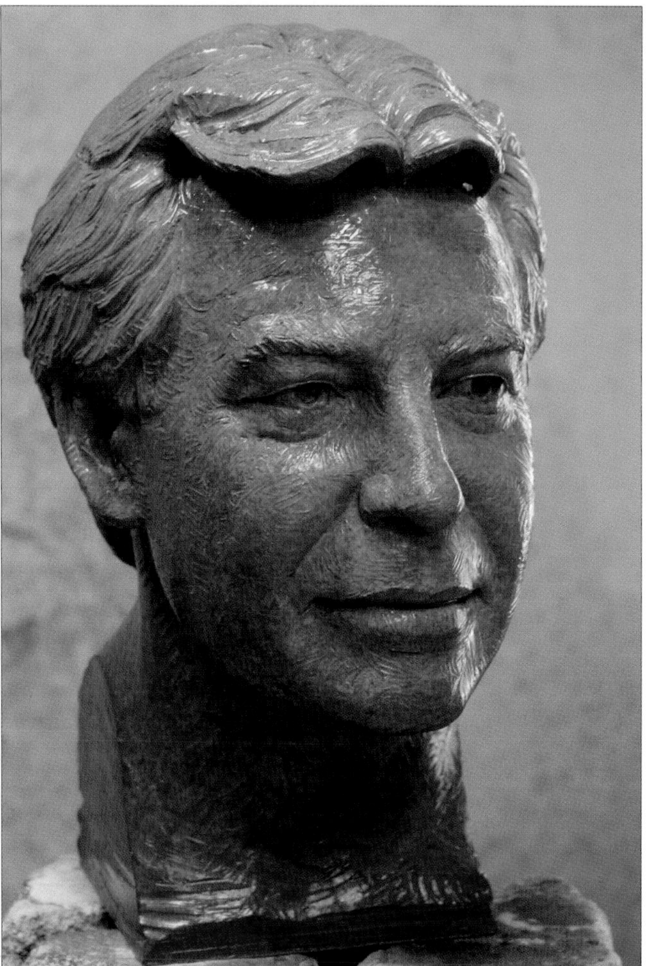

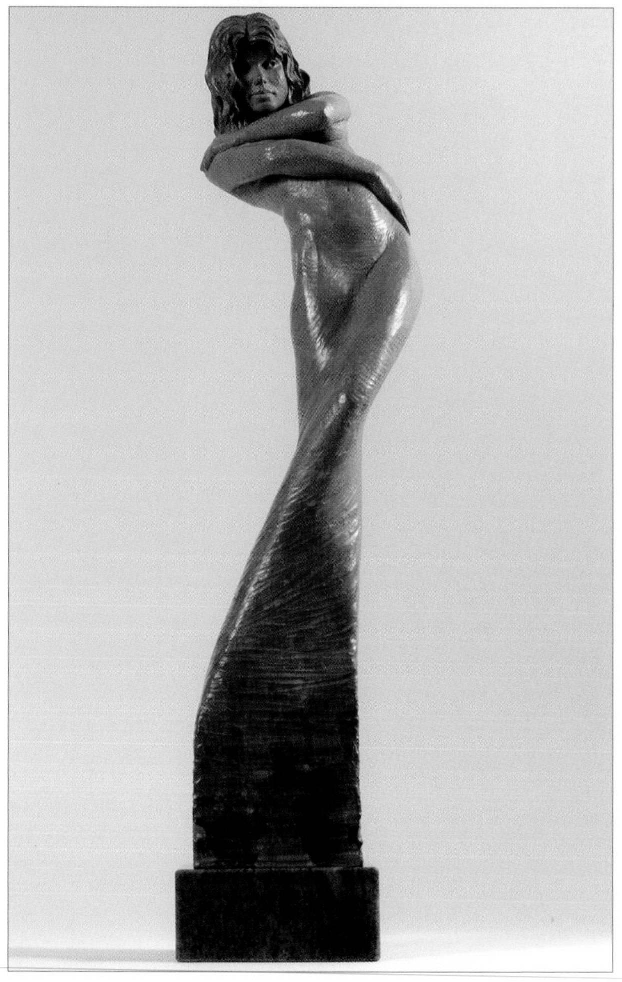

Top left: *Melody* (Repose), bronze edition, half life size. Top right: *Kneeling Figure Jenny*, limited-edition bronze, 12" x 10" x 6".
Bottom left: *Sam Linder*, bronze, life-size portrait head. Bottom right: *Coy* (the *Stance* series), bronze edition, 22" x 6" x 6".

STEVEN WHYTE SCULPTURE STUDIOS

700 CANNERY ROW SUITE GG ■ MONTEREY, CA 93940 ■ TEL/FAX 831-645-9953
TEL 831-521-6045 ■ E-MAIL SCULPTU@EARTHLINK.NET ■ WWW.STEVENWHYTESCULPTOR.COM

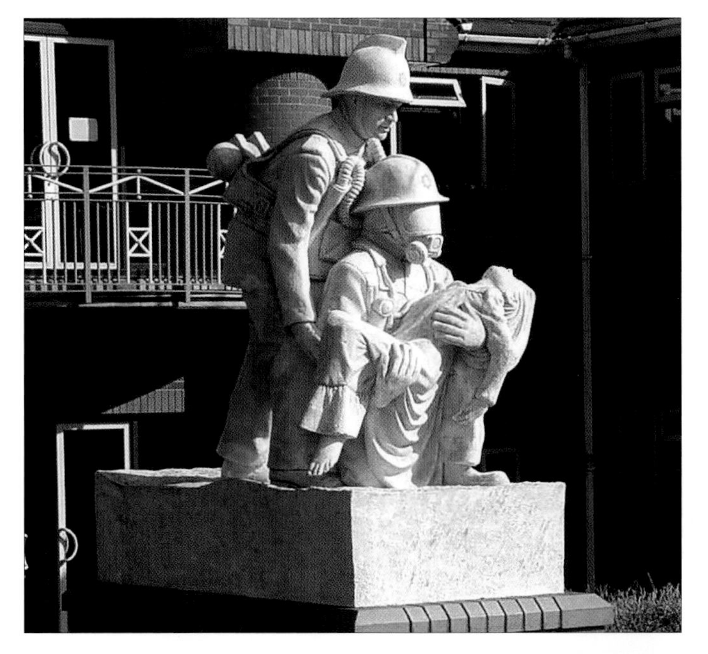

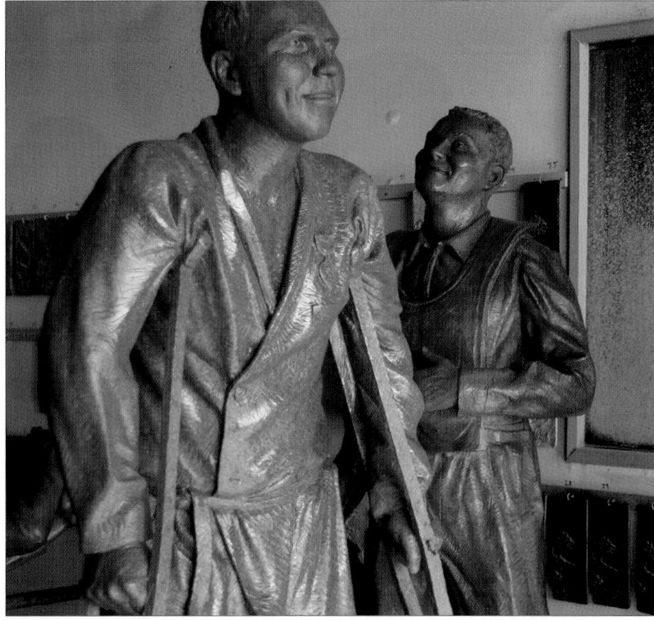

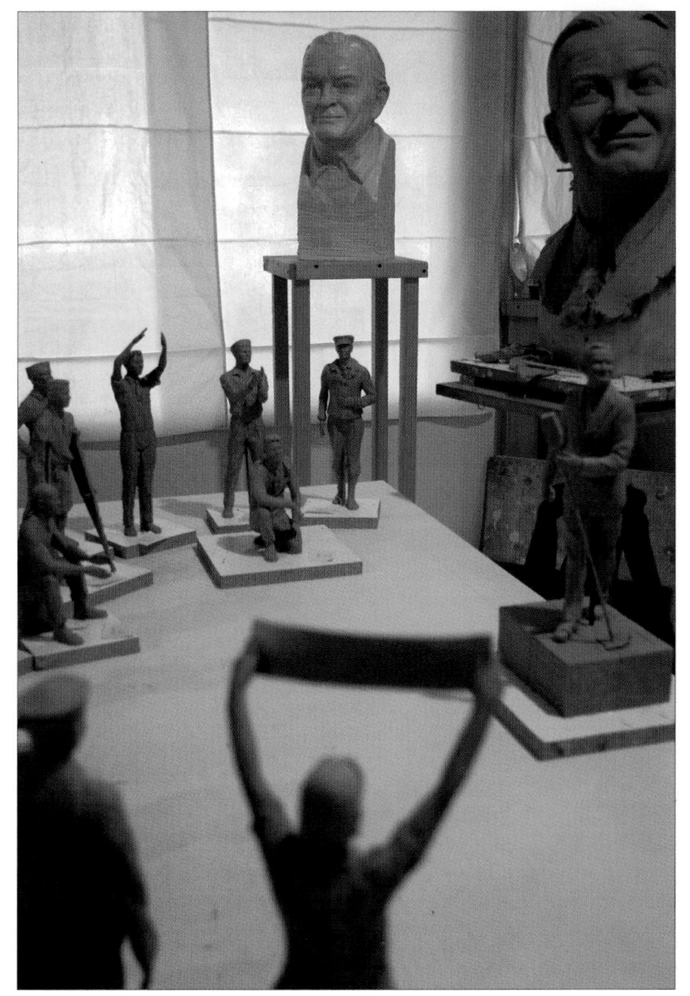

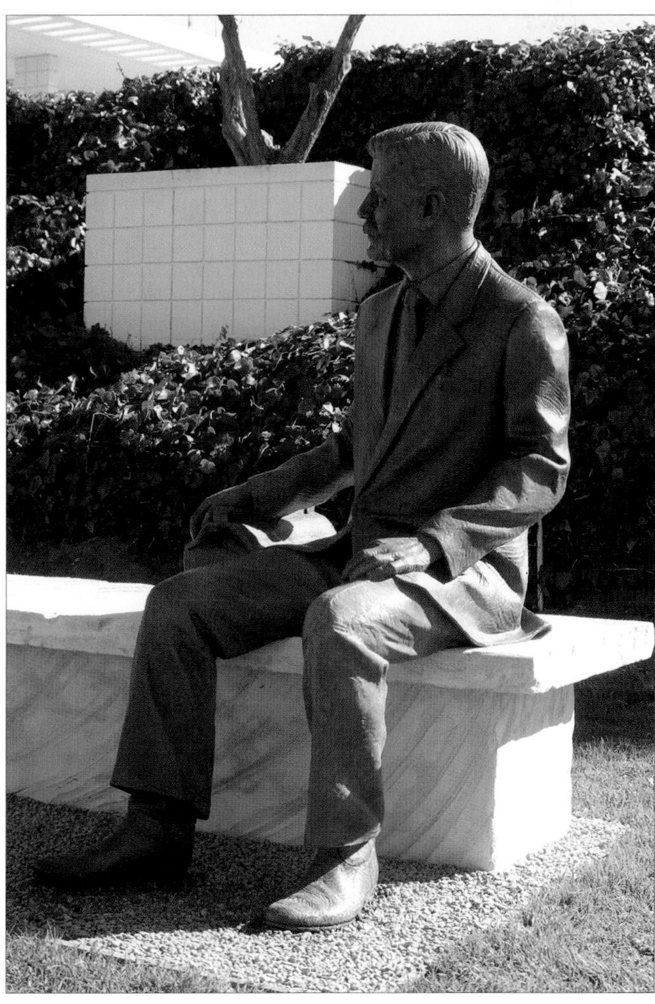

Top left: *Spirit of 1948*, Staffordshire, England, cast stone, 12' x 8' x 5'. Top right: *Joe and Jason*, bronze, life size, part of *A National Salute to Bob Hope and Our Military*. Bottom left: *A National Salute to Bob Hope and Our Military* maquettes, 2006, final sculpture to be unveiled in the Port of San Diego, CA, Oct. 2007. Bottom right: *Dr. John L. D. Roberts*, Seaside, CA, 7' x 4' x 5'.

KAREN R. STODDARD

ELEGANCE IN ART ■ 385 WEST BROADWAY ■ IDAHO FALLS, ID 83402 ■ TEL 208-523-7765 ■ TEL 800-523-7785
FAX 208-523-2171 ■ E-MAIL ELEGINART@AOL.COM ■ WWW.ELEGANCEINARTGALLERY.COM

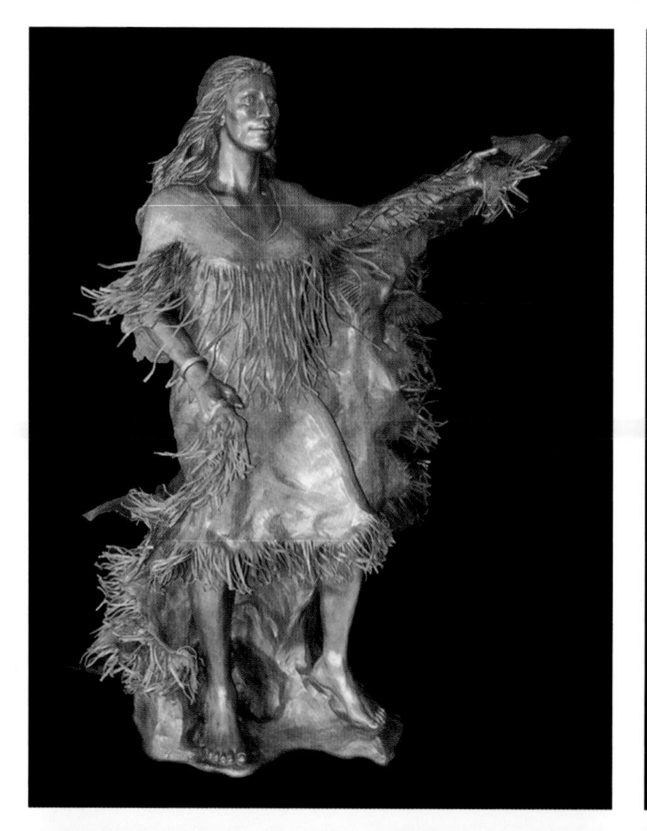

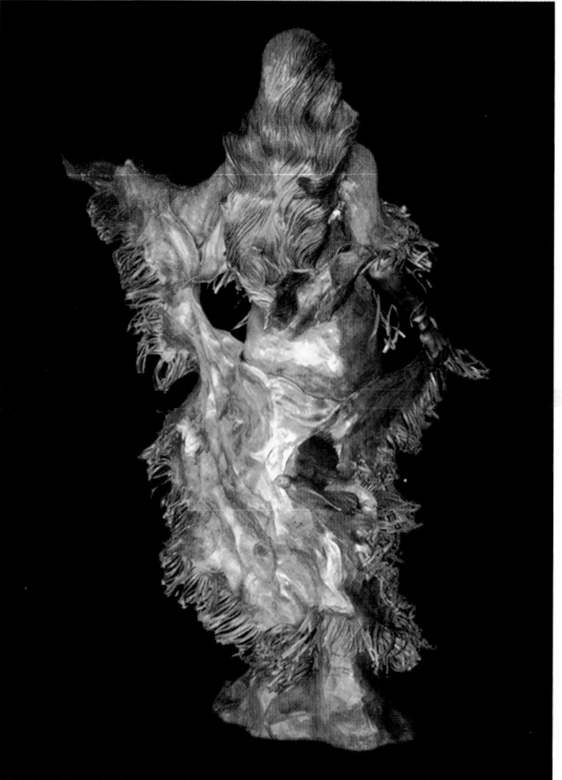

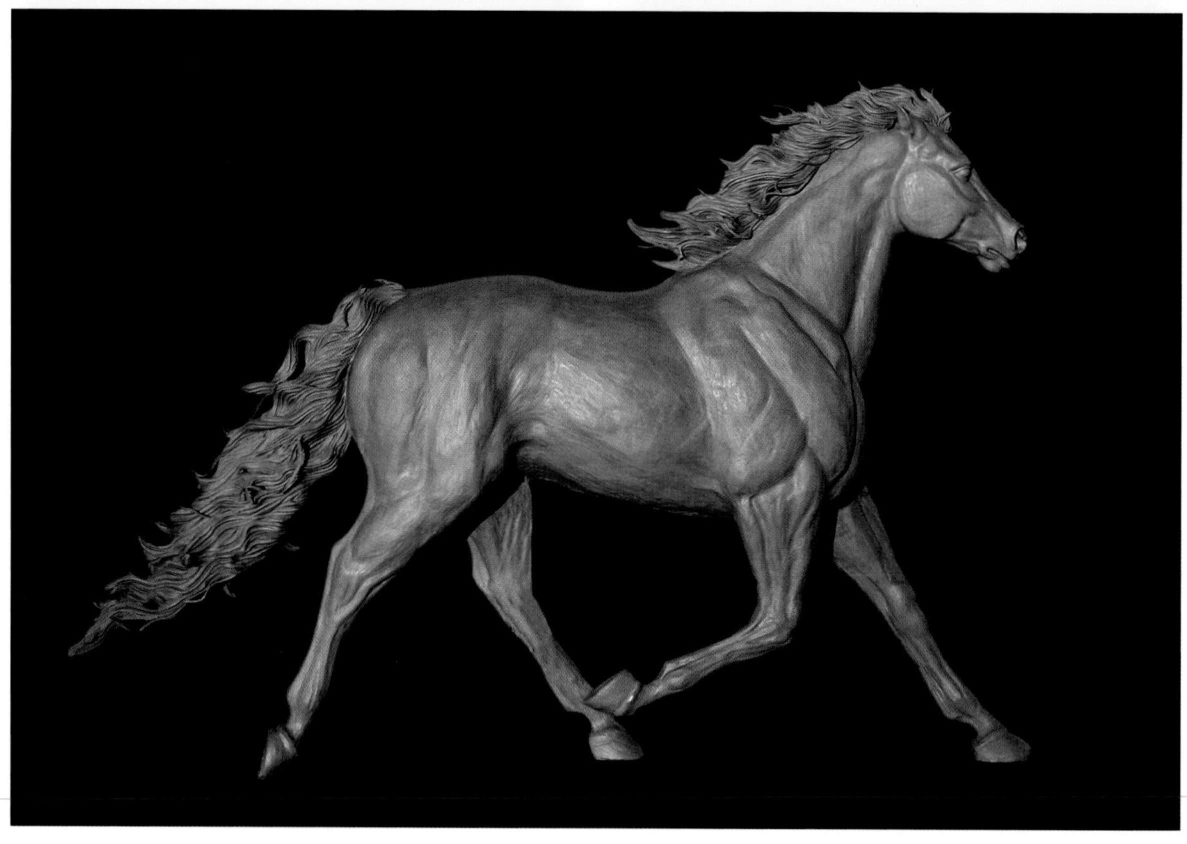

Top: *Indigenous Beauty—The Spirit of Sacajawea*, bronze, 70"H x 25"W x 58"L, edition of twenty-five.
Bottom: *Kudo—Lead Mare of Equus*, 72"H x 112"W x 28"D.

JAMES STONE

STONE AND GLASS ■ 13330 PASEO DEL VERANO ■ SAN DIEGO, CA 92128 ■ TEL 858-485-7701
FAX 760-294-4946 ■ E-MAIL JAMSTONE@COX.NET ■ WWW.STONEANDGLASS.COM

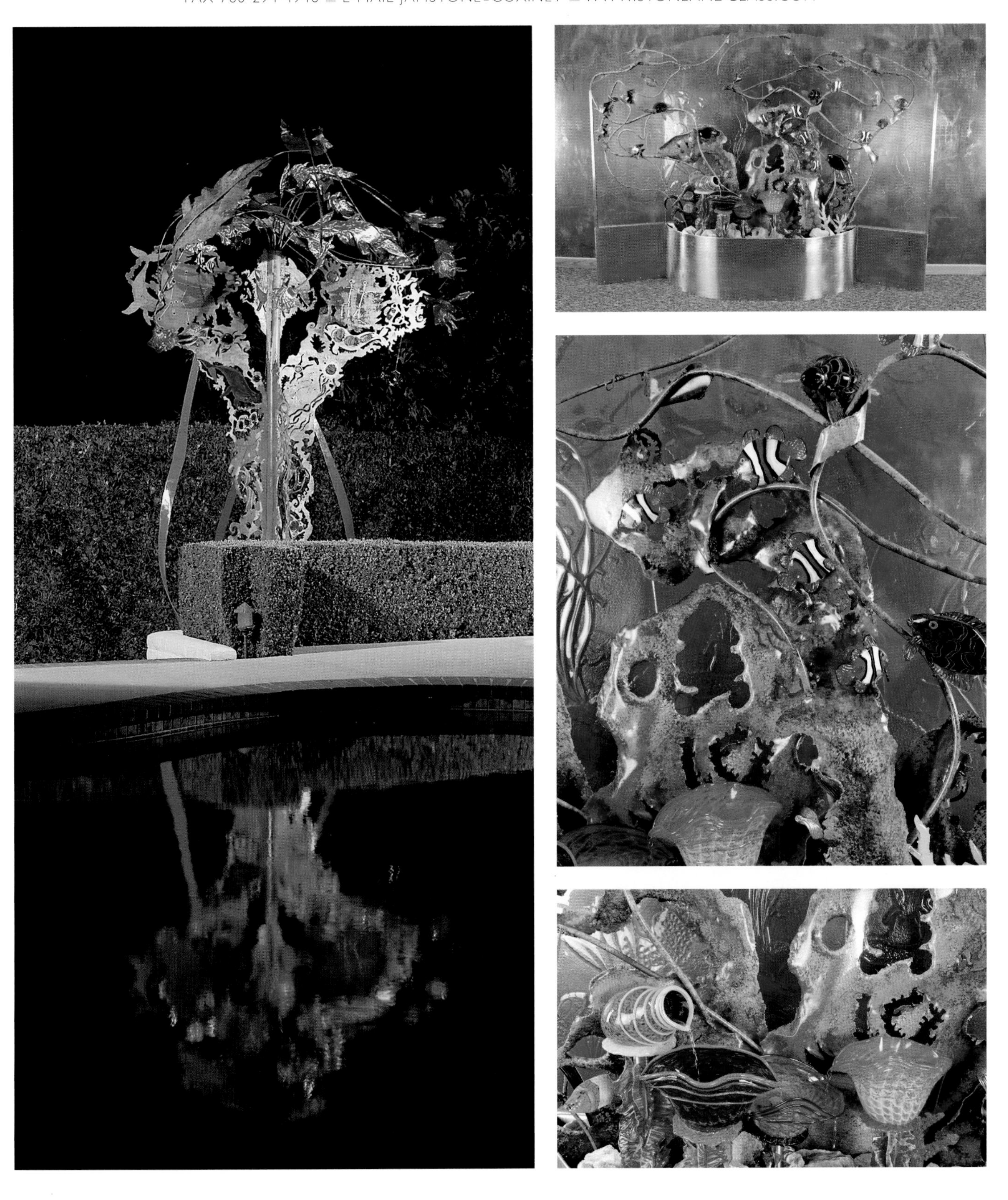

Left: *Neath the Sea*, steel with blown, sculpted, and cast glass, 16' x 6' x 6'.
Right: *Memories of the Sea*, forged copper and fabricated stainless steel with blown, sculpted, and slumped glass 8' x 12' x 20".

MARTIN STURMAN

STEEL SCULPTURES ■ 3201 BAYSHORE DRIVE ■ WESTLAKE VILLAGE, CA 91361-4933 ■ TEL 818-707-8087
FAX 818-707-3079 ■ E-MAIL MLSTURMAN@SBCGLOBAL.NET ■ WWW.STURMANSTEELSCULPTURES.COM

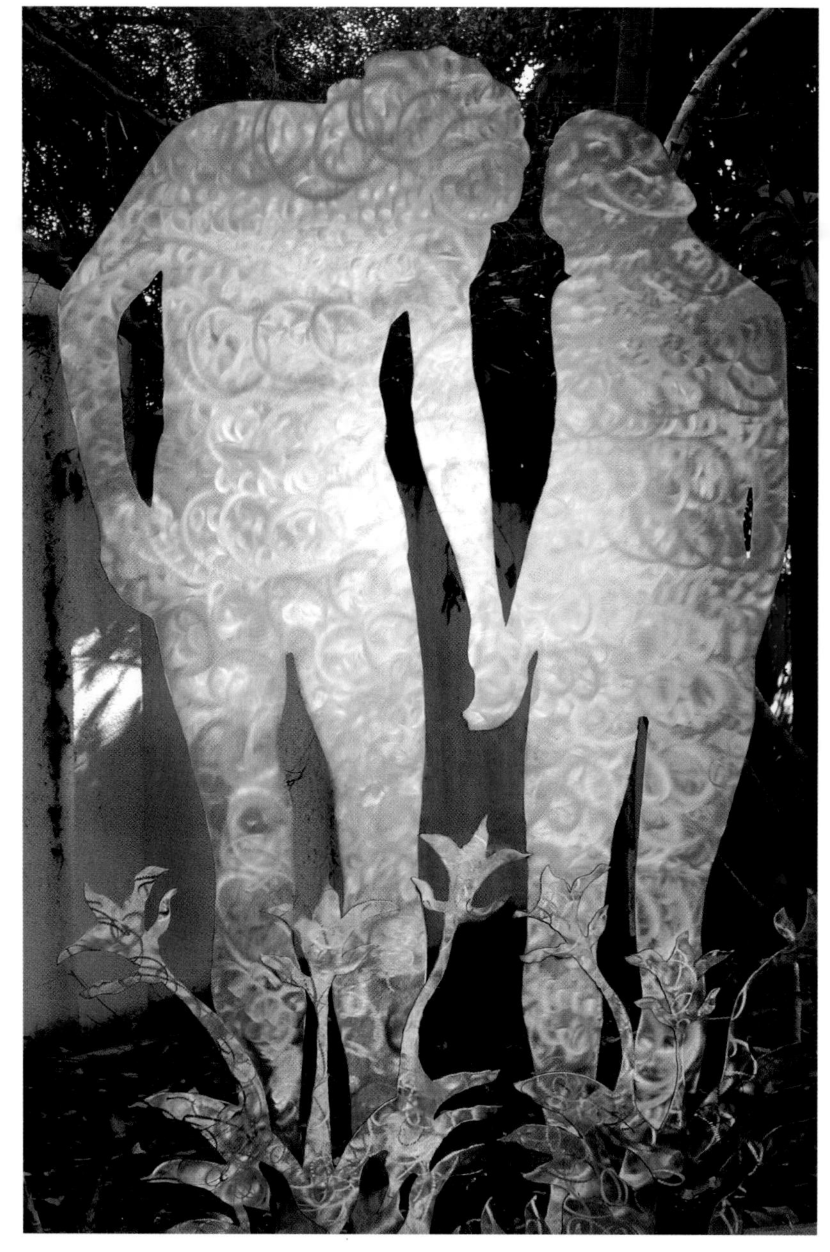

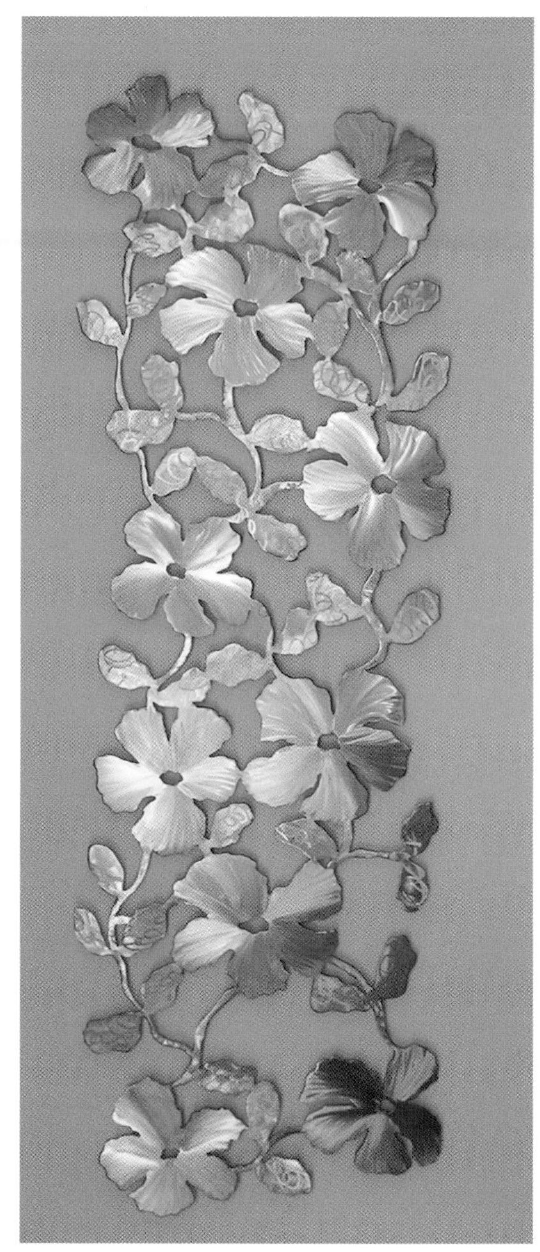

Left: *Lovers In Garden*, stainless steel, 72"H x 46"W x 19"D. Right: *Hibiscus*, stainless steel, 72"H x 24"W x 2"D.

GARY TILLERY

1142 FAIRVIEW AVENUE ■ LAKE FOREST, IL 60045 ■ TEL 847-707-1091
E-MAIL GARYTILLERY@HOTMAIL.COM ■ WWW.GARYTILLERY.COM

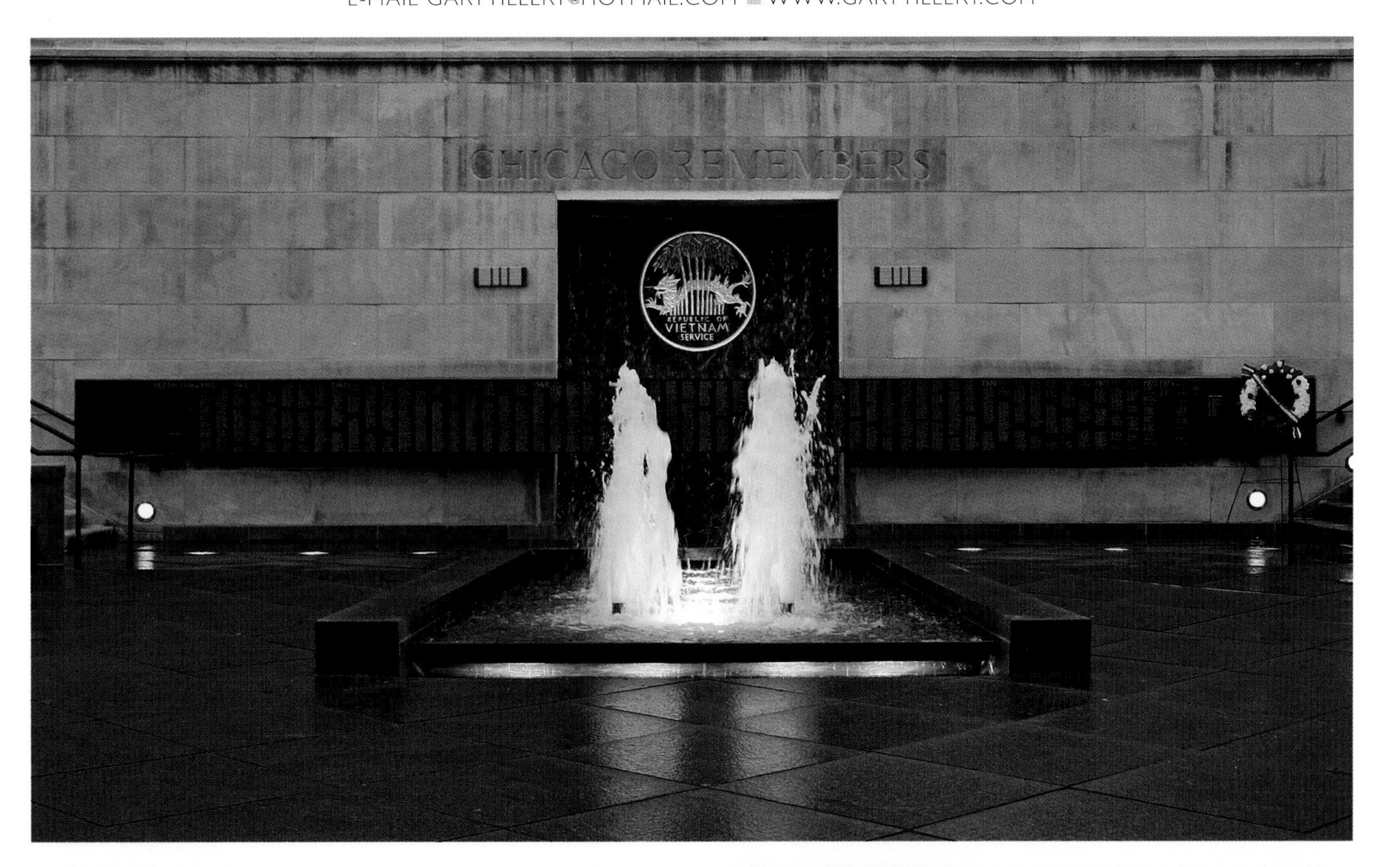

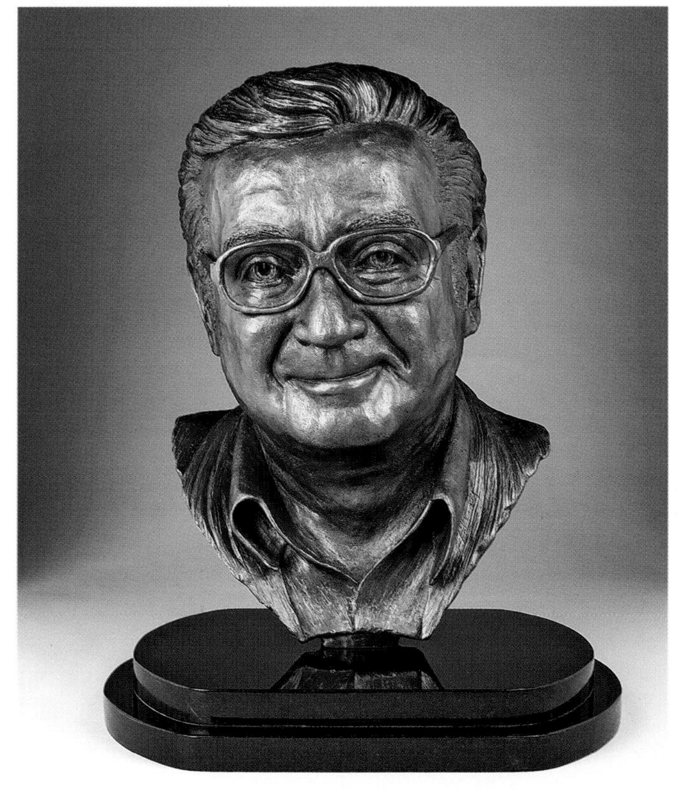

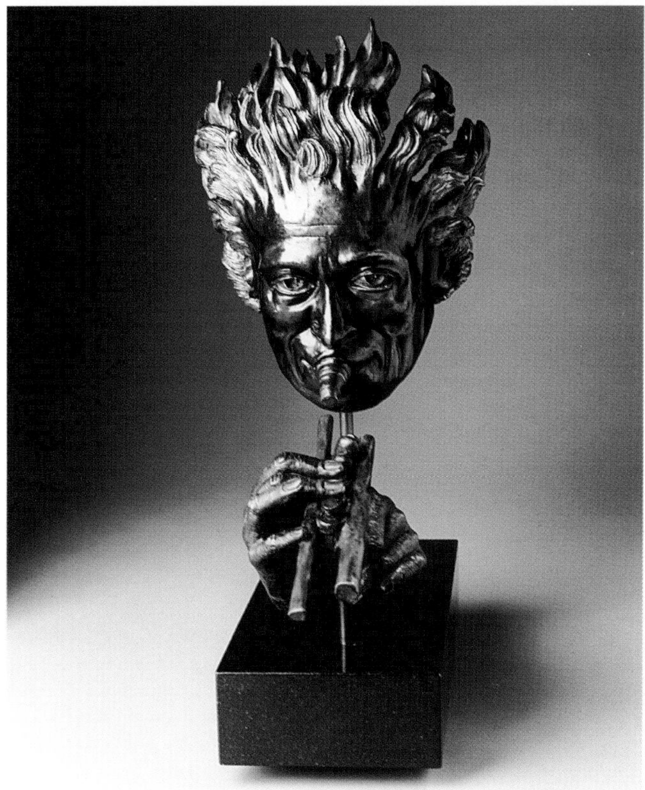

Top: *Chicago Vietnam Veterans Memorial,* 2005, bronze and enamels, 12' x 16'. Photograph: William M. Rausch, Rausch Construction, Inc.
Bottom left: *Steve Allen,* 2003, bronze, 20" x 13" x 12". Photograph: Robert Tolchin. Bottom right: *Jazz Man,* 2000, bronze, 25" x 13" x 20". Photograph: Robert Tolchin.

JOSHUA TOBEY

JOSHUA TOBEY STUDIOS ■ 15261 CARTAGENA COURT ■ CORPUS CHRISTI, TX 78418 ■ TEL 361-949-4638
TEL 361-222-0100 ■ FAX 361-949-7376 ■ E-MAIL JOSHUATOBEYSTUDIOS@YAHOO.COM ■ WWW.TOBEYSTUDIOS.COM

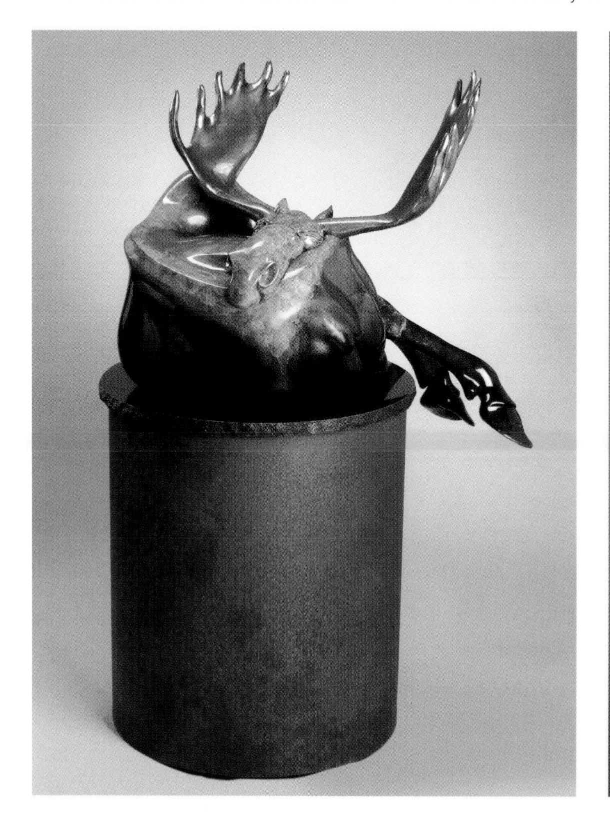

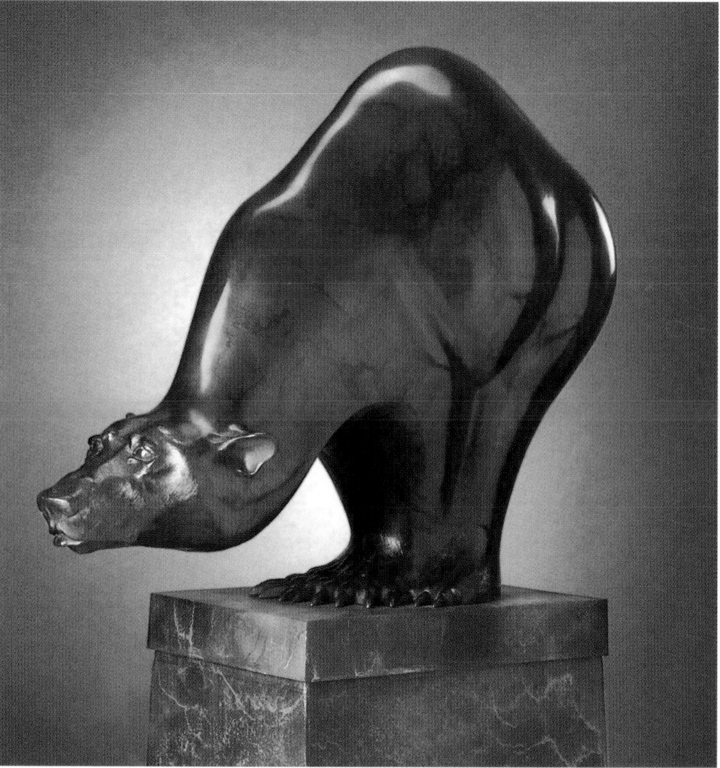

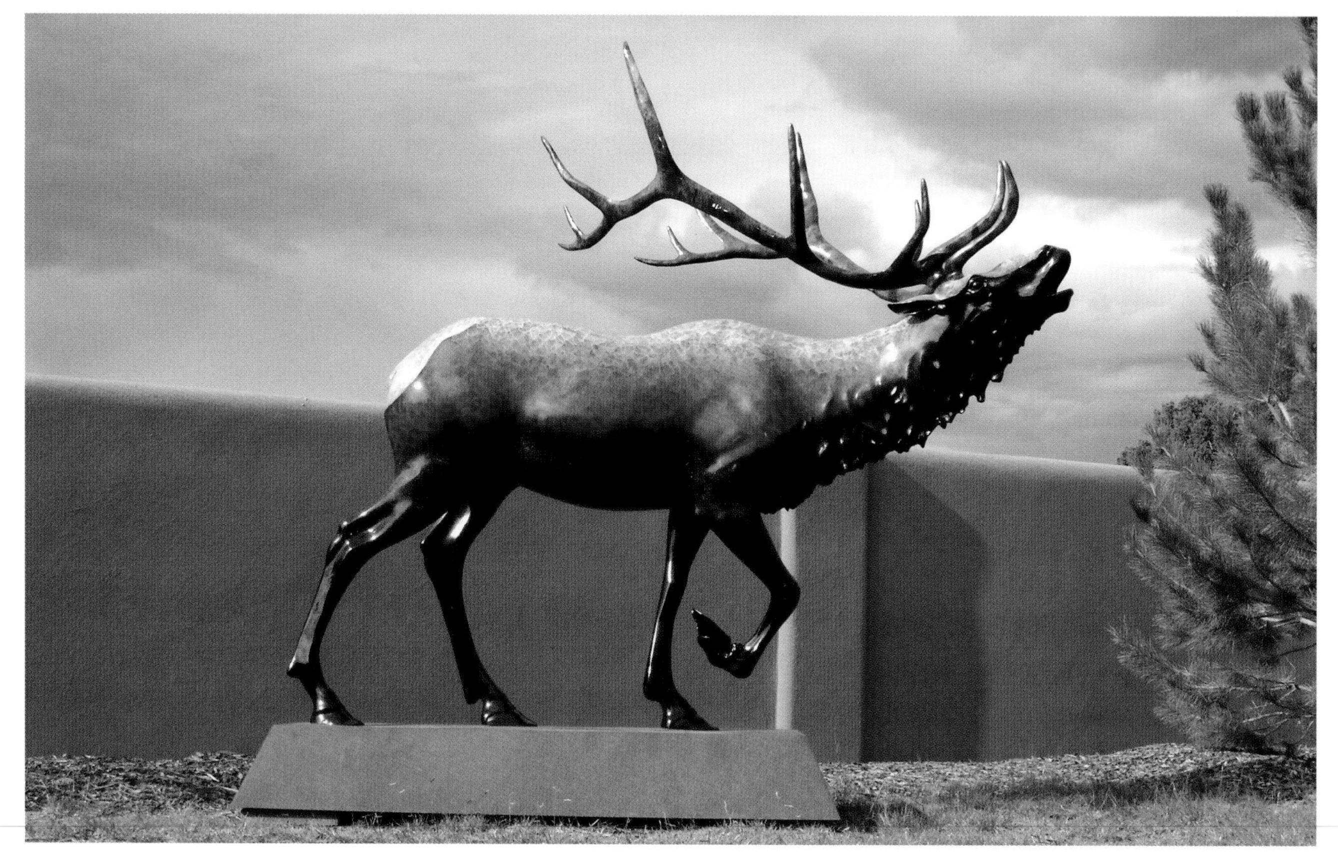

Top left: *The Enlightened One*, 57"H x 40"W x 40"D. Photograph: Marc Bennett. Top right: *Denali*, bronze, 32" x 41" x 18", with optional 36"H base. Bottom: *Heart of the Mountain*, 99"H x 56"W x 99"L. Photograph: Josephine Franklin.

WANNER SCULPTURE STUDIO

DAVID WANNER ■ JORDAN WANNER ■ 5828 NORTH 97TH STREET ■ MILWAUKEE, WI 53225
TEL/FAX 414-462-3569 ■ E-MAIL INFO@WANNERSCULPTURESTUDIO.COM ■ WWW.WANNERSCULPTURESTUDIO.COM

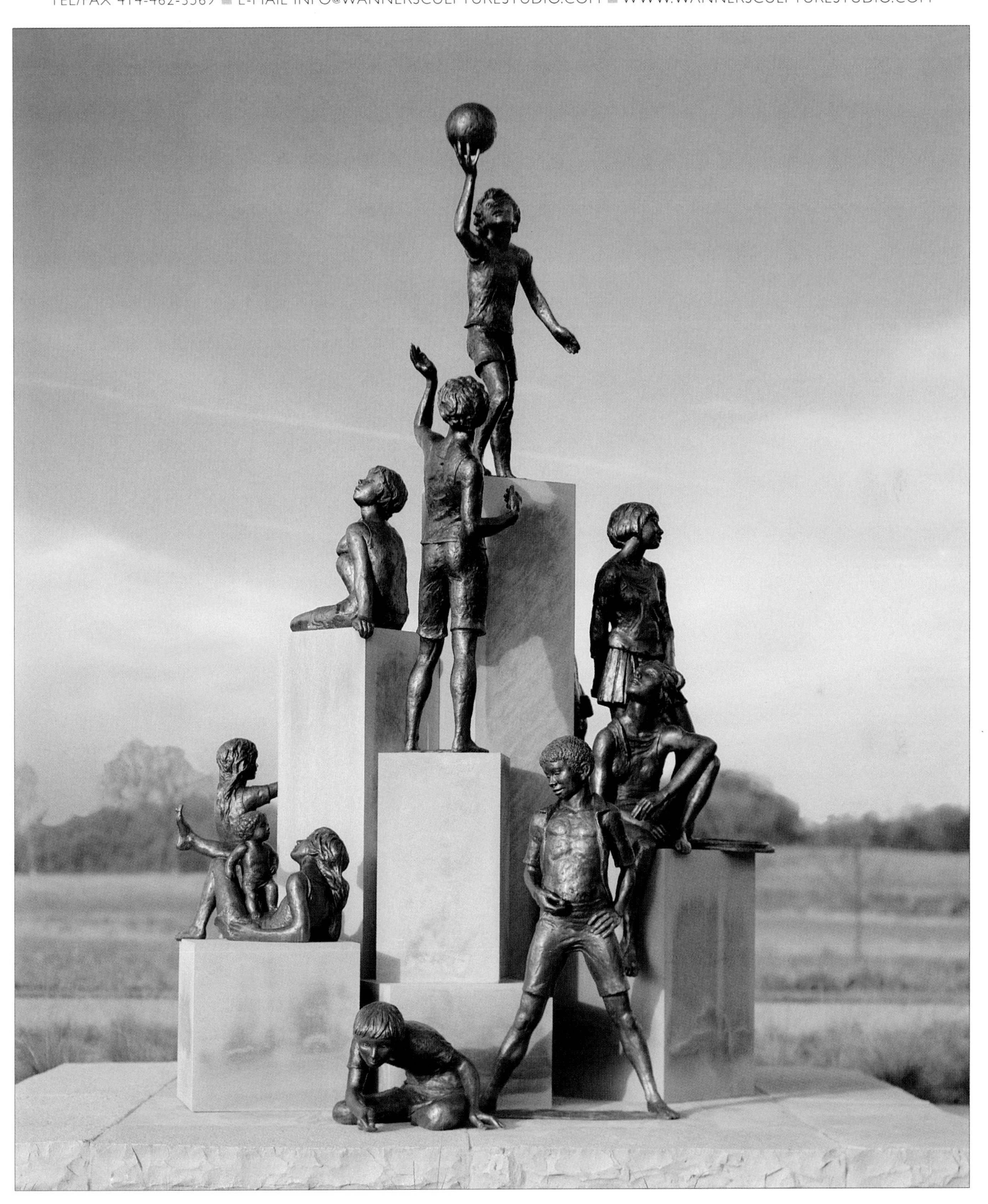

At Play, American Family Insurance World Headquarters, Madison, WI, bronze, life size.

BRUCE WOLFE

BRUCE WOLFE LTD. ■ 206 EL CERRITO AVENUE ■ PIEDMONT, CA 94611 ■ TEL 510-655-7871
FAX 510-601-7200 ■ E-MAIL LANDBWOLFE@EARTHLINK.NET ■ WWW.BRUCEWOLFE.COM

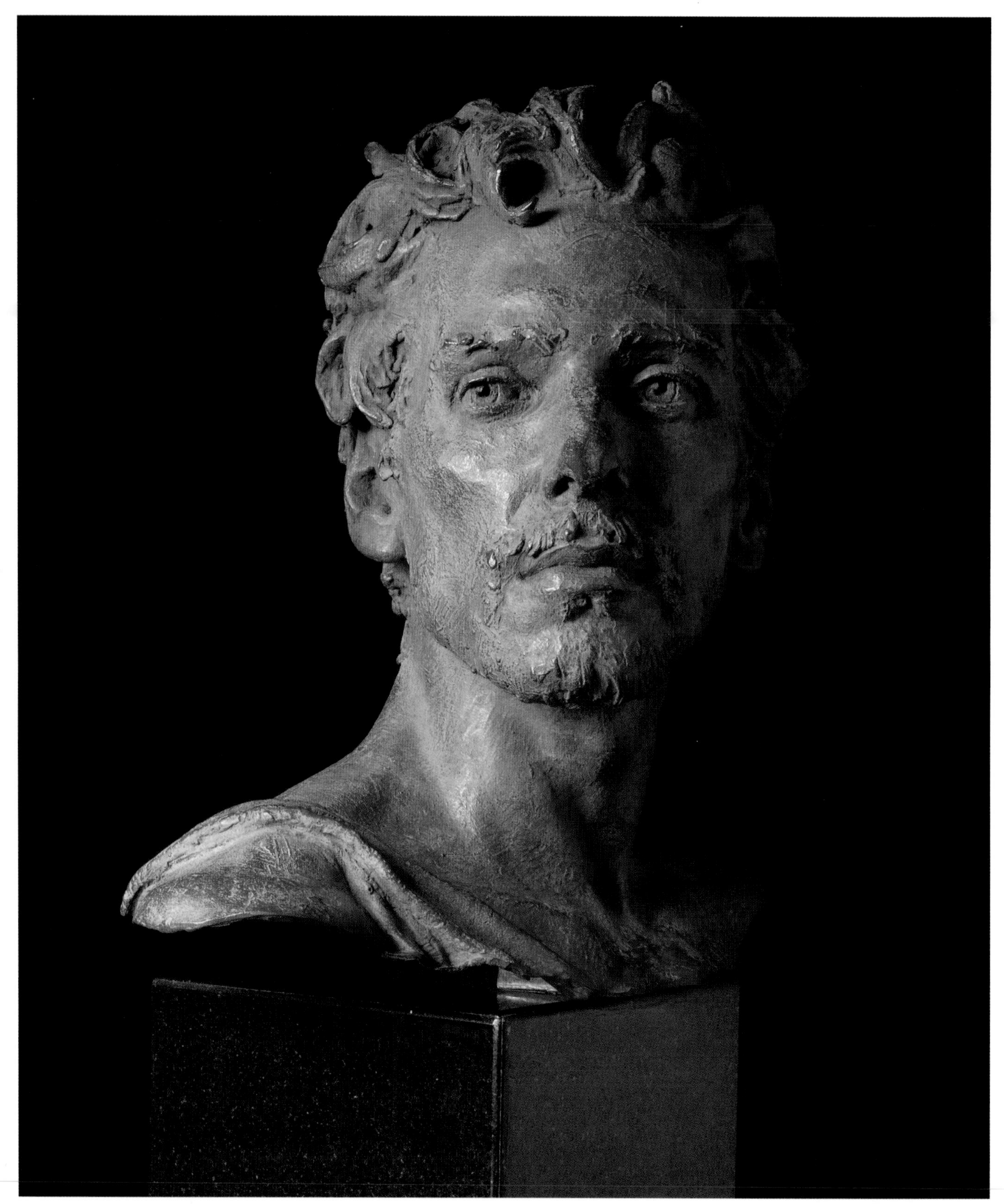

Claudio, bronze, 15"H x 18"W, first place winner of the Art of the Portrait conference of the Portrait Society of America. Photograph: Brian Mahany.

DERAN WRIGHT

3513 LABADIE DRIVE ■ FORT WORTH, TX 76118 ■ TEL 817-590-9598
E-MAIL DERANWRIGHT@GMAIL.COM ■ WWW.DERANWRIGHT.COM

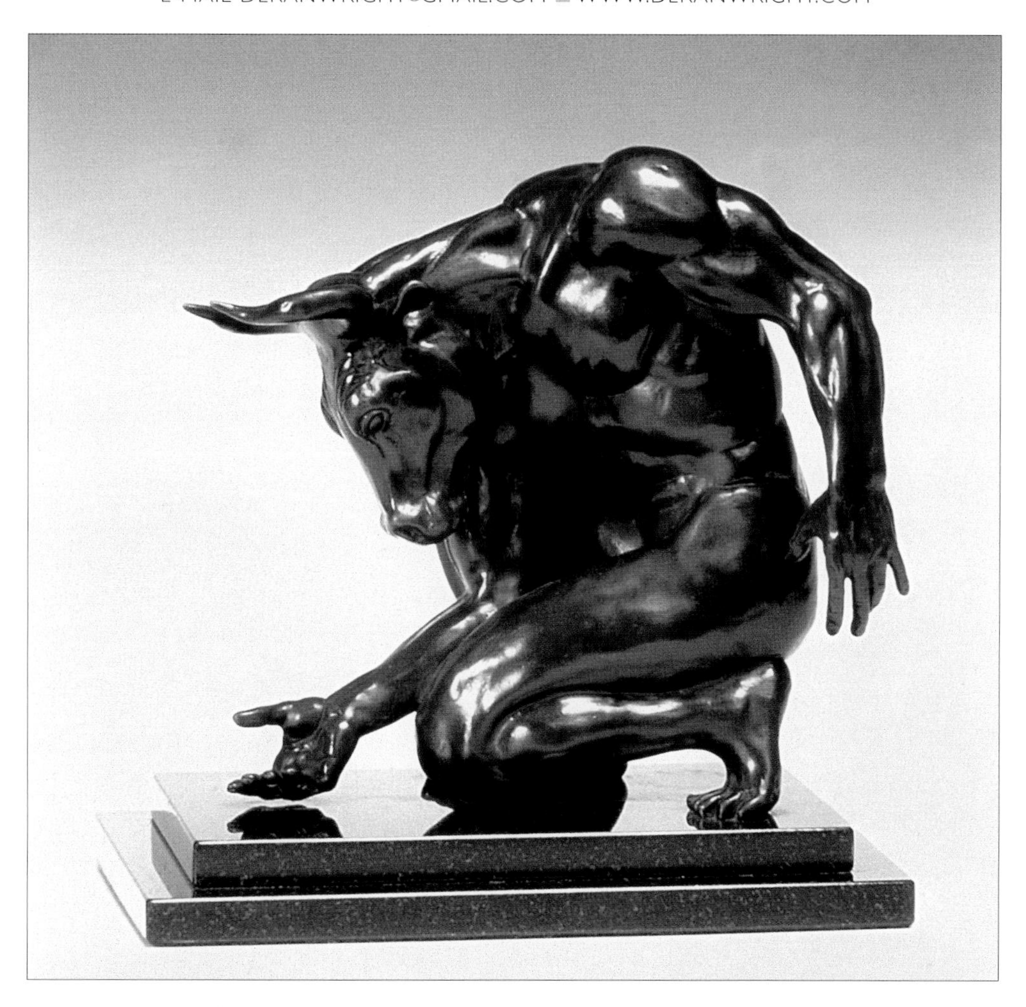

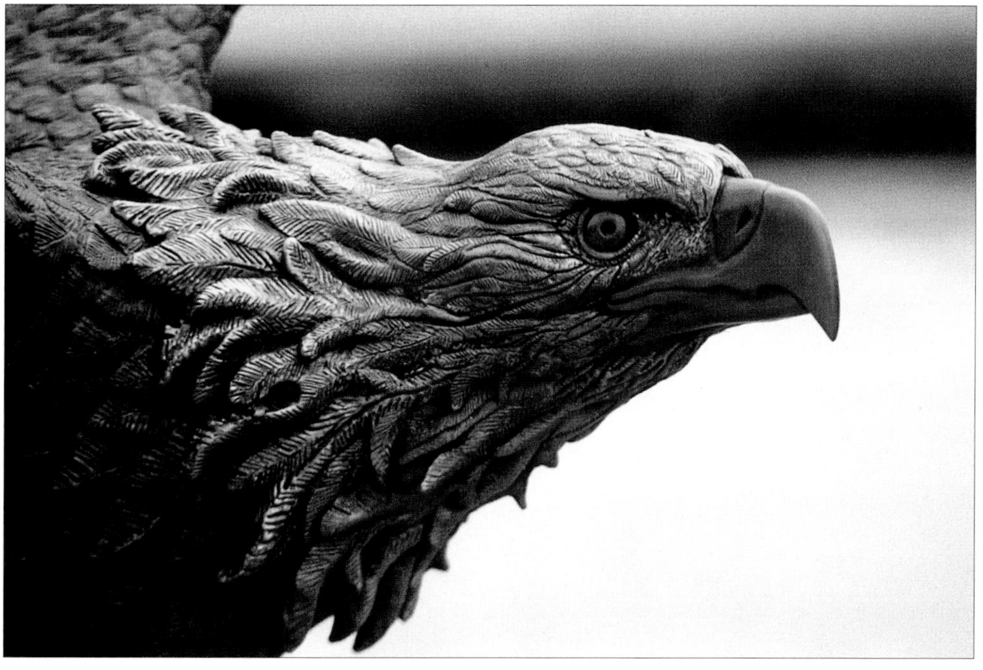

Top: *The Minotaur.* Photograph: B.J. Lacasse. Bottom: *Eagle Scout Memorial.*

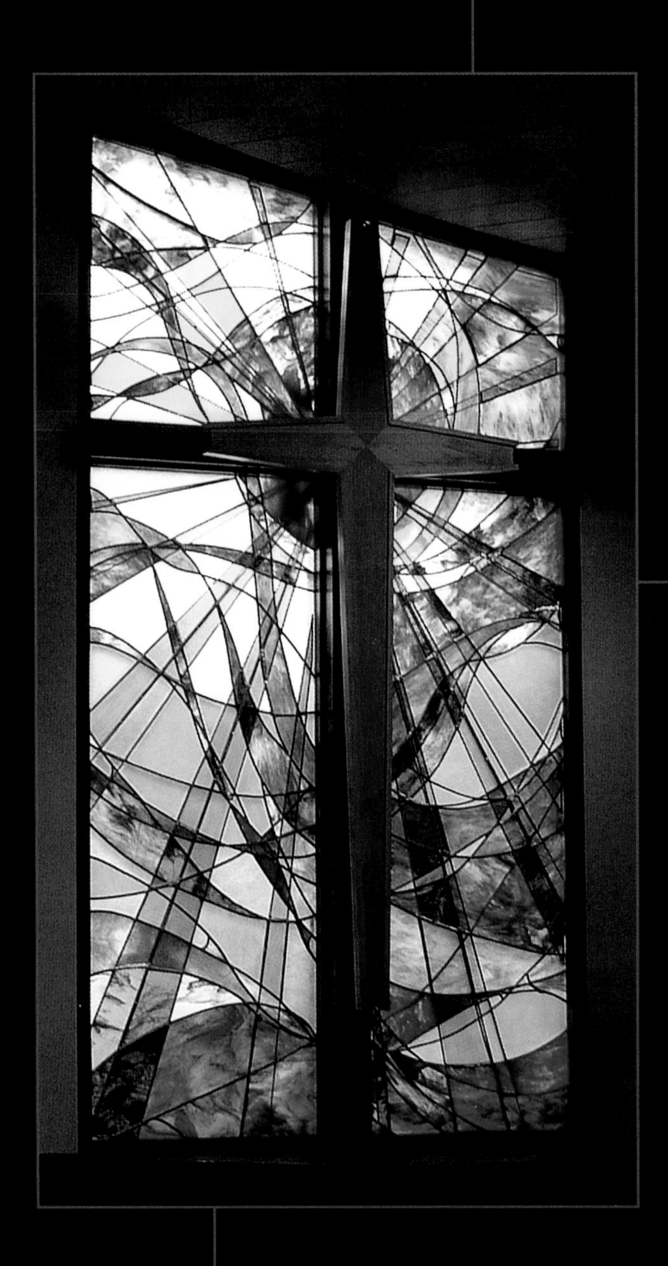

Liturgical Art

LEAH KRISTIN DAHLGREN

PO BOX 44 ■ TEMPLE, NH 03084 ■ TEL 603-878-0755
E-MAIL LK@DAHLGRENFINEART.COM ■ WWW.DAHLGRENFINEART.COM

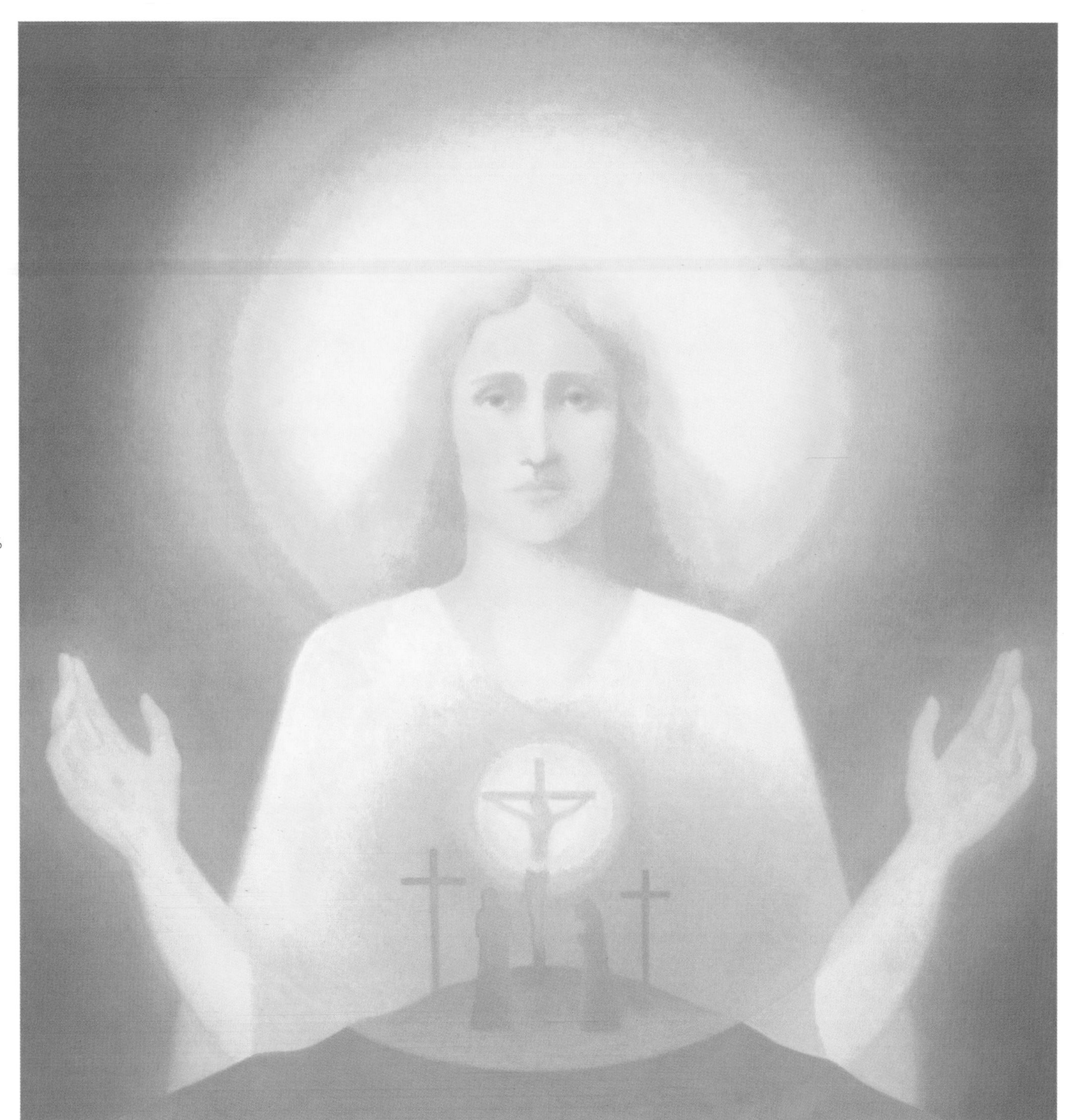

The Risen One, 36" x 34". Photograph: Rounds & Company.

FORMS IN METAL

LARRY LEWIS ■ 100 MELVIN AVENUE ■ CATONSVILLE, MD 21228 ■ TEL 410-747-8393
FAX 410-744-9070 ■ E-MAIL FORMSINMETAL@COMCAST.NET ■ WWW.FORMS-IN-METAL.COM

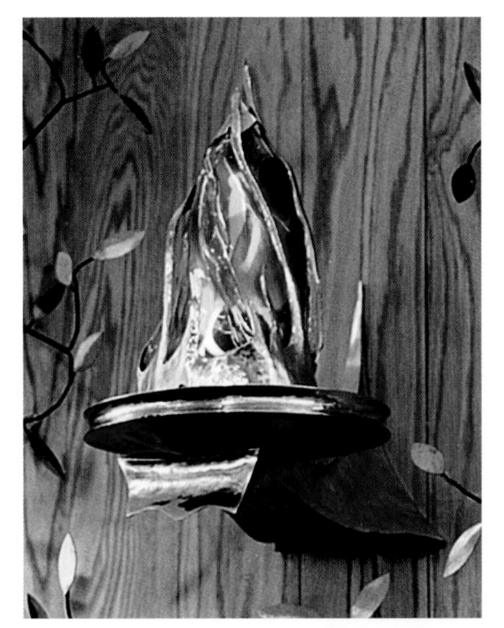

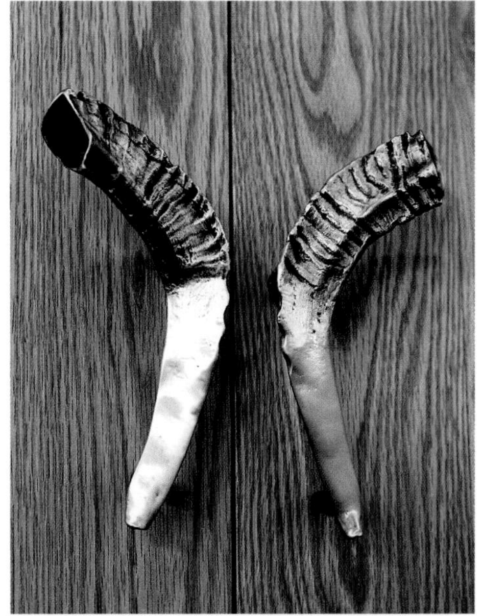

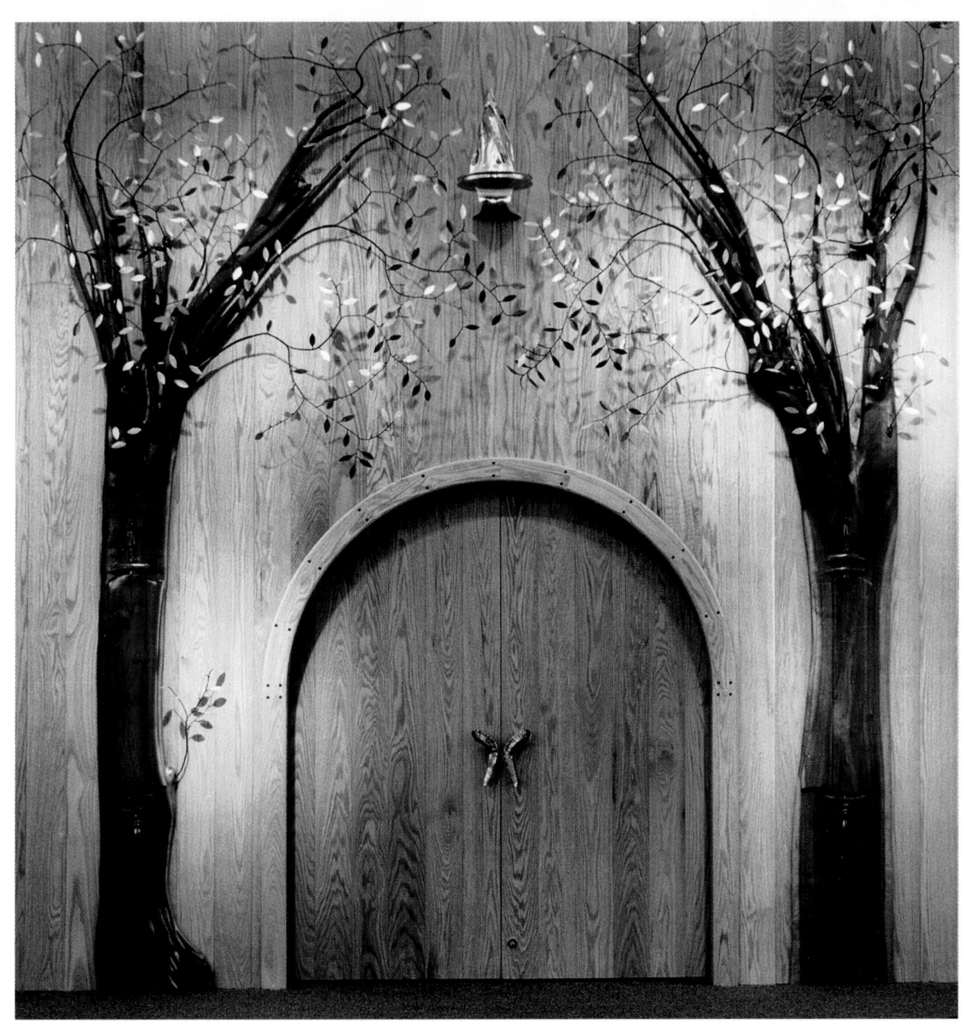

Top left: Synagogue Eternal Light (detail), brass and glass, 16"H x 12"W x 14"D. Top right: Synagogue door handles (detail), bronze, 10"H x 9"W. Bottom: Synagogue sanctuary, 1995, Gaithersburg, MD, brass and bronze, 15'H x 10'W.

PICTURES IN GLASS

PATRICIA DEERE ■ 10650 CARSON HIGHWAY ■ TECUMSEH, MI 49286
TEL 517-431-2271 ■ E-MAIL INFO@PICTURESINGLASS.NET ■ WWW.PICTURESINGLASS.NET

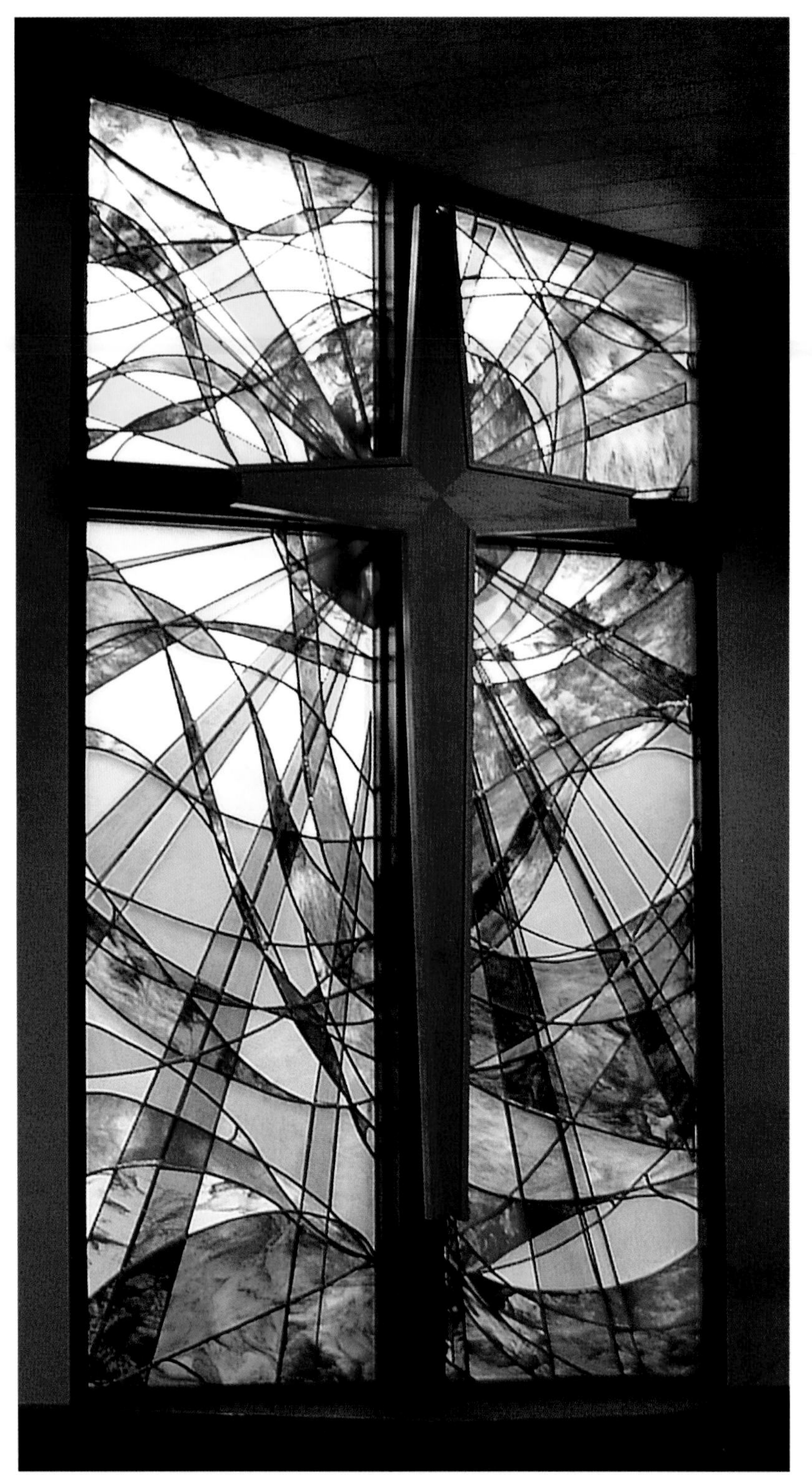

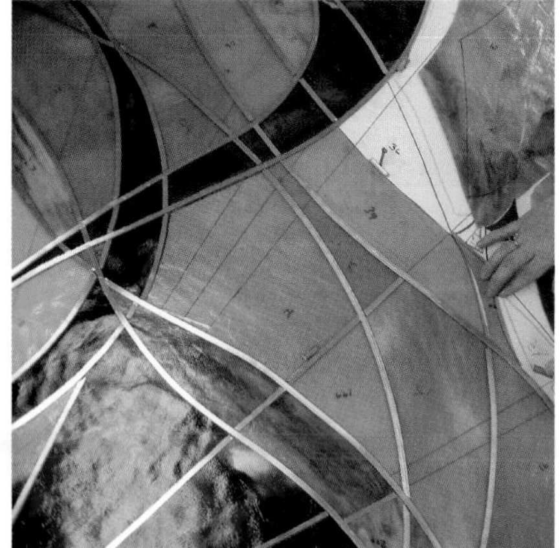

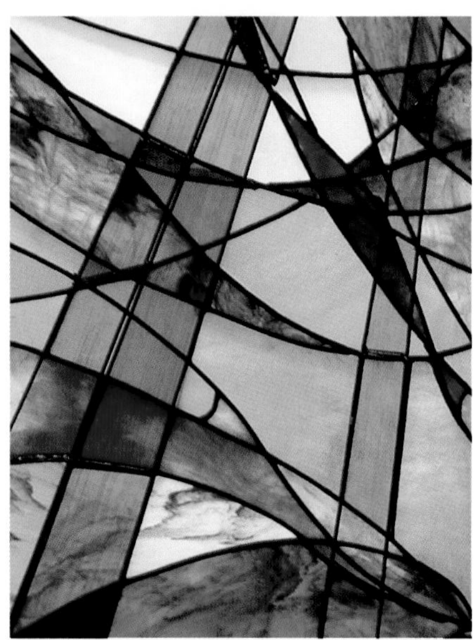

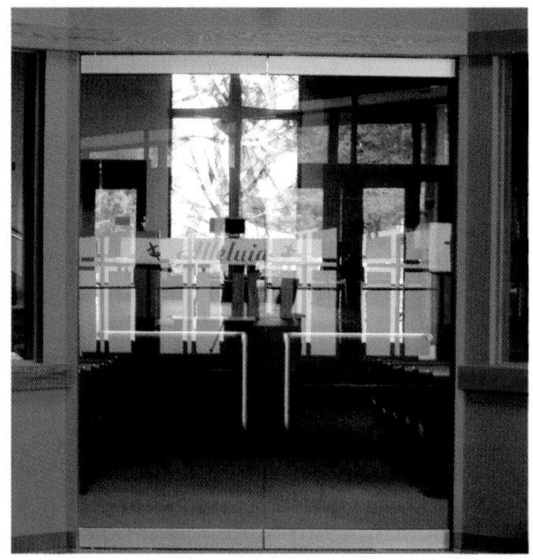

Window, St. John Lutheran Church, Farmington, MI, leaded glass with Youghiogheny stipple glass background and overlaid Uroboros fibroid sun rays, total size: 12'H x 6'W. Created in conjunction with artist Pamela Shapiro.

JUANITA YODER

148 MONMOUTH STREET ■ HIGHTSTOWN, NJ 08520
TEL 609-448-5335 ■ E-MAIL JUANITA@JYKART.COM ■ WWW.JYKART.COM

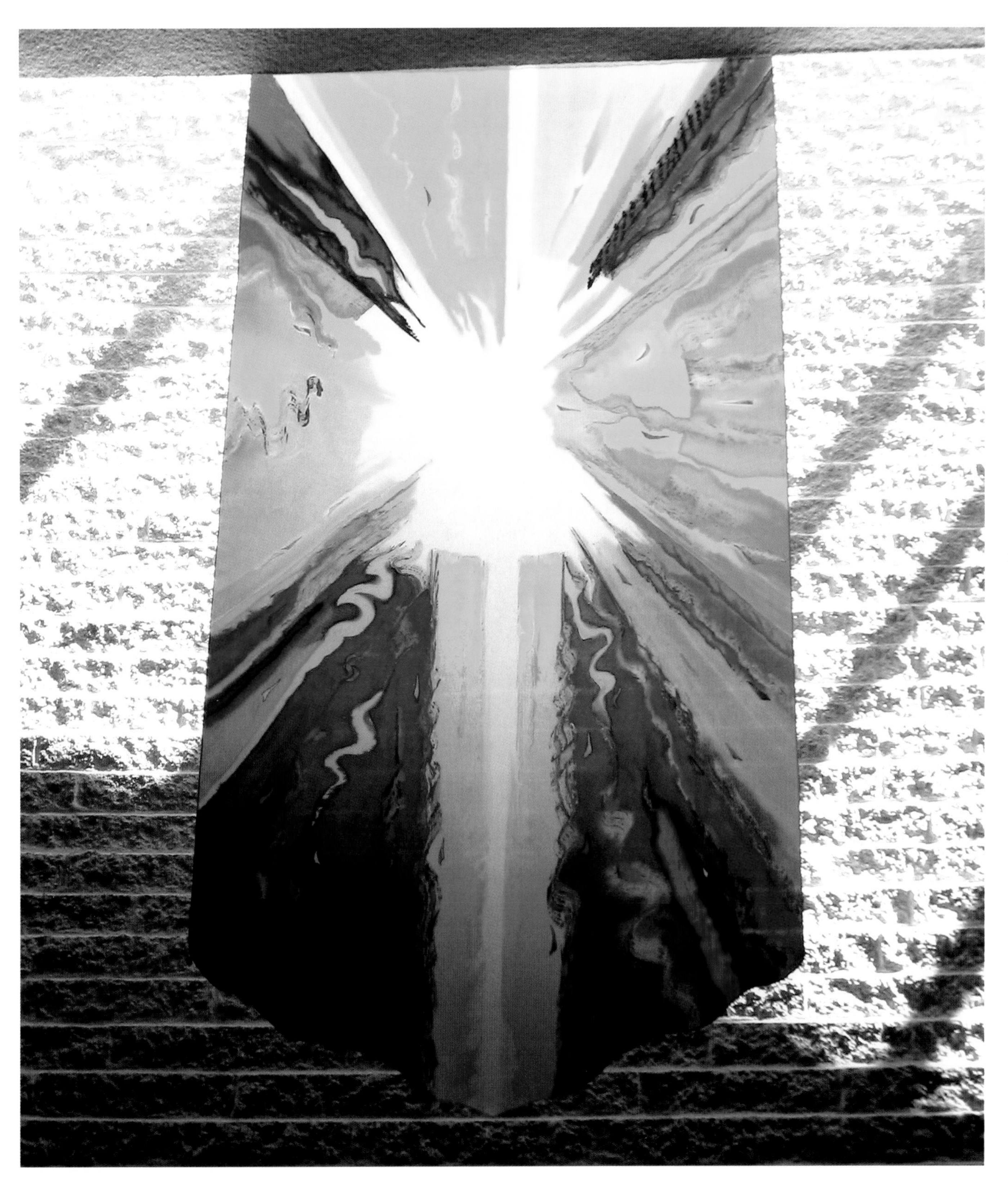

Resurrection: Station of the Cross 15, Church of St. Thomas More, Glendale, AZ, one of fifteen paintings on silk, each: 8' x 4'. Photographs: TaylorPhoto.com.

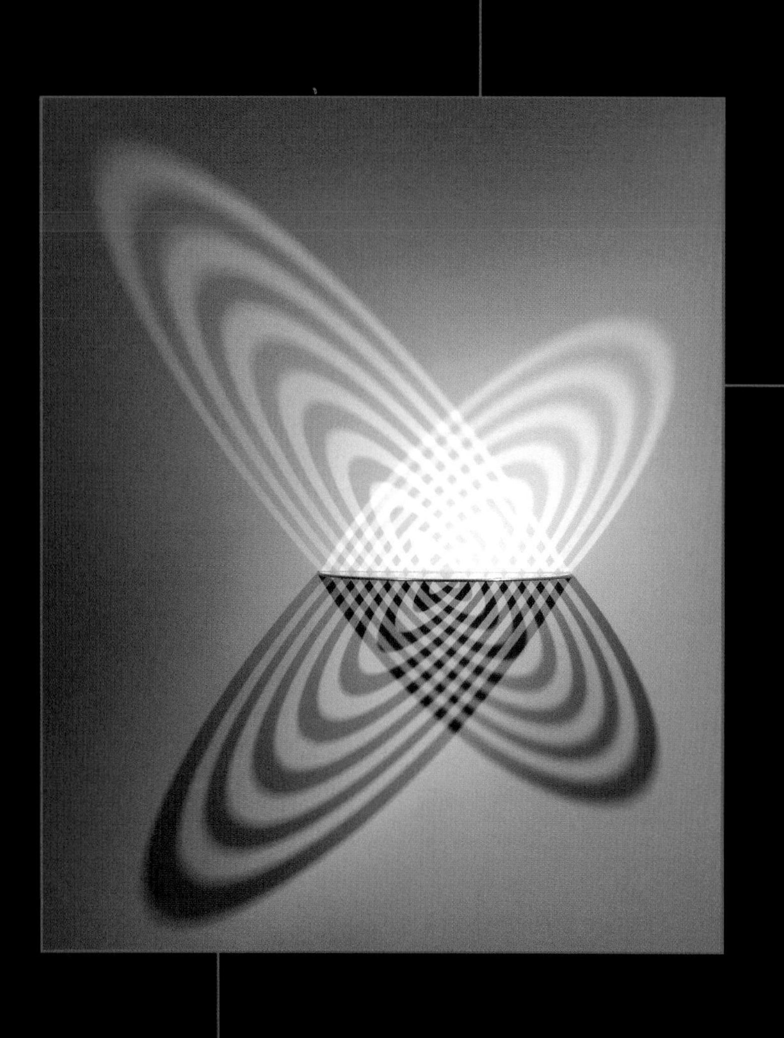

Lighting

ART OF BEING

CHARLES H. BARTHOLF ■ 5991 WESTPORT LANE ■ NAPLES, FL 34116
TEL 239-289-3362 ■ E-MAIL CBARTHOLF@EARTHLINK.NET ■ WWW.ARTOFBEING.US

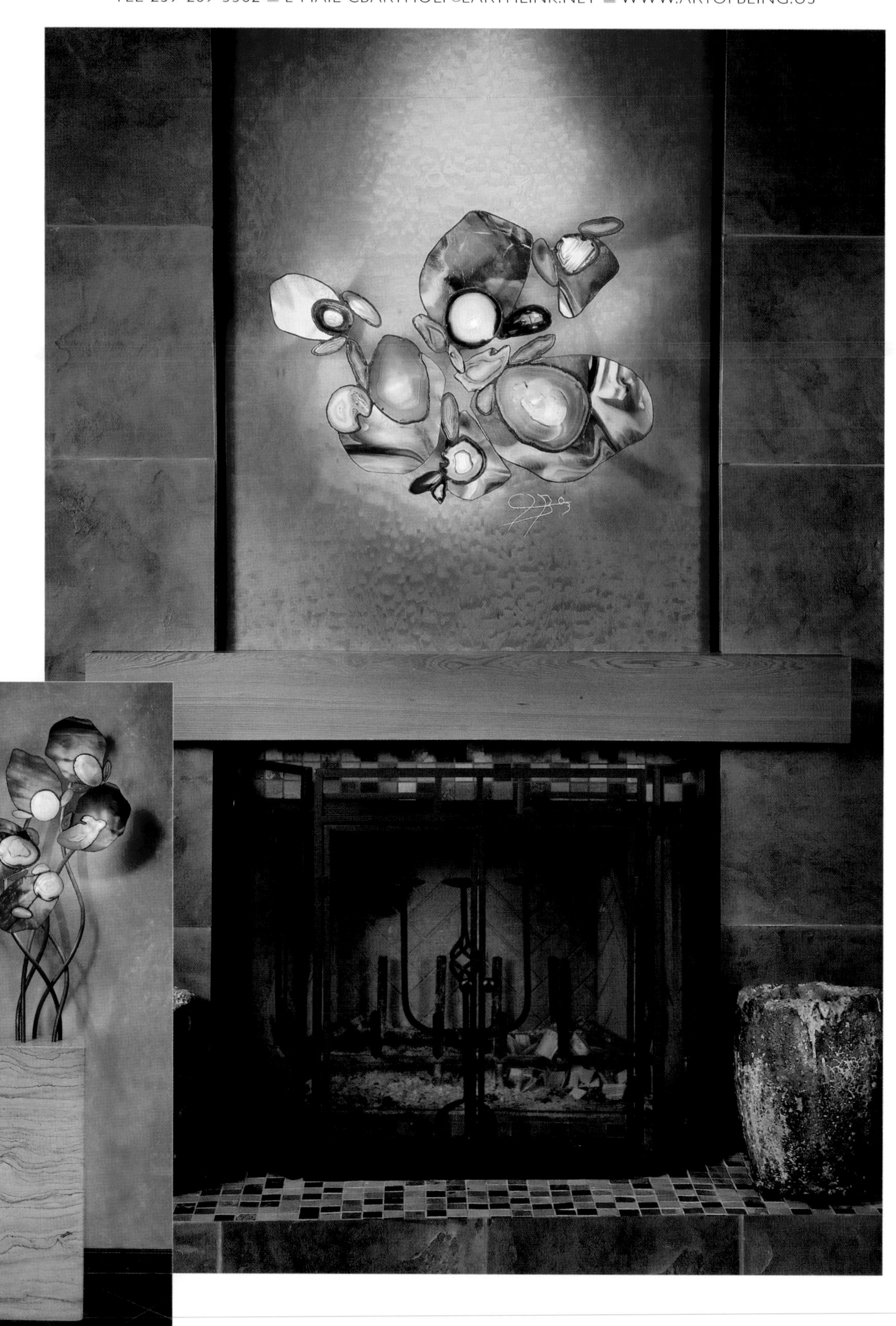

New Beginnings. Inset: *Into the Next Realm.* Photographs: John Sciarrino/Giovanni Photography.

SYDNEY CASH

72 RESERVOIR ROAD ■ MARLBORO, NY 12542 ■ TEL/FAX 845-236-7032
E-MAIL SCASH@HVC.RR.COM ■ WWW.SYDNEYCASH.COM

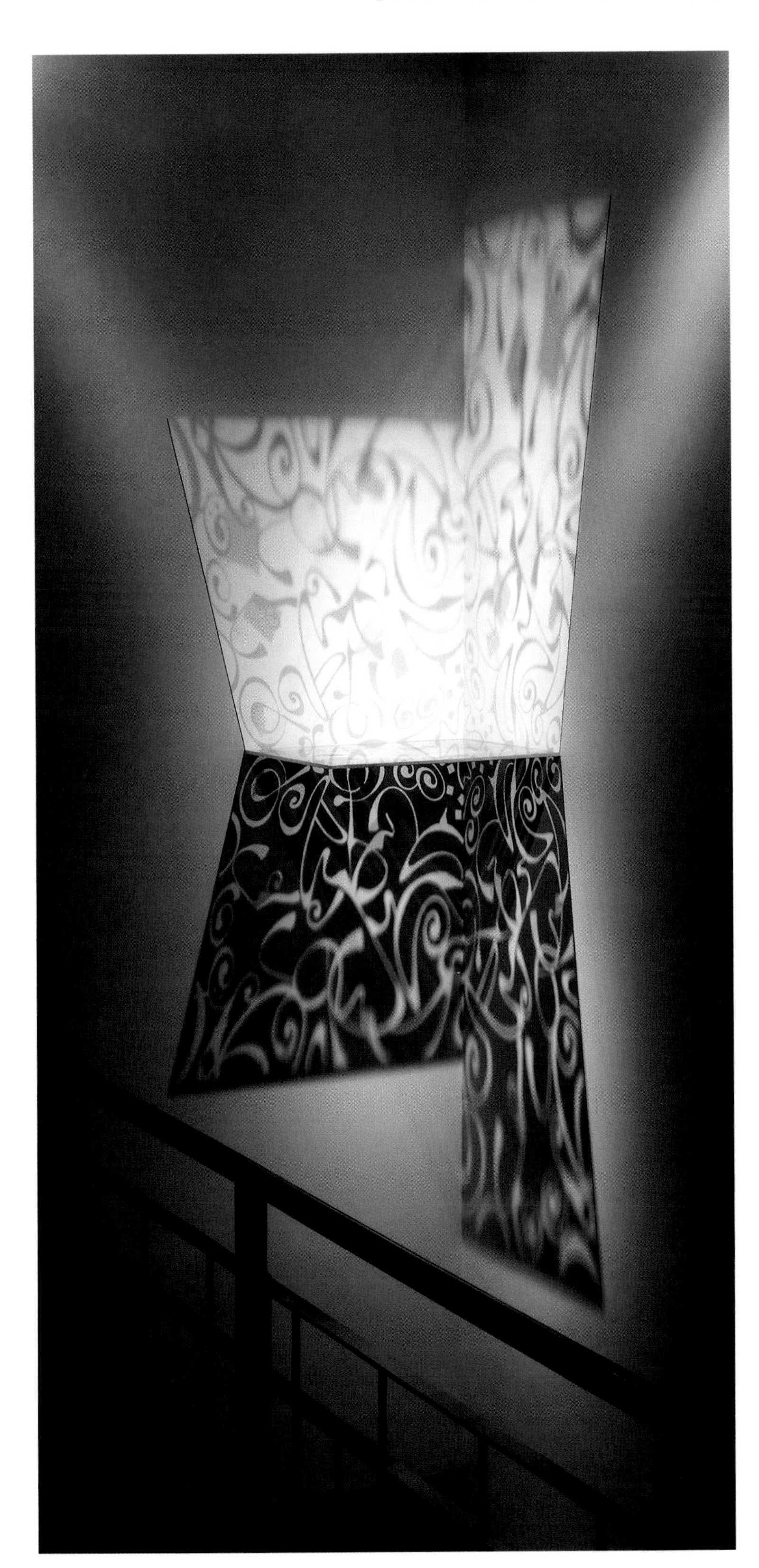

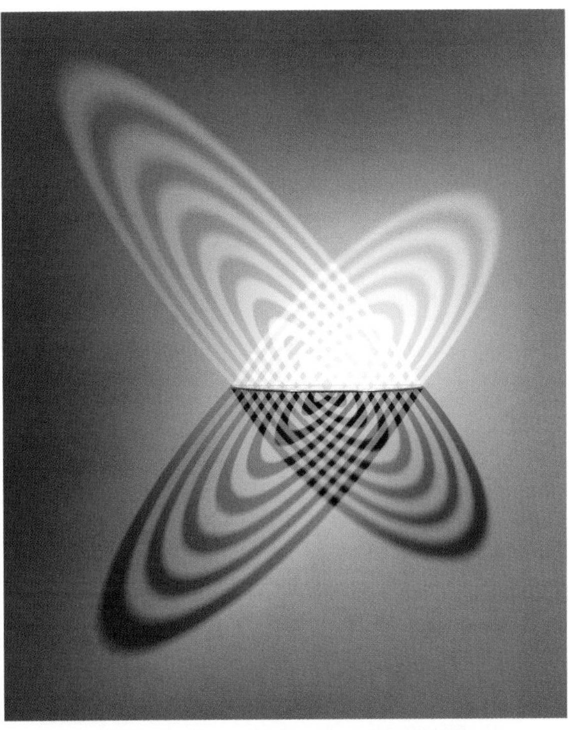

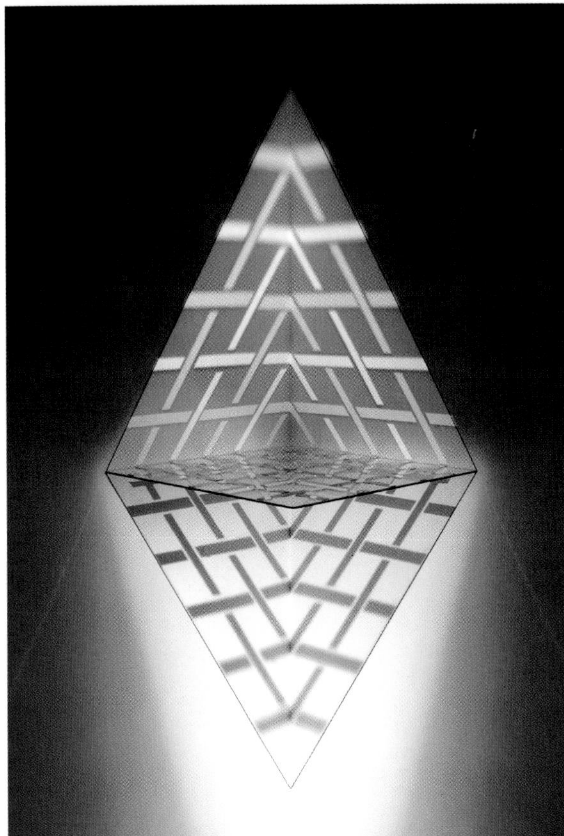

Left: *Jardin Des Fleurs*, 2006, stairwell corner in duplex loft, 78"H. Photograph: Todd Wienstein.
Top right: *Atomic*, 68"H. Photograph: Susan Jeffers. Bottom right: *Silver/Copper Weaving*, installed in wall corner, 61"H. Photograph: Laurel Smith.

SCOTT CHAMBERS

SCOTT CHAMBERS ARTIST INC. ■ 9844 25TH AVENUE SW ■ SEATTLE, WA 98106 ■ TEL 206-762-2009
E-MAIL PLAYINWITHFIRE9@AOL.COM ■ WWW.SCOTTCHAMBERSARTGLASS.COM

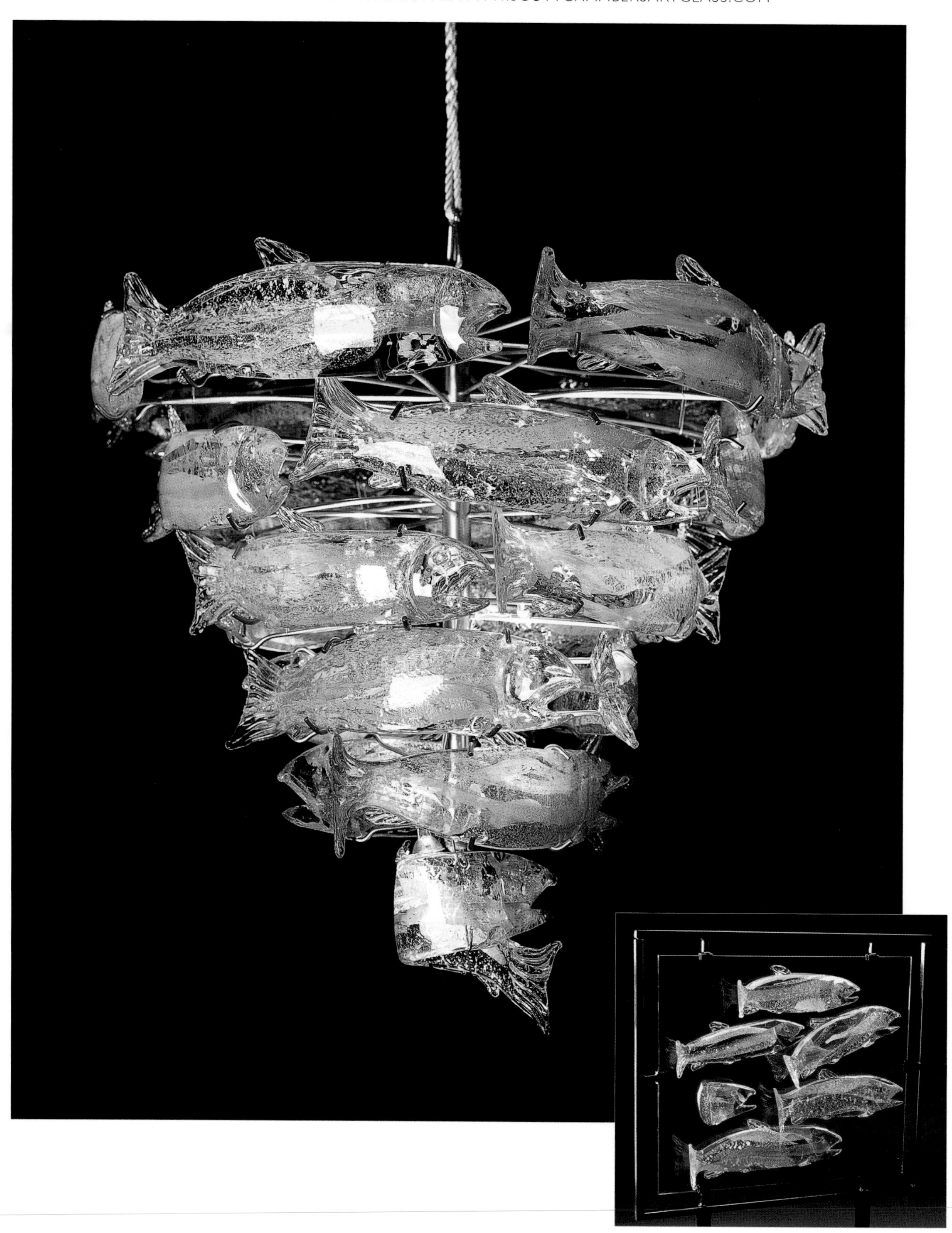

Top: *Salmon Chandelier,* hot-sculpted glass with sterling silver, 45"H x 40"W.
Inset: *Architectural Salmon Panel,* hot-sculpted glass with sterling silver, 36"H x 42"W on 0.5" plate glass. Photographs: Darrell Peterson.

JOLINE EL-HAI

BELLA LUZ STUDIO ■ 3737 NE 135TH STREET ■ SEATTLE, WA 98125 ■ TEL 206-364-8053
FAX 206-364-7235 ■ E-MAIL GLASS@BELLALUZ.COM ■ WWW.BELLALUZ.COM

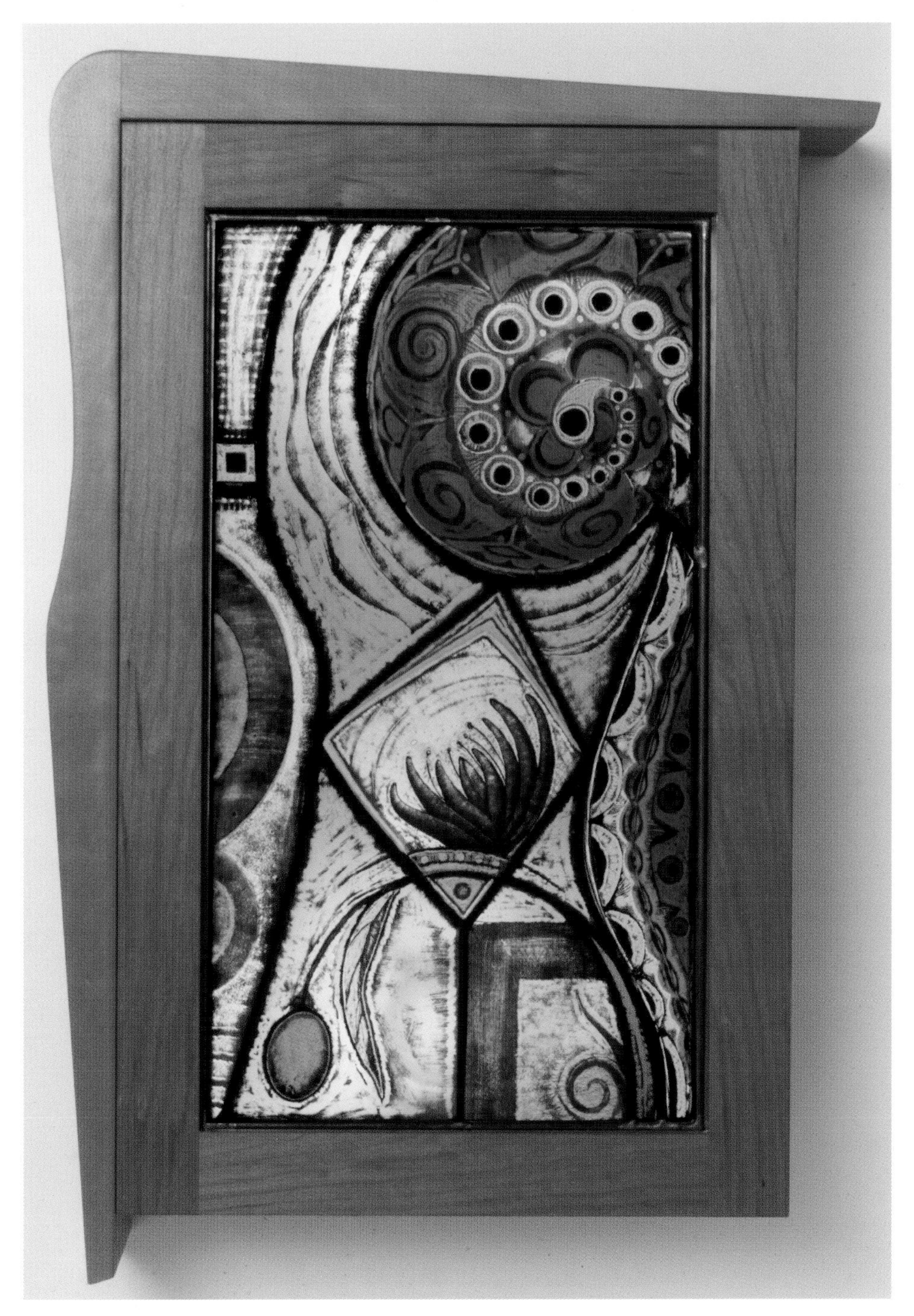

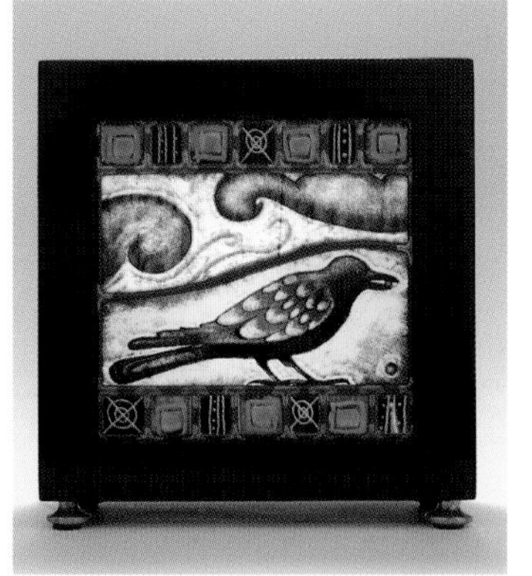

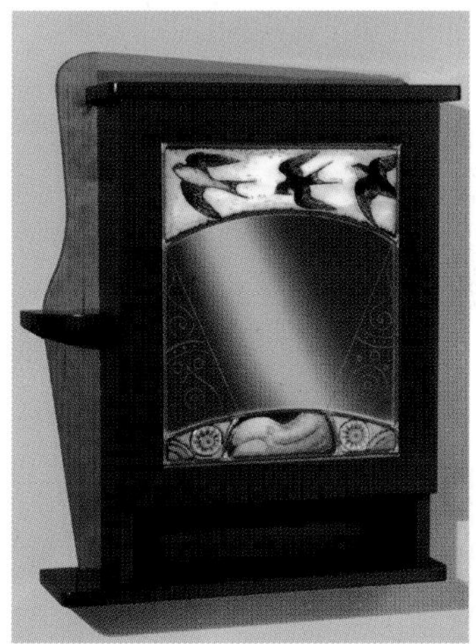

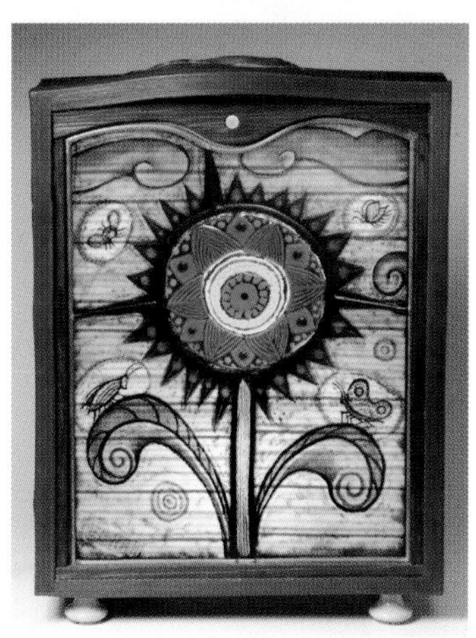

Left: *Youth Unfurling*, woodwork by Jeff Wasserman, 29" x 20" x 6". Photograph: Jeff Curtis. Top right: *Crow With Berry*, 12" x 11" x 5". Photograph: Lance Wagner. Center right: *Swallows*, 24" x 20" x 6". Photograph: Jeff Curtis. Bottom right: *Betsy's Flower*, 18" x 14" x 5". Photograph: Jeff Curtis.

GINI GARCIA

GARCIA GLASS ART, INC. ■ 715 SOUTH ALAMO ■ SAN ANTONIO, TX 78205 ■ TEL 210-354-4681
FAX 210-354-4688 ■ E-MAIL INFO@GARCIAARTGLASS.COM ■ WWW.GARCIAARTGLASS.COM

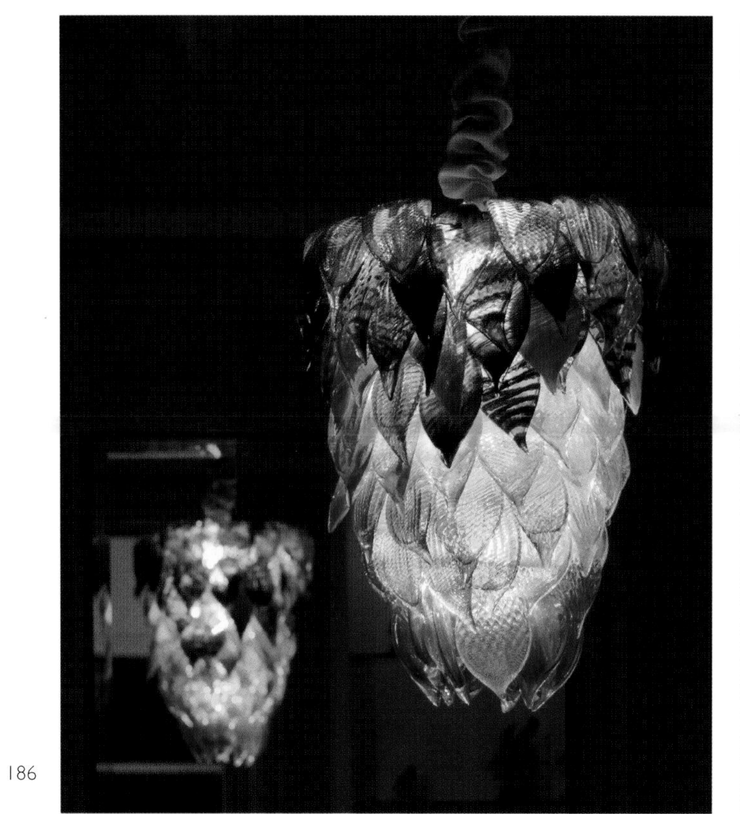

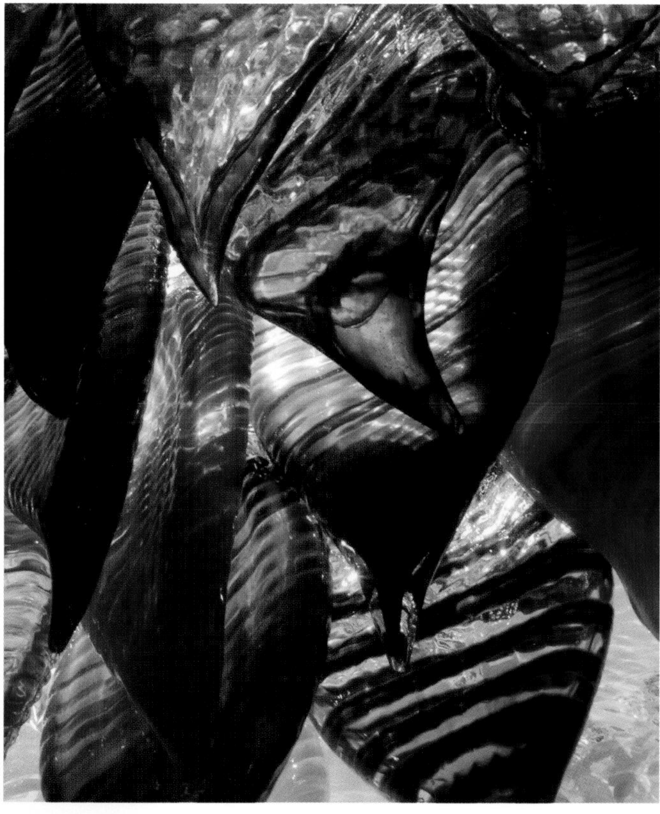

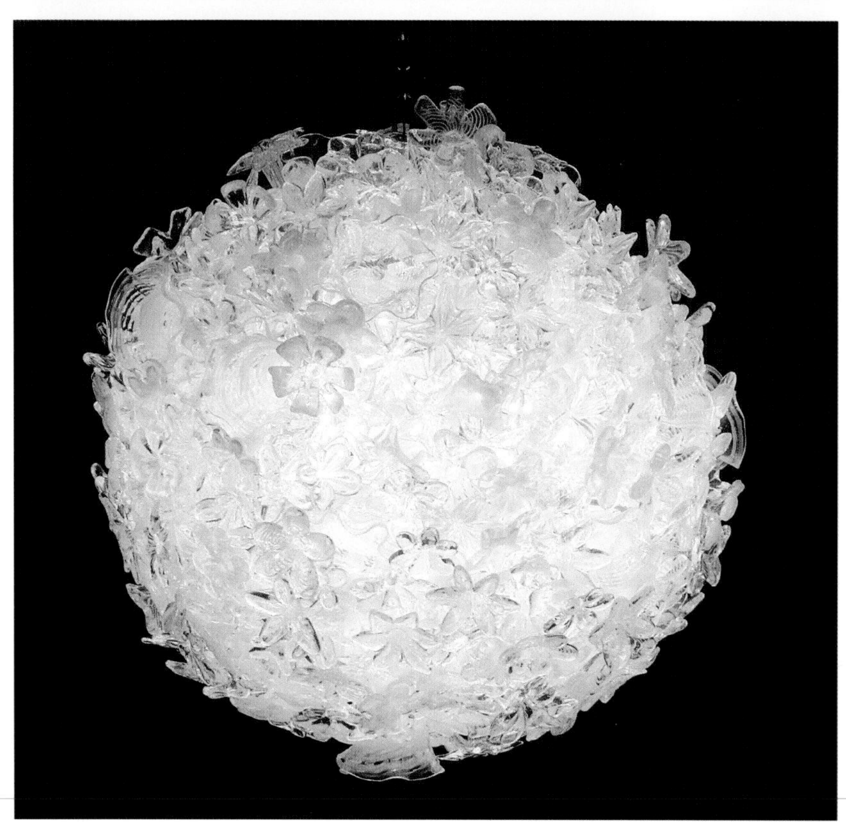

Top left: Site-specific custom chandelier, 38"H x 24"W. Top right: *Feather Chandelier* (detail). Photograph: Greg Harrison.
Bottom left: *White-on-White Custom Chandelier*, 30"Dia. Bottom right: *White-on-White* (detail).

GINI GARCIA

GARCIA GLASS ART, INC. ▪ 715 SOUTH ALAMO ▪ SAN ANTONIO, TX 78205 ▪ TEL 210-354-4681
FAX 210-354-4688 ▪ E-MAIL INFO@GARCIAARTGLASS.COM ▪ WWW.GARCIAARTGLASS.COM

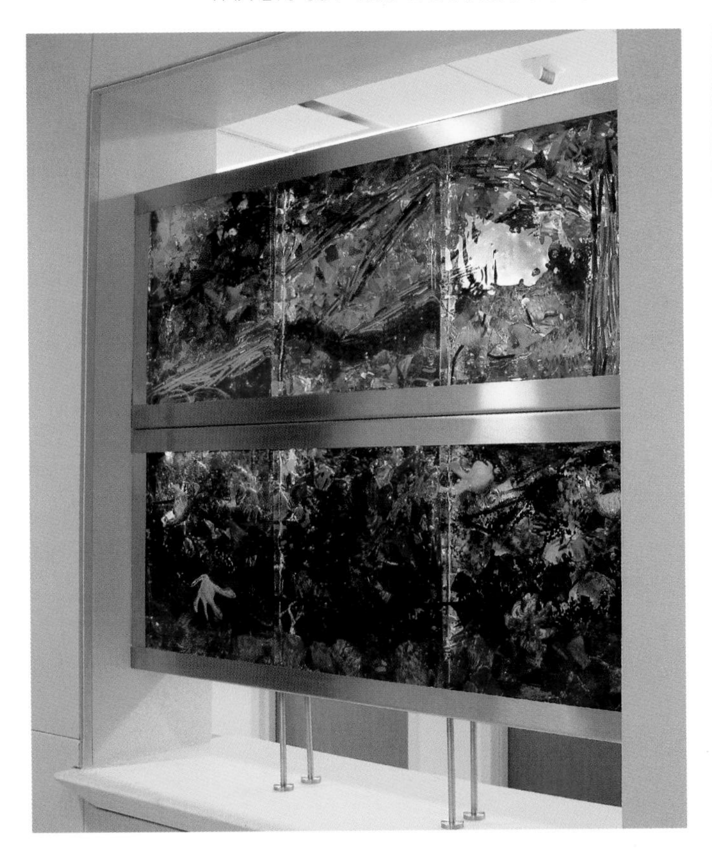

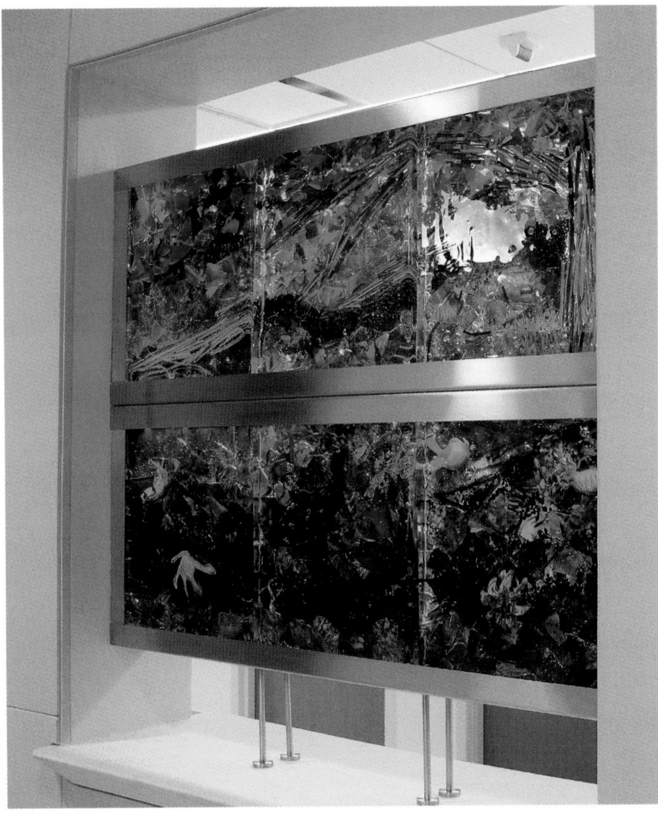

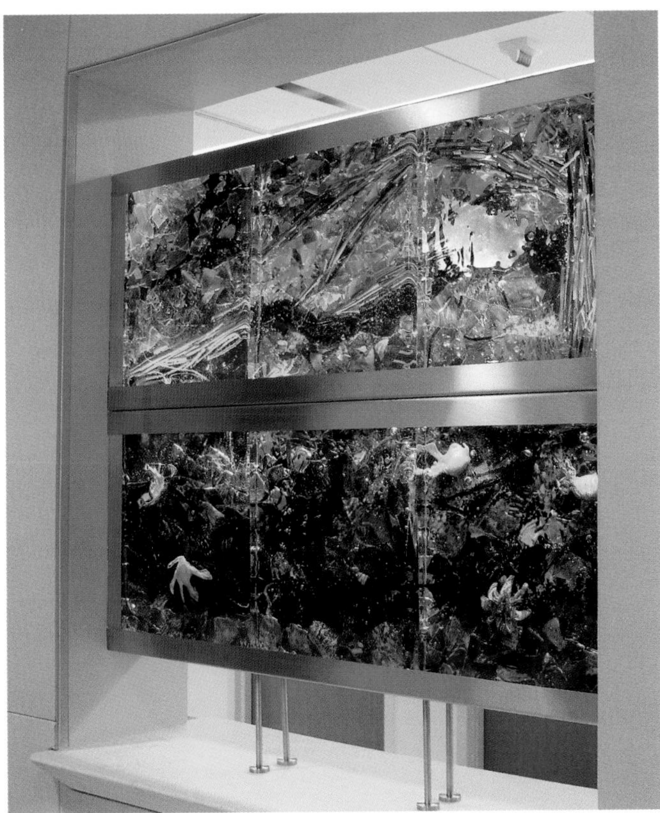

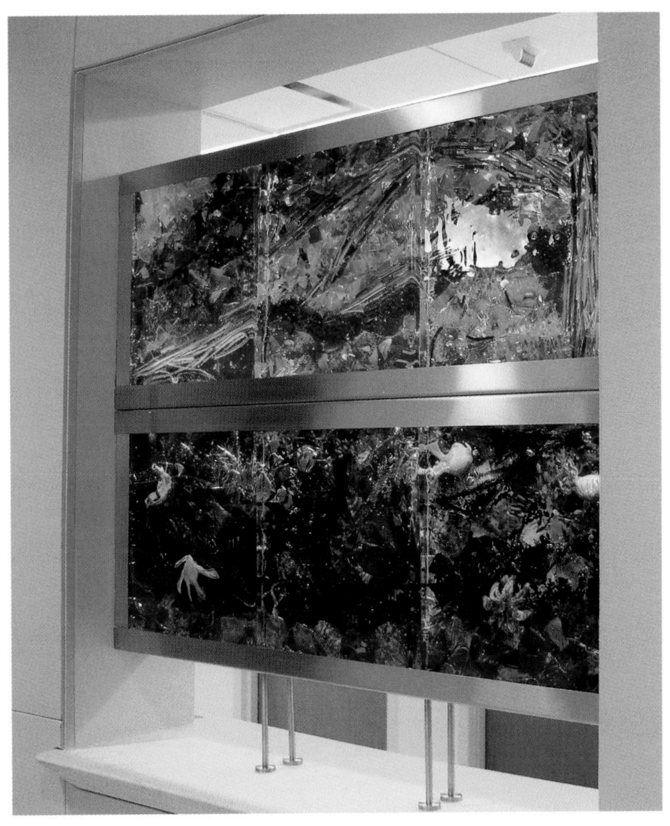

Virtual Aquarium, Memorial Hermann Hospital, Houston, TX, cast glass with changing color spectrum in orange violet, emerald cobalt, citron plum, and orange fuchsia, 28"H x 44"W. Fiber optics: Gerard Rendon, Stevens Lighting Company.

HUBBARDTON FORGE

154 ROUTE 30 SOUTH ■ CASTLETON, VT 05735 ■ TEL 800-826-4766
FAX 802-468-3284 ■ E-MAIL INFO@VTFORGE.COM ■ WWW.VTFORGE.COM

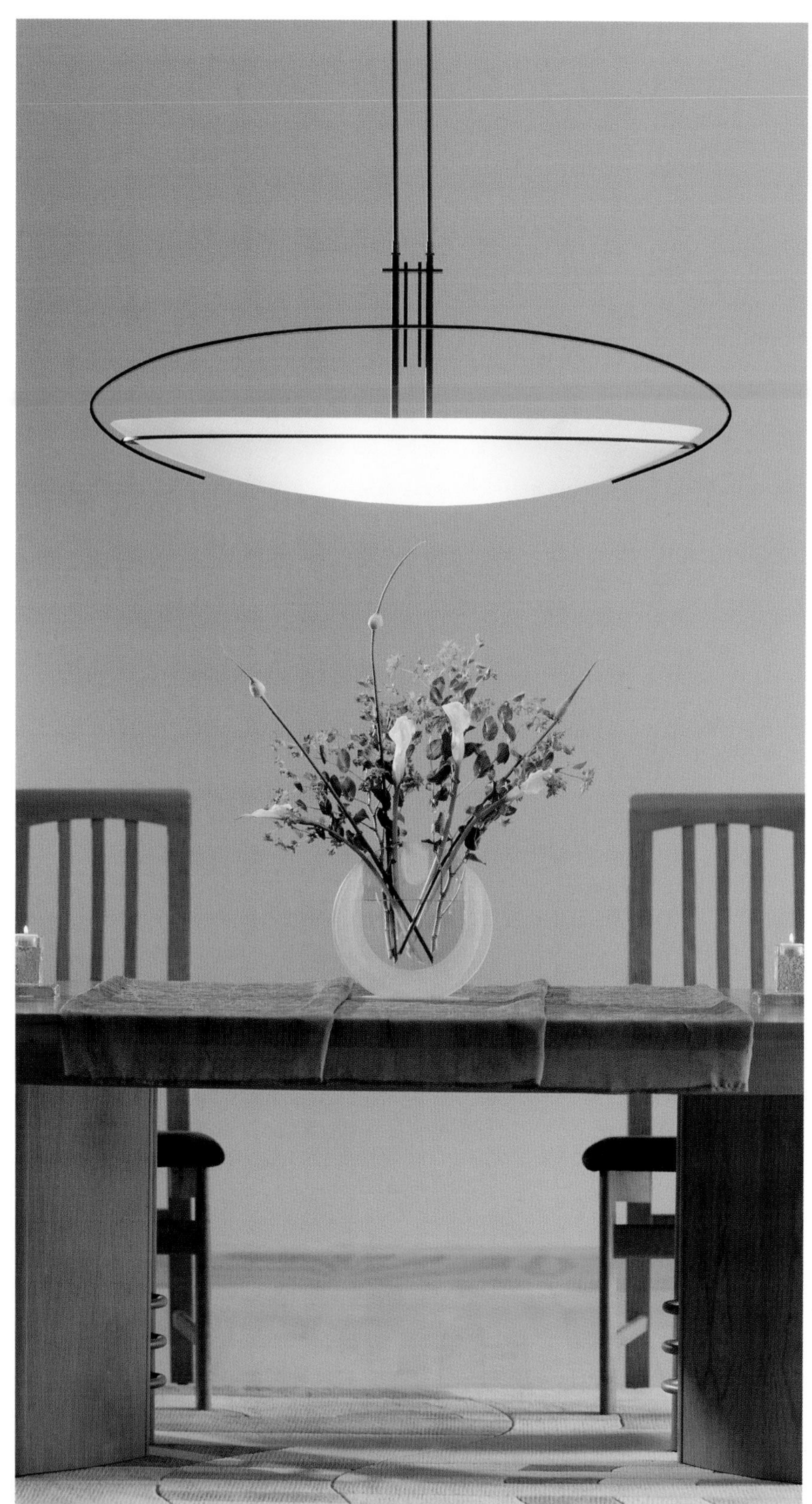

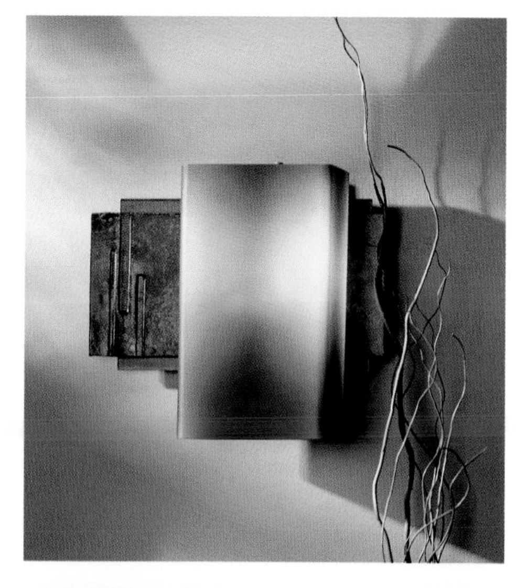

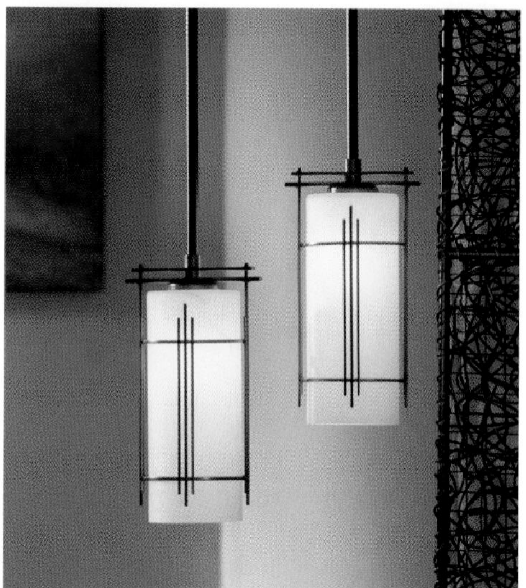

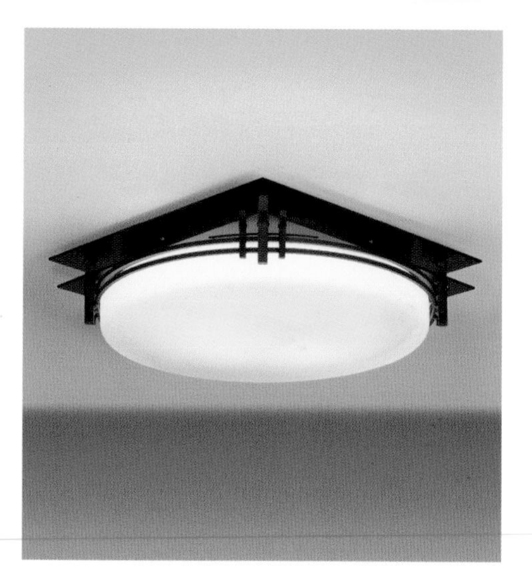

Left: *Adjustable Mackintosh Pendant* with opal glass bowl. Top right: *Fullered Impressions Wall Sconce* with matte dusk glass option.
Center right: *Adjustable Paralline Pendants* with stone glass option. Bottom right: *Banded Flush Mount* with stone glass option. Photographs: Jim Westphalen.

HUCK FISHER METALWORKERS

CHRISTOPHER HUCK ■ LAURA FISHER ■ SCOTTSDALE, AZ ■ TEL 480-946-3384
E-MAIL INFO@HUCKFISHER.COM ■ WWW.HUCKFISHER.COM

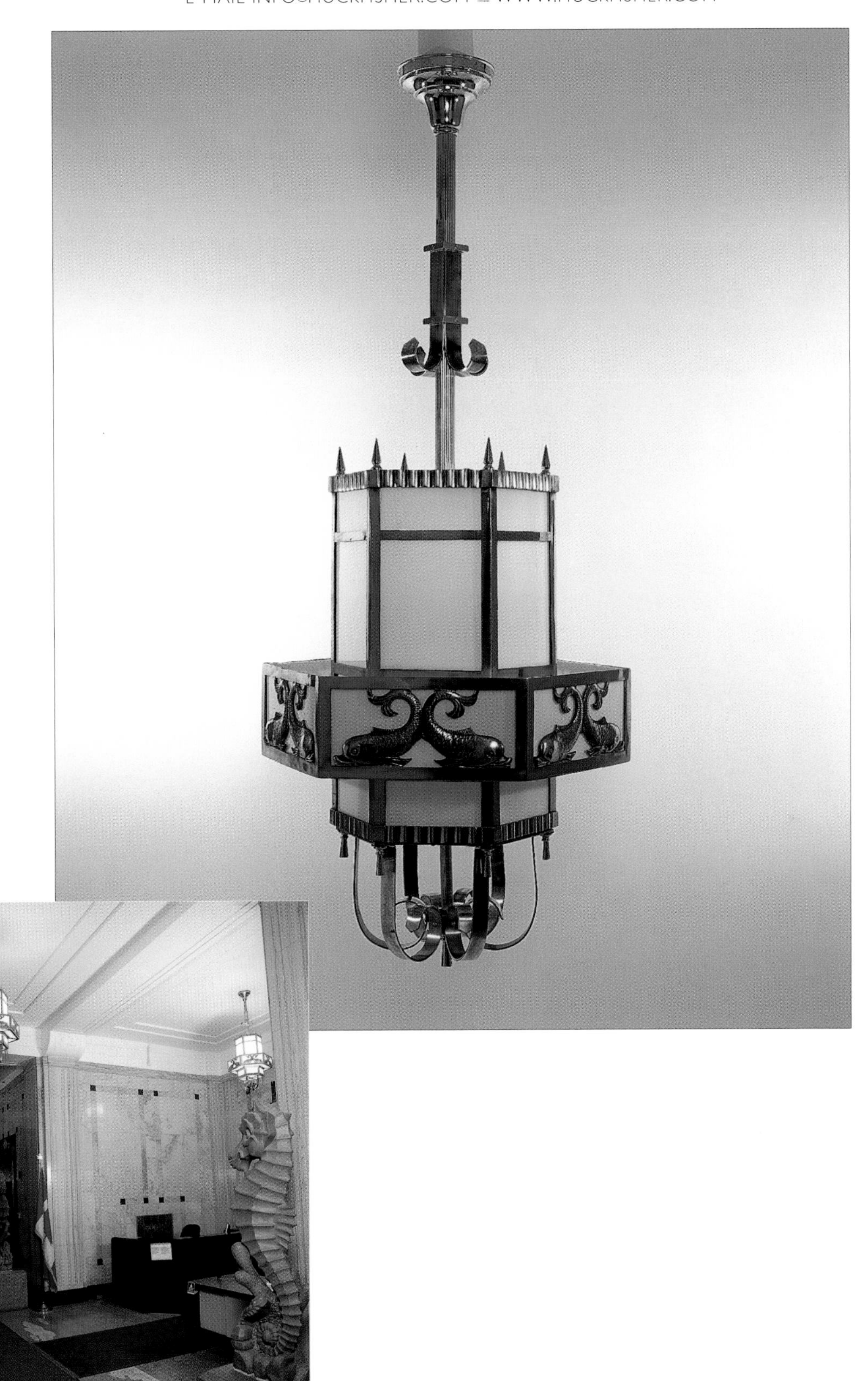

Pisces Chandelier, Bedford Row Building Lobby, Halifax, NS, bronze and stained glass, 55" x 42" x 42", commissioned by the Government of Canada. Photographs: Julian Beveridge Photography.

IVAN PAVLOVITS

ARTKONCEPTS ■ 841 NORTH KENTER AVENUE ■ LOS ANGELES, CA 90049
TEL 310-471-0990 ■ FAX 310-472-3148 ■ E-MAIL BUDAP@VERIZON.NET ■ WWW.AARTKONCEPTS.COM

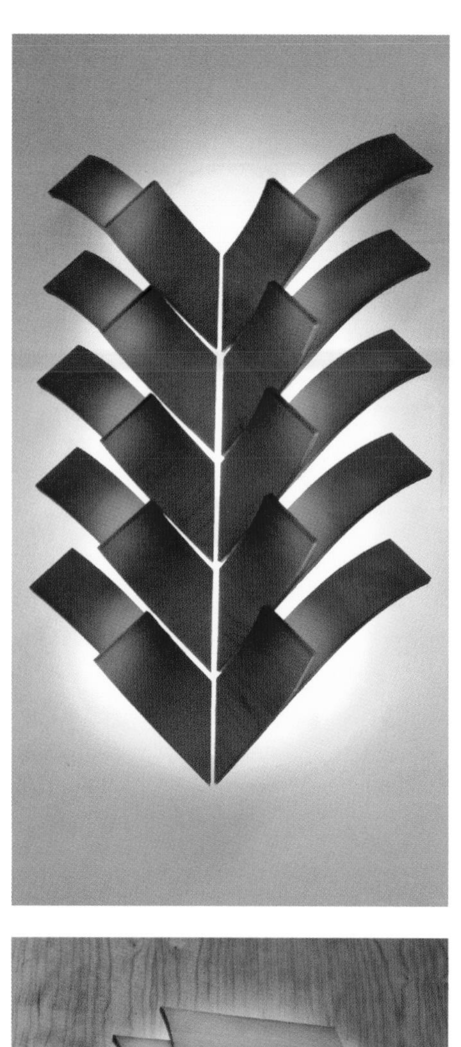

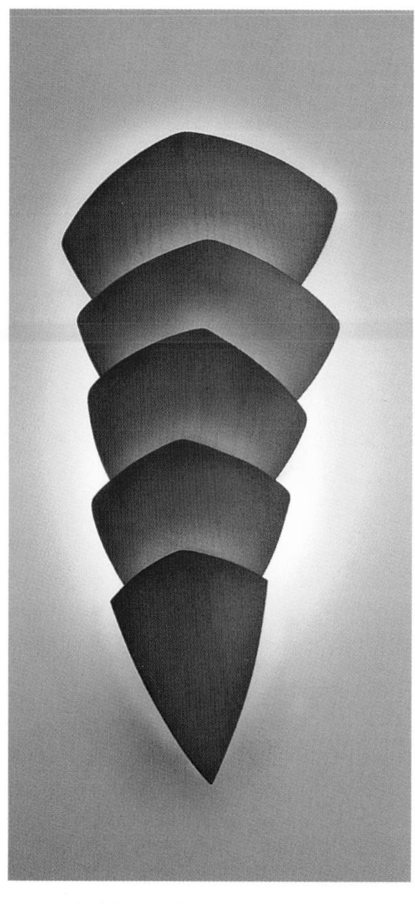

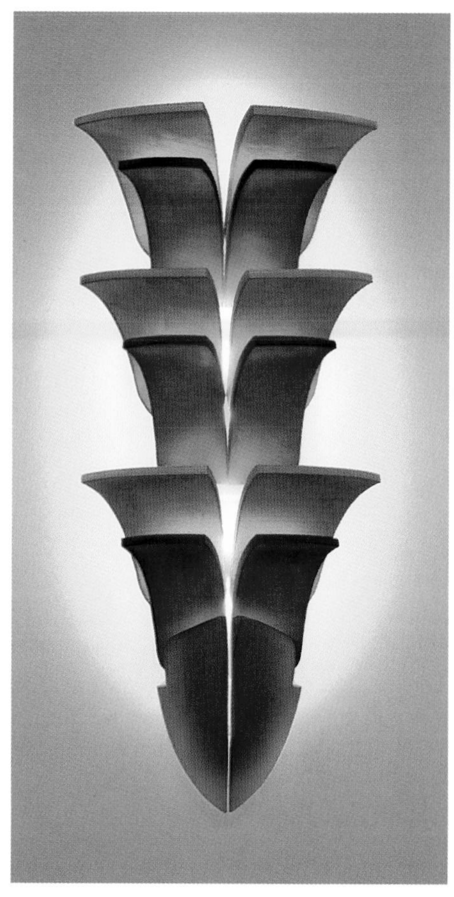

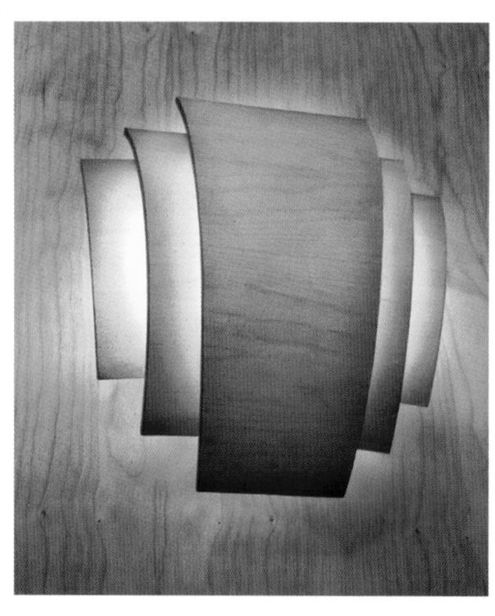

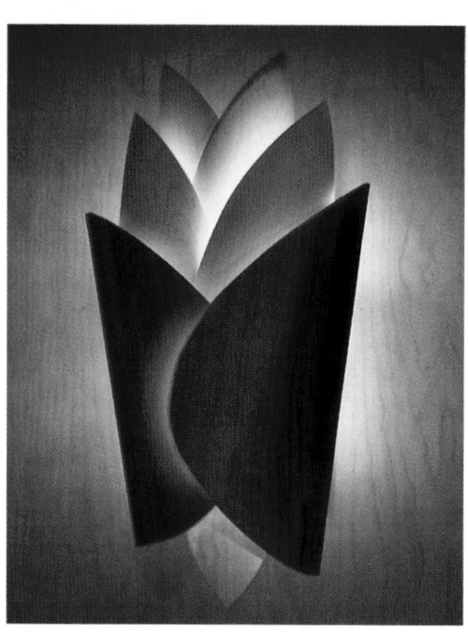

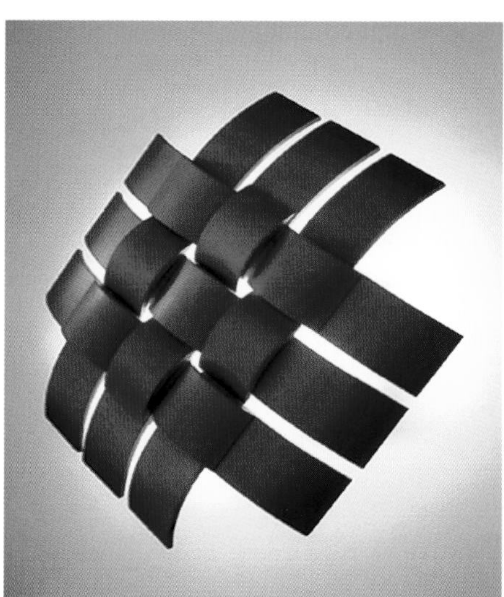

Sculptural Wood Lighting. All designs ©Artkoncepts.

TOM PHILABAUM

PHILABAUM GLASS, INC. ■ 711 SOUTH SIXTH AVENUE ■ TUCSON, AZ 85701 ■ TEL 520-884-7404
FAX 520-884-0679 ■ E-MAIL TPHILABAUM@QWEST.NET ■ WWW.PHILABAUMGLASS.COM

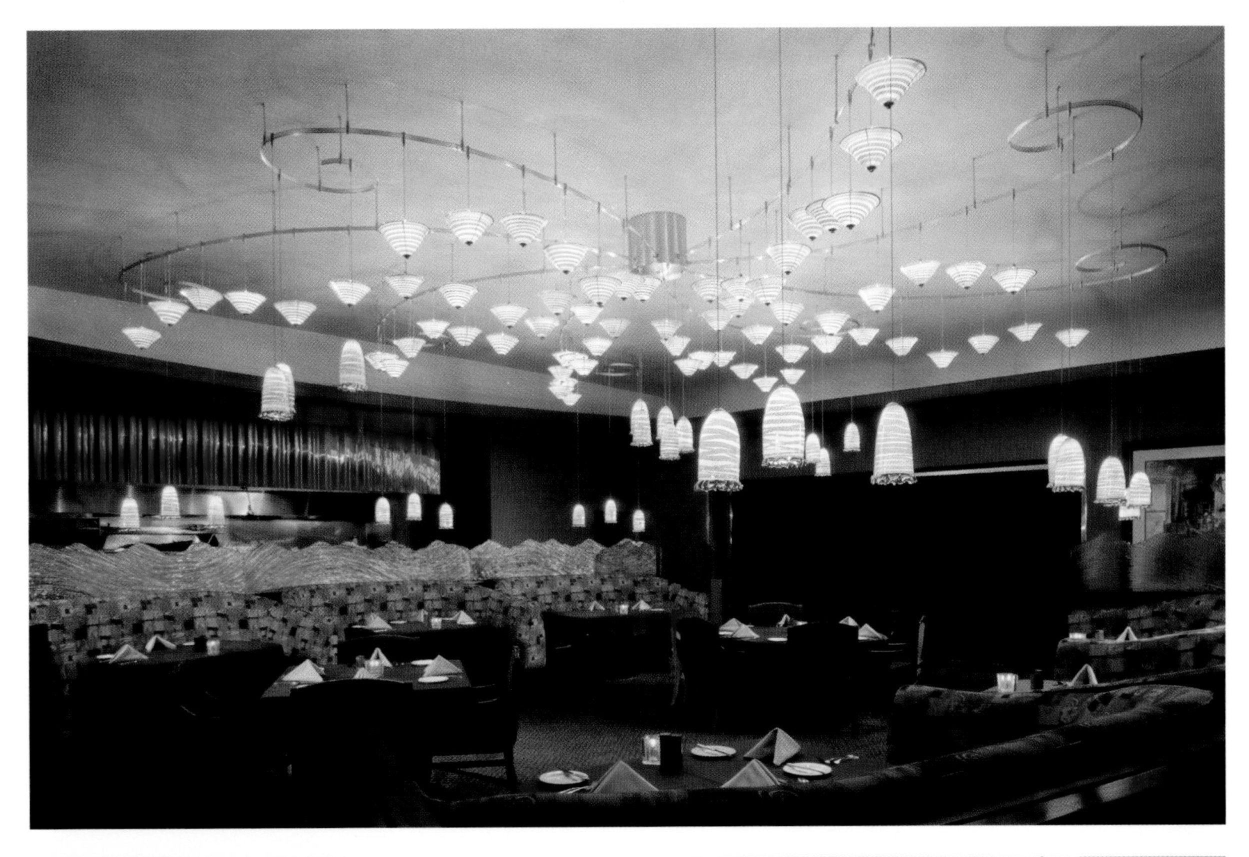

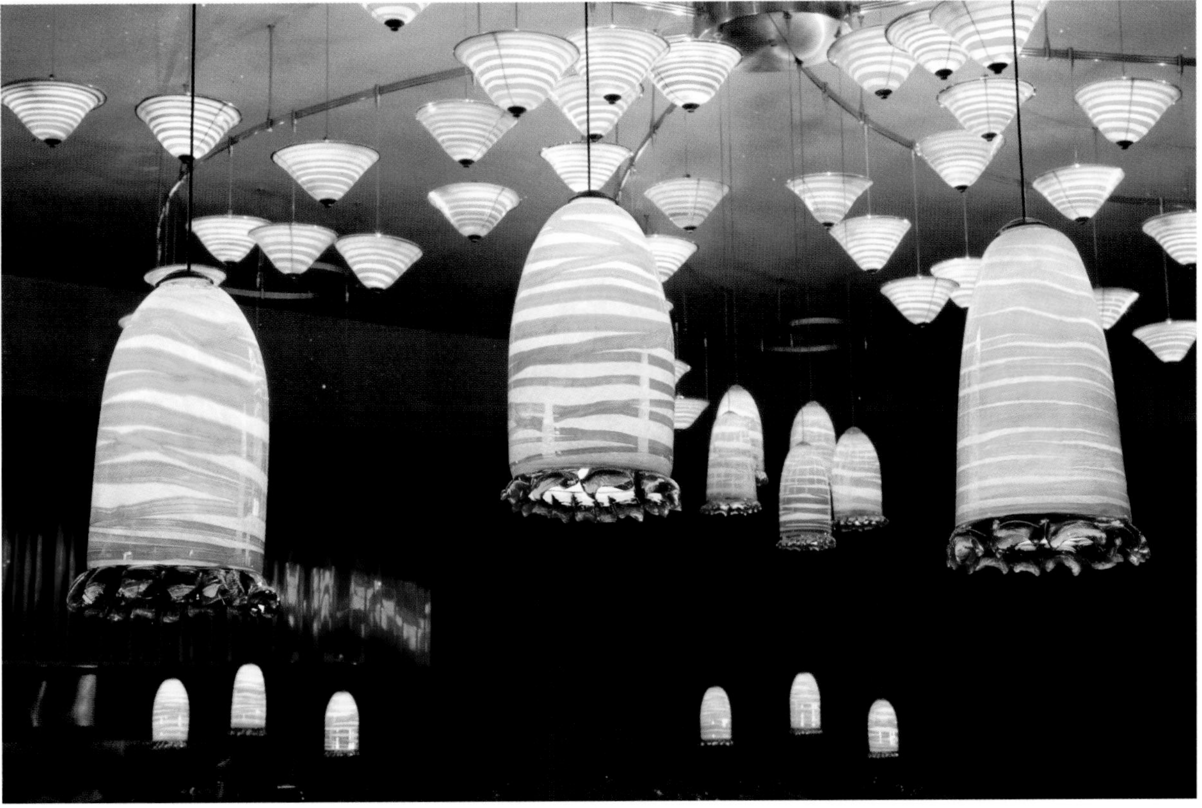

Lighting installation, McMahon's Restaurant, Tucson, AZ, blown glass and monorail system, 7' x 28' x 28'. Photograph: Steven Meckler.

ADAM JACKSON POLLOCK—FIRE FARM LIGHTING

FIRE FARM LIGHTING ■ PO BOX 458 ■ 104 FIRST STREET SOUTHWEST ■ ELKADER, IA 52043
TEL 563-245-3515 ■ FAX 563-245-3516 ■ E-MAIL INFO@FIREFARM.COM ■ WWW.FIREFARM.COM

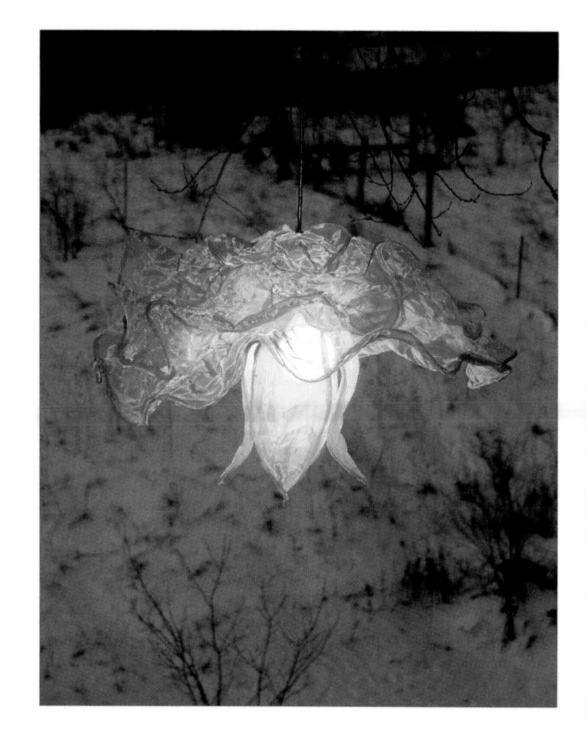

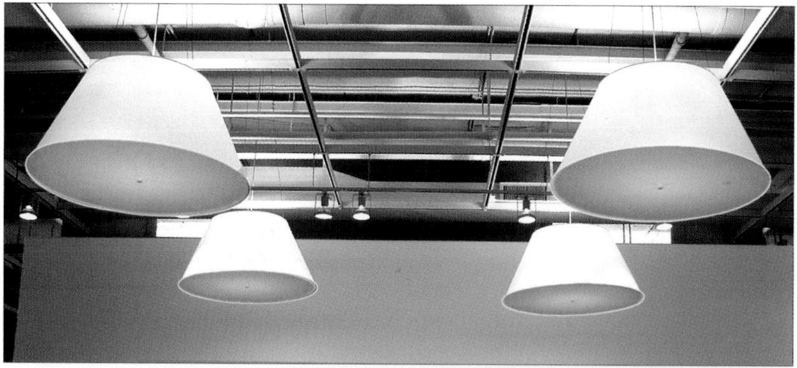

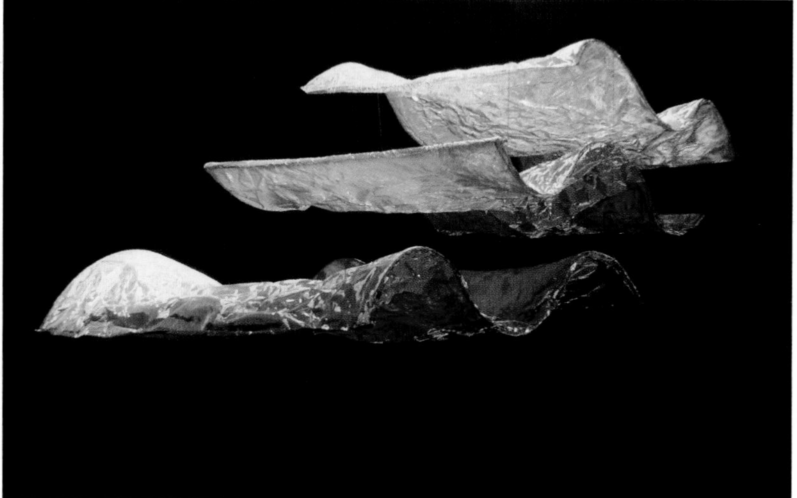

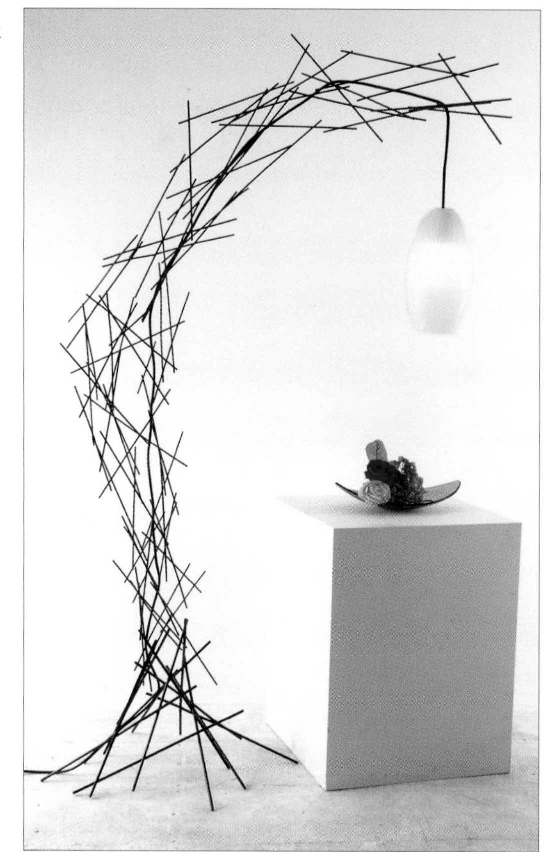

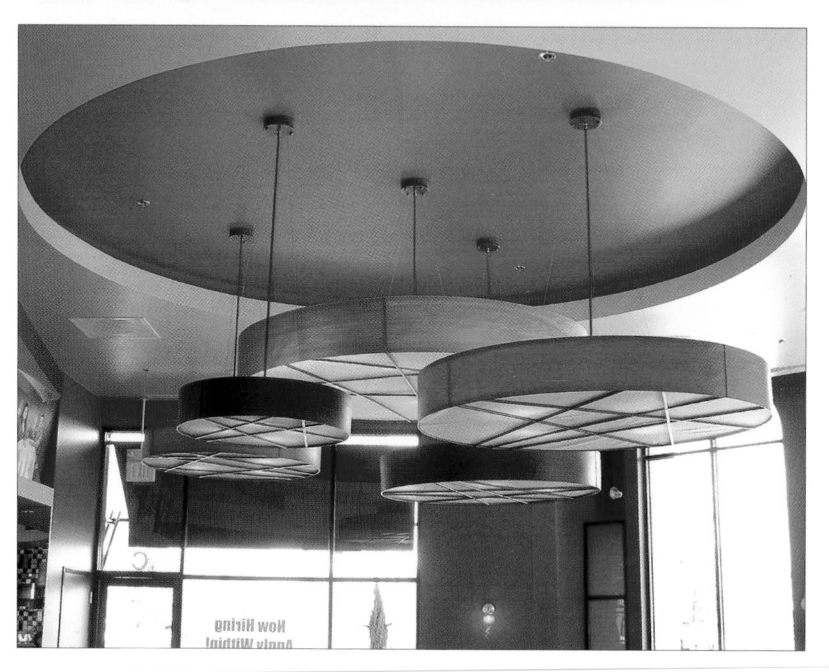

Top left: *Parnassus,* 2006, copper and brass wire cloth with electrical. Top right: *Luna,* 2004, linen, styrene, vinyl, and acrylic with electrical.
Center right: *Orion Wave,* 2006, stainless steel with dichroic film. Bottom left: *Twig Floor Lamp,* 2004, steel, powder coat paint, and lathed glass with electrical.
Bottom right: *Woven Drum,* 2001, wood veneer, powder-coated painted steel, and acrylic with electrical.

LEE PROCTOR

PROCTOR STUDIOS ■ 233 COVERDELL ROAD ■ BIGFORK, MT 59911
TEL/FAX 406-752-0726 ■ TEL 406-253-9607 ■ E-MAIL PROCTORSTUDIOS@CENTURYTEL.NET

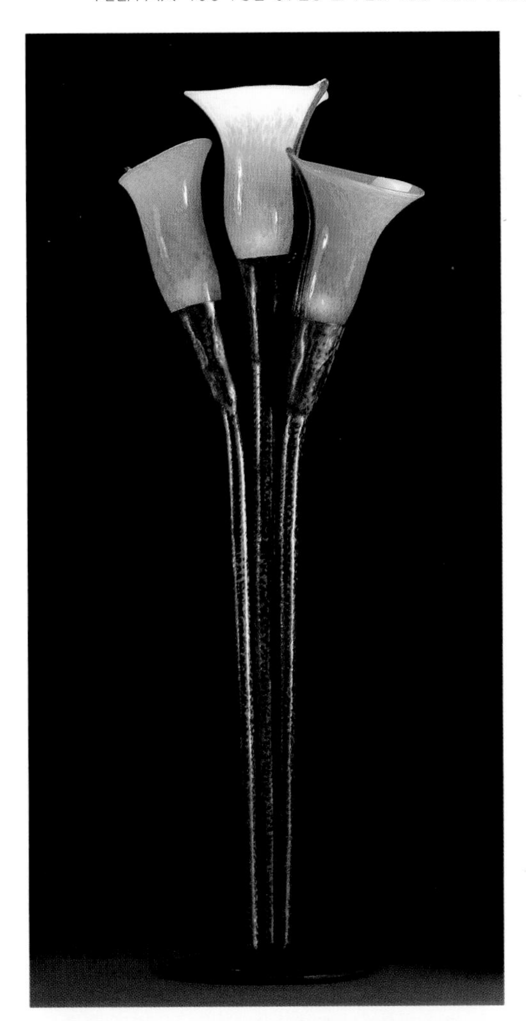

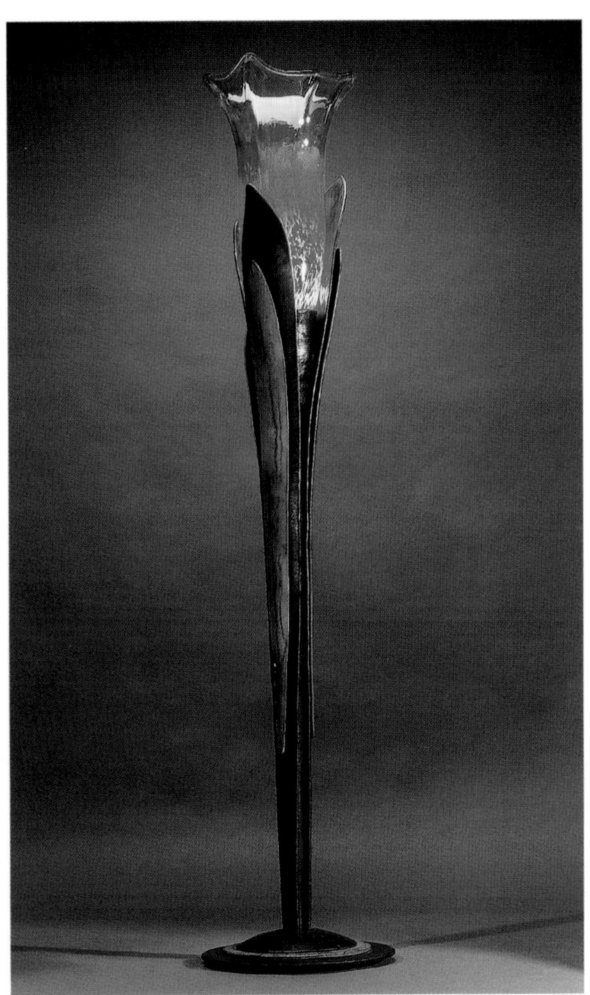

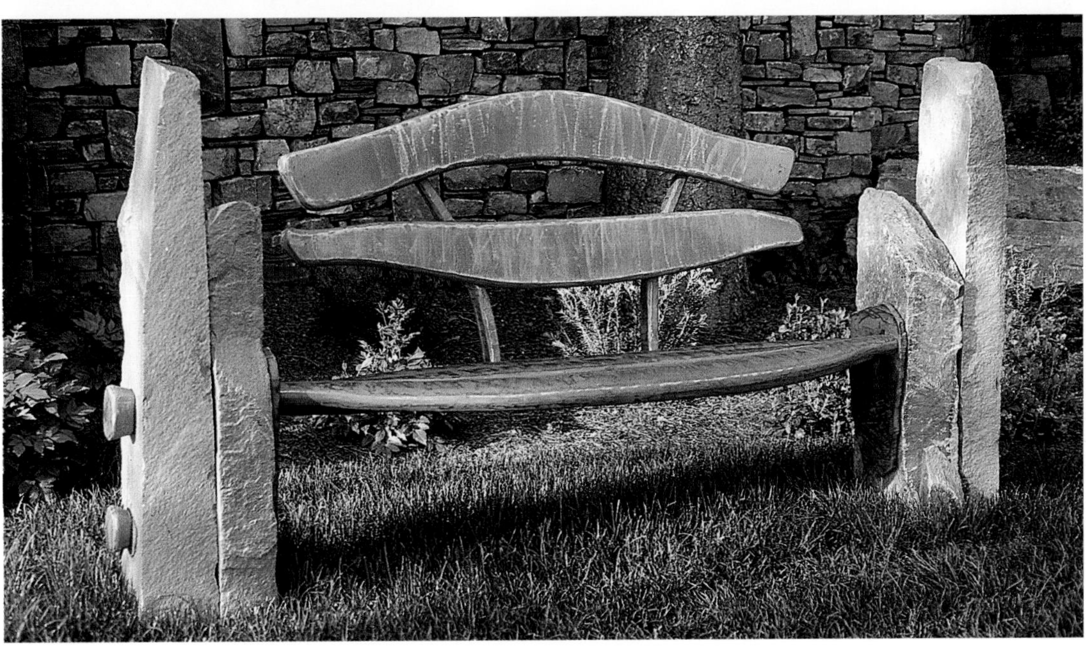

Top left: *Summer Nights Lamps*, 6'H x 2'W x 2'D. Photograph: Nicole Holdener, Wasabi Images.
Top right: *Passion Lamp*, 5'H x 1'W x 2'D. Photograph: Nicole Holdener, Wasabi Images. Bottom: *Birdwatching Bench*, 4'H x 7'W x 2'D.

DREW ADAM SCHNIEROW

DAS ART ■ SAN FRANCISCO, CA ■ TEL 888-307-8180
E-MAIL DREW@DASART.COM ■ WWW.DASART.COM

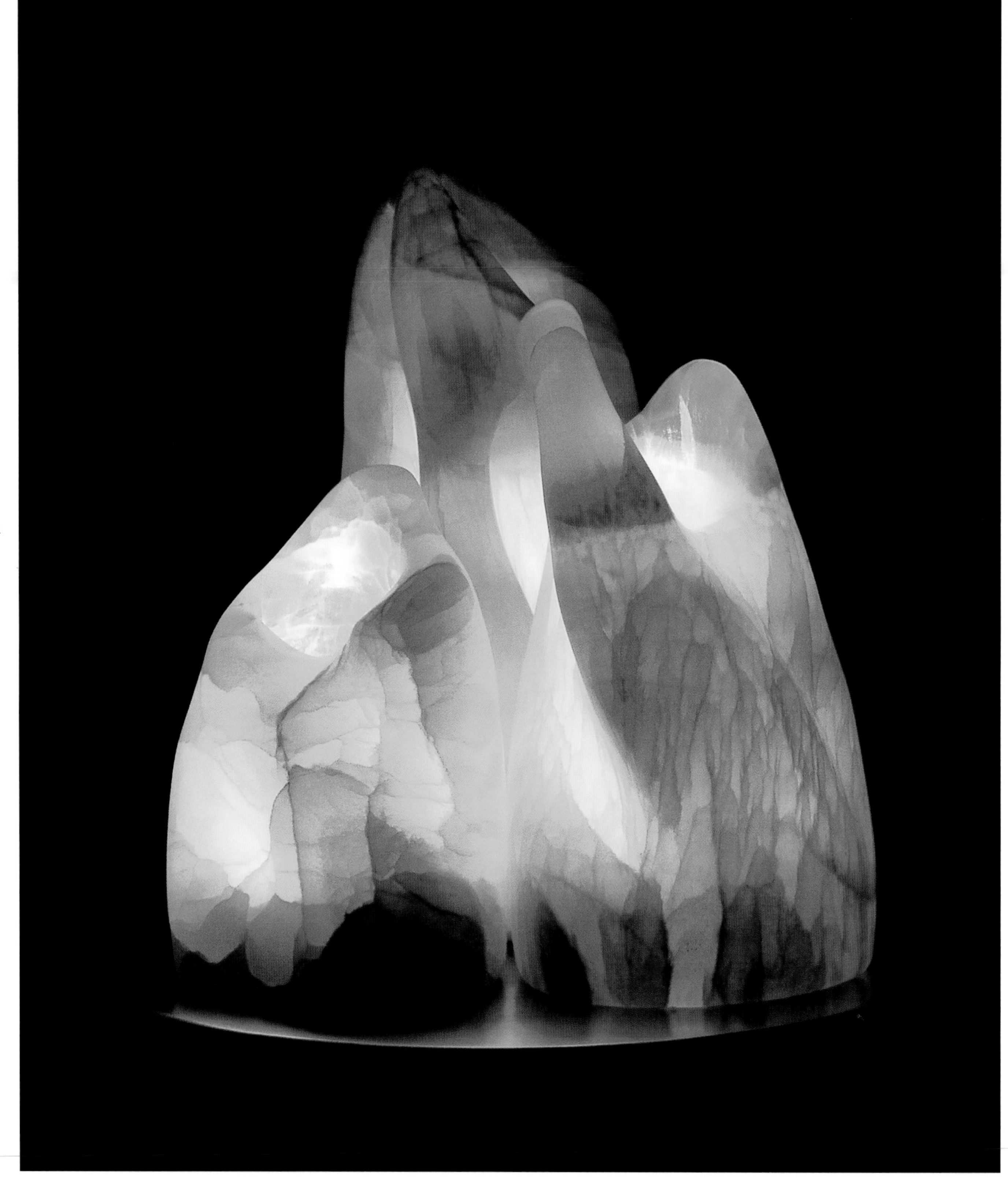

Eternal Flame, 2006, West End Synagogue, New York, NY, translucent honeycomb calcite, 16" x 14" x 14". Illuminated by LED lights.

GEORGE C. SCOTT

GEORGE C. SCOTT STUDIOS ■ 22220 SEVENTH AVENUE SOUTH ■ DES MOINES, WA 98198 ■ TEL 206-824-0464
FAX 206-824-0474 ■ E-MAIL GEORGE@GEORGECSCOTTSTUDIOS.COM ■ WWW.GEORGECSCOTTSTUDIOS.COM

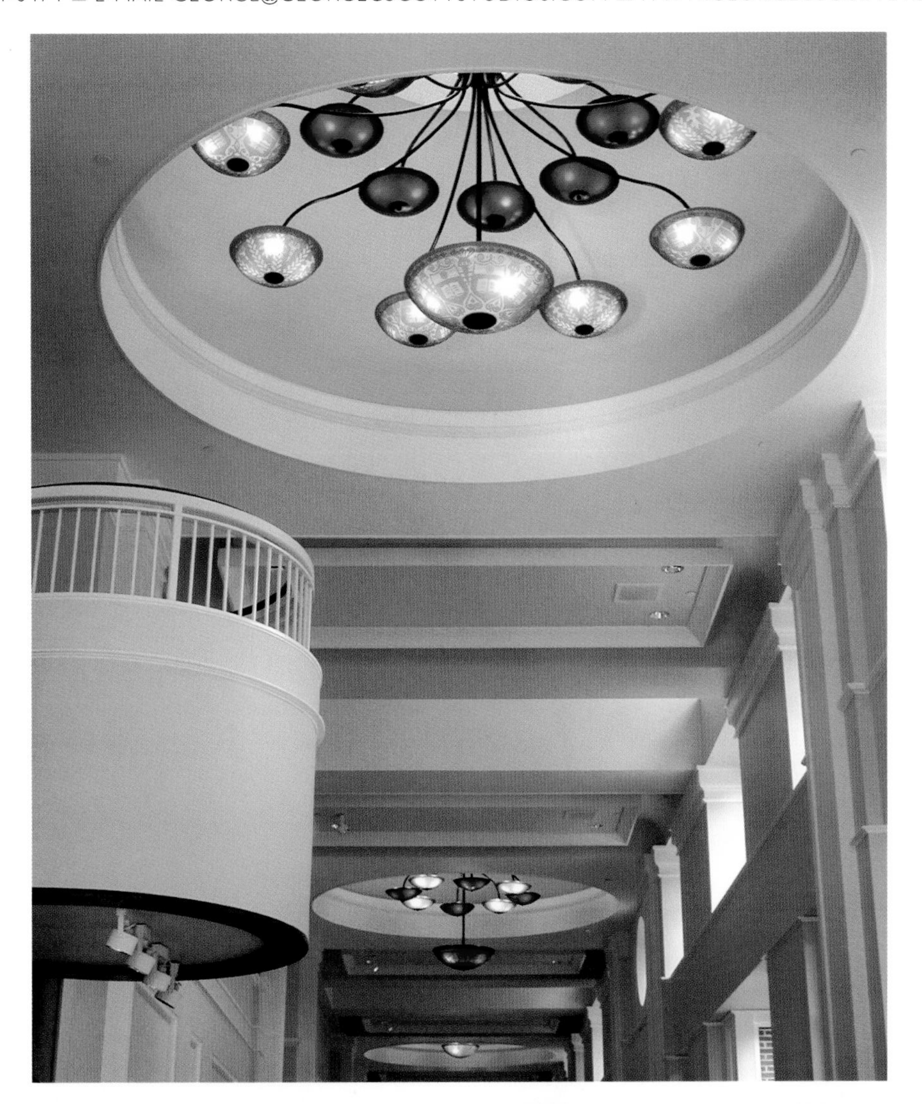

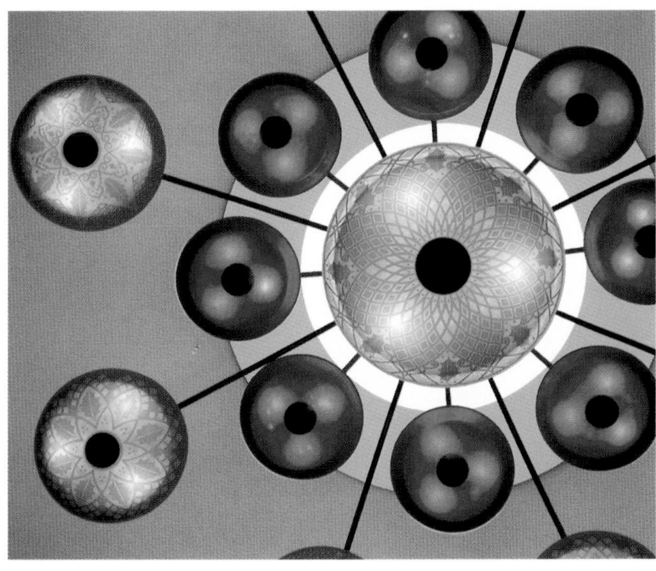

University of Delaware Center for the Performing Arts, fused, sand-carved, and slumped glass with aluminum armature, three chandeliers, each: 12'Dia x 18' drop.

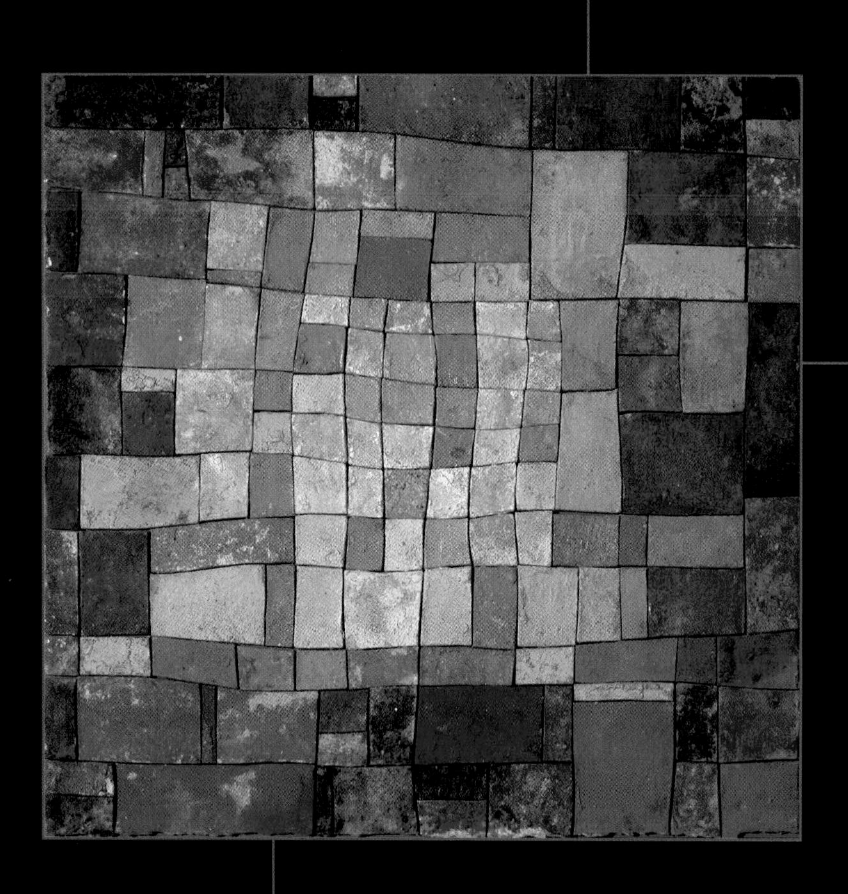

Murals, Tiles & Wall Reliefs

MARCUS AKINLANA

WON MURAL SOCIETY ■ NEW ORLEANS, LA ■ TEL/FAX 504-288-8368
E-MAIL AKIN1131@BELLSOUTH.NET ■ WWW.AKINLANA.NET

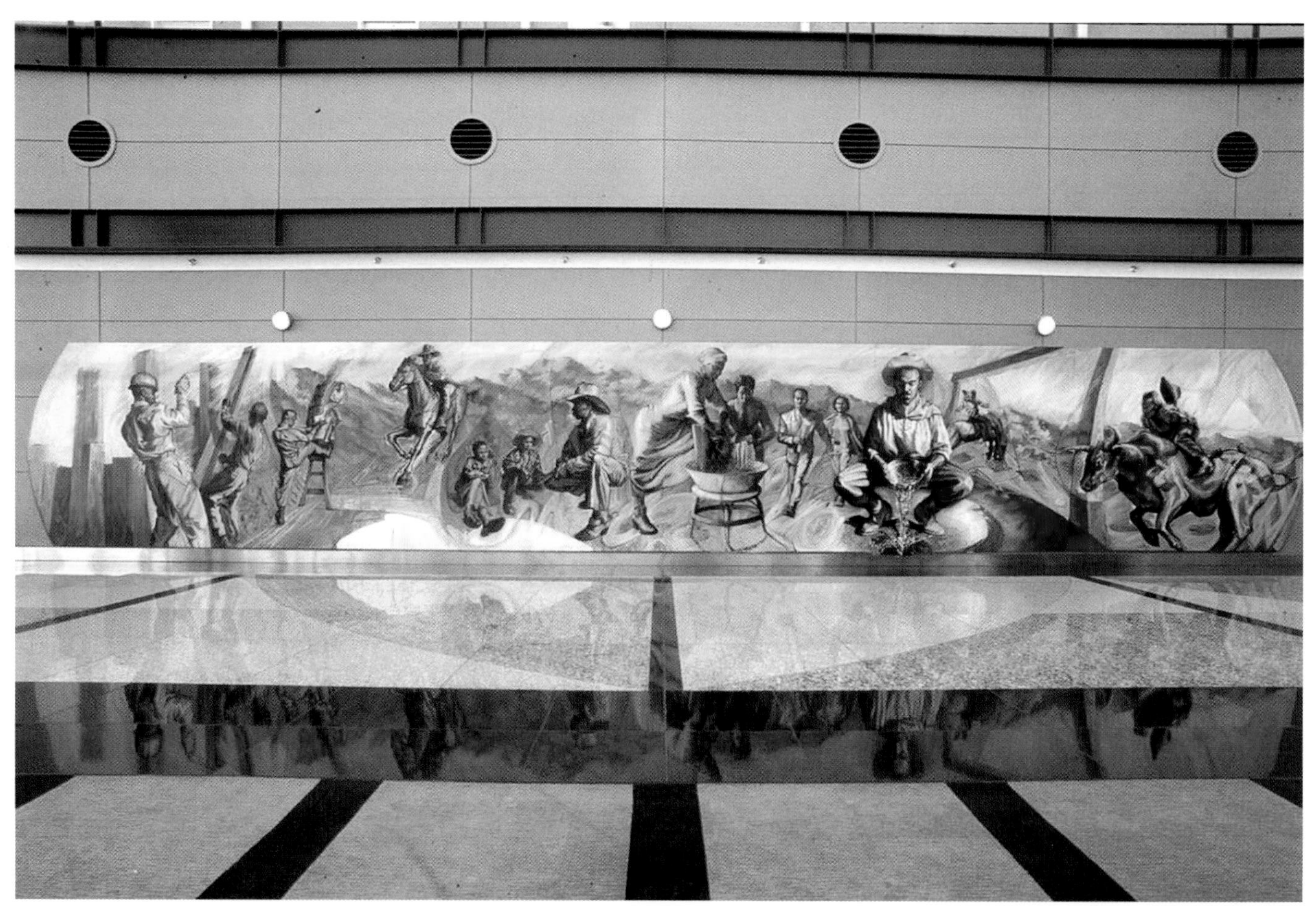

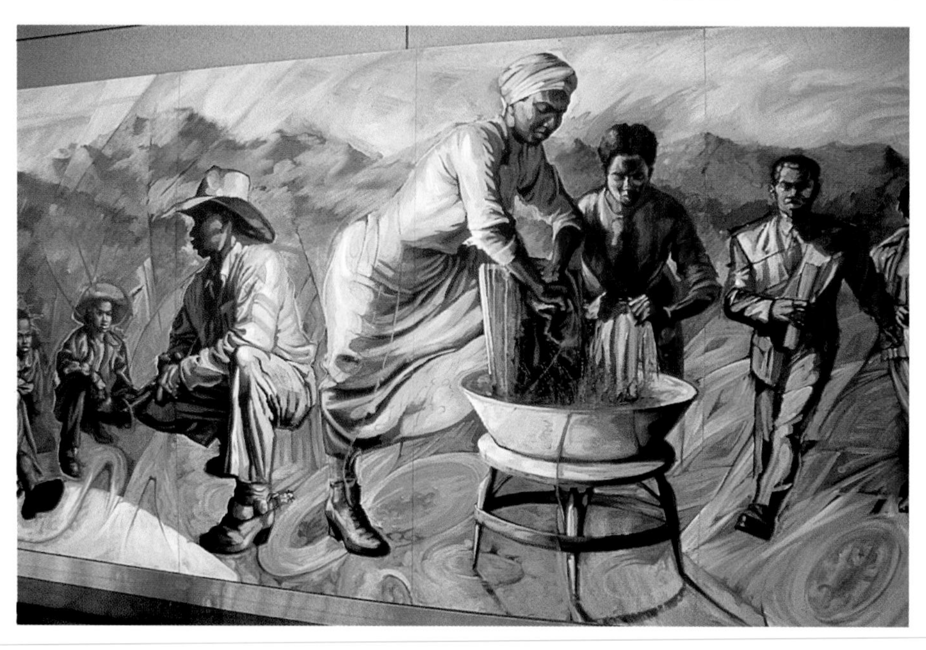

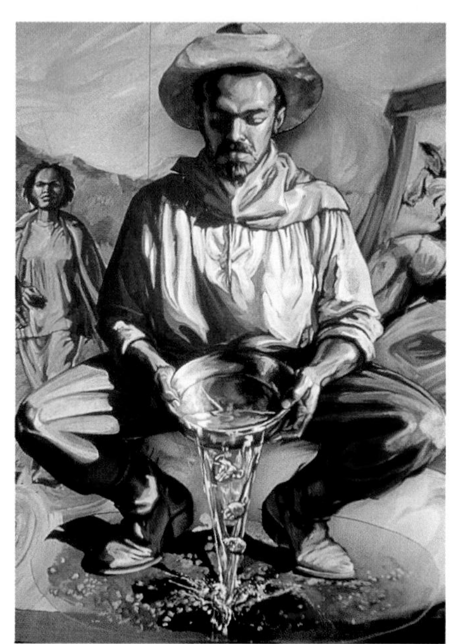

Mile High & Rising, 1999, Denver International Airport, Denver, CO, acrylic mural on panels with cut-out figure and brass sculptural relief, 8' x 52'.

ANNA CABO ARTGLASS TILES

ANNA CABO ■ 2568 STATE STREET ■ CARLSBAD, CA 92008
TEL 760-729-4631 ■ E-MAIL ANNACABO@AOL.COM ■ WWW.ANNACABO.COM

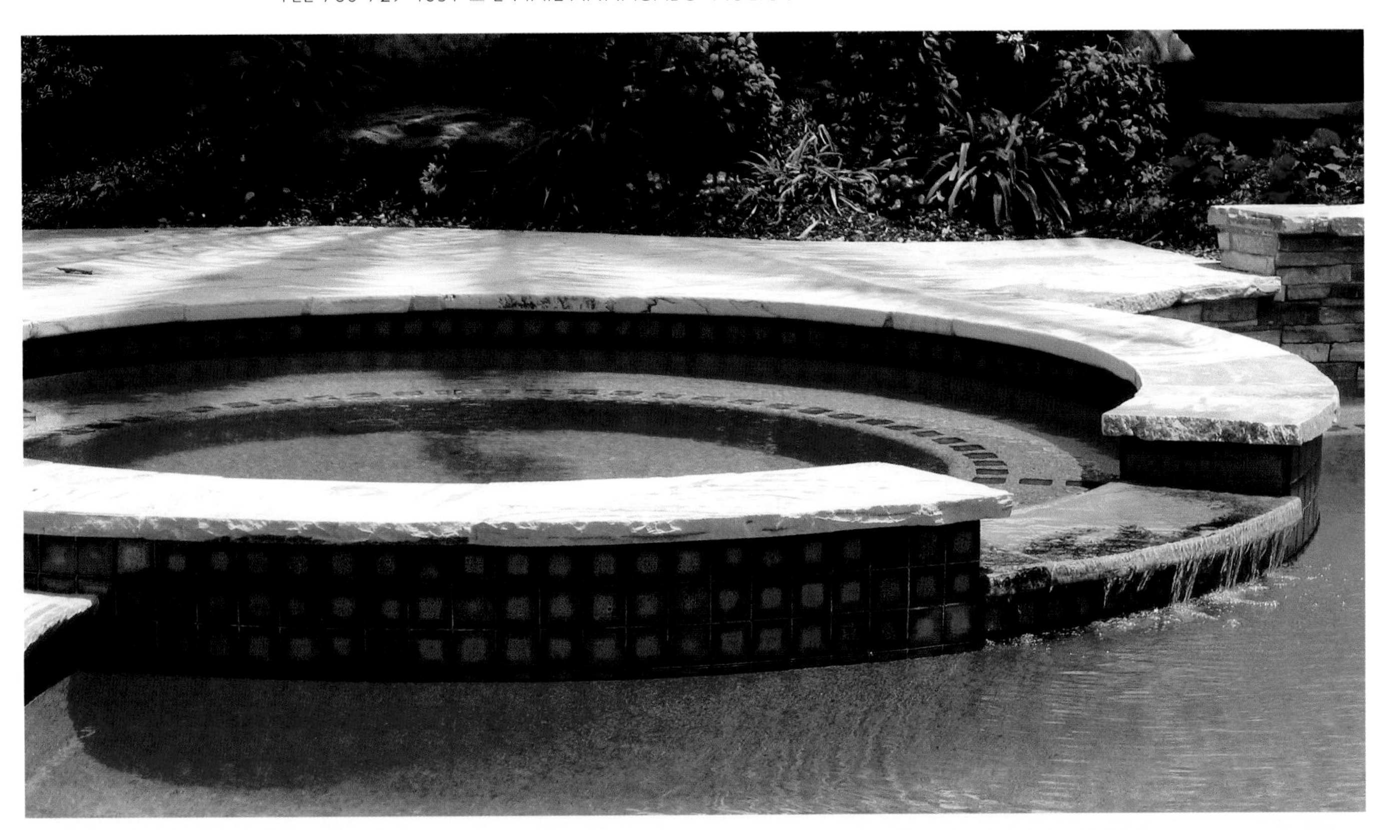

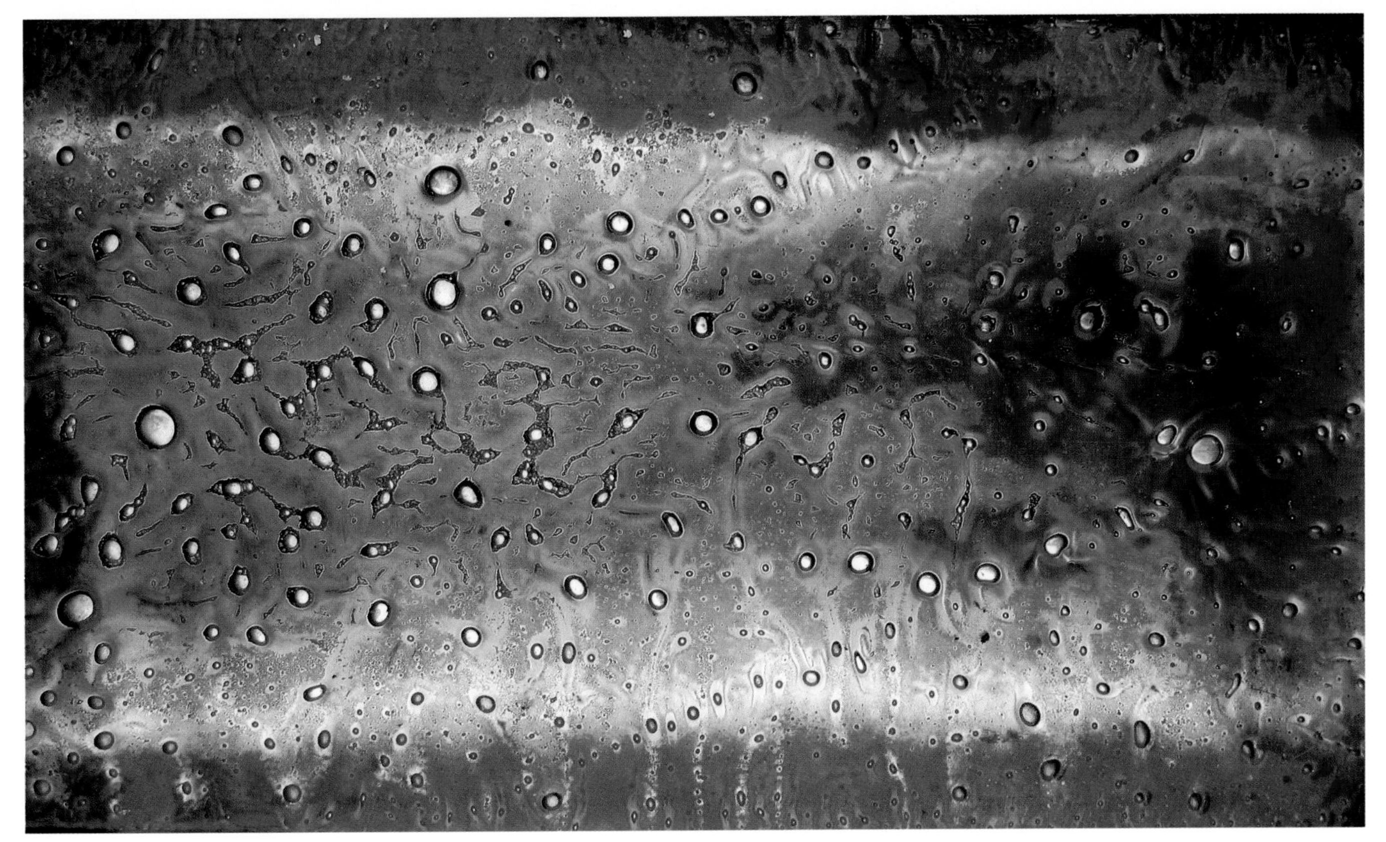

Top: Artglass pool tiles, private residence, Rancho Santa Fe, CA. Bottom: Artglass tile (detail). US Patent 6,837,073 B.

ARTECLETTICA

DOMINIC PANZIERA AND DANIELA GAROFALO ■ PO BOX 1907 ■ TRUCKEE, CA 96160
TEL 530-550-1076 ■ E-MAIL INFO@ARTECLETTICA.COM ■ WWW.ARTECLETTICA.COM

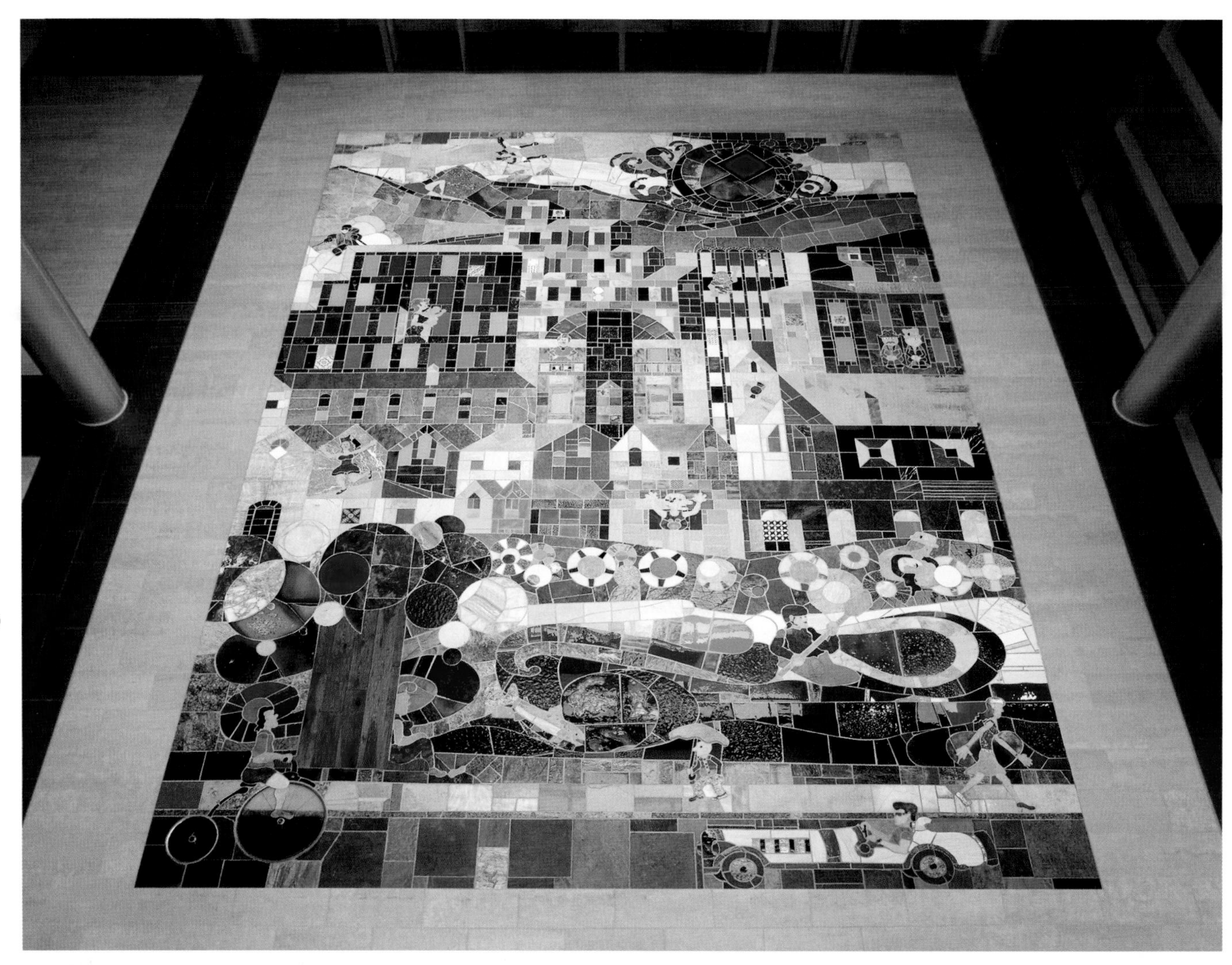

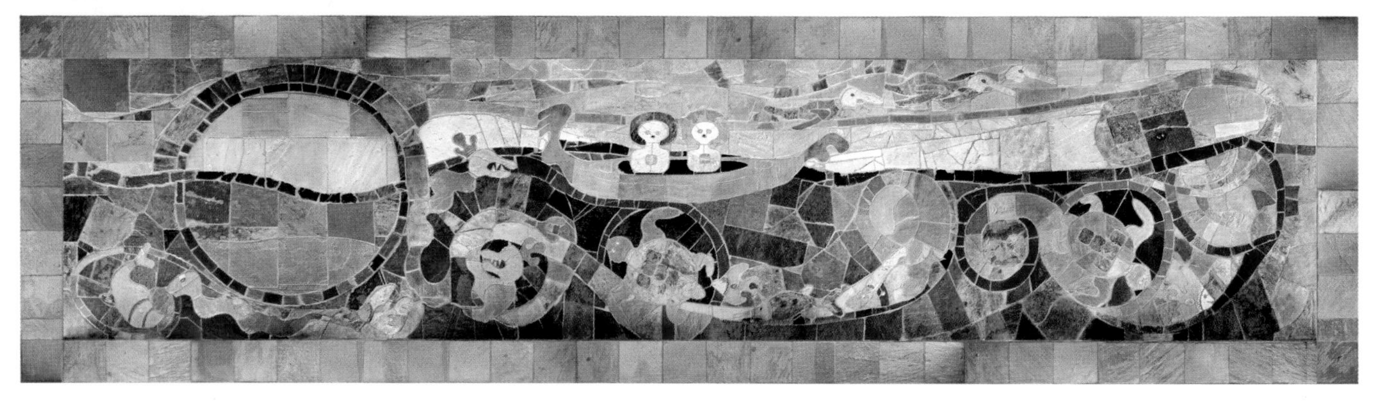

Top: *Society,* 2005, Reno Municipal Courthouse, NV, mosaic floor, 30' x 20'.
Bottom: *Flowing,* 2001, Home Concepts, Truckee, CA, mosaic floor, 8.5' x 31'.

CARL AND SANDRA BRYANT

FORBEY'S ART & TILE LLC ■ PO BOX 756 ■ LYNDEN, WA 98264
E-MAIL FORBEYSALES@FORBEYART.COM ■ WWW.FORBEYART.COM

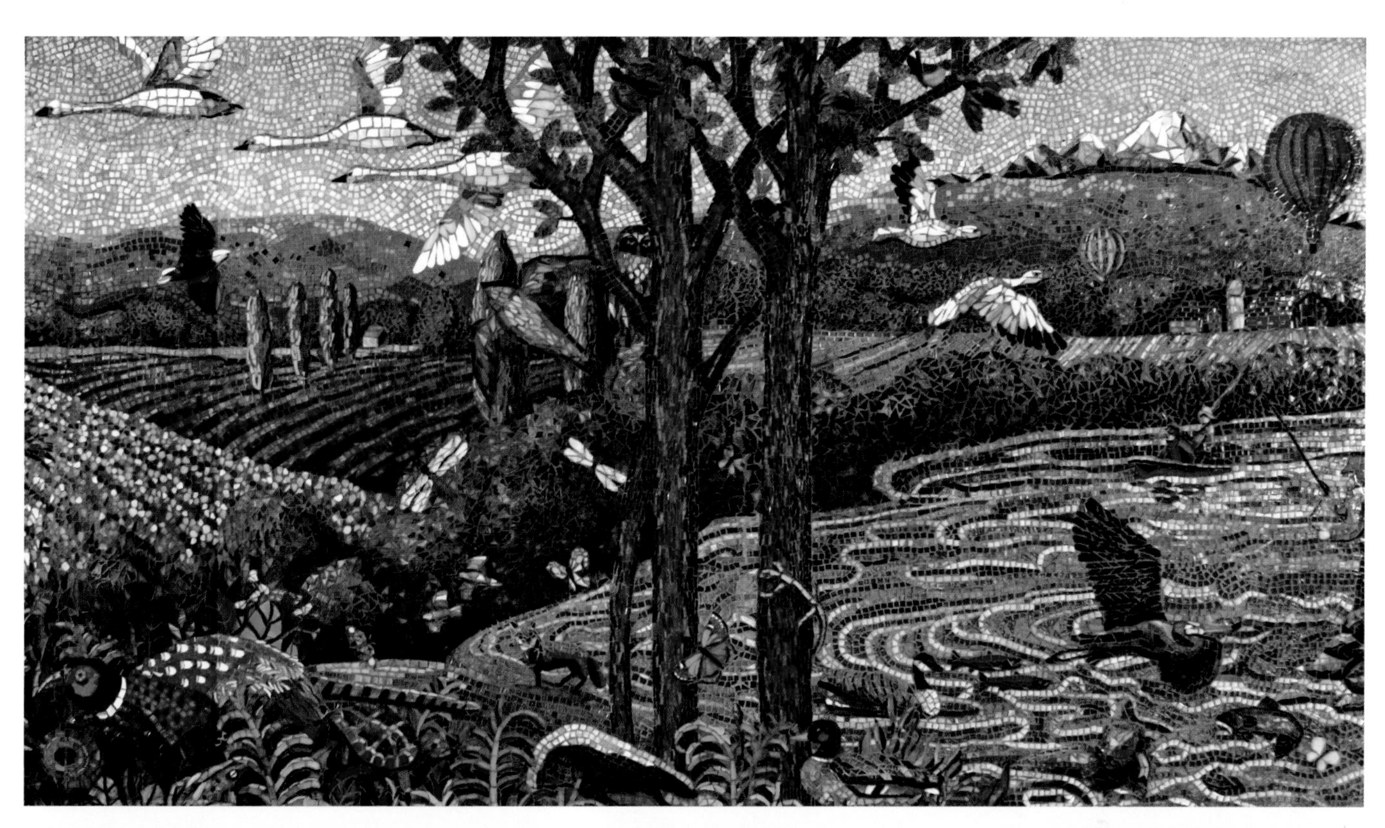

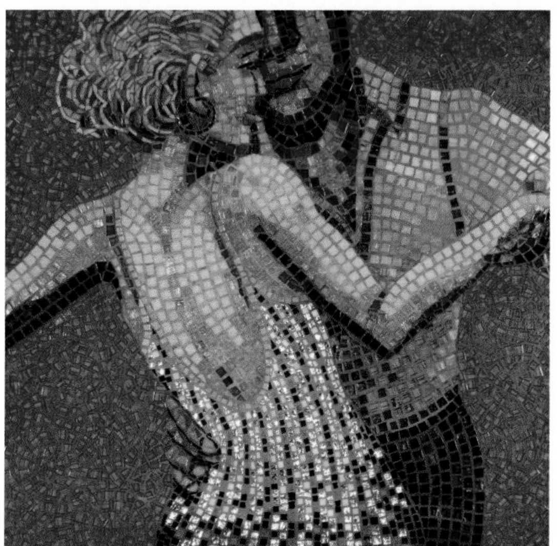

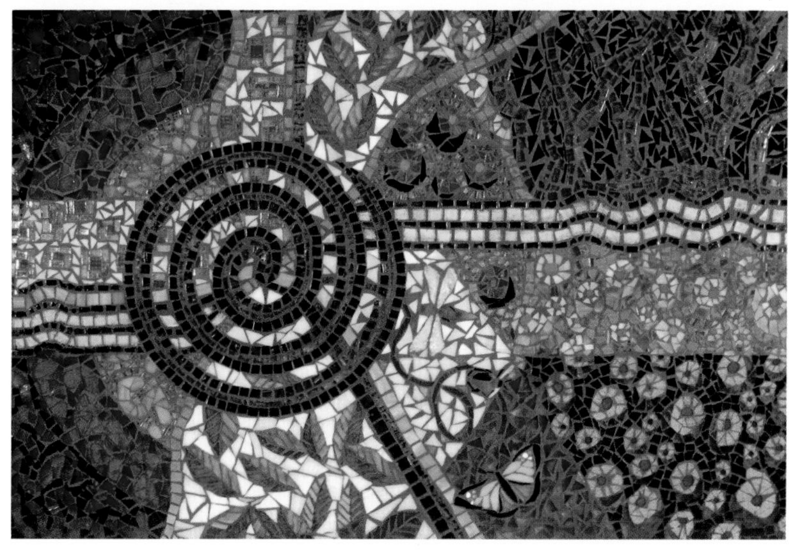

Top: *Skagit Valley* (detail), 2006, Lucille Umbarger Elementary School, Burlington, WA, glass mosaic, total size: 5' x 12'. Photograph: Kevin Clarke.
Bottom left: *The Dancers,* 2005, glass and gold leaf mosaic, 24" x 24". Bottom right: *Beneath The Surface,* 2006, glass mosaic, 24" x 36".

JAN BROWN CHECCO

BROWN CHECCO FINE ARTS ■ 360 RESOR AVENUE ■ CINCINNATI, OH 45220-1616
TEL/FAX 513-751-4783 ■ E-MAIL JAN@BROWNCHECCO.COM ■ WWW.BROWNCHECCO.COM

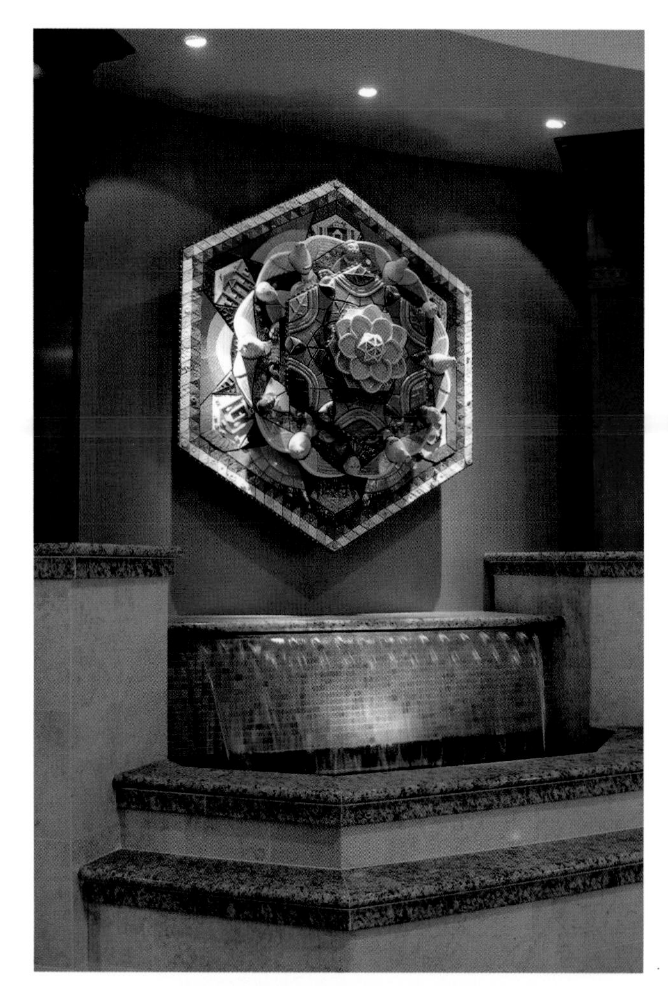

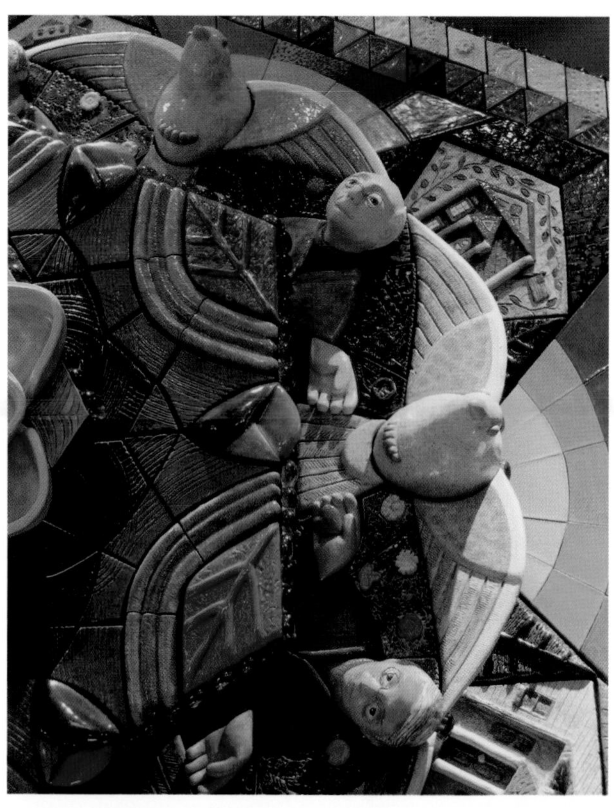

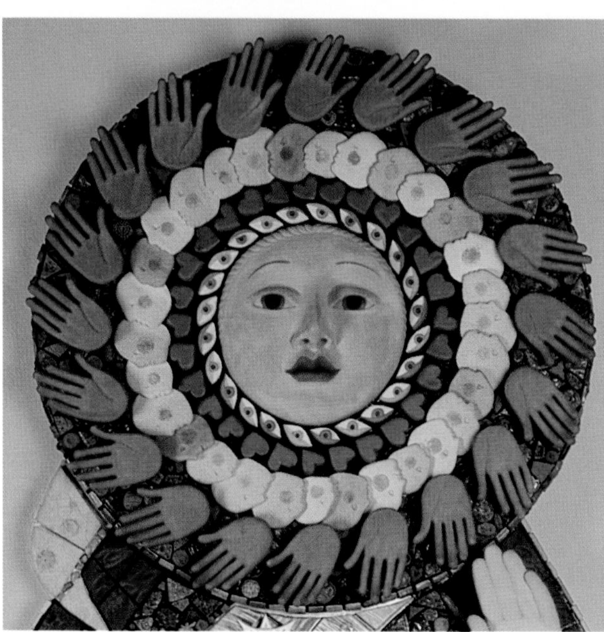

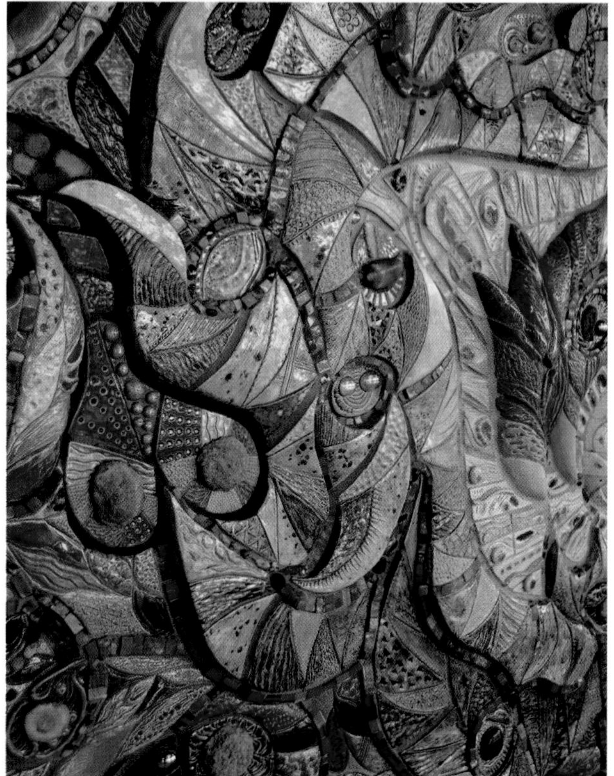

Top left: *Twin Lakes Fountain Mosaic,* 2006, Montgomery, OH, 60" x 48" x 16". Top right: *Twin Lakes Fountain Mosaic* (detail). Bottom left: *Spirit of Generosity* (detail), 2005, The Summit Country Day School, Cincinnati, OH. Photograph: Rick Norton. Bottom right: *Double Phoenix Hearth* (detail), 2003, International Friendship Park, Cincinnati, OH. Community-based artworks made in high-relief high-fired ceramic.

CLAYGAL

NAIRA BARSEGHIAN ■ 10600 SABLE AVENUE ■ SUNLAND, CA 91040 ■ TEL 818-353-1687
FAX 818-353-4803 ■ E-MAIL NAIRA@CLAYGAL.COM ■ WWW.CLAYGAL.COM

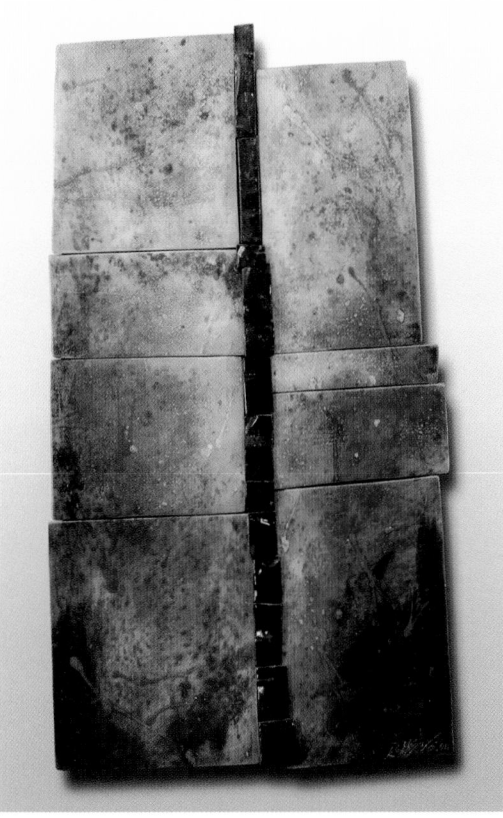

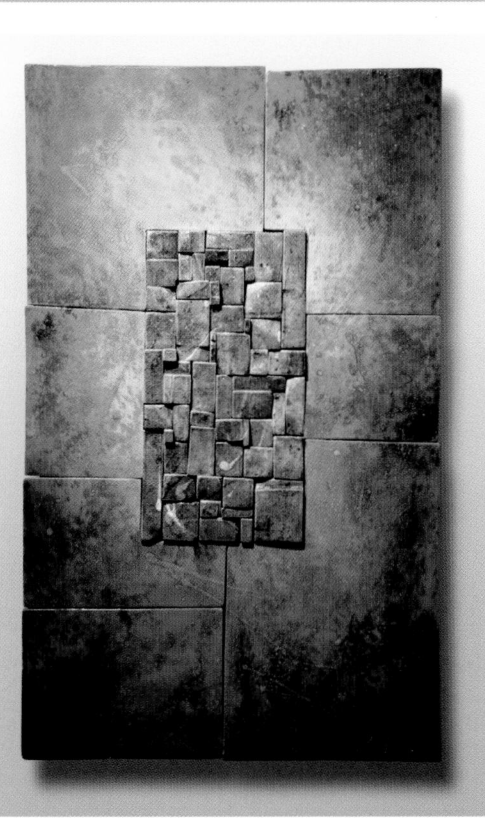

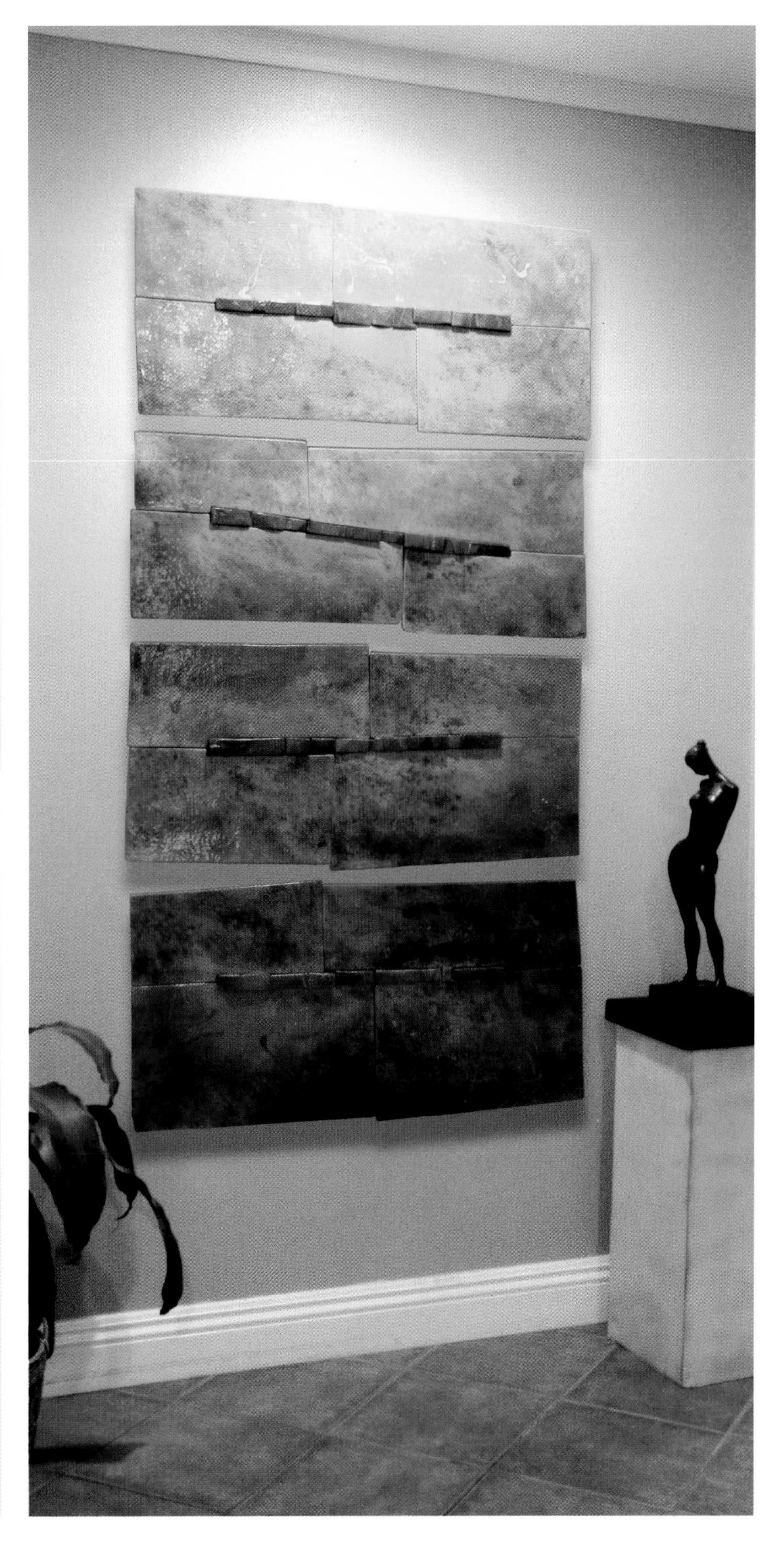

Top left: *Green Path*, ceramic wall piece, 40" x 28". Right: *Piano*, ceramic wall piece, total size: 60" x 32".
Bottom left: *Blue Wall*, ceramic wall piece, 40" x 28". Full-color catalog and price list available upon request. Photographs: Rafik Barseghian.

The Guild® Sourcebook of Architectural & Interior Art 22. © 2007 The Guild, Inc.

DORA DE LARIOS

DE LARIOS ■ 8560 VENICE BOULEVARD ■ LOS ANGELES, CA 90034
TEL 310-839-8305 ■ E-MAIL DELARIOS@CA.RR.COM ■ WWW.DORADELARIOS.COM

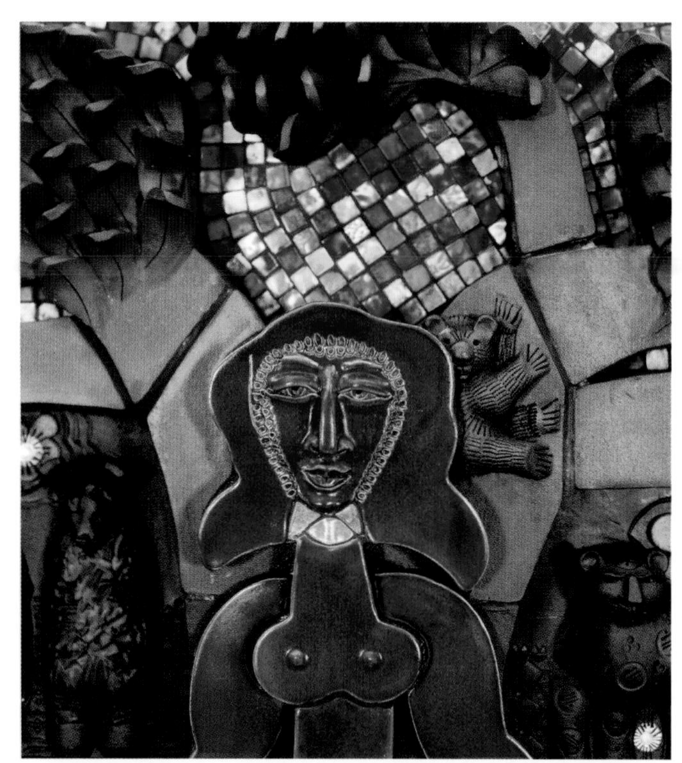

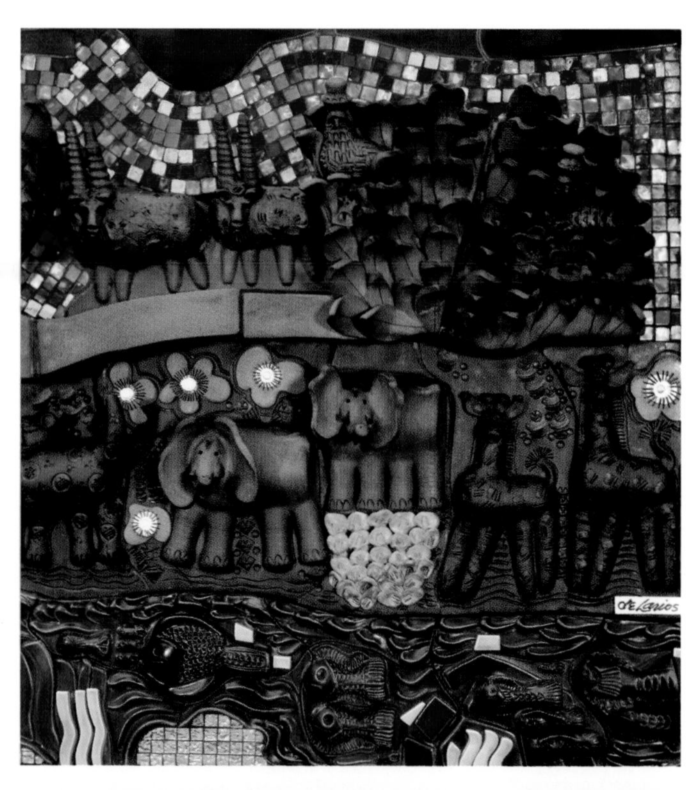

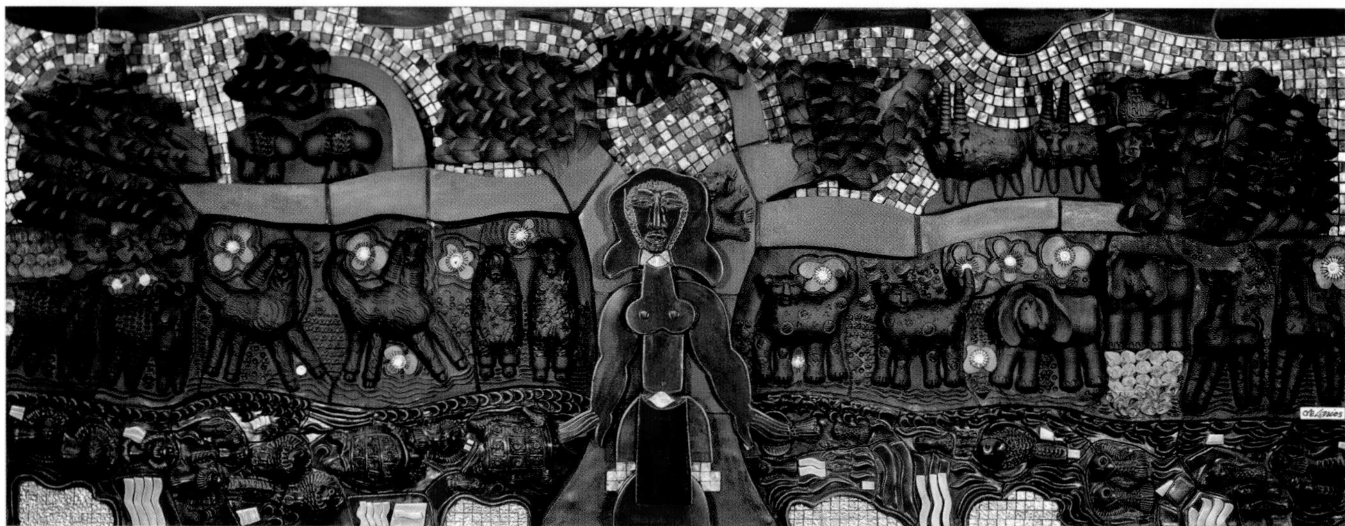

The World According to Dora, 4'H x 10'W x 6"D. Photographs: Chuck Bankuti.

ENANA & CO.

JOSEPH F. JACOB, PRESIDENT ■ 212 MENLO PARK ROAD ■ NISKAYUNA, NY 12309
TEL 866-79-ENANA ■ TEL 518-377-5742 ■ FAX 518-388-5148 ■ E-MAIL JFJACOB@ENANACO.COM ■ WWW.ENANACO.COM

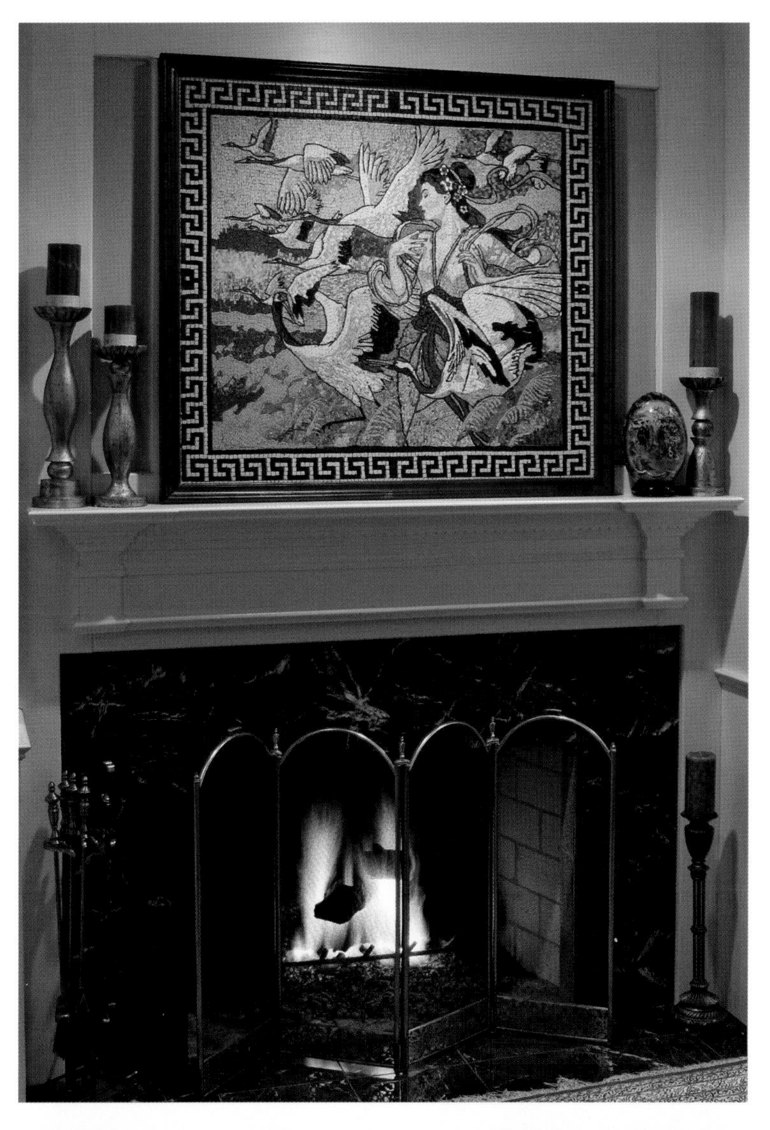

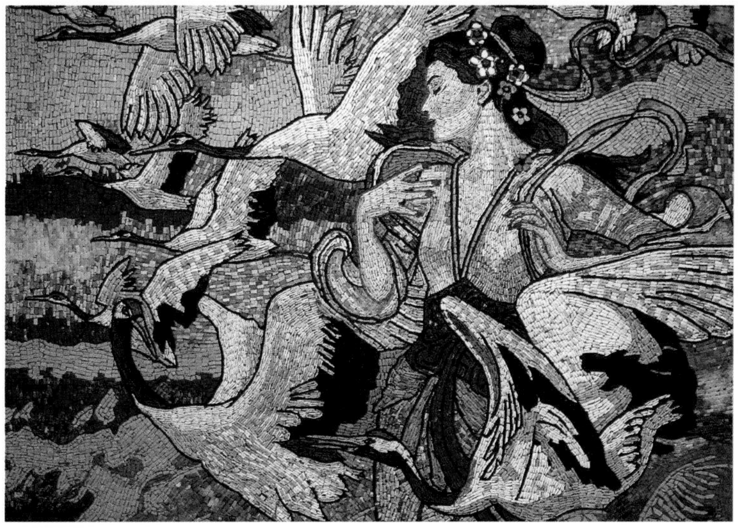

Swan Lady, Inspired, micromosaic natural color and natural stone mural, 48" x 48".

VIRGINIA GABALDO

VIRGINIA GABALDO FINE ART ■ 6724 CARNEY AVENUE NW ■ ALBUQUERQUE, NM 87120
TEL 760-567-2028 ■ FAX 760-369-2299 ■ E-MAIL VIRGINIA@VIRGINIAGABALDO.COM ■ WWW.VIRGINIAGABALDO.COM

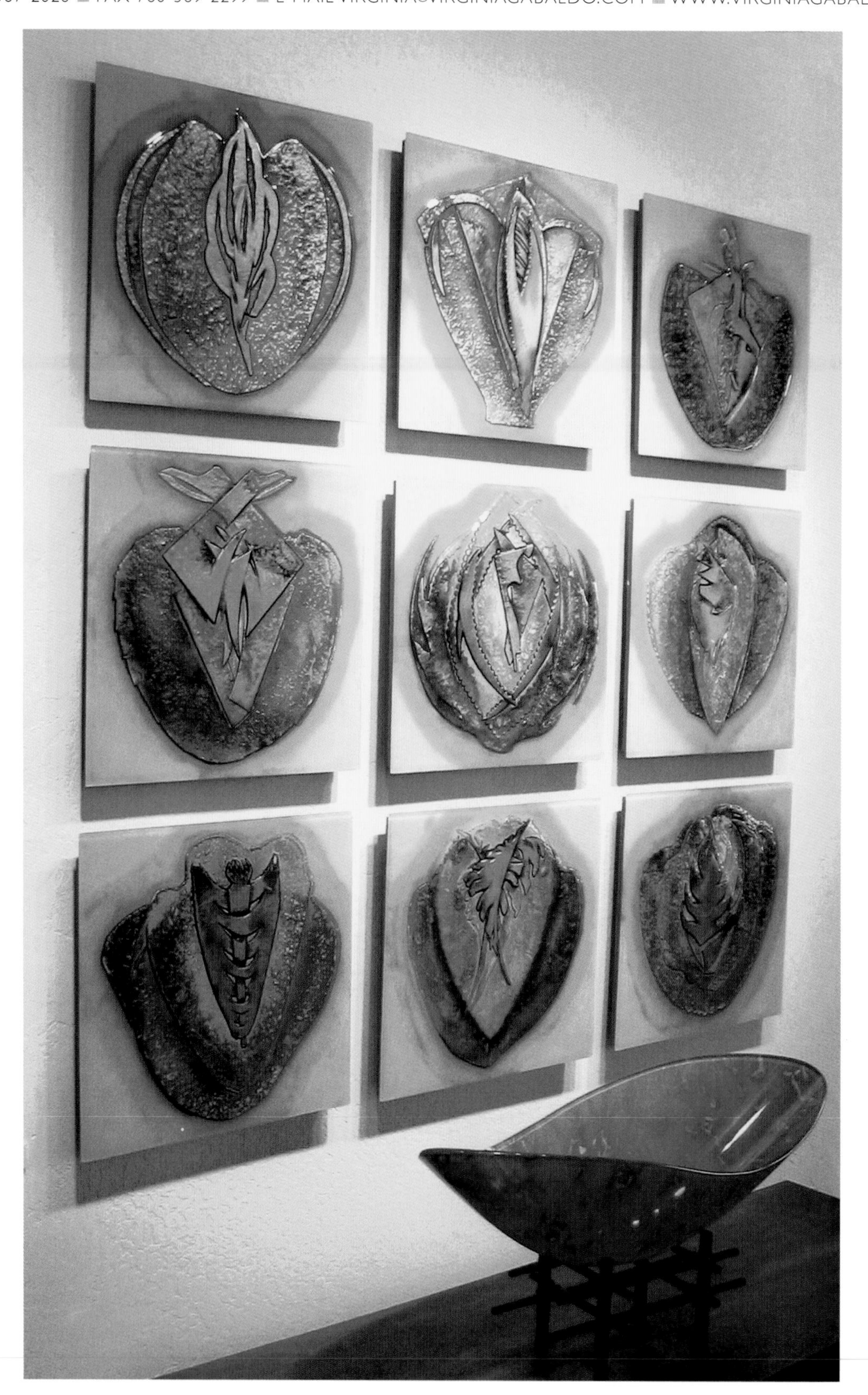

Drifting Seed Pods, 2006, 47" x 47" x 3" (14" x 14" x 3" each). Photograph: Donald K. Willis.

RUTH FRANCES GREENBERG

RUTH FRANCES GREENBERG MOSAICS ■ 1123 NE FREMONT STREET ■ PORTLAND, OR 97212 ■ TEL 503-235-2882
FAX 503-235-2883 ■ E-MAIL RUTH@RUTHFRANCESGREENBERG.COM ■ WWW.RUTHFRANCESGREENBERG.COM

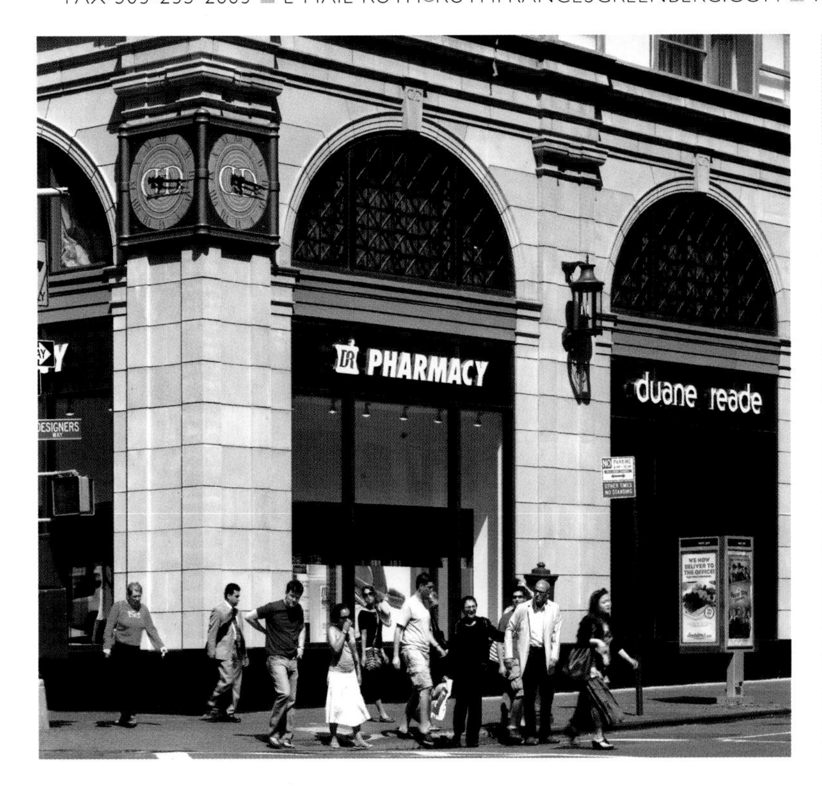

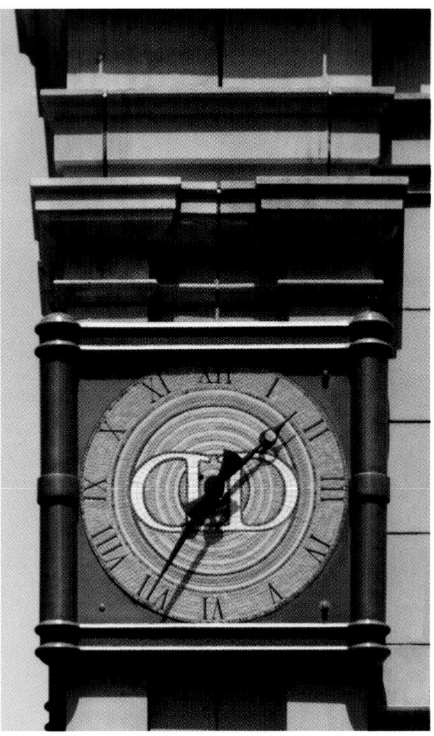

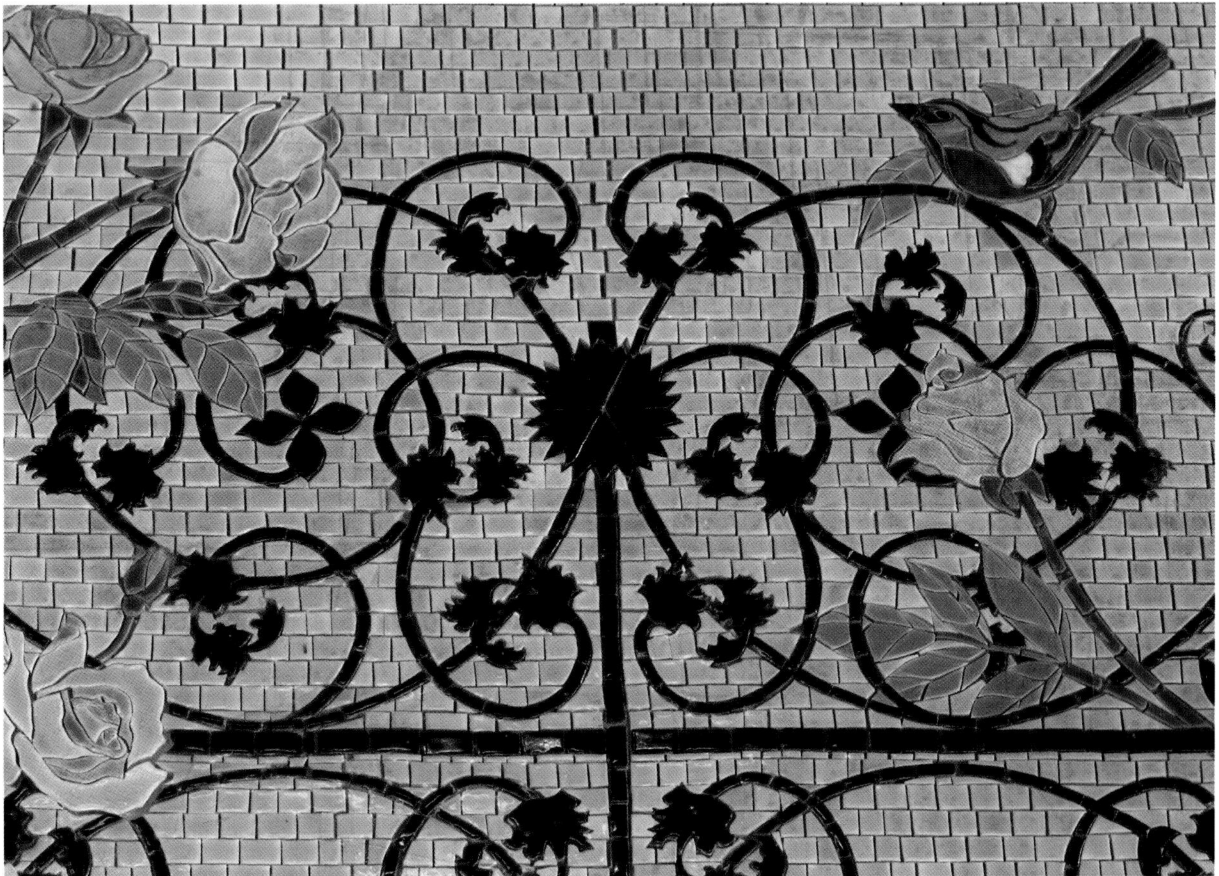

Top left and right: Clocks at the Design & Decoration Building, New York, NY. Photograph: Wade Zimmerman.
Bottom: *Rose Room Mosaic* (detail), installation in progress, private residence, New York, NY, 85' sq.

CHRISTOPHER GRYDER

METAMORPHEUS ■ 2718 CUMBERLAND STREET NORTHWEST ■ ROANOKE, VA 24012
TEL 540-366-9839 ■ E-MAIL CHRIS@CHRISGRYDER.COM ■ WWW.CHRISGRYDER.COM

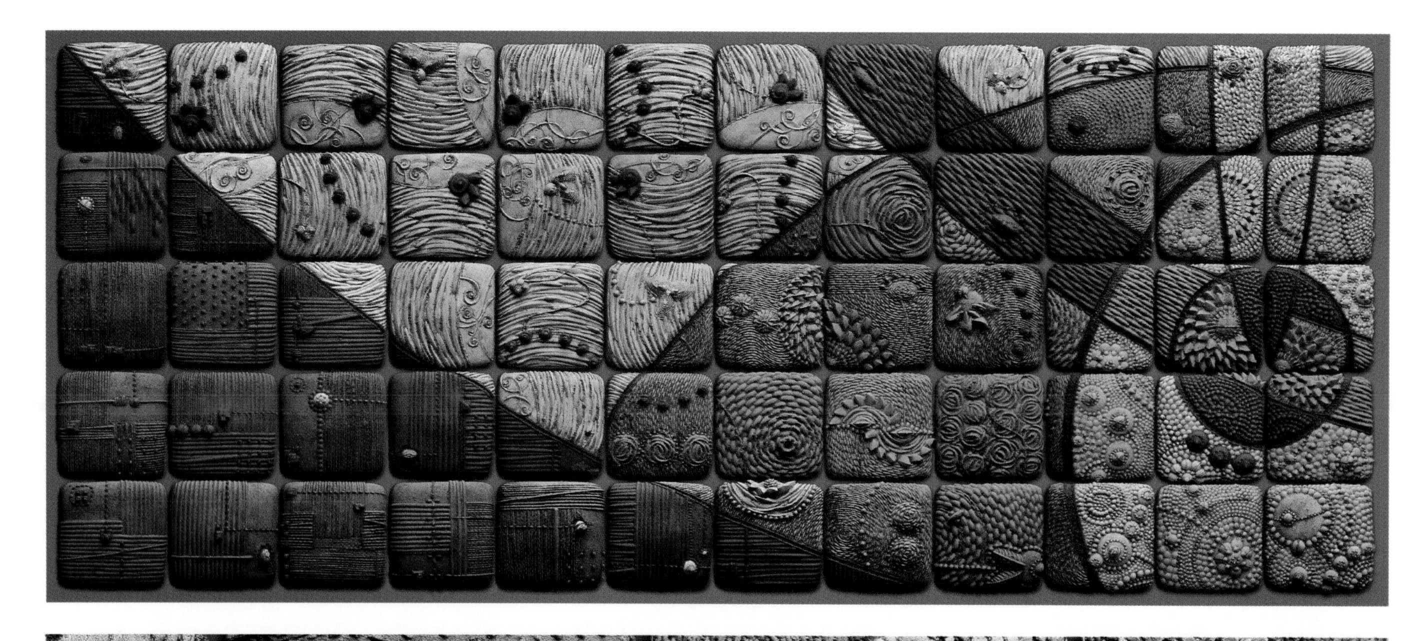

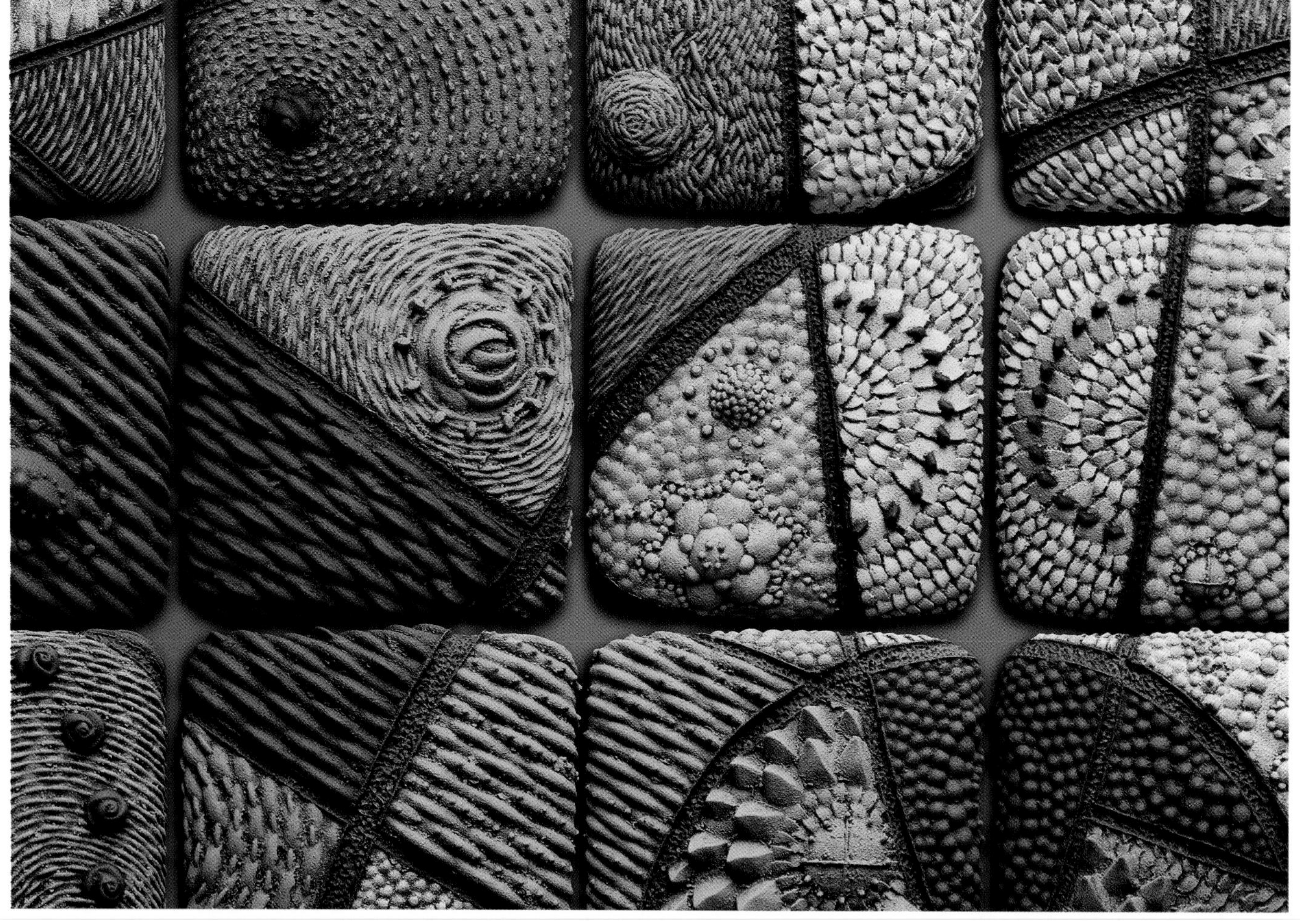

Marriot at River Cree Resort commission, 2006, ceramic relief tiles, 5' x 12'.

RHONDA HEISLER

RHONDA HEISLER MOSAIC ART ▪ 8 STONE MOUNTAIN COURT ▪ SKILLMAN, NJ 08558 ▪ TEL 609-466-2231
FAX 609-466-9043 ▪ E-MAIL RJHEISLER@PATMEDIA.NET ▪ WWW.RHONDAHEISLERMOSAICART.COM

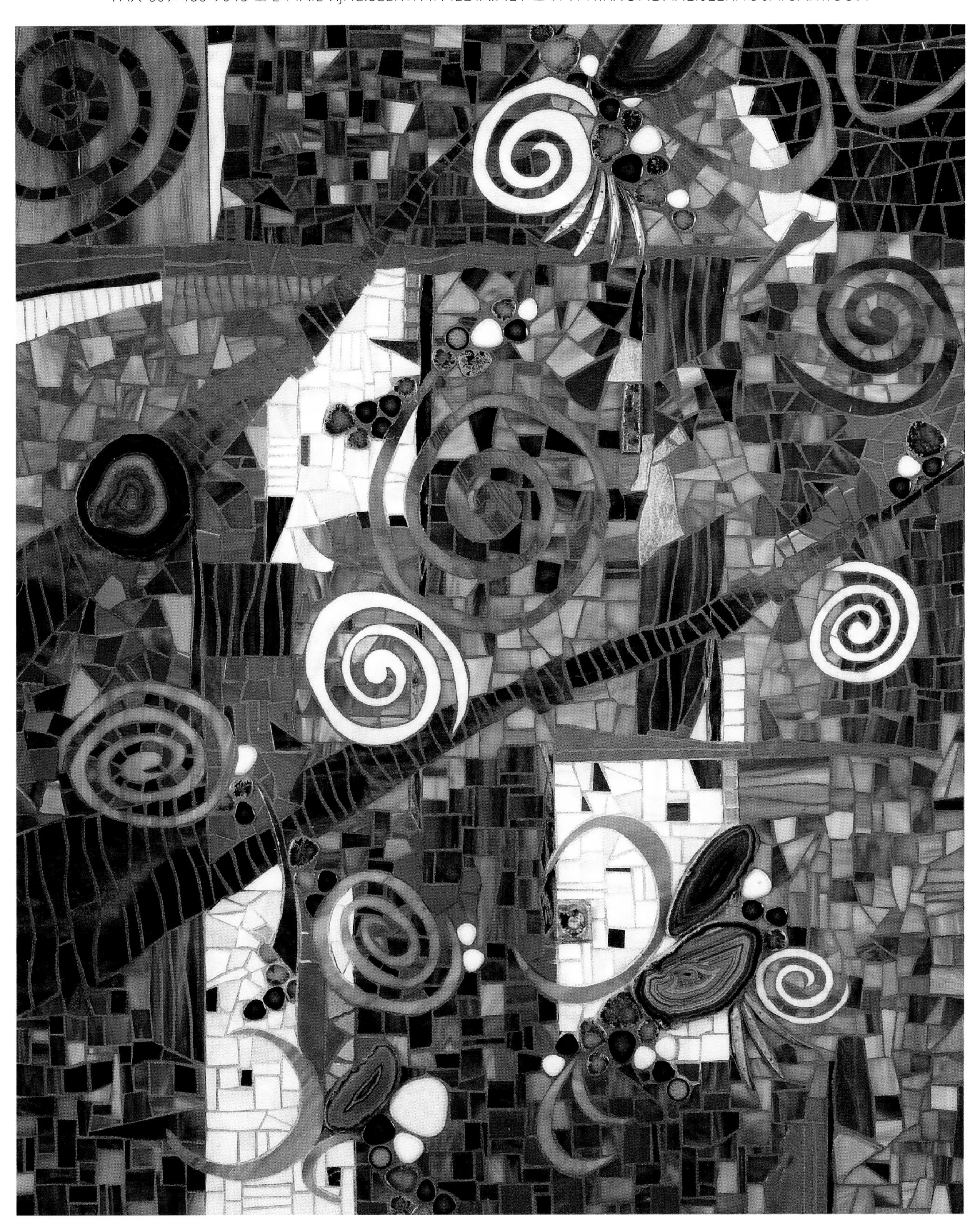

From This All Flows, 2006, stained glass mosaic, agates, shells, glazed and unglazed ceramic, and smalti, 35"H x 29"W. Photograph: Ross Stout.

KAREN HEYL

1310 PENDLETON STREET ■ CINCINNATI, OH 45202 ■ 907 SONIA PLACE ■ ESCONDIDO, CA 92026
TEL 513-421-9791 ■ TEL 760-489-7106 ■ E-MAIL KLHEYL@AOL.COM ■ WWW.KARENHEYL.COM

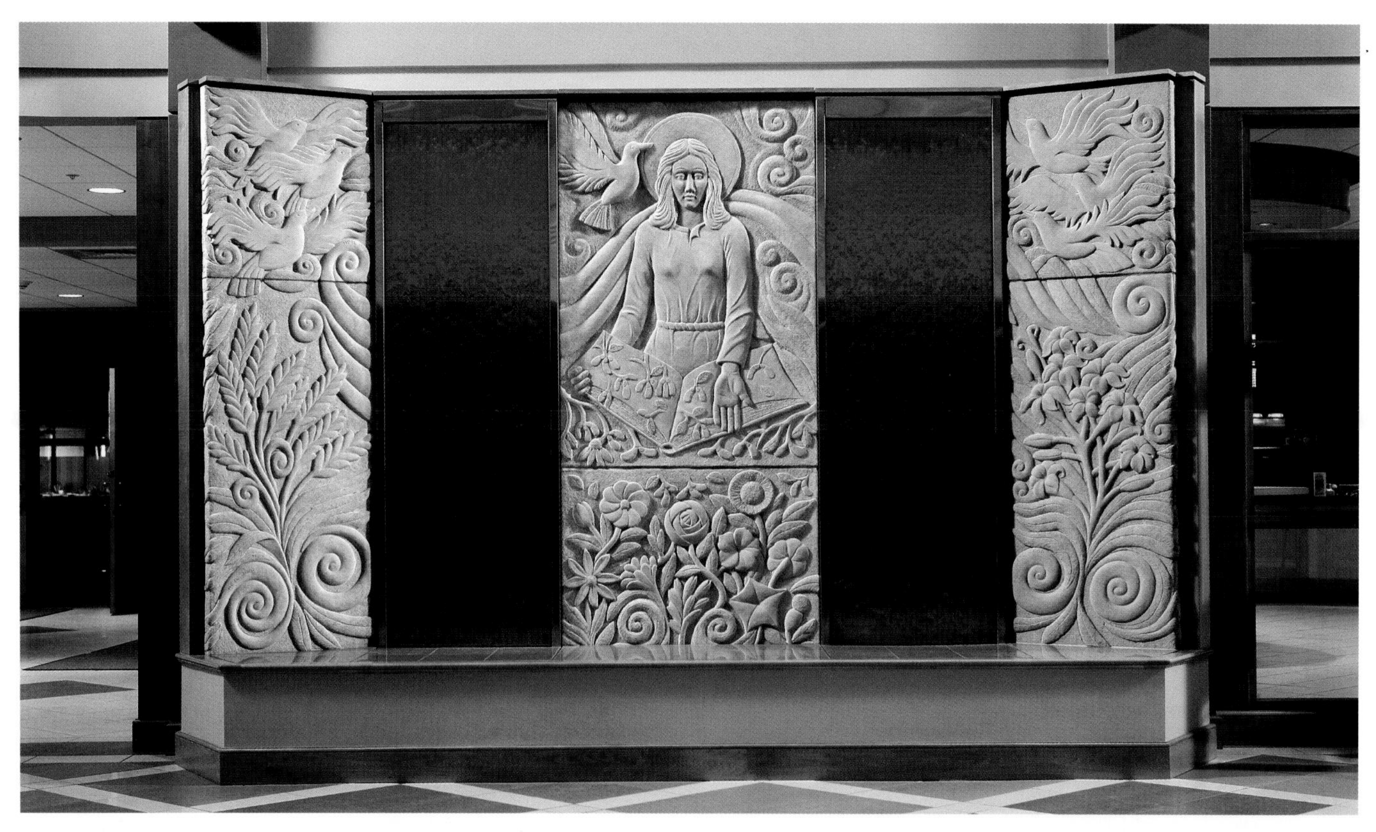

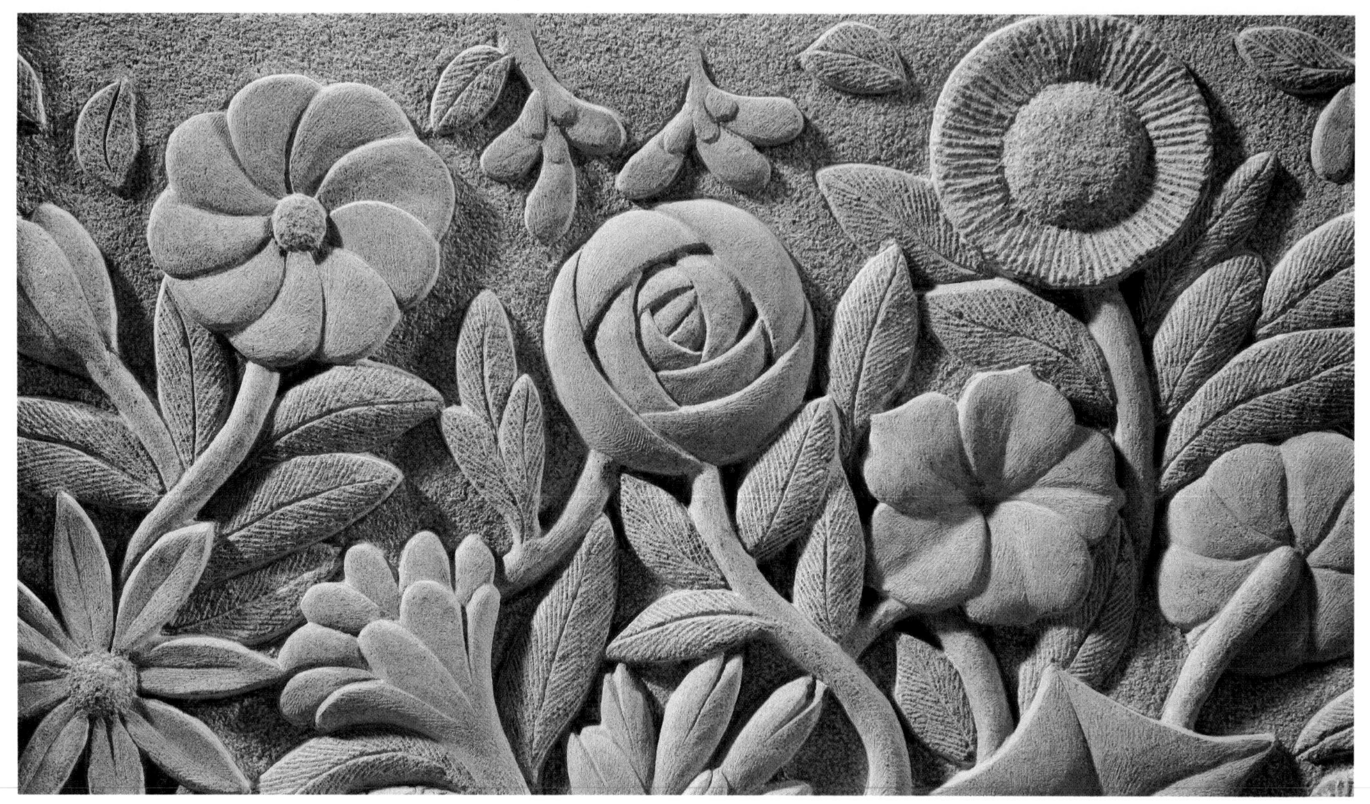

Mary, Seat of Wisdom, St. Mary's College, Notre Dame, IN, limestone, 30"H x 42"W. Photographs: Matt Cashore.

CLAUDIA HOLLISTER

PMB 158 333 SOUTH STATE STREET SUITE V ■ LAKE OSWEGO, OR 97034
TEL 503-636-6684 ■ FAX 503-636-0436 ■ E-MAIL CHD@EUROPA.COM

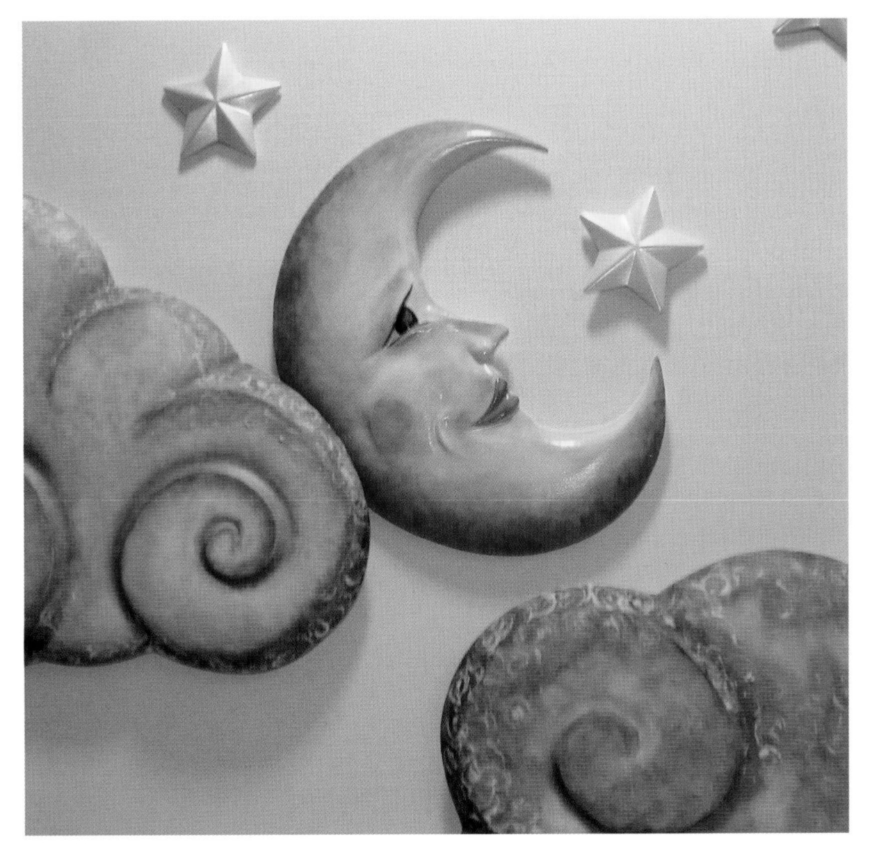

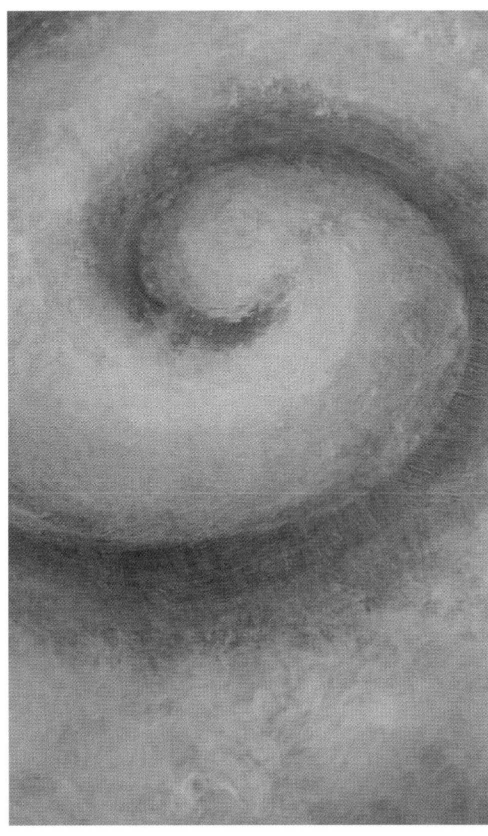

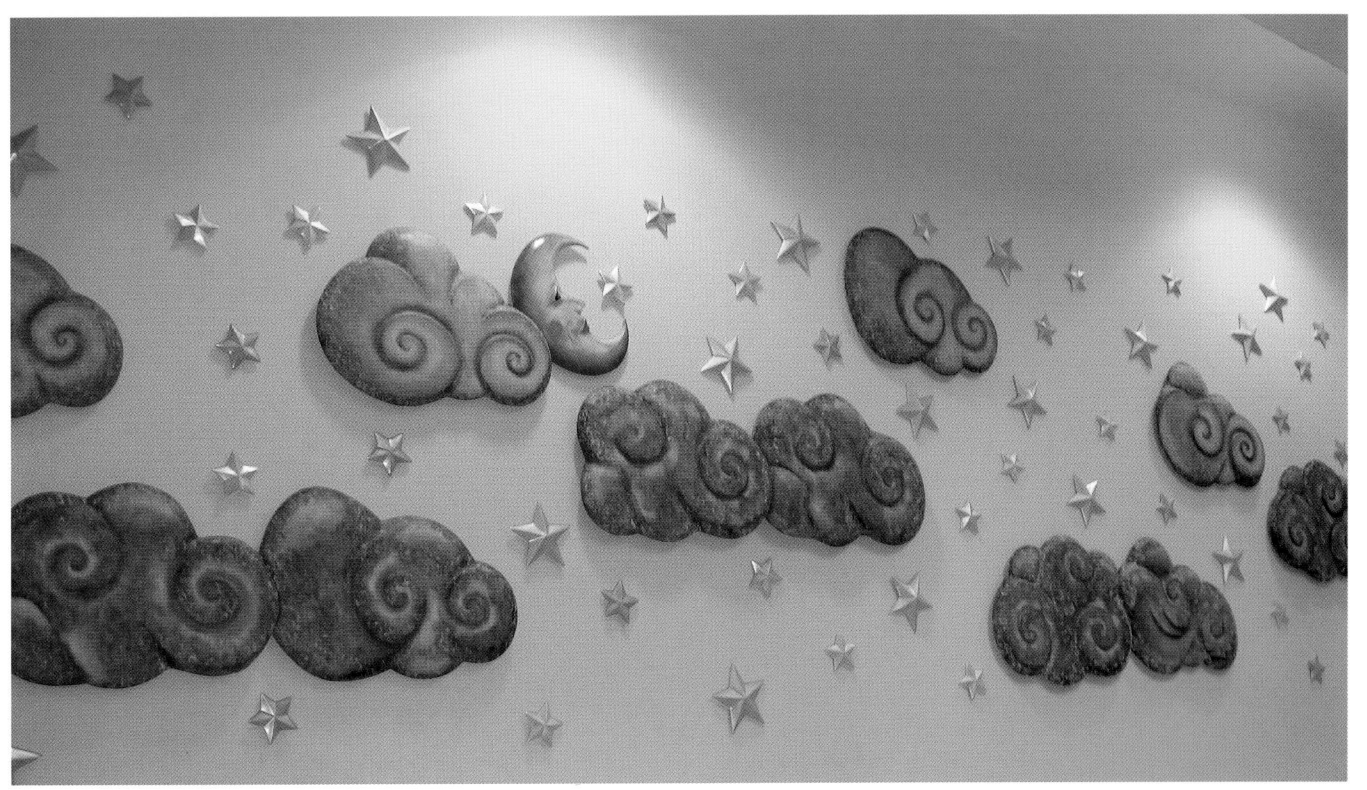

Sunrise Woman & Children's Hospital, Las Vegas, NV, total size: 4' x 23' x 2".

VICTORIA JENSEN

VICTORIA JENSEN STUDIO ■ 5132 SALEM HILLS ■ CINCINNATI, OH 45230
TEL 513-708-5618 ■ E-MAIL VJENSEN55@HOTMAIL.COM ■ WWW.VICTORIAJENSEN.COM

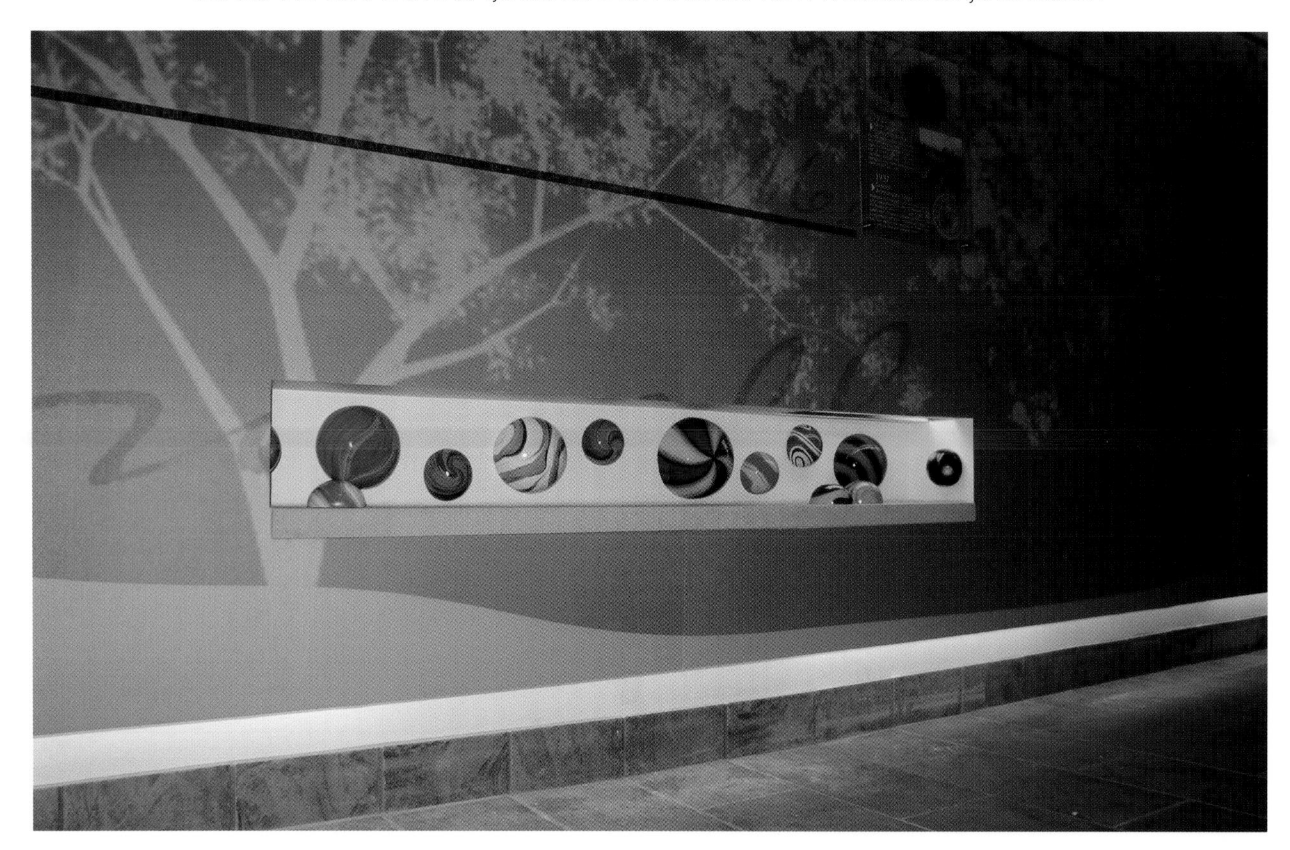

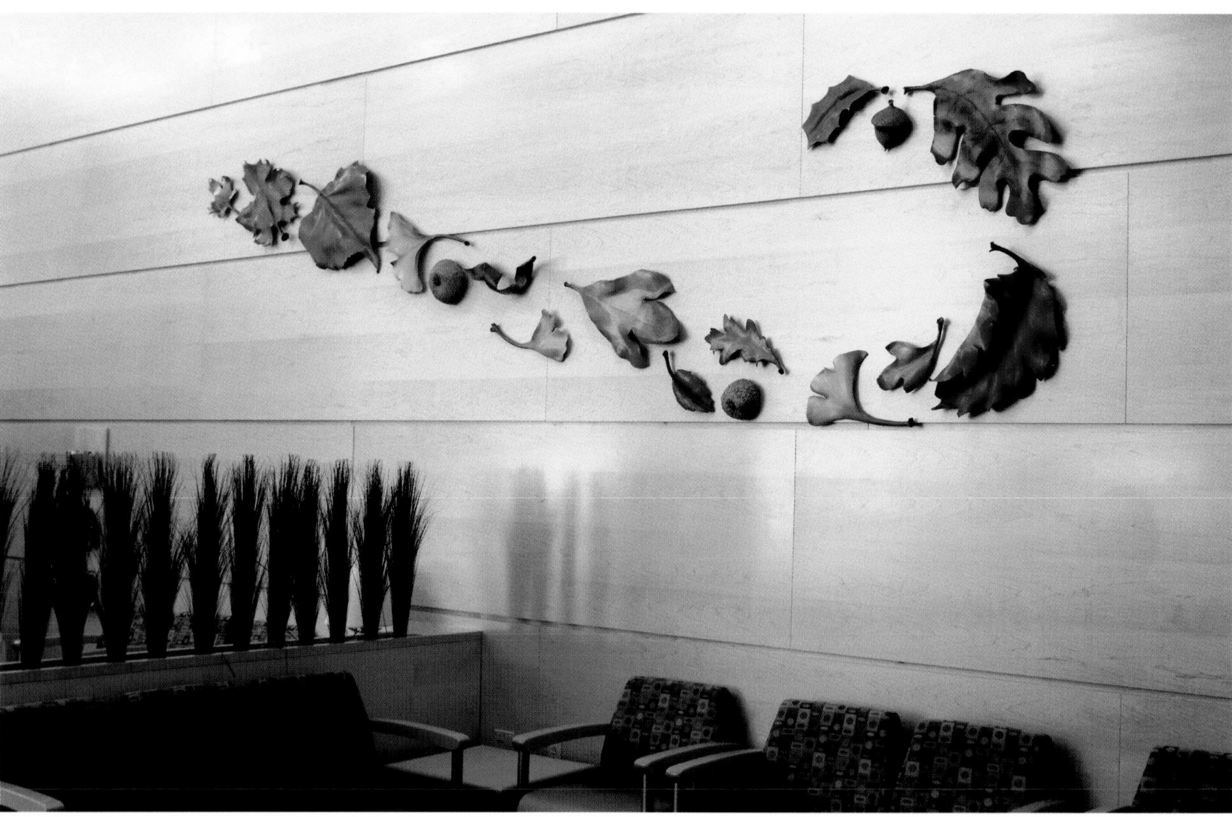

Top: *Blanchard Valley,* 7'L. Bottom: Mary Rutan Hospital, 15'L. Photograph: John Johnston.

ELLE TERRY LEONARD

ARCHITECTURAL CERAMICS ■ 1840 HYDE PARK STREET ■ SARASOTA, FL 34239 ■ TEL 941-362-9527
E-MAIL ETERRYLEONARD@AOL.COM ■ WWW.ELLETERRYLEONARD.COM

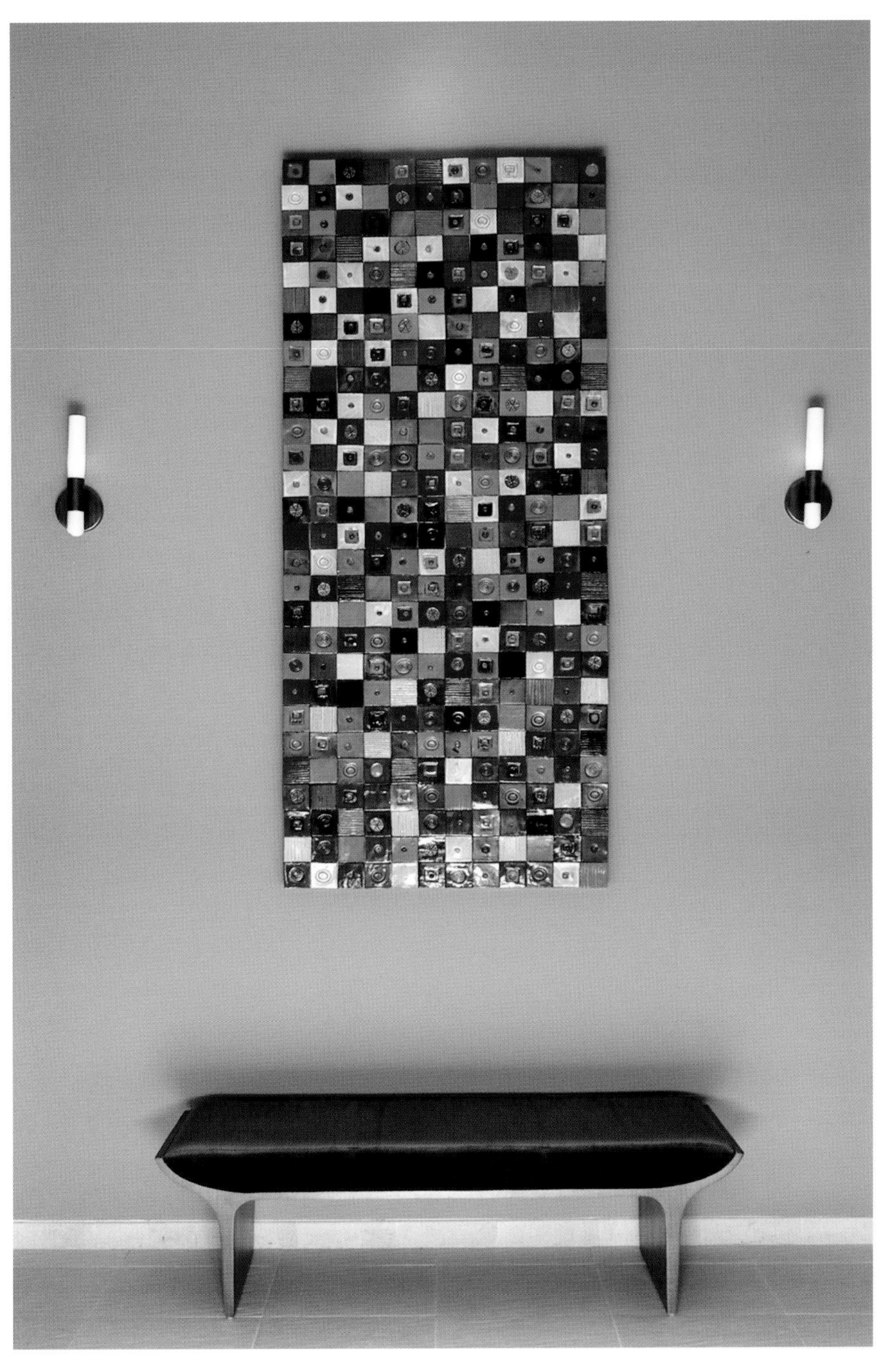

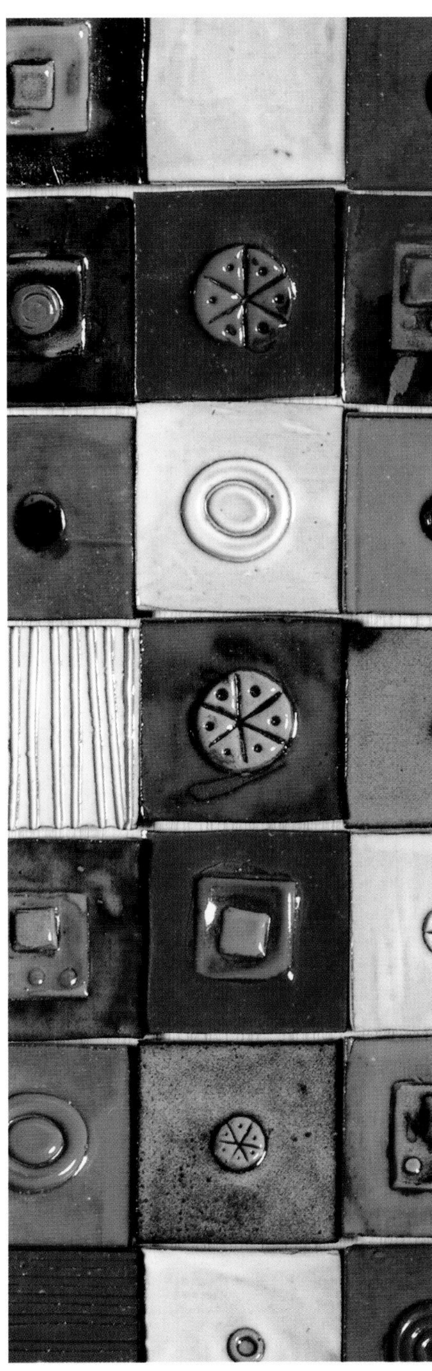

Ceramic Quilt, 2006, Whole Foods Centre, Sarasota, FL, 3' × 7'H. Photographs: Christopher Bunn.

A Commission Story

Arteclettica

TITLE
Garden (wall); *Flower* (floor); *Tea Table*, 2001-2002

COMMISSIONED FOR
Home Concepts Design Resource Center,
Truckee, CA

TIMELINE: 16 months

DIMENSIONS
Garden, 3'H x 4.25'W; *Flower*, 6'H x 7'W;
Tea Table, 1.5'H x 4'W x 2'D

TRADE PROFESSIONAL
Ruth Cross, Designer/Owner,
Home Concepts Design Resource Center

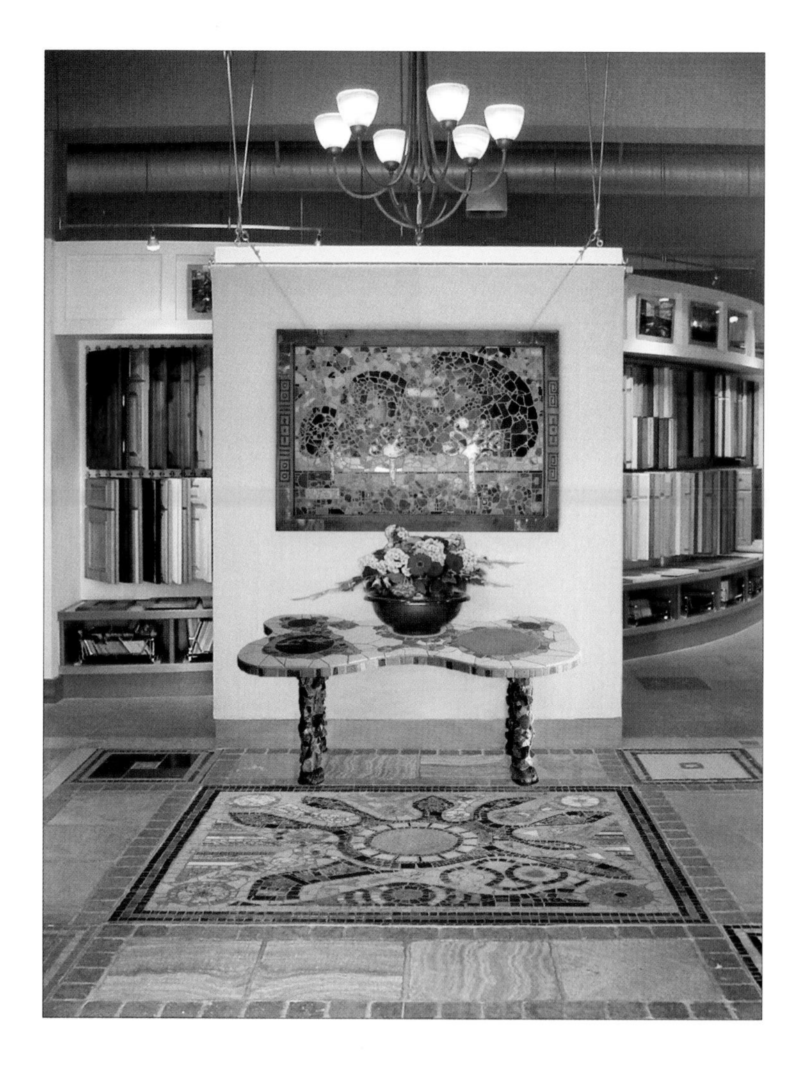

It all started on the basketball court, when a hoops-playing Italian architect/artist met the owner of a local lumber yard, and an unlikely but harmonious artistic alliance began. ■ When the lumber company launched a major renovation of its design resource center, Home Concepts, the owners turned to Arteclettica, tapping the combined talents of artists Daniela Garofalo and her partner, Dominic Panziera. The owners had confidence in the team's abilities, taking advantage of Garofalo's architectural acumen and knowledge of theatrical set design to transform the showroom interior, displays, and even some facets of the exterior. ■ Garofalo cites Ruth Cross, the owner of the showroom and a designer herself, as a supportive collaborator. "She was a great client, giving me an enormous amount of freedom," she explains. Cross was motivated by the challenge posed by big-box home improvement stores opening nearby. She wanted her showroom to have "an artist's perspective . . . to make it a creative place. But it also had to be functional. We had a very small space in which to show a lot of things. The artists really accomplished that." ■ The resource center's sensibility is emphasized by a large hanging canvas, which provides a perfect "wall" for a changing display of artwork by Arteclettica. The whimsical *Tea Table* by Panziera and a series of gorgeous floor mosaics, including *Flower*, by Panziera and Garofalo, dazzle customers with the intricacy and vibrancy of their tile and stonework. Beautiful yet practical, according to Cross, who says the colorful mosaics have stimulated the sales of tiles tremendously. ■ The bottom line is aesthetic and economic success, according to Cross, who is delighted by the artful impact of her showroom. "People come in and they feel comfortable buying here, not just looking."

MARILYN LINDSTRÖM

2528 PILLSBURY AVENUE SOUTH ■ MINNEAPOLIS, MN 55404 ■ TEL/FAX 612-825-1859
TEL 612-325-2114 ■ E-MAIL MURALS@BITSTREAM.NET ■ WWW.MARILYNLINDSTROM.COM

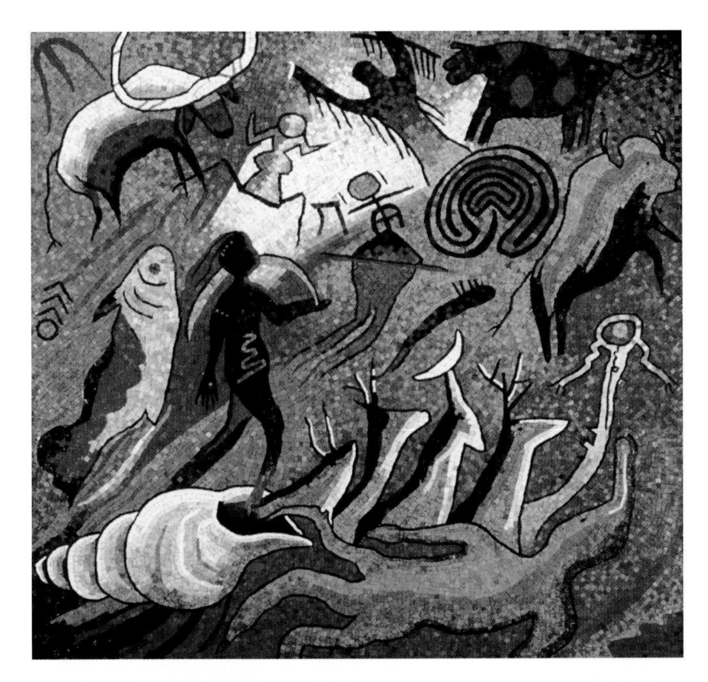

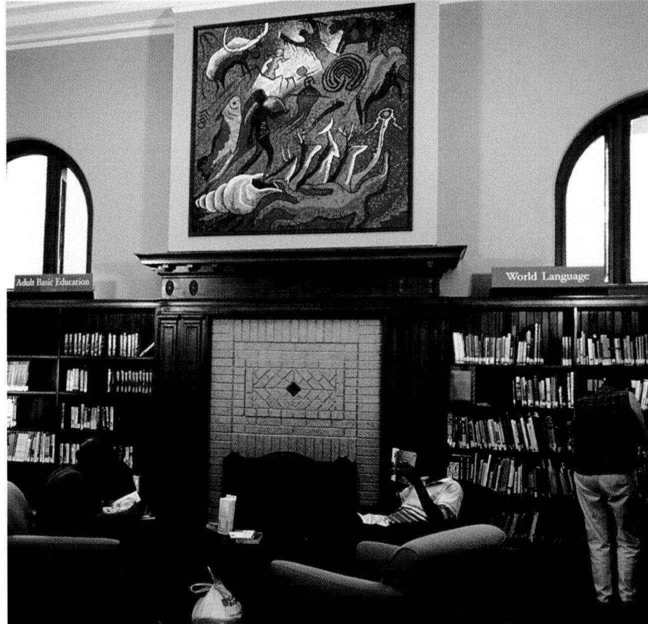

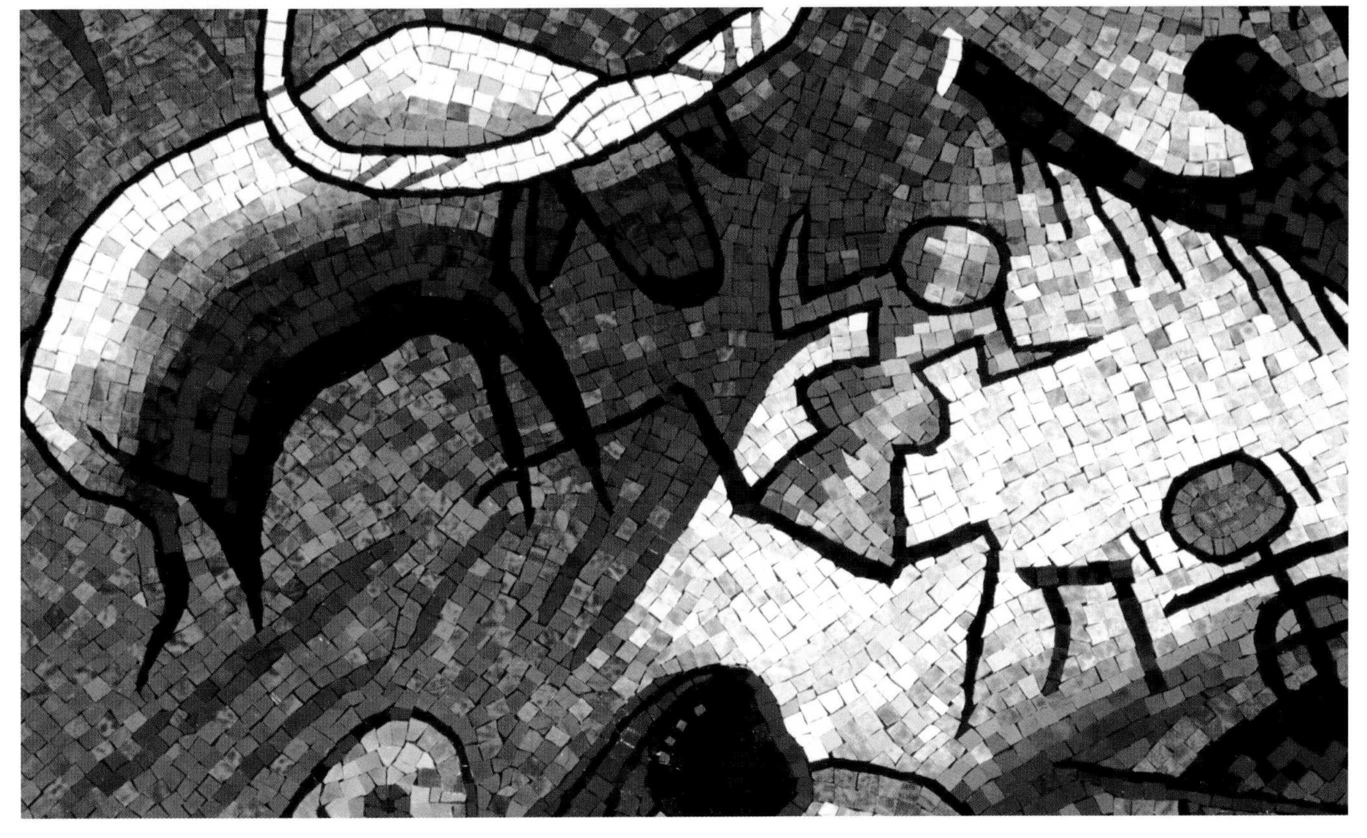

World Language, 2005, Franklin Library, Minneapolis, MN, Perdomo smalti glass mosaic, 6' x 6'. Photographs: Usry Alleyne, Inc.

ELIZABETH MacDONALD

PO BOX 186 ■ BRIDGEWATER, CT 06752 ■ TEL 860-354-0594 ■ FAX 860-350-4052
E-MAIL EPMACD@EARTHLINK.NET ■ WWW.ELIZABETHMACDONALD.COM

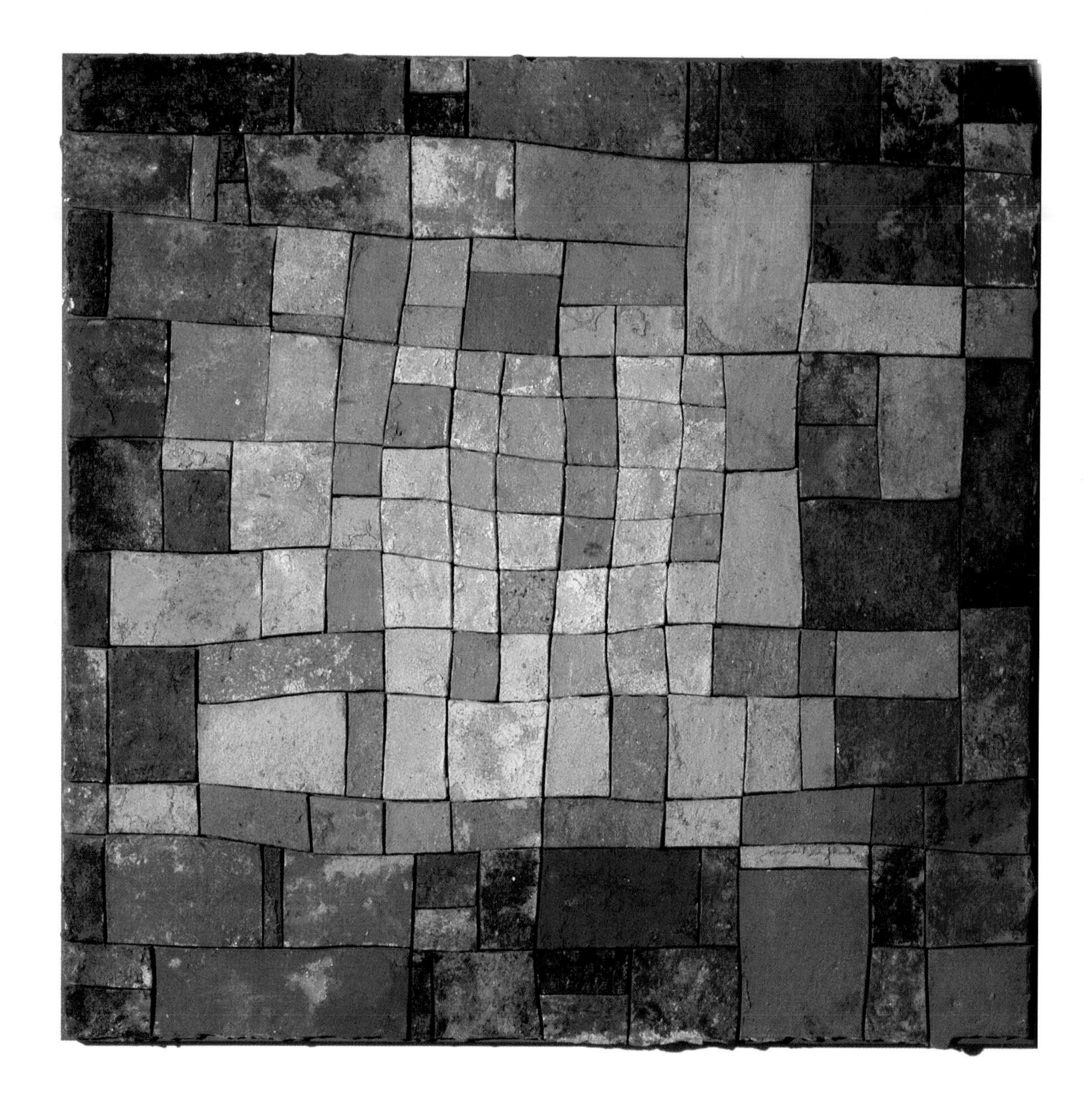

After Klee, 2005, ceramic, 21" x 21". Photograph: Randy Clark.

ANDI AND ROBERT MORAN

OBJECTS ■ 941 CAMPBELL ROAD ■ CHOUDRANT, LA 71227 ■ TEL 318-768-2479
E-MAIL INFO@MORAN-MORAN.COM ■ WWW.MORAN-MORAN.COM

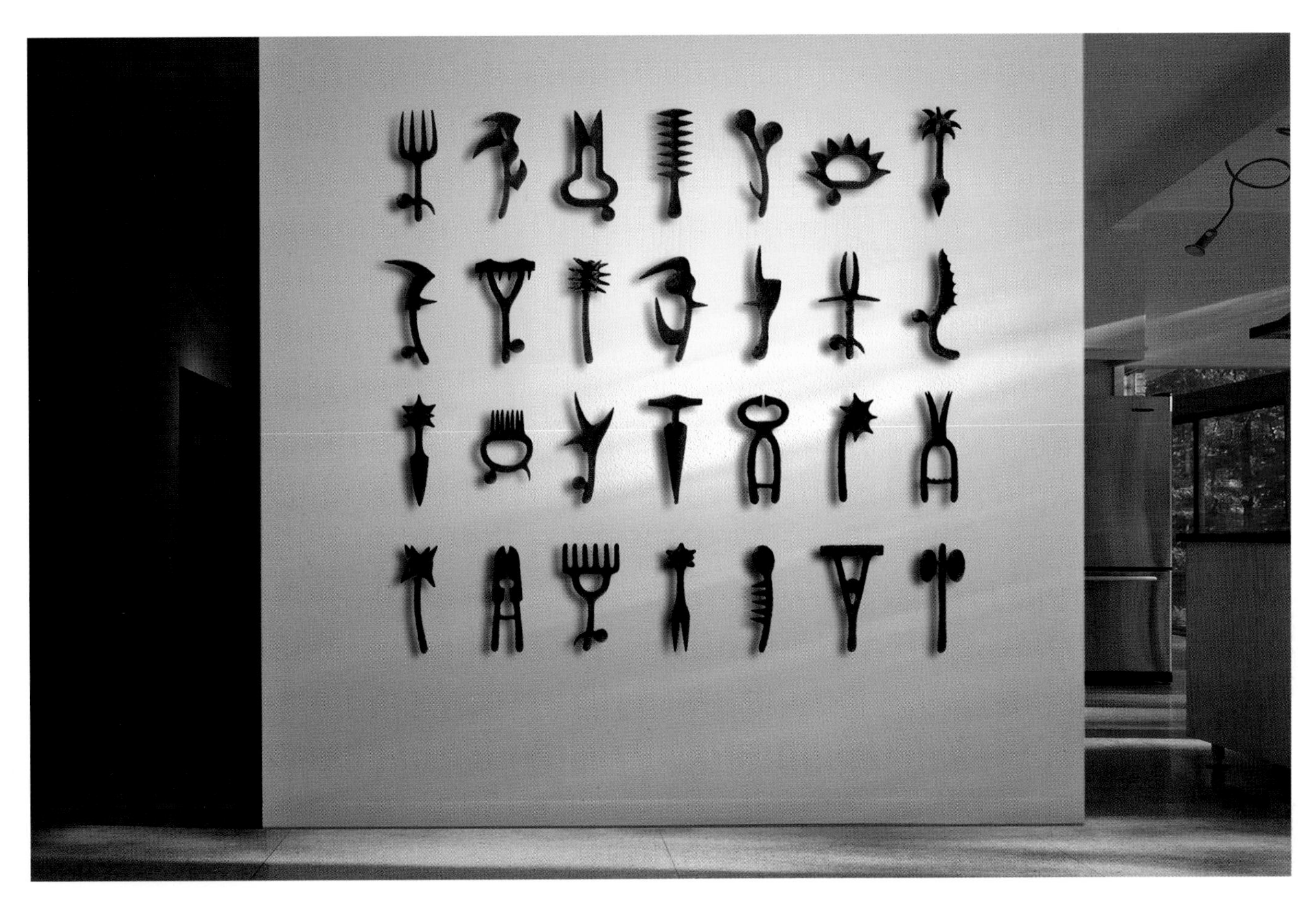

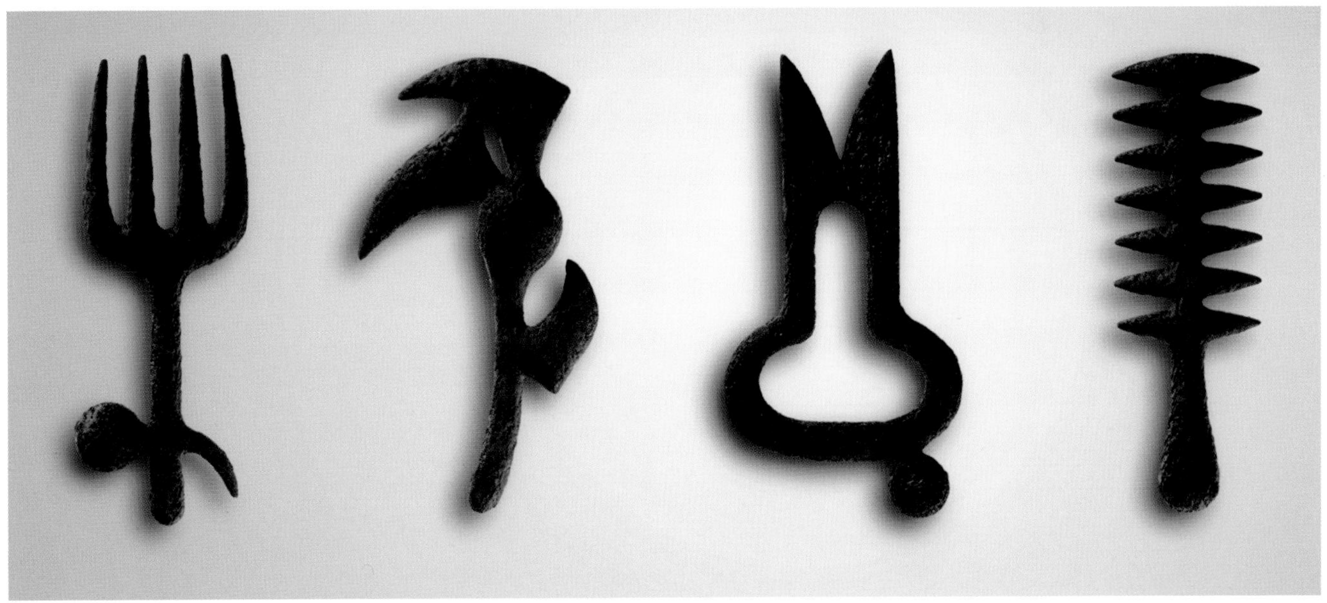

Top: *Implement* series installation, ceramic, 8'H x 8'W. Bottom: *Implement* series (detail). Photographs: Tom Joynt.

MASON NYE

MASON NYE MURALS ■ 423 ATLANTIC AVENUE #4P ■ BROOKLYN, NY 11217 ■ TEL/FAX 718-625-2330
TEL 917-566-4478 ■ E-MAIL MNYE@MASONNYEMURALS.COM ■ WWW.MASONNYEMURALS.COM

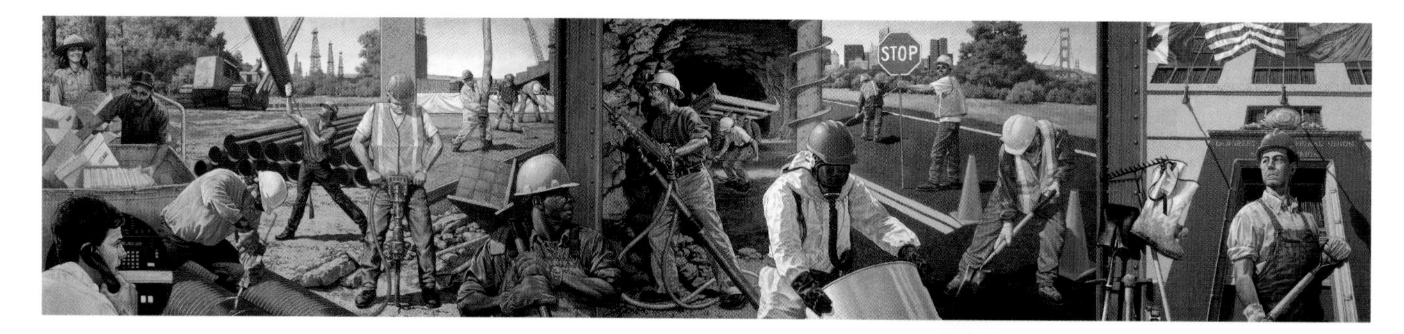

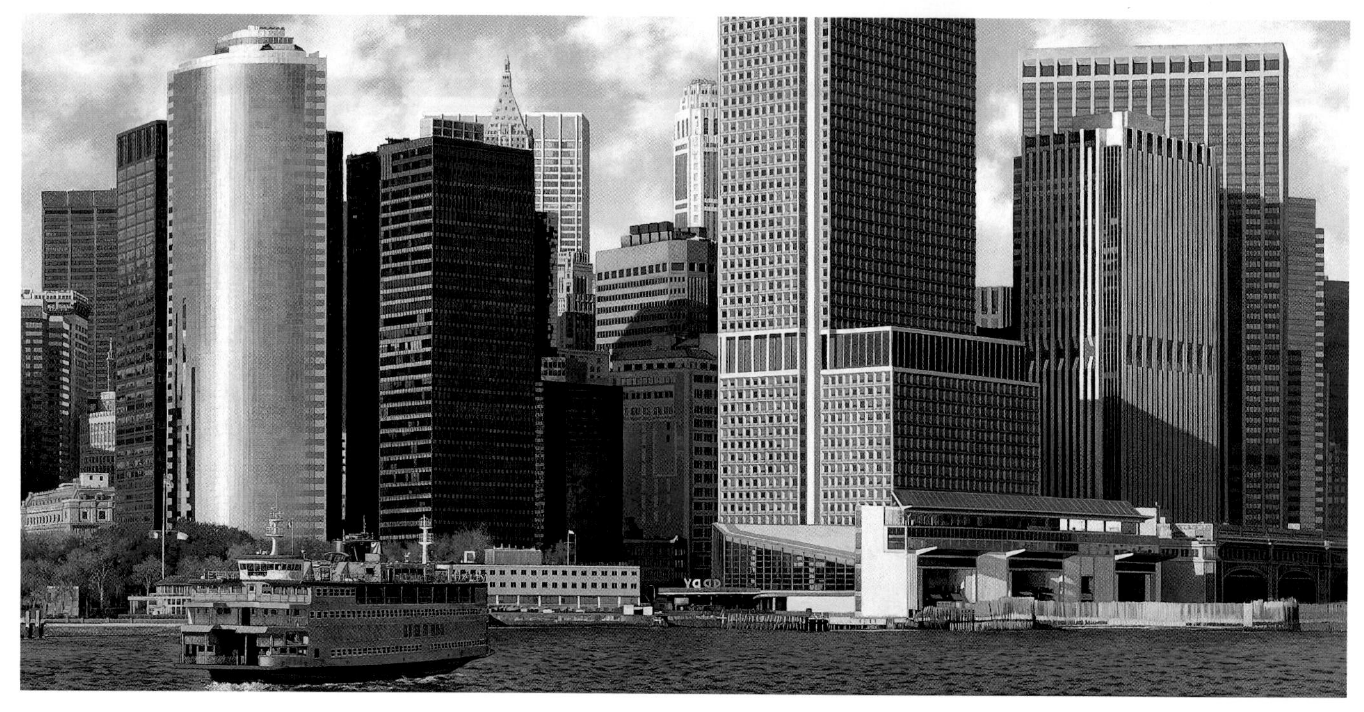

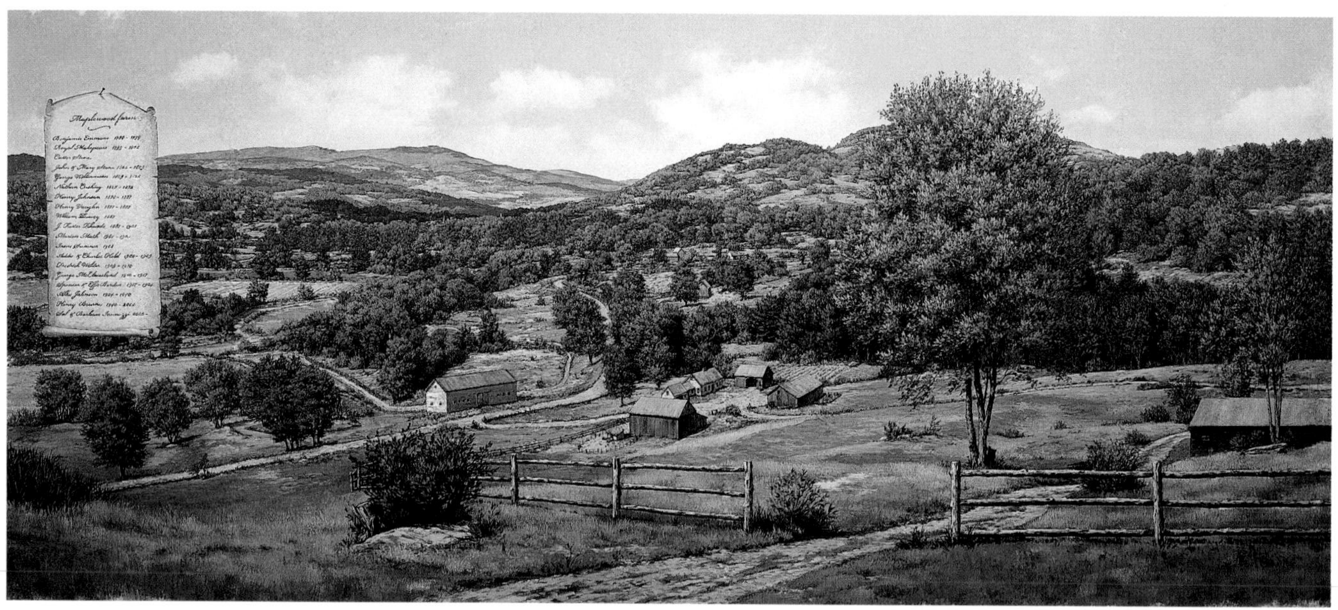

Top: *Laborer's International Union of North America,* Washington, DC, oil on canvas, 6'H x 28'W. Center: *Lower Manhattan,* Ambac Financial Group, New York, NY, oil on canvas, 48" x 96". Bottom: *Vermont Farm,* home office, Woodstock, VT, acrylic on canvas, 6' x 14'. Photographs: Micheal Imlay.

ALAN PEARSALL

ALAN PEARSALL ART AND DESIGN ■ 563 MAIN STREET ■ WEST NEWBURY, MA 01985
TEL 978-500-7315 ■ E-MAIL ALANPEARSALL@COMCAST.NET ■ WWW.ALANPEARSALL.COM

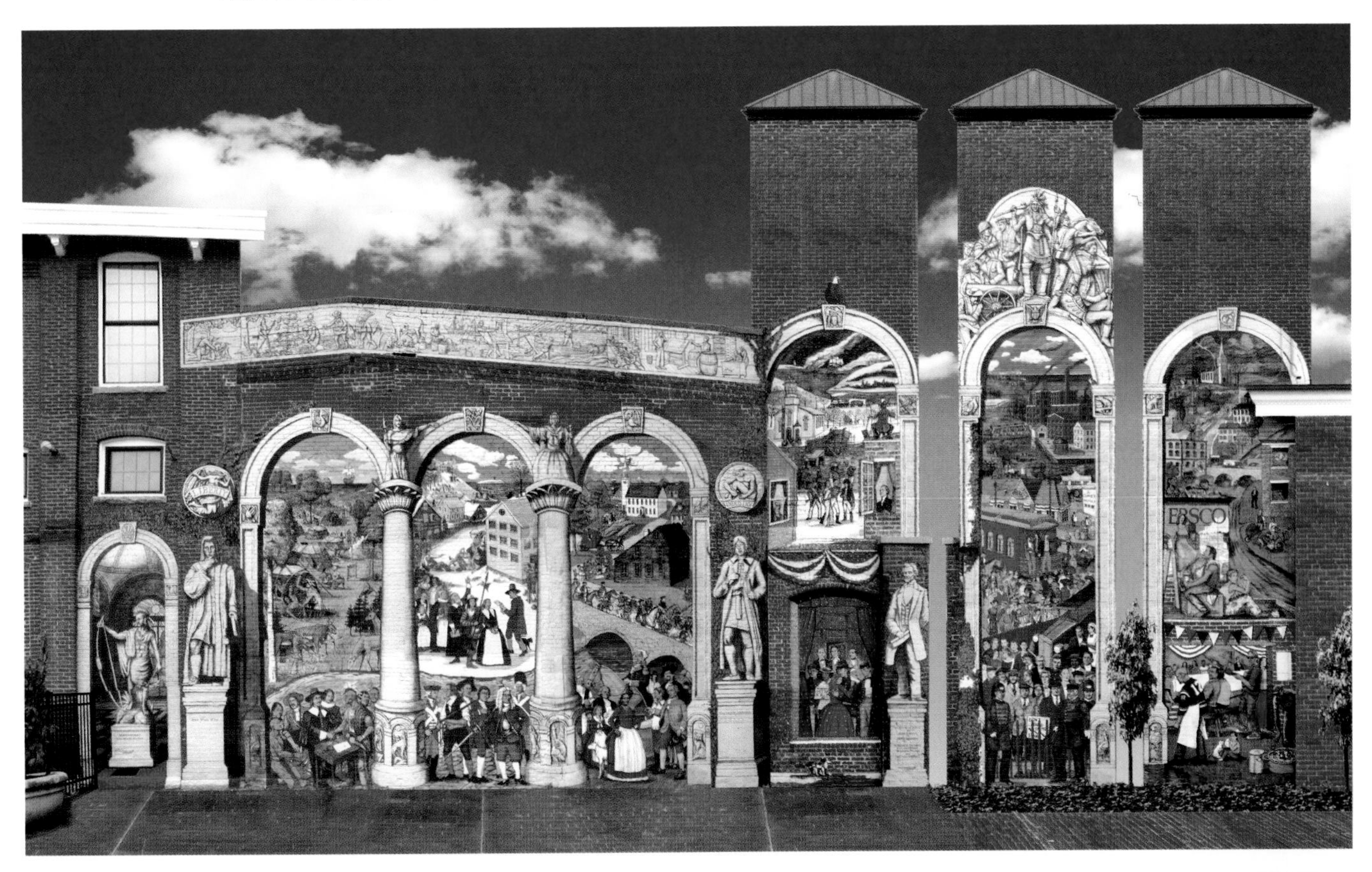

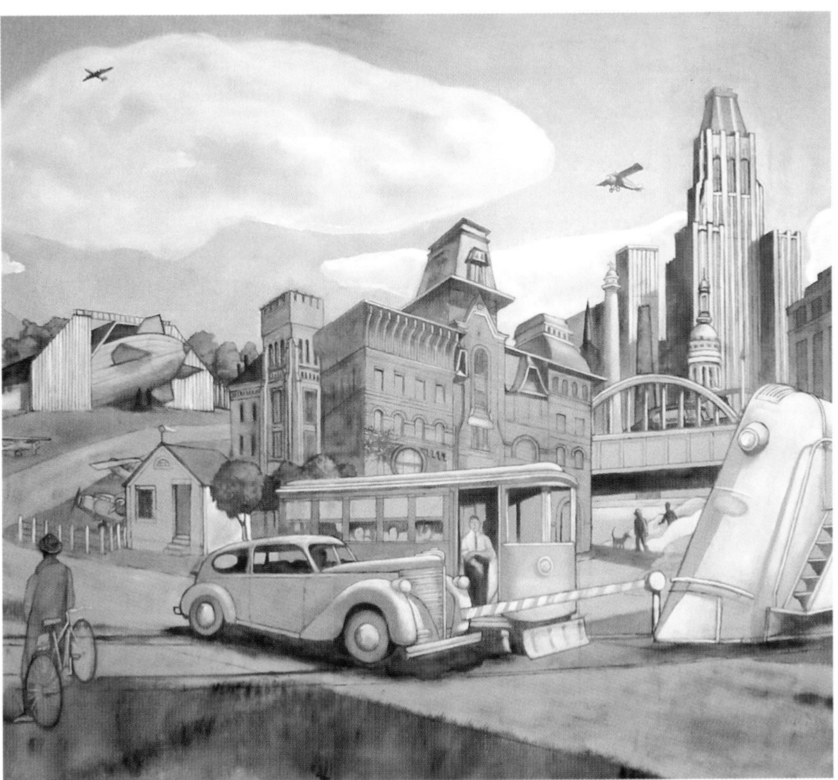

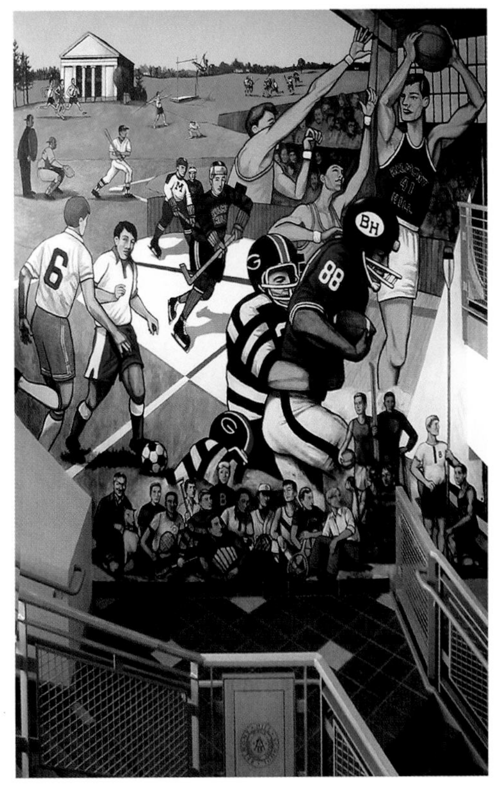

Top: *History of Ipswich Mural,* 2006, River Walk, Ipswich, MA, acrylic on brick, 1,700 square feet. Bottom left: *Transportation Mural,* 2005, Four Points Hotel lobby, Baltimore, MD, acrylic, 6' x 12'. Bottom right: *Sports Mural,* 2003, Belmont Hill School, Belmont, MA, acrylic, 22' x 20'.

PECK STUDIOS / CITY ARTS

G. BYRON PECK ■ 1857 LAMONT STREET NW ■ WASHINGTON, DC 20010 ■ TEL/FAX 202-331-1966
E-MAIL BYRONPECK@EARTHLINK.NET ■ WWW.PECKSTUDIOS.COM ■ WWW.CITYARTSDC.ORG

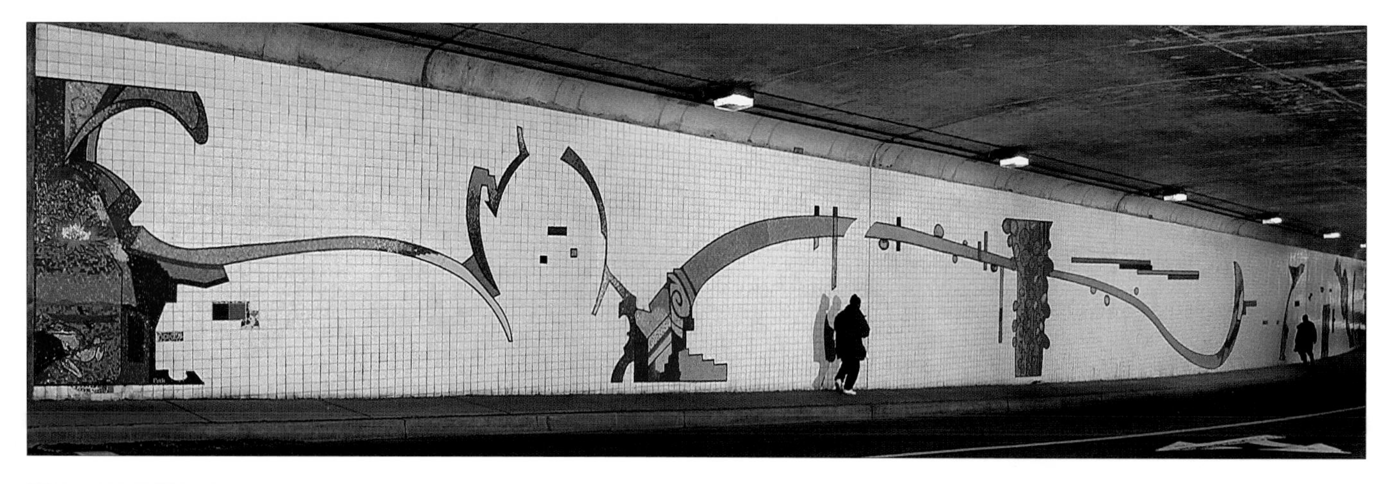

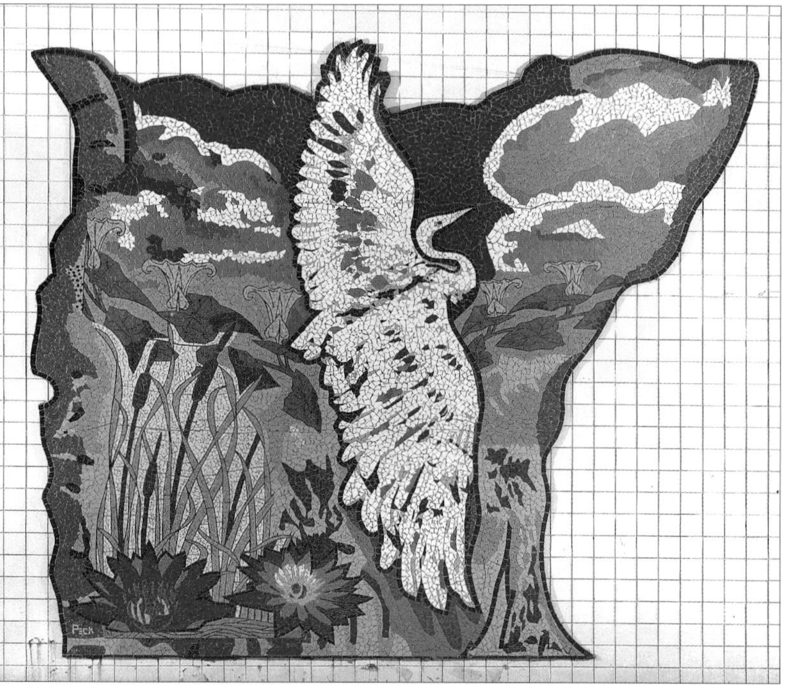

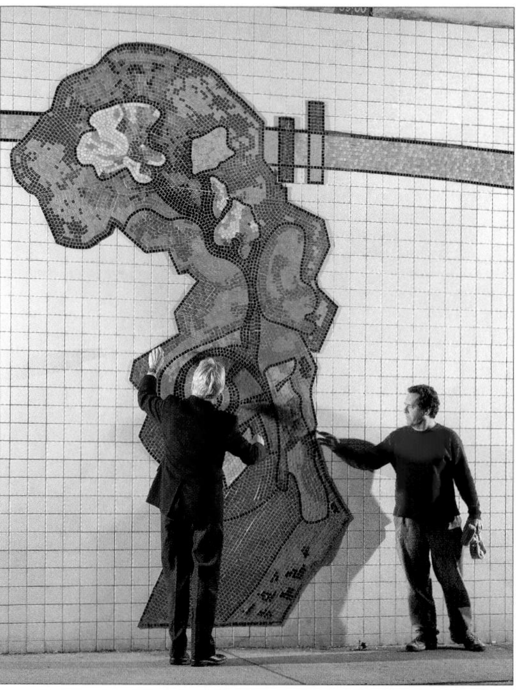

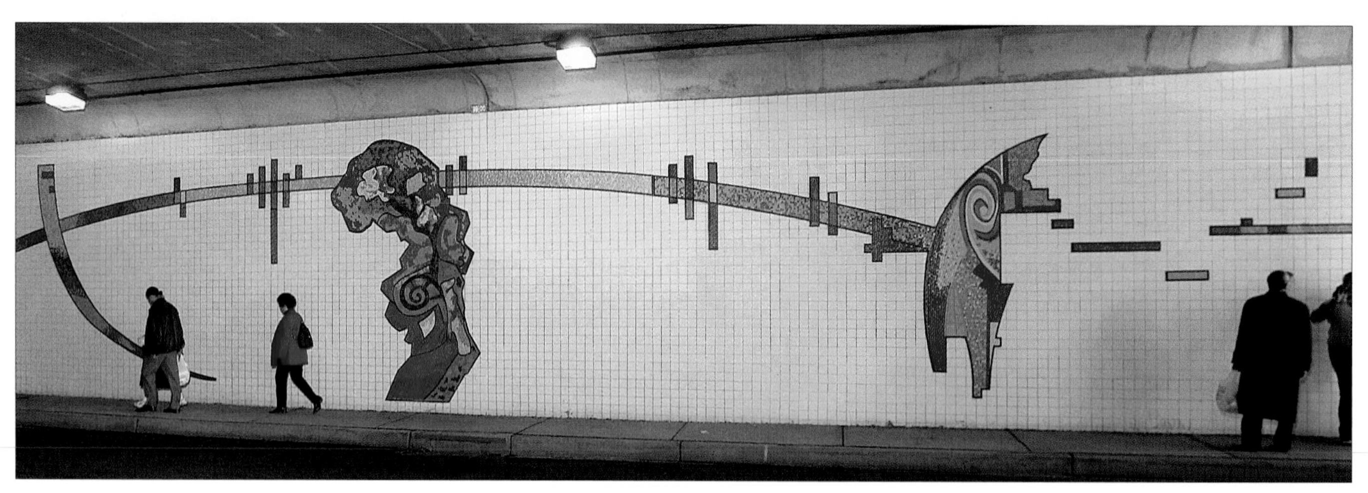

SW Gateway Mosaic Installation, SW Waterfront, Washington, DC, stainless steel, mosaic glass and tile, agate and cast concrete. Photographs: John Woo.

SUE KEANE STUDIO

SUE KEANE ■ 360 SUNSET AVENUE ■ VENICE, CA 90291 ■ TEL 310-562-5554
FAX 310-440-8516 ■ E-MAIL MISSUECLAY@AOL.COM ■ WWW.SUEKEANESTUDIO.COM

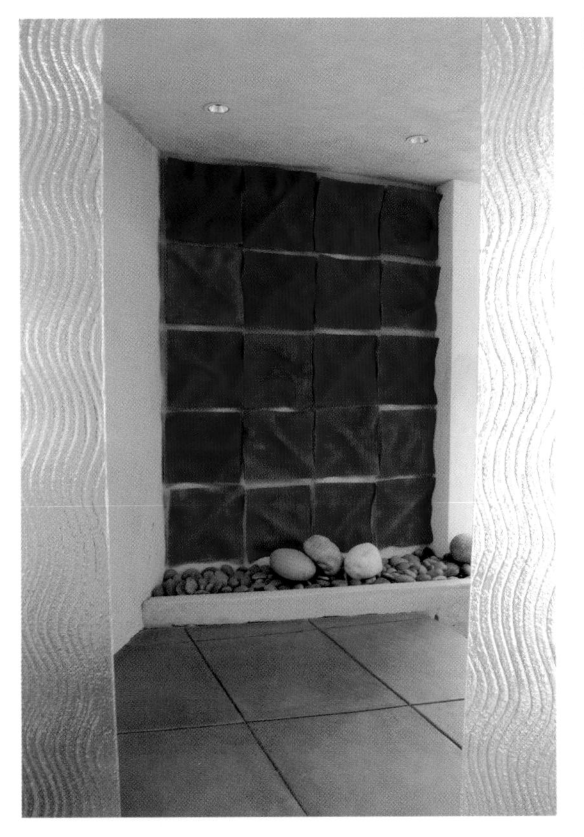

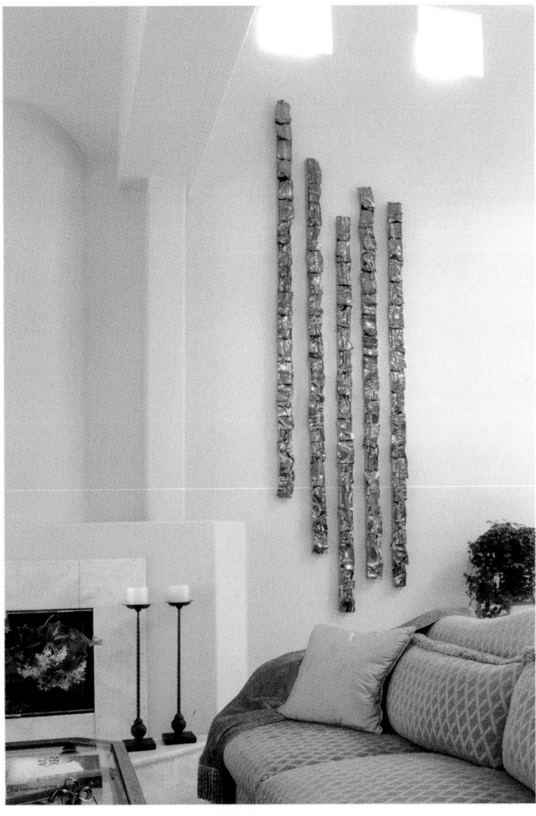

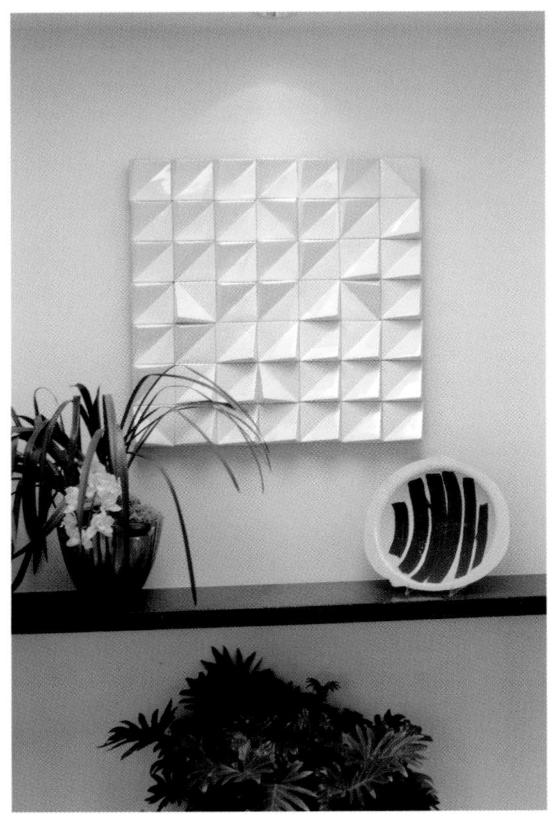

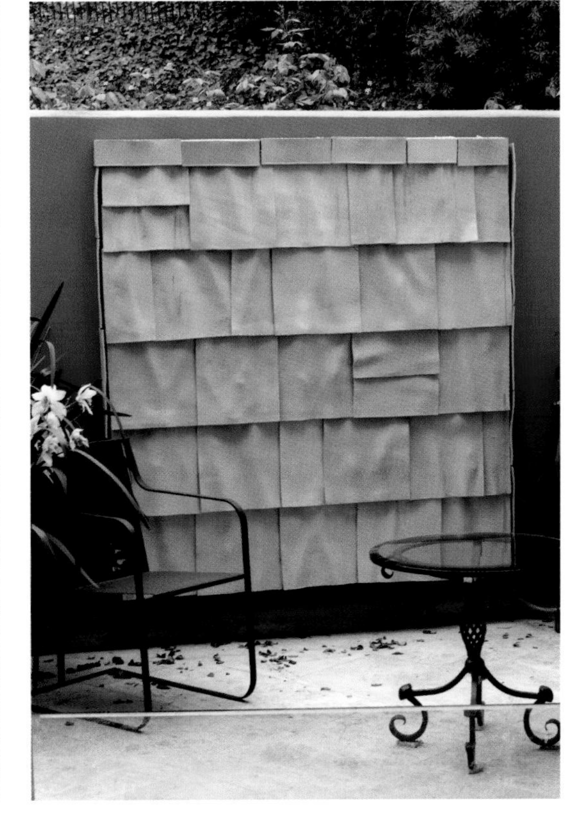

Top left: *Big Red Squares*, entry lobby, glazed ceramic, 9' x 6'. Top right: *Emporer's Pagoda*, glazed ceramic, each: 8' x 5".
Bottom left: *Formation*, entry lobby, glazed ceramic, 36" x 36". Bottom right: *Bungalow*, patio fountain, glazed ceramic, 6' x 6'. Photographs: Alan Shaffer.

LIBBY WARE

LIBBY WARE STUDIOS ■ 2005 POTTERY LANE ■ DAYTONA BEACH, FL 32128-6559
TEL 386-304-6102 ■ FAX 386-788-1641 ■ E-MAIL LIBBY@LIBBYWARE.COM ■ WWW.LIBBYWARE.COM

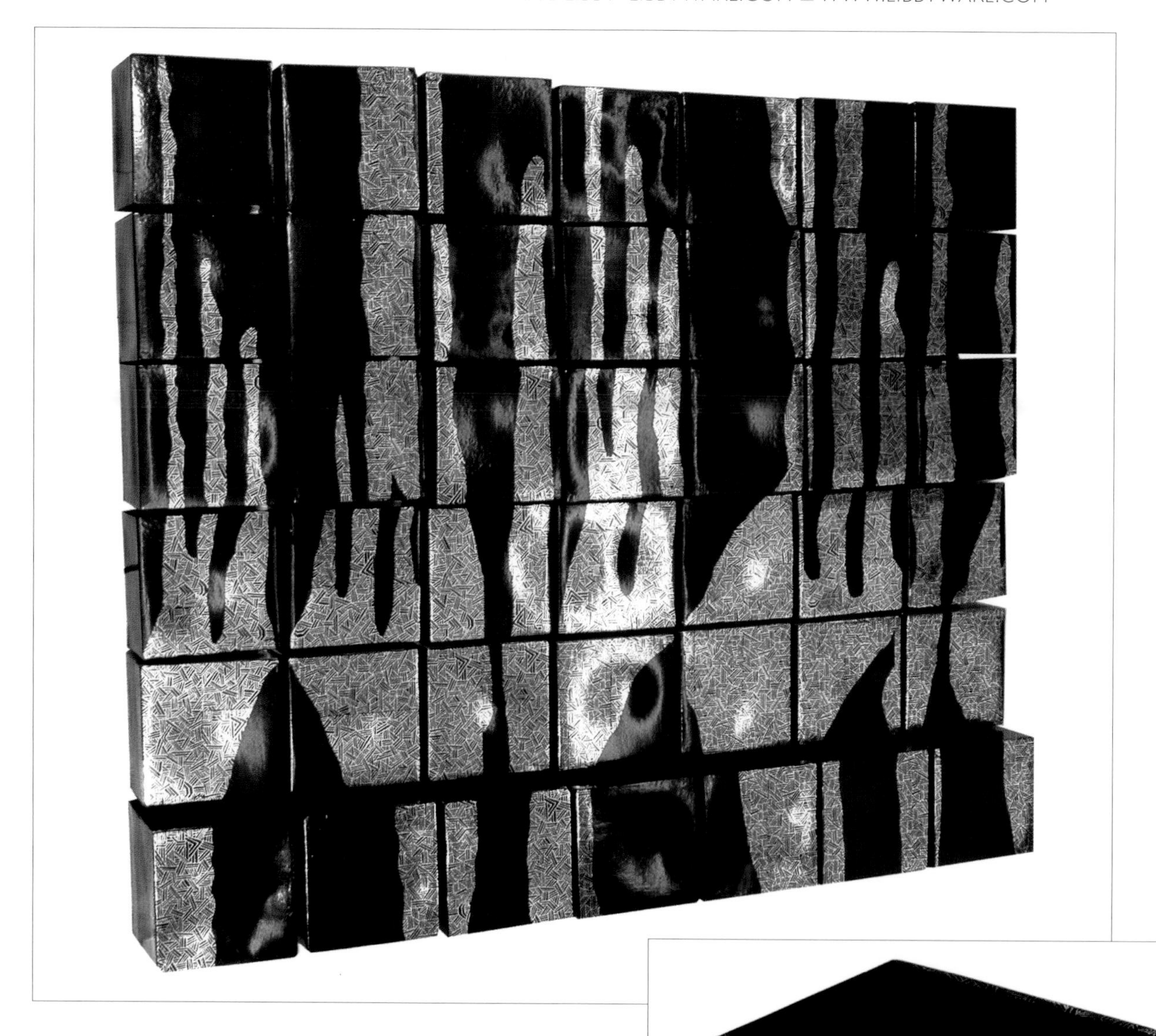

Serenity, 2007, forty-two multilevel porcelain cubes, each: 6" × 6", individually flushed-mounted to wall, total size: 3' × 4'.
Each shiny black glazed cube is detailed in bright gold luster. Photograph: Jack McCarty.

TRICIA ZIMIC

9 FAIRVIEW TERRACE ■ MAPLEWOOD, NJ 07040 ■ TEL 973-763-4668 ■ TEL 973-650-6106
FAX 973-761-6328 ■ E-MAIL CERAMICS@TRICIAZIMIC.COM ■ WWW.TRICIAZIMIC.COM

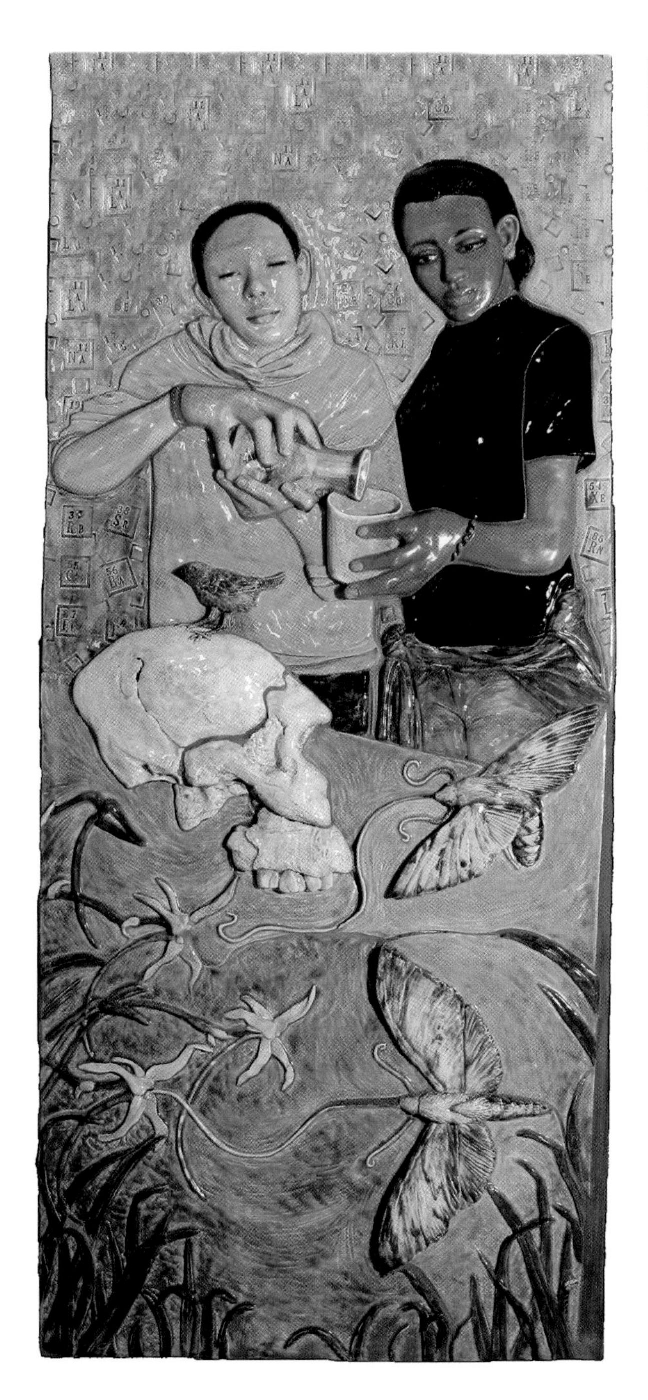

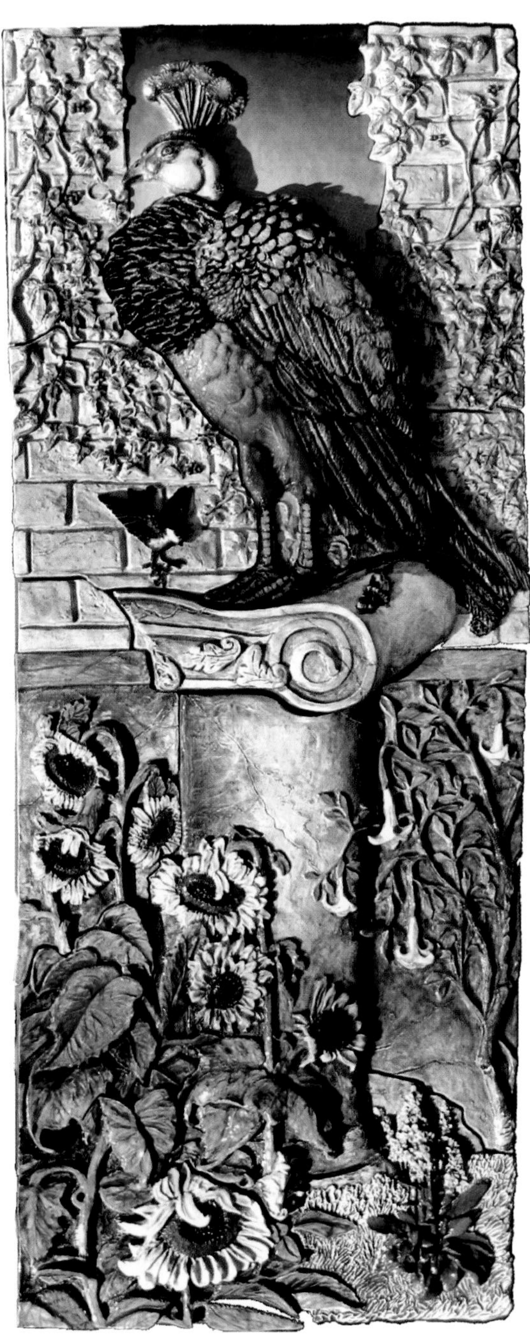

Left: Bas-relief glazed ceramic mural, 2007, Maplewood Middle School, Maplewood, NJ, one 4' x 2' section of 80 square feet.
Right: *Female Peacock*, bas-relief glazed ceramic mural, 2007, private residence, Bloomfield, NJ, 36" x 13".

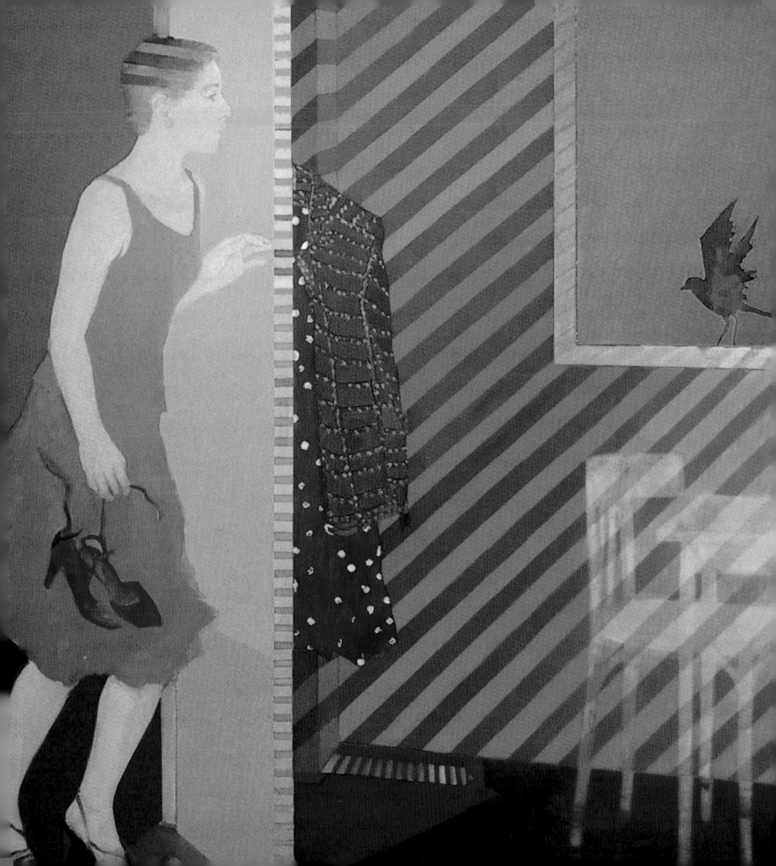

Paintings & Prints

BARBARA AMOS

AMOS FINE ART STUDIOS ■ 131 ROSERY DRIVE NW ■ CALGARY, AB T2K 1L6 ■ CANADA
TEL 403-560-4067 ■ FAX 403-289-4284 ■ E-MAIL BARBARAAMOS@SHAW.CA ■ WWW.BARBARAAMOS.COM

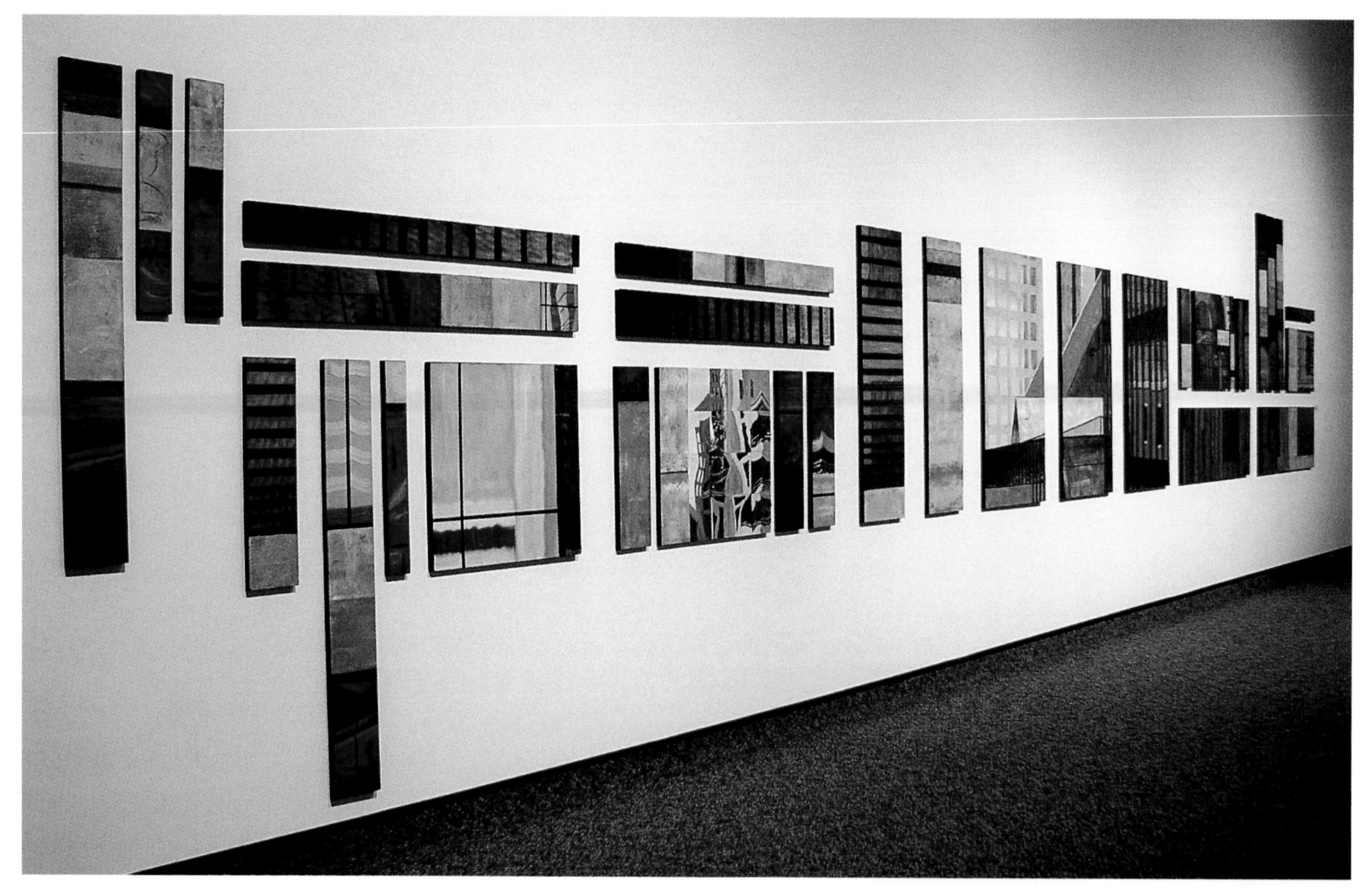

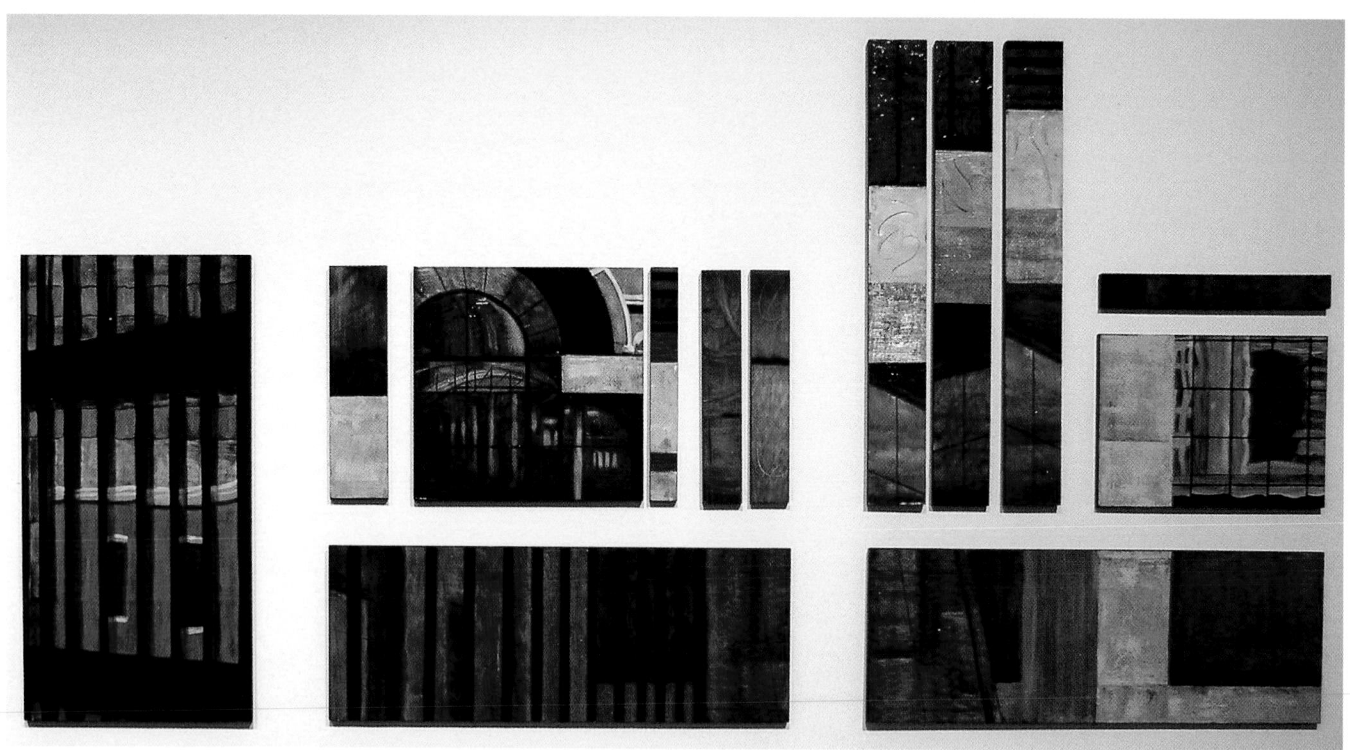

Cutting Up the Town, 2004, Burlington Art Centre, Burlington, Ontario, Canada, oil on panel, 6' x 32'.

BETH AVARY

STARFIREPRESS ■ 545 LODGE ROAD ■ BOULDER CREEK, CA 95006 ■ TEL 831-338-8362
FAX 831-338-9455 ■ E-MAIL BAVARY@STARFIREPRESS.COM ■ WWW.STARFIREPRESS.COM

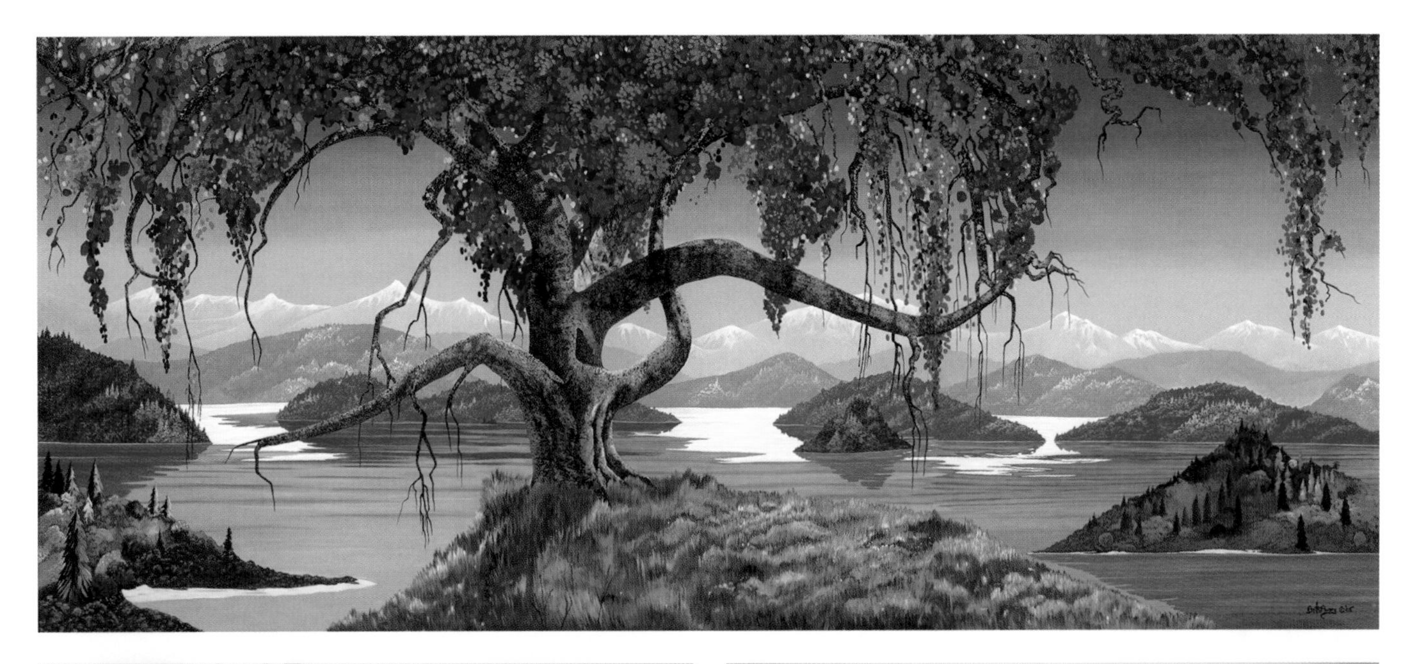

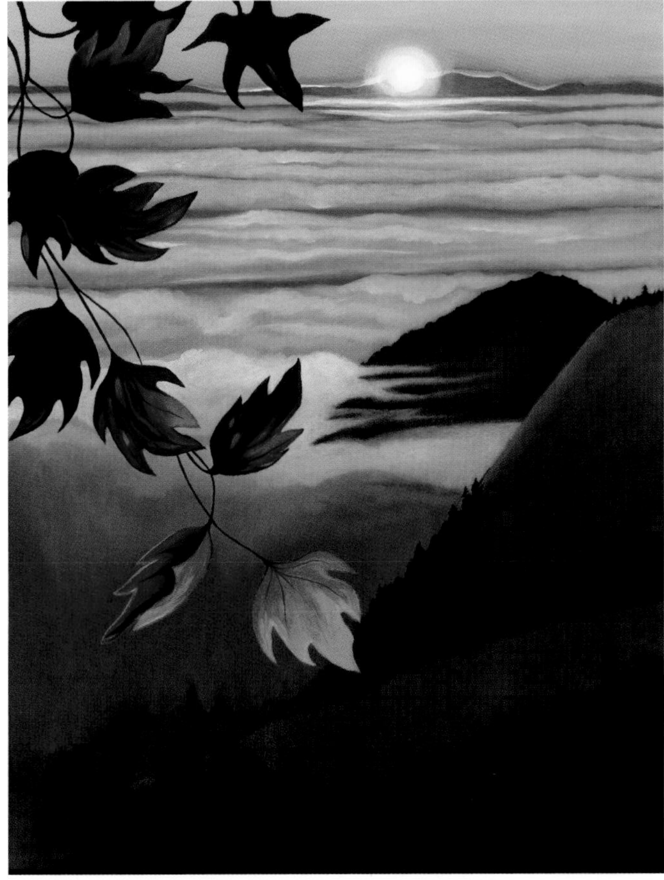

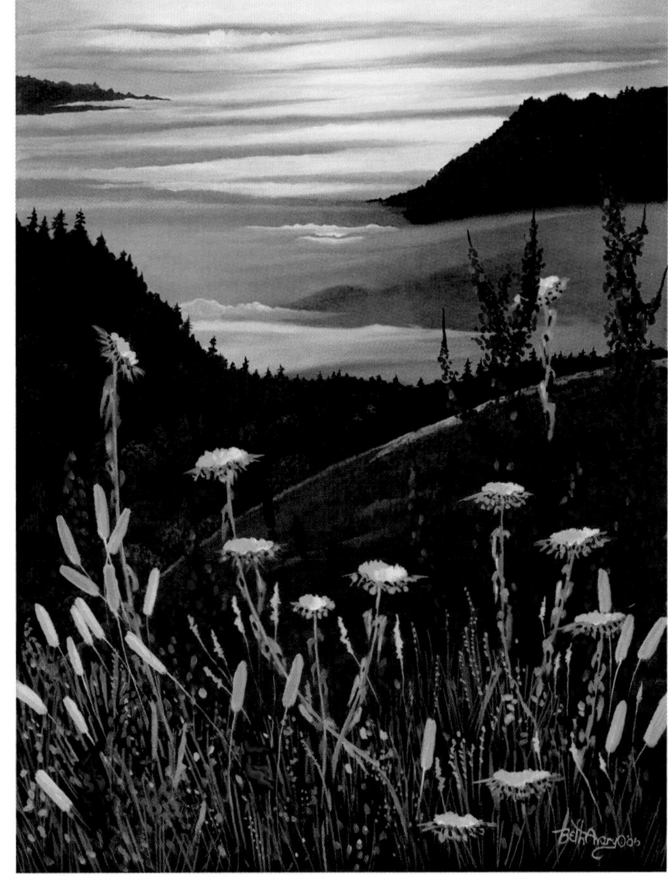

Top: *Autumn Tree*, hand-embellished giclée on canvas, 40" x 90", original: oil on canvas, three panels, giclée merged in Photoshop, limited edition of one hundred.
Bottom left: *Autumn Leaves Over Fog*, hand-embellished giclée on canvas, 24" x 18", limited edition of one hundred.
Bottom right: *Summer's End*, oil on canvas, 24" x 18", original on tour until 2009, giclées available, limited edition of one hundred.

FRAN BULL

FRAN BULL STUDIO ■ PO BOX 401 ■ BRANDON, VT 05733
TEL 802-247-0125 ■ E-MAIL FRANBULL@FRANBULL.COM ■ WWW.FRANBULL.COM

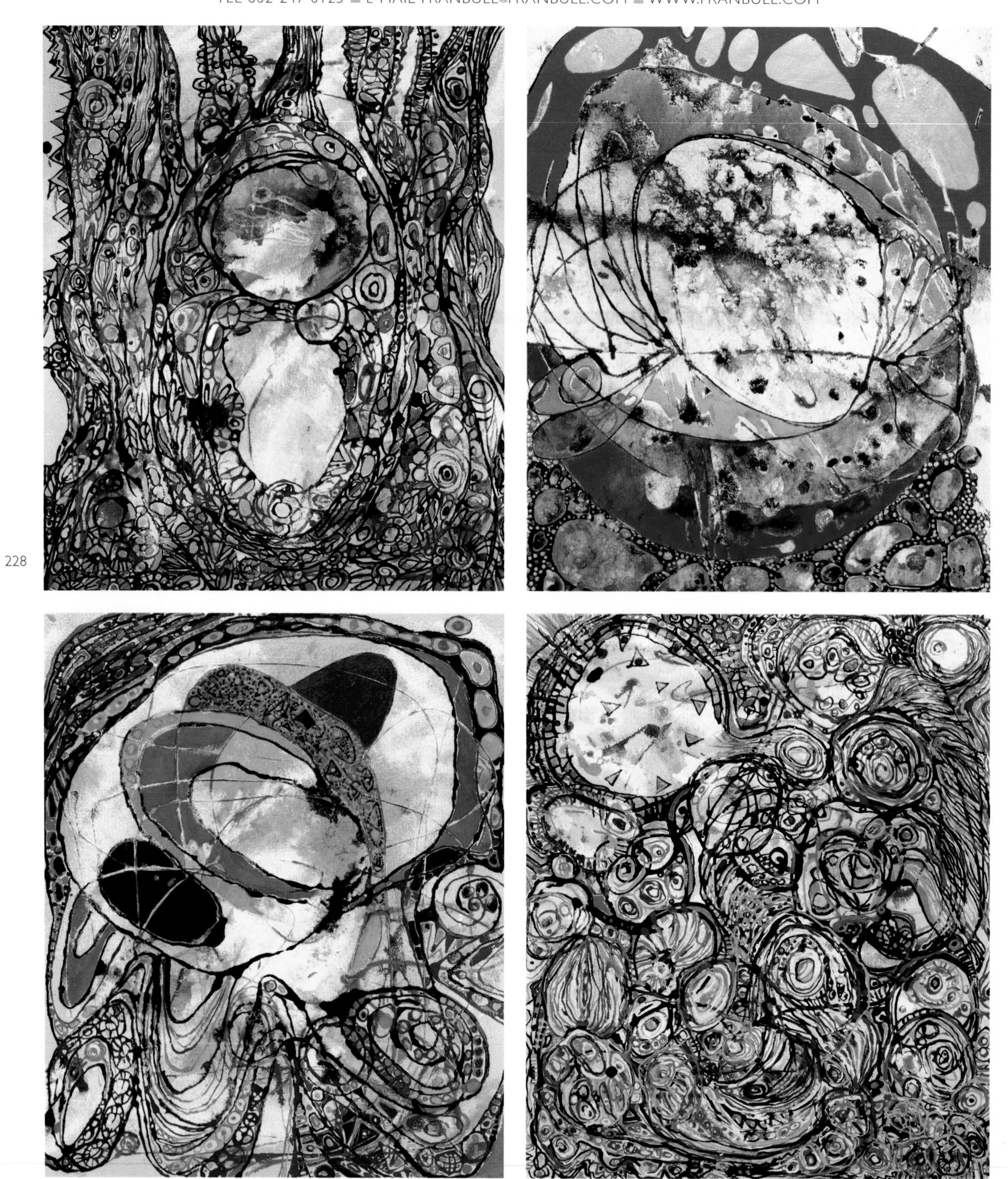

Top left: *Stones Only,* 2004, acrylic and ink on canvas, 36" x 30". Top right: *Such Howling Proportions,* 2004, acrylic and ink on canvas, 30" x 24". Bottom left: *And What Are Poets For in a Destitute Time,* 2004, acrylic and ink on canvas, 36" x 30". Bottom right: *The Immense Encyclopedia of Barbarism,* 2004, acrylic and ink on canvas, 36" x 30".

CHARLES CSURI

CSURIVISION LTD. ■ 110 AMAZON PLACE ■ COLUMBUS, OH 43214 ■ TEL 614-580-2571
TEL 614-292-1028 ■ E-MAIL CONTACT@CSURI.COM ■ WWW.CSURI.COM

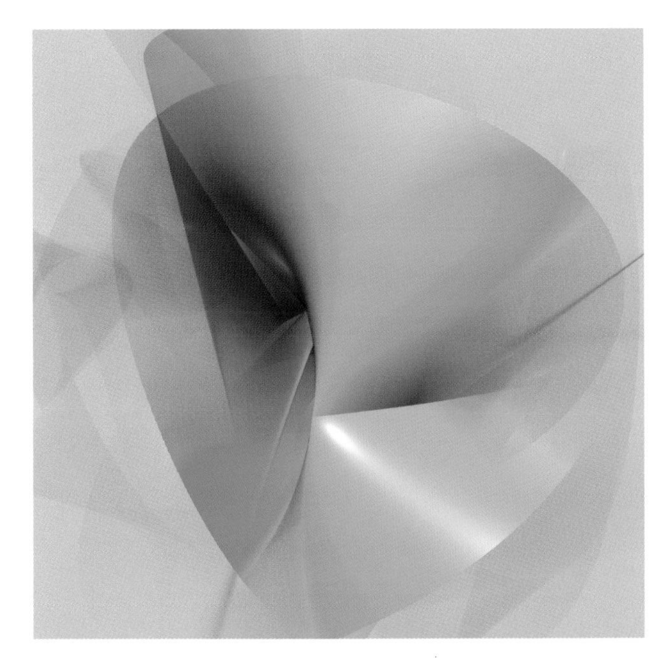

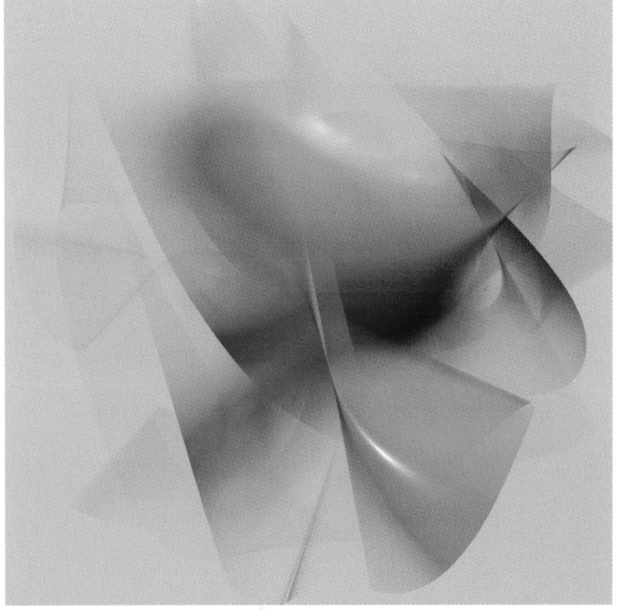

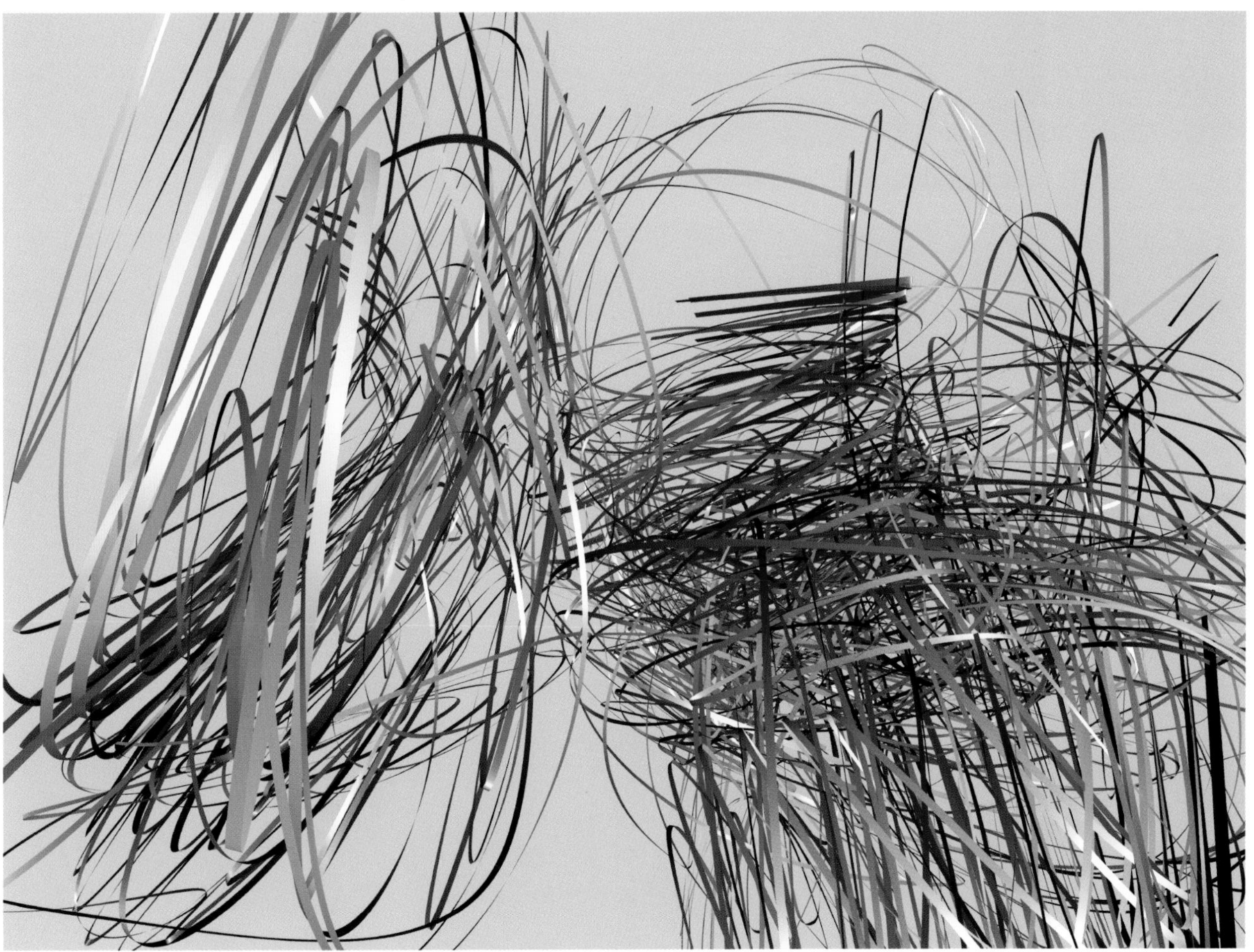

Top left: *Sunshadows Green*, dye-sublimated aluminum, 48" × 64". Top right: *Sunshadows Red*, dye-sublimated aluminum, 48" × 64".
Bottom: *Emily's Scribbles*, giclée on canvas, 48" × 65", aluminum and giclée editions of five. Prices and custom sizes available upon request.

CLAIRE EVANS

2810 WILDERNESS PLACE SUITE E ■ BOULDER, CO 80301
TEL/FAX 303-444-3839 ■ TEL 303-581-0168 ■ E-MAIL MCLAIREEVANS@EARTHLINK.NET

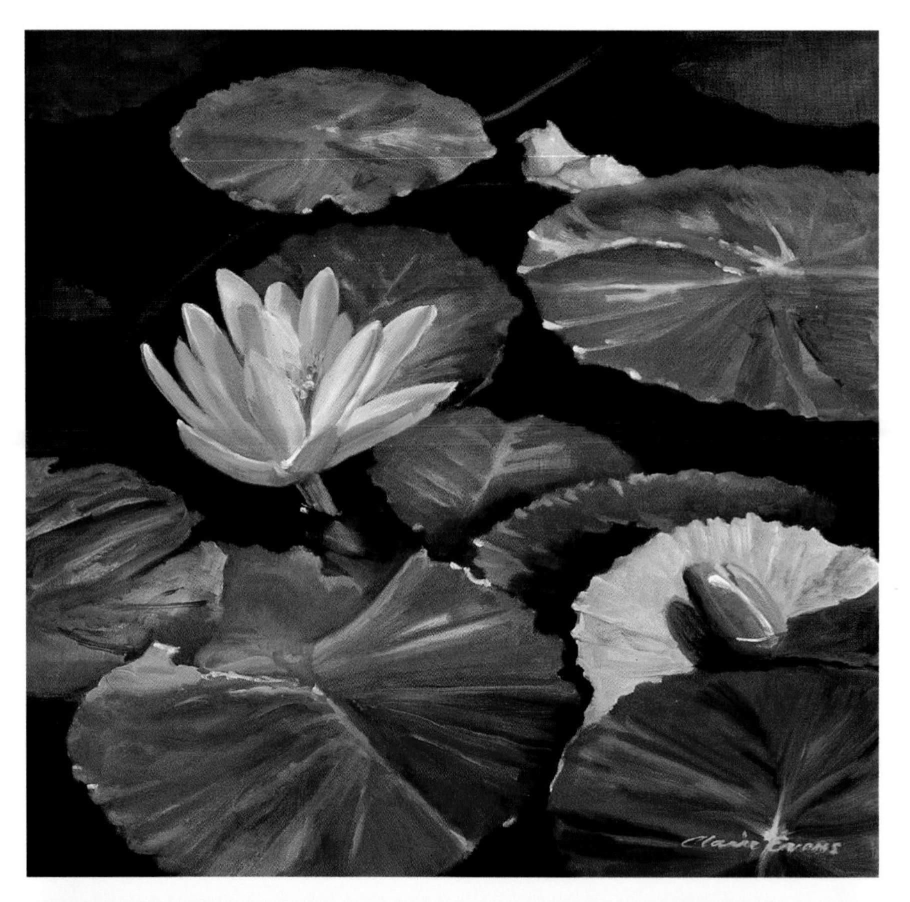

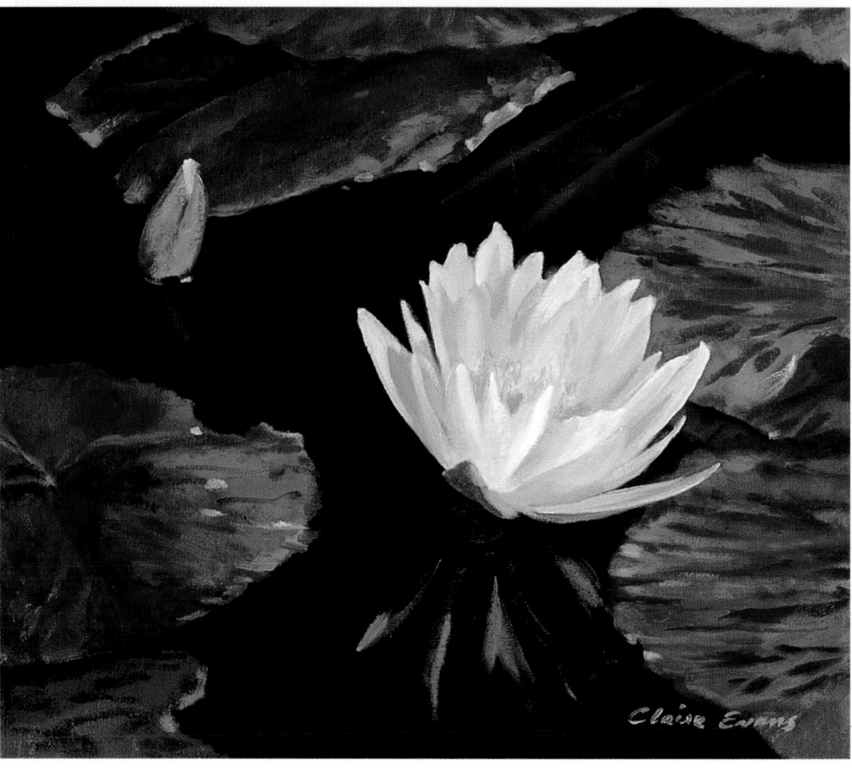

Top: *Flirtation*, oil, 24" x 24". Bottom: *Effervescence*, oil, 24" x 24". Photographs: Erik Arvidson.

MARY HATCH

6917 WILLSON DRIVE ■ KALAMAZOO, MI 49009 ■ TEL 269-375-0376
E-MAIL MARY_HATCH@SBCGLOBAL.NET ■ WWW.MARYHATCH.COM

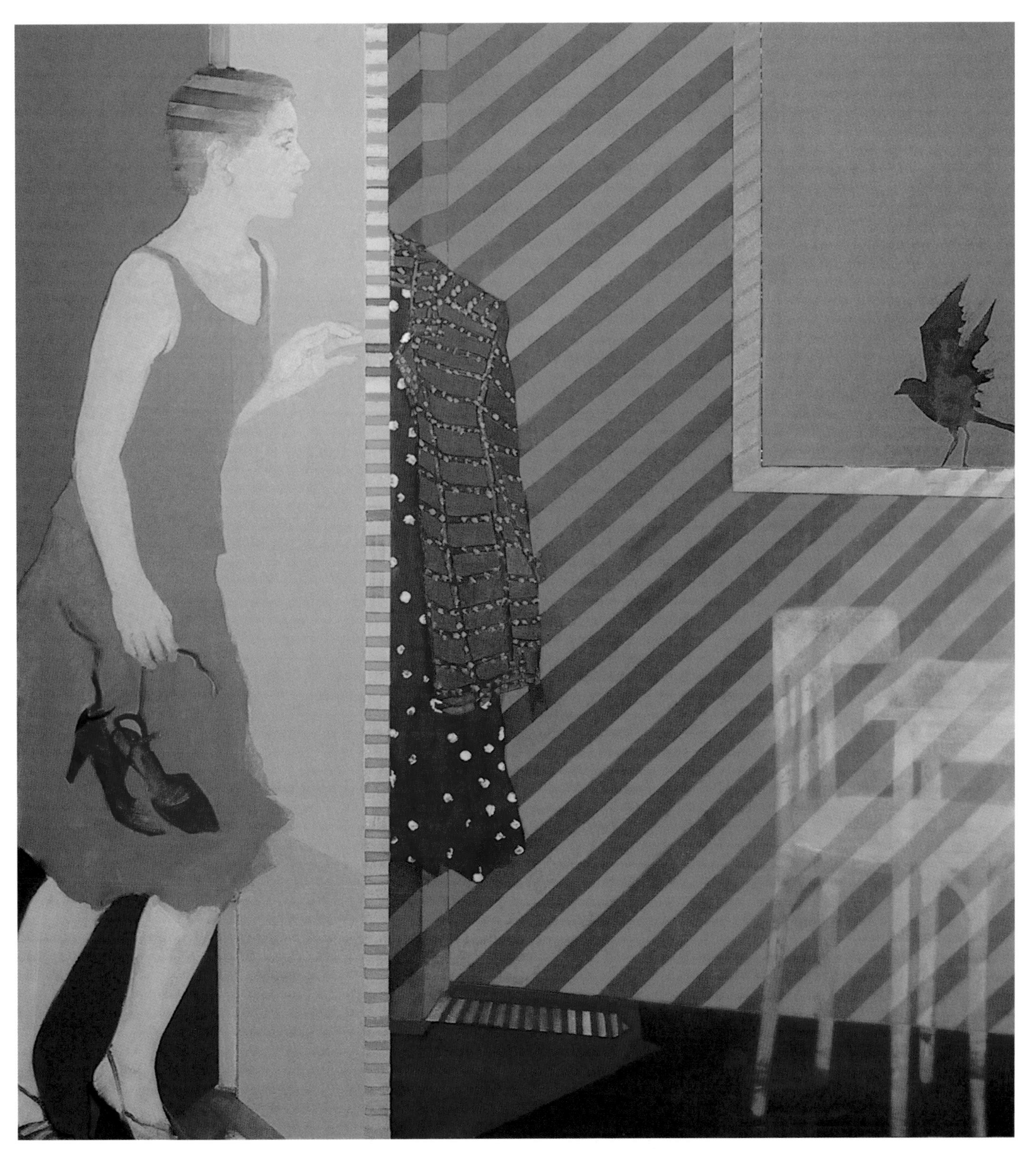

The Secret Room, inkjet on rag paper, paper size: 44" x 40", image size: 40" x 36", edition of one hundred.

YOSHI HAYASHI

255 KANSAS STREET #330 ■ SAN FRANCISCO, CA 94103 ■ TEL/FAX 415-552-0755
TEL 415-924-9224 ■ E-MAIL HAYASHI44@YAHOO.COM ■ WWW.YOSHIHAYASHI.COM

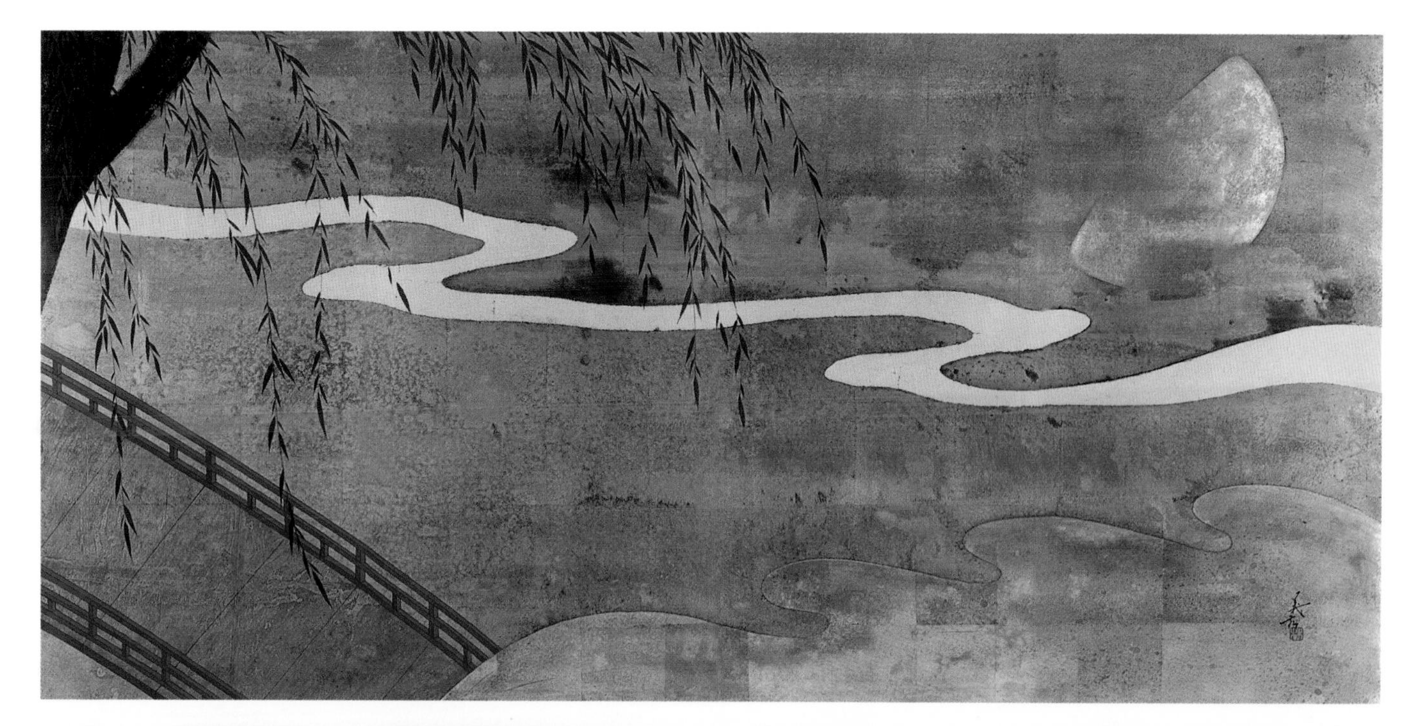

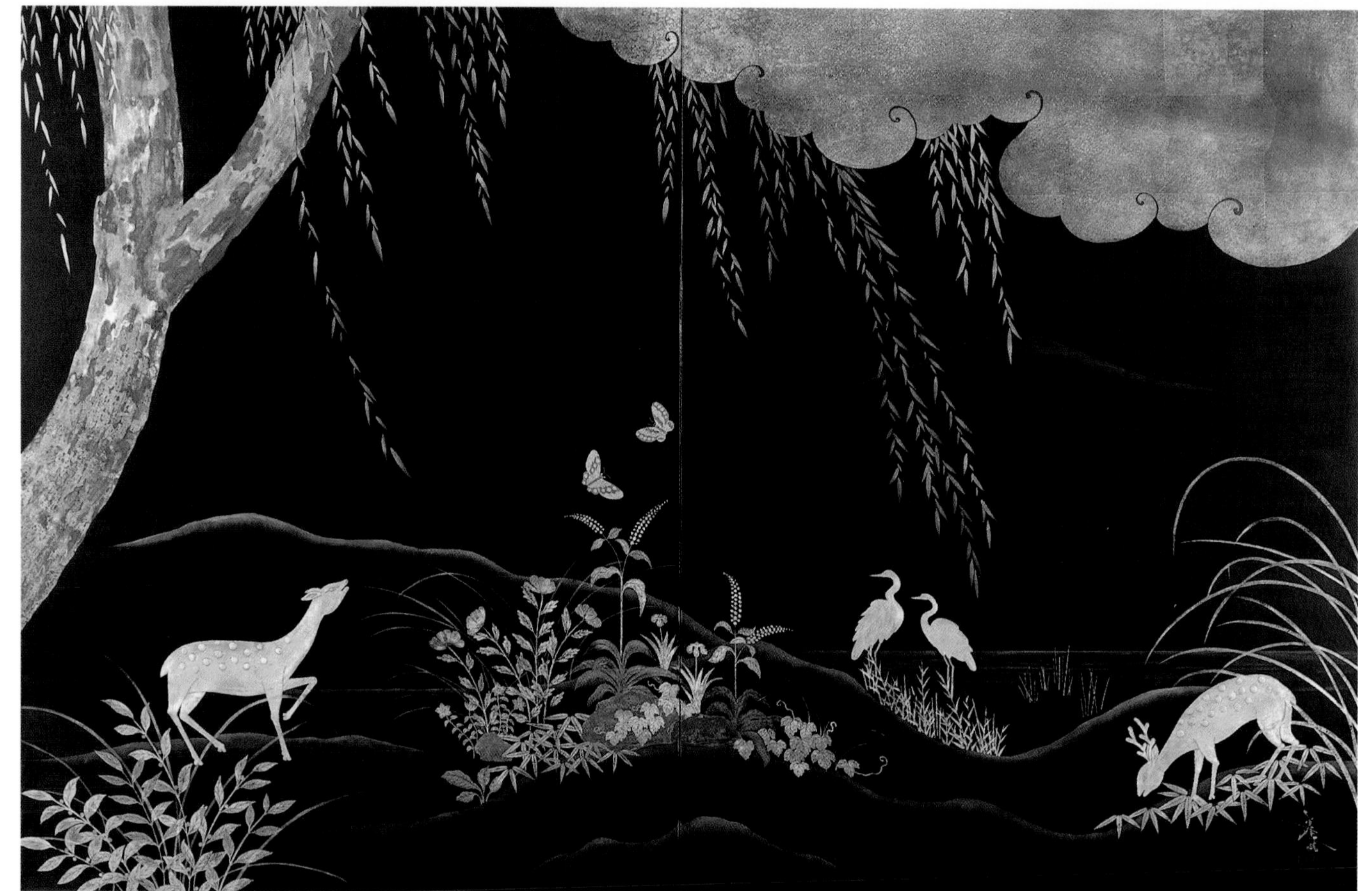

Top: *Tranquility,* 2003, private collection, San Francisco, CA, gold, silver, and copper leaf with oil paint, 36" x 72".
Bottom: *Serenity,* 2002, private collection, Japan, gold, silver, and copper leaf with oil paint, 40" x 60". Photographs: Ira D. Schrank.

CHARLES INGRAM

STUDIO 1100 ■ 2446 RIM OAK ■ SAN ANTONIO, TX 78232-2635
E-MAIL THEPAINTER@SWBELL.NET ■ WWW.STUDIO1100.COM

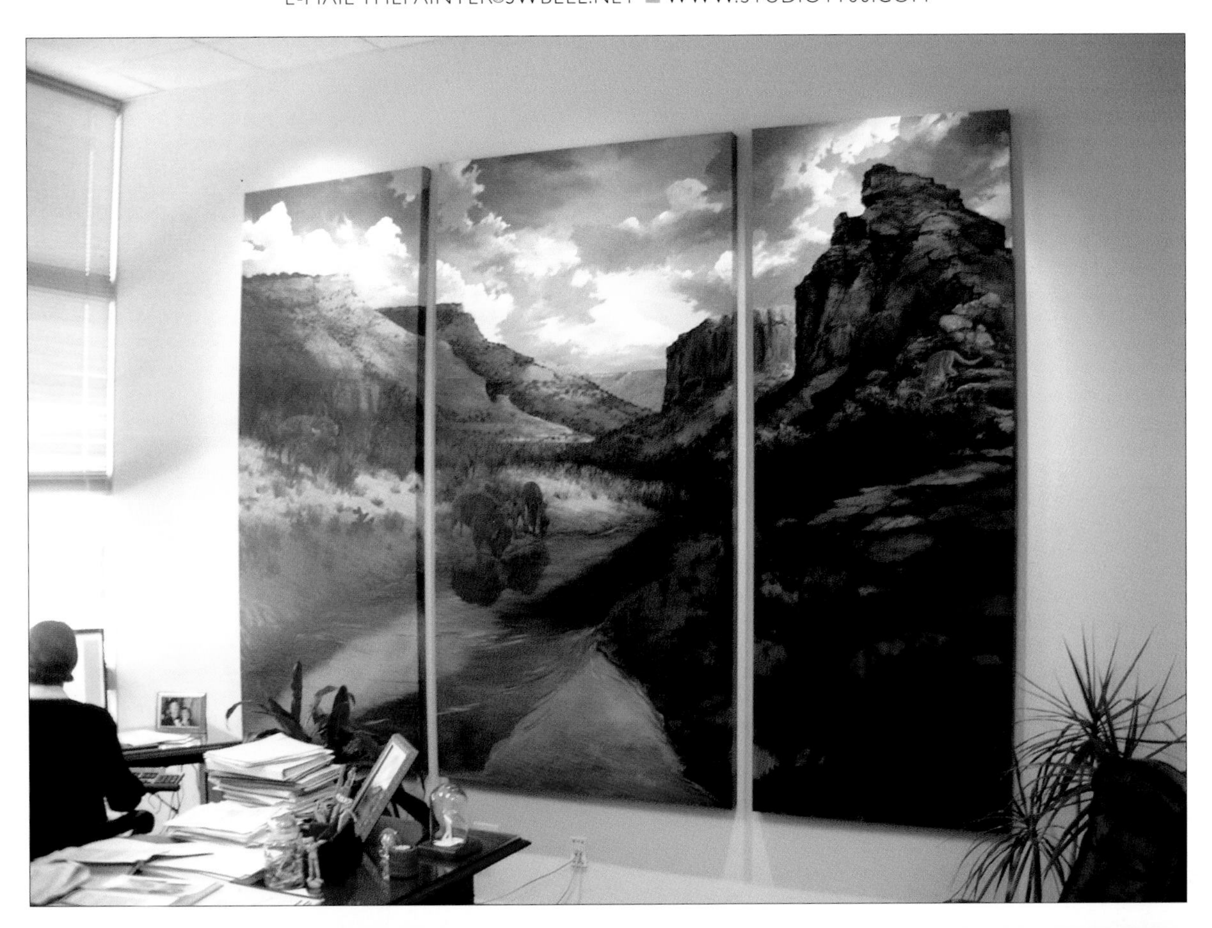

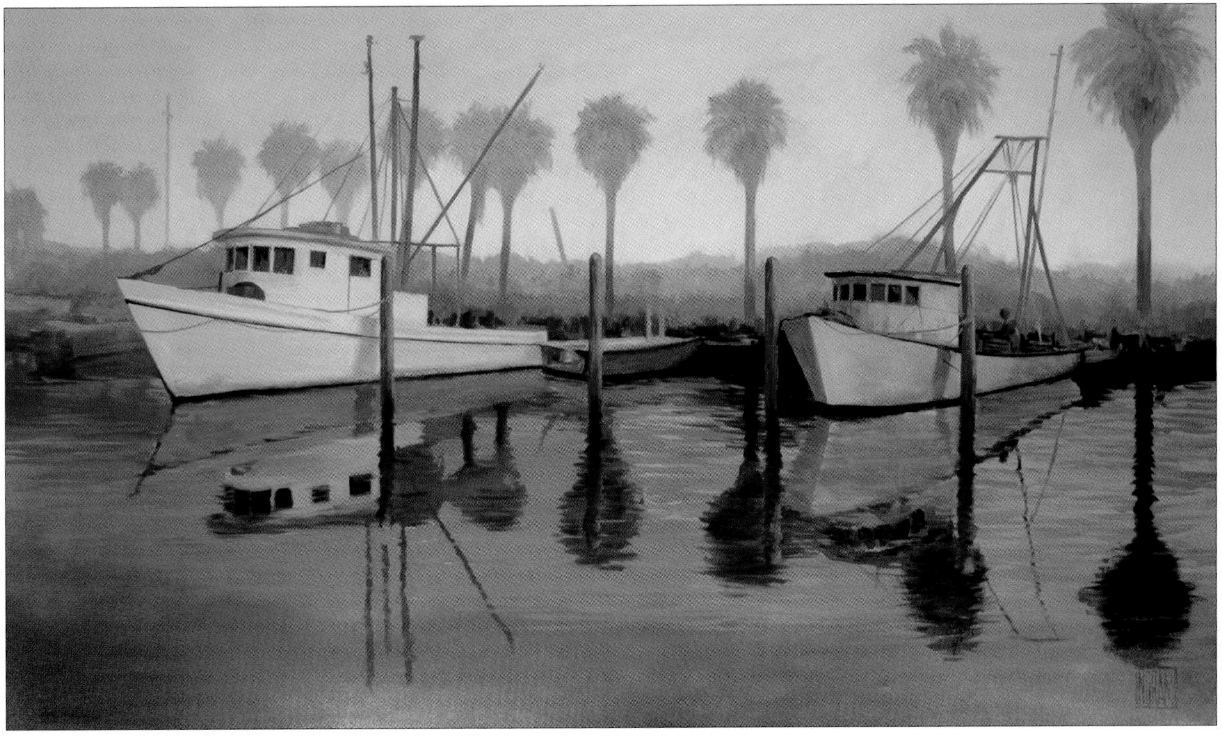

Top: *The Encounter*, oil on canvas, 120" x 72". Bottom: *Gulf Sunrise*, oil on canvas, 48" x 36".

CAROLINE JASPER

CAROLINE JASPER STUDIO ■ 796 BOUNDARY BOULEVARD ■ ROTONDA WEST, FL 33947
TEL 941-698-0718 ■ FAX 941-698-0801 ■ E-MAIL JASPERINC@MINDSPRING.COM ■ WWW.CAROLINEJASPER.COM

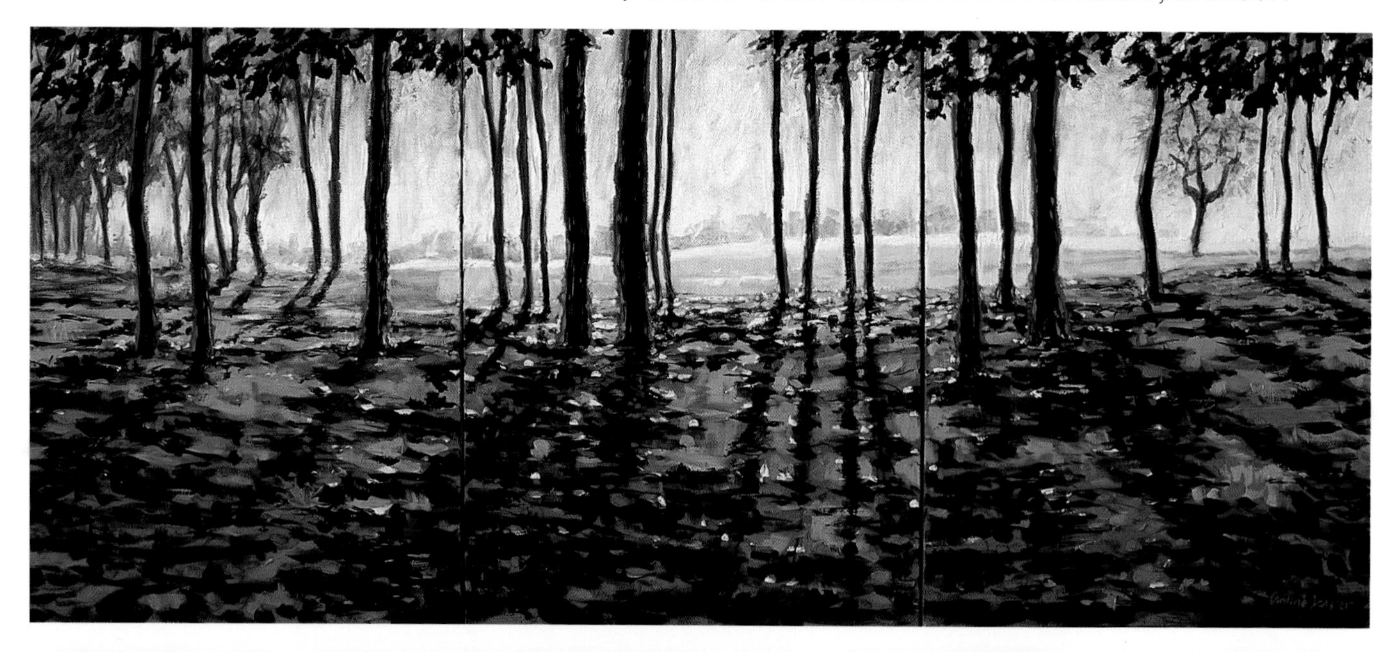

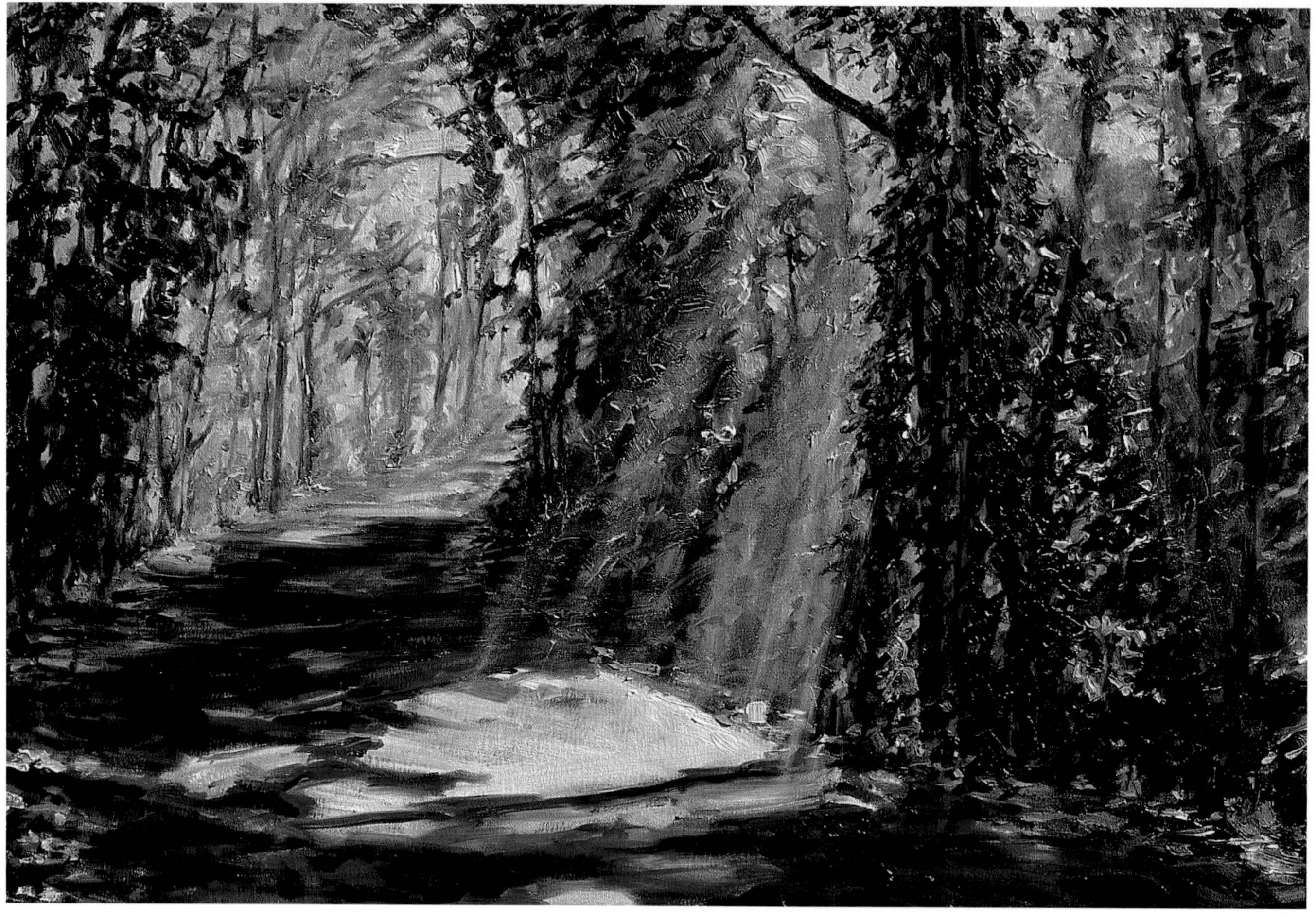

Top: *Spectraluxe*, 2004, oil on canvas, 32" x 72" (triptych). Giclée prints available.
Bottom: *Lumintice*, 2005 oil on canvas, 24" x 32". Giclée prints available.

SILJA TALIKKA LAHTINEN

SILJA'S FINE ART STUDIO ■ 5220 SUNSET TRAIL ■ MARIETTA, GA 30068
TEL 770-993-3409 ■ TEL 770-992-8380 ■ FAX 770-992-0350 ■ E-MAIL PENTEC02@BELLSOUTH.NET

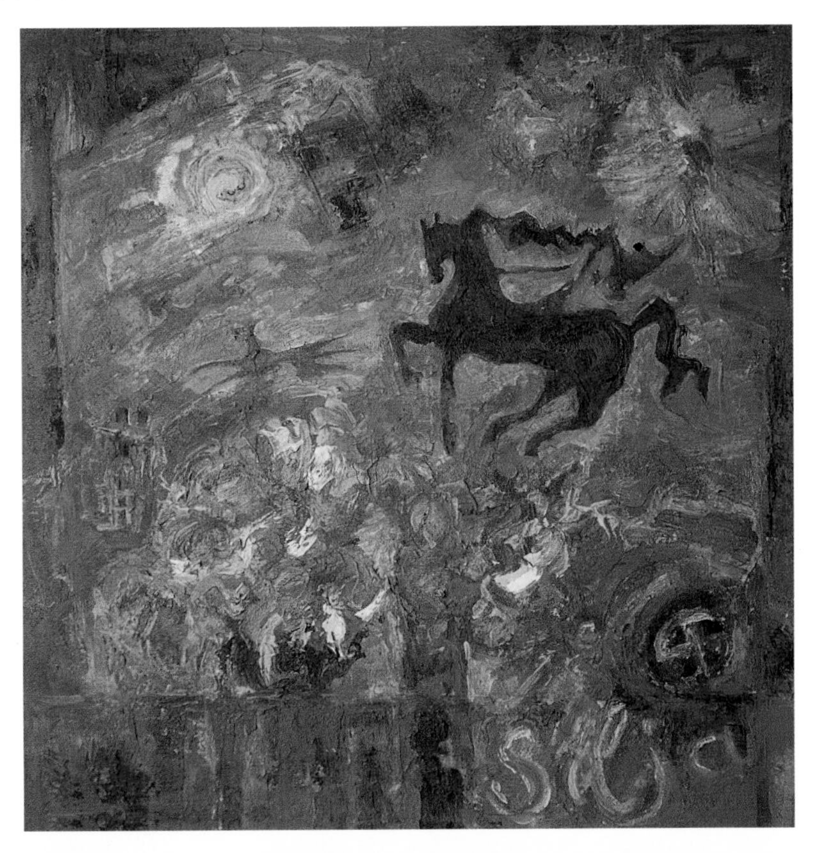

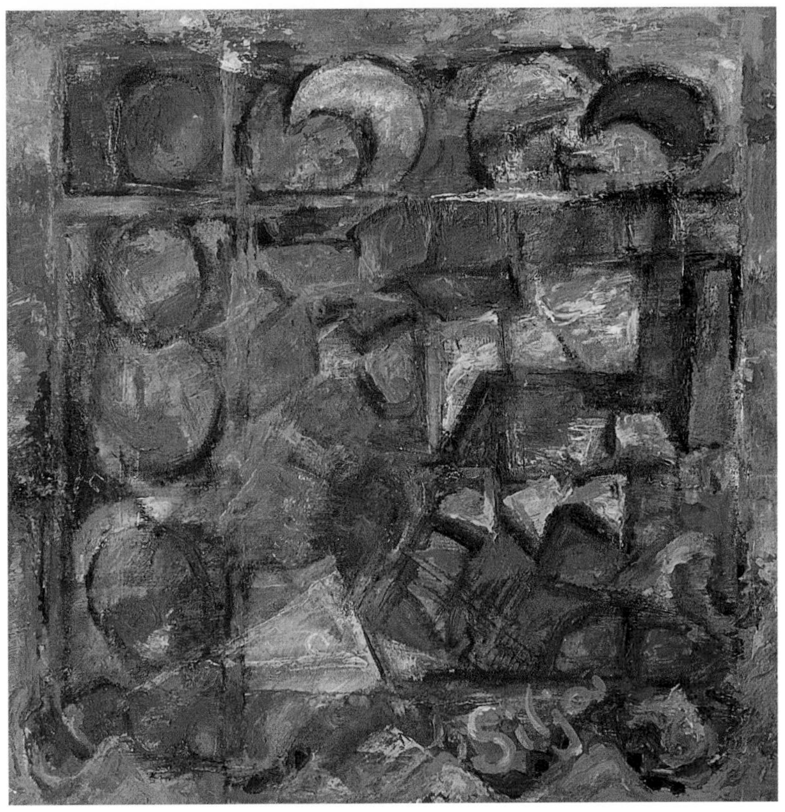

Top: *Summertime*, 2006, acrylic on canvas, 24" x 24".
Bottom: *All the World is Green*, 2006, acrylic on canvas, 24" x 24".

JACQUES LIEBERMAN

484 BROOME STREET ■ NEW YORK, NY 10013 ■ TEL 646-613-7302 ■ FAX 646-613-7305
E-MAIL JACQUESLIEBERMAN@MAC.COM ■ WWW.JACQUESLIEBERMAN.COM

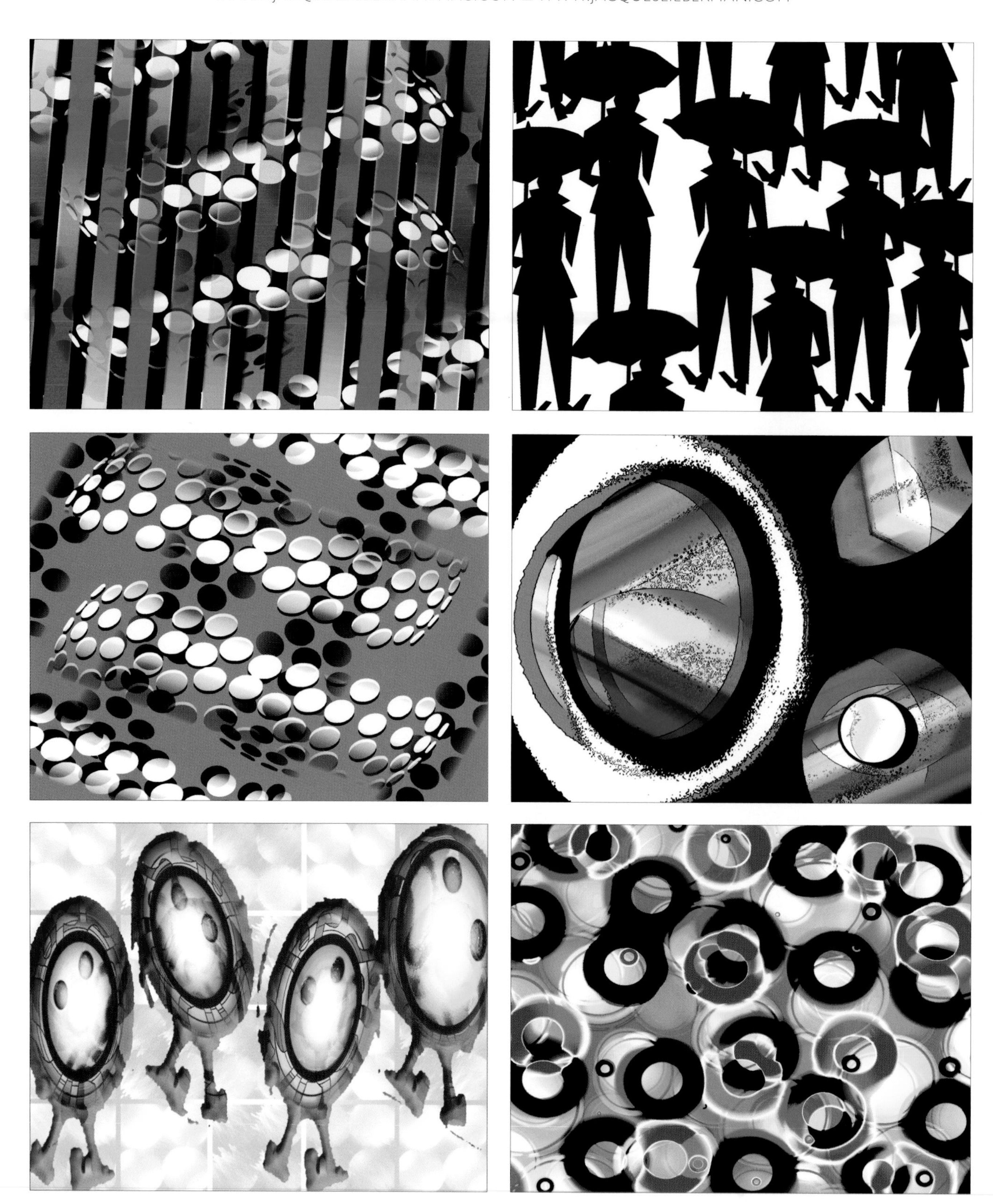

Six limited-edition prints, each: 40"H x 50"W.

CATHY LOCKE

STUDIO NORTH ▪ 560 TRUMBULL AVENUE ▪ NOVATO, CA 94947 ▪ TEL 415-893-9292
FAX 415-893-9464 ▪ E-MAIL CATHY@CATHYLOCKE.COM ▪ WWW.CATHYLOCKE.COM

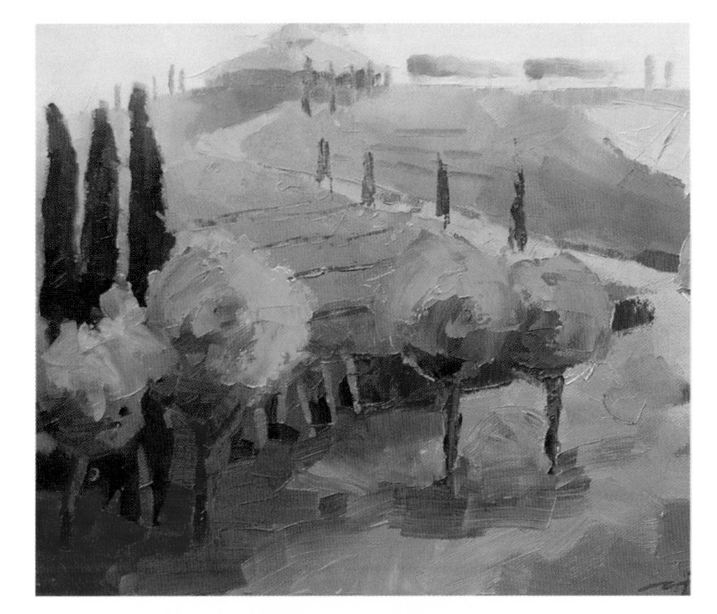

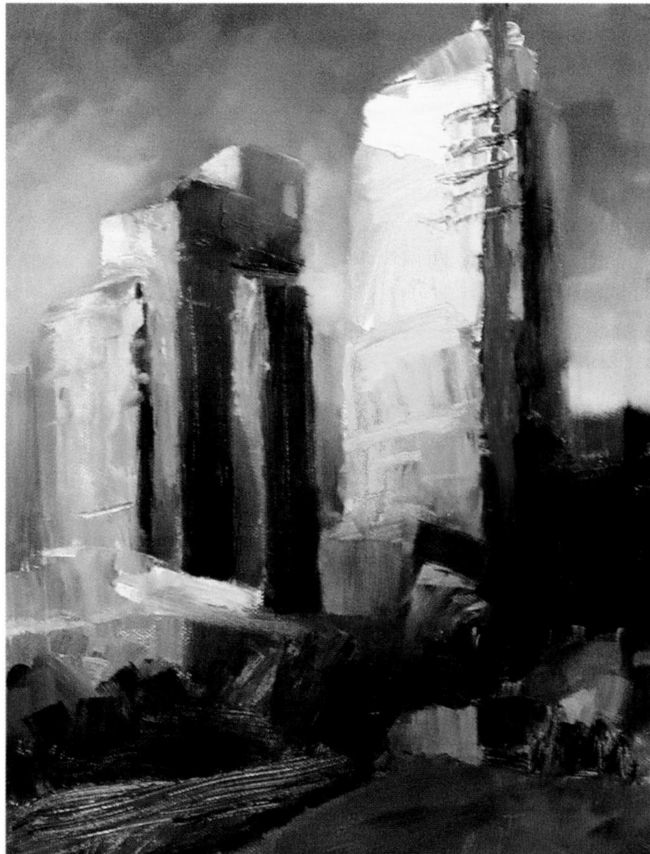

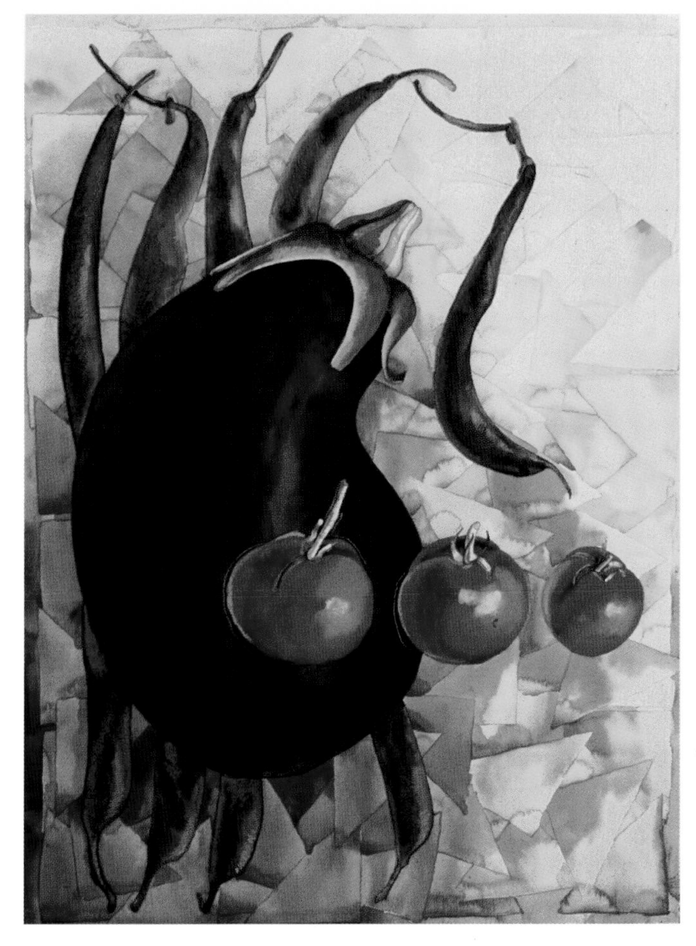

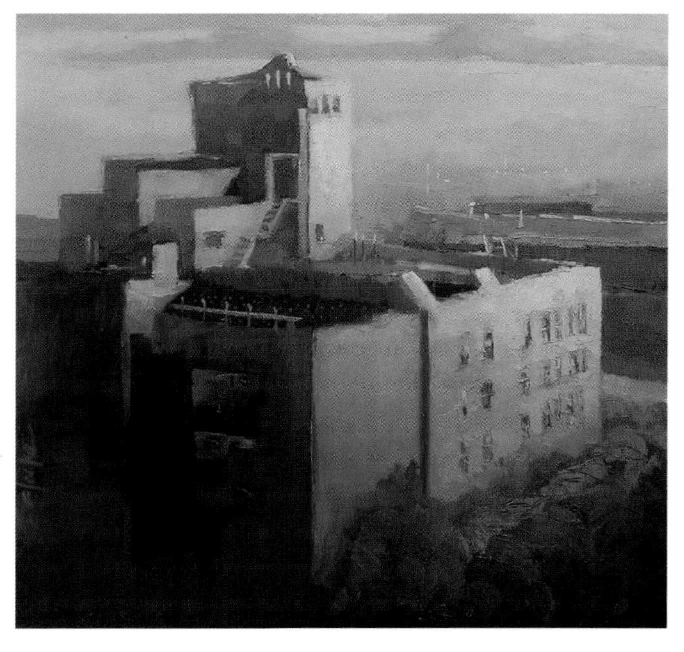

Top left: *Summer Heat,* Viansa Winery, Sonoma, CA, oil painting. Top right: *New Construction,* San Francisco, CA, oil painting. Bottom left: *Three Tomatoes,* Lou's North, Chicago, IL, original watercolor, 40" x 30", enlarged and installed onto the walls at 80" x 60". Bottom right: *Red Warehouse Dawn,* San Francisco docks, oil painting, 26" x 26".

SUSAN A. MASRI

JASMINE CO. ■ 8 LIKELY PLACE-GUESTHOUSE ■ SANTA FE, NM 87508 ■ TEL 505-982-9079
TEL 505-613-0046 ■ E-MAIL CONTACT@SUSANMASRI.COM ■ WWW.SUSANMASRI.COM

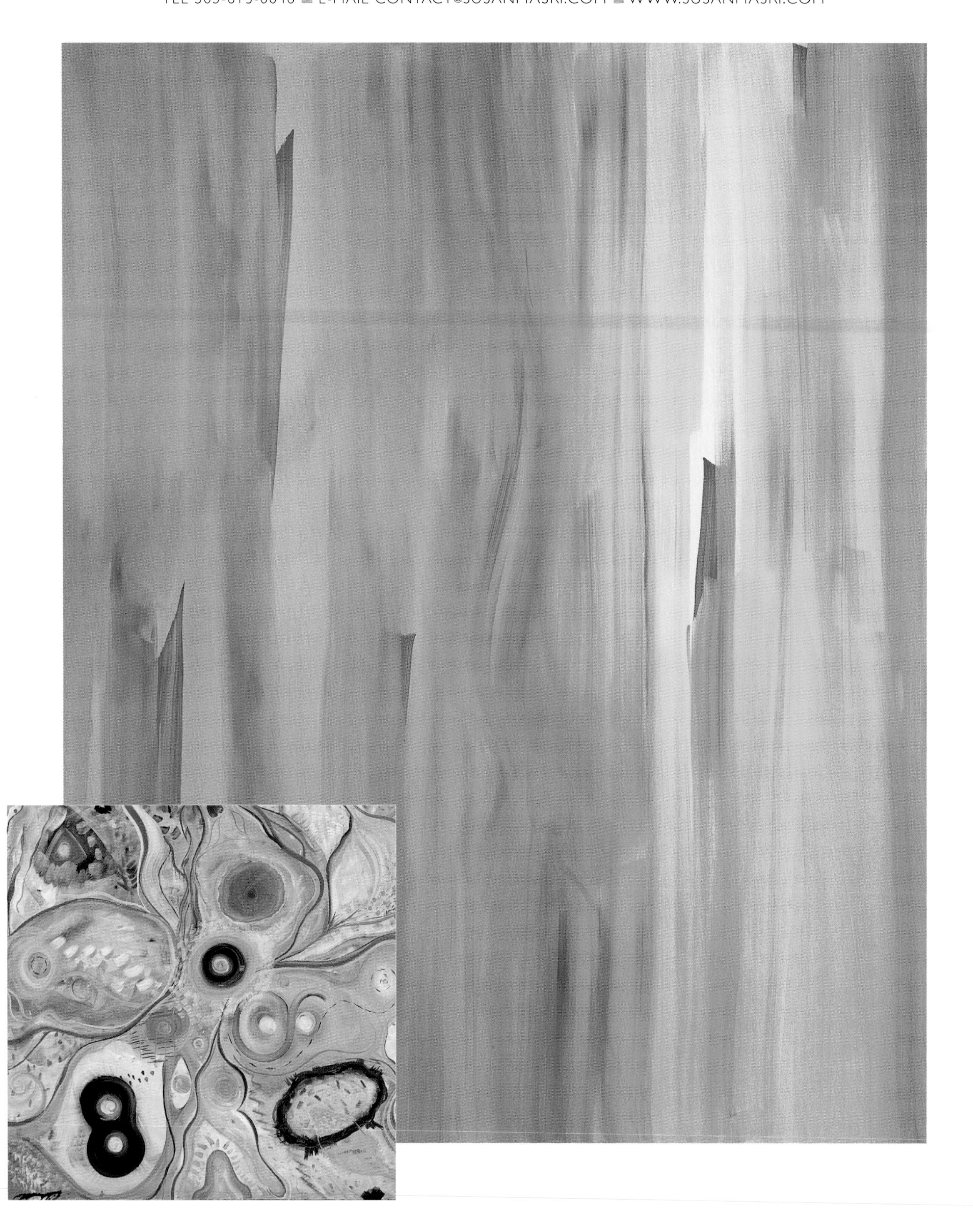

Hidden Virtue, 2005, oil on canvas, 60"H x 48"W. Inset: *The Light In Her Basket*, 2007, oil on canvas, 48"H x 48"W. Photographs: Mark Nohl.

TRENA McNABB

McNABB STUDIO, INC. ■ PO BOX 327 ■ BETHANIA, NC 27010 ■ TEL 336-924-6053
FAX 336-924-4854 ■ E-MAIL TRENA@TMCNABB.COM ■ WWW.TMCNABB.COM

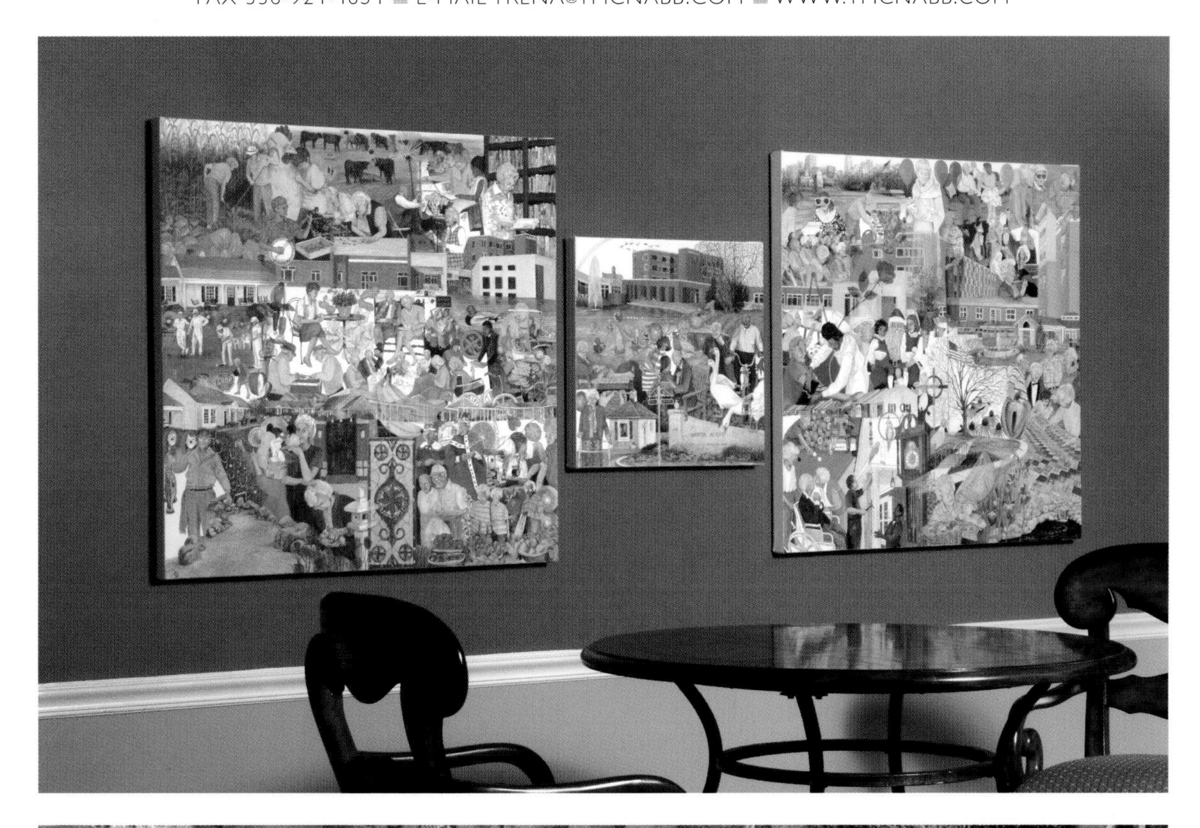

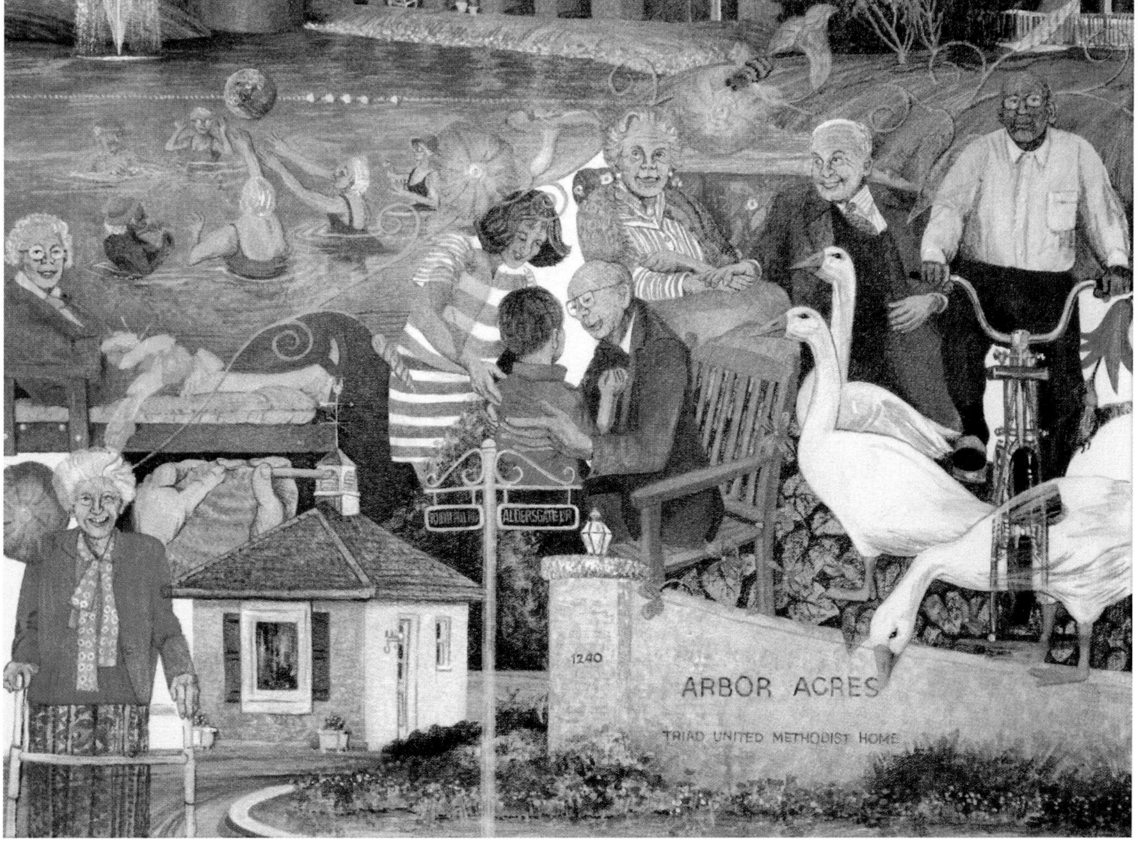

Arbor Acres Methodist Retirement Home, 2005, Winston-Salem, NC, three canvas panels, total size: 36" x 96". Photographs: Tommy McNabb

A Commission Story

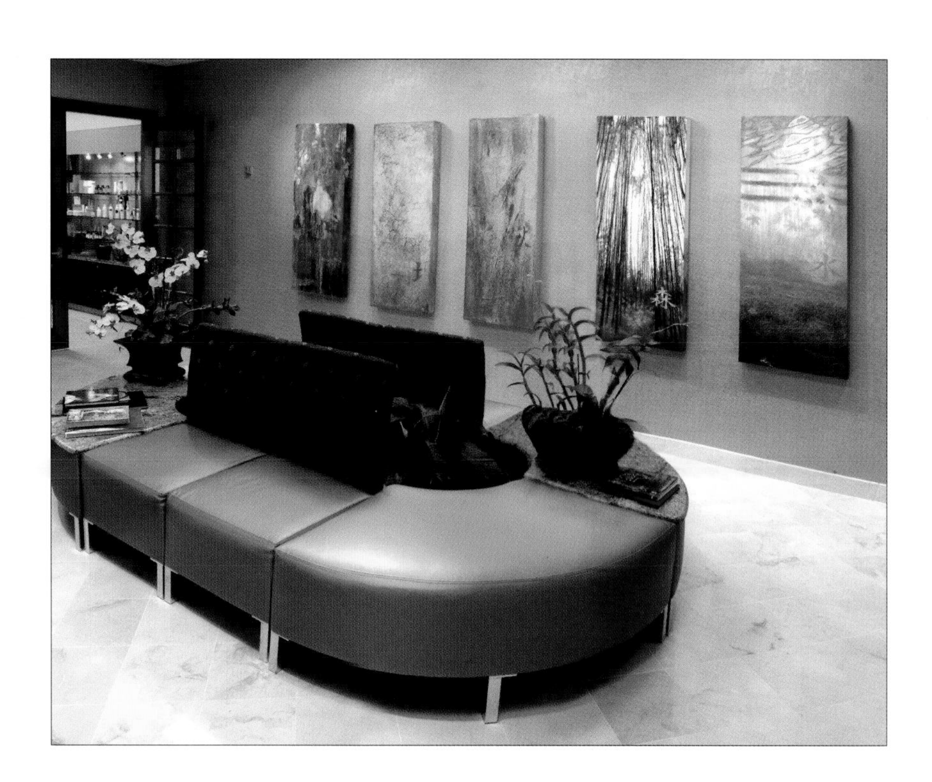

Imago Dei

TITLE
The Five Elements, 2006

COMMISSIONED FOR
Nikko Cosmetic Surgery Center,
Houston, TX

TIMELINE: 6 weeks

DIMENSIONS
Five panels, each: 60" x 24"

TRADE PROFESSIONAL
Diane Alexander and Rex Spencer,
Interior Designers,
Diane Alexander Designs

An office's all-important reception space sets the tone for the business, shaping the outlook of all who enter. ■ Houston's Nikko Cosmetic Surgery Center offered designer Diane Alexander an opportunity to compose an interior for a state-of-the-art clinic grounded in an ancient philosophy. "Our client was Japanese and asked us to develop a blend of earth-centered Zen design with contemporary overtones," Alexander explains. Together with Jamie and Jeremy Wells and their creative team at Imago Dei, Alexander developed a concept based on five elements: water, fire, earth, metal, and forest. Spanning a twenty-foot wall, five mixed-media panels explore and interpret each of the elements. Jeremy Wells recalls, "One of the things we looked for was abstract images of each of those elements. We then combined multiple imagery to create each unified piece." ■ Playing further with the concept, the artists then incorporated each of the actual elements as an art medium. "For instance, in the *Metal* piece, we used paints that actually have metal particles in them, then sprayed patina solutions on the surface to form oxidation processes such as rust," Jeremy Wells explains. Likewise, the *Forest* panel was rendered with handmade papers that have strips of wood and wood fiber woven into them. *Earth* is encrusted with soil and various earth-based plasters, while *Fire* is emblazoned with flames of gold leaf. ■ As a final touch, Imago Dei translated each element's name into its Japanese character and melded it into the surface of each panel. Diane Alexander adds, "Since Eastern artists often use chop marks as signatures, we wanted Imago Dei to develop an appropriate chop mark for their signature. They did and it is beautiful." ■ Jamie Wells articulates the artwork's Zen-infused potency: "We hope that as visitors are waiting they will have time to contemplate the textures, and try to figure out the characters, meaning, and symbolism in these paintings, which have produced an ambiance of rest and quiet meditation."

G. NEWMAN

GUDRUN NEWMAN STUDIO ■ 7429 PALMER GLEN CIRCLE ■ SARASOTA, FL 34240
TEL 941-320-8445 ■ E-MAIL GN@GNEWMANART.COM ■ WWW.GNEWMANART.COM

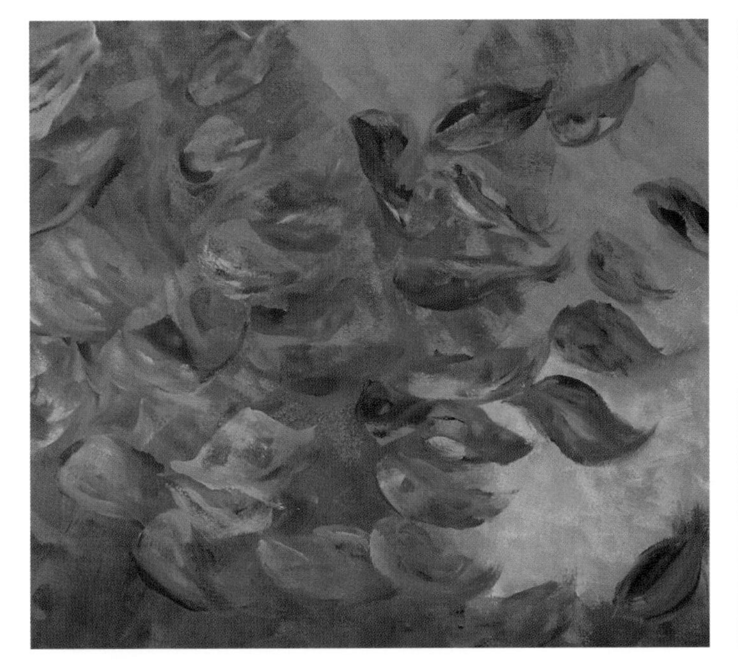

Top left: *Fall Leaves*, 2006, acrylic on canvas, 36" x 36". Top right: *Wave* series, 2006, mixed-media acrylic on canvas, 50" x 50". Bottom: *Blue Fusion*, 2006, acrylic, 40" x 58".

JOHNIENE PAPANDREAS

GALLERY VOYEUR ■ 444 COMMERCIAL STREET ■ PROVINCETOWN, MA 02657
TEL 508-487-3678 ■ E-MAIL INFO@VOY-ART.COM ■ WWW.VOY-ART.COM

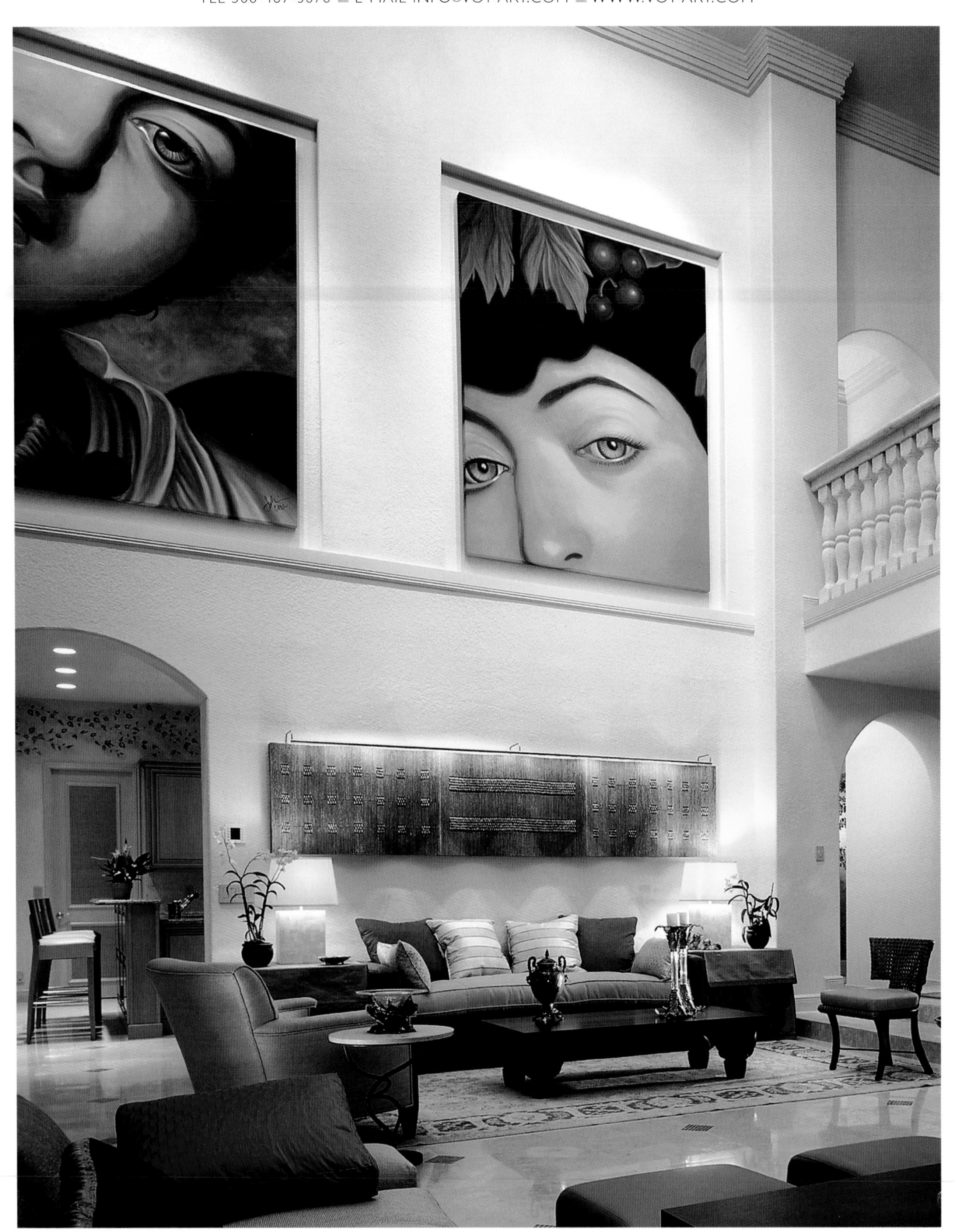

Poet and *Tell Me*, 2002, commissioned by Duffy Design Group, Boston, for private residence in Weston, FL, casein on muslin, each: 104" x 80". Photograph: Glenn Daidone, Glenn Daidone Photography.

JOHNIENE PAPANDREAS

GALLERY VOYEUR ■ 444 COMMERCIAL STREET ■ PROVINCETOWN, MA 02657
TEL 508-487-3678 ■ E-MAIL INFO@VOY-ART.COM ■ WWW.VOY-ART.COM

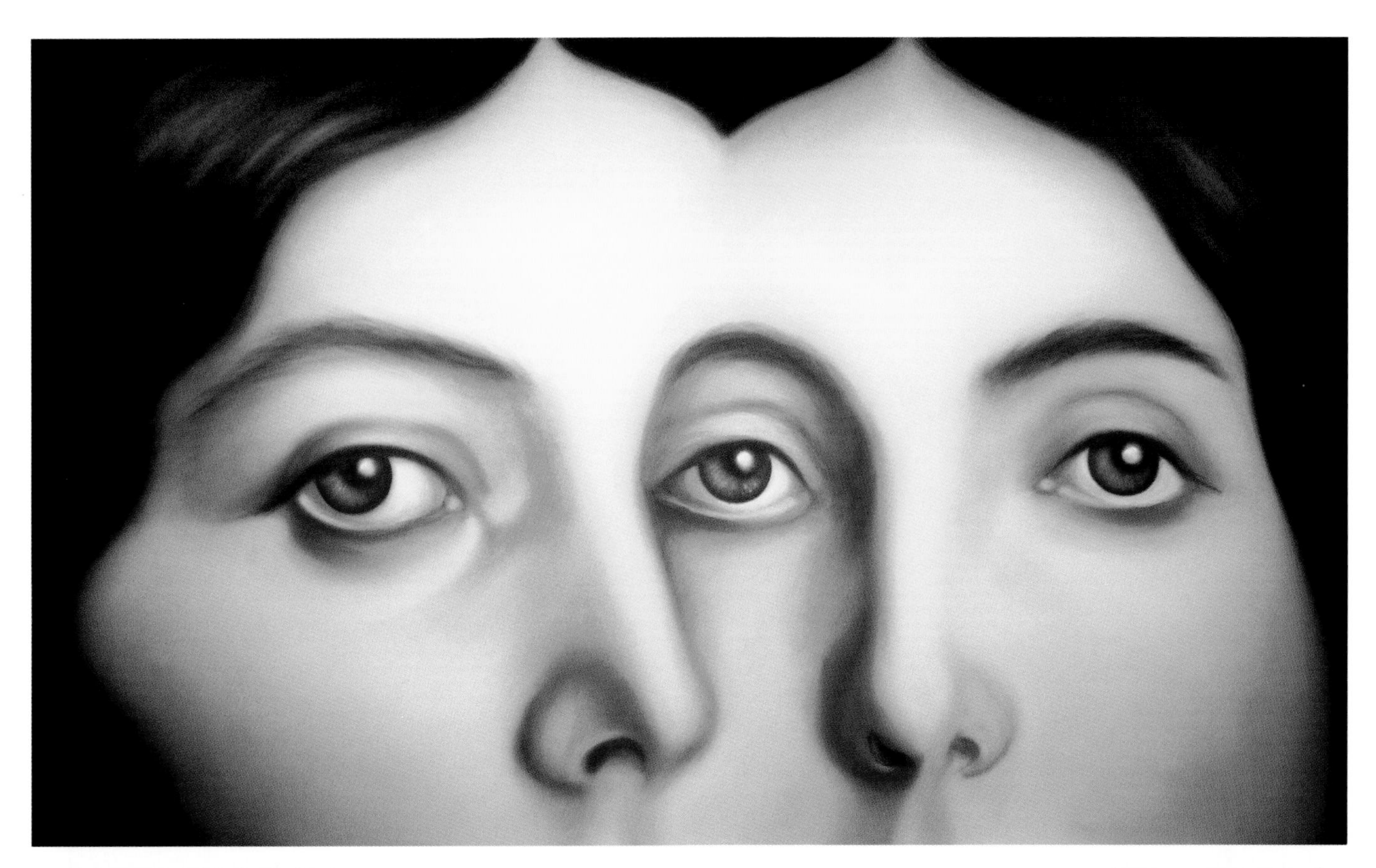

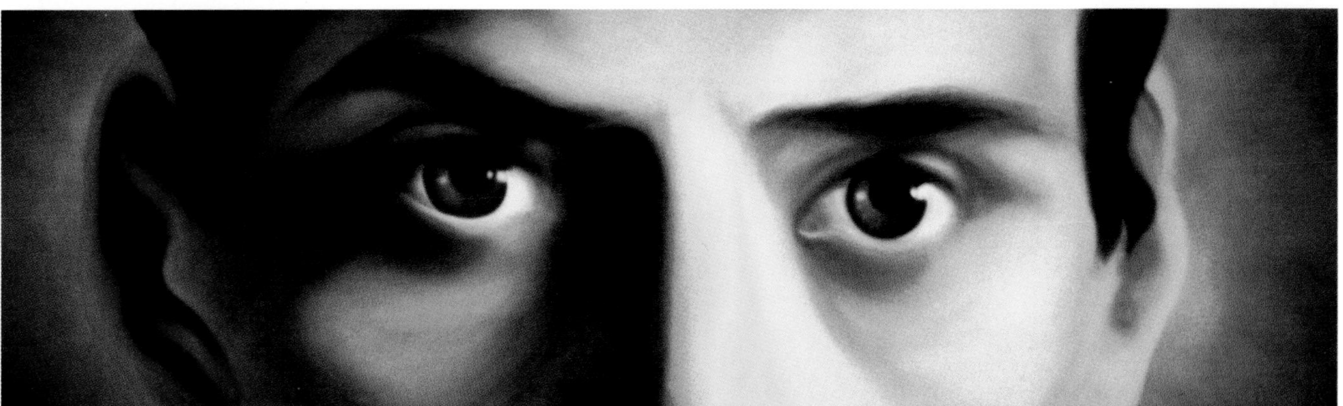

Top: *Like Mind*, 2005, casein on muslin, 48" x 78".
Bottom: *Priest*, 2002, private collection, casein on muslin, 28" x 94".

A Commission Story

Cathy Locke

TITLE
Celebration, 2006

COMMISSIONED FOR
Victoria Gardens Cultural Center,
Rancho Cucamonga, CA

TIMELINE: 6 months

DIMENSIONS: 10'H x 85'W

TRADE PROFESSIONAL
Michele Iacobucci, Design Principal,
Flying Colors Inc.

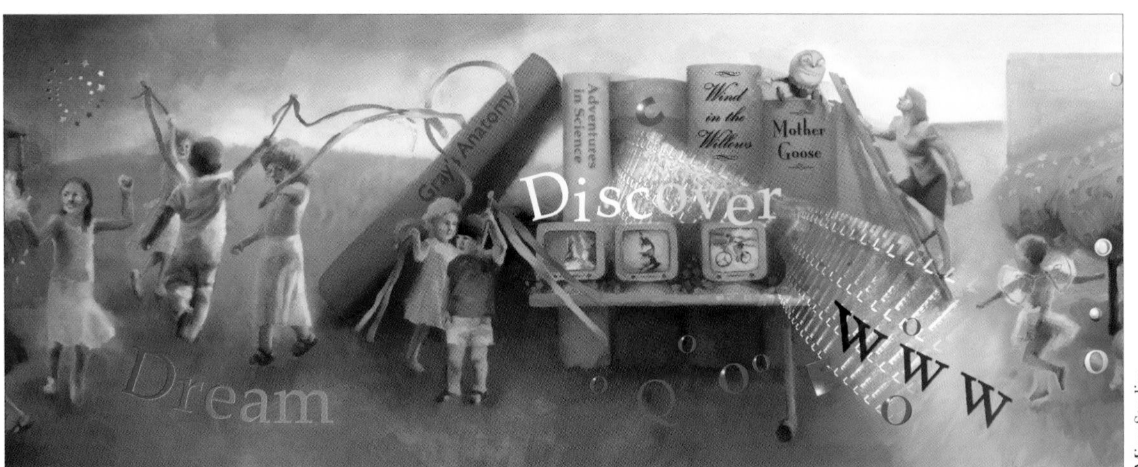

Ming Studios

The growing southern California city of Rancho Cucamonga is home to Victoria Gardens, a vibrant family-friendly retail center with plenty of dining and shopping options. When the city added a massive 80,000-square-foot cultural center to the mix, the party really started humming. ■ Michele Iacobucci of Flying Colors was called in to design and coordinate the interior theme of the huge complex, which houses a library and performing arts center connected by a spacious atrium. It was this atrium that was in need of a large mural. Having worked with Cathy Locke several times in the past, Iacobucci was confident that the artist had the ability to pull off this new, demanding commission. ■ A broad range of civic representatives had a vested interest in the building. "They put together a laundry list of things they wanted, and they each took a certain amount of wall space. It was our job to make all these different scenes flow from one to the next, and to make them look like they belonged together," Locke recalls. ■ Locke's sketches evolved into a multifaceted expression of the cultural center's theme: celebrating community. The delicately rendered scenes weave together five key concepts: create, imagine, discover, dream, and celebrate. ■ Locke explains her choice of light, fantasy-tinged imagery. "They were asking for such a vast variety of things. I thought we maybe needed to take this completely out of reality and start being very playful with it." Locke's compositional strategies are adept and elegant: In one instance, shimmering bubbles rise out of a cauldron to smoothly bridge a transition to dancers, then gently wind around a group of children. ■ Victoria Gardens Cultural Center embodies the joy of community. Michele Iacobucci enthuses, "It was a delightful project. It was nice to be able to create something that was fun, entertaining, visually beautiful, and full of lots of color and excitement. I think the mural was the culmination of all of that."

PINTER STUDIOS, INC.

DONNA PINTER ■ 480 KNOLLWOODS DRIVE ■ ROSWELL, GA 30075 ■ TEL 678-557-7871
FAX 770-992-1227 ■ E-MAIL PINTERART@EARTHLINK.NET ■ WWW.DONNAPINTER.COM

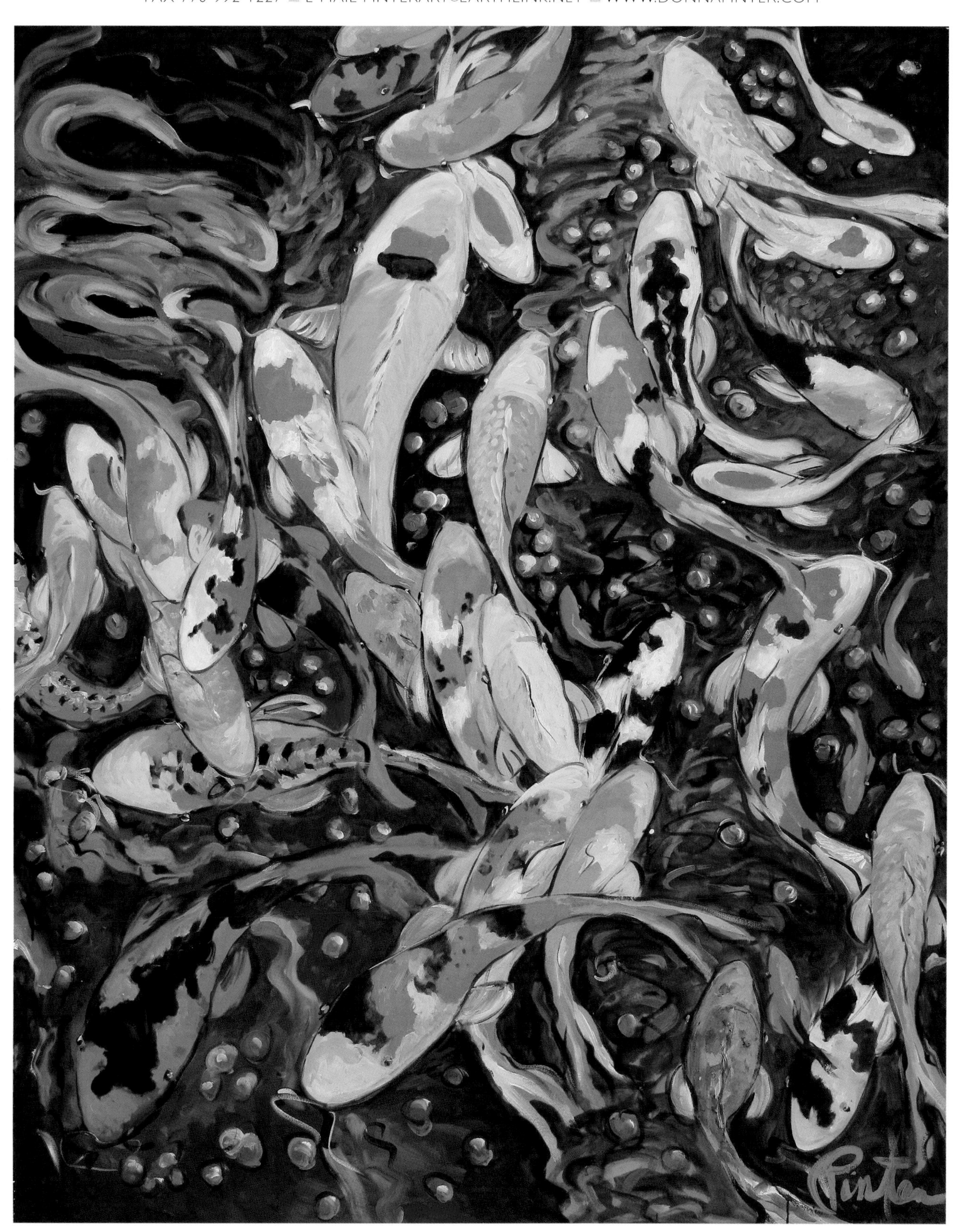

Tategoi: A Journey Not a Destination, oil on canvas 60" x 48". Photograph: Andrea Helms, Haigwoods Studios.

RICHARD POLSKY

660 PARK AVENUE ■ NEW YORK, NY 10021
TEL 212-988-4084 ■ E-MAIL VPOLSKY@AOL.COM

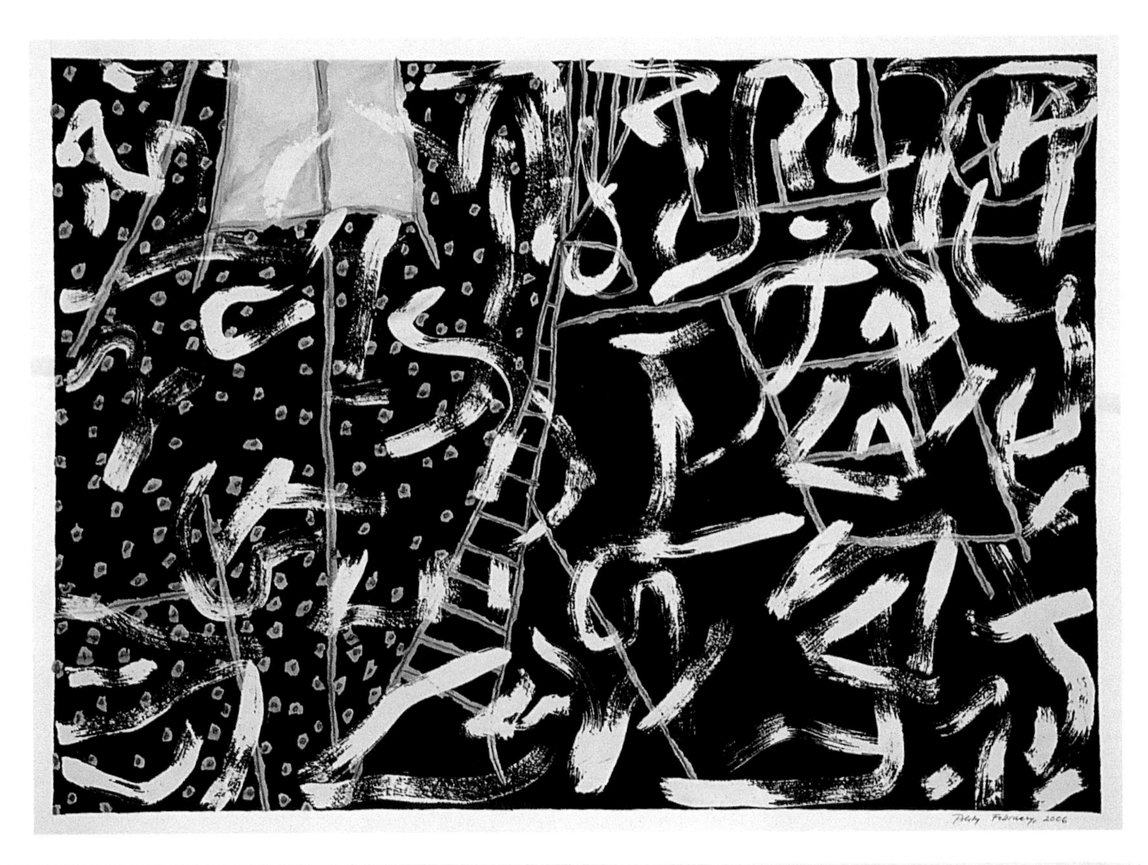

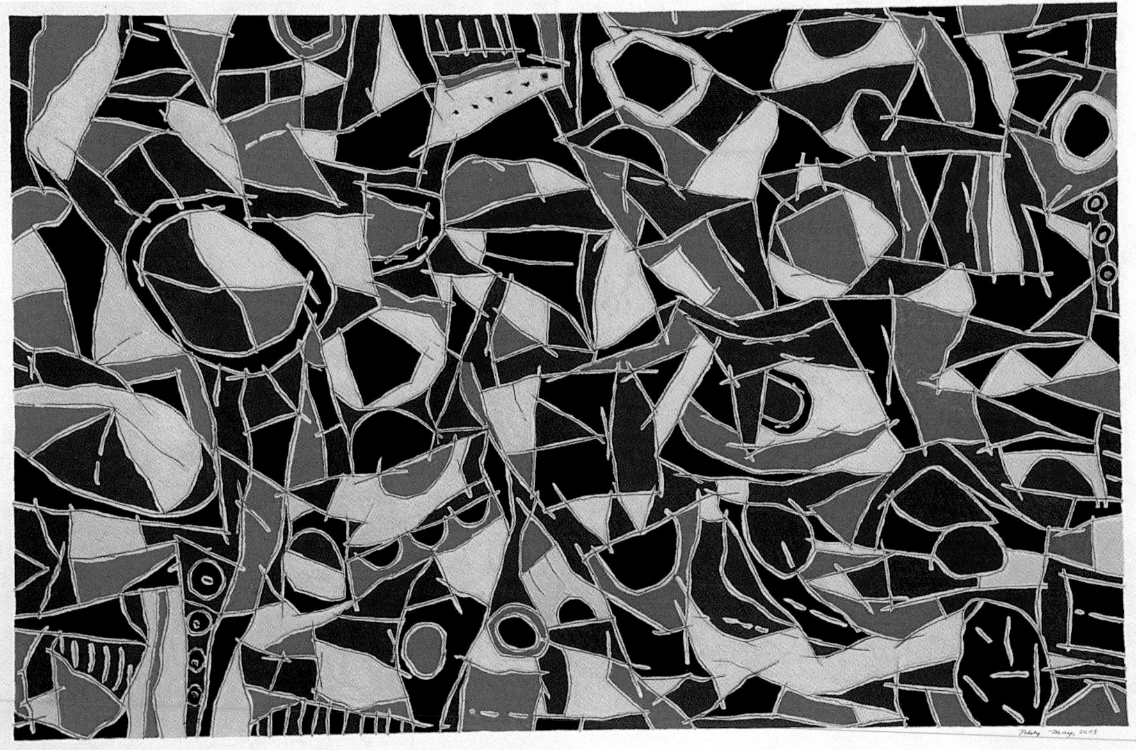

Top: *Untitled,* 30" x 40". Bottom: *Untitled,* 40" x 60". Photographs: John Beren.

RICHARD POLSKY

660 PARK AVENUE ■ NEW YORK, NY 10021
TEL 212-988-4084 ■ E-MAIL VPOLSKY@AOL.COM

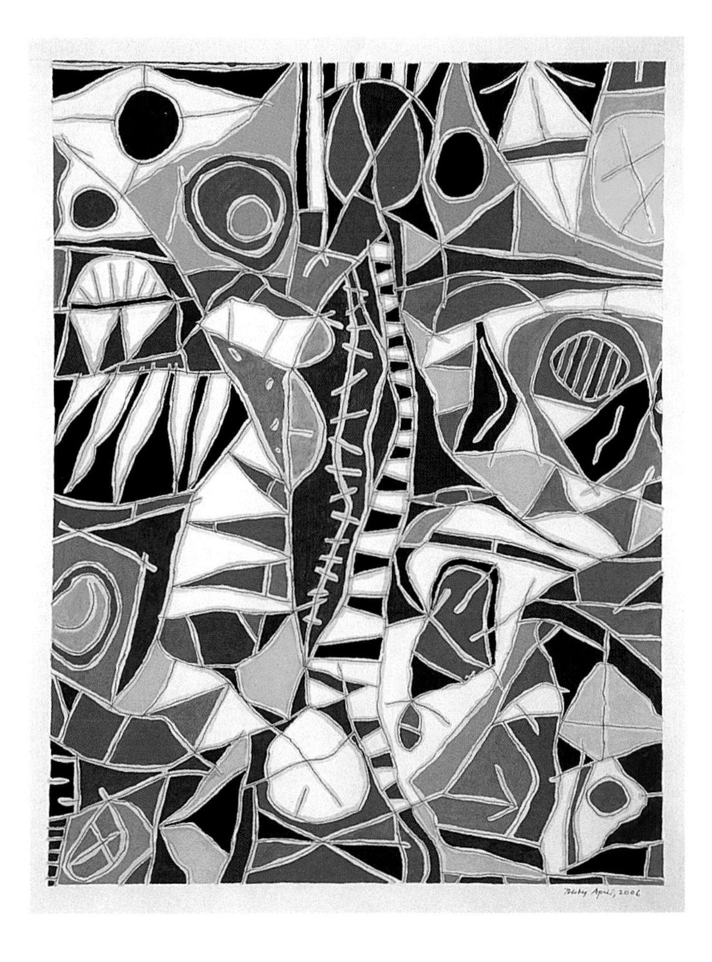

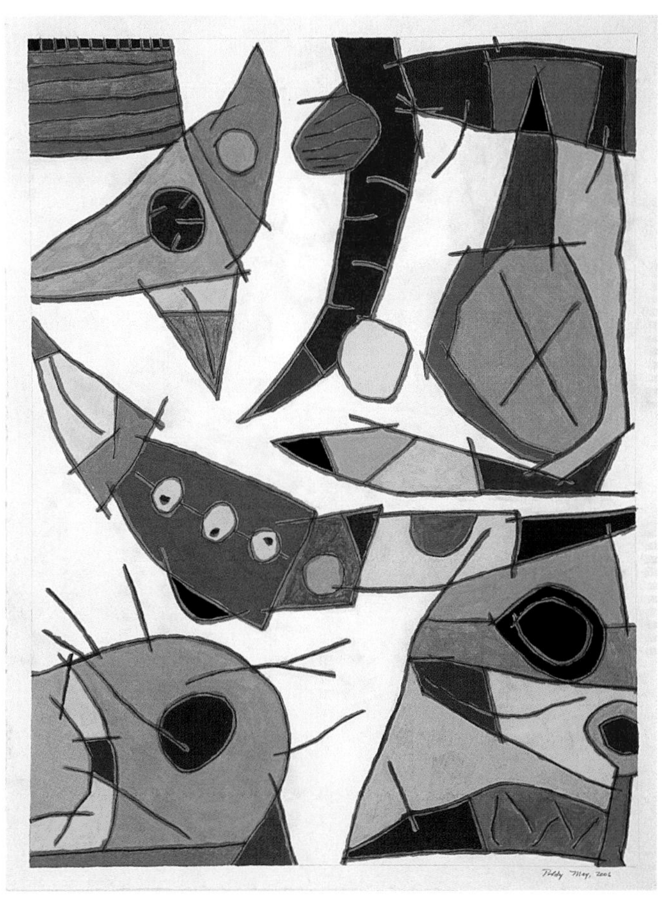

Left: *Untitled*, 40" x 30". Right: *Untitled*, 40" x 30". Photographs: John Beren.

PAUL ROUSSO

7520 VALLEYBROOK ROAD ■ CHARLOTTE, NC 28270 ■ TEL 704-965-2992 ■ TEL 704-366-7522
FAX 704-366-7577 ■ E-MAIL PAUL@ROUSSOPORTFOLIO.COM ■ WWW.ROUSSOPORTFOLIO.COM

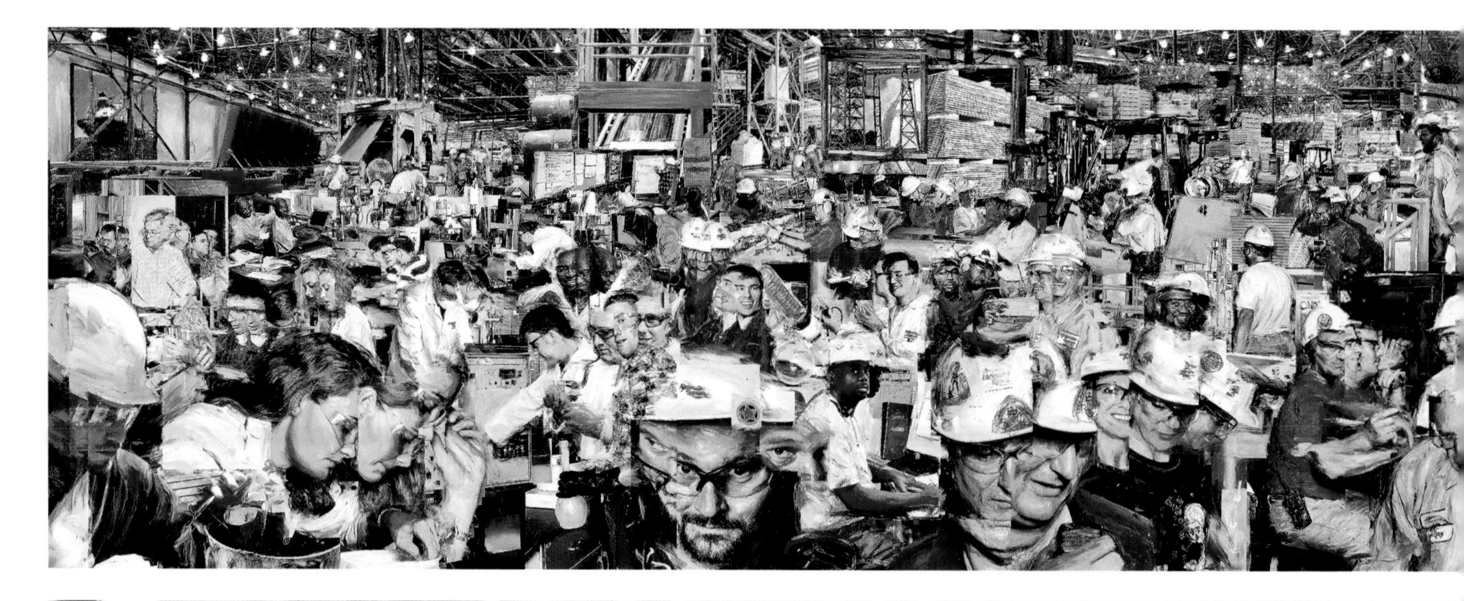

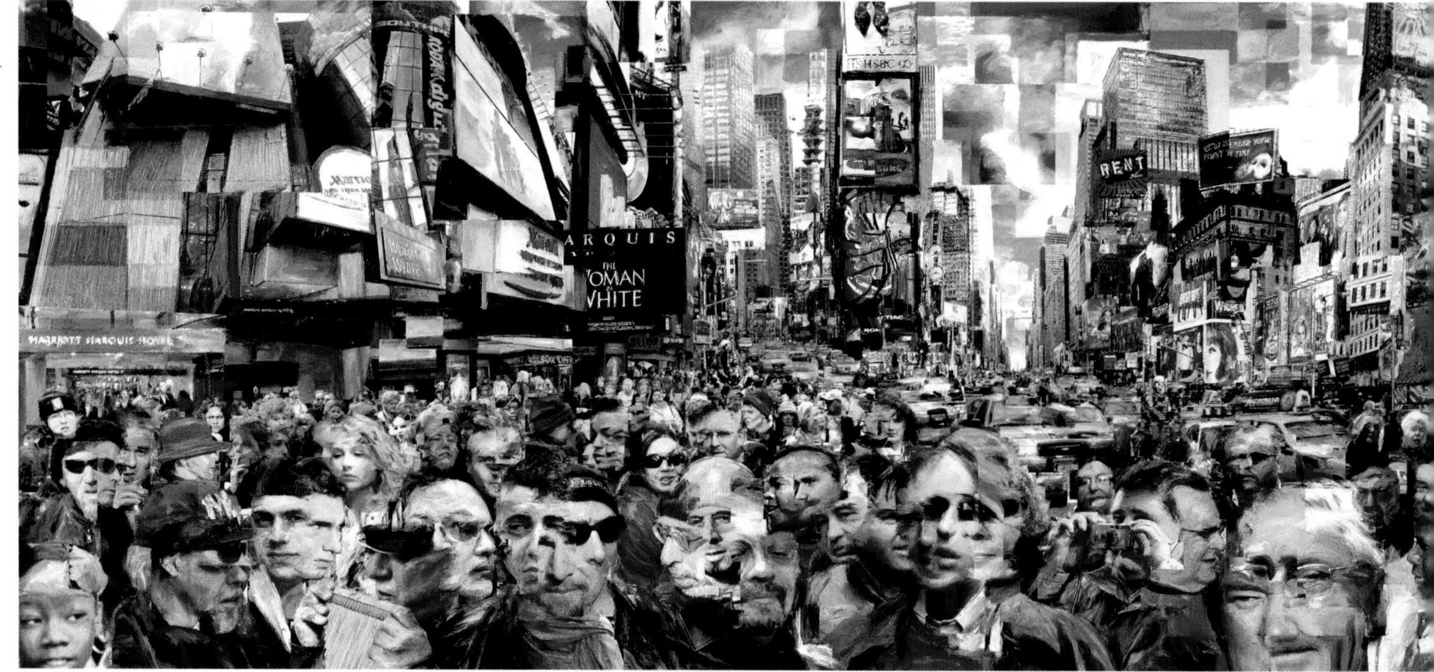

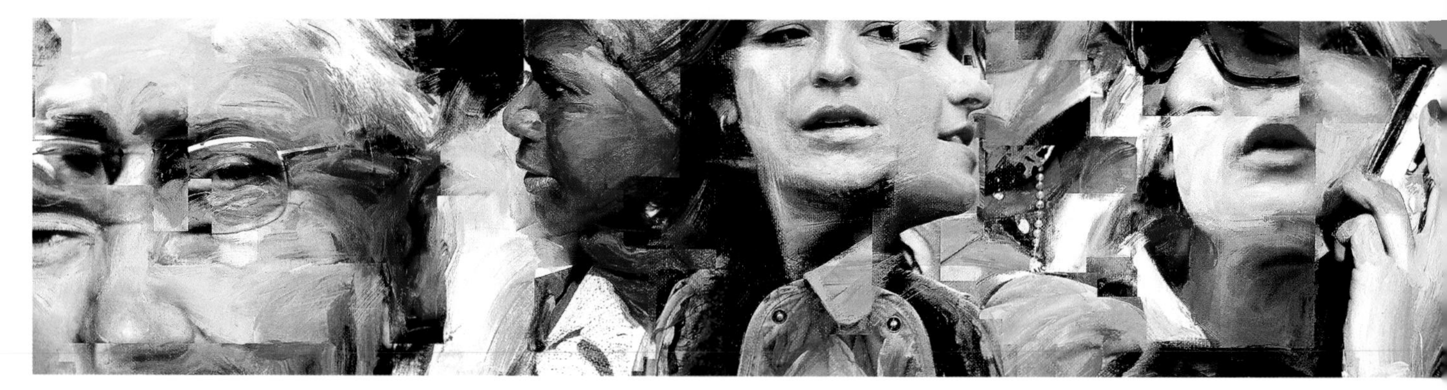

Top: *Portrait of National Gypsum*, 2006, acrylic and pigment on canvas, 44" x 18'. Middle: *Portrait of Times Square, December 2005*, acrylic and pigment on canvas, 38" x 15'. Bottom: *Portrait of Times Square* (detail).

PAUL ROUSSO

7520 VALLEYBROOK ROAD ■ CHARLOTTE, NC 28270 ■ TEL 704-965-2992 ■ TEL 704-366-7522
FAX 704-366-7577 ■ E-MAIL PAUL@ROUSSOPORTFOLIO.COM ■ WWW.ROUSSOPORTFOLIO.COM

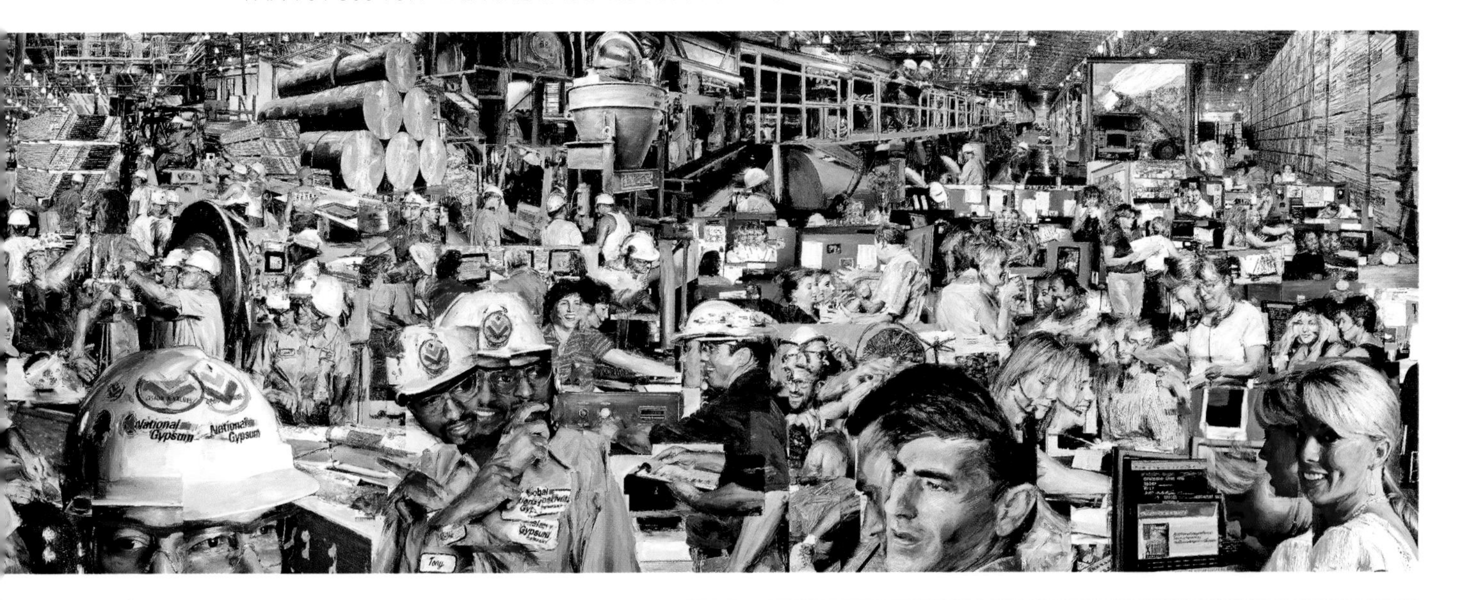

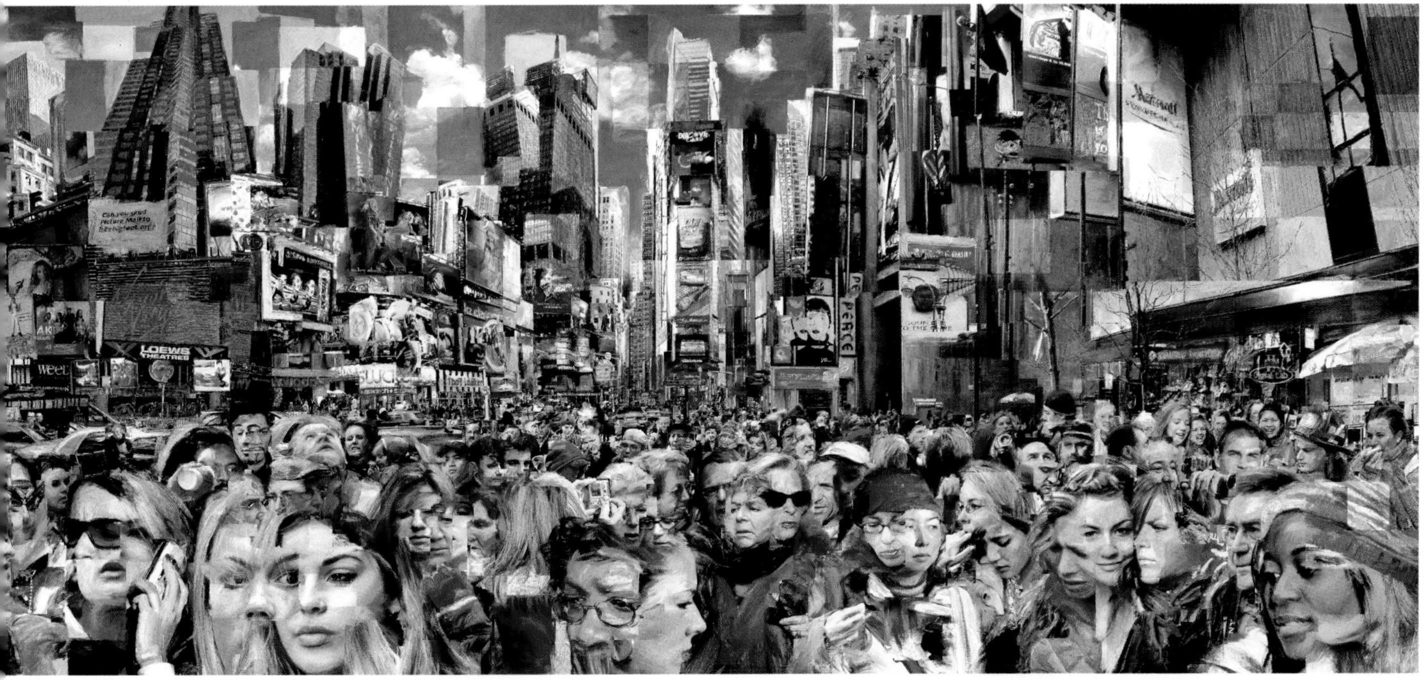

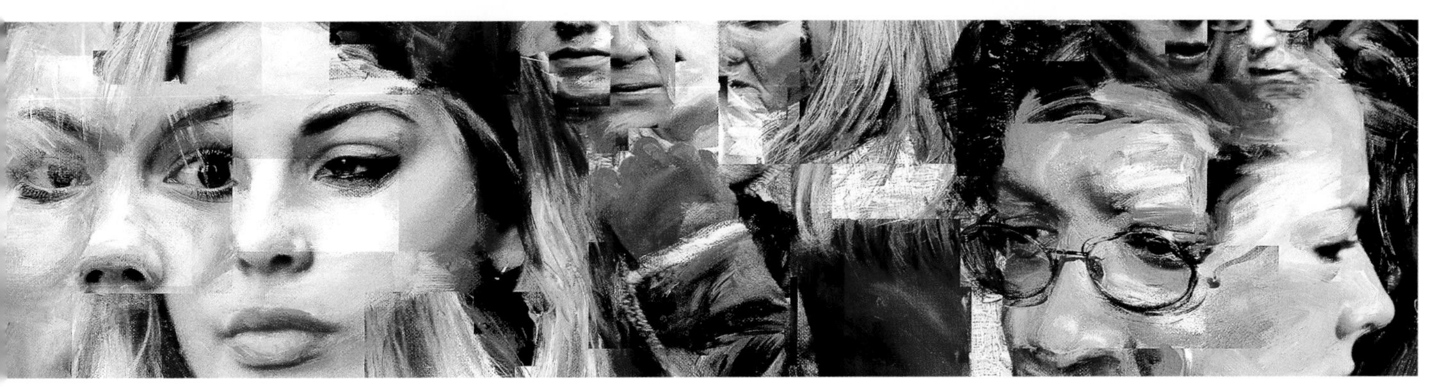

Top: *Portrait of National Gypsum*, 2006, acrylic and pigment on canvas, 44" x 18'. Middle: *Portrait of Times Square, December 2005*, acrylic and pigment on canvas, 38" x 15'. Bottom: *Portrait of Times Square* (detail).

The Guild® Sourcebook of Architectural & Interior Art 22. © 2007 The Guild, Inc.

JO ELLEN SIDDALL

JO ELLEN SIDDALL FINE ARTS ■ PO BOX 3179 ■ PONTE VEDRA, FL 32004-3179
TEL 904-826-3983 ■ E-MAIL JESFA@COMCAST.NET ■ WWW.JOELLENSIDDALLFINEARTS.COM

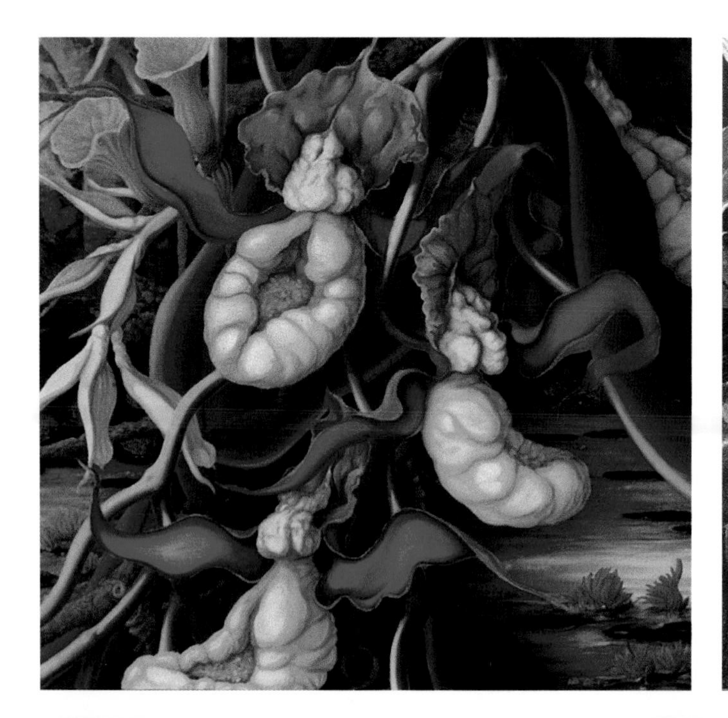

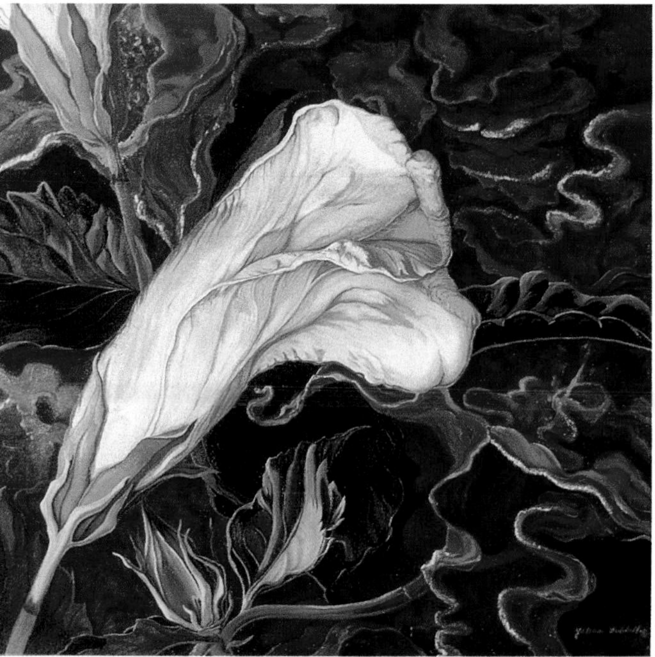

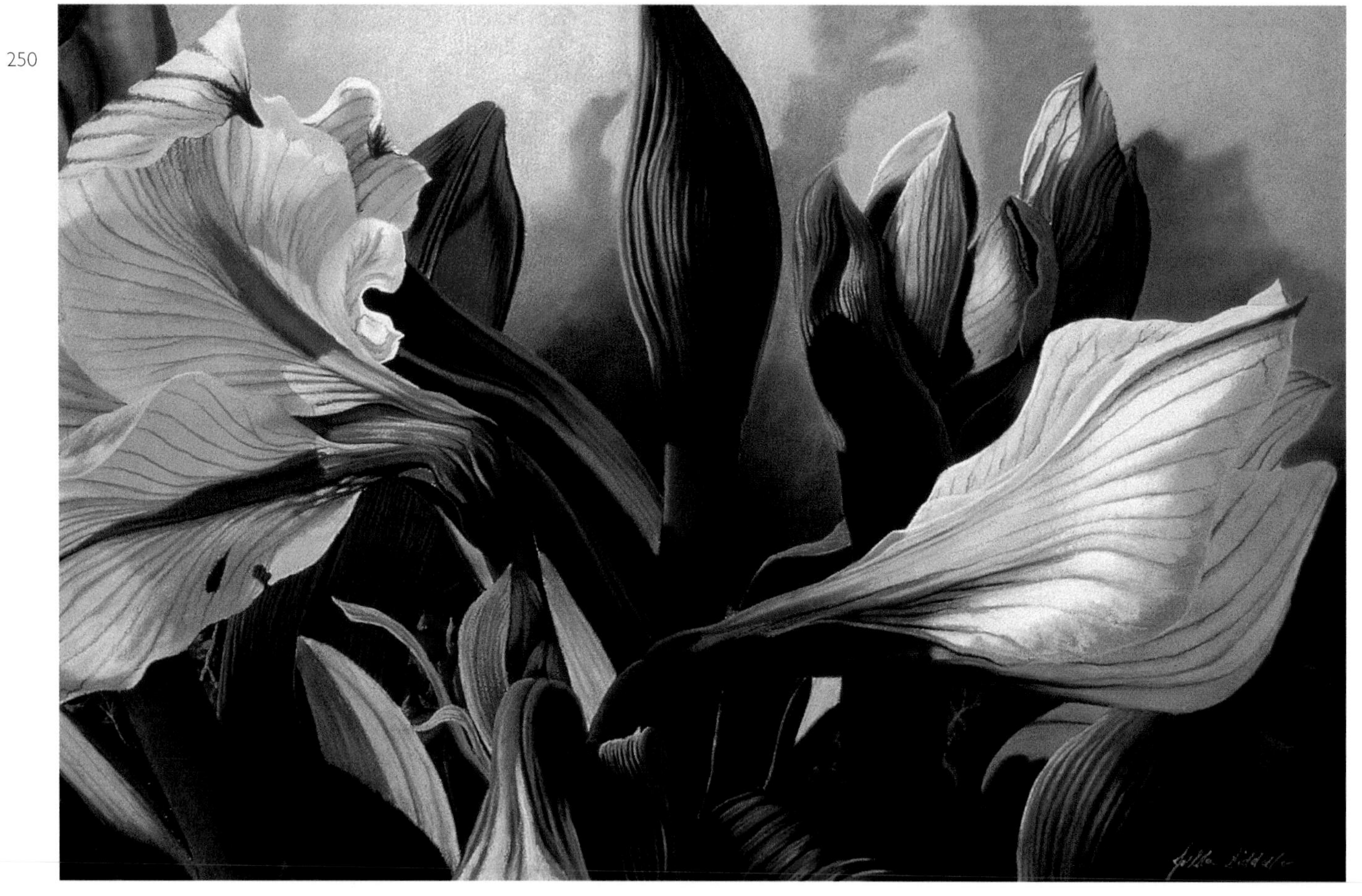

Top left: *It Flows from Within*, oil on canvas, 54" x 54". Top right: *Becoming the Spirit*, oil on canvas, 54" x 54".
Bottom: *Return of Light*, pastel, 35" x 51". Photographs: Daryl Bunn.

NICHOLAS WILTON

26 WEST NICASIO ROAD ■ PO BOX 473 ■ SAN GERONIMO, CA 94963 ■ TEL 415-488-4131 ■ FAX 415-488-4641
E-MAIL INFO@NICHOLASWILTONPAINTINGS.COM ■ WWW.NICHOLASWILTONPAINTINGS.COM

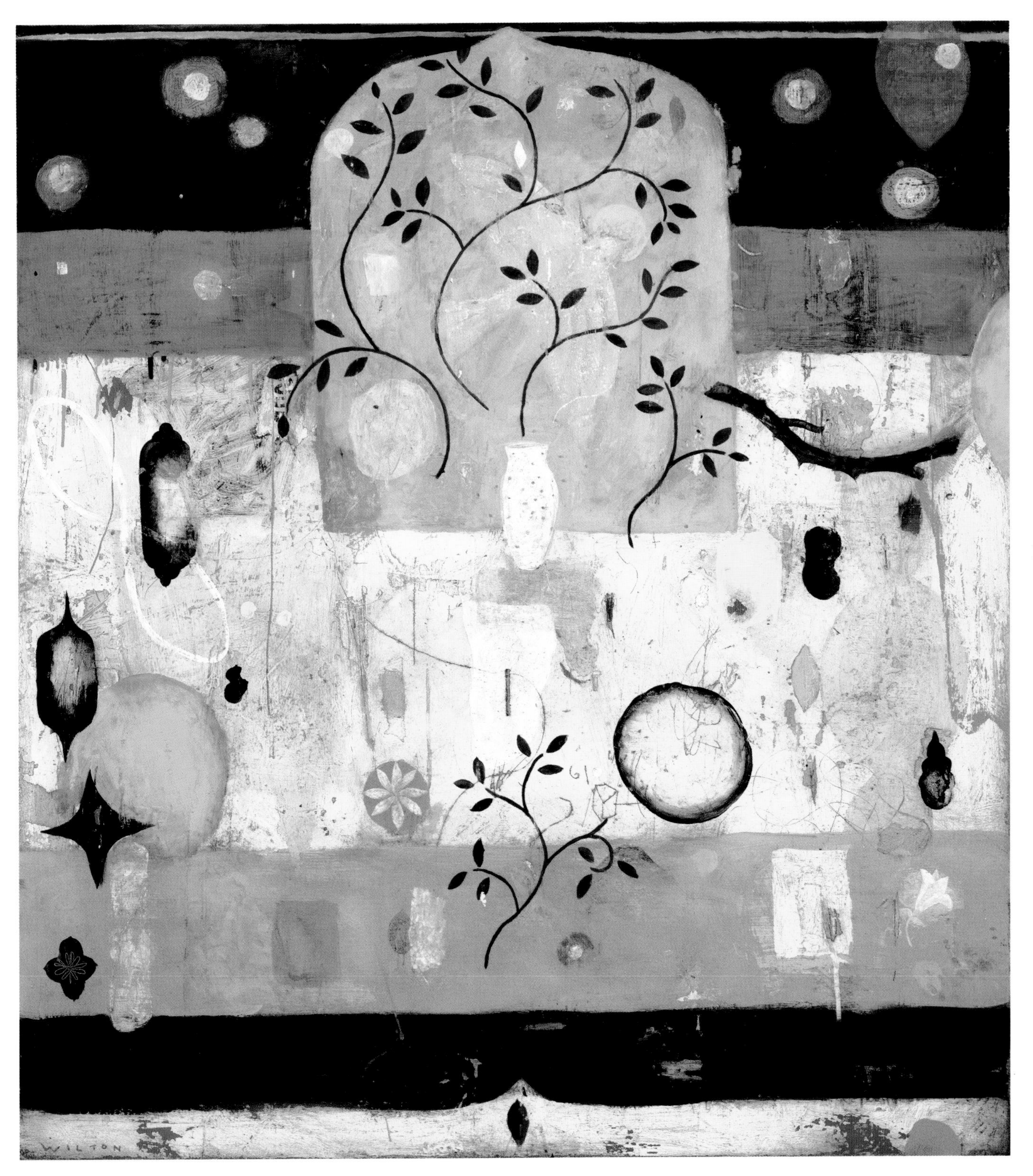

Sequence, 2006, mixed media on panel, 40" x 34".

A Commission Story

ThinkGlass

TITLE
Illumination, 2003

COMMISSIONED FOR
Our Lady of Mount Carmel,
Fairfield, CA

TIMELINE: 6 months

DIMENSIONS: 30'H x 15'W

TRADE PROFESSIONAL
Harry C. Hallenbeck, FAIA,
Vanir Construction Management

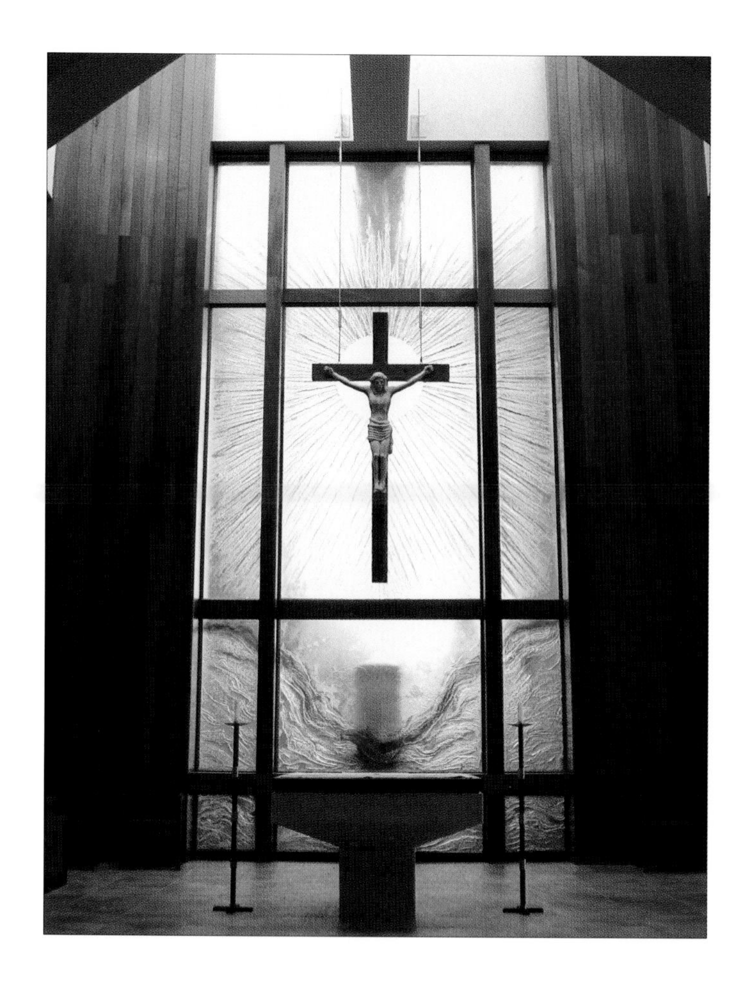

The design challenge was daunting: The cylindrical-shaped core of Our Lady of Mount Carmel's new church structure needed an internal element that would physically divide yet symbolically connect its two worship spaces. Fortunately, design architect Harry Hallenbeck happened upon the artists of ThinkGlass at an AIA conference in San Diego, and an elegant solution began to take shape—in glass. ■ ThinkGlass uses innovative thermoforming technology to mold glass into an infinite variety of rich textures and shapes, adding a dramatic sense of depth and liquid movement. "I thought this was really something that would work wonderfully," Hallenbeck remembers. "Stained glass is magnificent, but it is much more two-dimensional. Artist Michel Mailhot's [of ThinkGlass] work had a texture that really intrigued me—and it was interesting in what it could do, how free it was as artistry." ■ Serving a growing congregation, the large, contemporary-style Fairfield, California, church seats 1,000. Its semicircular main sanctuary space and Blessed Sacrament chapel adjoin one another, sharing a primary wall. And despite the obvious need for partitioning, the wall wasn't conceived as a conventional barrier. ■ Hallenbeck explains the complex demands of the commission: "It had to have a certain translucency, but not a great deal of transparency. And it had to be fairly neutral in color." Moreover, the two sides of the glass panel had to suit different purposes. "It had to speak of the glory of the risen Christ, as well as the call for more contemplation that goes on in the reservation chapel," the architect reports. Bertrand Charest of ThinkGlass recalls, "The client was looking for a very organic and luminous glass, representing the sun coming out of the clouds." ■ Hallenbeck gave Charest and ThinkGlass master glass artist Mailhot "a bubble diagram of emphasis points where transparency could occur and where it needed to be more opaque." Charest adds, "The proportions of the cross and the altar were also very important." ■ The serene radiance of the finished work is profoundly moving. Hallenbeck reports, "Everybody who sees it is intrigued. It achieved everything we hoped it would."

MARLENE SANAYE YAMADA

ARTWORK BY SANAYE ■ MANHATTAN BEACH, CA 90266 ■ TEL 310-435-7878
FAX 310-376-2695 ■ E-MAIL MARLENEYAMADA@YAHOO.COM ■ WWW.ARTWORKBYSANAYE.COM

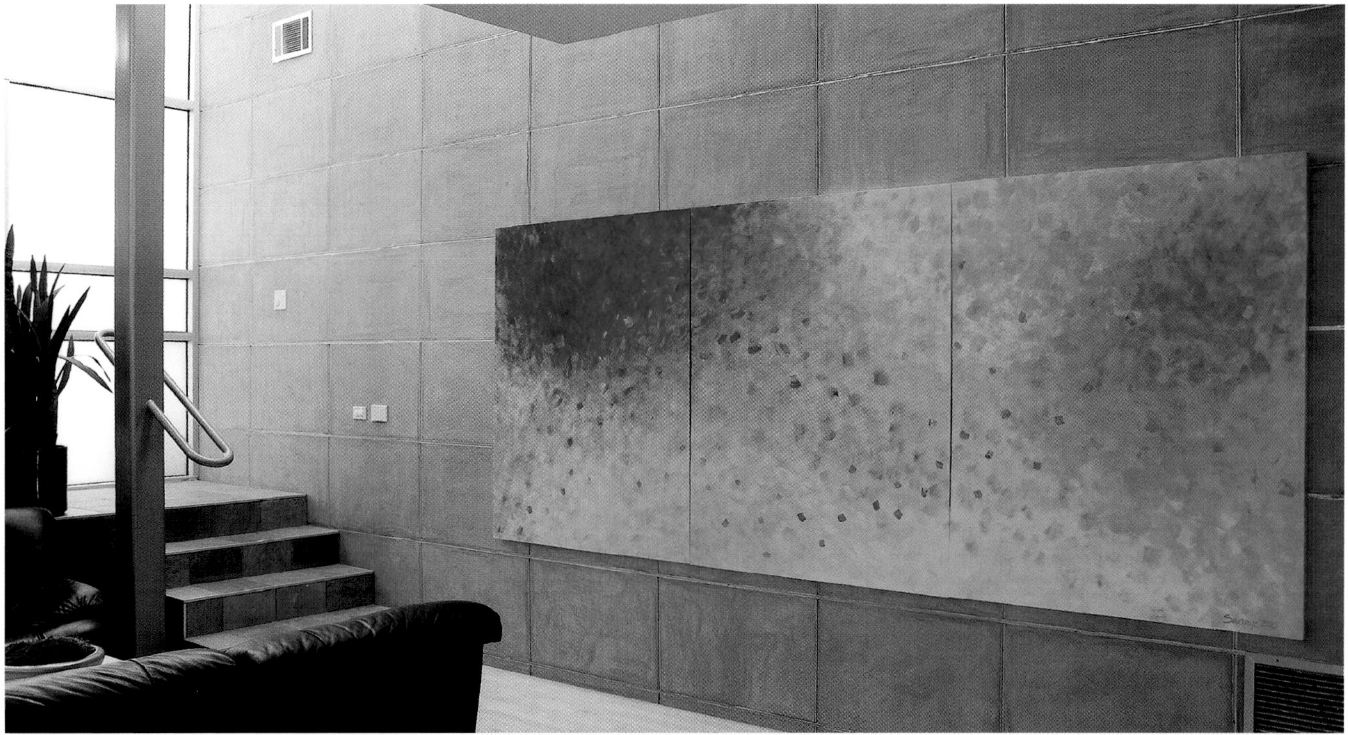

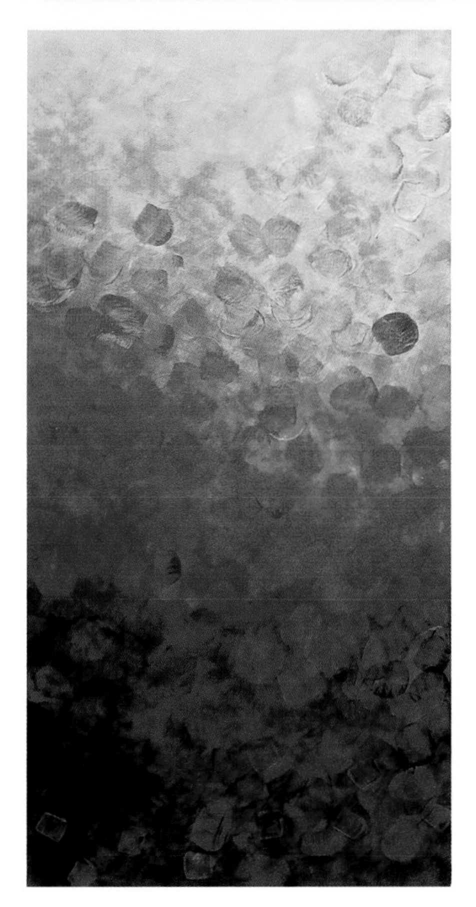

Top: *Transitions*, 2005, acrylic on canvas, 5' x 12'.
Bottom: *Spontaneous Combustion*, 2006, triptych, acrylic on canvas, each panel: 36" x 18".

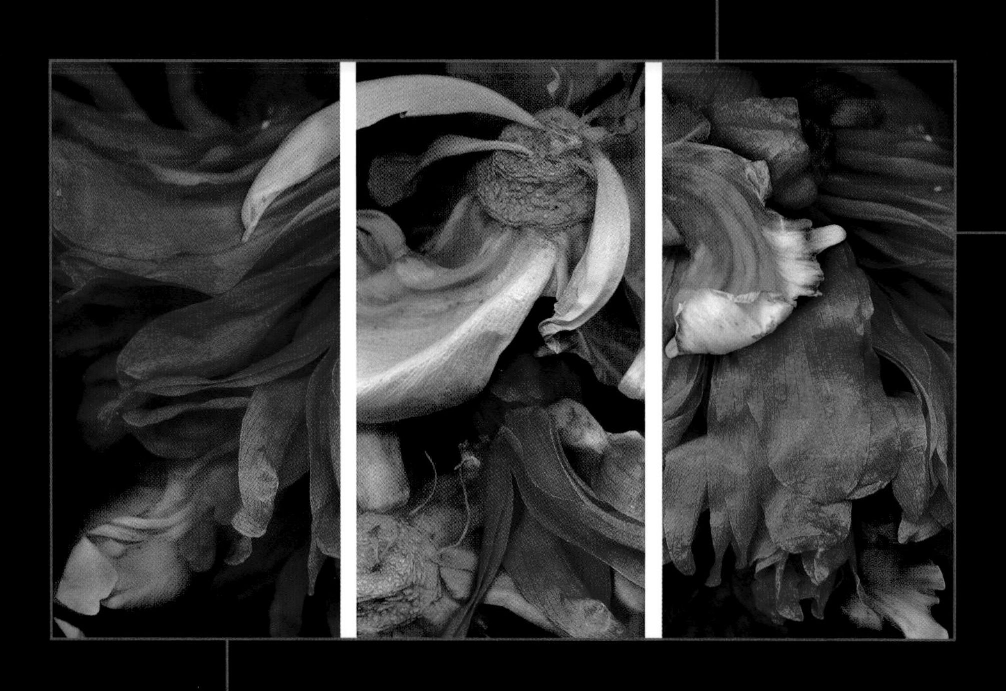

Fine Art Photography

ANDERSON CAPRON LTD./ADAMANTINE STUDIO

DAWN ANDERSON CAPRON ■ 38 NORTH LUMINA AVENUE ■ WRIGHTSVILLE BEACH, NC 28480
TEL 910-256-3855 ■ E-MAIL INFO@ANDERSON-CAPRONLTD.COM ■ WWW.ANDERSON-CAPRONLTD.COM

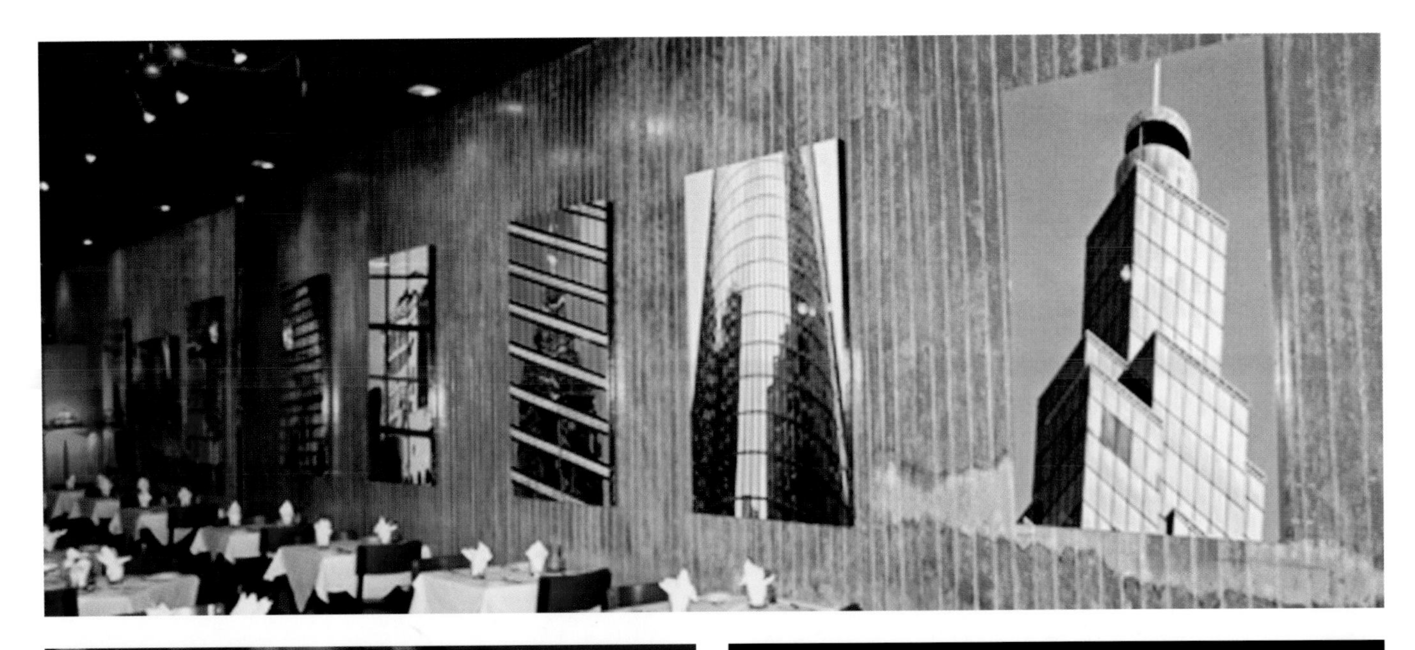

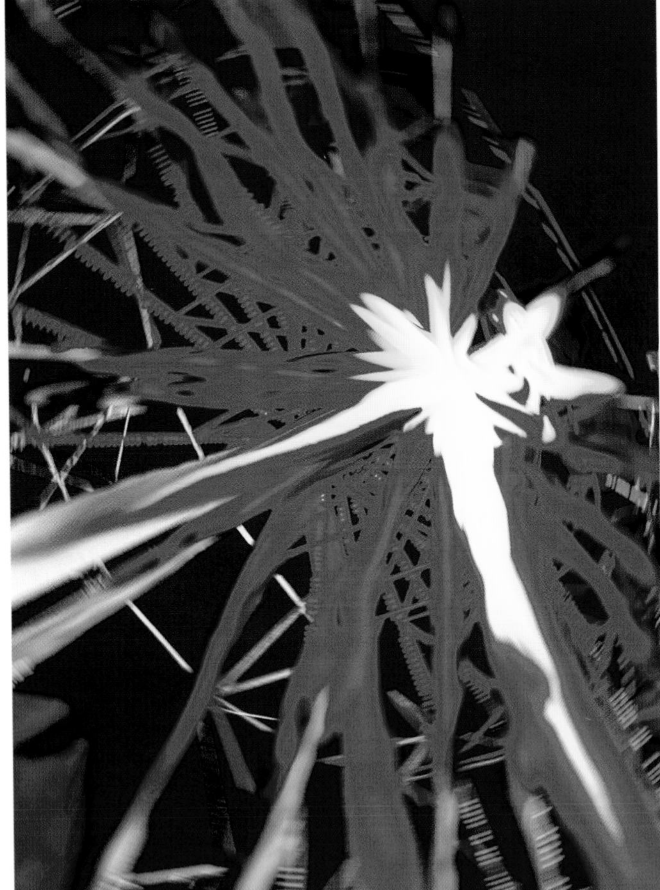

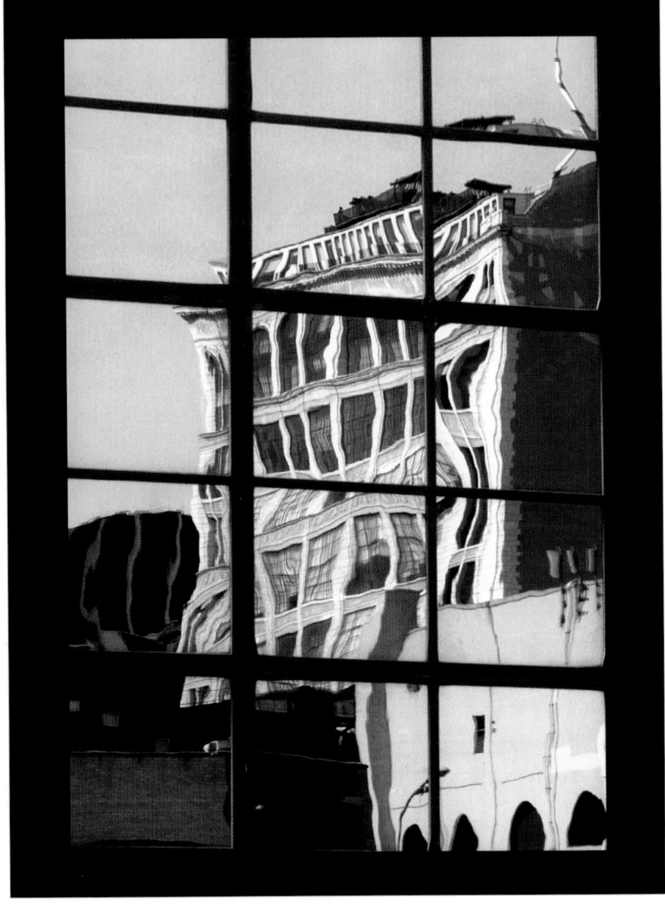

Top: Installation at Deluxe, Wilmington, NC. Bottom left: *Crazy,* 56" × 30". Bottom right: *Windows,* 62" × 38".

THE BARTELSTONE PHOTOWORKS COLLECTION

JAN BARTELSTONE ■ 2716 19TH NW ■ ALBUQUERQUE, NM 87104
TEL/FAX 505-344-3385 ■ E-MAIL JAN@EYESOFNEWMEXICO.COM ■ WWW.EYESOFNEWMEXICO.COM

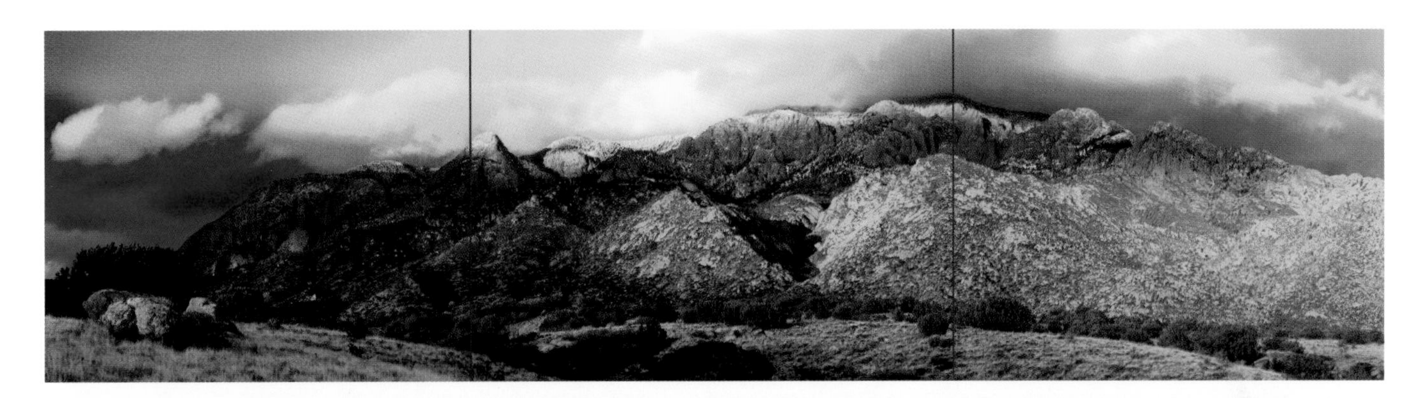

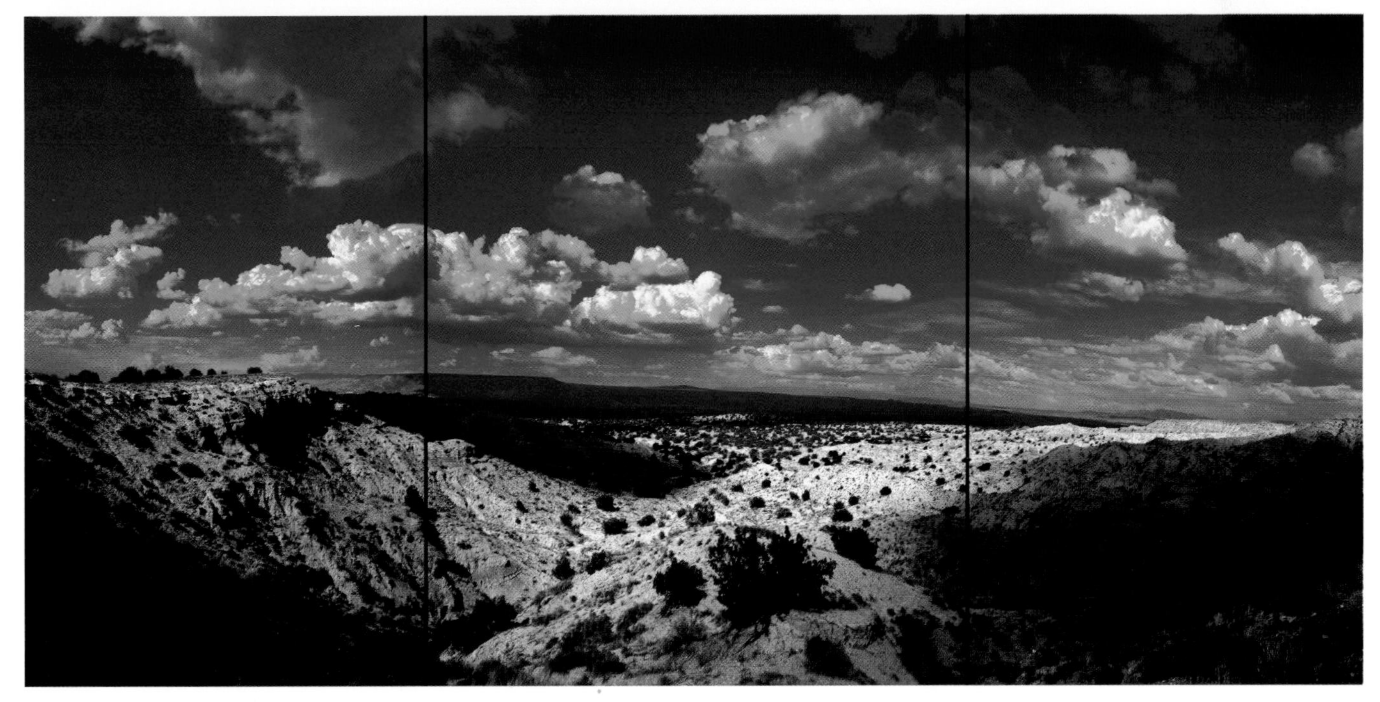

Top: *South Face*, 22" x 84", edition of fifty.
Bottom: *Star Mesa Suite*, 20" x 38" or 30" x 57", edition of twenty-five.

PIA DAVIS

PIA PHOTO ▪ 70 NORTH FRENCH PLACE ▪ PRESCOTT, AZ 86303
TEL 928-778-1227 ▪ FAX 928-443-1929 ▪ PIA@PIAPHOTO.COM ▪ WWW.PIAPHOTO.COM

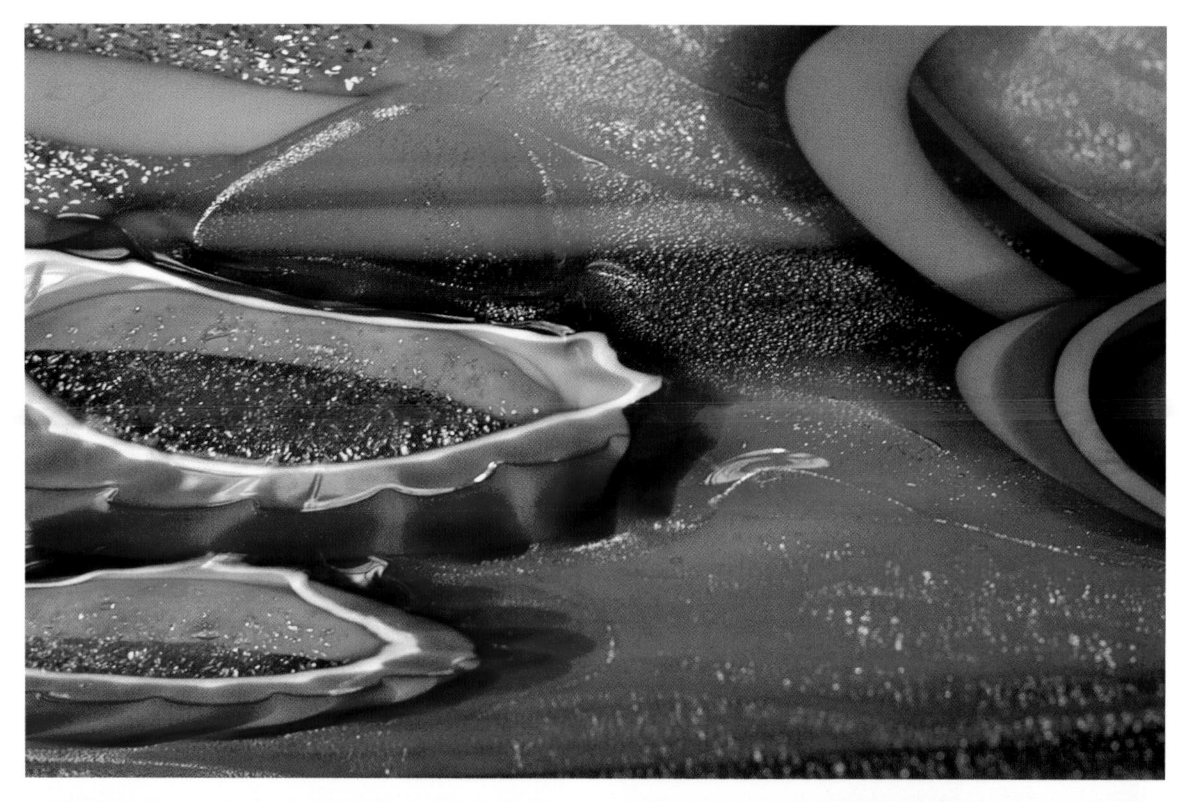

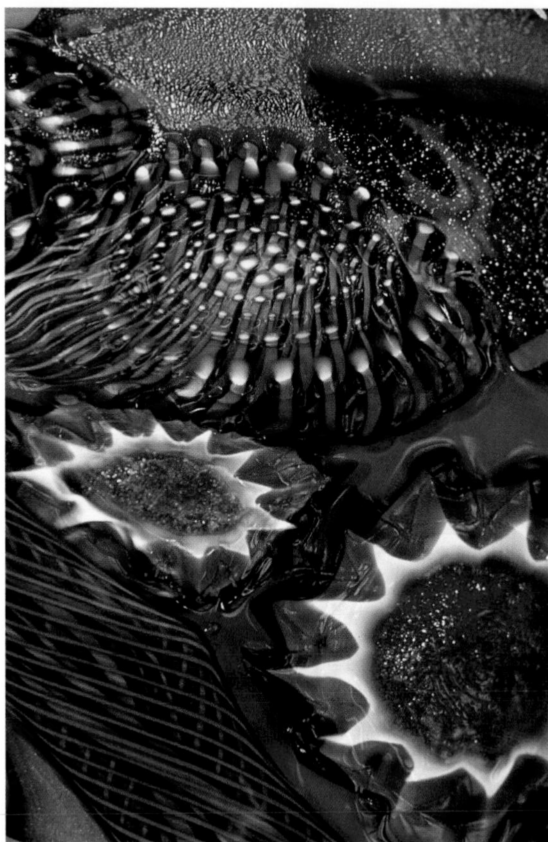

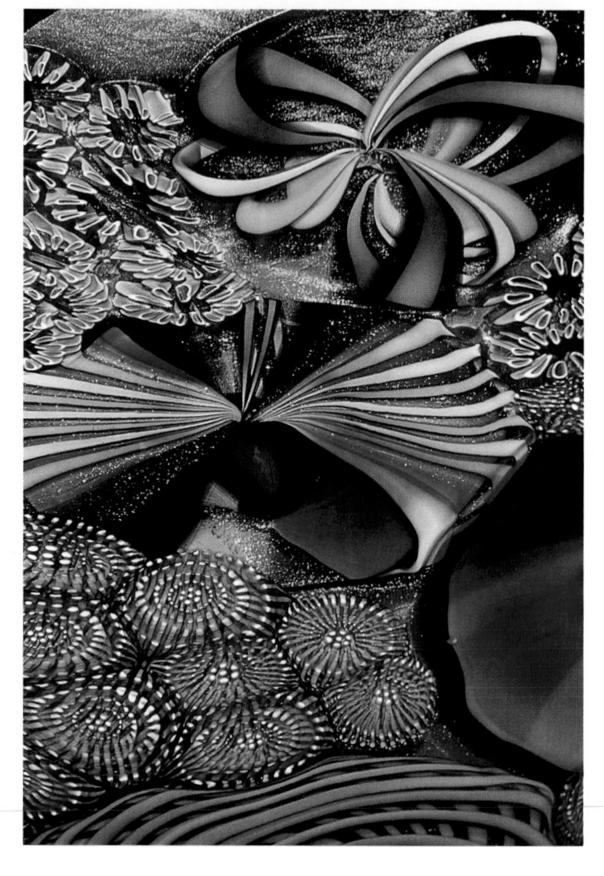

Top: *Magenta Gold.* Bottom left: *Deep Sea Pod.* Bottom right: *Rainforest.* Photographic interpretations of James Nowak's original glass art. Archival giclée prints up to 24" x 36" available individually or in mural combinations.

JOY DOHERTY

ORGANIC IMAGERY ■ 648 HYMETTUS AVENUE ■ ENCINITAS, CA 92024 ■ TEL 760-415-8285
FAX 760-942-0270 ■ E-MAIL JOY@ORGANICIMAGERY.COM ■ WWW.ORGANICIMAGERY.COM

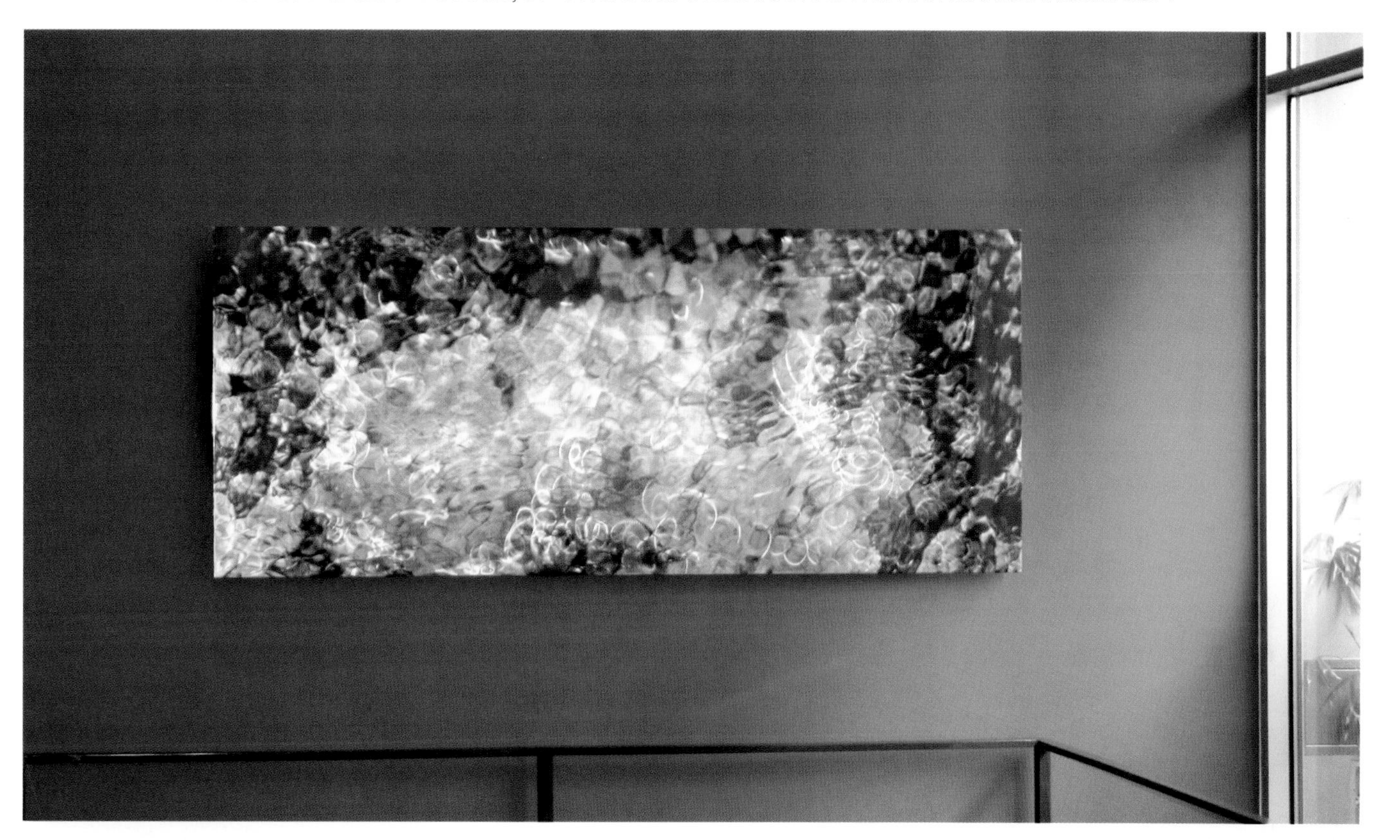

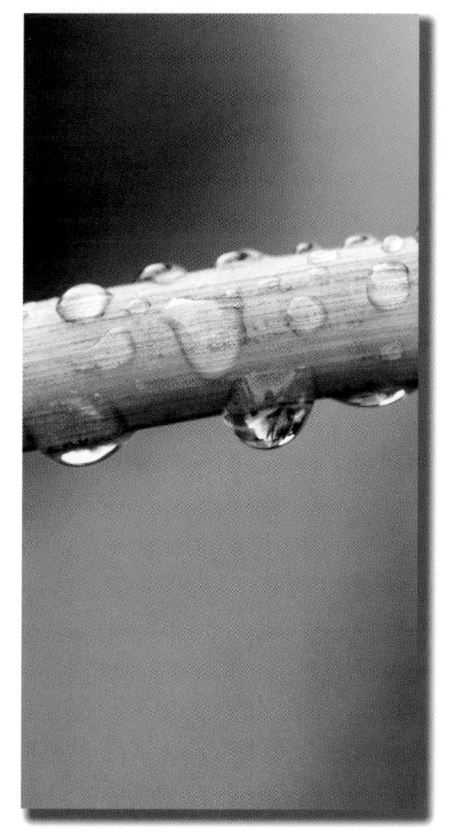

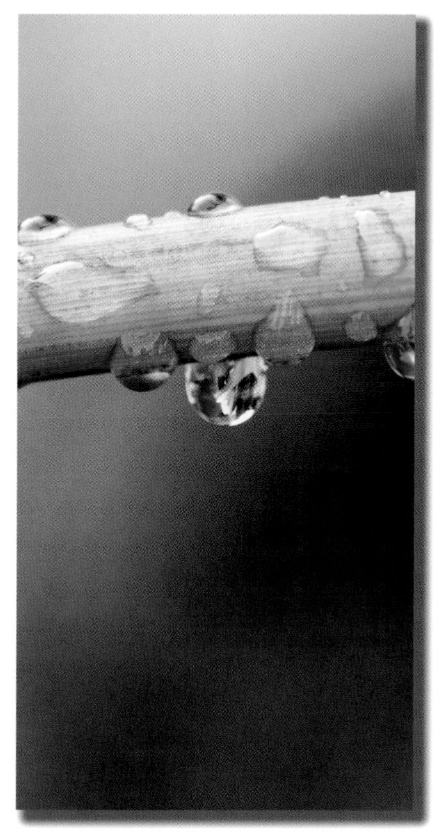

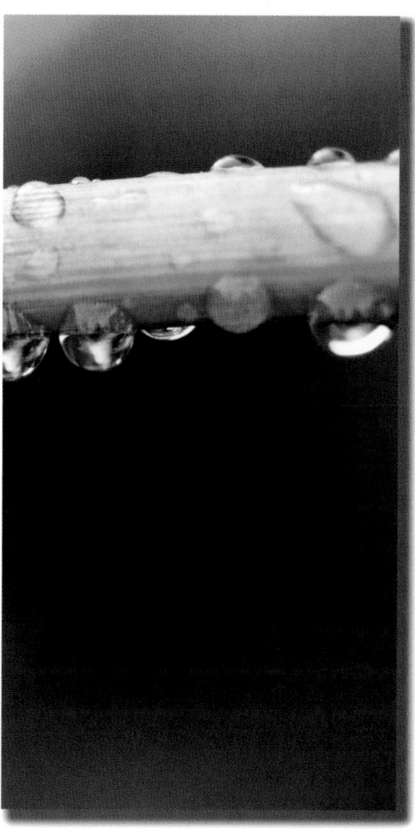

Top: *Yellowstone Ripples*, transparent laminate on textured metal, 30" × 90". Bottom: *Calla Water Drop Stem*, giclée on canvas, each panel: 32" × 16".

CHARLES GROGG

CHARLES GROGG PHOTOGRAPHY ■ 410 GRAND AVENUE ■ OJAI, CA 93023 ■ TEL 805-798-2989
E-MAIL GROGG@CHARLESGROGGPHOTOGRAPHY.NET ■ WWW.CHARLESGROGGPHOTOGRAPHY.NET

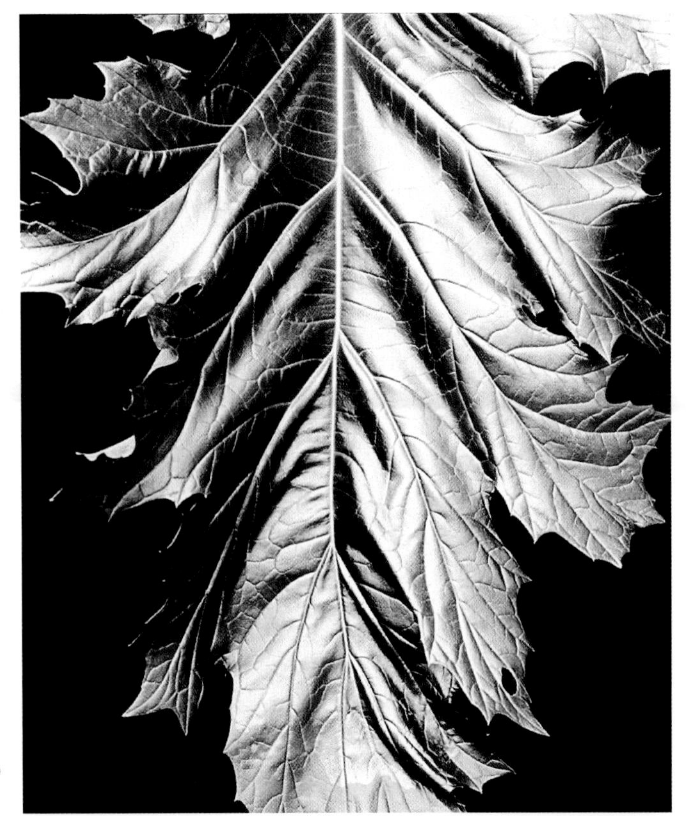

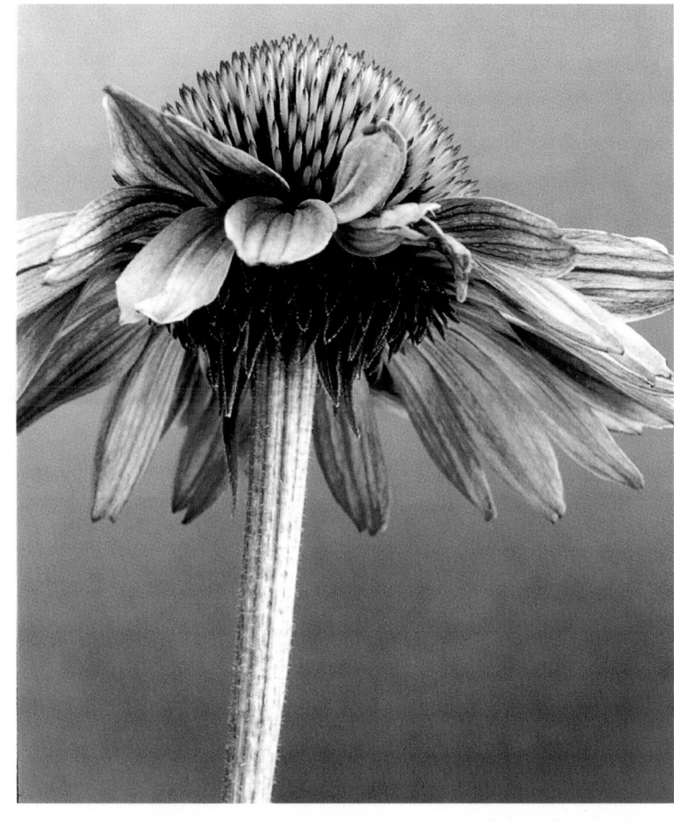

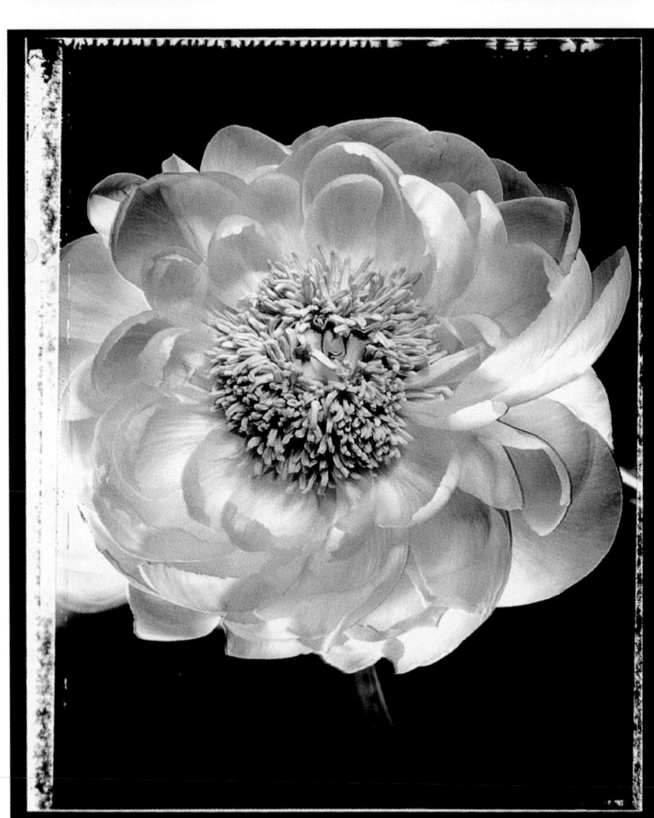

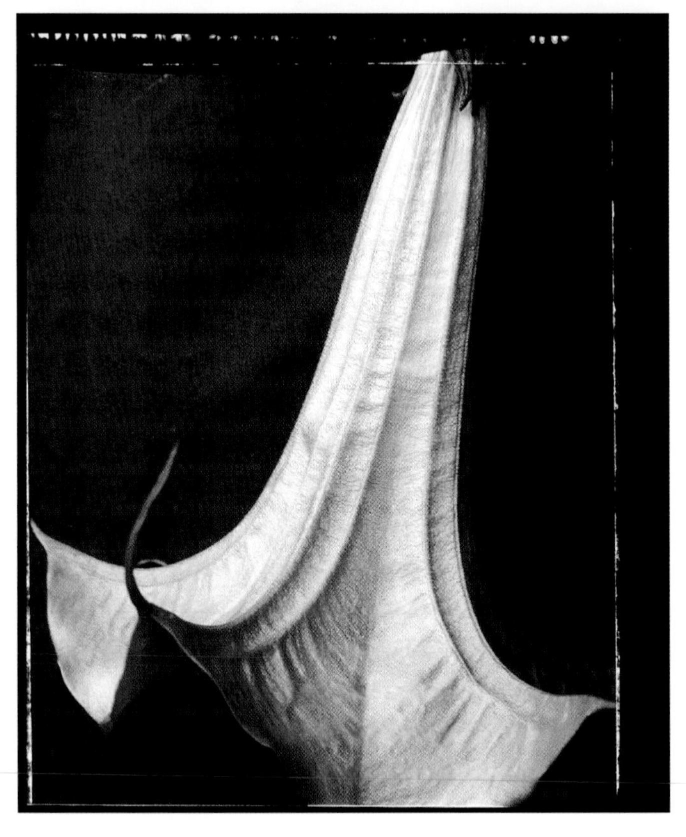

Top left: *Acanthus Leaf.* Top right: *Coneflower.* Bottom left: *Peony #1.* Bottom right: *Datura.*
All images available in 14" x 11" or 24" x 20" sizes.

HENRY DOMKE FINE ART

HENRY F. DOMKE ■ 3914 FOXDALE ROAD ■ NEW BLOOMFIELD, MO 65063
TEL 573-295-6349 ■ E-MAIL HENRY@HENRYDOMKE.COM ■ WWW.HENRYDOMKE.COM

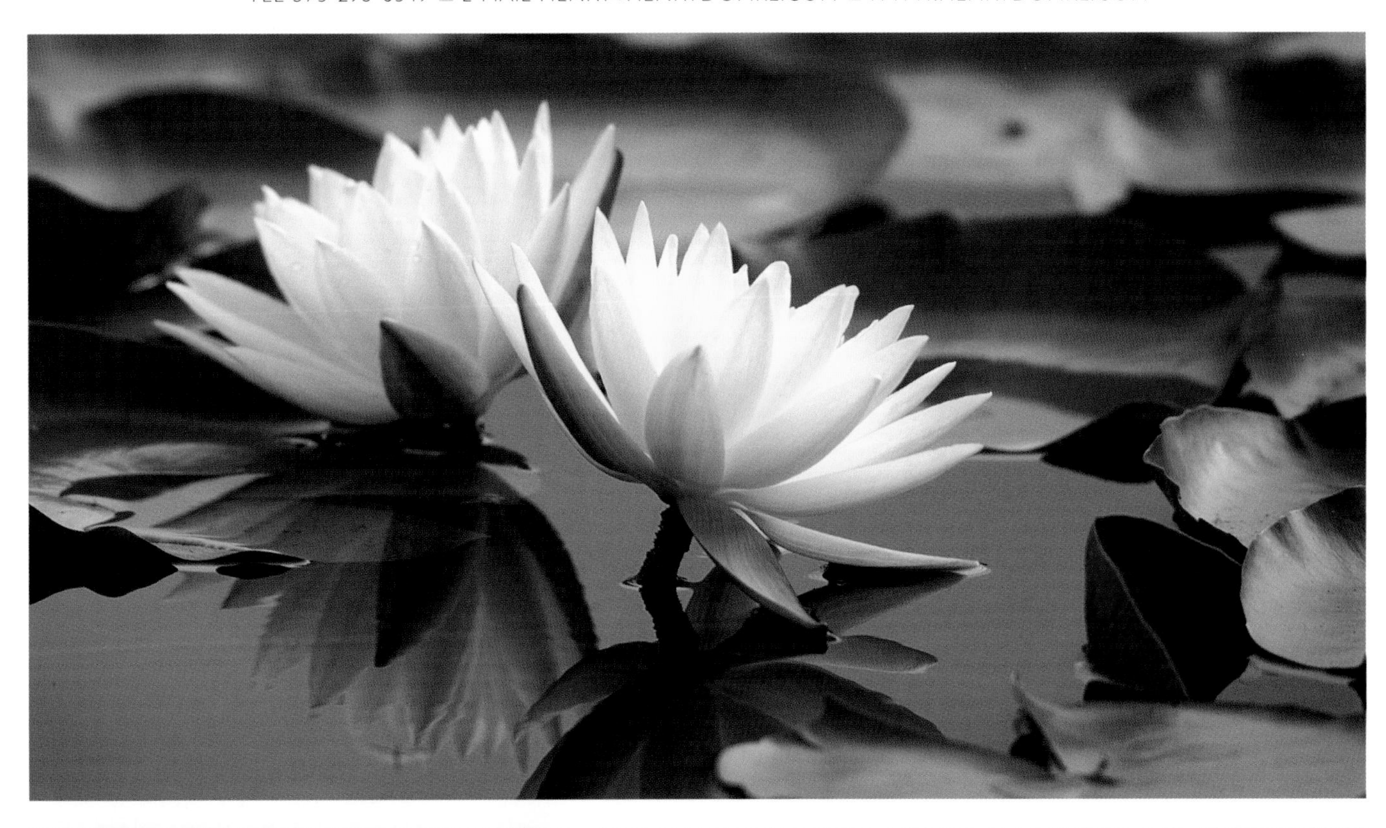

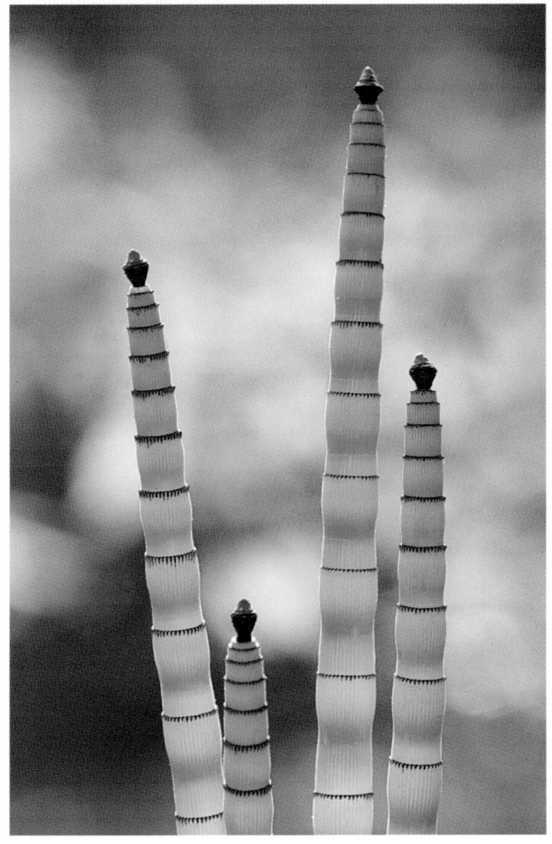

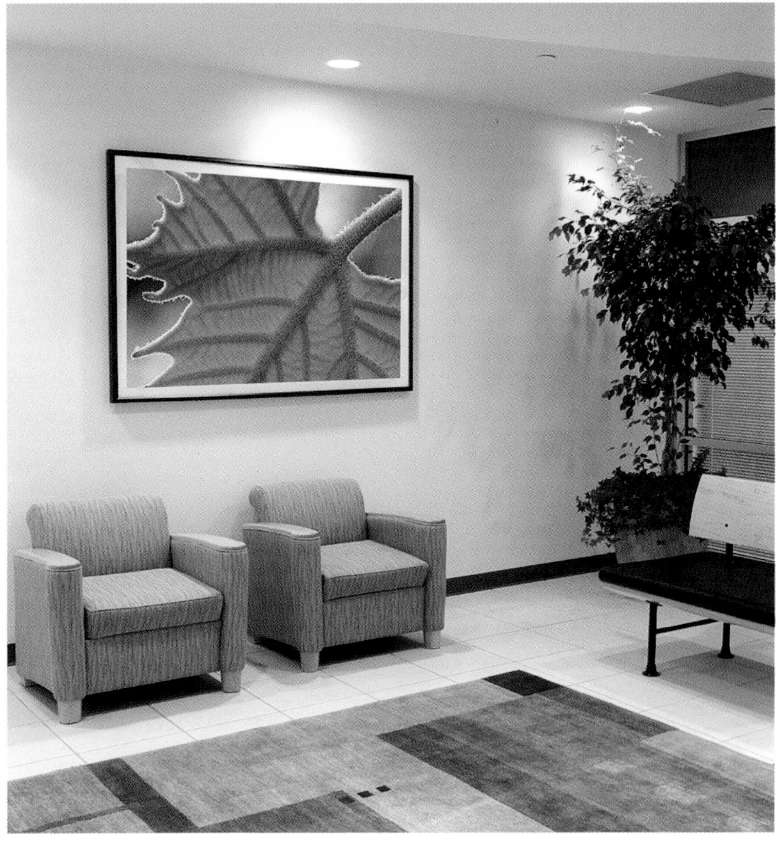

Top: *Water Lily 13548*. Bottom left: *Horse Tail 5723*. Bottom right: *Sycamore 8837*, Westminster College.

KIM ELLEN KAUFFMAN

SYNECDOCHE STUDIO ■ 712 TERMINAL ROAD ■ LANSING, MI 48906 ■ TEL/FAX 517-321-2815
E-MAIL KIM@SYNECDOCHESTUDIO.COM ■ WWW.SYNECDOCHESTUDIO.COM

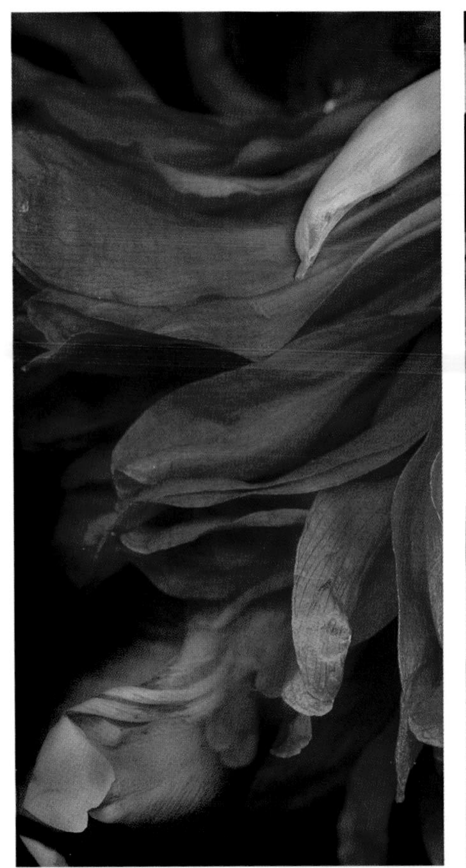

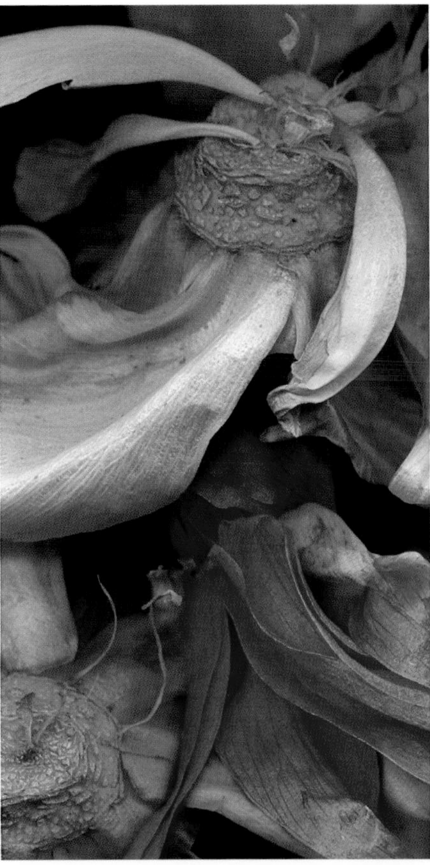

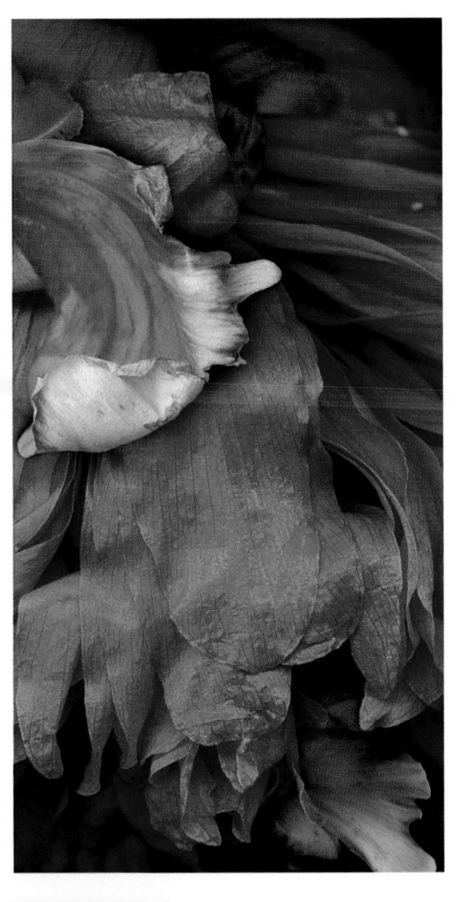

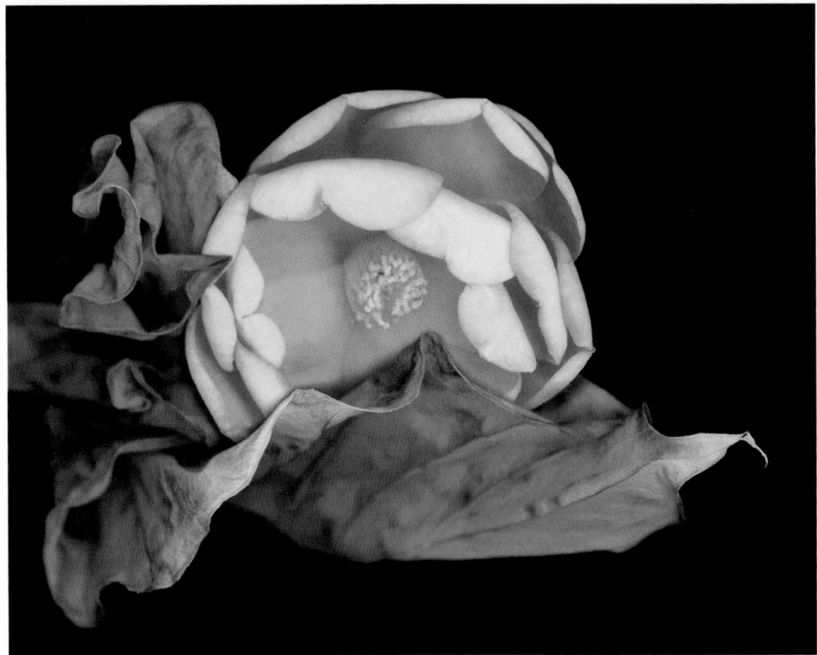

Flamenco and *Amor*, part of the *Florilegium* series of limited-edition photo collages from multiple scans of original objects.

PAULA STOEKE

2525 MICHIGAN AVENUE STUDIO A-6 ■ SANTA MONICA, CA 90404
TEL 310-573-1800 ■ FAX 310-264-2403 ■ WWW.PAULASTOEKE.COM

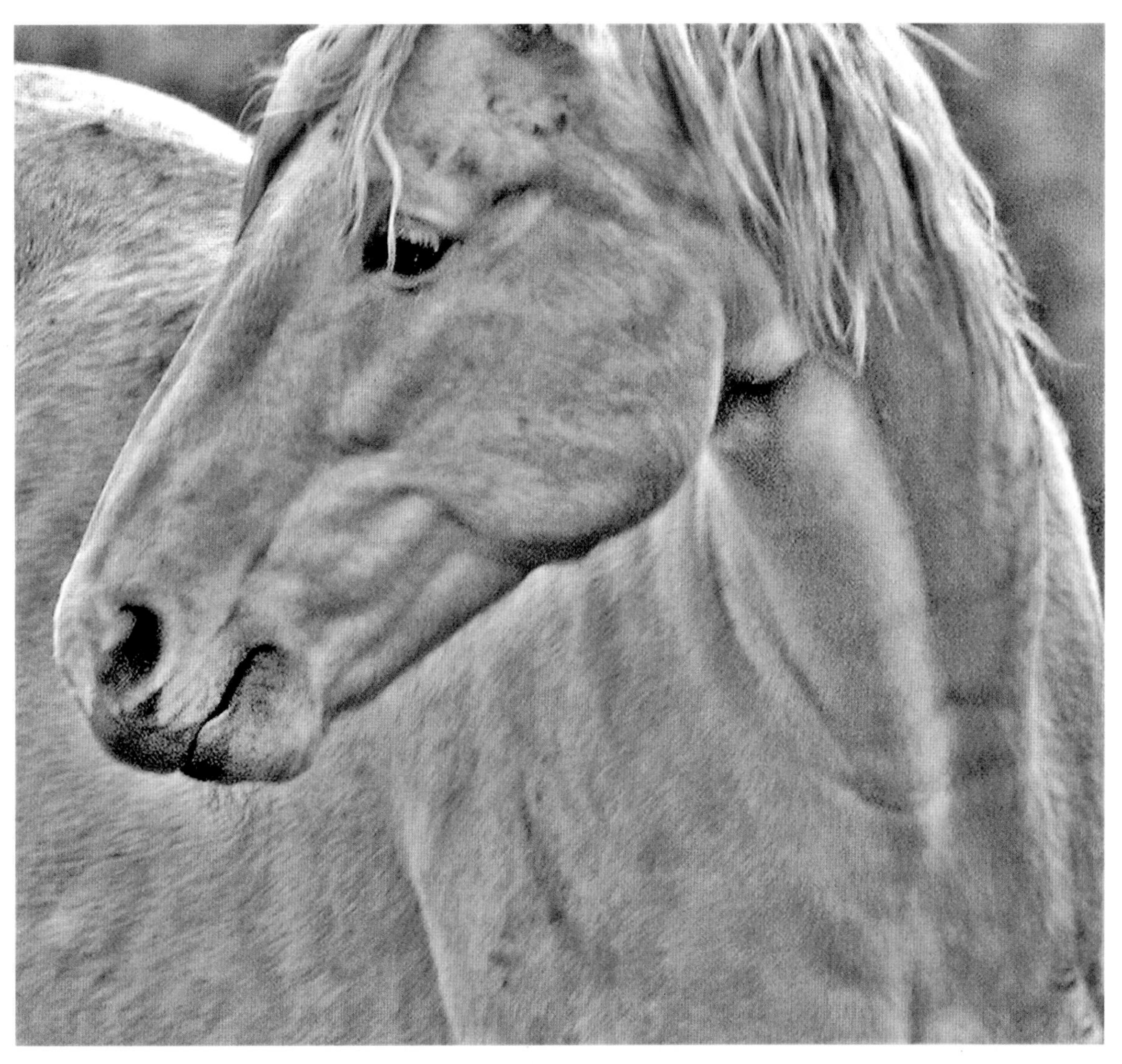

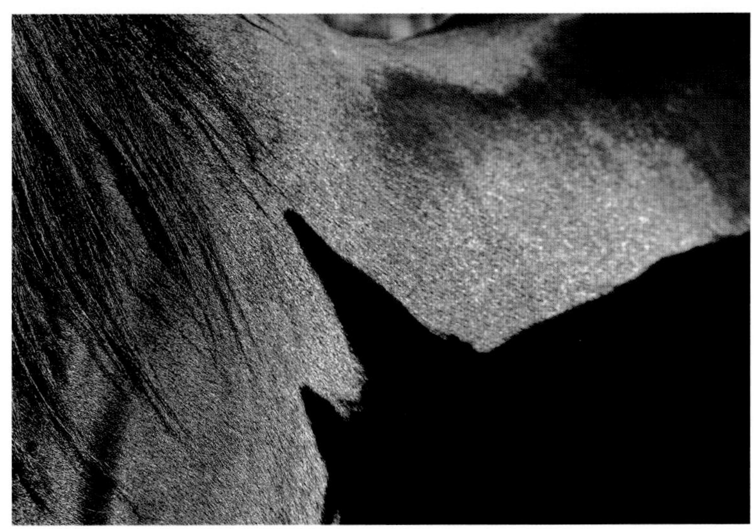

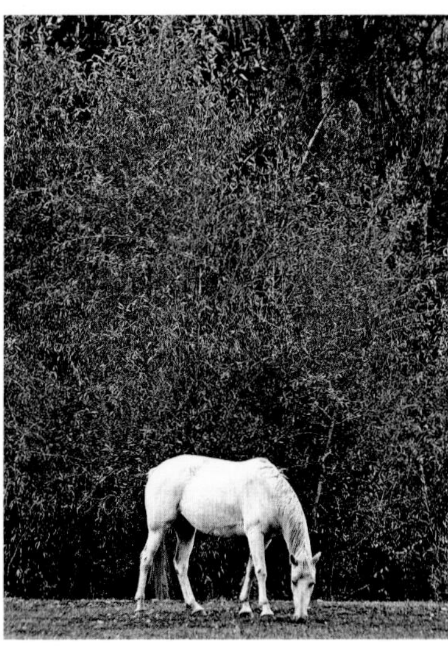

Top: *Emperor*. Bottom left: *Part of the Whole*. Bottom right: *Avalon*. All works are from the series *Horse: Messenger from Another Place and Time*, and are available as giclée prints.

©2005 Paula Stoeke *all rights reserved*

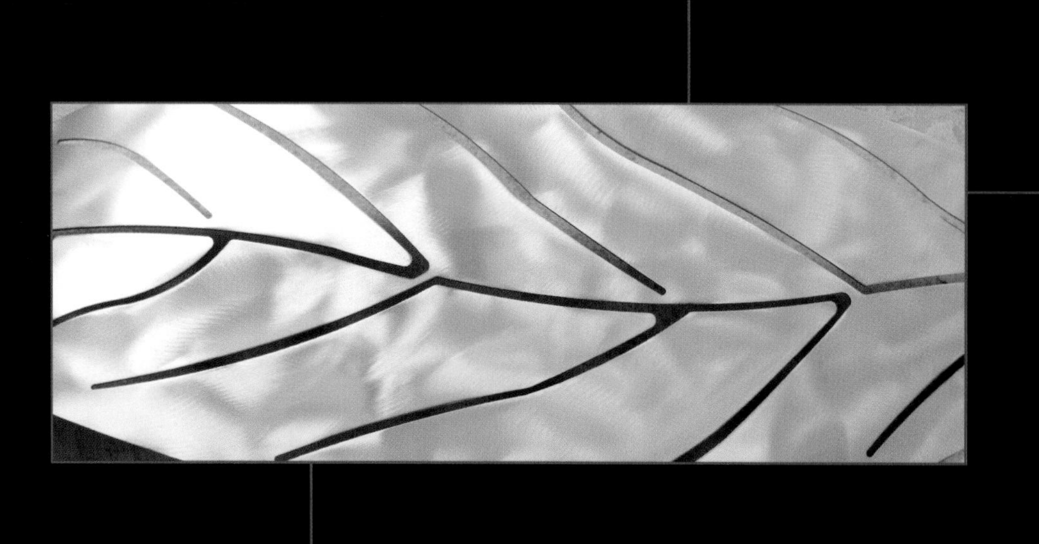

Metal Wall Art

RICARDO CABRERA

ARTESANO IRON WORKS GALLERY ■ 4446 CRESSON STREET ■ PHILADELPHIA, PA 19127
TEL 215-483-9273 ■ FAX 215-483-9274 ■ WWW.ARTESANOIRONWORKS.COM

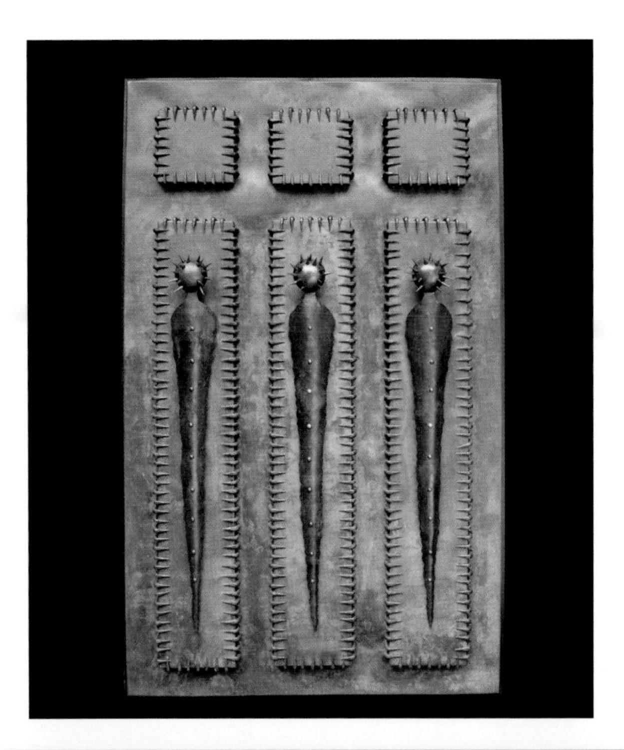

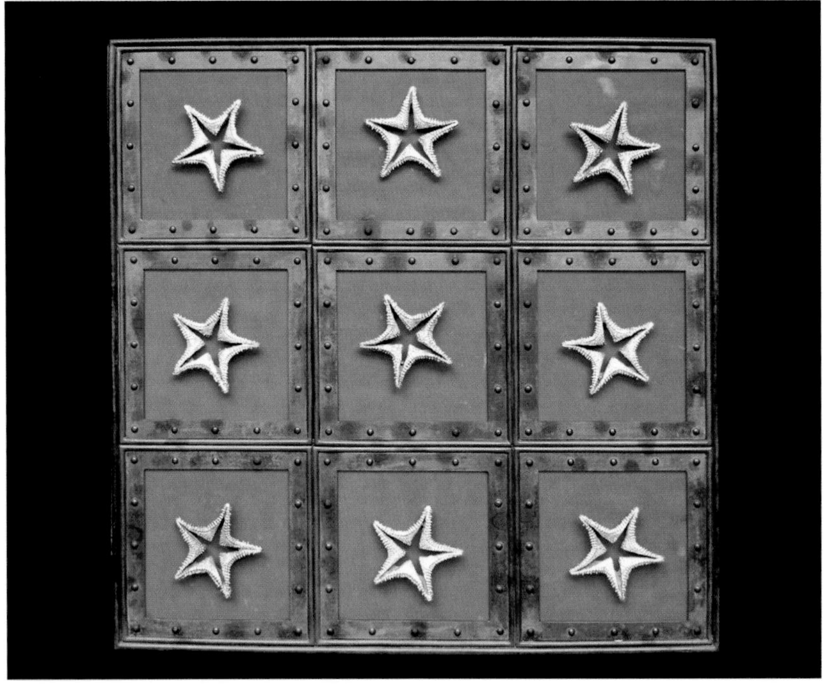

Top: *Three Graces*, iron on iron, 60" x 40". Bottom: *Depths*, bronze and oil on iron, 53" x 53".

LINDA LEVITON

LINDA LEVITON SCULPTURE ■ 1011 COLONY WAY ■ COLUMBUS, OH 43235
TEL 614-433-7486 ■ E-MAIL GUILD@LINDALEVITON.COM ■ WWW.LINDALEVITON.COM

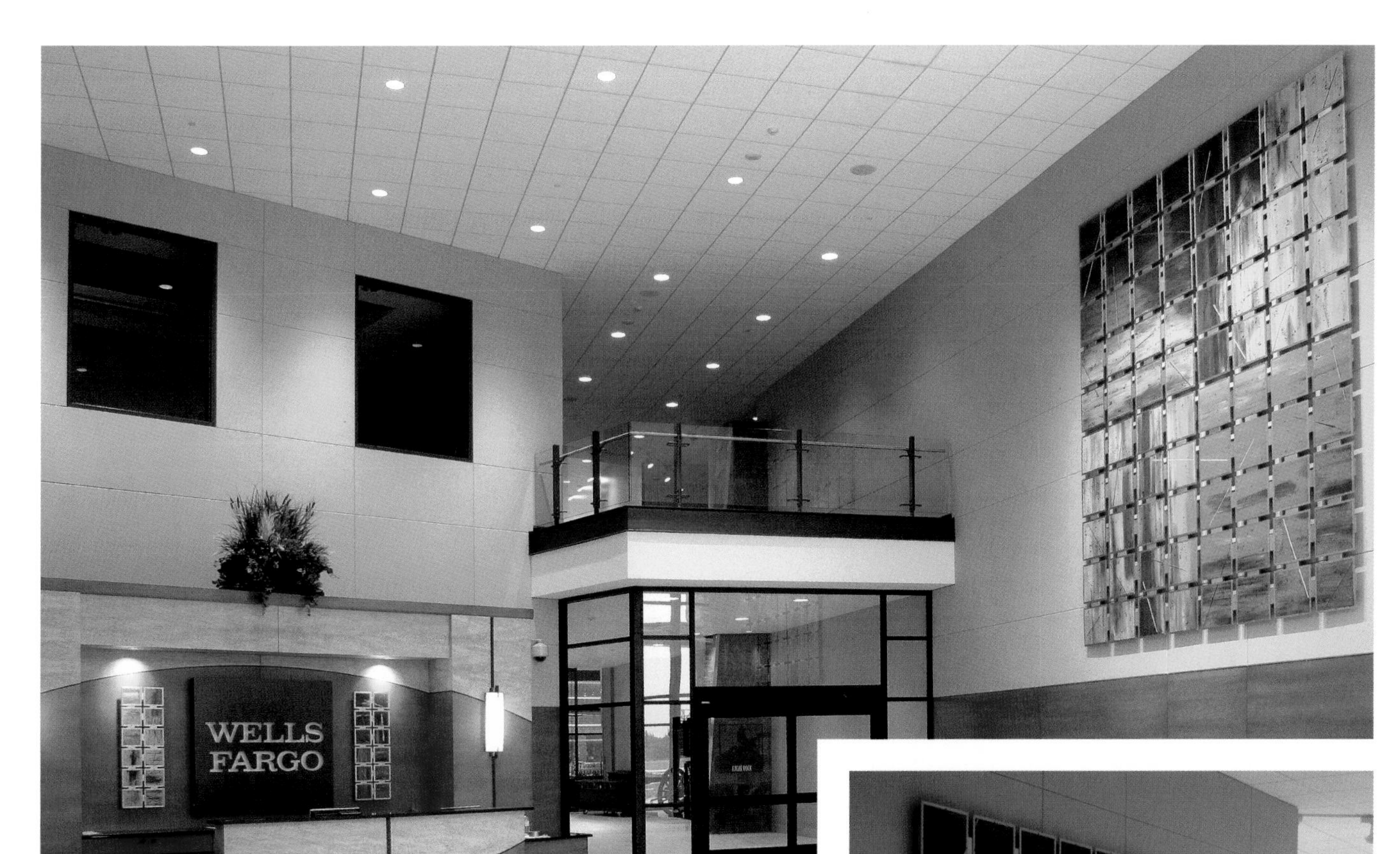

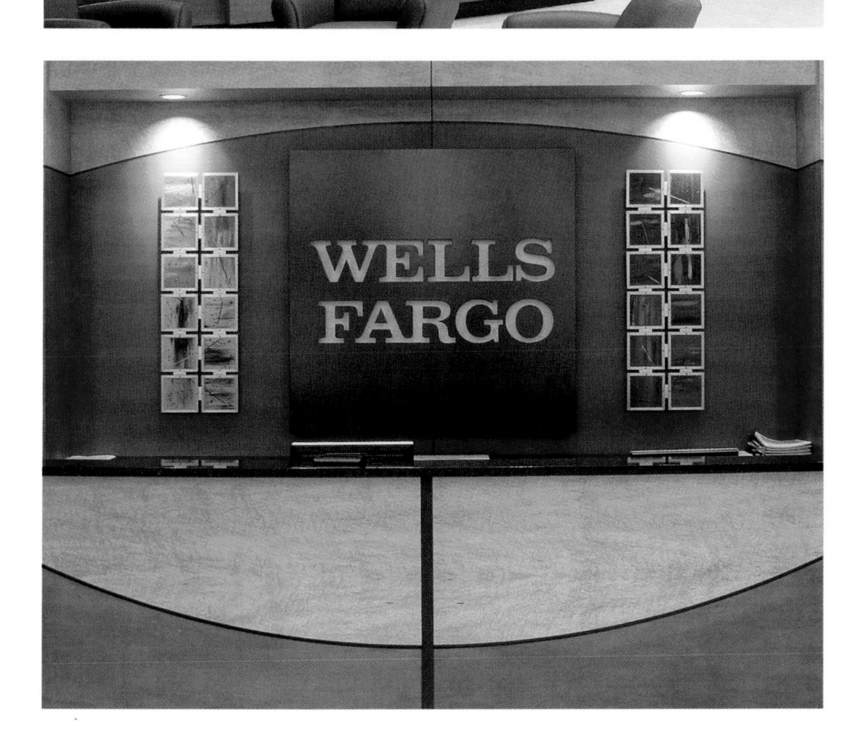

Pick-Up Sticks, copper, wood, paint, and patina, 15'H x 12'W x 3"D. Bottom left: Two panels, 14" x 44" each panel. Bottom right: View from balcony.

A Commission Story

Richard Taylor

TITLE
Blue Sky Between Footsteps, 2006

COMMISSIONED FOR
General Mitchell International Airport,
Milwaukee, WI

TIMELINE: 1 year

DIMENSIONS: Suspended portions (2): 10'H x 14'L x 2'D;
Wall-mounted panels (22): 2'H x 8'L

TRADE PROFESSIONAL
Edward A. Baisch, Acting Airport Engineer,
General Mitchell International Airport

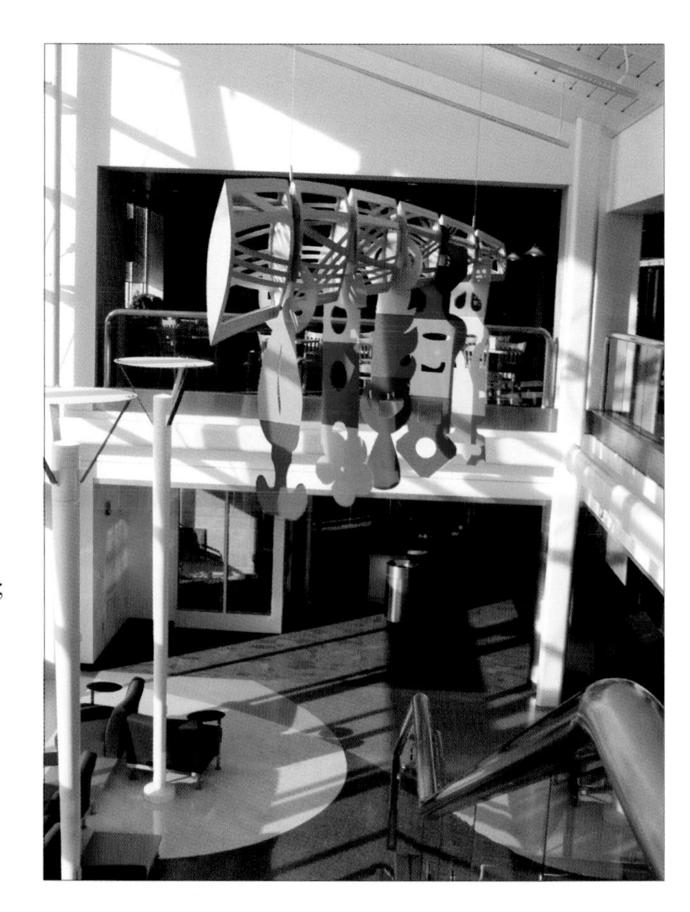

Richard Taylor enjoys a good challenge—and that's just what was presented to him when he won the commission to install his brilliant metal sculptures in Milwaukee's General Mitchell International Airport. ■ Acting Airport Engineer Ed Baisch recalls the situation: "We were significantly reconfiguring the layout of the stem portion of Concourse D," hub of hometown air carrier Midwest Airlines. "In the process of integrating art into the architectural design of the project, two areas were identified as good candidates: an existing wall of dark glass along a moving walkway, and the new two-story lounge areas." ■ Tasked with expressing what Taylor describes as "a hint of aeronautics," the artist responded with a lyrical interpretation of travel. "The two suspended pieces have a "backbone" reminiscent of aircraft wings, but I opened up the wings and have some flowing, linear patterns that to me could represent airflow, flying, music, rhythms of dance, many different things," he explains. "The colorful elements are composed of shapes of found objects that I've been collecting over the last five or six years during walks in places where I travel. There's certain poetry in these found objects; each one has its own story. They allow us to retrace steps, to take new ones, or to imagine those of others." ■ Taylor's enigmatic shapes reappear on twenty-two powder-coated aluminum panels, which enliven the formerly dreary black glass wall beside the moving walkway. The bright color palette was inspired more by emotion than the strict dictates of interior design. "I wanted something uplifting, fanciful, whimsical, a visual spark," Taylor explains. "The airport is either a spark for the beginning of someone's journey or a celebration of the end. It seemed appropriate to me to have bit of that celebration in the artwork itself." ■ Ed Baisch appreciates the tone Taylor's sculptural pieces set in this post-9/11 era, pointing out, "If you're a nervous flyer, the feeling that the artwork gives you is something easy, colorful, and calming."

SUSAN McGEHEE

METALLIC STRANDS ■ 540 23RD STREET ■ MANHATTAN BEACH, CA 90266 ■ TEL 310-545-4112
FAX 310-546-7152 ■ E-MAIL METALSTRANDS@AOL.COM ■ WWW.METALSTRANDS.COM

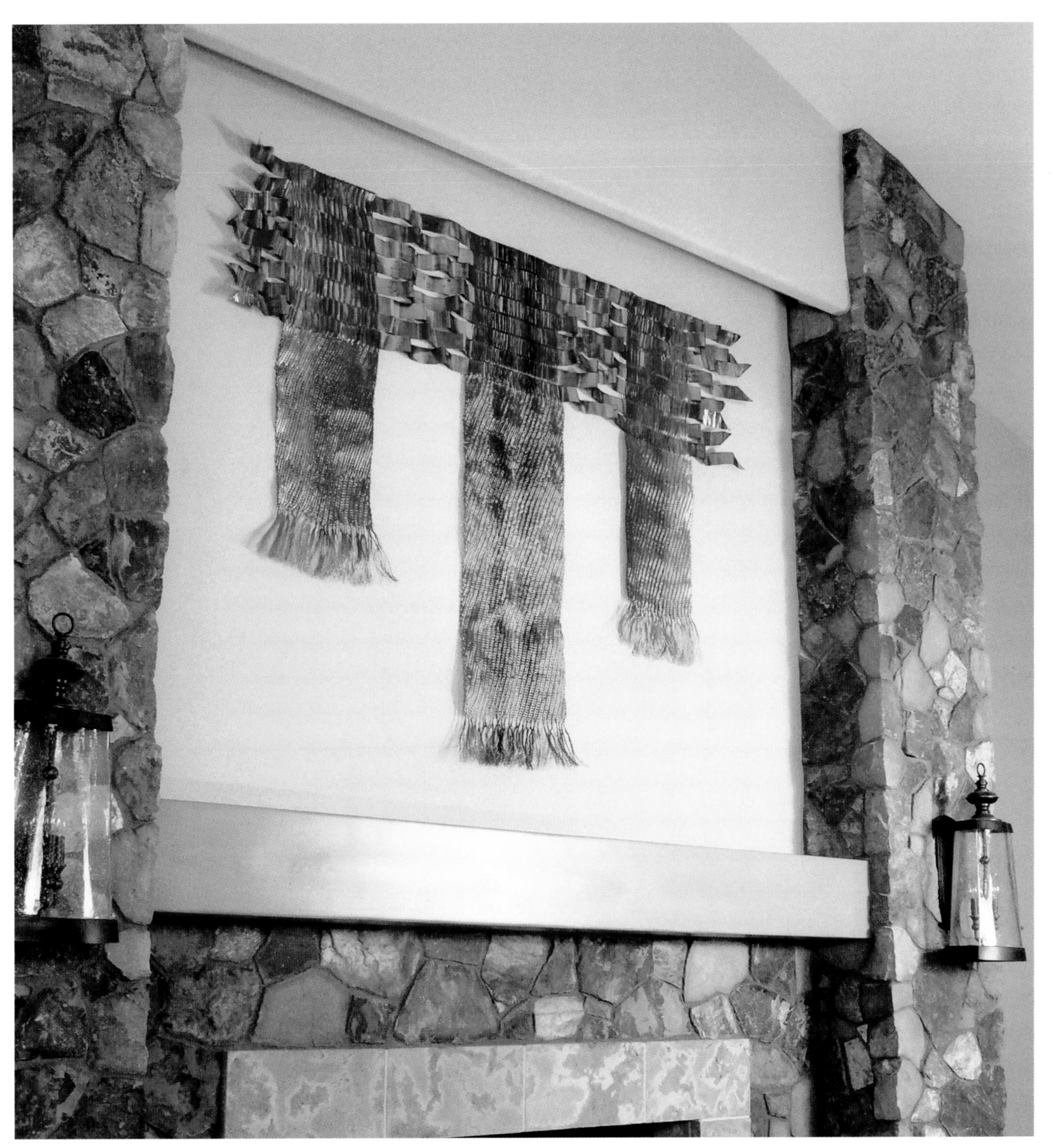

Commission for Pauma Country Club, Pauma Valley, CA, woven anodized aluminum wire and copper, 6' x 5.5'. Photograph: Andrew Neuhart.

BOB RICKARD

PO BOX E ■ TAOS, NM 87571 ■ TEL 505-770-8287
E-MAIL BOB@BOBRICKARD.COM ■ WWW.BOBRICKARD.COM

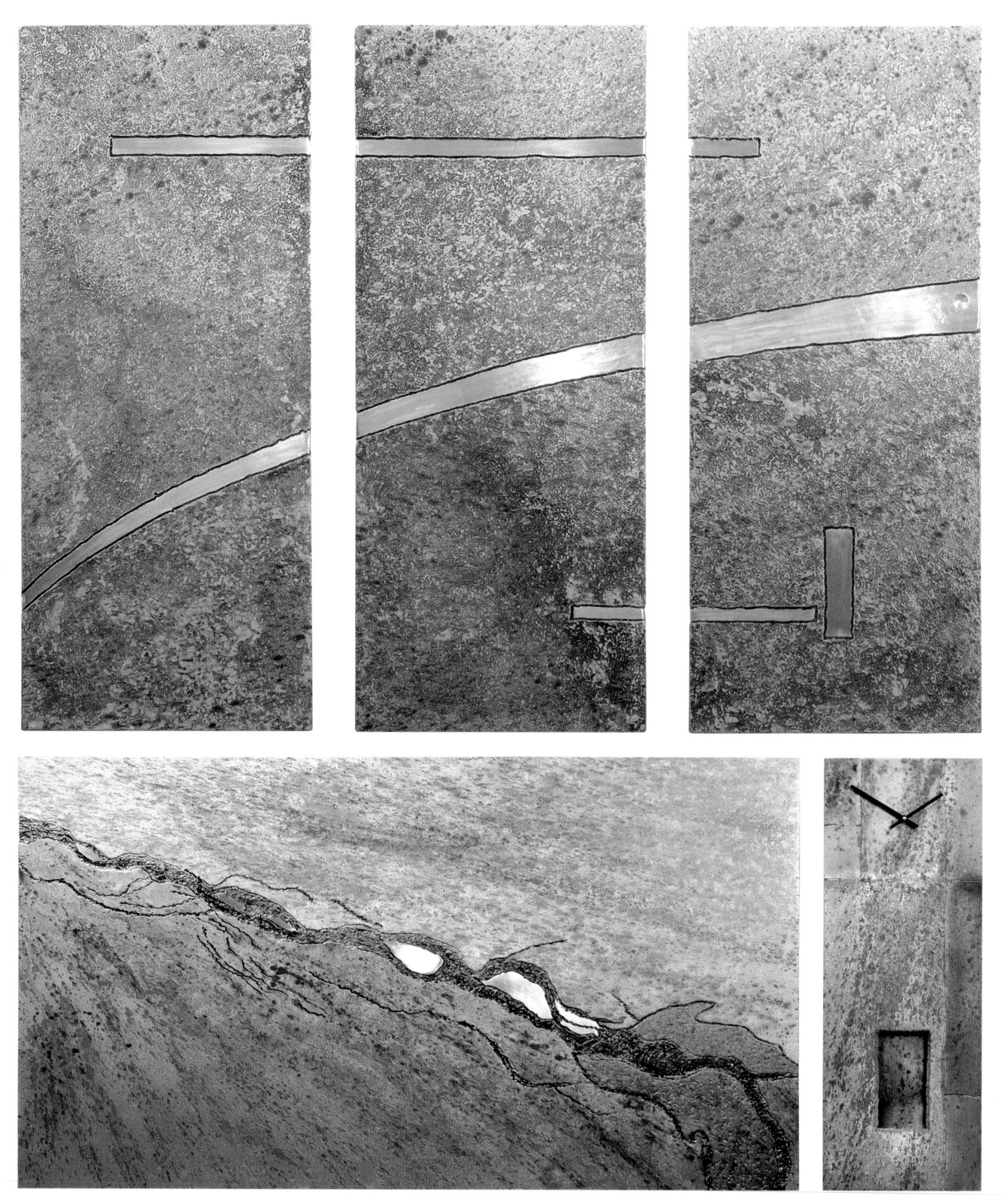

Top: *Valle Lindo,* 2006, patinaed and dyed copper, bronze, silver, and iron over aluminum, 38" × 52". Bottom left: *Tombouctou,* patinaed and dyed copper, bronze, silver, and iron over aluminum, 26" × 48". Bottom right: *Mondrian Redux,* pendulum wall clock, 2006, 28.5" × 10.5".

MARSH SCOTT

2795 LAGUNA CANYON ROAD #C ■ LAGUNA BEACH, CA 92651 ■ TEL 949-494-8672
E-MAIL MARSH@MARSHSCOTT.COM ■ WWW.MARSHSCOTT.COM

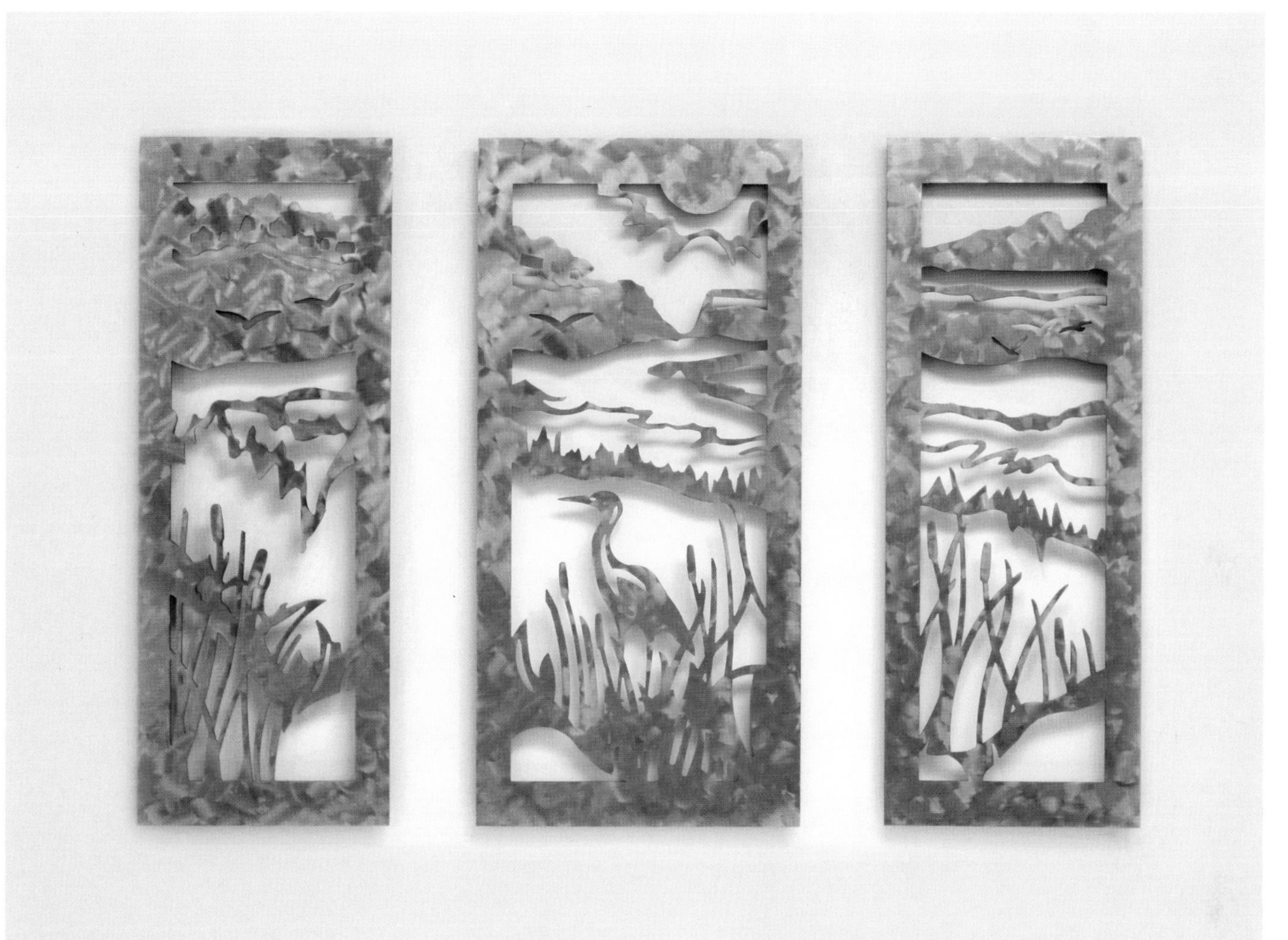

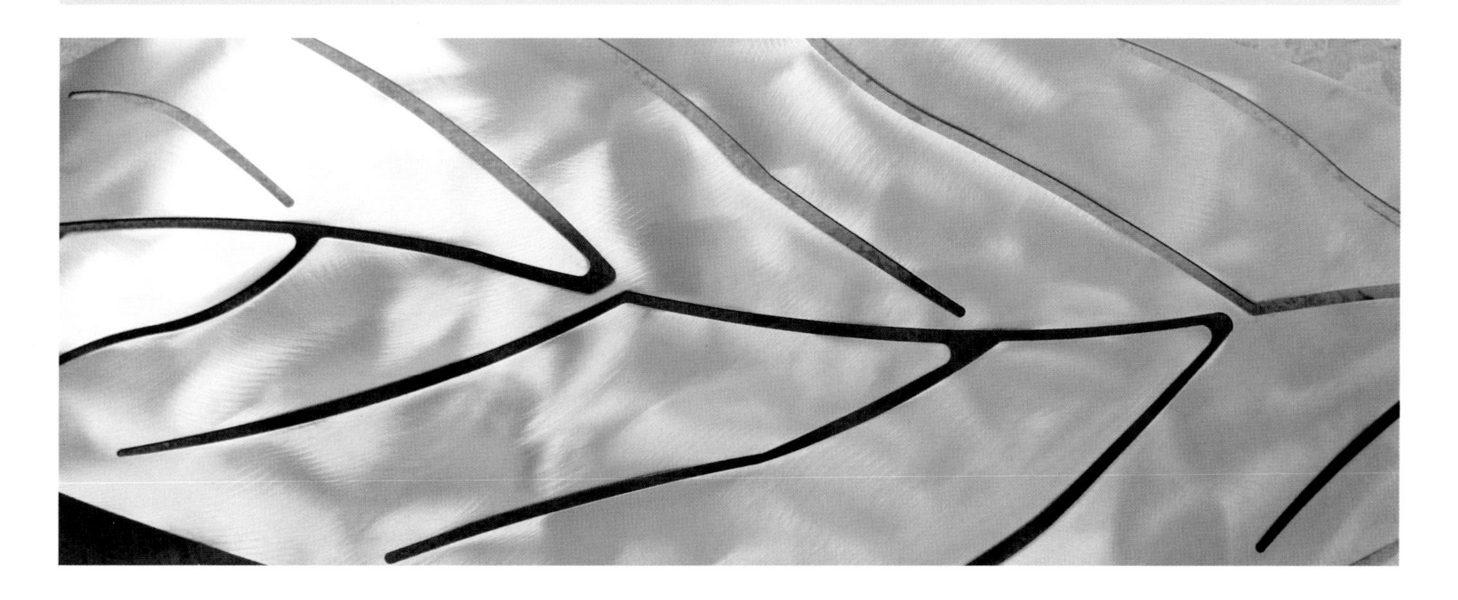

Top: *Back Bay Wandering,* Pfizer, Irvine, CA, stainless steel, 60" x 84".
Bottom: *Drifting Leaves* (detail), Flowers Hospital, Dothan, AL, suspended stainless steel sculpture, variable dimensions.

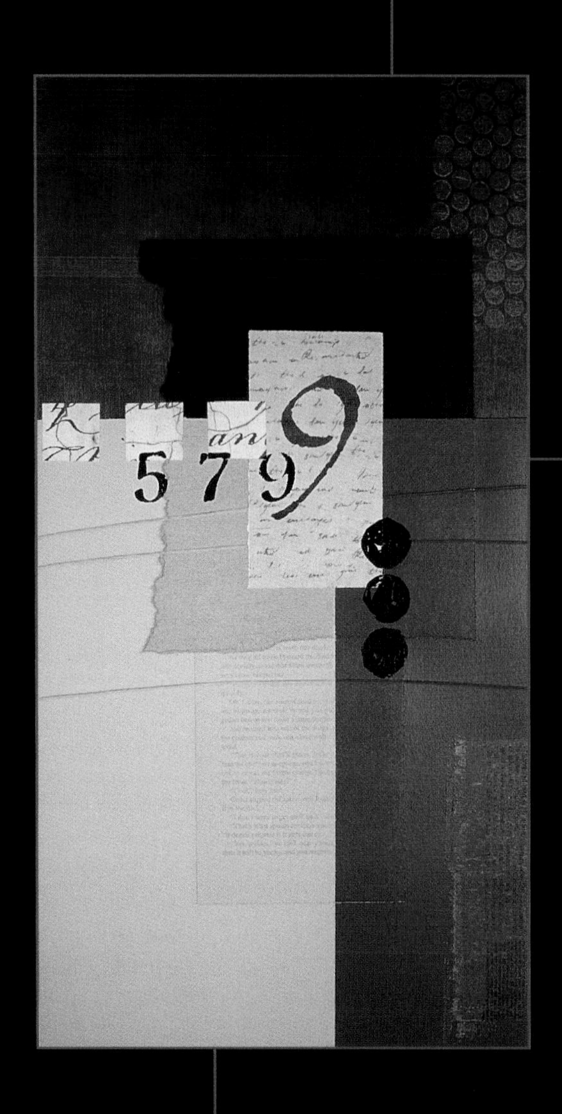

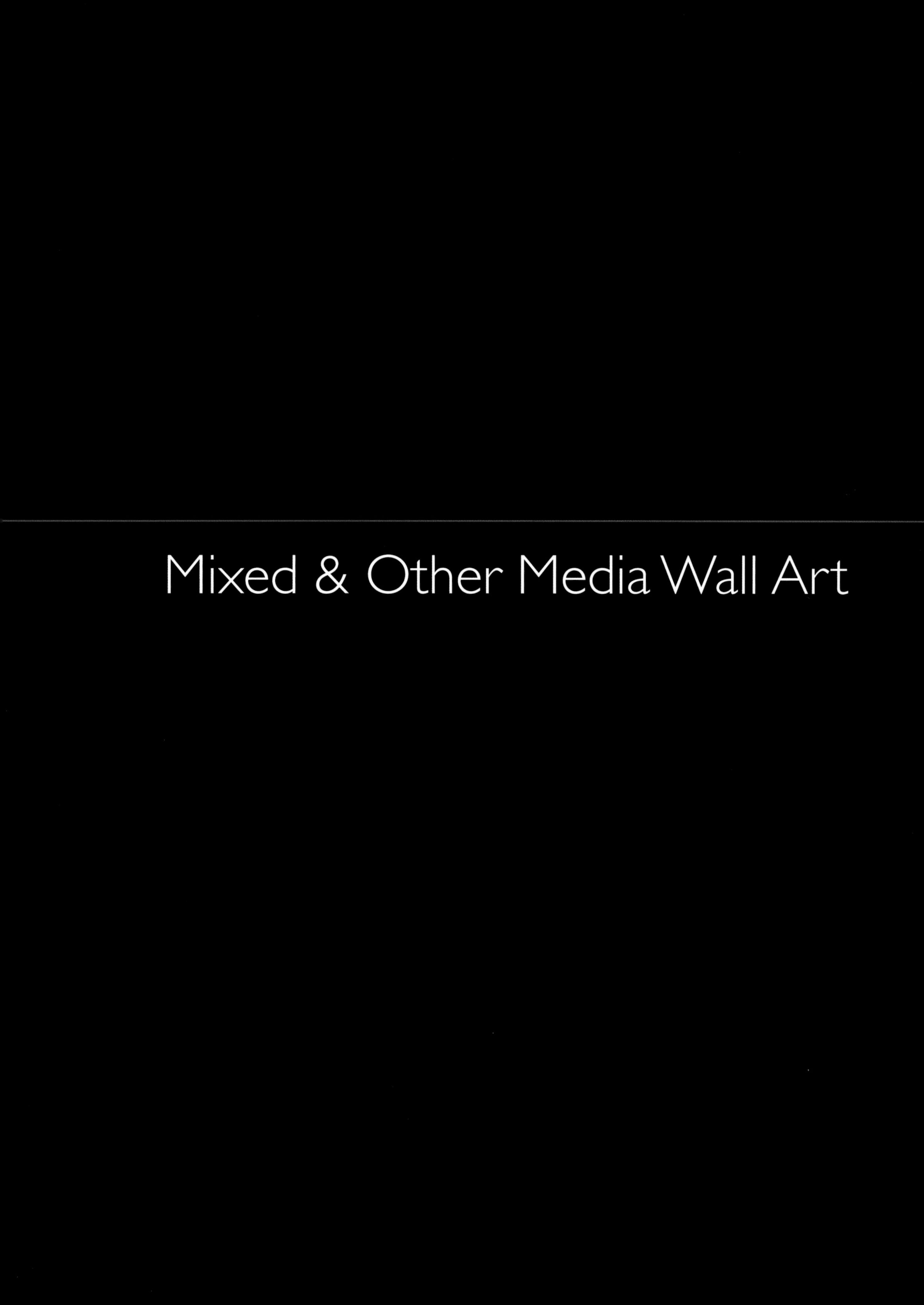

Mixed & Other Media Wall Art

CHRISTIAN BURCHARD

COLD MOUNTAIN STUDIO ■ 777 POMPADOUR DRIVE ■ ASHLAND, OR 97520
TEL/FAX 541-482-1916 ■ E-MAIL BURCHARD@HUGHES.NET ■ WWW.BURCHARDSTUDIO.COM

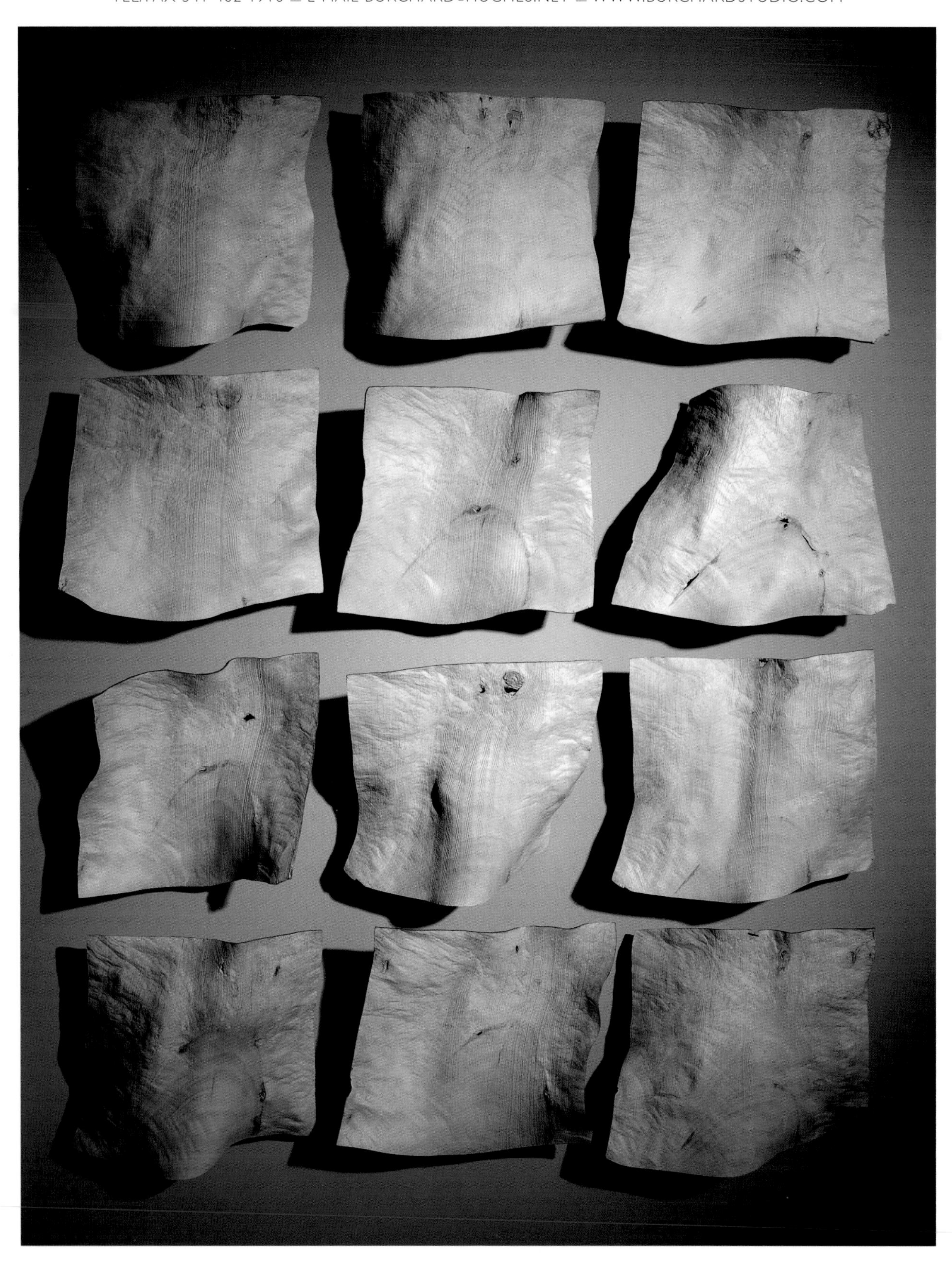

Fragments #2, bleached madrone burl, 72"H x 54"W x 6". Photograph: Rob Jaffe.

ALONZO DAVIS

4410 OGLETHORPE STREET #609 ■ HYATTSVILLE, MD 20781 ■ TEL 301-454-0433
E-MAIL ALONZODAVIS@YAHOO.COM ■ WWW.ALONZODAVIS.COM

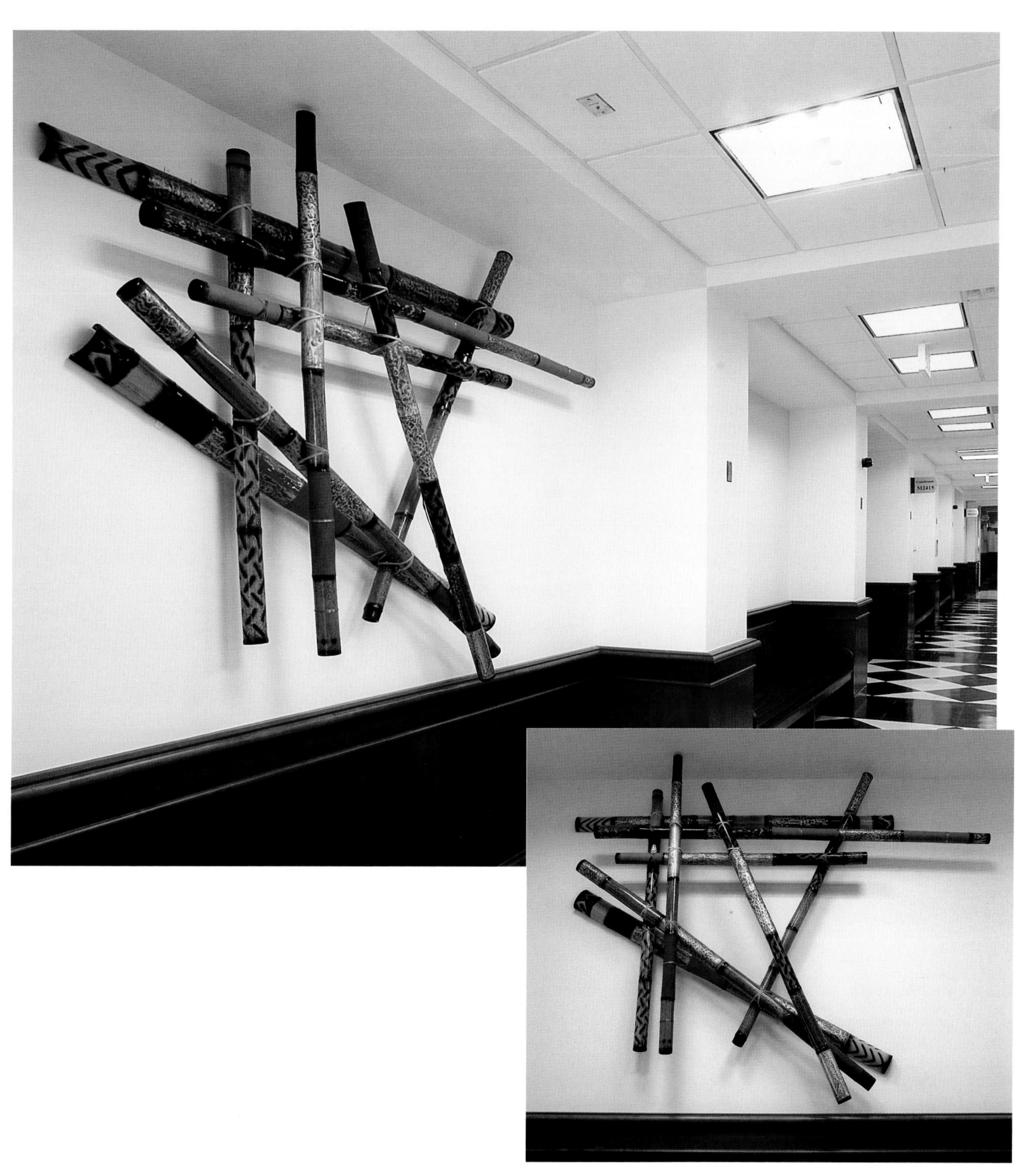

Judicial Balance. Photographs: Joseph Hyde.

RON FOSTER

379 LA PERLE PLACE ■ COSTA MESA, CA 93627 ■ TEL 949-650-0662
E-MAIL RON@RONFOSTERDESIGN.COM ■ WWW.RONFOSTERDESIGN.COM

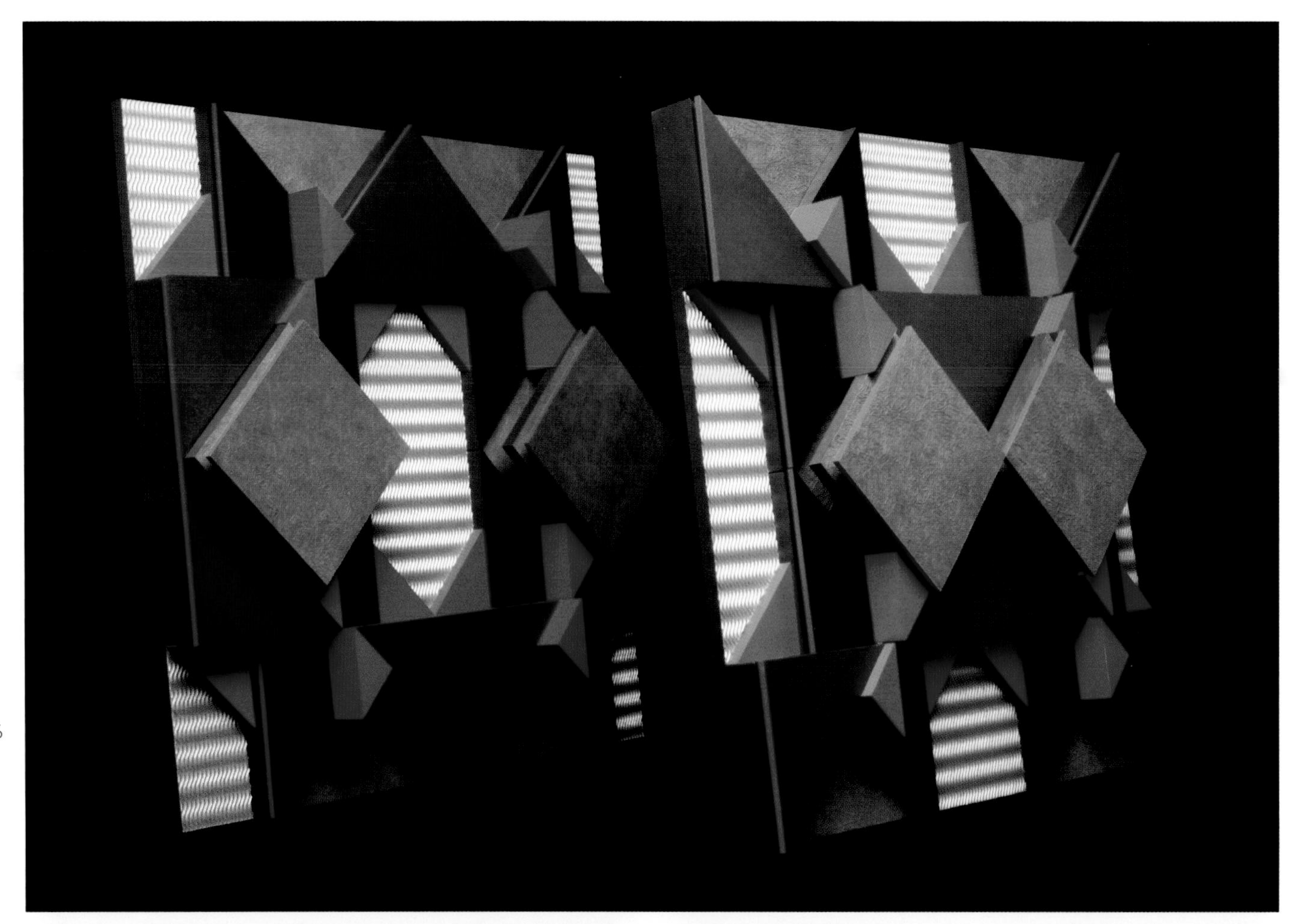

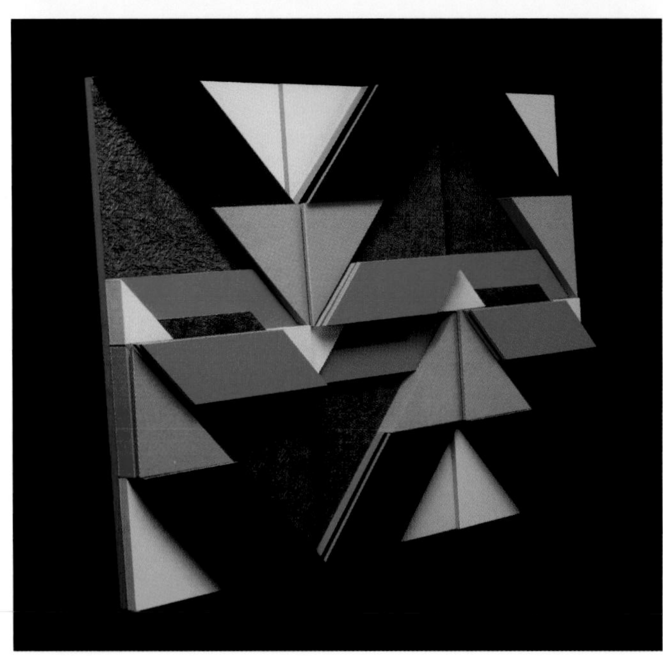

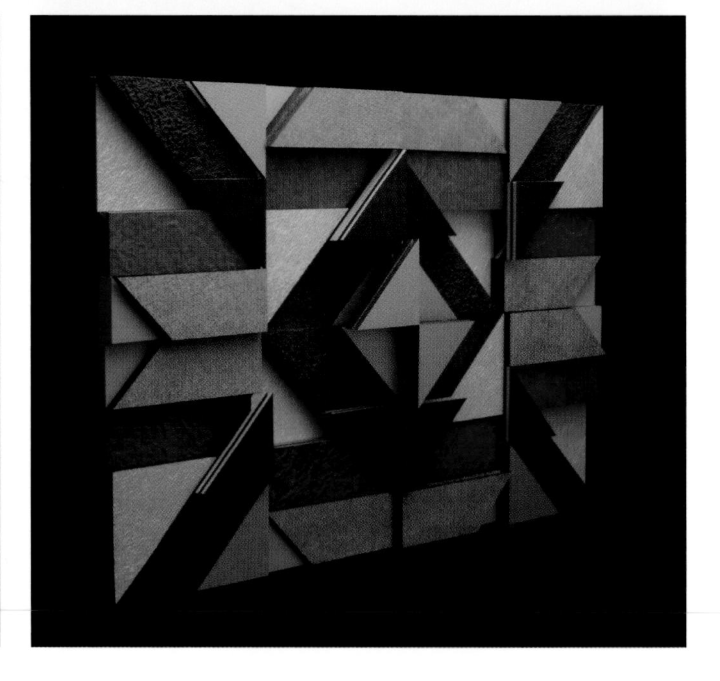

Top: *Purple Kaleidosculpture*™, mixed media: paper, fabric, wood, and foam core, each: 2' x 2'. Bottom left: *Teal Kaleidosculpture*™, mixed media: paper, fabric, wood, and foam core, 2' x 4'. Bottom right: *Orange Kaleidosculpture*™, mixed media: paper, fabric, wood, and foam core, 2' x 4'. Photographs: Bill Reiff.

NINA GABRIEL

18741 HATTERAS STREET UNIT 2 ■ TARZANA, CA 91356 ■ TEL 818-776-8526 ■ TEL 818-406-3579
FAX 818-450-0479 ■ E-MAIL NINAGABRIEL@SBCGLOBAL.NET ■ WWW.NINAGABRIEL.COM ■ WWW.NINAGABRIEL.NET

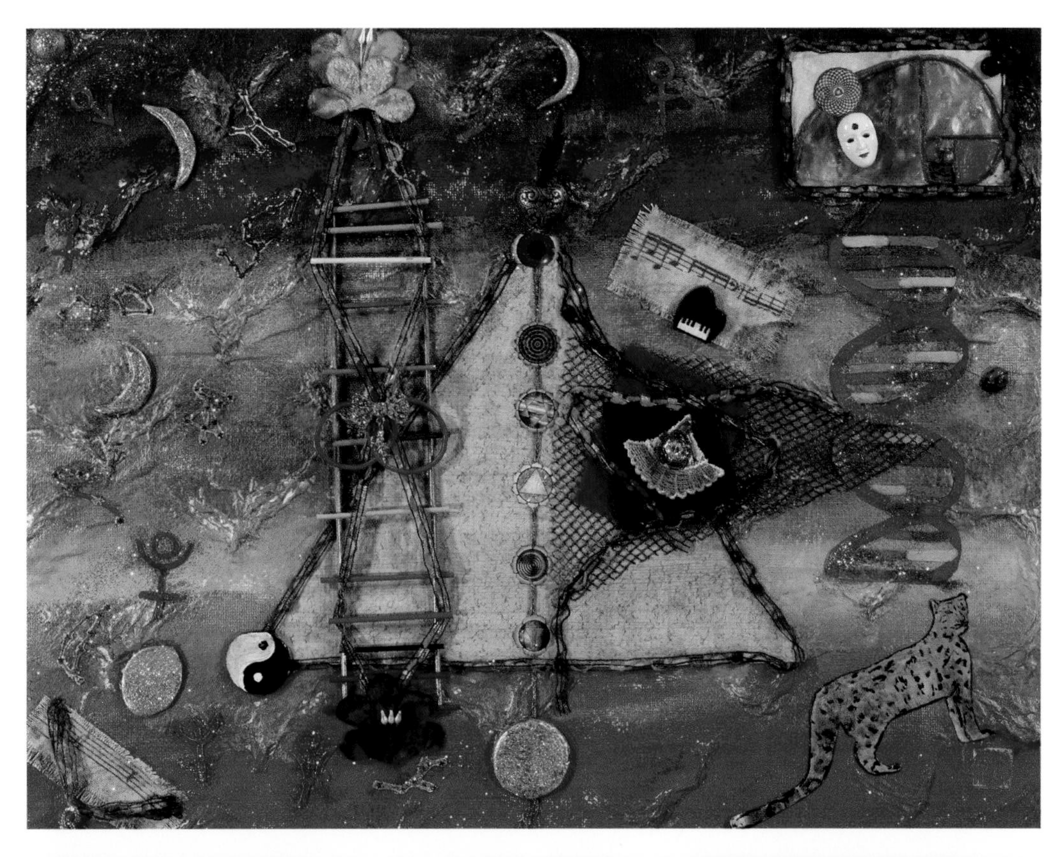

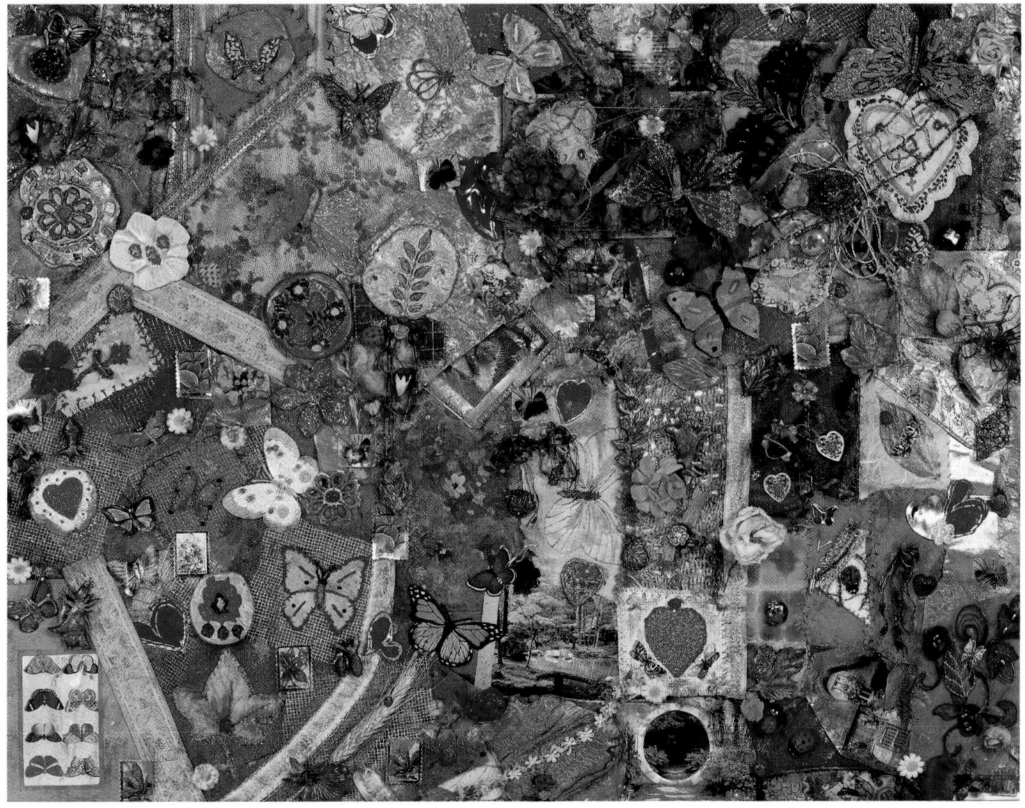

Top: *The Path of the Soul,* 2004, mixed media, 16" x 20"; framed: 19.5" x 23.5".
Bottom: *Metamorphosis #2,* mixed media, 26" x 32"; framed: 27" x 33". Photographs: Paul Jonason Photography.

GEORGE HANDY ARTWORKS INC.

2 WEBB COVE ROAD ■ ASHEVILLE, NC 28804 ■ TEL 828-254-4691
E-MAIL GEORGE@GEORGEHANDY.COM ■ WWW.GEORGEHANDY.COM

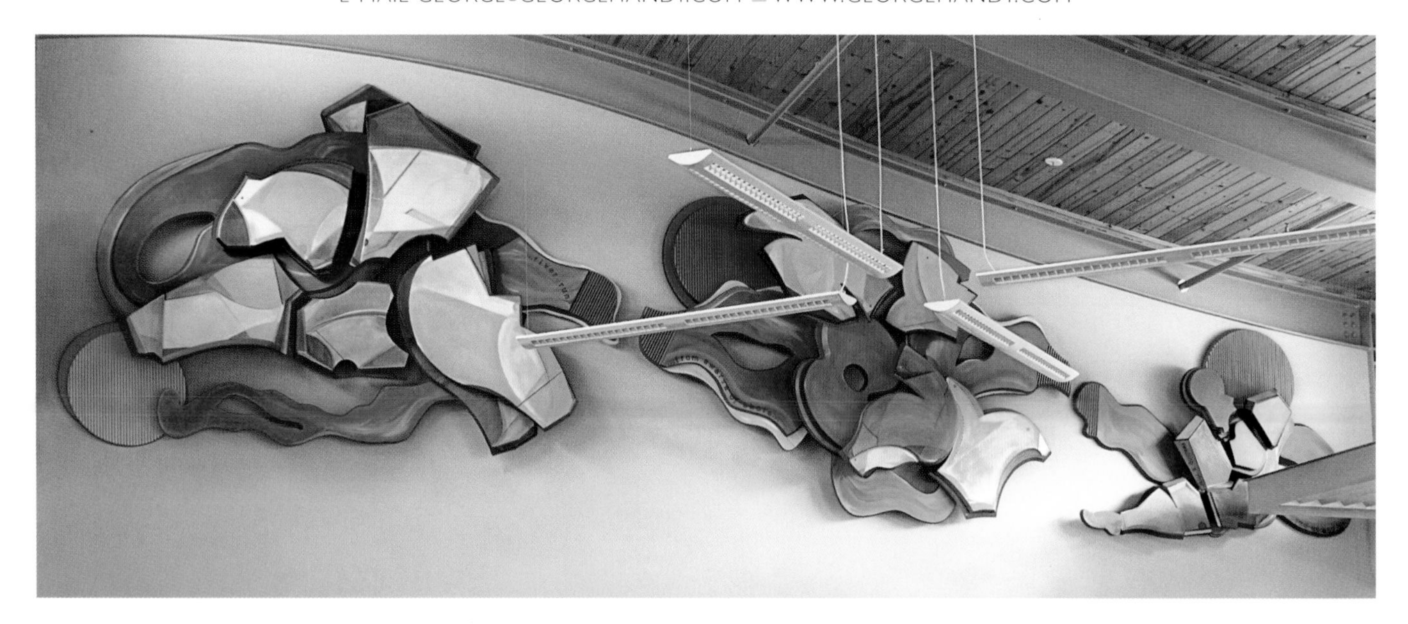

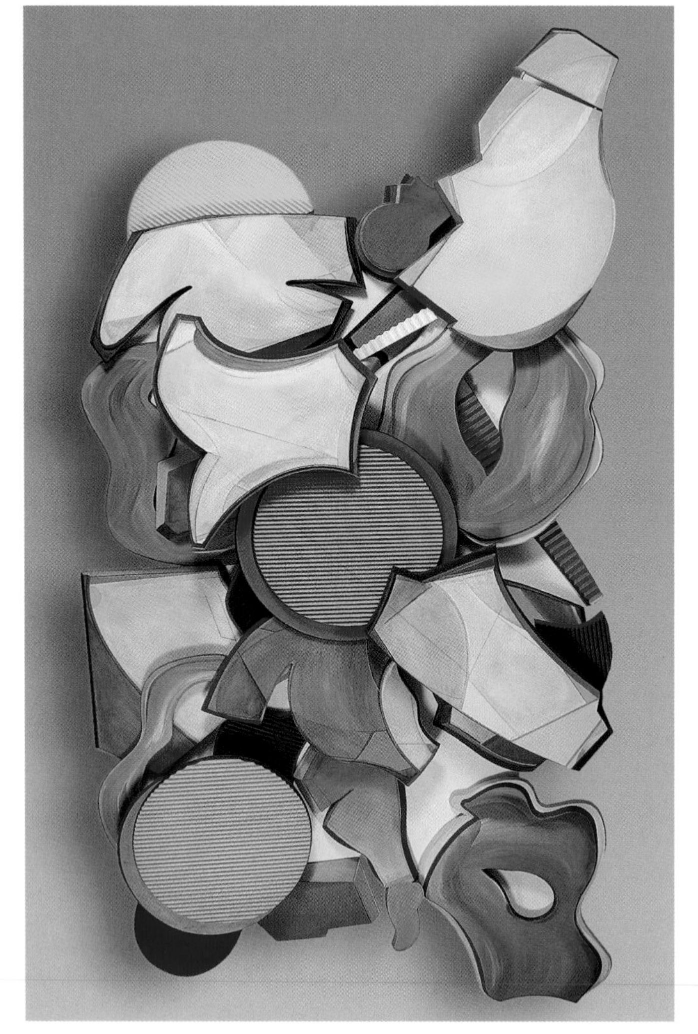

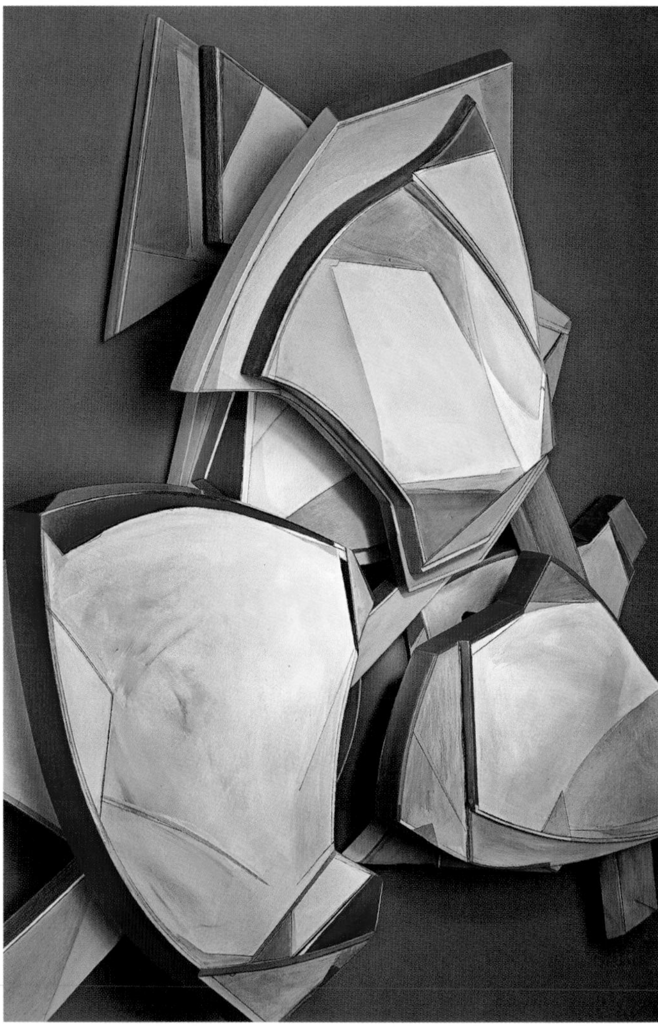

Top: *Reading A River,* 2007, Transylvania County Public Library, Brevard, NC, urethane archival board, aluminum, and acrylic, 10' × 37.5' × 2'. Photograph: Michael Justus.
Bottom left: *Five Strata* (detail), 2006, Liberty Trust Corporation, Greenville, SC, urethane archival board, 4.5' × 8' × 1'. Photograph: Steve Mann.
Bottom right: *Cubist Shards with Holographic Disks,* 2007, holographic color-changing disks, 18.5' × 8' × 1.5', design in progress. Photograph: Tim Barnwell.

BRYAN MARTIN

MARTIN STUDIOS ■ 4926 WEST EIGHTH STREET ROAD ■ GREELEY, CO 80634
TEL 970-590-4972 ■ E-MAIL BRYAN@MARTINSTUDIOS.COM ■ WWW.MARTINSTUDIOS.COM

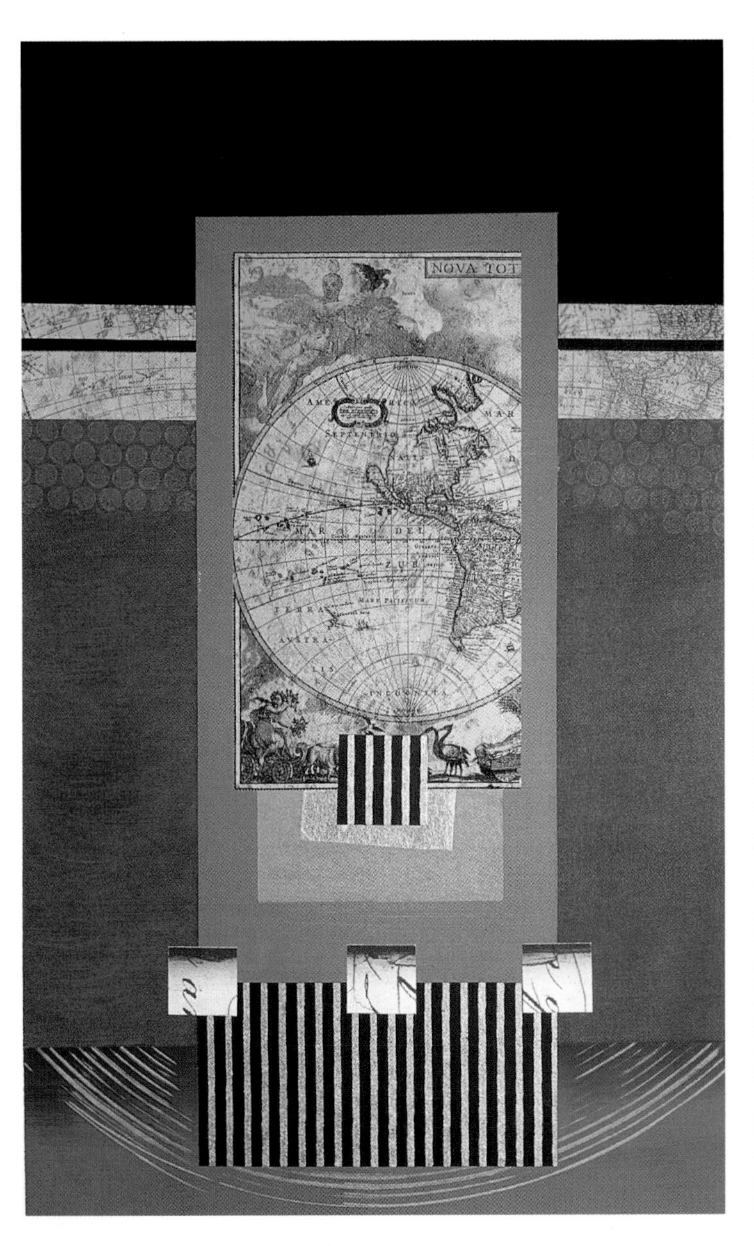

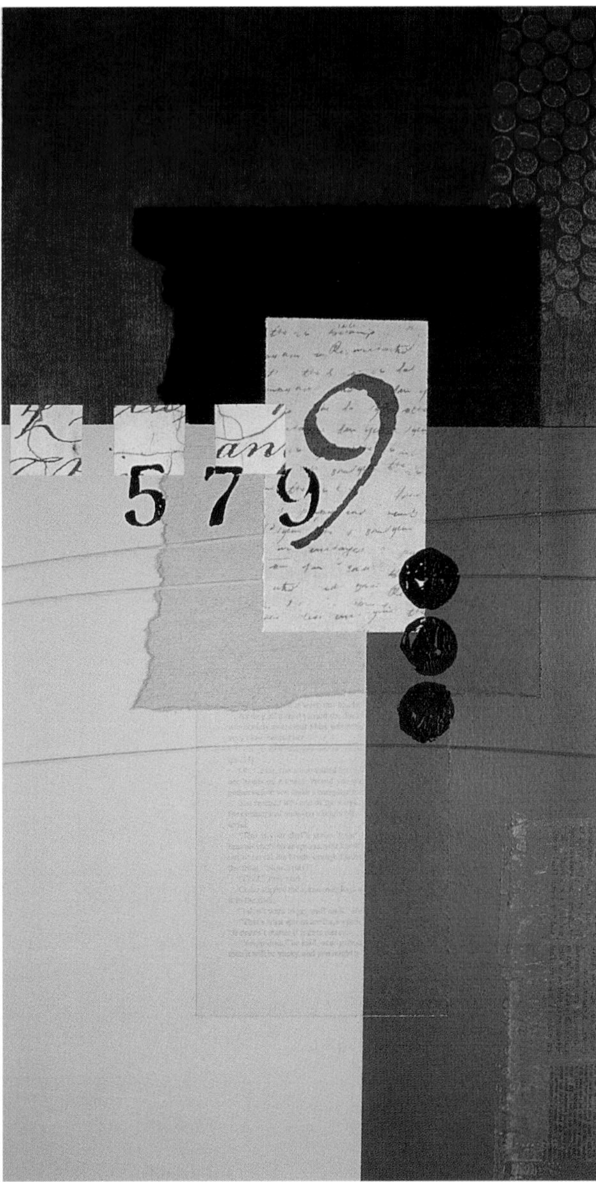

Left: *Globe 1*, mixed media on paper, 20" x 12". Right: *Unify*, mixed media on paper, 20" x 10".

AMY J. MUSIA

MUSIAN COLUMNS ■ PO BOX 18064 ■ EVANSVILLE, IN 47719 ■ TEL 812-985-7523
TEL 812-459-8833 ■ E-MAIL A.MUSIA@ATT.NET ■ WWW.MUSIANCOLUMNS.COM

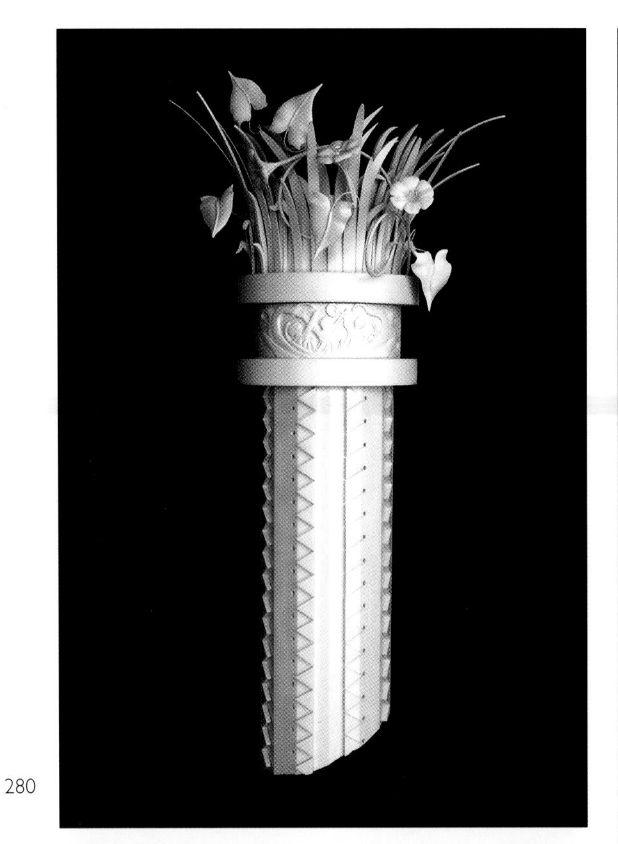

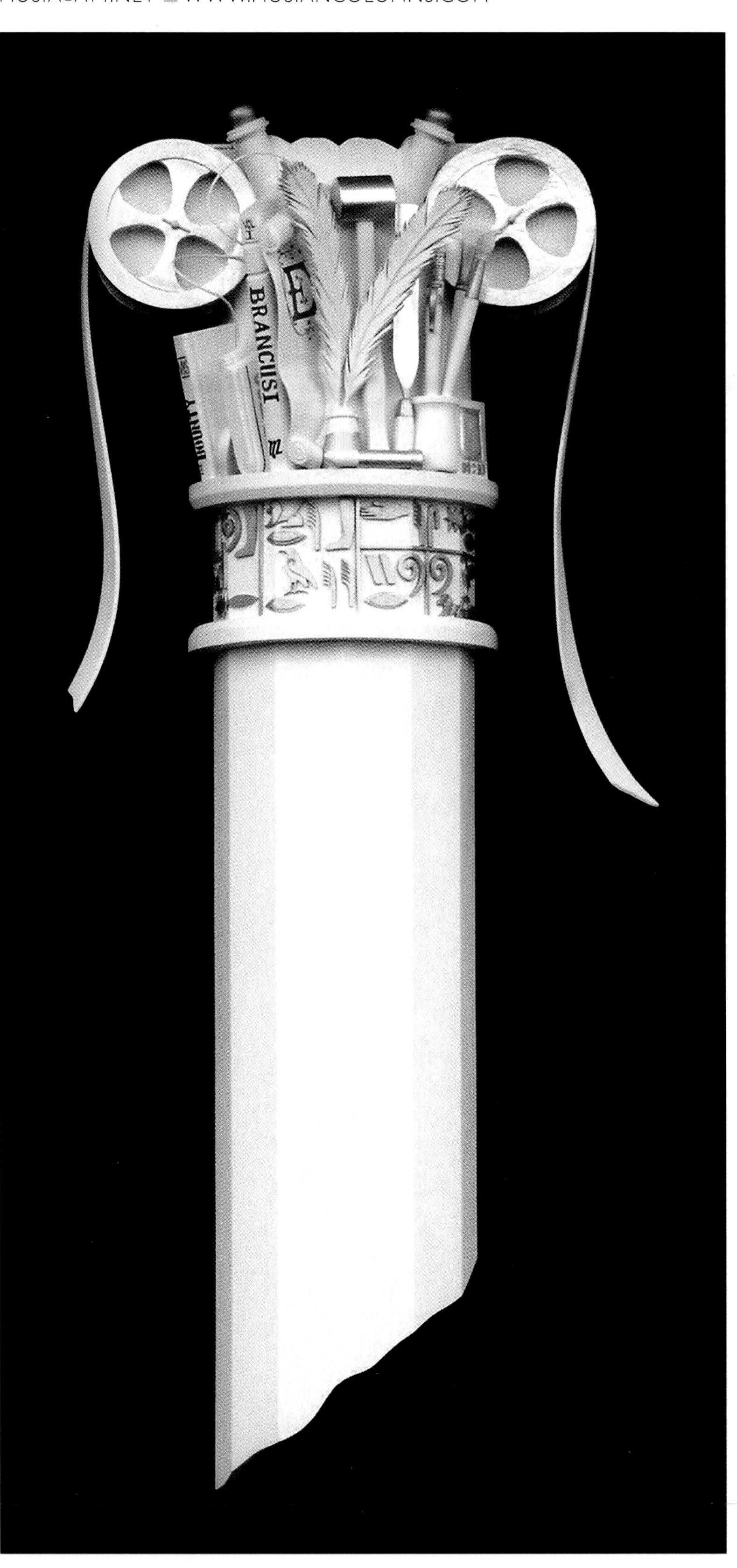

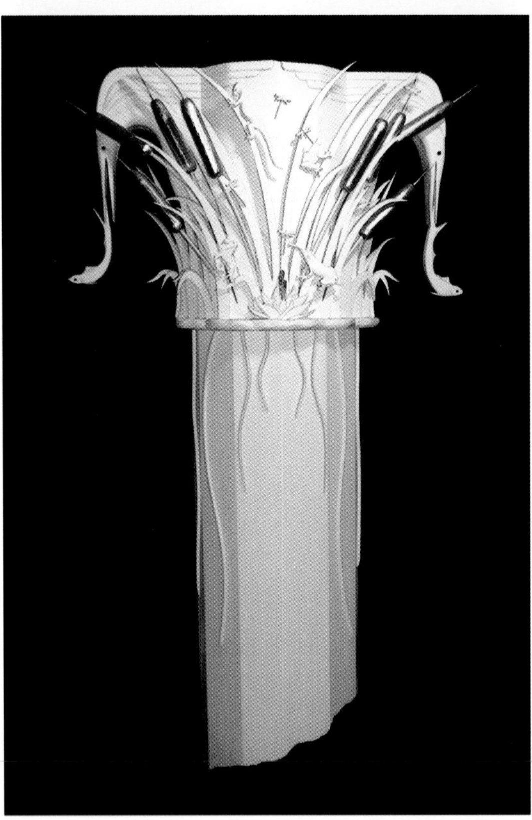

Top left: *Good Morning Glory,* 2006, wood, 50" x 24" x 12". Right: *Story Tools,* 2005, Evansville Vanderburgh Library, Evansville, IN, wood with 24K and silver gilding, 96" x 44" x 16". Bottom left: *Golden Tails,* 2004, Visiting Nurses' Association Hospice, Evansville, IN, wood with 24K gilding, 48" x 28" x 16".

JUNCO SATO POLLACK

11 POLO DRIVE NE ■ ATLANTA, GA 30309 ■ TEL/FAX 404-892-2155
E-MAIL JUNCO@JUNCOSATOPOLLACK.COM ■ WWW.JUNCOSATOPOLLACK.COM

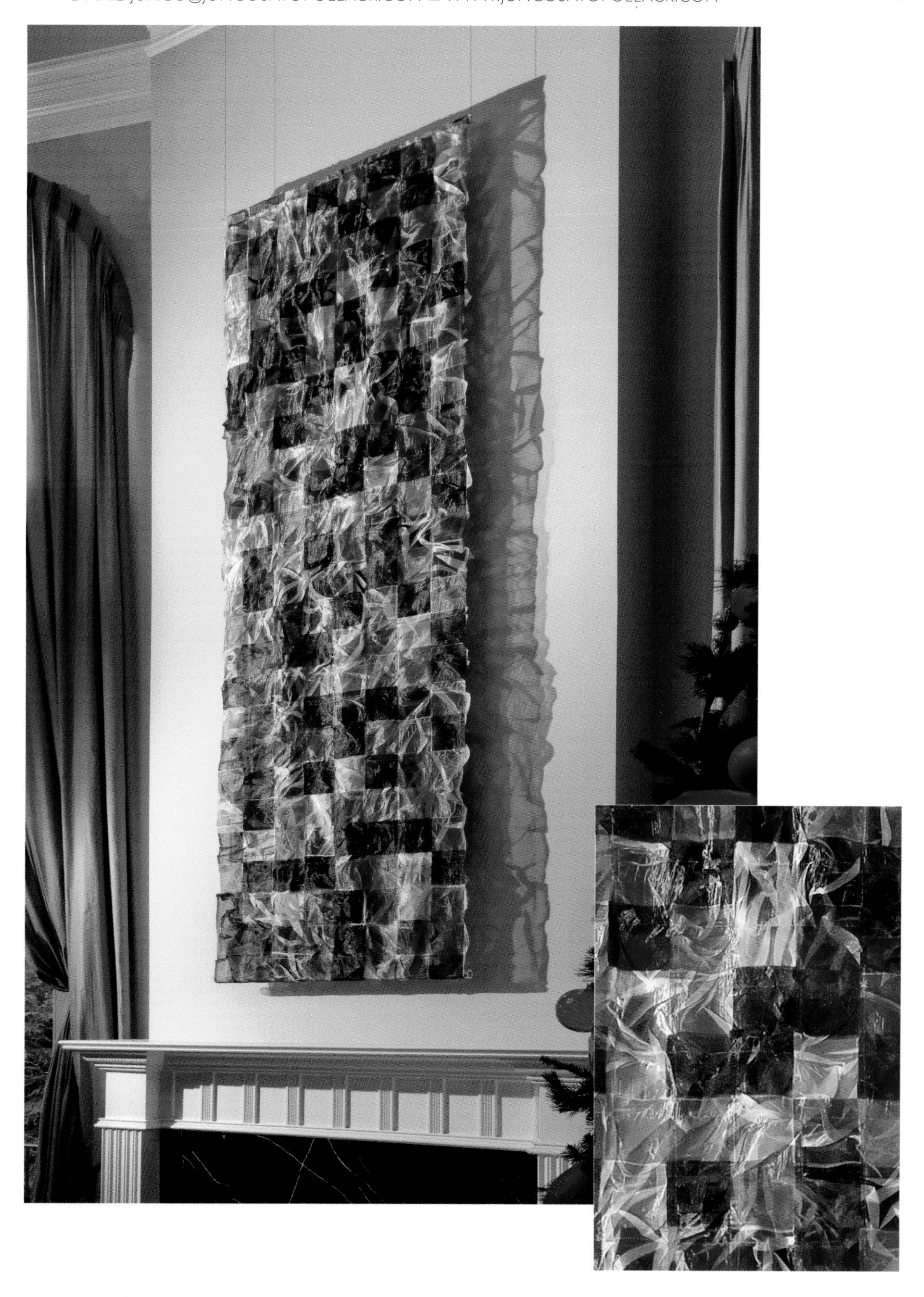

Origami #9, 2006, private residence, Atlanta, GA, double-layer looped hanging, heat compression with dye sublimation on polyester organza, 12'H x 40" x 2". Photograph: Departure 2007.

PRISCILLA ROBINSON

2811 HANCOCK DRIVE ■ AUSTIN, TX 78731 ■ TEL/FAX 512-452-3516 ■ TEL/FAX 505-758-2608
E-MAIL PJR@PRISCILLAROBINSON.COM ■ WWW.PRISCILLAROBINSON.COM

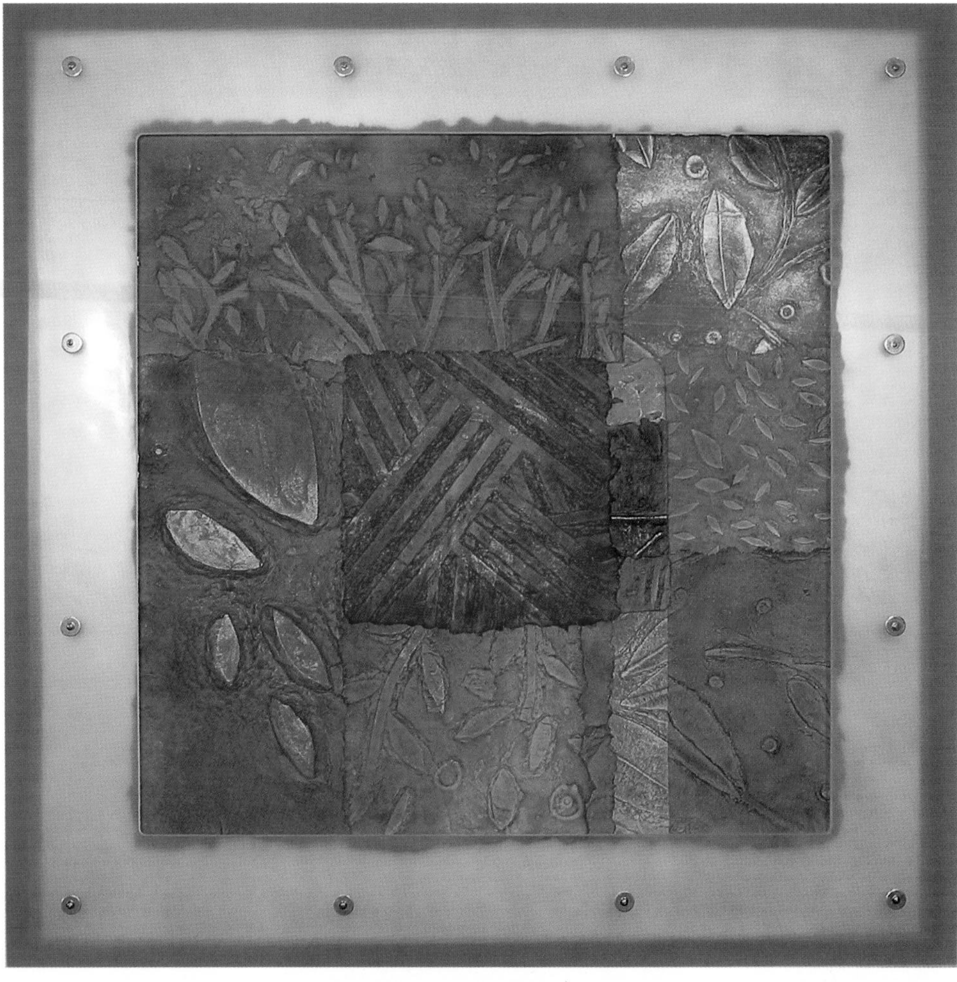

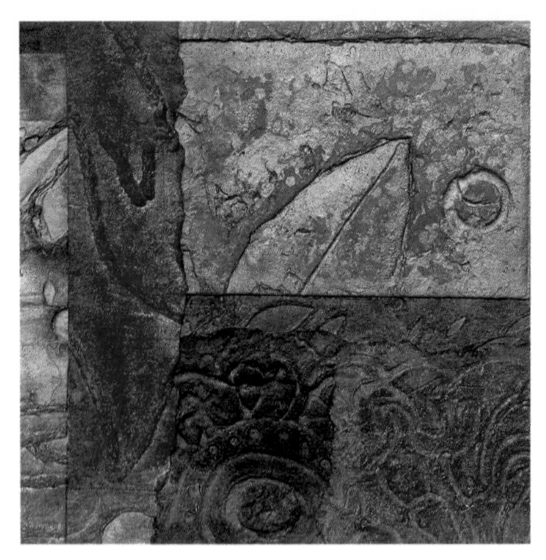

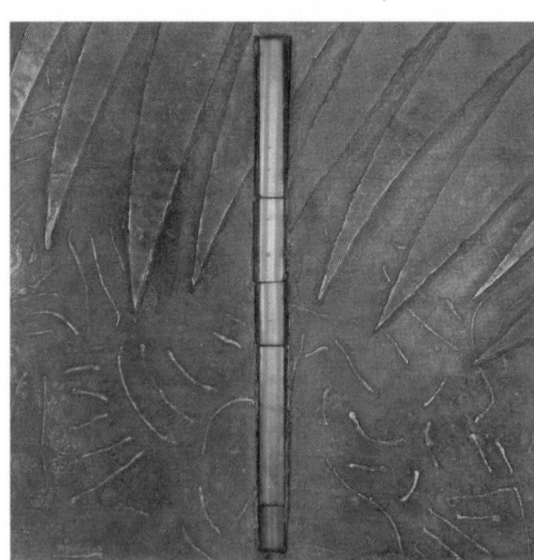

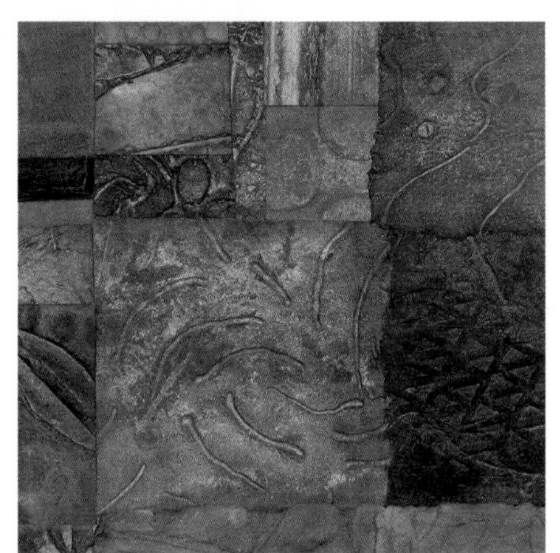

Top: *Harbor Series #3,* acrylic on embossed handmade paper mounted on lexan and aluminum, 36" x 36". Bottom left: *Abundant Fields,* acrylic on embossed handmade paper, 17" x 17". Bottom center: *In the Moment,* acrylic on embossed handmade paper and fused glass, 24" x 24". Bottom right: *Last Light,* acrylic on embossed handmade paper, 12" x 12".

DENISE M. SNYDER

3017 ALDERWOOD AVENUE ■ BELLINGHAM, WA 98225 ■ TEL 360-647-1152
E-MAIL DSNYDER@ARTSCAN.COM ■ WWW.ARTSCAN.COM/DSNYDER

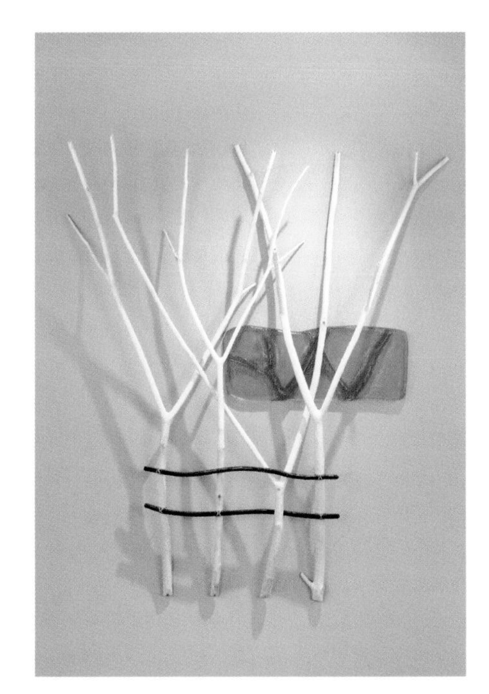

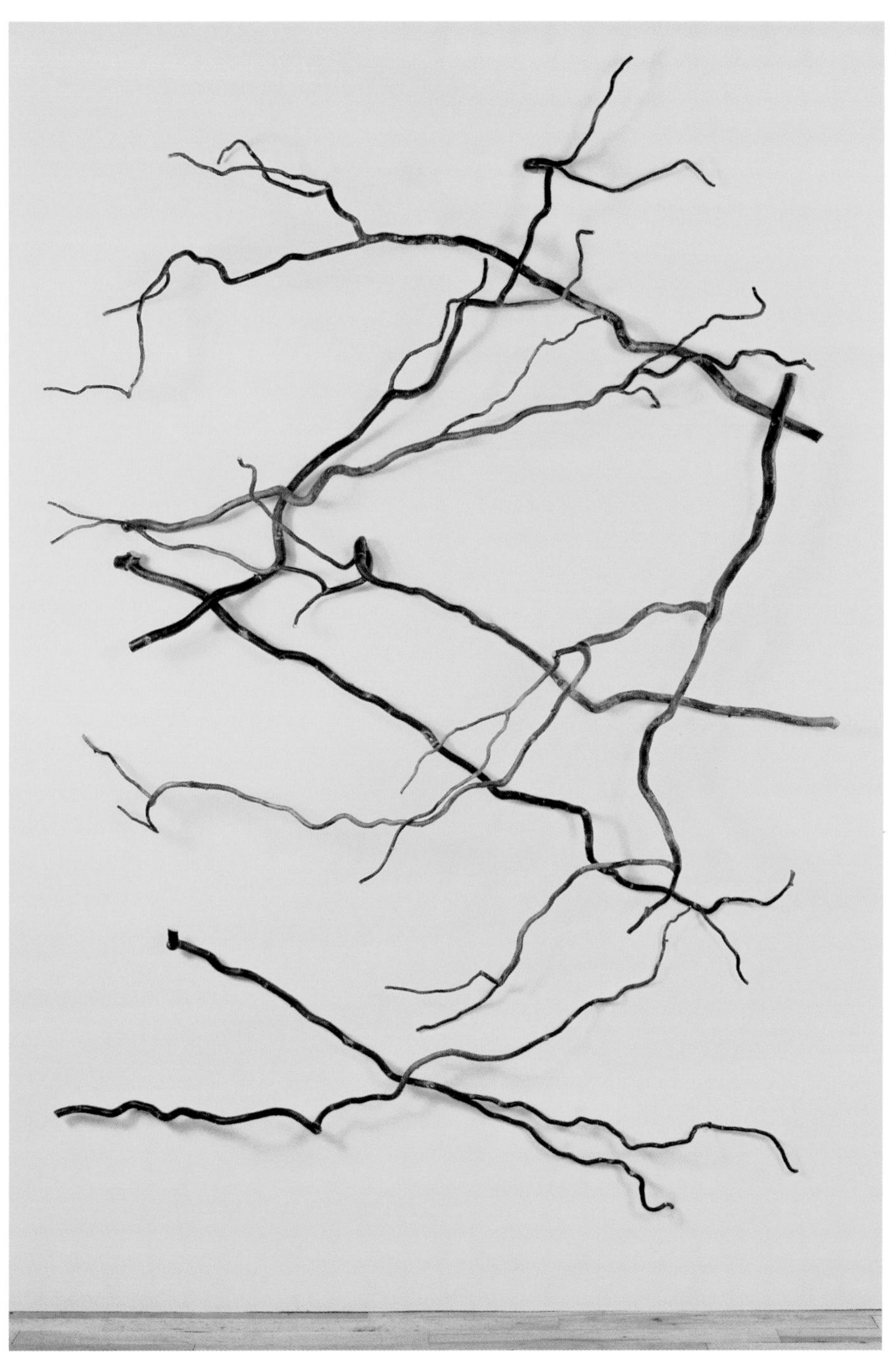

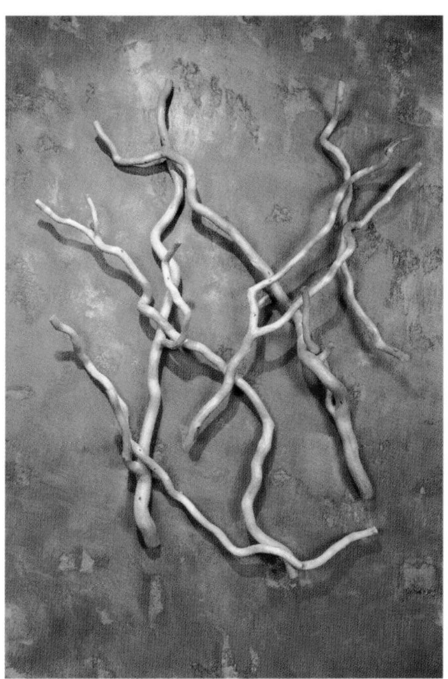

Top left: *Chestnut on Glass*, 2006, chestnut wood, steel, and cast glass, 33" x 28" x 5". Right: *Open Form Willow Wall*, 2006, unpeeled willow wood, 7' x 5' x 8". Bottom left: *Peeled Willow IV*, 2006, peeled willow wood, 47" x 36" x 7". Photographs: Brett Baunton Imagery.

RICHARD TAYLOR

RICHARD TAYLOR LLC ■ 3007 NORTH NEWHALL STREET ■ MILWAUKEE, WI 53211
TEL 414-967-1449 ■ TEL 414-961-0113 ■ E-MAIL RRTAYLOR@WI.RR.COM ■ WWW.TAYLORSCULPT.COM

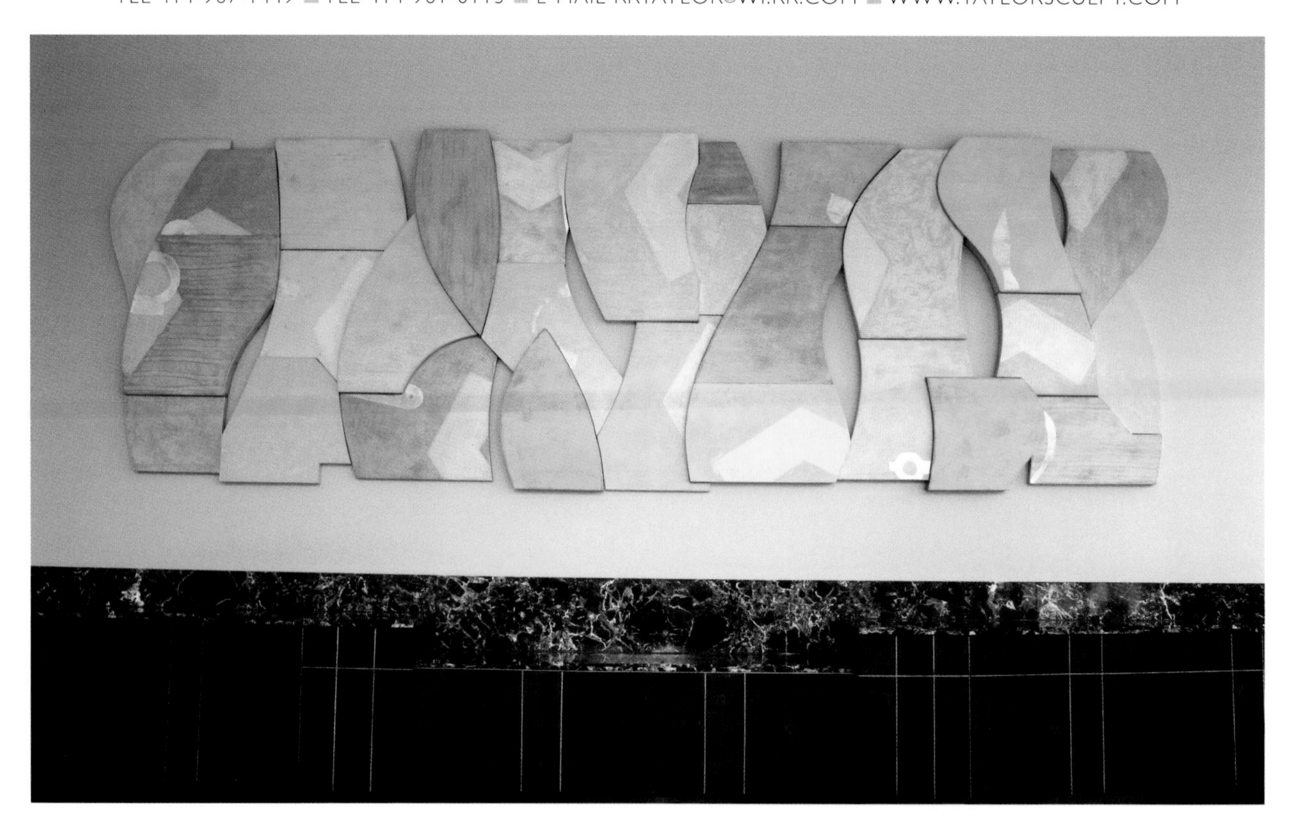

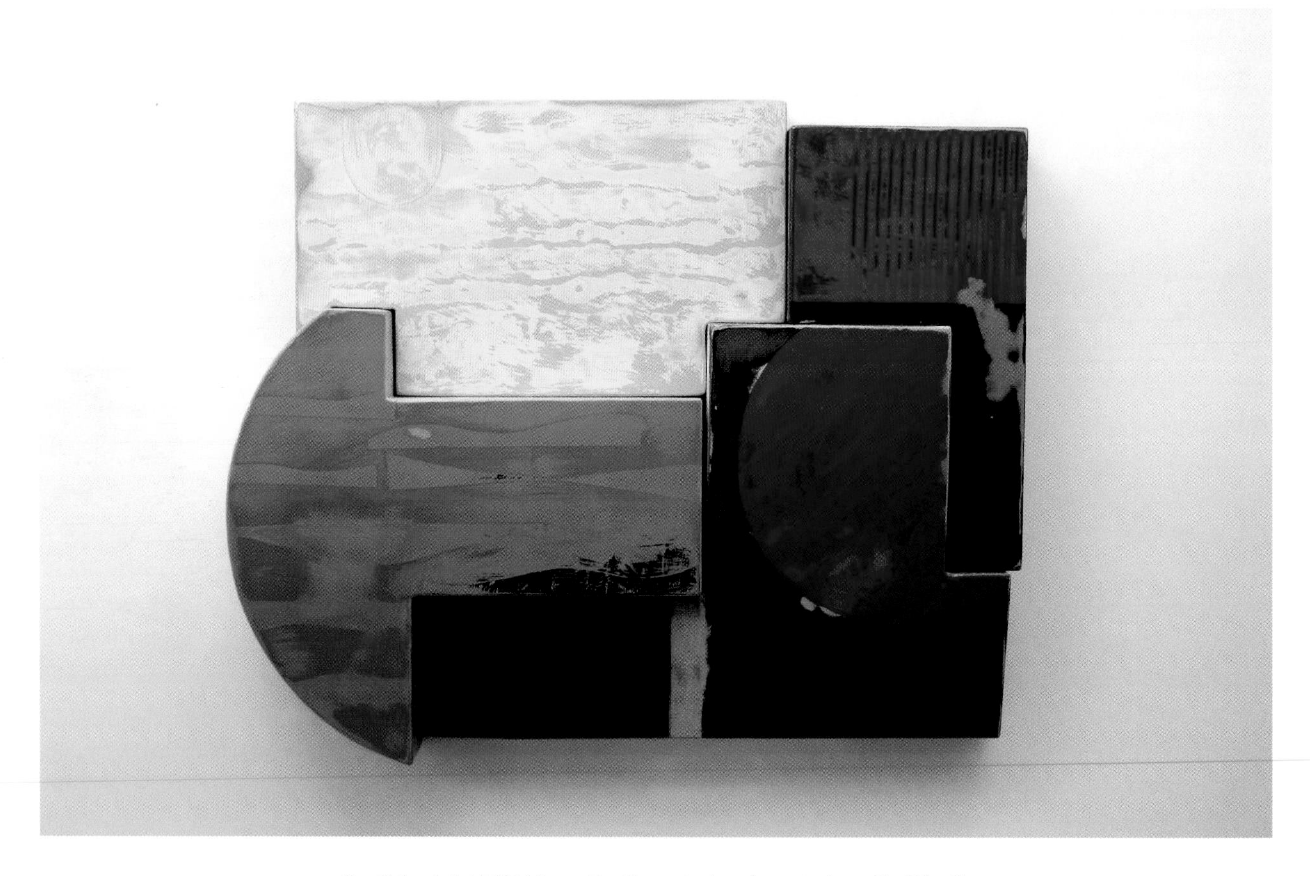

Top: *Rivière du Soleil,* 2006, State of Louisiana, mixed media on aluminum, 8' x 22' x 4".
Bottom: *Canyon de Chelly,* 2006, mixed media on aluminum, 29" x 35" x 4.5".

SUSAN VENABLE

VENABLE STUDIO ■ 2323 FOOTHILL LANE ■ SANTA BARBARA, CA 93105 ■ TEL 805-884-4963
FAX 805-884-4983 ■ E-MAIL SUSAN@VENABLESTUDIO.COM ■ WWW.VENABLESTUDIO.COM

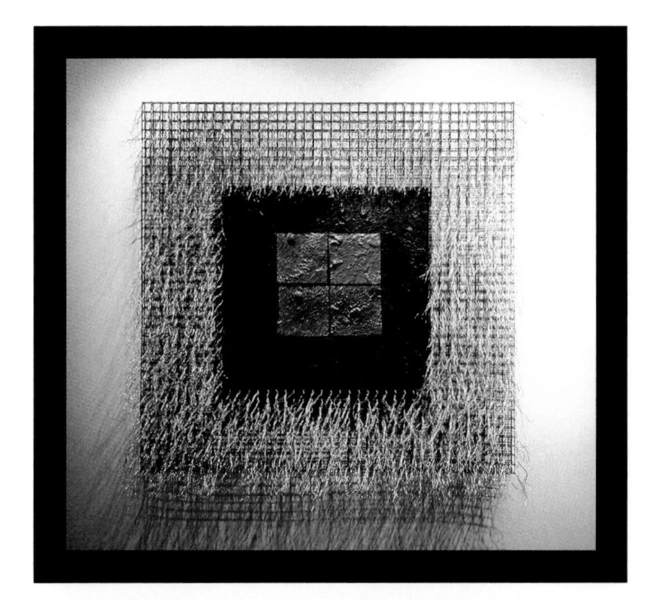

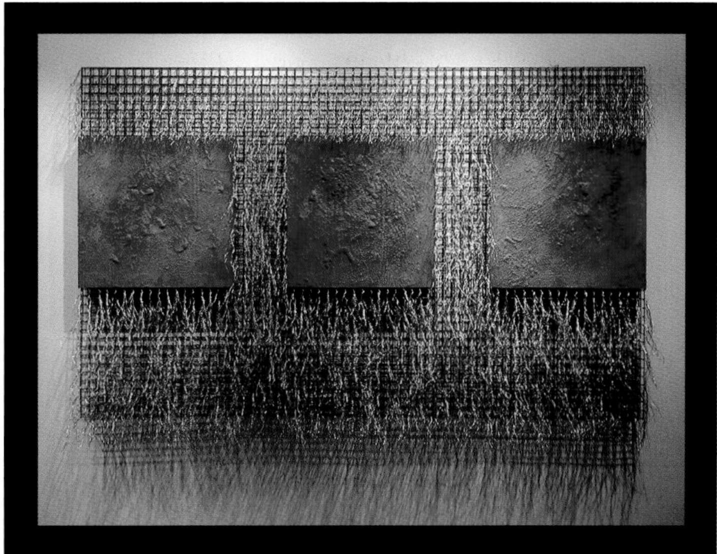

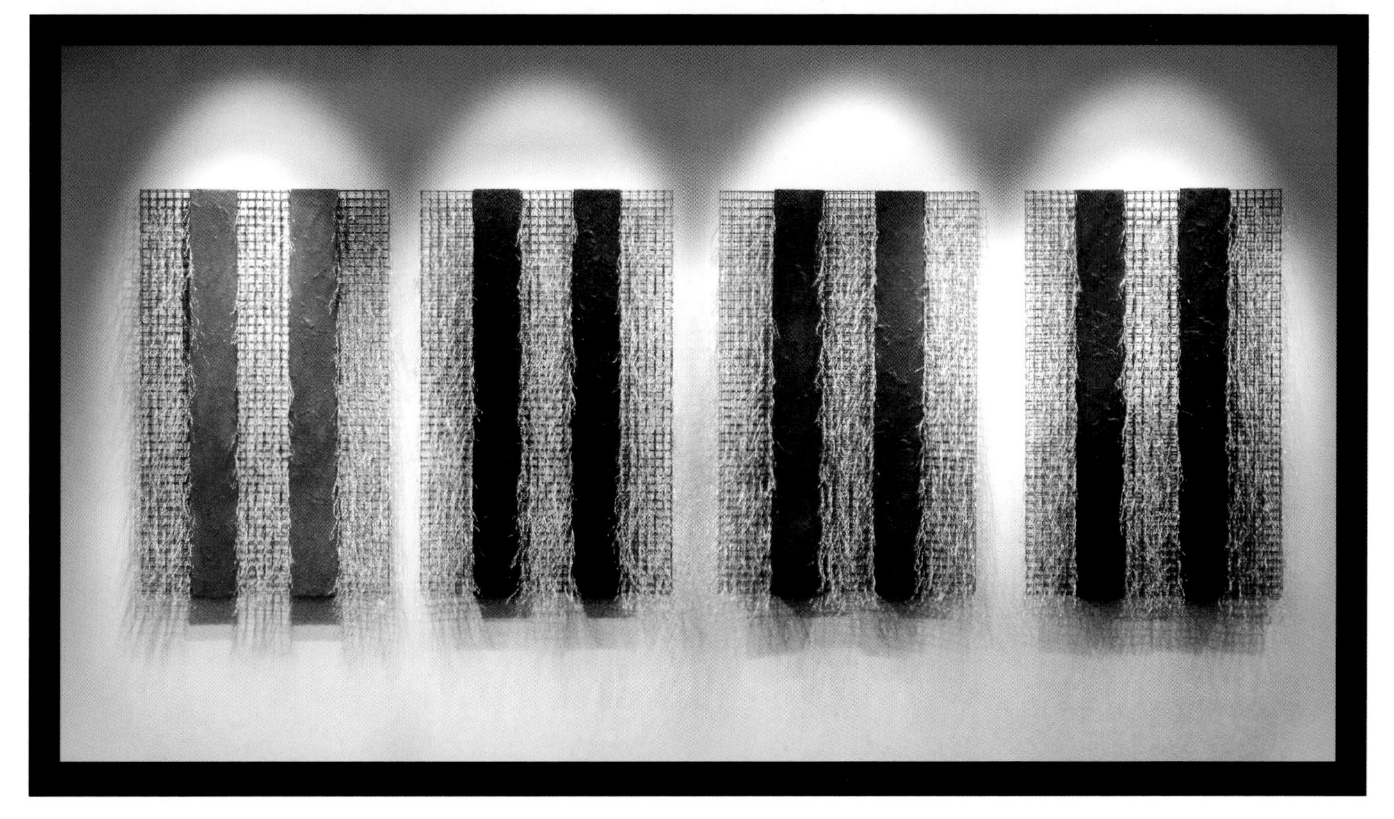

Top left: *silentSHADOW,* 2006. Top right: *redADAGIO,* 2006, Ryder Homes Corporation, Walnut Creek, CA, 42"H x 60"W.
Bottom: *mountainMAMBO,* 2006, Vail Marriott, Vail, CO, 4'H x 11'W. Photograph: William Nettles.

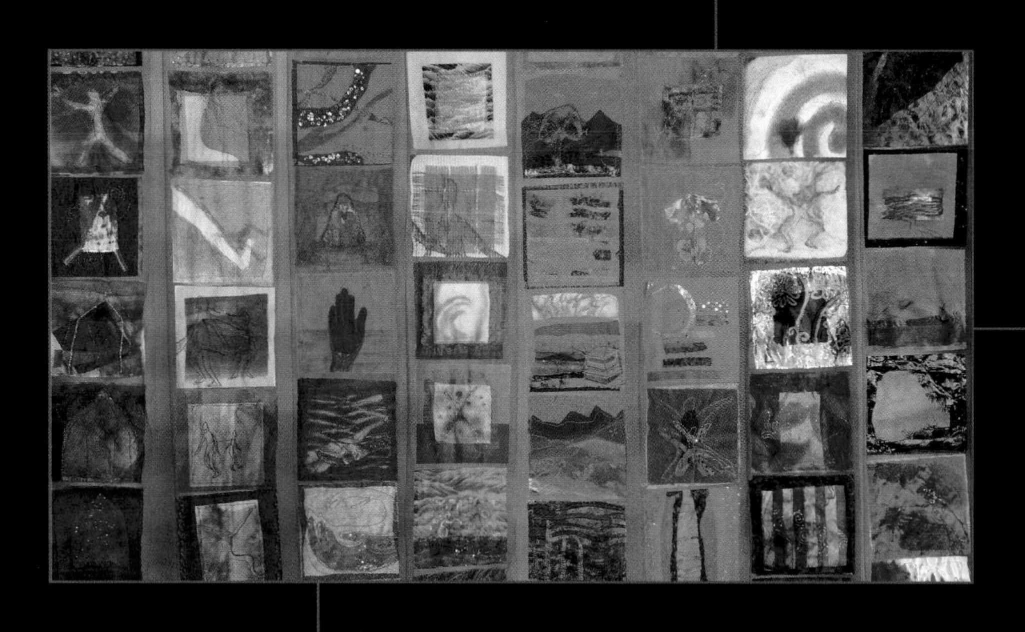

Fiber Wall Art

GEORGE-ANN BOWERS

1199 CORNELL AVENUE ■ BERKELEY, CA 94706 ■ TEL 510-524-3611
FAX 510-559-3152 ■ E-MAIL TMSLBWRS@EARTHLINK.NET

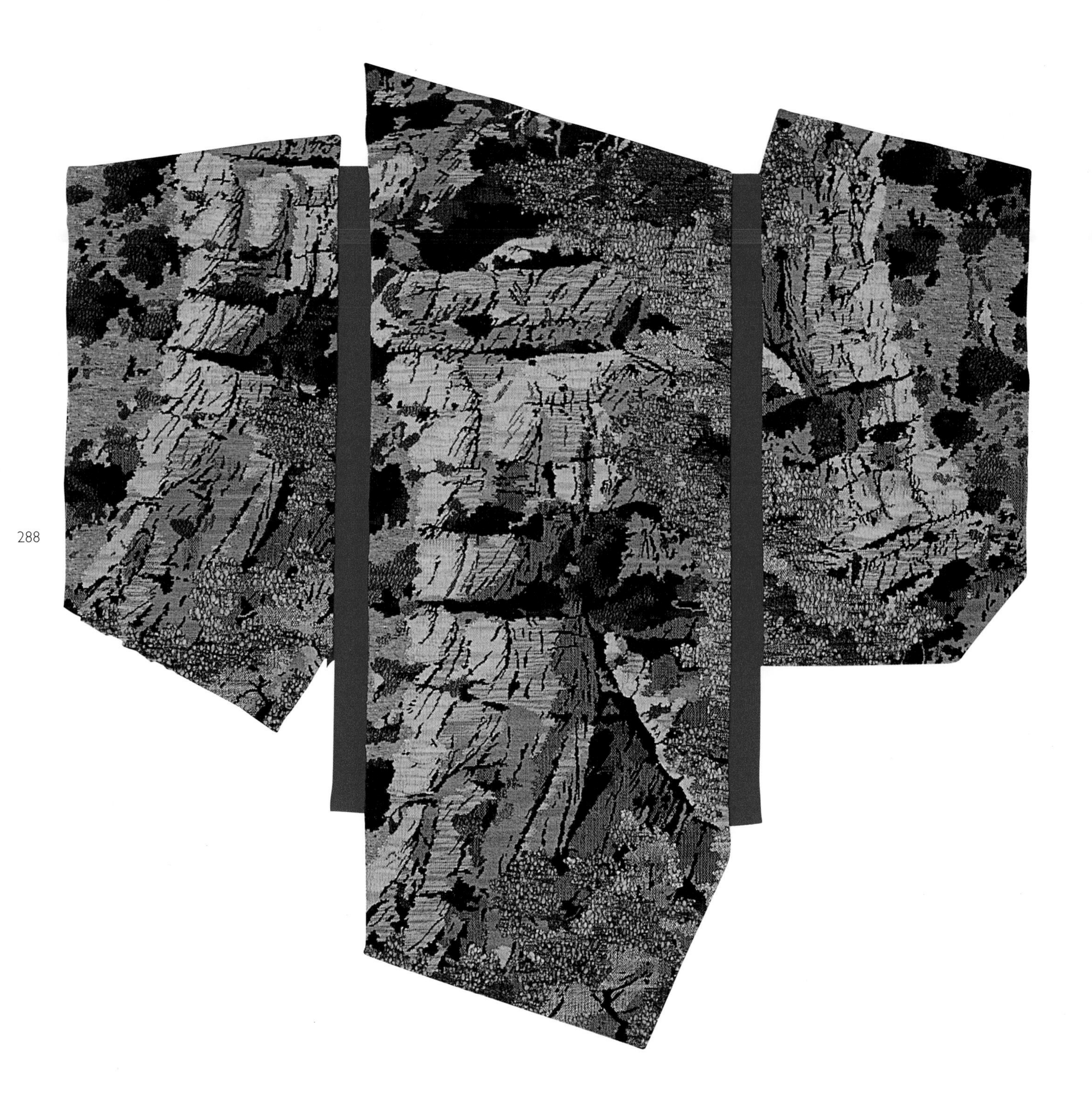

Canyon Kimono, 2006, triple-weave pick-up, cotton, wool, rayon, silk, acrylic, and silk noil, 59" x 58". Photograph: Dana Davis.

LAURA MILITZER BRYANT

PRISM ARTS, INC. ■ 3140 39TH AVENUE NORTH ■ ST. PETERSBURG, FL 33714
TEL 727-528-3800 ■ FAX 727-528-3308 ■ E-MAIL LAURA@PRISMYARN.COM ■ WWW.PRISMYARN.COM

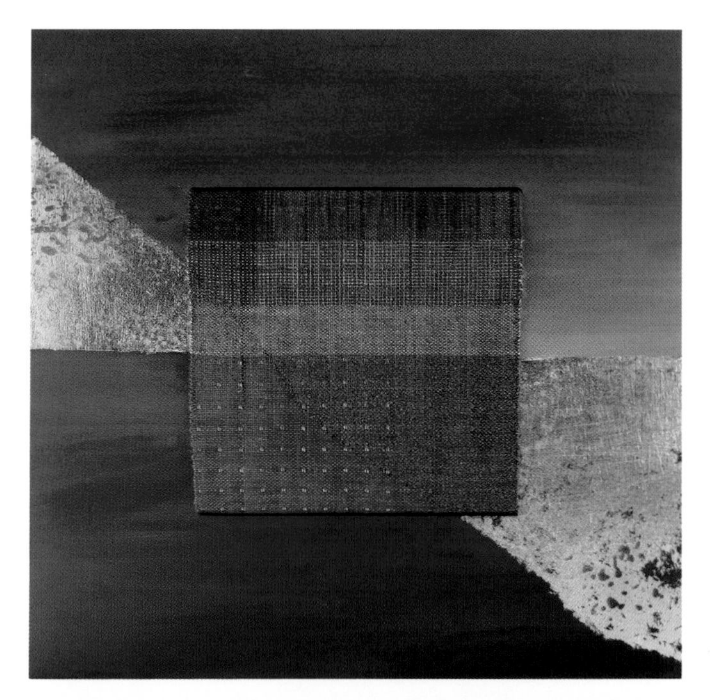

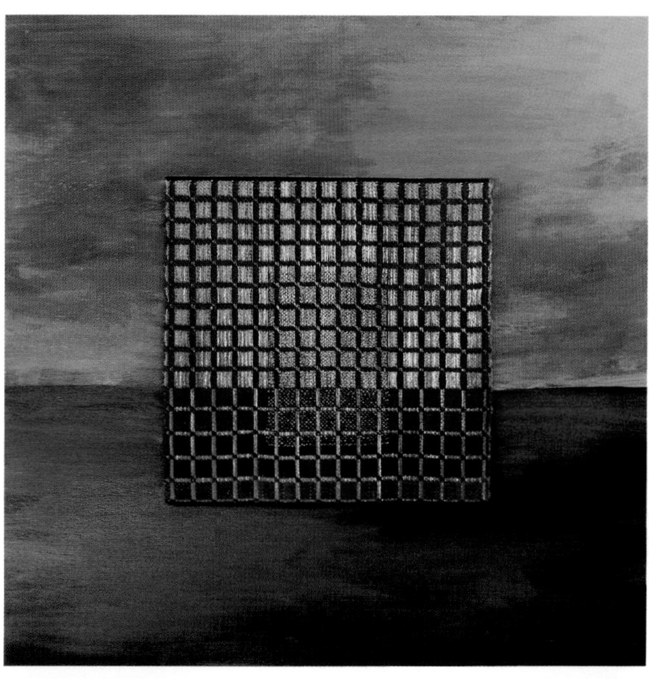

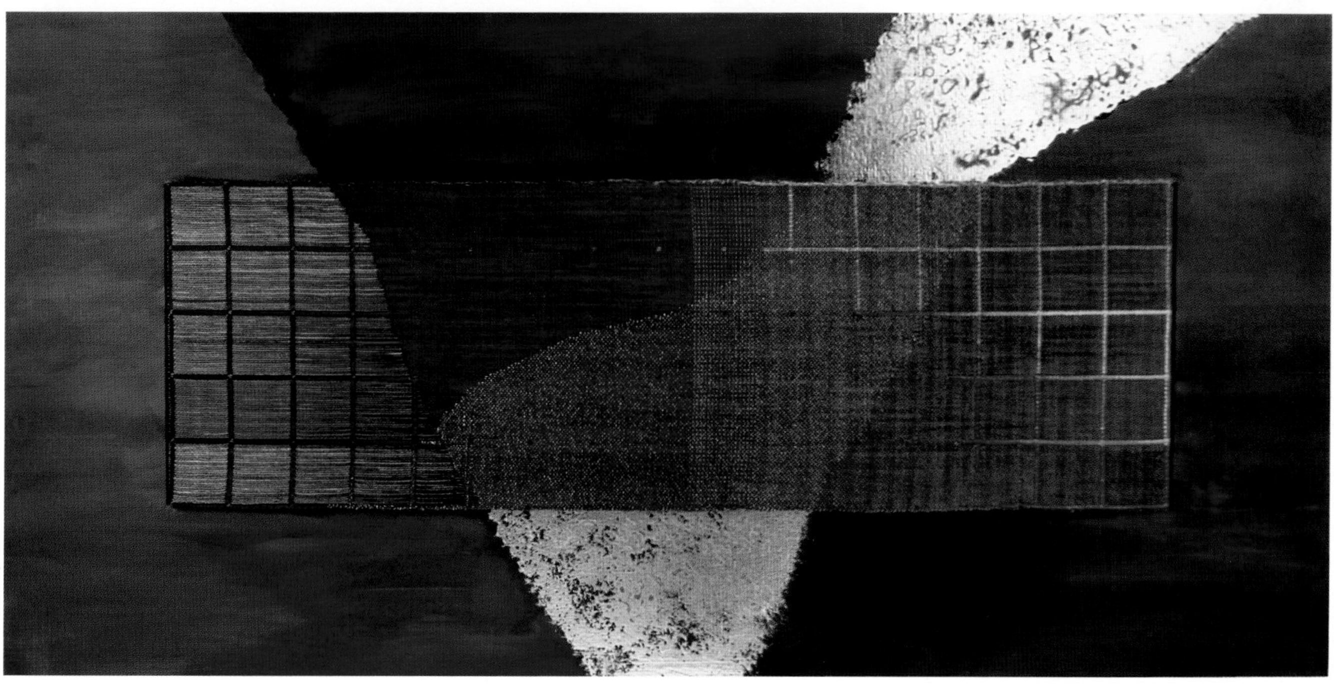

Top left: *Molten Sea,* weaving on wood with acrylic and copper leaf, 20" x 20". Top right: *Molten Sky,* weaving on wood with acrylic, 20" x 20". Bottom: *Crevasse,* weaving on wood with acrylic and metal leaf, 20" x 40".

MYRA BURG

171 PIER AVENUE #353 ■ SANTA MONICA, CA 90405
TEL 310-399-5040 ■ TEL 310-780-0666 ■ WWW.MYRABURG.COM

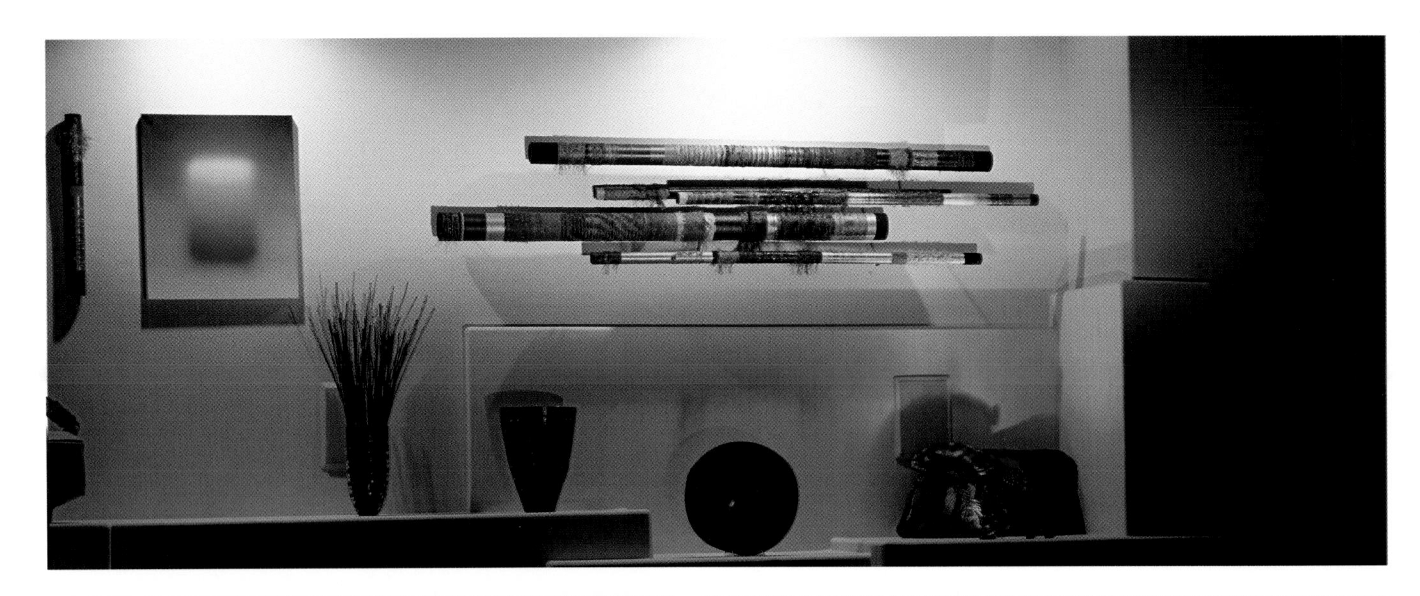

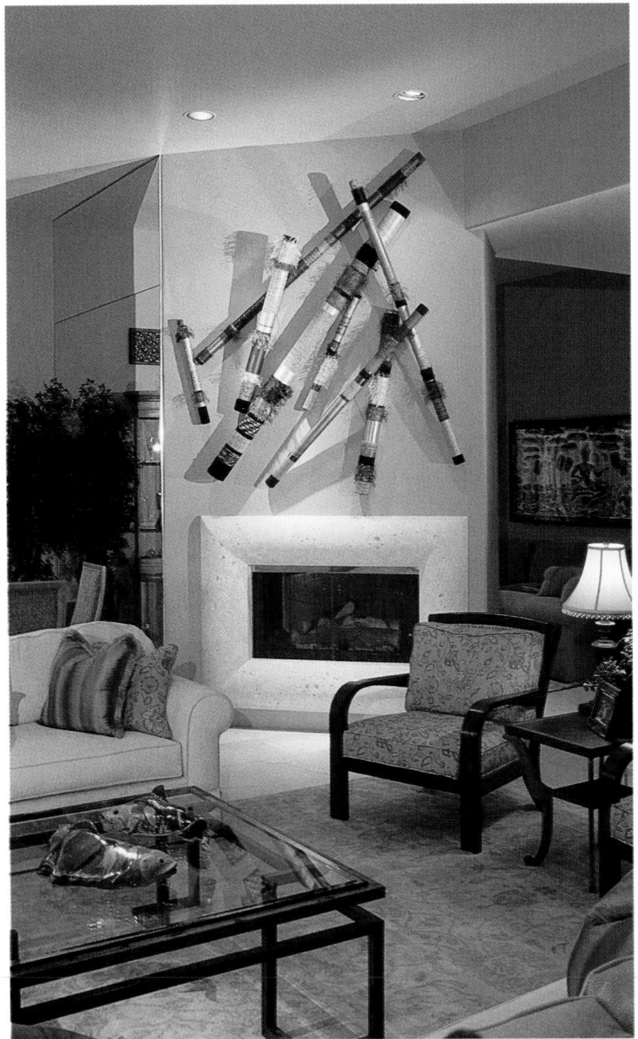

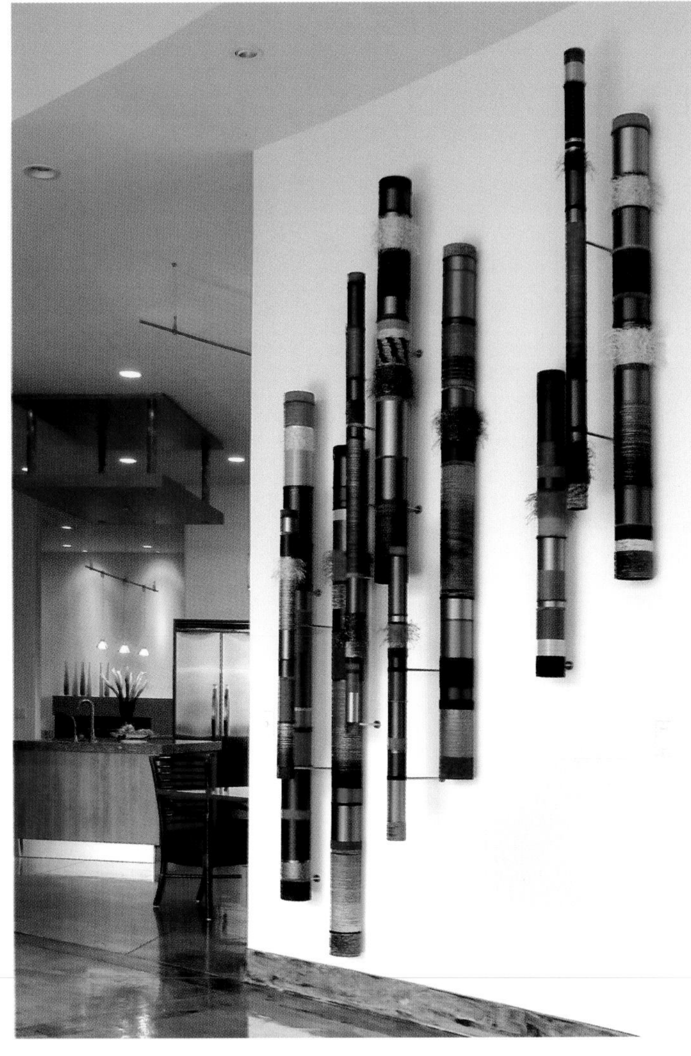

Top: *Quiet Oboes*, wrapped fiber, overall size: 2.5' x 7.5'. Photograph: Ron Luxemburg. Bottom left: *Indonesian Oboes*, wrapped fiber, overall size: 8'H x 7'W x 12"D. Photograph: Ron Luxemburg. Bottom right: *A Suite of Quiet Oboes in a Riot of Color*, overall size: 12'H x 10'W x 15"D. Photograph: Barry Blau.

MARLENE GLICKMAN

CREATIONS UNLIMITED ■ 2251 WILLOWBROOK DRIVE ■ CLEARWATER, FL 33764
TEL/FAX 727-524-6962 ■ E-MAIL MARLENE@123WEBMAGIC.COM ■ WWW.SILKDYES.COM

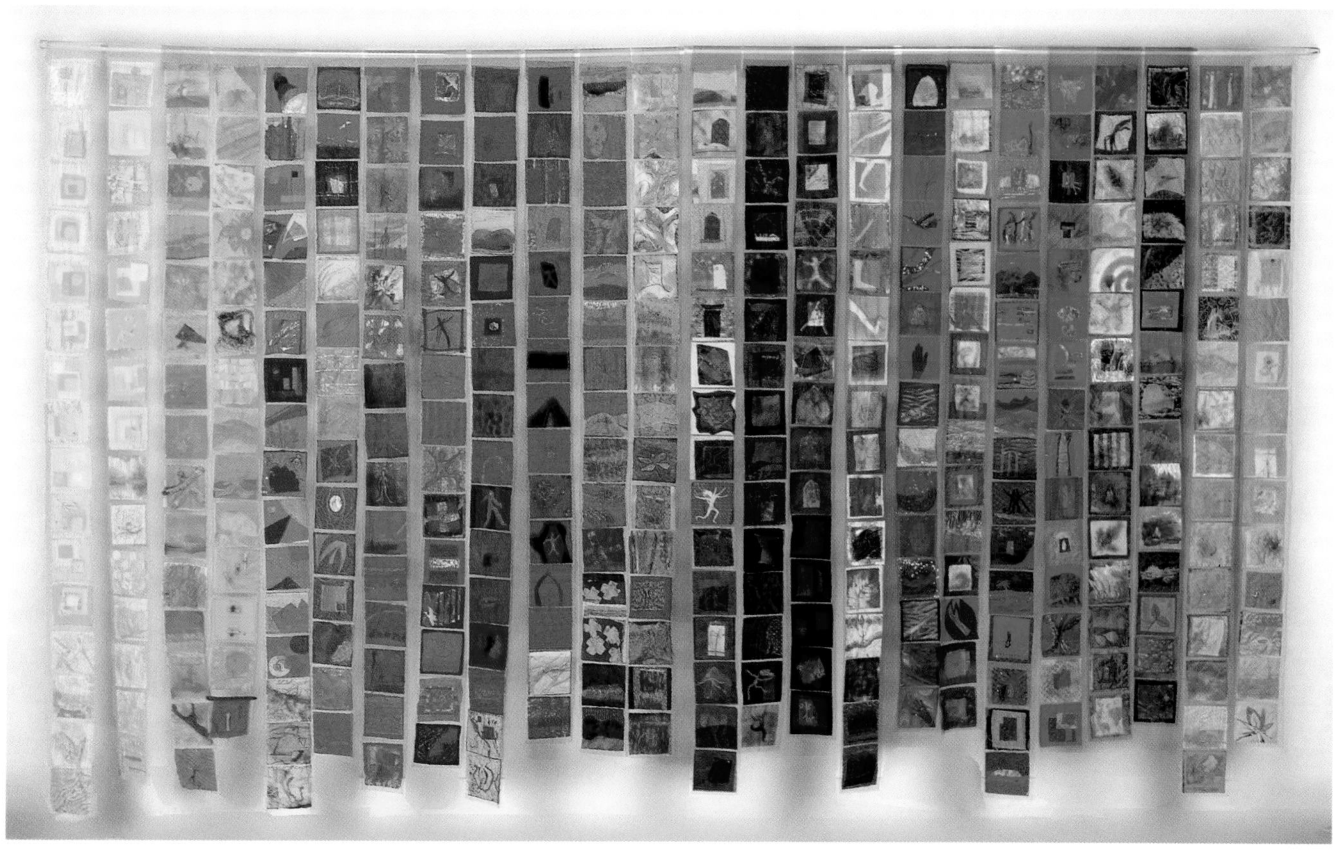

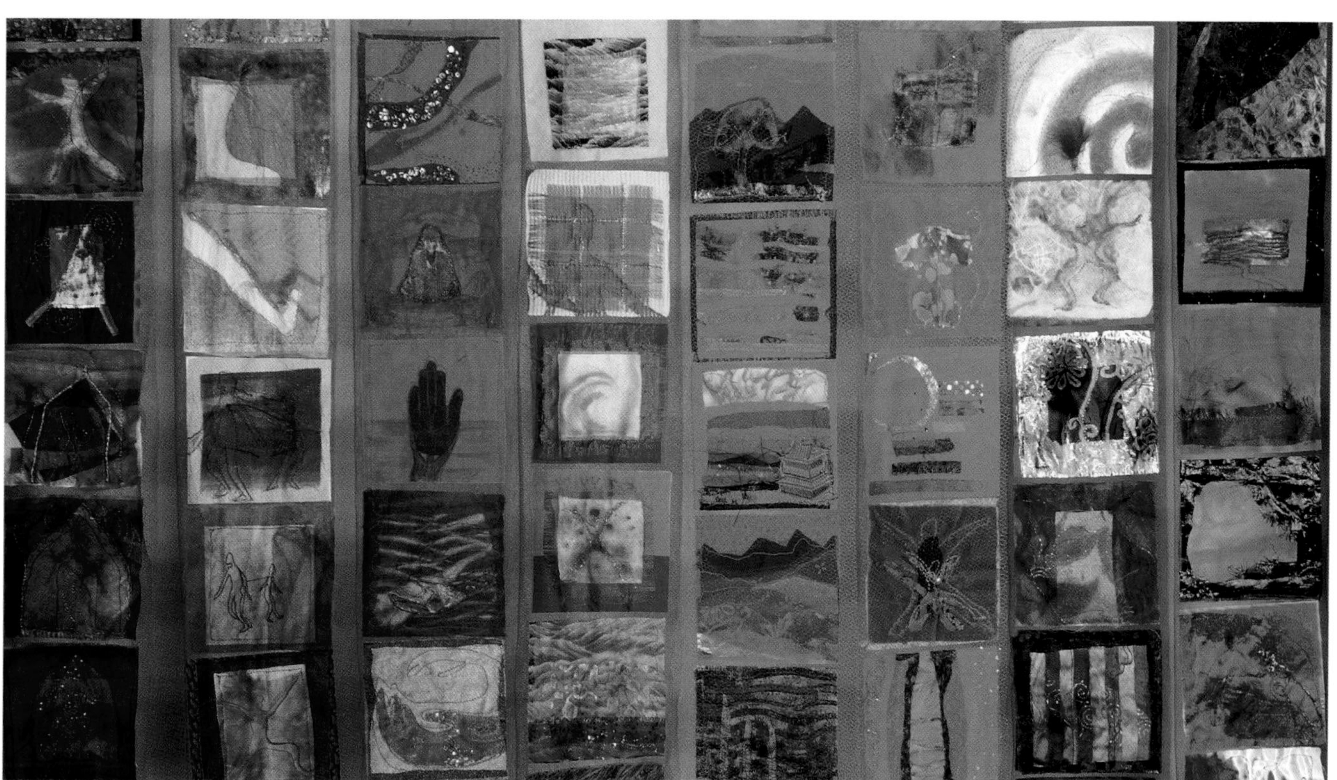

Top: *Day by Day: Pieces of Life*, 2004, fiber, 144"H x 102"W.
Bottom: *Indigo-Green of Day by Day: Pieces of Life* (detail). Photographs: Rob Moorman.

TIM HARDING

402 NORTH MAIN STREET ■ STILLWATER, MN 55082 ■ TEL 651-351-0383
FAX 651-351-1051 ■ E-MAIL TIM@TIMHARDING.COM ■ WWW.TIMHARDING.COM

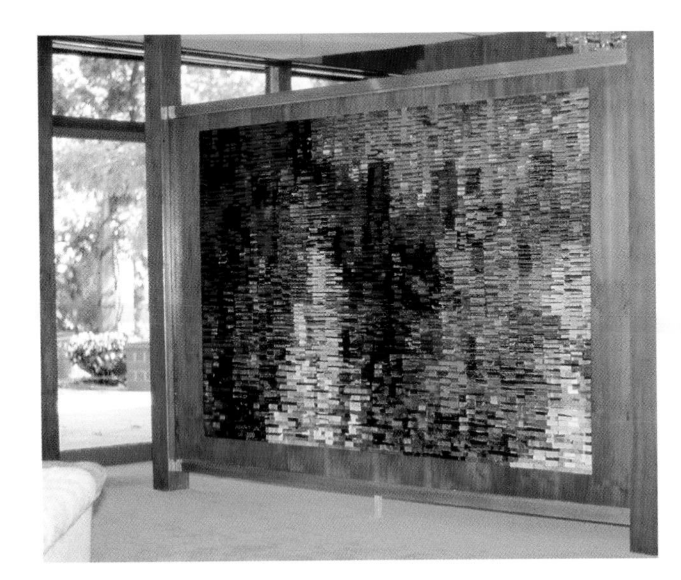

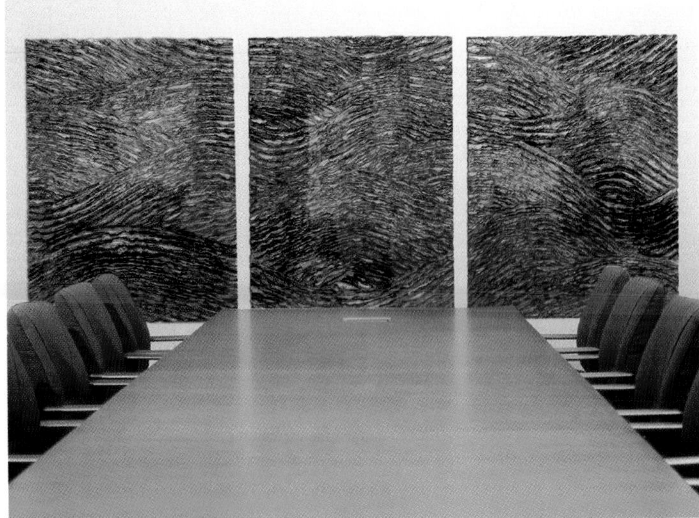

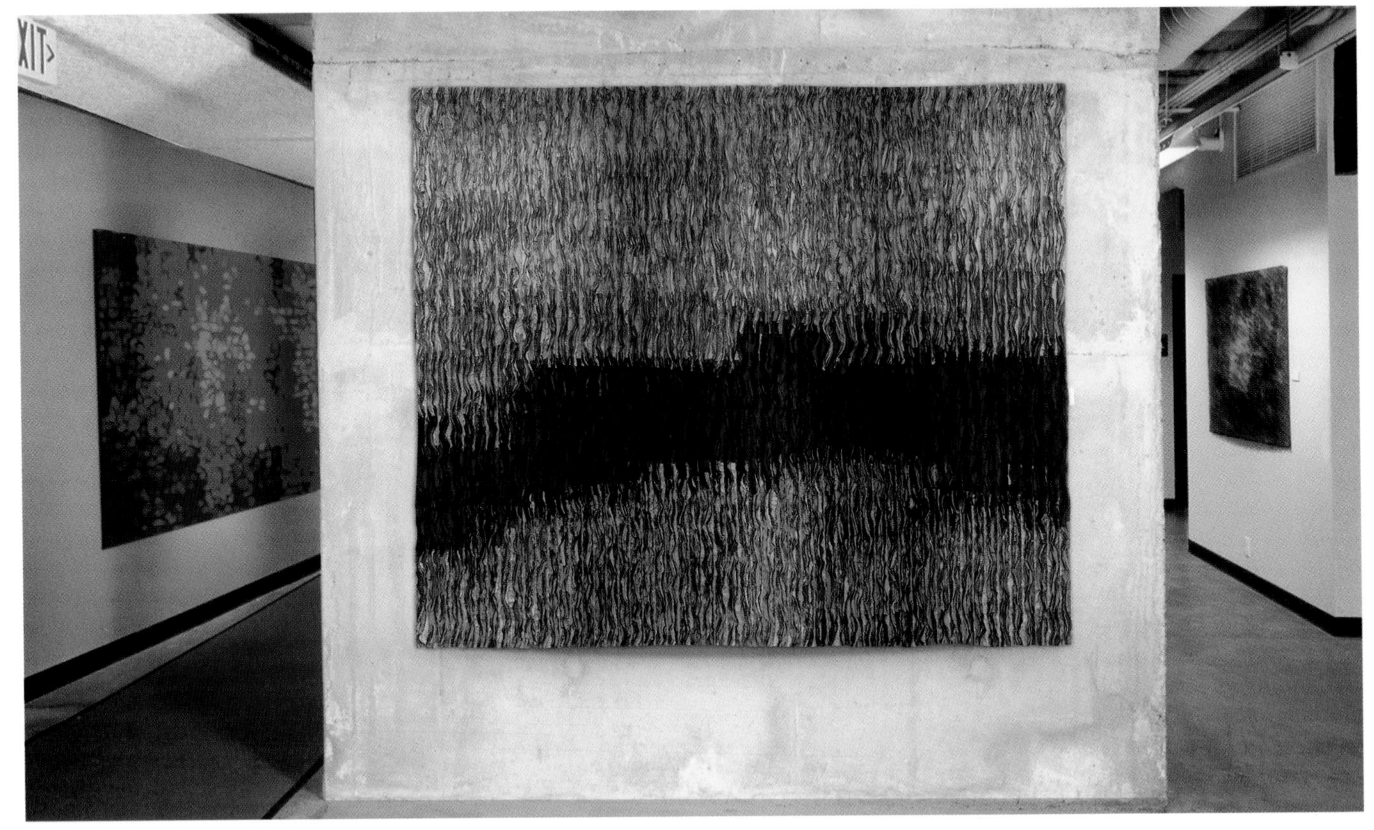

Top left: *Still Water Reflections,* 2002, private residence, Washington, DC, textured silk, 60" x 96". Photograph: T. Harding/C. Hooker.
Top right: *Sienna Fields Triptych,* 2004, Westlaw Inc., Minneapolis, textured silk, 56" x 138". Photograph: P. Ytsma/C. Hooker.
Bottom: *La Raya Negra,* 2006, GGLO Architects, Seattle, textured silk, 66" x 78". Photograph: P. Meyer/C. Hooker.

MARILYN HENRION

505 LAGUARDIA PLACE #23D ■ NEW YORK, NY 10012 ■ TEL 212-982-8949
E-MAIL MARILYNHENRION@MAC.COM ■ WWW.MARILYNHENRION.COM

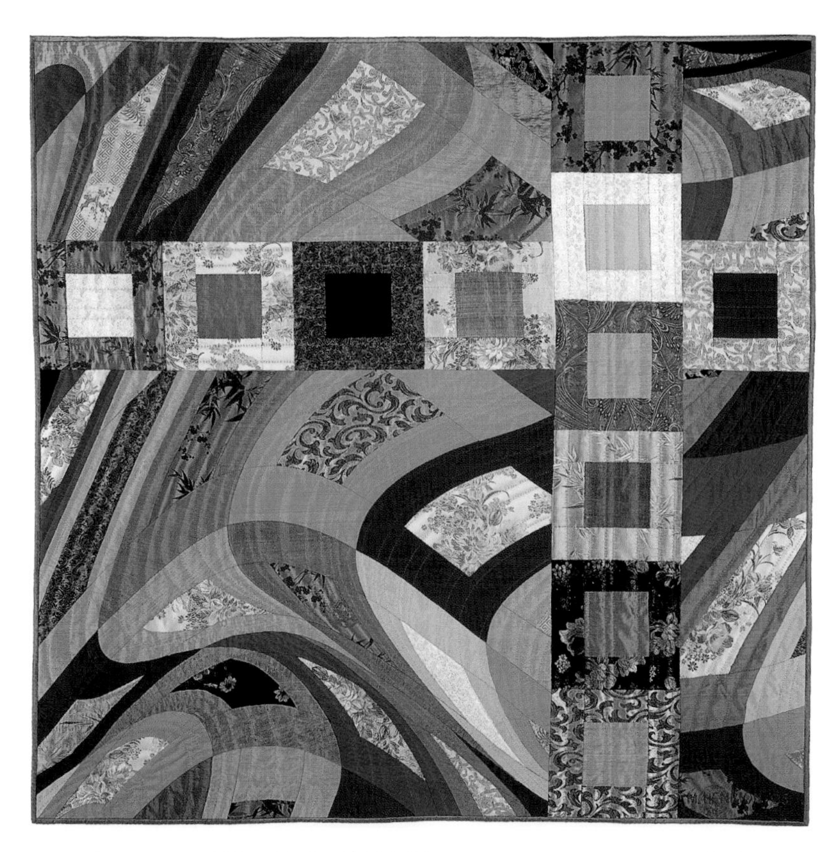

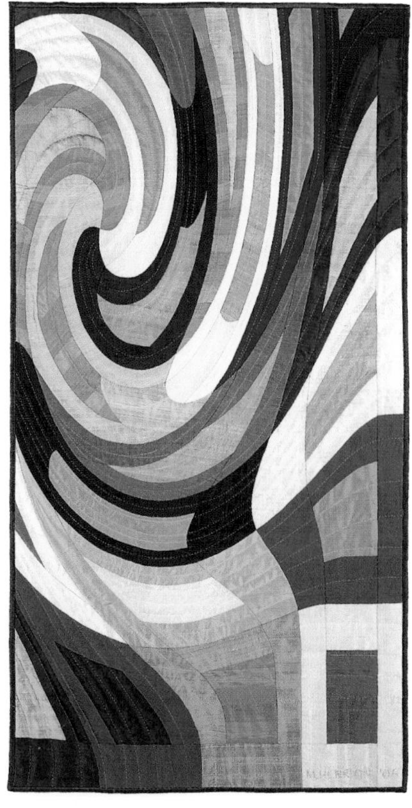

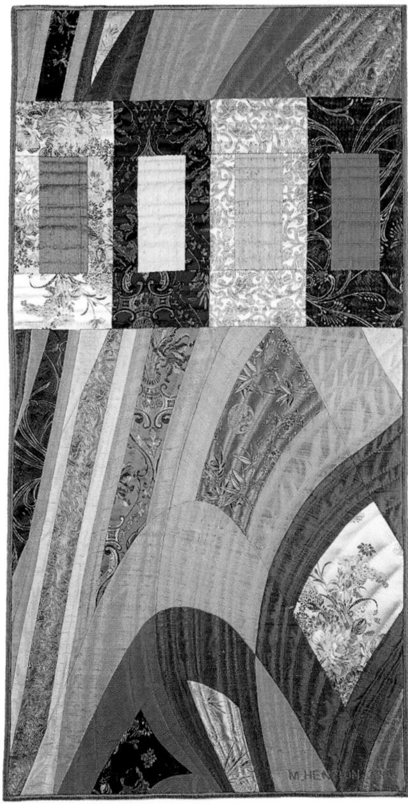

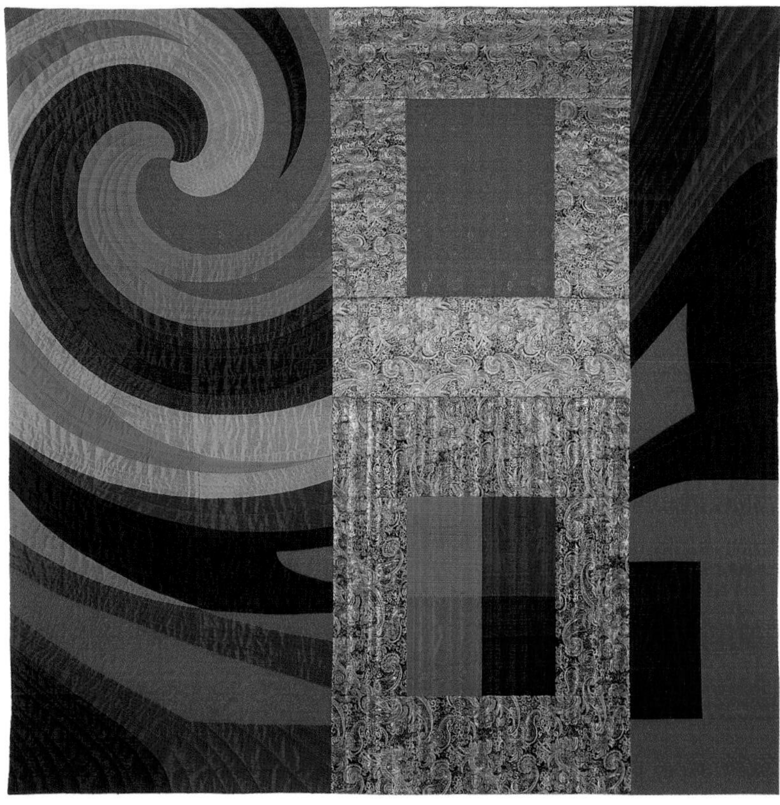

Top left: *Disturbances 4,* 2005, pieced silks, hand quilted, 48" x 48". Top right: *Disturbances 9,* 2006, pieced silks, hand quilted, 48" x 24".
Bottom left: *Disturbances 5,* 2006, pieced silks, hand quilted, 48" x 24". Bottom right: *Disturbances 7,* 2006, pieced silks, hand quilted, 66" x 65". Photographs: Karen Bell.

MARCIA HEWITT JOHNSON

SANTA FE STUDIO ■ 1104 PIEDRAS ROJAS ■ SANTA FE, NM 87501 ■ TEL/FAX 505-992-3273
E-MAIL ARTIST@MARCIAHEWITTJOHNSON.COM ■ WWW.MARCIAHEWITTJOHNSON.COM

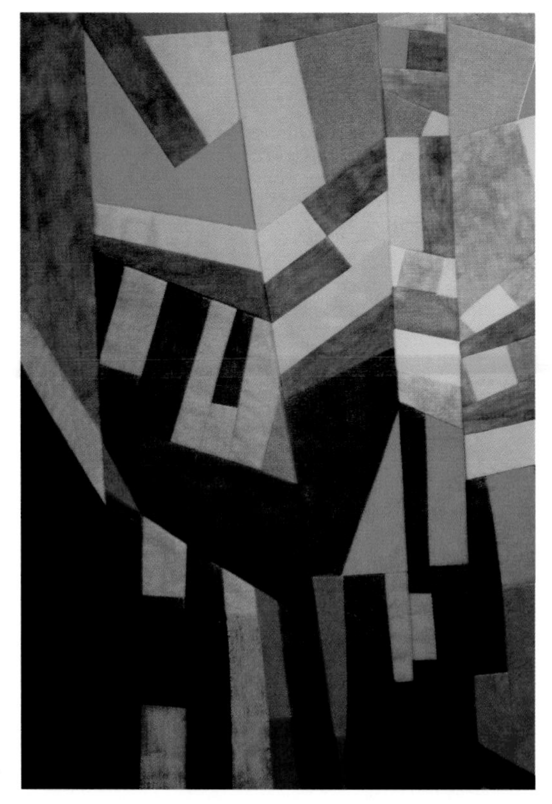

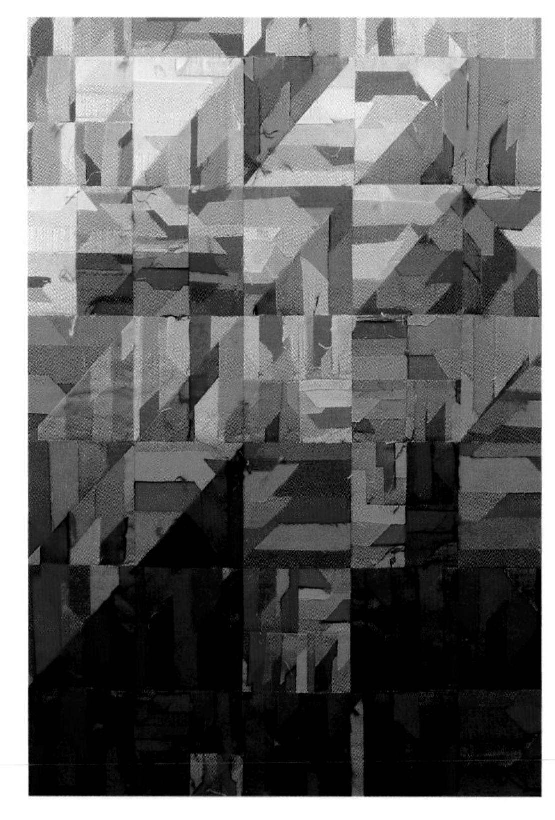

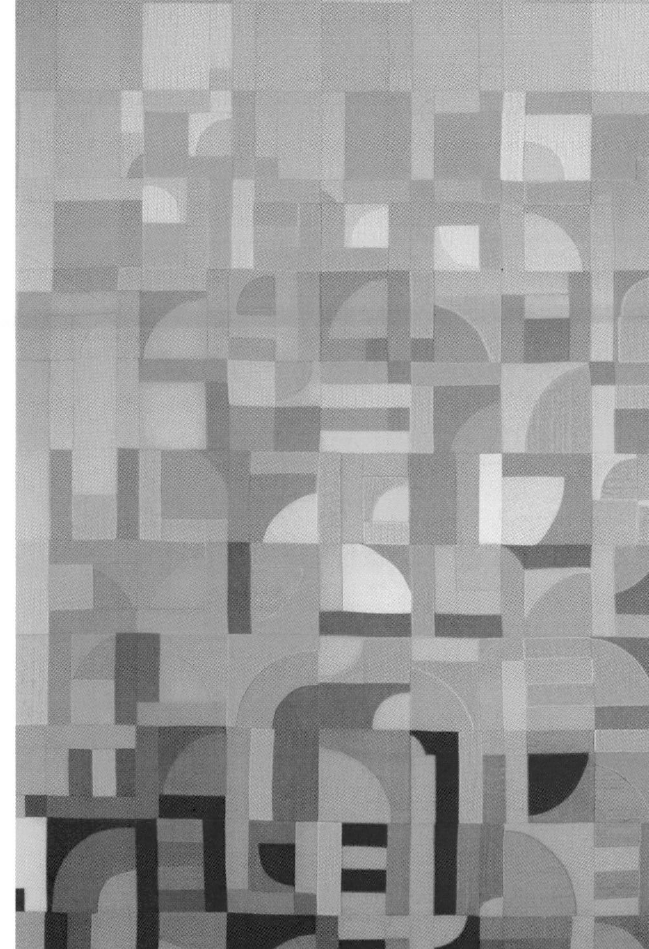

Top left: *High Road 2 Tobermory* (detail), 2006, art quilt, 40"H x 56"W.
Right: *Hacienda*, 2005, art quilt, 72"H x 36"W. Bottom left: *Alpineglow* (detail), 2004, art quilt, 60"H x 30"W.

JAMES KOEHLER

THE KOEHLER STUDIO ■ 7 ESTAMBRE ROAD ■ SANTA FE, NM 87508
TEL 505-466-3924 ■ E-MAIL JKOEHLER@NETS.COM ■ WWW.JAMESKOEHLER.COM

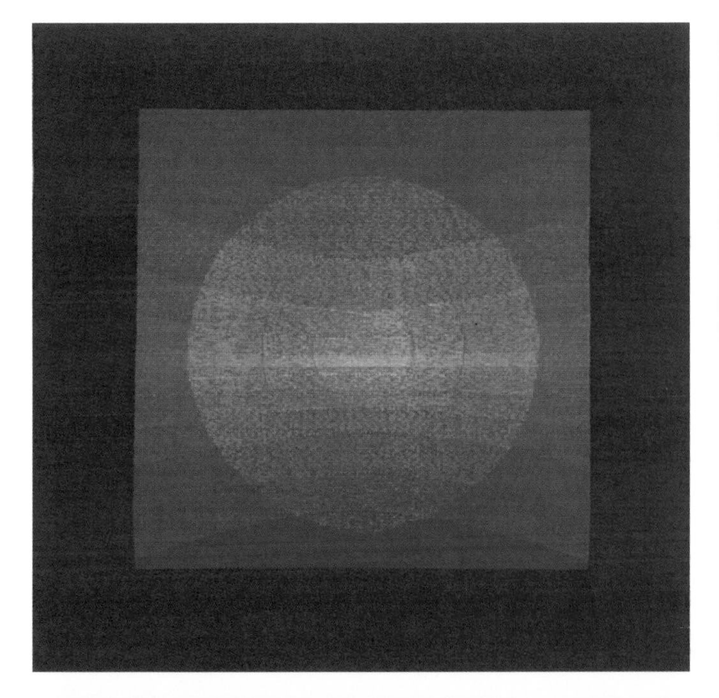

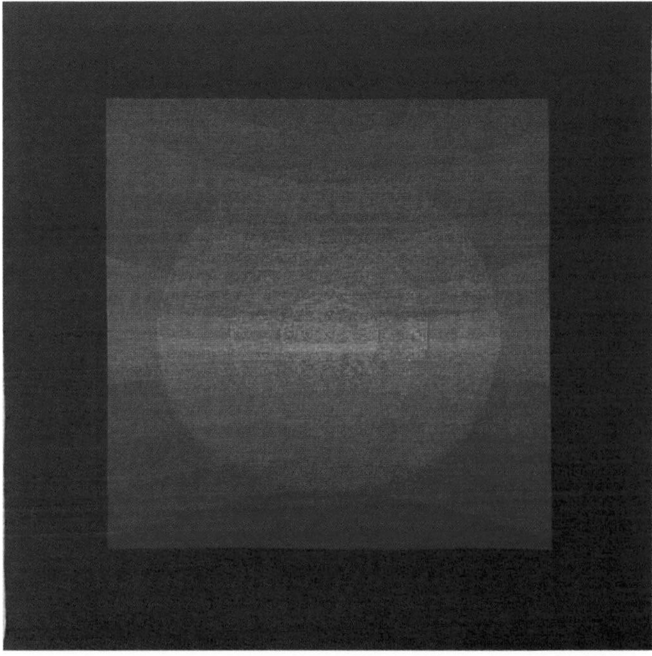

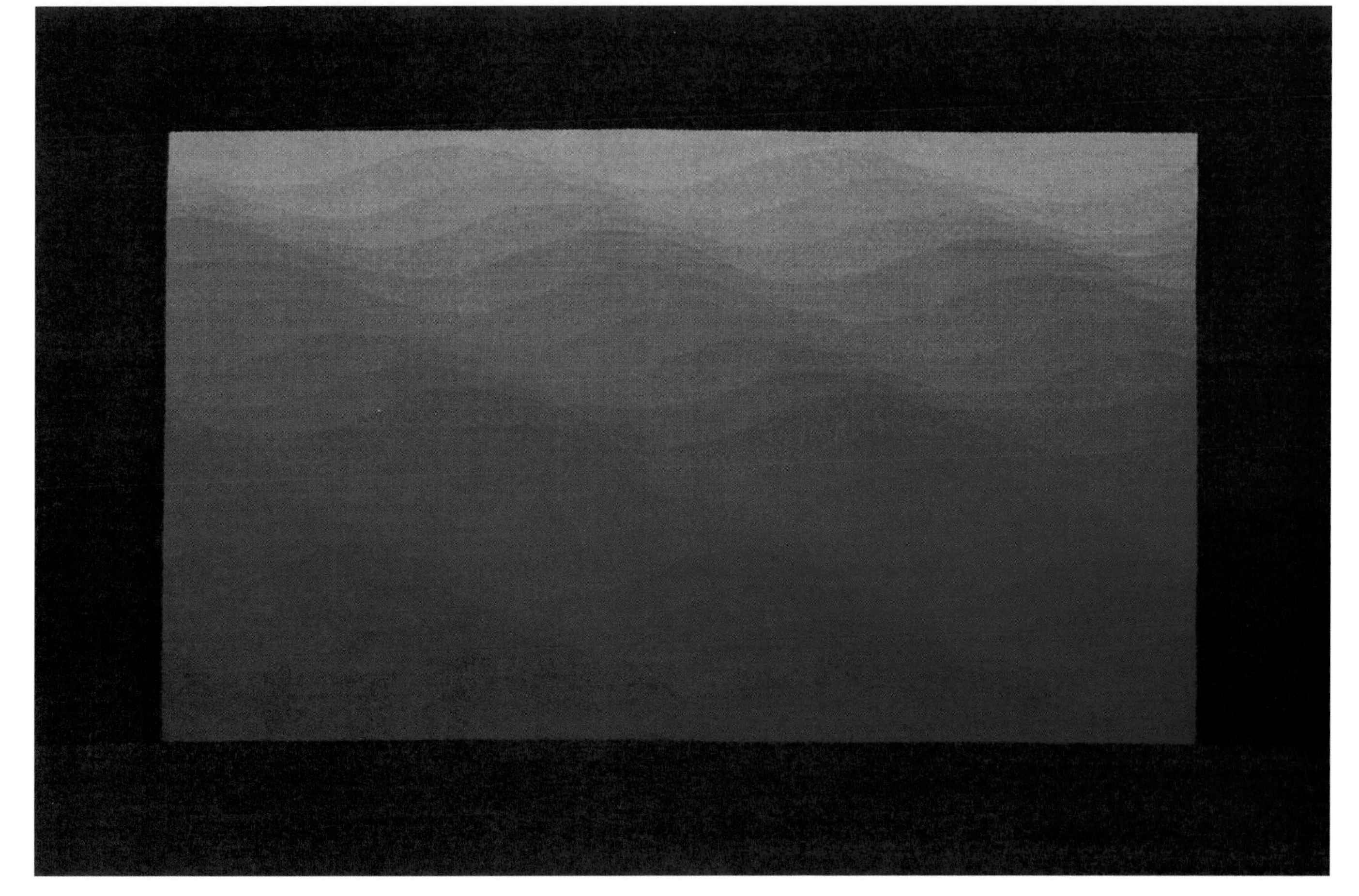

Top left: *Koan: Ensnared Light XII,* 2006, hand-dyed wool tapestry, 40" x 40". Photograph: James Hart. Top right: *Koan: Ensnared Light XIII,* 2006, hand-dyed wool tapestry, 40" x 40". Photograph: James Hart. Bottom: *Harmonic Oscillation XXXV,* 2006, U.S. Embassy, Reykjavik, Iceland, hand-dyed wool tapestry, 42" x 62".

OUT OF THE MAINSTREAM DESIGNS

CHRISTINE L. KEFER ■ 107 SOUTH SECOND STREET ■ PO BOX 725 ■ GENEVA, IL 60134 ■ TEL 630-232-2419
FAX 630-232-2491 ■ E-MAIL C.KEFER@ATT.NET ■ WWW.OUTOFTHEMAINSTREAMDESIGNS.COM

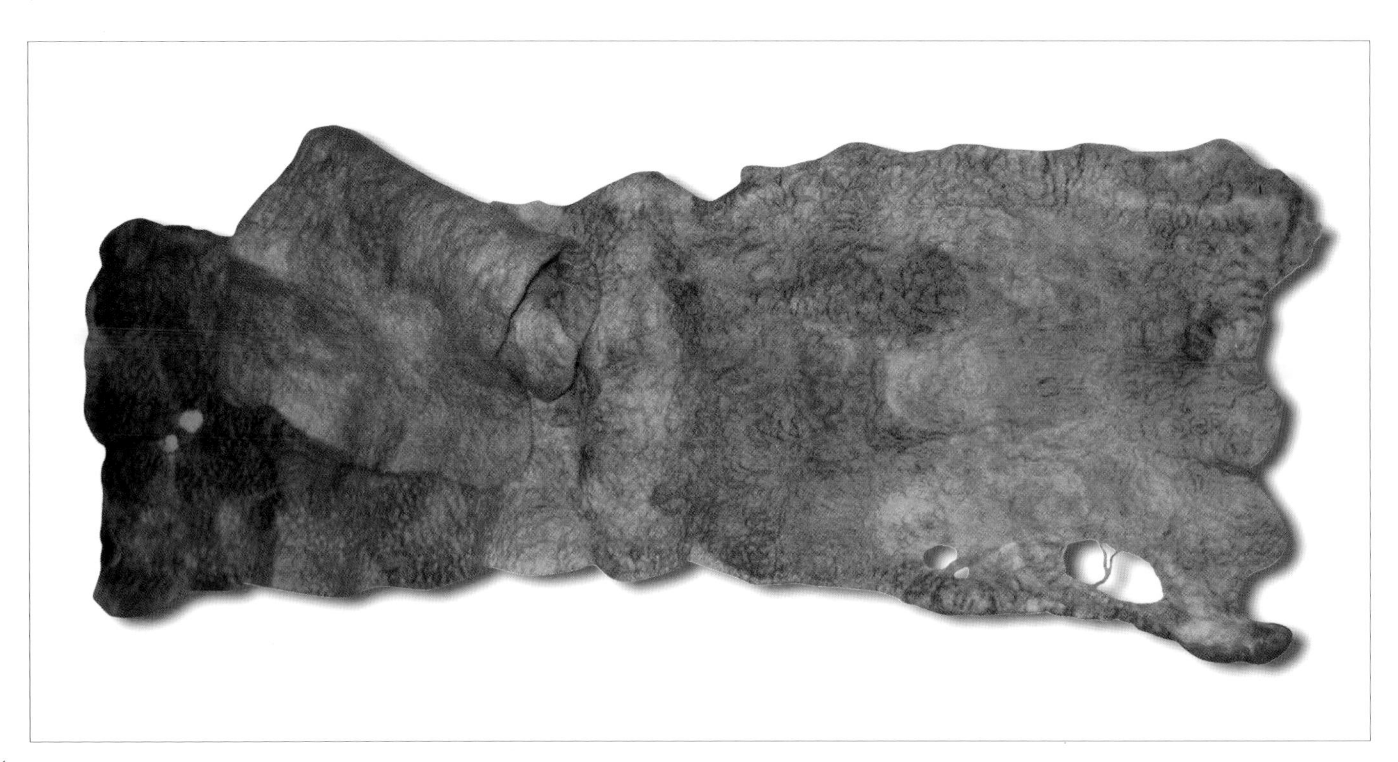

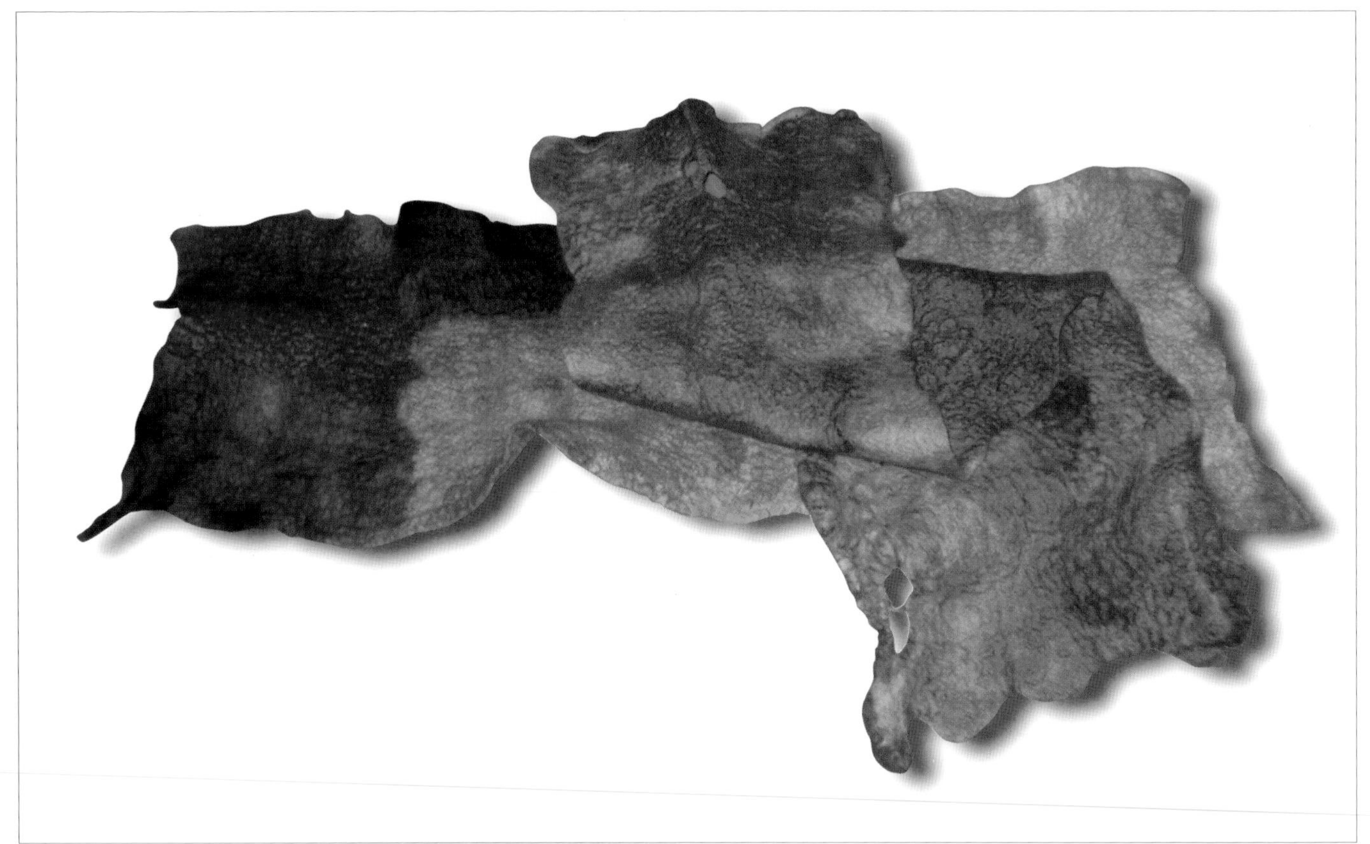

Goldenrod series, hand-felted merino wool landscape panel.

KAREN URBANEK

314 BLAIR AVENUE ■ PIEDMONT, CA 94611-4004 ■ TEL 510-654-0685 ■ FAX 510-654-2790
E-MAIL KU@KARENURBANEK.COM ■ WWW.KARENURBANEK.COM

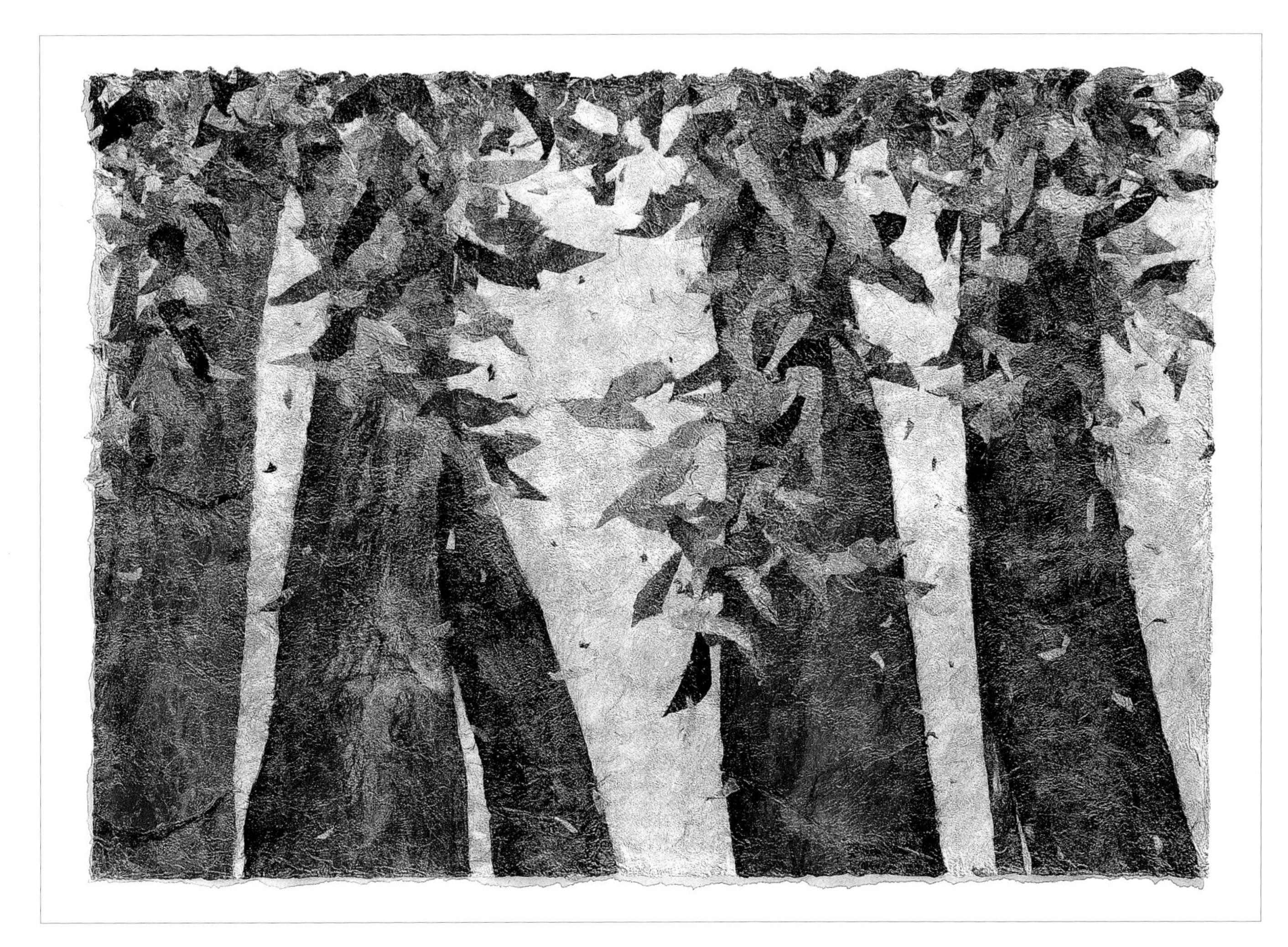

Culms 1 of 3, The Lodge at Woodloch, Hawley, PA, naturally dyed silk fiber and polymer, 42" x 60". Photograph: Don Tuttle Photography

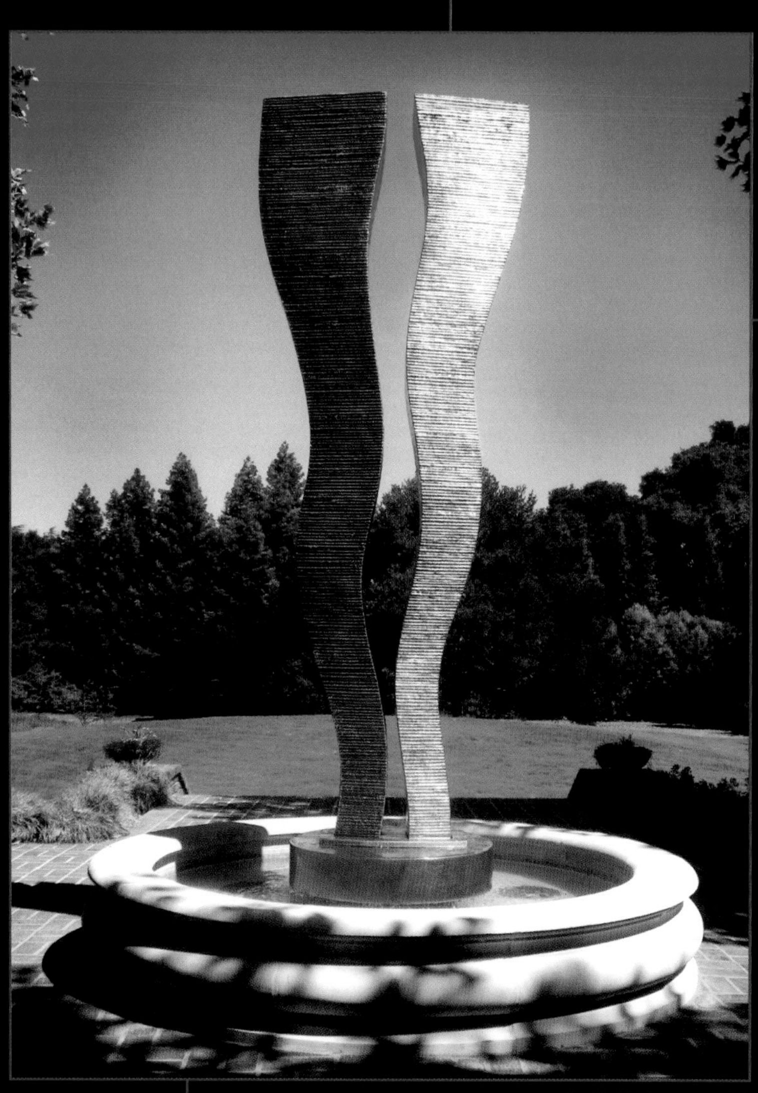

Archie Held, see page 85.

Resources

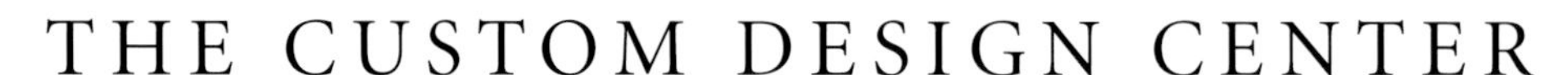

THE CUSTOM DESIGN CENTER

A feature of the Guild.com website

The Guild Sourcebooks give architects, designers, and art consultants the essential tools to find and commission original works of art. Within these pages you can find photographs showing a range of products, media, and art forms, as well as contact information so that you can connect directly with the artists who offer them.

But The Guild offers another avenue to find hundreds of other artwork options: the Custom Design Center, an online complement to The Guild's paper-and-ink sourcebooks. Best of all, it's free to use!

Available through the Guild.com website, the Custom Design Center features images of work by artists who have advertised in *Sourcebook 22* and others. In addition to artwork appropriate for corporate, public, and liturgical spaces, the Custom Design Center also features hundreds of unique residential pieces.

USE THE GUILD'S CUSTOM DESIGN CENTER TO:

- Search for the perfect work of art by art category or artist's name
- Post your project specifications to hundreds of artists through our online form
- Create an online presentation for a client by saving images or links
- Get help from one of our trade sales consultants by e-mail or phone

Visit The Guild's Custom Design Center at **www.guild.com/cdc**, or call 877-565-2002 to discuss your idea with one of our consultants. They can recommend candidates for a specific job, assess the qualifications of individual artists, or help draft letters of agreement.

Above: Markian Olynyk, three-story glass wall mural (detail), see pages 50 and 121. Photograph: Joaquin Pedrero.

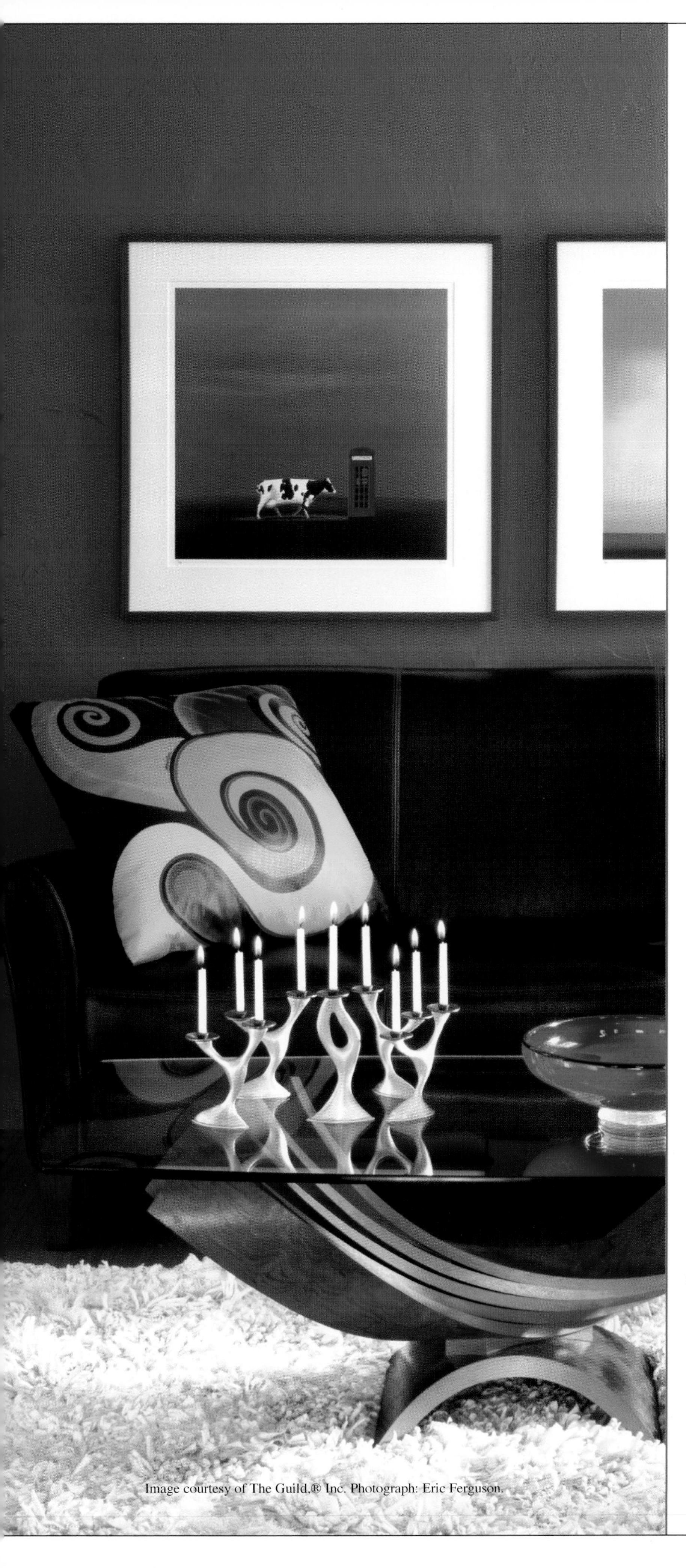
Image courtesy of The Guild,® Inc. Photograph: Eric Ferguson.

Indulge your Passion for Art

In every lavish issue, you'll find:

- Artist Profiles
- Savvy Collectors
- Interiors Showcase
- Arts Travel
- Private Collections
- Collector Tips
- Design Trends
- Museum Highlights
- Art Calendar

IT'S ALL IN AWARD-WINNING

AMERICANStyle

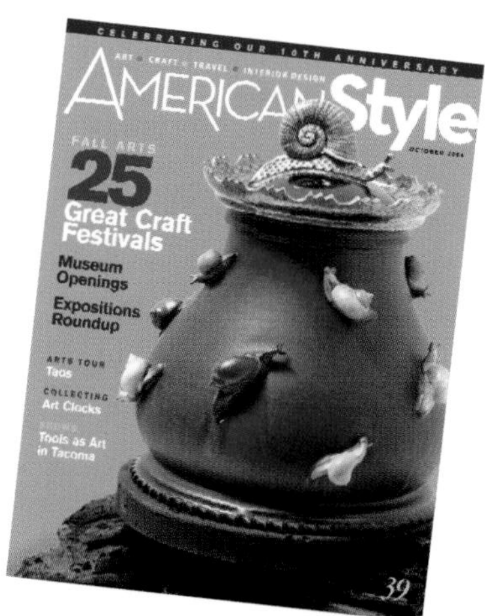

ORDER NOW!

One Year - 6 issues - Only $24.99
Two Years - 12 issues - Only $40.00

1.800.272.3893
www.AmericanStyle.com

Use Code GUILD to recieve $5 off the subscriber price.

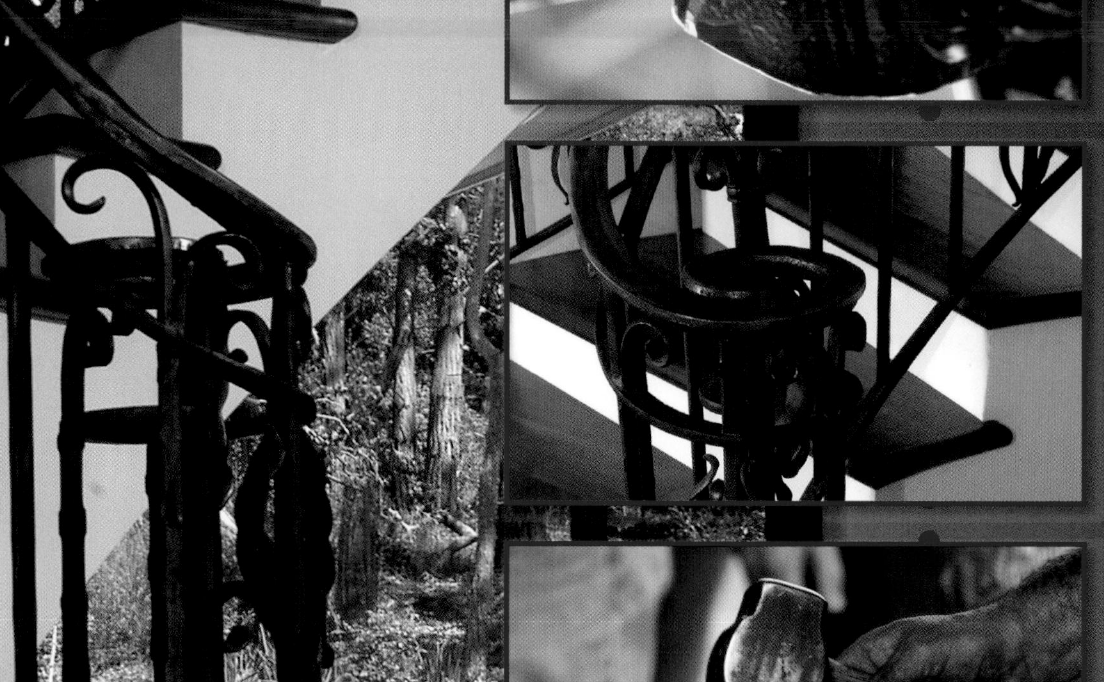

abana.org

Artist-Blacksmith's

Association of North America, Inc.

ABANA

PO Box 816

Farmington, GA 30838

(706) 310-1030

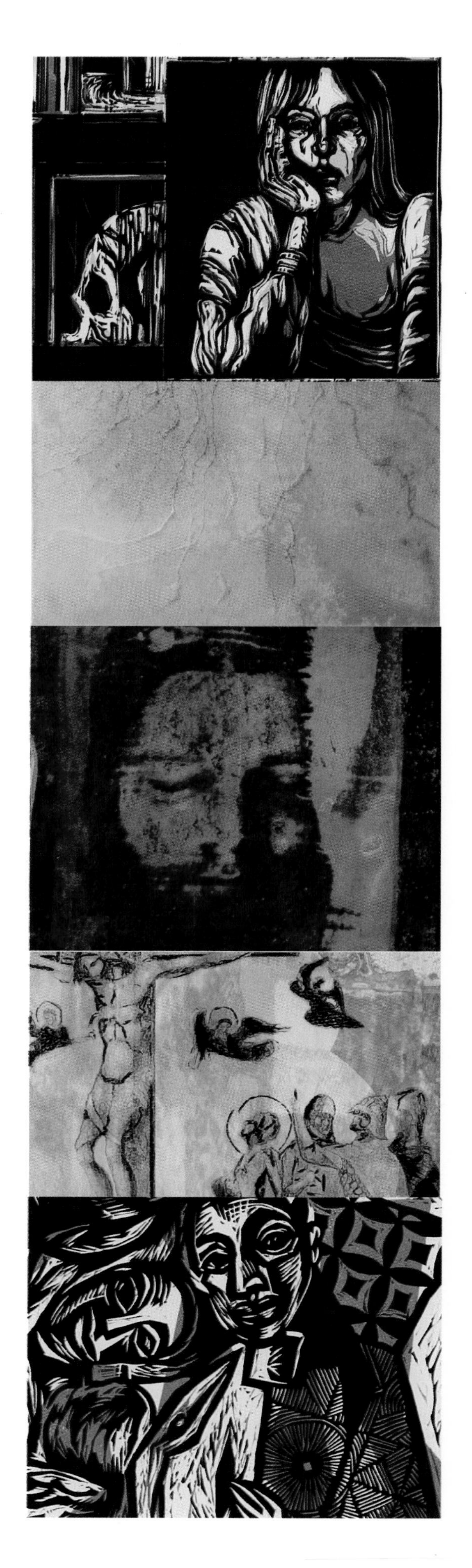

support the artist

serve the Church

engage the culture

Founded in 1979, Christians in the Visual Arts (CIVA) sets the standard for Christian non-profit organizations consisting of professionals in the visual arts. With nearly 1400 members and a network of over 9,000 individuals and organizations, CIVA connects artists, scholars, patrons, churches, and the culture. CIVA encourages Christians participating in the visual arts to develop their callings to the highest professional level; to learn how to engage specific issues within the field without compromising either faith or standards of artistic endeavor; to provide opportunities for sharing work and ideas; to foster understanding, trust, and cooperative relationships among those in the arts, Church and society. Our mission is to encourage and support a Christian presence within the art world.

CIVA is rooted at the core of a movement within the Church and culture. The past three decades have seen growth in the number of churches and seminaries introducing arts programs as a form of renewal of the visual within worship and theology. CIVA continues to support universities, colleges and seminaries; the work of local congregations; students enrolled in studio, art history, and art criticism programs; and finally, artists and art professionals currently shaping the cultural landscape.

CIVA Office
255 Grapevine Road
Wenham, MA
01984

(ph) 978-867-4124
(fax) 978-867-4125
office@civa.org
www.civa.org

Christians in the Visual Arts is the premier visual arts organization connecting the artist, the Church, and the culture.

Artists, top to bottom: M. Parker, M. Fujimura, K. Brimberry, J. Millet, and T. Butler. These original works and others are available at www.civa.org. Visit the site to find out about CIVA's conferences, workshops, exhibitions, publications, and more.

THE JOURNAL OF CERAMIC ART TRENDS, TOOLS, & TECHNIQUES

CLAY TIMES®

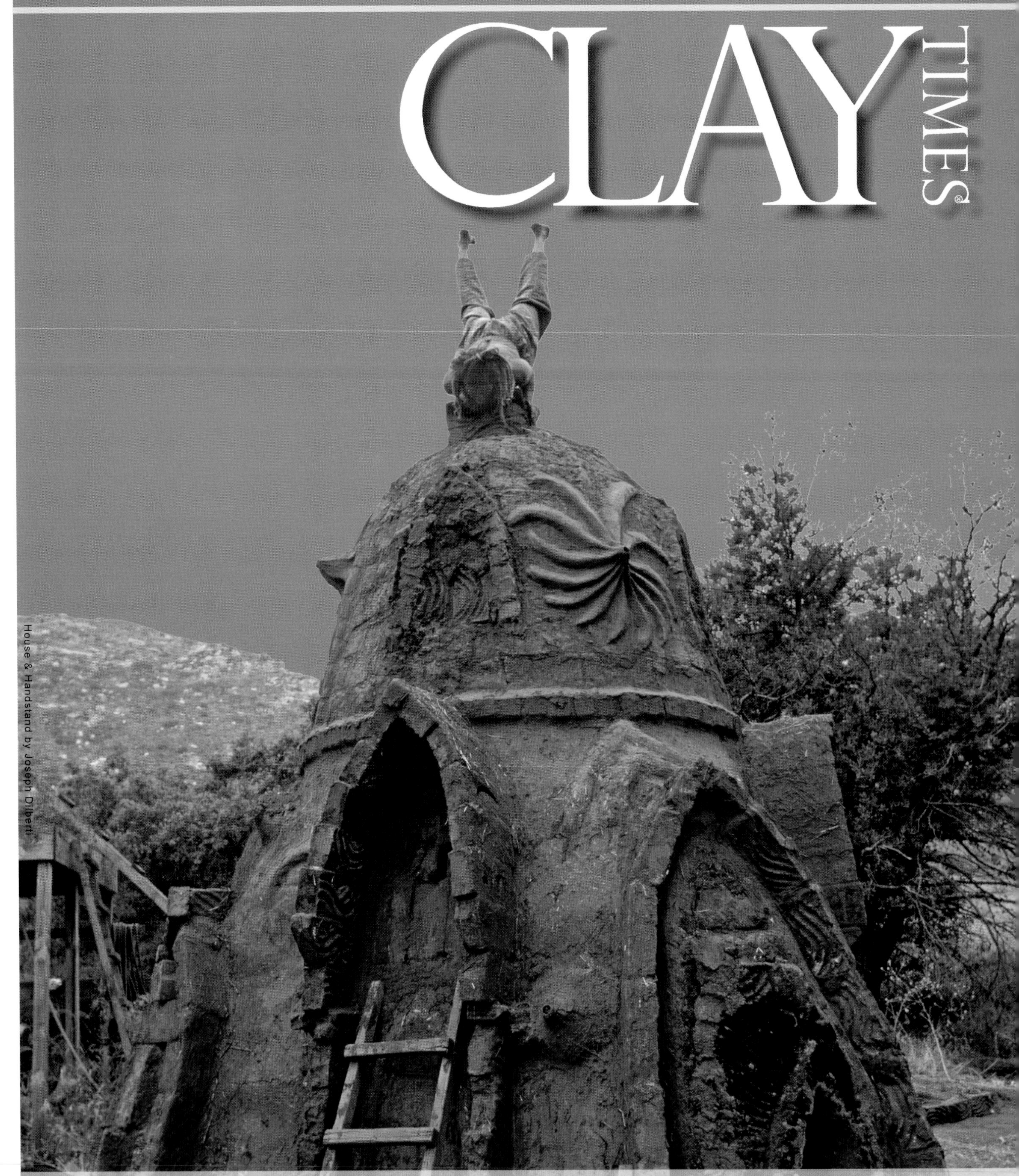

Call toll-free to subscribe (800) 356-2529 or visit www.claytimes.com

Inside every issue of CWB:

high-end projects ... custom niches ... amazing talent

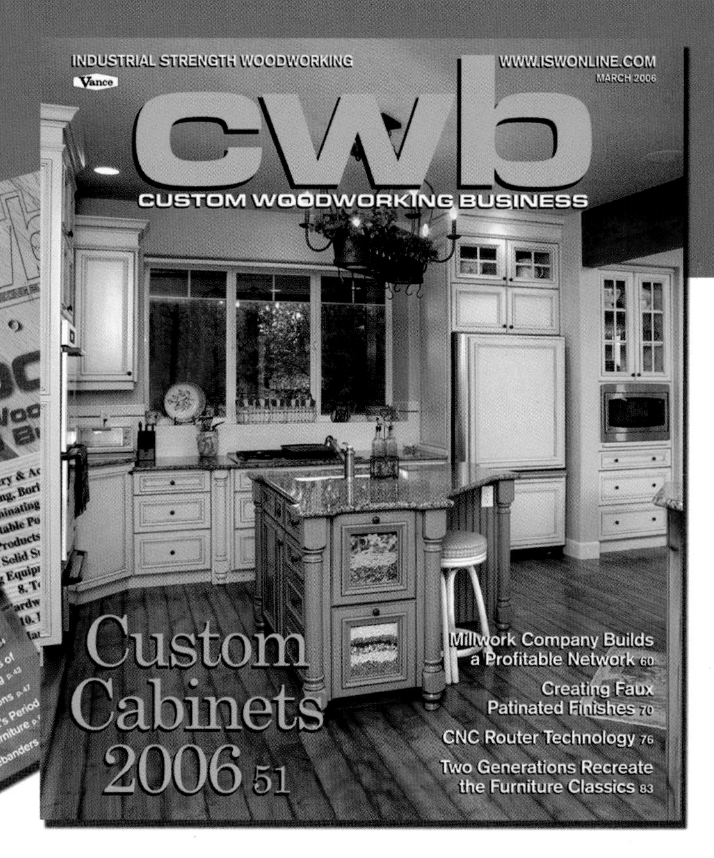

Custom Woodworking Business not only defines the custom woodworking market, it remains the only publication dedicated to serving it.

Custom Woodworking Business • CWB Illustrated Buying Guide • CWB Woodworking Expos & Cabinet Conferences

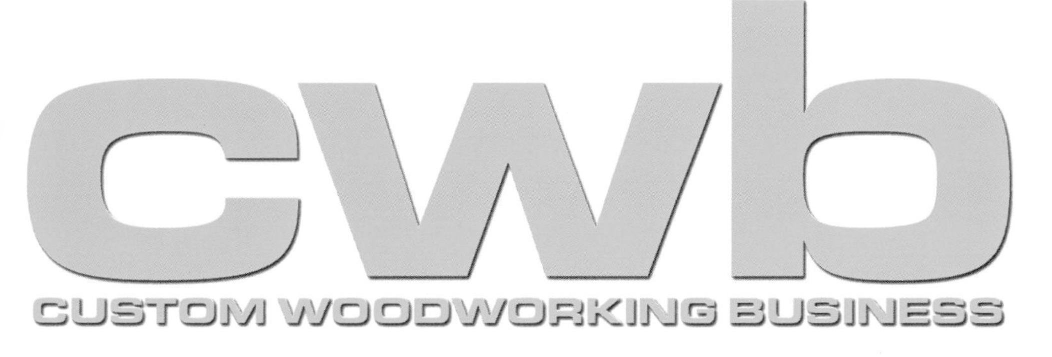

The right information is everything. And so is the right source.

800-343-2016 • Fax: 847-634-4374
industrialinfo@vancepublishing.com
www.iswonline.com

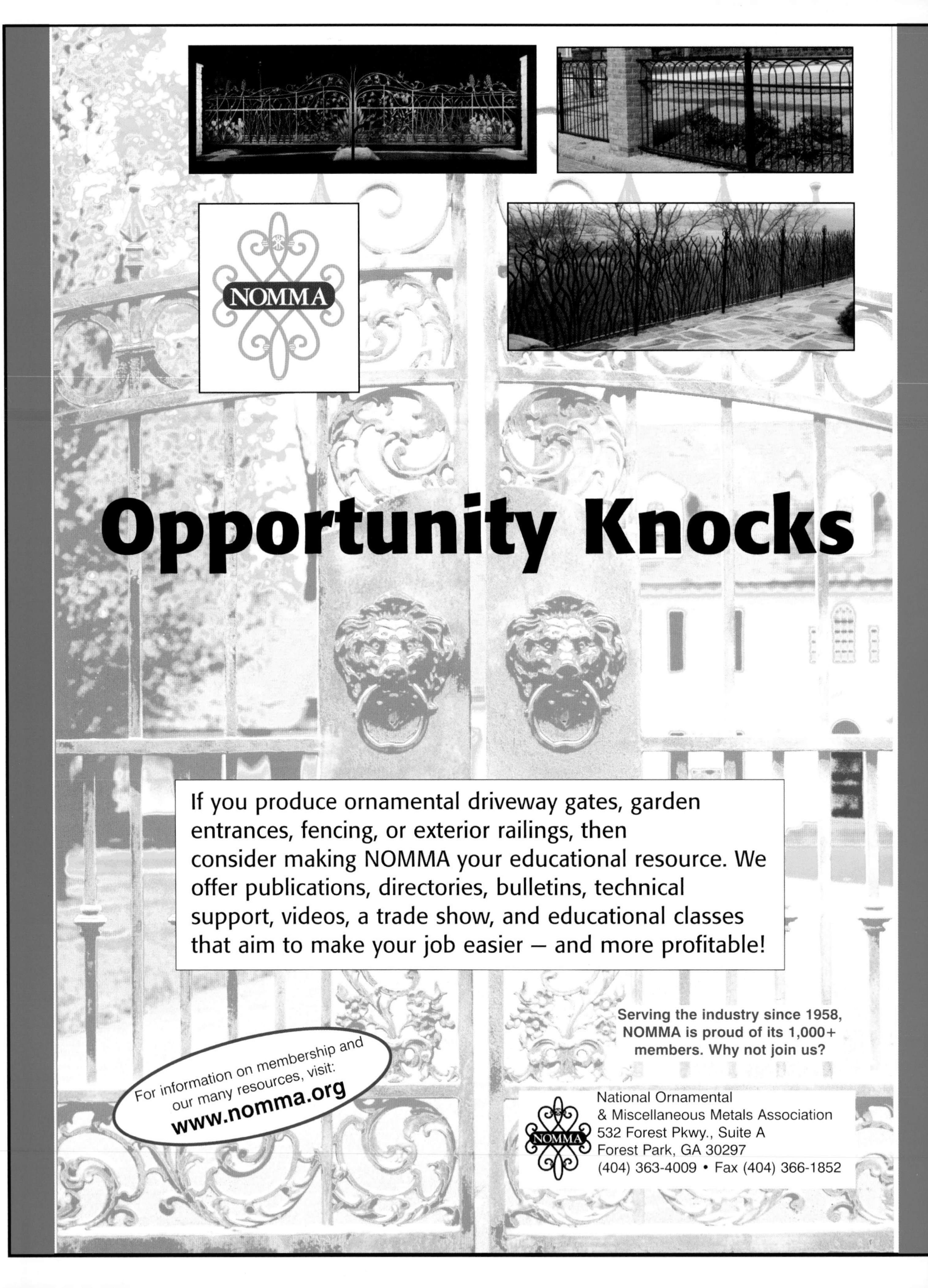
NOMMA
Opportunity Knocks
If you produce ornamental driveway gates, garden entrances, fencing, or exterior railings, then consider making NOMMA your educational resource. We offer publications, directories, bulletins, technical support, videos, a trade show, and educational classes that aim to make your job easier – and more profitable!
Serving the industry since 1958, NOMMA is proud of its 1,000+ members. Why not join us?
For information on membership and our many resources, visit:
www.nomma.org
NOMMA
National Ornamental
& Miscellaneous Metals Association
532 Forest Pkwy., Suite A
Forest Park, GA 30297
(404) 363-4009 • Fax (404) 366-1852

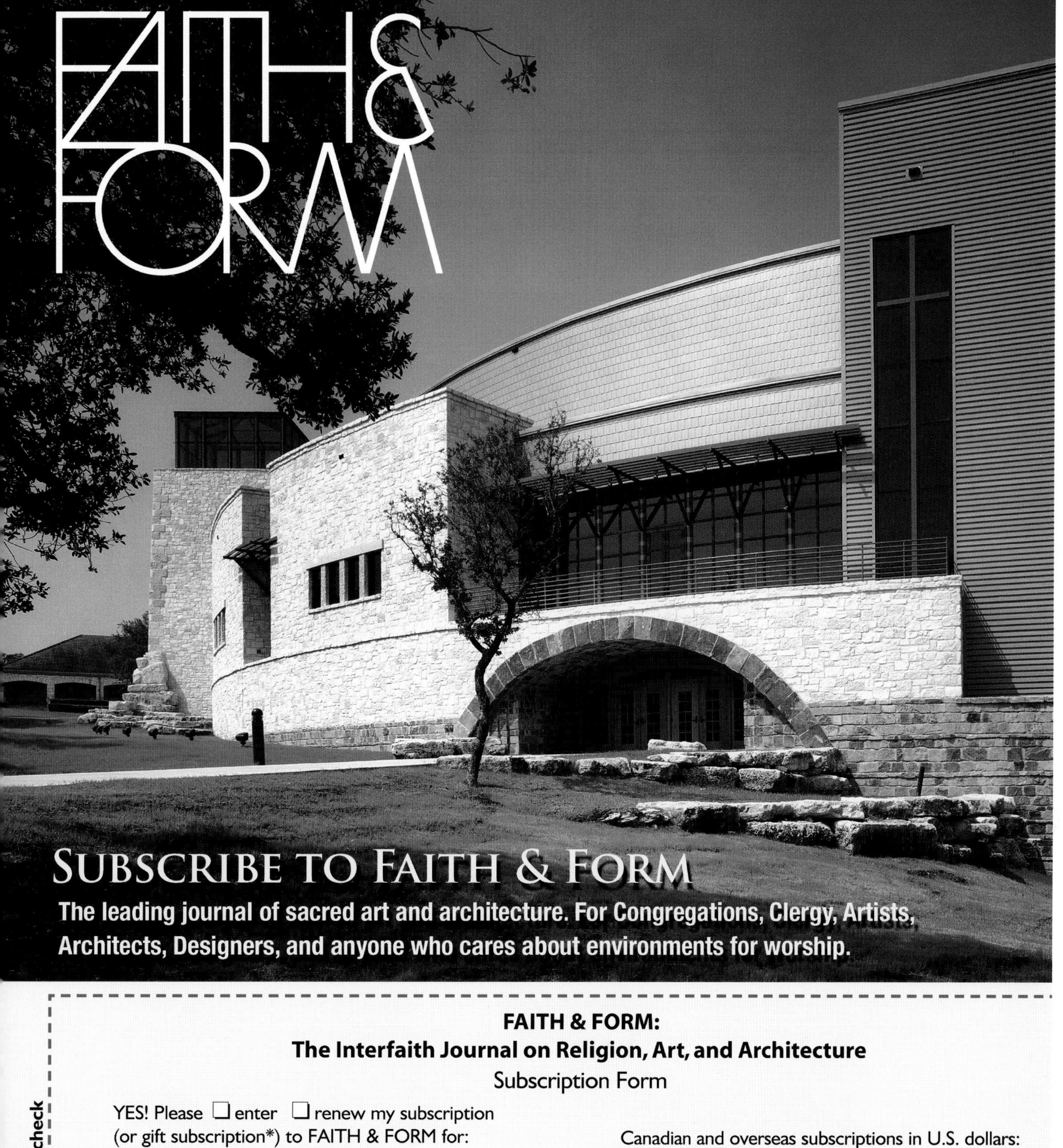

FAITH & FORM:
The Interfaith Journal on Religion, Art, and Architecture
Subscription Form

YES! Please ☐ enter ☐ renew my subscription (or gift subscription*) to FAITH & FORM for:

☐ 1 year, $36 ☐ 2 years, $60

Canadian and overseas subscriptions in U.S. dollars:

☐ 1 year, $46 ☐ 2 years, $70

☐ *Check here if this is a gift suscription and enclose name and address of your gift recipient. An attractive card will be sent in your name.

Name ______ Company/Organization ______
Address ______
City/State/Zip ______ Phone ______

cut and mail with check

GLASS ART Magazine

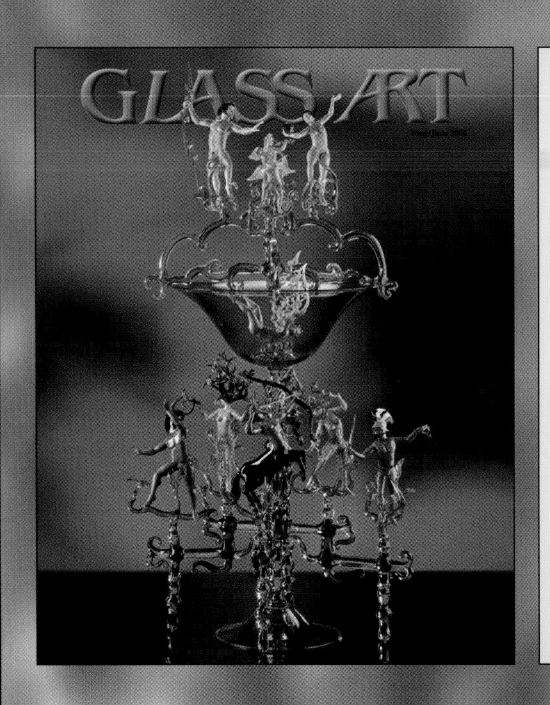

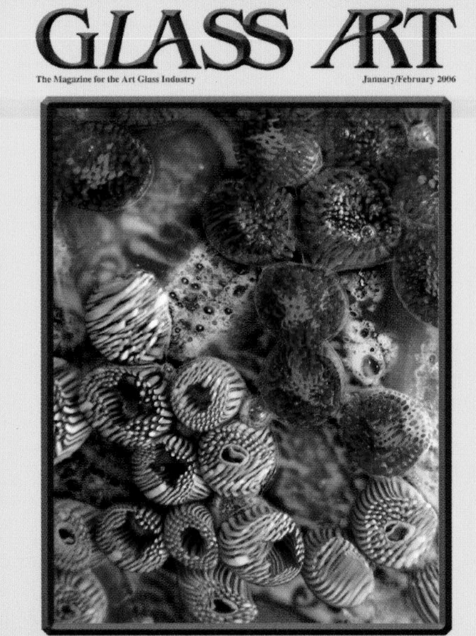

Subscribe Today!

United States:
Canada/Mexico: (U.S. Funds)
- ❑ **One Year (6 Issues) $30**
- ❑ **Two Years (12 Issues) $48**
- ❑ **Three Years (18 Issues) $60**

Foreign: (U.S. Funds)
- ❑ **One Year (6 Issues) $56**
- ❑ **One Year (AIRMAIL) $70**

Sample issues are available for $7.
Back issues also available for $7.

GLASS ART
P.O. Box 260377
Highlands Ranch, CO 80163-0377
(303) 791-8998 Fax: (303) 791-7739
info@glassartmagazine.com

www.glassartmagazine.com

Beautiful, four-color reproduction of glass works by the nation's finest artists and craftspeople.

Practical and easy-to-read technical articles on cold and hot glass processes.

Features on successful, professional artists, addressing their philosophies and lifestyles as well as their techniques and secrets for success.

Business articles for the retailer and professional studio.

The latest in Industry News, Products, Catalogs, Pattern Books and resource materials.

The annual Directory To Industry Supplies, intended to link products and services to people in the industry.

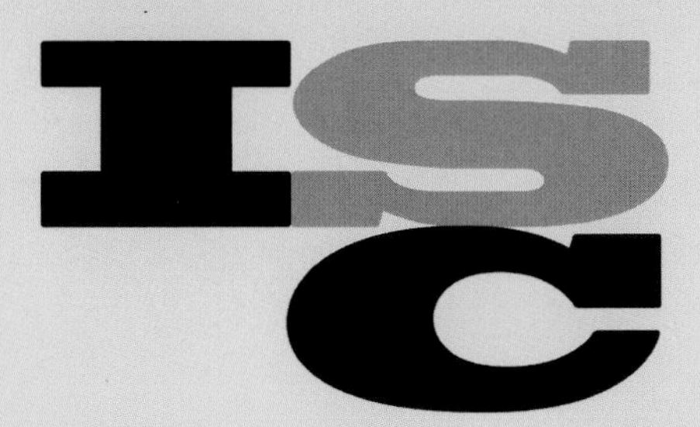

IN MEMORIAM:
ROB FISHER
1939-2006

Rob Fisher, a prominent sculptor and long-time member of the Board of Directors of the International Sculpture Center, died from sudden cardiac arrest on September 13, 2006, at the age of 67.

Rob's contributions to the science of art and architecture were tremendous, as evidenced by *The Design Continuum: An Approach to Understanding Visual Form,* a seminal book on visual design that he co-authored as a graduate student at Syracuse University. In 1979, Rob's interest in larger pieces led to his innovative use of computer visualization to model his work. A pioneer in computer-assisted art, he created works of art now considered formative for the field. One of Rob's many major public art commissions included *American Dream,* which was completed for the Philadelphia International Airport Arrivals Hall in 2003. *Solar Sails* was completed by Rob in 2006 and installed in 2007 by his studio, which will continue under the direction of Rob's daughter, Talley Fisher, who worked with Rob for many years.

The family requests that any memorial donations go to the International Sculpture Center. For further information on works continuing Rob Fisher's artistic legacy, contact: Rob Fisher Sculpture, LLC, 228 North Allegheny Street, Bellefonte, PA 16823. Tel: 814-355-1458, E-mail: robfishersculpture@yahoo.com.

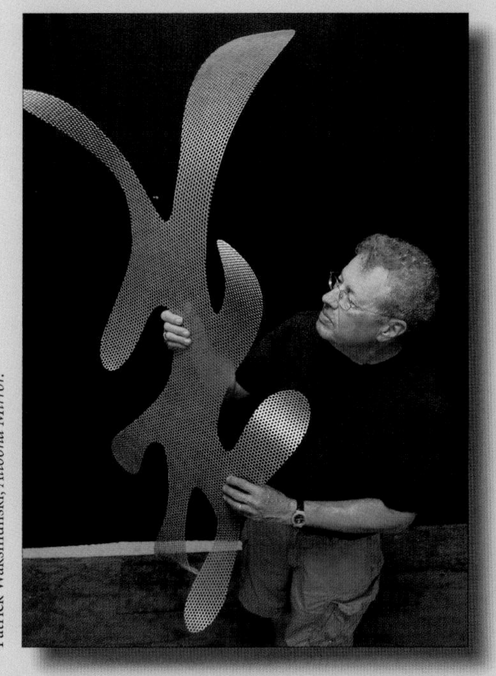

Patrick Waksmunski, *Altoona Mirror.*

American Dream. Photograph: Richard McMullin.

The International Sculpture Center (ISC) is a member-supported, nonprofit organization founded in 1960 to advance the creation and understanding of sculpture and its unique, vital contribution to society. Members include sculptors, collectors, patrons, architects, developers, journalists, curators, historians, critics, educators, foundries, galleries, and museums—anyone with an interest in and commitment to the field of sculpture. The ISC also publishes *Sculpture,* an international, monthly magazine dedicated to all forms of contemporary sculpture. It contains provocative criticisms, knowledgeable technical discussions, and timely exploration of new materials and techniques.

INTERNATIONAL SCULPTURE CENTER
19 Fairgrounds Road, Suite B
Hamilton, NJ 08619
P: 609.689.1051 F: 609.689.1061
www.sculpture.org

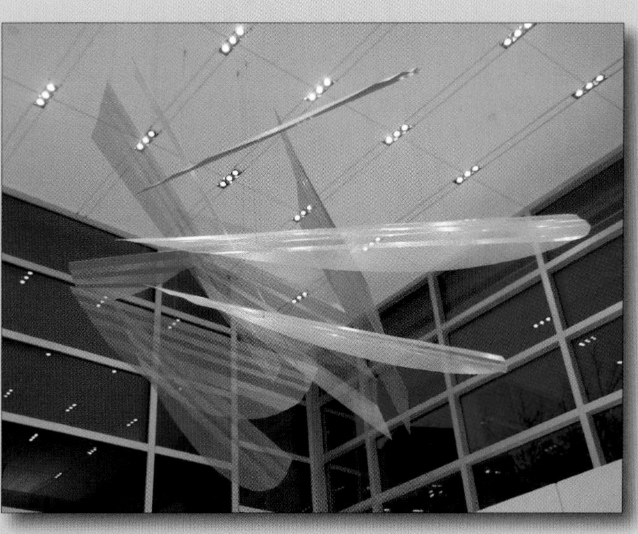

Solar Sails.

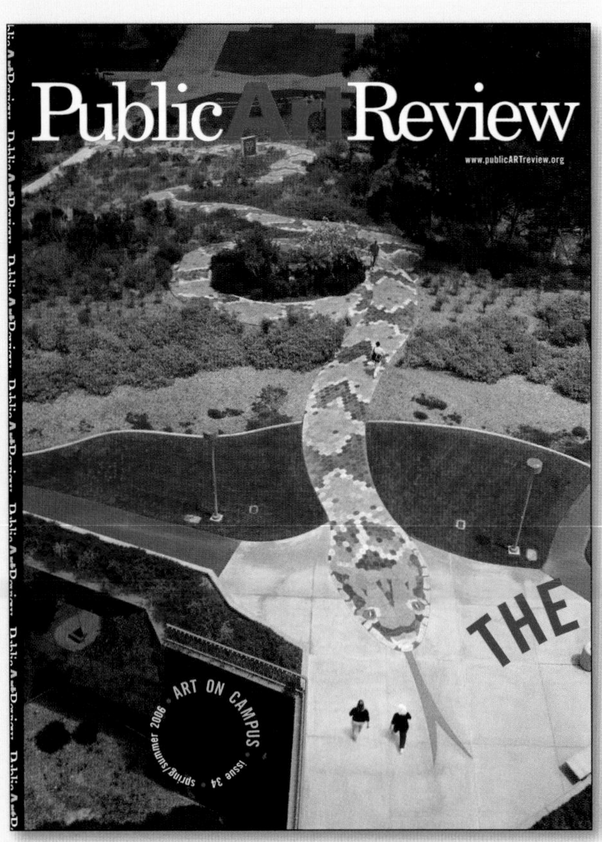

Each issue, focused on a different theme, is packed with insightful commentary, in-depth international coverage and innovative new projects. Published twice annually, the journal is enjoyed by thousands of readers in all 50 states and 20 foreign countries. Visit our website to learn more.

- **ORDER** / *from our catalog of 35 back issues.*
- **ADVERTISE** / *your work to a diverse audience.*
- **SUBSCRIBE** / *to an award-winning publication.*

THE ONLY JOURNAL IN THE WORLD devoted exclusively to public art.

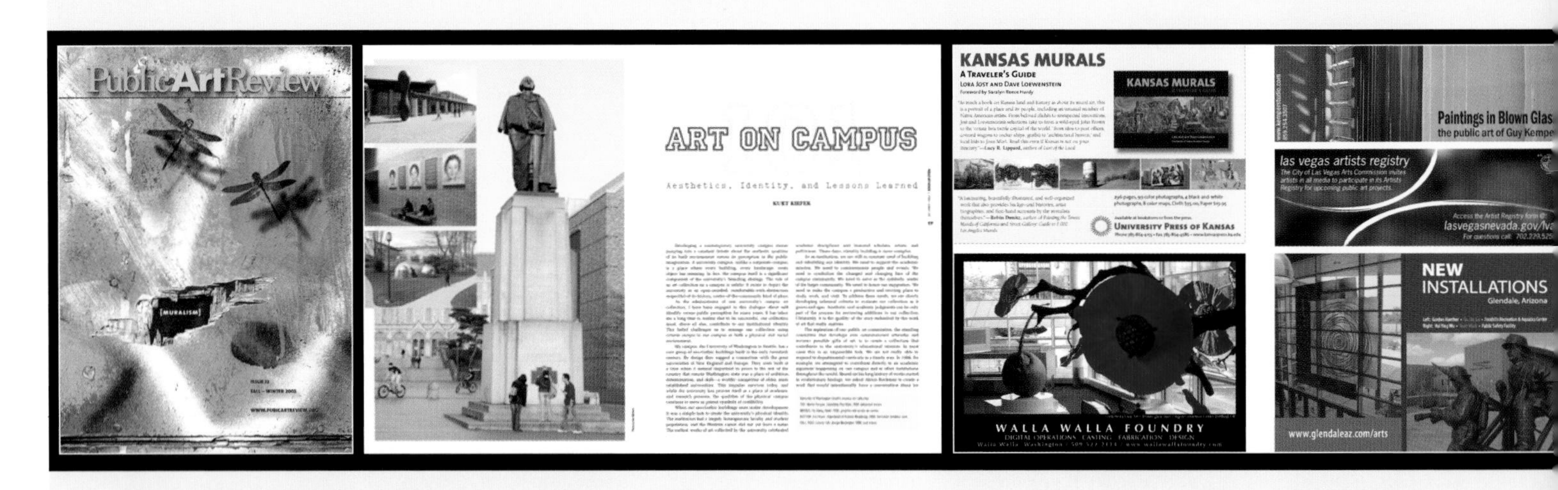

Public Art Review

Published twice a year since 1989 by FORECAST Public Artworks.

www.publicARTreview.org

sculpture

A publication of the International Sculpture Center

www.sculpture.org

Sculpture is the only international monthly publication devoted exclusively to the world of sculpture. It features lively dialogue, penetrating interviews, intimate studio visits and provocative criticism on both emerging and internationally renowned artists.

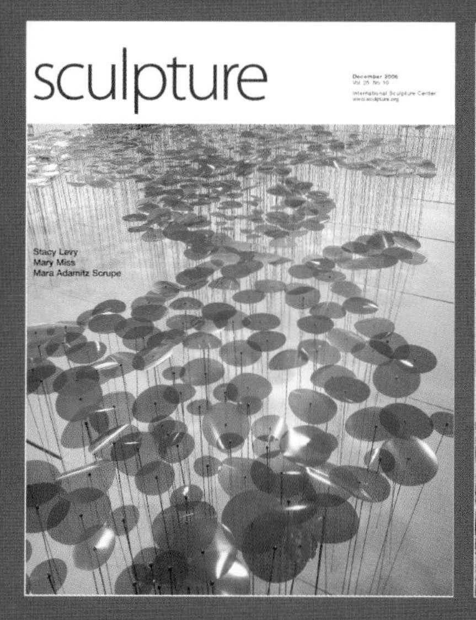

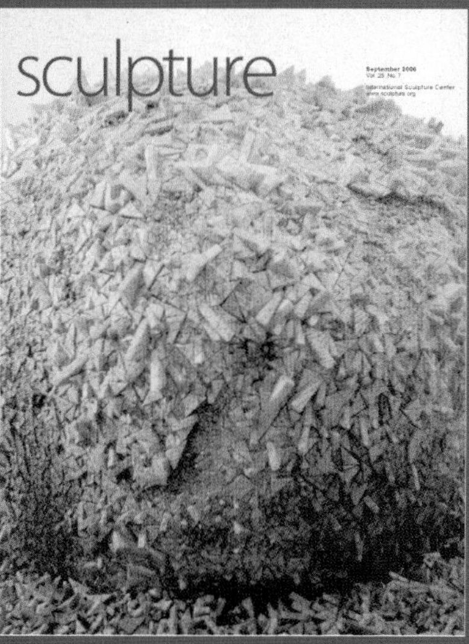

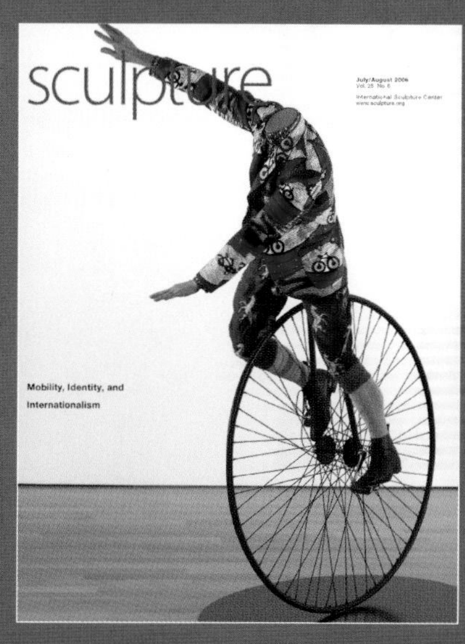

Sculpture magazine is published monthly (except February and August) by the International Sculpture Center (ISC), a not-for-profit organization founded in 1960 that advances the creation and understanding of sculpture and its unique, vital contribution to society. The ISC distributes *Sculpture* magazine as a member benefit and through subscription to non-members. Membership is open to anyone.

To become an ISC Member and subscribe to *Sculpture*:
phone 609.689.1051 ext. 301
fax 609.689.1061
email membership@sculpture.org
Or visit www.sculpture.org to join online.

To advertise in *Sculpture*:
phone 609.689.1051
fax 609.689.1061
email advertising@sculpture.org

Become a part of the
World Art Glass Community

World artGlass Quarterly

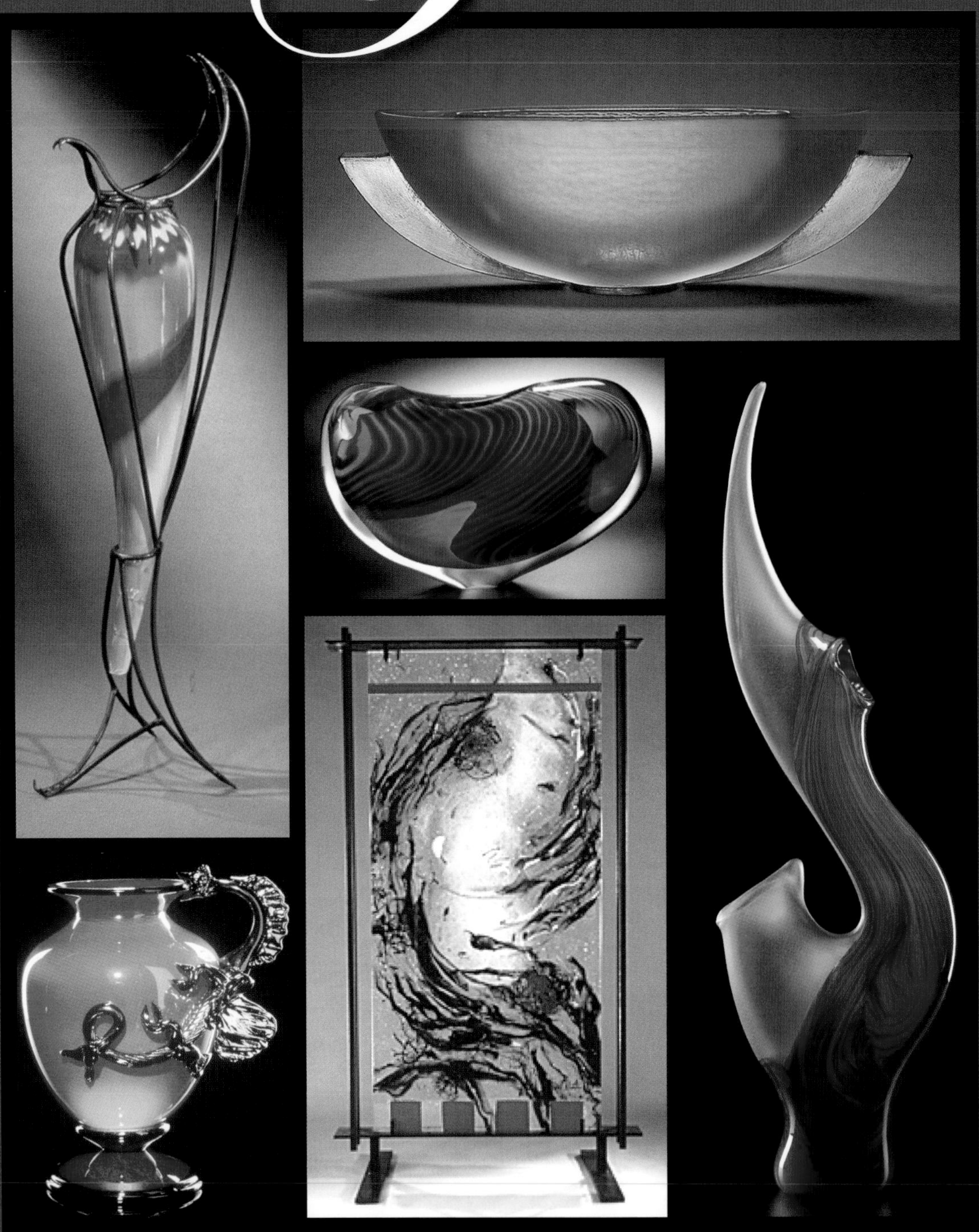

www.artglassquarterly.com

LISTING OF ART CONSULTANTS

As the scope of commissioned art has grown, so has the need for the technical mastery required to find, select, and place art. Art consultants have taken the job of matching art to environment, and developed it into a sophisticated profession that incorporates expertise in art, architecture, engineering, lighting, acoustics, law, human relations, and aesthetics. This establishes them as a uniquely qualified professional resource for the design trade in the execution of widely varied projects.

Consultants are particularly helpful when the scale of a project or the number of pieces demand assistance, or on large commissioned works that may involve design competitions. An experienced art consultant brings the know-how to orchestrate a project from conception to installation and beyond—from cataloging and maintenance to public relations.

The pages that follow provide a state-by-state listing of art consultants who stand ready to provide this expertise.

LISTING OF ART CONSULTANTS

ALABAMA

Corporate Art Source

Est. 1984
2960-F Zelda Road
Montgomery, AL 36106
CONTACT: Jean or Kevin Rainer
TEL 334-271-3772
FAX 334-271-3772
EMAIL casjb@mindspring.com
WEB www.casgallery.com

ARIZONA

C. Smith Fine Art Advisory

Est. 2002
1942 E. San Miguel Avenue
Phoenix, AZ 85016
CONTACT: Carly Smith
TEL 602-403-6469
FAX 602-283-5730
EMAIL info@csmithfineartadvisory.com
WEB www.csmithfineartadvisory.com

Niemann Hayden Fine Art

Est. 2000
1733 E. McKellips Road #103
Tempe, AZ 85281
CONTACT: Donna Niemann
TEL 480-315-1151
FAX 480-315-1116
EMAIL niemannhayden@earthlink.net

Niemann Hayden Fine Art is an art gallery and art consulting business. Depending on budget, projects have used poster art to fine original commission pieces. We work exclusively with commercial/residential designers, builders, and architects. We look forward to being a support affiliate to you in furnishing, art, and framing.

CLIENTS INCLUDE: Robson Ranch Clubhouse Casa Grande; Scottsdale Healthcare Shea—Women's Center; Aviano Community Center; Copperwynd Villas; Province Community Center; Scottsdale Conference Resort; Equiant Financial Services; DC Ranch, Gainey Health Club; Robson Ranch Clubhouse Denton, TX; Secille Country Club Clubhouse

ARKANSAS

art-exchange.com, Inc.

Est. 1998
804 Central Avenue
Hot Springs, AR 71901
CONTACT: Rodger Gipe
TEL 501-624-1044
FAX 501-624-2859
EMAIL pgipe@art-exchange.com
WEB www.artexchange.com

Simply the best place on earth to buy or sell fine art. We have wholesale and retail prices listed for your convenience. There is a full staff of professionals to aid the designer or just the art buyer. Give us a try, we have a satisfaction guarantee on all of our products.

CALIFORNIA

Aesthetics, Inc.

Est. 1980
301 Spruce Street
San Diego, CA 92103
CONTACT: Leah Goodwin
TEL 619-683-7500
FAX 619-683-7510
EMAIL goodwin@aesthetics.net
WEB www.aesthetics.net

The Art Collector, Inc.

Est. 1971
4151 Taylor Street
San Diego, CA 92110
CONTACT: Janet Disraeli
TEL 619-299-3232
FAX 619-299-8709
EMAIL janet@theartcollector.com
WEB www.theartcollector.com

Art Group International

Est. 1982
3216 Nebraska Avenue
Santa Monica, CA 90606
CONTACT: Erica Aris
TEL 310-315-2626
FAX 310-315-9226
EMAIL erica.aris@artgroupinternational.com
WEB www.A-G-I.com

Art Source L.A., Inc.

Est. 1984
2801 Ocean Park Blvd. #7
Santa Monica, CA 90405
CONTACT: Francine Ellman
TEL 310-452-4411
FAX 310-452-0300
EMAIL francinee@artsourcela.com
WEB www.artsourcela.com

Fine art consulting worldwide. Innovative collections for the discriminating private collector, corporate facilities, hospitality industry, healthcare, and public spaces. Our art resources include abstract, contemporary, and representational; works on canvas, paper, mixed media, photography, master prints, murals, sculpture, art commissions, and accessories. Custom framing, shipping, and installation services.

CLIENTS INCLUDE: Booz Allen Hamilton; CB Richard Ellis; Century City Doctor's Hospital, Century City, CA; East West Bank, CA; Miyako Hotel, Kyoto, Japan; St. Joseph's Hospital & Medical Ctr., BNI Tower, Healing Garden, Phoenix, AZ; USC Zilkha Neurogenetic Institute, Los Angeles, CA; Waters & Kraus LLP, El Segundo, CA; Western Asset Management, Worldwide; White & Case, LLP, Los Angeles, CA

Artspiration

Est. 2002
45775 Ocotillo Dr. #1
Palm Desert, CA 92260
CONTACT: Victoria Koutavas
TEL 760-776-4441
FAX 760-776-4441
EMAIL victoria@artspiration.com
WEB www.artspiration.com

Chandra Cerrito / Art Advisor

Est. 2004
626 Costa Drive
Napa, CA 94558
CONTACT: Chandra Cerrito
TEL 415-577-7537
FAX 707-257-0996
EMAIL chandra@chandracerrito.com
WEB www.chandracerrito.com

International Art Source

Est. 1994
8933 Lombard Place #221
San Diego, CA 92122
CONTACT: Nancy Hogstrom
TEL 858-457-2688
FAX 858-457-2688
EMAIL nhogstr1@san.rr.com

Lesli Pletcher Art Consultants

Est. 1998
6 Latham Lane
Sacramento, CA 95864
CONTACT: Lesli Pletcher
TEL 916-488-3163
FAX 916-488-3281
EMAIL lesli@pletcher.com
WEB www.lesli.pletcher.com

Paragone Gallery

621 West Knoll Drive
West Hollywood, CA 90069
CONTACT: Francie Kelley
TEL 310-659-0607
FAX 310-659-0895
EMAIL mail@paragonegallery.com
WEB www.paragonegallery.com

Paragone Gallery is a full-service Art Consulting business that provides a wide range of contemporary art for hotels, corporations, and residences. Owner Francie Kelley has been assisting Interior Designers in the selection, placement and acquisition of artwork for twenty years. Paragone offers unique custom framing and sees the projects through from art selection to frame design, delivery, and installation.

CLIENTS INCLUDE: Viceroy Hotels; The Bellagio Hotel; Borgata Hotel and Casino; The Mirage; Mandalay Bay; Four Seasons Hotels; Harrah's Hotels; Sheraton Delfina Hotel; The Hotel at Mandalay Bay; The Luxor

Regina Almaguer & Associates Art Consulting

Est. 1983
9 Pico Court
Orinda, CA 94563
CONTACT: Regina Almaguer
TEL 925-377-5531
FAX 925-377-5531
EMAIL ralmaguer@comcast.net

Regina Almaguer has been a public art administrator since 1983. She has extensive experience in managing complex and diverse projects for both public and private clients. Almaguer is recognized for her effectiveness in community outreach and for her ability to successfully integrate public input with client needs.

CLIENTS INCLUDE: Carpenter and Company, San Francisco, CA; John Portman & Associates, Atlanta, GA; Esherick Homsey Dodge and Davis Architects, San Francisco, CA; Bay Area Transit Consultants, San Francisco, CA; Shea Homes, Inc.; EDAW, San Francisco, CA; City and County of San Francisco, CA; San Francisco Bay Area Rapid Transit District, CA; City of Emeryville, CA; City of San Mateo, CA

Robin Ficara Fine Art

Est. 1999
269 S. Beverly Drive #417
Beverly Hills, CA 90212
CONTACT: Robin Ficara
TEL 323-651-4745
FAX 323-782-9989

Robin Ficara Fine Art represents emerging and established artists in all media and offers a unique selection of artwork that includes paintings, original works on paper, limited-edition prints, custom guestroom reproductions, photography, sculpture, murals, open editions, special commissions, mirrors and fine art glass, and ceramics.

CLIENTS INCLUDE: Bellagio, Las Vegas, NV; Borgata, Atlantic City, NJ; Grand Hyatt, Washington, DC; The Hotel at Mandalay Bay, Las Vegas, NV; Hotel Sofitel, Los Angeles, CA; Isle of Capri, Biloxi, MS; Palomar Hotel Dupont Circle, Washington, DC; Red Rock Casino, Las Vegas, NV; Spa Resort Casino, Palm Springs, CA

LISTING OF ART CONSULTANTS

Sylvia Greer Artworks

Est. 1985
PO Box 641579
Los Angeles, CA 90064
CONTACT: Sylvia Greer
TEL 310-474-6664
EMAIL sylvia@artwwworks.com
WEB www.artwwworks.com

Virginia Robinson, Art Consultant

Est. 2006
1120 Barlow Lane
Sebastopol, CA 95472
CONTACT: Virginia Robinson
TEL 707-824-1863
EMAIL gkollarik@hotmail.com

COLORADO

Easel Art Consulting

Est. 2004
1800 15th St. #203
Denver, CO 80202
CONTACT: Laura Reagan
TEL 303-564-2576
FAX 303-795-0955
EMAIL laura@easel-art.com

Fine Arts West, Ltd.

Est. 1998
1210 Atwood Street
Longmont, CO 80501
CONTACT: Jan Prokopenko
TEL 303-678-9970
EMAIL fineartswest@yahoo.com
WEB www.westernphotogallery.com

Fine Arts West Ltd. is a professional art consultancy providing art-related advisory and acquisition services for corporate clients. Tailored with convenience, project coordination, and an objective approach toward the aesthetic or collectors' interest in transforming space for a specific area, building, or outdoor setting. Specializing in a refined selection of innovative artwork, sculpture, and architectural details.

CLIENTS INCLUDE: CBiz Mayer Hoffman McCann; Denver Children's Hospital; Glacier Construction Co.; Horizon Banks, N.A.; Lockheed Martin; Parker Fire District; Promotech, Inc.; (Ventiv Health, Inc.); Saga Petroleum; Shaw Construction, Inc.; Western Gas Resources

Fryberger Art Consulting

Est. 1987
6662 South Hill Way
Littleton, CO 80120
CONTACT: Julie Fryberger
TEL 303-795-6523
EMAIL contact@frybergerart.com
WEB www.frybergerart.com

Fryberger Art Consulting works directly with corporations, real estate developers, architects, landscape architects, interior designers, and private collectors. We offer clients creative alternatives, incorporating artwork with various artistic styles and mediums. This includes indoor and outdoor sculpture, photography, works on canvas and paper, fiber art, tastefully framed posters, and more.

CLIENTS INCLUDE: Numerous private collectors; Conceptions—Fertility Clinic; SAFECO Corporation; Allstate Insurance; CarrAmerica Reality Corp.; Red Robin Gourmet Burgers, Headquarters; Grubb & Ellis Management Services, Inc.; Lockheed Martin; B2SJ Design Group; Vectra Bank Colorado

Hilary DePolo Visual Arts Consultants

Est. 1995
313 West Second Avenue
Denver, CO 80223
CONTACT: Hilary DePolo and Nathan Beard
TEL 303-722-8676
FAX 303-722-8674
EMAIL hilarydp@pcisys.net, nathanbeard@pcisys.net
WEB www.artconsultation.com

We have provided art consultation services in the Denver area for 25 years. We attend to each client's taste and corporate image while consistently meeting their budgets. Included in our services are framing, delivery, and installation. We also work with interior designers and architects to help meet their clients' needs.

CLIENTS INCLUDE: Arcadis; The Bailey Company—Arby's Restaurants; Beaver Run Resort; Cisco Systems, Inc.; Colorado Capital Bank; Copper Mountain Resort; First Data Corporation; Interior Architects; Lockheed Martin Corporation; Western Union

Joan Sapiro Art Consultants

Est. 1987
4750 E. Belleview Ave.
Greenwood Village, CO 80121
CONTACT: Kay Brouillette
TEL 303-793-0792
FAX 303-290-9204
EMAIL jsac@qwest.net

Parker Blake, Inc.

Est. 1980
7012 S. Revere Pkwy, Suite 120
Centennial, CO 80112
CONTACT: Robert Diaz
TEL 303-660-6079 x105 or x104
FAX 303-660-6079
EMAIL rdiaz@parkerblake.com, tyorke@parkerblake.com
WEB www.parkerblake.com

Parker Blake, a full-service art design and consulting firm, offers complete art sourcing solutions for interior designers and architects. We work with our clients at varying project stages to design customized, unique hospitality art programs that include theme research, concept development, commissioning or procuring of artwork, and supervision of installation.

CONNECTICUT

Contract Art International

Est. 1971
11 Halls Road PO Box 629
Old Lyme, CT 06371
CONTACT: Mac Thames
TEL 860-434-9799
FAX 860-434-6240
EMAIL info@contractartinternational.com
WEB www.contractartinternational.com

Contract Art International has been working within the professional design community providing unlimited art resources, custom fabricated art, and art features. Historically, our projects have been in the following industries: airports and airline clubs, casinos, cities/municipalities, city clubs, country clubs, conference centers, cruise lines/private yachts, hospitality, healthcare/assisted living, museums, schools, universities.

CLIENTS INCLUDE: Nashville International Airport; Hollywood Casino, Aurora, IL.; Barton Creek Country Club, Austin, TX; Westfield Conference Center, VA; General Electric; Celebrity Cruise Lines; Mary Black Hospital, Greenville, SC; Mandele Bay Resort, HI; Disney Resorts, U.S. and Europe; Mystic Seaport Museum, Mystic, CT; Essex Art Center, Essex, CT; Bucknell University, Lewisburg, PA

Susan Daniel Associates

Est. 1981
223 Deer Lane
Guilford, CT 06437
CONTACT: Susan Daniel
TEL 203-458-8558
FAX 203-458-2770
EMAIL susan@susandanielassociates.com
WEB www.susandanielassociates.com

FLORIDA

The Art Resource, Inc.

Est. 1979
2533 S. Park Road
Hallandale Beach, FL 33009
CONTACT: Fran Davidman
TEL 954-432-9242
FAX 954-966-1218
EMAIL fd@theartresource.com
WEB www.theartresource.com

Fogle Fine Art & Accessories

Est. 1994
3312 Beach Boulevard
Jacksonville, FL 32216
CONTACT: Leigh Fogle
TEL 904-296-1414
FAX 904-296-1310
EMAIL leigh@foglefineart.com
WEB www.foglefineart.com

Fogle Fine Art & Accessories is a full-service art consulting firm based in Jacksonville, FL. We offer services across the United States for residential, corporate, health care, and hospitality projects. The gallery showcases works from around the world, with an emphasis on Southeastern artists. In addition to two-dimensional paintings and prints, a large inventory of three-dimensional artists is available for purchase or commission.

CLIENTS INCLUDE: Amelia Island Plantation Inn; BB&T Bank; Baptist Medical Center—Northeast Florida; CIT Bank; Doctors Hospital, Augusta, GA; Mayo Clinic; PGA Tour—TPC Clubhouses Nationwide; Regions Bank; Shands Medical; Vistakon, a division of Johnson & Johnson

GEORGIA

Art Initiative Inc.

Est. 1999
887 West Marietta St., Ste. T-109 King Plow Arts Center
Atlanta, GA 30318
CONTACT: Kristen Rolando
TEL 404-874-3080
FAX 404-874-0606
EMAIL krolando@artinitiative.com
WEB www.artinitiative.com

Davis-Moye & Associates

Est. 1987
866 East Ponce de Leon Avenue
Decatur, GA 30030
CONTACT: Dorothy Moye
TEL 404-377-2116
FAX 404-377-4313
EMAIL davismoye@bellsouth.net

EDL & Associates

Est. 1986
56 East Andrews Dr., Suite 33
Atlanta, GA 30305
CONTACT: Emily Chamberlain
TEL 404-233-3602
FAX 404-233-3536
WEB www.edlart.com

Faulkner + Locke, Inc.

739 Trabert Avenue, Suite B
Atlanta, GA 30318
CONTACT: Sally Faulkner
TEL 404-367-8300
FAX 404-367-8788
EMAIL sally@faulknerlocke.com
WEB www.faulknerlocke.com

ILLINOIS

Accent Art

Est. 1986
166 Hilltop Lane
Sleepy Hollow, IL 60118
CONTACT: Robert Galitz
TEL 847-426-8842
FAX 847-426-8846
EMAIL robert@galitzfineart.com
WEB www.galitzfineart.com

Art Advisory, Ltd.

Est. 2002
5836 N. Christiana Ave.
Chicago, IL 60659
CONTACT: Susan Blackman
TEL 773-671-8624
FAX 773-588-8498
EMAIL susan@artadvisoryltd.com
WEB www.artadvisoryltd.com

Art Holdings

Est. 1980
111 N. State St. 8th Floor
Chicago, IL 60602
CONTACT: Christopher Holland and Ben Laskov
TEL 312-781-5708
FAX 312-781-5319
EMAIL christopher.holland@artholdings.com
ben.laskov@artholdings.com,
WEB www.artholdings.com

Arts In Health Ltd.

Est. 2002
28 Meadowview
Northfield, IL 60093
CONTACT: Monica Hork
TEL 773-671-2626
FAX 773-528-8788
EMAIL monicart26@aol.com
WEB artsinhealth.com

Billy Hork Galleries

Est. 1972
3033 North Clark Street
Chicago, IL 60657
CONTACT: Billy Hork
TEL 773-528-9090
FAX 773-528-8788
EMAIL bhgallerie@aol.com
WEB www.billyhork.com

Horizon Art Group

Est. 1984
1141 East Main Street Showroom #103
East Dundee, IL 60118
CONTACT: Steve Mosias
TEL National 800-278-4891, Chicago 847-649-3100
FAX 847-844-3074
EMAIL horizgrp@aol.com
WEB www.horizonartgroup.com

"WOW" is never a reaction from casual observation—it is created by a feeling you experience deep down and very emotional. If you seek to enrich your business environment, convey your vision, and display class and character, you can turn to Horizon Art and Design Group with confidence as your partner. Your business environment should express the character of the organization and positively influence the frame of mind of your visitor and employees. Professional offices for professionals. Artwork; furnishings; interiors; audio/visuals.

Murphy Rabb, Inc.

Est. 1991
400 S. Green Street Unit G
Chicago, IL 60607
CONTACT: Madeline Murphy Rabb
TEL 312-243-5070
FAX 312-243-5092
EMAIL madeline@murphyrabb.com
WEB www.murphyrabb.com

Madeline Murphy Rabb is president of Murphy Rabb, Inc., an art advisory firm. Rabb is nationally renowned for her expertise in curating art collections by national and internationally renowned African American artists. Relationships with artists, dealers, galleries, auction houses, and collectors enable her to build exquisite collections for her clients.

CLIENTS INCLUDE: Ariel Capital Management, Chicago; Brown Capital Management, Baltimore; Northern Trust Bank South Financial Center, Chicago; Capri Capital Advisors, Chicago; John H. Stroger Jr., Hospital of Cook County, Chicago

INDIANA

Sharon Eisbart Corporate Art

Est. 1992
6225 Constitution Drive
Fort Wayne, IN 46804
CONTACT: Sharon Eisbart
TEL 260-432-2252
FAX 260-432-2252
EMAIL secorporateart@yahoo.com

MARYLAND

The Art Resource, Inc.

Est. 1981
1106 N. Charles St., Ste. 303
Baltimore, MD 21230
CONTACT: Laura Siner and Leia McKenna
TEL 410-332-4644
FAX 410-332-4677
EMAIL leia@artresource.org
WEB www.artresource.org

The Art Resource, Inc. is a leading art dealership and consulting firm in Baltimore, Maryland, Washington, DC and South Florida. We represent hundreds of artists, including painters, printmakers, sculptors, weavers, mixed media, and several lines of limited-edition prints and reproductions. Our clients include architects, developers, interior designers, corporations, and private collectors.

Artists Circle Fine Art

13501 Travilah Road
North Potomac, MD 20878
CONTACT: Jack Devine
TEL 301-947-7400
FAX 301-947-9222
EMAIL jack@artcfa.com
WEB www.artcfa.com

Barbara Feeser Art Associates

Est. 1986
1810 A Yoek Road Suite 323
Timonium, MD 21093
CONTACT: Barbara Feeser
TEL 410-561-3901
FAX 410-561-3977
EMAIL barbfeeser@aol.com

Catherine Evans Fine Art

Est. 2001
16026 Carroll Road
Monkton, MD 21111
CONTACT: Catherine Evans
TEL 410-472-3096
EMAIL cefineart@aol.com

MASSACHUSETTS

Boston Art Inc.

Est. 2001
330 Congress Street
Boston, MA 02210
CONTACT: John Kirby
TEL 617-951-0900
FAX 617-951-0980
EMAIL info@bostonartinc.com
WEB www.bostonartinc.com

Boston Art Inc. is a corporate art consulting firm dedicated to creating professional and inspiring work environments of our clientele, including, corporate, heathcare, building owner, and hospitality industries. Our offices house a rotating art showroom and a professional multimedia conference room for presenting the very best artists available in the United States.

CLIENTS INCLUDE: AstraZeneca Pharmaceuticals LP; Blue Cross Blue Shield of Massachusetts; Boston Medical Center; Esec Lending; Goodwin Procter; Harvard Law School; Lenox Hotel; Massachusetts General Hospital; Ritz Carlton; Sherin & Logen LLC

Erdreich White Fine Art, Inc.

Est. 1987
145 West Newton Street
Boston, MA 02118
CONTACT: Christy Gillman & Elizabeth Erdereich
TEL 617-266-0644
FAX 617-266-0647
EMAIL ewfa@verizon.net

Art Consulting since 1987. Specialization: prestigious corporate projects on a national and international level. Services include: consultation and space analysis, art procurement, evaluation, restoration, framing, delivery, and installation. Resources include: over 1,400 artists representing an extensive variety of imagery and media to satisfy all budgetary and aesthetic needs.

CLIENTS INCLUDE: Clients include but are not limited to many of the leading law firms, financial firms, and entertainment firms.

Jacqueline Becker Fine Arts Consulting Services

Est. 1982
261 Franklin Street
Newton, MA 02458
CONTACT: Jacqueline Becker
TEL 617-527-6169
FAX 617-527-3116
EMAIL jacqui@beckerfinearts.com
WEB www.beckerfinearts.com

Award-winning firm supplies superb service and the perfect art for home or office. Acquisition of fine art and crafts; commissioned art work; presentations in the comfort and privacy of home or office; framing, restoration and conservation services; transportation and installation; documentation and curatorial services

CLIENTS INCLUDE: The many homeowners and designers whom I have been privileged to assist, and; Fidelity Investments; Federal Reserve Bank of Boston; Cubist Pharmaceuticals; Atria Software; Brigham and Women's Hospital; Tucker Anthony; Massachusetts Bar Association; Ares Serono International; Boston Federal Savings Bank

Masters Art Group—A Division of Horizon Art Group, Chicago

Est. 1984
15 Concord Road
Sudbury, MA 01776
CONTACT: Steve Mosias
TEL 978-443-8278
FAX 847-844-3074
EMAIL horizgrp@aol.com
WEB www.horizonartgroup.com

MINNESOTA

Art Holdings

Est. 1980
6210 Wayzata Blvd.
Minneapolis, MN 55416
CONTACT: Greg Hennes
TEL 763-567-2202
FAX 763-567-2201
EMAIL greg.hennes@artholdings.com
WEB www.artholdings.com

Art Holdings supports and enhances your design vision by providing art consulting, custom framing, and installation services for corporate and residential spaces. We seamlessly translate the project's needs into artwork while respecting the client's budget. From posters to originals in every style and medium, our expert staff can commission, frame, ship, and install artwork anywhere in the United States.

CLIENTS INCLUDE: Ameriprise Financial; RBC Dain Raucher; United HeathGroup; Blue Cross Blue Shield; Caribou Coffee; Macy's Furniture Galleries; Sheraton Hotels; Target Corporation; Wells Fargo; Numerous private residences

Art Partners Group

Est. 2006
11473 Valley View Road
Eden Prairie, MN 55344
CONTACT: Kim Cameron and Brian Knudsvig
TEL 952-548-6643
FAX 952-548-6641

Art Partners Group sources, sells, custom frames, and installs art for clients searching for a reliable, consultative "hands on" experience. We focus on client needs exclusively in the commercial real estate arena and deliver value with expert project management. Our national experience spans commissioned public pieces to value-based images.

Visual Arts

Est. 1994
275 Market St., Ste. 197
Minneapolis, MN 55405
CONTACT: Char Hovi
TEL 612-677-1244
FAX 612-659-1975
EMAIL visualarts@qwest.net
WEB www.visualartsltd.com

NEVADA

The Art Group

Est. 1986
9008 Opus Drive
Las Vegas, NV 89117
CONTACT: Carol Spiegel
TEL 702-896-2218
FAX 702-896-3488
EMAIL theartgroup@aol.com
WEB www.theartgroupllc.com

The Art Group helps clients articulate their personality, brand, and corporate identity. We draw from twenty years of experience in helping our clients identify their goals and objectives. It is our ability to integrate the universal language of art with the unique essence of our clients. Services: fine art, limited editions, sculpture, photography, limited-editions giclée.

CLIENTS INCLUDE: The Howard Hughes Corporation; Donald W. Reynolds Foundation; Summerlin Hospital Medical Center; The Andre Agassi Foundation; Kaufman & Broad Corporate Headquarters; Bellagio Hotel & Casino; Caesar Palace Hotel & Casino; MGM Grand Hotel & Casino; Trump Marina Hotel & Casino; Mandalay Bay Hotel & Casino

LISTING OF ART CONSULTANTS

NEW HAMPSHIRE

Art 3, Inc.

Est. 1986
44 West Brook Street
Manchester, NH 03101
CONTACT: Lee Forgosh and Joni Taube
TEL 603-668-6650
FAX 603-668-5136
EMAIL info@art3gallery.com
WEB www.art3gallery.com

NEW JERSEY

Art Resources, Inc.

Est. 1985
843 Nancyway
Westfield, NJ 07090
CONTACT: Linda Slove
TEL 908-400-1334
FAX 908-232-0061
EMAIL linart7@aol.com

Fieldstone Fine Art/ArtVue, Inc.

Est. 2006/1997
147 E. Main Street
Ramsey, NJ 07446
CONTACT: Mariana Maldonado
TEL 201-818-8913
FAX 201-818-4801
EMAIL mariana@artvue.com
WEB www.artvue.com, www.fieldstonefineart.com

Leader Associates Art Consulting

Est. 1987
7 Nottingham Road
Wayne, NJ 07470
CONTACT: Bernice Leader
TEL 973-969-1836
FAX 973-696-0163
EMAIL leadart@eptonline.net
WEB www.leaderartconsulting.com

NEW MEXICO

ARTWORKinternational, Inc.

Est. 1998
1816 San Felipe Circle
Santa Fe, NM 87505
CONTACT: Samantha Paige Furgason
TEL 505-982-7447
EMAIL artwork@artworkinternational.com
WEB www.artworkinternational.com

NEW YORK

Art Advice Corporate Art Consultants

Est. 1981
200 East 33rd Street, 24th floor
New York, NY 10016
CONTACT: Susan Greenberg
TEL 212-683-5611
FAX 212-683-1356
EMAIL info@artadvice-ny.com
WEB www.artadvice-ny.com

Art Consultants to the Trade

Est. 1982
429 E. 52nd St. 25C
New York, NY 10022
CONTACT: January Sarasohn
TEL 212-751-3133
FAX 212-682-7202
EMAIL arttothetrade@gmail.com
WEB www.artconsultantstothetrade.com

Art Consultants specializes in the induction of art programs, expanding existing collections, and supervising the selection, framing, placement, and installation of all types of art. We have experience presenting the full gamut of artworks, from investment paintings to offset posters, paying particular attention to the individual needs of the client.

CLIENTS INCLUDE: BUNGE; Endurance Reinsurance; Englewood Hospital; General Atlantic ; GHI; Gibson, Dunn and Crutcher LLP; Hitachi America; National Cable Corporation; Rabo Bank; Sebonack Country Club

Art Solutions

Est. 2005
PO Box 20519
New York, NY 10021
CONTACT: Debbi Schonberger-Pierce
TEL 917-837-1633
FAX 212-620-3734
EMAIL deb@art-solutions.net
WEB www.art-solutions.net

Art Solutions will develop an art program to enhance your corporate environment. Services include: art selection, design, and placement; custom framing; installation; and appraisal and inventory. Improve your surroundings with art solutions.

Novo Arts, Inc.

Est. 1975
57 East 11th Street, 10th Floor
New York, NY 10003
CONTACT: Marlaina Deppe
TEL 212-674-3093
FAX 212-979-5381
EMAIL art@novoarts.com
WEB www.novoarts.com

LISTING OF ART CONSULTANTS

Novo Arts is a fine art consulting firm with thirty-one years of experience providing art for corporate, hospitality, healthcare, and residential environments. We offer custom paintings, sculptures, photography, wall coverings, works on glass, large-scale prints on any surface, graphic services, ambient video production, wall surfacing, and environmental design.

CLIENTS INCLUDE: Bank of America; Bristol Meyers; Celebrity Cruises; Chase Manhattan Bank; Morgan Stanley Dean Witter; Walt Disney World; Ritz Carlton; Sony Electronics; Starwoods; Time Warner

NORTH CAROLINA

Ann Bourgeois Art Consultants

Est. 2005
2035 Queens Road West
Charlotte, NC 28207
CONTACT: Ann Bourgeois
TEL 704-488-5863
EMAIL ann.bourgeios@earthlink.net

ABAC is a full-service art consultancy that partners with architects, designers and clients. Offer complete objectivity as each project is custom. Assist in defining project specifications. Integrate existing artwork. Share unlimited access to artists nationwide, covering the art medium spectrum. From commissioned architectural elements to framed art prints—ABAC.

CLIENTS INCLUDE: Duke Energy Headquarters; Royal & Sun Alliance Headquarters; Mass Mutual Life Insurance Company; ESP Associates, P.A.; Carolina Family Eye Care

Art Source Fine Art Gallery & Framing

Est. 1990
4351-101 The Circle / 509-105 W. Whitaker Mill
Raleigh, NC 27609/27608
CONTACT: Sally Plyler & Gigi Johnson
TEL 919-787-9533 / 919-833-0013
FAX 919-787-9534 / 919-833-2210
EMAIL sally@artsourcefineart.com, gigi@artsourcefineart.com
WEB www.artsource-raleigh.com

Debra Rhodes Fine Art Services

Est. 1981
57 Pinewild Drive
Pinehurst, NC 28374
CONTACT: Debra Rhodes Smith
TEL 910-255-0570
FAX 910-255-0571
EMAIL drhodessmith@nc.rr.com
WEB www.debrarhodesfineartservices.com

Please visit my website to learn in an initial view, how integrity and a good eye have been the key to my success. Clients, genre, and media change with every project, but good quality art and dedicated service is a constant. Your expectations will be far exceeded. Debra Rhodes Smith.

OHIO

The Art Company

Est. 1983
700 W. Pete Rose Way Suite 130
Cincinnati, OH 45203
CONTACT: Patty Glass, Ed Capannari, Judy Mahan, Debbie Fredette, Callie Dudley
TEL 513-651-5092
FAX 513-651-5099
EMAIL theartcompany@fuse.net
WEB www.theartcompany.com

The Art Company provides full-service on-site art consultation and framing for corporate, healthcare, hospitality, professional, and residential interiors. Since 1983 excellent service, quality, and integrity have ben our trademark. From concept to completion, our goal is the right art for the right price for your space. Call us!

CLIENTS INCLUDE: Lexmark International; Anthem Blue Cross & Blue Shield; Givaudan Flavors; Proctor & Gamble; General Electric Aircraft Engines; Reynolds & Reynolds; Christ Hospital, Cincinnati, Ohio; Lexis Nexis; Mount Carmel Healthcare Systems, Columbus, Ohio; Indiana Wesleyan University

Art Resource Team

Est. 2000
16 Allen Avenue
Cincinnati, OH 45215
CONTACT: Inez Baird
TEL 513-662-1998
FAX 513-662-6977
WEB www.artresourceteam.com

PENNSYLVANIA

Art 4 Business

Est. 1978
161 Leveington Ave., Suite 101
Philadelphia, PA 19127
CONTACT: Christine Fields
TEL 215-222-2200
FAX 215-482-4572
EMAIL cfields@art4business.com
WEB www.art4business.com

Art4business, a business-to-business company, provides a full range of services for corporate art collections. We are experts at shipping, framing, art selection, and handling, and have developed internet-based collection management programs. Through us you can assemble, deliver, and manage a corporate art collection as a critical component of the project and as a valuable asset for the corporation.

CLIENTS INCLUDE: IBM; Novartis Pharmaceuticals; University of Delaware; Wyeth Pharmaceuticals; USAA McGraw-Hill Companies; Wharton School of Business; Liberty Property Trust; Merck & Co.; Boston University.

LISTING OF ART CONSULTANTS

Art by Design

Est. 1982
112 Wooded Lane
Villanova, PA 19085
CONTACT: Bonnie Paul
TEL 610-527-0139
FAX 610-527-0240 (call first)
EMAIL art.bydesign@verizon.net
WEB www.abdesign.us

Our firm has, in over twenty years in business, been involved in every aspect of art considerations in design projects. With our resources, we are able to adjust our services to the needs of the client. Our clients come from a wide and varied range of business types and specialties. They include financial services companies and banks, insurance corporations, hospitals, retirement and life care facilities, medical laboratories and offices, physician and attorney offices, and regional development companies.

CLIENTS INCLUDE: Trammell Crow Company; Reliance Insurance Company; Philadelphia Heart Hospital; Drexel University; Brandywine Realty Trust; Liberty Property Trust; Arc Properties; National Media Corporation; IBM; Comcast Cable

Hollander Associates

Est. 1986
220 W. Rittenhouse Sq. 18B
Philadelphia, PA 19103
CONTACT: Clara Hollander
TEL 215-545-8477
FAX 215-545-1636
EMAIL chollander@comcast.net

Marsha Moss Public Art Consultant

Est. 1980
220 Locust Street 27-D
Philadelphia, PA 19106
CONTACT: Marsha Moss
TEL 215-925-3384
FAX 215-925-3384
EMAIL marshamoss@aol.com

TEXAS

American Fine Art

1611 Dragon Street
Dallas, TX 75207
CONTACT: Ardell Zueger and David Zueger
TEL 214-749-7749
FAX 214-749-7324
EMAIL artsales@americanfineart.com
WEB www.americanfineart.com

Started consulting in 1980 and opened American Fine Art in 1982. 8,000 sq. ft. of original artwork on display. Curated art for corporations and private individuals. We are linked to other large professional art dealers and consultants in the art selection process. We have in-house certified picture framers for Museum mounting and re-framing of art. Bottom line—we are full service.

CLIENTS INCLUDE: Capstar, Austin, TX; Crossroad Group, Dallas, TX; Guidestone, Dallas, TX; Drive Financial Services, Dallas, TX; First Mercantile Bank, Dallas, TX; M/A/R/C, Irving, TX; Pomodoro Restaurant, Dallas, TX; Team Air Freight, Dallas, TX; 21st Century Dental, Irving, TX

Carter Nelson Fine Art

Est. 2005
6209 Greenway Road, #9
Fort Worth, TX 76116
CONTACT: Judy Nelson
TEL 817-763-0031
FAX 817-763-0197
EMAIL nelson@carternelson.net
WEB www.carternelson.net

Fenton Fine Arts

Est. 1985
1420 Shady Oaks Lane
Fort Worth, TX 76107
CONTACT: Phyllis Fenton
TEL 817-737-2252
FAX 817-731-3003
EMAIL ffa@sbcglobal.net
WEB listed in www.artnet.com

Gagnaire Art Associates

Est. 1984
9504 Summerhill Lane
Dallas, TX 75238
CONTACT: Leilani Gagnaire
TEL 214-343-8558
FAX 214-341-2292
EMAIL gagnaireart@tx.rr.com

Combining art history and business backgrounds, Gagnaire Art Associates specializes in customized art programs to fit image, décor, and budget requirements. Geographic or historical interests can be developed to provide a visual story. Services include art inventory, placement planning, special commissions, art consulting, custom framing, delivery, and installation.

CLIENTS INCLUDE: Available upon request

Image One International

Est. 1990
16126 Rainbow Lake Road
Houston, TX 77095
CONTACT: Genae Fields
TEL 281-856-8866
FAX 281-550-8618
EMAIL genae@ioiart.com or gfields@imageoneinternational.com
WEB www.ioiart.com or www.imageoneinternational.com

LISTING OF ART CONSULTANTS

UTAH

Lawrence Jeppson Associates Fine Arts

Est. 1958
241 N. Vine St., #1101 East
Salt Lake City, UT 84103
CONTACT: Lawrence Jeppson
TEL 801-532-1601 or 301-365-7400
FAX 801-532-1601
EMAIL acroeditions@yahoo.com

VIRGINIA

The Anderson Art Group

Est. 1998
12414 Seahaven Drive
Richmond, VA 23233
CONTACT: Lynn Anderson
TEL 804-357-2624
EMAIL lynn@theandersonartgroup.com
WEB www.theandersonartgroup.com

The Anderson Art Group works with corporations in the selection of artwork for offices and lobbies. Choosing the right piece for the right space while considering your budget and style is our specialty. We have a wide range of art resources, including genres from abstract to contemporary realism in paintings, prints, sculpture, glass, and installation pieces. The Anderson Art Group works on projects at any stage, from initial concepts and blueprints, to refurbishing of existing spaces.

CLIENTS INCLUDE: Richmond, VA, area: CB Richard Ellis; Genworth Financial; Hilb, Rogal and Hamilton; Land America Financial Group; Weinstein Properties; Williams, Mullen, Clark and Dobbins VA Beach area: Langley Federal Credit Union; Cox Communications Charlotssesville, VA area: First Bank, Hauser Homes

WASHINGTON

Art Consulting Services

216 First Avenue South
Seattle, WA 98104
CONTACT: Yvonne Banks
TEL 206-624-4352
EMAIL ybanks@aol.com

WISCONSIN

Artsource, Inc.

Est. 1990
5125 S. Towne Drive
New Berlin, WI 53151
CONTACT: Maggie Smith
TEL 262-860-4260
FAX 262-860-4278
EMAIL sales@artsourceonline.com
WEB www.artsourceonline.com

Nationally known art consultant and design service specializing in placement of decorative and fine art in healthcare, corporate, senior living, and hospitality markets. GSA contract for government purchasers. Comprehensive website with 15,000+ offerings. Gallery-quality custom framing. Specialists in national standards programs. Wholesale pricing for re-sellers.

Concepts in Art Ltd.

Est. 1980
310 E. Milwaukee St. / 3321 Lake Drive
Janesville / Hartland, WI 53545 / 53029
CONTACT: Joan Blackbourn
TEL 608-756-0333, 800-969-4484, 262-369-9403
FAX 608-756-3700, 262-369-9408
EMAIL concart@ticon.net
WEB www.conceptsinartltd.com

Joan Blackbourn and staff have worked with corporations, healthcare, and hotels for over twenty-six years. They work throughout the Midwest, traveling to the client, representing a vast number of artists from across the country. Happy to work within any specified budget, providing expert in-house custom framing and installation.

CLIENTS INCLUDE: Abbott Laboratories, Abbott Park, IL; Crown Plaza Hotel, Phoenix, AZ; American Family Insurance, Madison, WI, Phoenix, AZ, Regional offices; Johnson Banks, Milwaukee, WI, Racine, WI, Madison, WI, Regional offices; Sacred Heart Hospital, Eau Claire, WI; BDH and Young, Minneapolis, MN; Meriter Hospital, Madison, WI; A.C. Nielsen, Northbrook, IL; Edgewater Hotel, Madison, WI; Virchow Krause, Madison, WI, Detroit, MI, Regional offices

Erdman Art Group

Est. 1982
5117 University Ave.
Madison, WI 53705
CONTACT: Margaret LeMay
TEL 608-218-6308 or 866-848-4278
FAX 608-218-4461
EMAIL mlemay@erdmanart.com
WEB www.erdmanart.com

Gingrass Corporate Art

12605 W. North Avenue #262
Wauwatosa, WI 53005
CONTACT: Sarah Gingrass
TEL 414-607-7106
FAX 414-607-0176
EMAIL sarah@gingrasscorporateart.com
WEB www.gingrasscorporateart.com

Gingrass Corporate Art is a family-owned and operated business. Twenty years has led to a refined expertise in art consulting, design, and sales. Specializing in custom innovative art, framing, and installations. An unparalleled effect is promised on each project while staying within your budget. GCA collaborates with and can be requested through all top design/architectural firms in the Midwest.

CLIENTS INCLUDE: Please visit us at www.gingrasscorporateart.com to view our Exclusive Client list.

ARTIST STATEMENTS

The pages that follow provide important information on the artists featured in *The Guild Sourcebook of Architectural & Interior Art 22.*

Listings in the Artist Statements section are arranged alphabetically according to the heading on each artist's page. These listings include their contact information as well as details about materials and techniques, commissions, collections, and more. References to past Guild Sourcebooks are also included, so that you can further explore the breadth of a particular artist's work. Each listing includes a reference to the artist's page within the book.

As you explore *The Guild Sourcebook of Architectural & Interior Art 22,* use the Artist Statements section to enrich your experience. If something intrigues you while perusing the sourcebook—a shape, a form, an exotic use of the commonplace—we hope you'll give the artist a call. Serendipity often leads to a wonderful creation.

AIRWORKS, INC.

Atrium Sculpture

Page 62

The works we have created over a span of more than thirty years have been primarily influenced by aerial and atmospheric themes. As an artist team, we have installed numerous large-scale commissions both nationally and internationally for public spaces and corporate buildings. We work closely with the clients, artist agents, architects, and designers to develop integrated solutions for a unique proposal. We strive to make the works resonate with the architectural context or exterior site. The ideas are carefully researched and presented through photo illustrations and 3D computer modeling.

COMMISSIONS: Washington Metro Area Transit Authority, 2004, Washington, DC; McGraw-Hill Companies, London, 2003; Tokyo Bay Hilton, Tokyo, Japan 1999; AstraZeneca Pharmaceuticals, 2003, Wilmington, DE; San Diego Port Authority, 2004, Chula Vista, CA; University of Arizona, 2002, Tucson

GUILD SOURCEBOOKS: *Architect's 13, 14, 15, Architectural & Interior Art 16, 17, 19, 20*

MARCUS AKINLANA

Murals, Tiles & Wall Reliefs

Page 198

We endeavor to create entertaining public art that enthralls people and captivates their attention, fostering a sense of joy or evoking strong emotional responses. We have created and collaborated on over twenty large-scale public artworks. We enjoy working in different media in our public works and to date we have fabricated murals, reliefs, mosaic, freestanding sculpture, etched glass mirrors, and combinations thereof. We create work with a special emphasis on historical and political themes that reflect the specific history and values of the particular locale where the public artwork is placed. We aim to generate art that is technically superior and of high visual quality. We work both in monumental public art and more intimate scales. Our company, WON Mural Society, has seventeen years of experience successfully working with architects, engineers, communities, public art sponsors, and mural groups.

COMMISSIONS: *FlyVentures*, Philadelphia International Airport; *Aurora Eternal*, Aurora Municipal Center, CO; *Mile High & Rising*, Denver International Airport; *Monumental Intentions*, Denver Performing Arts Complex

BARBARA AMOS

Paintings & Prints

Page 226

Bold design, rich colors, and unusual modular formats define the paintings from my studios. Personal involvement in all phases of the project guarantees a timely and successful custom artwork. Past imagery has been thematically diverse, including urban night scenes, national parks, and historical postcards. A maquette is designed and approved in collaboration with the clients. The work is developed on wood, canvas, vinyl, or metal, in paint or photography, and can be shipped worldwide. High-quality materials, expert knowledge, and premium finishes combined with the time-tested techniques of the old masters, create artworks that are unique, contemporary and lasting.

COLLECTIONS: U.S. Library of Congress, Washington, DC; Civic Art Collection, City of Calgary, Canada; Alberta Art Foundation; RBC Dominion Securities; Norcen Energy Resources Ltd; Alberta Energy Corporation; Esso Resources Limited

COMMISSIONS: Cardel Place; Coe & Company International; Applied Communications; Auburn Saloon

PUBLICATIONS: *Legacy Magazine; Galleries West; Artichoke Magazine; Where Magazine; New York Times; Calgary Herald; Avenue Magazine*

ANDERSON CAPRON LTD./ ADAMANTINE STUDIO

Fine Art Photography

Page 256

A North Carolina artist, I begin my unique creative process with photographic images I capture myself—from my own beachfront neighborhood to the far exotic corners of the globe. I then alter and manipulate the images, making them distinctive personal expressions. Archival prints are then made on heavy canvas stretched on wooden frames. Then the magic begins, as the prints are enrobed in a deep crystalline overlayer. This proprietary technique brings detail and color to a rich, glowing life, adding depth and vibrance unlike anything ever seen. These breathtaking works will transform any space, charging it with energy and vitality. Fill your rooms with Dawn Anderson Capron's thrilling vision. Fill your rooms with Dawn's light.

ANNA CABO ARTGLASS TILES

Murals, Tiles & Wall Reliefs

Page 199

These handmade glass tiles are fused with metal and glazes to create one-of-a-kind art pieces that can be used indoors or outdoors. I make large- and standard-size tiles to fit many applications.

COMMISSIONS: Glass wall, Comix Club, New York, NY; Public restrooms tiles and sconces, Red Rock Casino, Las Vegas, NV; Steakhouse art tiles, Harrah's Casino, Las Vegas, NV; Lobby art tiles, Atlantis Hotel and Resort, Bahamas; Bus shelters and newspaper racks, City of Santa Monica, CA; Private gaming room glass wall, Barona Casino, CA; Art accents for outdoor bar, George's Restaurant, La Jolla, CA; Memorial Wall, Beth-El Zeder Synagogue, Indianapolis, IN; Front entrance glass tiles, Spago, Beverly Hills, CA

GUILD SOURCEBOOKS: *Designer's 11*

ROBIN ANTAR

Representational Sculpture

Page 140

My mission as a sculptor is to create a visual record of modern culture by capturing contemporary everyday objects in stone. By replicating the model on a life-size scale, along with marking and symbol details, I attempt to freeze the object in time as an artistic form of artifact. I achieve this high degree of realism through the use of such materials as pieces of the real object, custom-made stains, paints, plastics, and gold leaf.

COMMISSIONS: Dr. Martens Boots; Skechers Boots, U.S.A.; Chateau Haut-Brian Wines

EXHIBITIONS: MGM Grand Hotel, 2005, Las Vegas, NV; Diesel Jeans, 2002, New York, NY; *The Really Big Shoe Show*, 2002, City Museum, St. Louis, MO; *More Artistic License*, 1999, Nabisco Corporate Gallery, East Hanover, NJ

GUILD SOURCEBOOKS: *Architect's 14, 15; Designer's 14; Architectural & Interior Art 17, 21; Artful Home 2*

ART OF BEING

Lighting
Page 182

In a world where most of our time is caught in the doings of life, very rarely do we make time to allow ourselves to be in the moment. When creating works of art, I allow myself to be in the "space of being" in the moment. Bringing the elements alive by combining color, light, textures, and various media elements; together, these form unique works of art. For many years I have been assembling dimensional glass, agate, metal, and wood sculptural works of art to fulfill the diversified needs of the clientele with whom I work.

PUBLICATIONS: *Naples Daily News; Bonita Daily News; N Magazine; Gulf Shore Life; Coastal Magazine; Florida Design; Naples Illustrated*

COMMISSIONS: Various private collections

ARTECLETTICA

Murals, Tiles & Wall Reliefs
Pages 200, 214

Arteclettica embraces the idea of the complementarity of the arts. It is the uniqueness of a piece of art, stimulus of imagination and creativity, that enriches our existence. We are striving towards a global art, respectful of the past, projected to the future, thought out from the smallest detail. Our backgrounds in art, architecture, and engineering provide us with the ability to complete a project both artistically and successfully. Our original and modern mosaics are vibrant additions in both interior and exterior installations, and can be utilized as flooring, incorporated in or hung on walls, or used in sculptural pieces. All of our artwork is durable, low maintenance, and has the highest artistic quality. Our work includes mosaics, mixed media, sculpture, murals, portraiture, paintings, interior design, and architecture.

COMMISSIONS: Mixed-media bench; Artwork for *Arttown*; Mosaic floor, Municipal Courthouse, Reno, NV; Showroom design, mosaics & mixed-media sculpture, Home Concepts, Truckee, CA; House design, Truckee, CA

PUBLICATIONS: *Tahoe Quarterly; Reno Gazette Journal; Tahoe World*

BETH AVARY

Paintings & Prints
Page 227

I have shown my work throughout the United States in museums, festivals, galleries, corporations, and science fiction and fantasy conventions. I have also exhibited in Mexico, Japan, and Russia. My paintings are found in private collections throughout the world. I am interested in touching the underlying beauty and radiance of the world through my work. I hope to evoke a sense of deep connection to the natural world, creating an almost mystical feeling. For me painting is a search for beauty that inspires love and warms the heart. My work has received several awards, including First Place, Public Favorite, and Best of Show. To see more of my work, go to www.starfirepress.com.

GUILD SOURCEBOOKS: *Architectural & Interior Art 21; Residential Art 4, 5*

KATHY BARNARD

Architectural Glass
Pages 24-25

Kathy Barnard Studio designs and fabricates sculptural carved art glass, stained glass windows, deep-carved glass panels, and murals. My site-specific commissioned work is found in commercial, religious, and private environments throughout the country. A love of nature, a commitment to the client's vision, and a distinctive sense of design and detail are incorporated to produce representational and abstract installations in glass and granite.

COMMISSIONS: Adventist Hospitals, 2002–2007, Boulder, Littleton, and Denver, CO; Diocese of Wichita, Bishop's residence, 2003, KS; Stillwater National Bank & Trust, 2000, Tulsa, OK; Mormon Temple, 2000, Houston, TX; First USA Bank, 1997, Wilmington, DE; East Lawrence Recreation Center; Percent for the Arts Project, 1997, Lawrence, KS; RLDS Temple and World Headquarters, 1992, Independence, MO; Jewish Community Center and Jewish Federation Headquarters, 1988, Overland Park, KS; Midland Theatre, 1987, Kansas City, MO

AWARDS: AIA Allied Arts and Craftsmanship Award, 1990

GUILD SOURCEBOOKS: *THE GUILD 3, 4, 5; Architect's 8, 9, 10, 13; Architectural & Interior Art 16*

THE BARTELSTONE PHOTOWORKS COLLECTION

Fine Art Photography
Page 257

The surreal "Grand Landscapes" of this collection appear as much like large photographs as fine oil paintings. I photograph them all with a larger format film camera only and print them with state-of-the-art professional printers, using luxurious art paper and archival inks. They are available in very low edition numbers in image sizes ranging from 24" x 30" to 24" x 90". Inspired by the monumental geography of the West, I seek to create images that have a universal appearance. These pieces have a painterly, luminous detailed look that fools the eye. No digital alteration is used to create them. They have been sold to many corporate collections, five-star resorts, and homes across the country. I readily accept commissioned contracts for exclusive client usage. Packages of 14" exact reproductions are available for your resource files. My website is eyesofnewmexico.com.

MICHAEL BAUERMEISTER

Non-Representational Sculpture
Page 106

I think of these tall vessels as figures. As such, I'm interested in their personalities and how they relate to one another. These vessels are made from cabinet-grade hardwoods and are finished with lacquer so they will not warp or crack. Most range in price from $1,000 to $3,000. Collections include: Smithsonian Institution, Renwick Gallery, Washington, D.C.; University of Michigan Museum, Ann Arbor; Mesa Museum of contemporary Art, Mesa, AZ. Exhibitions include: Smithsonian Craft Show, 2003, 2002, Washington, DC; Wood Turning Invitational, 2000-2003, American Art Co., Tacoma, WA; Turned Wood Invitational, 2002, 1999, 1998, Del Mano Gallery, Los Angeles, CA; and *Nuances d'ete*, 2001, Carlin Gallery, Paris, France. Awards include: 25th Annual Contemporary Crafts Purchase Award, 2003, Mesa Arts Center, Mesa, AZ; Best of Wood, 2002, American Craft Exposition, Evanston, IL; Niche Award, 2002; and the Award of Excellence, 2000, American Craft Council, Baltimore, MD. Publications include: *Wood Art Today*, 2003; *Scratching the Surface*, 2002; *Object Lessons*, 2001; and *American Craft*, June 1995.

ARTIST STATEMENTS

SANDRA BELL

Public Art

Pages 5, 78

I am a full-time professional sculptor working in bronze. I work predominately in two areas, each complimenting the other: gallery exhibitions and public/private commissions. Gallery exhibitions allow me freedom of expression and also offer me the opportunity to exhibit the maquettes of the monumental works I produce. Monumental commissions channel. my work into particular directions, depending on the brief and the suggestions of clients. I find the interaction with those who commission my work of great benefit when creating site-specific work. It also makes the sculpture more personal for those who choose to live with it. My aim as an artist is to portray the essence of the human form and the tranquillity of the inner self by means of abstract figurative expression. My most recent projects combine animals, birds, and fish, incorporating these elements of nature into humanity.

BENNETT STUDIO

Public Art

Page 79

I specialize in classically rendered sculptures of human figures, animals, and wildlife. Works include more than fifty public works of art for parks, colleges, liturgical settings, memorials, corporate headquarters, hospitals, and private residences. Each design is personal and poignant to present a poetic and enduring perspective of those commemorated, or idea portrayed. Site-specific works relate to and inspire the community of origin. I have successfully worked in collaboration with architects and other professionals to implemented large-scale designs and site developments. All budgets are accommodated. Recently, $25,000–$250,000+.

COMMISSIONS: *Descending Strength, Ascending Peace,* 5th & Grand St intersection, 2006, Ames, IA; *Parade Route, Main Street,* 2007, Shoreline, WA; *Prairie Preening,* Butler Community College, 2007, El Dorado, KS; *Athletic Heroes of Iowa,* Iowa Events Center, Hall of Pride, 2006, Des Moines, IA; Douglas Hoeft Memorial, Riverside Park, 2005, Elgin, IL

PUBLICATIONS: *Traditional Building* magazine, Sept/Oct 2006

GUILD SOURCEBOOKS: *Architect's 12, 13, 14; Designer's 12, 13; Architecture & Interior Art 20*

MATTHEW BEZARK

Architectural Glass

Page 26

Growing up near Chicago, I gained a great appreciation for glass in architecture. Influenced in part by many visits to the Frank Lloyd Wright houses in the area, my exploration of glass design based on light and color began. A move to the foothills of Colorado added nature to the forces that inspire me to create. Building the Mountain Glassworks studio here has provided a place for this exploration to continue. The immediacy, movement, fluidity, and drama inherent in working with hot glass captivates me. This desire to work hot greatly influences my glass design. Typically, decorative glass used in architecture is kiln-cast or stained glass. Instead of these techniques where the glass is cut or stacked while cold, I hand pour molten glass to make glass castings that are used in place of the usual sheet glass. Hand poured castings are very dynamic. Color and surface texture work is done while the glass is still hot and helps ensure the uniqueness of these works. My creations often include sculptural metal or wood elements to complete the composition. One of my strengths is the ability to collaborate with other artists, as well as architects and designers, to exchange ideas and help a project become reality.

CHARLES BIGGER

Public Art

Page 80

As an artist it is inevitable that I bring my own personal aesthetic and vision to each and every project. As a public artist, it is my job to combine that personal vision with the needs of the host to create a piece of work that not only expresses aesthetic beauty, but presents and conveys ideas and concepts important to the local community. I have been very fortunate in the last few years to have the opportunity to create highly visible entry pieces for several community parks and additional large-scale pieces for private and commercial commissions. Please visit my website for a more detailed view of my public commissions and private studio work.

COMMISSIONS: Duwamish Campus Entry Piece, South Seattle Community College, in progress; Valley Bank Financial Center, 2005, Kent, WA; Canterbury Park, 2004, Kent, WA; Greenwood Park Entry, Seattle, WA; Wiggums Park, Everett, WA; Webster Park, Seattle, WA; Lincoln Park, Devil's Lake, North Dakota; Kake Elementary School, Kake, AK

GEORGE-ANN BOWERS

Fiber Wall Art

Page 288

Color, texture, pattern, and form as expressed in nature are my inspiration and the building blocks of my artwork. My subjects are the intimate details of trees, rocks, or landforms, visual evidence of biological processes and geological events colorfully rendered in textile form. Contrasts of light and shadow figure substantially in my work, creating the illusion of dimensionality in two-dimensional weavings and accentuating the shape of more sculptural pieces. My weavings enrich both residential and corporate settings, and range in size from intimate to monumental. Commissions welcomed.

EXHIBITIONS: *Tied Together: Textile Art in the 21st Century,* 2006, Chandler Center for the Arts, Chandler, AZ; *The Art of Seeing: Nature Revealed Through Illustration,* 2006, The Oakland Museum, Oakland, CA; Fifth International Textile Art Triennial, Tapisserie et Arts du Tissu, 2005, Tournai, Belgium

PUBLICATIONS: *Surface Design Journal,* Special Gallery Issue, 2006; *Fiberarts,* 2004

GUILD SOURCEBOOKS: *Designer's 11, 13, 14, 15; Architectural & Interior Art 18*

KATHY BRADFORD

Architectural Glass

Page 27

Sandblast carving and etching remain the major forces in my glass art. Over the years I have created many unique techniques to achieve certain imagery not found in the work of other glass artists. In the last few years, I have begun combining sand carving, etching and other glass detailing as appropriate to the composition. These compositions are unique, whimsical, energetic and powerful. I continually work with architects, designers and contractors to ensure proper and successful installations in many locations throughout the country. Everything possible is taken into account to create beautiful glasswork that will work in concert with the architecture of the location.

RECENT PROJECTS: Centura Health, Denver, CO; Aurora Firehouse #3, Aurora, CO; Oak Park Pavilion, St. Louis Park, MN; Russian Tea Room, New York, NY

ARTIST STATEMENTS

CARL AND SANDRA BRYANT

Murals, Tiles & Wall Reliefs

Page 201

We are a mosaic artist team that uses vitreous and stained glass, ceramic, and semi-precious stones to create beautiful art that will last indefinitely. We love the medium for its durability, resistance to graffiti, ability to withstand all kinds of weather, and suitability to so many settings. Mosaics can add unique style and color both as indoor fine art and outdoor installations. It's wonderful the way a piece will change as the glass absorbs the light that plays across its surface.

COMMISSIONS: Lucille Umbarger Elementary School mosaic in conjunction with the Washington State Arts Commission; Thirty-foot square commissioned mosaic for shower installation, private residence, Colorado; Pool surround project, California; Book cover art for *Mosaics in Communication*, Thomson Learning; *Beneath the Surface*, Chicago, IL; *A More Perfect Union: Mosaic Aspirations*, 2005, Arlington, VA; *Opus Veritas: Fragments of Truth*, 2004, Museo Italo Americano, San Francisco, CA

GUILD SOURCEBOOKS: *Architectural & Interior Art 20, 21*

LAURA MILITZER BRYANT

Fiber Wall Art

Page 289

I create richly layered and detailed complex double weaves of wool, rayon, nylon, and Lurex that reference both the natural world and structures of civilizations past and present. These landscape-inspired geometric images are interpreted in free-hanging large-scale weavings or as more intimate textiles floating on wood or metal panels. Visual integration of woven surface to panel involves processes ranging from patination on copper to acrylic paint and metal leaf on wood. All threads are hand painted and dyed with high-quality light-fast dyes; metal or wood surfaces are sealed. I welcome collaboration with clients to achieve the perfect enhancement for their environment, and enjoy the synergy that is created during the commission process.

GUILD SOURCEBOOKS: *Designer's 10, 11, 12, 13, 14, 15; Architectural & Interior Art 16, 17, 18, 19, 20, 21*

FRAN BULL

Paintings & Prints

Page 228

I have been exhibiting my art worldwide for over twenty-five years. My early work was associated with the New York-based Photorealist movement. Shown and sold through the Louis K. Meisel Gallery in New York City, this art is located in numerous public and private collections. In the early 1990s, I expanded my creative focus by exploring a more expressionistic approach to art, and with this, an expansion into other media. My drawings and paintings, performance art, sculpture, set design, and printmaking became investigations of the invisible worlds that lie beneath and within our own visible world. Over the past five years, I have been especially prolific in the area of printmaking, creating numerous bodies of etchings in collaboration with master printer Virgili Barbara in Taller 46, a printmaking studio in Barcelona, Spain. Today my art seeks to connect present-day scenarios with larger mythic and historical motifs, themes and narratives. Upcoming exhibitions include a solo exhibition of recent etchings and paintings in Montreal, a solo exhibition of paintings and etchings in Denver, CO, and a traveling exhibition of etchings in New York and Costa Rica.

CHRISTIAN BURCHARD

Mixed & Other Media Wall Art

Page 274

I create simple wall sculptures from single blocks of green wood. I use roots and burls from Pacific Madrone, which grows only in the Northwest. As the wood dries, a lot of changes happen. The wood shrinks, moves, and warps. I help this process along in many ways. I shape, sandblast, bleach, sand, burn, finish. As in black-and-white photography, I remove the color and focus instead on the spirit, the essence of the objects, and the material. I treasure their simplicity. Panels come in many sizes and shapes, sometimes reminiscent of torsos or other body parts, and can be arranged in many different configurations.

COMMISSIONS: Oregon Arts Commission 1997

COLLECTIONS: Museum of Art and Design, NY; L.A. County Museum, CA; Renwick Gallery, Smithsonian Institution; Mint Museum, NC

EXHIBITIONS: Patina Gallery, 2002, Santa Fe, NM; Del Mano Gallery, 2001, Los Angeles, CA; Sculpture Objects & Functional Art (SOFA) Chicago; Collect, London, England

PUBLICATIONS: *Craft Arts International* (Australia), 2005; *CRART* (South Korea), 2005; *Turning Wood into Art*, 2000; *American Craft*, 1997

MYRA BURG

Fiber Wall Art

Page 290

Somewhere between tapestry and jewelry, *Quiet Oboes* and sculptural installations adorn space in a free-floating, peaceful way. Hand-wrapped fiber and burnished metals are combined to create inspired sculptural pieces that meet clients' needs and wants within the requirements of the space. The bigger the challenge, the more the fun. Collaborations are welcome.

COMMISSIONS: Western Asset, London, England; Boston Children's Hospital; Japonaise, Universal Studios, Japan; Galactic Curve, Universal Studios, Japan; *Quiet Oboes*, Caribé Hilton, Puerto Rico; Travelocity, Dallas, TX

EXHIBITIONS: American Craft Council; SOFA, Chicago; Los Angeles County Museum of Art, CA; Howard Hughes Center, Los Angeles, CA; Orange County Museum of Art, CA

AWARDS: First place, 2002, Artfest of Henderson, NV; first place, 2001, 1999, 1998, Beverly Hills *Affaire in the Gardens*, CA

GUILD SOURCEBOOKS: *Designer's 10, 13, 14, 15; Architect's 14, 15; Architectural & Interior Art 16, 17, 18, 19, 20, 21; Artful Home 1, 2, 3, 4, 5*

RENATE MARGIT BURGYAN

Representational Sculpture

Page 141

Whether figurative or abstract, my sculptures invite you to experience an emotionally intimate expression of life. I strive to reach the viewer at a primordial level that ignites the fire of energy within. Although a graduate of The Ohio State University School of Journalism, I have found communicating through sculpture supercedes the written word. My twenty plus years' experience working in the lost wax method of bronze casting has been augmented by studies at the Columbus College of Art and Design, Johnson's Atelier, Columbia University, and patina workshops with Ron Young of Sculpt Nouveau. I have participated in all aspects of the bronze casting process, from bronze pour through outdoor installation.

COLLECTIONS: The White House; The Museum of Women in the Arts, Washington DC; Wendy's International; Charity Newsies; The Herb Society of America

PUBLICATIONS: *The Well Designed Mixed Garden; Midwest Living Magazine*, June 2001

ARTIST STATEMENTS

RIIS BURWELL

Non-Representational Sculpture

Page 107

My work is an exploration—emotional, spiritual, and physical—of what is seen and unseen in nature. Process and the gradual, though constant, change of things from one state of being to another fundamentally inform my artwork. The term "sculpture" has come to embody many things. My focus is to bring attention back to sculpture as a finely crafted object. Bronze, steel, and stainless steel are my materials of choice because of their permanence and inherent beauty. They lend themselves well to both tabletop and monumental sculpture, and are appropriate indoors and out.

COMMISSIONS: TCC International Holdings Ltd., 2006, Hong Kong; The MGM Mirage, 2005, Las Vegas, NV; Presbyterian Hospital of Denton, 2005, TX; SAS Institute World Headquarters, 2005, Cary, NC; The District at Green Valley Ranch Resort, 2004, Henderson, NV; Hyatt Hotel & Convention Center, 2002, Santa Rosa, CA

COLLECTIONS: Hotel Vue Plage, La Baule, France; Neuberg International Ltd., Hong Kong; Fresno Museum of Art, CA

GUILD SOURCEBOOKS: *Architect's 12, 13, 14, 15; Architectural & Interior Art 16, 17, 18, 19, 20, 21*

RICARDO CABRERA

Metal Wall Art

Page 266

My spiritual and inspirational journey led to my passion for forged iron. As a young man growing up in Bogotá, Colombia, I was surrounded by stunning examples of fine colonial architecture. As I develop as an artist, I constantly refer to the rich displays of color historically found in Spanish paintings and sculpture. For more than twenty years, I have been researching and developing techniques for handling metals with an emphasis on blacksmithing and cast iron projects. Every piece of art that I create is a modern portrayal of my cultural roots, of which I am so proud.

TERESA CAMOZZI

Architectural Glass/Atrium Sculpture

Pages 28, 63

Inspiration for my work is drawn from a passion for ecological ideals. In collaboration with architects and art and design professionals, I create intimate to monumental commissions for hospitals, hotels, and corporate collections. Working with nature photography, sculptural elements, painting, and chiffon mobiles, I am able to achieve a unique complexity that leaves a lasting impression. My work addresses the fragility of our environment, its beauty, and its desecration. My core belief is that the beauty of nature lifts us toward a higher state of spirituality and consciousness. My objective is to assist viewers in attaining inner equilibrium so that they may make wise choices in their everyday lives and salvage our ecology.

COLLECTIONS: St. Vincent's Hospital, Indianapolis, IN; Metropolitan Club, Chicago, IL; Four Seasons Hotels; Nemacolin Woodlands Resort, Farmington, PA; Fluor Daniel; Bellagio Hotel, Las Vegas, NV; Kaiser Permanente; Canon Corporation

PUBLICATIONS: *Photographer's Forum, Best of Photography Annual* 2006

GUILD SOURCEBOOKS: *Architect's 15; Architectural & Interior Art 21*

BOBBIE K. CARLYLE

Representational Sculpture

Page 143

I create monumental bronze sculptures that capture bold strength and provocative intelligence. My figures go beyond first impressions to challenge the intellect. My work reflects my love of classical sculpture, while presenting a modern approach and a psychological appeal for connection to the struggles and triumphs of life.

RECENT PROJECTS: Life-size figurative portrait sculpture; *Twilight*, life size; and *Self Made Man*, monumental sculpture, The Grand Del Mar Resort, San Diego, CA; *Aviator*, Rosecrans Memorial Airport, St. Joseph, MO; *For Love of the Game*, Parker, CO; *Hunter*, White Tail Club, McCall, ID

COLLECTIONS: University of North Carolina, Charlotte; Town of Parker, CO; City of Grand Junction, CO; City of Batavia, IL; Emir, Saudi Arabia; Lay Center, St. Louis University, Louisiana, MO; Indiana University-Purdue University, Columbus, IN; Manchester Grand Hyatt, San Diego, CA; City of Chinandega, Nicaragua; Western Bank, PR; MBI Institute, Austria; Nemacolin Woodlands, Hardy Family Collection, Farmington, PA

GUILD SOURCEBOOKS: *Architectural & Interior Art 20, 21*

SYDNEY CASH

Lighting

Pages 180, 183

A museum curator's initial response to this work: "I can't believe what my eyes are seeing!"

By directing lights through the patterned glass plane "lens," architectural and graphic imagery is magnified and projected onto flat walls, into corners, or onto ceilings. Developing these installations of light, reflection, and shadow has been a wonder-filled adventure. Concurrently, I design for Sydney Cash Jewelry.

COMMISSIONS: Light installations, Falcon Arts, Marlboro, NY; Sixteen 10'H glass panels, Queensborough Plaza Subway Station, New York City's Metropolitan Transit Authority; Collection of glass *Optical Vases* for MoMA

COLLECTIONS: Museum of Modern Art, New York City, NY; Le Musee des Arts Decoritifs, Paris; The Corning Museum of Glass, Corning, NY

EXHIBITIONS: Over forty solo exhibitions in the United States and Europe

AWARDS: Fellowship, The National Endowment for the Arts; Fellowship, The New York Foundation for the Arts; *Who's Who in America*, 2005

RIP H. CASWELL

Representational Sculpture

Pages 18, 142, 144-145

I was brought up surrounded by the wilderness of the Pacific Northwest, and, like the native people of the region, believe all living beings are connected to one another and to our Mother Earth. My goal as an artist has been to enrich communities through the installation of sculpture that embodies this belief. Throughout my sculpting career, I have collaborated with many architects, landscape architects, land developers, and public agencies to create work that is specific to a diverse collection of public, private, and corporate settings.

COMMISSIONS: *Wetland Wonders, Swift Pursuit, Temple Guardian*, 2002-2006, Park Plaza Buildings, Vancouver, WA; *Cougar on the Rocks, Upriver Challenge*, 2002, Hell's Gate State Park, Lewiston, ID; *The Battle*, 2006, High Desert Museum, Bend, OR; *Strength of America*, 2003, Pentagon, Washington, DC, and Belmont Firehouse, Portland, OR; *Christ's Family*, 2006, Southlake Church, West Linn, OR

PUBLICATIONS: "Discover the Wild," PBS documentary, Spring 2007; *Treasures of Western Oregon*, 2005

ARTIST STATEMENTS

SCOTT CHAMBERS

Lighting

Page 184

I build custom-designed chandeliers and lighting to any scale for commercial and residential applications. I own a glass studio and metal fabrication shop in Seattle, Washington. The ability to design and build the structural as well as the aesthetic components of a piece allows me to execute most design concepts. My *Migrating Salmon Architectural Panels* are available in any practical size. While the *Salmon Chandelier* is my signature lighting design, I am recognized nationally for my floral glass displays. Some of my lighting designs also incorporate these floral elements.

JAN BROWN CHECCO

Murals, Tiles & Wall Reliefs

Page 202

Community-based art is large scale, conceived of and fabricated by people who wish to live with work they help to create. I have been designing and leading such workshops since 1999, working with professional and amateur artists of all ages. The close-in "artist residency" aspect of these projects allows me to adapt materials and processes to the needs of each community, installation site, and client. The process builds relationships, affirms collective identity, and allows participants to experience creative expression beyond the usual small scale of personal artwork. The final product's aesthetic quality is insured by careful moderation of design, teaching, and building activities. The typical duration of a large project workshop runs three to seven months, depending on how much community participation is desired. Recent projects include: *A Friendship Tapestry,* 2006, fiber art, Liuzhou, PR China; *Our Daily Bread Mural,* 2006, 12' × 100' painted exterior mural, Cincinnati, OH; *Twin Lakes Fountain Mosaic*, 2006, handmade low-fired ceramic, Montgomery, OH; *Cincinnati Friendship Garden Mosaic,* 2005, six-foot circle of high-fired ceramic on plaza floor, Munich, Germany.

CLAYGAL

Murals, Tiles & Wall Reliefs

Page 203

It is difficult for an artist to pick out an absolute reason for making his or her art, but one of the most important reasons for me is that I enjoy doing it. Nine years ago while in college, I got hooked on clay; today I cannot imagine doing anything else. With a background in painting, I find my ceramic work consistently manifests itself in hybrid forms, with relationships to both painting and sculpture. I'm committed to quality, integrity of design, consistency, and a sense of professionalism. Color catalog is available upon request.

CLOWES SCULPTURE

Atrium Sculpture

Pages 60, 64

We design sculpture for healthcare, corporate, hotel/spa, cruising, and academic facilities, as well as private homes. We enjoy collaborating with architects, designers, and art consultants to achieve a balance of art, architecture, and interior design. We are skilled at developing the right design, in the preferred materials, and within budget. Our distinct shapes and flowing curves formed in wood, metal, or composite, contrast with the color and texture of blown glass, stone, and other materials. A Clowes Sculpture can be a powerful branding icon that endures for years, with gracious gestures that invoke the presence of serene seas and soft winds.

COMMISSIONS: Memorial Hermann Hospital; Kingsbury Cancer Center; Wells Fargo Home Loan; St. Vincent's Hospital; The Lodge At Woodloch; American Lawyer Media; White County Medical Center; Phelps Dunbar; Hope Hospice; Pfizer, International; Royal Caribbean International; Tokyo Hilton Hotel; Indianapolis Museum of Art; Visalia Convention Center; Monadnock Paper Inc; Manchester, NH, District Courthouse; Antioch New England Graduate School; The Retrovest Companies

GESSO COCTEAU

Representational Sculpture

Pages 146-147

One of the largest bronze sculptures in America, the fifty-one foot *Endless Celebration,* was a project that allowed me to understand the most intricate details of architectural sculpture. Working closely with structural engineers, architects, and developers, my studio produced *Endless Celebration* with attention to quality, deadlines, and budget. As our world of visual culture grows, I love meeting the challenges of architectural space on a large scale, while staying true to the disciplinary traditions of bronze sculpture. I like to embrace my inspiration with technical skill and close communication with my patrons. From the smallest sculpture to the monumental, Cocteau Studios excels at techniques of visual analysis so that when a sculpture commission begins, the patron has a vivid idea of what the outcome will be. For examples of Gesso's work, please visit www.gessococteau.com.

ZACHARY COFFIN

Public Art

Page 81

Kinetic on a grand scale, my sculptures interact with people, wind, or water. Drama, design clarity, and durability are the keys to my approach. I work with weights of thousands of pounds and measurements of thousandths of inches. For exterior installation, I use only the most rugged of materials such as galvanized steel, stainless steel, and granite. My kinetics conform to standard industrial practice and are designed to last lifetimes with little or no maintenance.

ARTIST STATEMENTS

RANDY COOPER

Representational Sculpture

Page 148

I am an internationally recognized sculptor with continuing exhibitions in galleries in France, Canada, Sweden, Mexico, China, Israel, and major art centers in the U.S., including NYC, San Francisco, Santa Fe, New Orleans, and Fort Lauderdale. My medium is wire cloth (steel, stainless steel, and bronze). I've created more than 3,000 hand-made *Shadow Sculptures*© in the past thirteen years. Recently, I've taken the graceful lines of my nudes and created mysteriously sensuous abstracts. I also play, as shown in my brightly colored clown fish (with personalities), sharks (with none), brains for brain surgeons, feet for podiatrists, a pug for my daughter, and wearable art. I also collaborated with a chocolate artist to create a chocolate gown that was modeled at the Chocolate Runway Show in NYC in 2003. I live for challenges and new projects!

RECENT EXHIBITIONS: Miva Galleri, Sept. 2005-2007, Malmo, Sweden; Galleri Scandinavia, 2007, Gotenborg, Sweden; Art Symbol Gallery, Nov. 2006, Paris, France; Nuances et Lumière, Sept. 2006, Lyon, France; Galleria Bella, April – May 2005-2007, New Orleans, LA; Wyland Gallery, June 2005 and May 2006, Niagara Falls, Canada; Jean Stephen Galleries, May 2006, Minneapolis, MN

LYNN CREIGHTON

Representational Sculpture

Page 149

Searching for the form of the woman in full celebration of life is my primary artistic purpose and delight. As a clay artist, I see in the clay's plasticity the potential for form. It is my yearning for the discovery of new possibility that pushes me forward. This discovery process is enhanced by the paddle I began to use after seeing the Japanese masters use them. The paddle provides a distance from the work and spontaneity. Now I take the form through molding and wax into bronze for the sensuous surface and the permanence. It is my intention that the power of these figures ignites an awakening of feminine energy. It is my belief that women aware of and experiencing their own core will speak with an authentic voice, revealing the secrets of how life can be sustained on this planet.

CHARLES CSURI

Paintings & Prints

Page 229

My worst enemy is the computer and the rigors it imposes upon me as an artist. I begin with a tentative vision in mind, realizing that it will evolve into something else. There is no single solution; there is no recipe for art. For me the possibilities are infinite. It's my sense of play with parameters, as well as the uncertainty, that gives the process life. It's important for me to use the unique capabilities of the computer as a guide to creating a dynamic, beautiful, intricate "living" environment. In my images there is inherent randomness—a spontaneous sense of movement, depth, gradation, and transparency of color and light. There are moments when reality becomes confused, and the visual surprise is what creates excitement as I search for meaning in an infinite black box.

LEAH KRISTIN DAHLGREN

Liturgical Art

Page 176

My painting career takes me in very engaging and enjoyable directions—portraiture, still life, and teaching. The impulse to create paintings of a spiritual or religious nature is of a unique impetus. In this work I strive to bring to the canvas works not only of grace and strength but those imbued with the energy and substance of meditative contemplation. In the scope of this subject, I especially hope to create paintings that will inspire and touch a deep inner chord in those who behold them.

GUILD SOURCEBOOKS: *Designer's 12*

DANZIGER DESIGNER GLASS STUDIO

Architectural Glass

Page 29

We are a multidisciplinary team of professionals who delight in exploring the creative use of glass as a design medium. It is our goal to demonstrate that glass transcends all media in its interplay with light and its environment. We are constantly developing new techniques and methodologies, and our creations benefit from our ability to combine cutting-edge technology with world-class artistry. Our projects grace the public spaces, offices, and homes of discerning clients all over North America. Whether the entire face of the building or the furniture, lighting, and sculptural work within—from spectacular entryways to interior feature walls, dividers, and stairways—our glasswork will produce stunning results in a cost effective and practical way. Our processes include laminating, fusing, kiln forming, sand carving, stained and blown glass, as well as other techniques. In handling each project from inception to installation, we pride ourselves on effectively interpreting our client's taste while strictly adhering to an established budget and schedule.

LUKE DAVID

Non-Representational Sculpture

Pages 104, 108

It is my desire to create works that are successful in appearance as well as concept through meaningful sculptures and fountains that incorporate strong visual imagery. Nature, human emotions, and manmade forms inspire me. I am continually generating new works in different scales and mediums. As well as creating original pieces, I also enjoy collaborating with others to design commissioned works that are site specific, taking into account the location where my sculpture will sit and those who will be viewing it. I design primarily with bronze and stainless steel, often adding water systems and lighting elements for further depth and movement. Every aspect of the fabrication technique I do completely hands-on in my own custom workshop and studio. I have years of experience building and installing large-scale public works in many different regions.

ARTIST STATEMENTS

DAVID WILSON DESIGN

Architectural Glass

Page 30

My work seeks to reinvent the ancient craft of stained glass and place it in the context of contemporary architecture as a visually integrated building component. Simplicity, restraint, changing light, projected image, and night view all inform design development. Together with architect and client, I encourage a reciprocal dialogue in a collaborative design process and offer, in association with WRW Studio LLC, a complete service of design, fabrication, and installation.

COMMISSIONS: Greystone Park Psychiatric Hospital, 2007, Morris Plains, NJ; St. Theresa Catholic Church, 2007, Tuckerton, NJ; Chapel, Society of Jesus of New England, 2005, Watertown, MA; St. Ignatius Chapel, 2005, University of Detroit Mercy, Detroit, MI

GUILD SOURCEBOOKS: *THE GUILD 1, 2, 3, 4, 5; Architect's 6, 7, 8, 9, 11, 13, 14, 15; Architectural & Interior Art 16, 17, 18, 19, 20*

ALONZO DAVIS

Mixed & Other Media Wall Art

Page 275

Bamboo insinuated itself into my life ten years ago as a medium I could not let go of. Lightweight but strong, bamboo lends itself to many facets of my art making. The variegated patterns and segmented structure inspire design decisions. *Bamboo Constructions*, arrangements of poles lashed together with cowhide strips, suggest abstract expressionist paintings. Dimensions range from 3'H x 2.5'W to wall size. *Bamboo Constructions* reflect the satisfaction I get from connecting with people and places. *Power Poles* and *Sky Ladders* are two other forms. *Power Poles* can be presented singly or in groups, propped against a wall, positioned over doorways, or suspended. *Sky Ladders*, poles joined by thin dowels arranged at irregular intervals and often interwoven with twigs, symbolize higher goals.

COMMISSIONS: U.S. Embassy, Togo; Marbury Wing, Prince George's County Courthouse, Upper Marlboro, MD; Memphis/Shelby County Public Library, Memphis, TN; Hartsfield International Airport, Atlanta, GA; Boston Blue Line Subway Station, MA

PIA DAVIS

Fine Art Photography

Page 258

Capturing patterns and saturated colors on film, particularly flowers and landscapes, has been a quest of mine for many years. More recently, my exploration of art glass through a macro lens has yielded uniquely beautiful perspectives of glass and saturated color, resulting in great richness and unusual, magical topographies to delight the eye and the soul. My photography is a labor of love. I am always in search of the beauty of nature and, in my glass series, my mission is to capture nature as interpreted by man. I work with 35mm and medium-format equipment. A self-taught photographer, I prefer shooting in natural light. Slides are scanned at high resolution, resulting in a precise rendering on giclée prints, using archival materials. Various sizes (up to 36" x 24") are available and many images also lend themselves to mural-style presentations. My work is held in private collections across Europe, the U.S., Australia, and Israel.

COLLECTIONS: Kaiser Permanente Medical Office Building, Oxnard, CA; Kaiser Permanente Replacement Hospital, Panorama City, CA; White Memorial Medical Center, Los Angeles, CA

GUILD SOURCEBOOKS: *Architectural & Interior Art 20*

DORA DE LARIOS

Murals, Tiles & Wall Reliefs

Page 204

The World According to Dora: The central Goddess figure forms the heart of the mural. She stands at the base of the Tree of Life and has created a joyful world imbued with all manner of animal, bird, and sea creature. Dark brown stoneware represents the earth, and porcelain was used for the Goddess and sea creatures. Gold and dichroic glass mosaics were incorporated in the ocean and sky. The gold mosaics are symbolic of the preciousness of the ocean, and the iridescent and multi-colored dichroic glass tile represents the luminous quality of the sky. The depth of relief is three to six inches; the scale is 4'H x 10'W. It is a fine work and is strong and vibrant in sculptural energy. The Salinas family commissioned the mural for their residence in Laguna Beach, California.

COMMISSIONS: Montage Resort and Spa, 2003, Laguna Beach, CA; Marriot Resort, 2000, Maui, HI; Bonaventure Hotel, 1997, Los Angeles, CA; Trammell Crow, 1993, Santa Fe Springs, CA.

SELECTED EXHIBITIONS: Lois Neiter Fine Art; Evalyn Daniel Fine Art; Japanese American Cultural Center, 2000, Los Angeles, CA

GUILD SOURCEBOOKS: *Architect's 10; Designer's 14; Architectural & Interior Art 20*

DERIX ART GLASS CONSULTANTS

Architectural Glass

Pages 31, 98

We work in collaboration with artists, architects, designers, and public arts organizations to organize the design, fabrication, and installation of unparalleled architectural art glass. Our studio, Derix Glasstudios, located near Wiesbaden, Germany, has been creating architectural art glass since 1866 and has earned a reputation worldwide for the highest quality craftsmanship and innovative techniques. In the last twenty years, we have advanced proportionally with this remarkable medium in both technique and design approach. These advances have liberated artists and designers from traditional limitations and sensibilities, and have dually made glass a truly contemporary material and applied art, suitable for modern architecture and aesthetics.

COMMISSIONS: Hung Liu's *Going Away, Coming Home*, Oakland Airport, CA; Michael Hammers & Swarovski Crystal, Observation Deck at Rockefeller Center, NY; Paul Marioni's *Consilience*, University of Houston, Clearlake, TX

AWARDS: *Ministry & Liturgy*, Honorable Mention, Linda Dabeau's *Daystar and Mary Windows*, Our Lady of Angels Catholic Church, Allen, TX

JOY DOHERTY

Fine Art Photography

Page 259

I am in love with and awed by the beauty of nature. My photographic images explore the limitless palette and mysterious play of light and form that nature offers. Once an image is chosen, it is processed onto unique and innovative substrates—hand-textured metal panels, archival gallery-wrapped giclée canvas, fabrics of varying density, plexiglass, and other plastics and resins. The resulting art has a fresh, contemporary look. The versatility of the materials gives clients the freedom to choose the shape, size, and substrate style that suits their project's unique requirements. My art is displayed in private collections, corporate offices, healthcare facilities, spas, and residential high rises.

GUILD SOURCEBOOKS: *Residential Art 5*

ARTIST STATEMENTS

BARBARA AND LARRY DOMSKY

Architectural Glass

Page 32

Working in the mediums of hot-glass, fused glass, and metal, we hold over thirty years' experience as professional artists. Our innovative use of these materials has produced a wide range of artworks, including hot-fusion glass panels, blown glass and fused glass sculptures, chandeliers, and architectural elements for both large-scale installations and one-of-a-kind art pieces. We welcome architects and designers to collaborate in creating site-specific residential and commercial commissions. Commission rates: $5,000 and up. National and International commissions welcomed.

COMMISSIONS: Nike, Mandalay Bay Hotel, Las Vegas, NV; Wynn Hotel, Las Vegas, NV; Cirque Du Soleil, Bellagio Hotel, Las Vegas, NV; City of Hope Hospital, Los Angeles, CA; Charlie Palmer Restaurants, Washington, DC, Las Vegas, NV, and New York, NY. International artworks in India, Australia, New Zealand, Germany and South Africa

THOMAS DONALSON

Representational Sculpture

Page 150

Raised as a rancher in the rich cultural diversity of the Rio Grande Valley, I have a respect and appreciation for God's creation, for love, family, freedom, and my fellow man. I have an excitement and anxiousness about my new work and the ability to execute an endless supply of ideas. I create sculptures out of steel, iron, and stainless. Most, monumental in size, are images that command respect and are symbolic to America and freedom. I manipulate these products with heat, welding, hammering, and physical energy using both old world techniques and new technology. It is only in the past four years that I have turned my full attention to a professional art career. Already I have established collectors across the United States and Canada. Sculptures range in size of six feet to over sixteen feet and $3,500 to $35,000.

COMMISSIONS: Public Work—9/11 Memorial, Belen, New Mexico. Fifty percent of my sculptures are private commissions.

EXHIBITIONS: Annual Loveland Sculpture Invitational; Sedona Sculpture & Art Walk; AZ Expo; New Mexico Expo; Route 66 Art Society; Thunder Bird Art Shows in Arizona

PUBLICATIONS: *Southwest Art Magazine*

PHILIP S. DRILL

Non-Representational Sculpture

Page 109

I am intrigued by natural forms. My sculpture combines structural integrity with the sensual curvilinear grace of found natural objects, such as leaves, shells, or bone fragments. A walk in the woods, a stroll on the beach or a city street, and even the remains of a meal have served as catalysts for my designs. An engineer by training, I began my career as an artist working with welded metal. My interest in organic form led me to explore the expressive possibilities of more plastic media such as clay, wax, or plaster, then casting each sculpture in bronze, acrylic, or stainless steel. My work has been exhibited in juried exhibitions, one-man shows, art festivals, museums, and universities. To view more of my sculpture, please visit my website at www.psdrill.com. I welcome the opportunity to discuss commissions.

ERIC EHLENBERGER

Atrium Sculpture

Page 65

I approach my sculptures as meditations of form and color. Using the vibrant colors and glows achieved by combining neon light with glass and brushed metal, I explore the emotional impact of luminous color and simple forms. The nature of my works extend from the use of simple geometric forms in contemplative abstractions to theme-based series of sculptures in which I explore a fantasy world of luminous flora and fauna, including the hanging neon and blown-glass *Jellyfish* sculptures. In the design of my work, I place importance on both practical installation and maintenance considerations as well as the aesthetics.

MARTIN EICHINGER

Representational Sculpture

Page 151

Even though most people see me as a figurative sculptor, I prefer being thought of as a narrative artist. It's this quality of my work that connects my heart and soul to others who are looking at it or, preferably, feeling it. By sharing story and emotion through the human form, I feel connected in a deeper way, both with the people that are viewing it and, perhaps most importantly, to the sculpture that I am working on. The art becomes a shared culture that is larger than the aesthetic experience alone. I strive to transcend Realism in pursuit of the more evocative Romanticism. Commissions and current work can be found at eichingersculpture.com.

EINO

Public Art

Page 82

As a sculptor for over forty years, I have completed in excess of 300 works. I am technically fluent in all types of stone, as well as bronze (doing my own bronze casting). My first public art commission was in 1964 for a sculpture in Mary Hotchkiss Park in Santa Monica, CA. More recent projects include a life-size bronze of former Cal Berkeley basketball coach Pete Newell, and a fifteen-foot diameter sphere of Brazilian blue quartzite as a memorial to the late environmentalist David Brower. I have had sculptures exhibited at two Olympic games (1996 & 2002), and another permanently installed in Athens, Greece, immediately following the 2004 games. One of my long-held beliefs is that art should influence society, rather than society influencing art. My work has always been "art for art's sake," and that is something of which I am very proud.

ARTIST STATEMENTS

JOLINE EL-HAI
Lighting
Page 185

I fill my glass panels with a sense of movement, rich coloring, and bold, detailed imagery of a narrative quality. The drama of the natural world often informs my designs. My reductive glass painting technique gives depth and mystery with a graininess reminiscent of mezzotints and old photographs. I incorporate glass fusing for complexity of color and texture. My glass panels, when internally-illuminated, range from large murals set into walls to small, intimate glowing sculpture for the table or shelf. I also design and fabricate naturally lit windows. I began creating leaded glass panels in 1975. Over the years I have expanded the scope of my work to include glass jewelry, fused glass wall sculpture, giclée prints of pastel drawings, and a nationally known and popular production line of decorative lights. My work has won awards and has been featured in group and solo shows in galleries and museums across the country.

ENANA & CO.
Murals, Tiles & Wall Reliefs
Page 205

The mosaic art of Enana & Co. is the blending of Mother Nature's abundance—color and stone—with human's passionate sphere, art. Natural stones, in natural color, hand picked, hand cut, and hand inlaid, translating an artist's vision into a magical piece of art. Patiently, one stone at a time, we capture the essence of our subjects, igniting the aspiration of our clients. We welcome your desires for commissioned work and invite you to unmask the splendor of our enchanting collection at www.enanaco.com. Enjoy the journey!

CLAIRE EVANS
Paintings & Prints
Page 230

I am a respected Colorado artist whose portraits, water lilies, and landscapes are included in private and corporate collections in the United States and abroad. My large oils express the spirit of the grasses, sunlit trees, and streams that surround me. I welcome the challenge of commissioned work in a variety of sizes and media. Prices range from $500 to $10,000.

COMMISSIONS: Marriott Hotels; U.S. West; Sapporo Hotel; KN Energy; Pinnacol Assurance; Meridian; Sky Across, Tokyo; and Hyatt Hotels

GUILD SOURCEBOOKS: *Designer's 9, 14; Architectural & Interior Art 16; Residential Art 1*

GAIL FOLWELL
Representational Sculpture
Page 152

Art can inspire, teach, and heal. I create sculpture to express physical and emotional energy through the abstraction of the human form. Anatomy, gesture, and the tactile handling of surfaces are essential components for manifesting my thoughts in these works. I work in large and small scale, bronze, clay, or styrothane for public and private collections. I have exhibited with The National Academy of Design and National Sculpture Society, New York, and have completed sculptural commissions for the National Hockey League, Vail Valley Foundation/Gerald Ford Amphitheater, and private collectors. I was honored by *Southwest Art*, July 2002, as one of twenty-five Leading American Sculptors. For gallery and portfolio information, please visit www.folwellstudios.com

FORMS IN METAL
Liturgical Art
Page 177

From the time I completed my first project in metal back in 1975, I was aware of the wide diversity of techniques, styles, and appearance of metals. My respect and love for that has been at the foundation of my work to this day. I enjoy combining traditional techniques with contemporary style, as well as the challenge of successfully combining different materials—both functionally and visually. My own expressions are usually contemporary and organic, showing the fluidity of the material, but my commissions over the years have covered the full spectrum of design—from traditional to contemporary—depending on the requirements of the project. Most of my works are custom-design commissions and restorations in bronze, brass, copper, and steel. I draw from a wide range of techniques, which allows me to review a project and to know that there is more than one way to execute a design, depending on the demands of the job.

RON FOSTER
Mixed & Other Media Wall Art
Page 276

I specialize in producing site-specific, mixed-media works of art to enhance architectural and interior design. I utilize kaleidoscope theory, bringing to life a three-dimensional effect that uniquely complements its surroundings. Beautiful surface treatments and precise workmanship provide extraordinary tactile and visual interest. This concept's originality is emphasized even further by its ability to use and combine a wide variety of materials, such as paper, fabric, steel, ceramics, wood, glass, and various laminates. Wall relief, leaded glass, murals, and free-standing works of virtually any scale are within my Kaleidosculpture™ repertoire.

DOUGLAS OLMSTED FREEMAN

Public Art

Page 83

I create sculpture and design spaces that invite the viewer to participate, to play, and to imagine. My focus is public art—particularly places for people—including fountains, memorials, plazas, and parks. The meaning and imagery is drawn from the place where the art will find a home. I have created traditional folk gods and animal messengers for the city of Tokyo, *Flying Pigs* for Cincinnati and *The Fountain of the Wind* for the city of Duluth on Lake Superior. We recently unveiled *The Lion's Fountain*, an interactive fountain in Culver City, California, and present with this book *The Mississippi Guardian Birds* and fountains on the river in Saint Paul, Minnesota.

GUILD SOURCEBOOKS: *Architect's 9, 10, 11, 12, 13, 14, 15; Architectural & Interior Art 16, 18, 21*

FUSIO STUDIO

Architectural Glass

Page 33

My glass work explores texture and pattern, transparency and opacity, and depth in glass. My training and experience as an architect strongly influence the design of my glass pieces. As an artist and an architect, I find inspiration in both the human-made environment and in the vast landscape of the American West where I grew up. Fusio Studio glass work includes architectural installations and design elements such as lighting, tiles, and windows; freestanding and wall hung panels; and functional objects.

COMMISSIONS: The Children's Hospital Chapel, 2007, Denver, CO; Bozeman Public Library, 2007, Bozeman, MT

EXHIBITIONS: New Work, 2007, Turman Gallery, Helena, MT; Design Elements, 2007, Shack Up, Bozeman, MT; Art Into Architecture, 2007, Bullseye Gallery, Portland, OR; Strata, 2006, Solo Exhibition, Bullseye Gallery, Portland, OR

AWARDS: Selected for the Corning Museum of Glass's *New Glass Review 27*, 2006; American Craft Council Award of Achievement, 2003

PUBLICATIONS: *500 Glass Objects, A Celebration of Functional and Sculptural Glass*, 2006

GUILD SOURCEBOOKS: *Residential Art 2*

GRT GLASS DESIGN

Architectural Glass

Page 34

Our artisans and craftsmen produce unique, high-end, custom architectural glass products to meet or exceed our clients' visual communication needs by adapting the medium of glass to any circumstance. Specializing in cast glass, we enjoy the challenge of diverse projects, including developing new ideas with glass. We can also include other materials such as metal and stone to produce quality pieces of functional glass art.

RECENT PROJECTS: Coca-Cola Museum Entry Vestibule, Atlanta, GA; Seamless Nightclub, Las Vegas, NV; Kalianas Spa, Boca Raton, FL; Lakeland Hospital, Kalamazoo, MI; Clarian North Medical Center; Clarian West Medical Center, Avon, IN; Fantasy Springs Resort Casino, Palm Springs, CA

EXHIBITIONS: HD Design Expo, 2007; NeoCon West Edge, 2006, 2005, Los Angeles, CA; HD Boutique, 2005, Miami, FL; AIA National Convention and Design Expo, 2004, Chicago, IL; NeoCon World's Trade Fair, 2005, 2004, Chicago, IL

PUBLICATIONS: *Glass Magazine*, 2007; *Doctor of Dentistry*, 2007

GUILD SOURCEBOOKS: *Architect's 8; Architectural & Interior Art 19, 20, 21*

VIRGINIA GABALDO

Murals, Tiles & Wall Reliefs

Page 206

I was born in Argentina and grew up in Southern California. This experience has enabled me to embrace diversity and has resulted in work that is as unique as my experiences. I studied fine art at the University of Southern California and also with my parents. My mother taught me painting and my father glass art. My reverse-painted glass bas-reliefs explore man's relationship with geologic time. These pieces appear to be ancient and fossilized, created by a process I call "sedimentation painting," which consists of applying layer upon layer of titanium and mica particles that have been stained with colors. My paintings can be hung in any type of lighting condition because the metal particles pick up any available light. Everyone who collects my work is amazed at the incredible textures and broad range of shifting color that my pieces display.

COMMISSIONS: Alaska Center for Facial Plastic Surgery, 2003, Anchorage, AK

COLLECTIONS: Capitol Arts Foundation, Santa Fe, NM

EXHIBITIONS: *Ahora: New Mexican Hispanic Art*, 2002, National Hispanic Cultural Center of New Mexico, Albuquerque

NINA GABRIEL

Mixed & Other Media Wall Art

Page 277

I have felt connected to nature and its boundless beauty since my childhood. My art and poetry represent many philosophies. I strive to understand the spirituality and the soul behind them. I often bring several ideas into one work, be that a collage or a poem. My art and poetry have contributed enormously to my own spiritual growth. It is my sincere wish that my work brings peace, happiness and joy to anyone that appreciates it. I also hope that it will bring forth many positive feelings, such as love, faith, and confidence, and truly all the good that life has to offer.

GINI GARCIA

Lighting

Pages 186-187

I founded Garcia Art Glass, Inc. in 1998. After receiving my B.F.A. in industrial and environmental design, I eventually opened a hot glass design and fabrication center that specializes in the creation of one-of-a-kind blown glass lighting and sculpture, including tablescapes and art for the wall. These creations, made to client specifications, range from the functional to the whimsical for homes, corporate offices, restaurants, and hospitals. Recently, I traveled to Murano, Italy, and studied the "Chandelier for the New Millennium." Using blown glass as a filter for light, each of my creations is designed with the overall environment in mind. Recent clients include AT&T, Wells Fargo, United Way, Volvo, and Warner Brothers, as well as numerous restaurants and hundreds of residential commissions. Garcia Art Glass, Inc. employs talented team members with a combined experience of fifty years in design, blown glass fabrication, lighting, metalwork, and installation.

ARTIST STATEMENTS

GEORGE HANDY ARTWORKS INC.

Mixed & Other Media Wall Art

Page 278

My relief wall sculptures combine cubist perspective and the painting style of abstract expressionism. The cantilevered and interwoven shapes of urethane board include a holographic feature in which surface colors alter in relationship to the viewer's perspective. Interactive art promotes viewer participation, and as my work has successfully generated dialogue, it fulfills my ultimate goal of creating public art, which brings people together. Urethane is archival and durable even for outdoor projects; square foot pricing is available for residential or corporate projects.

COMMISSIONS: Duke Auditorium; Charlotte Fire Dept., Health Dept., Parks Dept., NC; Mission Children's Hospital; Kohls; Petsmart; UNCA, Asheville, NC; Transylvania Public Library, Brevard, NC; Warner Brothers, *Batman Forever,* Charlotte Area Transit Authority; Duke Corporate Headquarters, Charlotte, NC

COLLECTIONS: Smithsonian Institution Permanent Collection, R.J. Reynolds

AWARDS: North Carolina Regional Artist Grant; Spartanburg, SC Museum of Art; Highlands NC Art Center, first prize

GUILD SOURCEBOOKS: *Architectural & Interior Art 19*

GLASMALEREI PETERS/ PETERS GLASS STUDIOS

Architectural Glass

Page 35

Established almost one hundred years ago, our artistic glass studio is one of Germany's most prominent workshops, offering excellence in everything from classical glass painting to contemporary glass fabrication. Our studio is dedicated to service, quality, and innovation, and it has built its reputation by working with architects, artists, and designers to develop creative solutions for the most challenging of proposals. We maintain extensive facilities for all kinds of glass fabrication work, including traditional leaded and painted glass, sandblasting, etching, screenprinting with paint or enamels, lamination, air brushing, adhesives, and safety glass. The studio and its staff have introduced many new techniques related to contemporary glass design and large-scale float glass painting for architectural settings. Located in the heart of Europe, our company works for clients and artists throughout the world.

GLASSIC ART

Architectural Glass

Page 36

True connoisseurs, collectors, curators, and discriminating buyers appreciate the outstanding quality of Glassic Art's creations—unique glass products developed from twenty-five years of experience. Our studio offers completion within deadlines, service beyond compare, and one-of-a-kind pieces that have been receiving rave reviews from investors and viewers for years. The "glassic art" created at the studio is a multi-dimensional medium made by sandblasting, painting, welding, fusion, kiln-formed glass, metal, and bonding techniques. From fine art to functional, our pieces are used for murals, bars and countertops, staircases, waterfalls, room dividers, entries, and free-form sculptures.

COMMISSIONS: Golden Door Spa, Puerto Rico; Red Rock Station/Casino, Las Vegas, NV; Golden Moon Casino, Meridian, MS; MGM High Limit Gaming, Las Vegas, NV; Bellagio Casino Resort, Las Vegas, NV

AWARDS: First place glass artist, 2005, Artv Awards; Gold, First place countertops, Designer's Home Excellence Awards

GUILD SOURCEBOOKS: *Architect's 12, 14, 15; Architectural & Interior Art: 16, 18, 20*

MARLENE GLICKMAN

Fiber Wall Art

Pages 286, 291

Whether I dye, paint with thread, manipulate, create 3D effects, or just simply wash and iron it, I am passionate about creating collages and sculptures with the sensual medium of fabric. Out of a daily design challenge that incorporated one color each month, my work evolved from small collaged units into large wall hangings. Each 5" x 5" fiber collage stands alone and can be framed or float from lucite rods in a series of panels. They are lightweight, easy to ship and hang. All pieces are one of a kind and can be designed for specific settings. Prices on application. Visit www.silkdyes.com for more information.

COMMISSIONS: First Night, 2004, St. Petersburg, FL; 300th Anniversary, 2005, St. Petersburg, Russia

EXHIBITIONS: *Daily: Courting the Muse,* 2005, Florida Craftsmen Gallery, St. Petersburg, FL; *My World in Black and White,* 2003, Museum of History & Art, Ontario, CA; *America: from the Heart,* 2001-2003, traveled U.S. and Spain

AWARDS: Artist Enhancement Grant, 2006, State of Florida, Division of Cultural Affairs

PUBLICATIONS: *I Remember Mama,* 2005; *Art in Embassies Program,* United States Embassy Yaounde, 2005, *The Roots of Racism: Ignorance and Fear,* 2003

GOLDSTEIN & KAPELLAS STUDIO

Atrium Sculpture

Page 66

We have collaborated with architects and designers for over twenty years on public, private, and corporate commissions of all sizes. Our site-specific sculptures and mobiles are lightweight, durable, and reflective. The kinetic pieces move gracefully and require minimal air currents to set them in motion.

COMMISSIONS: Mobile for Sallie Mae Corporation, Reston, VA; Mobile for California Department of Health Services, Richmond, CA; Mobile for AstraZeneca, Wilmington, DE

COLLECTIONS: Fine Arts Museums of San Francisco, CA; Art Institute of Chicago, IL; Brooklyn Museum, NY; California Department of Health Services, Richmond, CA; AstraZeneca, Wilmington, DE; Sallie Mae Corporation, Reston, VA

EXHIBITIONS: Durka Chang Gallery, 2002, San Francisco, CA; Brauer Museum of Art, 2000, Valparaiso, IN; Museum of Contemporary Religious Art, 1998, St. Louis, MO

PUBLICATIONS: *Beyond Belief: Modern Art and the Religious Imagination,* 1998; *Reliquaries,* 1994

GUILD SOURCEBOOKS: *Architect's 7, 8, 10, 13, 14, 15, 20, 21*

NANCY GONG

Architectural Glass

Page 37

The energy and spirit of living things have always intrigued me. It continues to be at the very core of my art. I constantly strive to capture grace, movement, and dimension of life in a simple yet powerful style. Facets of nature by way of lyrical abstractions are the soul of my art. With a rich personal style and an impressive command of my medium, I create sensitive, responsive, and enduring glass designs with quality craftsmanship for architectural installations and art collections.

COMMISSIONS: Lidestri Foods Inc.; Sharon Vermont Vietnam Honorial; American Institute of Architects; Constellation Brands Inc.; Cornell and Duke Universities; Corning Tropel.; Genencor Intl.; Garcia's Restaurant; NYS Appellate Court; ARTWalk Artistic Bus Shelter Competition Rochester, Port of Rochester

EXHIBITIONS: SOFA Chicago, 2004; Crafts National 38/27; ArtForm International, 2003

PUBLICATIONS: *Interiors and Sources, Contemporary Crafts for the Home, The Design Journal of Korea, Architect Design Collaborative, American Style Magazine, Stained Glass Magazine*

GUILD SOURCEBOOKS: *The Guild 3, 4, 5, 6, 8, 11; Architectural & Interior Art 18, 21; Residential Art 5*

ARTIST STATEMENTS

GORDON AUCHINCLOSS DESIGN, LLC

Atrium Sculpture

Page 6, 20

I build mobiles because it's soothing and because of what the mobiles create—a soothing, thoughtful space. Finding balance energizes me. I find creating a sculpture piece by piece, and watching it become alive, joyfully fulfilling. Forming relationships between the space, the sculpture, and the people using the space drives me further. Seeing how my work enriches environments and imparts complex, gentle, thoughtful feelings upon the people viewing my work is what it's all about. The materials I choose for specific projects are relative to the sites in mind, what my client requests, and what I am excited to work with at any given time. The place is paramount. Colors, shapes, and textures are all taken into account, as well as lighting, airflow, and structural engineering. Each project, in turn, builds upon itself and the dynamics of those to come. Communicating clearly with my clients and their representatives, be they designers or general contractors, is as much a part of getting my work installed in a streamlined fashion as building the sculptures themselves. My goal—and that of my clients—is to enhance a setting while triggering a creative, intriguing, and thoughtful stimulus from those who inhabit the space or happen through it.

RUTH FRANCES GREENBERG

Murals, Tiles & Wall Reliefs

Page 207

I am an artisan who is dedicated to elevating the medium of ceramic tile to a fine art. To realize my vision, I work with architects, individuals, and designers. My mosaics convey a personal narrative formed within the context of their environment and demonstrate a sensitivity to the unique personality of each project. Although my studio is rooted in the legacy of historical mosaics, I am constantly exploring new techniques and rediscovering ancient ways to illustrate and paint with tile. With the assistance of my team of five artists, I cut, glaze, fire, and assemble each piece of porcelain (tessera) by hand. This method of handcrafting the individual elements of my mosaics allows me tremendous freedom with color, form, and line, as well as a visceral connection to the materials. The result is the creation of customized surroundings and installations that will be cherished for generations.

COMMISSIONS: Heritage Square Shopping Center, 2007, Mishawaka, IN; *Rose Room Mosaic*, 2006, New York, NY; Private residence, 2006, Bedminster, NJ; Courtyard signage, 2006, Rice University, Houston, TX

GUILD SOURCEBOOKS: *Architectural & Interior Art 21*

MICHELLE GREGOR

Representational Sculpture

Page 153

As an artist my intention is to articulate something of the precious force that animates the human body and the lyricism of its movement. My sculptures in bronze and high-fire ceramic range in scale from large architectural installations to smaller works with subtle, delicate surfaces derived through multiple kiln firings.

COMMISSIONS: Olympic Club, 2004, San Francisco, CA; Pebble Beach Spa, CA; Residential installations, San Francisco, CA

EXHIBITIONS: Solo shows at Space 743, 2005, 2002, 2000, 1997, and 1995, San Francisco, CA; Michelle Gregor at Pence Gallery, Davis, CA; Garden Gallery Walk, 1996-98, Yerba Buena Center for the Arts, San Francisco, CA; California Clay Competition, 1993-97, Davis, CA

AWARDS: Second place award, 2001, City of Santa Clara Sculpture Competition

PUBLICATIONS: *Hands in Clay*, 2004; *Artweek*, 2001 and 1995; *Studio Potter Network News*, Spring 2001; *San Francisco Examiner Image Magazine*, 1993

GUILD SOURCEBOOKS: *Architectural & Interior Art 21*

CHARLES GROGG

Fine Art Photography

Page 260

Making images of flowers is like training one's eye on a moving target. They are alive, and alive they sit, move, fall over, wilt, and, often within minutes of cutting and trimming, lose too much of their transient luster to make beautiful subjects. I make these images on 4" x 5" negatives using natural light, light boxes, and flashlights. While I realize I ignore everything about a flower's origins or its historical use in pharmacology, and in its isolation cut it off from its environment, I still want to make images that look simple and honest. I want the lighting and the poses to speak to the emotion that caught me by surprise when I saw them, and that I wanted to preserve and to share.

CHRISTOPHER GRYDER

Murals, Tiles & Wall Reliefs

Page 208

The lineage of my meticulously carved ceramic relief tiles traces back to the architectural terra cotta tradition of organically inspired facades. My work reinterprets natural objects and processes into a new visual language of form. I have developed a sort of "dimensional drawing" technique that is incorporated within a modular tile framework to form elegant compositions at both the level of the individual tile and that of the larger assemblage. Suitable for both indoor and outdoor installations, the tiles come alive in strong light, creating a mesmerizing play of shadow. My skills as an artist and an architect allow me to seamlessly integrate my artistic vision with the unique needs of the space and client. I produce initial studies as detailed photorealistic images that allow others to have a clear understanding of what the artwork will eventually become.

RALF GSCHWEND

Public Art

Page 84

Kinetic art has been my passion for the last twenty-five years. I primarily design wind, water, or motor-driven sculptures for public places such as restaurants, hotel and corporate interior lobbies, or atriums. I also design for outdoor plazas, fountains, and parks. Custom commissions, as well as numerous ready designs, are available. My moving sculptures range from two-foot interior limited-edition models that start at $2,500 to large ceiling- or wall-suspended mobiles that start at $9,000 to monumental originals that start at $50,000. Ralfonso sculpture leasing is available. Please contact me for a free Ralfonso CD with videos, images, and descriptions of my work.

COMMISSIONS: *Moving on Up*, 15' sculpture for the New Star building in St. Petersburg, Russia; *Exo-Centric Spirits*, Royal Caribbean Cruise Line Center, Oregon, USA

EXHIBITIONS: *Art in Motion*, Biennale, Holland; Chinese Academy of Science, Beijing, China; *Grounds for Sculpture*, New Jersey, USA; Olympic Committee, Beijing, China

ARTIST STATEMENTS

MARK ERIC GULSRUD

Architectural Glass
Page 38

A self-employed artist/designer for twenty-nine years, I work primarily in architectural, cast, and laminated glass, with frequent mixed-media commissions incorporating stone, ceramic, wood, metal, and water. Site-specific commissions include public, corporate, and liturgical work. I am personally involved in all phases of design, fabrication, and installation. My primary concern is the sympathetic integration of artwork with environment and community. Accustomed to collaborating with clients, design teams, architects, and general contractors—often with different agendas—I strive for all to arrive at a unified goal without sacrificing the aesthetics of a commission. I expect to develop an approach to a site in consultation with other professionals, to benefit from their expertise as well as to share my own. I consider my artwork a visual point of departure, as each individual brings his or her own perspective. Like cloud watching, one is free to discover an unanticipated aspect, to see something new within the familiar.

GUILD SOURCEBOOKS: *GUILD 3, 4; Architect's 7, 8, 9, 10, 11, 12, 13, 14, 15; Architectural & Interior Art 16, 17, 18, 19, 20, 21*

SARAH HALL

Architectural Glass
Page 39

Art can open doors, illuminate the possible, and forge a connection with the spiritual. There is a point in every design project when all of the separate elements—material, practical, artistic, and spiritual—coalesce. The design takes on a life of its own and exists as a delicate bridge between ideas and feelings, physical thresholds and intuitive dimensions.

RECENT PROJECTS: Regent College, UBC, Photovoltaic Wind Tower, Vancouver, BC HQ, Union for Reform Judaism, Chapel Project, NYC; HQ, WYD, Chapel Window, Koln, Germany

EXHIBITIONS: *Das Farbige Licht,* Munich Succession Exhibition, 2005-2006, Pfarrkitchen, Germany; *Lumieres du Monde,* 2005, Musée Suisse de Vitrail, Romont, Switzerland; *Hot, Warm, Cold,* 2003, Glass Art Association, Harborfront, Toronto, Canada

AWARDS: Ministry & Liturgy, 2006, Outstanding Liturgical Art Award; Chalmers Arts Fellowship, 2005, Ontario Arts Council; Allied Arts Award, 1996, Ontario Association of Architects

PUBLICATIONS: *Windows on our Souls: A Spiritual Excavation with Bob Shantz,* 2007

GUILD SOURCEBOOKS: *Architectural & Interior Art 20, 21*

TIM HARDING

Fiber Wall Art
Pages 5, 292

My wall pieces are done in layered, stitched, and cut silks, and are characterized by vibrant, lustrous colors and richly faceted textures. These large-scale, semi-abstract compositions complement architectural interior spaces by adding a warm, inviting visual element. I have a great deal of experience working collaboratively with clients on their specific color requirements. The dense textural relief of my work also adds the important function of accoustic dampening. I am influenced by impressionists and color field painters, primarily for their ability to create luminous color. My use of their painterly techniques, such as simultaneous contrast, within my unique fiber medium, achieves a rich visual presence of intense color and texture with an almost lit-from-within quality.

COMMISSIONS: Mayo Clinic; MCI; SeaWorld; Kaiser Permanente; Neutrogena; Cargill; Nokia; Banner Aerospace; GMAC; Hyatt Regency Hotels; Lawson Software; Minneapolis Institute of Arts; St. Paul Companies; Westlaw; U.S. Embassy, Bangkok; Northwest Airlines; Wells Fargo; Ecolab

GUILD SOURCEBOOKS: *Architectural & Interior Art 16; Residential Art 3*

MARY HATCH

Paintings & Prints
Pages 224, 231

I'm in love with color, and the figure continues to fascinate me. My oil paintings often start with a figure inexplicably positioned "just so" or discovered residing in a picture, and the work evolves slowly as my mind picks up the threads. My interest is in the little fragments of life that are unintentionally stored away, tiny bits of memory—too insignificant to notice—that come together forming narratives, familiar, yet brand new. My work is included in over 300 public and private collections in the U.S. and Canada, and has been exhibited in more than thirty one-person shows in as many years. Please visit my website, www.maryhatch.com, for more prints, paintings, and a full resume. Select the "Guest Book/Contact" page to request a price list.

YOSHI HAYASHI

Paintings & Prints
Page 232

I was born in Japan and learned the rigorous techniques of Japanese lacquer art from my father. I carry the spirit, history, and inspiration of this process with me today as I reinterpret the ancient lacquer tradition for my screens and wall panels. My designs range from delicate, traditional seventeenth-century Japanese lacquer art themes to bold, contemporary geometric designs. By skillfully applying metallic leaf and bronzing powders, I add both illumination and contrast to the network of color, pattern, and texture. Recent commissions include works for private residences in the United States and Japan.

COMMISSIONS: Restaurant, 2003, San Diego, CA

EXHIBITIONS: *Lost Art for the Modern World,* 2004, San Francisco, CA; *Japanese Screens Revisited,* 2003, San Francisco, CA

GUILD SOURCEBOOKS: *The Guild 3, 4, 5; Designer's 6, 7, 8, 9, 10, 11, 12, 13, 14, 15; Architectural & Interior Art 16, 17, 18, 19, 20, 21; Artful Home 1*

RHONDA HEISLER

Murals, Tiles & Wall Reliefs
Page 209

My mosaic art is grounded in my fascination with the color, patterning, and textural properties of fine opaque and metallic stained glass. My technique is akin to painting in hand-cut art glass. I draw my inspiration from the material itself, and as I cut into the sheet, I edit the glass for the choicest bits, creating tesserae that vary in size and shape. In laying the tiles, I juxtapose surfaces that are matte, shiny, or iridescent; color that is solid, shaded, or streaky; textures that are smooth or irregular. In my abstract compositions, I sketch only minimally and work spontaneously and expressively, using modulated color progressions and variations in shape, scale, and texture to create visual metaphors for complex ideas. I often use several colors of grout to enhance the painterly effect.

ARTIST STATEMENTS

ARCHIE HELD

Public Art

Pages 85, 298

I work primarily in bronze and stainless steel, often incorporating water as a central element. I enjoy using contrasting materials, surfaces, and textures in my work. My many site-specific commissions require collaboration with design committees, architects, engineers, and building contractors to develop a piece of sculpture that is compatible with the site both aesthetically and technically. My philosophy of public art is one of inclusion. I have found it important to take a team approach and encourage input from all parties involved in the project. Through the simplicity and elegance of my sculptural designs, I strive to enhance and complement the environs and the architecture while making a dynamic statement that will draw people to the location and reward them with an exciting visual experience.

COMMISSIONS: Caesar's Palace, Atlantic City, NJ; City of Whittier, CA; San Mateo Public Library, CA; City of Brea, CA; University of Science and Arts, Chickasha, OK; Sacramento City Hall, CA; Beringer Vineyards, Napa, CA; Luis Vuitton Moet Hennessey, San Francisco, CA; Sky Tokyo Club, Japan; Bellagio Hotel and Casino, Las Vegas, NV; Hyatt Regency, Scottsdale, AZ; Harrah's Resort Casino, LA; Alliant Energy World Headquarters, Madison, WI

MARILYN HENRION

Fiber Wall Art

Page 293

I use color, line, and form much as a poet employs words to convey a particular emotion or idea. As in poetry, the images are meant to resonate, being both themselves and something they may suggest to the viewer. The works transcend the impersonal objectivity of geometric abstraction through the sensuousness of materials with which they are constructed. Paying homage to traditional techniques of hand piecing and hand quilting, these materials are transformed into expressive works of art. Clients include corporations, healthcare and government facilities, and private collectors. In addition to selling existing works, I have also worked with interior designers, architects, and art consultants to create site-specific commissions.

COLLECTIONS: Museum of Arts & Design, New York, NY; U.S. Embassy, Pnom Penh, Cambodia; Lucent Technologies, Denver, CO; Dana Farber Cancer Institute, Boston, MA, Carnegie Abbey Country Club, Portsmouth, MA

PUBLICATIONS: *Women Designers in the U.S.: 1900-2000*

GUILD SOURCEBOOKS: *Designer's 11,13; Architectural & Interior Art 17,19,20; Residential Art 1,3*

HENRY DOMKE FINE ART

Fine Art Photography

Page 261

I intended to major in art in college but switched to medicine instead. Today, as a family practice physician and fine artist, I combine both my life's passions in two careers. I live on 600 acres that includes the Prairie Garden Trust, a trust created by my parents. It's just out my door, so I can use it to show a fresh view of nature that's close to home but rarely seen. Designers like the strong graphic quality of the work, as well as its comforting appeal. Since natural scenes can enhance a sense of well-being, my art is especially suited to healthcare, hospitality, and commercial settings. My state-of-the-art digital equipment, inks, papers and canvas ensure high-quality archival art prints that will last for generations. My prints can go longer than 4' x 10' or combine to fill much bigger spaces. Clients have also printed my digital files on custom acrylic or vinyl pieces. My goal is to provide an escape to the natural world. I've had patients look at my photos and ask, "Were you at my grandfather's farm when you took that? It brings back a lot of childhood memories." That's what I like to hear.

SALLY HEPLER

Non-Representational Sculpture

Page 110

The themes of my handmade metal sculptures originate in the depths of my soul. I believe in the concept of collective consciousness, whereby like-minded individuals from different cultural backgrounds around the world can experience the same emotions and appreciate and respect the same things in life. This is why I choose to express my concepts through abstract movement and gesture. I believe that these combined expressions are closely linked to the human psyche.

COMMISSIONS: CNL Center II, Orlando, FL, 2005; Los Alamos County AIPP, Los Alamos, NM, 2002; Seagate Technologies International, 2001, Singapore

COLLECTIONS: JP Morgan International, London, England; Mayo Clinic, Scottsdale, AZ; University of Oklahoma, Norman; College of Santa Fe, NM; La Posada de Santa Fe Resort and Spa, NM; Trust Investments, Palm Beach, FL

PUBLICATIONS: *New Yorker Magazine*, 2005; *SANTA FEAN Magazine*, 2004; *The Collector's Guide*, 2002; *New Mexico Magazine*, 2001; *Sculpture Magazine*, 2000

GUILD SOURCEBOOKS: *Architectural & Interior Art 18*

KAREN HEYL

Murals, Tiles & Wall Reliefs

Page 210

My award-winning mural relief sculpture combines old-word stone carving techniques with contemporary design, lending itself to a variety of architectural applications, both monumental and small. Using varied textural surfaces, I create aesthetic sophistication with simplified, sensual form.

COMMISSIONS: *Ecological Sampler*, 2002, six limestone panels, each: 5' x 3.5' x 3", mounted on 30'H steel easel, Orange County Convention Center, Orlando, Florida; *Nature's Guardians: Endangered Land Animals, Endangered Sea Life*, 2003, limestone, each of two panels: 8' x 4' x 10", Art in Public Places Program; MBK Homes, Brea, CA; *Fight To Freedom*, 2004, six limestone panels, various sizes, The National Underground Railroad Freedom Center, Cincinnati, OH

GUILD SOURCEBOOKS: *Architect's 9, 12, 13, 14, 15; Architectural & Interior Art 16, 17, 18, 19, 20, 21; Residential Art: 1, 2, 3*

CLAUDIA HOLLISTER

Murals, Tiles & Wall Reliefs

Page 211

Using hand-built colored porcelain, I create site-specific architectural wall pieces for public, corporate, and residential environments. Highly textured and richly colored, my work is set apart by the combination of such intricate techniques as inlaying, embossing, and hand-carving three-dimensional elements on tiles.

RECENT PROJECTS: Comer Children's Hospital, University of Chicago; Bristol-Myers Squibb Children's Hospital at Robert Wood Johnson University Hospital, New Brunswick, NJ; Takashima residence, Portland, OR

COMMISSIONS: Air Pax, Indianapolis, IN; Beth-El Zedick Synagogue, Indianapolis, IN; General Instrument, Horsham, PA; Hewlett Packard, Fort Collins, CO; Humana Medical, Cincinnati, OH; Kelsey Seybold Clinic, Houston, TX; Longmont United Hospital, Longmont, CO; Marriott Denver Tech Center, Denver, CO

GUILD SOURCEBOOKS: *Designer's 8, 10, 11, 13, 14, 15; Architectural & Interior Art 16, 17, 18, 20*

ARTIST STATEMENTS

PAUL HOUSBERG

Architectural Glass

Page 40

I work primarily in fused and kiln-formed glass to create art glass features for hospitality, healthcare, corporate, and public spaces. Central to my work is the power of light, color, and texture to shape and define a space. I welcome inquiries regarding any planned or contemplated project. Please visit www.glassproject.com for additional projects and information.

COMMISSIONS: Ernst & Young, Boston, MA; Four Seasons Hotel, Boston, MA; Logan International Gateway, Boston, MA; Le Meridien Hotel, Minneapolis, MN; Temple Habonium, Barrington, RI; Peninsula Hotel, Chicago, IL; William J. Nealon Federal Building and U.S. Courthouse, Scranton, PA

GUILD SOURCEBOOKS: *Architect's 6, 7, 8, 9, 10, 11, 13, 15; Architectural & Interior Art 16, 17, 18, 19, 20, 21*

HUBBARDTON FORGE

Lighting

Pages 5, 21, 188

Thirty-two years ago Hubbardton Forge® was founded as a two-person craft studio located in an old barn in Hubbardton, Vermont. At that time, products were one of a kind, sold at craft fairs throughout New England. Though we have outgrown the barn, our products are still hand-forged by skilled craftsmen. Our designs are truly timeless–simple, classic, elegant, original–form and function inseparable in every piece. By blending time-honored blacksmithing techniques with environmentally friendly technology, Hubbardton Forge creates wrought-iron lighting and home accessories that sell through retail showrooms throughout North America. Visit us at www.vtforge.com. You can also find a selection of Hubbardton Forge products in The Artful Home catalog from The Guild, and at their web site, www.guild.com.

HUCK FISHER METALWORKERS

Lighting

Page 189

Our motto, "Attention to detail adds strength to design," is apparent in all our work, which includes large static and kinetic sculptures, garden sculptures, weathervanes, heirloom home furnishings, commercial and residential lighting, and exterior and interior forged railings and driveway gates.

RECENT PROJECTS: Streetscape design and creation of forty-four hand-painted aluminum fish placed throughout the seaport of the UNESCO World Heritage Site of Lunenburg, Nova Scotia; design and prototype of a grand entrance gate and peripheral hand-forged railing, Sculpture Court of the Art Gallery of Nova Scotia, Halifax

COMMISSIONS: Government of Canada, Halifax, NS; Coastal Flats Restaurant, McLean, VA; McKelvie's Restaurant, Halifax, NS; St. Francis Xavier University, Antigonish, NS

GUILD SOURCEBOOKS: *Architectural & Interior Art 20, 21*

IMAGO DEI, LLC

Public Art

Pages 86, 240

We are a creative arts firm in Houston, Texas, with clients and projects spanning the globe. Imago Dei was founded by husband-and-wife artists Jeremy and Jamie Wells, and has grown into a team of international artists who share a passion for collaborative creativity and a vision for excellence and integrity in all matters of business. Our creative works include an accomplished portfolio of fine art, custom murals, decorative finishes and large-scale art installations. We value our clients, who range from the individual collector, gallery, and design professional to city, hospitality, and corporate art committees. Recent commissions include a large-scale installation piece for the Chevron Art Collection that features over 2,500 sq. ft. of abstract fine art suspended by a custom-designed metal sculpture. If you're ever in Houston, please give us call to visit our showroom and studio. We would love the opportunity to create with you! Experience our online portfolio at www.ImagoDeiGallery.com.

CHARLES INGRAM

Paintings & Prints

Page 233

My hope is that the workmanship of my hands reflect the glory of my God.

J. GORSUCH COLLINS ARCHITECTURAL GLASS

Architectural Glass

Page 41

I produce works in leaded, fused, carved, cast, optically laminated, and beveled glass for corporate, health care, hospitality, public, and residential settings. Commitment to excellence and extensive dialogue with the client are distinguishing aspects of my work. Creative design solutions, often involving unique combinations of other materials with glass, provide a fresh approach to design and technique for each project and can result in a complete departure from prior work.

RECENT PROJECTS: Park Hyatt, Beaver Creek, CO; Kaiser Permanente Rock Creek, Lafayette, CO and Fontana, CA; Newmont Gold, Denver, CO; Mercy Hospital, Des Moines, IA: Marriott Hotel, Denver, CO

PUBLICATIONS: *House Beautiful's Glass House,* Hearst Books, 2006; *Colorado Expressions,* Aug/Sept 2006; *Sources + Design,* May/June 2006; *My House,* May/June 2005; *Fine Home Building,* Sept. 2005; *Architecture & Design of the West,* Spring,2004

GUILD SOURCEBOOKS: *THE GUILD 4, 5; Architect's 7, 8, 9, 10, 11; Architectural & Interior Art 20, 21*

CAROLINE JASPER

Paintings & Prints

Page 234

Using the language of color, my paintings focus on light and its intrinsic meaning. Colors express my feelings during an exact moment when the light, enriching an otherwise ordinary subject, caught my attention. I prefer the rich colors of early mornings or late afternoons, when the sun is low and shadows long. Each work starts on a red-hot canvas, the axis for impact dynamics. At close range subjects lose identity. Brushstrokes, denoting abstract color blocks, juxtapose bits of unpainted red ground, generating optical/psychological effects.

COMMISSIONS: The City of Bel Air, MD; The Community College of Baltimore County, MD; Harford Community College, Bel Air, MD; Philip Insurance Co, Bel Air, MD, The Ritz-Carlton; Orlando, FL

COLLECTIONS: The Circuit Court of Harford County, MD; Cisco Systems, Denver, CO; The Comus Inn at Sugarloaf Mountain, Dickerson, MD; Duncan Financial, Carlsbad, CA; HK Holbein, Inc., Williston, VT; Kilpatrick Stockton LLP, Washington, DC; McGraw Hill Publishers, Columbus, OH and New York, NY

GUILD SOURCEBOOKS: *Designer's 15, Architectural & Interior Art 16*

STEVE JENSEN

Non-Representational Sculpture

Page 111

My metal work is constructed from the highest quality aluminum for artistic uses. My images are based on waves, water, or the natural world. The tradition of carving is a universal cultural dialogue, and through this primitive form a number of images can be explored. I come from a long tradition of Norwegian fishermen and boat builders; the chisel I use has been passed from my grandfather. This body of work intends to honor our natural resources. This work can also be cast in bronze.

RECENT PROJECTS: *Compass,* four 12'H aluminum sculptures depicting North, South, East, and West for a traffic roundabout, City of Bend, OR; *Aqua Heart,* 13'H aluminum sculpture, memorial to a fallen officer, Pierce County Sheriff Office, Tacoma, WA; *Crane,* 16'H aluminum sculpture, Hekinan City, Japan; Edmonds Arts Commission, WA; Zoo Carving, Portland, OR, fence 7' x 27', drawn by youth of Portland, carved by artist

VICTORIA JENSEN

Murals, Tiles & Wall Reliefs

Page 212

My most recent commissions have been designed primarily for large public installations, where the beauty of nature is viewed in three-dimensional splendor. Sculptured ceramic productions of land and sea creations are individually and uniquely hand crafted, and then painted in brilliant oils with realistic magnificence. While some installations spawn from my own inspiration, others come at the request of the client and are refined in my studio. Allowing my lifelong love of art to influence my hands through sculpture and my eye through the oils provides me immense satisfaction. But the gratification of collaborating with a client in producing a timeless masterpiece in subject matter appropriate for the installation environment is almost equally exuberating.

COMMISSIONS: Blanchard Valley Hosp, 2007, OH; Mary Rutan Hosp, 2007, OH; Memorial Hosp, 2007, CA; St. Elizabeth Hospice, 2007, Edgewood, KY; Riverview Hospital, 2006, IN; Southeast Georgia Health System, 2005, Brunswick; Anthem, 2005, Louisville, KY; University of Cincinnati, 2005, OH; Sazeracs Grill, 2005, Ann Arbor, MI; Carson's American Bistro, 2005, Ft. Myers, FL

GUILD SOURCEBOOKS: *Architectural & Interior Art 21*

GREGORY JOHNSON

Representational Sculpture

Page 154

Everyone is a work of art, and within this context, my goals are to create lifelike, animated, and softly detailed figures that breathe—figures that connect with a concept larger than the work itself. I am dedicated to a sense of discovery in every work and every project, designing projects to fit a wide range of budgets. As I do not have exclusivities with galleries, you will be able to commission unique works at wholesale prices.

COMMISSIONS: *Bomb Technician Memorial,* Redstone Arsenal, Huntsville, AL; *President Madison-Gen. Daniel Morgan,* Bicentennial Park, Madison, GA; *Jules and Gwen Knapp,* University of Chicago, IL; *General George Washington,* Sandersville, GA

COLLECTIONS: Columbus Museum of Art, GA; State of Illinois Museum; Butler Institute of Fine Arts, OH; Southern Technical University, GA; Northwestern University, IL; Brenau University, GA; Illinois State University; AME of Paul Quinn College, TX

EXHIBITIONS: Loveland Sculpture Invitational 2005, 2003, 2001; Shidoni Sculpture Garden, 2004 to present, NM

GUILD SOURCEBOOKS: *Architect's 15; Architectural & Interior Art 16*

J. SEWARD JOHNSON

Representational Sculpture

Page 155

My art is an imitation of life. Realism has the capacity to reach everyone; there is no age barrier, no culture barrier. As the breadth of communication expands, so does the potency of a particular work. After an early career as a painter, I turned to the medium of sculpture. Since then more than 250 of my life-size bronze figures have been featured in private collections and museums around the world, as well as in public art placements including Rockefeller Center, NY; Pacific Place, Hong Kong; Les Halles, Paris; and Via Condotti in Rome. Best known for my life-sized sculptures of everyday people in contemporary situations, I have recently created a new series of life-size, three-dimensional tableaux of Impressionist masterworks. Now a solo museum exhibit, the national tour of *Beyond the Frame,* originally organized by the Corcoran Gallery of Art, continues throughout the U.S.

MARCIA HEWITT JOHNSON

Fiber Wall Art

Page 294

Using my photography as design models, I create abstract landscapes in fiber inspired by places all over the world. Color is all important in my fiber pieces, and I hand dye my own custom colors in graduated palettes, adding silks to create a dramatic contemporary statement. The resulting color shifts seen are more representative of painting techniques than traditional work in fiber. In choosing a color palette that I create myself, I am able to assemble an atmosphere or feeling about a specific place. Wall hangings come with easy-to-install hardware or can be framed or put on stretchers, bringing color and texture to private and public interiors. Please visit my artwork at www.marciahewittjohnson.com. I work with independent art consultants in major U.S. cities.

EXHIBITIONS: Fogel Fine Art, ongoing, Jacksonville, FL; Artreach, ongoing, Albuquerque, NM

COLLECTIONS: New Mexico Art in Public Places, 2004-2006, Albuquerque, NM; Memorial Sloan Kettering Cancer Center, 2001, New York, NY; Merck, 1998, Philadelphia, PA

GUILD SOURCEBOOKS: *Designer's 11, 12, 14, 15; Architectural & Interior Art 16; Residential Art 5*

ARTIST STATEMENTS

PATTIE AND MARK JOHNSON

Non-Representational Sculpture
Page 112

Inspired by the beauty of the Sonoran Desert and the Petroglyphs etched in its canyons, our collection offers an array of expertly crafted sculptures and glass designs utilizing stained, blown, fused, cast, and sand-carved glass. Whether for commercial, residential, interior, or exterior applications, our designs are unparalleled. We have been working in our studio located in Tucson, AZ, from fourteen years to seventeen years, always putting our clients first. Custom design services are available. Sculptures range in size from two feet to twelve feet and prices range from $500 to $15,000.

COMMISSIONS: *Guardian*, Ernst residence, Tucson, AZ; *Legacy*, Ernst residence, Tucson, AZ; *Fire Spirit*, Frank residence, Tucson, AZ; *Bear Spirit*, Kranhold residence, Tucson, AZ; *Sentry*, Wilkes residence, Scottsdale, AZ; *Near Man*, Wilkes residence, Scottsdale, AZ; *Ancient*, head office of First Magnus Financial Corp., Tucson, AZ; *Energy*, Bancroft and Associates, Tucson, AZ

PUBLICATIONS: *Arizona Collectors Guide, American Art Collector, Tucson Lifestyle, Tucson Guide*

GUILD SOURCEBOOKS: *Residential Art 3, Architectural & Interior Art 20*

BARRY WOODS JOHNSTON

Representational Sculpture
Page 156

My job is to visualize and then breathe life into inert clay, bronze, or stone. My sculptures, often light and lively in sentiment, are generally upbeat. I seek to complement an architectural setting while adding levity, movement, and humanity. Clothing is rendered in faithful detail, with flowing movement and compositional unity. My degree in architecture gives me a regard for aesthetics and the ability to integrate art into its architectural setting. I view public commissions as an opportunity to capture the vision of the community. My subjects are derived from mythology, religion, literature, psychology, and the contemporary dilemma.

COMMISSIONS: Govan's Presbyterian Church, Baltimore, MD; Catholic College of Notre Dame, Baltimore, MD; White River Medical Center, AR; City Hall, Hampton, VA; Lafayette Center, Washington, DC, Evanston Women's Hospital, IL

EXHIBITIONS: One-man show, 2005, Harrisburg Art Center, PA; One-man show, 2005, Rockville Arts Place, Gaithersburg, MD

GUILD SOURCEBOOKS: *Architect's 13, 14, 15; Architectural & Interior Art 16, 18, 19, 20, 21; Residential Art 3, 5*

BJ KATZ

Architectural Glass
Page 42

A fresh new milieu of art glass is emerging at my studio, Meltdown Glass, from the careful blending of creative vision with kiln-cast glass. Working from concept to completion, I coax an idea into being by molding, coloring, and shaping glass in large industrial kilns. Designs, form, and often stylistic use of color are imbedded through numerous firings until the desired effect is achieved. I begin each work with an overall concept and design, and intuitively follow the muse until vision becomes form. The nuances of each piece happen at the time of creation; thus, evocative, unique new works are created.

RECENT PROJECTS: Midwestern University Chapel, Chicago, IL; Sky Harbor Airport, Phoenix, AZ; Library, Jacksonville, FL; Methodist Hospital, Minneapolis, MN; American College Testing, Iowa City, IA; QVC Store, Mall of America, Minneapolis, MN; Phelps Dodge Corporate Headquarters, Phoenix, AZ; Texas Children's Hospital, Houston

PUBLICATIONS: Profiled on "Women Artisans" special on HGTV's *Modern Masters* show

GUILD SOURCEBOOKS: *Architect's 14, 15; Designer's 14, 15; Architectural & Interior Art 16, 17, 18, 19, 21; Artful Home 1*

KIM ELLEN KAUFFMAN

Fine Art Photography
Pages 254, 262

Flamenco and *Amor* are limited-edition photo collages created from multiple scans of original objects. They are from my botanically inspired body of work titled *Florilegium*, which utilizes a cameraless, filmless imaging technique. Cameraless images are as old as photography itself, begun with Henry Fox Talbot's photogenic drawings of plants (ca. 1830s) and Anna Atkin's cameraless studies of algae (1843). Today's tools have facilitated a new direction in this tradition. Begun in 1998, *Florilegium* is now eighty images and growing. Through it I hope to not only share the beauty of plants but also nurture in the viewer reverence for the natural world. See synecdochestudio.com for my vita, additional information, and to view the entire collection.

COLLECTIONS: Kresge Art Museum, East Lansing, MI; Umstead Suites Hotel, Cary, NC; North Ottawa Community Hospital, Grand Haven, MI; BGSU Firelands, Huron, OH; Northwestern Mutual Life Insurance, Milwaukee, WI; American Board of Emergency Medicine, East Lansing, MI

GUILD SOURCEBOOKS: *Residential Art 5*

KESSLER STUDIOS, INC.

Architectural Glass
Pages 19, 43, 56

For over twenty-five years, we have designed contemporary stained glass windows that soften and humanize the built environment. Our dramatic influence on the ambiance within a space is achieved by designing works that touch the human spirit, while respecting the architectural character of each site.

COMMISSIONS: McGuffey Hall, Miami University, Oxford, OH; Peru State College Library, Peru, NE; St. Mary's Hospital, Saginaw and Standish, MI; Central DuPage Hospital, Chicago, IL; Florida Department of Transportation, Miami, FL; Old St. Mary Catholic Church, Chicago, IL; Wheeling Hospital, Wheeling, WV; University Place Retirement Center, West Lafayette, IN; Ohio Department of Agriculture, Reynoldsville, OH; St. Michael's Catholic Church, North Canton, OH; University of Cincinnati, Cincinnati, OH; Good Samaritan Hospital, Cincinnati, OH

AWARDS: Religious Art Awards, 2004, 1994, American Institute of Architects; Visual Art Awards, 2004, 2003, 2002, *Ministry & Liturgy Magazine*; Best of Show, Bene Visual Art Award, 2003, *Ministry & Liturgy Magazine*; Ohio Artist Fellowship, 1998, Ohio Arts Council

DAVID KLASS

Representational Sculpture
Pages 157, 162

Nature and classical art have long been my twin muses—my guides and inspiration. After studying art and architecture at Pratt Institute, I attended Columbia College of Physicians & Surgeons, where I acquired an intimate knowledge of anatomy. It is because of this experience that my work achieves the powerful naturalism for which it is known. Indeed, my artistic aim is to create works that might come alive—that might step off the pedestal and take flight. In this way, I am indebted to the sculptural advances of the Renaissance and the exemplary works of the nineteenth century. My understanding of anatomy, coupled with my solid structural know-how, allows me to create human and animal figures with a high level of expertise. Thus, in 1991, the Metropolitan Museum of Art in New York City commissioned me to create life-size horses for its Arms and Armor wing. I also create site-specific functional work for religious institutions, public spaces, and private patrons, and am a member of the prestigious National Sculpture Society.

JAMES KOEHLER
Fiber Wall Art
Page 295

Tapestry focuses on the creative constructive process. My creative process is one of mixing dye, blending dyed fibers, and weaving them into a richly textured surface to create abstract images that convey meaning. I am influenced by the extraordinary landscape and the unique cultures of New Mexico, and by an aesthetic of simplicity and purity, portraying only what is essential. My tapestries can be found in several museum, corporate, and private collections, including the Renwick Gallery of the Smithsonian American Art Museum. Publications include: *Fiberarts; American Craft; Shuttle, Spindle and Dyepot;* and *Handwoven.* Site-specific commissions are accepted. Prices range from $450 to $550 per square foot.

ANTHONY KRAUSS
Public Art
Page 87

In my exploration of the precise power of the triangle and rectangle, I have evolved my sculptural concepts into pyramidal forms on the diagonal with circular shapes, creating dynamic kinetic illusions. By using mirrored surfaces, the sculptural forms are at once solid and transitory as they reflect changing light patterns and abstract glimpses of the rural and urban environments. The viewer is also captured in the reflective surfaces, thus becoming an integral part of the sculpture.

COMMISSIONS: Miyagi University, Sendai, Japan; The Daimaru, Inc., Kobe, Japan; Frontier Insurance Co., Rock Hill, NY

COLLECTIONS: Whitney Museum of American Art, New York, NY; Hirshhorn Museum and Sculpture Garden, Washington, DC; JPMorgan Chase, New York, NY; Metro Goldwyn Mayer, New York, NY; Pitney Bowes Corporation, Shelton, CT

AWARDS: Pollock-Krasner Foundation Grant, New York, NY; Lorenzo IL Magnifico Sculpture Medallion, Biennale Internazionale, Florence, Italy

PUBLICATIONS: *New Art International,* 2006, 2004

GUILD SOURCEBOOKS: *Architectural & Interior Art 21, 20; Residential Art 5, 4*

SILJA TALIKKA LAHTINEN
Paintings & Prints
Page 235

My work draws from the myths, landscape, folk songs, and textiles of my native Finland. I am especially inspired by Lapland Shamanism in my paintings, collages, wall panels, prints, and drums. I am always trying to do a better painting today than what I did yesterday. Prices range from $400-$30,000.

EXHIBITIONS: One-person show, 2006, Viljamakasiini, Ruovesi, Finland; Kennesaw College, 2003, Atlanta, GA; Elevations Gallery, 2003, Atlanta, GA; Ward-Nasse Gallery, 2003-2004, New York, NY

AWARDS: Diploma Di Merito by Galleria D'Arte Moderna "Alba," 2004; Ferrara, Italy; Award of Merit, *Not Just Another Pretty Face,* WCA Show, 2003, Sanford, FL

PUBLICATIONS: *New Art International,* Vol X, 2005-2006; Print World Directory, 2002; *Encyclopedia of Living Artists,* 2004, 2006; *Who's Who of American Artists; Who's Who of Women Artists*

GUILD SOURCEBOOKS: *GUILD 1, 2, 3; Designer's 9, 10, 11; Architectural & Interior Art 17, 19, 20, 21*

COLIN LAMBERT & PETER ADAMS
Public Art
Page 88

When Russell Page advised us to "approach each site anew with neither momentum nor agenda . . . allow it to disclose to you what it wants . . . impose nothing," we were given a master's formula for successful site-specific design. We are committed professionals who have collaborated for the past twenty-five years. We are both classically trained and formally educated, and have discovered our individual and joint voice through representational and figurative work. Our many years of experience have taught us to raise our vision above the current horizon, aiming for a relevancy beyond the immediate time or fashion. We are inspired and willingly guided by the magic of beautiful architecture. It has been said of us that we make jewelry for beautiful buildings.

COMMISSIONS: *ROSE WAVE,* Ocean View Park, City of Albany, CA; Sacramento City Hall, CA; Stamford Forum, Stamford, CT; London United Insurance Group, City of London, England; Market Centre, Warminster, Wiltshire, England

DEBORAH LEFKOWITZ
Public Art
Page 89

I create kinetic light installations to enhance the experience of place in public and corporate buildings. These site-specific works combine subtly changing light (achieved with computer-programmed lighting control), sculptural elements, and the movement of passersby. I use aluminum screening, fabric, plexiglass, and other materials to catch light or image projections in mid-air and sculpt them into three-dimensional forms, thereby transforming ordinary interiors into landscapes of shifting light and color. My outstanding record of professional accomplishments extends over twenty-five years and includes numerous installations for galleries and museums in the U.S. and abroad. I am currently completing a public art commission using fiber optic technology to illuminate the windows of a fire station in Los Angeles.

COMMISSIONS: Los Angeles Cultural Affairs Department, 2003-07, Percent-for-Art Program

AWARDS: Artists Fellowship, 2001-02, California Arts Council

PUBLICATIONS: *Women Making Art,* 2003; *World Sculpture News,* Summer, 2003; *Los Angeles Times,* Aug. 23, 2002; *Fiberarts,* Sept./Oct., 2001

ELLE TERRY LEONARD
Murals, Tiles & Wall Reliefs
Page 213

My ceramic work is created as an integral part of an architectural structure. My specialty is relief murals. Beautiful and durable, pieces are suitable for interior and exterior application. A full-service studio that works primarily with the trade, Architectural Ceramics produces site-specific commissions for corporate and residential clients.

RECENT PROJECTS: Whole Foods City Centre, Sarasota, FL, Plaza at Five Points, Sarasota, FL

COMMISSIONS: Esalen Institute, Big Sur, CA; Tampa International Airport, Tampa, FL; Johns Hopkins Hospital, Baltimore, MD; Worldgate Marriott Hotels, Reston, VA; Kaiser Permanente, Silver Springs, MD; Arvida Corporation, Longboat Key, FL; Chamber of Commerce, Sarasota, FL; Venice City Hall, Venice, FL

PUBLICATIONS: *Ceramics in the Environment; An International Review,* 2006

GUILD SOURCEBOOKS: *The Guild 1, 2, 3, 4, 5; Architect's 6, 8, 9, 10, 11, 12, 13, 14, 15; Designer's 13, 14, 15; Architectural & Interior Art 16, 17, 20*

ARTIST STATEMENTS

LINDA LEVITON
Non-Representational Sculpture/Metal Wall Art
Pages 113, 267

Creating sculpture that evokes the color and texture of nature is central to my art. *Patterns of Nature-Totem* combines etched metal and curved wood frames that stack atop one another making a modern totem pole. *Pick Up Sticks* is a copper wall sculpture based on a quilt concept. An oil painting done on eighty copper squares makes up the 12' x 15' piece.

COMMISSIONS: Wells Fargo, Des Moines, IA; The Hartford Insurance Company, Hartford, CT; Abbott Northwestern Hospital, Minneapolis, MN; Shades of Green, Walt Disney World, Orlando, FL; Symantec Corp., New York, NY; Ross Heart Hospital, Columbus, OH; Kaiser Permanente, Pasadena, CA; Northwestern Mutual, Milwaukee, WI; Nestle/Ralston, St. Louis, MO; State of Ohio, Columbus, OH; Med Central Hospital, Mansfield, OH; Akron/Summit County Public Library, Akron, OH; St. Vincent's Hospital, Indianapolis, IN; Northwest Airlines, Detroit, MI

PUBLICATIONS: *Color on Metal*, 2001

EXHIBITIONS: SOFA Chicago, 2006

MARK J. LEVY
Architectural Glass
Page 44

For twenty-nine years my architectural background and design philosophy have been instrumental in the publication, both nationally and internationally, of my award-winning works. Glass's wonderful quality of light transmission allows me to paint with its shape and kinetic energy. Keenly aware of how my work will be encountered, I make glass choices to reflect my belief that each piece can be as individualized as a brush stroke. In the same manner that a sculptor seeks to choose just the right piece of stone for a sculpture, I also know how important the nuances of glass can be. In both the private and public art sector, my ability to listen well is key to successful collaborations, where the goals of all are exceeded. Working in partnership with community groups, architects, and city agencies is an important element of public art; my experience in that area has taught me to be responsive to their goals. Professional Affiliations: A.I.A. and S.G.A.A. Clients include the Cities of Los Angeles and La Quinta, CA; Disney; A&M Records; and Hilton Hotels.

GUILD SOURCEBOOKS: *Architect's 9, 12, 14, 15; Architectural & Interior Art 16, 21*

JACQUES LIEBERMAN
Paintings & Prints
Page 236

The human spirit has an infinite capacity to absorb universal elements and restructure them into fresh compositions; thus, my yearning, indeed compelling exigency to envision, dissect, enlarge, reduce, alter, recombine shapes, contrasts, colors, etc. Giving birth to a new creation. It is when a forceful shiver emanates from within me, announcing the infusion of a soul into my new creation, that I quiver and know it has a life. Then I bask in my new creation's warmth. A continuum as basic to me as breathing. One additional component is a part of this cycle: sharing. A viewer's visceral, exuberant, direct response to my creation completes the experience. I adapt and apply my digitally created original images to various media. My work has been included in television shows, and has been reviewed by professional publications. It can be found around the world. Let each viewer's soul interact with my work in its own way. There is no correct or prescribed interpretation. Enjoy!

MARILYN LINDSTRÖM
Murals, Tiles & Wall Reliefs
Page 215

After more than thirty years of making community public art as a mural painter, I've discovered an affinity for the eternally stunning, light like mosaic art form. I see mosaic as a kind of lingua franca, transcending different concepts of art; accordingly, the imagery of *World Language* comes from petroglyphs/rock art—the first visual languages of the world. My approach to mosaic is much like the technique of mosaic; the tesserae of my life and community life are tessellated to make the larger artwork—further tessellating with the surrounding spaces, structures, and communities of place.

COMMISSIONS: *Homage*, 2006, Perdomo smalti mosaic, Heritage Commons Public Housing, Minneapolis, MN; *World Language*, 2005, Perdomo smalti mosaic, Franklin Community Library, Minneapolis, MN

AWARDS: Committee on Urban Environment Award, 2004, 1999, City of Minneapolis, MN; Leadership Initiatives in Neighborhoods Fellowship, 2000, St. Paul Companies, St. Paul, MN

CATHY LOCKE
Paintings & Prints
Pages 237, 244

My paintings are driven by light, and specifically, how light affects a subject matter. For this reason I tend to paint a broad range of subjects—from people to cityscapes. I am more interested in capturing a feeling than staying with one subject matter. Whether it's the early morning light on city rooftops or the way the light hits a glass vase, I am searching for a special moment. I describe light in my paintings through a strong color and value theme, building layers to create depth. Though I primarily work in pastels and oils, I have used every type of medium at one point in time. As an artist I believe it is important to always explore new ways of translating that special feeling that turns a canvas into poetry. Clients include American Express, Bank of America, Kaiser Permanente, and ITT. My work has received accolades from the Pastel Society of America, the Art Directors Club of New York, the Society of Illustrators, *CAMagazine*, and Campaign Papers.

ROB LORENSON
Non-Representational Sculpture
Page 114

My studio produces works in stainless steel, Cor-Ten, painted aluminum, and bronze. The scale ranges from small tabletop works to pieces over sixteen feet high. The methodology behind my work is to create a compositionally rich interplay of modernist elements that are exceptionally crafted, removing the hand of the artist. The purpose of this is to further emphasize the compositional qualities of the work. I also intend to make the work look manufactured, as though it was itself an industrial product, like the industrial forms that originally influenced it. Works have been placed in over seventy-five collections in residential, corporate, municipal, and educational settings. My scope of services includes design, fabrication, transportation, and installation of all works that I produce. The wholesale price range of my works is from $1,000 to $100,000. Call for a printed catalog.

COMMISSIONS: Boca Raton, FL; Sarasota, FL; Arlington, MA; and Culpepper, VA

ARTIST STATEMENTS

GRETCHEN LOTHROP

Non-Representational Sculpture

Page 115

I think of my work as haiku writ large. I am fascinated by the paradox of capturing instants of insight with insistently permanent materials such as stainless steel and bronze. Although my inspiration is often poetry, music, and dance, in fact, much of my work has gone to places having to do with life sciences. I enjoy designing to specific sites or concepts for public and private clients.

COMMISSIONS: Dempsey Student Center, 2005, and Meyer Hall Science Building, 1999, Sandhills Community College, Pinehurst, NC; Health and Public Affairs Buildings, 2004, University of Central Florida, Orlando; Life Science Building, 2003, Spartanburg Technical College, Spartanburg, SC; Centennial Plaza, 2002, Appalachian State University, Boone, NC; Newman Catholic Student Center Parish, Garden: 2006, Church: 2000, Chapel Hill, NC; Inaugural Sculpture in Public Places, 1996, Columbia, SC

COLLECTIONS: Bank of America; Eli Lilly; Quantum Radiology; Caldwell Memorial Hospital; First Union National Bank; BTI Services; H & R Associates; Barrett Kays; Practice Resources

GUILD SOURCEBOOKS: *Architectural & Interior Art 21*

ALEKSANDRA LUGOWSKA

Architectural Glass

Pages 22, 45

Glass connects us to and separates us from the world. It protects and exposes. It can hide an unwanted view or reveal a beautiful landscape. It creates a unique verge of symbiotic existence for both the material and illusive. Through my glass art, the viewer participates in a mystical performance of light and color, and it is conveyed to a peaceful and fulfilling place. My progression of line, form and color has helped me leap from the "real" world into the abstract, into a suggestion of movement and gesture, and into the kinetic relationship between all these elements. I use a compassionate approach to integrate art glass with its surrounding architecture—developing harmonious ways of expression to compel modern aesthetics.

ELIZABETH MacDONALD

Murals, Tiles & Wall Reliefs

Pages 196, 216

I produce tile paintings that suggest the patina of age. Layering color onto thin, textured stoneware achieves a surface that combines the subtlety of nature with the formality of a grid. These compositions are suitable for either in- or outdoors and take the form of freestanding columns, wall panels, or architectural installations. Attached to .25" luan with silicone, the tiles (often 3.5" square) weigh approximately 1.75 pounds per square foot, are durable, and require a minimum of maintenance. I enjoy working with the requirements of clients and can produce small- or large-scale work. In 1999 I was presented with the Governor's award for visual art. During the last twenty years, my commissions have included private installations as well as the following: Dartmouth-Hitchcock Hospital, Lebanon, NH; Conrad Hotel, Hong Kong; Mayo Clinic Chapel, Scottsdale, AZ; and Nobu Restaurant, New York, NY.

MICHEL MAILHOT

Architectural Glass

Pages 46, 252

For three decades my passion has been to push the artistic and technical boundaries of glass, to master the powerful process of thermoforming. By combining these fields of expertise, I express the feeling and demands of any design possible using this rich, chameleon-like material. My fascination is understanding and appealing to the relationship between architecture, art, and individual perception. My inspiration is derived from nature, expressed by the beautiful, organic touch of our glass creations. My passion is driven by my desire to continually transform this material into new applications and new forms. Be it a sculpture, mural, lighting fixture, or even countertop, I strive to make each piece achieve its best. I have introduced our unique glass expressions to five continents, where they have found their place in commercial and public spaces, churches, high-end residences, and more. This work combines color, texture, and imagination with individual pieces as delicate as a quarter-inch deep, as powerful as 12 inches thick, or large as 84" x 152".

COMMISSIONS: Jean-Philippe Patisserie, Bellagio, LV; Sidley Austin LLP, One South Dearborn, Chicago, IL; Montreal Congress Center, Montreal; Bella Luna, Bella Rio Development, AL

ELLEN MANDELBAUM

Architectural Glass

Pages 16, 47

Established in 1981, Ellen Mandelbaum Glass Art produces original glass for private and public spaces. I am an award-winning artist known for my ability to personalize design for special projects. I have been delighted to be commissioned to make architectural work that is creative and non-traditional. At the same time, I am always aware of the seriousness of architectural purpose and that I am helping to create a permanent prayerful environment or secular space for people's real use. I want my client to be happy.

"Recent work by one of America's foremost glass artists . . . Mandelbaum started as an expressive painter; in the mid-seventies she discovered and fell in love with stained glass and began to work in this medium. Using the expression, line, color, and form she developed as a painter, and creates distinctive free work in glass" (Light Listened Exhibition, Queens College Art Center, New York, NY).

BRYAN MARTIN

Mixed & Other Media Wall Art

Pages 272, 279

Layers of rich, earthy colors and diverse textures characterize my work. Both visual and tactile textures are inspiring to me, and therefore very prominent in the art I create. I strive to add a sense of visual depth by using layers of handmade papers, metallic foils, photographs, and texture mediums.

EXHIBITIONS: New York Art Expo, 1999-2005; Greeley Arts Festival, 2005, 2000, 1999, CO; Atlanta Art Expo, 1999-2005, GA; Thompson Valley Art Festival, 2005, Loveland, CO; London Contemporary Art Fair, 1999, England

AWARDS: First Place mixed media, Merit Award mixed media, 2005, Thompson Valley Arts Festival, Loveland, CO; City Purchase Award, 2000, Greeley Arts Festival, CO

PUBLICATIONS: Cover, *Décor,* Dec 2005; *Décor,* Aug 2005; *Art Trends,* Mar/Apr 2001, May/June 2000; *Art Expo Preview,* Feb 2005, 2001

GUILD SOURCEBOOKS: *Architectural & Interior Art 21*

SUSAN A. MASRI
Paintings & Prints
Page 238

My paintings are about the spiritual side of experience. I also try to give the process of thought a material character with paint. I want to represent those layers of perception as a physical space, and I want to do that as a prayer. If I translated my paintings into words, they would represent my life philosophy. I now paint with oils because they let me suggest subtler qualities of dimension. I am grateful for the direction I received from painters Lucio Pozzi, Doug Huebler, Michael Asher, Jeremy Gilbert-Rolfe, and John Baldessari, who worked hard to help me bring mindfulness to art-making, to be true to my own process. After receiving my B.F.A. at CalArts in 1984, I proceeded into a business career. Returning to art as my mainstay is a dream come true. Please see more of my paintings at www.susanmasri.com.

SUSAN McGEHEE
Metal Wall Art
Page 269

Instead of fiber, I weave with wire and metals. I continue to employ the traditional tools, techniques, and patterns from when I worked in fiber. Weaving metals allows me to form a piece into a dimensional shape that will retain its form and undulating vitality. I primarily weave with anodized aluminum wire because even though a piece looks like copper, the anodized aluminum wire has the advantage of being lightweight while maintaining a vibrant color and shine. The pieces are easy to install and maintain. I enjoy the fact that people will assume a piece is fiber and then are astonished to discover it is woven metal.

COMMISSIONS: Nokia, Burlington, MA; Wells Fargo, Minneapolis, MN; American Family Insurance, Madison, WI, and Phoenix, AZ; Lawson Commons lobby, St. Paul, MN; St. Joseph's Medical Center, Milwaukee, WI; Fantasy Springs Convention Center, Indio, CA; Pauma Valley Golf Club, Pauma Valley, CA.

GUILD SOURCEBOOKS: *Designer's 12, 13, 14, 15; Architectural & Interior Art 16, 17, 18, 19, 20, 21; Residential Art 1, 3, 4, 5*

CYNTHIA McKEAN
Non-Representational Sculpture
Page 116

I grew up in the West—Montana and Wyoming. The West is where there are so few people that everyone counts. It is also where one is inclined to be more in tune with one's own natural environment because one is closer to it. The horizon there is chiseled out against the sky. Lines are sharp. Space is forever. Colors are strong. I believe that all of this influences my art. In my work I dream of natural and built environments, and how they might interact. Sometimes the results lean toward Mother Nature and sometimes they are meant to complement Her. Many ideas frolic without particular meaning, but a few are very serious. I think in terms of cutting through space, blocking space, and what the results might be. Sometimes I see the object, sometimes it's the space around the object, but it's usually a combination of the two. Steel is a marvelous medium. Strong and pliable, it speaks to me. If I work it, respect it, and treat it gently, it will reward me by telling my story to others as well. If people walk around, touch, and occasionally climb my work, I consider it a success. It means they have connected with it. It is talking to them.

TRENA McNABB
Paintings & Prints
Page 239

My art is a visual form of storytelling that is both real and yet surreal. I paint both small and large site-specific paintings of allegorical scenes, uniting stylized shapes with a unique concept of beauty. These compositions are a multi-layered montage of brightly lighted, realistically rendered, thematically related scenes and images. Dimensionality is achieved in many ways: sectional pieces wrap around a corner or suspend from the ceiling on swivels; unexpected materials such as extra canvas, plexiglass, twine, or sawdust are often sewn or adhered to the canvas. Different textures, such as matte and gloss, can be found on a single painting. These pairings, combined with the repeated applications of the white on natural canvas, result in an unusual vibrancy in a contemporary technique. Because of my wide experience, I am able to tailor size and price to fit the scope of a specific project without ever sacrificing artistic content or integrity.

PETER W. MICHEL
Public Art
Page 90

My work represents a stand for the possibility that art is for the expression of joy, aliveness, love, and relationship. Through color, humor, the play of ideas, and the effects of light and space, the viewer is invited to access his own spirit of playfulness and relatedness. From small tabletop and wall pieces to monumental outdoor public art, my work is refined with the aid of computer software and produced with computer-controlled waterjet or laser-cutting methods.

COLLECTIONS: Oakton Sculpture Park, Des Plaines, IL; Wandell Sculpture Garden, Urbana, IL

EXHIBITIONS: Art In Public Places—Stamford Downtown, 2006; Sculpture Internationale, Atlanta, 2002; Pier Walk, Chicago, 2000, 1999; Chesterwood Museum, Stockbridge MA, 1994

PUBLICATIONS: *Educational Psychology,* 8th Edition, 2002

GUILD SOURCEBOOKS: *Architectural & Interior Art 16, 20*

KARI MINNICK
Architectural Glass
Page 48

Masterful in the medium and passionate about design, I create glass art for architecture. Successfully integrating art with its environment is an exciting and essential part of the creative process. My work in glass involves the use of line, language, and mark making, a fascination for graphic design and the power of placement. My kiln-formed pieces are infused with drawings and calligraphic imagery occurring on many layers within a work. This painterly expression in glass breaks new ground artistically, yet retains my core aesthetic concerns of expressive use of line and the transmission of light. My work is collected internationally and is exhibited in galleries nationwide.

COMMISSIONS: Holy Cross Hospital, 2005, Silver Spring, MD; Embassy Suites Hotel, 2005, Washington, DC; Hampden Square, 2003, Bethesda, MD

COLLECTIONS: Sheppard Mullin Richter & Hampton LLP, Washington, DC; Samek McMillan & Metro, Rockville, MD

GUILD SOURCEBOOKS: *Architectural & Interior Art 21*

PETER MITTEN

Non-Representational Sculpture

Page 117

My background is in bronze casting and fabrication. I often incorporate cast and welded aluminum, concrete, steel, and granite in sculptures and wall pieces. Artistic awards include two California Art Council grants and a Pollock-Krasner Foundation Grant. Public commissions include the Dallas Area Rapid Transit and the Escondido, CA, Transit Center. My work has been collected nationally and internationally. It has been recognized in various publications, including *50 San Diego Artists, The Boston Globe, L.A. Times,* and *Sculpture Magazine*. The sizes range from maquettes (ten inches or more) to public works over ten feet tall and twenty feet long. I enjoy hiking through and observing various canyon, desert, and woodland habitats. Notations from these experiences often become subjects of sculpture, with rhythmic patterns of erosion, slopes and crevices, majestic outcroppings, and layered surfaces. I produce sculpture for interior and exterior application in architectural, garden, residential, and public spaces.

MONUMENTAL-SCULPTURES.COM, INC.

Public Art

Page 91

We are known for our original artwork as well as being the "Artist's Artist" for our services to the worldwide art community in the area of bronze and granite enlargements and custom fabrications in acrylic and stainless steel. As a combined team studio, we have completed representational bronze to nearly 300 feet in height, granite bas relief columns to 150 feet tall, and stainless steel spheres to eighty feet in diameter. Spheres of all materials and sizes have been requested from us; however, we have become world famous for the most remembered water features in the world, the interactive floating *Granite Sphere Fountains,* with spheres weighing as much as 85,000 pounds. In the realm of monumental sculptures, our capabilities are virtually unlimited.

COMMISSIONS: Worldwide public and private art in granite and bronze

MERRILEE MOORE

Public Art

Page 92

I have been a glass artist and sculptor since 1996. By integrating materials such as stone, metal, and wood into my glass sculptural compositions, I try to utilize the unique properties that each material offers. I also like to create synergy by combining the concept of dance and physical gesture with stainless steel and glass. My ongoing study of how color, form, texture, and implied motion can convey emotion allow me to express my visions.

COLLECTIONS: Elton John, 2006, London, England; Ann Geddy, 2006, Los Angeles, CA; The Boeing Company, 2000, Chicago, IL

EXHIBITIONS: West Edge Sculpture Invitational, 2003-2006, Seattle, WA; Bellevue Sculpture Invitational, 2006, Bellevue, WA

ANDI AND ROBERT MORAN

Murals, Tiles & Wall Reliefs

Page 217

The ceramic *Implement Series* illustrated in this volume is inspired by ancient tribal weapons and antique cultivation tools. The complete series includes over thirty different pieces; they are attached to the wall by machined metal standoffs and may be edited or combined to accommodate various settings. The illusion of a time-wrought patina is created by a sequence of hand-applied layers of textured and colored slips, stains, and glazes. Dimensions of the individual implements vary. All pieces are made to order, and surface finishes can be adapted to fit the requirements of specific environments. For more information about our work, please visit our web site at: www.moran-moran.com.

EXHIBITIONS: SOFA, Chicago; Smithsonian Craft Show

AWARDS: Artist Fellowship (Design Arts) Louisiana Arts Council/NEA; Artist Fellowship (Visual Arts) Louisiana Arts Council/NEA; Roger Ward Ranger Fund Prize, The National Academy of Design

PUBLICATIONS: *American Craft,* January 2007; *Teapots Makers & Collectors,* 2005; *Smithsonian,* 1999; *The Washington Post,* 1999; *The Ceramic Design Book,* 1998; *Ceramics Monthly,* 1997

AMY J. MUSIA

Mixed & Other Media Wall Art

Page 280

For over thirty years, I have worked with private and public art committees, architects, engineers, and designers to create a multitude of successful commissions for private and corporate clients. Noted as a versatile designer/craftsman in many mediums and styles, I have focused on contemporary columns and capitals for the last four years. Individually designed, each wall, half or full column translates dreams, beliefs, aspirations, and loves into glamorous and thought-provoking works of art. They are commissioned as a unique focal piece or as an anthology. Working closely with clients, pieces are created that reflect their vision. At times, corporate philosophies are interpreted into exclusive pieces of fine art. Using traditional woodworking techniques, each site-specific piece, indoors or outdoors, is hand carved and constructed in my Evansville studio. Pieces are finished in white with 24K, silver, and/or copper gilded embellishments. Other mediums available.

COMMISSIONS: Evansville, IN: Vectren, Evansville-Vanderburgh Public Library, Old National Bank, VNA Hospice

COLLECTIONS: City of Evansville, IN; City of Tochigi, Japan

NATIONAL SCULPTORS' GUILD

Public Art

Page 93

Since 1992 the National Sculptors' Guild has consulted private and public collectors in the placement of fine art for the interior and exterior. Specializing in limited-edition and site-specific sculpture in bronze, steel, and stone, the National Sculptors' Guild is an association of its design team and nationally recognized sculptors chosen for their outstanding artistic abilities and varied style. Our primary objective is to place Guild members' artwork publicly—from conception to completion. Headed by Executive Director John W. Kinkade, the NSG has installed monumental-scale work in municipal, corporate, and private collections throughout the world. Guild members include: Gary Alsum, Kevin Box, Kathleen Caricof, Chapel, Tim Cherry, Dee Clements, Jane Dedecker, Carol Gold, Bruce Gueswel, Denny Haskew, Mark Leichliter, Leo E. Osborne, Louise Peterson, Sandy Scott, and C.T. Whitehouse.

GUILD SOURCEBOOKS: *Architect's 9, 10, 11, 12, 14, 15; Architectural & Interior Art 16, 17, 20, 21*

ARTIST STATEMENTS

BASHA RUTH NELSON

Public Art

Page 94

The hallmark of my sculpture is the relationship between form and the volume in which the work lives. Recent commissions in aluminum, copper, and stainless steel gracefully engage the viewer through surface, texture, and scale. My vertical and circular themes are elegant, pure, and some of the simplest and strongest in nature. I have exhibited widely in the United States and abroad.

COMMISSIONS: Collaborations with architects and collectors in New York (Corporate Office), Maryland (Yoga Retreat Center), the Bahamas (National Institute of the Arts), Maryland, Florida, and England (private residences)

COLLECTIONS: Robins Collection of Contemporary Art, Miami, FL; United States Embassy, Nassau, Bahamas; Woodstock Historical Society, NY

AWARDS: Lorenzo IL Magnifico Award for Sculpture, Biennale, Florence, Italy; Welfred McGibbon Award, Norton Gallery and Museum, FL

PUBLICATIONS: *New Art International, Gallery Guide,* and *Who's Who in American Art*

GUILD SOURCEBOOKS: *Architectural & Interior Art 20, 21; Residential Art 4, 5*

G. NEWMAN

Paintings & Prints

Page 241

My abstract expressions are painted in acrylic and mixed media to obtain texture. The *Fusion* series was born to capture the rhythms of color. Each painting has many layers of paint applied in a playful, almost musical fashion. The colors blend together with certain motion to form a colorful combination and skillful integration of abstract. This series is available in any color combination. The *Wave* series comes from my love of the ocean. Born near the Icelandic coast, I remember the view from my window where the color of the mountains and the ocean would change throughout the day. These paintings have a strong degree of texture, which adds depth and dimension, showing all the colors in the rainbow, similar to the reflections on the ocean surface. Some of my abstract paintings will reflect the nature that surrounds us like *Fall Leaves*. My varied styles and experience make it easy to work within any customized project, and I welcome commissions. My painting sizes range from 10" x 10" to 80" x 120". I also love to work with diptych or triptych combinations. A portfolio of paintings is available upon request.

PUBLICATIONS: *Florida Design; Art Galleries and Collectors*

BRUCE A. NIEMI

Non-Representational Sculpture

Page 118

The stainless steel and bronze sculptures I create are characterized by an uplifting positive nature of aesthetically powerful, graceful forms that create the illusion of movement. My purpose is to stimulate the mind of the viewer, as well as to create a sculpture that complements and harmonizes with its environment. Craftsmanship, structural strength, and public safety are also important elements. The size of my sculptures range from small tabletop pieces to large-scale public art. Currently, I have placed twenty-two public sculptures and have five more in outdoor public exhibitions. I work well with architects, designers, and developers, and am able to meet budgets and timelines.

COMMISSIONS: Escena Golf Club, Palm Springs, CA; Northern Illinois University, DeKalb, IL; Liberty Property Trust, Hunt Valley, MD; Wausau Hospital, Wausau, WI; Chicago Heights City Hall, Illinois; Synopsys, Inc., Sunnyvale, CA

GUILD SOURCEBOOKS: *Architect's 9, 10, 11, 14, 15; Architectural & Interior Art 16, 17, 18, 19, 20, 21*

NORIKAZU

Public Art

Page 95

The appeal of public sculpture is its potential for emotional connections with many people. I strive for this in each of the various sculpture types I design. The challenge of public sculpture is to complement the aesthetics of its setting. The sculptures of Cincinnati Reds ballplayers are depicted playing an imaginary game at Great American Ball Park's main entrance. People enjoy interacting with these life-size bronzes, posing for photos as an umpire or a player stealing a base. The High Street Bridge medallions show historical scenes of Hamilton, Ohio. Each relief is composed of both large-scale patterns and detailed components so one can appreciate the designs whether crossing the bridge by car or by foot. The scale and uncluttered appearance of the ten-foot high Cleveland Parker Memorial help anchor this sculpture in its vast park setting. At night, the memorial announces its presence with gently pulsating internal LED lights.

MASON NYE

Murals, Tiles & Wall Reliefs

Page 218

The grand scale of murals and the extended narrative possibilities inherent in their design offer the ultimate opportunity to me as an artist. Many of my works have been commissioned not only to add dramatic visual impact to a site, but also to capture the spirit of a client organization, its identity and mission, its work environment and civic context. I have created murals and large easel paintings for a wide variety of public, commercial, retail and residential spaces. This has enabled me to develop a diverse knowledge of painting styles and technical approaches to suit the requirements of each project. I work closely and collaboratively with interior designers, architects, art consultants and the clients to realize a specific vision for each site. Clients include: Marriott Hotels; Ambac Financial Group; The Doe Fund; Laborer's International Union; British Airways; Bloomingdale's; Macy's; Metropolitan Life; Bristol-Myers Squibb; Tulsa Transit Authority; Columbia University; First Manhattan Co.

GUILD SOURCEBOOKS: *Architect's 8, 9*

DANIEL OBERTI

Non-Representational Sculpture

Page 119

Art is a gift that presupposes the dignity of its recipient. My works embrace concepts about time, space, light, and shadow. They reveal humanity's relationship to symbols, archetypes, and forms that uplift our spirits and instill a sense of contemplative solace. I am part of a lineage that defines the artistic self by forming works that inform and inspire inquiry within. I work to unveil the elusive and seek an audience and affinity with others who recognize the value of this pursuit.

COMMISSIONS: Spheres and Circumagi, 2004, Biogebidec Campus, San Diego, CA; Venus (the world's largest scale model of our solar system), 2004, Royal Technical Institute, Stockholm, Sweden; Three Spheres, 2002, Vineyard Creek Hotel, Santa Rosa, CA; Time Peace, 2000, South Carolina Governor's School for the Arts and Humanities, Greenville; Sphaera Palermo, 2000, Osservatorio di Palermo, Palermo, Italy

ARTIST STATEMENTS

JANINE S. ODY

Architectural Glass

Page 49

I have been a commissioned glass artist since 1983, working with architects, designers, and private individuals to create site-specific artwork, secular and sacred, while pursuing my own fulfillment in glass art. I have a particular interest in traditional painted and fired glass, true "stained glass," a technique that became a vehicle for figurative pictorial communication in the Middle Ages.

COMMISSIONS: Medical University of Ohio, Ohio Percent for the Arts; Inverness Country Club, Toledo, OH; Notre Dame Academy, Provincial Center Chapel, Toledo, OH

AWARDS: The Stephen Bridges Scholarship, 2002, Advanced Techniques of Stained Glass Painting with Dick Millard in Antrim, NH

PUBLICATIONS: Featured on back covers of *Glass Art,* Jan/Feb, 2006; *Glass Craftsman,* No. 193, 2006; *Profitable Glass Quarterly,* Winter, 2005; Published in *Creative Stained Glass: Modern Designs & Simple Techniques,* 2004; *Professional Stained Glass Magazine,* Spring 2001, Fall 1998

GUILD SOURCEBOOKS: *Architect's 13*

THE OLANA GROUP

Public Art

Page 96

Ann Adams: I have a degree in ceramic design and have maintained a fine arts studio for over three decades. I use a variety of materials for my installations, including handmade ceramic tile, glass, and stone and commercial tile. Through this direction I have developed a strong working relationship with architects and other public works designers, accepting commissions on all scales. My work deals with structure, pattern, and color, combining the formality of geometry with the flow of nature. It may be flat or three dimensional. My works have been exhibited widely across the United States and in Japan and Israel, receiving numerous awards.

Twyla Arthur: I create art that is often functional and always respectful of its environment. My M.F.A. training at Mills College, in Northern California, allowed me the opportunity to begin my career doing site-specific mosaic work around the San Francisco Bay area. I like to see my work as a natural part of the landscape or architecture that it is designed to embellish and hope it evokes a feeling or memory, as well as an invitation to touch.

ERIC O'LEARY

Non-Representational Sculpture

Page 120

I am an internationally acclaimed ceramic artist and designer. Trained in the tradition by my father, master craftsman Jack O'Leary, I have worked in ceramics for more than forty-five years. Our studio has history of working with landscape architects, architects, and designers as a team approach to sculpture placement and integration to site. We have our own site design capacity and will work with the client to create a total environment for the artwork.

COMMISSIONS: Sculptural gate and bridge for private residence, 2006, Norwich VT; Totem sculpture and patio area for private residence, 2005, Newton MA; Water sculpture for courtyard at Pinnacle Health Care Center, 1995, Harrisburg, PA

COLLECTIONS: Museum of Fine Arts, Boston, MA; New Britain Museum of American Art, CT; Currier Museum of Art, Manchester, NH

EXHIBITIONS: *Architectural Ceramics,* 2006, Cross Mackenzie Ceramic Arts, Washington, DC; *Gateway to Sculpture,* 2005, The Fells, Newbury NH; *Creations in Clay: Contemporary New England Ceramics,* 2004, Currier Museum, Manchester NH

MARKIAN OLYNYK

Architectural Glass/Non-Representational Sculpture

Pages 50, 121, 136, 300

My artwork has been featured in public spaces throughout North America. Exploring the versatile properties of glass, my elaborately worked pieces are a balance between simple geometric structure and the elemental beauties of nature. I am a self taught artist who employs a wide variety of leading-edge techniques, many of which have been developed in my studio. Selected projects include: HSBC Bank Canada, University of North Florida, Port Moody Recreation Complex, New England Biolabs, University of British Columbia Faculty of Dentistry, Renfrew Library, and St. Elizabeth Regional Medical Center.

OUT OF THE MAINSTREAM DESIGNS

Fiber Wall Art

Page 296

I have been designing and weaving for over twenty-five years, and work in traditional and non-traditional fiber techniques. My focus for many of the last fifteen years has been commissioned tapestries and rugs. I enjoy research in historic textiles, graphic design of the past century, and architecture. Each piece is created with the client's needs, location, and architectural space in mind. Framed wall pieces may include layered fabric that has been hand dyed and/or hand felted, as well as handwoven silk that is embellished with vintage and antique buttons or glass beads. I am currently designing woven tapestries for private and corporate clients, as well as a series of Renaissance-inspired fabrics in bold colors for use in home or office. Recent projects include handwoven and hand-felted fabrics for a corporate installation to soften a large glass atrium and reception area. Please contact the studio for additional information.

GUILD SOURCEBOOKS: *Residential Art 3, 4, 5; Architectural & Interior Art 20, 21*

ULRICH PAKKER

Public Art

Pages 14-15, 97

I was fourteen when I began my apprenticeship in Germany as a sheet metal worker, learning skills that would allow me to create the complex geometries of my art. I am a self-taught artist. During the 1980s I discovered stainless steel, now the primary medium for my artwork (although I also create works in titanium, silicon bronze, silver, and gold). Patinas allow me to add startling colors to my work, from turquoise to coffee to jet black. Each work of art begins in my mind's eye as geometrical shapes, shifting and aligning themselves. Circular forms stretch and curve, bending together and apart, creating the voids—or negative spaces—and the curvilinear forms I see in nature. I start with large, flat pieces of metal and transform this stubborn medium into flowing curves and sweeping silhouettes, mimicking the natural geometries around me, playing with universal shapes and primordial materials. Different textures layer my work: velvet finishes contrast with mirrored reflections and swirling surfaces, while rough bronzes lay next to clean, clear stainless steel. In my fountains I add the element of water, joining the lines of the piece with thick ropes of weaving waters. My art pieces counterbalance the impermanence of nature's creations. These sculptures will last for centuries.

PANED EXPRESSIONS STUDIOS
Architectural Glass
Page 51

The richness and beauty of ever-changing light streaming through the textures and colors of stained glass make a wonderfully satisfying medium in which to work and create. The challenge we set for ourselves with every window is to capture the essence of our subject without allowing the image or idea to be compromised by technical difficulties inherent to stained glass. We think of our methods as painting with glass. While we work we have a large variety of glass spread around us on light tables, like a palette, and by choosing each piece carefully we get subtle variations of shade and hue. We are also able to enhance the design detail and beauty of the glass through the use of etching, carving, and fired painting techniques. For nearly thirty years, we've worked with galleries, designers, agents, architects, and individual clients creating site-specific works for public, corporate, and residential spaces.

JOHNIENE PAPANDREAS
Paintings & Prints
Pages 242-243

I have a fascination with subtext, reading between the lines, tuning in to the unspoken. Mine are portraits of imagined selves—damaged, passionate, hidden selves—expressions from a moment thought private, unobserved, before the walls go back up. Guided by past masters, passionate in their revelation of the human condition, I seek out the souls that populate their paintings, their complex expressions, hidden agendas—faces stripped of artifice, laid bare by ecstasy. I lift them out of their place and time to take them as my models. I listen carefully and translate, unlocking something completely new. Your eyes meet theirs and something is familiar; you connect, and across the centuries spirits speak. I transformed a design career in the New York theater into a business designing corporate theater and events before returning to fine art. My travels in the heightened world of theater and the sometimes surreal world of corporate America contribute largely to the insights into human nature I explore in my work.

COLLECTIONS: Numerous private national and international collections

POKEY PARK
Representational Sculpture
Page 158

Life needs to be celebrated! My work is influenced by the parallel beliefs and the artistic symbols that create repetitive patterns in history and the natural world. Everything has serious and whimsical dimensions. I see these characteristics in the uninhibited play of wild animals and children's quiet moments of introspection. I look for underlying joy in the world to express in my sculpture.

COMMISSIONS: Vineyard office, MA; Arboretum, PA; Bank lobbies, PA

EXHIBITIONS: 2007: *ArtExpo*, New York, NY; *Women's Perspective*, National Association of Women Artists, Marco Island, FL; *Sculpture Walk*, Sioux Falls, SD; 2006-2007: *Sculpture in the Streets*, Mesa, AZ; Pyramid Hill, Hamilton, OH; Loveland, CO; Historical Museum, Aiken, SC; *Sculptors Dominion*, San Antonio, TX; *Avenue of Art*, Gillette, WY

AWARDS: 2006, Aiken County Historical Museum, Sculpture Competition; *Sculptural Pursuit Magazine*, Sculpture Only Competition

PUBLICATIONS: *Telluride Style Magazine*, Fall-Winter, 2005-2006

GUILD SOURCEBOOKS: *Architectural & Interior Art 21*

SHELLEY PARRIOTT
Public Art
Page 99

Color Field Sculpture redefines public and private spaces. My unique site-specific installations are polychromes of transparent steel mesh layered to create prismatic patterns of color and light.

Reviews:

"The beauty of these works is their ability to assert themselves without obscuring the marvelous views of land and riverscapes visible through the sheer mesh." *Kingston Daily Freeman, NY*

"Parriott's work is ethereal. Colorful wire mesh multiples interact with their surroundings as sunlight dances through the sculpture and beckons the viewer to take part." *Saugerties Times, NY*

EXHIBITIONS: *LS3P Architecture and Design*, Charleston, SC; Courthouse lawn, Pittsfield, MA; DeSanti Plaza Sculpture Project, Hartsdale, New York, NY; Max Planck Institute, Berlin, Germany; Galerie im Turm, Cologne, Germany

AWARDS: U.S. Embassy, Berlin, Germany; Lorenzo il Magnifico Sculpture Medallion, Biennale Internazionale, Florence, Italy; Best in Show, *Art of the Northeast*, Silvermine Guild, New Canaan, CT, (juried by Leo Castelli Gallery); New York Foundation for the Arts

IVAN PAVLOVITS
Lighting
Page 190

I have been in the hospitality design business for approximately three decades, after receiving a degree in interior architecture. My body of work accumu-lated during my years in hotel interior design demonstrates my versatility for understanding and designing together with the client to achieve the greatest solution. Having recently developed a fresh new type of sculptural wood lighting, I have pieces that can be placed in any environment imaginable. From residential to commercial projects, these sculptural objects give life to any space, day or night. My mission is to provide a special tool for all creative clients in making their projects unique and memorable. This innovative line encompasses all environments by providing custom dimensions and color schemes, helping to create important focal points within each distinct space. Individual lighting objects are produced by ©Artkoncepts.

PEARL RIVER GLASS STUDIO
Architectural Glass
Page 52

Pearl River Glass Studio is committed to pursuing the craft of stained glass as an art form. We work in a broad range of styles and employ a wide variety of methods. Central to our mission is the principle of applying creative solutions to complex problems where thoroughness and quality count.

COMMISSIONS: Lobby window, St. Dominic's Hospital, Jackson, MS; Church windows, Christ United Methodist Church, Jackson, MS

EXHIBITIONS: *Made in USA: Contemporary Crafts*, 2003, Peoria Art Guild

AWARDS: Governor's Award for Excellence in the Arts, 2002, Mississippi

PUBLICATIONS: *The Stained Glass Association of America Sourcebook* 2004, 2003, 2002, 2001, 2000, 1999, 1998; *Stained Glass Quarterly*, Winter 2002

GUILD SOURCEBOOKS: *Designer's 15; Architectural & Interior Art 16, 17, 18, 19, 20, 21*

ARTIST STATEMENTS

ALAN PEARSALL
Murals, Tiles & Wall Reliefs
Page 219

Seven years ago I opened a studio specializing in murals and large-scale artwork. I have painted murals for public spaces, hotels, corporate lobbies, and private homes. My latest and largest mural, at 1,700 square feet, is the EBSCO Mural, an exterior mural celebrating the history of Ipswich, MA. The historically accurate mural is located in a public space and took two years to paint. The research continues as I have been commissioned to create a book on the town's history using the images from the mural. Long before the Pope hired Michelangelo to paint the images of the Bible on the ceiling of the Sistine Chapel, murals were used to record our culture and history. The WPA murals of the 1930s told the story of America in post offices, and Diego Rivera used murals to tell the history of America and Mexico. I follow in this proud tradition.

PECK STUDIOS / CITY ARTS
Murals, Tiles & Wall Reliefs
Page 220

Full-service studios for the production of public art, murals, and mosaics for large-scale artwork or intimate private murals. Our studios have twenty-five years of experience working with architects, designers, and organizations to create solutions for any environment.

RECENT PROJECTS: 1,500' mosaic on the Potomac River waterfront, Washington, DC; 100' mural for the City of Los Angeles, Cultural Affairs Department; Two murals for the newly built visitors center at historic Mount Vernon, Alexandria, VA; 60' mural for main subway station, Washington, DC

COLLECTIONS: The Kennedy Center for the Performing Arts, Washington, DC; Chamber of Commerce, Washington, DC; U.S. Embassy, Santiago, Chile; U.S. Embassy, Georgetown, Guyana; U.S. Nuclear Regulatory Commission, Rockville, MD; Marriott Corporation, Bethesda, MD

GUILD SOURCEBOOKS: *Architect's 6, 7, 8, 9, 10, 11, 12, 13, 14, 15; Architectural & Interior Art 16, 17, 18, 19, 20, 21*

ERIC PELTZER
Non-Representational Sculpture
Page 122

My subject is simply the human form, abstracted and distilled to elemental shapes, poses, and gestures. Stripped of personalizing detail, space is lined with the essence of what defines the body and the soul within. The entire three-dimensional canvas is used to the fullest. Moving around each piece, the form changes subtly, then often dramatically. A number of different compositions can be found in a single sculpture. Recently, I've turned to actual moving (kinetic) sculptures, carefully balanced to move in the wind or by hand. But I strive to imbue even the non-moving works with an unmistakable flow and energy. Rhythm and motion are implied in cascading and graceful curves.

COLLECTIONS: Advancial Federal Credit Union, Dallas, TX; BF Goodrich Corp., Phoenix, AZ, Ford Motor Credit Corp., Dearborn, MI; Beth Israel Synagogue, Fayetteville, NC, Gottschalks Corp., Visalia, CA; Target Marketing, St. Johns, Newfoundland, Canada; Price Costco Corp., Bellevue, WA; Roland America Corp., Los Angeles, CA; Harbor View Hotel, Hong Kong

GUILD SOURCEBOOKS: *Architect's 10, 13*

TOM PHILABAUM
Architectural Glass/Lighting
Pages 53, 191

My first contact with glass was in 1971, at the University of Wisconsin-Madison. Since that time I've made my living primarily as a glassblower, starting with art fairs in the 70s and early 80s. Soon, however, my work turned more toward one-of-a-kind pieces for gallery representation. I have always been mindful of the economic role that "production" work played in the development of my personal work. I have also been a student of monadology and believe in the power of parts. My waterfalls are comprised of at least 1,000 parts, and lighting and installation pieces also celebrate the impact that numbers can create.

RECENT PROJECTS: BIO5 Research Center, University of Arizona, 30' × 7' × 7' hanging atrium sculpture; McMahon's Restaurant, Tucson AZ, 28' × 28' lighting installation; *Baseline Bouquet,* South Mountain Community College, Lobby of Performing Arts Center, 30' × 30', 210 parts.

PICTURES IN GLASS
Liturgical Art
Pages 174, 178

My inspiration comes from life experiences and my interpretation of them. My goal, when working with clients, is to make sure they are left with feelings when entering a room that they didn't have before my glasswork was installed. Glass is my medium. The play of light on it, how the sun affects the colors and textures throughout the day, the story told within, and the feeling derived from it cannot be duplicated by any other source. With twenty-five years of experience and whether designing or fabricating new windows, repairing or restoring old stained glass, sandblasting, or creating a mosaic design, I am inspired by the people I work with and the journey they are on. Their project will be a reflection of who they are, communicating their beliefs, expressing their thoughts without words. Commissioned projects can be found in churches, public buildings, and private residences throughout Michigan.

RECENT PROJECTS: St. Johns Lutheran Church, Farmington, MI; St. Joseph Catholic Church, Adrian, MI; St. Dominic Catholic Church, Clinton, MI; Blessed Savior Lutheran Church, Blissfield, MI

PINTER STUDIOS, INC.
Paintings & Prints
Page 245

I create original painted canvases ranging from intimate views of pools and ponds to more ornate abstracted underwater environments for private and corporate clients. A working artist for over twenty-five years, I have mastered a variety of materials, including ceramic and glass, but I always consider myself a painter. I am most recognized for my bold color use and gestural style. My love of koi began during my first trip to Japan; the resulting series is transformative, effervescent, and provocative. These initial creations have evolved to become the dynamic aqueous environments you see in my work today. Commissions include: Hughes Spalding Children's Hospital, Atlanta, GA; McDonalds Corporate Headquarters, Chicago, IL; HBO Corporate Headquarters, New York, NY; RCA Corporate Staff Center, Princeton, NJ; Portland Museum, Portland, ME; and Canton Museum, Canton, OH. Exhibitions include: Quinlan Visual Arts Center, Gainsville, GA; Vibrantz Gallery, 2006, Half Moon Bay, CA; City Art, 2005, York, PA; and Riverview Gallery, 2005, Portsmouth, VA. Publications include: *Koi USA*, Jan/Feb 2005; *Southern Homes;* and *Arts Southwest.*

JUNCO SATO POLLACK

Mixed & Other Media Wall Art
Page 281

I am a maker of art textiles that float as architectural accent in atriums and on walls. Incorporating the natural elements of light, air, and shadow, I endow the urban environment with the sense of space my work evokes. Through my intuitive use of heat-compressed folds and light, I create Zen-inspired "shadow brush painting," on the wall, fusing Eastern artistic sensibility with Western kinetic energy.

COMMISSIONS: Hotel Mandarin Oriental, Miami, FL; Pittsburgh Airport, Pittsburgh, PA; Georgia Tech Conference Center and Hotel, Atlanta

COLLECTIONS: Museum of Art and Design, New York, NY

EXHIBITIONS: Kuanos Art Biennial Textile, 2005; The 11th International Lace Biennial: Contemporary Art, 2004; Crafts Now: Twenty-one Artists from America, Europe, and Asia, 2003; Defining Craft: Collecting for the New Millennium, 2000

AWARDS: Twenty-First Century Award for Achievement, International Man of the Year, 2000

GUILD SOURCEBOOKS: *Designer's 7, 14; Architectural & Interior Art 18*

ADAM JACKSON POLLOCK—FIRE FARM LIGHTING

Lighting
Page 192

I am the primary designer and artistic director for Fire Farm Lighting. Working in avant-garde theatrical lighting and as a light sculptor prior to establishing Fire Farm in 1991, I now manufacture and distribute artistically designed lamps and light fixtures. Fire Farm is a respected supplier of lighting solutions to residential, commercial, hospitality, and healthcare facility clients throughout the world. We explore a wide range of materials in our work. While we are sensitive to the form of the lamp, we are equally focused on the emotive qualities of the light created. This experience enables us to offer unique services including a varied stock product line, small-run custom production, and custom fabrication of large-scale chandeliers. We are happy to work with your designs or provide you with original sculptural solutions. Manufacturing and distribution is from the U.L.-certified factory in Elkader along the banks of the Turkey River in Northeast Iowa.

RICHARD POLSKY

Paintings & Prints
Pages 246-247

I make art because it gives me pleasure, and because it is part of a self-realization process. The visual arts communicate non-verbally. My art is non-objective. There are no overt or subliminal social, political, or moral messages in it. It is not about anything other than what it is: an abstract painting, drawing, or print. A viewer who looks at a given work of mine can see what my artistic concerns were at that particular moment in my life.

PRESCOTT STUDIOS

Representational Sculpture
Page 159

Life and art join to reveal a dynamic partnership in my art. The joy and animation seen in my sculptures result from my outpouring of individual perception of the world around me, leading to the creation of a captivating, multidimensional art form. Using the visual and emotional impact of brilliant color on moving steel, I produce sculptures that reflect my singularly fantastic interpretation of the world around me. My work is seen as a blend of folk art, pop art, and technically advanced construction. Those who find joy in my work come from every walk of life. A vast audience, including sophisticated art collectors, museums, and corporations, makes my work a part of their lives.

LEE PROCTOR

Lighting
Pages 17, 193

It seems I have always worked with fire, first in metals and now in combination with hot glass techniques. Working with these heated materials demands a focus that encourages an "in the moment" intuitive approach. For years I have worked on commission, mostly in the private sector, creating one-of-a-kind, site-specific installations. These projects have ranged from gates, railings, furniture, benches, etc., to large outdoor sculpture, including sculptural lighting solutions. With time the scale of my work has been increasing, and I have become more interested in public art opportunities. I truly enjoy the collaborative process; exploring new ideas and bringing them to light. I am constantly pursuing new ways to combine metal and glass. It is a humbling experience to work with such transformational mediums with the realization that I have just scratched the surface, seeing that the possibilities are endless.

PUBLIC ART COMMISSIONS

Public Art
Pages cover, 3, 100

It is my observation that the best working climate for creating works of art is when the intentions of the artist, architect, and interior designer are well met, and each assists others in their mutual goals. It is then that high moments of art occur. I choose to realize these works in the use of the monumental approach, with my expressions taking shape in a richness of forms and colors. I choose to create this through my palette of creativity. My woven Aubusson-type tapestries, Venetian glass mosaics, translucent glass panel forms, and bronzes reflect my efforts to elevate the spirit. My installations are found worldwide, from Rome to Beverly Hills, from Saudi Arabia to China. Please contact me through the information printed in this book—or by using Google's search engine. Your inquiries are welcomed.

ARTIST STATEMENTS

TANYA RAGIR

Representational Sculpture

Page 160

All of my work is figurative in origin. For years I have been exploring the sensual relationship between landform and human form. By framing details of the figure as if through a lens, then changing the scale, one can have both a more intimate relationship to the form and separation from its human reference. When sculpting people I am interested in the essence of the person. I perceive beauty as authenticity, not perfection. In all the work, I have a great reverence for grace and attempt to find a balance between sensuality and power. I graduated from the University of California at Santa Cruz in 1976 with a B.A. in art and dance. My work is in permanent collections of the Total Art Museum, Seoul, Korea; Rose Museum at Brandeis University; Columbia College of Dance; and Cerro Cosa College. My work has been internationally collected and is represented in the Frederick Weisman collection, among others. *Moment in Time*, a large public commission for the City of Brea, CA, was recently installed, and I am currently working on a site-specific project for the Joffrey Ballet Company of Chicago.

GUILD SOURCEBOOKS: *Architectural & Interior Art 16, 17; Residential Art 4, 5*

BOB RICKARD

Metal Wall Art

Page 270

I am fortunate to work in a mountain studio surrounded by the natural beauty of Taos, New Mexico. This lends my work a certain quiet and calmness. I use industrial tools to challenge the immutable properties of metal. I use a hand-held plasma cutter to carve my designs into aluminum. I then coat the aluminum with other metals, typically copper, bronze, and iron. Each of these metals reacts differently to the chemical patinas and dyes with which I finish the pieces. My work reflects my love of geometry, movement, and color. I enjoy having clients spend time with me in the studio collaborating on the design and execution of my large pieces. This not only gives them a personal involvement with the creation of their work, but the rich culture of Taos provides a wonderful background for their visit.

ROB FISHER SCULPTURE, LLC

Atrium Sculpture

Pages 69, 309

Seaform and *Norwegian Spring* are sculptures that Rob Fisher completed and installed before his death in 2006. *Solar Sails* was completed by Rob in 2006 and installed by our studio in 2007. Rob Fisher Sculpture, LLC continues under the direction of Talley Fisher, who worked with Rob for many years. Our studio produces artworks in aluminum, stainless steel, light, and color that honor my father's artistic legacy and are inspired by his design direction, aesthetic, and creative sensibility. My master's degree in Landscape Architecture has honed my skills in concept development, computer simulations and presentations, and collaboration with architects, designers, fabricators, engineers, and installers.

COMMISSIONS: In 2007 the studio oversaw the installation of Rob's glass art project, *Skybridge*, at the University of Utah. We are creating suspended artworks for Reid Hospital, Indiana, and Byrd Alzheimer's Institute, Florida, and have commissions for a hotel atrium and new airports in Indianapolis (2008) and Las Vegas (2009).

GUILD SOURCEBOOKS: *Architect's 9, 11, 12, 13, 14, 15; Architectural & Interior Art 16, 17, 18, 19, 20, 21*

KEVIN ROBB

Non-Representational Sculpture

Page 123

I have made my mark on the national and international art scene with my unique, free-flowing sculptural expressions in bronze and stainless steel. These contemporary pieces work equally well in intimate environments or large-scale public areas. My natural curiosity and integral understanding of how positive/negative space and shadow/light work together manifests itself in these pieces, bringing life, energy, and beauty to the spaces they occupy. I pride myself in the high quality of craftsmanship as evidenced in the smooth to the touch edges and seamless metal intersections.

RECENT PROJECTS: University of Kentucky Art Museum, 2006, Lexington; Value Home Loans, 2006, Woodland Hills, CA; Cities of Edmond, OK and Keller, TX, 2006; JW Marriott, 2005, Palm Springs, CA

EXHIBITIONS: *Sculpture In the Park*, 2006, Loveland, CO; Ventana Fine Arts, 2006, Santa Fe, NM; Knox Galleries, 2006, Denver, CO; Sculpture Along Bear Creek, Keller, TX; Rand/Workman Fine Motor Auction/Luxury Lifestyles Expo, 2005, New York, NY

GUILD SOURCEBOOKS: *Architectural & Interior Art 16, 17, 18, 19, 20, 21*

PRISCILLA ROBINSON

Mixed & Other Media Wall Art

Page 282

My art pieces are about texture and color, and are created from handmade paper and kiln cast glass. Inspired by nature, the work is a personal voice exploring translucency, contrasts of materials, and chroma saturation within the motifs of land, leaves, and light. Because my unique techniques work well for specific requirements of size and color, I have created a wide rage of commissions from residential to large public art installations. The acrylic-saturated, embossed fibers are durable and suitable for public spaces. I welcome the opportunity to create unique artwork for commissioned projects.

COMMISSIONS: Boston University, Lobby, School of Hospitality, Boston, MA; Denver Health Center, Denver, CO; First Capital Bank, Corpus Christi, TX; Holmes Medical Center, Melbourne, FL, Broadwing, Austin, TX; Frost Bank Plaza, Lobby, Austin, TX

COLLECTIONS: Chevron Pipeline, Houston, TX; The Royal Library, The Hague, The Netherlands; The Abbey at Spineto, Tuscany, Italy; Komazawa House, Setagaya, Tokyo, Japan

GUILD SOURCEBOOKS: *Designer's 14; Architectural & Interior Art: 16, 17, 20; Residential Art 3*

ROSETTA

Representational Sculpture

Page 161

My subjects are animals, but it is their life force in all of its visual splendor, rather than their realistic physical form, that inspires my stylized interpretations. My work ranges from miniature to monumental and has been exhibited nationally and internationally in museums and galleries, and in numerous juried and invitational exhibitions.

RECENT PROJECTS: The Shops at Walnut Creek, Westminster, CO; Meridian Commons Retail, Parker, CO; *Flight of Falcons*, Dubai, UAE; Chapman University, Orange, CA; Brookgreen Gardens, Pawleys Island, SC.; *Pumas on Parade*, Durango, CO

COMMISSIONS: Florida Institute of Technology, Melbourne, FL; Lincoln Park Zoo, Chicago, IL; Hewlett-Packard, Loveland, CO; Champaign-Urbana Mass Transit District, IL; The Cities of Steamboat Springs, Lakewood, and Loveland, CO, and Dowagiac, MI

AWARDS: People's Choice Sculpture, 2006 and 2005, Western Rendezvous of Art; Silver Medal, 2003, National Sculpture Society; Award of Excellence, 2001, Society of Animal Artists; Gold Medals & Purchase Awards, 2001 and 2000, Bosque Conservatory Art Council

PAUL ROUSSO

Paintings & Prints

Pages 248-249

What happened to the commissioning of huge, intricate, engaging paintings? Paintings that truly capture the imagination of everyone no matter their age or background. Paintings that are specifically created for the interiors of great public and private spaces. Paintings that are definitive, visual statements of complex subjects. Paintings that have so much to say you never grow tired of them. This is what I offer. I like to call my work "maximum-ism". Others define it as a unique form of portraiture. When I capture a subject (i.e. a city, a sport, a corporation, etc.) I cover every single aspect of a concept as if it were happening all at once, right before your eyes. It's like viewing choice moments from a film on one canvas. After a great deal of research and discussion, I shoot literally thousands of photographs and collage them together, creating the final composition. The client sees exactly what he or she will get before the painting ever begins. To really comprehend one of these pieces, it is best to see a huge reproduction from my portfolio or the original. The next best thing is my website, www.roussoportfolio.com, where you can see the vast scope and variety of public and private projects I have completed. You can also see my groundbreaking gallery work at www.paulrousso.com.

BARTON RUBENSTEIN

Public Art

Pages 76, 101

I create indoor and outdoor sculpture with and without water for public and private spaces. These include corporate, commercial, and academic institutions, as well as private residences. I typically work with bronze, stainless steel, stone, and glass. Fascinated with various elements of nature, I focus on water, kinetics, light, and suspension to create sculpture that surprises and challenges the viewer.

COMMISSIONS: National competition-awarded commissions: Summit Behavioral Healthcare, 2006, Cincinnati, OH; Owens Community College, 2005, Findlay, OH; Boone County National Bank, 2005, Columbia, MO; Jefferson at Congressional Village, 2004, Rockville, MD; University of Central Florida, 2003, Orlando. Other commissions: Sidwell Friends School, 2007, Washington, DC; Somerset Elementary School, 2005, Chevy Chase, MD; Temple Emanuel, 2003, Charleston, SC; Weizmann Institute of Science, 2003, Rehovot, Israel; Mount Vernon Unitarian Church, 2002, Alexandria, VA; Avalere Health, LLC, 2002, Washington, DC; Millennium Building, 2002, Washington, DC; Neurovision, Ltd., 2001, Ramat Gan, Israel

BRIAN F. RUSSELL

Non-Representational Sculpture

Page 124

I create works that will live harmoniously in the world as independent functionaries of society. I draw inspiration from forms and rhythms in nature, the human body, ancient artifacts, mathematics, and science, distilling these influences into abstract points of intersection. My aim on a public scale is to involve the viewer, to interject into the world points of beauty, interest, and spontaneity. I want people to use my sculpture as an excuse to mentally shift to another level of consciousness, above the daily hubbub, even for a moment, and to reconnect with themselves via that primal, emotional, cortex-controlled spasm of an encounter with an unexpected oasis in a visual desert.

COLLECTIONS: Cafesjian Museum, Minneapolis, MN; Rhodes College, Memphis, TN; Tennessee State Museum, Nashville

EXHIBITIONS: Solo exhibitions at Eleonore Austerer Gallery, 2005, Palm Desert, CA; Tobin Hewett Gallery, 2005, Louisville, KY; Jerald Melberg Gallery, 2004, Charlotte, NC; David Lusk Gallery, 2005, Memphis, TN

JAMES T. RUSSELL

Non-Representational Sculpture

Page 125

The concept of my sculpture is based on the juxtaposition of contrasting contours. Opposites attract opposites. I use highly polished stainless steel because it is alive with reflective energy. Through this medium I transform my inner emotion into permanent form. I have edition sculptures that range from $5,000 to $50,000. Monumental sculptures start at $60,000.

COMMISSIONS: Coast Aluminum and Architectural, 2003, Santa Fe Springs, CA; Astra Zeneca Pharmaceuticals, 2002, Wilmington, DE; Chico Municipal Airport, 2001, Chico, CA

COLLECTIONS: Four Seasons Hotel, Hong Kong; City of Cerritos, CA; Bellagio Hotel, Las Vegas, NV; Motorola Corporation, Beijing, China; Riverside Art Museum, Riverside, CA; A.T. Kearney Inc., Chicago, IL

EXHIBITIONS: *Impact,* 2004, Tadu Contemporary Art, Santa Fe, NM; *Miniatures,* 2004, Albuquerque Museum of Art, NM

PUBLICATIONS: *Santa Fe Reporter,* October 2004; *Leaders* magazine, September 2004

GUILD SOURCEBOOKS: *Architect's 7, 8, 12, 14; Architectural & Interior Art 16, 17, 18, 19, 20, 21; Residential Art 1, 3*

SABLE STUDIOS

Atrium Sculpture

Pages 68, 70-71, 355

Sable Studios has been creating kinetic mobiles and stabiles for over forty years. Collaborating with art consultants, architects, and designers, our custom-designed sculpture has enhanced private, corporate, and public spaces. Whether transforming an interior atrium or an exterior location, the artwork integrates color, light, and movement to create a multidimensional experience. Our studio creates work that truly graces the world with exquisite beauty.

RECENT PROJECTS: Children's Hospital Boston, Waltham and Boston campuses; Union City Senior Center, CA; Lucent Technologies, CO; Boys Town National Research Hospital, Omaha, NE

COMMISSIONS: Metro Plaza Building, San Jose, CA; Syntex Corporation, Hayward, CA; Berklee Performance Center, Boston, MA; Quantum Corporation, San Jose, CA; 3 Comm Corporation, Sunnydale, CA; Cadence Corporation, San Jose, CA

GUILD SOURCEBOOKS: *Architect's 11, 12, 13, 14, 15; Architectural & Interior Art 16, 17, 18, 20, 21*

JOANIE SAN CHIRICO

Atrium Sculpture

Page 72

My atrium sculptures are site-specific and inspired by the environment and the area surrounding the installation. I'm capable of working closely with architects, designers and developers. I use dye sublimation technology with heat to infuse dye into the fabric, the result is an extraordinarily vibrant image that can be used without concern that the colors will fade. Wall mounted pieces are also available, using either the technology above or with your choice of materials and techniques. I employ various pigments, dyes, stitching and manipulation of cloth, paper and paint to achieve the illusion of a natural patina.

COLLECTIONS: Ocean County Library Main Branch, 2006, Toms River, NJ; Amalgamated NYC, 2004, New York, NY; Loan to Norvo Nordisk Pharmaceuticals, 2004, Princeton, NJ; Beardsworth Consulting, 2002, Flemington, NJ; and many private collections in the US and Europe

EXHIBITIONS: Signature artist, 2007, Noyes Museum of Art, Oceanville, NJ; NorDys Gallery, 2006, Birmingham, AL; Pringle Gallery, 2005, Philadelphia, PA; Solo Exhibit, 2004, Brodsky Gallery, Princeton, NJ

ARTIST STATEMENTS

CRAIG SCHAFFER

Non-Representational Sculpture

Pages 126-127

My sculptures are inspired by the shapes formed by natural processes over time. I try to emulate, but not copy, the rhythms and proportions found in dynamic systems. Nature is non-linear, and I am fascinated by the ways different reflexive processes create similar complex patterns, such as fractals and spirals. Partly because these shapes are universal, my sculpture is found in many types of art venues. I have completed commissions for universities, research centers, hospitals, religious institutions, corporations, and private homes. I create sculpture in all materials and sizes, for indoor and outdoor placement. Prices vary with size and material.

COMMISSIONS: Brown Hall Math Tower, The Ohio State University, Columbus; Princeton Institute for Advanced Studies; Robins Center for Philanthropy, Columbus, OH; Baptist Hospital DeSoto, Memphis, TN; Mathematical Association of America, Washington, DC; Hualien Cultural Center, Hualien, Taiwan

DREW ADAM SCHNIEROW

Lighting

Page 194

I sculpt using light and translucent stone. My illuminated stone sculptures are inspired by the evolving landscape, life forms, and contemporary design. This synthesis of attention allows my art to be both timeless and contemporary. My process of discovering the unique relationship of each stone to its particular illuminating qualities is a constant play between aesthetics and lighting functionality. Creating the *Eternal Flame* (commissioned by Susan and Mark Beckerman for the West End Synagogue of New York City) was a recent commission, which balances all the elements that I strive to create in the perfection of my sculptures. Working with both public and private clients, I have work in collections throughout the United States and Europe. Please visit my website, www.dasart.com, for a comprehensive viewing.

GEORGE C. SCOTT

Lighting

Page 195

When I was a boy, the allure of beach glass inspired vast, decorative ornament on sand castles on the beaches of Southern California. Some things don't change much. Although the scale has dramatically changed, I continue to adorn architecture with glass embellishments. The restrictions of working with found random gems of the sea has given way to the more deliberate disciplines of fusing, casting, slumping, and blowing glass elements. The means may have changed, but the process remains. If only I could get the kilns onto the beach. Please visit www.georgecscottstudios.com for more details of past work and inspiration for future work.

COLLECTIONS: University of Delaware; Yakima Valley Community College; City of Seatac Community Center; Sunset Station Casino; St. Charles Station Casino; Kansas City Station Casino; St. Louis Station Casino; Providence Hospital, Seattle, WA; Crown Plaza Hotel; Mr. Jack Nicholson; Ms. Angelica Huston; Ms. Bette Midler; Mr. Kenny Loggins; Ms. Michele Philips; Mr. and Mrs. Elias Alvord; Mr. and Mrs. Steve Balmer

MARSH SCOTT

Metal Wall Art

Pages 264, 271

Working in pierced metals allows me to combine the narrative, symbolic, or abstract in a sculptural context. My work is often a collaborative expression reflecting geographic and cultural diversity to provide a site-specific installation. The positive and negative piercing defines the design while creating dynamic shadows. The hand-brushed surface reflects the colors of the surrounding environment.

COMMISSIONS: Public Art: Brea CA; Laguna Beach, CA; Kaiser Permanente, various locations, CA; Hoag Memorial Hospital, Newport Beach, CA; Pfizer, Irvine, CA; Canal Plus US, CA; Discovery Museum, CA; Edison, NY, CA; Flowers Hospital, AL; Four Seasons, NY; Orange County Airport, CA; Torrance Memorial Hospital, CA; Verizon, CA; Viking Components, CA

EXHIBITIONS: *Affaire in the Gardens,* Beverly Hills, CA; Sawdust Art Festival, Laguna Beach, CA.; Los Angeles County Museum of Art, Los Angeles, CA; *Design for Living,* Millard Sheets Gallery, a Smithsonian Affiliate, Pomona, CA; Festival of Arts, Laguna Beach, CA

GUILD SOURCEBOOKS: *Architectural & Interior Art 17, 18, 19, 20, 21*

ALI SHAHVALI

Non-Representational Sculpture

Page 128

My art pieces are testament to my ongoing love of glass, and I am continually fascinated by the ability of glass to transform an environment from the ordinary to the wondrous. Glass, despite its constant presence in our modern world, remains mysterious. It interacts with light in a manner unlike any other medium. Like other materials, it can cast shadows creating a sense of drama, yet its ability to both reflect and transmit light is unparalleled. Most captivating still is the process of its creation, from a molten liquid state into a solid finished work of art. My blown glass art is created in my studio, Viccolo Glass, where I enjoy working closely with clients to create unique custom glass installations for indoor and outdoor spaces. My work has been featured in private, public, and corporate spaces.

KURT SHAW

Atrium Sculpture

Page 73

I have been creating custom artwork for corporate spaces, healthcare facilities, and the hospitality industry since 1992. My work includes some of the largest wall-mounted sculptures in the United States, ranging from an atrium filled with multiple sea-themed pieces in Toms River, NJ, which I completed in 1995, to a massive clock I built for a corporate multi-use space in Westerville, OH, and installed in the spring of 2006. I attended both Carnegie Mellon University in Pittsburgh, PA, graduating summa cum laude with a B.F.A. in 1989, and the Hobart Institute of Welding Technology in Troy, OH, where I received G.M.A.W. certification in 1995. In addition to studio work, I have published hundreds of art reviews on regional, national, and international art exhibitions primarily in the capacity of art critic for the *Pittsburgh Tribune-Review,* where I have been a regular twice-weekly contributor since June of 2001.

GUILD SOURCEBOOKS: *Designer's 9, 10, 12, 13*

ARTIST STATEMENTS

JO ELLEN SIDDALL
Paintings & Prints
Page 250

As a native of Florida, I have spent my life in and around the ocean and inland waters, so prevalent in my state. These waterways, abundant with many beautiful forms of life, have played a large part in shaping my personal aesthetic. The sense of joy, freedom, and spirituality I receive while exploring in the water is so strong, I feel compelled to share it. My desire is to convey these same emotions to others. I attempt to evoke these feelings through the use of rich colors, lyrical line, and sensual forms.

COMMISSIONS: Cummer Museum of Arts and Gardens, Jacksonville, FL

COLLECTIONS: Bank of America, Jacksonville, FL; Bank of America, Tampa, FL; Hope Haven Children's Hospital, Jacksonville, FL; Merrill Lynch, Jacksonville, FL

EXHIBITIONS: Solo Exhibition, 2006, City Hall, Hollywood, FL; Juried Exhibition, 2006, Ponte Vedra Cultural Arts Center, Ponte Vedra, FL; Impressions of Northeast Florida Juried Exhibition, 2005, Haskell Gallery, Jacksonville International Airport; Invitational Exhibit, 2004, Cummer Museum of Art and Gardens, Jacksonville, FL; Solo Exhibition, 2003, Ponte Vedra Cultural Arts Center, Ponte Vedra, FL; Solo Exhibition, 2003, Bethel Gallery, Ponte Vedra, FL

SCOTT SNIBBE
Public Art
Page 102

I create interactive media art for public spaces that directly engages viewers' bodies. Within these works people experience an incredible sense of engagement where they can, for a short while, stop regretting the past, stop anticipating the future, and become completely absorbed with each other in a social work of art that fosters a sense of warmth, humor, and interdependence.

COMMISIONS: Cité de Science, Paris; New York Hall of Science; Yahoo Corporation, CA; Phaeno Wolfsburg, Germany; Jerusalem Museum, Israel; Mills College, CA; London Science Museum

EXHIBITIONS: London Institute of Contemporary Arts; SFMOMA; Whitney Museum of American Art; Tokyo Intercommunications Center; South Korea Media Arts Biennial

AWARDS: Ars Electronica 2003, 1998, 1996, Austria; Rockefeller Foundation; National Endowment for the Arts

PUBLICATIONS: *Artforum; New York Times; Artweek; Responsive Environments,* 2006; *Digital Art,* 2003

DENISE M. SNYDER
Mixed & Other Media Wall Art
Page 283

My wall sculptures add sophistication and a personal element to interiors. I employ natural and man-made materials in my bold designs, which reflect the natural world and create a dynamic flair. I work directly with private individuals, interior designers, and corporate clients to create works that best suit their needs. I have received awards and have shown in national and international competitions since 1989.

GUILD SOURCEBOOKS: *Designer's 12, 14; Architectural & Interior Art 19; Residential Art 5*

CHERSTIN SPARKS
Representational Sculpture
Page 163

I sculpt to capture life, to make personal and real for us scenes and people who are worlds away from our own experience, to bring into new focus the world around us, and to make us aware of undiscovered facets within ourselves. My sculpture should be an eye-opening and world-expanding experience. I take my subjects from both the familiar and the unknown: the common people and animals of today, as well as characters of mythology, history, and legend. But independent of my source of inspiration, I strive to capture honest reality through an intense study of my subject, a practice that never fails to unfold new understanding and appreciation for the depth, breadth, and beauty of life.

JOHN E. STALLINGS
Non-Representational Sculpture
Page 129

My work is about the search for the infinite. For the past several years, I've concentrated my efforts toward creating modern minimalist sculpture with a timeless quality—clean lines and surfaces blended to create constant movement and balance within the occupied space. Infused with the concept of continuous motion, the designs neither begin nor end. "Powerful in their reflection of surroundings and in their sublime and clean geometric volumes." Mariana Bego, Ezair Gallery, NYC. "The polished surfaces of many of his sculptures blur the borders of matter and its surrounding environment. The viewer is left wondering which aspect is visual and which is physical. Thus each piece, at once autonomous and boundless, has a dialectical relationship with its setting. It is in this way that Mr. Stallings' minimalist approach to abstraction continuously proves itself to be among the most engaging and effective sculpture available today." Ruthie Tucker, Amsterdam Whitney Gallery, NYC. More of my work can be seen at my website, www.stallingsart.com.

STANTON GLASS STUDIO, LLC.
Architectural Glass
Pages 54-55

For more than twenty-five years, Stanton Glass Studio has been creating distinctive, one-of-a-kind architectural stained glass pieces for a broad range of clients, including churches, hotels, resorts, restaurants, and homeowners. Working in a centuries-old craft, our talented staff has produced masterpieces in glass, ranging from large church windows to many decorative elements at the landmark Driskill Hotel in Austin, TX. In the residential realm, our company handcrafts unique, custom-stained beveled glass elements—from doors, windows, domes, and ceilings to stunning light fixtures. Everything is custom tailored to the client. Our craftsmen also specialize in the preservation, restoration, and repair of historic stained glass windows. Recent restoration projects include The Guadalupe Cathedral in Dallas, TX; St. Patrick's in Ft. Worth, TX; and St. David's in Austin, TX. Our craftsmen practice the latest conservation and restoration techniques used in the preservation of historic stained glass. Working from our facility in Waco, Texas, we collaborate with other highly skilled and gifted blacksmiths and craftsmen to produce hand-forged ironwork to frame our windows, suspend light fixtures and domes, and set off our decorative glasswork.

ARTIST STATEMENTS

ARTHUR STERN

Architectural Glass

Page 57

I create site-specific architectural glass installations, primarily in leaded glass, as well as other art glass techniques. Specializing in the collaboration with clients and design professionals, my studio currently has installations in thirty-six states, Canada, Japan, and Hong Kong. Commissions range from residential work to large public art projects and churches. I have been widely published and have won numerous awards, including several American Institute of Architects design awards, as well as honors from the Interfaith Forum on Religion, Art & Architecture, The Construction Specifications Institute, and *Ministry & Liturgy* magazine's BENE Awards. Each project receives the same thorough attention to detail and fine craftsmanship. I also work in other media, including wood and glass bas-relief sculpture, mixed-media works on canvas, and works on paper.

STEVEN WHYTE SCULPTURE STUDIOS

Representational Sculpture

Pages 164-165

Celebrated for my work's expressiveness, authenticity and effectiveness, I am an accomplished figurative sculptor with a growing reputation for public works of varying scale. A noted portrait sculptor, I am former Vice President of the prestigious London-based Society of Portrait Sculptors. During my career I have completed dozens of portrait commissions and nine public monuments, including the soon-to-be-unveiled multi-million dollar *National Tribute to Bob Hope and Our Nation's Military.* I have established a reputation for authenticity and professionalism, and I regard public commissions as a responsibility to the past and future legacies of the communities involved. I am experienced in collaborating with civic organizations and local governments, and at ease working within budget and schedule parameters. I also appreciate the creative challenges and rewards of site-specific installations; I work frequently with architects, designers and developers. With my in-house studio team, I provide my clients and collectors with the highest-quality fine art bronze to suit the needs of communities, homes, offices, congregations, collections, and public spaces.

KAREN R. STODDARD

Representational Sculpture

Page 166

I feel the ability to sculpt is a gift to be used, honed, and shared. I am very receptive to commissions. It gives me a great feeling of accomplishment to bring to existence the vision of another, to fill a void with the perfect piece, to accept the challenge.

EXHIBITIONS: Fifteenth Annual Loveland Sculpture Invitational, 2006, Loveland, CO; Western Design Conference Juried Exhibitor, 2006, Cody, WY; Fourteenth Annual Loveland Sculpture Invitational, 2005, Loveland, CO; *Affaire in the Gardens,* 2005, Beverly Hills, CA

PUBLICATIONS: *InformArt Magazine,* Winter & Summer 2005; *Cowboys and Indians,* June 2005; *Southwest Art,* May 2005; *Jackson Hole Magazine,* Summer/ Fall 2005

GUILD SOURCEBOOKS: *Architectural & Interior Art 21*

PAULA STOEKE

Fine Art Photography

Page 263

As a photographer and a painter, I seek to express elusive events that happen just outside my field of vision. I'm drawn to recreating memory, dreams, and life's subtleties. This current exhibition explores the soul-to-soul connection between horses and humans. A portion of the proceeds from the series is being donated to a wild horse rescue ranch that generously provides sanctuary for displaced herds. The horse, as symbol, is rich in metaphor and plays an evocative role in our universal subconscious. Nobility, mythology, strength, and grace are among the associations I've chosen to honor and to study within this context. Living in California affords me the natural beauty of the coast, as well as easy access to the Western states where I often shoot. I have been honored to have images appear in numerous U.S. galleries and private collections, as well as in solo exhibitions in Rome and Monte Carlo. I invite you to view additional work at www.paulastoeke.com.

JAMES STONE

Representational Sculpture

Page 167

My art today is the convergence of my experiences living around water from my earliest years though my adult life. As a boy I was fascinated with the mysteries of underwater existence. The liquid crystal quality of water (which resembles glass) and the never-ending study of the strange and wonderful creatures that live within it became a life-long passion. Creating illusions of underwater environments in glass, copper, and steel infuses the work with the life force of fire and forge. It is my hope that as viewers become lost in the sight, sound, and feel of the work, they become gently charged with that same life force.

COMMISSIONS: Chabad of Poway, San Diego, CA; Montefiore, Cleveland, OH; Red Bull, Santa Monica, CA; Santa Monica Medical Center, Santa Monica, CA

EXHIBITIONS: Highland Fine Arts, 2006; Whittier Art Gallery, 2005; Hilton La Jolla Torrey Pines, 2003

AWARDS: Beverly Hills Affair in the Garden, Mayor's Choice Award, 2006; One of a Kind, Chicago, People's Choice Award, 2006

PUBLICATIONS: *Beverly Hills Courier,* May, 2006; *Orange County Jewish Journal,* September 2005; *San Diego Union Tribune,* July 2005; *Salt Lake Tribune,* June 2005; *Décor & Style Magazine,* February, 2005

CHARLES STRAIN

Non-Representational Sculpture

Page 130

I draw my imagery from nature and from life experience. The human figure and human emotions are the basis of most of my compositions. Happiness, sadness, a moment in time, a familiar experience, a celebration—these events and emotions serve as catalysts for my sculptures. My dedication to mastering the lost wax method of casting bronze and a "labor of love" approach to art making serve to transform each bronze into a timeless statement. My sculpture can be installed indoors or outdoors. I enjoy working with clients who have the creative vision to transform outdoor spaces into works of art. I accept commissions in a broad range of sizes and can install sculpture on freestanding bases, or in fountains or ponds. Size range from 6" to 120".

GUILD SOURCEBOOKS: *Architectural & Interior Art 20; Residential Art 3, 4, 5*

MARTIN STURMAN

Representational Sculpture

Pages 11-12, 168

My contemporary sculptures and functional art are created either in carbon steel or stainless steel and are suitable for indoor or outdoor placement. Stainless steel surfaces are hand burnished to create an incredible vibrancy when viewed from different angles. Carbon steel surfaces are acrylic painted with a polyurethane overlay to preserve color vitality. I encourage site-specific and collaborative efforts to achieve maximum client and artistic satisfaction.

COMMISSIONS: Royal Caribbean Cruise Lines, Springfield, OR; Hyatt Westlake Plaza Hotel, Westlake Village, CA; McGraw-Hill Publishing Companies, Columbus, OH; McDonald's, Oakbrook, IL; Bascom Palmer Eye Institute, West Palm Beach Gardens, FL; Tesoro Galleries, Beverly Hills, CA; Grant & Weber, Calabasas, CA

GUILD SOURCEBOOKS: *Architect's 12, 14; Designer's 7, 8, 9, 10, 11, 12, 13, 14, 15; Architectural & Interior Art 16, 17, 18, 19, 20, 21; Artful Home 2*

SUE KEANE STUDIO

Murals, Tiles & Wall Reliefs

Page 221

I mold, bend, and fold clay to form abstract wall or freestanding works. Each sensitive design is a one-of-a-kind creation. These clay pieces may also incorporate wood, metallic lusters, paint, glass, and light to complete the artistic statement. I hold degrees from the Parsons School of Design, New York, NY, and from Otis College of Art and Design, Los Angeles, CA. Commissions are welcomed for private residences, corporate environments, and public spaces. Slides of current works are available upon request. Exhibitions include: Raiford Gallery, Roswell, GA; Gallery Eight, La Jolla, CA; TAG-Artist Gallery, Santa Monica, CA; and Roche-Bobois, Los Angeles, CA. Recent projects include: A Community of Angels, public art project, Los Angeles, CA.

METTJE SWIFT

Atrium Sculpture

Page 74

I seek beauty and grace in my translucent fabric mobile sculptures. I bring in an outdoor spirit of sun and wind to energize the sculptures, which revolve in interior air currents and balance from one point. The fabric catches both natural and artificial light, and transforms it into shades and tints of its own transforming interior ambiance. My work is as bright and exciting as stained glass, yet lightweight and safe to hang overhead. My focus is suspended installations for architectural spaces, including atriums, entryways, and corridors. My design inspiration developed from iconographic images, primitive and modern, that represent the natural world. Each new project challenges me to invent new forms and functions, empowering me to animate the human environment through light and motion.

COMMISSIONS: *Crossroads of the World,* Jakarta, Indonesia; *Kite Shapes,* Oklahoma University Children's Hospital, Oklahoma City; *Grace in Flight,* Crystal River Elementary School, Carbondale, CO; *Interlocking Striae,* Cincinnati, OH; *Playful Geometrics,* Graceland University, Lamoni, IA

RICHARD TAYLOR

Mixed & Other Media Wall Art

Pages 268, 284

My work is a distillation of life experiences, often seen through the influences of music and poetry. I allow the cadences, rhythms, and syncopations of the musical and the poetic to resonate within and inform the spirits of my pieces.

COMMISSIONS: General Electric Medical Systems, SC Johnson Company, Milwaukee Public Central Library, Rockwell International, State of Louisiana, State of Wisconsin

COLLECTIONS: General Electric Medical Systems, Quad/Graphics, Southwestern Illinois College, VISA

EXHIBITIONS: OK Harris, New York, NY; Fresh Paint, Culver City, CA; Mary Bell Galleries, Chicago, IL; Tucson Art Museum; Sylvia Schmidt Gallery, New Orleans, LA; Chicago Navy Pier Sculpture Exhibition, 2001 & 2002, IL; Tory Folliard Gallery, Milwaukee, WI

AWARDS: Kajima Sculpture Exhibition, 2006, Tokyo, Japan

PUBLICATIONS: *Paint on Metal* 2005

GUILD SOURCEBOOKS: *Guild Sourcebook of Architectural & Interior Art 13, 16, 20*

GARY TILLERY

Representational Sculpture

Page 169

I came to art along an unconventional path, which included service in Vietnam, work on oil rigs in Indonesia, and a twenty-year business career in advertising. Incurably fascinated by sculpture, I finally left the corporate world behind to devote my energy and time to art. I have always been an internationalist at heart, visiting or living in more than fifty countries. One benefit of wide travel is direct exposure to the world's great art, and my influences range from Native American to Japanese brush painting to Rodin. Drawing on these eclectic influences, I favor the traditional mediums of metal and stone, though using them to express contemporary ideas. While I gravitate toward the representational approach to art, I am happiest stretching its limits. The full spectrum of my work can be seen on my web site: www.garytillery.com.

RECENT PROJECTS: Chicago Vietnam Veterans Memorial, Chicago, IL; Luis Aparicio for the Chicago White Sox

COLLECTIONS: National Vietnam Veterans Art Museum; Patricia Dupont; General and Mrs. Tommy Franks

GUILD SOURCEBOOKS: *Architect's 14*

JOSHUA TOBEY

Representational Sculpture

Page 170

I grew up in Santa Fe, New Mexico, the son of a man whose desire and talent to create works of art surpassed every artist I have ever known. My true passion is the outdoors and the wildlife in it. I enjoy inventing rather than replicating, and I create wildlife that is stylized and simplified in all sizes. I use all the colors of the natural world to create my own images of wildlife that a person can appreciate not only for their beauty in bronze, but also for their sensitivity. I always impart an aspect of the human element to make the animal more accessible to human emotions and feelings. Through this journey of creative invention, I have always maintained that my artwork would stand alone as my own invention from my own desire to create. I now create works in bronze with the inspiration of my father/mentor Gene Tobey, who passed away last year. His talent and creative spark help to drive me today.

KAREN URBANEK
Fiber Wall Art
Page 297

I build painterly images and sculptural forms—both abstract and representational—in luminous layers of complex color and texture. My extensive color palette comes from natural sources and environmentally responsible working methodologies. Constructed primarily of compacted tussah silk, flax, and bamboo fiber with a penetrating coating that adds crispness and strength, surfaces range from smooth and translucent to dense, high relief. Works may be double sided and hang freely, or may be composed of separate layers and elements. Recent work also incorporates wire and new construction techniques, including three-dimensional sculpture. Light in weight, easy to ship, mount, maintain, and clean. Framing is optional. Commissions accepted. Visuals/pricing available upon request.

COLLECTIONS: Lockheed Martin Corp.; Aspect Communications; Kaiser Hospitals; McGraw-Hill Publishing Co.; Grace Cathedral, San Francisco, CA

GUILD SOURCEBOOKS: *Designer's 13, 14, 15; Architectural & Interior Art: 16, 17, 18, 19, 20, 21*

AARON P. VAN DE KERCKHOVE
Non-Representational Sculpture
Page 131

I create large-scale metal sculptures that are often kinetic and interact with the viewer and the environment, either by moving in the wind or by human touch. With a strong sense of spatial relationships, I enjoy sculpting steel forms that compliment both the urban landscape and the natural environment. I have made sculpture for architects, designers, galleries, city councils, and private collectors. Created from powder-coated steel, stainless steel, Cor-ten®, or bronze, my work is meant to withstand the test of time; as a certified welder, I pay much attention to quality and technique. My studio in Watsonville, CA, is able to produce work from a few feet high to monumental public sculpture. Prices for small to mid-sized work begins around $10,000. Commissions include a public sculpture for Mission Gateway Housing, Union City, CA; a kinetic sculpture for Saks Fifth Avenue, Santa Barbara, CA; and private commissions all over the U.S.

SUSAN VENABLE
Mixed & Other Media Wall Art
Page 285

My work is an exploration of structure, surface, and the relationship between the two. The constructions are bas-reliefs of stacked steel grids woven with copper wire and juxtaposed with encaustic paintings. I want to maximize the physicality of the materials, seeking an energy field through structure and surface. My exploration, on a perceptual and tactile level, is to create a transcendent reality, not to recall a specific place or object. Archaeology, rituals, repetition, ruins, magic, and the art of indigenous societies all strongly influence my creative process. My work can be seen in public spaces, homes, and museums. The commissions/installations have involved collaboration with collectors, architects, and designers throughout the world. The materials are durable, low maintenance, and suitable for installation in public areas.

GUILD SOURCEBOOKS: *Designer's 10, 11, 12, 13, 14, 15; Architectural & Interior Art 16, 17, 18, 19, 20, 21*

SERANDA VESPERMANN
Architectural Glass
Pages 5, 8, 58

Simply put, I love glass. I fell in love with it at age five, fascinated by how a beveled piece of clear glass broke up the sun's rays into a rainbow of light. The colors, the textures, even the smooth outlines of lead speak volumes to me. These are the messages I seek to reveal to others.

RECENT PROJECTS: 96" x 68" triptych for the entrance of a private residence; Six panels on three floors (for a total of 18), Chattanooga City Hall Renovation, Chattanooga, TN

GUILD SOURCEBOOKS: *Architect's 14; Architectural & Interior Art 18, 20, 21*

KENNETH F. VonROENN, JR.
Atrium Sculpture
Page 75

For the past several years, we have been developing techniques for suspended metal and glass sculptures using a support system of tensile structures to carry glass elements, primarily dichroic and holographic diffraction grating glasses. The tensile structures allow for a light and delicate support system, while the dichroic and holographic glass create a very dynamic visual experience, casting and reflecting a variety of colors as the angle of light or the viewing perspective changes. We focus on diverse applications of glass, thereby expanding the role of glass in architecture. Using a broad range of new techniques, we are able to meet the functional and aesthetic requirements of diverse architectural applications. These techniques have been developed and refined from new and emerging technologies, creating dynamic opportunities for glass to enhance architecture.

COMMISSIONS: Clarian Hospital, Indianapolis, IN; Manchester College, Science Building, North Manchester, IN; Orlando Federal Courthouse, Orlando, FL

SCOTT WALLACE
Public Art
Page 103

Past public art projects include large-scale freestanding sculptures, hanging sculptures and, wall reliefs produced in bronze, stainless steel, and painted aluminum. Given the sometimes whimsical and optimistic nature of my work, I am especially interested in developing artwork for spaces where the public will welcome interaction with forms that evoke positive emotions. I recognize the special concerns involved with integrating durable artwork into public spaces and am open to working with architects, landscape designers, and interior designers.

COMMISSIONS: City of Minneapolis, MN; Center for the Arts, Whitewater, WI; University of Central Florida, Orlando; Arizona Cancer Center, Tucson; Bay Colony Technology Center, Tucson; McCormick Place Convention Center, Chicago, IL; Student Recreation Center at the University of Arizona, Tucson

GUILD SOURCEBOOKS: *Architectural & Interior Art 19*

ARTIST STATEMENTS

WANNER SCULPTURE STUDIO

Representational Sculpture
Page 171

We have created figurative sculpture for over 200 architectural settings throughout the United States. Our sculpture spans secular and religious themes, and ranges from small to over life size in scale. We have worked successfully with architects, art consultants, designers, and contractors for over thirty-five years on projects for hospitals, cathedrals, churches, government buildings, corporations, and more. Our in-house foundry has enabled us to maintain a strong competitive advantage. Please visit our website at www.wannersculpturestudio.com for more information about our work and us.

GUILD SOURCEBOOKS: *Architect's 9, 10; Architectural & Interior Art 17, 20*

LIBBY WARE

Murals, Tiles & Wall Reliefs
Page 222

I create limited-edition and one-of-a-kind porcelain objects. I began as a two-dimensional artist and, in 1976, began to paint three-dimensional objects. I work in clay and use a number of techniques (thrown, altered, built by hand, poured) to create an object. As each piece is constructed, I visualize the surface. Some objects are masked prior to glazing in order to produce the rhythm of the surface. Some surfaces are achieved through the use of underglaze, which is applied by hand or airbrushed onto the piece. Some objects are hand painted after they have been glazed and before their final firing. I am fascinated by how surface alters the perception, emotion, nature, and material of an object.

EDWIN C. WHITE

Non-Representational Sculpture
Page 132

My fascination with origami, coupled with a background in both graphic and product design, often challenges me to treat metals as one would paper. I normally choose sheet stock for material and rely on multiple and often parallel cuts, perforations, and a lot of "tugging" to coax a shape from its two-dimensional source. As a result the forms have an innate simplicity that is difficult to duplicate in my other, more involved welded or mixed-media assemblies. When I began "expanding" works that incorporated this abundance of cuts, moiré patterns naturally evolved that I now attempt to incorporate in my designs.

COMMISSIONS: Glenwood North, Raleigh, NC; Preston Hotel, Nashville, TN; Migration: A Gallery, Charlottesville, VA; Proposal for Hilton Hotel Beijing, China; Proposal for Terminus Atlanta, Atlanta, GA; Commission for Atlantis Development, Paradise Island, Bahamas

EXHIBITIONS: Florida Outdoor Sculpture Competition, Lakeland, FL; Garden Art Sculpture Invitational, Hillsborough, NC; Time Warner Headquarters, Charlotte, NC

C.T. WHITEHOUSE

Non-Representational Sculpture
Page 133

The intent of my work with bronze is simply to express the nature and the beauty of the material itself. My choice to use simple forms invites a closer connection to the creative process and frees the viewer to see the qualities of bronze without concern for subject or involved detail. Exhibitions and honors include: Art in the Embassies Program, 2006, U.S. Embassy, Brunae; National Sculpture Society Exhibit, 2005, New York, NY; American Craft Exhibition, 2004, Evanston, IL; Arts in the Embassies Program, 2002-2004, U.S. Embassy, Vienna, Austria; Philadelphia Craft Show, 2001, PA; and Washington Craft Show, 1999-2004, Washington, DC. Galleries carrying my work include: National Sculptors Guild, Loveland, CO; Columbine Gallery, Santa Fe, NM; Karats Gallery, Vail, CO; Rhodes Stringfellow Gallery, Cannon Beach, OR; Edgewood Orchard Gallery, Fish Creek, WI; and Savage Fine Art, Carmel, CA.

NICHOLAS WILTON

Paintings & Prints
Page 251

Rich in color, texture, and symbols, my paintings reference a personal vocabulary of botanical forms, patterns, and abstract designs. The many layers and worn surfaces of the paintings reveal a history and give evidence of the passage of time in their creation. I work with interior designers, art consultants, and galleries. For a complete listing of available paintings, prints, upcoming shows, and painting workshops, visit www.nicholaswiltonpaintings.com.

COMMISSIONS: Private residence, Sausalito, CA; Jewish Community Foundation, Los Angeles, CA; Seattle Opera, WA; Beringer Wines, Napa, CA

COLLECTIONS: Shinsei Bank, Tokyo, Japan; Birkenstock, San Rafael, CA; Celebrity Cruise Lines, Miami, FL; Circle Bank, San Rafael, CA; The Irvine Foundation, San Francisco, CA

EXHIBITIONS: Solo show, 2006, Gallatin River Gallery, Big Sky, MO; Solo show 2005, Selby Fleetwood Gallery, Santa Fe, NM; Solo show, 2005, Kyobashi Center, Tokyo, Japan

PUBLICATIONS: *Southwest Art Magazine*, March 2007, *Focus Magazine*, July 2005

GUILD SOURCEBOOKS: *Artful Home 1, Architectural & Interior Art 21*

BRUCE WOLFE

Representational Sculpture
Page 172

I am interested in creating classic, contemporary figurative sculpture with a strong sense of the individual, as well as the appearance of fluid movement to the clothing and the figure. Making my pieces fit and enhance the landscape and surrounding architecture is of the utmost importance. The philosophy behind my work is to reflect the high values, integrity of the character, and attitude of the fine person we are honoring. I want the sculpture to be timeless, not trendy—a quality piece. Too often, monuments are simply lifeless metal. Sculpture needs movement and mood. I like the natural beauty of the human form. I like the truth of concentrated observation. I enjoy working with clients, collectors, galleries, architects, and project planners.

RECENT PROJECTS: *Crucifix*, 7'H, Our Mother of Confidence, San Diego, CA; Bust, Schermerhorn Symphony Center, Nashville, TN; *Harry Truman*, 26'H bronze, Union Station Building, Kansas City, MO

COMMISSIONS: *Mayor Ilus Davis*, 9'H bronze, Ilus Davis Civic Center Park, Kansas City, MO; *President John Hannah*, 7.5' bronze, Michigan State University, Lansing; *Barbara Jordan* sculpture, 7'H, Austin-Bergstrom International Airport, TX

ARTIST STATEMENTS

JEAN WOLFF

Non-Representational Sculpture

Pages 134-135

I create sculptures in wood, bronze and papier-mâché, combining these mediums into abstract sculptures, from six-foot totems to small table-size sculptures to wall pieces. My inspiration comes from the spirituality of Buddhism and twelve-step personal improvement programs. Meshing my philosophy with meditation leads me to express a series of sculptures to achieve a connection between art and spirit. I seek to have my sculptures aimed at the stimulation of the viewer's sensitivity and sensuality. I desire to place unique sculpture within the broadest reach of emerging and established collectors. To view more of my sculptures, please visit my website, Sculptjean.com.

COMMISSIONS: Plaza Center Project, Pasadena, CA; Park Center Financial Plaza, San Jose, CA; San Jose Hilton and Towers, San Jose, CA

EXHIBITIONS: L.A. Municipal Gallery, Ontario, CA; Gallery C. Hermosa Beach, CA; Gensler and Associates, Santa Monica, CA; Venice Art Forum, Venice, CA

COLLECTIONS: Private and public collections throughout the United States

DERAN WRIGHT

Representational Sculpture

Pages 138, 173

I began to experiment with three-dimensional sculpture at the age of fifteen. After twenty-seven years of creating original bronze sculpture—from small scale to larger than life—for clients corporate, public, and private, I am still experimenting. Having created custom commissions on request since 1979, I have learned that there are only two people who must be pleased with what I create. The first is the client, of course. The second is myself. To make sure these two people are happy requires good communication. And when they are happy, then chances are good that many others will like it too.

COMMISSIONS: Harris Methodist Hospital, 2006, Fort Worth, TX; The Haltom City Public Library, 2004, Haltom City, TX; Founders Park, 2003, North Richland Hills, TX; Civil Courts Building, 2002, Fort Worth, TX; Beth-El Congregation, 2000, Fort Worth, TX; Cessna Aircraft Company, 2000, Wichita, KS

EXHIBITIONS: Brookgreen Gardens, 2005, SC; *Art is the Preservation of the City*, 2005, Fort Worth, TX; Park Avenue Atrium, 2004, New York, NY; Evelyn Siegel's Gallery, 1997, Fort Worth, TX

AWARDS: The Tallix Award, 2004, National Sculpture Society

MARLENE SANAYE YAMADA

Paintings & Prints

Page 253

Artwork to revitalize your senses. I was enchanted with the simple beauty of my color palette when I was blending colors to paint landscapes. My *Just Colors* collection was inspired by that observation. Instead of painting from a palette onto a canvas, I predominantly use the canvas itself as the palette. I find it exciting to see the unique and unexpected essence that emerges with each new creation. The gentle shade variations are peaceful and soothing. The bold, bright colors are rejuvenating. Each piece develops its own personality, and I follow its lead until it feels complete. I hope that my artwork stirs your emotions, lifts your spirits, and inspires you to reach new heights. I invite you to collaborate with me on new commissions. My work has been featured in gallery exhibits, private and public collections, and has appeared on the television show *CSI: Miami*. Please visit www.artworkbysanaye.com for additional samples of my work.

RICHARD YASKI

Non-Representational Sculpture

Page 137

I studied art at the prestigious Chouinard Art Institute in Los Angeles. For the past forty-two years, I have been creating metal sculptures at my studio and residence in Little River, CA, near Mendocino. Much of my work is displayed here, interspersed among the redwood trees, fern gardens, and waterfalls in the Shibui Sculpture Garden, a five-acre landscaped sculpture garden sitting adjacent to a 400-acre nature conservancy. My work, although grand in scale, reflects the spirit and philosophy of the Japanese Shibui: simple, subtle, unobtrusive, and beautifying with age, timeless in design and feeling. In addition to creating metal sculptures, I work in stone, creating water fountains and sacred spaces. My sculptures range in size from monumental outdoor pieces to tabletop and wall pieces. My work can be found in the Kremlin, Moscow; Istanbul, Turkey; the Detroit International Airport, as well as in synagogues, and private and corporate collections throughout the U.S. I have worked extensively with architects, engineers, and design teams, and welcome collaboration for site-specific commissions for residential, commercial, and ecumenical sites. Please visit www.yaski.com for more information.

GUILD SOURCEBOOKS: *Architect's 10*

JUANITA YODER

Liturgical Art

Page 179

Suspended paintings on silk for liturgical, public, and private spaces comprise my commissioned work. I create work of spiritual and artistic integrity that melds personal expression with liturgical and architectural considerations. Suspension sets up a kinetic relationship between the viewer and the art, while color and movement express an essence for the environment. My commissions have included seasonal liturgical pieces and permanent installations of paintings, altar cloths, and the Stations of the Cross. My work is also available as kinetic processional kites (used at national Catholic and Presbyterian conventions and cathedrals) or stained glass.

RECENT PROJECTS: Laguna Beach Presbyterian, CA, Princeton Academy, NJ, Daytona First Presbyterian, FL, Church of St. Thomas More, Glendale, AZ

COMMISSIONS: Lawrenceville School Chapel, NJ; Good Shepherd Catholic Community, Colleyville, TX, Our Lady of Mercy Church, Potomac, MD; Princeton University Chapel, NJ

AWARDS: Ministry and Liturgy 2006 Bene Award

GUILD SOURCEBOOKS: *Architectural & Interior Art 20* (as Juanita Yoder), *16* and *15* (as Juanita Y. Kauffman)

LARRY ZGODA

Architectural Glass

Page 59

Stained glass has captivated me for my entire adult life. Much art has resulted from a willingness to explore possibilities within the parameters of the stained/leaded glass format. This exploration has led to conceptual and technical breakthroughs: stainless glass, beveled wire glass, architonomous art glass and Clovis glass. Designs are simple and straightforward while sympathetic to the architecture. Color is a quality that I regularly discover. It is amusing to take a cliché, design, or color dogma and breach it while still achieving aesthetic success. Works in stained/leaded glass are easily maintained, durable, and beautiful. The juxtaposition of glasses with different optical qualities makes visually interesting works. In contrast to trendiness often seen in architecture and related arts, I advocate "genuine and permanent beauty in the built environment." What we make today should look as good in one hundred years as on the day of installation.

ARTIST STATEMENTS

TRICIA ZIMIC
Murals, Tiles & Wall Reliefs
Page 223

Creating images in clay evolved naturally from my earlier career as a book illustrator. I enjoy designing and creating colorful scenes and images that bring an area to life. My unique bas-relief murals create an aesthetic beauty that is both durable and maintenance free. These "high-relief" murals are custom-designed to fit a specific location. I work closely with clients providing detailed drawings and watercolors. Sculpted ceramic tiles may include decorative elements, including 24K gold leaf, jewels, glazes, and oil paint. Murals range from smaller portable works for the home, office, or public building to large, permanent wall installations for lobbies, entranceways, libraries, schools, hospitals—any space in need of artistic focus and colorful expression.

COMMISSIONS: Maplewood Middle School entrance hall; Jersey Animal Coalition lobby; Numerous private collections

COLLECTIONS: Avid Tile, Clinton, NJ; Dragonfly Gallery, Martha's Vineyard

PUBLICATIONS: *Millburn-Short Hills Magazine*, 2005; *News-Record*, Jan and Oct 2006

Location Index

LOCATION INDEX

LOCATION INDEX

MASSACHUSETTS

MICHIGAN

MINNESOTA

MISSISSIPPI

MISSOURI

MONTANA

NEVADA

NEW HAMPSHIRE

NEW JERSEY

NEW MEXICO

NEW YORK

NORTH CAROLINA

OHIO

OREGON

PENNSYLVANIA

RHODE ISLAND

TENNESSEE

LOCATION INDEX

TEXAS

VERMONT

VIRGINIA

WASHINGTON

WISCONSIN

CANADA

GERMANY

Index of Artists & Companies

INDEX OF ARTISTS & COMPANIES

INDEX OF ARTISTS & COMPANIES

INDEX OF ARTISTS & COMPANIES

R

S

T

U

V

W

Y

Z